# THE GREENHOUSE

**A wide variety of plants can be grown in a small greenhouse.**

# THE GREENHOUSE

*A Complete Guide to the Construction and Management of Greenhouses of all kinds, from the Cold House to the Tropical House; and to the Cultivation of Greenhouse Plants, including Orchids, Cacti and Hot House Species*

Edited by

## F. G. PRESTON, M.A., V.M.H., A.H.R.H.S.

### FORMERLY IN CHARGE OF
### THE UNIVERSITY BOTANIC GARDEN, CAMBRIDGE

16 PLATES IN COLOUR
126 PHOTOGRAPHS AND MANY
CONSTRUCTIONAL PLANS AND DIAGRAMS

WARD, LOCK & CO., LIMITED
LONDON AND MELBOURNE

© WARD, LOCK & CO., LIMITED, 1951

*Second impression 1956*
*Third impression 1960*
*Fourth impression 1962*
*Fifth impression 1964*
*Sixth impression 1967*

MADE IN ENGLAND

PRINTED IN GREAT BRITAIN BY RICHARD CLAY (THE CHAUCER PRESS), LTD.,
BUNGAY, SUFFOLK

# CONTENTS

CHAPTER                                                                                   PAGE

I. THE GREENHOUSE . . . . . . 13
Reasons Governing Design—Types of Greenhouses—Metal and Concrete Houses—Construction—Heating—Maintenance—Frames.

II. FERTILIZERS . . . . . . . 55
Organic and Artificial—The Uses of Lime

III. METHODS OF PROPAGATION . . . . 60
Plants from Seed—Division of Roots—Offsets—Cuttings — Layering — Runners — Root-Cuttings — Leaf-Cuttings—Ringing—Grafting.

IV. POTTING AND RE-POTTING . . . . 79

V. FORCING . . . . . . . . 93
Early Vegetables—Fruit—Flowering Plants—Plants for the Cold or Unheated Greenhouse—Plants for the Cool Greenhouse—Plants for the Warm Greenhouse—Plants for Baskets—Some Winter Flowering Greenhouse Plants—Greenhouse Plants from Seed—Annuals in the Greenhouse—Hard-wooded Greenhouse Plants—Climbers and Twiners—Greenhouse Plants for Scent.

VI. BULB CULTURE. . . . . . . 118
Bulbs grown in Pots—Bulbs grown in Fibre.

VII. GREENHOUSE FOLIAGE PLANTS . . . 124

VIII. GREENHOUSE FERNS . . . . . . 130

IX. ROOM PLANTS . . . . . . . 136

X. CACTI . . . . . . . . . 138

XI. THE ALPINE HOUSE . . . . . . 141
Selection of Suitable Plants—Bulbs, Corms and Tubers—The Inside Aquarium.

XII. ORCHID-GROWING . . . . . . 153

XIII. FRUIT UNDER GLASS . . . . . 178

XIV. FRUIT-GROWING IN POTS . . . . 181

XV. THE CULTURE OF PARTICULAR FRUITS—UNDER GLASS . . . . . . 190

XVI. ALPHABETICAL LIST OF GREENHOUSE PLANTS 233

XVII. DISEASES AND PESTS . . . . . 600

INDEX . . . . . . . . 621

# CONTENTS

CHAPTER

I. THE GREENHOUSE . . . . . . . . 13
  Season—Aspect—Design—Types of Greenhouses—Metal and Concrete Houses—Construction—Heating—Ventilation—Frames.

II. IMPLEMENTS . . . . . . . . 55
  Organic and Artificial—Fresh use of Lime.

III. METHODS OF PROPAGATION . . . . 60
  Plants from Seed—Division of Roots—Offsets—Cuttings—Layering—Runners—Root-cuttings—Leaf-Cuttings—Budding—Grafting.

IV. POTTING AND RE-POTTING . . . . 78

V. FORCING . . . . . . . . . 93
  Early Vegetables, Fruits, Flowering Plants—Plants for the Cold or Unheated Greenhouse—Plants for the Cool Greenhouse—Plants for the Warm Greenhouse—Plants from Bulbs—Some Winter-flowering Greenhouse Plants—Greenhouse Plants from Seed—Annual in the Greenhouse—Late-worked Greenhouse Plants—Climbers and Twiners—Greenhouse Plants for Scent.

VI. BULB CULTURE . . . . . . . 113
  Bulbs grown in Pots—Bulbs grown in Fibre.

VII. GREENHOUSE FOLIAGE PLANTS . . . 114

VIII. GREENHOUSE FERNS . . . . . . 130

IX. ROOM PLANTS . . . . . . . 135

X. CACTI . . . . . . . . . 138

XI. THE ALPINE HOUSE . . . . . . 141
  Suitable Alpine Plants—Bulbs, Corms and Tubers—The Rock Aquarium.

XII. ORCHID-GROWING . . . . . . 184

XIII. FRUIT UNDER GLASS . . . . . . 178

XIV. FRUIT GROWING IN POTS . . . . 181

XV. THE CULTURE OF PARTICULAR FRUITS—UNDER GLASS . . . . . . 190

XVI. VEGETABLES AS GREENHOUSE PLANTS 212

XVII. DISEASES AND PESTS . . . . . . 300

INDEX . . . . . . . . . 

v

# COLOUR PLATES

A WIDE VARIETY OF PLANTS CAN BE GROWN IN A
SMALL GREENHOUSE . . . . *Frontispiece*

FACING PAGE

A HYBRID HIPPEASTRUM (EQUESTRIAN LILY) . 14

A GIANT-FLOWERED MARIGOLD (CALENDULA) . . 64

FLOWER-HEAD OF A CLIVIA . . . . . 81

A FULLY-GROWN COLEUS (FIRE NETTLE) . . . 96

THE DOUBLE GLOXINIA "QUEEN OF HEARTS" . 113

A SINGLE-FLOWERED GLOXINIA . . . . . 144

"LADY WASHINGTON", AN ATTRACTIVE VARIETY OF
PELARGONIUM . . . . . . . . 161

A VARIETY OF PELARGONIUM WITH STRONGLY
VARIEGATED LEAVES . . . . . . 240

A POT OF SAINTPAULIA (AFRICAN VIOLET) . . 257

SAINTPAULIA (AFRICAN VIOLET) . . . . . 336

IMPERIAL HYBRIDS OF SCABIOSA . . . . 353

"FLORADALE BEAUTY", A VARIETY OF VERBENA . 464

"CHERRYTIME", A VARIETY OF CACTUS-FLOWERED
ZINNIA . . . . . . . . . 481

"SNOWTIME", A VARIETY OF CACTUS-FLOWERED
ZINNIA . . . . . . . . . 528

THE MAGNIFICENT BLOOM OF A POT-GROWN
BEGONIA . . . . . . . . . 545

# LIST OF ILLUSTRATIONS

FACING PAGE

A Well-constructed Greenhouse—The Greenhouse and Garden 20

An Attractive Lay-out of Garden and Greenhouse—Greenhouse at Side of House . . . . . . 21

Streptocarpus—Colour in the Greenhouse . . . . 28

Fuchsias in the Greenhouse—Tulips in the Greenhouse . . 29

A Well-constructed Lily-pond under Glass—Lily-pond in the Greenhouse . . . . . . . . 32

Anemone blanda—Iris reticulata *var.* " Cantab " . . . 33

Carnations in the Greenhouse . . . . . . 48

Muscari armeniacum—Tulipa tarda (T. dasystemon) . . 49

Close-up of a Modern Paphiopedilum (Cypripedium) hybrid . 52

Oxalis enneaphylla—Vanda suavis . . . . . 53

Propagating Pelargoniums . . . . . . . 60

Sowing Seed in Boxes and Pans . . . . . 61

How to Pot-up . . . . . . . . 84

Bulbs in Pots . . . . . . . . 85

Propagating Violas and Phlox . . . . . . 92

The Culture of Fuchsias . . . . . . . 93

Calceolaria herbeohybrida in the Greenhouse—Single Begonias 116

Clusia grandiflora—Agapetes macrantha . . . . 117

Senecio grandifolius . . . . . . . . 124

Aristolochia kewensis and elegans . . . . . 125

Cheilanthes californica—Adiantum pedatum . . . 132

Adiantum cuneatum *var.*—Polystichum *var.* . . . 133

Corner in the Cactus House—Cacti under Glass . . . 140

Coleuses in the Greenhouse—Alpine House at Kew . . 141

Phaius Marthæ—Cypripedium Reginæ (C. spectabile) . . 176

# LIST OF ILLUSTRATIONS

FACING PAGE

Cymbidium Lowianum—Dendrobium aggregatum . . 177

Cherry Bigarreau Noir-de-Guben . . . . . 192

A Pine-apple . . . . . . . . . 193

Grapes in the Greenhouse . . . . . . . 208

Pruning and Training the Grape Vine . . . . 209

Peach " Princess of Wales " . . . . . . 224

Strawberries in the Greenhouse . . . . . . 225

Achimenes—Auriculas—Acroclinium and Aquilegias (long
spurred) . . . . . . . . . 272

Camellias in an Unheated Greenhouse. . . . . 273

Layering Carnations . . . . . . . . 288

Campanula pyramidalis—Campanula Medium—Celmisia insignis—Calceolaria herbeohybrida . . . . 289

Annual Chrysanthemum — Chrysanthemum (The Melba)
Calendula (Double)—Crocus . . . . . 304

Chionodoxa Luciliæ — Eustoma Russellianum — Cyclamen
persicum " Triumph "—Cineraria stellata . . . 305

Conandrum ramondioides—Chlidanthus fragrans . . . 320

Dicentra spectabilis—Acocanthera spectabilis . . . 321

Cephalotus follicularis — Echium plantagineum — Chimonanthus præcox . . . . . . . . 368

Eranthis cilicica—Eranthis Tubergenii . . . . 369

Hippeastrum rutilum *var.* fulgidum . . . . . 384

Gloxinias and Hybrid Cineraria grandiflora in the Greenhouse 385

Hibiscus Manihot — Helichrysum bracteatum — Fuchsia —
Gloxinia " Triumph " strain . . . . . 400

Incarvillea Delavayi —Delphinium Gayanum (Larkspurs) —
Brodiæa uniflora (Tritelia)—Ixias—Fritillaria Meleagris . 401

Hæmaria discolor . . . . . . . . 416

Jasminum primulinum—Jeffersonia . . . . . 417

Lewisia Howellii and L. Tweedyi . . . . . 432

Monstera deliciosa . . . . . . . . 433

x

# LIST OF ILLUSTRATIONS

FACING PAGE

Nelumbium Nelumbo (N. speciosum) . . . . . 448

Giant Mimulus — Linum rubrum — Tropæolum (Golden
Gleam)—Myosotis alpestris . . . . . . 449

Nigella Miss Jekyll—Petunia (Single)—Nemesia strumosa—
Petunia (Double)—Dimorphotheca hybrids . . . 496

Primula obconica — Phacelia campanularia — Phlox paniculata—Double Begonias—Ranunculus . . . 497

Primulas : stellata, obconica, malacoides, japonica, sinensis,
Double and Single . . . . . . . 512

Salpiglossus sinuata—Gloxinia (sinningia speciosa) . . 513

Silene orientalis—Hyacinth " Queen of the Pinks "—Schizanthus—Lychnis Cœli-rosa (Viscaria) . . . 560

Sparaxis " Fire King " — Polianthes tuberosa (Tuberose) —
Scabiosa atropurpurea (Sweet Scabious) — Viburnum
Opulus sterile . . . . . . . . 561

Strobilanthes isophyllus—Reinwardtia trigyna . . . 576

Saxifraga " Tumbling Waters "—Ramonda Myconi (R.
pyrenaica) . . . . . . . . 577

Platyclinis glumacea . . . . . . . 592

Nerine hybrid Nena . . . . . . . 593

Passiflora Allardii . . . . . . . 608

Amaryllis Belladonna var. " Hathor " . . . . 609

# CHAPTER I

## REASONS FOR THE GREENHOUSE

A GREENHOUSE can be used for almost any kind of plant life—flowers, vegetables, ferns, palms, etc.—and can give to these plants the kind of conditions which suit them best. In a greenhouse most of the natural conditions of each plant can be reproduced, for water, sun, air, and soil can be controlled. The greenhouse is used for plants of other climates, for plants grown out of season, and for the cultivation of many flowers and vegetables which would probably spoil under less controlled conditions.

A greenhouse is also used for propagation, forcing, and storing, and for starting into growth half-hardy plants that are destined for summer borders.

In this country a greenhouse is specially useful for controlling atmospheric conditions, as our weather is too variable to be relied upon. Heavy showers of rain, early unexpected frosts, poisonous fogs, and biting winds can be ignored if plants are in a greenhouse—preferably, of course, a heated greenhouse.

The vegetable crops grown out of season with the aid of a greenhouse ensure a variety throughout the year. Such crops as beans, peas, lettuce, tomato, and cucumber can be carefully timed to give a continuous twelve-month succession.

Grapes and peaches, early strawberries, and other fruits are available from the greenhouse when out-of-door fruit is still in the bud stage.

Flowers from warmer climates and flowers from cooler climates are both possible under glass, for control of all conditions is practicable. Alpines are as frequently grown in a glasshouse as are orchids, begonias, and African lilies.

So with careful management and an understanding of the essential conditions needed to grow plants to perfection, much pleasure and profit are obtained from the use of areas under glass.

## REASONS GOVERNING DESIGN

There are many different shapes of glasshouses, and they vary greatly in size. Areas of glass in commercial districts are usually of the simplest design, because the art of growing each crop has been reduced to the most simple and economical

13

methods. Houses to take a mixed collection of plants are constructed to cover varying cultural conditions, and are in consequence more varied in their architecture.

**Crop Houses** must be draught-proof, and need plenty of light and ventilation. The heating system should be efficient. Points in connection with these factors are :—

1. Heating apparatus must be placed to give the maximum results and be as out-of-the-way as possible.
2. Doors should be wide and easy to open, to allow for the passage of sterilising apparatus, trolleys, etc., and the easy removal of soil, when this is necessary.
3. Paths should be preferably of a temporary nature and well placed, so that it is easy to get at the borders for cultivation purposes.
4. Tanks should be large and clean, and there should be high pressure on the water, to allow for quick and thorough watering.

The design of a crop house is governed by the utilitarian requirements of the crops, which may be of differing types, such as tomatoes, cucumbers, lettuce, rape, and cress, vines, or flowers, such as bulbs or carnations.

**Show or Plant Houses,** besides being designed with the growing conditions in mind, must also show the plants to the maximum advantage. Plant houses need plenty of staging to hold the standing pots, and this staging should be tiered when displaying the plants, so that banks of flowers can be arranged without the pots showing. Concrete paving is also a necessity, so that it can be washed down and kept spotlessly clean. The house must, of course, be of strong construction, and high enough to give a feeling of spaciousness. The plant house must also be designed from the æsthetic point of view, and must be set gracefully into the general garden picture. The relationship to nearby buildings needs to be considered. Often a carefully chosen group of shrubs or flowering trees can be used to make an effective link.

Situation and aspect affect the size and design of all types of glasshouse to a certain extent. If houses are to be built on a slope they may have to be shorter in length than anticipated, as, with heavy watering, the slope may cause flooding at one end of the house. The height may be partly determined by the surrounding trees. If the garden is small and a range of plant houses is desired to grow many kinds of plants, a choice will probably have to be made between having several small houses to form a range, or one large house partitioned off to provide the varying conditions needed.

14

**PLATE 2**
A hybrid *Hippeastrum* (Equestrian Lily). This
plant is often known under the name Amaryllis.

# TYPES OF GREENHOUSES

## ESSENTIALS OF A WELL-DESIGNED GREENHOUSE

Whatever the aspect, site, or purpose of a greenhouse, there are certain essentials which must be borne in mind and which are connected with every type of glasshouse. They are the basis of healthy plant cultivation.

There must be the maximum light available, and the greenhouse should therefore be positioned to catch the most sun, the best direction normally being from north to south. Shade may be temporarily needed, and blinds or other shading device must be considered.

There should be shelter from strong winds, for where the greenhouse is exposed to prevailing winds there is great loss of heat from the surface of the glass. Strong winds also drive rain under the panes, and are likely to rip off and break the glass from the framework. A shelter belt of small trees is often advisable. Larger trees, however, cast shadows, and the roots may upset the construction, crack the brickwork, and make the floor uneven.

There should be adequate provision for ventilation and an adequate water supply, with tanks for storage; the heating system must be in good working order and of the correct size to heat the house properly. Guttering is important, and should be in good repair. Paths should be smooth and well positioned to admit of easy working. Sun-blinds should be provided if possible.

A potting-bench is a vital adjunct to the plant house, and should be near to the house. When pot plants need any kind of treatment, they are taken to the potting-shed bench. If they are hot- or warm-house plants, a sudden change of temperature may retard them badly, so if possible the potting-shed should be directly connected with the plant houses. With large ranges of glasshouses, a potting-shed is generally incorporated into the general design. Small all-purpose houses have a potting-bench provided in one part of the house, or they can have a prefabricated potting-shed attached to one end.

If it is not possible to provide a potting-bench or shed attached directly to the plant house it should be situated on the leeward side of the house and not very far distant.

## TYPES OF GREENHOUSES

There are three main types of greenhouses : span, lean-to, and three-quarter span. These types have been modified to give intermediate types for special purposes.

**The Span Type** is mostly used where there is plenty of room

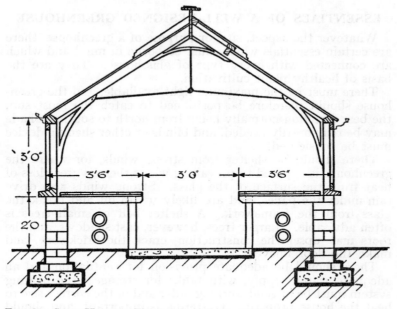

FIG. 1.—Span House. The brick walls are well bedded on to the concrete foundations and the 4-inch pipes under the staging ensure a steady rise of warm air to the plants.

and light, but can be erected in confined spaces with satisfactory results. The span roof enables full benefit to be obtained from the sun, both before and after noon. Maximum use can also be made of the whole space available. The span house is generally no more costly than the half-span or lean-to, as more strengthening is needed to support a half-span roof.

**The Lean-to** is very useful for crops that need a lot of sunshine for ripening purposes—*e.g.*, vines, peaches, and nectarines. As its name suggests, it is a half-span house that leans against a wall. Frequently in a walled garden, lean-to or even " peach cases " (narrow lean-to glasshouses) are useful for making the most of the sunshine and the existing walls. The lean-to is often expensive because of the extra bracing needed for support, and except for the certain crops cited above which the lean-to grows to perfection, it is not an economical proposition. For ordinary mixed crops a span or three-quarter span is more desirable, except where space is very limited. In a big range of greenhouses, however, a lean-to facing north is very useful for ferns and to rest summer-blooming, exotic plants, while a lean-to facing south is advantageous for propagation.

16

# TYPES OF GREENHOUSES

When constructing a lean-to it is essential to have the slope of the roof at an angle of not less than 26°, otherwise the water will work up through the glass and drips will cause damage to the plants.

**The Three-quarter Span House** is useful for some crops, as it possesses a wall, as well as two roof surfaces to trap the sunlight. As with the lean-to, existing walls can be utilised, thus minimising the costs.

**The Sunken Span House or Pit** is suitable for special purposes. The construction and measurements, etc., correspond to those of an ordinary span house, but the pit is sunk into the ground up to the eaves, and is reached by a flight of steps.

The ground helps to keep the house very warm, and the full-span roof gives good light. The heated pit house is used for propagation (owing to the humidity and shelter), and for cucumbers and other crops demanding great quantities of heat and humidity. A pit can also be cold, and it then provides the conditions suited to such pot plants as cyclamen and primula in the summer.

## SIZES AND PURPOSE

The span house may vary in size from 15 feet in length to over 200 feet. The small garden greenhouse averages 20 feet × 10 feet up to 40 feet × 10 feet. The width hardly varies with the small greenhouse, as 10 feet is convenient to take the staging and paths with due comfort for the worker, and without leaving parts of the house unused. Larger houses up to 200 feet are wider, generally 30 feet, although cucumber houses may measure 100 feet × 15 feet.

A small greenhouse can be used for either flowers alone or vegetables alone, or it may be needed for many purposes. In

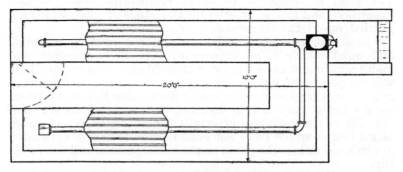

Fig. 2.—Plan of Span Roof House illustrated on page 16.

B

a small garden the greenhouse may be needed to start early flowers and vegetables for later planting. It may also be used for chitting potatoes, forcing bulbs and early flowers for the house, for propagating dahlias, chrysanthemums, etc., for forcing early strawberries, and for the storage of dahlia and other roots. The size of such a house will vary according to the space available, cost, and the demands that are to be made on it.

The three-quarter span, by reason of its position, does not vary so much in size as the full-span house, and is generally from 20 feet to 40 feet in length and 10 feet or 12 feet wide.

The three-quarter span can be used as an ordinary general plant house or to grow peaches and vines, and is useful to house chrysanthemums in the autumn or to grow arums in the spring. The size usually depends on other circumstances, and the use of this type of house will be controlled by its size.

The lean-to greenhouse is nearly always from 20 feet to 40 feet in length and 10 feet to 12 feet wide, as its size is governed by the length of wall, and this is rarely more than 40 feet. The lean-to can be used as a general plant house, but it is more usual to find it growing vines or peaches. Lean-to's facing north are used as ferneries and for storing roots and chitting potatoes.

## METAL HOUSES

Many types of metal and concrete houses are now available. These are all of a prefabricated nature, to be quickly fitted together on the site. The three most popular kinds of new materials are special-type steel, aluminium, and concrete. All these greenhouses tend to have as little framework as possible, and great areas of glass. There is little puttying or brickwork. The steel is tempered to resist temperature changes and expansion, and has no grooves for the panes of glass, which are puttied on to the framework.

The advantages of these houses are that erection is simple and quick, there is no expansion, very little painting and maintenance and the extra large areas of glass ensure that there will be plenty of light in the house. On the other hand, a greater area of glass means greater fluctuation in temperatures, houses being very hot in summer and cold in winter; also draught is unavoidable, especially where putty is not used. Metal houses which have not been treated for extra expansion are inclined to lose the glass, as the metal shrinks and the panes slip.

It is difficult to introduce adequate ventilation where there is no framework, and lack of a wooden surface means extra condensation and drip.

Steel, iron tension, and aluminium-type houses are all on a moderate scale, and suitable for vegetables or flowers. Staging is additional for potted plants, and tanks and potting-benches can also be added.

## CONCRETE HOUSES

Concrete houses are mostly constructed of precast strips, and the glass panes are riveted to the strips with asbestos, from beneath, to prevent draught and rain-water leakage.

Steel, concrete, or composite houses can take any form of heating : a hot-water system, electricity, or oil. With large expanses of glass, electricity is very useful, as fluctuating temperatures can be easily controlled.

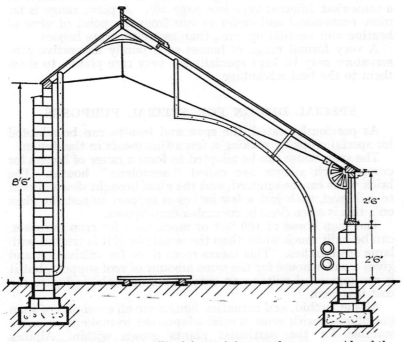

FIG. 3.—The wall can be utilised for training peaches on one side of the house, while the other has a special wired bracket to train the peaches against. The pipes near the outside wall give heat to the trunk and branches, while the slatted path can be rolled away when thorough cultivation of the border is necessary.

19

# THE GREENHOUSE

## DIFFERENCES BETWEEN THE TYPES

Ranges of greenhouses are frequently found in small gardens as well as on large estates, if many different plants are cultivated under glass. Before building a range it is best to work out in broad outline just what is needed, and try to relate this to the amount of space and general arrangement of the rest of the site. In this way every inch of ground available can be put to the best use, and all the features needed can be planned together to give an interesting and pleasing appearance to the range of houses (see diagram, pages 24 and 25).

A plant-house range may consist of a cool house, stove house, show house, and potting-shed. These various features must be planned so that the warmest house is nearest to the stokehole and boiler and the cooler houses have more ventilation and different staging and paving, etc.

Vegetable and flower crops are grown in house ranges of a somewhat different type (see page 26). A plant range is far more economical and easier to run from the point of view of heating and ventilating, etc., than many separate houses.

A very formal range of houses or a purely decorative conservatory may be kept specially for very rare plants, to show them to the best advantage.

## SPECIAL DESIGN FOR SPECIAL PURPOSES

As previously stated, the span and lean-to can be adapted for special crops by making a few adjustments in the design.

The span house can be adapted to form a range of houses for crops. Such ranges are called " aeroplane " houses. The brick walls can be omitted, and the glass brought down almost to soil level, with just a few inches of support to rest the glass on : this is often done in cucumber crop houses.

The span house of 100 feet or more, used for crop purposes, can be built much wider than the usual size if it is trussed with large steel arches. This leaves more room for cultivation and gives a wider house for the same amount of roof support, but it is recommended only on an extensive crop scale, owing to the cost involved.

Alpine, orchid, and carnation houses are all examples of span greenhouses with some special adaptation to make them more suitable for the particular plants grown within. Alpines require little heat, practically no humidity, and plenty of ventilation. Therefore the house has a small heating system and plenty of working ventilators. The staging is usually high, to allow for massing of the alpines on show.

A Well-constructed Greenhouse

*Photos*] [*Humphrey and Vera Joel*

An attractive Lay-out of Greenhouse and Garden

An Attractive Lay-out of Garden and Greenhouse

*Photos*]

[*Humphrey and Vera Joel*

Greenhouse at Side of House

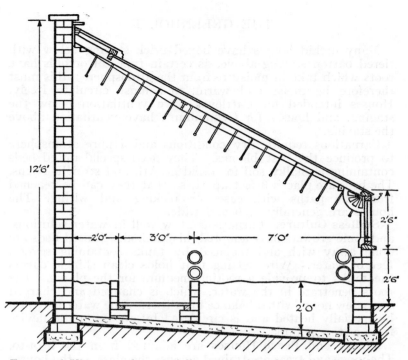

FIG. 4.—A Vinery needs a specially prepared border which should be at least 2½ ft. deep and have plenty of drainage incorporated in the subsoil. A slatted path is useful as it can be rolled up when the borders are being cultivated in the winter. A rain tank should be provided and gutters kept clean.

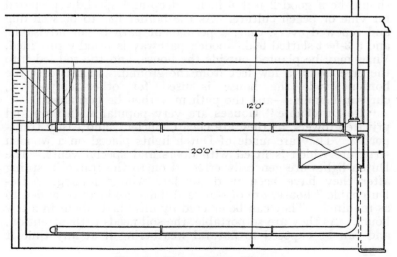

FIG. 5.—Plan of above Vinery.

Many orchid houses have boxed brick staging below with tiered batton staging above, as certain types of orchids have roots which take in moisture from the atmosphere; this must therefore be moist and warm, and must circulate freely. Houses intended for Cattleyas have ventilation below the staging, and houses for Cymbidiums have ventilation above the staging.

Carnations require airy conditions and a pure atmosphere to produce the best blooms. They need special raised beds containing a chalky soil for rapid growth and straight stems. The beds are placed 3 feet apart, so that they can be reached from the paths with ease for picking and wiring. The houses are generally high and wide.

**Soilless Culture.** Carnations grow well in water solutions, and some growers have adopted this method. Raised beds are done away with and replaced by tanks containing several feet of water. Wire netting that holds clean shingle covers the tanks to provide a rooting medium for the plants. The roots penetrate in the water, which is changed and charged every few hours with a balanced fertiliser. The water may also be specially heated and is circulated by an automatic device from a storage tank.

**Vinery and Peach Houses** are adapted from the lean-to. The vines and trees are trained against the glass, so the houses must be specially wired and the cross-bars slotted or holed to take these wires. The gutters are moulded to take the rain-water down into the rain-water tank within the house. The hot pipes are near the soil on both sides of the border, which should be a good 2 feet 6 inches deep and specially prepared for vine or peach culture. As the border has to be well dug and renewed every year, a permanent path is not advisable, and a 3-feet slatted teak wooden pathway is usually provided. Vines may be planted outside the house, and the rod led into the greenhouse a few feet from the ground. In this case the border inside the house is used for other crops—*e.g.*, chrysanthemums—and the path may then be permanent.

**" De-Dutchable "" Houses** are very popular with crop and private growers, as they are cheap, efficient, and easily transported. They are made of Dutch lights placed on a wooden structure which is fitted with doors and special vents. The Dutch lights are generally errected on to the frame in spring after they have been used for late winter forcing. " De-Dutchable " houses are of standard units, and can be added to as required. They can be erected by unskilled labour in a few hours. As they are so portable, the soil needs little attention, and can be exposed to natural weathering if at any time it suffers from excess cultivation of one crop. The " Dutchman " greenhouse is then moved to a new site, while the old soil is refreshed. These houses can be heated by electrical units. They are usually 12 feet wide, and a useful length is 30 feet, which means twelve units of four Dutch lights.

## CONSTRUCTION

### SOIL AND ASPECT

A Greenhouse should be built where there is good drainage. Good drainage depends on the subsoil, which should be sandy, chalky, or gravelly, as these subsoils warm up quickly and drain well. It is best to avoid a high water table, for there will be risk of a water-logged soil and occasional flooding. Where there are to be several large greenhouses, it is important to consider the drainage of the soil especially, as artificial watering under glass calls for a more exacting runaway than does soil in the open, where wind helps to keep the soil moisture evenly distributed.

If a full span greenhouse runs from north to south, the sun travelling from east to west will give the maximum of light without scorching. At noon it will be over the ridge-bar, and the rays will be dispersed. If the span house runs from east to west, one side of the house gets very little sun and the other side will have no respite from its direct rays. This will mean a poor distribution of solar energy.

It is important that there shall be as much light as possible reaching the plants, so as to harden the growth, otherwise forcing conditions will exist and many plants will become yellowish and spindly; they will also be prone to disease. The greenhouse should not be overshadowed by trees, although protection from the prevailing wind is useful to prevent unnecessary loss of heat from the surface of the glass.

Where there is a stretch of glass of more than 100 feet, the greenhouse should be on a gradient of 1 foot in 100 feet, to help the drainage, and get the maximum sunshine.

With a small " many-purpose " house, points to remember are that the position of the greenhouse should be where it catches the most sun and where all parts of the house will benefit equally, and also there should not be overhanging trees near the house, though a windbreak of some kind is desirable.

### FOUNDATION AND STRUCTURE

Before laying the concrete foundations which are essential for every house, the depth of soil to be taken out must be decided by an experienced worker, as it will depend on the size and

23

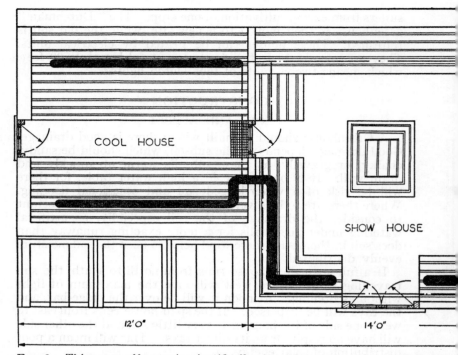

COOL HOUSE

SHOW HOUSE

12'0"

14'0"

FIG. 6.—This range of houses is scientifically planned to conserve heat and distribut and the cool house farthest away. The potting bench is near the warmth one house to another without causing draughts. Wing frames are a great ass warmth provided.

weight of the greenhouse and the type of soil. This is so that the structure will be completely rigid. The top soil which is removed from the trenches should be put on one side for cultural use. The subsoil is then consolidated and rammed hard and a 6-inch hard core of broken bricks and rubble is laid down before the concrete foundation. Cement concrete consisting of 1 part cement, 2 parts sand, 4 parts broken brick is used for the foundation, and should be from 4 to 6 inches thick. It is best to build this foundation several inches below the soil level, so that the brick or concrete wall built on to the cement concrete, and holding the structure, is well embedded.

In a conservatory type of greenhouse or a show house the floor will be laid down with the foundations. Other houses will only have concrete paths, and some commercial houses will have concrete only under the walls.

Bricks, or concrete blocks, or even timber in some cases, form the lower walls of the greenhouse. This is to conserve heat, to

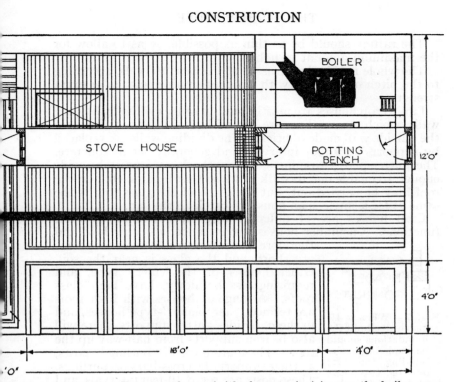

t to the right parts. The stove house (with close staging) is near the boiler room
hat no shock is given the plants during treatment and it is possible to walk from
and when built in close to the houses they benefit greatly from the shelter and

prevent frost entry, and to support the top structure. Bricks
are the warmest material, and when used should be standard
9 inch × 4½ inch, and built up so that the wall is 9 inches or
4½ inches thick. A 9-inch wall is preferable, but if a 4½-inch
wall is used, the first two rows of bricks should be put head-on
to give the 9-inch width.

The concrete blocks in use are 2 feet 6 inches × 6 inches
thick. Timber frames are also supplied for general use, but
are not so warm as bricks or concrete. The average height of
the wall from ground level is 2 to 3 feet, and it is topped by a sill,
which can be of pitch pine, oak, or teak. To this sill, solid
pieces of timber called mullions are bolted on very securely.
On these mullions rests a light eaves-plate, which receives the
roof-bars and rafters and carries the gutters. The ridge-bar
runs along the top of the greenhouse and supports the ridge-bar
ventilators. A wooden " capping " over the ridge bar helps to
keep the whole structure waterproof.

The rafters should be as thin as possible, so as to allow for the maximum amount of light.

The whole roof is then trussed at various intervals, according to the pitch of the roof, with wrought-iron principals for extra strength.

Large crop houses are mostly built in ranges without dividing walls, which means there are several houses together with only the outside wall made of brick. The dividing walls are replaced by supports at 9 foot intervals and generally set in concrete. The gutter-plates running between the houses must be wide enough to enable one to walk along so that repairs, etc., on the roof may be carried out, but the pitch of the glass roof is the same as for a single-span house, to catch all the sun.

Crop houses are of different heights, according to their functions. Cucumber houses, for instance, are very low, and therefore the intermediate gutter supports are short, and the glass is near the soil. Other houses of the vinery type, and requiring less humidity, have high glass roofs. A range of houses with high roofs are termed " aeroplane "-type houses, and in these, besides gutter supports, there will also be iron supports from half-way up the roof. These are termed " purling " posts, as they support the cross-bars or purlings. These posts are set at 10-feet intervals, and they are bedded in concrete blocks of 9-inch-square base.

WALL
HEADER
CONCRETE

FIG. 7.—When a 4½-inch wall is built the foundations should be made secure by building the first one or two rows of bricks 9 inches thick.

Even though there should be plenty of light and air, it is also important that the house should be draught-proof. The slightest cold draught will greatly reduce the average temperature and affect the plants, and if the average temperature is reduced by draught, more fuel is needed to keep up the temperature. Draughts, especially if from the north and east are very inhibiting to plant growth.

After the foundations and lower walls have been carefully laid down, the wooden structure is erected on top. It is best if frames are sectioned together as a whole before erection. There are various ways of putting up these sections, but if the two end sections are erected first, they can be " tied " together by the ridge-bar and the middle sections. Thus small errors in construction can be avoided. The rafters should be as far apart as possible—20 feet or more—to allow for the maximum amount of light. The ridge-bar across the middle must be of a good thickness, and well jointed, as it supports the rafters and glass.

# CONSTRUCTION

## WOODWORK

As there is an extraordinary amount of moisture within a greenhouse, measures should be taken to prevent the woodwork from rotting too quickly. There are several kinds of wood to choose from. These each give different performances, and need different treatment.

Teak, oak, deal, Douglas Fir, Western red cedar, red deal, and pitch pine are all woods that can be used in the structure of a greenhouse, the first and last being the most general. Teak has strength and durability, and because of this, thin scantlings

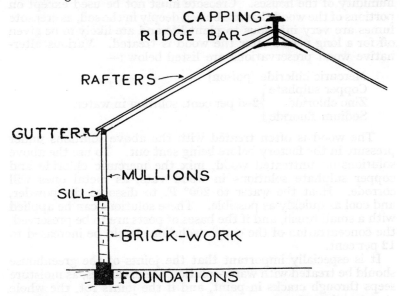

Fig. 8.—The above section through a house shows the principal structures and how they connect with each other.

can be used, the advantage being that a more slender framework allows for more light. It is an expensive wood and should be oiled with linseed oil rather than painted, as this will preserve it. Oak is also expensive when it is straight-grained : non-straight-grained wood is less expensive, but is inclined to distort. Deal and Douglas Fir especially are inclined to split on nailing, and they are both harder to finish. Western red cedar is soft, durable, and light, and contains essential oils, which helps preservation. There are two types used : the " merchantable " type for gutter plates and posts, and " select merchantable " or " clear " for the scantlings and bars.

27

Pitch pine, which is in general use, is very durable and straight-grained wood. It is moderately inexpensive but, on the other hand, it is fairly heavy. It is especially used for gutters and boards, even where other woods are used for the main structure.

### Preserving the Woodwork

As has been stated above, teak and sometimes red cedar are oiled with linseed, but other woods must be thoroughly safeguarded against premature rotting, owing to the high humidity of the houses. Creosote must not be used except on portions of the wood that are buried deeply in the soil, as creosote fumes are very injurious to plant life and are likely to be given off for a long period after the wood is treated. Various alternative wood preservations are listed below :—

Mercuric chloride (poison)
Copper sulphate ⎫
Zinc chloride ⎬ 2–5 per cent. solution in water.
Sodium fluoride ⎭

The wood is often treated with the above solutions under pressure in the factory before being sent out. To use the above solutions on untreated wood, mix the mercuric chloride and copper sulphate solutions in wood vats, as metal ones will corrode. Heat the water to 200° F. to dissolve the powder, and cool as quickly as possible. These solutions can be applied with a small brush, and if the bases of posts are to be preserved, the concentration of the copper solution should be increased to 12 per cent.

It is especially important that the joints of the greenhouse should be treated with water-solution preservatives, as moisture seeps through cracks in paint, and if the joints rot, the whole structure is useless.

White paint is used on greenhouses to allow for the reflection of light. Darker paints would absorb the rays from the sun, and thus prevent them from reaching the plants. The wood is treated with red-lead paint or " priming " before the final coats are given, as the " priming " fills the cracks and helps preservation. Then the house is painted and given several coats (three to four) on the inside and one to two on the outside. This additional amount of painting is to help against the high humidity. The greenhouse should be painted at least once a year inside following its construction, and once in three years on the outside. If the woodwork is carefully looked after from the very beginning, much expense on repairs and much time will be saved, and the life of the greenhouse will be greatly lengthened.

Streptocarpus in the Greenhouse

Colour in the Greenhouse

Fuchsias in the Greenhouse

*Photos*]  [*R. A. Malby*

Tulips in the Greenhouse

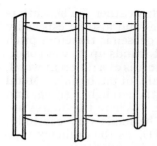

FIG. 9.—"Anti-drip" device. Rounded panes of glass carry water down the centre and keep it away from the joints.

White lead paint should always be used in preference to zinc paint, as zinc sulphide, produced with sulphur from the air, scorches the plants, and also turns the paint black. Aluminium paints are more recent in introduction and very satisfactory, although slightly more expensive than the foregoing ones.

It is also advisable to paint the iron-work to prevent rust. Nails and screws should not be used for Western red cedar or oak, as they tend to rust; galvanised or coppered iron nails, or even wooden pegs are suitable.

Steel hinges are best preserved by means of a red-paint dressing or linseed oil.

## GLASS

A special " horticultural " type of glass is used in greenhouses, as this lets through all the rays in the spectrum and is also light in weight. The standard weight is 21 oz. per square foot, and the usual size of the pane is 24 inches × 18 inches, or 24 inches × 12 inches. The panes are slid into the scantlings and puttied in place, overlapping one another by an inch, so that the water runs away quickly to the gutter, and does not drip on the inside of the house. A perpetual drip on the plants inside the house is extremely bad for them, and to counteract this an " anti-drip " pane has been devised. This has rounded corners, so that the moisture runs away from the sides of the bars and down the centre of the panes of glass to the gutter.

The texture of the glass is important, as the smallest air bubble may act as a lens and scorch the plants beneath. The best-made glass is carefully rolled out to get an even thickness and to avoid air bubbles or flaws which would damage the plants. This faultless glass is the type to choose.

### RIDGE-BOARDS AND GUTTER-BOARDS

The ridge-bar runs along the top of the greenhouse and supports the framework. It must therefore be strong and durable enough to bear a great

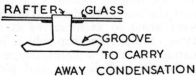

FIG. 10.—Another " anti-drip " device in a metal house. Grooves run down either side of each rafter and lead water away.

deal of weight and stand up to rough weather. The gutter-boards must also possess these qualities and also be especially impermeable to moisture. The timber chosen is therefore pitch pine, which is durable and strong and stands up to wet conditions well. Even if the rest of the structure is of a different wood, the ridge- and gutter-boards are generally of pitch pine. Metal is also available for this purpose, but although light, strong, and waterproof, it is not yet in general use. Where the houses are long, the joints in the timber should be made very carefully, and splice joints should be used (Fig 11), as the ordinary type of joint (Fig. 11) does not take the strain sufficiently.

Timber 2 inches thick and $1\frac{1}{2}$ inches wide is mostly used. These pieces are made into a V-shape for the guttering, which is positioned under the edge of the framework, so that the frame overlaps an inch, thus enabling the rain to be quickly carried

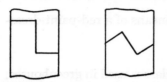

away. There should be a slight fall from one end of the house to the other. A metal pipe is fixed to take the water away from the guttering to a drain or storage tank. If stored properly, this rain-water can be used inside the house, but, of course, it must be clean and tepid, not cold. Rain-water is preferable to tap-water, as the latter is often hard, with a high percentage of chalk.

FIG. 11.—The joints in the timber must be carefully made to take the strain, especially in ridge-bars and sills.

Rain-water may also possess a small percentage of nitrogen dissolved out of the air, and this is good for the growth of the crops.

As previously stated, in the case of all woods, the timber used for gutters should be impregnated with a preservative to prolong its life.

### VENTILATION

The chief problems confronting greenhouse management are the control of the heat available and the control of moisture. The air quickly becomes saturated through regular watering, and the humidity rises. This humidity is adjusted by careful ventilating so as to arrive at the correct atmosphere for the type of plant or crop which is being grown. For example, carnations need a warm, dry, moving atmosphere, so they are grown in high houses, and plenty of ventilation is allowed. Cucumbers, on the other hand, need a very hot, humid atmosphere, but stagnant air will quickly spread disease, consequently ventilation has to be thorough, but most carefully controlled, and adjusted with the watering, so that the air is

30

always humid and warm, yet always moving. It is true to say that a stagnant atmosphere will encourage disease, as well as certain pests, therefore a current of fresh air is a vital necessity, but it must never become a cold draught.

There are three main types of ventilator in every span house —ridge, side, and box. This means there are ventilators from the ridge-bar, above the brick wall at the staging level, and beneath the staging. The box ventilation is in the brick or concrete wall beneath the staging.

The top or ridge ventilators are on both sides, and can be continuous or in sections of one or two panes. If the ventilators are separate, as in a small house, they are generally controlled by sashes and rack-and-pinion gearing. Where the ventilator is not more than 4 feet wide, one stay is sufficient, but with wider ventilators two must be provided, to take the weight and prevent the glass from breaking.

It is more usual to have the ventilators in sections geared together for easy opening. The gearing can be controlled by a handle a few feet from the ground at one end of the house or outside the house. This gearing is far more efficient and less liable to break down than sash-cord or window-stays.

Side ventilators are opened by means of an ordinary notched stay, or in large houses these can be geared, as for the ridge ventilators. Side ventilators are not always present in hot houses. Box ventilators are so called because they need not be made of glass; timber will do as well, if not better. The box vents are erected on all houses under the staging. They are approximately 9 inches × 4½ inches, and slide open, leaving a gap one brick wide. The air, on entering, is warmed by the pipes before reaching the house.

Since hot air rises, vents are opened in this order : ridge, side, and box. When the ridge vents are open it is also advisable to have a little side ventilation to enable the air to circulate properly. More information about ventilation control will be given later. It is important to stress here, however, the necessity of having adequate means of ventilation, and of having it in good working order and draught- and water-proof. A faulty ventilator may drip badly and will also upset the greenhouse routine and management.

## SHADING

This is used in summer for soft and thin-leaved plants and for plants with a slow intake of moisture. These categories include both flower and vegetable crops, *e.g.*, cyclamen, primula, and hot-house plants, as well as crops of tomatoes, lettuce, etc. Shading helps to keep the temperature down, so when shading is used, adjustments are made with the ventilation and humidity control.

There are two types of shading : temporary and permanent. Temporary shading is of the kind that can be used only when needed. So-called permanent shading is present all the summer. The temporary kind is preferable because where there is permanent shade there is too much loss of sunlight on dull days.

### Temporary Shading

This may consist of wooden-slatted blinds, or of blinds made from scrim or hessian. Both kinds can be used on a roller and worked by means of pulleys. Hessian blinds can be put up in spring and removed in the autumn, but wooden (teak) slatted blinds are generally left up permanently, although in winter there is some danger of snow bringing them down and breaking the glass. The slats used are $\frac{3}{4}$ inch in width, but these do not actually rest on the glass, but on steel supports. The blinds roll up into a box fixed on the ridge-bar. These shades are more expensive than permanent kinds, but last from ten to fifteen years, and are far more useful, as they can be rolled away in dull weather.

### Permanent Shading

There are several ways of shading a greenhouse permanently. By the term " permanent " we mean shading which is put on in the spring and taken away in the autumn and, therefore, the same amount of shade is cast in dull and brilliant weather throughout the summer months. Although they will probably need renewing after heavy rain, the advantages of these shades are, that they are cheap and little skill or labour is needed in putting then into position. Here are some washes for permanent shading :

*Lime* (Slaked). This is quite a common wash. It is made by mixing lime and water together into a thin paste and then adding a handful of salt or alum to every two gallons to make the lime adhere to the glass.

*Flour and Water* adheres better and casts a better shade.

*Distemper* is not advisable, as it washes off too easily.

" *Summer Cloud* " is a patent wash for glasshouses, and is very effective. It is more expensive than the above washes, but is very economical when applying, and resists the weather. " Summer Cloud " is a pale green, and gives a good light in the house.

There are two good methods of applying the above washes : (*a*) by stippling and (*b*) by syringeing. Stippling is more

A Well-constructed Lily-pond under Glass

*Photos*]                             *[Humphrey and Vera Joel*

Lily-pond in the Greenhouse

Anemone blanda

*Photos*]

Iris reticulata *var*. "Cantab"

[*F. G. Preston*

economical and reaches the corners better, but it is the slower method.

If the weather is dull for long periods, it is advisable to wash off the permanent shading until more sunny conditions ensue. The washes can be added to in periods of heat-wave.

## WATER SUPPLY

Water is needed both for the heating system and for plant growth. The water used in connection with hot-water systems is dealt with later. Water supply for the growing crops may be from the main supply or from natural sources. Wherever the water comes from, it must be in good supply, *i.e.*, plentiful in times of drought.

Main-water supply is generally the best, and there is no need for large storage tanks. The cost, however, is fairly heavy, varying with the district. Other sources of water are : (*a*) drainage from the house roofs, (*b*) wells or ponds, and (*c*) streams. In the case of roof drainage there may be some disadvantages to counteract obvious advantages. For example, plant material may be brought down with the water, and this may infect the supply to the greenhouse. Storage tanks are needed, and must be closed. Cleanliness is essential. Wells or ponds are a good source of water, but it is doubtful whether they and the other natural sources of water will hold out in times of drought. Wells and ponds may also be infected with disease from old plant remains. Water from a well is also very cold, and it has to be pumped up, and stood in tanks to be aerated and warmed before use.

Sometimes artesian wells are used, but the capital outlay is very heavy—approximately £1 per 1 foot drop.

With these natural sources power is also needed to pump the water through the pipes ; electricity needs to be in the district and at a low rate before wells and streams are of much practical value. The question of pressure is already taken care of when you use company's water.

Streams to be of any practical value have to be fairly fast and so free of plants and diseases.

In the greenhouse itself there should be taps fitted with good washers, a hose, and a fairly large metal tank. The hose is used for syringeing, watering, and damping down. The tank is for storing water before use on the plants, as in this way the temperature of the water becomes nearer that of the house and is not a shock to the plants. If the tank is fitted with a ball-tap from the main pipe, the tank will fill up as the water is used, and the water will have plenty of time to stand before a further supply is used.

C

In many commercial houses it is a common practice to have automatic irrigation both below soil level and above it. In underground irrigation there are 1-inch drain-pipes 4 feet apart and 9 inches below the surface level. The drain-pipes connect up with a 6-inch main. Water from an overground tap is allowed to flow into an underground reservoir connected with the underground system. This is very good for lettuce, needing plenty of underground moisture, for if lettuce are watered from above, the atmosphere tends to get too humid, and *Botrytis* and other rotting diseases set in. It is not certain yet whether this method is equally good for tomatoes and other crops.

Overground irrigation is carried out by means of pipes perforated at intervals, the height varying with the house and crop. The whole house is thus watered and damped down by a single tap, but in hot weather this type of irrigation is usually supplemented by hosing the borders and the paths. Overhead sprays can be permanent or temporary.

Good pressure is needed for both overhead and underground automatic watering.

Where there is a gradual slope in houses over 100 feet long, " terracing " may be necessary to take the extra moisture resulting from heavy watering. The terracing is done with straw at intervals of 15 to 20 feet. The straw is cut to the lengths needed, laid on top, and forced down with a spade so that it is 6 inches above the soil level. This terracing is done in the winter time, and lasts two–three years. Besides holding the water and preventing the soil from " eroding ", straw helps to lighten the soil and prevents soil sickness.

As watering under glass is necessarily very heavy to produce tender and quick growth, drainage must also be considered. The ground must have a pervious subsoil and the drains must be of adequate number and gradient.

## BORDERS AND PATHS

The amount of paving in a greenhouse varies with the type of house, but the average width is 2 feet 6 inches. In a house where there are wide borders the path is usually beneath the ridge-bar, partly because this situation is the easiest for operations, but also because this is the coldest part of the house and the drips from the ridge-bar and ventilators make it the least useful for plant cultivation. A house that is mostly used for show will have a larger proportion of the floor space devoted to paths.

In a small span-type greenhouse, where the centre is needed for plants, the paths may run round the outside of the central staging.

# CONSTRUCTION

Where the paths are permanent, concrete is laid down. In houses where the cropping scheme is changed frequently and the paths are also altered, they are generally made of some movable material, *e.g.*, clinkers, or slatted boards.

A permanent concrete path has a proper foundation, as for the walls of the building (see previous remarks). The soil is taken out to form a trench, and coarse concrete poured in to within 3 inches of the surface of the soil. A finer concrete is then bedded on top and levelled.

Temporary clinkers used as a path are laid on a shallow foundation and rolled. Boards laid down at the sides will prevent the clinkers from spreading on to the borders. Slatted boards can also be laid down on the soil to form a path, and be taken up quickly when not needed.

The borders in a house are made up specially to suit the peculiar conditions under glass. To be in fertile condition, soil must be well drained, well aired, and of a good texture, and this is more difficult to achieve in a closed greenhouse than in an outdoor border. Because of the added heat and lack of a natural rainfall, it is essential once a year to flood the borders until they are saturated, and to water heavily at times all through the growing season. This means that the subsoil must be of a kind through which this surplus moisture can pass rapidly, but the top soil must also be capable of holding water long enough for the plants to benefit fully. Where the subsoil is clay, broken bricks should be incorporated in the border at a depth of 18 inches to 2 feet.

Top soil is generally brought in specially, and should be a good-quality loam. " Cranleigh " and " Kettering " loams which can be bought by the yard are two good types of soil for greenhouse borders. Ordinary good garden loam should be used if a new stock of soil is not thought necessary.

The border soil should be *dark* for early heating up and for absorbing the sun's rays, *rich in humus*, *sticky*, to hold moisture, and fairly porous. A greenhouse soil tends to go " sick " from lack of healthy soil organisms, ventilation, and excess of one crop. It should be completely renewed every five years, and dug out to a depth of 18 inches and put to weather out of doors during the third winter.

The addition of dung and straw is also very important, as this helps to keep the soil fertile and sweet.

Greenhouse soil needs very careful management, and will not yield good crops if allowed to stagnate. Therefore a depth of 18 inches to 2 feet of the best soil possible should be incorporated and maintained by good cultivation.

# THE GREENHOUSE

## STAGING

There are many uses to which staging can be put, and consequently there are many kinds of staging. Open staging is built of iron or wood, with angle-iron bearers at intervals to hold slats or corrugated iron. The iron is punched at intervals to allow good drainage, and covered with gravel or coke breeze. Open staging is the best type of staging for pots, as the gravel makes a smooth bed for them to stand on and acts as an absorbent of surplus water. This water evaporates and helps to prevent the pots from drying out.

Slatted staging is not so good for standing pots as open staging, but it is often used for this purpose in cold houses. It is also used for seed-trays or boxes. Slatted staging is made of battens 1 inch × 3 inches thick, the slats being 1 inch apart. Pots are inclined to dry out when on slatted staging in a warm house.

Box staging is built of brick with iron sheeting on top.

The usual height of the staging, *i.e.*, up to the level of the brickwork, at the house sides, is 2–3 feet from ground level. Brick (or box) staging contains hot pipes with holes at intervals to enable the hot air to escape. Its main uses are for tropical and hot-house potted plants and for propagation.

Slatted and boxed staging together are used for orchid houses. The box staging has tiers of slatted staging above it. The pot plants stand on the slats; the boxed staging below gives a wet, airy condition necessary to their survival.

Tiers of slatted staging can be used in ordinary houses, so as to take as many pot plants as possible. It is especially useful to have tiers where there are hundreds of small pots needing as much light and air as possible, *e.g.*, when many bedding plants have just been potted up from seed-trays. Some kinds of slatted staging are removable, and so are doubly useful, as they can serve in temporary or permanent positions.

The wood used should be of the same kind as that used for the house, *e.g.*, pitch pine, and painted with several coats of white-lead paint. The battens should be very firmly screwed in place.

Corrugated iron or open staging is usually made in sheets, for easy handling. The sheets overlap one another to take pea shingle, gravel, or breeze approximately 3 inches thick. Shingle can be raked smooth occasionally with a small rake, specially made for the purpose; this keeps the shingle free from weeds and moss.

## HEATING

In the past the main type of heating has depended on a hot-water system, using various types of coal fuel for this purpose.

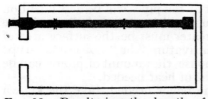

FIG. 12.—By altering the length of piping in a house the temperature can be altered to give different conditions for different types of plants.

Water enclosed in pipes gives an even warm temperature without harmful fumes or danger. In the last few years, however, electrical heating in the air and soil has been developed and become popular, although it is still prohibited by the price of electricity in some districts. The essentials of a good heating system are that the temperatures produced are even and reliable, that there shall be no harmful fumes, and that the atmosphere shall not be dried out. It should also need the minimum of upkeep. All these conditions are fulfilled by hot-water pipes and also by direct electrical heaters. Electricity used for direct soil and air heating has many other advantages, chiefly that very little labour is needed to control the heating, as a thermostat keeps the temperature even, and no stoking is required. Electricity is very reliable, and when used with a thermostat, the greenhouse can be left with complete confidence throughout the twenty-four hours, as unforeseen changes of outside temperature are automatically balanced. Electricity is often used to heat hot-water systems, giving the advantages of no stoking and cleanliness, but the temperature control is obviously not so complete as with direct heating.

FIG. 13.—Note additional length of piping.

Any heating system should keep the maximum and minimum temperature steady for the whole twenty-four hours, including night hours, and there must be little danger of a breakdown, which might, in frosty weather, lead to damage and possible loss of a whole house of plants. In case of any breakdown, the system should be easily repairable, and spare parts should be inexpensive and readily available.

Where a solid fuel is used in conjunction with a hot-water system, the boiler should be as simple and re-

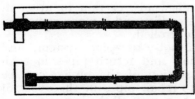

FIG. 14.—The piping in Fig. 13 is greatly extended.

37

liable as possible. The layout of the pipes will be dependent on the use to which the greenhouse will be put, and obviously the higher the temperature the greater must be the surface area of the pipes. When a small " cultivatum " or " horseshoe "-type boiler is used in a small greenhouse, the amount of piping can be varied according to the amount of heat needed.

In estimating the size of the boiler needed, take the known length of pipe and multiply by 185. This gives the size of the boiler needed in B.Th.U (*i.e.*, British Thermal Units). Add 25 per cent. as a safety margin, as cold spells necessitate more coal or other fuel. A 4-inch piping is the size usually used, as this gives an even temperature without wastage. The pipes should be supported by brick tiers or hooks. The higher the temperature the more pipes are needed, *e.g.*, in a small cold house one flow and one return pipe are sufficient, whereas in a hot house two flow and two return pipes are needed.

## HOT-WATER SYSTEMS

With low-pressure boilers the hot-water system works on the principle that cold water sinks and hot water rises. The boiler is therefore at the lowest point, and there should be a gradual rise to the highest point in the house. The same water is used for many years, and it should be chalk-free, to prevent the pipes from furring up. They also become furred if the water is changed often, and for this reason water should not be drawn from a hot-water system. Also, change in pressure may cause damage, and excess water may expand and cause the pipes to burst. To prevent this, a storage tank is fitted with the boiler, and this allows for the expansion of water, and replaces losses through leakage. This supply tank is at the end of the hot-water system, and should have a ball valve to allow extra water through as needed. The tank must be large enough to allow the water to expand one-twenty-third of its volume.

The gradient from boiler to the highest point in the house should be 1 foot in 120 feet, and for this and other reasons the boiler should be below ground level. When the boiler is below ground level and solid fuel is in use, it is far easier to control the fire—there are no draughts, high winds, or rain to upset it. The fuel burns more easily and steadily, and is more economically used where the draught is controlled.

Valves are all-essential in a hot-water-pipe system, and should be positioned on the flow and return pipes in each house. In this way a single section of the piping can be drained should it be necessary to repair pipes in the event of leaks, etc., and it is unnecessary to run off all the hot water.

Air-taps are also essential, and are found at the highest

point in every hot-water system. Where there are several houses, they must be at the highest points in each of the houses. These taps are to allow for the escape of air that collects in the water and might cause an air-lock if allowed to remain there. Air may get into the pipes when the water is allowed to boil or through leaks in the castings or joints. It is usual to open the air-taps every week and leave them open until water bubbles out; the taps should then be tightly screwed down again.

Where loss of heat to the outside air is likely to occur the pipes should be lagged with felting or one of the special cements which are on the market. Boilers and stoke-holes should be several feet away from the houses, so that no poisonous fumes contact the plant life, and all the pipes to and from the house and boiler should be underground if possible, and well lagged where they enter the greenhouses. The boilers themselves should be covered with special cement and bricked in.

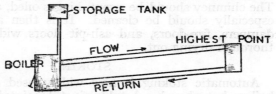

Hot-water systems, as stated previously, are run by solid fuel, gas, or electricity. The most general form of fuel which

Fig. 15.—A hot-water system. The boiler is placed below ground level and pipes rise steadily to warmest part of house and then fall back to boiler.

has been used up to now has been coal, and there are several kinds suitable for boilers, anthracite and small boiler coke being the two most economical kinds. Anthracite gives a slow, steady fire which needs little stoking, but is expensive. Coke gives a bright, hot fire which needs more attention, but compensates by being less costly. It is not wise to mix the fuels, as the fire burns unevenly if this is done. The boiler is really only a fire-bed with fire-bars beneath and pipes all round the fire, and containing the water which circulates in the pipes. The pipes, plus water, are heated by both the fire-bed and hot fumes which come from the burning fuel. The stoke-hole is made deep enough to take the boiler. Different sizes of boiler are supplied to suit the depth decided upon. A larger-size boiler than that actually required is always recommended, as it is unwise to work the boilers to their full capacity.

Tubular and sectional boilers are in general use for plant-house ranges and large greenhouses, " cultivatum " and " horseshoe " boilers for smaller greenhouses. In certain cases the sectional boiler is preferred to the tubular, by reason of its ready adaptability as regards extension. Sections of pipe can be added to the same fire-bed for additional capacity requirements. The "sectional" boiler is also easier to repair. A boiler should always be kept in good repair, with all doors fitting well. The flue damper is made with a 10 per cent. clearance, to allow for its being shut completely, and to help keep the draught even, and most chimneys are fitted with a chimney-draught stabiliser. There are also two air-dampers : the primary air-damper on the ash-pit door, which when wide open gives rapid combustion, and the air-damper on the boiler door, called the secondary air-damper, which is rarely used in normal routine.

At the end of the season, in the spring, when the boilers are put out of action, there are several things to do to preserve the heating system. First, the fire-box should be emptied, as half-burnt fuel causes corrosion, and the ash-pit should be cleaned. The chimney should be swept, hinges oiled, and movable parts especially should be cleaned. It is then advisable to leave dampers, fire-doors, and ash-pit doors wide open to permit thorough drying out.

### STOKING

Automatic stoking is now widely used even with small boilers, but where hand stoking is still maintained it is important to have a stoking routine and keep to it, because irregular draught and irregular stoking lead to a great wastage of heat and fuel, besides giving uneven conditions within the houses themselves. The fire should be kept in for the whole twenty-four hours if possible. Here is an example of fuelling routine :—

7 or 8 a.m. (The smaller the boiler the earlier it needs attention.)
Open chimney and ash-pit damper.
Rake through fire-bed and remove clinker.
Rake through fire GENTLY to sift out ash.
Refuel if necessary. A slight slope to the chimney gives a better draught.
12 noon. Look at boiler and refuel if necessary.
2 p.m. Look at boiler and refuel if necessary.
6.30 p.m. Clean fire thoroughly for the night. Remove clinker and ash. Rake fire-bed and make up a good fire.
Open dampers only SLIGHTLY.
At night time aim at getting the fire to burn slowly.
9–10 p.m. Bank down the fire for the night.
Remove clinker if necessary.
Fill fire-box really well with small fuel.
Close dampers as soon as possible.

**40**

### IDEAL THICKNESS OF FIRE-BED

| | | | | |
|---|---|---|---|---|
| Coal . | . | . | 1–2-inch diameter | 9-inch bed |
| Coke . | . | . | 2-inch ,, | 12–18-inch thickness |
| Anthracite . | . | 1–2-inch ,, | 6–10-inch ,, |
| ,, | . | . | 3–4 inch ,, | 8–15-inch ,, |

Automatic stokers are in general use for large boilers, and can be fitted on to an old boiler for a reasonable sum. There are two main types of automatic stoker : the power-driven hopper and the gravity feed. The hopper is attached to an ordinary boiler, and a " worm " feeds the fuel into the boiler.

FIG. 16.—An automatic stoker can be attached to an existing boiler. Coal in the hopper is worm fed to the boiler.

The gravity feed is automatic stoker and hopper combined and the old boiler cannot be utilised.

The dampers and draught are controlled.

The tubes carrying the water are heated by the hot gases, and not by the fire itself. The advantages of a gravity-feed boiler are that cheap graded fuel can be used and there is a slow fire, so very little clinker and ash accumulate. The advantages of automatic stoking are that the stoking does not need attention and cleaning operations are not so heavy, because a lighter fuel is used and a slow draught maintained. Automatic stoking reduces labour costs on a large scale and is a great convenience on a small scale. Breakdown possibilities are guarded against by the setting up of warning electric bells in the home, and temperature is controlled by a thermostat. Therefore, no fuel is burnt unnecessarily and an even temperature is maintained.

### OIL-BURNERS

These are used for a low-pressure hot-water system, and work

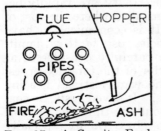

FIG. 17.—A Gravity Feed. The coal falls from hopper to the fire bed.

on the same principle as solid-fuel boilers—the hot water rises by convection and the cold water circulates past the burner to become heated in its turn. The advantages of oil are that it needs less attention, makes less hard work, and less dirty work. The maintenance costs, however, are heavy.

An oil-burner of the Valor type is sometimes used for direct heating on a small scale, but it is an expensive

**41**

and, unless carefully managed, dangerous method. Oil-burners are very useful in time of boiler and electricity breakdown, however, or during a severe frost when extra heat is needed.

The most satisfactory type of burner is that in which the hot water in the pipes is heated by the fuel gases. The gases are led up long stack-pipes, and in this way the danger of poisonous fumes is lessened. Copper is used for the pipes, to prevent rusting and excessive loss of heat, while the whole is painted for appearance and protection. The smallest heater will heat a house 9 × 6 feet, and uses paraffin oil.

When there is a critical breakdown of the heating system in cold weather, and the plants are liable to be killed if there is no other means of heating available, protect them by means of candles placed in flower-pots. Eight-hour candles at the rate of twelve to fourteen per 18-foot × 12-foot house will keep the temperature just above freezing. Newspaper will also help to protect the plants if laid over them several sheets thick.

## GAS

This is also used for heating the water in a hot-water system, but the disadvantage of fumes, danger of fire, and expense outweigh the advantages of cheaper maintenance. Gas-stoves that burn outside the house are now a possibility. They can be thermostatically controlled. Enquiry should be made of the local Gas Company's offices for particulars of new systems and costs before installation.

## ELECTRIC IMMERSION HEATERS

These are also used, and where electricity is cheap and there is a hot-water system already installed it can be modernised by the installation of electric heaters. Direct tubular electrical heaters are most useful, however, and will be discussed later.

## ELECTRIC CABLE IN SOIL AND AIR

Soil heating and air heating by electricity are rapidly becoming more popular, and are being installed where the cost of electrical power is not too heavy. It is economical to have electrical heating installed where electricity costs $\frac{1}{2}d.$ to $\frac{3}{4}d.$ a unit.

Greenhouse heating costs must be carefully considered, as fuel constitutes approximately a quarter of the total expenses.

In Germany and France before the war electrical heating was very common in large crop houses. It saved costs, as coal supplied to the power stations was about one-third the price of that supplied to the private consumer. In Germany especially glass-houses were built near the power-stations to reduce overheads and produce crops cheaply. In America certain crops are grown on matting dipped into electrically heated tanks containing plant nutrients in water solution. Small firms in this country have also experimented in this way, but these methods are not being rapidly adopted.

Soil heaters are used for shallow-rooting crops, *e.g.*, lettuce in frames, and for portable " De-Dutchable " houses. Soil heating is especially useful also for propagating frames and for early crops grown in frames or under hot-bed conditions. A complete soil-heating outfit is supplied by most electrical firms, and consists of standard 230-volt A.C. cable, a transformer, and bare wire for use in the soil itself. The cable can be run from the nearest power point, the transformer being needed to reduce the voltage to twelve or less volts, suitable for the bare wire which is in actual contact with the soil.

When there are cuttings in a propagating frame, 6 inches of sand is recommended to cover the cable, and 12 inches of soil should cover this.

To prevent loss of heat it is advisable to insulate the sides of the frame and paint them with bitumen. A 6-inch layer of clinker at the bottom of the bed beneath the cable, and extending 1 foot either way, will also help to conserve heat.

The number of watts needed to heat a square foot of soil is five for a border and four or less for a frame. A frame 6 feet × 4 feet will therefore use a loading of 90–100 watts and burn approximately one unit of electricity per day, and therefore the cost will be $\frac{3}{4}d$. to 1$d$. per day.

Air can be treated by direct tubular heaters; the advantage of these is that they can be put where wanted, but they are generally bracketed on the wall. Heaters are supplied by electrical firms in sizes from 2 feet upwards and from 100 watts. The size and wattage of the heater will depend on the amount of air to be heaped and to what temperature.

A house 18 feet × 12 feet × 8 feet is a cubic measure of 1,728 cubic feet, and at 1·25 watts per cubic foot, the amount of wattage will be 2,162. Using 100-watt heaters, it will be seen that twenty-two heaters will be needed, or two heaters of 1,500 watts. Where sizes do not exactly fit requirements it is usual to take the nearest size, but in this way the wattage may be higher, and more electricity used.

A thermostat is essential, and costs very little. The thermostat cuts off the electrical supply when the maximum temperature is reached and switches on again when the temperature falls. The thermostat can be set at a certain minimum for night, and it should be attached to an alarm bell so that if there is a breakdown, the bell will waken whoever is responsible for the heating.

# THE GREENHOUSE

The advantages of electrical heating are fairly obvious, because this type of fuel is clean, quiet, fumeless, and controllable. It is used only when wanted, and is easily installed at specified points. Labour costs are low, and so also are maintenance and repair costs. Electricity can generally be relied upon, and does not involve so much time as do stoking and cleaning boilers. The cost of installation is not excessive and is soon recovered, and where electricity costs less than one penny a unit it is very economical. It is advisable, however, to call in a reliable electrical contractor to install the outside wiring and fuse-boxes, etc. A well-established electrical system should last five years at the minimum without serious trouble.

## POSITION OF HEATING IN THE HOUSE

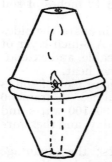

Fig. 18. — Emergency Heating. Candles in flower-pots.

The position of the heating in the greenhouse varies with the size of the house and the type of crop grown. The type of heating system also has an influence on its position.

In a small-span greenhouse used as a plant house, and where the heating system is low-pressure hot water, the pipes are generally placed under the staging. See diagram on page 16.

The number of flow and return pipes depends on the amount of heat needed. The hot air from under the pipes rises through the staging and warms the pot plants standing on the benches.

In a vinery or peach house, where the trees are trained against the wall or glass, the pipes are bracketed to the inner and outer walls, so that the heat is available to the growing trees.

In large crop tomato and lettuce houses the pipes are near the soil, to warm both soil and air.

Crop houses which are designed for forcing bulbs or chrysanthemums need overhead heating, because the air should be of an even temperature and it is not essential to heat the pots or soil borders.

The pipes should be supported by brick tiers or hooks, and nothing should be put on the pipes.

Electrical heaters are bracketed on the walls of the greenhouse as near to the soil as possible.

## USES OF GREENHOUSES

Greenhouses may be heated or unheated, according to the availability of fuels, the crops which are to be grown, and the amount of money to be spent. It may be found that the railway station is too far away to make the extra costs involved in cartage economical, or there may be no local labour to keep the fires going from 6 a.m. to 10 p.m. at night. On a large cropping scale these and other factors are considered before the erection of the ranges.

Cold houses are useful in many ways, as they give protection against varying temperatures and cold winds and will bring plants on earlier than is normal. Therefore it is possible to bring bulbs and early spring flowers into bloom for massed effect in the greenhouse or the living house. Also many half-hardy plants are kept in a cold house during the winter, and bedding plants can be started or sown earlier. In the summer the house can be utilised for cucumbers or tomatoes, and there is a variety of lettuce—Cheshunt, Early Ball—which will only grow in a cold house.

The heated greenhouse is infinitely more useful than the unheated greenhouse, for there is practically no plant which cannot be grown there, as the conditions in the house are controlled completely. Flowers and fruit from every climate can be attempted, and will give satisfaction.

For convenience, heated plant houses are divided into several categories, depending on the maximum and minimum temperatures, the general run of heated houses being as follows :—

|  | *Winter Temp.* | | |
|---|---|---|---|
|  | *Min. Night Temp.*<br>° F. | *Day Temp.*<br>° F. | *Summer Temp.* |
| Stove . . . | 65–70 | 75–80 | |
| Cool stove . . | 60 | 65–70 | |
| Intermediate . | 50 | 55–60 | 5° F. higher than |
| Cool . . . | 40 | 50–55 | winter temp. |
| Cold . . . | Just above 32 | 45–50 | |
| Conservatory . | 32–40 | 50–60 | |

The temperatures cover the range of plants grown in greenhouses and provide the conditions needed for each section of plants. The temperatures are kept even by careful ventilation, watering, and control of artificial and solar heat.

These houses can be built as separate units, but are usually found connected together in a range, so that the heating is conserved by having fewer outside walls.

If the show house is in the centre, it can be reached from the outside without causing draughts or discomfort to the other plants, and it can also be used as a conservatory.

The amount of ventilation and watering necessary depends on the temperature range, and the cooler the house the more ventilation is needed and the less watering.

# THE GREENHOUSE

Large crop houses and houses used for one crop only have the temperatures regulated for that particular crop.

## USES OF BORDERS, STAGING, AND WALLS

Where there are borders in the house, they are generally used for growing quick one-season crops, or for plants which need many years to complete their growth. Small exotic plants needing very careful attention are grown in pots so that this attention can be accurately carried out.

The borders are, therefore, used for cucumbers, tomatoes, lettuce, bulbs, and where only a part of the plant is used, *e.g.*, fruit, flower, or leaf, and the whole crop is then scrapped and the border cleaned.

Vines, peaches, roses, asparagus, and other plants which do not require disturbance, and which crop year after year, are also grown in specially prepared borders.

Staging is used for potted plants, seed-boxes, and supporting climbers. Many exotic climbing plants are grown in pots on the staging, and are trained up the cross-bars and across the house.

Walls support peaches, vines, apricots, and climbing flowering plants. Where these plants are supported by walls, the borders should be specially prepared.

## PROPAGATING CASES

It is important to have a special house for propagating or if this is not possible, a " case " can be erected in the warmest house. The conditions needed for ready rooting are warmth, good drainage, and plenty of moisture overhead as well as in the soil. Soft-wood cuttings, leaf-bud cuttings, and leaf cuttings can be taken and grown into new plants with the help of a propagating case. It resembles a garden frame in construction and size, and usually stands on an iron staging. There is a covering, which is usually an ordinary garden light, to let in sun and prevent moisture from escaping. It should also be possible to shade the case to prevent scorching.

The case is usually filled up with a very light loam and sandy compost with a certain amount of leaf-mould. This is packed down and covered with an inch or two of sharp sand or ground pumice. This compost is put over a layer of ash, for better drainage.

Where really hot conditions are needed at the roots, electrical heating panels can be put in the bottom of the case, or the case can be supported on bricks over a hot pipe.

On a small scale, cuttings can be put into special sandy compost in a pot, and this pot put into a larger one, the space

46

in between being packed with peat or sphagnum moss, which is kept damp.

The sand is to provide good drainage, as the cuttings are watered continuously. Sand and moss keep the propagating case free from disease.

## MAINTENANCE

### HEAT

The heat supplied to plants is both from the sun and by artificial means, and this must be controlled to give the right temperature. If the weather is dull and much heat is being lost to the air, fire heat or electrical heat must be increased, and vice versa. In summer the greenhouse is warmed by solar heat only, except when temperatures of over 100° F. are needed, and the sun's heat is controlled by shading in hot weather or by close ventilating in cool.

The most important fact to bear in mind is to keep the temperature even, and this means continual attention. If the wind changes, or there is no sun, or there is a shower of rain, the vents may need altering, and the artificial heat must be increased or decreased. There should be a maximum or minimum thermometer in every house, and this should be in constant use.

Hot-water pipes should never get so hot that they cannot be touched.

### WATERING

Watering pot plants is a very exacting task. It is extremely easy to over-water them and this causes more failures than any other factor. It is better to keep plants UNDER-watered rather than OVER-watered. Each plant needs individual attention, and the requirements should not be judged by the surface of soil alone. It is advisable to have a small tapper and to tap each pot with it. If the pot gives a ringing sound then water is needed; if a dull sound, no water is required. This test, combined with the general appearance of the plant, should be adequate in judging its requirements. When watering, fill the pot up to the top and let the water soak through. Water infrequently and thoroughly rather than give a sprinkle every day. The state of the weather also has a bearing on watering, as on dull days the plants will need less water. Sickly or diseased plants also require less water.

When potting up, leave a watering space at the top of the pot, which will, of course, vary with the requirements of the plant. The soil of a newly-potted plant should be allowed to settle for a day before watering (the soil should be thoroughly moist before potting), and when the soil is watered, a rose should be used on the can, so as not to disturb the surface soil.

The majority of pot plants have a " resting " period, which varies with the country of origin. During this resting period leaves die and the plant becomes dormant. Most pot plants should not be watered in this condition, but allowed to dry out until signs of fresh growth appear. Deciduous shrubs, *e.g.*, fuchsias and hydrangeas, should be given only a small amount of water, if any, during the resting period.

The times of watering pot plants in the winter (October–April) are as follows : in the morning as soon as the temperature is beginning to rise and, if necessary, again at two o'clock ; in the summer (April–September) ; in the morning as before, and also late in afternoon or evening. This should be the heaviest watering, when the plants will not lose so much by transpiration.

Syringeing is also important, to get a moist atmosphere, and to lower the temperature. It also checks insects, washes the foliage, softens dormant buds, and helps young leaves to stand up to warm atmospheric conditions. Syringeing is carried out only in warm or hot houses—once a day in winter and twice or four times a day in summer. Syringeing helps humidity control.

Plants grown in the borders need great quantities of water, but watering them is not so exacting a task as watering pot plants. When the borders are double-dug and prepared in the winter, it is usual to flood the subsoil at the same time. Where large crops of tomatoes are grown, 300,000 gallons of water may be used to flood the borders—100,000 gallons at a time. This heavy watering provides a reservoir to give the plants a good start in the spring. Vineries and peach houses are watered in the spring when growth is commencing, and the soil is kept moist the whole growing season.

Growing crops should be watered daily, the amount varying with the temperature. Borders should never be just lightly watered, however, as this does more harm than good. The times for watering are as for pot plants.

The reason for keeping the atmosphere moist or humid is to prevent excess evaporation from the plants, and therefore the humidity must increase as the temperature rises higher. Humidity control must be combined with watering and ventilation : for example, excess watering is bad for the plants if the atmosphere is too damp and they cannot lose the water, and under-watering is to be avoided if the air is too dry so that they transpire too freely and flag. Where there is plenty of ventilation, water vapour is quickly lost to the air, and must be replaced frequently.

So the humidity of the greenhouse is mainly regulated by

Carnations under Glass

*Photos*]                                                                *[Humphrey and Vera Joel*

Carnations in the Greenhouse

Muscari armeniacum

*Photos*]

[*H. Smith*

Tulipa tarda (T. dasystemon)

watering and syringeing the air. When a high humidity is required, as in a tropical house, the air and plants are syringed, and thus the atmosphere is charged with water vapour. All houses are filled with water vapour to a degree, but in the cooler houses damping down the paths, staging, and pipes is sufficient to charge the air with moisture, without additional syringeing. Damping down is regulated by the weather : if it is dull, and water is not evaporating readily, damping down is limited to the pipes only; if the outside temperature is very high, the pipes will be watered several times a day. In warm houses an iron trough, full of water—which is evaporating all the time—is often kept over the pipes. Normal times for damping down and syringeing are in the morning and evening when watering is being done, and several times in between should the necessity arise.

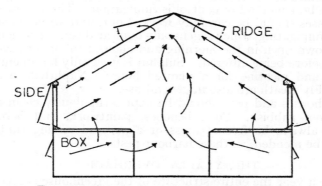

Fig. 19.—Hot air rises. Air circulation when box, side and ridge ventilators are open.

VENTILATION

The objects of ventilating are to regulate the temperature and to freshen and dry the air. The houses should be ventilated on a rising temperature, by degrees, to keep the temperatures rising. Close down as the temperatures fall, or at sundown if they have been high all day. As it is imperative to avoid draughts, houses are usually ventilated on the leeward side. Ventilating should be done a crack at a time, so that there is no sharp fall in the temperature.

The order in which the ventilators are opened is top vents first, then side, and then box. In houses which need a moist atmosphere and plenty of ventilation open the top ventilators a crack and use the box ventilators, so that there is plenty of air circulating, but it is warmed by the pipes before reaching the plants.

D

# THE GREENHOUSE

The houses should be closed while still warm, so that the heat can be utilised during the night.

In foggy weather ventilate fully for a while and force the fire heat; then close the whole house to keep the air pure.

In modern greenhouses, where temperature is kept even by thermostatic control, ventilating is only necessary to change the air, and does not need to be regulated so carefully.

## CONTROL OF PESTS AND DISEASES

The fight against pests and diseases goes on daily because the conditions which suit the various plants to perfection are also ideal for pests and diseases (see Chapter XVII).

## FUMIGATION

Baits and insecticides can be used against pests under glass, but the best method of control is fumigation. The volumes of the houses should be carefully worked out, and all vents shut before fumigating, which is generally done at dusk. The houses are thrown open in the morning and allowed to air for several hours before being entered. Sulphur is used only for an empty house, and nicotine for a planted house. Naphthalene and White Fly Death are also in general use.

The houses and pots should be kept scrupulously clean and free from rubbish. Pots, benches, paintwork, and borders should always be free of moss or algæ, and rotting timbers should be mended, as these harbour pests.

## THE YEARLY OVERHAUL

Once a year the entire structure of the greenhouse is given a thorough overhaul, this is usually done in January, when the houses are empty. If there is a crop present, then the overhaul can be carried out later in the spring, before summer planting. The paintwork should be cleaned thoroughly with hot water and disinfectant or cresylic acid. The glass should be scrubbed inside and out. If it is necessary, paint the woodwork with a good white paint and the ironwork also, to prevent rust. Clean the benches well underneath, where pests are liable to hibernate, and treat the brickwork under the staging with hot quicklime to clean and sterilise it. Pipes are also painted, not with blacklead or paint, as these give off fumes, but with a mixture of vegetable black and linseed oil.

At this time of the year needed repairs should be carried out on doors and vents. Glass is also repaired and putty renewed.

Tanks are scrubbed, and taps fitted with new washers if necessary. All the pots and boxes should be scrubbed with hot water and disinfectant, and the gravel on the staging

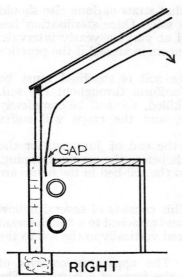

FIG. 20.—Arrangement of Staging. The warm air rises through gap.

removed and washed, and the stages scrubbed before it is put back.

This is also a good time to check up on boilers, to see that there are no leaks or that the pipes are not furred up. Also make sure that the supply tank has enough water and that all doors and dampers on the boiler are working and fit well.

Every five years the borders should be removed to a depth of 18 inches to weather out of doors. Whether removed or not, the soil should be thoroughly double-dug and manure incorporated during the winter. It is a common practice on a commercial scale, and advisable on a small scale, to flood the borders while being double dug, so that the subsoil is saturated.

This can be effectively carried out by means of a small irrigating "Rainmaster", which works on a swivel system, and which covers many square yards at a time.

### SOIL STERILISATION

Soil sterilisation is carried out at the beginning of the year. This may be done by steam, electricity, or, on a small scale, by baking. Many crops fail because the roots are attacked by pests or diseases, or because the soil is in a poor physical condition owing to the conditions peculiar to artificial greenhouse culture or to excess of one crop. Soil sterilisation will destroy the organisms responsible for disease and leave the useful bacteria alive, and it will also improve the condition

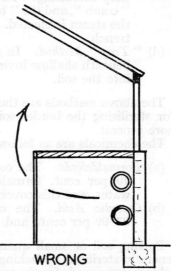

FIG. 21.—Where there is no gap the hot air is lost to plants on staging.

of the soil. It is recommended that straw or dung also should be incorporated to " open " the soil. Once sterilisation has been begun it must be continued at varying yearly intervals, for the effects will be lost and dangers increased if the practice is discontinued.

The temperature at which the soil is sterilised must be between 210 and 212° F., and uniform throughout the soil, otherwise vital bacteria will be killed, the soil be completely sterilised and rendered infertile, and the crops will suffer badly.

It is advisable to sterilise by the end of January, for the border must be flooded afterwards before the spring cropping.

The methods used for STEAMING the soil-bed in the house are as follows :—

(a) *Hoddeston Pipe System.* This consists of several hollow tubes bracketed together and attached to a 2-inch steam main. The pipes are placed vertically in the soil to the depth required.

(b) *The " Harrow " Method.* The apparatus consists of hollow pipes arranged in the form of a harrow. The pipes are pushed into the soil, and the steam ejected through the ends.

(c) *The " Small-Grid " Method.* This is especially useful for deep sterilising. The apparatus is in the shape of a " comb ", and the " teeth " possess holes through which the steam is ejected. The apparatus must be put in a trench.

(d) *" Tray " Method.* In this case the steam is introduced beneath shallow inverted trays, and the steam diffuses into the soil.

The above methods are those generally used on a large scale. For sterilising the border soil on a small scale, chemicals are more general.

The chemicals are as follows :—

(a) *Formaldehyde.* The concentration used is one gallon of 40 per cent. formaldehyde to forty-eight gallons of water, and this covers 15 square yards of soil.

(b) *Cresylic Acid.* The concentration of cresylic acid is 97–99 per cent., and one gallon does 9 square yards.

Potting soil or small quantities of soil from the border are generally sterilised by baking or electricity. There are special baking-ovens made for the purpose, and on a small scale the soil can be baked in a copper or in a tray over a bunsen burner.

52

Close-up of a Modern Cypripedium hybrid

Oxalis enneaphylla

Vanda, tricolor, *var.* suavis

# FRAMES

Baked soil should be left for six weeks before use. Soil when electrically sterilised must be wet to enable the current to flow through the soil. Small sterilising bins run by electricity are much in evidence, and are of good design. Those supplied by electrical firms can take from ½ cwt. up to several cwts. of soil at a time. Soil sterilised by electricity only needs heating to a temperature of 180° F., which should be maintained for forty minutes.

It must be remembered above all when sterilising that the process must be THOROUGHLY carried out, or more harm than good will result. The temperature must not rise above 212°. Open, dry soils steam better than wet ones. Over-baked soils can be rendered infertile. Sterilisation is well worth while if carried out with a knowledge of what is happening, and with care.

## FRAMES

It is always advisable to have a few frames, even if the green-house is very small, because, used in conjunction with the greenhouse, they make it more profitable. "Wing" frames attached to the greenhouse itself will be protected from the weather, and close at hand for transfer of plant material. These and other cold frames take surplus material for resting in the summer, and are useful for cuttings and for growing early vegetables. For instance, after pot plants have finished blooming in the greenhouse they can be rested in the frame (primulas, cyclamen, etc.) during the summer months. Soft-wood cuttings can also be raised in frames (violas and lavender).

Early lettuce, turnips, radish, and carrot for the house can be grown in cold frames, but are most successful where the bed has been specially prepared with hot manure or is heated with an electric cable.

Plants for the herbaceous border and for summer bedding can be raised from seed in a greenhouse and hardened off in the cold frame. The cold frame is the counterpart of the greenhouse, and is used to harden off plants before they are put out in the garden.

Frames should face south and be sheltered. Where there are several frames, they are best constructed together in rows in a specially sheltered part of the garden, called the "frame yard". Wing frames are built on to the greenhouses under the sills. To protect them from direct sunshine in summer and frost in winter the frames should be provided with matting which rolls up. This matting may be of hessian or canvas. Straw mats are also placed over the frames in winter to keep out the frost.

# THE GREENHOUSE

Permanent hot and cold frames are constructed of wood or brick and have properly-fitting lights. Hot frames constructed in this manner are usually those supplied with pipes or electric cable. Hot-bed frames are temporary—*i.e.*, they are constructed in January over hot manure and weathered soil-beds. They grow forced spring crops, and are dismantled in late spring.

## ENGLISH, FRENCH, AND DUTCH " LIGHTS "

There are three types of " light " which is the glass frame that covers a wooden or brick structure to form a cold or hot frame—English, French, and Dutch lights. The latter is the most valuable, as it is of light weight, and can be used for many purposes. Permanent frames usually have French lights, which are more durable than the Dutch, and constructed to take smaller panes of glass, so that breakages can be replaced more easily and cheaply.

English lights are the heaviest, and therefore less popular than the other kinds.

The frames may be lean-to types or span, and the lights are made to slide on and off the lean-to, or are hinged on to the span. The hinged lights are opened by stays, the sliding lights have handles at either end.

## HEATING FRAMES

The general methods of heating frames are : (1) by hot bed made in January, (2) by hot pipes under the soil, or (3) by an electric cable. Hot manure is the most favourable, as it gives a gentle, natural, non-drying heat and adds to the fertility of the soil.

## WATERING FRAMES

Frames need careful watering, as the space between the soil and glass is not considerable, and therefore very quickly becomes saturated. In cold weather, frames should be kept dry, and in hot weather the lights should be removed completely, as the glass would draw the plants, dry the air, and upset the water balance. When ventilating lean-to frames, open every other light at the top and the in-between ones at the bottom, to get an even flow of air.

Cuttings need close conditions—*i.e.*, little ventilation and a good deal of watering. The lights over propagating frames should therefore be shaded in hot sunshine.

All frames should be kept clean and should be painted as often as the greenhouse. It is a good plan to include the yearly overhaul of the frames with that of the greenhouses, then the materials for painting, puttying, and whitewashing are at hand.

**54**

# CHAPTER II

# FERTILIZERS : ORGANIC AND ARTIFICIAL

MANURES play an important part, particularly in greenhouses where crops are grown in beds or borders. They are also essential for the success of some plants grown in pots.

In the first place, they are a source of actual food elements, which they directly contribute to the plants' necessities, and secondly—and this is true particularly of so-called organic manures, such as farmyard manure—by reason of the fermentation which takes place in the manure, chemical changes are brought about in the soil which liberate materials required by the plants. In light, sandy soils the farmyard manures also act like a sponge in holding moisture, and they also keep the soil well aerated, so that the useful soil bacteria can live and supply valuable food for the plants.

## ORGANIC MANURES

It is because it fulfils these functions that farmyard manure, or its equivalent, is so specially valuable.

Not only does it directly add to the soil constituents needed for the healthy life of plants, but also through the fermentation which it undergoes, and the acids produced thereby, it liberates from the soil itself plant foods which would not otherwise be available.

Moreover, by its texture, and by the gases produced in the process of its fermentation, it tends to lighten the soil and keep its texture open. For similar reasons there is considerable value in such manurial substances as leaves, lawn cuttings, road sweepings, vegetable refuse, fish guano, and seaweed. All organic waste, indeed, has some manurial value. It is very great in the case of such substances as cow manure, fowl manure, pig manure, and night soil. Wood-ash and soot are also useful, the former largely on account of the potash it contains, the latter for its ammonia.

### Natural Manure

Whenever possible, natural, rather than artificial manure, should be employed in the garden. The rubbish-heap, composed of turf parings, soft vegetable matter, and clearings from the garden, forms a compost which puts heart into the land.

Artificial manures are to the land what stimulants or tonics are to the human being, useful for a season, but imparting no lasting and enduring benefit, and incapable of rendering the soil fit to keep up a sustained effort over a considerable period of time. Artificial manures, useful as they may be for the crop that immediately follows on their introduction, are soon exhausted, and leave no traces of their influence if not constantly renewed.

In its dissolution the contents of the rubbish-heap adds to the humus, or vegetable mould, which forms so essential a part of fertile soils, and supplies, or is the means of supplying, all growing plants with the food that is so absolutely necessary to their growth and well-being.

## The Compost Heap

The gardener who is anxious to have a good display, or to secure bumper crops should always have at hand :—

All the leaves which can be got together, except those in the shrubberies, which should be dug in.

A heap of clean road-grit (from non-tarred roads).

A heap of sand, silver or river.

A good stack of turves cut from some pasture.

A heap of cow-dung.

A heap of stable-dung.

A stack of turfy peat.

The compost of the rubbish-heap *must* have reached a sufficient stage of decomposition before it is mingled with the soil. In the suburbs of large towns, where ground is valuable and space limited, it often happens that kitchen gardens are severely overtaxed, through a prevailing notion that good cultivation and abundant manuring make up for lack of room. This is true to a certain extent, but it has its limits, for instances are not wanting to show that serious results are traceable to this cause. The ground becomes filled with insects, undecomposed manure is worked into the soil after each crop —it is trenched in, dug in or sometimes laid on the surface as mulch—and all kinds of half-rotted rubbish and garden refuse are trenched in 2 or 3 feet deep. The result is obvious, for where decomposition takes place, many agencies hasten the work; insects are bred in vast numbers, club root and canker are prevalent, and good gardening becomes impossible. The remedy for this state of things is a copious dressing with unslaked lime, burning the soil, or the substitution of new soil, if the surface-parings of a pasture are conveniently obtainable. But prevention is better than cure, and although this warning does not affect the greenhouse to any extent, one always has a rubbish heap in a garden, so this note is not altogether out of place.

## INORGANIC ARTIFICIAL FERTILIZERS

It is, however, not always convenient to obtain a sufficiency of stable or farmyard and organic manure for the requirements of one's garden. In such cases resort must be had to various chemical manures, most of which provide plant food in a highly concentrated form. These, for the most part, have but little effect—at any rate directly—on the structure or chemical activity of the soil itself. They add no humus to the soil and do not affect the tilth, and for this reason, if for no other, they cannot entirely replace organic manures.

The three elements which it is generally necessary to add to soil in the form of manure if crops, whether vegetable, fruit, or flowers, are to be raised year after year on the same ground, are phosphates, potash, and nitrogen. And it must be remembered that these have not only to be added to the soil, but to be added in such a form that they are, or readily become, soluble, and so capable of being absorbed by the finer rootlets of plants.

## NITROGENOUS FERTILIZERS

The most expensive of these elements is nitrogen—that is to say, nitrogen in a form available for plant food. Apart from guano and other mixed-element manures, the most useful nitrogenous manures are *nitrate of soda* and *sulphate of ammonia*, the latter should be applied early in the spring at the rate of 1 lb. to the square rod. The former fertiliser is often applied at the rate of 1 lb. to the square rod as a top-dressing during the growing season. *Nitrate of potash* is also good, but is much more expensive. Nitrogenous manures act very rapidly, and appreciable growth is often visible a few days after application. The plants become noticeably greener and more vigorous. Nitrates must, however, not be added to excess, or rank growth will follow, accompanied by lack of flowers and fruit and susceptibility to attack by fungoid diseases.

## POTASH FERTILIZERS

These help the development of sugar and starch in seeds, tubers, and fruit, and improve the colour and size of the blooms. Of potash manures, *kainit* is, on the whole, the cheapest and most useful; it should be dug well into the soil at the rate of $2\frac{1}{2}$ lb. to the square rod early in the spring. On heavy soils, *sulphate of potash* applied at the rate of $1\frac{1}{2}$ lb. to the square rod in the early spring is also valuable. *Note.*—2 lb. to the square rod = 1 oz. to the square yard. A simple way of

57

providing potash for pot plants or a small plot of ground in a greenhouse is to add wood ashes and the ashes from burnt weeds in generous quantities.

## PHOSPHATIC FERTILIZERS

These assist the correct development of the plant, its fruit or seed, and its roots. The three commonest forms of phosphatic manure are *superphosphate of lime, dissolved bones,* and *basic slag.* Superphosphate is the quickest acting, whilst basic slag is the cheapest, slowest acting, and therefore most enduring. It is best applied in autumn. Superphosphate is usually applied just before the plants are mature, at the rate of 5 lb. to the square rod, and should be thoroughly mixed with the top 4 inches of the soil.

Basic slag is a chemical manure much used of late years, consisting largely of lime, phosphoric acid, and various iron oxides. It contains other constituents as well as these, but in small proportions. Its effects are much the same as those of superphosphate, but almost twice the quantity is required to produce a given result. It does not succeed mixed with ammonia salts, as it sets free the ammonia and wastes valuable material, but is useful with nitrates. It is most useful on medium or heavy soils which are deficient in lime, or are too wet and stiff; but to obtain the full advantage the soil must already be fairly well provided with organic matter. As a manure it is good for flowering shrubs, roses, and fruit trees.

Phosphates encourage the formation of fibrous roots, cause earlier development of the plants, and counteract rank, sappy growth caused by excess of nitrogen in the soil. They should be applied every third year.

Where chemical manures are applied to trees and plants which have made full root-growth, so that the soil is filled with roots, the best plan, in order to avoid injury to the plants, is to scatter the manure where it is required, and then lightly to " point it in " with a small fork, placing the manure only just under the surface of the ground should the plants be in beds or borders in the greenhouse or by means of watering for pot plants. In this way the manure is protected from loss by wind or rain, while the delicate roots are not liable to suffer, as they are if the manure is dug in with a spade.

## JOHN INNES COMPOSTS

Two excellent composts which will be found to be ideal for greenhouse use have been developed by the John Innes Horticultural Institution. They are the John Innes Seed Compost,

58

for seed-sowing, and the John Innes Potting Compost, for potting and general plant growing. These composts can be successfully used for the majority of greenhouse plants.

*John Innes Seed Compost* is made up as follows : 2 parts by bulk loam, 1 part by bulk moss peat, and 1 part by bulk coarse sand or grit. To each bushel of the mixture should be added 1½ oz. superphosphate (18% phosphoric acid) and ¾ oz. chalk.

*John Innes Potting Compost* is made up as follows : 7 parts by bulk loam, 3 parts by bulk moss peat, and 2 parts by bulk coarse sand or grit. To each bushel of this compost should be mixed ¾ oz. of chalk and ¼ lb. of John Innes base fertilizer. The base fertilizer consists of : 2 lb. hoof and horn (⅛ grist, 13% nitrogen), 2 lb. superphosphate (18% phosphoric acid), and 1 lb. sulphate of potash (48% pure potash).

Both these composts will keep in good condition for several weeks but storage for longer periods is not recommended. It should be remembered that thorough mixing of the contents is most important.

## THE USES OF LIME

The nitrates, phosphates, and potash supplied by manures are quite inaccessible to most plants in a soil deficient in lime. Lime, too, assists the bacteria which render organic matter in soil available to crops, and is itself an essential plant food. It makes heavy soil more porous, and therefore better drained and warmer, cleanses the soil of insect and fungoid pests, and sweetens sour soil, which has become deficient in lime.

In greenhouses that grow crops on commercial lines, the soil in due course becomes sour, this state should be rectified as soon as possible by the application of hydrated lime at 10 oz. to the square yard, the dressing being repeated every four to five years. If the soil is not sour, but merely deficient in lime, dressings of slaked lime, 6 oz. to the square yard for heavy soil, or 10 oz. to the square yard of carbonate of lime on light or sandy soil, will be sufficient. Lime must never be applied at the same time as farmyard manure. When applied it should be perfectly dry and powdered as finely as possible, must be evenly dusted over the ground, and immediately well pricked into the top 3 to 4 inches of the soil, which must also be dry. Whether the lime is applied in the form of slaked lime or carbonate of lime depends on the nature of the soil, and the time of the year.

# CHAPTER III

# METHODS OF PROPAGATION

THERE are several methods by which plants may be propagated : they may be raised from seed ; cuttings may be
taken ; they can be layered ; with a great number, especially
herbaceous perennials, the roots may be divided ; of some,
root-cuttings can be secured ; a few can be propagated by leaf-
cuttings ; while others, mostly fruit trees, roses, and many
trees and shrubs, are propagated by budding or grafting.
Below we describe in detail the various processes.

## PLANTS FROM SEED

Generally speaking, seeds retain full vitality for one or two
years only in ordinary circumstances. From this we gather
it is better to sow seeds as soon as convenient after ripening
or in the spring of the following year.

### Preserving and Storing Seeds

Seed should be stored in a dark, cool place ; it should be
kept dry and, above all, in an even temperature. It is best
placed in tins with tightly fitting lids, in thoroughly clean
glass bottles, if kept in the dark, or in glazed paper impermeable to moisture. Soft absorbent paper is bad, as the seeds
will either dry and shrivel up or, if kept in too moist a place,
will get damp and will rot. Do not leave the seeds in their
pods, as is so often advised, for after a time the pods dry up
and draw both moisture and vitality from the seeds.

When saving seeds from the garden, they should not be
gathered too early, but must be allowed ample time to ripen.

The seeds of such trees as the chestnut, oak, walnut, and
magnolia are oily in nature and, unless carefully stored in
slightly moist sand or fibre, are apt to shrivel. They are therefore best sown as soon as they are ripe, but the seeds of most
other shrubs are better sown under glass, in well-drained boxes
of sandy soil, in February or March, and when germinated and
sufficiently high, should be thinned-out to $1\frac{1}{2}$ to 2 inches apart ;
the less hardy kinds being hardened-off in a cold frame and
the hardy kinds planted out in nursery beds in the open.
The seeds of most shrubs and trees germinate in a month or
two ; some, however, like the rose and thorn, take a year and

## Propagating Pelargoniums

1. Suitable plant from which cuttings may be taken, preferably in June and July. The cuttings should be kept dry for 24 hours before potting. 2. The plant after the cuttings have been removed. 3. The cuttings, showing the straight cut just below a joint. 4. The cuttings struck, 1½ in. deep, round the sides of a 4-in. pot of light sandy soil. The pot should be placed in a shady position under glass. See page 488.

## Sowing in Boxes and Pans

1. The ingredients of the compost correctly proportioned previously to mixing. 2. "Crocking" the seed box. 3 & 4. The seeds in position. 5. Covering the seed with fine soil. 6. The box covered with glass and paper to keep off the sun. 7. Seedlings placed up near the glass to keep them short-jointed and sturdy.

even more.  The smaller the seed, the finer should be the soil in which it is grown.  The soil in which seed is sown should be tolerably dry—dry enough to crumble lightly when worked with the hand.  It must not clot together in a pasty mess.  Place or position—whether in the open air or under protection— is also an important factor with regard to time.

## SOWING UNDER GLASS

The less hardy plants must be raised under glass, and can generally be sown in a temperature that is slightly higher than that in which the parent plant grows.  The soil for the seed-pans or boxes should consist of a composition of two-thirds good loam and one-third leaf-mould, together with a good sprinkling of sharp silver sand.  The compost should be sieved through a $\frac{1}{4}$-inch mesh, and the soil for covering the seeds through another sieve even finer.  Mix the compost thoroughly, press it gently into the pot or box, and make a level surface just below the rim of the pot.  The seed-pans or boxes should be drained by means of " crocks " or broken pots, an inch of crocks being required in a box or pot 5 inches in depth.  Earthenware pots or pans are preferable, as the earthenware keeps the soil more evenly moist than does the wooden box.  The seeds must be sown thinly in February or March, being watered afterwards, not with a can, but by the pots or pans being immersed nearly to their brims, the water being in this way able to soak up from the bottom.  Set the seed-pans in a frame or greenhouse in moderate but steady heat (about 60° F.).  A sheet of glass should be placed over the boxes, the glass in turn being covered with a sheet of brown paper to keep out the light.  Each day the glass must be lifted so that the condensation may be wiped off, otherwise the seeds will be kept too moist.  No further water need, as a rule, be given until the seeds have germinated.  As soon as the seeds are up (in about three weeks' time), the glass and paper may be removed, and the boxes must be lifted by gradual steps up to within 6 inches of the lights of the house.  If the box is left some distance from the glass, weak, straggling seedlings will result. .  In warm weather it is wise to water the seedlings in the evening, but in the colder weather the watering must be done before lunch time, or there may be a danger of the seedlings " damping off."

### Sowing in a Frame

The seeds may be sown in a frame in exactly the same way as described for sowing in pans or boxes.  The frame should be in a sheltered position, for it is essential to ventilate as much as possible when the weather is sunny and calm.

61

### Pricking-off the Seedlings

When the seedlings are large enough to handle easily, they must be pricked-off, a wooden label being used in place of a small hand-fork. They should be transplanted into boxes of light sandy soil, being set from 1 to 3 inches apart, so that the leaves do not touch (strong-growing kinds 6 inches apart). After this they should again be put in position some 6 inches from the lights. When pricking-off, the wooden label should be inserted in the soil an inch or so from the seedling, whose roots may then be gently levered up without damage—never should seedlings be pulled up between the finger and thumb, as this will badly damage the roots. The seedlings should be planted so that the first pair of leaves show just above the soil. They must be planted firmly, and should have the soil pressed tightly down round the roots and stems, though care must be taken not to injure any part of the seedling. A thin dibble about the size of a pencil should be used to make the holes for the seedlings, and these must not be made too deep, otherwise the roots of the seedlings will not reach the bottom, and the air-pockets left under them will wither their roots. Do not " firm " the seedlings by pressing the earth round the stems with the fingers, but use the dibble, inserting it into the soil in three or four places round the seedlings, about half an inch from them, and to the same depth as when preparing the holes. This will firm the soil all round the seedlings, right down to the bottom of the roots ; the fingers would only press in the top, and the roots would be left loose in the soil. Strongly growing seedlings can be potted up at once, the process of pricking-off being unnecessary. In the case of seeds that germinate irregularly, the first batch of seedlings should be pricked-off as soon as they can be handled, and the seed-boxes should then be replaced, so that the remaining seeds may germinate.

Such treatment is necessary with plants like the Anemone, Auricula, Polyanthus, or Primula. After pricking-off, keep the seedlings in a close atmosphere and shade from the sun for a few days until they are established.

### Hardening-off and Planting-out

In March or April the seedlings should be transplanted into the cold frame, which should contain soil similar to that in the seed-boxes. There they are hardened-off by being gradually allowed more and more air until they are planted out very firmly in the reserve garden in May or early June. Annuals will, of course, be placed in their flowering position.

# METHODS OF PROPAGATION

## Protection in Winter

Half-hardy biennial and perennial seedlings, however, will require protection during the coming winter, and in early October must be lifted, then replanted close together in light sandy soil in boxes, to be stored in the greenhouse in a temperature of about 50° F., or in a cold frame. As much air as possible should be given when the weather is fine and dry, to prevent the plants from "damping-off." Should there be any signs of this, every opportunity should be taken of thoroughly ventilating on dry warm days, the soil being sprinkled very finely with powdered charcoal. In the following spring, the biennials should be set out in their flowering positions, and the perennials must again be placed in the reserve garden. Half-hardy perennials will require protection during each winter, and will again have to be lifted in October and wintered under glass.

It is as well to look at the thermometer the last thing at night and to cover the lights with sacking if the frost is likely to be severe. These mats should not be removed too early in the morning.

Half-hardy perennials or biennials can, of course, be sown in the open in May or June and wintered as stated above. The seeds of hardy plants are frequently sown under glass to procure early and sturdy plants for bedding-out in the spring.

## DIVISION OF ROOTS

There are very few plants for the greenhouse propagated in this way, although there are a few, such as Ferns, Canna, Hedychiums, Bananas, and some of the herbaceous plants, that are useful for conservatory work and have been growing in the open ground, most of which are best divided in March and April. The clumps should be lifted with their roots as entire as possible, that is, with a good "ball" of earth round the fibres. This is done by inserting two forks vertically downwards, one on either side of the plant, with their backs facing each other, and then by levering the clump and its roots gently upwards. When the plant has been lifted, do not, as is so often done, use a spade to cut the roots apart, but carefully divide the plant into as many crowns as possible by means of a sharp knife; this will do the minimum injury to the roots. The strong new outer crowns are those that should be retained, and replanted, the old inner roots being removed.

The stems that have already borne flowers should be cut away from the new crowns, so that only the young and vigorous shoots from the base remain.

# THE GREENHOUSE

## PROPAGATION BY OFFSETS

Offsets afford yet another means of propagation suitable to many herbaceous perennials and to many rock plants. These offsets are growths forming young crowns round the older central crown, and when large enough may be carefully separated from the parent crown and can be potted up into small pots and in some cases should be kept in a cold frame during the winter or transplanted out in the open ground. About a month after the plant has flowered will be found the best time to accomplish this.

## RAISING PLANTS FROM CUTTINGS

### Preparing the Cuttings

Cuttings should be taken of shoots that have ripened or which are beginning to ripen, because in wood which is attaining or has attained maturity the callus so necessary to root formation is more readily induced to show itself. The side-shoots of plants, low down on the stem, are the best for cuttings, and should be taken when the sap is in full motion, because its return by the bark tends to form the callus, or ring, of granular matter from which the roots proceed. The leaves of a cutting must never be cut off, except in so far as may be necessary at its base in order that it may be inserted in the soil. The foliage is the lungs of the plant, and if it is cut, the sap that it contains will be lost to the cutting and prevented from passing downwards to form the callus. Cuttings of plants that are difficult to strike may frequently be induced to do so if a ring is made round them, or if a piece of string is tied round them for a short time before they are taken from the parent plant. The downward flow of the sap is arrested by the tightened ligature and a swelling is caused, which forms a callus from which roots are soon emitted. The cutting must be severed from the parent plant just below the ring or band, and the callus formed should be covered when the cutting is inserted in the soil.

In taking cuttings, strong, sturdy shoots varying from 3 to 12 inches in length should be removed from the plant, with a very sharp knife, by a clean, straight cut just below a joint. If it is possible to take a " heel " or small wedge-shaped portion of the old wood and bark with it, so much the better, and it is then not essential to cut immediately below a joint. The joint need not necessarily be the junction of two stems; it may equally well be the " eye " from which a pair of leaves has sprung. When no " heel " is taken, the cut must be especially clean and just below a joint, but the joint itself

64

**PLATE 3**
A giant-flowered marigold *(Calendula)*.

must be left intact; in fact, about an eighth of an inch of wood should be left below the joint. The " heel," from which all ragged edges should be trimmed, when placed in contact with the ground, provides a larger surface on which roots can form. The length of cuttings is decided by the distance between the joints; when these are, say, an inch apart, the cuttings must be 12 inches long, and over half this length must be buried in the soil. Where the distance between joints is less, the cuttings may be shorter, but all hard-wooded cuttings should have at least 6 inches in the ground, and all cuttings must be inserted right to the bottom of the hole prepared for them.

### Cuttings of Hard-wooded and Soft-wooded Plants

Cuttings of hard-wooded shrubs, such as the Heath or Myrtle, are more difficult to strike than those of soft-wooded plants, such as the Geranium, and for this reason on hard-wooded cuttings the " eyes " on the part of the stem that will be placed underground should be carefully cut out. This will encourage the formation of roots at these places. The position for all cuttings should, of course, be sheltered and shaded from full sun, and although not necessary with hardy plants, most cuttings when planted in the open do better if covered by a hand light until the roots have formed. The less hardy and less vigorous plants should be struck in pots or boxes in a cold frame or under hand lights, while the more delicate still require artificial heat or the bottom-heat of a propagating box. It may be taken as a general rule that cuttings of soft-wooded plants require more heat than those of hard-wooded plants. " Soft " cuttings, as a rule, should not be struck in the open, for, apart from a little heat being desirable, the wind and sun would dry the moisture from their leaves and the roots would never form. A glass covering is, therefore, necessary. Cuttings of soft-wooded plants, such as the Geranium, strike best when they have not too much foliage to bear, and should have the stems shortened to two or three joints beneath the point from which the foliage springs. Never make the cuttings longer than necessary. In the case of the less hardy plants, the soil should be stored in a warm greenhouse for a few days before the cuttings are inserted, and rooting will be more certain and prompt if the cuttings are watered with lukewarm water.

### Hollow-stemmed Plants

There are several plants, like the Pansy or the Honeysuckle, whose stems, when mature, are hollow and useless for ordinary cuttings. In such cases the young shoots must be struck,

E

or with the Honeysuckle both ends of the cutting may be inserted in the soil. There are other plants, such as Dahlias and Lupins, whose cuttings must be taken at the junction of the stems and the roots. These require a glass covering.

## Greenhouse Plants

Cuttings of nearly all the less hardy and greenhouse plants require a propagating case, placed over the hot-water pipes. With the more hardy kinds no artificial heat is needed, except that provided by the glass, but the soil must be kept uniformly warm and moist.

## Shrub Cuttings

This is undoubtedly the most popular method of propagating shrubs. It provides larger plants in a much shorter time than most other means, and ensures that the new plants shall be true to type, which cannot always be relied upon when raising from seeds. This method is resorted to especially when propagating popular varieties and rare shrubs.

Shrub cuttings may be taken at three distinct periods: first in autumn, when the wood has hardened and is quite mature; secondly in September or August, when the shoots have half-matured; and thirdly when the shoots are beginning to ripen in early summer. The last time is, perhaps, the best of the three. Healthy shoots varying from 3 to 6 inches in length should be taken. During these periods, most shrub cuttings may be struck in a close propagating frame in a greenhouse, preferably with slight bottom heat. A gritty sand provides a suitable medium for rooting most cuttings. During August and September a bed of sandy soil in a cold frame, or under hand-lights, cloches, or bell-glasses, provides a medium for rooting cuttings of brooms, double gorse, heaths, etc. During October and November cuttings of very many shrubs may be inserted in sandy soil in a sheltered border outside. These, as a rule, should be longer than the cuttings inserted under glass. They should be fully ripe wood and average 9 to 12 inches in length, from one third to one half being inserted in the soil. Half-matured cuttings, even of hardy shrubs, must, however, be treated like those of the less hardy natures and be struck under glass. The cuttings of most conifers and many evergreens require the protection and moist atmosphere that glass provides. Cuttings inserted in the autumn remain inactive through the winter and do not usually form roots until the following spring. They must, therefore, not be disturbed until the next autumn, when they may be planted-out 12 to 18 inches apart in a nursery bed.

When cuttings are struck in pots or boxes, the latter should be well drained by an inch layer of crocks at the bottom, and must be clean. If they are dirty, the mould will be likely to stick to them when the cuttings are turned out for transplanting and the tender new root fibres may be torn.

## Preparing the Compost

Coarse sand is perhaps the best medium in which to strike cuttings. A light soil through which the air can pass freely is essential to the well-being of all cuttings. That aeration is necessary is proved by the fact that cuttings will strike readily in coco-nut fibre, a material that is extremely pervious to air and which retains moisture for a considerable period. Powdered charcoal also forms a good medium. Perhaps the free access of air through the excellent drainage in such a position is the reason why cuttings root more freely when placed close to the side of the pot.

A good compost for striking the cuttings of most plants can be made by mixing equal quantities of leaf-mould and well-sieved loam and by adding to this a good proportion of coarse sand, and then sieving the whole mixture through a $\frac{1}{4}$-inch mesh. It is always well to sprinkle the surface of the soil which is to receive the cuttings with a layer of coarse sand about 1 inch thick, so that when the dibble is pressed down to form the hole for the cutting, some of the sand will trickle into it and be ready to encourage the production of roots. The sand keeps the soil porous and prevents the base of the cutting from rotting. The soil should be firmed down and the slips inserted at least $1\frac{1}{2}$ inches apart. They must not be placed too close together, or they may " damp-off." Press the earth well down round the cuttings, as they will not root if standing loosely in the soil. If the cuttings can be fairly easily pulled up, it may be taken as an indication that they are not planted sufficiently firmly.

## Setting the Cuttings in the Soil

As has been said, cuttings strike more readily when placed at the side of a pot, than when inserted in its centre. Of ordinary plants about seven cuttings can be placed in a 4-inch pot. No cutting should be set too deeply, but, as in the case of seeds, the depth will depend mainly on the size of the cutting. A good general rule is to set about two-thirds of the length of hard-wooded cuttings in the soil; with soft-wooded cuttings only one-third or one-half should be inserted. Leaves should not be permitted to touch the soil; if they do, they will " damp-off." Water well after insertion.

**67**

When using pots or boxes, it is better, but not necessary, to sink these nearly to their brims in ashes or coco-nut fibre. This will keep the soil at an even temperature. Whether the cuttings are covered by plates of glass, glass bells, or the lights of a frame, the condensation must be wiped off each morning. Once the cuttings have struck, ventilation must be given whenever possible, and decaying leaves must be removed to avoid any possibility of " damping-off." The great thing is to keep the soil at the same temperature as the surrounding air.

### Shade and Ventilation

Too much light, air, water, heat, or cold are alike injurious to cuttings freshly inserted under glass. A close, equable temperature, and a moderate degree of moisture should be maintained until the cuttings have " rooted." This condition is best attained by covering them with a bell-glass or hand-light and by shading them if not placed in a shady situation. Once they have struck, which will be in about three weeks, the cuttings should be gradually given more ventilation and hardened-off until they can be potted up singly for the greenhouse, or planted out into the open.

### Transplanting and Potting-off

Soft-wooded cuttings soon form roots, and can often be potted-off in a month or so's time; cuttings of hard-wooded shrubs, however, take root less quickly and should not be disturbed for at least a year (sometimes 18 months) after being struck. To give the cuttings ample room to grow they are usually planted at least 6 inches from each other in rows 10 inches to a foot apart.

### LAYERING

This is an easy and very sure method of propagation, usually effected about July, though it may be satisfactorily carried out at any season of the year. It consists in the production of roots on one or more of the lower shoots of the plant to be reproduced. An upward cut, just below a joint, is made in the layer or shoot; the incision passes from the underside through to the centre of the shoot, and is from about 1 inch to 3 inches in length, according to the size and nature of the plant to be propagated. The aim is to produce a " tongue " of bark and wood that can be wedged open and pegged down into the soil; the more the tongue is kept open when placed in contact with the earth, the better are the chances of rooting. The shoots chosen for layering must be perfectly healthy, and should be semi-matured. It is usual to layer several shoots at a time, and when the cuts have been made, as described above, the earth all round the plant is stirred up to a depth of 3 inches and the layers are pegged down firmly, so that the open tongues come well in contact with the soil. Little mounds of earth some 6 inches high are then piled up over the layers, which are pressed firmly down into the earth, and well watered. An addition of coarse sand to the soil (often in the proportion of 50 per cent. of its volume), as in the case of cuttings, helps the layers to root. The outer end of the shoot, beyond the cut, should be turned upwards to check the flow of the sap, and all buds not required to form shoots in the new plant should be removed. When the layers have rooted firmly, they may be cut away from the parent plant, being potted up or planted out, preferably in autumn. The layers of soft-wooded plants, such as the carnation, will be found to root in six weeks or so, shrubs like the laurel or veronica will take two or three months to form roots; while with hard-wooded shrubs, like the daphne or rhododendron, it will be a year or more.

## PROPAGATION BY RUNNERS

This is perhaps the most simple method of propagation, though possible only with certain plants, namely those that throw out long, thin stems or runners which grow out over the surface of the ground, although not generally adopted for many greenhouse plants. The strawberry is a well-known example of the runner-producing plant; also Saxifraga sarmentosa. At intervals along the stems will be found joints, and wherever one of these joints comes in contact with the soil and so remains for some time, roots form and foliage is thrown up.

To assist in this method of propagation, the earth should be stirred up to a depth of 2 or 3 inches all round the plant and the runners must be firmly pegged down into it at the required number of joints. Young roots will form, and after a few weeks they will be strong enough to support the new plant, which may be cut away from its parent, and potted up or transplanted. A better method, but one entailing a little more work, is to sink to their brims pots of good sandy soil exactly under the joints of the runners and to peg the latter down firmly to the soil in the pots. This operation provides an easier way of transplanting.

## ROOT-CUTTINGS

This is another and easy method of propagation eminently suitable in the case of plants with fleshy roots. If the roots

69

of plants of this nature are examined in the early spring, they will be found to be covered with small, whitish knobs or shoots; these are the " eyes " from which the new growth will spring. Cuttings of these roots from 2 to 8 inches in length, in accordance with the virility of the plant, and each having an " eye," are taken. They are planted 1 inch deep and 8 inches apart in light sandy soil in partial shade, or in a cold frame with a warm, close atmosphere. The cuttings are inserted vertically with that part of the root which was nearest the stem uppermost.

In propagating plants whose roots are fleshy, but rather more fibrous in nature, the larger root-stems should be cut away from the crowns with as many of the smaller fibrous roots as possible adhering, and should be planted as advised above, but should be left intact, and not be cut up into small pieces. In the case of plants whose roots creep horizontally just below the surface of the soil, cut the roots into pieces from 1 to 6 inches in length, each piece having an " eye " or bud from which shoots can spring, and plant them horizontally at the same depth as they were before being dug up.

The root-cuttings will require frequent watering during the following few months, and will be benefited by the occasional application of a little weak manure water. It is essential to keep the surface of the soil loose. The cuttings can be planted out in the autumn or in the following March or April.

## PROPAGATION BY LEAF-CUTTINGS

Propagation by leaf-cuttings is a very interesting method not often resorted to, and then only in the case of plants with succulent or thick spongy leaves and soft veins. A healthy leaf is taken and planted, stalk downwards, and with the leaf proper just clear of the soil, in a propagating case in equal parts of sandy loam amd leaf-mould. Roots will soon form and a young plant will grow from them. In the case of a large and thick leaf, the veins on the back may be slit at their junctions. The stalk is then planted in sandy soil, and the whole leaf is pinned firmly backside-down, so that it cannot move, on to the mould in the propagating case (temperature 70° F.), and allowed plenty of moisture, though the bed must be well-drained and should not be permitted to become stagnant, or the leaves will rot. In a short time plants will grow wherever the veins have been slit. The little plants can be transplanted or potted up as soon as they have roots strong enough to support them. This method, which may be resorted to at any season when fully-matured leaves are available, is particularly suitable in the case of such plants as the

Achimenes, Begonia, Gloxinia, also with some shrubs—*i.e.*, Camellias, Viburnum, and many others.

## RINGING

A number of plants which are difficult to propagate by other methods may be increased by a process known as ringing, and which consists in removing a small narrow ring of bark. This is especially useful for tall, lanky plants in pots—*i.e.*, Crotons, Dracænas, Condylines, and Pleomeles—by either placing two half pots filled with sandy soil round the stem where the ringing has been done, or binding moss round and keeping it damp, when roots soon appear, the top is then cut away below the pot or moss and potted up, and placed in a warm, moist house.

## GRAFTING

This is a subject that is more in keeping with outdoor gardening, but as it is also applied to certain plants under glass —*i.e.*, Clianthus Dampieri, Double Cherries, Crabs, some Grevilleas, Rhododendrons, etc.—a few remarks will not be altogether out of place, as a nursery ground is a great asset to grow-on young trees and shrubs for the greenhouse.

Grafting has been spoken of as " ennobling," the branch which is transferred being spoken of as the " scion," and the tree to which it is attached as the " stock." The scion becomes, as it were, parasitic upon the stock, and by carefully removing all branches which spring from the stock below the point of union, gardeners are enabled to divert to the scion all the energy produced by the roots of the stock. It is only possible to graft a scion on to a stock of a nearly-allied species. Thus quinces, apples, pears, and medlars can all be mutually grafted on to one another, so also can plums, peaches, apricots, and almonds, but it would be impossible to graft an apple on to an oak or a plum on to a willow.

## PURPOSES OF GRAFTING

### Alteration of Habit

Much valuable time may be saved by grafting; it might take some fifteen or twenty years before a tree raised from seed would bear fruit, whereas by grafting, fruit might be had in three or four years. Better results are also often obtained by grafting a tree on to a stock and roots other than its own.

Another purpose for which grafting is employed is for the

altering of the habit of a tree. Thus, pears and apples are dwarfed by grafting them respectively on the quince and the paradise stock, and dwarfed weeping trees are converted into tall standards by attaching a scion from the weeping variety to a tree with a tall, upright trunk.

### Restoration and Development

Grafting is also occasionally employed to bring about the development of flowers or fruit from parts of a tree that is lacking in them. Sometimes, again, it is made use of for the purpose of restoring an exhausted tree; and lastly it is employed to bring together on one stock the two sexes of diœcious plants—that is to say, plants which bear their male and female flowers on different trees—and so to facilitate their fertilisation and consequent fructification.

### Times for Grafting

In order to effect a successful union by grafting, it is necessary that the sap shall be flowing in the portions of the wood used for the operation, and it is therefore possible to graft in the open between the first signs of growth in the buds at the beginning of spring until about midsummer, when the sap has risen fully. The greenhouse propagating case, with slight bottom-heat, is of great assistance in grafting evergreen shrubs like the Rhododendron and choice or delicate trees and shrubs, including Hamamelis mollis and the hybrid brooms. It is very desirable to pot up the stocks in autumn in order to have them well established in pots before grafting. Under glass the time for grafting is somewhat earlier, the operation being possible any time from January to March, and again from July to September. The operations of budding and grafting are not unlike, being, indeed, identical in theory, but whereas in budding just a single bud of the current year's growth is employed, in grafting whole branches are used, while their buds are still dormant or nearly so. The time for grafting trees will therefore vary with the time of their breaking into leaf, those kinds which bud early being the first to be dealt with. Plums are generally the first to be ready in late March, next come quinces and pears, followed by cherries and apples in this order; but as the time of leafing varies with certain varieties, the order is not without exceptions. To ascertain whether the stock is ready for grafting, the bark should be slit, and if it is easily raised to expose the polished surface of the wood beneath, the stock is ready. If the bark tends to tear, the stock must be left for a week or so longer.

## Preparing the Scions

Grafting needs a certain amount of previous preparation. The stock or tree which is to receive the graft should be cut back or beheaded at about the end of January. Where the frosts are still very hard, it is well to defer the operation till the weather loosens a little, but no risk must be run of movement having begun in the sap. The object of the preparation of the grafts and scions beforehand is that the last year's ripened sap shall still be in them, to supply life to the severed scion until union has been effected, and to this end the scions, which must be well-ripened one-year-old wood and taken from prolific and healthy trees only, should be cut in winter before there is any chance of movement, and while the buds are still absolutely dormant. Grafting must be carried out when the scion is in the same state of vegetation as the intended stock. It is necessary, therefore, where the grafts selected are in a more advanced state of vegetation, to detach them from the parent stems and to lay them with their stems three parts buried in moist soil under a north wall until stocks and grafts are in a similar state. In this position the grafts will remain stationary while the stocks are advancing. When the weather is so mild as to appear likely to cause movement of the sap, the scions should be pulled up occasionally, and left exposed to the air for a little while in order to check growth. The scions should be cut at about the same time as the stock is cut off.

## Cutting Off the Stock

This process consists in removing from the stocks, which should be three-year-old plants planted at least a year before grafting, all the side branches together with the tops, and cutting down the main stock to just above a bud within about 7 or 8 inches of the soil. Enough wood should always be left to allow of the removal of a further portion, as this will be necessary when the actual grafting is proceeded with. If this cutting back is not done until the actual time of grafting, the junction is seldom so good, and where the trees employed are stone-fruit trees—particularly liable to this accident—gumming is very likely to result, with consequent weakening of the trees. Stocks to be used as standards must be allowed to grow to the height required. The time of grafting varies according to the stock used. It should be ascertained with accuracy that the sap is really rising, and it is better for that reason to be a little too late than too early, when there is a chance that it has not yet begun to move. Usually the end of March or April will be found the best time for grafting on mature trees, and March for those which are only in their third year.

### Suitability of the Stock for the Soil

In the selection of a suitable stock, attention should be paid not only to the readiness with which connection is able to be established between the scion and the stock, but also to the soil in which the trees are to be grown. Thus, for example, in light soils, plums grown on their own roots rarely do well, but when grafted on the peach they usually thrive. *Vice versa*, peaches on their own roots rarely do well in heavy soils, and may often be made to succeed by grafting them on the plum. Again, on chalky soil, where the peach usually does badly, it can often be made to grow and fruit by grafting it on the plum. It is certain, also, that in some cases the flavour of fruit can be modified by the stock on which the variety is grafted. Apples occasionally become more acrid by being grafted on to the crab, and the Angoulême pear is improved by being grafted on the quince.

## THE PRINCIPLE OF GRAFTING

Except when standard or half-standard trees are to be formed, the stock should be grafted, as in the case of budding, as near to the ground as possible. To effect a union, the inner edges of the inner bark of the two parts must meet and remain in contact, this inner layer of bark being the only portion of the wood that is capable of uniting. The process consists in cutting the bark of the two portions so that this inner layer shall be in contact when the two pieces are pressed together, and in keeping them together and excluding air, which might dry the tissues, by means of wax or clay and ties of thread and wool.

### Materials and Tools

When grafting is to be undertaken, all materials should be got in readiness beforehand. The stocks and grafts should be prepared and at hand, together with a few tools, such as a strong knife for cutting back the stocks, a saw, a small knife with a narrow blade for fine operations, woollen thread and soft string for tying, and the wax or clay required. The clay needs careful preparation, and should be obtained some weeks before it is required for use, being beaten up with water into the consistency of mortar. This moistening and beating should be repeated every day for a fortnight, and a day before the clay is to be used it should be mixed with one-third of its own bulk of cow manure and about the same amount of hay. The

74

hay should be cut into lengths of about **3** inches, being thoroughly mixed into the other ingredients. It will prevent the clay from cracking off as it hardens, and will also materially assist in keeping it moist.

It is simpler for the amateur to buy a good grafting wax than to prepare it for himself, and he is advised to obtain some such good cold grafting wax as Mastic l'Homme Lefort, an excellent French cold wax. A good substitute for grafting wax is the quick-drying varnish called " knotting." This is very quickly dry, and is impervious to wet and weather. It is applied with a brush over the part to be protected.

## FORMS OF GRAFTING

### Whip- or Tongue-grafting

The method of grafting employed depends largely on the size and other conditions of stock and scion. Where the stock is a young one, and about the size of the finger, the kind known as tongue-grafting is the most suitable. With this method of grafting, the stock must be more advanced in its state of growth than the scion. The scion is prepared by taking a well-ripened one-year-old shoot some **6** inches long, and selecting a place on it where two good buds come on opposite sides of the shoot, one a little higher than the other. Beginning just below the upper of the buds, make a clean cut at one sweep through the wood in a downward slope, coming out just below the lower bud. It is essential that there should be a good bud just above the cut at each end. Now, beginning at the top of the cut just under the top bud, with a perfectly sharp knife cut a hollow curve in the wood, sloping the cut from the inner end of the curve down in a straight line to the tip of the cut by the lower bud. The bottom of the shoot, seen sideways, should now have a section like the letter **J** turned upside down. It is important that these cuts should be made firmly and without unevenness, otherwise the scion will not fit closely to the stock, and its chance of a perfect union will be lessened. Having prepared the scion, attention should be turned to the stock. This, as will be remembered, was cut back late in January to about 8 inches from the ground. Remove all side growth from the base and, selecting a good smooth place about 3 or 4 inches from the surface of the ground, cut the stock cleanly off just above a good healthy bud. This bud's chief function will be to draw up the sap into the top of the cut parts while they are healing together, just as do the buds on the scion, but while the latter are allowed to grow and, indeed, become the real tree, the former should not be permitted to outlive its utility, and when perfect union has taken place, it should only be allowed to grow two or three leaves, and then should be stopped out. Having cut down the stock, its top should be carefully measured against the scion, and cut in a curve corresponding with the curve on the scion. Where the scion has a long " tail "—the tail of the " J " shape—a strip of wood and bark should be peeled from the side of the stock, with the greatest care to adjust it, so that the stock and scion, when placed together, may fit with accuracy. The tail of the scion will be found to fit on to the peeled strip of the outside of the stock, though, owing to the different angle of the section, a narrow strip of the inner bark of the stock will show round the edge of the scion when applied. The important thing to arrive at is that the cut surfaces of the inner bark of both stock and scion shall touch as much as possible. If it is found impossible to make these layers of bark meet on both edges, make them meet perfectly on the one. The tail of the scion should not in any case come below the end of the peeled piece of the stock; if anything, it should err very slightly on the other side.

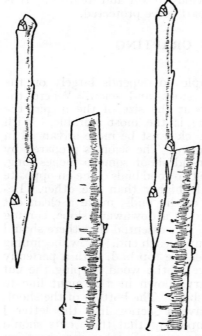

FIG. 22.—Whip or Tongue Grafting.

When both scion and stock fit perfectly, a further security should be obtained by making a small upward cut in the tail of the scion, in order to obtain a slip projecting towards the stock. In the stock itself, opposite this slip, an incision should be made into which the slip will exactly fit, thus holding stock and scion together during the operations of tying and covering with wax. This slip should be thin, or it may cause the junction to bulge and the scion to be pushed away from the stock. When these two latter are fitted closely together, and it is found that their layers of inner bark are fitting closely and neatly the junction should be made firm by tying with raffia,

76

woollen thread, or soft string; the ligature being made firm enough to prevent movement, but not tight enough to prevent the proper circulation of the sap beneath the bark.

The last process is the secure covering of the whole junction —scion, stock, and ligature—with grafting wax of clay—and the graft is complete. The label should always be attached to the stock, not to the scion, as otherwise there would be an added risk of the scion being caught accidentally and pulled off before a union has been effected.

## Saddle-grafting

Saddle-grafting is a kind much used for stocks of about half-an-inch in diameter, and generally the method adopted for Rhododendrons, the scion in this case being about the same thickness as the stock and cut with two tails, the one below the upper bud being shorter than that below the lower bud.

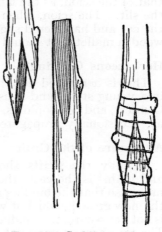

The whole of the inner part of the wood below the buds is removed, and at the top the cuts are ended by a cross-cut beginning just behind the upper bud and sloping slightly upwards. The scion will now have two tails of unequal length, the shorter one having a bud at its upper extremity, and the longer one having a bud midway up its length. The stock should then be taken, and its top cut to slope slightly at an angle corresponding with that of the cross-cut of the scion. A slip should

FIG. 23.—Saddle-grafting.

be peeled corresponding with the long tail of the scion, and the latter laid over the stock, saddle-wise, the long tail fitting its peeled slip, and the top angle of the stock fitting into the top angle of the cross-cut. The short tail of the scion will be found to cross the top of the stock and project a little. A slip should be cut off the side of the stock to fit this projecting piece of the tail, which should then be bent down on to it, and the graft is ready for tying and waxing. This system has the advantage that the scion unites on both sides of the stock, and is therefore not so liable to an accidental break during the healing process.

## Slit- or Notch-grafting

Notch-grafting is rather difficult, but is excellent when well done, and is used when the diameter of the stock is some four times greater than that of the graft. In this method the stock is first cut clean across as in the other ways, and is then pointed, wedge-shaped incisions being made in the bark and wood, beginning at the cut edge of the bark and sloping downwards and outwards. The scions are prepared by making sloping cuts on two sides of the wood, making an angle corresponding with that of the wedge-shaped incision in the stock, so that the scion, when fitted into the stock, fills the space closely, the outer layer of the bark of the scion being slightly lower—because thinner—than that of the stock. The best way of doing this is to make the first cut in the stock with a widely-set saw, and then sloping the sides of the cut slightly outwards with a sharp knife. The angle of the cut in the stock should not be quite so wide as that of the scion, as the latter will in this way be held tighter in the slit. The scion, when properly shaped, should be set into the cut and hammered slightly down into position with a small wooden mallet. It should then be tied and waxed as described.

### Herbaceous Grafting

This is a method adopted for such plants that are grafted in a young stage, and is usually adopted for such as Clianthus, Conifers, and Gypsophilas, while such as Clematis, Pæonia, etc., are occasionally propagated by root grafting.

### After-care of the Graft

In May the grafts should have begun to make growth, and if this is the case, the clay or grafting wax should be removed so that the binding may be undone before it " throttles " the new growth, which it will do if left in position. If the graft is not yet secure, the binding must be replaced, but more loosely. The clay or wax must not be replaced.

The graft should also be supported by a stake firmly bound to the stock.

Laterals that form on a graft should be pinched off to encourage a good straight single shoot from the graft, and any shoots forming on the stock below the point of graftng must be rubbed off, once they have served their purpose in drawing sap up to the graft.

The wax may be found difficult of removal, and in such a case care is required in order to get it off without damaging the junction. This is best done by placing a block of wood or some other firm object on one side of the lump of wax, and then lightly hitting the other side with a hammer, no unnecessary force being employed. The wax will crack off, and may be removed with ease.

THE GREENHOUSE

HOW TO POT UP

## CHAPTER IV

# POTTING AND RE-POTTING

### THE POTTING-SHED

TO every greenhouse of sufficient size a potting-shed should be attached. It should be quite near, so as to be handy, and in order that the more delicate plants shall not be harmed by a long journey through the cold air when taken from the house to be potted-up, and if connected to the greenhouse so much the better. The shed must be roomy and above all should have ample head-room. The door must be wide enough to admit the hand-barrow, for it greatly increases labour if materials have to be handled more than is absolutely necessary. Another important point in designing the potting-shed is, if possible, to avoid any steps; these are very awkward obstacles when pots are being carried about. Lighting is another important question. Side windows in the two shorter ends of the shed are quite good, but if possible the windows or one long window should be along one side, where the bench is, thus allowing plenty of light; this leaves the other side for the door, shelves, and cupboards. If possible, arrangements should be made for a headlight in the roof directly over the bench, and artificial light is invaluable for working in winter. The hot-water system from the greenhouse boiler should be carried into the shed, not only for the comfort of the gardener, but also in order that composts may be dried and warmed.

### The Bench

The shed should be furnished with a shelf or stage of suitable height on which plants can be potted or re-potted, as the case may be, before removal to the greenhouse. This should be large and strong enough to hold sufficient potting soil to complete a good batch of plants before it is again necessary to mix more compost, and must be of sufficient height to obviate stooping. In a potting-shed it is convenient to place bins below the shelf or stage to contain a sufficient supply of potting materials for immediate use : silver sand, peat, loam, coco-nut fibre, crocks, etc.

The great thing to aim at in designing the potting-shed is to have all materials and implements as handy as possible, so as to avoid all unnecessary waste of time and energy.

# HOW TO POT UP

## CLEANING THE POTS

Pots that have been used should always be washed, otherwise any disease or fungus present in the old potting soil will be transferred to the next inhabitant of the pot. Besides, a dirty pot will not be porous, as it should be, to allow the air to permeate the soil. Even new pots should be put in water for at least half an hour, for a dry pot will draw away the moisture from the potting soil. The pot, however, must not be actually *wet* when used, as this would be almost as bad as using a dirty pot, for the soil, and eventually the roots, would stick to it. For the winter, always store pots in a dry, frost-proof place : if they are dry, the frost will not hurt them ; if they are wet, however, when the frost comes, it is almost certain that many of them will be ruined.

## PREPARING THE POTTING SOIL

When it is considered that the compost is the medium whereby the roots receive nutrition, water, and air, it will be realised what an important part it plays in the life of the plant, and for this reason every effort should be made to provide the compost best suited to the needs of each plant. In the *Alphabetical List of Flowering Plants*, Chapter XVI, details as to the most suitable individual composts are given.

When potting-up, it is just as easy to include two, three, or even more ingredients in the compost, provided certain arrangements are made, as it is to use plain loam.

The most usual ingredients of potting composts are : loam, which generally forms the greater part ; leaf-mould ; sand ; old mortar rubble ; well-rotted manure ; and charcoal. The gardener should have small heaps of these handy on his potting bench, or in the bins below it ; the compost can then be made up of the varying ingredients in the required proportions.

Before going on to describe how the compost should be made up, it may be advisable to give a brief account of each ingredient, so that the gardener may have some idea of their natures and functions, and may be able to select good and useful samples of each kind.

### Coconut Fibre Refuse

This can, to some extent, be described as a possible constituent of a potting compost, since with loam it may be used instead of peat or leaf-mould, but it is not so satisfactory. It is, however, for its other uses that it is chiefly

**PLATE 4**
**Flower-head of a *Clivia*. This beautiful
evergreen plant can be grown as a room plant.**

useful to the gardener. If mixed with sand and kept moist, cuttings can be struck in it, but since it provides little plant food, they must be potted up in the ordinary way as soon as roots have formed. Bulbs can also be successfully raised in this fibre (see page 122), which is likewise used for " starting " the tubers of such plants as begonias.

## MIXING THE COMPOST

If the gardener has not the time or inclination to prepare his own potting composts, he may purchase them quite cheaply already mixed. This has the disadvantage that, with a standard mixture already prepared, the amateur is encouraged to use this one compost for plants, all and sundry, irrespective of their special needs as to soil. If, on the other hand, the soil is mixed by the gardener, each kind of plant can be given the compost most suitable for it.

The potting soil must be moderately moist, that is to say, if a handful is taken up and gripped firmly, it should become moulded to the shape of the hand, but at the same time it should be dry enough to crumble as soon as it is disturbed. If too dry it should be watered, but should be allowed at least a day in which to absorb the moisture, otherwise the compost will be patchy and not evenly moist all through. Mix the ingredients well together, but do not sieve the compost; this would rob it of much of its plant food and most of its porosity, large lumps must, of course, be broken up. Only for seeds and cuttings should the compost be sieved, and in this case through a $\frac{1}{4}$-inch mesh. Young plants with fine fibrous roots need a compost much finer in texture than do mature and vigorous plants being potted-on into their final pots.

As has already been said, the proportions in which the various ingredients are added to the compost vary in accordance with the requirements of individual plants and with the nature of the loam used, but the following may be taken as a suitable compost for the general run of the more common soft-wooded plants grown in our greenhouses.

$\frac{1}{2}$ part fibrous loam.    $\frac{1}{8}$ part well-rotted manure.
$\frac{1}{4}$ part leaf-mould.    $\frac{1}{8}$ part coarse silver sand.

The compost should be stored in the potting-shed, and where greenhouse subjects are to be potted-up, the compost should, if possible, be kept in the warm house for at least twenty-four hours previously to potting so that it may be warmed up to the temperature of the house.

*Loam.* As a warning note it may first be stated that ordinary

F           81

garden loam should not be used for the potting compost; it may be good enough for most plants grown in the open, but it will not be suitable for the choicer greenhouse varieties, and seedlings and cuttings will not thrive in it to full advantage.

The reason for this may not be immediately apparent, but a little thought will soon make the matter clear. In the open ground the rain drains down through the soil gradually as it falls, but when hot, dry weather comes, it is gradually drawn up again, and keeps the roots of plants moist and cool. In a pot, however, the small quantity of soil presents a comparatively large surface to the drying influence of air and sun, and is soon relieved of all its moisture. This means that if the soil is to be kept at all moist, it will have to receive frequent doses of water. Now, if the soil used is ordinary garden loam, the constant watering will soon render it sticky, and eventually sour—in addition, should watering be neglected for a short time in hot weather, the soil will bake into a compact mass which will parch up the roots and exclude all air from them. Leaf-mould, however, is spongy by nature, will absorb a large quantity of water, and will retain it for the use of the roots. But, as this water gradually drains away, or is used by the roots, the leaf-mould contracts, and this creates a system of minute cells throughout the soil by means of which the air can permeate to the roots and at the same time keep the soil sweet and clean. Sand also helps to keep the compost porous; and it is for this reason that it should, if possible, be added, with leaf-mould, to every potting compost, however fibrous the loam may be. Garden loam usually contains too large a percentage of clay, and is therefore too sticky by nature to be used as an ingredient in a potting compost; its place should, whenever possible, be taken by good fibrous loam from the meadows.

The best loam is found in the upper layers of the top-spit, just under the turf on meadows on which sheep or cattle have been grazed for a considerable number of years.

Some of the best comes from the downs in Berkshire, Kent, and Sussex, and the gardener would do well to buy a little through his nurseryman. Kettering, in Northamptonshire, is also noted for good loam. If the soil from a local meadow is preferred, make a stack of the upper 3 inches of the top-spit, turf intact and upside down, place decayed stable manure between each layer, and let the whole settle for at least a year. The grass will die, and its fibrous roots will make a good, porous mould. Loam should be moderately adhesive, but should crumble if rubbed between the fingers. It contains a large proportion of clay; if this is in excess, rather more leaf-mould or peat will have to be added to the compost to balance this,

82

or it will become too sticky and retentive. Good fibrous loam is the foundation on which the compost for nearly all soft-wooded plants is built up, and where the other usual ingredients are lacking, it is quite possible to grow the more common soft-wooded plants, such as geraniums, in a compost consisting purely of fibrous loam, provided the latter is good. It should not be sieved, but large pieces must be broken up into lumps not greater than an inch in diameter. Ordinary garden loam, as explained above, cannot thus be successfully used as potting soil.

*Leaf-mould.* This, like loam, enters into almost every compost, and is, as a rule, used in quantities up to one-third part of the whole bulk. Its function is to make the soil porous, so that air and water can permeate freely through it, but at the same time to retain a certain amount of moisture in the soil. It must therefore be light and open in nature; not black and soil-like, as it so often becomes after rotting in damp, boggy woods. As its name implies, leaf-mould consists of the decayed leaves of trees; those of the beech and oak undoubtedly form the best mould. If leaf-mould is to be good, care must be taken in collecting and storing the leaves; they should be kept in the dry; if allowed to lie about and rot in the wet—as in ditches, for example—the resultant mould will be of very little value, if not actually harmful to the plants. The leaves should be collected in a heap early in autumn, and should be covered with a board, or metal sheet to keep them dry. They should be allowed to decay for a year or eighteen months, and should be turned over every two or three months during this period. All sticks and other rubbish must be picked out, as these are liable to shelter pests and fungus spores. The decayed leaf-mould should be passed through a $\frac{1}{4}$-inch sieve, that not passing through the mesh being returned for further decomposition. Bake it for a short time, if possible, or sprinkle it with boiling water to kill any pests present.

*Sand.* This is included in the compost to make it porous, and should form a large portion—at least a tenth part—of any compost prepared for plants with fibrous and fine roots. For this reason it is an important constituent in composts used for sowing seeds and for striking cuttings. Coarse silver sand is excellent for the purpose; sea-sand may be used if it has had all its salt washed out of it. The ordinary reddish sand contains iron, is harmful to most plants, and cannot be used.

*Old Mortar Rubble.* Mortar rubble is a constituent in many composts; not only does it help to keep the soil open, but it supplies lime so necessary to many plants. The older it is the better; it should be stored in the dry, as damp will rapidly rob it of its properties.

*Manure.* New and crude manure should never be used in a potting compost; it will burn the tender roots of most pot plants. Manure for this purpose should be well-decayed, and should be stored in the dry where the rain cannot wash away its manurial value. Any farmyard manure may be used, although most gardeners prefer cow or sheep manure for potting purposes. The better the animals have been fed the more valuable will be their manure—it always pays to buy good manure, even if it is a little more expensive. Potting manure must be dry, and must be passed through a $\frac{1}{2}$-inch sieve before being incorporated in the compost; if it is possible to bake it for a short time before it is used, no anxiety need be felt about attacks from eelworms, wireworms, and other soil pests. When the manure can be stacked with the loam as described on page 82, it will ensure its being well decayed. It can then be sterilised with the loam. Manures should be added to composts only for vigorous and mature plants, and even then the proportion should never exceed one-sixth part of the whole compost. Seedlings and cuttings should not be given any animal manure when first potted up, a compost of loam, leaf-mould, and sand proving quite adequate for most of them. Artificial manures should never be incorporated in the compost; they may be added later as top-dressings when the flower-buds are forming. See also Manure, page 57.

*Peat.* This is composed chiefly of sand and decayed vegetable matter, and is very porous. Rubbed through a $\frac{1}{2}$-inch sieve and mixed with loam it forms a well-drained compost suitable to such plants as ferns, palms, heaths, azaleas, some orchids, and many others. For all the first-mentioned plants the peat should be sandy and of fairly close texture, but orchids prefer it more open and fibrous. Dark peat from bogs is useless in the potting compost. Stack peat under cover. Acid peat should be used, alkaline peat being useless for many plants.

*Charcoal.* This is an invaluable ingredient of the compost as it helps to keep the soil sweet. It should be crushed up very fine and mixed with the compost at the rate of one part to every fifty parts of compost, or it can be used in small lumps as drainage matter in lieu of crocks. When used in this latter way, it also keeps the soil sweet.

## TIME FOR POTTING AND RE-POTTING

The time at which a plant should be re-potted depends on whether the " ball " is to be broken up, as for instance when a plant from the open ground is to be potted-up or when a plant has to be re-potted because the soil is old and sour, or whether the " ball " is to be left practically intact as when a growing

## How to Pot Up

1. The plant (left) potted up, showing the "ball" of the roots, the fine potting compost round it, the coarse soil below it, and the drainage; (right) the plant, pot-bound and requiring a larger pot. 2. Washing the pots.    3. Inserting the "crocks".    4. Removing the plant from the old pot. 5. Working the fine soil round the roots.

### Bulbs in Pots
1. Amaryllis.  See page 243.  2. Tulip.  See page 579.  3 and 4. Hyacinth.  See page 402.

# HOW TO POT UP

plant is to be " shifted " into a slightly larger pot. In the latter case the operation can be performed at any time when the plant is in fairly active growth, as the roots will at once go ahead and take possession of the new soil. Where the " ball " is to be broken up, however, re-potting can only be undertaken just as the roots are beginning to come into active growth, at which time they will be able to penetrate the new compost. If the " ball " were broken up when the roots were not in their most vigorous state, the young root-matter could not fail to be badly damaged, and in consequence would be unable to recuperate in sufficient time to penetrate the fresh compost before the " resting " period set in, and the new soil would become sour before it could be occupied.

During the growing season a plant or two of each batch of a similar kind, whether they are biennials being grown on for greenhouse use, soft-wooded perennials, or hard-wooded plants, should be turned out of their pots, so that it may be seen whether re-potting is necessary. As soon as the roots begin to wind round the sides of the pot, a larger one should at once be given, unless the " resting " season is approaching, when potting should be held over till the plants again become active. They make most growth in April and May and again in August and September. The best time to re-pot, therefore, is just before this growth commences, that is to say, about March and again in July or August. March is the better time at which to re-pot established plants, as growth in spring is more vigorous than in autumn, and new material will then be of more use to them.

## THE SIZE OF THE POT

Pots are generally made in what are termed " casts "—that is to say, a certain quantity of clay is taken, from which one pot is made, or two, four, six, eight, twelve, sixteen, twenty-four, thirty-two, forty-eight, sixty, or eighty; and pots are, therefore, known to gardeners as ones, twos, fours, etc., according to the number of pots made from a single cast.

The following table shows the inside measurements of the pot-sizes in general use.

| Sizes. | Diam. Top in Ins. | Depth in Ins. | Sizes. | Diam. Top in Ins. | Depth in Ins. |
|---|---|---|---|---|---|
| Thimbles | 2 | 2 | Sixteens | 9½ | 9 |
| Thumbs | 2½ | 2½ | Twelves | 11½ | 10 |
| Sixties | 3 | 3½ | Eights | 12 | 11 |
| Fifty-fours | 4 | 4 | Sixes | 13 | 12 |
| Forty-eights | 4½ | 5 | Fours | 15 | 13 |
| Thirty-twos | 6 | 6 | Twos | 18 | 14 |
| Twenty-fours | 8½ | 8 | Ones | 20 | 16 |

It is always advisable to put a plant in a pot slightly too small rather than too large. Unless the plant is very pot-bound, or is required to grow very quickly (as in the case of many young and growing plants), put the plant back in the same-sized pot if possible. Many gardeners like to have 1 inch of soil between the " ball " and the sides of the pot.

It is fatal to try to save work or to force a plant on by putting a small subject into a pot too large for it. The small roots will be unable to make use of all the moisture and plant food in the soil; this hangs about in the compost and it is a long time before any fresh air is able to enter, so that the soil becomes clammy and finally sour. For this reason pot-up into small pots, re-potting frequently as the plants grow and the roots become pot-bound. It is rarely necessary to move a plant into a pot more than two, at the most three, sizes larger than the old one. As soft-wooded plants are, as a rule, vigorous growers, they may usually be put into pro-portionately larger pots than would be advisable for the slower-growing hard-wooded plants.

## DRAINING THE POT

In potting it is always necessary to make provision for the escape of surplus water—that is to say, water which, when given to the plant in the pot, cannot be retained by the soil in which it grows. For the purpose of providing drainage, every gardener keeps by him a store of fragments of broken pots and saucers, oyster shells, and even pieces of soft brick. The oyster shell is useful for placing over the hole at the bottom of the pot, and surrounding this and above it may be placed small pieces of broken pots, technically called " crocks." For cuttings, which are not intended to remain in the pot for any length of time after they have rooted, a single piece of crock, convex side uppermost, is sufficient, but when the time of tenancy is likely to be prolonged to months, and perhaps even years, it is necessary to fill one-sixth, and in some cases as much as one-fourth, of the entire depth of the pot with broken potsherds. If possible, it is desirable to give a conical form to the crocking placed in the pot.

## FILLING IN THE POTTING COMPOST

The pot being crocked, some gardeners like to place a little moss or coco-nut fibre, or even a few leaves (although leaves are not to be recommended), over the crocks before putting in the soil. This prevents the interstices between the crocks from being choked by the finer particles of earth that may be carried down from time to time during the process of watering. There is, however, no absolute need to do this if the pot is crocked properly, as the very presence of the shells and potsherds at the bottom of the pot secures the escape of the surplus water, even though a little earth is carried down among them.

The crocking being done and a little coarse soil thrown over them, some fine mould should be put in and shaken together by gently knocking the edge of the bottom of the pot against the potting-bench, or by striking the sides of the pot gently with the hand. This soil at the bottom of the pot should be just sufficient to lift the plant so that the top of the "ball," when set in the new pot, is within $1\frac{1}{2}$ inches of the rim—when firmly planted and covered with $\frac{1}{2}$ to 1 inch of new soil, it should be 1 inch below the rim in a large pot and $\frac{1}{2}$ inch in a small one.

## REMOVING THE OLD POT

The most suitable times for re-potting the various kinds of plants will be found in the individual articles in the Alphabetical List of Flowering Plants, page 233.

The plants to be re-potted should, if necessary, be watered an hour or so before the work is to take place, so that the "ball" of earth round the roots may be just moderately moist; if too wet the fibrous roots may be torn; if over-dry the small roots will find great difficulty in becoming established in the new compost. Now turn the pot upside-down, placing the first and second fingers of the left hand so that the stem lies between them while the palm and fingers lie across the top edges of the pot, and grasp the bottom of the pot, which is now uppermost, with the right hand. Next tap the rim of the pot gently on the edge of the potting-bench, and the roots and soil will come out complete, being supported by the left hand, as the pot is removed with the right. Care must be taken that the plant and soil do not drop from the pot. Should the plant "ball" not come out of the pot, the finger or a small blunt-headed stick should be inserted through the drainage hole at the bottom, and gentle pressure applied.

## POTTING-UP THE PLANTS

Soft-wooded plants are not, as a general rule, kept in the pot for more than two or three seasons. It is therefore not necessary to remove all the old soil from the "ball," which can be kept intact. If it is necessary to give the plant an entire change of soil, the operation should be carried out as advised for re-potting on the next page. We may assume here, however, that the "ball" is to be left intact.

The crocks, any sour soil and dead roots must be carefully removed so that the roots are not bruised, and some of the thickest roots should be drawn out from the " ball " with a pointed stick; these will establish themselves in the new soil round the sides of the larger pot. Now place the " ball " on the soil already in the pot so that the plant will be quite central, and pack the soil with the hand or potting-stick between the " ball " and the sides of the pot, consolidating the earth by knocking the pot from time to time on the bench, and pressing the compost down round the sides with a potting-stick, or the thumb, which is more convenient when dealing with the smaller sizes of pots. Press the new soil firmly about the collar of the plant with the thumbs. Keep the new soil *level* with the top of the old " ball." The collar should not be raised above the general level, but to depress it beneath is certain death to hard-wooded plants. All plants, however hardy, should be kept warm and moist for a few weeks after re-potting, especially if they have received a large shift. The growth of the roots is thus promoted—a point of great importance at this stage.

Only remove from the " ball " that soil that is really sour; it is a mistake to disturb the roots when the soil is still fresh. If, however, the compost has become very sour, all the soil must be removed and the roots well washed through with luke-warm water, any dead or diseased parts being cut away.

## POTTING-ON SEEDLINGS AND CUTTINGS

Cuttings and seedlings are best potted-up in the house in which they have hitherto been grown. They are delicate, and if transferred to a cold draughty shed, may receive a set-back. Once established in their new pots, they can gradually be hardened off to stand the temperature of their new house.

The size of the pot to be used naturally depends on the kind and size of the plant, but as a general rule 3- or 4-inch pots are suitable for the first potting-up of seedlings that have previously been pricked-off into boxes, round the sides of the pots, or into thumb pots; the new pots should be just large enough to take the roots without their touching the sides; a larger pot will be needed with each shift as the plants grow. The size of the pot in which the plant is ultimately to be flowered bears closely upon the dimensions of the pot used for the first potting-up. If the ultimate pot is to be 8 inches in diameter, the first pot should usually be a $3\frac{1}{2}$-inch one, the pot for the second shift being a 5-inch one. A 3-inch is generally large enough as a first pot when the eventual size is to be 6 inches, the intermediate shift being into a 4-inch pot. For the general run of biennials potted-on for greenhouse use, three pottings in all (excluding the seed or cutting boxes and the pricking-off) are all that the gardener can afford to give, though in some cases more frequent potting is beneficial, when possible. Perennials are potted-on as they increase in size and as they become pot-bound.

The procedure is the same as for the potting-up of maturer plants, but the stem of the seedling must be buried nearly up to the two small seed-leaves or cotyledons. The young roots are very brittle and tender, so that the soil must not be pressed down with the thumbs and fingers, as when potting maturer plants; the tapping of the pot on the bench and the watering afterwards should render the compost quite firm enough. Seedlings grown in boxes or close together in pots should be potted-off early, before the roots begin to intertwine.

## DEGREE OF FIRMNESS IN POTTING

With most plants it is desirable to pot firmly, not to ram the earth down hard, but sufficiently firm for the plant to offer resistance if slight pressure is applied to it to pull it upwards. The degree of firmness necessary varies with the age of the plant, the nature of the roots, and the character of the compost. Young plants of all kinds, whose roots will expand, need planting only moderately firmly, the soil being packed just tight enough to hold the plants in position; each potting must, however, be firmer than the previous one. When mature, fibrous-rooted plants should be planted very firmly, the more sandy the compost the firmer must the planting be. Plants with large fleshy roots require a much looser compost. Between these two extremes there are roots of varying sizes and characteristics, and in each case the gardener must use his discretion. Although it may be necessary to firm the soil firmly round the roots, do not pack the surface down hard, or the air will be excluded. Lastly, never fill a pot with soil right up to the edge, but only to about half an inch below the edge of smaller pots, and 1 inch for larger pots. This should be done in order to afford sufficient room for watering. This must always be given through a fine rose directly after potting-up, so that the soil may settle round the roots, after which the plants should be kept rather dry in a close atmosphere for a week or so until established. Soft-wooded plants should also be shaded from the sun. Plants which are rather top-heavy, or whose roots do not grip the soil firmly, must be staked—the stick should be thin, but strong, and should be pushed into the compost down the side of the pot to avoid piercing and damaging the roots.

## Liquid Manures for Pot Plants.

These cannot strictly be said to come under the head of potting, but since it is in this liquid form that manure is generally applied to pot plants, a few words on the subject of liquid manures may not be out of place. As has been said, no artificial fertilisers and only a comparatively small proportion of animal manure should be added to the compost when potting-up, so that the plants will later need some stimulant; this is usually supplied in the form of liquid manure, and is best given when the flower-buds are beginning to form. As soon as the flowers open, the manure water must be discontinued. The manure should only be given once a week or every ten days; it must not be too strong, and if dry the soil must be moistened with clear water before the liquid manure is applied. Newly potted-up plants, whose roots have had no time to become established, and weak sickly flowers should not be given stimulants; they should receive clear water only. Manure water would not help them; in fact, it would do far more harm than good, and would probably prove fatal.

## STERILISATION OF SOILS

There are many methods of sterilising soil for the destruction of insects and other forms of animal life in the soil, the spores of diseases which attack crops, and the seeds of weeds which are troublesome to cultivators. Scarcely any of the under-mentioned methods of sterilisation can be said to be complete on a large scale, but are sufficiently so to exterminate a large proportion of the harmful life in the soil and, by thus destroying competition, give the succeeding crop a better chance.

In practice, the sterilisation is accomplished either by heat applied by live steam, or by a chemical process employing a formalin drench. In either case the work must be thoroughly performed if satisfactory results are expected. Steam sterilisation is of two methods : by buried perforated pipes, and by a pan inverted over the soil and under which the steam may be conveyed and applied for an hour or more. The perforated-pipe method is a system or set of perforated pipes with cross head and high-pressure boiler connections. These pipes are connected and buried in the soil of the bed either with or without partial banking up of the soil. The surface of the bed is then covered with canvas or other covering, and the steam passes into the system for such a period as is required to heat the soil to the necessary temperature—say from 180 to 212° F.—and this should be maintained for a period of an hour or more. $1\frac{1}{2}$-inch pipe is used with $\frac{1}{8}$-inch holes bored in a straight line about 1 foot apart. These pipes are buried in the bed 12 to 16 inches apart.

For the inverted-pan method the apparatus consists of a galvanised-iron pan or box 10 feet × 6 feet × 6 inches. Lay it on the soil prepared for growing, and push it down 1 or 2 inches, then blow steam in at 80 to 100 lb. for forty minutes. On the principle of the warming-pan the soil speedily becomes heated.

The advantage of this method is that it does not necessitate moving the soil from the house and is suitable for greenhouses where plants are grown in beds or borders.

Any soils to be treated by any method of sterilisation, should be prepared for use by the addition of manures with the soil before treatment, whether by steaming or drenching.

For the formalin drench some of the following may be useful.

Formalin at the rate of 1 pint to 20 gallons of water, a 5 per cent. solution of Lysol, or Jeyes' Fluid at the rate of 1 oz. to 1 gallon of soft water, may be used for watering the soil a week before planting or sowing.

Permanganate of potash is a powerful disinfectant. About 1 oz. to 5 gallons of water makes a rose-red solution which may be applied to the soil.

Carbolic acid applied to the soil at the rate of 1 part carbolic acid to 20 parts of water three times at intervals of a fortnight before planting or sowing, and 1 teaspoonful to 4 gallons of water after planting, kills the spores of many fungoid diseases.

Naphthaline at the rate of 2 oz. per square yard, and well mixed with the soil for the destruction of insect life in the soil.

Toluol may also be used, in which case the soil should be thoroughly moistened with it, then spread out in a fairly thin layer, and raked over from time to time until the sterilising substance has evaporated.

Frost also destroys a large amount of animal life in the soil, so that greenhouse soil wheeled outside and exposed to hard frost, and afterwards limed, is in a much better condition for plant growth.

A simple method on a very small scale is the burning or baking of soil, in which the soil is placed in an old saucepan and stood over a fire until the temperature should reach 180 to 200° F. It should be kept at this for at least an hour. Or soil can be placed in vessels and boiling water poured over it, afterwards covering up the soil to prevent any foreign spores collecting on it; of course leaving the soil to get cool before attempting to use it.

Electricity is now used for sterilisation. The electric heaters consist of a bin wherein a metal plate at the bottom is lined with electric cable. The soil is tipped in on the cable, and a current of electricity passed through the soil raising the temperature to 200° F. It is kept at this temperature for thirty minutes. Afterwards the current is switched off and the soil left in the container for another thirty minutes before removing. The soil must never be dry when placed in the container— moisture is absolutely necessary for the passage of the electric current.

A number of books have been written dealing entirely with soil sterilisation, and are worth consulting for more details on the subject.

## Propagating Violas and Phlox

1. Viola cuttings; cuttings should be taken of new but vigorous growth from the centre of the plant, preferably in September, and struck in a shady frame. See page 586. 2. Phlox are best propagated by division of roots in March or October; root divisions ready for planting. 3. Dividing the roots of phlox; a sharp knife should be used so as to damage the roots as little as possible; never divide them with a spade. See page 498.

## The Culture of Fuchsias

1. Fuchsia cuttings; they should be taken from plants started in heat in February or March and struck, in a bottom heat of 60° F., in pots of two-thirds fibrous loam and one-third leaf-mould, well-rotted manure and old mortar rubble. Cuttings can also be taken of semi-matured wood in August.
2. A fuchsia cutting rooted. 3. Training a standard fuchsia; all side-shoots are removed. See page 376.

# CHAPTER V

# FORCING

THE process of making a plant flower or fruit out of its natural season is known as forcing. To effect this, a suitable glass shelter and a means of applying artificial heat are necessary. The heat of the sun's rays alone is not usually sufficient, and additional heat has to be applied either by means of a hot-bed or by the aid of hot-water pipes. Electricity is still in its infancy as regards this purpose, and although experiments show that it is quite successful, it is apt to prove costly.

## EARLY VEGETABLES

Vegetables may be forced in a heated frame, or in borders and boxes in the warm greenhouse. The following paragraphs will show not only what may be done to produce early crops, but how it is possible to have supplies of many choice vegetables all through the winter.

**Asparagus.**—An early spring supply may be obtained by means of forcing. Place glass cloches or small frames over the crowns in the permenent beds early in February. Three-year-old plants are the best for forcing. Bottom heat is useful, though not essential. If it is available, lift and replant the plants in January in a mild hot-bed in a frame with 3 inches of soil over the crowns. Keep the frame dark and the soil moist.

**Beans, Broad.**—Very early crops may be grown by means of forcing. Sow in pots or boxes in a compost consisting of two-thirds fibrous loam, one-third well-rotted and finely-sifted manure and leaf-mould. Place in a frame in January or February (temperature 50° F. or below), and grow under glass in as natural a manner as possible. In the case of the later batches, they may be hardened off and set out in the open with their boxes plunged nearly to their rims in the soil.

**Beans, French.**—To obtain the earliest possible supplies, sow at intervals in December, January, and February in a compost of loam, well-rotted manure, and coarse sand in 6-inch pots (three seeds in each), and stand the pots 15 inches apart in an ordinary hot-bed made in the same way as for cucumbers. Water sparingly until the seeds are up, and grow close to the glass. The temperature should not fall below 60° F. Grow in as natural a manner as possible under glass.

**Beans, Runner.**—An early supply may be obtained by means of sowing in boxes in April (equal parts of loam and leaf-mould, with a little sand), and planting out at the end of May. They should be grown in as near to natural conditions as possible under glass.

**Beetroot, Globe.**—To obtain successional crops of early beetroots, sow batches of seed in a mild hot-bed in a frame from the beginning of January to the end of March and grow under glass.

**Brussels Sprouts.**—In order to obtain an early supply, sow seeds in boxes in a frame at the end of February and in March, and grow under glass in as near to natural conditions as possible.

**Capsicums.**—To force capsicums, sow in pots in February and place in cucumber frame (temp. 65° F.). Pot-off when big enough, two or three in a 5-inch pot. When large enough shift into 7-inch pots, and stand in cold frame. Harden-off and plant out in warm sheltered position protected with hand glasses, end of May, or shift into 10-inch pots and grow under glass.

**Carrots, Stump-rooted.**—For a successional supply of early carrots, sow seed in shallow drills 10 inches apart in 2–3 inches of finely-sifted soil over a mild hot-bed in frame early in January and at intervals until the first sowing outdoors is made.

**Cauliflower.**—To obtain an early supply, sow seed of an early kind on a mild hot-bed in February or early March and cover with hand glasses. Thin the seedlings when fit to handle, and plant singly in 3-inch pots, harden off, and plant out in a warm, sheltered situation or under glass in April. Seed may be sown in frames in August and September, the seedlings being pricked out as soon as they are up. Autumn-sown plants in the open may be pricked out under frames and forced under glass to obtain an early supply.

**Celery.**—To force celery, sow over a heat of about 70° F. in light, sandy soil in shallow boxes or pans under glass in February or March. Prick out singly in 3-inch pots when fit to handle, and discontinue the bottom heat. Shift to a cold frame or cool greenhouse, and into bigger pots, preparatory to planting out in May. Never let the plants become too dry at the root.

**Chicory.**—Treat this in the same way as advised for seakale.

**Cucumber.**—Cucumbers may be had at any time by sowing seed in a hot-bed or under glass about 3 months before the fruit is required.

**Endive.**—To obtain an early supply, sow in the open early in August. Prick out in sheltered position, and transfer the plants to a pit or cold frame in October for the winter.

**Leeks.**—For an early supply, sow seed thinly in a finely-sieved compost of two-thirds loam and one-third leaf-mould and sand in 3-inch-deep boxes towards the end of January or early in February, and keep in moderate heat (55–60° F.). When 3 inches in height, prick off the seedlings into boxes (2–3 inches apart). Give ample light and air, and transfer to a cold frame about the middle of April. Harden off and plant out in May.

**Lettuce.**—To obtain early plants, sow batches of seed in a frame from January to March, and raise indoors, or plant out in the open in a warm, sheltered position when fit to handle. Autumn-sown plants outdoors should be pricked-off in October and transferred to a frame for the winter. Ventilate as freely as possible.

**Mint.**—An early supply of mint may be had by propagating by means of division of roots and planting in boxes in March. Stand the boxes in a heated frame.

**Mushrooms.** *Soil and Situation.*—Mushrooms merely require a supply of horse manure, and a certain degree of warmth and moisture. If the manure when crushed in the hand binds, but no excess liquid is pressed out, it contains the required proportion of moisture. During the months of summer and autumn, mushrooms may, perhaps, most conveniently be grown in the open air, but during late autumn, winter, and spring, some building or frame is necessary.

*Making the Bed.*—As a rule, about six to nine weeks must be allowed from the commencement of operations to the gathering of a crop. The longest litter should first be shaken out of the manure, all up to the length of about a foot being retained. This should then be made up into a heap about 2 or 3 feet high and from 4 to 6 feet wide, and is best made on a gentle slope. In winter-time this heap should be made up under cover, or the heat will too quickly evaporate. Every second day the heap should be thoroughly turned, so as to bring the central portion to the surface and the surface to the centre, and during this process all lumps should be broken up. This turning should be continued for about a week in winter and for about two weeks in summer. The manure should then be placed in position, being well trodden down. The temperature of the heap should be taken by means of a thermometer plunged to a depth of about 8 inches.

*Sowing the Spawn.*—As soon as this temperature **reaches** about 75 or 80° F., the spawn, which must be fresh and which is bought in bricks composed of a mixture of manure and soil, containing dry mycelium of the mushroom, should be inserted in pieces about 2 inches square. These pieces should be firmly planted by means of a trowel, about 2 or 3 inches deep in the manure and about 8 inches apart. The heap of manure is then at once covered with about 2 inches of well-sieved, sandy loam. Old garden soil is totally unsuitable for the purpose. This soil should be just, and only just, moist enough to hold together, and should be beaten firm with the flat of the spade. The whole must then be covered with a layer of straw, 15 inches in thickness, or with other material to exclude all light. If the spawn is planted in winter additional protection should be afforded by mats or sacking.

*Care of the Bed.*—Little or no water should be given to the bed until the mushrooms begin to come up. As soon as the mushrooms appear, however, a moderate supply of tepid water may be given once a week, and it will be found that a little common salt, or, better still, saltpetre, will be beneficial. So far as possible, the temperature of the air of the building in which mushrooms are being grown should be kept at from 55 to 60° F. If the bed is to retain its health, mushrooms should not be cut, but should be twisted off, separating the stalks as near the base as possible. Fresh soil must be added to fill the holes made by picking, and the bed must again be covered with straw.

*Pests.*—Woodlice play great havoc in mushroom beds. Traps baited with carrot or potato will do much to keep this pest down.

**Mustard and Cress.**—To obtain a continuous supply, make sowings in boxes in the greenhouse from October to March.

**Onions.**—To obtain an early crop, sow in a compost of two-thirds loam and one-third leaf-mould and sand in boxes in January (temp. 60° F.). Reduce the heat and thin out to 3 inches apart when the seedlings are fit to handle. Give ample light and air, and transfer to a cold frame in April. Harden off and plant out early in May.

**Parsley.**—Early supplies of this may be had by transferring plants from outdoors to the cold frame in August, September, or October.

**Peas.**—In order to have an early supply, sow in December, January, or February, placing nine or ten seeds in each 5-inch pot, or say five seeds in a $3\frac{1}{2}$-inch pot, and standing them in cold frames. A compost of loam, leaf-mould, and sand suits peas well. Thin out the seedlings to six plants in each pot. Give as much light as possible and ample air, harden off, and plunge the boxes nearly to their rims in rows in the soil in the open in a warm, sheltered position about the second week in March, or, if space permits, grow entirely under glass.

**Potatoes.**—To obtain early potatoes, plant sprouted " seed " potatoes of an early variety in boxes, small tubs, or large pots, towards the end of January or early in February (temp. 50° F.). The pots should be only half filled with soil, so that top-dressings may be added as the haulm grows. A suitable compost is two-thirds well-decayed leaf-mould and one-third fibrous loam. If more convenient, plant them 4 inches deep and 9 inches apart in the above compost on a gentle hot-bed or in an old melon pit in February and grow under glass.

**Radishes.**—A continuous supply may be obtained by sowing seed in a frame or on a gentle hot-bed between rows of potatoes or other crops, from October to February, and growing under glass.

**Rhubarb.**—To force early rhubarb, cover young shoots in early spring with seakale pots or drain-pipes, and surround them with rotted manure, etc., or lift the roots of plants two or more years old, and pack in boxes in a warm, dark place in October or November.

**Seakale.**—Lift the roots about the end of November or early in December. and pack them closely in light soil, and place in a dark, warm position. Water liberally. Fresh roots should be lifted and treated weekly to provide a succession.

**Tarragon.**—Propagate by means of division of roots in March, and plant in boxes in a heated frame.

**Tomatoes.**—To obtain a continuous supply, seed may be sown from September to March in pots, pans, boxes, etc., covered with glass and placed close to the glass in warm frame or greenhouse (temp. 60° F. night to 70° F. day). Prick off singly into small pots or boxes when fit to handle, and move into larger pots or boxes when necessary. Grow under glass.

**Turnips.**—An early supply may be obtained by means of seed sown early in February in drills, 8 inches apart, on a hot-bed in a frame. Thin the seedlings to 3 inches apart when fit to handle, harden off, and plant out in drills in May.

**Vegetable Marrow.**—These may be treated in exactly the same manner as cucumbers. Sow seed singly in small pots in a heated frame in February. Re-pot into 9-inch pots with a rich compost in April or May, or if preferred, plant out on a gentle hot-bed.

## FRUIT

For forcing fruit a greenhouse is necessary; cucumbers, figs, grapes, nectarines, peaches, and tomatoes require a warm green-house, most other fruit can be forced in a cool greenhouse and is generally grown in pots. For cultural details and for the temperature required at the various seasons the reader is referred to the articles on the cultivation of the different fruits in the chapter on *Fruit in the Greenhouse*.

## FLOWERING PLANTS

### Flowers

Among the flowers most suitable for forcing are those of a woody and shrubby nature and those with bulbous or large, fleshy roots. All plants to be forced must be vigorous and fully matured, or no blooms will result.

**PLATE 5**
A fully-grown *Coleus* (Fire nettle).

# FORCING

## Bulbs

Bulbs for forcing must be firm and plump, and are best of medium size. For cultural details, *see* Bulbs in Pots, page 120. After forcing, the bulbs should be placed in a cold frame for a fortnight or three weeks to harden-off and allow the foliage to die down. Bulbs are useless for forcing a second year, but if naturalised in the wild garden or in grass, they will soon regain their vigour and will bloom for many years.

The following are the bulbs and corms most usually forced : *Alliums, Crocuses, Freesias, Fritillarias, Gladiolus, Hippeastrums, Hyacinths, Lachenalias, Lilies, Narcissus, Scillas, Snowdrops, Tritonias, Tuberoses,* and *Tulips.*

## Flowering Shrubs

Shrubs for forcing must, above all things, be vigorous, and the shoots should be firm, well ripened, and must show plenty of flower-buds. Heat should be applied gradually, and too little rather than over-much should be given. The shrubs are usually potted up in September and early in October, and are plunged outdoors until required. Early potting is essential. About the middle of November some of the earlier-flowering subjects may be transferred to the greenhouse and placed in a temperature of about 45° F. for the first fortnight; during this period, syringing overhead twice a day will be necessary in fine weather. After the first couple of weeks the temperature may be raised to 60° F., and as soon as the plants break into active growth the temperature can be increased by another ten degrees. When the colour of the buds begins to show, lower the temperature by five or ten degrees, and maintain this level while the plants are flowering. After forcing, some of the old wood that has borne flowers should be cut away and any weak shoots should be cut right back; the aim being to let the air and light into the centre of the plant, so that the shoots shall become thoroughly ripened and be able to produce buds for the following season. After trimming, let the plants remain in the warm for three weeks or so, and syringe overhead in fine weather with tepid water, and feed once a week with weak liquid manure. Following this treatment they should be stood in the cold house or cold frame for a fortnight or three weeks to be gradually hardened-off, preparatory to being set out in the open for the summer early in June. Nearly all shrubs are the better if forced every alternate year only, and with lilacs this is essential. Roses, however, can quite successfully be forced for several years in succession.

For details of pruning and special cultural requirements of individual shrubs, *see Alphabetical List of Plants.*

G

The following is a selection of hardy shrubs for forcing :—

*ACER japonica, Negundo variegata*
*AMELANCHIER canadensis*
*AZALEA mollis*
CEANOTHUS
*CHOISYA ternata*
CLEMATIS
*CYTISUS Andreanus*, etc.
*DEUTZIA gracilis* and *Lemoinei*
EXOCORDAS
*FORSYTHIA spectabilis*
*HYDRANGEA paniculata, grandiflora* and Mme. Mouillère
*ITEA virginiana*
*KALMIA latifolia*
*KERRIA japonica plena*
LABURNUM
LILAC (see Syringa)
*MAGNOLIA stellata*, etc.

*MALUS floribunda* var. *atrosanguinea, purpurea* and *spectabilis*
PHILADELPHUS
*PIERIS floribunda*
*PRUNUS Persica, sinensis, subhirtella* and *triloba fl. pl.*
RHODODENDRONS
*RIBES sanguineum*
ROSES
*SPIRÆA arguta, media* and *Thunbergii*
*STAPHYLEA colchica*
SYRINGA, " Charles the Tenth " or " Marie Legraye," etc.
*VIBURNUM Carlesii, plicatum* and *Opulus sterile*
WEIGELAS
WISTARIA

## Roses

The treatment of roses differs slightly from that of other shrubs, in that they must be established in their pots for at least twelve months before forcing is to take place ; that is to say, they must not be lifted straight from the open ground to be forced. They can, however, be re-potted in October, if need be.

Early in November they must be placed in a cold frame, pruned about the middle of December, and transferred to the greenhouse. About a fortnight later the forcing heat should gradually be applied.

## Other Plants

Other plants valuable for forcing are : *Astilbe japonica* and its varieties, *Convallaria* (Lily of the Valley), *Dicentra spectabilis* (Bleeding Heart), and *Polygonatum* (Solomon's Seal).

These roots should be potted-up at the end of October or early in November, being kept in a cold, but frost-proof, frame to be transferred to the greenhouse, in batches as required, at any time from December to March or April.

Gradually remove the pots farther and farther from the glass as the days grow longer and the sun stronger, and to increase the time that they remain in flower, shade the plants while they are actually in bloom.

## PLANTS FOR THE UNHEATED OR COLD GREENHOUSE

In arranging an unheated greenhouse it should be remembered that plants which have their roots under the surface of the ground can stand cold far better than those whose roots are in a pot and above the surface of the earth. Plants in the border will stand many degrees more cold with less damage than exactly similar plants standing beside them in pots. It follows that in the unheated house plants should, as far as possible, be grown in the soil, or at least as many pots as possible should be plunged in the ground. Permanent groups of such plants as Azaleas or Camellias, for example, are a beautiful feature in such a house, and should be planted straight in the soil. Rhododendrons, Palms, and Dracænas all do well in the unheated house, while the Japanese Lilies are lovely additions.

Among suitable shrubs for growing in this house are the Myrtles, the Camellias, the Oleanders, various Jasminums, Tree Carnations, Rhododendrons, Veronicas, and the Azaleas. Laurustinus, and *Daphne Mezereum* will enliven it in the depth of winter. Among other plants suitable are the Agapanthus, both white and blue, *Fatsia japonica, Arundo Donax,* the *Aspidistra lurida variegata,* the various Bamboos, the various Cannas, *Clematis balearica, C. indivisa, Coronilla glauca, Coronilla viminalis, Dicentra spectabilis, Edwardsia grandiflora,* all the Fuchsias, the Fan palms, Hydrangeas, the white and red Lapageria, *Mandevilla suaveolens, Phormium tenax variegatum,* Lilies, and *Solanum jasminoides.* Added to these are most of the hardy and nearly hardy garden plants which do well in pots, including the Primulas, Wallflowers, Brompton Stocks, Columbines, Christmas roses, and Anemones, all of which do well and flower freely in the unheated house. All the bulbs do well, as do the hardy Cyclamen and Lily of the Valley. With these may be included such hardy evergreen ferns as the Hart's Tongue, and an infinite variety of Alpines (*see* page 146). The best arrangement for such a house is on the whole to group a selection of the shrubby plants together, planted permanently in the soil, and to arrange the pot plants harmoniously around and among them, using staging and shelves as supports.

If the house is sufficiently large a very charming effect is produced by arranging it almost in the manner of a garden border, with the plants grouped just as they would be in a herbaceous border, with a winding path running between them as in the open garden. If the plants and shrubs are well arranged, a real winter garden may be produced.

It should be remembered, however, in such a case, that the soil is not exposed to the purifying effects of the rain and air, as in the open, and that the compost in the borders must be renewed occasionally to make good its losses in plant food and fertility.

# THE GREENHOUSE

## A SELECTION OF FLOWERING PLANTS SUITABLE FOR THE COLD OR UNHEATED GREENHOUSE

NOTE.—*For Cultural Details, Colour of Flowers, Time of Flowering, Height,* see *Alphabetical List of Plants page* 233.

### Spring

*AQUILEGIA cærulea*
*ASTILBE japonica*
AURICULAS (Alpine)
*BERGENIA (Saxifraga) ciliata*
CARNATIONS (Perpetual)
*CONVALLARIA majalis* (Lily of the Valley)
LARKSPUR
*MYOSOTIS sylvatica* (Forget-me-not)
PANSIES
POLYGALA
*POLYGONATUM multiflorum*

*PRIMULA vulgaris* (Primrose), *Auricula.*
*variabilis* (polyantha), etc.
SAXIFRAGAS
SEDUMS
SEMPERVIVUMS
*TIARELLA cordifolia*
*TROLLIUS asiaticus, europæus*
*VIOLA odorata* (Violet)
VIOLAS
WALLFLOWER

### Summer

AGAPANTHUS (African Lilies)
ALONSOA
*ARISTOLOCHIA
BEGONIA (tuberous), *semperflorens* vars.
BROWALLIAS
CALCEOLARIA (herbaceous and shrubby)
*CAMPANULA pyramidalis,* etc.
*CANNA indica*
CARNATIONS (Perpetual)
CELOSIAS
*CELSIA cretica,* etc.
*CENTAUREA gymnocarpa, ragusina*
CHINA ASTER (*Callistephus chinensis*)
*CHRYSANTHEMUM arcticum, frutescens hispanicum Mawii,* etc.
*CLARKIA elegans* varieties
COLLINSIA
*COTYLEDON chrysantha, Pestalozzæ spinosa*
DELPHINIUMS
*DIANTHUS Heddewigii*
*DICENTRA spectabilis*
DROSERA
FUCHSIAS
GERANIUM (Crane's Bill) (see also Pelargonium)
HELIPTERUM (Rhodanthe)

HIBISCUS
*HUMEA elegans*
*HYMENOCALLIS calathina*
*HYPERICUM Moserianum, patulum*
*LOBELIA cardinalis*
MATTHIOLA (Intermediate Stocks)
NICOTIANA (Tobacco Plant)
ŒNOTHERA
OXALIS
PELARGONIUMS
MARTYNIA
PETUNIAS
PICOTEES
SALPIGLOSSUS
*SCABIOUS atropurpurea, caucasica*
*SCHIZANTHUS pinnatus*
SEDUMS
SEMPERVIVUMS
SENECIOS
*SISYRINCHIUM Bermudianum, strictum*
*SWEET PEAS
*THALICTRUM dipterocarpum,* etc.
*THUNBERGIA alata*
TORENIA
*TRICHINIUM Manglesii*
VERBENA
VISCARIA
WAITZIA
ZINNIA

### Autumn

CARNATIONS (Perpetual)
CHRYSANTHEMUMS
KNIPHOFIAS
*LAPAGERIA rosea*

*PHILESIA buxifolia*
*SCHIZOSTYLIS coccinea*
SEDUMS
SEMPERVIVUMS

* Denotes climbers. Many of the annuals can be had in bloom at other seasons by sowing at various intervals.

100

# PLANTS FOR THE COLD GREENHOUSE

## LIST OF PLANTS FOR THE COLD OR UNHEATED GREENHOUSE—contd.

### Bulbs, Corms, and Tuberous-rooted Plants

#### Spring

*ANEMONE blanda,
  fulgens
BRODIÆA
*BULBOCODIUM vernum
*CHIONODOXA Luciliæ, var. sardensis
*CROCUS
*CYCLAMEN coüm
DAFFODILS (Narcissi)
ERANTHIS cilicica,
  hymalis
*FRITILLARIA aurea,
*  Meleagris
GALANTHUS (Snowdrop)

*HYACINTHUS azurea
*IRIS reticulata
*MUSCARI botryoides
*NARCISSUS Bulbocodium,
*  cyclamensus
  Horsfieldi, etc.
ORNITHOGALUM arabicum
*SCILLA bifolia,
  peruviana
*  sibirica
TECOPHILÆA cyanocrocus
TRILLIUM grandiflorum
TULIPS

#### Summer

ACHIMENES
ALLIUM
ALSTRŒMERIAS
ANTHERICUM Liliago
BABIANAS
BLOOMERIA
BRAVOA geminiflora
BREVOORTIA (Ida Maia)
CALOCHORTUS
CHLIDANTHUS fragrans
CRINUM Moorei,
  Powellii
*ERYTHRONIUM Dens canis

FERRARIA (Black Iris)
IXIA
LILIUM auratum,
  candicans regale
PANCRATIUM illyricum, etc.
PHÆDRANASSA chloracra
SPARAXIS
TIGRIDIA Pavonia
VALLOTA purpurea (Scarborough Lily)
WACHENDORFIA paniculata
  thrysiflora
WATSONIA Meriana var. Ardernei

#### Autumn

AMARYLLIS Belladonna
CYCLAMEN europæum
EUCOMIS punctata
GLADIOLI
HOSTA grandiflora
HYACINTHUS candicans (Galtonia
  or Cape Hyacinth)
KNIPHOFIA Macowani
LAPEYROUSIA cruenta

LILIUM speciosum, etc.
MONTBRETIA (Tritonias)
NERINE
*STERNBERGIAS
TRITONIAS (Montbretia)
ZEPHRYANTHES atamasco,
  candida
  carinata
  rosea

#### Winter

*CYCLAMEN neapolitanum
FREESIA

IRIS alata,
*  unguicularis
ZANTEDESCHIAS (Richardias)

### Flowering Shrubs

#### Spring

BERBERIS Darwinii,
  linearifolia
CAMELLIA japonica, reticulata
CLETHRA alnifolia
CORONILLA glauca

CORYLOPSIS pauciflora
CYDONIA japonica,
  lagenaria
  sinensis
CYTISUS Ardoinii,

* Denotes bulbs and corms suitable for culture in the Alpine House. All small bulbs are best grown in shallow pans—not pots.

101

# THE GREENHOUSE

## LIST OF PLANTS FOR THE COLD OR UNHEATED GREENHOUSE—contd.

### Flowering Shrubs

#### Spring

CYTISUS Beanii,
  kewensis
  sessilifolius
  supranubius
DAPHNE Cneorum
DEUTZIA gracilis,
  Lemoinei
EPACRIS
ERICA mediterranea
ERIOSTEMON pulchellus
FATSIA japonica

FORSYTHIA intermedia var. spectabilis
  suspensa
MAGNOLIA stellata, etc.
MALUS floribunda,
  Lemoinei
MYRTLE communis
PRUNUS japonica fl. pl., etc.
  nanus
RIBES sanguinea
SPIRÆA arguta, etc.
VIBURNUM Carlesii

#### Summer

ANDROMEDA polifolia
AZALEA mollis
BUDDLEIA asiatica,
  alternifolia
  caryopteridifolia
  Colvilei
CEANOTHUS rigidus
CHOISYA ternata
*CLEMATIS Jackmanii
CLETHRA alnifolia
CORONILLA valentina,
  viminalis
CORREA speciosa
DESFONTAINEA spinosa
DESMODIUM tiliifolium
DIERVILLEA
*ECCREMOCARPUS scaber
ERICA arborea,
  lusitanica
  Veitchii
EUCRYPHIA glandulosa
FABIANA imbricata
FATSIA japonica

HYDRANGEA macrophylla (hortensis)
  vars.
LIPPIA (Aloysia) citriodora
MITRARIA coccinea
MUTISIA decurrens
NERIUM Oleander
PERNETTYA mucronata
PIERIS floribunda,
  japonica
RHODODENDRONS (various)
ROMNEYA Coulteri
ROSES
SOLANUM jasminoides
STAPHYLEA Coulombieri,
  pinnata
*SWAINSONIA galegifolia
SYRINGA vulgaris (Lilac)
VERONICA Hulkeana
WISTARIA floribunda,
  sinensis
ZENOBIA pulverulenta
ZIZYPHUS sativa

#### Autumn

*BIGNONIA capreolata
BUDDLEIA alternifolia,
  asiatica
  caryopteridifolia
  Colvilei
*CAMPSIS (Bignonia) grandiflora
CLERODENDRON fragrans
*ECCREMOCARPUS scaber
FATSIA japonica

*PASSIFLORA cærulea
PERNETTYA mucronata
PUNICA Granatum nana
ROSES
SALVIA Grahamii,
  Greggii
SOLANUM jasminoides
TECOMA (see Campsis)
VERONICA speciosa

#### Winter

ERICA carnea,
  mediterranea
FATSIA japonica
*JASMINUM nudiflorum,
* primulinum

SOLANUM Capsicastrum
VIBURNUM fragrans,
  grandiflora
  Tinus (Laurustinus)

* Denotes climbers.

102

# PLANTS FOR THE COOL GREENHOUSE

## A SELECTION OF PLANTS FOR THE COOL GREENHOUSE

Summer Temperature = 55–65° F.; Winter Temperature = 45–60° F.

### Flowering in Spring

*ACACIA dealbata* (Mimosa)
*AGATHÆA cœlestis*
*AZALEA indica,*
  *mollis*
BORONIAS
*BRACHYSEMA lanceolatum,*
  *subcordatum*
BROWALLIAS
*CAMELLIA japonica* vars.
CARNATIONS (Perpetual)
CINERARIAS
*CLEMATIS indivisa lobata*
*CLIANTHUS Dampieri,*
  *puniceus*
*CLIVIA miniata* and Hybrids
*CONVALLARIA majalis* (Lily of the
  Valley)
*CYTISUS canariensis,*
  *racemosus*
  (*Genista fragrans*)
*DEUTZIA gracilis*
*DICENTRA spectabilis*
ERICAS (S. African Heaths)
EUPATORIUMS

FREESIAS
*HIBBERTIA dentata,*
  *volubilis*
*KALMIA glauca*
*KERRIA japonica* fl. pl.
*LABURNUM anagyroides*
LACHENALIAS
LILIUM (various)
MALUS (various)
*MORÆA iridioides*
MYOSOTIS (Forget-me-not)
*PELARGONIUM Domesticum [Regal]*
  *zonale*
PRIMULA (various)
PRUNUS (various)
RHODODENDRONS
*RIBES aureum,*
  *sanguineum*
*TROPÆOLUM azureum,* etc.
*VIBURNUM plicatum*
*WISTARIA sinensis*
*ZANTEDESCHIA* (Richardia) *æthio-*
  *pica* (Arum Lily)

### Flowering in Summer

ABELIA
AGAPANTHUS
BALSAM (see Impatiens)
BEGONIAS
BERBERIDOPSIS
BOUGAINVILLEA
CALCEOLARIAS
CALLISTEMON
*CAMPANULA isophylla,*
  *pyramidalis*
  *Vidallii*
*CANNA indica* vars.
CARNATIONS (Malmaison) (Perpetual
  Flowering)
*CELSIA Arcturus,* etc.
*CLEMATIS Armandii,*
  *hybrids*
*COBÆA scandens*
*CORYDALIS thalictrifolia*
*CRINUM Moorei,*
  *Powellii*
*DATURA* (Brugmansia) *suaveolens* and
  var. *Knightii*
*ERLANGEA tomentosa*
*ERYTHRINA Crista-gallii*
*EUSTOMA Russelliana*
*FABIANA imbricata*
*FRANCOA ramosa*
FUCHSIAS
GAZANIAS
*GOMPHRENA globosa*

*HABRANTHUS pratensis*
*HEBENSTRETIA comosa*
*HELIOTROPIUM peruvianum*
*HYDRANGEA opuloides* vars.
IMPATIENS
*KALMIA latifolia*
*KENNEDYA Becksiana,*
  *rubicunda*
*LANTANA Camara,*
  *salvifolia*
*LEPTOSPERMUM scoparium* var.
  *Boscawenii,*
  *scoparium* var. *Nichollsii*
LILIUM (various)
*LOBELIA cardinalis,* etc.
*LOTUS Bertholetii*
MESEMBRYANTHEMUMS
MIMULUS (Musk)
*NERIUM Oleander*
OLEARIAS
OXALIS
*PELARGONIUM domesticum* (P. Regale),
  *zonale*
PETUNIAS
PHILADELPHUS
SCHIZANTHUS
*STEPHANOTIS floribunda*
*STREPTOSOLEN Jamesonii*
*TRACHELIUM cœruleum*
VERBENAS
ZINNIAS

# THE GREENHOUSE

## A SELECTION OF PLANTS FOR THE COOL GREENHOUSE—*contd.*

### Flowering in Autumn

ABUTILONS
*AMARYLLIS Belladonna*
BIGNONIAS
BROWALLIAS
CHRYSANTHEMUMS
CLEMATIS (Late)
*CLERODENDRON ugandense*
*FATSIA japonica*
GAZANIAS
*GERBERA hybrids*

*LAPAGERIA rosea*
MIGNONETTE (*Reseda*)
NERINES
*PLUMBAGO capensis*
*POLIANTHES tuberosa*
SALVIA (various)
*SCHIZOSTYLIS coccinea*
STREPTOCARPUS hybrids
*VALLOTA purpurea* (Scarborough Lily
*ZINNIA elegans* var.

### Flowering in Winter

BEGONIAS, fibrous rooted
BOUVARDIAS
CARNATIONS (Perpetual)
*CHEIRANTHUS kewensis*
CHRYSANTHEMUM (Japanese)
CINERARIAS
*CYCLAMEN persicum*
*DAPHNE indica (odora)*

EPACRIS
ERICAS (S. African Heaths)
*EUPATORIUM vernale*
*HELLEBORUS niger* (Christmas Rose)
*SPARMANNIA africana*
*TROPÆOLUM Lobbianum*
WALLFLOWERS

### Flowering Almost All the Year

BEGONIAS
CARNATIONS (Perpetual)
CHORIZEMAS
*CHRYSANTHEMUM frutescens* (Marguerite)
*FATSIA japonica*
*GREVILLEA Thelemanniana*

*LAPAGERIA alba,*
  *rosea*
PASSIFLORAS
*PELARGONIUM zonale*
*RAPHIOLEPIS Delacourii,*
  *indica*
*RESEDA odorata* (Mignonette)
STOCKS

# THE WARM GREENHOUSE

## A SELECTION OF PLANTS FOR THE WARM GREENHOUSE

NOTE.—*For Cultural Details, etc.*, see *Alphabetical List of Greenhouse Plants, page* 233.

### The Warm House

Summer Temperature = 60–75° F.; Winter Temperature = 55–70° F.

### Flowering in Early Spring

*ACACIA armata*,
  *Baileyana*
  *Drummondii*
  *lineata*
  *platyptera*
  *Riceana*
ARUM
*AZALEA indica* vars.
  *mollis*
*CAMELLIA japonica* vars.
CINERARIAS
*CONVALLARIA majalis* (Lily of the Valley)
CARNATIONS (Perpetual flowering)
*CHORIZEMA cordatum*,
  *ilicifolium*
*CORONELLA glauca*
*CYTISUS canariense* (*Genista fragrans*)
  *racemosa*
*DIERVILLA rosea* (Weigela)
*EPACRIS hyacinthiflora*,
  *miniata*
EPIPHYLLUMS (*Phyllocactus*)
*ERICA gracilis*,
  *hyemalis*
  *melanthera*
*EUPATORIUM atrorubens*,
  *glandulosum*
  *riparium*

*FREESIA refracta alba* and the many coloured varieties
*KERRIA japonica* fl. pl.
*LABURNUM anagyroides* (*L. vulgare*)
LACHENALIAS
*MALUS Eleyi*,
  *floribunda atrosanguinea*
  *purpurea*
  *spectabilis*
*PRIMULA floribunda*,
  *kewensis*
  *malacoides*
  *sinensis* vars.
*PRUNUS Amygdalus* (Almond),
  *persica* vars. (Flowering Peach)
  (*Cerasus*) *serrulata* vars. (Flowering Cherries)
  *triloba* fl. pl.
*RIBES aureum*,
  *sanguineum*
*SCHLUMBERGERA Gærtneri*,
  *Russelliana*
*SPIRÆA arguta*,
  *Van Houttei*
*SYRINGA vulgaris* (Lilac) vars.
*VIBURNUM plicatum* (Japanese Snowball)
*ZYGOCACTUS truncatus*

### Flowering in Late Spring

*AOTUS gracillima*
BEGONIAS
*BORONIA megastigma*,
  *tetrandra*
*CALCEOLARIA Banksii*,
  *Clibranii*
  *herbeo hybrida* (*herbacea*)
  hybrids
CINERARIAS
*DEUTZIA gracilis*,
  *rosea*
*DICENTRA spectabilis*
*EUPATORIUM petiolare*
*EUSTOMA Russelliana*

*EXACUM affine*
GLOXINIAS
HIPPEASTRUMS
*KALMIA glauca*
*LEPTOSPERMUM Nichollsii*,
  *scoparium*
*LILIUM longiflorum*
*PELARGONIUM domesticum* (*P. Regal*),
  *zonale*
*PENTAPTERYGIUM serpens*
*PHILADELPHUS Lemoinei erectus*
SCHIZANTHUS
*WISTARIA sinensis*

### Flowering in Summer

ACHIMENES
*AGAPANTHUS umbellatus*
BEGONIAS
BOUVARDIAS
*CALLISTEMON linearis*,
  *speciosus*
*CAMPANULA isophylla*,
  *pyramidalis*
*CANNA indica* vars.
*CELSIA Arcturus*

*COBÆA scandens*
*CRASSULA* (*Rochea*) *coccinea*,
  *falcata*
*CRINUM Powellii*,
  *Moorei*
*DATURA* (Brugmansia) *sanguineum*,
  *suaveolens*
*ECHEVERIA secunda glauca*
FUCHSIAS
GLOXINIAS

105

# THE GREENHOUSE

## A SELECTION OF PLANTS FOR THE WARM GREENHOUSE—contd.

### Flowering in Summer

HEDYCHIUM flavum,
  Gardnerianum
HELIOTROPIUM peruvianum and vars.
HYDRANGEA macrophylla (hortensis) vars.
IMPATIENS Balsamina,
  Hostii
  Oliveri
  sultani
Lilium auratum,
  speciosum, etc.
LIPPIA (Aloysia) citriodora
MIMULUS (Diplacus) glutinosum,
  moschatus
NERIUM Oleander (cool house)

OLEARIA stellulata
OXALIS
PASSIFLORA Banksii,
  cærulea
  racemosa
PELARGONIUM domesticum (P. Regal),
  zonale
PETUNIA violacea
PLUMBAGO capensis
SCHIZANTHUS
STREPTOCARPUS
STREPTOSOLEN Jamesonii
SWAINSONIA galegifolia
VERBENA

### Flowering in Autumn

BEGONIAS
BOUVARDIAS
BROWALLIAS
CANNAS
CHRYSANTHEMUMS
CUPHEA ignea,
  micropetala
  pubigera
EXACUM affine
POLIANTHES tuberosa

RESEDA odorata (Mignonette)
SALVIA gesneriflora,
  involucrata var. Bethellii
  patens
  rutilans
  splendens vars.
SPARMANNIA africana
STREPTOCARPUS
VALLOTA purpurea (Scarborough Lily)

### Flowering in Winter

AZALEA indica vars.
BEGONIA Glorie de Lorraine
BOUVARDIAS
CARNATION (Perpetual flowering)
CHRYSANTHEMUM frutescens
CHRYSANTHEMUMS (Japanese)
CELOSIA
CINERARIAS
COLEUS Fredericii,
  thyrsoides
CYCLAMEN
DÆDALACANTHUS nervosus
ERICAS (S. African)
EUPATORIUM micranthum (E. Wein-
  mannianum),
  vernale
EUPHORBIA fulgens,
  pulcherrima (Poinsettia)
FREESIA

GARDENIAS
HYACINTH, etc.
LEONOTIS Leonurus
LEUCOPOGON Lucyanum
LINDENBERGIA grandiflora
NARCISSUS Tazetta var. papyraceus
  (Paper-white Narcissus)
PELARGONIUM zonale vars.
PRIMULA Forbesii,
  malacoides
  sinensis vars.
PYCNOSTACHYS Dawei
REINWARDTIA (Linum) trigyna
SOLANUM Capsicastrum (Winter
  Cherry)
SPARMANNIA africana
TROPÆOLUM Lobbianum
ZANTEDESCHIA æthiopica (Arum
  Lily)

### Flowering Almost All the Year Round

ABUTILON
AGATHÆA cœlestis (Blue Marguerite)
ARDISIA crenulata (Berried shrub)
BEGONIA (fibrous-rooted)
CARNATION (Perpetual flowering)
CASSIA corymbosa
CESTRUM aurantiacum,
  elegans
  (Habrathamnus) Newellii
CHRYSANTHEMUM frutescens

DIANTHUS (Perpetual-flowering Car-
  nation)
HELIOTROPIUM (Cherry Pie)
LAPAGERIA alba and rosea
PELARGONIUM quercifolium (Geran-
  ium, Oak-leaved),
  zonale and Cape species and hybrids
PRIMULA obconica
RESEDA odorata (Mignonette)
SOLANUM jasminoides

NOTE.—Cuttings and seeds of nearly all warm greenhouse plants should be placed under glass in a temperature of 50° F. Light, sandy, well-drained soil is essential.

All shrubs that have been forced on in a warm house must be carefully pruned after flowering. They must be forced only alternate years.

## PLANTS FOR BASKETS
### (see also Ferns)

| Name | House | Flowering |
|---|---|---|
| ACHIMENES | Cool | June, July, Aug. |
| *ASPARAGUS asparagoides* (*Myrsi-phyllum asparagoides*), | ,, | All the year |
| scandens | ,, | ,, |
| Sprengeri | ,, | ,, |
| BEGONIA (some vars.) | Warm | Summer and autumn |
| CACTI (some vars.) | Cool | Spring and summer |
| *CAMPANULA fragilis*, | ,, | Summer |
| isophylla | ,, | ,, |
| Mayi | ,, | ,, |
| COLUMNEA | Stove | March and April |
| *CONVOLVULUS mauritanicus* | Cold | Summer |
| *DISSOTIS plumosa* | Warm | ,, |
| EPISCIA | Stove | ,, |
| FERNS | Stove, warm, cool, and cold | All the year |
| FUCHSIA | Cool | Summer and autumn |
| GERANIUMS (see Pelargoniums) | ,, | |
| HEERIA (see Schizocentron) | | |
| HOYA | Warm and cool | Summer |
| *ISOLEPIS gracilis* (see *SCIRPUS cernuus*) | | |
| *LINARIA Cymbalaria* | Cold | Spring to autumn |
| *LOBELIA Erinus* vars. | Cool | Summer and autumn |
| tenuior | ,, | ,, |
| *LOTUS Bertholetii* syn. *pelio-rhynchus* | ,, | May and June |
| *LYSIMACHIA nummularia* | Cold | Summer and autumn |
| *MACLEANIA speciosissima* | Cool | March and April |
| *MAURANDIA Barclaiana* | ,, | Summer |
| MIMULUS (Musk) | Cold | ,, |
| *MYRSIPHYLLUM asparagoides* (see Asparagus) | | |
| NASTURTIUM (see Tropæolum) | | |
| NEPENTHES (Pitcher plant) | Stove | Summer foliage |
| *NEPETA hederacea variegata* | Cool | All the year |
| NEPHROLEPIS | Warm | ,, |
| *NIEREMBERGIA gracilis* | Cold | Summer |
| *OTHONNA crassifolia* | Cool | All the year |
| *OXALIS lasiandra* | Cold | ,, |
| *PELARGONIUM peltatum* vars. (Ivy-leaved Pelargoniums) | Cool | Spring, summer, autumn |
| *PENTAPTERYGIUM serpens* | ,, | April and May |
| PETUNIAS | ,, | Summer and autumn |
| *SAXIFRAGA sarmentosa* | Cold | June and July |
| *SCHIZOCENTRON elegans* | ,, | Summer |
| *SCHLUMBERGERA Gærtneri* | ,, | Winter |
| Russelliana | ,, | ,, |
| *SCIRPUS cernuus* | Cool | All the year |
| SEDUM | Cold | Summer and autumn |
| *SELAGINELLA Galeottei*, | Warm | All the year |
| uncinata | ,, | ,, |
| *SIBTHORPIA peregrina* | Cool | June |
| SMILAX (see *Asparagus medeoloides*) | | |
| *THUNBERGIA alata* | ,, | Summer and autumn |
| TROPÆOLUM | ,, | Spring, summer, autumn |
| *ZEBRINA pendula* | Warm and cool | All the year, foliage plant |
| *ZYGOCACTUS truncatus* | Cool | Winter |

# THE GREENHOUSE

## SOME WINTER FLOWERING GREENHOUSE PLANTS

| Name | House | Flowering |
|---|---|---|
| ALONSOA | Cool | Oct. to Dec. |
| *ANEMONE blanda* | Cold | Feb. to March |
| BEGONIAS (Winter-blooming) | Warm | Nov. to March |
| BOUVARDIA | ,, | Nov. to April |
| CARNATIONS (Perpetual) | Cool | ,, |
| *CENTROPOGON Lucyanus* | ,, | Nov. to Feb. |
| *CHIMONANTHUS præcox* (*C. fragrans*) | Cold | Dec and Jan. |
| CHIONODOXA | ,, | March |
| CHRYSANTHEMUM | Cool and cold | Oct. to Jan. |
| CINERARIAS | Cool | Jan. to April |
| *COLEUS Fredericii, thyrsoideus* | Warm | Feb. and March |
| CROCUS (some vars.) | Cold | Feb., March, April |
| *CONVALLARIA majalis* | Warm and cool | Dec. to March |
| *CYCLAMEN persicum* var. | Warm | Dec. to April |
| DAPHNE | Cold | Jan. to March |
| *ERICA gracilis*, etc. | Cool | Dec. to March |
| EUPATORIUMS | ,, | Nov. to April |
| *EUPHORBIA fulgens,* (*jacquiniæflora*) | Warm | Dec. to April |
| | Cool | All the winter |
| *pulcherrima* (Poinsettia) | Warm | Dec. to Feb. |
| *splendens* | Cool | All the winter |
| FREESIA | ,, | Jan. to March |
| GALANTHUS (Snowdrop) | Cold | Jan. to Feb. |
| GARDENIA | Warm | Sept. to Jan. |
| HAMAMELIS | Cold | Dec. to Jan. |
| *HELLEBORUS niger* | ,, | ,, |
| HIBISCUS | ,, | Nov. to March |
| HYACINTHUS | Cool | Dec. to April |
| IRIS (Early) | Cold | April to March |
| *JASMINUM nudiflorum, primulinum* | ,, | Dec. to March |
| *LIBONIA floribunda* | Cool | ,, |
| *LINDENBERGIA grandiflora* | Warm | Nov. to Feb. |
| *LONICERA fragrantissima, Standishii* | Cold | Dec. to March |
| MATTHIOLA (Stocks) | Cool | Winter |
| *NARCISSUS Tazetta* var. *papyraceus* (Paper White) | ,, | Dec. to Feb. |
| *PELARGONIUM zonale* | Cool | Nov. to March |
| POINSETTIA (see *Euphorbia pulcherrima*) | | |
| *PRIMULA malacoides*, etc. | Cool | Dec. to March |
| *PYCNOSTACHYS Dawei* | ,, | ,, |
| *RESEDA odorata* (Mignonette) | ,, | Jan. to April |
| *RICHARDIA africana* (see *Zantedeschia*) | | |
| *SALVIA splendens* | Cool | Autumn |
| SAXIFRAGAS | Cold | March |
| *SCHIZOSTYLIS coccinea* | ,, | Oct. to Dec. |
| *SOLANUM Capsicastrum* | Cool | Nov. to March. |
| *SPARMANNIA africana* | ,, | Jan. to April |
| *TROPÆOLUM Lobbianum* | ,, | Nov. and Dec. |
| VIBURNUM | Cold | Dec. and April |
| VIOLETS (Neapolitan) | ,, | Jan. to April |
| WALLFLOWERS (Cheiranthus) some vars. | Cool | Jan., Feb., March |
| *ZANTEDESCHIA æthiopica* (Arum Lily) | ,, | Jan. to April |

# PLANTS FROM SEED

## SOME GREENHOUSE PLANTS FROM SEED

| Name | Flowering | House | Sow Seed |
|---|---|---|---|
| ABUTILON | Summer | Warm and cool | March and April |
| ACHIMENES | ,, | Warm | Sept. |
| AGERATUM | ,, | Warm and cool | March |
| ALONSOA | April, July | ,, | Sept. or March |
| AMARANTUS | Summer | Cool | March |
| AMARYLLIS | April to June | ,, | Sept. and Jan. to March |
| ANAGALLIS | Summer | ,, | March |
| AQUILEGIA | April and May | Cold | June |
| BALSAM (Impatiens) | June to July, Sept. | Cool | Feb. to May |
| BEGONIA | Summer | Warm | Feb. |
| BOUVARDIA | Winter | ,, | Feb. to May |
| BRACHYCOME | April and June | Cold | Sept. and Feb. |
| BROWALLIA | ,, | Cool | ,, |
| CALADIUM | Summer | Cold | Jan. to March |
| CALCEOLARIA (herbaceous) | May to July | Cool | May to July |
| CALENDULA | April, June, July | ,, | Sept. and March |
| CALLISTEMON | Spring | | March |
| CALLISTEPHUS chinensis (China Aster) | Sept. | Cold | ,, |
| CAMPANULA | April to Aug. | Cool | May to July |
| CANNA | July to Oct. | Warm | Jan. |
| CELOSIA | June, Sept. | Cool | Feb. to May |
| CENTAUREA gymnocarpa, ragusina | Summer | Warm | Feb. and March |
| CHORIZEMA | Feb. to April | Cool | Feb. to April |
| CHRYSANTHEMUM frutescens (Marguerite), etc. | Summer | ,, | ,, |
| CINERARIA | Dec. to April | ,, | May and June |
| CLARKIA | May to Aug. | ,, | Sept. to March |
| CLIVIA | March to May | ,, | June |
| COLEUS | Summer | Warm | Feb. to March |
| COLLINSIA | April to July | Cool | Sept. and March |
| CORONILLA glauca | March, April | Cold | Feb. and March |
| CUPHEA | Summer | Cool | March |
| CYCLAMEN | Dec. to April | Warm | Oct. to Jan. |
| DATURA (Brugmansia) | Aug. and Sept. | Cool | Feb. and March |
| DELPHINIUM (Annual) | April, June | Cold | Sept. and Feb. |
| DIASCIA Barberæ | ,, | Cool | ,, |
| DIDISCUS (see Trachymene) | | | |
| DIMORPHOTHECA | June and July | ,, | Feb. and Mar. |
| DIPLACUS glutinosus | April to Sept. | ,, | Feb. to May |
| ERLANGEA | April to May | ,, | Feb. to April |
| EUPATORIUM | ,, | ,, | Feb. |
| EVERLASTING FLOWERS (see Helichrysum, Helipterum, Statice, etc.) | | | |
| FRANCOA | April | ,, | March and April |
| GERBERA | Summer | Cool | Feb. to April |
| GILIA | April, May to July | Cold | Sept., Feb. to April |
| GLOBE AMARANTH (see Gomphrena) | | | |
| GLOXINIA | Spring and summer | Warm | Feb., Jan. to Mar., and June or July |
| GODETIA | July and Aug. | Cool | Feb. to April |
| GOMPHRENA (Globe, Amaranth) | April, June, and July | ,, | Sept., Feb. and March |
| HELICHRYSUM | June to Aug. | ,, | Feb. to April |
| HELIOTROPIUM peruvianum | Summer | Warm | ,, |
| HELIPTERUM (Rhodanthes) | April and June to Aug. | Cool | Sept., Feb. to April |

109

## SOME GREENHOUSE PLANTS FROM SEED—*contd.*

| Name | Flowering | House | Sow Seed |
|---|---|---|---|
| HELLEBORUS (Christmas Rose) | Dec. and Jan. | Cold | May and June |
| HOSTA (Funkia) | June and July | Cold | Sept. and March |
| HUMEA | Summer | Cool | May and June |
| IBERIS (Candytuft) | June to Aug. | ,, | Feb. to April |
| *IMPATIENS Sultani* | Summer | ,, | March |
| IPOMŒA | ,, | ,, | Feb. to April |
| KALANCHOË | April, May | Warm | March to May |
| KALOSANTHES (Crassula) | April to Oct. | ,, | Feb. to May |
| *KENNEDYA* | April to June | Cool | March to May |
| *KOCHIA tricophylla* | Summer | Cold | March and April |
| LANTANA | ,, | Cool | Feb. to April |
| LAPAGARIA | April to June | Cold | Sept., Feb. to May |
| LARKSPUR (see Delphinium) | | | |
| *LATHYRUS odoratus* (Sweet Pea) | April to July | Cool | Sept., or Feb. and March |
| LINARIA | June and July | ,, | March and April |
| *LIPPIA citriodora* | Summer | Cold | Feb. to April |
| LOBELIA | ,, | Cool | Jan. to March |
| MARTYNIA | May to July | ,, | |
| MATTHIOLA | April and June | ,, | Sept. and Feb. |
| MAURANDIA | Summer | ,, | Feb. to April |
| MIMULUS | ,, | Cold | |
| NEMESIA | April, June, July | Cool | Sept., Feb. to May |
| NICOTIANA | ,, | ,, | ,, |
| NIGELLA | ,, | Cold | ,, |
| NYCTERINA | ,, | ,, | |
| ŒNOTHERA | Summer | ,, | May and June |
| OXALIS | May to July | Cool | Feb. to April |
| PANSIES (see Viola) | | | |
| PELARGONIUM | Summer | ,, | Jan. and Feb. |
| PETUNIAS | ,, | ,, | Sept., Feb. to Apr. |
| PHACELIAS | June and July | ,, | Feb. and March |
| PHLOX | Summer | Cold | Feb. to April |
| POLYANTHUS | April and May | ,, | May and June |
| PRIMULA (Auricula) | April | ,, | May and June |
| PRIMULAS | Dec. to April | Cool | April to June |
| RESEDA (Mignonette) | April to Sept. | ,, | Sept., Feb. to May |
| SALPIGLOSSIS | April to July | ,, | ,, |
| SALVIA | Sept. and Oct. | ,, | Feb. to April |
| SAPONARIA | April, June, and July | Cold | Sept., Feb., and April |
| SAXIFRAGA | March and April | Cold | Sept. and Feb. to April |
| SCABIOUS | April, July, and Aug. | Cool | Sept., Feb. to April |
| SCHIZANTHUS | | | ,, |
| SEDUM | April to June | Cold | ,, |
| *SOLANUM Capsicastrum* | Winter (berried shrub) | Cool | Feb. to April |
| STATICE | Summer | | ,, |
| STREPTOCARPUS | March to May | Warm | April to June |
| STOCKS (see Matthiola) | | | |
| SWEET PEAS (see Lathyrus) | | | |
| THALICTRUM | April and May | Cold | June to Aug. |
| THUNBERGIA | Summer | Warm | Feb. to May |
| TORENIA | ,, | Cool | ,, |
| TRACHYMENE | April, June, and July | ,, | Sept. and Feb. to April |
| VERBENA | Summer | | Feb. to May |
| VERONICA | July to Oct. | Cold | ,, |
| VIOLAS | April to June | ,, | May and June |
| VISCARIA | April, June, and July | Cool | Sept. and Feb. to April |
| WALLFLOWER | March and April | Cold | May and June |

# GREENHOUSE PLANTS

## ANNUALS IN THE GREENHOUSE

Quite a number of beautiful annuals may be used with striking effect to provide masses of colour in the greenhouse. If sown at intervals they will give a display over a long period. They should all be grown in a cool temperature, particularly autumn sown seed. For detailed culture, *see* Alphabetical List of Greenhouse Plants.

| Name | Height, inches | Colours | Flowering | Sow seeds |
|---|---|---|---|---|
| AGERATUM (Floss Flower) | 6–18 | Blue, lavender, white | May to Sept. | March to June |
| ALONSOA (Mask Flower) | 12–18 | Scarlet | Summer and autumn | March, June, Sept. |
| AMARANTUS (Love-lies-bleeding) | 12–36 | Crimson | Summer and autumn | March to May |
| ANAGALLIS (Pimpernel) | 2–6 | Blue or red | Summer | March to May |
| BALSAM (Impatiens) | 18 | White, rose, scarlet, violet | Summer | March to June |
| BRACHYCOME (Swan River Daisy) | 9 | White, blue, red | Summer | March to May |
| BROWALLIA | 12–18 | Yellow, bluish violet | All the year | March, June, Aug., Oct. |
| CALENDULA (Pot Marigold) | 18 | Yellow, orange | March to Oct. | Sept., March, May |
| CHINA ASTERS (*Callistephus chinensis*) | 6–24 | Various | Autumn | March to May |
| CARNATIONS (Marguerite) | 18 | Various | Winter, spring, and summer | June, Sept., March |
| CELOSIA (Prince of Wales' Feathers) | 18–30 | Crimson, scarlet, or gold | Summer and autumn | March to July |
| CENTAUREA (Sweet Sultan, Cornflower) | 20 | White, yellow, rose, purple | March to Oct. | Sept., March, June |
| CLARKIA | 18–24 | Rose, red, orange, purple, white | March to Oct. | Sept., March, June |
| COLLINSIA | 12 | Purple, blue, white, etc. | March to Oct. | Sept., March, June |
| CORYDALIS | 12 | Yellow | March to Sept. | Feb. to May |
| CUPHEA *miniata* | 24 | Reddish violet, purplish violet | Summer and autumn | March to June |
| DELPHINIUM (Larkspur) | 12–40 | White, pink, scarlet, mauve to purple | Spring and summer | Sept., March to May |
| DIASCIA *Barberæ* | 12 | Rosy | Spring, summer, and autumn | Sept., March, June |
| DIMORPHOTHECA | 12 | Orange-yellow, black centres | July to Sept. | April to June |
| GILIA (Ipomopsis) | 5–12 | Scarlet, white, yellow, purple | June to Oct. | March to June |
| GODETIA | 6–24 | White, pink, red-and-white, mauve | June to Oct. | March to June |
| HELICHRYSUM (Everlasting Flower) | 6–36 | White, brown, red, pink, yellow | June to Oct. | March to June |
| IBERIS (Candytuft) | 6–12 | Various | June to Oct. | March to June |
| KOCHIA | 24–36 | Crimson foliage | July to Oct. | April to May |
| LINARIA (Toad Flax) | 12 | White, red, purple | Summer | April to June |
| MALOPE | 24–30 | Red, rose, white | April to Sept. | Sept., March to May |
| MARTYNIA | 10–20 | Orange-yellow, violet, orange | July, Aug., and Sept. | April to June |

**111**

# THE GREENHOUSE

## ANNUALS IN THE GREENHOUSE—*contd.*

| Name | Height, inches | Colours | Flowering | Sow seeds |
|---|---|---|---|---|
| MIGNONETTE | 9–18 | Cream, gold pink, buff, red | Almost all the year | Sept., Feb., April, June |
| *MIMULUS brevipes* | 9–18 | Yellow | Summer | April |
| NEMESIA | 12 | White, pink, red, orange, yellow, blue | March to Sept. | Sept., March, June |
| NICOTIANA (Tobacco Plant *Perennial, treated as annual*) | 18–36 | White or red | Jan. to March and summer | Sept., Jan., March to June |
| NIGELLA (Love-in-a-Mist) | 18 | Various, blue to white | June to Sept. | Oct., March to June |
| PERILLA | 12–24 | Dark purple foliage | Summer | March |
| PETUNIA | 12 | White, rose, carmine, magenta, purple | Summer and autumn | Sept., March to May |
| PHACELIA | 8–20 | Mauve and blue | Summer | March to June |
| *PHLOX Drummondii* | 6–12 | Various | Summer | March to May |
| *RICINUS communis* | — | Decorative foliage and fruits | Summer | March and April |
| SALPIGLOSSIS | 18–20 | Violet, purple, crimson, gold to white | May to Sept. | Jan. to May |
| *SAPONARIA Vaccaria* | 6–20 | Rose, red-and-white | May to Oct. | Jan. to June |
| SCABIOUS | 24–36 | Yellow, pink, red, maroon, etc. | Spring, summer, and autumn | Sept., March to May |
| SCHIZANTHUS | 18–48 | Various | March to Oct. | Sept., Jan., March, June |
| STOCKS | 12–18 | Various | Practically whole year | March, May, July, Oct. |
| SWEET PEAS | 48–60 | Various | Summer | Sept., Feb. to April |
| *THUNBERGIA alata* (Black-eyed Susan) | Dwarf Climber | White, yellow, orange | June to Sept. | Feb. to May |
| TORENIAS | 8 | Yellow, brown throat and violet-blue, yellow-and-white throat | March to Oct. | Oct., March to June |
| VERBENA (*Treated as annual*) | 6–24 | Various | Summer and autumn | March to June |
| VISCARIA | 9–12 | Red to pale rose | April to Sept. | Sept., March, June |
| WAITZIA (Everlasting Flower) | 20 | Golden yellow | Summer | March and April |
| *ZEA Mays* | 36–40 | Foliage, etc. | Summer | March and April |
| ZINNIA | 9–40 | Various | Spring, summer, and autumn | Sept. to Oct., and March to May |

## HARD-WOODED GREENHOUSE PLANTS

| Name | House | Flowering |
|---|---|---|
| ABELIAS (E. & D.) | Cool | Spring and summer |
| ABROMA (E.) | Stove | June |
| ABUTILON (E.) | Warm | All the year |
| ACACIA (E.) | Cool | Feb., March, and April |
| ACALYPHA (E.) | Stove | All the year |
| ACOKANTHERA (E.) | ,, | Spring |
| ACRADENIA (E.) | Warm | Aug. |
| ADAMIA (E.) | ,, | Summer |
| AGAPETES (E.) | ,, | Feb. to May |
| ALBIZZIA (E.) | Cool | Spring and summer |

112

**PLATE 6**
The double *Gloxinia* 'Queen of Hearts'. There are
many hybrids ranging from pure white to deep crimson.

## HARD-WOODED GREENHOUSE PLANTS—*contd.*

| Name | House | Flowering |
|---|---|---|
| AMASONIA (E.) | Stove | May and June |
| AMERSTIA (E.) | ,, | May |
| ANDROMEDA (E) | Cool | April, May, and June |
| ANOPTERUS (E.) | ,, | April and May |
| ANTHYLLIS (E.) | ,, | March and April |
| AOTUS (E.) | ,, | April and May |
| ARALIA (E.) | Stove | All the year, foliage plant |
| ARDISIA (E.) | Cool | Winter-berried |
| ASYSTASIA (E.) | ,, | June |
| AZALEAS (E. & D.) | Warm | Winter and spring |
| BELOPERONE (E.) | Stove | Summer |
| *BERBERIDOPSIS corallina* | Cool | June to Sept. |
| BERBERIS (E. & D.) | ,, | Winter and spring |
| BORONIA (E.) | Warm | Spring and early summer |
| BOUVARDIA (E.) | ,, | Summer, autumn |
| BRUNFELSIA (E.) | Stove | Most of the year |
| BUDDLEIAS (E.) | Cool | Autumn and winter |
| BURCHELLIA (E.) | Warm | March, April |
| CALLISTEMON (E.) | Cool | Spring and Summer |
| CAMELLIAS (E) | ,, | Winter and spring |
| CANTUA (E.) | Warm | April, May |
| CARPENTERIA (E.) | Cool | June and July |
| CASSIAS (E.) | ,, | Summer |
| CEANOTHUS (E. & D.) | ,, | ,, |
| CERASUS (D.) | Cool or warm | Feb. to May |
| CESTRUM (Habrothamnus) | Cool | June and July |
| CHÆNOMELES (D) | Cool | Feb. and May |
| *CHIONANTHUS virginica* (D.) | ,, | April and May |
| *CHOISYA ternata* (E.) | ,, | June and July |
| CHORIZEMAS (E.) | ,, | March to July |
| CITRUS (Orange) (E.) | ,, | All the year |
| CLERODENDRONS (E.) | Warm | Summer and autumn |
| CLETHRA (E. & D.) | Cool | Summer |
| CLIANTHUS (E.) | ,, | March to May |
| CLUSIA (E.) | Stove | May and June |
| COLEONEMA (E.) | Cool | Autumn and winter |
| *CORONILLA glauca* (E.) | ,, | Spring and summer |
| *valentina* | ,, | ,, |
| CORREA (E.) | ,, | Summer |
| CORYLOPSIS (D.) | ,, | Feb. and March |
| CROTOLARIA (E.) | ,, | June and July |
| CROTON (E.) | Stove | All the year |
| CYTISUS (D.) | Cool | Spring and early summer |
| DAPHNE (E.) | ,, | Spring |
| DARWINIA (E.) | ,, | April to July |
| DATURA (Brugmansia) (E.) | ,, | Summer and autumn |
| *DESFONTAINEA spinosa* (E.) | ,, | Aug. |
| DESMODIUM (E.) | ,, | July and Aug. |
| DEUTZIA (D.) | ,, | March to June |
| DIERVILLA (D.) | ,, | April to June |
| DIZYGOTHECA (Aralia) (E.) | Stove | All the year |
| DOMBEYA (E.) | ,, | Winter |
| DRIMYS (E.) | Cool | April and May |
| EMBOTHRIUM (E.) | ,, | Summer |
| EPACRIS (E.) | ,, | Jan. to June |
| ERICA (E.) | ,, | All the year |
| ERIOSTEMON (E.) | ,, | April to June |
| ESCALLONIA (E.) | ,, | May and June |
| EUCALYPTUS (E.) | ,, | All the year, foliage plant |
| *EUCRYPHIA glutinosa* (E.) | ,, | Summer |
| *pinnatifolia* (E.) | ,, | |
| EUGENIA (E.) | ,, | May to July |

(E.) = Evergreen ; (D.) = Deciduous

H

# THE GREENHOUSE

## HARD-WOODED GREENHOUSE PLANTS—*contd.*

| Name | House | Flowering |
|---|---|---|
| EUPATORIUM (E.) | Cool | Autumn and winter |
| *EUPHORBIA fulgens, pulcherrima* (*Poinsettia*) | Warm | Sept. to March |
| *EURYA japonica* (E.) | Cool | Winter |
| FABIANA (E.) | ,, | April and May |
| *FATSIA japonica* (E.) | ,, | All the year, foliage plant |
| FICUS (E.) | Stove | All the year |
| FORSYTHIA (D.) | Cool | Feb. and March |
| FREMONTIA (E.) | ,, | April and May |
| FUCHSIA (D.) | ,, | Summer |
| *GARDENIA florida* (E.) | Stove | Aug. |
| *radicans* (E.) | Warm | June |
| *Thunbergii* (E.) | ,, | Winter |
| GOETHEA (E.) | Stove | July and Aug. |
| *GREVILLEA robusta* (E.) | Cool | All the year, foliage plant |
| HABROTHAMNUS (E.) (see Cestrum) | | |
| HELIOTROPIUM (E.) | Warm | All the year |
| HIBISCUS (E.) | ,, | Spring and summer |
| HOHERIA (D.) | Cool | June and July |
| HYDRANGEA (D.) | ,, | Summer and autumn |
| ILLICIUM (E.) | ,, | May to July |
| IXORA (E.) | Stove | Summer |
| JATROPHA (E.) | ,, | May to Aug. |
| KALMIA (E.) | Cool | Summer |
| LABURNUM (D.) | ,, | April to June |
| LAGERSTRŒMIA (E.) | Warm | July and Aug. |
| LANTANA (E.) | Cool | Summer and autumn |
| LEPTOSPERMUMS (E.) | ,, | Summer |
| LESCHENAULTIA (E.) | ,, | ,, |
| *LIPPIA citriodora* (D.) | ,, | |
| LUCULIA (E.) | Warm | Autumn |
| MAGNOLIAS (E. & D.) | Cool | March to July |
| MALUS (D.) | Cool or Warm | Feb. to May |
| MEDINILLA (E.) | Stove | Spring |
| *MIMULUS glutinosus* (E.) | Cool | Nearly all the year |
| MYRTUS (E.) | ,, | Spring and summer |
| NAPOLEONA (E.) | Stove | May |
| NERIUM (E.) | Cool | June to Oct. |
| NIEREMBERGIA | ,, | May to July |
| OLEARIA (E.) | ,, | Aug. to Oct. |
| OSBECKIA (E.) | Stove | Summer |
| OSTEOSPERMUM (E.) | Cool | Spring and summer |
| OXERA (E.) | Warm | Winter |
| PENTAPTERYGIUM (E.) | | April and May |
| PERNETTYA (E.) | Cool | May to July, berries autumn and winter |
| PHILADELPHUS (D.) | ,, | April to June |
| PIMELIA (E.) | ,, | May to June |
| POINSETTIA (E.) | Warm | Winter |
| PROTEA (E.) | ,, | Summer |
| PRUNUS (D.) | Cool or Warm | Feb. to May |
| RHODODENDRONS (E.) | Cool | Feb. to July |
| *RIBES aureum,* etc. (D.) | ,, | March and April |
| RONDELETIA (E.) | Stove | Summer |
| ROSES (D.) | Cool | ,, |
| SANCHEZIA (E.) | Stove | Foliage |
| SKIMMIA (E.) | Cool | May and June, berries autumn and winter |
| *SOLANUM Capsicastrum* (E.) | ,, | Berries winter |
| SPARMANNIA (E.) | ,, | Spring and summer |
| STIFFTIA (E.) | Stove | Spring |

(E.) = Evergreen ; (D.) = Deciduous

114

# GREENHOUSE PLANTS

## HARD-WOODED GREENHOUSE PLANTS—*contd.*

| Name | House | Flowering |
|---|---|---|
| *SWAINSONIA galegifolia* (E.) | Cool | July and Aug. |
| *SYRINGA* (Lilac) (D.) | Warm or cool | Feb. to May |
| *TALAUMA* (E.) | Stove | Summer |
| *VERONICA* (E.) | Cool | Summer and autumn |
| *VINCA rosea* (E.) | Warm | Spring and summer |
| *VIBURNUM fragrans* (D.) | Cool | Winter to April |
| *WIGANDIA* (E.) | Stove | April |
| *YUCCA* (E.) | Cool | Chiefly foliage plant |
| *ZIERIA* (E.) | ,, | Spring |
| *ZIZYPHUS* (D.) | ,, | April to Aug. |

(E.) = Evergreen; (D.) = Deciduous

Many of those grown in a cool house can also be grown in a cold house.

## CLIMBERS AND TWINERS

| Name | House | Flowering |
|---|---|---|
| ABUTILON | Warm | Nearly all the year |
| ALLAMANDA | Stove | June and July |
| *ARAUJIA sericifera* | Cool | Summer |
| ARISTOLOCHIA | Stove | Summer |
| *ASPARAGUS medeoloides*, (Smilax), *plumosus* | Cool | All the year, foliage plant |
| | ,, | ,, |
| *BERBERIDOPSIS corallina* | Cold | July to Sept. |
| BIGNONIA | Stove and warm | Summer and autumn |
| BOMAREA | Warm | Spring and autumn |
| BOUGAINVILLEA | ,, | Spring and summer |
| BRACHYSEMA | Cool | March to May |
| CESTRUM | ,, | Spring, summer, and autumn |
| CISSUS | Stove and warm | Summer |
| CLEMATIS | Cool | Spring and summer |
| *CLIANTHUS puniceus* | ,, | Spring |
| *CLITORIA Ternatea* | ,, | July |
| *COBÆA scandens* | ,, | May to Oct. |
| COMBRETUM | Warm | May to Aug. |
| DIPLADENIA | Stove | May to Sept. |
| *ECCREMOCARPUS scaber* | Cool | Summer |
| *FICUS pumila* (*repens*) | Stove and warm | All the year, foliage plant |
| GLORIOSA | Warm | Summer |
| HABROTHAMNUS (see Cestrum) | Cool | Spring, summer, and autumn |
| HARDENBERGIA | ,, | March and April |
| *HIBBERTIA dentata, volubilis* | ,, | Spring and summer |
| *HIDALGOA Wercklei* (Climbing Dahlia) | ,, | Summer |
| *HOYA carnosa* | ,, | ,, |
| IPOMŒA | Warm | Summer and autumn |
| JASMINUM | Warm and cool | Spring and summer |
| KENNEDYA | Cool | March to June |
| *LAPAGERIA rosea* and var. *alba* | ,, | Spring and summer |
| LITTONIA | Warm | |
| *LONICERA sempervirens* | Cool | Spring and summer |
| *MANDEVILLA suaveolens* | ,, | Summer |
| *MANETTIA bicolor, inflata* | Warm | Spring and summer |
| *MAURANDIA Barclaiana, scandens* | Cool | Summer |
| MUTISIA | ,, | June till Aug. |
| *MYRSIPHYLLUM asparagoides* (see *Asparagus medeoloides*) | | |
| PASSIFLORA | Warm and cool | Summer |
| PERESKIA | Cool | Oct. to Jan. |

## CLIMBERS AND TWINERS—*contd.*

| Name | House | Flowering |
|---|---|---|
| *PLUMBAGO capensis* | Cool | Summer and autumn |
| *RHODOCHITON volubile* | ,, | Summer |
| RHYNCHOSPERMUM (see Trachelospermum) | | |
| *SOLANDRA grandiflora* | Cool | March and April |
| *SOLANUM jasminoides, Wendlandii* | ,, | Summer ,, |
| *SOLLYA heterophylla* | ,, | July |
| *STEPHANOTIS floribunda* | Stove | May to July |
| *STREPTOSOLEN Jamesonii* | Warm | Summer |
| *SWAINSONIA galegifolia* | (Semi) cool | July |
| TACSONIA | Cool | Summer and autumn |
| TECOMA | ,, | Summer |
| TECOMARIA | ,, | Autumn |
| *THUNBERGIA coccinea, Gibsonii* | Warm | Summer |
| TRACHELOSPERMUM *jas-minoides* | ,, Cool | June and July |
| TROPÆOLUM (Nasturtium) | ,, | Spring and summer |
| VINES | Warm and cool | Spring and summer, foliage plants |

## SOME GREENHOUSE PLANTS FOR SCENT

| Name | House | Flowering |
|---|---|---|
| *ACACIA dealbata* (Mimosa) | Cool | Dec. and Jan. |
| *ACHIMENES tubiflora* | Warm | April and May |
| *ACOKANTHERA spectabilis* | ,, | March and April |
| *ALOYSIA citriodora* (see Lippia) | | |
| ANDROPOGON | Cool | All the year |
| BAROSMA | ,, | Feb. to June |
| BOUVARDIAS | Warm and cool | Summer and autumn |
| CALYCANTHUS | Cold | May to June |
| CARNATIONS | Cool | All the year |
| *CEDRONELLA triphylla* | Cold | Summer |
| *CENTAUREA moschata* (Sweet Sultan) | Cool | May and June |
| *CHEIRANTHUS Cheiri* vars. (*kewensis*) | ,, Cold | Early spring to summer ,, |
| *CHOISYA ternata* (Mexican Orange Blossom) | ,, | June and July |
| *CHIMONANTHUS praecox* (C. *fragrans*) | Cold | Dec. and Jan. |
| CITRUS (Orange, Lemon, etc.) | Cool | Nearly all the year |
| CONVALLARIA (Lily of the Valley) | Warm and cool | Dec. to May |
| *CYTISUS canariensis, racemosus* | Cool | Feb., March, May ,, |
| DAPHNES | Cool and cold | Dec. to March |
| *DATURA suaveolens* | Cool | Summer |
| ELETTARIA *Cardamomum* | Warm | Most of the year, foliage plants |
| EUCALYPTUS | Cool | ,, ,, |
| *EUCHARIS amazonica* | Cold | Summer |
| *FREESIA refracta* | Cool | Jan. to April |
| *GARDENIA florida* | Warm | Autumn |
| GERANIUM (scented leaves) see Pelargonium | | |
| *HEBENSTRETIA comosa* | Cold | Summer |
| *HEDYCHIUM coronarium* | Cool | Summer |
| HELIOTROPIUM *peruvianum* vars. | ,, | Spring and summer |
| *HOYA carnosa* | ,, | Summer |
| *HUMEA elegans* | Cold | ,, |

Calceolaria herbeohybrida in the Greenhouse

By courtesy of ]                    [Sutton & Sons Ltd.
Single Begonias in the Greenhouse

G                                                             H*

Clusia grandiflora

Agapetes macrantha

## SOME GREENHOUSE PLANTS FOR SCENT—*contd.*

| Name | House | Flowering |
|---|---|---|
| *HYACINTHUS orientalis* | Cool | Winter and spring |
| *ITEA virginica* | Cold | June |
| JASMINUM (White) | ,, | Summer |
| *LATHYRUS odoratus* (Sweet Pea) | ,, | Spring and summer |
| LAVANDULA | ,, | Summer |
| *LIPPIA citriodora* | Cool and cold | ,, |
| LONICERAS | Cold | Jan., May, and June |
| *LUCULIA gratissima* | Cool | Autumn |
| *MANDEVILLA suaveolens* | ,, | Summer |
| *MARTYNIA fragrans* | ,, | ,, |
| MATTHIOLA (Stocks) | Cool and cold | Spring and summer |
| MIGNONETTE (see Reseda) | Cool | Spring, summer, and autumn |
| *MITRIOSTIGMA axillare* | Warm | Spring |
| *MYRTUS communis* | Cold | June and July |
| *NARCISSUS Tazetta* var. | Cool and cold | Dec. to March |
| *NICOTIANA affinis* | Cool | Spring and summer |
| *OSMANTHUS fragrans* | Cold | Summer |
| PELARGONIUM (Cape or Sweet-scented) | Cool | Spring, summer, and autumn |
| PHILADELPHUS (Mock Orange) | Cool and cold | April and May |
| *POLIANTHES tuberosa* | Warm | Autumn |
| POLYANTHUS | Cold | Spring |
| *RESEDA odorata* | Cool | Spring and summer |
| ROSES | Cool and cold | ,, |
| *SALVIA rutilans* | Cool | Autumn and winter |
| *SPIRONEMA fragrans* | ,, | May |
| *STEPHANOTIS floribunda* | Warm | April, May, and June |
| STOCKS (see Matthiola) | | |
| SWEET PEAS (see *Lathyrus odorata*) | | |
| SWEET SULTAN (see Centaurea) | | |
| SYRINGA (Lilac) | Cool | March to June |
| *TRACHELIUM cœruleum* | Cold | May and June |
| TRACHELOSPERMUM | Cool | June and July |
| VIOLETS | Cold | Jan. to April |
| WALLFLOWER (see *Cheiranthus Cheiri*) | | |

**117**

# CHAPTER VI

# BULB CULTURE

D ETAILS of the special management of all the more important bulbs and corms, such as the Crocus, the Hyacinth,
Daffodil, Tulip, and the Gladiolus, are given under their respective headings. The general treatment of bulbs is much the same,
however, and it will be sufficient for our present purpose to
describe this broadly, any of the special points being discussed
under their separate headings.

## WHAT ARE BULBS AND CORMS?

A *bulb* consists of a short, conical, fleshy stem surrounded by
fleshy scale-leaves. These may all be arranged individually
on the fleshy stem, as in the genus *Lilium*, or they may be
arranged concentrically around the stem, as in the case of the
Onion. The stem of the Hyacinth, for example, grows in
successive coats superimposed one over the other; the stem of
the Lily is formed of scales growing one over the other, as tiles
are placed on the roof of a house. Bulbs following the formation
of the Hyacinth as said to be " tunicated " bulbs, and those
following the formation of the Lily are said to be " imbricated ".
From this it is evident that Snowdrops, Daffodils, etc., which
are similar in construction to the Hyacinth, and all that possess
the scale-like formation of the Lily are genuine bulbs, and the
term *bulb* is really applicable only to such as these.

A *corm* is a fleshy stem with the growing point on top, and is
usually surrounded by a few remains of the withered bases of
the old leaves. The stored nutriment in a corm is all in the
fleshy stem, whereas in a bulb it is mostly stored in the fleshy
leaves. The Crocus, Gladiolus, Cyclamen, Freesias, etc., all
come under this classification, but, having the exterior appearance of bulbs, they are commonly, though erroneously, accepted
as such. If a cross-section of a corm is taken, either longitudinally or transversely, it will be seen that it consists of a fleshy
stem without any division whatever in the interior, like the
Hyacinth, but consists of one mass throughout. From this it
must not be confused with the potato, which is an underground
stem or tuber. Corms differ from tubers, in that the roots by
which nourishment is drawn from the soil are sent forth anew
each year from a ring or circular patch at the base of the stem,
and not from the eyes, as in tubers, from which stalk and roots

both proceed, the former in an upward direction and the latter downwards.

## BULBS GROWN IN POTS

These should be planted in autumn, and the crowns should just appear above the surface of the soil, which must come up to within $\frac{3}{4}$ inch of the top of the pot. After planting, the pots should be well soaked in water and placed in the open on boards or slates, so that worms cannot get up into the soil. The pots should be surrounded and covered with a layer of 5 inches of fibre or ashes, which maintains equable conditions at the root, and does away with the necessity for frequent watering. They should then be left for seven to nine weeks, by which time the roots will have formed and the tops have made an inch of growth, when they may be moved to a frame or a cold greenhouse, if the roots have made sufficient growth, and should be liberally supplied with water, but not saturated. The less forward plants should be put back in the ashes, and will furnish a succession of later blooms if brought into the greenhouse at successive intervals. The darkness encourages good root growth, which is so essential. Bulbs should never be forced on before their roots have developed sufficiently.

The pots must not be subjected to full light until two or three days after the covering of fibre has been removed—that is, until the pale yellow shoots have turned green. When this has happened, the pots should be placed close to the glass, and should be brought on gradually till the flower-buds are well advanced, when liquid manure-water may be given and the plants forced on with moderate heat. A good compost consists of a mixture of equal parts of loam, leaf-mould, and well-rotted cow-manure, together with a little sand.

As to the number of bulbs that may be planted in a pot, this, of course, depends on the species of bulb and on the size of the pot used. Snowdrops, Crocuses, and Scilla may be planted so that they practically touch one another—that is, about nine bulbs in a 5-inch pot—larger bulbs, such as those of the Daffodil and Tulip, may be planted six in a 5-inch pot; while only three Hyacinths should be grown in a 6-inch pot.

### Depth to Plant

The bulbs of the Daffodil, Hyacinth, Tulip, and similar flowers should be potted so that their tips are just above the surface of the soil; a few other bulbs should only be half-buried; while others, again, must be set 1, 3, or even more

**119**

inches below the surface. Crocuses and Scilla, for instance, should be just covered with soil.

After forcing, which cannot be done for more than one year running, bulbs may be planted out in borders or used for naturalising. They should be dried off and planted out in July or August. The year after forcing, the bloom may not be very fine, but in subsequent years a wealth of bloom will be provided.

## SOME BULBS, CORMS, AND TUBERS FOR GROWING IN POTS

| Name | Pot-up | Bring into house | House |
|---|---|---|---|
| ACHIMENES | Feb. till April | In warm house | Cool |
| AGAPANTHUS | Early spring | In warmth | ,, |
| ALLIUM neapolitanum | Sept., Oct., and Nov. | As required | ,, |
| ALSTRŒMERIA | Spring | In flower | Cold |
| AMARYLLIS Belladonna | June and July | ,, | ,, |
| *ANEMONES (tuberous) | Sept. to Nov. | When well rooted | ,, |
| ANTHERICUM Liliago | Early spring | When growth commences | ,, |
| BABIANA | October | Place in cool house | Cool |
| BEGONIAS (tuberous) | In heat in Feb. | Harden off later | ,, |
| BLOOMERIA | Autumn | Grow on in cool house | ,, |
| BRAVOA geminiflora | ,, | Grow on in cold house | ,, |
| *BREVOORTIA | ,, | ,, ,, | Cold |
| *BRODIÆA | ,, | ,, ,, | ,, |
| *BULBOCODIUM | Sept. and Oct. | Place in cold frame | ,, |
| CALOCHORTUS (various) | Autumn | ,, ,, ,, | ,, |
| CANNA | Spring | Grow in warm house, harden off | Warm and cool |
| *CHIONODOXAS | July, Aug. to Sept. | Put in cold frame | Cold |
| CHLIDANTHUS fragrans | April | Place in cool house | Cool |
| CLIVIA miniata | Spring | After flowering place in warm house | ,, |
| *COLCHICUM | July and Aug. | Autumn | Cold |
| CONVALLARIA majalis | At intervals | Autumn and winter | Cool and cold |
| CRINUM Moorei, Powelli | Spring and early summer | Grow on in cool house | Cool |
| *CROCUS (various) | July till Oct. | When in flower | Cold |
| CYCLAMEN persicum, etc. | July and Aug. | Winter | Warm |
| DAFFODILS (see Narcissus) | | | |
| *ERANTHIS | Sept. to Nov. | End of Dec. | Cold |
| *ERYTHRONIUM Dens canis | Aug. and Sept. | March and April | ,, |
| EUCOMIS punctata | March and April | Summer and autumn | Cool |
| FERRARIA | Autumn | Grow on in cool house | ,, |
| FREESIA (various) | Aug. and Sept. | Jan. and Feb. | ,, |
| *FRITILLARIA Meleagris, etc. | Sept., Oct. | March and April | Cool and cold |
| FUNKIA (see Hostea) | | | |
| *GALANTHUS (Snowdrop) | Sept. and Oct. | Jan. to March | Cold |
| GALTONIA candicans | Spring | When in bud | ,, |
| GLADIOLI (various) | April | When in bud | Cool |
| nanus type | | | Warm |
| GLOXINIA | Jan. to April | From May to Oct. | ,, |

* For growing in pans for the Alpine House.

# BULB CULTURE

## SOME BULBS, CORMS, AND TUBERS FOR GROWING IN POTS—contd.

| Name | Pot-up | Bring into house | House |
|---|---|---|---|
| HABRANTHUS pratensis | From Feb. | Grow on in warm house | Cool |
| HÆMANTHUS | After flowering | Place in warm house | „ |
| HIPPEASTRUM | Feb. | „        „ | Warm and cool |
| HOMERIA | Oct. | Place in cool house | Cool |
| HOSTEA | Autumn | When in bud | Cold |
| HYACINTHUS azureus, orientalis (Hyacinth) | Sept. and Oct. | Dec. to Feb. | Cool |
| IMANTOPHYLLUM (see Clivia) | „ | „ | „ |
| IRIS (various) | Sept. and Oct. | From Feb. as buds appear | Cool and cold |
| IXIA speciosa, etc. | Oct. and place in frame | In spring | Cool |
| IXIOLIRION montanum | Feb. and March | May and June when in bud | Cool and cold |
| LACHENALIA | Aug. and Sept. | Grow on in cool house | Cool |
| *LAPEYROUSIA cruenta | Feb. and March | Grow on in cool or cold house | Cool and cold |
| LEUCOJUM | Aug. and Sept. | When in bud | Cold |
| LILIUM (various) | Autumn or spring | Grow on in cool house as required | Cool and cold |
| MIRABILIS longiflora, | Feb. and March | Grow on in cold house | Cold |
| Jalapa | „ | „        „ | „ |
| MONTBRETIA (see Tritonia) | | | |
| *MUSCARI botrioides | Sept., Oct., place in cold frame | When in flower | „ |
| *NARCISSUS (various) | Aug. to Oct. | As required from Dec. onwards | Cool and cold |
| NERINE (Guernsey Lily) | Autumn after flowering | When in flower | Cool |
| ORNITHOGALUM arabicum | Sept. and Oct. | Place in cool house | „ |
| OXALIS Bowei | Spring | Grow on in cool house | „ |
| PANCRATIUM illyricum, etc. | Feb. and March | „        „ | „ |
| PHÆDRANASSA chloracra | „ | „        „ | „ |
| POLIANTHES tuberosa (Tuberose) | At intervals from Jan. | „        „ | Warm |
| *RANUNCULUS asiaticus, etc. | Sept. and Oct. and Feb. | Grow on in cold frame till in bud | Cold |
| RICHARDIA (Arum) (see Zantedeschia) | | | |
| *SCHIZOSTYLIS coccinea | March and April in cold frame | In cold house in autumn | „ |
| *SCILLA bifolia, | Sept. and Oct. | Keep in cold frame till in bud | „ |
| *   peruviana | „ | „        „ | „ |
| *   præcox | „ | „        „ | „ |
| *   sibirica | „ | „        „ | „ |
| *   verna | „ | „        „ | „ |
| SPARAXIS grandiflora, tricolor | Sept. and Oct. | Keep in cool house | „ |
| *STERNBERGIA lutea major | May and June in pan outside | Put in cold house in flower | Cold |
| *TECOPHILÆA cyanocrocus | Aug. and Sept. | In pans in cold frame till in bud | „ |
| TIGRIDIA, | „ | „        „ | „ |
| Pavonia, etc. | „ | „        „ | „ |
| *TRILLIUM grandiflorum | „ | „        „ | „ |

# THE GREENHOUSE

## SOME BULBS, CORMS, AND TUBERS FOR GROWING IN POTS—contd.

| Name | Pot-up | Bring into house | House |
|---|---|---|---|
| *TRITELIA | Sept. and Oct. | In cold frame till in bud | ,, |
| TRITONIA (Montbretia) | Feb. and March | In autumn | ,, |
| TUBEROSA (see Polianthes) | | | |
| TULIPS | Aug. to Oct. | Bring in warm house in spring as required | Cool |
| VALLOTA (Scarborough Lily) | June and July | Grow on in cool house | ,, |
| WACHENDORFIA | Jan. and Feb. | ,, ,, | ,, |
| WATSONIA Meriana var Ardernei, O. Brienii (W. iridifolia) | ,, | ,, ,, | ,, |
| WINTER ACONITE (see Eranthis) | | | |
| ZANTEDESCHIA (Arum Lily) | Aug. and Sept. | ,, ,, | ,, |
| ZEPHRANTHES candida | Feb. and March | Sept. | Cold |

NOTE.—For cultural details see Chapter XVI.

## BULBS GROWN IN FIBRE

When growing bulbs in this way in small numbers, it is obvious that it is false economy to buy any but the best bulbs for treatment. It is waste of time, labour, and space to grow small weak plants, some of which may not flower at all. In ordering the bulbs, it is best to tell the people from whom they are procured that they are required for this form of culture, and they will then select suitable bulbs. At the same time order the fibre, which will be found on experiment to be the best material for filling the bulb-bowls. These latter should be simple in shape and colour, so that they will not distract attention from or clash with the flowers growing in them, and should be shallow—some 5 inches deep—and glazed. Porous bowls are not good. Mixed with the fibre will be found a certain proportion of lumps of charcoal, and a few of them should be placed at the bottom of the bowl. If the fibre is · at all lumpy, pick it over and rub out the lumps between the fingers, then soak it for a day or so and drain it thoroughly until only a drop or two of water comes out when the fibre is squeezed in the hand. Then fill the bowls to a depth of about one-half for large bulbs, such as the Narcissus and Hyacinth; three-quarters for the smaller, such as Crocuses and Scillas. On this layer, which should not be pressed down too tightly, place your bulbs.

If the bowl is very large, group them in small clumps, do not space them regularly over it; if it is small, the bulbs may almost, but not quite touch. Then fill the bowl nearly to the top with the fibre, so that the extreme tips of the bulbs just show above it.

122

# BULB CULTURE

For the first six weeks the bowls should be kept in a dark place, preferably an airy one, and certainly not near a fire. A cool, airy cupboard or cellar will do. Once a week or so examine the bowls to see whether the fibre is dry, and if it shows signs of dryness, plunge the bowls in a tub or basin of luke-warm water, which should cover them completely. When the fibre is well soaked, take out the bowls and turn them carefully sideways, so that any superfluous water may drain off.

While this is being done, care must be taken that the whole of the contents of the bowl do not fall out; the fibre should be supported by the open hand during the operation. The fibre should be just damp, never sodden. When the bulbs have made shoots about an inch long, the bowls should be brought out into the light, but they should not be exposed to full air and sunshine until the shoots have turned a healthy green.

While this is happening the bowls should be kept in a shady corner of the room. When the shoots are green, the more light and air they have the better; but when they are placed in a window they should always be removed to the middle of the room if there is the smallest likelihood of a frost during the night.

It should also be remembered that the plants will naturally grow towards the light, so that, to ensure good straight plants and flower-stalks, the bowls should be turned each day. No manure should be used.

Crocuses, Daffodils, Tulips, Hyacinths, Chionodoxas, Fritillarias, and Grape Hyacinths may all be successfully grown in fibre, as described above, each kind being raised in a separate bowl.

**123**

# CHAPTER VII

## GREENHOUSE FOLIAGE PLANTS

THERE has been a great increase in late years in the number of foliage plants grown for greenhouse and indoor decoration. Half a century ago the use made of plants indoors was very limited, the cottager's window Pelargoniums, so often spoken of as Geraniums, or Cactus being almost the sole examples. Foliage plants now enjoy a high degree of popularity for indoor use. They are beautiful thoughout the year, or nearly so—an advantage which the flowering plant does not possess; they can be used at various stages of their growth in numerous ways, and they are usually fairly easy of cultivation.

### Palms

The greatest increase in popularity is undoubtedly in the case of the Palm family. These plants are now used more than any others for indoor decoration, and the fact that they vary so enormously in size makes them useful in a number of ways. The smallest kinds are excellent for table decoration, and from these dainty specimens we can ring the changes on all sizes up to the 20- or 30-foot giant which lives in the big conservatory or palm-house. Half-way up the scale we find many specimens which do well in the milder spots of the garden during summer. One kind, *Trachycarpus excelsa*, will, if well looked after and protected in winter, do fairly well out of doors, but the majority of species are house plants. For general purposes, *Syagous (Cocos) Weddelliana* is an excellent palm : its elegant, fern-like leaves, together with the fact that it shows its full beauty while still in a small state, making it an almost ideal foliage plant for the table. Besides these two, useful palms for the greenhouse include the Howeas, often known as Kentias, notably *Howea (Kentia) Belmoreana* and *H. (Kentia) Forsteriana*, *Chamærops humilis*, *Areca sapida*, *Arecastrum Romanzoffiana*, *Livistonia australis*, *Livistonia chinensis*, *Latania borbonica*, *Phoenix canariensis*, *Ph. Ræbelenii*, *Ph. rupicola*, *Verschaffeltia splendida*, and *Washingtonia filifera*.

To grow palms successfully the pots they are grouped in should be well drained, with a plentiful supply of water, both winter and summer. They are peculiar in that they do best with their roots somewhat restricted as to space, so they should

124

[G. H. Preston

Senecio grandifolius

Aristolochia elegans

Aristolochia kewensis

never be put in too large a pot. Many of the species need a considerable amount of heat, and often moisture as well, though these are not the best for the amateur to select. Those named above do well in a house merely protected from frost. During spring and summer the Palms should be syringed morning and evening. In a warm house the evaporation from sprinkled walls and staging will be sufficient during the winter. Partial shade in the hottest part of the day should be provided. In the cool house the temperature for palms should vary from between 45° and 55° F. in winter to between 55° and 65° F. in spring and summer.

Palms are propagated from seed sown at any time in boxes in a compost of finely sieved loam and sand. The temperature of the house in which they are raised should be from 50° to 60° F. As soon as the seedlings have made two leaves they should be potted up singly into well-drained pots. Slight bottom-heat is a great advantage, and the atmosphere of the house must be kept moist.

Palms are, however, usually bought by the amateur as small plants, as they are cheap enough, and are rather troublesome to raise. When purchased they should be re-potted in pots of the same size in a good mixture of yellow fibrous loam and silver sand, or, if preferred, of fibrous peat and grit. The spring or early summer is the best time to re-pot. The pots used should be of a size just to contain the roots without injury, and in potting it is most important that no part of the stem is buried in soil. The earth should be well rammed with a hand rammer. The base of the stem should be set so as just to rest on the surface, and any injury to or cutting of the roots may easily prove fatal to the more delicate palms, so care is needed in the re-potting process. Palms should be inspected at fairly frequent intervals to see whether re-potting is necessary, but it should not be done until the roots are really crowded. In potting, the ball of soil and roots should be lifted intact, the old crocks removed, if the roots are matted round them, and a little soil substituted for them. The ball should then be placed, still intact, in another pot, of such a size as to allow about 2 inches all round of new soil, which will in many cases keep the plant in health for a couple of years. Where the plants are small in size, the increase in size of the new pot should be as little as possible, or the roots will have too much running room. Palms are the better for a little liquid manure, preferably a manure-water made from cow-manure and soot, and where their foliage has a tendency to yellowness or pallor, a small lump of sulphate of iron, placed on the surface of the soil and allowed to dissolve slowly, will often work wonders. (*See also* PALMS, page 483.)

### Cycads

With the Palms we should consider the Cycad family as greenhouse and sheltered garden plants. They are useful and beautiful, though, as their growth is somewhat slow, they are not so popular as the Palms. They like a fairly dry atmosphere, which makes them suitable in some cases where Palms cannot be used. The variety *C. revoluta* is excellent in a sheltered spot in the open garden, and may be left there from May until September. This species and *C. circinalis* are the two most useful for the small house, as the others differ from them only in minor details. They enjoy much the same conditions as do the Palms, liking a mixture of strong loam and river sand, and needing good and thorough drainage.

### Other Foliage Plants

The greenhouse Yuccas are good foliage plants, and although they are slow of growth, the fact that they are equally decorative in a small state counterbalances the defect, as they may serve various uses at various stages. Their varieties are endless, and comprise both hardy and stove plants. Also useful are the Dracænas, some of which are sometimes known as Pleomeles. Some of the Musa (Banana) family are fine foliage plants. The Dasylirions are a useful family of evergreen foliage plants, with fine flowering heads, but are rather large for the small greenhouse. Their flower-stems, in well-grown specimens, are sometimes 10 and 12 feet in height, and make magnificient ornaments in a house large enough to show them well. They enjoy a compost of one part each of peat and sand with two parts of loam, while, as with the above-mentioned plants, good drainage and a plentiful supply of water in the summer are essential. There are numerous forms and varieties of Caladiums, some of the leaves being of the most delicate tints or shades of colouring, while the Marantas are very beautiful. For culture and other treatment of all these see Alphabetical List.

Of beautiful plants, far too rarely seen, perhaps the best is *Miconia magnificum,* one of the most lovely foliage plants in cultivation. The fine colouring of its leaves—velvety green above, reddish-purple below, with ivory veins and midribs—gives it a most striking appearance. It is equally good used in a small state as a table plant or as a fine specimen in the greenhouse. It likes a somewhat more moist atmosphere than the foregoing plants, for the leaves are apt to become deformed if allowed to get too dry when immature. Otherwise the cultural directions are the same, the plants thriving best in equal parts of fibrous peat and leaf-mould, with one-fourth part of silver sand added.

**126**

The silver-foliaged plants are worthy of a place in all greenhouses and among them the best are *Eulalia japonica variegata*, *Pandanus Veitchii*, *Cyperus alternifolius variegata*, and *Anthericum argenteo-lineare*. The Eulalias are nearly hardy, and do not require much heat, indeed, some of them make good border plants. They will do well in any good garden soil. Pandanus requires some heat, and does best in sandy loam, mixed with a little charcoal and leaf-mould. In winter it needs but little water, but in summer should have a liberal supply. In watering during the winter care must be taken that no water remains in the axils of the leaves, as this is very injurious to the plant. Cyperus likes moisture, with a soil of loam and sand, mixed with a little peat. The Anthericums do best in a rich, light soil, composed of fibrous loam and either leaf-mould or well-decayed manure, with some coarse sand. They should be potted in pots about a foot across, and kept well watered while flowering; after that time the water may be lessened, but the roots should never be dry. This family is largely hardy, and the plants therefore do well in cool houses, or in a room.

### Plants for Table Decoration

Where plants are required to serve as table decorations—where they are often most successful—the grower should select dwarf-growing plants, which give their full effect while still small enough to be suitable. Among them he should place the Fittonias, *F. argyroneura* and *F. Pearcei*; *Selaginella uncinata*, sometimes known as *S. cæsia*; and *Oplismenus hirtellus* (*Panicum variegatum* of florists). These make pretty dinner-table decorations, grown either in thumb-pots or in the shallow pans used for growing Orchids. The Fittonias have prettily variegated leaves, and enjoy partial shade and a liberal water supply. The best soil for them is a compost of loam, peat, and silver sand. Selaginellas like the same conditions as do ferns, and thrive well in light ordinary soil, to which charcoal or small potsherds have been added and freely mixed, so as to keep the texture very open. Moisture and shade suit them. *Oplismenus hirtellus* is a grass, variegated with pink and white, and does well in ordinary light garden soil. It is nearly hardy, but in winter should be kept in heat.

### For Greenhouse Decoration

For the actual decoration of the greenhouse the foliage plants are most useful. The dwarf varieties may be used in small pots to cover and decorate the fronts of the stagings, and others, a trifle higher, as an undergrowth to larger specimen plants. Where, as is often the case, there is a damp wall which will not retain whitewash or other colour, and is always patchy and untidy, the maidenhairs and other ferns, such as *Pteris longifolia*, *Dryopteris molle*, and *Nephrolepis cordifolia*, can be used to clothe them. Climbers, if used with discretion, help enormously in the look of a greenhouse, among them the varieties of Asparagus, some being suited to the warm and others to the cool house. *Aristolochia elegans*, *Gloriosa superba*, and the Passion-flower, Passiflora, are all useful and beautiful. For a quite cool house the African Asparagus is admirably suited, as it can stand a temperature as low as 40°. Another climber which can stand a low temperature is *Lygodium scandens*, but this is less hardy than the foregoing. *Asparagus (Myrsiphyllum) asparagoides* is so good for cutting that it should be included wherever possible. *Cissus (Vitis) discolor* is one of the most handsome of all greenhouse foliage climbers.

Ferns can be established on the wall itself with very little trouble, wherever the surface is not cement. A little soil rammed into crevices will help the plants to get a foothold, or the face of the wall can be covered with fine wire netting, behind which lumps of fibrous peat and loam have been placed, and small ferns planted in it. In this way the wall will be covered with decorative foliage, which also provides good material for cutting.

For baskets many ferns are admirably suited, notably *Adiantum Moorei (A. amabile)* among the maidenhairs, and with it *Ceropteris schizophylla gloriosa*. *Asparagus deflexus* is a good basket plant. Many basket plants get an insufficient supply of water, and look dwarfed and poor in consequence. This fault should be avoided, and this can easily be done. At least once a week each basket should be stood in a tub of rainwater to have a good soaking, standing the basket out to drain before hanging it up.

Rockwork is far too little used in conservatories and ornamental greenhouses. It has quite a unique utility in hiding unsightly walls and filling useless corners, and may be utilised for growing such things as the Ferns, variegated Grasses, and the foliage Begonias. Many of the hardier of the exotic ferns may be grown in this way in the cool house without any artificial heat, the filmy ferns in glass cases, in particular, doing well in this manner. (*See* FERNS, page 130.)

# FOLIAGE PLANTS

## GREENHOUSE FOLIAGE PLANTS
### (See also Ferns)

*ACANTHUS spinosus
AGAVE americana, var. variegata
ALOE variegata
AMARANTUS ruber
ANTHERICUM variegatum
ARAUCARIA excelsa
ASPARAGUS plumosus nanus,
  Sprengeri
* verticillatus
ASPIDISTRA lurida, var. variegata
*AUCUBA japonica
BEGONIA Rex in its many coloured
  varieties
CANNAS (various)
*CAREX japonica variegata
CENTAUREA gymnocarpa,
* ragusina
CHLOROPHYTUM elatum
CHRYSALIDOCARPUS lutescens
*CINERARIA maritima
CODIÆUMS in var.
COLEUS Blumei vars.
CORDYLINE australis
CORYPHA australis
CYANOPHYLLUM magnificum
CYPERUS alternifolius
DRACÆNAS in vars.
ECHEVERIAS
EUCALYPTUS citriodora,
  globulus
EUGENIA buxifolia
EULALIA japonica variegata, etc.
EURYA japonica
FATSIA japonica (syn. Aralia Sie-
  boldii)
FERNS (see list)
FICUS elastica and the var. variegata

FITTONIAS
GREVILLEA robusta
GYNURE aurantiaca
HOSTA (Funkia) Sieboldiana
HOWEA Belmoreana
HUMEA elegans
IRESINE (vars.)
KOCHIA tricophylla, etc.
LATANIA Verschaffeltii
  borbonica
LIRIOPE spicata variegata
MICONIA
OPHIOPOGONS
OPLISMENUS hirtellus
PANDANUS Sanderi,
  Veitchii
PANICUM plicatum
PHOENIX
PHORMIUM tenax and var. variegata
PLEOMELE
RHOPALOSTYLIS Baueri,
  sapida
RICINUS communis
SALVIA argentea
SANCHEZIA nobilis
SANSEVIERIA zeylanica var. Laurentii
SCIRPUS cernuus
SELAGINELLA uncinata (cæsia)
SENECIO Cineraria
STROBILANTHES Dyerianus
SYAGRUS Weddelliana
*THALICTRUM adiantifolium
TRADESCANTIAS
VACCINIUMS
YUCCA aloifolia and its var. variegata
* filamentosa
ZEA Mays var. quadricolor

* Denotes plants requiring no artificial heat in winter.

# CHAPTER VIII

# GREENHOUSE FERNS

OWING to their beautiful forms of foliage and their diverse colouring, ferns are very popular greenhouse plants. Many of them bear foliage all through the year and can be used as a set off, and as a background, to flowering plants. The pendulous nature of many makes them excellent subjects for hanging baskets.

The position of the fernhouse should be exactly opposite to that of the greenhouse—that is to say, it should face to the north, north-east, or north-west.

## Atmosphere and Temperature

Nearly all the half-hardy ferns may be grown in a greenhouse unheated in the summer, but slight artificial heat is necessary to keep the temperature to about 40° F. in winter. Tender ferns, of course, need a temperature on a winter's night of at least 60° F., and must therefore be grown in the warm house.

Ferns at all times, especially in summer, need a moist atmosphere, and should be shaded from the direct rays of the sun. From October until April most varieties are more or less dormant, and at this time require to be kept cooler than during their period of growth in summer, and also considerably drier at the roots, although no ferns should ever be allowed to become " dust-dry ". The atmosphere, too, should be less humid at this period.

## Ventilation

Ventilation is of great importance. In summer give a good circulation of fresh air, guarding always against a draught. Give bottom ventilation if possible. Top ventilation allows the atmosphere to become dry, and should be given carefully, but it is always advisable to give a little top air in the early part of the morning for a short time only to allow sour air to escape. Keep the atmosphere cool by bottom ventilation and damp floor and staging. In late autumn, winter, and early spring, ventilation should be somewhat curtailed, and given only when the outdoor conditions are fine and not too windy. Close the ventilators early in the afternoon during winter to sustain the necessary night temperature. (*See also* Ventilation, page 30.)

## Potting

Spring, just when the new growth is starting, is the best time for this. For most ferns two parts fibrous loam, and the remaining part composed of well-sieved rotted manure, sifted leaf-mould, coarse sand, and some powdered charcoal, forms an excellent compost.

It is essential that the soil shall be porous and well-drained. The compost must be pressed firmly about the roots when potting. In order that the roots shall be thoroughly moist, the plants should be immersed in water for an hour or two before potting-up; this must be done, as it is almost impossible to make the water permeate to the close fibrous roots once the plants are potted-up, and excessive watering immediately after potting tends to turn the compost sour.

The plants may be divided at re-potting time, one large plant being split up to form several smaller ones. Rather than pull the roots apart, which is liable to damage them, it is advisable to cut right through the " ball ", soil as well, with a sharp knife. All dead leaves must be cut away when re-potting, and the ferns should be kept in a warm, close atmosphere for a fortnight to three weeks until thoroughly established in the new pots. Shade carefully, and do not water much until the roots are established. To encourage growth, young plants should be re-potted, each time into a slightly larger pot, several times a year. For information as to pot sizes, how to pot, and treatment after potting, *see* Chapter IV.

## Watering

The foliage of nearly all ferns, whether grown under glass or out of doors, must be kept moist, and some, such as the Royal Fern (*Osmunda regalis*), will thrive best when exposed to the constant splash of falling water. To afford the proper amount of moisture by artificial means, the best thing that can be done is to spray the ferns with a syringe having the finest possible rose. Certain ferns should never have their fronds moistened. These include those whose fronds are covered with fine hairs, as in the case of the Elephant's Ear Fern (*Elaphoglossum crinitum*), or those covered with farina, such as the Gold and Silver Ferns, *Ceropteris*, sometimes known as Gymnogramma. The roots of all ferns must be watered regularly.

Ferns grown in baskets require more frequent watering than those kept on the staging, and must be examined regularly, as they dry up rather quickly. When they need moisture it is best to immerse the whole basket in a pail or tub of tepid water. The baskets should be lined with a thick layer of turf to prevent the compost, which is the same as that used for pot ferns, from falling through the wire mesh.

## THE PROPAGATION OF FERNS

### Spores

Ferns may be increased by several methods, the most general is by means of " spores " which are contained in small capsules (sporangia), usually on the underside of the fronds. When these capsules are ripe—that is, just beginning to burst—the fronds should be picked and wrapped in smooth, white paper. If these are undone after a day or so, the paper will be found to be covered with fine brown dust, which looks like brown pollen, and is composed of millions of tiny " spores ". The spores are sown in the same way as seeds (*see* Sowing Seed under Glass, page 61), but the compost used—*e.g.*, equal parts of loam, peat, leaf-mould, and sand—must be first sterilised with boiling water (*see* page 90), and then allowed to cool. When sown, the pans should be stood in a saucer of water in a shady place. It is fatal to let pans get dry. The saucers should be kept filled with water, as the pans should never be watered on the top. They should have a pane of glass placed over the top of each to keep the soil moist and to prevent foreign spores, etc., getting in the soil. Ferns may be propagated by spores at any time, but preferably as soon after the spores are ripe as possible, although the early spring is quite a good time.

### Division of Roots

This method is best carried out in March or April, just as growth is about to commence, but before the young fronds have made much growth, or they may be damaged during the operation. The division should be potted-up, and kept in a close, warm atmosphere for a time till the roots begin to get active. (*See* Division of Roots, page **63**.)

### Trailing Roots

This is the simplest of all methods, and consists in cutting off an inch or so of the tuberous root, strictly rhizome, of such ferns as the Polypody and *Davallias*, and potting them up. The rhizome must, of course, have a frond sprouting from it.

### Minute Plants on Fronds

On Shield ferns and some others there appear from time to time small replicas of the parent plant. The frond bearing these may be pegged down on pots of sandy soil standing by

132

Cheilanthes californica

*Photos*] Adiantum pedatum [*R. A. Malby*

Adiantum cuneatum

Polystichum *var.*

the side of the parent plant, or may be cut off and pegged down on to shallow boxes or pots filled with light, sandy, well-sieved, and smooth soil. The little plants will soon root, when they can be cut apart and potted-up. A close, moist atmosphere will encourage rooting.

## SOME HARDY FERNS FOR A COLD HOUSE

(D.) = deciduous; (E.) = evergreen

*ADIANTUM pedatum* (D.)
*ALLOSORUS crispus* (see *Cryptogramma crispa*)
*ASPIDIUM acrostichoides* (see *Polystichum acrostichoides*)
   *aculeatum* (see *Polystichum aculeatum*)
   *Lonchitis* (see *Polystichum Lonchitis*)
*ASPLENIUM Adiantum-nigrum* (Black-Maidenhair Spleenwort) (E.)
   *fontanum* (Smoothrock Spleenwort) (E.)
   *Ruta-muraria* (Wall Rue) (E.)
   *septentrionale* (Forked Spleenwort) (E.)
   *Trichomanes* (Maidenhair Spleenwort) (E.)
*ATHYRIUM Filix fœmina* (Lady Fern), vars. *cristatum, depauperatum, multifur-catum, plumosum elegans* (D.)
*BLECHNUM penna marina* (Alpine Hard Fern)
   *spicant* (Hard Fern)
*CRYPTOGRAMMA crispa* (Mountain Parsley Fern) (E.)
*CYSTOPTERIS alpina* (Alpine Bladder Fern) (D.)
   *bulbifera* (D.)
   *fragilis* (D.)
   *montana* (Mountain Bladder Fern) (D.)
*DRYOPTERIS æmula* (Hay-scented Fern) (E.)
   *dilatatum* (see *D. spinulosa*) (D.)
   *Filix-mas* (Common Male Fern) (D.), var. *cristata*
   *Linnæana* (Oak Fern) (D.) see *Phegopteris polypodioides*
   *montana* (see *D. oreopteris*)
   *oreopteris* (Mountain Buckler Fern), vars. *cristata, gracilis, ramo-coronans* (E.)
   *Phegopteris* (Beech Fern) (D.)
   *remotum* (Remote Bucklers Fern) (D.)
   *rigida* (Rigid Bucklers Fern) (D.)
   *Robertiana* (Limestone Bucklers Fern) (E.)
   *spinulosa* (Prickly Bucklers Fern) (E.)
   *Thelypteris* (Marsh Buckler Fern) (E.)
*HYMENOPHYLLUM tunbridgense* (Filmy Fern) (E.)
*LASTREA* (see *Dryopteris*)
*LOMARIA alpina* (see *Blechnum penna-marina*) (E.)
   *spicant* (see *Blechnum spicant*) (E.)
*MATTEUCCIA Struthiopteris* (Ostrich Fern) (D.)
*NEPHRODIUM* (see Dryopteris)
*ONOCLEA sensibilis* (Sensitive Fern) (D.)
*OPHIOGLOSSUM vulgatum* (Adders Tongue Fern) (D.)
*OSMUNDA cinnamomea* (Cinnamon Fern) (D.)
   *regalis* (Royal Fern), vars. *cristata, gracilis,* and *palustris* (D.)
*PHEGOPTERIS polypodioides*
*PHYLLITIS Scolopendrium* (Harts Tongue), many varieties
*POLYPODIUM calcareum* (see *Dryopteris Robertiana*) (E.)
   *Dryopteris* (see *Dryopteris Linnæana*) (E.)
   *Phegopteris* (see *Phegopteris polypodioides*) (E.)
   *vulgare* (Common Polypody) (E), var. *cambricum* (Welch Polypody) (E); *cornu-biense* (Cornish Polypody) (E.)
*POLYSTICHUM acrostichoides* (Christmas Fern) (D.)
   *aculeatum* (Hard-shield Fern) (E.)
   *Lonchitis* (Holly Fern) (E.)
*PTERIDIUM aquilinum* (Bracken) (D.)
*PTERIS aquilina* (see *Pteridium aquilinum*) (D.)

**133**

## SOME HARDY FERNS FOR A COLD HOUSE—*contd.*

(D.) = deciduous; (E.) = evergreen

*SCOLOPENDRIUM vulgare* (see *Phyllitis Scolopendrium*) (E.)
*SELAGINELLA helvetica* (E.)
*STRUTHIOPTERIS germanica* (see *Matteuccia Struthiopsis*) (D.)
*WOODSIA alpina* (D.)
    *ilvensis* (D.)
    *hyperborea* (see *Woodsia alpina*) (D.)

Hardy ferns thrive in sheltered and shady positions in moist but well-drained deep loam with plenty of leaf-mould, peat, and coarse sand in it. Half-hardy kinds require slight artificial heat in winter. Propagate, preferably in March or July, by means of " spores " sown under glass in the same manner as seed. Increase also by division in March. Pot-up in spring in a compost of two parts fibrous loam and one part well-sieved manure, leaf-mould, and coarse sand, keep moist and syringe.

## SOME STOVE AND GREENHOUSE FERNS

*ACROSTICHUM aureum,*
    *crinitum* (see *Elaphoglossum crinitum*)
    *latifolium* (see *E. latifolium*)
ADIANTUMS (Maiden-hair Ferns)
*ANEMIA Phyllitidis* and *A. rotundifolia*
*ANGIOPTERIS evecta*
*ASPIDIUM aristatum* (see *Polystichum aristatum*)
    *capense* (see *Polystichum adiantiforme*)
    *caryotideum* (see *Cyrtomium falcatum* var. *caryotideum*)
    *falcatum* (see *Cyrtomium falcatum*)
    *Fortunei* (see *Cyrtomium falcatum* var. *Fortunei*)
*ASPLENIUM bulbiferum,*
    *caudatum*
    *esculentum* (see *Diplazium esculentum*)
    *lunulatum*
    *Nidus* (Bird's-nest Fern)
    *sylvaticum*, etc. (Spleenworts)
*BLECHNUM brasiliense,*
    *gibbum*
    *Moorei*
    *occidentale*
*CAMPTOSURUS rhizophyllus*
*CERATOPTERIS thalictroides* (Horned or Water Fern)
*CEROPTERIS calomelanos,*
    *peruviana* (Gold and Silver Ferns)
    *tartarea* ,,
*CHEILANTHES gracillima* (Lace Fern)
    *tomentosa*
*CIBOTUM Barometz* (Scythian Lamb)
    *glaucum* (Tree Fern)
*CONIOGRAMME japonica*
*CYATHEA dealbata* (Tree Fern)
    *medullaris* (Tree Fern)

*CYCLOPHORUS lingua*
*CYRTOMIUM falcatum* and vars.
    *caryotideum, Fortunei* (Shield Ferns)
*DAVALLIA bullata,*
    *canariensis* (Common Hare's-foot Fern)
    *elegans* (Hare's-foot Fern)
    *fijiensis* ,,
    *solida*, etc. ,,
*DENNSTÆDTIA cicutaria,*
    *cornuta*
*DICKSONIA antarctica* (Tree Fern)
    *Barometz* (see *Cibotium Barometz*)
    *cicutaria* (see *Dennstædtia cicutaria*)
    *cornuta* (see *Dennstædtia cornuta*)
*DIDYMOCHLÆNA truncatula*
*DIPLAZIUM esculentum*
*DOODIA aspera,*
    *caudata*
    *media*
*DRYMOGLOSSUM carnosum,*
    *heterophyllum*
*DRYNARIA propingua,*
    *quercifolia*
*DRYOPSIS cana,*
    *crenata*
    *decomposita*
    *dissecta*
    *effusa*
    *parasitica*
    *patens*
    *setigera*
*ELAPHOGLOSSUM crititum* (Elephant's Ear Fern)
    *latifolium*
*GLEICHENIA circinnata,*
    *flabellata*

## SOME STOVE AND GREENHOUSE FERNS—*contd.*

*GYMNOGRAMMA calomelanos* (see *Ceropteris calomelanos*)
*peruviana* (see *Ceropteris peruviana*)
*tartarea* (see *Ceropteris tartarea*)
*HEMIONITIS arifolia,*
*palmata*
*HYMENOPHYLLUM caudiculatum* (Filmy Fern)
*demissum* (Filmy Fern)
*dichotomum* „
*pulcherrimum* „
*LASTREA membranifolia* (see *Dryopteris dissecta*)
*patens* (see *Dryopteris patens*)
*LEPTOPTERIS hymenophylloides* (Filmy Fern)
*superba* (Filmy Fern)
*LOMARIA ciliata* (see *Blechnum Moorei*)
*gibba* (see *Blechnum gibbum*)
*LYGODIUM circinnatum,*
*japonicum* (Climbing Fern)
*MARATTIA fraxinea*
*NEPHRODIUM decompositum* (see *Dryopteris decomposita*)
*patens* (see *Dryopteris patens*)
*NEPHROLEPIS cordifolia* and var. *compacta*
*exaltata* and vars. *elegantissima, Piersonii, todeoides,* etc.
*NOTHOCHLÆNA* (see Notholæna)
*NOTHOLÆNA*
*lanuginosa*
*Parryi* (Lace Fern)
*sinuata*
*ONYCHIUM japonicum*
*OSMUNDA cinnamomea,*
*javanica*
*regalis* var. *japonica* (Royal Fern)
*PELLÆA cordata,*
*hastata*
*rotundifolia* (Cliff Brake Fern)
*PHYLLITIS Delavayi,*
*hemionitis*
*PLATYCERIUM æthiopieum* (see *P. Stemaria*)
*alcicorne* (see *P. bifurcatum*)
*bifurcatum* (Stag's-horn Fern)
*grande* (Elk's-horn Fern)
*Stemaria*

*POLYPODIUM appendiculatum* (see *Dryopteris cana*)
*aureum* and vars. *glaucum,* Mayi Knightiæ
*Lingua* (see *Cyclophorus Lingua*)
*subauriculatum*
*POLYSTICHUM adiantiforme,*
*aristatum*
*PTERIS cretica* and its vars. *albolineata Alexandræ, cristata*
*heterophylla* var. *internata*
*longifolia*
*quadriauurita* var. *argyræa*
*serrulata* and its vars.
*SCOLOPENDRIUM Delavayi* (see *Phyllitis Delavayi*)
*rhizophyllum* (see *Camptosorus rhizophyllum*)
*TODEA barbara* (Crape Fern)
*superba* (see *Leptopteris superba*)
*TRICHOMANES radicans* (Killarney Fern)
*reniforme* (Filmy Fern)
*WOODWARDIA radicans* and its vars. *orientalis* and *plumosa,*
*spinulosa*

Selaginellas, although not strictly ferns, but closely allied, require the same cultural conditions and may be grown in the same house.

*SELAGINELLA atroviridis,*
*caulescens*
*Emiliana*
*flabellata*
*hæmatodes*
*Kraussiana*
*Martensii*
*pilifera*
*uncinata*
*Vogelii*
*Willdenovii* (Climbing Selaginella)

**135**

FERN CULTURE

SOME STOCK AND CULTURE OF FERNS

CYMOGLOSSUM

RODIULA

CHAPTER IX

# ROOM PLANTS

ROOM plants are so generally used, and so deservedly
popular, that it seems time that their cultivation and care
were more widely studied. Most people who keep a plant or
two in their rooms have little or no knowledge of their needs,
and so long as the plants have water at stated intervals, cannot
understand why they frequently wither and die off leaf by
leaf. Now, plants living in an ordinary sitting-room are
living under what are to them highly artificial conditions, and
care and watchfulness are needed if they are to adapt themselves to these conditions and flourish as they do in their
natural surroundings. First, perhaps, of the necessities to a
room plant is an ample supply of fresh air, though this must
not be supplied in the form of a draught. More room plants
die of draughts than of anything else, though frost is also
a danger. The presence of a valued pot plant in a living-
room is often the cause of good health in its owners, as the
fresh air which it needs is equally necessary to human beings,
and without its presence would often be excluded. A pot
plant should never be left between open door and open window,
especially in a time of drying winds. It is through draughts
that most of the hall plants perish.

## POSITION IN THE ROOM

The best place for a room plant is in the window, where
the maximum of light and sun are obtainable, but in cold
weather the plants should be moved from the window at night
and placed in a corner sheltered from draughts, further protected if necessary by a light screen covered with tiffany or
newspapers, if any severe degree of cold is expected.

Dust is another of the powerful enemies of room plants.
Anyone who knows anything of the structure of plants will
realise that the pores in the leaves, fulfilling as they do the
functions of the lungs in the human body, must never be
allowed to become clogged with dust. It is through these
pores that the plant breathes and perspires, and the little
apertures must always be in a condition to work freely. This
is best ensured by careful washing or spraying. Where the
character of the foliage renders it possible, as in the case of

136

# ROOM PLANTS

Palms, Aspidistras, India-rubber plants, and all plants with thick-textured leaves, actual sponging with a soft sponge and warm water two or three times a week, the frequency varying with the degree of dust present in the room, should be carried out. Rain-water should be used, and not cold.

Most of the plants usually grown in rooms will thrive well in a soil composed of two parts of a fibrous loam to one part each of sand and leaf-mould. The cacti like a good proportion of broken brick-rubble, sometimes as much as one-half of the whole, added to their mixture, while the heaths will do best if peat is substituted for the leaf-mould. All the ferns enjoy a large proportion of peat. (*See also* Potting, page 87.)

## WATERING ROOM PLANTS

Watering must be carefully regulated to the needs of the plant, and good drainage is most essential. If the drainage is not absolutely free, the soil will become waterlogged and sour : conditions under which no plant will thrive. (*See also* Watering, page 47).

## BUYING PLANTS

In buying plants for use in rooms, it is always well worth while to get good plants from a good grower. The difference in price is trivial in the long run, and care is wasted upon a sickly, ill-grown plant, forced for the market, the kind that are mostly dealt in by the travelling hawker.

## PLANTS THAT WILL THRIVE IN A ROOM

Although almost any greenhouse plant may be brought indoors and used for decorating a room so long as it is returned periodically to the greenhouse to recuperate, the following is a list of plants which may be grown continuously in rooms, withstanding the effects of gas, fires, and dust.

*ADIANTUM Capillus-veneris* (Maidenhair Fern)
*APORACACTUS flagelliformis* (Rat-tail Cactus)
*ARAUCARIA excelsa* (Norfolk Island Pine)
ASPIDISTRA (Parlour Palm)
*ASPLENIUM bulbiferum* (Carrot-leaved Fern)
*BEGONIA Rex,*
*weltoniensis*
\*CAMPANULA isophylla* and var. *alba* (Hanging Bellflower)
*CHAMÆROPS-humilis* (Fan Palm)
\*CLIVIA miniata*
*CORYPHA australis* (Fan Palm)
*CYPERUS alternifolius*
*CYRTOMIUM falcatum*
*DAVALLIA canariensis* (Hare's-foot Fern)

*DRACÆNA stricta* (Cordyline) (Small)
*FATSIA* (syn. Aralia) *japonica* (Japanese Aralia)
*FICUS elastica* (India-rubber Plant)
*KENTIA Forsteriana*
*NEPHROLEPIS exaltata*
\*OXALIS cernua,*
*floribunda*
*PHŒNIX Rœbelinii*
\*PHYLLOCACTUS* (Flowering Cactus)
*PLATYCERIUM bifurcatum*
*PTERIS cretica* (Ribbon Fern)
*serrulata*
*tremula*
*SAXIFRAGA sarmentosa*
*SYAGRUS Weddelliana*
*TRACHYCARPUS excelsus*
\*VALLOTA purpurea* (Scarborough Lily).

\* Indicates flowering plants. In addition to these, there are, of course, numerous bulbs which may be utilised for indoor decoration.

# CHAPTER X

## CACTI

CACTI are well worth growing because of the brilliance and size of their blooms and on account of the interest afforded by their curiously shaped stems and bristling spines. A great number of the plants have the additional advantage of being quite small, so that as many as a hundred specimens can often be accommodated in quite a small greenhouse. The majority are of slow growth, and once potted-up in suitable soil need not be re-potted for a considerable time.

Nearly all the species of cacti may be easily grown in a moderately-heated greenhouse. For most kinds a winter night temperature of about 45° F. and a summer temperature of 60–80° will be found suitable. Those species which come from tropical regions should be accommodated in the warmer parts of the house, and should be kept very dry throughout the winter. Coming as they do from desert regions, the cacti require practically no watering during half the year (October–March), they thrive in the sunniest parts of the greenhouse, and only the Epiphyllums, the Rhipsalis, and the Schlumbergera require slight shade to ward off the strongest rays of the sun at the hottest part of the year. These three species also need just a little water through the winter—only sufficient to prevent them from shrivelling. For shading, a roller-blind, that may be run up as soon as the strongest rays have passed, will be found the most suitable appliance. Although loving the hot sun, cacti require ample ventilation, and a free circulation of air must be given in summer and in warm, fine weather. Cacti may also be grown to advantage in frames, and a large number of varieties do well if kept in an ordinary dwelling-room, if placed in the window.

### Soil and Potting

The soil used should consist of one-half fibrous loam, and one-half an equal mixture of sand, broken bricks, and lime rubble, the pots being filled to about one-third of their height with broken pots and other sorts of drainage material. Dwarf-growing plants like the Mamillarias may even have their pots filled three-quarters full of crocks. This will prove a great saving in potting compost. In this soil, in an almost dry condition, the plants

138

should be firmly potted, preferably during February or March. Epiphyllums, Rhipsalis, and Schlumbergera again require treatment different from the rest and need a compost of two-thirds fibrous loam and one-third sand, peat, and brick-rubble. Cacti thrive best when left in the same pots for as long as possible, and should only be re-potted every three or four years, when their roots become over-crowded, or if the plants appear to be doing badly owing to stale and exhausted soil. Use the smallest pots that will comfortably accommodate the plant, and shake out and wash away the old soil from the roots. Fill the pot to about one-third its height with broken crocks, prepare the compost mentioned above. Insert the plant in the compost so that the base of the stem is about 1 inch below the rim of the pot, and press the soil moderately firmly round the roots to keep the plant steady. Tall plants will, of course, have to be staked, as the stems of most cacti are heavy, and may snap if allowed to carry too much weight unsupported. Water in moderation for the first few weeks after potting. A few pieces of charcoal sprinkled in the compost will help to keep the soil sweet. (*See* Potting, page 87.) When the roots have filled the pot, a little diluted liquid manure given, say, once a fortnight, will be found very beneficial to the plants. Some growers prefer to make a miniature rock-garden with suitable soil in the greenhouse and to plant the cacti in the crevices of the rockwork, where they certainly look better and grow more freely than in pots.

## Watering

In the cultivation of cacti watering is most important, the great danger being the giving of too much rather than too little. When the plants are in active growth—from April to September in most cases—they may be watered twice a week, the amount of water given increasing as the weather becomes hotter, and on hot, fine days the stems should be syringed and the floors damped down twice a day. In September give more ventilation to ripen off the wood, stop the syringing gradually and decrease the water supply till in winter—that is, from October to April— water is not given oftener than once a week, or even once a fortnight, and then only sufficient to keep the stems from shrivelling. Always use tepid water, and do not let the stems of the plants remain unduly wet after watering.

## Propagation

Propagation is generally managed by cuttings, the lengths varying from 1 inch to 1 or 2 feet, according to the size of the plant. These cuttings should be taken off with a sharp knife, and laid on a shelf for two to three days to dry out some of the moisture, or they will rot. They must then be inserted in single pots in sandy soil, very little water being given until the roots are formed. Summer is the best time for this method of propagation. Cacti can also be raised from seeds. These should be sown as soon as received in soil consisting of one part loam and one part sand with a liberal admixture of crushed brick-rubble. The top layer of the soil should be finely sifted and sprinkled with a little powdered brick dust. A thorough drainage of broken crocks is essential. After sowing cover the pot with glass and keep the temperature at 65–75° F. Keep the seedlings just moist, or they will be scorched, and as soon as they can be handled prick them off into sandy soil and place in a sunny position near the glass. Grafting, in the case of cacti, is an easy operation. The graft, with the bottom cut like a wedge, is firmly fixed in a cut in the stock, and rarely gives any trouble, provided both scion and graft are healthy and in full growth. Cacti may also be propagated by offsets, which must be carefully removed from the parent plant with the hand, and not cut away; they are then potted up in single pots in soil as recommended for cuttings.

**Diseases**

The succulent and thick stems are often damaged in transit; the injured portions must be cut away with a sharp knife and the cut allowed to dry-up for a day or so in the sun before planting. Painting at intervals with a weak solution of carbolic acid will help to staunch the bleeding. As a general rule cacti are not much troubled with insect pests. Mealy Bugs are their worst enemies, as they hide and feed among their spines and tufts of hair. Red Spider, Scale, Woodlice, Ants, Mason Bee, Mice, and Snails also may put in an appearance and must be dealt with. (*See* Greenhouse Pests, page 600.)

Epiphyllums, Rhipsalis, and Phyllocacti require rather different treatment from the ordinary run of cacti.

Their cultural details are, however, given with the other species, Anhalonium, Cereus, Echinocactus, Echinocereus, Echinopsis, Leuchtenbergia, Mammillaria, Melocactus, Opuntia, Pelecyphora, Pereskia, and Pilocereus; in the Alphabetical List of Greenhouse Plants, page 233.)

**Succulents,** other than Cacti, such as Agave, Aloe, Cotyledon, Crassula, Echeveria, Euphorbia, Haworthia, Kalanchöe, Kalosanthes, Mesembryanthemum and allied genera, Sedum, Sempervivum, and Stapelia are all dealt with in detail under the Alphabetical List of Greenhouse Plants.

Corner in the Cactus House

Cacti under Glass

Coleuses in the Greenhouse

*Photos*]                                                  [*H. Smith*

The Alpine House at Kew

CHAPTER XI

# THE ALPINE HOUSE

THERE are some choice alpines that cannot be cultivated to the best advantage in the open in our uncertain
climate. To say that they are choice does not necessarily
mean that they are delicate, but that the blooms of many
are apt to be spoilt by inclement weather; it is to these subjects
that the alpine house affords protection while they are in
bloom; it will also prolong their season of flowering. Most
of the inmates can be brought on during the summer in pans
sunk to their rims in ashes in the open, or in sunny frames,
until they are about to flower, when they should be transferred
to the house, to be removed again to the open after flowering.
After the beginning of October all the plants should be housed
in a frost-proof frame, and must be removed to the cold house
as the blooms become visible. While the plants are in the frame
ample air must be provided, but frost must be excluded. The
choicest *Saxifrages*, however, are usually kept in the house
the whole year through, as their neat and compact foliage is
pleasing and interesting even after the flowers are over, and
does not get ragged and untidy.

### Culture of Alpines in Pans

The culture of alpines under glass is a comparatively new
hobby with the amateur, but one whose popularity is rapidly
increasing. The plants, except the bulbs, which should be
planted again each autumn, require but little attention, and
only need re-potting every second or third year; this is best
carried out in July or the early part of August. Although the
house is as a rule unheated artificially, the plants will furnish
a mass of interesting and brilliant bloom, while the neat, and
in many cases unusual, foliage of such subjects as the *Shortias*,
*Achilleas*, *Sedums*, and *Saxifrages* will provide unbounded
interest in the off season. Great variety of bloom may be had,
since a large number of specimens can be kept in quite a small
space. The alpine house does not necessarily require artificial
heating, although a row of hot-water pipes round the sides
is an advantage. In such a case care should be taken to
keep them away from the plants, as scorching is instant death
to alpines. They are required only during the dark, damp days
(especially in cities) or very severe weather of winter.

141

The alpine house is best of the low span-roof type, so situated that it runs north and south; both sides then get their fair share of the sun. If, as suggested, a span-roof type of house is used, it will be found most convenient to have a centre path and stagings down both sides that will raise the plants up near the glass; the plants will then be easily accessible. The stagings should be covered with a ½-inch layer of shingle, ashes, small breeze, or coke.

## Ventilation

Ample provision must be made for ventilation, for the plants require a fresh, cool atmosphere and plenty of air, but no cold draughts. Upon the proper ventilation much of the success of the alpine house depends. It is very easy to kill, or at least gravely to injure, a house full of plants by injudicious opening or closing of the ventilators. Only in summer when the temperature is too high should top and side ventilators be opened simultaneously, and then only in moderation, as a chilly draught between the two openings may cripple the less hardy plants. Only ventilators on the side opposite to that from which the wind is blowing should be opened.

The amount of air admitted depends, of course, on the nature of the plants; young, growing plants and seedlings require a warm and moist atmosphere, while plants in bloom require the air to be drier. It is important to have ample top ventilation, perhaps less important to have side ventilation, although it is advisable to have it when possible, for emergency, during very hot weather, for it is wiser to have too much ventilation than too little in an alpine house. Side ventilation under the staging is also advisable when possible. It is important that the temperature of the house should be watched, especially in the morning, when the sun will often come out suddenly with surprising power, and unless the ventilation is regulated in time, the heat will become intense. In order to avoid the risk of scorching, the ventilators should be opened early in mild weather, beginning with a small aperture, which is gradually increased as the sun becomes more powerful, reversing the process towards evening as the temperature falls. Violent changes of temperature are as harmful to plants as to people. Frost and fog must also be carefully excluded.

## Shading

Some means of shading the house should be devised. No definite dates or hours when shading should be commenced can be given, as everything depends on the weather prevailing. The alpine house, however, usually needs shading from about

# THE ALPINE HOUSE

the end of April, and should be shaded each day as soon as the direct rays of the sun fall on the house. The blinds may be removed as soon as the fiercest rays are passed. Moderate sun will not hurt the great majority of alpines; it is only the fiercest rays of mid-summer that must be warded off. Protection from only the direct rays of the sun should be provided. Where constant attention can be given, an arrangement of roller blinds is, of course, the best, as the amount of light can be better regulated, and the blinds may be left up on dull and sunless days. Where blinds are not possible, however, and the alpine house must of necessity be left to look after itself for a good part of the day, the simplest, and the most satisfactory, method is to wash the glass over with a mixture of whiting and milk, care being taken to cover all small air bubbles, etc., so common in the cheaper glass, for these act as lenses and intensify the sun's rays. The whiting solution is easily washed off when cloudy weather sets in. Shading is rarely necessary after the end of September.

## Compost and Potting

Most alpines thrive in gritty, well-drained soil. Two-thirds fibrous loam and leaf-mould with one-third coarse, gritty sand makes an excellent compost for most of them. Many of the finer *Saxifrages* like a little splintered limestone or some old lime-rubble, similar to that used in carnation culture, in their soil. Individual tastes must be studied. (*See* lists, pages 536–538.) Pot-up in pans from 6 to 9 inches in diameter and about 5 inches deep; and since ample drainage is required, place 2½–3 inches of broken crocks in the bottom of the pans for plants like the *Androsaces* and the *Saxifrages*. For subjects of a more vigorous nature and for bulbs, 1 inch of crocks will suffice.

## Watering

Alpines require ample water during their growing period and while in bloom; but care must be taken to see that the drainage is adequate, for a stale, stagnant soil is the alpine's greatest enemy. Plants will need most water in the spring and summer. Water at least once a day, sometimes twice, at this season. Dormant plants and those freshly potted are best kept rather dry until growth begins. A watering once a week, or even less frequently, will suffice for most plants in winter time; but the soil must be prevented from becoming dust-dry.

In the summer the watering should be done when the sun's heat is at its lowest, early in the morning or in the early evening,

**143**

but in spring, late autumn, and in winter it is essential to water in the morning, so that excessive moisture may have drained off before the evening, otherwise there is great liability to " damping-off ". The more tender alpines should be stood in a shallow tray with 1–2 inches of water in the bottom, so that the water may percolate up by way of the drainage without damping the foliage ; this is especially necessary in the case of those plants with dense, downy, or waxy foliage which nestles close to the soil.

Plants should never be allowed to become so dry as to droop, for this may cause irreparable damage ; but if this has occurred, the whole plant, pan as well, should be stood in water deep enough to cover the pan. When thoroughly soaked, it should not at once be replaced on the staging, but should be put in the shade for an hour or two to recover. Many plants, especially those that have not recently been re-potted, will be the better for a watering with liquid manure every ten days while the buds are forming. This must be discontinued as soon as the flowers are out.

### Cleanliness in the House

Cleanliness inside the house is most essential. Aphides, Thrips, Red Spiders, Mealy Bugs, Scale insects, and Woodlice are the chief pests met with here. The manner of countering them is shown in the chapter on *Diseases and Pests*, where fumigation and sterilisation are described. Keeping every corner of the house and the stem and foliage of every plant as clean and free from rubbish as possible will do a great deal to keep down insect and fungus attacks.

### Propagation

The plants are increased by seed, of which many kinds are best sown as soon as ripe.

They may also be increased by cuttings of young growths, which usually appear after the plants have done flowering. These cuttings should be planted in sand or sandy soil, and kept close in a frame or hand-light, and syringed several times during the day. When rooted they should be potted-up. Division of the roots is also possible. It is best done immediately flowering is over.

The newly-potted plants should be kept in a close frame, shaded from the sun, until the roots are established ; usually in about fourteen days.

For treatment of bulbs, *see* Bulbs in Pots, page 119. *See also* chapter on Propagation, page 60.

**PLATE 7**
A single-flowered *Gloxinia*. Some varieties
of this plant make excellent room plants.

# A SELECTION OF SUITABLE PLANTS FOR THE ALPINE HOUSE

*ACANTHOLIMON* (Prickly Thrift). Plant in shallow pans in rich sandy soil and stand in sunny position.
  *acerosum.* Rose, 6 inches.
  *venustum.* Rosy pink, 8 inches.
*ACHILLEA* (Milfoil or Yarrow). Plant in shallow 5–6-inch pans of light, dry, rather poor soil in July and stand in a sunny position. Propagate by means of seed in March or division in spring or autumn.
  *ageratifolia.* White, May–September, 6 inches.
  *Kellereri.* White, May–September, 12 inches.
  *umbellata.* White, May and June, 5 inches.
*ADONIS.* Plant in July or September in 4–5-inch pans of rich, deep loam and stand in sun or semi-shade. Rest in summer. Propagate by means of seed in March or division of roots in September.
  *amurensis.* Yellow, February–April, 12 inches.
  *vernalis.* Yellow, February–April, 12 inches.
*ÆTHIONEMA.* Plant in September in 5–6-inch pans in well-drained soil. Propagate by seed in March, or cuttings in July.
  *armenum.* Pink, April and May, 4 inches.
  *iberideum.* White, May and June, 5 inches.
  *pulchellum.* Pink, April–June, 4 inches.
*ANDROSACE* (Rock Jasmine). Plant from July to September in 4–5-inch pans of loam and peat with 30 per cent. grit and limestone and stand in a sunny position. Keep fairly dry and do not water overhead in winter. Propagate by means of seed sown in March, cuttings in September, or division in April.
  *carnea.* Rose and rose-pink, April and May, 3 inches.
  *ciliata.* Rose-pink, May and June, 1 inch.
  *cylindrica.* White, May–June, 1 inch.
  *pyrenaica.* White, May–June, 1 inch.
  *sarmentosa.* Rose, white eye, April and May, 3–4 inches.
*ANEMONE.* Several species are suitable for culture in 5–6-inch pans, see p. 245.
  (Wind-flower). Many suitable for growing in 5–6-inch pans in rich, sandy loam. Increase by seeds in July, or March by division as soon as flowers are over. Tubers should be planted in the Autumn.
  *alpina.* White, purple outside, April and May 5 inches.
  *alpina* var. *sulphurea.* Yellow, April and May, 5 inches.
  *Hepatica.* Blue and coloured forms, March–April, 5 inches.
  *vernalis.* White, tinged purplish-violet, April, 4 inches.
*AQUILEGIA* (Columbine). Charming in 5–6-inch pans in rich, well-drained soil. Sow seeds in autumn or spring, prick out in small pots, and pan-up in spring.
  *flabellata.* Lavender and white, April and May, 10 inches.
*ARABIS* (Rock Cress). Pot-up in September in 5–6-inch, well-drained pans of ordinary soil or sandy loam. Stand in the sun. Winter in a cold frame with plenty of air. Propagate by means of seed sown in the open in April, cuttings in August or root division in September.
  *alpina.* White, May–July, 6 inches.
  *androsacea.* White, April, 3 inches.
*ARMERIA* (Thrift). Pot-up after flowering or early spring in 5-inch pans in sandy soil. Seed sown in spring, or divisions in early spring, or as soon as flowering is over.
  *cæspitosa.* Pink, May–June, 4 inches.
*ASPERULA.* Plant from June–September in 4–5-inch pans of gritty loam and leaf-mould. Keep on the dry side, and do not water overhead in winter. These plants are impatient of damp. Propagate by means of seed sown in the open in April or root division in April.
  *arcadiensis.* Rosy pink, summer, 4 inches.
  *Gussonii.* Rose, summer, 4 inches.
*CALCEOLARIA.* A number of choice species suitable for the alpine house grown in pans in rich soil and kept in a shady, cool place. Divide in early spring or autumn, seeds sown in autumn.
  *Darwinii.* Yellow and chestnut, 3 inches.
  *tenella.* Yellow, summer, 3 inches. (See also in Alphabetical List of Plants.)
*CALLIANTHEMUM.* At one time included under Ranunculus. Should be grown in scree mixture in 5–6-inch pans, well watered during growing season. Seed should be sown as soon as ripe.
  *Kernerianum.* Lilac-white, April–May, 3 inches.

K                                                                                        **145**

*CAMPANULA* (Bell-flower). In rich, well-drained soil in 4–5-inch pans. Division early spring or early autumn, seed sown as soon as ripe, or in spring.

*Allionii.* Satiny purple, June–July, 3 inches.

*arvatica.* Violet, June–July, 4 inches.

*cenisia.* Greyish blue, July–August, 3 inches.

*Raineri.* Blue, July–August, 2 inches.

*Zoysii.* Pale blue, June–July, 2 inches. (See also in Alphabetical List of Plants.)

*CASSIOPE tetragona.* White, June–July, 5 inches. (See also page 294.)

*CRASSULA sarcocaulis.* For culture, see page 328.

*CYTISUS Ardoinii.* Yellow, June–July, 6 inches.

*DAPHNE petræa (rupestris).* For culture, see page 338.

*DIANTHUS* (Pink). Plant in September in 4–5-inch pans of gritty loam (without lime), and winter in a cold frame. Give ample air and keep on the dry side. Propagate by means of seed sown in April, cuttings in June, or layering in July.

*alpinus* (Alpine Pink). Rose, June, 5 inches.

*Freynii.* Rose or white, June–July, 3 inches.

*glaucus (cæsius).* Rose-pink, June, 6 inches.

*neglectus.* Rose, June, 3 inches.

*DRABA* (Whitlow Grass). Pot-up in April–May in 4-inch pans of well-drained, gritty loam. Keep on dry side, and winter in a cold frame. Give ample air. Propagate by means of seed sown in April or division in April.

*Aizoön.* Yellow, March–April, 3 inches.

*imbricata.* Yellow, 3 inches.

*pyrenaica.* Rosy pink, 2–3 inches.

*DROSERA rotundifolia* (Sundew). For culture, see page 352.

*DRYAS* (Mountain Avens). Pot-up in July–September in 4–5-inch pans of cool, gritty, limed loam, and stand in sun or partial shade. Propagate by means of seed sown in April or cuttings taken in August–September.

*octopetala.* White, June and July, 3 inches.

*ERICA carnea.* Peaty soil, increased by cuttings or division after flowering. Pink, January–April, 6 inches. (See also in Alphabetical List of Plants.)

*ERIGERON* (Flea-bane). In 5–6-inch pans, using well-drained soil. Increase by division as soon as flowers are over, or in the autumn, or by seed when ripe.

*aurantiacus.* Orange, May, 7 inches.

*leiomeris.* Lavender-blue, May, 4 inches.

*ERINACEA.* Should be grown in a warm, dry position in well-drained soil, a charming little bush for pans. Increased by cuttings about midsummer, or by seed sown as soon as ripe, but usually imported from its native land.

*pungens* (Hedgehog Broom). Lavender-blue, May–June, 5–8 inches.

*ERINUS.* Plant in 5–6-inch pans in well-drained soil, chiefly increased by seed sown when ripe, or early spring, or by division after flowering, or early spring.

*alpinus.* Various shades of rose and white, May and June, 3 inches.

*ERODIUM* (Heron's Bill). Pot-up in September in 4–6-inch pans of well-drained, sandy loam and stand in a sunny position. Propagate by means of seed sown in spring, cuttings in July, or division in July.

*amanum.* White, April–July, 6 inches.

*chrysanthum.* Yellow, May–August, 5 inches.

*petræum.* White, May–August, 3 inches.

*GENTIANA* (Gentian). Pot-up in July to October in 4–5-inch pans in a compost of two parts loam to one part each of grit and coarse sand. Stand in the open during summer. Propagate by means of seed sown in a frame in March or division in May.

*GENTIANA acaulis (Gentianella).* Deep blue, February–May, 4 inches.

*saxosa.* White, July–August, 5 inches.

*verna.* Deep blue, April–May, 3 inches.

*GERANIUM* (Crane's Bill). For culture, see page 381.

*argenteum.* Pink, April–May, 6 inches.

*Farreri.* Pale pink, June–July, 6 inches.

*napuligerum.* Deep rose, June–July, 6 inches.

*Traversii.* Rosy pink, June–July, 4 inches.

*GLOBULARIA.* Pot-up in early spring or autumn in 5-inch pans in good but well-drained soil. Increased by division or cuttings taken in July or by seed sown as soon as ripe, or in the spring.

*incanescens.* Greyish blue, June, 3 inches.

*GYPSOPHILA.* Pot in 5–6-inch pans in early spring or autumn. Easily increased by cuttings of shoots or of roots, or by seed sown in March or August.

*aretioides.* Pale pink, summer, 2 inches.

*repens.* Rose and white, summer, 4 inches.

146

# THE ALPINE HOUSE

*HELICHRYSUM* (Everlasting Flowers). For culture, see page 393. Some dwarf growing kinds are charming for growing in pans in light, open soil, readily increased by cuttings taken after flowering, or by division in early spring.

*bellidioides.* White, June–July, 3 inches.

*frigidum.* Snow-white flowers, silvery foliage, June–July, 3 inches.

*HEPATICA triloba.* See *Anemone Hepatica*, p. 400.

*HOUSTONIA cærulea.* Pot-up in pans early spring in good loam and peat and granite chippings. Blue and white, May, 3 inches.

*IBERIS.* Pot-up in April or October in 4–6-inch pans of loam, leaf-mould, and sand. Keep in a cool frame until June. Give liquid manure when the buds appear. Propagate by means of seed sown from March to May or division in April or October.

*corifolia.* White, April and May, 8 inches.

*saxatilis.* White, tinged purple, April, 3 inches.

*sempervirens* (Evergreen Candytuft). White, May and June, 6–12 inches.

*IRIS.* Several dwarf species are charming for the alpine house. Pot in 5–6-inch pans in good open soil. Increase by division as soon as flowers are over, or by seed, which should be sown as soon as ripe.

*cristata.* Lilac or lavender, with white and orange markings, May, 3 inches.

*gracilipes.* Lilac or pinkish mauve, orange crest, May, 6–8 inches.

*lacustris.* Dark lavender with white and orange, May, 3 inches.

*verna.* Lilac-blue, orange centre, April–May, 5 inches.

*JANKÆA.* Pot-up in April or September in 4–6-inch pans of fibrous peat, loam, and silver-sand. Stand in the shade under a north wall in summer. Propagate by means of leaves placed in sand in July and grown in heat, or seeds from March to April.

*Heldreichii* (syn. *Ramonda*). Pale blue (grey foliage), June–July, 3–4 inches.

*LEWISIA* (Bitter-wort). Pot-up in April in 4–5-inch pans of sandy loam and peat. Give a little water now and then in dry weather. Keep fairly dry in winter. Propagate by means of seeds sown in March or April in a frame.

*Cotyledon.* Pink, striped with buff or white, May and June, 4 inches.

*Howellii.* Pink, striped white, May and June, 4–6 inches.

*LINUM* (Flax). Plant in 5–6-inch pans in well-drained soil, giving plenty of water during the growing season. Cuttings should be taken in July, or seeds should be sown as soon as ripe, or in early spring.

*alpinum.* China-blue, April and May, 4 inches.

*arboreum.* A small shrub, yellow flowers, May–June, 9–12 inches.

*monogynum.* White, summer, 9 inches.

*LITHOSPERMUM.* Plant in 6–8-inch pans in good gritty loam, most of the species are readily raised from seed, or cuttings may be taken in July.

*canescens.* Orange-yellow, May–June, 6 inches.

*diffusum (prostratum).* Blue, May–June, 8 inches.

*oleifolium.* Violet and blue, May–June, 6 inches.

*MECONOPSIS* (Himalayan Poppy). Pot-up in March in 5–6-inch pans of light, sandy loam, and peat. Transplant in April and keep inside until June. Water well while growing, but keep fairly dry in winter. Propagate by means of seed sown in March or April.

*aculeata.* Blue, May–June, 24 inches.

*puniceus.* Red, May–June, 12–18 inches.

*quintuplinervia* (Harebell Poppy). Pale purple, April.

*MERTENSIA.* Pot-up in April or September in 3–4-inch pans of moist, ordinary soil with a little gritty peat added. Stand in a well-drained position. Keep fairly dry during winter. Propagate by means of seed sown in March or September, or division in April or September.

*maritima.* Purplish blue, white centre, April–May, 6 inches.

*MORISIA* (Mediterranean Cress). Pot-up in March or October, in 3–4-inch pans of moist, gritty loam and stand in moderate sun. Keep fairly dry during winter. Propagate by means of seed or root cuttings in March or division in March or October.

*monanthos (hypogæa).* Deep yellow, March–June, 2–3 inches.

*MYOSOTIS* (Forget-me-not). Pot up in 5-inch pans in autumn or early spring in gritty loam. Seeds should be sown in June, July, or Spring.

*azorica.* Purplish violet, summer, 3 inches.

*rupicola.* Blue, May–June, 4 inches.

*NERTERA depressa.* Forms a carpet of bright green covered with scarlet coral-like berries, should be grown in shade in 5-inch pans in a damp, sandy loam.

*NIEREMBERGIA rivularis* (White Cup). For culture, see page 472.

*ŒNOTHERA pumila.* See page 475.

# THE GREENHOUSE

*OMPHALODES Luciliæ.* Plant in 5-inch pans in light, rich loam with some old mortar-rubble. With care can be divided in early spring, but best grown from seed sown in the autumn or early spring. Porcelain-blue and rose, summer, 5 inches.

*verna* (Blue-eyed Mary). Azure-blue, March–April, 3 inches.

*ONOSMA.* Pot-up in March in 6–8-inch pans of well-drained loam with some mortar-rubble. All can be raised from seed sown in the spring or autumn, or from cuttings in July.

*albo-roseum.* White and red, May–July, 8 inches.

*nanum.* White, May–June, 4 inches.

*tauricum* (Golden Drop). Golden yellow, May–July, 6 inches.

*OXALIS adenophylla.* See page 482.

*PENTSTEMON.* Many of the dwarf kinds are charming for pans, in good loam. Propagated by division in early spring, but cuttings in July and August, or by seed sown as soon as ripe, or in the spring.

*angustifolius.* Azure-blue, May–July, 8 inches.

*Davidsonii.* Reddish mauve. May–June, 3 inches.

*Jamesii.* Blue and white, May–June, 6 inches.

*Scouleri.* Lilac-rose, April–May, 12 inches.

*PHLOX.* Pot-up into 5–6-inch pans, either in early spring or autumn in good, rich, gritty loam. Propagate by division or by cuttings in July–August.

*amœna.* Pinky lilac, May–June, 5 inches.

*Douglasii.* Lilac, May–June, 4 inches.

*mesoleuca.* Rosy pink, May–June, 6 inches. This species is readily increased by root cuttings.

*subulata* (Moss Pink). See page 498.

*PHYTEUMA* (Horned Rampion). Pot-up from November to March in 4–5-inch pans of rich loam, limestone, grit, or old mortar and leaf-mould. Keep fairly dry during winter. Propagate by means of seed sown in summer. Transplant the seedlings in April or May.

*comosum.* Blue, July, 3–6 inches.

*PINGUICULA* (Bog Violet or Butterwort). Pot-up in March or April in 4–5-inch pans of moist, rich, peaty loam and Sphagnum moss. Stand in the shade. Propagate by means of division in March or April. Seed sown as soon as ripe.

*vulgaris.* Purplish violet, April and May, 4 inches.

*POLYGALA Vayrediæ.* Crimson, June–July, 4 inches.

*POTENTILLA.* In well-drained soil in 6-inch pans, increased by division in early spring or autumn, or by seed, sown as soon as ripe.

*megalantha.* Yellow, May–June, 4 inches.

*nitida.* Rose-pink, June–July, 3 inches.

*PRIMULA.* For culture, see page 510.

*Allionii.* Various shades of rose to white, 3 inches.

*Auricula* vars., *farinosa, Forrestii, hirsuta.* Pink or mauve, 4 inches; *marginata.* Blue, 4 inches; *minima,* and *nutans, pubescens* and vars., *Palinuri.*

*Winteri.* Lavender-lilac, 4 inches.

*RAFFENALDIA primuloides.* Deep yellow, May to June, as *Morisia.*

*RAMONDA.* Pot-up in April, using 4–5-inch pans and a compost of fibrous loam and limestone chips, and stand in semi-shade. Propagate by means of seed sown in March or division in April.

*Myconi* (Pyrenean Primrose). Pale purple-blue, orange centre, May to July, 3 inches.

*RANUNCULUS.* Some of the choicest kinds are attractive for pans; they require good well-drained soil. Some can be divided in early spring, or seeds sown as soon as ripe.

*glacialis.* White, April, 3 inches.

*gramineus.* Yellow, April, May, 5 inches.

*montana.* Yellow, April, 3 inches.

*RAOULIA australis.*

*RHODODENDRON ferrugineum.* Deep rose, May and June.

*hirsutum.* Rosy pink.

*intricatum.* See page 521.

*ROSA Roulettii.* Rosy pink, summer, 5 inches.

*SAPONARIA* (Soapwort). Pot-up in 5–6-inch pans in early spring or autumn in sandy loam and a small portion of old mortar-rubble.

*cæspitosa.* Pink, April–May, 3 inches.

*lutea.* Pale yellow, April–May, 3 inches.

*pulvinaris.* Pink, 2 inches.

# THE ALPINE HOUSE

*SAXIFRAGA* (Rockfoil). Divide in spring and summer and plant closely in 4–6-inch pans of gritty loam and leaf-mould (limed), with small pieces of stone between. Water carefully in winter. Propagate by means of seeds or offsets in spring or division in April or summer.

*apiculata.* Pale yellow, March–May, 4 inches.
" *Arco-Valleyi.* " Rosy pink, March–April, 1 inch.
"*Boydii.*" Pale yellow, March–May, 3 inches.
*Burseriana.* White, March–May, 4 inches.
" *bursiculata.* " White, March, 3 inches.
*dispensioides.* White, April–May, 3 inches.
" *Faldonside.* " Yellow, March–April, 2 inches.
*Grisebachii.* Crimson, April–May, 6 inches.
   var. *Wisleyana.* A fine form of the above.
" *Irvingii.* " Pale pink, March–April, 1 inch.
*longifolia.* Creamy white, May–June, 20 inches.
*Macnabiana.* White spotted with pink dots, April–May, 10 inches.
*moschata.* White, May–June, 6 inches.
   var. *versicolor* and its many forms. Crimson to rosy pink, 6 inches.
*oppositifolia.* Purplish crimson, May, 2 inches.
   var. *alba.* White, May, 2 inches.
*retusa.* Rose-carmine. June–July, 4 inches.
*Rocheliana.* White or yellow. March–May, 4 inches.
" *Salmonii.* " White, April, 3 inches.
*sancta.* Yellow, April–May, 4 inches.
*sarmentosa* (Mother of Thousands). Pink and white, June–September, 10 inches.
*scardica.* White, May, 3 inches.
*Stribrnyi.* Purple, May, 6 inches.
*thessalica.* Red and yellow, May, 6 inches. See also *Saxifraga*, page 535.

*SEDUM* (Stonecrop). Divide and plant closely in spring or summer in 4–6-inch pans of sandy and gritty loam with small pieces of stone in between. Water carefully in winter. Propagate by means of seeds sown in March or division in April.

*brevifolium.* Pink or white. March to May. 1 inch.
*Kamschaticum.* Orange. July and August, 6 inches.
*pulchellum.* Rosy purple, summer, trailer.
*spathulifolium.* Bright yellow, June–September.

*SEMPERVIVUM.* Divide and plant closely in spring or summer in 4–6-inch pans of limed, sandy loam. Water carefully in winter. Propagate by means of seed sown in March, cuttings in summer, or division in April.

*arachnoideum* (Cobweb Houseleek). Reddish pink, June–August, 5 inches.
*calcareum.* Pale red, summer, 6–10 inches.
*ciliatum.* Pink, April–June, 5 inches.

*SENECIO incanus.* Sow seeds as soon as ripe, grow on and put in 5-inch pans when large enough. Yellow with silvery foliage, May–June, 3 inches.

*SHORTIA* (Crimson Leaf). Pot-up in autumn (*S. galacifolia*), April (*S. uniflora*), in 5–6-inch pans of compost of two-thirds sandy peat to one-third loam, and stand out in north frame during summer. Water carefully in winter. Keep fairly moist at all times. Propagate by means of division in April.

*galacifolia.* White, May–June, 6 inches.
*uniflora.* Pale pink, May–June, 5 inches.

*SILENE.* Pot-up in April in 4–5-inch pans of moist, gritty loam and stand in sunny open position. Propagate by seed in July or August or cuttings in summer.

*acaulis* (Moss Campion or Cushion Pink). Pink, June–August, 2 inches.
*Hookeri.* Pink, May–June, 3 inches.
*Schafta.* Rosy magenta, July–August, 5 inches.

*SOLDANELLA.* Pot-up in March in 5-inch pans in good sandy loam with addition of a little peat and granite chips. Seeds should be sown as soon as ripe, or divide old plants as soon as flowers are over.

*alpina.* Violet, April–May, 2 inches.

*STACHYS.* Some of the dwarf kinds are charming for pans. Pot-up in March or the autumn in good open soil. Seeds should be sown as soon as ripe, cuttings taken of young shoots in July or August.

*corsica.* Creamy, tinged flesh-pink, May, 2 inches.
*lavandulæfolia.* Purplish red, summer, 3 inches.

*TEUCRIUM marum.* Pot-up in good gritty soil in 5–6-inch pans. Increased by cuttings of young shoots in July or August or by seed sown in the early autumn or spring. Pink, June–July, 6 inches.

**149**

# THE GREENHOUSE

*THYMUS membranaceus.* Plant in a well-drained 5–6-inch pan in good open soil in early spring. Seed should be sown as soon as ripe and the pot kept in a little warmth. White, June–August, 10 inches.

*VIOLA.* A number of these, both of the true violet type as well as Pansy, are charming for pans, they require good well-drained soil in which there is a proportion of leaf-soil; they can be divided after flowering by cutting of the freer-growing kinds during the early autumn, or by seed sown as soon as ripe.
    *alpina.* Purple, April–May, 4 inches.
    *cuculata.* Blue, April–June, 3 inches.
    *gracilis.* Purple, April–July, 6 inches.
    *Patrinii.* Lavender-blue, April–May, 4 inches.

*WAHLENBERGIA.* Pot-up in March in 5–6-inch pans of sandy loam and peat Keep on the dry side in winter. Propagate by means of seed in March, cuttings in summer, or division in spring.
    *pumilio.* Lilac-lavender, May–June, 3 inches.
    *serpyllifolia* (Thyme-leaved Harebell). Violet-blue, May–June, 3 inches.

Other plants suitable will also be found in Alphabetical List of Plants.

## SOME BULBS, CORMS, AND TUBERS FOR THE ALPINE HOUSE

*CHIONODOXA sardensis*
CROCUS (various)
*CYCLAMEN coüm,*
  *ibericum*
  *neapolitanum*
*FRITILLARIA aurea*
*HYACINTHUS azureus*
*IRIS persica,* var. *Tauri*
  *histrioides*
  *reticulata*
  *Danfordiæ*
  *Histrio*

*MUSCARI botryoides*
*NARCISSUS asturiensis,*
  *Bulbocodium*
  *cyclamineus*
  *sibirica*
  *triandrus*
  *Watieri*
*SCILLA bifolia*
*TULIPA Clusiana,*
  *montana*
  *persica*
  *silvestris*

For cultural details see under Alphabetical List of Plants.

## THE INSIDE AQUARIUM

The growing of aquatic plants under glass is quite an interesting and fascinating type of gardening. There are many beautiful plants that can be grown in the water, such as true aquatics, while tender bog plants can be grown in the mud around the edge, in sections set off for such plants, or in pots submerged in water.

To grow them successfully a tank is required, and this should be carefully made and a good foundation secured for anything except a very small tank. The masonry should be at least 12 inches in thickness and laid in cement, the bottom of which should have at least 2 inches of good concrete.

A large tank of course allows for a larger variety of plants, also for them to develop more, but even a small tank can be full of interest.

The tank can be any shape. A round, basin-like tank, partly built in the ground, such as the water-lily house in the Royal Botanic Gardens, Kew, is as suitable as any and quite effective. This water-tight receptacle in a square-built greenhouse allows for the corners of the house to be used for bog plants or those which grow in mud in a few inches of water, such as *Thalia*, *Nelumbo*, *Pontederia*, *Cyperus*, *Hydroclea*, *Sagittaria*, etc.

The depth of the main tank should be from 3 to 4 feet, so that at least 6 to 12 inches of water are above the crown of the plants. There should be an outlet at the bottom for emptying the tank, also an overflow, which can be in the form of hollow piping fitted in the outlet, the water flowing down the pipe from the top, the pipe being as long as the required depth of the water.

The temperature of the water should be 65° F. minimum in spring and summer, and sufficient 4-inch pipes should be fitted in the tank to ensure attaining that temperature, and this should not be allowed to fall below 50° F. in the depth of winter. The temperature of the house should never fall below 60° F.

For such as *Victoria regia*, a temperature of not less than 85° should be maintained, and this requires 1 foot of 4-inch piping to 12 cubic feet of water. The *Victoria regia* (*see* page 585) should be grown alone, although a few tropical *Nymphæas* or other plants may be cultivated should space allow, but the *Victoria* must on no account be crowded. *Eichornias*, *Pistia*, *Vallisneria*, and *Limnocharis* can properly occupy the outside spaces in order to occupy or help dress the tank. Aquatic plants, particularly *Victoria regia*, usually require the maximum amount of light. They should not be overshadowed by the leaves of palms or other heavy foliage, although a few light creepers trained to the roof add effect, giving a tropical effect to the coloured water-lilies beneath.

Although it is only rarely that a natural arrangement for the culture of tropical aquatics is attempted, there is no reason why such should not be a success. A sunken tank of irregular outline could be formed with stones as for rock-work, and thus form various bays for bog plants or plants that grow in shallow water, while the slopes of the banks could be furnished with *Begonia rex*, *Pellionias*, *Selaginellas*, and such-like choice dwarf plants, which would give a very fine effect; while in the background *Aroids*, *Nepenthes*, and such plants could be arranged, all of which thrive in a warm, moist atmosphere.

What has been mentioned so far is somewhat extensive and not always possible, but many kinds of plants may be grown in a much smaller tank with hot-water pipes passing through, while many kinds of *Nymphæas* and other plants may be grown in tubs, and the small aquatics may be effectively grown in small glass vessels, such as inverted bell-glasses.

The re-potting or transplanting of the indoor aquatics is best carried out in the spring, just as new growth is about to start. The tank should be emptied and given a good scrub down, first

# THE GREENHOUSE

removing to a safe place all it is desired to retain, including such as gold-fish, which are very beneficial to the plant, as they eat the algæ, the aphis, and other pests that attack the plants.

The plants are best grown in large pots or tubs. These can be stood in their respective places and the tank gradually filled, so as to allow the water to reach a certain temperature, rather than rush too much cold water in at once. The water supply is of the highest importance. Few aquatics require or like a swift flow, although a sufficient flow to keep the water circulated is beneficial. In suitable weather ventilation must be given, and a dry atmosphere avoided by damping the paths, etc., and a liberal syringing of the plants. This also helps to keep the plants free from insect pests such as Water-lily Aphis and the Caddis Fly Worms both of which are destructuve to water-lilies. As already mentioned, some gold or other ornamental fish should be kept in the tank.

Should the water become cloudy, or thick with algæ (Flannel-weed) it can be destroyed with copper sulphate. Total the cubic contents of water by multiplying together the length, breadth, and average depth in feet. Then multiply the result by six, which will give approximately the number of gallons of water in the tank. For every 4,000 gallons put 1 oz. of copper sulphate into a bag and continually move it about the tank until all is dissolved and well mixed with the water. This does not affect the plants or ordinary gold-fish.

## SELECTION OF SUITABLE PLANTS

ACROSTICHUM aureum
APONOGETON distachyus, fenestralis
AZOLLA filiculoides
BRASENIA Schreberi
CABOMBA aquatica, caroliniana
COLOCASIA antiquorum, var. esculentum
CERATOPTERIS thalictroides and the var. cornuta
COIX Lacryma-Jobi
CYPERUS alternifolius, Papyrus
EICHORNIA azurea, crassipes
ELODEA crispa, densa
EURYALE ferox
HESPESTIS Monnieria
HETERANTHERA reniformis
HYDROCLEA spinosa
HYDROCLEIS nymphoides
JUSSIÆA species
LIMNOBIUM Spongia, stoloniferum
LIMNOCHARIS Commersonii (see Hydrocleis nymphoides)
MYRIOPHYLLUM proserpinacoides
NELUMBIUM (see Nelumbo)

NELUMBO lutea, nucifera
NEPTUNIA oleracea
NYMPHÆAS, many species, varieties, and hybrids
ONOCLEA sensibilis
ORYZA sativa
OSMUNDA regalis
OUVIRANDRA fenestralis (see Aponogeton fenestralis)
PISTIA Stratiotes
PONTEDERIA cordata and var. lancifolia
SAGITTARIA montevidensis
SALVINIA auriculata, natans
THALIA dealbata, geniculata
TRAPA natans
TRINEA bogotensis (see Limnobium stoloniferum)
TYPHONODORUM Lindleyanum
UTRICULARIA prehensilis
VALLISNERIA spiralis
VICTORIA Cruziana, regia
VILLARSIA reniformis
XANTHOSMA violaceum
ZIZANIA palustris

152

# CHAPTER XII

# ORCHID-GROWING

THERE is a popular notion that orchid-growing is a hobby solely for millionaires, and that it is futile for the amateur to attempt it. This is far from being the case. There are many orchids, and these by no means among the least beautiful, that can well be grown by the amateur in a cool greenhouse. It must, however, be borne in mind that it is impossible to grow orchids successfully in a house in which other plants are also accommodated. They need a separate house, and if a miscellaneous assortment is to be kept in one house, care must be taken that all subjects selected will thrive in a similar temperature. If both warm and cool houses are available there is, of course, no difficulty. Exactly what is meant by the hot, the warm, and the cool house is to a large extent arbitrary, but care must be taken that suitable conditions are provided for the inmates. In our list of plants that will thrive in the hot, the warm, or the cool houses we have assumed the respective temperatures to be as follows :—

| | | | |
|---|---|---|---|
| HOT HOUSE . . . . . | *Summer* | Day | 70–85° F. |
| | | Night | 65–75° F. |
| | *Winter* | Day | 65–75° F. |
| | | Night | 60–70° F. |
| WARM (INTERMEDIATE) HOUSE . | *Summer* | Day | 65–75° F. |
| | | Night | 60–70° F. |
| | *Winter* | Day | 60–70° F. |
| | | Night | 55–65° F. |
| COOL HOUSE . . . . | *Summer* | Day | 60–65° F. |
| | | Night | 55–60° F. |
| | *Winter* | Day | 55–65° F. |
| | | Night | 45–50° F. |

## THE ORCHID HOUSE

The best house in which to begin orchid-growing is one of the lean-to kind, with a north or north-west aspect, and not more than 12 feet high at the back. The front lights should not be made to open, but ventilation must be ensured by letting shutters, working on a central pin, into the low front wall, and so placed that the incoming air may be warmed by passing over the hot-water pipes. The top ventilators should run the whole length of the house. In the cool house the pipes will only be required in order to keep out the frost in hard weather, so that little piping is needed. The winter temperature should never fall below 40° F., nor should it rise much above 60° F.

## Ventilation

Correct ventilation is essential to orchid-growing, and in all the houses, especially the cool house, fresh air must be admitted as freely as possible, taking care never to cause a draught and not to lower the temperature suddenly. In the warmer houses, where a humid atmosphere is necessary, the top ventilators should be used sparingly, and the air should be admitted through the side ventilators so that it passes over the hot pipes and is warmed as it enters. If opened too freely the warm moist air is apt to escape over-rapidly. Provided the weather permits, ventilation must be given throughout the night. Each ventilator should be covered with gauze to keep out insects and dirt. It is preferable to open all the ventilators a little rather than have one or two of them wide open and the others shut; the plants near the wide-open ventilators are sure to suffer. Regulate the ventilation by the outside weather conditions, exclude north-east winds, and do not try to work to a rigid time-table drawn up to suit the season of the year.

Never must the orchid-grower allow the temperature of the house to fall suddenly when the air contains a large amount of moisture and when the paths and stagings are damp. Equally fatal is it to allow the hot pipes to dry-up all the moisture from the air. To prevent this latter state, and to provide the warm and moist atmosphere so necessary to the plants in their growing season, the staging and paths should be liberally sprayed two or three times each day when the weather is fine and warm and the temperature of the house is at its highest. The hotter the day the more liberal the " damping-down ". This " damping-down " is often necessary even in cold weather; the cold will necessitate strong artificial heat, which must not be allowed to dry-up the plants. When the weather is hot, the plants themselves should be syringed once or twice a day with rain-water brought to the same temperature as the atmosphere of the house.

## Shading

The orchid house should never be allowed to get too hot in summer, and for this purpose outside blinds will be required, made of some material substantial enough to keep out the heat and yet excluding as little light as possible. The blinds should not lie close to the glass, but should be fixed to iron runners parallel to the roof, so that when pulled down there may be an

154

air-space of about 9 inches between the glass and the blinds. This space will provide a cooling current of air, and will help to afford an even temperature winter and summer, as the blinds can also be employed as a shield from frost. The glass must be kept as clean as possible, to allow ample light to enter.

Permanent shading should never be used. It is, of course, quite impossible to lay down rigid rules as to dates and times when the houses should be shaded—everything of course depends on the weather prevailing. It is generally advisable to have the blinds ready by the end of February. The cool house should be shaded as soon as the sun actually begins to fall on the plants; the shading should be removed immediately the sun has passed. Care should be taken not to neglect the shading of the cool house, even in early spring, as the foliage of the plants is very delicate and easily scorched by the sun. With the warm house, whose inmates require more heat and sun, the sun may be allowed to play on the plants for a short time before protection is given, and the shading should be removed about three-quarters of an hour before the sun leaves the house.

## Watering

Hard water is injurious to orchids, and soft water is required, so that a tank should be provided to catch the drainage from the roof. It is best to have the tank inside the house, so that the water may be at a temperature equal to that of the air within.

An ash floor, with a wooden lattice for a path down the middle, is the best and most economical, and when well damped will give out enough moisture to keep the atmosphere in the state which orchids enjoy.

The stages should be about 4 feet wide, running along both front and back of the house. The back one must be slightly higher than the front, which should be on a level with the bottom of the front lights. Slate or, if slate is too expensive, iron galvanised sheets, covered with a layer of broken shells, shingle, or coke breeze 2 inches deep, should form the shelves.

For suspended plants a few wires should be firmly stretched along the roof.

## Soil for Orchids

Soil is one of the things to study for those orchids which root in the earth, while the fact that special pots with extra openings are provided shows how essential is good and thorough drainage. In addition to these provisions, the pot destined for an orchid should be thoroughly washed and then dried for several hours before use. It must next be half filled with drainage crocks, instead of receiving a layer at the bottom only, the rest of the pot being filled with a layer of fibrous peat mixed with an equal proportion of Sphagnum moss, which must be fresh. These proportions, however, are by no means unvarying. (*See* tables, pages 160–177.) This compost is all the better for a liberal admixture of charcoal in lumps, together with some pieces of broken pot pounded finely, and coarse sand. Peat is not an altogether successful ingredient to the compost; it is rather wasteful in use, as it is necessary to break it up into small pieces an inch or so in diameter, and the bracken roots have to be removed. A.1 fibre and Osmundo fibre are often used instead of the peat. These fibres are chopped up into short lengths and used in the same way as the peat.

The Sphagnum moss must be thoroughly cleaned and moistened, and must have any extraneous matter or weeds taken out before it is incorporated in the compost. There are, however, many vigorous varieties of orchids which do not require the above rather complicated compost; for them fibrous loam, from which all but the fibre has been removed by careful sieving, will serve excellently. The addition of charcoal, pounded broken pots, and coarse sand as above will usually be found beneficial.

The aerial or ephiphytical orchids, such as the *Phalænopsis*, do not grow in soil, most of them doing best when their roots are spread between layers of Sphagnum moss and are fixed by copper wire to a block of some such hard wood as teak, a foot or so in length and a few inches wide, which does not readily decay and which is placed near the glass. Orchid-baskets for suspension are also made of this hard wood, though in the case of such orchids as send their flower-spikes downwards through the soil the wire baskets must be used.

**Re-Potting**

The best time for re-potting is soon after the blooms have faded; at this time new growth will be forming and the roots will establish themselves easily. With a varied assortment of orchids, potting will therefore go on more or less throughout the year, though spring and early autumn will be the busiest times. Though not necessary every year occasional re-potting is good for orchids, as the compost is apt to become stale and lose its nourishment, and as the roots are prone to die off. On an average it is advisable to re-pot every other year. At times a slightly larger pot is required, but on no account put in a larger pot than is required. This must be decided by the amount of live roots the plant possesses. When re-potting, carefully scrape away the old compost from the roots, cut off all bulbs having no roots, also dead and decayed roots. Each crown should have about four bulbs attached to it when re-potted. Potting should be carried out so that the " crown " or base from which the roots spring shall be just above the compost, which should be pressed firmly round the roots and raised to the rim of the pot; pieces of moss that project after potting should be cut off with the scissors. Keep the plant well in the centre of the pot and spread the roots out, taking care not to injure them or the bulbs; the fewer the roots the less the quantity of compost required. Little water should be given, and the plants should be well shaded for a fortnight to three weeks after potting, to allow the roots to become established. If too much water is given before the roots can utilise it, the soil will become stagnant.

## PROPAGATION

Orchids are propagated at the time of re-potting—that is to say, when new growth is forming. Those that have pseudo bulbs should have the roots cut through, allowing three to four bulbs to each piece of root potted up. Some species, such as the Dendrobium, in which the pseudo bulbs are large, are increased by cutting up the bulbs into lengths of $1\frac{1}{2}$ inches, and these are inserted round the side of the pot. The Paphiopedilum is divided in the same way as an ordinary herbaceous plant, and those species which throw out young shoots and roots from their stems are propagated by having these growths removed and potted up in the ordinary way. The young plants should be kept in a warm, moist atmosphere, must be sparingly watered, and carefully shaded until the roots are established. Orchids may also be raised from seed; hybrids, of course, must be propagated vegetatively. To be successful, however, considerable knowledge of the individual plant's habits is essential. Space will not permit us here to go sufficiently fully into the process to make the instruction of practical value, and the reader is referred to a work devoted solely to orchid-growing.

### Diseases

Orchids are on the whole very free from disease, but constant vigilance is necessary, as once a disease grips a plant it usually spreads rapidly, and can only be eradicated by drastic measures. " Spot " is perhaps the most common disease. It is caused by faulty ventilation and temperature; generally by too low a temperature in conjunction with excessive moisture. Its prevention and cure are obvious. In winter the leaves of species with pseudo bulbs sometimes turn dark brown and die off; this is because moisture settles in the interstices between the leaves and at the base of the plant over the bulbs. All decayed leaves should be cut away, likewise the affected parts of the pseudo bulbs, and then the plants must be liberally dusted with powdered charcoal.

It is very unwise to allow orchids to over-flower themselves, for it is easy to kill a strong plant by allowing it to bear too many flowers or to keep them on the plant too long. If you have room, have two plants of each kind, and allow them to flower in alternate years only, and where the plant is at all delicate, cut its flower-spike as soon as it has reached perfection and place it in a tube of water beside the parent plant. This preserves the flower just as well, and for as long a time as if it had been left on the plant, while it relieves the orchid of a great strain.

During spring and summer is the growing period of most orchids, and at this time they require liberal watering and occasional doses of weak manure water. In autumn and winter the majority of the plants will be dormant, and will require very little water. This refers chiefly to the deciduous kinds; the evergreens need little rest and require moderate watering at all times.

Orchids are freakish plants, and will often take likes and dislikes to particular positions in the greenhouse, flourishing freely on one shelf and pining on another. Take notice of these whimsies, and humour them. If a plant seems ailing, move it about the house, leaving it long enough in each place to give it a chance of settling down, but removing it if it does not seem happy. When once the ideal spot is found, leave the plant there, and do not allow it to be removed.

## ESSENTIALS OF ORCHID CULTURE

There are three things to remember in growing orchids if success is to be obtained. The first is proper watering; this should be regular, but not overdone. While the plants are making growth, the supply should be liberal; when the growth has finished and the bulbs are fully developed, only sufficient water to prevent their shrivelling-up must be given. In watering, the soil only, not the foliage, should be moistened, unless the weather is hot and dry, when gentle spraying each day is beneficial, but it must be done early enough to allow the foliage to dry before nightfall. The second essential is the correct temperature, and the third cleanliness of air, house, pots, soil, and water. If the latter conditions are observed, pests will trouble the orchid house very little, but they must be watched for with great care. The commonest of them is thrips, and the

158

# ORCHID CULTURE

Orchid Thrip is so small that it will often be overlooked unless sought for with the magnifying glass. It should be made a rule to examine each plant for thrips at least once every three weeks, and the inspection should be directed chiefly to the axils of the young leaves. The best weapon against thrips is a soft, camel-hair brush, dipped in an insecticide, and poked gently into all hollows and cavities about the plant. The foliage should be washed with weak soap and water, special attention being given to the underside of the leaves, where the eggs are usually laid.

Slug-traps are needed in the orchid house, and should consist of small pieces of turnip, orange peel, or carrot. Slugs are very fond of climbing the stems and devouring the young flower-buds, which they enjoy extremely. A band of cotton wool fastened round the base of the flower-stalk will prevent them from securing this feast. Fumigate with pure tobacco at once should greenfly appear in the house. Cockroaches, red spider, scale, and woodlice are other prevalent pests. (*See* Pests and Fumigation, page 600.)

Grown in this way and with careful treatment, as perfect blooms may be grown by the amateur as by the professional with his range of heated houses. It all lies in the selection of the varieties of plant which enjoy the conditions you are able to provide, and in then setting yourself to provide these conditions in their most perfect form.

## SELECTING THE STOCK

The best, and by far the most " sporting " plan is to buy unflowered plants from the importers, either at sales or direct, this being the cheapest as well as the most exciting method of obtaining them. The element of chance in these purchases is pleasantly stimulating, as among a lot of good ordinary flowers there is always a chance of getting a really choice specimen; while many of the orchids which are despised by the professional orchid-growers are far more decorative and useful for the amateur than their show cousins. The following lists of species for the hot, warm, and cool houses include all the best and most suitable kinds for the amateur to grow, and will furnish him with ample choice. Cultural details applicable to other individual species are given in the Alphabetical List of Greenhouse Plants and will supplement the necessarily general information given in this chapter.

## ORCHID PESTS

The following pests may prove troublesome in the orchid house. A constant and keen look-out for these must be kept,

159

# THE GREENHOUSE

and, at the first sight, the necessary steps taken to destroy the pests, see our chapter devoted entirely to Diseases and Pests.

| | |
|---|---|
| Aphides | Red Spider |
| Ants | Root Fly |
| Boring Insects | Scale |
| Cattleya-fly | Slugs |
| Cockroaches | Thrips |
| Crickets | Woodlice |
| Mealy bug | |

## ORCHIDS FOR THE HOT OR STOVE HOUSE

*Temperature :* Summer—Day  70–85° F.  Winter—Day  65–75° F.
   „   —Night 65–75° F.     „   —Night 60–70° F.

**Acriopsis.**—A pretty group of epiphytal orchids requiring similar treatment to **Vanda.**

**Ærides** (Air Plant).—Pot-up when blooms are over, in a compost of sphagnum and a little charcoal, half the pot having previously been filled with crocks. Water liberally in spring and summer. Propagate by means of division in August.
*Species.—A. multiflorum (affine)* [India] (white, dark-red spots, May–July, 15 in.); *A. crispum* [S. India] (white, flushed purple, amethyst lip, May–July, 30 in.); *A. odoratum* [Tropical Asia] (creamy, striped purple, May–July, 40 in.).

**Ancistrochilus** (see **Pachystoma**).

**Angræcum** (Bourbon Tea Plant).—Pot-up in March in pots half filled with crocks and half sphagnum, with a little charcoal. Water liberally in summer. Propagate by means of division in March.
*Species.—A. modestum (Sanderianum)* [Comoro Islands] (white, June–July, 12 in.).

**Ancœctochilus.**—Attractive foliage plants for the hot or stove orchid house. Plants should be grown in small pots in chopped sphagnum, a little good fibrous peat and silver sand well mixed, and the plants should have plenty of drainage ; they can then be plunged in a pan and covered with a bell-glass. Plant in February and March, increase by cutting the plant in pieces just below the first joint, with roots attached to each piece, and at least two eyes. These should be put in soil as recommended above and placed under a bell-glass. Pot-up when rooted.
*Species.—A. argyroneurus* [Java] (bright green with darker hues, and silvery veins forming a network); *A. intermedius* [Ceylon] (dark-olive leaves, striped and veined with gold); *A. regalis* [Java] (one of the handsomest species, with leaves of a beautiful velvety green, covered with a network of gold).

**Ansellia.**—An orchid with tall, thickened, leafy stems  Use a compost of turfy loam and peat in equal proportions with good drainage. Propagated by division when growth commences.
*Species.—A. africana* [Fernando Po] (brownish-purple spots on greenish yellow, Feb., 20–24 in.); *A. gigantea (Cymbidium Saundersonii)* [Natal] (yellowish brown, Feb.–March), differs from the above in the smaller flowers.

**Arachnanthe.**—Will thrive in pots or pans three parts filled with crocks and living sphagnum. Increased by division with roots attached, when growth commences.
*Species.—A. moschifera* [Malaya] (creamy white or lemon colour, with purple spots). The flowers are sweetly scented, and last in perfection a long time. They bloom in May and June.

**Bifrenaria.**—A group of pretty orchids somewhat allied to **Maxillaria.** They thrive in a compost of good fibrous peat and chopped sphagnum in equal parts. During the growing season an abundance of water is essential. In the winter less water is required, but it is not advisable to dry off entirely, but temperature should be reduced by 10°. Propagated by division in spring.
*Species and Varieties.—B. aurantiaca* [Guiana and Trinidad] (deep yellow, or orange spotted with purple, Oct., 15–18 in.); *B. Hadwenii* [Brazil] (large flowers, yellowish green, mottled rich brown, with broad white lip, spotted rose, 18 in.); there is also a beautiful variety of this *B.H.* var. *bella*, tinted cinnamon ; *B. Harrisoniæ* [Brazil] (ivory-white or cream, with purple lip, Sept., 16–20 in.); *B. inodora* [Brazil] (sepals apple-green, with either white, yellow, or rose-coloured lip, autumn, 15–18 in.).

160

**PLATE 8**
'Lady Washington', an attractive variety of *Pelargonium*.

# ORCHIDS FOR THE HOT OR STOVE HOUSE

**Brassia** (see **Brassia** in Cool House List).

*Species.*—*B. Gireoudeana* [Central America] (greenish yellow and reddish brown, summer, 24 in.); *B. longissima* [Costa Rica] (orange-yellow, spotted purple, summer and autumn, 24 in.).

**Broughtonia sanguinea.**—An orchid from Jamaica, allied to **Epidendrum,** and sometimes included with it. It can be grown in the stove house in fibrous peat and crocks, well raised above the pot, or on a block of wood suspended from the roof. It requires a free supply of moisture and heat in the summer, with temperatures of 65–75° F., but needs cooler and drier conditions in the winter. It is increased by division. Flowers are crimson, August, 18 inches.

**Bulbophyllum.**—Pot-up when growth commences in April or May in shallow pans containing a compost of three parts of chopped Osmunda fibre to one part of sphagnum moss and some broken crocks, or top dress with new soil. Grow near the glass, but shade from strong sun in summer. Water well while growing, and increase by means of division of rhizomes.

*Species.*—*B. Dearei* [Borneo] (tawny-yellow, streaked and stained purple, summer, etc., 9 in.); *B. fascinator* [Brazil] (white, tinged purple, late autumn, 12 in.); *B. Lobbii* (buff-yellow, marked purple-red, summer and autumn, 9 in.); *B. reticulatum* [Borneo] (white, striped inside with purple, lip spotted same colour, summer and autumn, 9 in.).

**Burlingtonia fragrans** (see **Rodriguezia venusta**).

**Calanthe.**—Pot-up in March when new growth starts, using a compost of half peat and half fibrous loam, with a little sphagnum, dry cow-manure, and coarse sand, the pot first being a third full of crushed crocks. A 6-inch pot is big enough for an average-sized bulb. Give plenty of light and a moist, buoyant atmosphere while growing. Dry off after flowering. Propagate by means of division in March.

*Species.*—*B. Veitchii* [garden hybrid] (bright rose with white throat, Dec–Feb., 10–15 in.); *B. vestita* [India] (white with crimson blotch, Dec.–Feb., 10–15 in.). There are several beautiful hybrids and varieties.

**Camarotis rostrata.**—This stove, tree-growing orchid from India, with aerial roots, similar to **Epidendrum,** is best grown on a piece of wood or shallow pan, where the plant is raised about it, in a well-drained mixture of peat and moss. (Temperature 55–65° F. winter, 65–80° F. summer.) Rose-purple, 24–36 in.

**Catasetum.**—Pot-up annually in spring in well-drained, shallow pans containing a compost of two to three parts of chopped Osmunda fibre to one part of sphagnum moss. Grow up near the glass. Water regularly and well while growing, and keep only just moist in winter.

*Species.*—*C. Bungerothii* [Venezuela] (ivory-white or creamy, with ochreous blotch, 12–15 in.); *C. macrocarpum* [Tropical America] (greenish yellow, spotted brown-yellow lip, 16–20 in.); *C. pileatum* [Venezuela] (white, large, shell-like lip, 12–15 in.).

**Cirrhopetalum.**—Pot-up in shallow pans, hollow pieces of cork or tree-fern stems, when new roots form, in late spring or early summer, using a compost of equal parts of sphagnum moss and Osmunda fibre. Water regularly while making growth and hang up near the glass, but shade from strong sun.

*Species.*—*C. appendiculatum* [Sikkim] (pale yellow, tinged purple, late autumn, 10 in.); *C. longissimum* [Malay Peninsula] (dull pinkish with yellow lip, uncertain, 8–10 in.); *C. Makoyanum* [Tropical Asia] (yellow and red, winter, 12 in.); *C. psillacoides* (*gracillimum*) [Malaya] (bright red, uncertain, 8–10 in.); *C. Rothschildianum* [N. India] (greenish yellow, tinted and striped red, winter, 12 in.)

**Cœlogyne.**—Pot-up when new growths are forming, using a compost of half live sphagnum and half fibrous peat, the pot first being half filled with broken crocks. Grow near the glass, but shade from strong sun. Water liberally in spring and summer. Propagate by means of division in March.

*Species.*—*C. Massangeana* (Chain Orchid) [Assam] (light yellow, dark brown lip, Feb.–April, 12–15 in.); *C. pandurata* (Fiddle Orchid) [Malaya] (green and black, Aug.–Sept., 12–18 in.); *C. speciosa* [Malaya] (blush-salmon and yellowish brown, spring, 12–15 in.); *C. Veitchii* [New Guinea] (white, spring, 20–24 in.).

**Cycnoches** (Swan Orchid). Pot-up in spring in shallow pots or pans of chopped Osmunda fibre and sphagnum moss, in the proportion of one part of the former to two parts of the latter, and a little loam added. Grow high up near the glass but shaded from direct sun. Water well and preserve a moist atmosphere.

*Species.*—*C. chlorochilon* [British Guiana] (greenish yellow, 24 in.); *C. Loddigesii* [French Guiana] (purplish brown with red marks on lip, 20–24 in.); *C. peruvianum* [Peru] (purplish brown, red marks on lip, 24 in.).

**Dendrobium** (Rock Lily).—Pot-up when young shoots are from 2 to 3 in. long in well-drained pots and a compost of three parts Osmunda fibre to one part of sphagnum and a little charcoal. Give ample light, and water liberally from March to August, sparingly while dormant (though not completely dried), and keep cool. Propagate by means of division in March. Most of the species are evergreen.

L                                                                                      161

*Species.*—*D. aggregatum* [N. India] (orange-yellow, spring, 12 in.); *D. bigibbum* [Australia] (magenta, spring, 12–18 in.); *D. fimbriatum* [N. India] (orange-yellow, spring, 30–40 in.); *D. moschatum* [N. India] (pale yellow, spring, 40–60 in.).

**Dendrochilum.**—see **Platyclinis.**

**Elleanthus.**—Pretty stove terrestrial orchids from tropical America. They are of easy culture in an ordinary orchid house, and require a compost of fibrous loam, peat, and sand.

*Species.*—*E. Caravata* [Guiana] (bright yellow and purple, Nov., 12–15 in.); *E. Kermesina* [Guiana Mariquita] (bright carmine, Jan., 5–6 in) ; *E. xanthocomus* [Peru] (yellow, May, 12 in.).

**Eria**—Pot-up in March in shallow pans or pots in a mixture of three parts Osmunda fibre to one part of sphagnum moss. Grow up near the glass in a moist atmosphere, shading from strong sun. Water well while growing and gradually dry off after flowering.

*Species.*—*E. obesa* [Malayan Peninsula] (white, tinged pink, Feb., 8 in.); *E. stellata* [Java] (yellowish red, March–April, 12–15 in.).

**Eulophia.** Pot-up in spring as soon as new growth commences. They like a compost of half Osmunda fibre and half sphagnum moss and fibrous loam mixed. Water the soil carefully while growing, dry off gradually after flowering. The treatment of **Calanthes** applies to this genus.

*Species.*—*E. guineensis* [Sierra Leone] (white lip with purple marks, autumn, 12 in.); *E. guineensis* var. *purpurea* (purplish green, crimson-purple lip, autumn, 12 in.); *E. maculata* [Brazil] (reddish brown, white, or pale rose, autumn, 12 in.).

**Eulophiella.**—Pot-up, when necessary, in April, in well-drained pots containing a compost of one part of sphagnum moss and a few dried beech leaves to two parts of Osmunda fibre. Grow high up near the glass on small rafts, but shade from strong sun. Water well while growing, and preserve a moist atmosphere. Propagation is carried out by means of division of the rhizomatous growths when re-potting.

*Species.*—*E. Elizabethæ* [Madagascar] (white and purplish, spring or early summer, 24 in.); *E. Hamelinii* [Madagascar] (white, tinted pink, spring or early summer, 30–36 in.); *E. Peetersiana* [Madagascar] (rose-purple and white centre, golden blotch, spring or early summer, 30–40 in.).

**Galeandra.**—Terrestrial orchids that require either the stove or warm greenhouse. They should be grown in fibrous peat with some sharp sand, surfaced with sphagnum. They require plenty of water in the growing season, but very little during the winter, and they should be kept near the glass. They are subject to red spider and thrip, so that the plants will benefit from a syringing with warm water twice a week. They are propagated by division.

*Species.*—*G. Baueri* [Mexico] (yellowish and purple, June–Aug., 6–8 in.); *G. Devoniana* [Rio Negro] (reddish brown and green lip, whitish, veined crimson, June, 15–18 in.); *G. nivalis* (Tropical America) (olive-green, lip white with purple blotch, March, 15 in.).

**Gongora** (Punch-and-Judy Orchid) [S. America]. Pot-up when necessary in early spring in shallow pots or pans or orchid baskets, using a compost of one part sphagnum moss to three parts of Osmunda fibre and grow high up near the glass. Water well while growing and preserve a moist atmosphere. Dry off gradually after flowering.

*Species.*—*G. atropurpurea* [Trinidad] (rich purplish brown, spring and summer, 18 in.); *G. quinquenervis* (*maculata*) [Trinidad] (yellow, marked red, spring and summer, 18 in.); *G. tricolor* [Central America] (reddish purple and golden yellow, spring and summer, 15–18 in.).

**Grammangis.**—Pot-up in shallow pots or pans or in orchid baskets, using a compost similar to that recommended for **Gongora,** and follow the subsequent cultural details.

*Species.*—*G. Ellisii* [Madagascar] (yellow, with pale pink lip, summer, 24 in.); *G. Huttonii* [Java] (light brown, greenish lip with chocolate markings, June, 12–15 in.).

**Grammatophyllum.** Pot-up in spring in a compost of three parts of Osmunda fibre to one part each of fibrous loam and sphagnum moss, and add a little crushed brick. Water well while growing, and preserve a warm, moist atmosphere.

*Species.*—*G. Fenzlianum* [Isle of Amboina] (green, flushed yellow, and marked brownish red, 36 in.); *G. Rumphianum* [New Guinea, Borneo] (green, spotted brown, 24–48 in.); *G. speciosum* [Malaya], "Giant Orchid" (green, spotted brown, 6–10 ft.).

**Habenaria** (Rein Orchis).—Although a number of this genera are hardy and very suitable for growing in the bog garden, and for naturalising in moist places, there, are others, including some from the East Indies, which should be grown in a moderately warm house, with a fair amount of water and a good light. After resting they should be re-potted in a mixture of two parts peat, one part loam, with some live chopped sphagnum, and crock dust, the tubers being placed upon the crocks so that the crowns are just below the soil level. They should then have a fair amount of water

**162**

until after flowering. They are increased by division of the rootstock either after growth has finished, or before it begins in the spring. They should be potted up and placed in a close propagating case.

*Species.*—*H. carnea* [Penang] (pale pink, fading to white, leaves spotted white, summer, 10 in.); *H. cinnabarina* [Madagascar] (orange, spotted red, summer, 12 in.); *H. Elwesii* [India] (greenish yellow, 14–18 in.); *H. longecalcarata* [India] (white to greenish yellow, Sept.–Nov.); *H. Susannæ* (*H. gigantea*) [India] (greenish white, July, 4–6 in.). The following are suitable for the cool or alpine house, grown in pans with compost similar to the above. Keep the pans plunged in ashes in a partially shaded cold frame when not in flower. *H. ciliaris* (Fringed Orchis) [N. America] (brilliant orange, with fringed petals, summer 18–24 in.); *H. fimbriata* [N. America] (lilac, occasionally white, summer, 12–15 in.); *H. psycodes* [N. America] (lilac, sometimes white, fragrant, July–Aug., 10–12 in.); *H. Suzannae* [India and Malaya] (white, summer and autumn, 15–18 ins.).

**Hæmaria.**—A small group of terrestrial orchids with attractive foliage, requiring similar conditions to **Anœctochilus,** although more easily grown. They thrive in a warm, moist atmosphere in pans with their rhizomes creeping in a compost of fibrous peat and sphagnum. They are increased by cuttings taken with a piece of root attached, and kept close with bottom heat until they begin to grow. *H. discolor* [China] has white flowers with crimson bracts. The leaves are crimson underneath, and green above, with a white line down the centre. This line disappears when the leaf gets old and the plant flowers. *H. Dawsoniana* (*Anœctochilus Dawsonianus*) [Burma] has flowers like the previous species. The leaves are green, beautifully veined with blood-red and yellow.

**Houlettia.**—A group of stove house summer flowering orchids. They are best grown in baskets in a mixture of fibrous peat, sphagnum and charcoal. When growing, plenty of heat and moisture should be given, reducing the water and temperature when growth is complete. Increase by careful division just as growth commences.

*Species.*—*H. Brocklehurstiana* [Brazil] (brownish red and yellow, dotted brownish purple, 18–20 in.); *H. chrysantha* [Colombia] (yellow with chocolate blotches, lip spotted crimson); *H. picta* [Colombia] (yellow and brownish purple, or red with crimson veins, 20 in.).

**Isochilus linearis.**—These epiphytic stove orchids, originating in the regions from Mexico to Brazil, have spikes of curiously shaped purple flowers 12–15 inches high, in the spring. When growth commences, re-plant them in the basket or pan in fibrous peat and broken crocks. When growing they require a liberal amount of water, syringing in the mornings during hot weather and air to dry up the extra moisture. Shade from the bright sun.

When growth is finished in the autumn reduce the heat and moisture, and cease watering in the winter. They may also be fastened to tufts of peat or pieces of fern stem and suspended from the roof.

**Lacæna.**—Stove epiphytic orchids which should be grown in baskets, or on blocks of wood, for, like **Stanhopeas,** they throw their racemes downwards, and may possibly get buried. They require fibrous peat and chopped sphagnum in equal proportions, with some sand. At the end of October water should be almost entirely withheld for a time. They are propagated by division at the time of potting.

*Species.*—*L. bicolor* [Guatemala] (greenish yellow, streaked, and spotted with violet and dark purple). The vars. *alba* and *glabra* grow to a height of 12 inches and have creamy-white flowers in the summer; *L. spectabilis* [Costa Rica], has pinkish-white flowers dotted with purple in early summer, and grows to a height of 10 in.

**Lælia.**—Pot-up when new roots are forming at the base of new shoots, using a compost of half live sphagnum and half Osmunda fibre and a little charcoal. Ventilate freely in summer, and expose to the sun. Water liberally while growing, and syringe two or three times daily in fine weather, but not too late to allow foliage to dry before nightfall. Propagate by means of division in March.

*Species.*—*L. cinnabarina* [Brazil] (orange-red, Feb.–March, 12–15 in.); *L. harpophylla* [Brazil] (orange-scarlet, Feb.–March, 10 in.); *L. superbiens* [Guatemala] (pink, crimson lip, Dec., 12–18 in.).

**Læliocattleya.**—Bigeneric hybrids between **Lælia** and **Cattleya,** requiring the same cultural treatment.

*Species.*—*L. Dominiana* [garden hybrid] (light purple, dark purple-labellum, summer, 24 in.); *L. Duvaliana* [garden hybrid] (light mauve, dark maroon-crimson, summer, 24 in.); *L. radiata* [garden hybrid] (violet-red, deep reddish purple and white, summer, 24 in.).

**Limatodes rosea.**—An attractive winter flowering orchid from Burma. It is allied to **Calanthe,** and succeeds with the same cultural treatment. It should not be watered until the roots are well advanced, and then only sparingly, until the leaves

# THE GREENHOUSE

are well started. Afterwards they appreciate copious watering and syringing, and occasional feeding with weak liquid manure. This species hybridised with **Calanthe vestita** gave rise to **Calanthe Veitchii,** a plant common in cultivation.

**Liparis.**—Plant in pans in a compost of fibrous peat, sphagnum, and charcoal, with small pieces of crock. Increase by divisions of plant when growth commences.

*Species.—L. atropurpurea* [Ceylon] (dark purple, June, 10–12 in.) ; *L. longipes* var. *pendula* (whitish green, July, 12 in.).

**Lissochilus.**- Terrestrial orchids, chiefly from South Africa, some of which are very handsome.

*Culture.*—They can be grown in a compost of fibrous peat, loam, leaf-mould, and sand. During the growing season they require a high temperature, plenty of light, and a liberal supply of water ; but during the winter they should be given a lower temperature, kept dry, and rested.

*Species.—L. Horsfallii* [Old Calabar] (purplish brown, white, suffused with rose, summer, 30–36 in.) ; *L. Krebsii* [Natal] (green with purple blotches, bright yellow, summer, 30–36 in.; *L. Sandersonii* [Natal] (green, white, mauve-purple, summer, 30–40 in.); *L. speciosus* [S. Africa] (bright yellow, purple lines, June, 20–30 in.) ; *L. stylites* [Tropical Africa] (purple, green, tinged lilac, and white, summer).

**Listrostachys.**—Attractive free-flowering orchids, allied to **Angræcum,** and sometimes included with that genus. They succeed with precisely the same cultural treatment.

*Species.—L. bidens* [W. Tropical Africa] (flowers sweet scented, white or pinkish, May–June, 10–15 in.) ; *L. pertusa* (*A. Pescatoreanum*) [Sierra Leone] (white, tinged yellow, May–June, 12 ins.); *L. tabularis* [Penang] (purple, summer, 12 in.).

**Lockhartia.**—A group of interesting stove orchids. They can be wired on to rafts or blocks of wood, with fibre and some sphagnum, and placed in a hot, damp atmosphere. They are propagated by side shoots, used as cuttings.

*Species.—L. elegans* [Trinidad] (yellow, spotted red, June, 6–8 in.) ; *L. verrucosa* [Guatemala] (bright yellow, barred and spotted red, 10–12 in.).

**Macodes.**—Attractive plants with variegated foliage similar to **Anœctochilus** requiring the same cultural treatment.

*Species.—M. javanica* [Java] (flowers orange-red, tipped white; leaves velvety green with pale green and white markings, deep red beneath, 6–8 in.) ; *M. Petola* [Java] (greenish flowers, leaves green, with network of golden-yellow veins).

**Miltonia.**—Pot-up when new roots are formed at the base of young shoots, in a compost of half live sphagnum and half fibrous peat and a little charcoal. Ventilate freely in summer and subject to strong light, but shade from direct sun. Water liberally while growing and syringe two or three times a day in fine weather, but not too late to allow foliage to dry before nightfall. Propagate by means of division in March.

*Species.—M. candida* [Brazil] (yellow, reddish brown, purple, autumn, 12–18 in.) ; *M. Endresii* [Costa Rica] (white, yellow and rose, Feb. 12–15 in.) ; *M. spectabilis,* [Brazil] (pink, purple lip, June–July, 8 in.).

**Pachystoma** (*Ancistrochilus*).—Pot-up in March or April in well-drained pans in a compost of half sphagnum moss and half fibrous loam and chopped Osmunda fibre. Grow near the glass and water regularly. Propagate by means of division in spring.

*Species.—P. Rothschildiana* (white, flushed pink, winter, 7–9 in.) ; *P. Thompsoniana* [W. Tropical Africa] (white, green and purple lip, late autumn, 6–8 in.).

**Paphinia.**— Pot-up in well-drained small pots or pans in early spring as soon as new growth is visible, using a compost of shredded sphagnum moss and Osmunda fibre in equal proportions, with a sprinkling of good leaf-mould. Grow up near the glass in a moist, warm atmosphere, but shade from direct sun. Keep the soil moist while growing. Gradually dry off after flowering and rest in winter.

*Species.—P. cristata* [British Guiana] (yellow and purplish brown, summer, 6 in.) ; *P. rugosa* [Colombia] (reddish pink, summer, 6 in.).

**Paphiopedilum** (Lady's Slipper).—Pot-up in March, using a compost of two parts of turfy peat to one part of sphagnum and coarse sand, the pots first being a third full of broken crocks. Water liberally in summer, and keep moist always. Propagate by means of division in March.

*Species.—P. Lawrenceanum* [Borneo] (white, veined purple, March–May, 10 in.) ; *P. Spicerianum* [Assam] (crimson-purple and green, speckled red, Dec., 10–12 in ). There are many beautiful hydrids of garden origin.

**Peristeria** (Dove Orchid or Holy-Ghost-Flower) [Central America].—Pot-up in March in a compost composed of two parts of turfy loam to one part peat (brown), and one part charcoal and sphagnum. Keep the roots and air moist from March to September. Water sparingly when dormant. Propagate by means of division in March.

*Species.—P. elata* (white, Aug.–Sept., 40 in.).

# ORCHIDS FOR THE HOT OR STOVE HOUSE

**Phalænopsis** (Moth Orchid).—Pot-up in March in a mixture of half turfy peat and half sphagnum, charcoal, and crocks. Grow on raft, but shade from direct sun. Water liberally in spring and keep air moist in summer. Propagate by means of division in March.

*Species.*—*P. amabilis* [Malaya] (white, stains of deep yellow, a few purple spots, summer–autumn, 6–9 in.); *P. Aphrodite* [Philippines] (white, spotted yellow and red, summer, 6–9 in.); *P. violacea* var. *Schrœderiana* (light yellow and purple, summer, 9 in.).

**Phragmopedilum.**—They require plenty of heat and moisture in the growing season, March to November. Give good drainage. Use chopped sphagnum with broken crocks, and a little leaf-soil, raising the material as high above the rim of the pots as possible.

*Species.*—*P. caudatum* (pale yellow and white, shaded brown, April–May, 30 in.); *P. Sedenii* (greenish white, purplish crimson, spring, 18–24 in.).

**Platyclinis** [**Dendrochilum**] (Chain Orchid).—Pot-up in spring as soon as new growth is visible, in shallow pots or pans, using a compost of one part sphagnum moss to three parts of chopped Osmunda fibre with a little sand and leaf-mould added. Grow high up near the glass, but shade from strong sun. Water and syringe regularly and preserve a moist atmosphere.

*Species.*—*P. cucumerina* [Philippines] (golden yellow, tinged green, late autumn, 10 in.); *P. filiformis* [Philippines] (golden yellow, early summer, 8 in.); *P. glumacea* [Philippines] (cream, late winter, 10 in.).

**Podochilus.**—Pot-up in peat and sphagnum in well-drained pans during the growing season. Increase by division when growth commences.

*Species.*—*P. longicalcaratus* [Borneo]. White and purple, summer, 24 in.

**Renanthera.**—Pot-up in early spring as new growth is visible, using well-drained pots and a compost of shredded sphagnum moss and Osmunda fibre in equal proportions. Grow up near the glass in a warm, moist atmosphere, but shade from hot sun. Water regularly while making growth. Reduce the quantity and gradually dry off after flowering.

*Species.*—*R. annamensis* [Annam] (yellow, marked red, summer, 12 in.); *R. coccinea* [Cochin China] (reddish (semi-climber), summer, 8–10 ft.); *R. Imschootiana* [Assam] (reddish, early summer, 12 in.); *R. pulchella* [Burma] (yellow and red, summer, 12 in.); *R. Storiei* [Philippines] (reddish (semi-climber), summer, 10–12 ft.).

**Rhyncostylis.**—Grow in well-drained orchid baskets in a compost of equal parts of sphagnum moss and Osmunda fibre, and renew the soil, without undue disturbance of the roots, annually in early spring when new growth is visible. Grow well up near the glass in a warm moist atmosphere, but shade from strong sun. Give ample water when making growth and never allow the roots to become dry.

*Species.*—*R. cœlestis* [Siam] (white, tipped violet, summer); *R. retusa* (Tropical India and Malay Is.] (white, spotted bluish violet, purple lip, summer).

**Rodriguezia.** Pot-up in spring as soon as new growth is visible, in well-drained pans containing a compost of equal parts of shredded sphagnum moss and Osmunda fibre. Grow up near the glass in a moist, warm atmosphere, but shade from direct sun. Water well and regularly while making growth, and never allow the roots to become dry.

*Species.*—*R. decora* [Brazil] (white, marked red (semi-trailer), May–June, 10 in.); *R. secunda* [Trinidad] (rose-pink, summer, 6 in.); *R. venusta* (*Burlingtonia fragrans*) [Brazil] (white, yellow on lip, summer, 8–10 in.).

**Saccolabium.**—Pot-up in February, using a compost of half sphagnum and half crocks, with a little charcoal. Keep close to the glass, but shade from strong sun. Water liberally in spring and summer. Keep the atmosphere warm and damp, but the leaves dry in winter. Propagate by means of offsets in March.

*Species.*—*S. ampullaceum* [N. India] (deep rose, white, June, 6–8 in.); *S. bellinum* [Burma] (yellow, blotched purple, March–June, 5 in.); *S. Hendersonianum* [Borneo] (summer, 4–6 in.).

**Schomburgkia.**—Stove orchids with showy flowers somewhat resembling **Lælia.** They will succeed in the Cattleya house, either in baskets or on blocks of wood, suspended from the roof in chopped moss and fibre, or peat, or in pots if preferred. They require plenty of heat and a liberal supply of water during the growing season, but after growth is completed they should be given a lower temperature (50–55° F.), and water should be withheld until the flowers begin to show. Propagation is by division.

*Species.*—*S. crispa* [Demerara] (yellowish brown and white, winter, 30–40 in.); *S. Lyonsii* [Jamaica] (yellowish brown, white, with purple spots, Aug. 30–40 in.); this is one of the prettiest of the genus. *S. tibicinis* (*Epidendrum tibicinis*), " Cow-horn Orchid " [Honduras and Cuba] (pink, speckled white, red, white, and deep rose, May–June, 50–60 in.); the var. *grandiflora* has larger flowers with more yellow on

**165**

the lips. Both the species and the variety do best on a block, as they require less compost.

**Scuticaria.** Pot-up in early spring when necessary to renew soil, in well-drained pans, or pieces of cork, bark, or wood, in a compost of equal parts of shredded sphagnum moss and Osmunda fibre. Grow up near the glass in a warm, moist atmosphere in a slightly tilted position. Water and syringe regularly and shade from direct sun.

*Species.—S. Hadwenii* [Brazil] (yellow, green, and deep brown, all seasons, 20–30 in.); *S. Steelii* [British Guiana] (yellow, green, and deep brown, all seasons, 30 -48 in.).

**Selenipedilum** or **Selenipedium.**—Now generally included under **Phragmopedilum,** which see.

**Spathoglottis.**—Pot-up in early spring as soon as new growth is visible in well-crocked pots containing a compost of sandy loam with the addition of a little sphagnum moss and Osmunda fibre. Grow in a warm, moist atmosphere, up near the glass, but shade from strong sun. Water regularly while growing, reduce the quantity gradually after flowering.

*Species.—S. aurea* [Malaya] (golden yellow, lip spotted red, summer and autumn, 36 in.); *S. plicata* [Malaya]. Deep rose to rose-purple, summer, 36–48 in.; *S. Vieillardii* [Polynesia] (white, tinted rose, orange, summer, 36 in.).

**Stanhopea.**—Grow in a mixture of Osmunda fibre and sphagnum moss, in the proportion of three parts of the former to one part of the latter, in orchid baskets, and renew the compost when necessary in spring. Grow in a moist, warm atmosphere well up near the glass. Water regularly while growing and keep just moist during winter.

*Species.—S. Bucephalus* [Mexico] (yellow, summer, 16 in.); *S. devoniensis* [Mexico] (pale yellow, marked red, summer, 16 in.); *S. eburnea* [Guiana] (white, summer. 10–12 in.); *S. graveolens* [Guatemala] (greenish white, yellow, summer, 10 in.); *S. insignis* [Brazil] (yellow, spotted purple, summer, 10 in.); *S. oculata* [Mexico] (pale yellow, marked purple, summer, 12 in.); *S. tigrina* [Mexico] (yellow mottled with blotches of purple, summer, 10 in.).

**Stauropsis.**—Pot-up in well-drained large pots in spring in a compost of equal parts of sphagnum moss and Osmunda fibre and add a few small pieces of charcoal. Renew some of the compost annually without undue disturbance of roots. Grow in a warm, moist atmosphere, but shaded from strong sun, and water regularly. Little water is needed when dormant.

*Species.—S. gigantea* [Burma] (yellow, brown spots, summer, 24 in.); *S. lisso-chiloides (Vanda Batemanii)* [Philippines] (reddish purple and yellowish purple, summer, 30–40 in.).

**Tainia.**—Pot-up, when necessary, in early spring, as soon as new growth is visible, in a compost of three parts of sandy loam to one part each of sphagnum moss and Osmunda fibre, with some dried cow-manure, or renew some of the top compost without undue disturbance of roots. Grow in a warm, moist atmosphere near the glass, but shade from strong sun. Water well while growing, gradually reduce quantity and almost dry off in winter.

*Species.—T. Hookeriana* [N. India] (greenish brown, spring and summer, 24 in.); *T. latifolia* [N. India] (greenish brown, spring and summer, 24 in.); *T. penangiana* [Penang] (spring, 18 in.).

**Thunia.**—Pot-up annually in March when the young growths are 2 to 3 in. tall, using a compost of half sandy peat and half fibrous loam, with some dried cow-manure. Give ample light and sun, and water liberally while growing, but sparingly while dormant. Propagate by means of division in March.

*Species.—T. Bensoniæ* [Burma] (purplish pink, July, 20 in.); *T. Marshalliana* [Burma] (orange and white, July, 30 in.).

**Vanda** (Cowslip-scented Orchid).—Pot-up in March in sphagnum, the pots being previously half filled with broken crocks. Keep the atmosphere close and warm while growing, but shade from strong sun. Water liberally from April to September. Propagate by means of offsets in March.

*Species.—V. teres* [Borneo] (white, tinged rose and crimson (climber), summer, 50 in.); *V. tricolor* [Java] (cream, marked reddish brown, April–June, 30 in.); *V. tricolor* var. *suavis* (white, spotted purple and lip, March–June. 30 in.).

**Vanilla.**—Pot-up in a rather small-sized but well-drained pot containing a compost of two parts sphagnum moss to three parts Osmunda fibre, and replenish the top layer annually in spring without undue disturbance of the roots.

Raise the pots up near the glass in a warm, moist atmosphere, and train the plants on wires or other supports. Water well and syringe while growing, but shade from strong sun.

*Species.—V. planifolia* (Common Vanilla, Vanilla Bean) [Mexico], bears fragrant, dull-coloured flowers in spring and summer. If these are hand fertilised the long,

# ORCHIDS FOR THE HOT OR STOVE HOUSE

bean-like seed-pods from which Vanilla is obtained will be produced; *V. pompona* [Tropical America]. A climber bearing greenish-white flowers.

**Zeuxine regia.**—A dwarf stove terrestrial orchid from Borneo. It bears spikes of white and green flowers, and handsome dark-green foliage with a lilac or whitish band down the centre. It requires the same cultural treatment as **Anœctochilus.**

In addition to the species and varieties given in these lists there are innumerable lovely hybrids available, raised by growers here—in fact, the production of new hybrids by inter-crossing is one of the most attractive features of orchid-growing and those really interested should visit an orchid-grower's collection or a leading nursery and study the works devoted exclusively to this most interesting subject.

## ORCHIDS FOR THE WARM OR INTERMEDIATE GREENHOUSE

*Temperature :* Summer—Day  65–75° F.  Winter—Day  60–70° F.
„  —Night 60–70° F.  „  —Night 55–65° F.

**Acanthophippium.**—These orchids thrive in sandy peat with a quantity of broken pots or gravel, warmer conditions during growing period. Increase by division of the pseudo bulbs when growth commences.

*Species.*—*A. bicolor* [Ceylon] (purple and yellow, June, 9 in.); *A. Lavanicum* [Java] (yellow and red with stripes, spring, 18 in.).

**Acriopsis.**—A pretty group of epiphytal orchids requiring similar treatment to **Vanda.**

**Anguloa** (Bull's Head or Cradle Orchid).—When new shoots break, pot up in well-drained pots in a mixture of turfy peat with a little charcoal added. Shade and water liberally in summer. Propagate by means of division at potting time. If brown scale attacks plants, sponge with soap and water. Care should be taken not to injure young leaves.

*Species.*—*A. Clowesii* [Colombia] (lemon-yellow, summer, 20–24 in.); *A.C.* var *eburnea* (ivory-white flowers); *A. Rückeri* [Colombia] (yellow and red, June–July. 20 in.); *A. uniflora* [Peru and Colombia] (creamy white, flushed pink, summer, 20 in.).

**Arundina.**—Pot-up in early spring in good, rich, fibrous loam, silver sand, and rough peat. The plant is increased by dividing it at that time. It requires a good supply of water during the growing season, and the soil must be kept moderately moist even when the plant is at rest.

*Species.*—*A. bambusæfolia* [Tropical Asia] (magenta, rose, and orange lines, July, 18–24 in.).

**Bollea.**—An attractive group closely allied to **Zyogpetalum,** and requiring the same treatment. Pot-up in rough peat and sphagnum with a lump of charcoal, and water freely during the growing season. When resting they should be supplied with only sufficient moisture to prevent them from shrivelling, and they should never be allowed to get quite dry.

*Species and Varieties.*—*B. cœlestris* [Colombia] (bluish violet and yellow, June and July, 18–20 in.); *B. Lalindei* [New Granada] (yellowish white with orange and brown markings); *B. violaceum* [British Guiana] (deep rich violet, tipped with greenish yellow).

**Bonatea speciosa.**—A handsome terrestrial orchid from the Cape of Good Hope. It is allied to the **Habenaria,** and succeeds in fibrous loam and peat. It is propagated by division of the roots when new growth commences. It bears green and white flowers in May and June, and grows to a height of 20–24 inches.

**Brassia.**—Pot-up in February triennially in shallow pans or on blocks of wood in a compost of one part of sphagnum moss to three parts of chopped Osmunda fibre. Grow up near the glass and water regularly.

*Species.*—*B. brachiata* [Guatemala] (green with purple spots, summer—vigorous and spreading, best grown in a basket); *B. maculata* [Tropical America] (greenish yellow, spotted brown, summer, 18 in.); *B. verrucosa* [Guatemala] (green, white lip, spotted green, spring and summer, 12–18 in.).

**Cattleya.**—Pot-up very firmly from March to April when new roots are forming at the base of young shoots, using well-drained pots and a compost of one part of live sphagnum to three parts of Osmunda fibre and charcoal. Grow near the glass. Water liberally while growing, but sparingly when dormant. Propagate by means of division in March. Each root must have three to four bulbs.

*Species.*—*C. bicolor* [Brazil] (purple and greenish brown, Aug.–Sept., 18 in.); *C. citrina* [Mexico] (yellow, April–May, 9–12 in., pendant); *C. Dowiana* [Costa Rica] (yellow and purple, gold stripe on lip, Sept., 15 in.); *C. Harrisoniana* [Brazil] (mauve,

July–Sept., 15 in.) ; *C. labiata* [Brazil] (rose and purple, Oct.–Nov., 15 in.) ; *C. maxima* [Ecuador and Peru] (pink, crimson-veined lip, Dec., 15 in.) ; *C. Mossiæ* [La Guayra] (mauve and crimson, yellow on lip, June 12–15 in.) ; *C. Rex* [Peruvian Andes] (cream, crimson lip, June–July, 15–18 in.) ; *C. Skinneri* [Guatemala] (purplish rose, May–June, 15 in.) ; *C. Warneri* [Brazil] (rose and purple, June–Aug., 12 in.). There are many beautiful varieties and hybrids of these.

**Chysis.**—Pot-up annually or bi-annually in spring in well-drained shallow pans containing a compost of three parts of Osmunda fibre and one part of sphagnum moss. Grow up near the glass and shade from strong sun in summer. Water well while growing, dry off gradually, and rest in winter.

*Species.*—*C. aurea* [S. America] (buff-yellow, lip marked red, 18–24 in.) ; *C. bractescens* [Mexico] (whitish yellow, lip marked red, spring and early summer, 20–26 in.) ; *C. lævis* [Mexico] (buff-yellow, lip marked red, early spring, 18–24 in.).

**Comparettia.**—A little group of graceful orchids, with small but brightly coloured flowers which retain their beauty for a considerable period. They can be grown on blocks of wood or in pots or baskets. Use a compost of fibrous peat and live sphagnum in equal parts, with plenty of crocks. They should be placed in the intermediate or warm house where they will not be fully exposed to the sun, and at no time should they be allowed to become too dry. The inflorescence is usually pendulous, and the plants should always be kept well above the surface of the pot or basket. They are propagated by division when the new growth starts.

*Species.*—*C. coccinea* [Brazil] (scarlet, white, and crimson, Nov., 9–12 in.) ; *C. falcata* [Peru] (rosy purple, Oct., 6 in.) ; *C. macroplectron* [New Granada] (pale rose, red spots, Oct., 12 in.).

**Coryanthes.**—A group of orchids allied to **Stanhopea**, remarkable for the peculiar form of their flowers, which are of a very delicate texture. They collapse almost as soon as out. They succeed in orchid pots or baskets in well-drained fibrous peat, and chopped sphagnum in equal proportions, with the addition of small crocks mixed in. They require a moist atmosphere and a growing temperature of 60–70° F., with a resting temperature of 50–60° F.

*Species.*—*C. macrantha* [Caracas] (rich yellow, dotted with red and brownish red, May and June, 12 in.) ; *C. maculata* [Demerara] (pale yellow, blotched with dull red, June, 12 in.) ; *C. m.* var. *punctata* (bright yellow, speckled with red) ; *C. m.* var. *Cobbii* (unspotted form) ; *C. speciosa* [Brazil] (pale yellow, May, 15 in.).

**Cryptochilus.**—Pot-up in spring in a chopped-up mixture of one part of sphagnum moss to three parts of Osmunda fibre and one part of loam.

*Species.*—*C. sanguinea* [Himalayas] (deep rich red).

**Dendrobium** (Rock Lily).—Pot-up from March to April when growths are from 2 to 3 inches long, using well-drained pots and a compost of three parts of Osmunda fibre to one part of sphagnum moss and a little charcoal. Water liberally from March to August. Give plenty of light, but shade from strong sun. Water sparingly and keep cool when dormant. Propagate by means of offsets at any time in heat.

*Species.*—*D. aureum* [Tropical Asia] (amber-yellow, March, 12–18 in.) ; *D. crassinode* [Burma] (white, purple edge, April, 18–24 in.) ; *D. formosum giganteum* (white, May–July, 12–18 in.) ; *D. monile* (*japonicum*) [Japan and China] (white, May, 10 in.) ; *D. nobile* [N. India and China] (rose, maroon, and white, Feb.–April, 18–24 in.) ; *D. thyrsiflorum* [Burma] (white and orange lip, March–May, 18–24 in.). There are many beautiful forms and varieties of these.

**Dichæa picta.**—An interesting and elegant little orchid from Trinidad, bearing bright-green flowers with purplish dots. It thrives in the stove house on a block of wood with some moss and fibre.

**Epicattleya.**—These are a cross between **Cattleya** and **Epidendrum**. They require similar treatment to that recommended for **Cattleya**.

**Epiphronitis.**—These are a cross between **Sophronitis** and **Epidendrum**. They require similar treatment to that recommended for **Sophronitis**.

**Eriopsis.**—Pot-up in fibrous peat and sphagnum moss, with good drainage, and allow an ample supply of water when growing. Increase by dividing the plant when growth commences.

*Species.*—*E. biloba* [Colombia] (yellow, with orange-red, brown spots, 6–8 in.) ; *E. rutidobulbon* [Peru] (similar to the above, but with larger and deeper-coloured flowers, 18 in.).

**Galeandra.**—Terrestrial orchids that require either the stove or warm greenhouse. They should be grown in fibrous peat with some sharp sand, surfaced with sphagnum. They require plenty of water in the growing season, but very little during the winter, and they should be kept near the glass. They are subject to red spider and thrip, so that the plants will benefit from a syringing twice a week with warm water. They are propagated by division.

*Species.*—*G. Baueri* [Mexico] (yellowish and purple, June–Aug., 6–8 in.) ; *G.*

# ORCHIDS FOR THE WARM HOUSE

*Devoniana* [Rio Negro] (reddish brown and green lip, whitish, veined crimson, June, 15–18 in.); *G. nivalis* [Tropical America] (olive-green, lip white, with purple blotch, March, 15 in.).

**Geodorum.**—Should be planted in pans in fibrous peat and sphagnum moss in a hot, damp stove. Increased by division in March.

*Species.*—*G. citrinum* [E. Indies] (yellow, Oct.–Dec., 12 in.); *G. furcatum* [Ceylon] (pink, July, 12 in.).

**Goodyera.**—Pot-up in pans in spring in a compost of well-drained peat and sand with sphagnum moss and a little loam. Propagated by pieces of stem with eyes and some roots attached placed under a bell-glass in the spring.

*Species.*—*G. rubicunda* [Manilla] (reddish, July), velvety leaves with red bands; *G. velutina* [Japan] (white, summer), velvety purplish leaves.

**Hexisea bidentata.**—This attractive little orchid from Panama is closely related to and somewhat resembles **Epidendrum**. It is useful for the warm orchid house, and requires a compost of fibrous peat and sphagnum. It is increased by division. It grows to a height of from 6 to 8 inches and bears scarlet flowers in June.

**Holothrix.**—Warm greenhouse orchids which die down to the ground annually. They succeed in fibrous peat, sphagnum, and charcoal, with plenty of drainage.

*Species.*—*H. Lindleyana* [S. Africa] (white, 6–8 in.); *H. villosa* [S. Africa] (yellowish green, fragrant, 9–10 in.).

**Inobulbon munificum** (*Dendrobium muricatum* var. *munificum*).—An attractive epiphytic orchid for the intermediate house, requiring an abundance of light and a fair supply of air. It succeeds in a mixture of Osmunda fibre and fibrous peat with broken crocks, and a little fresh sphagnum. Its flowers are greenish with brown spots and reddish-purple and yellow markings. It flowers from July to August, and attains a height of from 12 to 16 inches.

**Ipsea** (Daffodil Orchid).—Pot-up in early spring in a well-drained mixture of three parts of loam to one part of leaf-mould and sphagnum. Water regularly while growing, and give ample light and ventilation. Gradually dry off after flowering, and rest during winter.

*Species.*—*I. speciosa* [Ceylon] (golden yellow, winter or early spring, 18 in.).

**Lælia.**—Pot-up in March in pots more than half full of crocks, using a compost of half live sphagnum and half fibrous peat, and a little charcoal. Water liberally while growing, but sparingly while dormant. Give plenty of light. Propagate by means of division in March.

*Species.*—*L. anceps* [Mexico] (dark pink, purple lip, Dec., 5–10 in.); *L. Dayana* [Brazil] (rosy purple, April–May, dwarf); *L. Digbyana* [British Honduras] (greenish white with cream lip, July–Aug., 9–12 in.); *L. glauca* [Mexico] (greenish white, cream lip streaked red, spring 12 in.); *L. pumila* [Brazil] (rose, purple lip, Sept.–Oct., dwarf); *L. pumila* var. *præstans* (rose and purple, April–May, 6 in.); *L. xanthina* [Brazil] (yellow, orange, July, 9–12 in.).

**Læliocattleya.**—Hybrids of two attractive genera, some of them being natural hybrids and others having been raised artificially. Pot-up very firmly in pots more than half full of crocks, using a compost of half live sphagnum and half Osmunda fibre and a little charcoal. Water liberally while growing, but sparingly when dormant. Propagate by means of division in March.

*Species.*—*L. Dominiana* [garden origin] (rose and purple, July–Sept., 18 in.); *L. Dormaniana* [Brazil] (olive-brown, red spots, purple and white, summer, 14–16 in.); *L. elegans* [Brazil] (bright rose, whitish and purple, summer, 16–20 in.); *L. radiata* [garden origin] (violet, red, purple, and white, summer, 10–12 in.); *L. Schilleriana* [Brazil] (white, purple, yellow, June–July, 16–20 in.).

**Leptotes bicolor** (*Tetramicra bicolor*).—A pretty orchid from Brazil, with white and rose flowers in racemes during the winter. It requires the same cultural treatment as **Lælia.**

**Macradenia.**—A small group of orchids, perhaps more interesting than beautiful. They require the same cultural treatment as **Oncidium.**

*Species.*—*M. Brassavolæ* [Colombia] (cinnamon, yellow, and white, with purple stripes, 5–7 in.); *M. lutescens* [Trinidad] (yellow with brownish spots, Nov., 5–6 in.).

**Macroplectrum sesquipedale** (*Angræcum sesquipedale*).—This native of Madagascar is one of the grandest of winter-flowering orchids, blooming from November to January. It has fleshy, ivory-white flowers from 6 to 8 inches across, with a long, whip-like spur, or tail-like appendage, often from 10 to 15 inches long. It should be grown in fibrous peat, sphagnum and broken crocks, mixed with pieces of wood. It requires moisture and heat when growing in the summer, but only warmth when coming into bloom, and should be kept cool and dry during the winter It is propagated by offsets or by seed.

**Maxillaria.**—A large group of orchids showing a considerable range of variation. A number are quite showy, and deserve a place in all collections.

*Culture.*—They are of easy cultivation, and usually succeed when treated as pot plants. They should be potted in a compost of equal parts of good fibrous peat and chopped sphagnum. During the growing season they should have a temperature of 60–70° F., and an abundant supply of water. In the winter the temperature should be 10–15° lower, but on no account should the plants be allowed to get dry in the winter. One or two species with creeping rhizomes may be placed on tree-fern stems or blocks of wood. Shade is essential during bright weather, more so than in most orchids.

Propagation is carried out by division of the pseudo bulbs in the spring.

*Species.*—*M. grandiflora* [Peru, etc.] (white, striped with purple and yellow, Aug., 12–16 in.); *M. Houtteana* [Guatemala] (yellow and reddish purple, April, 10–12 in.); *M. picta* [Brazil] (deep orange, spotted purple, white with purple spots, winter, 12–16 in.); *M. Sanderiana* [Ecuador] (pure white).

**Microstylis.**—Pot-up annually in early spring in well-crocked pots containing a mixture of rich loam (three parts) with a little dried cow-manure, leaf-mould, and shredded sphagnum moss (one part). Grow up near the glass in a warm, moist atmosphere, but shade from strong sun until the flowering period is over, then gradually dry off and rest. Propagate by means of division in early spring.

*Species.*—*M. calophylla* [Malaya] (yellow, summer, 9–12 in.); *M. discolor* [Ceylon] (yellow, shading to orange, summer, 9–12 in.); *M. Lowii* [Borneo] (purple, summer, 9–12 in.); *M. metallica* [Borneo] (purplish pink, yellow markings, summer, 9–12 in.); *M. Wallichii* [Burma] (greenish yellow, summer, 9–12 in.).

**Miltonia.**—Pot-up in March when new roots are forming at the base of shoots, in well-drained pots, using a compost of two parts of live sphagnum to one part of fibrous peat and a little charcoal. Water liberally while growing, and give ample light, but shade from strong sun. Propagate by means of division in March.

*Species.*—*M. vexilliaria* (lilac, rose, or white, May–June, 9–12 in.).

**Moorea irrorata,** *Orchidaceæ.*—A handsome warm greenhouse plant from Colombia. It should be potted in a compost of fibrous peat, sphagnum, and some fibrous loam. After growth is completed it should be rested. It is an easily grown, free-flowering orchid which succeeds in the Cattleya house. It bears reddish-brown, yellow, purple, and white flowers in the summer and grows to a height of from 15 to 24 inches.

**Neogyne Gardneriana,** *Orchidaceæ.*—A winter flowering species from the Himalayas. It bears white flowers marked with yellow. It is sometimes included under **Cœlogyne** and requires the same cultural treatment as the warm greenhouse Cœlogyne.

**Nephelaphyllum.**—A group of orchids for the warm greenhouse, attractive both in flower and foliage, the latter being usually purple beneath, spotted or mottled above. They thrive in a mixture of peat and fibre, among which should be mixed some pieces of porous sandstone and charcoal. They require a similar treatment to that of **Anœctochilus,** and are increased by division at the time of potting-up.

*Species.*—*N. pulchrum* [Java] (small white and green flowers, leaves beautifully mottled dark green, 3 in.); *N. scapigerum* [Borneo] (flowers white, with purple and yellow, 4–5 in.).

**Oncidium.**—Pot-up in September when new bulb begins to form, using well-drained pots and a compost of half live sphagnum and half fibrous-peat with a little charcoal. Water with soft water. Keep cool and damp after potting. Water liberally in summer, but in winter give only sufficient moisture to keep the bulbs plump. Shade from strong sun.

*Species.*—*O. crispum* [Brazil] (brown and yellow, Aug., 9–12 in.); *O. flexuosum* [Brazil] (yellow and red, July–Aug., 9 in.); *O. Forbesii* [Brazil] (brown, edged with yellow, Oct.–Dec., 10–12 in.); *O. Kramerianum* [Central America] (yellow and cinnamon-brown, any season, 24–30 in., somewhat resembles *O. Papilio*); *O. Marshallianum* [Brazil] (yellow and brown, May and June, 9–12 in.); *O Papilio* (Butterfly Orchid) [W. Indies] (yellow and brown, any season, 24–36 in.); *O. sarcodes* [Brazil] (orange-yellow, spotted crimson, Jan.–March, 6–9 in.).

**Paphiopedilum** (Lady's Slipper).—Pot-up in April in well-drained pots (about one-third full of crocks), using a compost of one part turfy loam, two parts turfy peat, and one part sphagnum moss, with a little coarse sand and crushed brick. Water liberally and syringe overhead in summer. Always keep moist, but water sparingly in winter. Propagate by means of division in April. The mottled-leaf kinds require a slightly higher temperature.

*Species.*—*P. barbatum* [Malay Peninsula] (white, striped purple, June, 6–9 in.); *P. bellatulum* [Burma] (white, spotted purple, July–Aug., dwarf); *P. callosum* [Cochin China] (white, crimson, and brown, March–May, 9 in.); *P. Charlesworthii* [Upper Burma] (white, pink, and brown, Oct.–Nov., 9 in.); *P. Druryi* [S. India] (greenish yellow, dark lines, Dec.–Feb., 9–12 in.); *P. Lathamianum* [garden hybrid] (light brown, dark lines, Dec.–Feb., 12 in.); *P. Leeanum* [garden hybrid] (brown and white, spotted purple, Dec.–Feb., 9–12 in.); *P. Maudiæ* [garden hybrid] (light green, broad white band, June–July, 9 in.) ; *P. nitens* [garden hybrid] (light brown, dark lip, Jan.–March, 9–12 in.) ; *P. niveum* [Langkawi and Tambilan Islands] (white, June, dwarf) ; *P venustum* [Himalayas] (greenish white, striped purple, April, 6 in.). There are also many other beautiful varieties and hybrids.

**Pescatoria.**—A group of orchids sometimes included under **Zygopetalum,** requiring the same cultural treatment.

*Species.*—*P. cerina* [Chiriqui] grows 12–15 inches high, and is coloured variously, pale straw-yellow, deep yellow, and deep purple, according to the season. *P. Dayana,* [Colombia], grows 8–10 inches high, and bears in late autumn flowers whose sepals and petals are white, tipped green, and the rest of the flower purplish violet, yellow, and red. In the variety *rhodacra* the sepals and petals have rose tips, and the labellum is suffused crimson.

**Phaius.**—Pot-up in April, using three parts of fibrous peat to one part of sandy loam. Keep the atmosphere warm and damp while growing. Water sparingly, and keep cool while resting. Propagate by means of division in April.

*Species.*—*P. grandifolius* [Tropical Asia and Australia] (brown and white, Feb.–April, 30 in.) ; *P. mishmensis* [Himalayas] (rose, spring, 20–30 in.) ; *P. Wallichii* [Tropical India] (purplish yellow and white, spring, 30–40 in.).

**Pholidota** (Rattlesnake Orchid).—Pot-up annually in March, using well-drained pots or pans and a compost of two parts of sphagnum moss to three parts of Osmunda fibre, with one part of old dried cow-manure. Grow up near the glass in a warm, moist atmosphere. Shade from hot sun. Water regularly while growing, but dry off gradually and keep almost dry during the winter.

*Species.*—*P. articulata* [India] (yellowish white, summer, 15–18 in.) ; *P. imbricata* [India] (pale yellow, with a shade of violet, summer, 12 in,) ; *P. ventricosa* [Java] (yellowish white, summer, 18 in.)

**Phragmopedilum**—This group of orchids, together with **Paphiopedilum,** was at one time included in **Cypripedium.** Phragmopedilums enjoy plenty of moisture and a temperature of 65–80° F., in the growing season, which is March to the end of October. Such good drainage do they require that the pots should be half-filled with drainage, and with species and hybrids such as *P. Dominianum, P. Schlimii,* and *P. Sedenii* they should be three parts full.

*Culture.*—Fill the pot to the rim with Osmunda or A1 fibre, then place the plant on top of this and build up round the plant with a compost of chopped sphagnum, broken clinkers or crocks, and leaf-mould mixed with some sand, to a height of 2½–3 inches or even more above the rim of the pot. This will be found excellent treatment for young or divided plants. Use rain-water to keep moss in a growing condition. Water sparingly until growth commences.

Propagation is carried out by means of division when the new growth starts, or by seed.

*Species.*—*P. caudatum* (*Selenipedium caudatum*) [Peru] is a remarkable orchid, with pale yellow creamy-white flowers, veined green, borne in April and May. The petals, which are twisted, sometimes attain a length of 20–30 inches, and are yellowish red at the tips. *P. Dominianum* (*Selenipedium Dominianum*) is a beautiful garden hybrid, with yellowish-green flowers tinged with coppery brown, and having dark-purple spots. The petals are long and twisted. *P. Hartwegii* (*Selenipedium Hartwegii*) has flowers which are pale green, rosy, and white, tinged with brown. *P. Schlimii* (*Selenipedium Schlimii*) [New Granada] has white flowers, mottled and striped dark rose. *P. Sedenii* (*Selenipedium Sedenii*) is a garden hybrid with greenish-white, purple, or rich crimson flowers, with crimson spots.

There are also many interesting and beautiful hybrids of those mentioned, as well as of others.

**Pleione** (Indian Crocus).—Pot-up one month after blooming, placing five bulbs in a 5-inch pot in a compost of one part each of sphagnum moss, peat, fibrous loam, and sand. Water well, and keep warm while growing. Keep well up near the glass. Water sparingly, and keep cool while resting. Propagate by means of offsets in late autumn.

*Species.*—*P. humilis* [N. India] (pink and white, purple spotted lip, Feb., dwarf) ; *P. maculata* [N. India] (white and purple, Oct.–Nov., dwarf) ; *P. præcox* [N. India] (purple and yellow, Nov., dwarf) ; *P. yunnensis* [China] (rosy purple, Dec., 6–10 ins.).

**Rhynchostylis.**—A small group of epiphytic orchids with dense racemes of flowers coming from the axils of the leaves. They are closely allied to **Saccalobium** and succeed with the same cultural treatment.

*Species.*—*R. cœlestis* [Siam] has white flowers with a blue marking. *R. retusa* [E. Indies] has white flowers blotched with pink or violet in June and July ; there are several beautiful varieties. *R. violacea* [Philippines] has white flowers spotted with pale mauve and dark violet. Although the type is said to have an unpleasant odour the var. *Harrisonianum* with white flowers is fragrant.

**171**

# THE GREENHOUSE

**Saccalobium.**—Pot-up in February in well-drained pots containing half sphagnum moss, half crocks, and a little charcoal. Keep close to the glass, but shade from strong sun. Water liberally in spring and summer. Keep the atmosphere warm and damp, but the leaves dry in winter. Propagate by means of offsets at any time.
*Species.*—*S. ampullaceum* [India] (deep rose, May–June, 12–15 in.); *S. cœleste* [Siam] (white and blue, July–Aug., 10–12 in.); *S. Hendersonianum* [Borneo] (bright rose, summer, 5–7 in.).

**Satyrium.**—Pot-up in spring when new growth is visible in clean, well-drained pots of sandy loam, with a little leaf-mould added. Grow near the glass in a warm, moist atmosphere, and keep well watered. Shade from strong sun. Withhold water gradually after flowering, and rest in winter.
*Species.*—*S. candidum* [S. Africa] (white, summer, 18 in.); *S. carneum* [S. Africa] (pale pink to white, summer, 18–24 in.); *S. coriifolium* [S. Africa] (red and yellow, summer, 12 in.); *S. erectum* [S. Africa] (orange, tinted purple, summer, 18–24 in.).

**Sobralia.**—Pot-up in March, giving plenty of room, in a pot half-filled with crocks, and using a compost of two parts of fibrous loam to one part of charcoal and grit. Cut away old stalks if overcrowded. Keep moist at roots and give ample light. Propagate by means of division in March.
*Species.*—*S. leucoxantha* [Costa Rica] (white, yellow throat, Aug., 25–30 in.); *S. macrantha* [Mexico] (crimson, July–Aug. 70 in.); *S. virginalis* [Colombia] (white, shaded yellow, summer, 30–36 in.); *S. xantholeuca* [Guatemala] (lemon-yellow, lip deeper shade, summer, 20–24 in.).

**Sophrocattleya.**—These orchids are the result of a cross between **Cattleya** and **Sophronitis**. Their cultivation is similar to that given for **Cattleya**.

**Sophrocattllælia.** These orchids are the result of crossing **Cattleya, Sophronitis,** and **Lælia**. Cultivation is as for **Cattleya**.

**Trichocentrum.**—Dwarf-growing, free-flowering, epiphitic orchids. As they suffer from too much water at the roots, they are best grown on blocks of wood. They should be given a warm greenhouse temperature, and are increased by division when new growth starts.
*Species.*—*T. albo-purpureum* [Brazil] has flowers 2 inches across, maroon, tawny-yellow, or green, and a white lip with purple spots. *T. fuscum* [Mexico] has purplish-green flowers, blotched and spotted with rose and red. *T. panamense* [Panama] has light green and white flowers with a reddish-purple blotch. *T. tigrinum* [Central America] has flowers nearly 3 inches in diameter, yellow speckled with red, white with rose.

**Trichopilia.**—Pot-up in March when new shoots appear, using a compost of equal parts of sphagnum moss, turfy peat, crocks and charcoal. Keep the atmosphere moist. Water moderately in spring and summer, and keep almost dry in winter. Propagate by means of division in March.
*Species.*—*T. fragrans* [Colombia] (greenish white and yellow, summer, 10–12 in.); *T. marginata* [Central America] (white and reddish purple, May–June, 6–8 in.); *T. suavis* [Central America] (cream, rose, and purple, April 4–6 in.).

**Vanda** (Cowslip-scented Orchid).—Pot-up in March in new soil annually, using a compost of Osmunda fibre and half sphagnum moss (alive) and plenty of broken crocks. Grow in pans near the glass, but shade from strong sun. Syringe liberally in warm, bright weather and generally keep moist while growing. Keep moderately dry and cool when dormant. Propagate by means of offsets in March.
*Species.*—*V. cœrulea* [N. India and Burma] (light blue, Oct.–Nov., 20–30 in.); *V. Kimballiana* [Burma] (white, tinged purple, Oct.–Nov., 12 in.).

**Xylobium.**—Warm greenhouse epiphytic orchids with racemes of flowers rising from the base of the pseudo bulb. They are closely allied to, and sometimes included with **Maxillaria**, and require the same cultural treatment.
*Species.*—*X. brachystachyum* [Brazil] (dull purple and yellow, spotted purple, spring, 12 in.); *X. decolor* (*Maxillaria decolor*) [W. Indies] (sulphur and white, spring, 12 in.); *X. elongatum* (*Maxillaria elongata*) [W. Indies] (yellowish white and purplish brown, 12 in.); *X. leontoglossum* (*Maxillaria leontoglossa*) [Colombia] (yellow, spotted with maroon and purplish brown); *X. squalens* (*Maxillaria squalens*) [Venezuela] (yellowish white, marked purple, spring, 12 in.).

**Zygopetalum.**—Pot-up in March, when essential, using a compost of equal parts of sphagnum moss, peat, loam, and charcoal. Grow in summer in a cool, moist house. Water liberally and shade from strong sun. Propagate by means of division in March.
*Species.*—*Z. crinitum* [Brazil] (greenish yellow, with white lip, Nov.–Dec., 10–12 in.); *Z. Mackaii* [Brazil] (greenish yellow, with white lip, Nov.–Dec., 10–12 in.).

# ORCHID CULTURE

## ORCHIDS FOR THE COOL HOUSE

*Temperature :* Summer—Day   60–65° F.   Winter—Day   55–60° F.
         „    —Night 55–60° F.      „    —Night 45–55° F.

**Ada.**—Pot-up in March as soon as new growth is visible in a compost of half peat and half sphagnum moss, in a pot previously half filled with broken crocks. Water liberally from May to October. Propagate by means of division in March.

*Species.—A. aurantiaca* [Colombia] (orange-scarlet, Jan.–March, 10 in.).

**Anguloa** (Bull's Head or Cradle Orchid).—Pot-up in spring when new roots form at the base of young shoots, using a compost of two parts of peat to one part of sphagnum moss. Keep in the warmest part of the house. Water well while growing, but sparingly when mature, and give a short rest. Propagate by means of division at potting time.

*Species.—A. Clowesii* [Colombia] (golden yellow and white, March–May, 20 in.) ; *A. Ruckeri* [Columbia] (green, yellow, red, spring, 20–24 in.) ; *A. uniflora* [Columbia] (white, tinged pink, June–July, 20 in.).

**Bletia.**—Pot-up in March when new shoots appear, using a compost of half sandy loam and half leaf-mould. Keep cool and in partial shade from May to September, and water liberally. Water sparingly while resting. Propagate by means of division in June.

*Species.—B. hyacinthina* [China and Japan] (carmine-purple, May–April, up to 12 in.).

**Brassavola** (see **Lælia** in Orchids for the Intermediate House).

**Brassia.**—Pot-up in February triennially in shallow pans or on blocks of wood in a compost of one part of sphagnum moss to three parts of chopped Osmunda fibre.

*Species.—B. brachiata* [Guatemala] (green with purple spots, summer (vigorous and spreading. Best grown in a basket) ; *B. maculata* [Tropical America] (greenish yellow, spotted brown, summer, 18 in.) ; *B. verrucosa* [Guatemala] (green, white lip, spotted green, spring and summer, 12–18 in.).

**Calypso borealis.**—An almost hardy terrestrial orchid from North America, which, although it may be grown in a sheltered shady spot in the rock garden, is suitable for the cool greenhouse or alpine house. It should be grown in pans in a compost of peat, leaf-soil, and sand, and kept in a cool pit or frame in a shady position. It is increased by offsets in the autumn. (Flowers rose and brown, March and April, 6 in.)

**Chondrorhyncha.**—A small group of cool stove epiphytal orchids. For treatment see **Odontoglossum crispum.**

**Cochlioda.**—A group of South American orchids requiring the same treatment as **Odontoglossum,** to which they are closely allied.

*Species.—C. Noetzliana* [Andes] (scarlet, spring, 12 in. ; the var. *aurantiaca* has orange flowers) ; *C. rosea* [Peru] (rose-coloured, winter, 6–8 in.) : *C. sanguinea* [Ecuador] (bright rose, June–Aug., 6–8 in.).

**Cœlogyne.**—Pot-up in March or replace top soil, using a compost of half live sphagnum moss and half turfy peat. Twelve bulbs should be included in each clump potted-up, and the pot or pan should first be half filled with crocks ; or they may be grown on rafts. Grow near the glass, but shade from strong sun. Water liberally during spring and summer. Propagate by means of division in March.

*Species.—C. cristata* [Himalayas] and vars. (white, with golden-yellow lip, Feb. and March, 6–9 in.).

**Cryptophoranthus.**—A small group of cool greenhouse orchids allied to, and sometimes included in, **Masdevallia** and **Pleurothallis,** requiring precisely the same treatment.

*Species.—C. atropurpureus* [W. Indies] (purple, summer, 6 in.) ; *C. Dayanus* [Colombia] (yellowish white with purple spots, July–Oct., 6–8 in.) ; *C. Moorei* [Tropical America] (reddish purple, yellowish or light green, 5–6 in.).

**Cymbidium.**—Re-pot as necessary when young shoots are 2–3 inches long. They require ample drainage and plenty of room. A compost of half fibrous loam and half peat, sphagnum moss, dried cow-manure, and crocks suits them well. Give ample light, but shade from strong sun. Water well while growing. Keep moist and cool in summer. Reduce water supply for a few weeks after flowering. Propagate by means of division in March.

*Species.—C. Alexanderi* [garden hybrid] (rose, March–May, 30 in.) ; *C. eburneum* [Khasia Hills] (ivory-white, March, 30 in.) ; *C. giganteum* [Annam] (greenish yellow and yellow, striped red, Feb.–March, 30 in.) ; *C. insigne* (*Sanderi*) [Annam] (rose and white, March–May, 30 in.) ; *C. Lowianum* [Burma] (greenish yellow and dark-red lip, March–April, 30 in.) ; *C. Traceyanum* [Burma] (yellow, striped brown, dark-red lip, March–May, 30 in.).

There are many other beautiful hybrids of garden origin.

# THE GREENHOUSE

**Cyperorchis.**—Pot-up in February or March in well-crocked pots in a mixture of three-quarters loam and one-quarter Osmunda fibre, with a sprinkling of broken brick and sphagnum moss. Give ample light, but shade from strong sun. Water carefully and regularly while growing.

*Species.*—*C. elegans* [Himalayas] (pale yellow, autumn, 20 in.); *C. Mastersii* [Sikkim and Khasia Hills] (white, spotted pink, 30 in.).

**Cypripedium** (Lady's Slipper).—Attractive, hardy, herbaceous, terrestrial orchids, usually grown outside, but which are valuable when grown in pans for the alpine or cold greenhouse. (At one time the greenhouse species of Lady's Slipper were included in **Cypripedium,** but, as they are slightly different botanically, they are now separated and known as **Paphiopedilum** and **Phragmipedilum,** which see.)

*Culture.*—When grown in pans for the alpine house they should be planted in the spring in a compost of good fibrous loam and fibrous peat in equal proportions, with some sphagnum moss and broken sandstone mixed in ; a little charcoal may also be added. The pans should be plunged in ashes in a cool position in a cold frame, and although they require less water when resting than when growing, they should never be allowed to become dry. Division is the usual method of increase, but it is desirable to disturb the plants as little as possible.

*Species.*—*C. acaule* [N. United States] (pinkish-purple solitary flowers, May–June, 6–8 in.); *C. Calceolus* [N. Asia and Europe] (a rare British species, reddish browny yellow, June, 9 in.); *C. candidum* [N. America] (greenish brown and white, June, 12 in.); *C. japonicum* [Japan] (pink and white, tinged with crimson, June, 8–10 in.); *C. macranthum* [Siberia, N. Asia] (purple, May and June, 9–12 in.); *C. montanum* [California] (white, veined with purple, June, 18–24 in.); *C. reginæ* [*C. spectabilis*] (rose and white, June, 15–20 in.).

**Dendrobium** (Rock Lily).—Pot-up when new shoots are from 2 to 3 inches long, using well-drained pots and a compost of three-quarters Osmunda fibre to a quarter of charcoal, in a temperature of 60–65° F.—cooler when at rest. Water liberally from March to August, but sparingly when dormant. Give ample light. Propagate by means of off-sets or cuttings in heat all the year round.

*Species.*—*D. infundibulum* [Burma] (white, April–July, 12–15 in.); *D. infundibulum* var. *Jamesianum* (white, red-tinged lip, April–July, 12–15 in.).

**Diacrium bicornutum.**—An attractive orchid from Tropical America. It is closely allied to **Epidendrum,** and has been included in that genus. It requires the same cultural treatment. The loose racemes of flowers, which are white with small crimson spots on the tip, are borne in May and June. It requires a light position in a very moist house.

**Disa** (Table Mountain Orchid).—Pot-up from November to December in well-drained coarse sand. Ventilate freely while growing. Keep moist, and shade from direct sun. Syringe overhead in spring and summer. Propagate by means of seed sown under glass in living sphagnum moss in March, or by division of the roots in November.

*Species.*—*D. grandiflora* [S. Africa] (scarlet and crimson, veined pink, May–Aug., 20 in.); *D. kewensis* [garden hybrid] (pink, May–Aug., 20 in.); *D. Luna* (garden hybrid) (pink, May–Aug., 20 in.).

**Diuris.**—Interesting and attractive Australian orchids. They should be grown in fibrous loam and peat, half the pot being filled with crocks in equal proportions with some sand. They appreciate a little shade when making their growth and flowers. Propagation is by division when growth commences.

*Species.*—*D. longifolia* (yellow and purple, summer, 12–24 in.); *D. maculata* (yellow, spotted with purple or brown, March, 12 in.); *D. punctata* (blue or purplish, occasionally spotted, but not blotched, spring, 12–16 in.).

**Epidendrum** (Dragon's Mouth Orchid).—Pot-up in March in well-drained pots containing a compost of half live sphagnum and half fibrous peat and charcoal. Grow on a raft suspended near the glass. Water liberally while growing, but very sparingly when dormant. Propagate by means of division in March. Some species, such as *E. radicans,* which are ramblers, need support.

*Species.*—*E. evectum* [Colombia] (rose-purple, summer, 30 in.); *E. radicans* [Guatemala] (scarlet-orange, summer, 50–60 in.; *E. vitellinum majus* [Brazil] (orange-red, July–Aug., 12 in.); *E. xanthinum* [Brazil] (yellow, summer, 20–30 in.).

**Epilælia.**—Bi-generic orchids obtained by hybridising **Epidendrum** and **Lælia.** They succeed under the same treatment as **Epidendrum.**

*Species.*—*E. Charlesworthii* [*E. radicans* X *L. cinnabarina*] (orange-scarlet, July, 18 in.); *E. radico-purpurata* [*E. radicans* X *L. purpurata*] (rosy red, purple, and yellow, July, 18 in.).

**Eriochilus.**—A group of Australian terrestrial orchids which succeed in a cool house in sandy peat and fibrous loam, in equal proportions with good drainage. They may be increased by division of the roots.

**174**

# ORCHIDS FOR THE COOL HOUSE

*Species.*—*E. autumnalis* (pink, Oct., 6–8 in.) ; *E. multiflorus* (pink, March, 8–10 in.

**Hartwegia.**—Tropical American orchids allied to **Epidendrum,** requiring precisely the same cultural treatment as **Odontoglossum.** The leaves are spotted with blackish violet.

*Species.*—*H. gemma* [Central America] (a beautiful flower of amethyst-purple, July) ; *H. purpurea* [Mexico] (small purple flowers, Aug., 12 in.).

**Liparis.**—A group of orchids of herbaceous habit. some of which are hardy. Others require greenhouse treatment, either cool, medium, or warm.

*Culture.*—The greenhouse kinds require a compost of fibrous peat, sphagnum, charcoal, and finely broken crocks, and are very suitable in open baskets. They should be kept on the dry side when resting, but never allowed to get quite dry. They are propagated by division when new growth starts.

*Species.*—*L. lilifolia* [N. America] (brownish purple, July, 10 in.). This is hardy and will grow in well-drained, lime-free soil, in a shady position in the rock-garden or woodland. It is an attractive plant in pans for the cool greenhouse or alpine house.

**Lycaste.**—Pot-up when young growth appears, in well-drained pots containing a compost of sphagnum moss, loam, and Osmunda fibre in equal proportions. Water liberally and syringe overhead while growing. Give ample light. Rest after flowering, but do not allow bulb to shrink for want of water. Propagate by means of division in March.

*Species.*—*L. Skinneri* [Guatemala] (pink, lip white, spotted crimson ; also has numerous other coloured varieties from pure white to deep crimson ; Dec.- Feb., 10 in.).

**Masdevallia** (Spectral-flowered Orchid).—Pot-up in September in well-drained pots, in a compost of two parts of sphagnum moss to one part of fibrous peat and charcoal. Ventilate freely. Syringe and shade in summer. Water liberally while growing and flowering. Keep slightly moist while dormant. Propagate by means of division in September.

*Species.*—*M. amabilis* [Colombia] (purplish crimson to yellow, May–June, 6–10 in.) ; *M. caudata* [Colombia] (green and yellow, streaked purple, spring, 6–10 in.) ; *M. coccinea* [Colombia] (crimson magenta and white, May, 8–10 in.) ; *M. coccinea* var. *Harryana* (rosy crimson, early June, 6–10 in.) ; *M. muscosa* [Colombia] (yellow, brown lines, spring, 6–10 in.) ; *M. rosea* [Peru] (rose, spring, 6–10 in.) ; *M. triangularis* [Colombia] (brown and yellowish purple spots, spring, 6–10 in.) ; *M. Veitchiana* [Peru] (vermilion and purple, April–June, 6–10 in.).

**Maxillaria.**—Pot-up when new shoots break, using well-drained pots, and a compost of two parts of sphagnum moss to one part of fibrous peat and charcoal, and sand. Syringe and water well while growing ; moderately while resting. Give ample light and ventilation in summer. Propagate by means of division in May.

*Species.*—*M. grandiflora* [Peru] (white, lip yellow, crimson markings, March, 10 in) ; *M. venusta* [Colombia] (white, lip yellow, Dec.-Feb., 10 in.).

**Mesospinidium sanguineum.**—An evergreen cool-greenhouse orchid from the Peruvian Andes, somewhat resembling a slender **Odontoglossum.** It succeeds in baskets of peat and moss, and requires the same cultural treatment as **Odontoglossum** and **Cochlioda**.

**Mormodes.**—Epiphytal deciduous orchids, with long, stem-like, pseudo bulbs. They resemble **Catasetum.** The flowers are thick and fleshy in dense spikes from the side of the pseudo bulb.

*Culture.*—They should be grown in baskets half filled with crocks and charcoal, and a compost of equal parts of chopped fibre, sphagnum, and fibrous loam, with some charcoal. They do not require an abundance of water at any time, although occasional applications of weak cow-manure or soot-water is beneficial, and it is advisable to allow the compost to dry out occasionally during the growing season. As the leaves decay, the plants should be given a cooler and airier position to ripen the growth. When at rest they should be watered occasionally, just to keep the soil moist and the pseudo bulbs from shrivelling.

Mormodes are subject to thrip, which should be kept under by a light fumigation from time to time. This treatment should also be given if green- or black-fly appears.

Propagation is effected by division when growth commences in the spring, when basketing is done, or by imported plants.

*Species.*—*M. Buccinator* [Mexico] (pale green and ivory-white, April, 15–24 in.) ; the var. *aurantiaca* has golden yellow flowers. *M. Colossus* [Central America] (pink and yellow, with pink dots, March, 15–24 in.) ; *M. pardina* [Mexico] (yellow, spotted reddish purple, fragrant, July–Aug., 12–18 in.). The var. *aurantiaca* has golden-yellow and light-yellow flowers ; while the flowers of the var. *unicolor* (*M. citrina*) are lemon-yellow.

**Nanodes.**—Pot-up in March in well-drained pots in a compost of half sphagnum moss and half turfy peat. Grow on a raft suspended near the glass, and water liberally in spring and summer. Propagate by means of division in March. This genus is sometimes included under **Epidendrum.**

*Species.*—*N. Medusæ* [Ecuador] (purple, green, and brown, fringed lip, Feb.–Oct., 10 in.).

**Nasonia punctata** (*Nasonia cinnabarina*).—A dwarf, creeping, cool-greenhouse orchid from Peru, with bright orange-scarlet and golden-yellow flowers during April. It requires the same cool greenhouse treatment and culture as **Masdevallia.**

**Neobenthamia gracilis.**—This native of Zanzibar bears flowers in terminal racemes, white with a yellow centre, and two rows of red spots, in February. It grows 30–40 inches high, and requires the same cultural treatment as **Cymbidium.**

**Odontioda.**—Pot-up in September when new bulb begins to form, using well-drained pots and a compost of half live sphagnum moss and half fibrous peat and charcoal. Water with soft water, and keep cool and damp after potting. Later water moderately to avoid damping-off. Ventilate freely, shade, and keep cool in hot weather. Give plenty of light while flowers are forming, and keep the atmosphere moist when warm and fine. Stand pot on inverted pot, and water liberally during summer, but give only sufficient water to keep bulbs plump in winter. Propagate by means of division in September. Each division must have three to four bulbs. They are of bi-generic origin, being hybrids of **Odontoglossum X Cochlioda.**

There are many beautiful named forms and varieties with crimson, scarlet, orange, yellow, white, etc., flowers, March–May, 9–14 in.

**Odontoglossum.**—Pot-up in September when new bulb begins to form, using well-drained pots and a compost of half live sphagnum moss and half fibrous peat and charcoal. Water with soft water, and keep cool and damp after potting. Later water moderately to avoid damping-off. Ventilate freely, shade and keep cool in hot weather. Give plenty of light while flowers are forming, and keep the atmosphere moist when warm and fine. Stand pot on inverted pot and water liberally during summer, but give only sufficient water to keep bulbs plump in winter. Propagate by means of division in September. Each root should have three to four bulbs.

*Species.*—*O. Cervantesii* [Mexico] (white, striped red, April–May, dwarf); *O. citrosmum* [Mexico] (pink and white, May and June, 6–9 in.); *O. coronarium* [Colombia] (brown, spotted yellow, May–June, 9–12 in.); *O. crispum* [Colombia] (white, with pink tinge, Feb.–May, 9–12 in.); *O. grande* [Guatemala] (yellow and brown, Nov.–Feb., 6–9 in.); *O. maculatum* [Mexico] (brown and yellow, April–May, 12 in.); *O. pulchellum* [Guatemala] (white, Feb.–March, 9 in.); *O. Rossii* [Mexico] (white, tinged pink, spotted brown, Nov.–Feb., dwarf); *O. triumphans* [Colombia] (gold and brownish red, March and April, 10 in.).

There are many beautiful varieties, particularly of *O. crispum.*

**Oncidium.**—Pot-up in September when new bulb begins to form, using well-drained pots and a compost of half live sphagnum and half fibrous peat and charcoal. Water with soft water, and keep cool and damp after potting. Later water moderately to avoid damping-off. Ventilate freely, shade, and keep cool in hot weather. Give plenty of light while flowers are forming, and keep the atmosphere moist when warm and fine. Stand pot on inverted pot, and water liberally during summer, but give only sufficient water to keep bulbs plump in winter. Propagate by means of division in September. Each root to have three to four bulbs.

*Species.*—*O. concolor* [Brazil] (bright yellow, April–May, 30 in.); *O. incurvum* [Mexico] (purple, edged white, Oct., 30 in.); *O. macranthum* [Tropical America] (yellow and brown, purple and white lip, May and June, 50 in.); *O. ornithorhynchum* [Mexico] (rose purple, Sept.–Nov., 15–20 in.); *O. tigrinum* [Mexico] (yellow and brown, Nov.–Dec., 30 in.); *O. varicosum* [Brazil] (green, reddish brown, and yellow, Nov.–Dec., 30 in.)

**Paphinia.**—A pretty group of orchids somewhat resembling **Lycaste,** which can be grown with that genus. They should be planted in fibrous peat and moss, and require a liberal supply of water during the growing season, and should at no time be allowed to get dry.

*Species.*—*P. cristata* [Trinidad] (whitish ground with deep crimson or chocolate markings, summer, 5–6 in.); *P. grandiflora* [Brazil] is a curious orchid, bearing greenish yellow, cream, and dark-purple flowers in October, and growing 5 to 8 inches high. *P. rugosa* [Colombia] is a dwarf growing orchid, remarkable and attractive. It has waxy flowers, which are creamy white with red spots and blotches.

**Paphiopedilum** (Lady's Slipper or Sandal Orchid).—Pot-up in March in well-drained pots, using a compost of two parts of fibrous peat to one part of sphagnum moss, coarse sand, and crushed bricks. Water liberally, especially during summer, and syringe overhead. Propagate by means of division when new roots are forming on young growths, and shade from sun until established.

Phaius Marthæ

 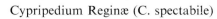

Cypripedium Reginæ (C. spectabile)

Cymbidium Lowianum

Dendrobium aggregatum

# ORCHIDS FOR THE COOL HOUSE

*Species.*—*P. insigne* (greenish yellow and white, spotted purplish brown, Nov.–April, 10 in.); *P. insigne* var. *Sanderæ* (yellow and white, Dec.–Feb., 10 in.); *P. villosum* [Burma] (green and brown, Feb., 10 in.).

**Pterostylis.**—A group of tufted, greenhouse, terrestrial orchids with upright solitary flowers and small underground tubers. They are best grown in leaf-mould with a little sand added. Good drainage is essential and one-third of the pot should be filled with broken crocks. They are propagated by division as new growth is about to start.

*Species.*—*P. acuminata* [Australia] (green flowers, April, 6–9 in.); *P. Baptistii* [Australia] (green marked with white and brown, winter, 12 in.); *P. nutans* [Australia] (green and white, Sept., 8–10 in.).

**Scaphosepalum.**—A small group of orchids somewhat resembling and requiring the same cultural treatment as **Masdevallia.** They were at one time included with this genus.

*Species.*—*S. gibberosum* [Colombia] (red, green, and yellow, spotted red, summer, 6–9 in.); *S. punctatum* [Colombia] (dull yellow, speckled crimson, autumn, 3–5 in.).

**Sophronitis** (Scarlet-flowered Orchid).—Pot-up in March when new roots form at base of young shoots, using half live sphagnum and half fibrous peat, plus a little charcoal. Grow in pans hung near the glass. Water liberally in summer and shade from strong sun.

*Species.*—*S. grandiflora* [Organ Mountains] (orange, scarlet, Dec.–March, dwarf).

**Trichosma** (Hair Orchid).—Pot-up when necessary in spring in well-drained pots in a compost of three parts Osmunda fibre to one part of sandy leaf-mould, or renew top soil. Grow in a moist, cool atmosphere near the glass, water regularly while growing, and shade from direct sun. Keep just moist during winter. Propagate by means of division when repotting.

*Species.*—*T. crispa* [Central America] (brownish yellow, crimson, and white, May–June, 8–10 in.); *T. suavis* [Central America] (white, lip marked red and yellow, March–May, 10 in.); *T. tortilis* [Mexico] (brownish yellow, white with crimson spots, summer, sometimes winter, 8–10 in.).

**Warscewiczella.**—A small group of orchids, suitable for the cool house, with large solitary flowers. They are sometimes included under **Zygopetalum,** and require the same cultural treatment.

*Species.*—*W. aromatica* (*Zygopetalum aromaticum*) [Costa Rica] (white, azure-blue, and purple, strongly perfumed); *W. discolor* (*Warrea discolor, Zygopetalum discolor*) [Central America] (white, yellow, and purple, winter, 12–18 in.); *W. Wendlandii* (*Zygopetalum Wendlandii*) [Costa Rica] (greenish white, and violet-purple Aug.–Sept.).

## CHAPTER XIII

# FRUIT UNDER GLASS

FRUIT may be grown under glass, either planted in borders or in pots, in lean-to or span-roofed houses, the latter being the more suitable form of house for fruit-culture in pots, while some fruits, such as the melon, may be grown in frames.

### The Border

The border may be entirely in the house, all outside, or half in and half out. For early forcing, however, the whole border should be under glass.

A border 3 feet in depth will accommodate any kind of tree, and 3½–4 feet will be found quite wide enough for the first year. It may be made 18 inches to 2 feet wider each succeeding year, up to 12–15 feet in width, as the roots extend. This is a better plan than making the border the full width the first year, as by extending it annually new soil is supplied to the young roots, whereas if the whole border were made up together, the soil at the extreme edge would probably be stale by the time the roots reached it.

Drainage must be perfect, and 9–12 inches of broken brick is usually rammed into the bottom of the border to ensure this.

Instructions for preparing the borders and composts to suit the various trees will be found in the following paragraphs on the cultivation of each particular fruit.

### Aspect and Site of the House

If the glasshouse is to be used for fruit, it should stand in full sunlight. Daylight and shelter from north winds are essentials.

Lean-to and hip-roof houses can be built with any aspect from south to west, the east being not so good, the worst of all being north.

### Ventilation

Ventilation, from which temperature or heat cannot be divorced, is an art that can be acquired only through experience. Hardy fruits such as those referred to in this section, will do well without any artificial heat. Success or failure in growing fruit under glass depends more frequently on sound ventilation than on any other factor. The plant will vitiate the air in a badly-ventilated house, just as a crowd of people will use up

178

the air in a crowded room. The plant's vitality, the composition of its substance, and the functioning of its organs, are seriously affected by inadequate ventilation. Again, ventilation controls the atmospheric moisture in a glasshouse, and this in turn controls the transpiration of the plants. If the ventilation is inefficient, the atmosphere becomes saturated. The plant cannot get rid of its moisture, and transpiration slows down. The young growth becomes soft and is susceptible to diseases, and wood grown under such conditions will never ripen, however the conditions may improve at a later period. Further, since ventilation and temperature are the two most important factors in the management of a glasshouse and cannot be dissociated from one another, they must be considered together and applied proportionally, always having regard to the plant, and to its condition and stage of development. Every glasshouse is to some degree a forcing house, and a forcing temperature is merely a relative one. For example, we would start early peaches in a temperature of 45–50° F. We would ventilate the house at 50°, as we are growing hard-wooded plants and the temperature must be kept low, air being given whenever it is possible. A temperature of 50° F. with ventilation during the period of growth to which we refer will produce the desired results; while a temperature of 60° F. without air would prove fatal.

It is impossible to give a general rule that can be applied to the ventilation of all plants. The amount of air given must vary with the nature of the plant, the stage of growth and the season of the year.

It is well to remember that it is extremely rare to find a crop that has been spoiled by excessive ventilation, while a hot, vitiated atmosphere in glasshouses is as common to-day as it used to be in a dwelling-house.

Except in very small houses, side ventilators are always desirable where hard-wooded plants are grown.

If the top ventilation is ample, side ventilation is of less importance, but it must be remembered that the air which escapes from the top of the house must be replaced from somewhere. The draught bogey exists largely in the imagination only. *See also* page 30.

## Temperatures of the Houses

It is not possible to give any definite figures for the temperature of the glasshouse. This must of necessity vary with the plants grown, and instructions in this matter will be found under the headings of the different plants in Chapter XV. *See also* page 45.

# THE GREENHOUSE

## THE UNHEATED OR COLD HOUSE

This house depends solely on the heat of the sun for its warmth. Thus its temperature varies enormously at different times of the year. It requires no artificial heat, even in winter. It must, however, be remembered that glass of itself will not keep out frost, and the plants grown in the cold house must necessarily be hardy and able to stand a few degrees of frost. For management, *see* Chapter I.

### Shading from the Sun

Shading is a difficult subject. Speaking generally, the less of it the better. The amount required depends largely upon the facilities available for keeping sufficient atmospheric moisture during the very sunny periods. If the house is efficiently ventilated and the ventilators are used to the best advantage, there are few plants that will not winter in a cold house and that are not better without shading.

An unheated house should be provided with ample ventilation. Other things being equal, a plant which will not burn in the sun out of doors will not burn under glass, providing the atmosphere is not allowed to get too dry.

Actually, ordinary glass, to a certain degree, forms a barrier against the sun. *See also* page 32.

A point to remember is that a plant that has been heavily shaded in the summer will winter badly.

### Training

Strong galvanised wire should be stretched along the roof, some 18 inches to 2 feet from the glass; it must not be closer, or the foliage will be scorched by the sun, but wire can be fixed 12–15 inches at the front or sides of the house. The wires must be about 9 inches apart; and on these the trees will be trained.

### Fumigation

Shut all ventilators, and cover with damp matting all broken or cracked lights and all roof ventilators which are likely to leak. Most gardeners will find the fumigating or vaporising materials sold ready for use, with the necessary apparatus for burning, highly satisfactory; the makers give detailed instructions which should be closely followed.

Where the house is badly infested with any insect pest, it should be dealt two or three times on successive evenings; this is almost always necessary when extirpating the red spider. *See also* page 600.

# CHAPTER XIV

# FRUIT-GROWING IN POTS

IN certain conditions it may be impossible or inexpedient to grow the more delicate kinds of fruit-trees in a suitable situation against a wall. Where, for example, the garden is enclosed, not with walls, but with hedges, and where these hedges, for some reason of beauty or age, are required to be preserved, a difficult problem presents itself to the gardener who wishes to grow peaches, nectarines, apricots, or late pears, with the better kinds of dessert plum. Where a moderate supply of fruit only is required, and where there is some glass available, an excellent plan is that of growing trees in pots, placing them in the open for a certain part of the year, and bringing them into the fruit house in succession as they require shelter and warmth.

Pot trees in a house have the advantage over planted-out trees of providing a greater variety of fruit from a given space. A supply of apples, apricots, cherries, currants, figs, gooseberries, nectarines, peaches, pears, and plums can be produced in one house, while strawberries of good quality can be grown on shelves where they can receive abundance of light, being introduced in March and removed outside as soon as the fruit has been gathered. Moreover, the trees in pots are portable, and therefore can be removed whenever desired.

Success or failure with these trees depends entirely on the management, attention, potting, watering, syringing, top dressings, supplemented by concentrated or liquid manure, in order to sustain health and fertility. So that trees in pots entail more work than those planted out.

In a mixed house some fruits can be kept constantly in the house from the beginning of February—apricots, figs, nectarines, and peaches; while apples, pears, and plums only need to be placed in the house to ensure the safety of the blossoms and young fruit from spring frost and can be given a favourable position out-of-doors from the beginning of June to the beginning of February, if desired. Currants, cherries, and gooseberries, come under the latter group of fruits, but these are best left in the house till after the fruit has been gathered. By removing those last mentioned, more light and air are admitted to the kinds first referred to.

Early varieties of apricots, nectarines, and peaches can be re-

# THE GREENHOUSE

moved to a warm position outdoors as the trees are cleared of the fruit; this allows space for any plums or other kinds which it may be desirable to return to the house for perfecting or preserving the fruit in unfavourable weather.

## The House

The best house for the purpose is one not less than 20 feet wide, and about 6 feet high at the sides, rising to 12 feet at the ridge. The "run" of the house does not much matter, some people preferring a north-to-south house, others liking it to lie east and west. The latter is perhaps slightly preferable, as it exposes a smaller surface to the easterly winds, which are most prevalent when the fruit-trees are in blossom. The doors should be in both ends, and should be double, allowing ample space for the entrance of the trees. All the sides of the house should be made to open panel-wise, as free ventilation, whatever the wind, may be necessary. Sufficient heating should be allowed to keep out frost in March and April, though where the difficulties seem insuperable this may be dispensed with. It has the advantage, however, of making the house far more generally useful, as it may then be used during winter for such things as chrysanthemums, while the trees are wintering outside. A floor of beaten ashes is the best.

## Selecting the Trees

The trees selected for this purpose should preferably have been grown in pots from the time they were first budded or grafted, should be three or four years old, and must have a good show of fruit buds.

Varieties suitable for pot culture are :—

### Apples

| | | |
|---|---|---|
| Calville Blanche | Lady Sudeley | Patricia |
| Charles Ross | Laxton's Exquisite | Peasgood Nonsuch |
| Cox's Orange Pippin | Laxton's Fortune | Rev. W. Wilks |
| Ellison's Orange | Laxton's Premier | Wealthy |
| Irish Peach | Melba | White Transparent |
| James Grieve | Miller's Seedling | |

### Apricots

| | | |
|---|---|---|
| Blenheim | Hemstirk | Moorpark |
| Gros Peach | Kaisha | |

### Cherries

| | | |
|---|---|---|
| Bigarreau Napoleon | Early Rivers | Governor Wood |
| Black Tartarian | Frogmore | May Duke |

### Currants

| | | |
|---|---|---|
| Raby Castle (Red) | Laxton's No. 1 | White Dutch (White) |

182

# FRUIT-GROWING IN POTS

Varieties suitable for pot culture are :—

## Figs

| | | |
|---|---|---|
| Brown Turkey | St. John | White Marseilles |
| Osborne Prolific | | |

## Gooseberries

| | | |
|---|---|---|
| Broom Girl | Leveller | White Lion |
| Leader | Lord Derby | Whitesmith |

## Nectarines

| | | |
|---|---|---|
| Early Rivers | Elruge | Lord Napier |

## Peaches

| | | |
|---|---|---|
| Barrington | Hale's Early | Sea Eagle |
| Duke of Cornwall | Princess of Wales | Violette Hative |
| Duke of York | Royal George | |

## Pears

| | | |
|---|---|---|
| Beurré Giffard | Doyenné d'Eté | Marie Louise |
| Citron des Carmes | Doyenné du Comice | Souvenir de Congres |

## Plums

| | | |
|---|---|---|
| Coe's Golden Drop | Early Transparent | Late Transparent Gage |
| Denniston's Superb | Jefferson | Reine Claude de Bavay |

## Strawberries

| | | |
|---|---|---|
| Dr. Hogg | Royal Sovereign | Sir Joseph Paxton |
| King George | Sir Douglas Haig | Waterloo |

## The Compost

An important part of the process is the preparation of the compost in which the plants are to grow. This should be prepared in September, and have a clear month in the open, under cover, to amalgamate. It should be composed of a barrow-load of leaf-mould, one of coarse sand, one of old mortar rubbish, one of rotted manure, and five of yellow loam. This is further enriched by the addition of two gallons of bonemeal and another gallon or so of some good fertiliser or vine manure. A bushel of quarter-inch bones is also mixed in the compost for drainage purposes.

## Re-potting

Every year, in about the middle of October, when the leaves commence to drop, the trees should be overhauled, as annual potting is not necessary. Healthy trees only need the removal of loose surface soil, also a little from the sides of the ball, with a pointed stick.

The trees should be taken out of their pots, while the soil is fairly dry, so that their roots may be easily freed from it.

When a tree requires re-potting, a strip of board is placed

across a barrow, and the tree is lifted out of its pot ; the drainage crocks are loosened and fall back into the pot, which, with the crocks, is taken away to be washed and dried. The ball of roots and soil is then lifted on to the board, while the operator stands between the handles of the barrow with the head of the tree turned from him. The latter thus has free room, and there is less danger of injury either to shoots or bloom-buds. The stem of the tree is held in the left hand, while with the right a short, pointed stick is used among the roots to loosen the soil as much as possible, taking great care not to break the root-fibres.

The ball of roots should be shaken from time to time during this process.

When the roots are as free as possible from soil they should be carefully looked over, all woody and long, fleshy roots being removed with clean cuts with a sharp knife, leaving all the useful fibrous ones untouched.

It is better, if anything, to err on the side of over-severity with the larger roots, as with strong growers such as pears and apples these long roots would soon take the tree beyond the possibility of pot culture.

The pots used should always be large enough to allow of the fibrous roots lying out horizontally in the soil, but so long as this is possible the smaller the pot the better. Pot-grown fruit-trees ought never to exceed a 16-inch pot, and smaller sizes—the twelves and fourteens—are used extensively. While the trees are young, it will usually be found advisable to give a larger-sized pot each re-potting, but with older trees this is seldom needed, the trees going back into a pot of the same size as before. Composts best suited to each kind of tree are given in the sections devoted to the culture of the individual plants.

All pots should, of course, be clean and dry, as should the crocks for drainage. A good layer of these latter is placed in the bottom of the pot, and covered with a little soil. The ball of the tree is set firmly in the centre, and the upper two-thirds of the fibrous roots are held upwards with the left hand, while with the right compost is rammed down very firmly and evenly over the bottom third in the pot. A wooden rammer is used for this purpose. A few more roots are then laid out, and covered with firmly-rammed soil, and so on until the pot is almost full, a space of 2 inches being left at the top for future top-dressings.

### Wintering in the Open

The trees, when potted, should be watered well and plunged to the rims of the pots in ashes in the open, the pots being covered with a layer of litter from 6–10 inches in depth to exclude the frost.

This should be done not later than the first week in November, and, if possible, a fortnight earlier.

They will then require little further care or attention until February, when they are moved into the house, except that in January they will need looking over, and the pruning of the pears and plums should be completed.

Before bringing in the trees, at the end of January, the orchard house should be thoroughly cleaned, and the brickwork lime-washed.

## Moving into the House

The peaches and nectarines should come into the house between February 1st and March 1st, and should be given the sunniest part of the house.

The exact date must be determined by the weather, and they should not be brought in whilst the ground is very wet, nor when there is hard frost. A time should be chosen when there is a spell of bright, open weather, fairly dry, and the trees brought in while it lasts.

If cherries are grown, they must be placed on the shady side. The various kinds of fruit should be grouped together in batches, and should not be placed piecemeal all over the house. The house need not be heated at all until the blosson appears, but ample fresh air is required, for which the ventilating facilities of the house will be all called into play.

## Watering in the House

A watering with clean water is also needed occasionally. During the whole period of the indoor life of the trees, with the exception of the period in which the fruit is colouring, they should be syringed daily in all dull weather; twice daily, night and morning, on fine and sunny days, with rain-water.

Early in the season only a little water is required, but as the hot weather comes on, watering must be more frequent— as often as four times a day in the middle of summer may be necessary.

## Forcing

If heat is available, some of the trees can be forced : apples, cherries, pears, and similar fruits may be taken into the house with a temperature of between 40° and 50° F. As little heat as possible should be used when forcing these fruits. Nectarines and peaches can endure a greater amount of heat than the fruits mentioned above—namely, 45° and 50° F.

**185**

## Fumigation

When the blossoms of the peaches and nectarines in the house are showing pink, which is generally about the middle of March, and just about a couple of days before they open, the pears and plums are moved in. This is a good opportunity to fumigate the house, to destroy any young green-fly that there may be. These are destructive to the peach-blossom.

Two successive nights should make the fumigation effective. (*See also* page 600.)

When the peach-blossom is opening it is well to give a little heat at night, but only just sufficient to keep out possible frost. This night heat should be continued until the fruit is set, or even, should the frosts still be hard at night, longer still. In damp weather, whilst the bloom is out, a very little heat during the day, also, will help to keep the air dry and assist the diffusion of the pollen. As soon as the fruit has set, a moister atmosphere is again necessary.

## Pollination

The pollen question is an important one where indoor trees are concerned, owing to their isolation from insects and wind, and where an especially choice specimen or variety is being dealt with it is usually worth while to go round the trees with a small camel-hair brush or rabbit's tail and cross-pollinate by hand. Where, however, the blossom is abundant, as it usually is in orchard houses, the best plan is to go round the house morning and afternoon and give the stem of each tree a sharp, firm blow with the side of the hand. This jerk will set the pollen flying, and in all ordinary cases is enough to secure a good supply of set fruit.

Pears, which have heavier, stickier pollen, will not fertilise in this simple way, and generally need attention with the camel-hair brush or rabbit's tail.

It is a good plan to put a plant or two of cytisus among the pear-trees to attract the bees, which will very materially help in the operation. Some fruit-growers place a hive of bees in the house during the blossom season. This is a method worth adopting if a hive is available, but it should be removed during the time that any fumigating is being done; it can be replaced later.

Between the setting of the fruit of the peaches and nectarines and the blossoming of the pears and plums, it is as well again to fumigate the house, the operation being of sufficient importance to warrant the removal of any precocious trees which may have broken a few blossoms into a neighbouring shed for the night whilst the smoking is in progress.

**186**

## Thinning the Fruit

The next important step is the thinning, and this must be done with a stern hand, as almost every tree will have set far more fruit that it can possibly carry. The trees should be gone over as soon as the blossom drops, and at least two-thirds of the fruit taken out at once, leaving a final thinning to be done when the fruit has " stoned ".

This last operation needs firmness again, or too much fruit will be left. Young trees should not be permitted to bear more than from ten to a dozen fruits.

## Pruning and Disbudding

All fruit-trees in pots need careful pruning. In the case of nectarines, peaches, and plums, the main shoots are cut back by about one-half and laterals to within two or three buds of their base. Nectarines and peaches produce their fruit on the previous year's growth, which must therefore be preserved.

All unfruitful wood not needed for the extension of the tree should be cut out. When the young shoots have put out eight good leaves they should be pinched back to five while the shoot is still soft and immature. This will have the effect of checking the shoot only enough to throw all the buds into flower-buds except the last one, which will again shoot out, and should again be pinched back later on.

Plums are pinched back and pruned in much the same way, longer leaders and shorter side-shoots being left.

Apples, pears, cherries, currants, and gooseberries are summer pruned in July and August.

## Manuring

When the young fruit on the trees is making good progress, the trees should be helped by feeding them. A rich compost is prepared, consisting of a couple of barrow-loads of turfy loam, one of well-rotted, rather sticky manure, and one of mortar-rubble, pounded fine, the whole enriched with two gallons of bonemeal and two gallons of fertiliser or vine manure. This compost is banked up round the trees to as much as 3 inches above the rim of the pot, being shaped and moulded with the fingers into a steep rim or dyke, steep on its outer side and sloping more gradually towards the stem, so as to afford a shallow basin or cup for watering. Between setting and stoning, each tree is banked in this way with the compost, and as soon as the stoning is over weak liquid manure is used for watering instead of plain water previously used.

As much air and light as possible must be given while the fruit is ripening, and heavy fruits, as apples and pears, should be secured to the trees with bass or raffia. At this time it is essential to exclude wasps; this may be done by placing close-meshed netting over the ventilators.

In the middle of September all the trees are moved out of the house on to a spare piece of ground, where they remain, plunged to the rims of the pots in ashes, until the overhauling or re-potting again takes place. They must be shaded from the strong sun when first put out in the open, but after a week or so they will enjoy all the sun they can get. Watering must still be carefully attended to.

In securing a supply of plums, at least three times as many trees are grown as there is accommodation for in the house. One-third are taken in for blooming, while the rest are plunged in a spot sheltered alike from the east wind and the morning sun. When their fruit is three-quarters grown, that of the trees in the house is ripe, and the first lot comes out, to give place to a set from outside. In this way three gatherings of plums is obtained, and the season much prolonged.

**Bruises**

Care should be taken, when working with tools among the branches of fruit-trees, that the bark is not bruised or rubbed off by accident. Such bruises and grazes are very apt to give entry to the spores of one of the wound fungi, and canker may result, or, in the case of peaches, plums, and apricots, gumming may be caused.

Instead of repeating our remarks on heating, ventilation, and the general management of the glasshouse, we refer the reader to the chapters I and XIII, where temperature, ventilation, and cultural requirements are discussed.

Full cultural details for all fruit grown in pots will be found in the paragraphs in the following section devoted to each particular fruit.

## DISEASES AND PESTS IN THE GLASSHOUSE

Cleanliness is the most important factor in successful glass-house work. Dead leaves and other rubbish harbour pests and diseases and, if allowed to remain, give rise to endless trouble. Fungus spores and small insects get into crevices in the timber and brickwork; dirt and growths of green algæ accumulate on the glass, robbing the plants of valuable light. Every year, there-fore, the glass should be washed, the bars scrubbed, and the inside of the house thoroughly cleaned. For this soap and water have no equal, though if the house be empty it is wise to finish up by spraying the inside of the structure with cresylic acid or formalin.

A house that can be completely emptied periodically, if only once a year, is very much easier to keep clean than one that houses plants—particularly a mixture of various kinds—all the year round.

## Treatment of Empty Houses

In treating an empty house where disease has been prevalent, all benches, pipes, and floors, as well as the glass, walls, and woodwork should be well wetted with a 2 per cent. solution of formalin. It is advisable to start at the far end and finish at the door. The house should then be closed up for twenty-four hours and the temperature raised—to 70° F. if possible. It must then be freely ventilated until no smell of formalin remains. This may take two weeks or more, but is a wise precaution, for formalin fumes are fatal to many plants.

## Pots, Boxes, and Pans

Pots, boxes, and pans should be thoroughly cleaned before use. It is advisable to sterilise them, either by bringing them to the boil in water or by soaking in 2 per cent. formalin, not omitting to air them until no smell remains.

## Sterilisation of Soil

The sterilisation of the soil of the glasshouse, so necessary for the profitable cultivation of fruits such as the tomato, is scarcely necessary for the hardier fruits that are dealt with here. For pot work, however, it is advantageous to sterilise the soil, and this can readily be done either with steam or with formalin. A compost should never be sterilised as such, unless it is not required for a considerable time. Ingredients such as loam or turf should be sterilised beforehand and mixed with the other ingredients (lime, fertilisers, peat, etc.) afterwards. For steam sterilising some form of apparatus is required in which the temperature of the soil can be raised to 180° F. and maintained there for ten to fifteen minutes. Many types, some electrically operated, are available, ranging from the large vertical steam-boiler type down to a domestic copper.

The most elaborate precautions to ensure a clean house and clean soil can readily be brought to naught by failure to ensure that the plants brought inside are equally clean. Many of the pests that attack fruit-trees and bushes out of doors can, if allowed to do so, become established in a glasshouse, and give rise to a great deal of trouble. For this reason it is necessary to dip dormant trees and bushes in a tar-oil wash to prevent outbreaks of the various species of aphis, *Apple Sucker*, *Tortrix* caterpillars, and the like, and in a petroleum wash to destroy *Capsid*, *Red Spider*, and *Winter Moth* caterpillar. If both dips are given, the first should be allowed to dry on before the second is given. Potted strawberries should receive a warm water bath.

# CHAPTER XV

# THE CULTURE OF PARTICULAR FRUITS —UNDER GLASS

## APPLES, PEARS, PLUMS, CURRANTS, AND GOOSEBERRIES

THESE need no artificial heat, and may well all be successfully grown in the cold glasshouse, in the same way as described below for the apricot. Cultural details are here unnecessary, and the reader is referred to the chapter on Fruit-growing in Pots, page 181.

## APRICOT

The apricot will hardly bear forcing, and, being more sensitive to heat than almost any of the half-hardy fruits, a confined atmosphere, or the slightest excess of heat, brings its blossoms off in showers, and so mars the prospect of fruit, so that it requires a cool house with plenty of ventilation. If planted in the border along a wall, fan-trained trees must be used, fastened to wires 6 inches apart. If the house is of sufficient height, standards or half-standard trees can be planted in the centre and sides of the house and excellent crops obtained. For pots, pyramid trees are best. Place these in 11-inch pots with good drainage, on this put a layer of half-inch bones, using a compost of three parts good turfy loam, torn into pieces the size of a walnut, one part of decayed horse manure, one part of old mortar-rubble. Shorten the strong roots so that the tree can be placed in the pot, with uppermost roots $1\frac{1}{2}$ inches below the rim and the side roots 1 inch from the sides; place some rough soil in first, ram it firmly with a stick, and press the soil well about the roots, which should be spread out evenly. Water at once, moistening the soil through to the drainage; the pots can then be either plunged in ashes outside or stood in a cool house. The trees can be frequently syringed before and after the flowering period. During all the earlier stages of growth, and until fruits have stoned, an artificial temperature of 45° F. should not be exceeded. After that stage the fruit will stand 5° higher, but not more, for unless abundance of air is given, a temperature of, say, 55° F. may bring off the fruit. There must on no account be any closing of the house, such as is practised for peaches or grapes. The apricot loves a warm day and a cool night. Attention must be given to watering and damping, an occasional syringing up to the time of the fruit changing colour is beneficial, it helps to keep away red spider, but when ripening commences, syringing should be discontinued. In dry weather damp the floor, borders, etc., instead. When the fruits are developing, an occasional watering with liquid manure will greatly assist the plants.

After the fruit has been gathered, the heat should gradually be reduced, then full air admitted regularly, and when the wood is ripe, give all the air possible for the trees planted out, and those in pots can be stood outside.

Packing and marketing are the same as for peaches and nectarines, while the pruning is similar.

## Diseases and Pests

Very few diseases affect the apricot, the chief trouble being what is termed " die-back " or " branch-dying ". This disease is sometimes apparent from the presence of gum, in some instances there is no outward indication of that disease beyond the shrinkage in the branches and the smallness of the foliage, or perhaps a few small holes may be seen in the branch where it dies off. It, however, provides evidence of the channels of the wood being closed by the gum, preventing the nourishment of the branch above the point of infestation. Gum is induced by planting in over-rich soil, and by severe cutting back of the growths in summer.

Mildew is also a pest, and infests the leaves and young growths, causing the former to curl and the young growth to be distorted. Mildew may result from a confined and damp site and over-wetness of soil, or the opposite extremes of exposure, poverty, and dryness. Thorough syringings will wash off the fungus spores, and a good dusting of every affected part with flowers of sulphur will keep the parasite in check.

## Varieties Suitable for Growing as Trained Trees under Glass

(*See* page 182.)

### BANANA (*Musa Cavendishii, paradisiaca,* etc.)

This is a native of the hilly districts of India and Bermuda. It was introduced into this country about 1729, but only in large, lofty houses can this fruit be grown successfully under glass. There are several varieties : *paradisiaca* (Plaintain), *Champa* (Lady's Fingers), *Location,* etc.

The one most cultivated under glass in this country is *Musa Cavendishii,* the Chinese Dwarf Banana, introduced here in 1829, and requiring less heat than many others. It is a native of South China, but is now extensively cultivated in the West Indies and in parts of the southern United States and large quantities of its fruit are sent from Jamaica annually to Europe. Good crops of this plant can be grown in this country, fruit being borne from fifteen to eighteen months from the time of potting up the young suckers.

The chief requirements in banana cultivation are : a rich compost in a limited area, giving complete control over the growth ; high feeding at the right time; proper space for development; unobstructed light in close proximity to the glass without touching; free ventilation, and ample heat, maintaining a temperature of 65° F. by night, 70–75° F. on a dull day, and 10° higher when sunny.

All the varieties are readily increased by strong suckers, these being allowed to attain a good size and become well rooted before being detached from the parent plant. These suckers should then be taken off when ready and placed in suitable pots, being potted on from time to time until they are finally potted on into a large pot or tub not less than 2 feet deep and 3 feet in diameter. It should have plenty of drainage in the bottom, a mixture of good loam (three parts), with equal portions of old manure, mortar-rubble, and sand being used; and to every three bushels of compost a quarter of a peck of bonemeal, a quarter of a peck of soot, and half a peck of wood ashes should be added. When suckers begin to come up from the base and the stem of the plant thickens at the top, we know that the fruit is forming. A stimulant can then be given in the form of a liquid manure or soot-water. Liquid manure can be made from 1 lb. of guano in twenty gallons of water; one peck of cow or sheep manure in twenty-five gallons of water; or one peck of soot in 100 gallons of water.

Larger clusters and finer fruit are obtained if the bananas are cultivated in beds; the beds should be well drained with rubble 1 foot deep and covered with a 3-inch layer of gravel or mortar-rubble and a layer of turf, allowing for 2 feet of soil, the beds being filled up with the same mixture as that used for pot or tub culture. Although plants from 2 to 3 feet high and with good leaves are best for planting out, the plants should be sturdy and well rooted. The middle of February is the best time for planting. Bananas delight in a rich mulch, and whether in tubs or in a border, they benefit from top dressing when they are well established, the dressing being repeated at monthly intervals, and a good watering being given after each dressing. The top dressing should consist of one bushel of turfy loam, one peck of decayed manure, and half a peck of wood ashes. The bananas enjoy a good genial atmosphere and

Cherry Bigarreau Noir-de-Guben

[R. A. Malby

A Pine-apple

suffer from checks. The plants should be syringed every afternoon during the growing season, and from February to September the walls, floors, and beds must be damped when they become dry. Damping in the morning and early afternoon provides sufficient moisture during the winter months. When the plants thicken in the centre, syringing must stop, for if the water enters the hearts of the plants, it will cause the young fruit to decay. When the bunch of young fruit appears expose it to the sun by drawing the leaves aside, and if the plant is some distance from the glass it may be necessary to remove some of the leaves. When the fruit is set and commences to swell, the barren end of the inflorescence should be cut away to assist the growth. The richest-flavoured fruits are those which ripen on the plants, which are kept rather dry at the root in a warm, freely ventilated house.

## CHERRIES (*Prunus avium*)

Cherries may be grown planted permanently in a border in the cool house and trained as fans or as cordons, or they may be grown as bushes or pyramids in pots.

### Soil

This fruit thrives best in a compost of two-thirds loam and one-third old mortar-rubble, wood ashes, bonemeal, and charcoal. Potting or planting should be done firmly in October, the roots being covered with at least 6 inches and not more than 9 inches of fine soil. Good drainage is essential; ample crocks should therefore be provided in the pots or, if planted out, the bottom of the border must be filled with some 9 inches of broken bricks well rammed in. After planting, give the trees a liberal watering.

### Temperatures

Only slight heat should be applied, and that very gradually. Until the flowers open, the thermometer should not be allowed to drop below 40° F. at night, but it must not rise above 50–55° F. by day. Once the fruit has set, the temperature may be allowed to rise to between 45° and 50° F. by night and 55–60° F. by day.

Ventilation is all-important. Give a free circulation of air whenever the weather outside will permit, but do not allow sudden drops and rises in the temperature.

### Pollination

When the flowers are out, dust them over daily about noon, when the air is driest, with a rabbit's tail to ensure good pollina-

N

tion; this is an important point. (*See* page 186.) While the fruit is setting, syringe the trees twice daily in fine weather, and keep a good look-out for insect pests.

As soon as the fruit has set, the trees may be assisted by the application of diluted farmyard manure or soot-water. This may be varied by guano or a compound fruit manure.

When applying manure it is important not to use it when the soil is dry. If dry, the plants should be first watered with clear water; this applies to all plants, especially to pot-grown subjects.

## Summer Pruning

Young shoots should be pinched back to five or six leaves to encourage good fruiting spurs, the laterals being again shortened to three or four buds in October.

The cherry easily forms fruiting spurs, and when the tree has a sufficient number of these to ensure a good but not exhaustive crop, it should be left alone, and the knife used as little as possible.

## Re-potting and Wintering

Once the fruit has been gathered, all possible air should be afforded the trees, those in pots being stood out in the open, in the sun, on a hard ash floor. As soon as the wood begins to ripen up, re-potting should be commenced. The pots are then plunged to the rim in ashes and wintered in the open.

*See also* Fruit-growing in Pots, page 181.

## Cherries—Varieties Suitable for Growing under Glass

| Variety | Season | Colour | Variety | Season | Colour |
|---|---|---|---|---|---|
| Early Rivers . . | Early | Black | Roundel . . | Mid | Black |
| Elton . . . | Early | White | Bradbourne Black . | Late | Black |
| Ronald's Late Duke | Late | Red | Bigarreau Mezel . | Late | White |
| Noble . . . | Late | Black | Reine Hortense . | Early | Red |
| Royal Duke . . | Mid | Red | Impératrice Eugénie | Early | Red |
| May Duke . . | Early | Red | Triaux . . . | Mid | Red |
| Bigarreau Napoleon | Late | White | Waterloo . . | Mid | Black |

## CUCUMBER (*Cucumis sativa*)

The cucumber is a native of southern and central Asia. There does not seem to be any record of its introduction to Great Britain, but it has been in cultivation here for several centuries, as an article of food. Strangely enough, it is only quite recently that it has definitely been classified as a fruit. Whether the cucumber is grown in the open or under glass, it is necessary to raise the seedlings in a hot-bed, and for this purpose a hot-bed should be prepared early in March. (*See* page 212.)

# THE CUCUMBER

## Sowing

In a few days, when the steam generated by the hot-bed has been allowed to escape, seeds may be sown in the bed, rather more being sown than plants are required. The seedlings will make their appearance above ground in two or three days.

## Cultivation and Training

As soon as the plants appear, a day temperature of about 70° F. and a night temperature of 60° F. should be aimed at. Should the night temperature much exceed 60° F., it is well to wedge up the lights about ½ inch when shutting for the night, and during hot weather this amount of night ventilation may be increased. When the plants are grown in a frame and have made two leaves in addition to the cotyledon leaves, pinch out the point above the second; each plant will then send out two lateral shoots above the second leaf on each shoot; pick off the top. After that, stop them above every fruit, and as the plants grow, add fresh soil to keep the roots covered till the whole bed is level, taking care that the soil is of the same temperature as that in the bed. If the cucumbers are grown under glass, it should be in the hot-house, although useful fruit can be grown in the warm house. Stakes should be placed to lead the stems up to the first wire, and until this is reached all side-shoots must be pinched out. The main-stems must be stopped when the top of the roof is reached. The common practice to-day is to stop laterals first at the second fruit and then stop the sub-laterals at the first leaf. We prefer to stop laterals at the leaf beyond the second fruit, which on young plants is usually the third leaf. We then rub out the sub-lateral buds which appear after the one nearest the stem of the plant, and stop that one at the second leaf. The practice simplifies pruning immensely, in the later stages of growth. Liberal supplies of tepid water are essential, but the leaves should be watched, as, should they turn yellow, it is an indication that the temperature is too cold. The borders and paths in a cucumber house should never be dry at any time. It is not desirable to put too much water on the foliage, because it is almost impossible to do so without drenching the under side of the leaves. It is essential that the atmosphere shall always be saturated. This also helps to keep Red Spider in check. Twice, or, in hot weather, three times a day, the plants and bed should be well damped, either from the watering-pot by means of a fine rose, or by means of a garden syringe. Liberal dressings of a nitrogenous fertiliser are very beneficial.

## Cutting the Cucumbers

As soon as the cucumbers attain adequate size, those ready

should be cut for use; malformed ones should be removed at once. When grown on a large scale for market, the cut fruits are placed in padded trays or in specially constructed shallow boxes with one side removed.

The fruit should be cut early in the morning, so as to permit of grading, packing, and despatch in time for the next morning's market, and should be handled in the process as little as possible. Thence the trays are conveyed, with the minimum of jolting, to the grading and packing-room or shed.

## Grading

Under the Agricultural Produce (Grading and Marking) Regulation, 1930, definite standards are laid down, and a chart is supplied to assist packers in grading cucumbers.

A1 grade may include sound, straight, unblemished fruits only, of any size over and above $\frac{1}{2}$ lb. in weight and up to $1\frac{1}{4}$ lb. each.

Under the National Mark, A1 grade, however, must contain only sound, straight, unblemished fruits of even colour and even size, not more than a 3-oz. variation being allowed between individual fruits in flat baskets (36 lb.) and boxes (18 lb.) and a 2-oz. variation in the case of fruits in trays (7–12 lb.). Those fruits below these grades are sent up as " Smalls " and " Crooks ".

## Marketing

Cucumbers are sent to market in flat baskets, wooden boxes, and trays. Flat baskets contain four layers of fruit, packed between soft hay or wood wool and blue tissue paper, each layer containing a minimum of 9 lb. of cucumbers. The wooden box usually contains two rows only, packed in the same way and of similar weight, viz. 9 lb. per row or over. The tray contains a layer only of eight to fifteen fruits, weighing from 7–12 lb. (about 90 per cent. go up in unreturnable wooden boxes). Trays are used chiefly for early crops and extra-special cucumbers. They may be returnable or non-returnable. Small cucumbers and crooks are sent up in flat baskets or boxes only, and all packages must bear identification labels.

The adoption of any regulation is optional. Copies may be had from the British Glass House Marketing Association. It should be remembered, however, that buyers never purchase any fruit haphazard. They buy on inspection and on the grower's mark or name. They know the grower's brand, and they buy the type that suits their customers.

## Varieties

The best varieties to grow for market are : *Butcher's Disease Resister*, a favourite in the Lea Valley area; a long, straight, dull-green fruit with a short handle; it travels well, is a splendid cropper, and is highly resistant to " Spot " disease. *Rochford's Market Favourite*, another Lea Valley favourite; a long, straight, deep-green fruit with a short handle; a fine cropper and travels well. *Telegraph*, the well-known, long, smooth-skinned, dark-green cucumber with short handle; a heavy cropper and a favourite for early market.

## Diseases and Pests

The chief troubles of the cucumber are of a fungoid nature : Cucumber Leaf-blotch, Wilt, Mildew, and Leaf-spot. While of the pests, Red Spider is the most troublesome.

Diseased plants should be destroyed as soon as the fruit has been gathered, and the house should be thoroughly cleaned and fumigated. For treatment of Red Spider and Thrips, *see* Diseases and Pests, page 600.

## Diseases and Pests : Diagnosis Table

### The Cucumber

| SYMPTOMS | PROBABLE CAUSE |
|---|---|
| *Foliage and Stems* | *Pests* |
| Turning colour, rusty patches | Red Spider |
| Turning colour, silvery patches | Thrips |
| | *Fungi* |
| Pale green spots, turning brown and falling | Cucumber Leaf-blotch |
| Browning and yellow spots | Cucumber Leaf-spot |
| White, powdery mildew | Cucumber Mildew |
| Yellow patches, mottled and wrinkled | Cucumber Mosaic or Chlorosis |
| Turning yellow and dying | Cucumber Wilt |
| *Fruit* | *Pest* |
| Wilts and dies off for no apparent reason | Eelworms |
| | *Fungus* |
| Spotted brown and yellow | Cucumber Leaf-spot |

## FIG (*Ficus Carica*)

The fig is an excellent fruit for forcing, and very easy to grow and under glass most varieties will easily produce two or three good crops in the year. The first crop is borne on the shoots of the previous year, the second on the growth of the current year, and the third on the sub-laterals which spring from the current year's shoots. The third crop, however, unless the plants are in expert hands and are started very early, is rarely of much value, and to avoid unduly weakening the plants, amateur growers usually prefer to pick this off before it develops. When doing this, however, care must be taken to remove only those fruits that would partially develop and would not remain

**197**

dormant through the winter; the smaller fruits towards the points of shoots must on no account be removed, as these produce the first crop of fruit for the following year. A clever grower will get his third crop off every time. Success depends largely on starting the trees sufficiently early, correct practice, and perfectly matured wood. To get three crops of figs, the first crop must be ripe in May, and for such early work the plants must be started early in December, and are more easily controlled in pots. Plants started in January will yield their first crop in June, the second in August, and the third crop is then too late to be of much value, and is best treated as described above. A temperature of from 75–80° F. during the day is necessary, and it must not be allowed to fall below 60° F. at night. Any form of house is suitable for forcing figs, but if the figs are to be grown in pots, the span-roofed house will be ound the most suitable. Ample light is essential.

## Compost and Planting

Figs are usually propagated by means of cuttings, taken from one-year-old wood, 4–6 inches long, and inserted in pots in September, but the amateur may prefer to buy his plants from the nurseryman. They should be bought in 6- to 8-inch pots already shaped as bushes or fan-trained trees. As figs are very vigorous growers and " gross " feeders, the roots must be confined, or the plants will run to wood and produce little fruit. Small pots should therefore be used, and the plants remain in the pots, and not be planted out in the glasshouse border.

Good drainage is essential, and the compost should consist of fairly rich fibrous loam, broken mortar-rubble, and burnt earth. The addition of a little lime every second or third year is very helpful.

## Watering

Until the plants break into active growth little moisture is required, but, once moving, ample moisture must never be lacking, even in winter, or the fruit will shrivel up and drop. During the ripening period the water must be withheld somewhat, or the fruit may crack. If this happens, ventilation should be more freely given and the floor of the house be sprinkled instead of the foliage being syringed.

## Pruning

Fig-trees planted under glass may be trained as fans, allowing ample room between the fan ribs for training in new fruit-bearing shoots, or as horizontal trees.

198

# THE FIG

Pruning appears much more simple if one keeps in mind the fact that the spring crop of fruit develops from the tiny fruit that have remained dormant on the young wood during the previous winter, and that the second crop comes on the young shoots which grow while the spring crop is maturing. The third crop comes on a young shoot which grows while the second crop is maturing. This is the shoot which carries at the point the dormant fruit which forms the spring crop. Care must be taken not to cut these points back, and so reduce the spring crop in the following year. For this reason the points of these shoots must not be cut off, but as soon as it is possible to decide which fruit forming the third crop will ripen, and which are sufficiently undeveloped to remain dormant—say, the size of large peas—the intervening fruit which will be too late to ripen and too far advanced to remain dormant should be picked off. Having decided upon the shoots that may, with ample room, be left for fruit production, the remainder may be removed by dis-budding, and the fruiting shoots should be stopped beyond the fruit.

## Thinning

As soon as the fruits are the size of a pea they should be thinned out so that, on an average, not more than three remain on each shoot. Once the fruit commences to ripen, syringing should be discontinued and more ventilation given. About nine weeks after the first crop has been gathered, the second should be nearly ripe.

## Gathering

The fruit is gathered as it ripens for dessert, or, if for market, just before it is ripe. Choice selected early fruits are sent up in small wicker " handles " containing four figs. The later crop is marketed in trays containing a dozen or in boxes holding up to four dozen figs. Early fruit is always the most profitable.

## Re-potting and Wintering

After all the fruit has been gathered, fruit grown in pots should be taken out and stood in the open on a bed of hard ashes. When the leaves begin to turn in colour, the trees should be re-potted, if necessary, and before the frosts become severe the pots should be plunged to the rim in ashes and then covered with 6–9 inches of litter to exclude all frost. Where the trees are planted permanently in the borders in the house, as free a circulation of air as possible should be given, except when there is danger from frost; never give such ventilation as to cause the temperature to drop suddenly.

**199**

## Varieties of Figs

| Name | Colour | Size | Qualities |
|---|---|---|---|
| Black Ischia | Purplish black | Medium | Sweet and juicy. Hardy |
| Bourjasotte Grise | Reddish brown | Medium–large | Excellent flavour. Sweet and rich |
| Brown Turkey | Brownish purple | Medium–large | Prolific. Good under glass, and best for outdoor culture. Excellent flavour |
| Brunswick | Brownish red-purple | Very large | Excellent flavour. Forces well, and good outdoor sort |
| Castle Kennedy | Light brown | Large | Hardy. Good and early bearer |
| Negro Largo | Brown-red | Large | Not hardy enough for outdoor. Good flavour |
| Osborne's Prolific | Brown-red | Medium | Free bearer. Best for pot culture under glass |
| St. John's | White-fleshed | Large | Excellent. Early bearer under glass |
| White Ischia | Pale yellow | Small | Prolific and well adapted for forcing. Not hardy. Sweet and delicious |
| White Marseilles | Pale yellowish green | Large | Hardy and prolific. Good pot sort. Forces well. Excellent flavour |

## Diseases and Pests

The fig suffers little from pests. Scale insects and Red Spider, should they appear, can be checked with petroleum-oil emulsions.

## Diseases

### Canker (*Phomopsis cinerescens*)

This fungus disease sometimes attacks the branches, gaining entry through wounds. It may cause death of an affected branch, the bark of which is roughened at the seat of the canker, often reminiscent of the markings of an oyster-shell. In damp weather the spores of the fungus are released in whitish tendrils from tiny points scattered over the surface of the canker, from whence they can be splashed about by rain.

*Control.*—Removal and burning of cankered branches, and painting of all wounds with white-lead paint. Branches should be cut out flush, so that no snags are left.

### Die-back and Fruit Rot (*Botrytis cinerea*)

This common fungus, the cause of Grey Mould disease in many plants, sometimes attacks the young shoots and fruits. The young shoots wilt and the developing fruits rot and usually drop off, though they may become mummified and remain on the tree through the winter, producing spores in the following spring for further infections. The fungus can be recognised by its greyish, fluffy felt produced on affected parts in wet weather.

*Control.*—Affected shoots and fruits should be removed and burnt.

## Diseases and Pests : Diagnosis Table

### The Fig (Under Glass)

| DAMAGE CAUSED | PROBABLE CAUSE |
|---|---|
| *Branches and Twigs* | *Pests* |
| White, mealy-looking patches | Mealy Bug |
| Encrusted with scale-like formation | Scale |
| | *Fungus* |
| Twigs die off, patches and cracks in bark, red dot-like fungus | Canker |
| | |
| *Foliage* | *Pests* |
| White mealy-looking patches | Mealy Bug |
| Leaves turn yellow, then silvery, falling early | Red Spider |
| Wilt and curl, infested with whitish fly | White Fly |
| | |
| *Blossom* | *Pests* |
| Injured and infested with blackish-grey insects | Thrips |
| | |
| *Fruit* | *Pest* |
| Damaged | Ants |
| Eaten | Wasps |
| Stolen | Mice |

## GRAPE (*Vitis vinifera*)

The grape is said to be a native of Asia Minor, particularly of the country to the south of the Caucasus and of the Caspian Sea. The introduction of the grape into this country is generally credited to the Romans, during the reign of the Emperor Augustus, about A.D. 10. It is certainly one of the oldest of domesticated fruits, and it is a well-known fact that the food values of fresh grapes and fresh figs, reckoned in calories, are higher than those of any other of the fruits cultivated generally in northern climes.

By careful selection of suitable varieties, grapes of a high quality may be grown in glasshouses of the simplest construction. In suitable conditions really excellent grapes can in most seasons be obtained without any artificial heat at all, though, of course, where this is available, much better results may be counted on.

### Form of House

The best form of house is in general that known as the lean-to, providing that a wall facing south is to be had. For a cool vinery much is to be said in favour of a three-quarter-span against a south wall. Otherwise a span-roof house must be used, in which case the house should run north to south, so as to obtain the maximum amount of sunshine. The situation chosen should be a high one, so that there may be no possibility of stagnant water in the borders. Where artificial heat is provided it is desirable to have much more piping than is usually afforded, since thus it is unnecessary to heat the pipes to excess in order to get the average temperature to the required degree.

The requirements of the grape-vine, however, are such that it is not possible to grow it successfully in a glasshouse with numerous other plants. Only those plants which are grown out of doors in summer and need little heat in winter, such as the Chrysanthemum, should be kept in the vinery.

**Soil and Site**

The border in which the vines are to be planted should be dug out to a depth of from $2\frac{1}{2}$–3 feet, because although the vine is not very particular as to soil, it is very particular as to drainage. The borders should, where space is available, be about 10 feet wide. Still, where choice can be had, there is no doubt the vine thrives best when the sub-soil is of chalk or limestone.

A suitable compost is composed of five parts of turfy loam, one part wood-ash charcoal and burnt garden refuse, one part stable manure, one part of old mortar-rubble and broken brick, and about 1 lb. of broken-up bones added to every barrow-load. The soil should be thoroughly mixed and trodden firm before planting.

In the case of quite small houses a narrow border about 2 feet wide may be constructed on lines similar to those suggested immediately within the front wall of the house. In this border the vines are to be planted, and their roots should be able to make their way into a wide, similarly-prepared border outside. In the case of wide, span-roofed houses, beds can be prepared on similar lines anywhere within the house.

**Planting**

The vines are best planted 3–4 feet apart, if grown as single stems, $1\frac{1}{2}$–2 feet from the front wall, and about 1 inch deeper in the soil than the old planting mark. A good time to plant indoors is early in January, when the canes should be cut back to about 18 inches long. As vines for planting are usually purchased in pots, they should, before planting, be washed free of all soil. This allows the roots to be spread out evenly. The extent to which they should be shortened depends on the height of the glass in front of the house. It is best to cut back to ripe wood. Choose a time when the soil is not too adhesive. See that the soil is carefully filled in amongst the roots, and cover the surface roots with about 4 inches of soil; then tread the plant in. If the vines are planted in the front of the house they have a clear run up the wall and up the slope of the roof to the back.

An eye struck in the spring will be well developed in a 6-inch pot to go out in the late autumn. Or it may be transferred into a 10-inch pot and carried over for planting in the following year. They should not remain in the pot sufficiently long for the roots to become matted. At the same time, the ball of earth should, when carefully removed from its pot, remain practically coherent until slightly squeezed by the hand. This should be done at the moment of planting, in order to break up the soil about the roots a little and to bring about a more ready extension of the rootlets into the adjacent soil. Before removing the plants from the pots, holes should be dug at the required intervals, ready to receive them. The surface of the ground should be covered with about 3 inches of short manure as soon as planting has taken place. Although the soil should be well broken up it should be made firm as soon as the plants are in position.

### Training, Pruning, and Disbudding

During the first year, the main shoot only should be allowed to grow to its full length. Side shoots may be run out to 2 feet to encourage root action ; they should then be stopped. These side shoots will be cut off in the winter pruning. The leading shoot, if the vine is well grown, will reach the top of the house during the second year, and at the winter pruning it should be cut back to a point where it is well developed and the wood is ripe and hard. This will be at about 6–8 feet from the ground. The following year's leader will ripen to the top of the house, where it may be cut back and definitely stopped on the top wire. After the first year of growth, side shoots are allowed to form on the wood that has been cut back the previous winter ; these laterals are pruned to one bud from the base to form spurs. When the main shoot is sufficiently strong and has reached the top of the house, no young growth is allowed to form at the top of the main stem, but is rubbed off to promote vigour in the fruiting spurs below ; these are annually cut back to one bud shooting outwards. Only one shoot is desired from each of these spurs, therefore, when the young shoots push out in spring ; the most vigorous one only is retained, the others being pinched off. The inexperienced gardener, however, should wait until the small bunches of fruit are visible on these shoots ; then he should select the best bunch and discard all the other shoots. When a rod has not been fruiting well, it is a good plan to train in another shoot from the bottom to take its place, the old rod being cut out when the young growth has reached the top of the house. The young shoot should be cut back to hard, ripe wood and then be treated as advised for the young vine.

The above method of training is applicable when several vines are grown in one house. Where only one vine is planted, instead of training one shoot to run vertically up the glass, two shoots are grown horizontally, running in opposite directions to each other, and are pruned as for the single vertical stem. Laterals are allowed to form from the upper side of these stems and are trained vertically upwards at intervals of 3–4 feet, these eventually being pruned and trained as for the single main shoot. The vines should be tied to wires, fixed 9 inches apart, and kept 18 inches from the roof-glass. The rods frequently produce shoots from their tops before any young growth has formed near the base. To encourage this lower growth, the rods must be unfastened from the wires and should have their heads bent down towards the ground. This will arrest the flow of sap, and young growth will soon form at the base. When the laterals all up the rod are in an even state of growth the rods may again be tied to the wires in an upright position. Vines should not be allowed to bear grapes the first year. If the vine is a strong one, a few branches of fruit may be taken off during the second year, but not until the third season should anything like a crop be allowed to mature. At this time each lateral may be permitted to carry one bunch.

The rule against over-cropping must be rigidly enforced. Flavour, size, and colour will be sacrificed if the vine is over-loaded. There is no known cultural practice that will adjust the balance. The weight of fruit that a vine will mature to perfection varies with the variety. Generally the less fine flavoured will colour the greatest weight, but in such cases the result is to make what a connoisseur would call bad, worse. (*See* Thinning, page 206.)

As an unlimited extension is undesirable, when a lateral has produced two leaves beyond the bunch, the end should be nipped off. Laterals that have not borne fruit should be left the same length as those that are fruiting. Sub-laterals that result from this stopping should be pinched back to one leaf. After fruiting, each lateral is cut back to one-half its length when the bunch is cut, and in winter to the basal bud close to the main rod. The next spring three or more laterals will shoot from this bud, and the strongest of these should be retained for fruiting, while the others must be pinched off so that the shoot bearing the grapes may be as vigorous as possible.

### Temperatures

Newly-planted vines should be allowed to become well established before any unnecessary heat is employed, but it is only in an exceptionally good summer that well-ripened wood can be obtained without artificial heat. The economy of fuel is not worth the loss of time. Indeed, the best results can never be obtained in an unheated house. The finish of a grape, its flavour and colour, provided the vines are properly grown and not over-cropped, depend on warmth and sun. Choice grapes such as *Cannon Hall* and *Muscat of Alexandria* are not worth growing without artificial heat. Temperatures must vary with the requirement of the variety grown. *Hamburgh* and *Muscat*, for example, started in January in a temperature of 50–55° F., with the increase that the sun, as the season advances, will give, will progress together through the increased night temperature of 60° F. with the day temperature of 70° F. until just before the bunches come into flavour. Then, however, the difference in the variety begins to assert itself. The *Muscat* prefers a temperature 10° higher than the *Hamburgh* after this, and must be indulged to that extent if the crop is to approach perfection. Another example may be taken from late *Colmar*. For winter grapes *Colmar* may be allowed to start with the weather in an unheated house, but the period without artificial heat is very short. The grapes must be ripe by the first of October. After that time there is not sufficient sun to complete the ripening, and the grapes will not keep if not ripe. It is quite possible to get a good berry even though the heat has been stinted, and with the aid of a few chilly nights some colour may be obtained, but grapes are not eaten for the sake of their appearance, although because of their appearance sometimes they are not eaten.

When the fruit is required in July or August, the temperature may be raised to a minimum of about 55° F. early in March, and from the middle of April onward the temperature from sun-heat alone may be allowed to rise to 70–75° F., a night temperature of about 55° F. being afforded. From the time the young leaves are fairly developed until the grapes are in flower a night temperature of 55–60° F. should be given.

When grapes are in bloom, the night temperature should not fall below 60° F. In the case of *Muscats*, not below 70° F. Some very successful growers maintain 80° F. at night during the setting period of *Cannon Hall Muscats*. It is the practice in some nurseries to fertilise this last-mentioned grape with a rabbit's tail. We have never found artificial pollination necessary at any time. The trouble with most grapes is that they set too freely. Those varieties that are shy will set as much fruit as they will carry if the borders are sufficiently wet and a reasonable amount of atmospheric moisture is maintained. A dry house and a dry atmosphere are inimical to vines in bloom.

The two most necessary factors making for successful grape culture are moisture and ventilation. The air in the house must be fresh and sparkling—what is known as " buoyant "

205

among grape-growers—and this can be secured only by efficient ventilation and by keeping the soil moist and by syringing the foliage frequently as soon as growth starts and until the flowers open. The house should be well ventilated at all times, but especially when the sun is shining brightly, since otherwise the berries may be scalded and the leaves scorched.

Ventilation should always be started just before the sun rises, and should be increased as the temperature rises, until noon. With the setting of the sun, and with an eye on the temperature, the ventilation should be diminished, and the house should be finally closed just before the maximum evening temperature is reached. During very hot weather, and when the grapes are beginning to colour, a little top ventilation should be afforded at night. Should the weather be cold and dull while the grapes are ripening, heat should be given, but ventilation should be provided. Except when the grapes are colouring, when the heat must be somewhat reduced and more air given, the floor and walls should be freely damped during the hot weather. When the grapes are colouring, however, a good damping twice a week is sufficient. As soon as the grapes are well coloured, more ventilation may be given and the heat must be reduced to the minimum.

The different varieties of grape vary in the amount of heat they require. The *Muscat of Alexandria*—a finely-flavoured yellow fruit—needs the highest temperature of all. As soon as the crop has been gathered, the heat should be reduced to that degree which will ensure the frost being kept out, ample ventilation being given.

As the laterals grow, they must be gradually bent down, a little at a time, before they touch the glass, and should be first loosely tied to the wires with raffia, being later more securely fixed when the wood has toughened and they have become more used to the position. Great care must be exercised when the loose tie is put on, because a shoot will tie down with perfect safety when the sun is shining, but the cool night will stiffen the shoot and it will break off hours after it was tied down. The shoots must be evenly distributed over the wires so that each receives ample sun and air. Water when the vines are " starting ", shortly before the flowers open, while the fruit is stoning, liberally while the grapes are swelling, and after the fruit has been harvested.

## Thinning

As soon as the bunches have set their berries, it should be decided how many bunches are to be left, and how many grapes on each bunch. It has been estimated that each foot of rod of a well-matured vine should bear about 1 lb. weight of grapes. Thus a fully-established vine about 20 feet long, of such a variety as *Muscat of Alexandria* or *Black Hamburgh*, should not be allowed to bear more than about twenty bunches, averaging 1 lb. a bunch, whilst of such varieties as *Trebbiano* or *Grosse Guillaume* not more than sixteen bunches, each averaging 1¼ lb. in weight, are as much as it should be permitted to hold. No lateral should be allowed to carry more than one bunch, and the bunches retained should be compact and neat in form, not long, straggling ones. Surplus bunches should be removed as early as possible, and on the bunches that are allowed to remain the grapes should be thinned out at an early stage, so as to make shapely bunches.

Grape-thinning is an art which is quickly acquired, but hard and fast rules, particularly as to spacing, cannot be set down on paper. Even if the size of the berry were accepted as a guide for spacing, the ultimate issue is affected by the long or short shank varieties. *Colmar* gives a big berry, has a short shank, and requires double the space that should be given to *Alicante*, which is a smaller berry but a thicker setter. *Alexandria*, on the other hand, with a berry of size about midway between the former two, has a long shank and an oblong berry. Neither *Colmar* nor *Alicante* can be used for comparison in such a case. The thinner must thin with the facts and peculiarities in mind, otherwise the grapes will be flappy, shapeless bunches. It is a good plan to get on to a few of the earliest bunches in good time and so accustom the eye to the results. Generally, terminal berries should be retained, shoulders must be left well-furnished and the whole of the thinning done within the frame of the bunch. The centre especially should be thinned. Failure to thin the bunches sufficiently will result in flattened berries in the centre of bunches when ripe. This occurs particularly in the case of *Colmar*. On the other hand, over-thinning will result in slack bunches of mature fruit. Experience will soon teach the grower how to secure the desired result. Grape-thinning scissors and a forked stick some 10 inches long to separate the grapes should be used, as on no account must the grapes be touched by the hand. Care must be taken not to injure the grapes.

## Supporting the " Shoulders "

With some varieties that produce large, heavy berries it is necessary to support the top two bunches with raffia looped to the wires ; this relieves the pressure on the lower fruit, and should be done before the berries become very heavy. For market work, bunches of this type and size are seldom required, and it is the usual practice at the time of thinning to cut off such shoulders as would require support, with the object of reducing the weight of the bunch. Varieties bearing smaller and lighter berries are better without this support. After thinning has been completed, the border should be dressed with a layer of farmyard manure 2–3 inches in thickness, or with a dressing of good fertiliser, since farmyard manure is difficult to obtain.

**Propagation**

The grape-vine is grown on its own roots, as is the case with the majority of soft fruits, and may be propagated either from buds or dormant cuttings in January. The amateur, however, is advised to leave this work to the professional, since better results are obtained when a vine is bought in autumn or winter.

To propagate, several eyes or buds—that is, short pieces of the previous year's side growth some 2 inches in length, each with one good bud upon it, and having a slanting cut half an inch long directly under the bud—are planted in January horizontally, with the bud just above the soil in small pots, in a compost consisting of loam with one-third leaf-mould and a liberal addition of sand. The pots are placed in a mild hot-bed and the soil is kept moist and shaded. The eyes start growth under these conditions, and should then be moved to a cooler, but light position. As soon as the roots have well filled the pot, the plants should be re-potted singly into 6-inch pots. As the vines grow, they must be carefully staked, and by mid-summer the plants will be about 6 feet in height. They should be moved into 8-inch pots, then again into 10-inch pots, being kept in the open from September to November, and planted in the house in January.

**Inarching of Vines**

This is a process whereby new and vigorous shoots may be grafted on to an old and perhaps useless vine. Two growing shoots in close proximity (the plant bearing the scion or graft is usually potted-up and stood close to the stock on which it is to be grafted) are selected, and a thin strip, some 3 inches long, is cut away from the stems of each shoot. The shoots are then bound firmly together with raffia or soft cloth so that the cut surfaces come into contact and so that the outer side or bark of one shoot coincides with that of the other stem ; on both sides if the shoots are of similar diameter, or on one side at any rate should there be a difference in the thickness of the stems. Cover the graft thickly with clay or grafting wax to exclude the air. The union should be complete in six weeks or so, when the portions of the old vine above the graft may be cut back.

208

Grapes in the Greenhouse

G

O

## Pruning and Training the Grape Vine

1. A vine spur before pruning.  2. After pruning.  3. A vinery cleared and pruned in readiness for starting, and showing the tops of the vines bent down to ensure an even flow of sap.  See page 203.

When the graft is quite firm—usually the following autumn—it may be severed from its mother vine, and will in future be supported by the roots of the formerly useless vine. Inarching is best carried out when the vines are in vigorous growth.

## Bottle-grafting

Bottle-grafting is similar in its principles to inarching, but does not necessitate having the root bearing the graft or scion in close proximity to the stock. Bottle-grafting is most successful if effected when the vine is just coming into growth. The graft must be cut from its parent in the previous autumn and should be stored buried to half its depth in earth in a cold, but frost-proof position. A few days before the operation is to be effected—that is, when the vine breaks into growth—place the graft in the vinery so that both graft and stock may assume the same state of growth. The stems are grafted together as described under inarching, but the lower end of the graft is placed in a bottle of rain-water, so suspended that its weight shall not be borne by the graft. The bottle must not be removed until the graft is finally established and has grown to a fair length.

## Storing Grapes

Cut the grapes, when quite ripe, so that the laterals remaining below the bunches are about 9 inches long. These should be inserted into wine-bottles almost filled with water containing a few lumps of charcoal to keep it sweet. The bottles are then placed in racks or secured to the wall at an angle of 40° so that the grapes will hang naturally, as if still on the vine.

The room in which they are stored must be kept cool and dark, but well aired. Bunches so kept will last almost into the new year.

## Cutting, Grading, and Packing

Ripe bunches of grapes only should be cut, one at a time, as they become ready, cutting with each bunch (except in the case of early *Hamburghs*) 2–3 inches of the lateral from which the stalk springs. In the case of early *Hamburghs*, however, this seems detrimental to the subsequent development of the vine, and the main stalk itself should be cut close to the lateral, without injuring the latter. Each bunch must be carefully examined and any imperfect or diseased berries snipped out. The bunch is then graded direct into its prepared package for market. These packages (*see* page 210) are usually ready padded and papered and placed on a movable stand in the vine house. In grading, the size and shape of the bunch are important points, also the colour and size of the grapes them-

o

selves, and the general quality of the fruit. Some black grapes, such as *Alicante*, must be quite black when ready; the others, such as *Hamburghs* and *Colmar*, show reddish tints when fully ripe. They are usually graded as : " Extra Selected " (symmetrically shaped bunches of 1 lb. or over of fully coloured, even-shaped, large-sized berries) ; " Selected " (symmetrically shaped bunches of ¾ lb. or over of good-sized, uniformly mature berries) ; and " Medium " (bunches of ½ lb. or more of sound, ripe grapes). Great skill and care are necessary in packing. All packages should be carefully padded with wood wool and lined with tissue (white in the case of black grapes, and pink for other kinds). Some growers send the fruit to market in shallow baskets, unpadded, the bunches being secured in position by means of string, 8–10 lb. in a basket. The grapes must be comfortably tight in their baskets and not be allowed to shake about. Muscats are frequently sent up two or three bunches in a handled basket.

## Marketing

Grapes are sent to market chiefly in returnable flat baskets, containing a shallow tray and oval cross-handle baskets (Nos. 6, 8, 10, and 12). A package that has gained favour in recent years is the " Climax " chip-basket (non-returnable), with curved ends, and this is to be recommended especially when sending up a few early " Selected " bunches. All packages should be clearly marked " GRAPES " and labelled with full details.

## GRAPES

### Indoor Varieties

| Name | Colour | Size | Season | Qualities |
|---|---|---|---|---|
| *Black Alicante (Mixed vinery) | Black | Large, oval | Late Oct. to March | Of good flavour if lightly cropped, otherwise much inferior to Colmar |
| *Black Hamburgh (Hot or cool house) | Black | Large, roundish | May–Nov. | Vigorous and productive. Excellent flavour. Forces well. For Pots |
| Buckland Sweetwater (Mixed vinery) | Amber | Large, round | Early | Does not keep well. Must be started early. Cool house |
| *Cannon Hall Muscat (Hot house) | White | Very large, good | Later than Alexandria | Excellent flavour. For pot culture |
| Foster's White Seedling (Cool house) | White | Large, round | May–Nov. | Vigorous and productive. Inferior flavour to Muscat of Alexandria. Cool house |
| Gros Colmar (Warm house) | Black | Large, round | Late Aug. to Feb. | Poor flavour. Very sweet, requires heat to finish |
| Gros Maroc (Warm house) | Black | Large, round, oval | Late | Vigorous and productive. Showy fruit but poor flavour. Flavour like that of a sloe |
| Lady Downes (Mixed vinery) | Black | Large, roundish-oval | Late | Keeps well |
| Mrs. Pearson | White | Good | Late | Excellent flavour |
| *Muscat of Alexandria (Hot house) | Amber | Large, oval | Early and Late | Superior flavour, but requires more heat than Black Hamburgh, etc. For pot culture |

* Best grapes to grow for market.

210

# THE GRAPE

## Diseases and Pests

The chief insect pests of the vine are the mealy bug, red spider, and thrips. As these are mainly glasshouse pests, the reader is referred for their control to the section on Diseases and Pests, page 600.

## Powdery Mildew (*Uncinula spiralis*)

This is the most common fungus disease of indoor and outdoor vines in this country. Its chief characteristic, like that of the powdery mildews as a class, is the presence of a white, mealy fungus growth over affected leaves, shoots, flowers, and fruits. The disease is common in heated vineries in spring, when equable ventilation is difficult and the vines are making quick growth. Sometimes over-dryness of the roots will induce mildew, both in indoor and outdoor vines.

*Control.*—The disease can usually be avoided on indoor vines by adequate moisture and ventilation. Dusting with sulphur powder or spraying with a colloidal or dispersible sulphur preparation will check infection.

## Shanking (*functional*)

This is common in over-cropped or under-fed grapes; in fact, among all those that are water-logged or improperly grown in some way. The fruit develops well for a time, when the stalk begins to shrivel and becomes discoloured, while the berries themselves shrink up and grow sour and uneatable. Thorough remaking and enrichment of the vine border, together with the avoidance of over-cropping, will get rid of the tendency.

## Diseases and Pests : Diagnosis Table

### Grapes

| SYMPTOMS | PROBABLE CAUSE |
|---|---|
| *Branches and Twigs* | *Pests* |
| White, mealy patches | Mealy Bug |
| Scales on bark | Scale Insects |
| *Foliage* | |
| White, mealy patches | Mealy Bug |
| Leaves turn yellow, then silvery-grey and fall early | Red Spider |
| Spotted, infested with small, blackish or yellow insects | Thrips |
| Leaves infested with whitish fly | White Fly |
| Patches eaten out of leaves | Vine Weevil |
| Leaves spun together, eaten by caterpillars | Tortrix Moths |
| | *Fungi* |
| White, mealy mould | Grape Powdery Mildew |
| *Buds and Young Shoots* | *Fungi* |
| White, mealy mould | Grape Powdery Mildew |

211

## Diseases and Pests: Diagnosis Table—*contd.*

### Grapes

*Blossom*
  Infested with small, blackish or yellow insects

*Pests*
  Thrips

*Fungi*

  White, mealy mould      Grape Powdery Mildew

*Fruit*
  White mealiness      Mealy Bug
  White, mealy mould      Grape Powdery Mildew
  Berries shrivel      Shanking

### MELON (*Cucumis Melo*)

The melon, which is closely related to the cucumber, is said to be a native of the milder parts of Asia. It was originally introduced into this country from Jamaica in 1570, and has long been cultivated under glass. *C. Melo*, at one time known as the Musk Melon, is quite a different variety from *C. Citrullus*, the Water Melon, so largely imported from abroad. The latter's cultivation is rarely attempted here.

The home-produced melon is much superior to its imported rival, possessing a far better flavour. It is distinguished from the imported melon by its skin, which may be either green or yellow.

Melons are best grown in houses heated by hot-water pipes. But in most gardens, frame culture will necessarily be resorted to, and in frames, carefully managed, melons of the highest quality can undoubtedly be grown. The cultivation is somewhat similar to that of the cucumber, but it should be remembered that, whereas the cucumber is picked in the green stage, the melon is of value only when it is fully ripened. Consequently, a high temperature is needed, and it is hopeless to attempt to ripen the melon after the month of October. A firmer soil and less water are needed in the case of the melon than in the case of the cucumber. Also, a stronger light and more air are necessary for the successful growing of the former. Stiff loam, with an admixture of a little old mortar-rubble, makes an excellent compost.

### Preparing the Bed

Not less than a two-light frame should be employed, and a three-light frame is to be preferred, as it is easier to maintain an even heat with a larger body of fermenting material. For a three-light frame six loads of farmyard manure should be laid in a heap, and turned two or three times in the course of a fortnight, so as to let out a little of the heat. Fresh manure is necessary, and it is important that fermentation should be in active progress. At the end of the fortnight the manure should be pressed down firmly with the fork, but not trampled upon, and it should be covered with about 6 inches of good, ordinary garden loam with an admixture of a little old mortar-rubble, sand, and a few handfuls of crushed charcoal. The top of the bed should be brought up to within 24 inches of the glass to afford the plants full sun. This should bring us to about the end of March. Melons are better grown on heaps of soil, each heap amounting to about two pecks of compost. A hole is opened in the centre of the heap and the soil rammed down firmly and hard. When stable manure is unobtainable, the bed may be heated by means of hot-water pipes or electricity.

## Sowing

Seed may be sown in the bed itself, or young plants may be raised in a pot, in a temperature of about 70° F. early in March, being planted out, 2 feet apart, as soon as an even temperature of about 80° F. may be counted upon.

Double as many seeds should be sown as plants ultimately required.

As the fumes generated by the hot-bed are liable to injure the young seedlings, for the first few days the lights should be left very slightly open, to allow the gases to escape. Cover the lights with matting or sacking at night to exclude frost, gradually reducing the covering as the weather becomes warmer.

## Pruning

Very little pruning is necessary, the cutting and slashing so commonly resorted to being very harmful. If grown in a frame, the main shoot should be pegged down on to the soil and stopped when about 2 feet in length. Three or four laterals should be permitted to form. These should be trained evenly over the bed, being pinched back when sufficient flowers are visible.

No plant should be allowed to bear more than four fruits, and these should be kept off the earth by means of a tile or slate.

In a house the plant should be allowed to grow up as a single cordon supported by a cane until it reaches the wires, being stopped back when 4 feet high. Laterals will be thrown out, and should be trained along horizontal wires 10 inches apart, being stopped when some 18 inches long. The female flowers have small, globular growths at their base, and four or five of these on each plant require " setting ". This is done by picking the male flower, which has no globular formation at its base, removing the yellow petals, and by pressing the pollen-covered stamens into the female flower. The best time to do this is

**213**

early in the morning when the sun is shining and the plants are dry. The female flower will close, and in a few days' time will commence to swell. A dry atmosphere is not essential while the fruits are setting. While the fruit is ripening it is essential to allow the shoots from beyond the fruits to thrive, in order that nourishment may be drawn out to the fruit; all unnecessary side growth, however, must be stopped to avoid crowding. Only one fruit must be allowed on a lateral.

### Watering and Ventilation

During the early periods of growth the plants must never be allowed to be dry at the root; in bright weather the leaves should be syringed with water, preferably in the morning and again when closing the house for the night. Tepid water should always be used. When the flowers open, less water may be given, but the plant must never be allowed to suffer for want of it. Red spider, fly, thrips, and mildew are all associated with scarcity of water. Water at the roots should be given, and the plant should not again be syringed overhead until the fruits begin to swell. In watering melons great caution must be used in supplying only the quantity wanted, as an excess of water at the roots only tends to increase the size and deteriorate the quality of the fruit. The kind of structure the plants are grown in will have some effect on the quantity of water they will require. In lofty pits or houses, where the foliage attains a large size, and where a much drier atmosphere is obtained than in frames and low pits, more water will be necessary, and the whole surface of the soil should be frequently sprinkled. During the whole period of growth, air should be liberally afforded, a careful eye being, of course, kept on the temperature, which should not fall below 60° F. at night, or below 70° F. by day. Should the thermometer rise above 85° F. while the sun is shining, a little more ventilation should be afforded until the temperature has dropped. It will be difficult to maintain these temperatures when frames are used, but much may be done by covering the lights closely with mats and sacking on cold nights. Throughout their whole lives melon plants require free ventilation and an abundance of light, and this is especially true during the period of fruit ripening. Once their roots are established, they cannot have too much sun. It is almost impossible to give a melon too much heat. After the fruit has commenced to ripen, a temperature of 90° F. will enhance the flavour.

### Ripening the Fruit

Fruit sown in March takes some four months from the time of

214

sowing to ripen, later-sown fruit will require only three months. As soon as the fruits begin to swell, fertilisers may be applied or tepid liquid manure may be given at intervals. As the fruits swell, more water, which must be tepid, is needed until they begin to ripen, when the syringing and water supply must be diminished and more air given, but the plants must never be allowed to flag.

Three melons on a plant are as much as can be expected to do well; never more than four should be allowed to remain. Pinch off all the rest and every unnecessary growth. It is important that the plants shall not be allowed to ramble after the fruit has begun to swell, for this will require the whole strength of the plants. Three or four laterals in addition to those carrying the fruits are sufficient, and after the first stopping, at, say, the fourth leaf, these should be stopped again at the first leaf that appears.

The fruit is heavy, and when the size of a tennis-ball, arrangements should be made for supporting it by means of small wooden " rafts ", or nets, suspended from the wires. Ample sun is required during the ripening period. The fruit takes some four or five weeks, occasionally more, from the time of setting to the time of ripening, which is indicated by the stalk appearing to separate from the fruit. Melons should be cut and used on the day this takes place or very soon after, and a melon should be dead ripe before it is cut.

Melons, while ripening their fruit, are liable to crack when exposed to moisture or when water is applied too freely to their roots. This is more likely to happen with the higher-flavoured ones owing to the thinness of their skin. But a melon that has not been deprived of sufficient water when it required it will not crack when it is ripening. In ordinary frames some difficulty will be found in keeping the air sufficiently dry. To prevent this, in moist weather air must be left on at night, both back and front, to admit of a slight circulation. By turning over linings, a little extra heat should be thrown into the bed to keep the temperature up. Where, however, melons are grown with the assistance of hot-water pipes, an atmosphere can be maintained which will fully carry out the ripening process of this delicious fruit even in unfavourable weather.

## Second and Third Crops

As soon as the fruit is cut—if it is intended that the plants shall bear a second crop—prune back the shoots to where the fresh growth commences. Two or 3 inches of fresh loam should be spread over the surface of the bed, which should at the same time have a good soaking with manure water in order to assist the plants to make fresh growth. At the same time an additional stimulus should be given to the roots by means of slightly increased bottom heat. It is never worth while, except in extraordinary circumstances, to attempt a second crop on old plants.

Where artificial heat is available, by planting a strong young plant as soon as the fruit has been gathered from the old one, three crops of melons may often be obtained in one season. Seed sown in January will bear fruit in June, the plants put in at this time will ripen their fruit in August, and the last crop should ripen off by October.

### Varieties

*Green-fleshed.*—Emerald Gem, Monarch, and Ringleader.
*Scarlet-fleshed.*—Blenheim Orange, Cantaloup, Golden Beauty, King George, and Superlative.
*White-fleshed.*—Hero of Lockinge and Universal.
These all do well in the glasshouse.
*Munroe's Little Heath* and *The Earl's Favourite* are fairly hardy, and may be successfully grown on hot-beds in a frame.

### Gathering and Marketing

There is only one important rule about gathering melons. Never be tempted to cut one off until it is ripe. Marketing is equally simple. Melons of quality are usually packed in shallow handle baskets with moderately coarse wood wool to support them. They are good travellers and need only to be prevented from rolling about. Sizes vary immensely, so that the number in a basket varies according to size. Very big fruit will be placed two in a basket, and the smaller up to six together. The scarlet-fleshed variety usually sells better than the green- or white-fleshed varieties.

### Diseases and Pests

The melon, when carefully attended to, is not subject to a lot of trouble. But a sharp look-out must be kept for Aphides, Woodlice, and Red Spider. Eelworms may attack the roots and cause the plants to wilt and die off without any apparent cause.

The two chief diseases to which the melon is subject, Canker (sometimes called Foot Rot), caused by a bacterium that rots the base of the main stem near ground level, and Downy Mildew, caused by a fungus that gives rise to greyish patches on the foliage and may be severe enough to prevent proper ripening of the fruit, are each largely brought about by too moist conditions. Good ventilation is the best safeguard against attack, and it will check either disease if noticed in the early stages. Excessive " free moisture " should be avoided, though the plants need plenty at the roots.

The plants may safely be lightly dusted with copper-lime dust to prevent the spread of infection.

Diseased plants should be destroyed as soon as the fruit is gathered, and the frame thoroughly cleaned and fumigated.

For Pests, *see* Diseases and Pests, page 600.

## SWEET ORANGE (*Citrus Sinansis*)

Orange-trees were first brought to Great Britain, and planted with little success, in 1595. They are said to have been planted at Beddington Park, near Croydon, Surrey. Later their cultivation under glass was attempted. But it is apparently no use trying to grow the orange for commercial purposes in Great Britain, as the large-fruited palatable kinds when grown under glass require far too much room.

As ornamental plants some of the smaller, dwarf-fruiting kinds, such as *C. taitensis*, the Otaheite Orange, which may be grown in 6–7-inch pots, are very attractive. The smaller fruits, however, are very unpalatable.

To grow these ornamental oranges, ripe pips should be sown in pots filled with light, rich soil and subjected to brick-bottom heat. The pots should further be kept under glass, and when the seeds have sprung up, the plants should be kept in an atmosphere both close and warm.

When about 12–18 inches in height the seedlings should be grafted or budded with grafts or buds from an established flowering and fruiting tree. The temperature of the green-house in which they grow must not fall below 45° F. during the winter, and this temperature should be raised about 10° in early spring. Artificial heat must be discontinued during the warm summer weather.

Young plants should be re-potted annually in early spring when the winter temperature of the house is raised. Older plants, and particularly those in large tubs, need a top dressing with rich new soil.

The growing plants require plenty of air and light, but must be shaded from the hottest rays of the sun. They should be given careful watering and periodical syringing until the blossom breaks, when syringing must cease until the fruit has set.

### Pruning

Very little pruning is necessary, except just to stop back an over-vigorous shoot here and there to keep the plant shapely, and this is best done in late spring.

**217**

## PEACHES AND NECTARINES (*Prunus Persica* [**Peach**] and *P. P.* var. *Nectarina nucipersica* [**Nectarine**])

The nectarine is a smooth-skinned variety of the peach. Nectarines will grow from peach stones and peaches from nectarine stones. Of Chinese origin, there is no authentic record of the introduction of the peach into England, although it is said to have been brought from Italy in 1524 by Wolf, gardener to Henry VIII. It is mentioned by Tusser in the list of fruits growing in this country in 1557.

Under glass the cultivation of these fruits is essentially similar to their outdoor culture.

The house must be kept very cool until the first or second week in February, when a temperature of 45–50° F. should be given. The border must be watered, and on fine days the trees should be syringed twice daily with lukewarm water. After ten days the temperature should be raised by about 10°. Ample ventilation should be given when outside conditions are suitable. A temperature of 50–60° F. and plenty of air should be given during the flowering season. In order to ensure pollination, the flowers must be dusted over about noon with a soft camel-hair brush or a rabbit's tail. No syringing should be done while the trees are in bloom, but should be continued daily with soft water as soon as the fruit has set, when the temperature should be raised to 65° F. The ground should also be sprinkled with water while the fruits are forming and swelling; but no syringing and damping should be done while the fruit is ripening. Not more than one fruit for every 12 inches square of wall space should be allowed.

### Soil and Planting

Next to the grape, the peach and nectarine have been the fruit most generally grown under glass in this country, and it is certainly one of the most profitable crops, for the success of which it is essential to see that the soil is suitable and well drained, it being most important that the roots do not come in contact with water that is either percolating through or stagnant. If the soil is poor and sandy the trees will not find nourishment to enable them to support a good crop, yet, as it can afterwards be enriched by suitable composts, it is preferable to soil that is too adhesive. Clay soils are most unsuitable, and the most difficult to deal with; in fact, neither the peach nor the nectarine should ever be planted in such. The best method is to remove the whole of the clay and substitute a suitable compost, or, if this is too expensive an item to undertake at once, it is best to provide sufficient good soil for planting the trees, and additional suitable soil can then be substituted for the bad soil, in advance of the root-growth, of course. Soil that is removed should be replaced by some good, mellow, turfy loam of a substantial, but not of a binding nature. If it is strong and adhesive, then add some mortar-rubble and burnt earth.

The types of trees to be planted depend on the positions for which they are required. For the front of the glasshouse dwarf trees trained on wires 12–15 inches from the glass; better-flavoured peaches and nectarines are obtained from trees that are grown not far from the glass.

The best season for planting is the autumn, but if it should happen that the planting cannot be done before vegetation commences in the spring, the trees should be lifted and heeled in in a cool, shaded place to retard growth till the final planting can be performed.

## Forms of Tree for Planting under Glass

In high houses fan-trained heads on half-standard or standard stems, according to the height of the back walls, may be used. The most usual form, however, is the low-stemmed fan tree. The training of this form of tree is essentially a slow process, needing patience and experience to obtain uniformly successful trees, and one which for that reason is best left to the skilled nurseryman.

## Pruning and Disbudding of Trained Trees of Peach and Nectarine

On peaches and nectarines the best fruits are borne on good shoots of the previous season's growth. Good fruits are sometimes produced on comparatively short and weak growths, but attention should be devoted mainly to shoots from 15–18 inches long, bearing in winter mixed fruit- and wood-buds. These shoots are referred to in the following pages as fruit-bearing shoots.

*Fruit-bearing Shoots.*—The fruit-buds on these shoots will blossom and carry fruits which in due course must be drastically thinned out. The wood-buds on the same shoots, if allowed to grow unchecked, will starve the fruit and smother in the tree, so it is important to know how to deal with them by means of disbudding. The expression " disbudding " in this connection does not mean the actual rubbing out of the bud between finger and thumb, but it means pinching out the tip of the embryo shoot when it is not more than an inch long. This process is vital to the successful control of all wall-trained trees, especially apricots, peaches, and nectarines. Disbudding should

**219**

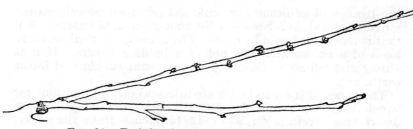

FIG. 24.—Fruit-bearing shoot after fruit is picked, showing
replacement shoot ready to replace it.

begin at the top of the tree as soon as the wood-buds begin to
push out into shoots in the late spring. All "fore-right"
shoots—namely, those growing straight outwards from or
inwards to the wall—are disbudded first. After that the principle is to restrict the number of shoots, so that when these are
ultimately tied in to the supporting wires there will be a clear
5-inch lateral space between each. Most trees on walls are
allowed to carry far too many shoots, especially at the top.
the only way to avoid this is to lay down a "rule of thumb"
regulation for the pruner somewhat as follows :—

*Wood-bud for Replacement Shoot.*—At the base of every fruit-
bearing shoot on which fruit either has or has not set at least
one good shoot must be left to grow. This must be situated at
the base of the fruit-bearing shoot, and is known as the "replacement shoot". By the end of the season, the fruit-bearing
shoot, having done its work and being of no further use, will be
cut off just above the replacement shoot, which will then be tied
in its place to carry out the same function—namely, carrying
fruit the next season.*

*Extension Shoot.*—In early years, when there is plenty of room
on the wall, one wood-bud at the end of the fruit-bearing shoot
is also retained to form an extension shoot growing in the same

FIG. 25.—Same as above after fruit-bearing shoot has been cut
off at base, and replacement tied in to take its place.

* Some pruners like to leave two wood-buds at the base of each fruit-bearing shoot
in order to make certain of having something to replace the old shoot.

direction as the fruit-bearing shoot, its subsequent treatment being the same as described for the replacement shoot.

*Shoots next to Fruits.*—Shoots growing next to fruits left from the final thinning should not be disbudded. These, however, must be pinched out later, as described later under Summer Pruning.

*All Other Shoots Growing from Fruit-bearing Shoots.*—All other shoots except those mentioned above should be disbudded over a period of two to three weeks. When the process is complete each fruit-bearing shoot should be seen to have either one (or occasionally two) shoots growing strongly away from its base, and one at or near the tip, *where space allows.* No other wood shoots should be tolerated with the exception of those actually next to a fruit. At this stage the fruit-bearing shoot should look something like the first of the diagrams on page 220.

### Summer Pinching

*Replacement of Extension Shoots.*—Should these grow too strongly, showing signs of much exceeding 18 inches in length, they should have their tips pinched out at this length. Where wall-space is limited, extension shoots on established trees should be pinched out above the fifth good leaf when they have attained that length. As a result of summer pinching, especially if rainy weather follows, the buds below the pinch are likely to send out one or more " secondary " shoots after a week or two. These should be pinched or " stopped " above the first good leaf.

*Shoots next to Fruits.*—Shoots that have been allowed to grow next to fruits should be pinched above the second good leaf, and secondaries above the first leaf.

### Pruning and Tying-in after Fruiting

The next pruning operation takes place after the fruit has been picked. Where there is plenty of wall-space available, the extension shoot is tied in, carrying on the direction of the fruit-bearing shoot, and the replacement shoot is tied in beside last year's fruit-bearing shoot. In an established tree, or where wall-space is limited, the old fruit-bearing shoot with its terminal extension shoot is cut off at the base immediately in front of the new replacement shoot. The replacement shoot is then tied in to the space formerly occupied by the fruit-bearing shoot. Thus the replacement shoot of this season becomes the fruit-bearing shoot for next season, and in this way the whole tree is refurnished annually. The pinching programme we have described may be expressed in tabular form as follows :—

## Summer Pinching Programme—Peaches and Nectarines

*Replacement Shoot.* (At base of fruit-bearing shoot.)
    (1) Terminal bud pinched out at about 18 inches.
    (2) Secondaries stopped at first leaf.

*Extension Shoot.* (At end of fruit-bearing shoot.)
  (a) *On Young Trees where Wall-space is Plentiful.*
    (1) Terminal bud pinched out at about 18 inches.
    (2) Secondaries stopped at first leaf.
  (b) *On Established Trees where Wall-space is Limited.*
    (1) Terminal shoot pinched out above fifth leaf.
    (2) Secondaries stopped at first leaf.

## Subsequent Treatment of Shoots

  (a) *On Young Trees where Wall-space is Plentiful.*
    (1) Extension shoot tied in in the same direction as the fruit-bearing shoot.
    (2) Replacement shoot tied in alongside old last-season's fruit-bearing shoot.
  (b) *On Established Trees where Wall-space is Limited.*
    (1) Fruit-bearing shoot cut back to base.
    (2) Replacement shoot tied in in its place.

The method of disbudding and pinching here described is only one of various systems employed by gardeners, and does not attempt to deal exhaustively with the treatment of all the shoots which may grow in the course of the season. For the sake of simplicity, it has been thought best to concentrate on the treatment of the fruit-bearing shoots, since these are the most important. Shoots arising in other parts of the tree which are not disbudded, and which are clearly not going to be required are best dealt with by cutting them clean out after the fruit has been picked.

In peaches and nectarines, when tying in, a space of not less than 4–5 inches should be left between all fruit-bearing shoots. In plums and cherries this space may be reduced to about 2 inches.

## Fruit Thinning

Thinning should start when the fruits are the size of a hazel nut, leaving twice as many fruits as will ultimately be required. A natural process known as " stoning " begins when the fruit is about an inch in diameter, and in the course of which many drop off. After stoning, the fruits again begin to swell, and thinning should then be continued, leaving the fruits approximately 9 inches apart for peaches, and rather less for nectarines. In the final thinning only the largest and best-placed fruits should be left on the tree, spaced at about one to every 12 square inches, but leaving more at the top of the tree and less at the bottom.

## Ripening the Fruit

As the fruit approaches the ripening period it should be fully exposed to the sun and given as much ventilation as possible. The shoots should be kept laid in closely, obstructing leaves being removed, and a mulch of manure given. Syringing should cease as soon as the fruit begins to colour, as a drier atmosphere is needed at this period. Some growers suspend nets supported by short stakes beneath the trees to catch any falling fruit, with some soft material in the net to soften the fall. But fruit should be picked before it falls. If the trees have been well grown, the fruit will not fall before it is quite ripe. Netting of a fine mesh is also used successfully to keep off the attacks of flies and wasps. Strong shoots that have been stopped and that have thrown out laterals should be thinned to the number required to cover the allotted space so that the wood may be thoroughly ripened in the sun. Once the fruit is gathered, the roots must be given ample water and the border dressed with lime. The foliage should be syringed and ventilation freely given.

## Gathering and Marketing

In picking a peach considerable art is required. The fruit must be ripe before it is gathered. A peach that is picked only partly ripe is deprived of all its bouquet and half its sweetness. Although ripe, if it has been well grown it will still be attached to the tree with a considerable degree of tenacity, and because it is ripe, its delicate bloom and tender, succulent substance are readily injured by the slightest uneven pressure. The fruit must be gripped by every muscle in the hand. The palm must be in close contact with the peach, the fingers and thumb each exerting the minimum of necessary pressure all round the fruit that will remove it from the plant. When the fruit is picked it must be placed in shallow boxes lined with cotton wool or very soft wood wool. These are carried into the packing-shed, where the fruit is graded with as little handling as is absolutely necessary and placed in shallow boxes, usually twelve fruit in a box. The fruit is well supported with wool so that it will not move when travelling, but is sufficiently exposed to allow buyers to appreciate the quality. Grading is carried out, having regard to size and colour. A good colour is the best indication of a good flavour. Although this is not an absolutely invariable rule, colour counts more in a peach than anything else.

# THE GREENHOUSE

## Peaches Suitable for Forcing under Glass

| *Early* | *Mid-Season* | *Late* |
|---|---|---|
| Dr. Hogg | Royal George | Barrington |
| Duke of York | Violette Hative | Princess of Wales |
| Duchess of Cornwall | | Sea Eagle |
| Hale's Early | | |

## Nectarines Suitable for Forcing under Glass

| *Early* | *Late* |
|---|---|
| Early Rivers | Pine-apple |
| Elruge | River's Orange |
| Lord Napier | Spenser |

## Insect Pests of the Peach and Nectarine

Peaches and nectarines sometimes suffer from attacks of greenfly, the Green Peach Aphis (*Myzus persicæ*) and the Leaf-curling Peach Aphis (*Anuraphis amygdali*), feeding on the young leaves (causing leaf-curl) and on the blossoms. These can be kept in check with a tar-oil wash in December or with nicotine or derris and soap in spring and summer. Peach Scale (*Lecanium*) may also occur, but can be killed with strong lime-sulphur or with tar-oil washes. Red Spider (*Tetranychus telarius*) is the chief pest. The same species attacks hops and is troublesome on almost all glasshouse plants; it hibernates as an adult, and emerges in the spring and soon causes silvering or browning of the foliage. The lime-sulphur applied at bud-break for Peach Leaf-curl will also destroy Red Spider.

## Diseases of the Peach and Nectarine

### Leaf-curl (*Taphrina deformans*)

This disease is commonly found on peaches grown in the open, and, to a less extent, on those grown under glass. It also attacks nectarines and almonds. Chiefly the leaves are affected. These become crinkled and swollen and, when young, are yellowish in colour with tinges of red. The older the leaf, the more pronounced are the symptoms and the more striking is the red coloration. When the fungus is producing spores, affected leaves develop a whitish bloom mostly on the upper surface. Diseased leaves ultimately wither and die prematurely, and this saps the vitality of the tree, and in bad cases, causes the immature fruits to drop. The shoots are sometimes attacked.

Infection of the leaves in early spring is believed to arise from spores that have passed the winter dormant on the tree, possibly entangled in the bud-scales; the disease is favoured by a wet spring. Affected leaves produce large numbers of spores throughout the spring and early summer, and these serve to spread the disease to healthy leaves.

[*R. A. Malby*

Peach "Princess of Wales"

[R. A. Malby

Strawberries in the Greenhouse

*Control.*—Good control can be obtained by spraying with lime-sulphur at 3 per cent., or with Bordeaux Mixture at 8–12–100, just as the buds are bursting. The collection and burning of diseased leaves are also helpful.

## PINE-APPLE (*Ananas sativa*)

This fruit is a native of tropical America, and was first introduced into Great Britain at the end of the seventeenth century. Its cultivation is now rarely attempted, as imported fruit is usually obtainable; while cultivation here is costly. Where a quantity is desired, it is usual to set apart structures for the plants in various stages of growth.

In all cases provision must be made for plunging beds, where there should be plenty of hot-water pipes for keeping a high temperature without the need to overheat them and so produce a dry atmosphere. Provision should be always made for admission of ample light. This is a most important factor in the cultivation of pine-apples, as it is conducive to keeping the plants dwarf and sturdy.

The plunging beds should be arranged so that the plants are nearly touching the glass when fixed in position. Hot-water pipes should pass beneath the staging of slate or wood which supports the plunging beds, which should consist of good oak leaves or tin and should be from 2–3 feet deep, so as to maintain heat for a long period. Ventilation should be given chiefly from the top, but where possible provision should be made to admit side air near the pipes in case it should be necessary during the summer.

The soil should consist of light fibrous loam to which should be added about one-fifth part of fibrous peat. Some charcoal and crushed bones to the extent of half a bushel to about five barrow-loads of the compost should also be included. This should be prepared beforehand, and should always be made warm before it is used. Pine-apples will never succeed in a compost that becomes at any time close and retentive or in the least sour from being over-wet. They need never be placed in a pot larger than a 12-inch, and require an average minimum temperature of from 70–75° F. both by day and night. Watering should always be conducted with great care, particularly in the winter, and sufficient should always be given thoroughly to soak the " ball ". The water should be of a temperature equal to that of the house. Syringing should be done throughout the season the plants are growing, and should be carried out at closing time in the afternoon. As the fruit commences to ripen, water must be withheld and a much dryer atmosphere maintained, otherwise the flower will be affected.

P

## Propagation

This can be carried out by seeds, which should be sown in shallow pans of light, sandy soil and placed in a bottom heat of about 85° F. and covered with bell-glasses, the seedlings being pricked out when large enough to handle. Crowns—that is, the top of the fruit—can be utilised, or suckers that are produced just below the fruit. These should be inserted in sandy soil and placed in a close, warm temperature, say 75° F. Cuttings of the stem, with dormant eyes, may be taken when suckers are scarce. These should be cut into pieces, or can be laid intact in shallow boxes, being covered with at least an inch of light soil. The dormant buds will break into growth, and they can be removed carefully when large enough, being treated as seedlings and potted-up in clean pots.

## Diseases and Pests

Mealy Bug and White Scale are the most destructive pests the pine-apple is subject to. One method of dealing with them is to place the affected plants head-downwards over a bed of fermenting horse manure, in a frame that is kept closed for an hour; or paraffin may be applied in the proportion of a wine-glass of paraffin to a gallon of warm soft water, the plants being laid on their sides and the mixture syringed carefully into the plant. The whole of the paraffin must afterwards be carefully washed off with warm water and with some force.

## Varieties

For winter fruiting: *Smooth-leaved Cayenne,* and *Black Jamaica.* For summer fruiting: *The Queen* and its sub-varieties *Ripley Queen* and *Fairy Queen.*

## STRAWBERRY (*Fragaria*)

Forced strawberries are usually the first of the new fruit of the year.

Strawberries are forced in pots in the glasshouse. In forcing them half the battle can be won by getting runners as early as possible and growing them on for all they are worth. Runners should be taken from maidens growing in the open and which were planted the previous year. All the bloom should be picked off the plants from which runners are to be taken, and the runners should be pegged down to the soil in sunken 3-inch pots in June. Time is one of the most important factors. The little plant has to be grown and matured, with a well-ripened crown, within about three months. As soon as the roots are showing well round the ball on the 3-inch pot, the plants should be potted into 6-inch pots.

# THE STRAWBERRY

## Compost and Potting

A strawberry revels in a strong loam, from a pasture of this nature, dug 5 or 6 inches deep, and chopped fine, not sifted. This makes an excellent potting soil for a 6-inch pot, and is better used freshly dug. Add *well*-rotted dung and a 6-inch pot of good, fine bonemeal to each barrow-load of soil. If the soil is well-chosen—i.e., is not too heavy and adhesive—brick-rubble and lime can be dispensed with. Pot very firmly and keep the " ball " well down. The crowns will form upwards. Keep the soil 1 inch down from the rim of the pot. Strawberries are thirsty subjects in August, and in the forcing house. These plants will grow very fast, but they will do their best work towards the end of September. Space them out as they increase in size. Light and air must get all around them. Ultimate success depends on a well-grown, well-ripened crown.

With the fall of the year, watering may be eased off; but the plant must never be dry while it is growing. By the middle of October the plants will have finished their work and soakings of rain, which were invaluable in September, will not be helpful in the winter.

## Wintering

The plants may be turned on their sides, or placed in a cold house or frame, preferably the former. A plant that is to be forced must be properly rested. *For this reason the dormant period is of as much importance as the growing*. Frost plays a very important part in the scheme. There is a diversity of opinion amongst growers as to the value of frost in such cases, but in the experience of many advanced growers 8° or 10° degrees of frost at the end of October or beginning of November on the plants that are to be forced early is invaluable. It fixes a definite and early date to the resting stage, and the plants start better and grow stronger as the result.

It stands to reason that the roots, protected only by the thin walls of the pot, will not resist frost, and the pots must of necessity be protected with litter. If the winter is severe the plants are better removed to a cold house.

## Temperature and Ventilation

Bottom heat for a strawberry plant is unnecessary and useless. It is a full hardy plant, and will stand intense frost, and thrives best in a cool soil.

If the plants are brought into the forcing house on the 1st of January—a very good time for starting the work—a night temperature of 45° F. with a day temperature of 50° F. for the first fortnight should be the maximum. This may be increased

227

during the next fortnight by 5°, allowing a further rise of 5° during sunshine. Air is of great importance, and the ventilators should never be closed when these temperatures can be maintained with them open. These temperatures may be sustained until the plants bloom, when a minimum day temperature of 60° F. increasing to 70° F. with the sunshine and ample air, and a night temperature of not less than 55° F. will be correct. It might be well to mention here that the brightness of the fruit and the quality of the colour depend immensely upon temperature and a liberal supply of water. A strawberry grown too slowly or slightly short of water—not necessarily actually dry— will be dull and seedy. The flavour of the fruit depends largely on sunshine. The water supply must be ample. If the plant really suffers once from dryness it will almost invariably mildew. The strawberry in its native element lives near the ground. Soaked by the dews, it sets its fruit abundantly.

The atmosphere should be kept reasonably moist. It is not necessary to make a special effort to keep a dry atmosphere during the pollination period. Ample ventilation will do all that is required. An arid atmosphere is, indeed, fatal to fertilisation. Rabbit tails need seldom be resorted to at this period of the year.

Spider will not attack the plant if the house is clean and the plant is not deprived of water at the roots.

Plants placed out of reach against the glass are invariably neglected at some time or other. They are much better grown on stages.

## Thinning and Ripening

Should more than twelve berries have formed on any plant, they must be thinned out, only the largest and best-shaped berries being retained. Once the fruits commence to swell, weak liquid manure should be applied once a week. As soon as the fruit begins to turn colour, the temperature must be gradually lowered, freer ventilation should be given, and syringing and the application of manure water must stop.

The berries may be prevented from becoming soiled by contact with the soil by each being supported on a short prong of wood pushed into the soil below the berry.

### TOMATO (*Lycopersicum esculentum*)

This is a native of Mexico and South America, also found in the East Indies, but was probably introduced there by the Spaniards.

In the southern parts of England, in favourable seasons, tomatoes can be grown in sheltered situations in the open

228

air, preferably against a south wall or fence, and with suitable varieties, in average seasons in almost all districts quite good crops can be obtained in the open.

The majority of tomatoes imported from abroad are picked before they are ripe, and the ripening which takes place on the voyage yields a result very different from that consequent on the natural ripening which takes place on the plant itself.

The tomato is a half-hardy plant, and requires an abundance of light and a moderate degree of heat to ripen it properly. At the same time a close atmosphere is fatal to success, and whatever structure is employed, a free supply of air is necessary.

## Sowing

Seed may be sown in September, December, February, and March. The beginner would do well to sow seed in February and March, $\frac{1}{4}$ inch deep and 1 inch apart, in pans of fine soil covered with glass and placed close to the glass in a warm greenhouse or moderately warm frame (night temperature, 55° F.; day temperature, 60° and 65° F.). The pans should be shaded from the strong sun till the seeds germinate. Seed sown in February should produce fruit in July. As soon as two leaves appear on the seedlings they should be pricked-off into seed-boxes, about twenty plants in each box, and when they are well rooted they should be potted-up singly into 3-inch pots, with the roots $\frac{1}{2}$ inch below soil level. Seed may also be sown in June and July to furnish tomatoes throughout the winter.

## Soil

The soil for potting should consist of turfy loam and one-eighth part of well-rotted dung with a little bone flour. This compost must be stored for some days previously in the greenhouse, so that it may acquire the same temperature as that from which the plants are taken. The seedlings should be watered sparingly until the roots are established, otherwise they are liable to " damp-off ".

In a small greenhouse it is well that these young seedlings should be kept near the glass, to keep them short-jointed. As they grow, they should be moved on into larger pots, and in about ten or twelve weeks they should be ready for planting out into borders, 18 inches apart in the row, or into the final pots, some 10 inches in diameter, in which they are to be fruited. The first truss of bloom must be formed before the plants are finally planted out. Potting should be very firm. Very early crops must be grown in 10-inch pots. In order that the fruit shall ripen quickly, only three or four trusses of bloom should be carried.

**229**

## Manuring

Over-manuring definitely tends to unfruitfulness, and no manure which has not fully fermented must be used. It is desirable to add a pinch or two of kainit or nitrate of potash at intervals through the growing season.

## Watering

Generous watering is essential at every period of growth, though a permanently saturated condition of the soil is, of course, undesirable. Insufficiency of water during the growing period is likely to make the skins crack. If proper drainage is afforded and the atmospheric conditions are suitable, over-watering is unlikely. In any case, it is useless merely to sprinkle the surface of the soil. Sufficient water should be given to saturate down to the roots, and no more should then be given until another soaking is called for.

## Training

In the ordinary tomato house the plants are almost invariably supported with string. The string is either tied to the stem of the plant near the ground or to a short stake adjacent to the plant, and is then attached to an overhead wire about 6 feet high. The string is twisted around the stem of the plant during the early growth, and the later growth is tied to the string just as if it were a stake. In small houses wires should be stretched 9 or 10 inches from the glass, and the plants may be trained along these under the glass. All side shoots may be nipped off, only the flower-trusses being allowed to break from the main stem. When tomatoes are trained on wires near the glass, it is customary to remove side shoots on the early parts of the growth but as the season advances, side shoots are invariably trained in. The plants should have their heads pinched out as soon as they reach the top of the wires. The flower is cleistogamic, and " shaking " is often advised to aid fertilisation.

## Temperature and Ventilation

Although warmth is necessary, over-heating is to be avoided. A night temperature of 55–60° F. and a day temperature of 60–70° or 75° F. should mark the extremes. Ample ventilation must be given, and air should always be admitted when it is possible to maintain the required temperature with the ventilators open. In hot weather ventilation may be given all day and all night.

## Picking

As soon as tomatoes have reached a certain stage of develop-

230

ment—that is to say, are mature and ripening—picking may commence. The fruit should be picked with the stalk intact. Fruit that is required for immediate sale or consumption should be quite ripe before it is gathered. Fruit that has to travel some distance to market should be picked, in warm weather, early in the morning, when reddish yellow. Blemished, mal-formed, and small fruits, if ripe, should also be removed.

### Grading and Packing

Tomatoes are graded by hand and eye, except in the case of large growers, who employ special grading machines. Under the Agricultural Produce (Grading and Marketing) (Glasshouse-grown Tomatoes) Regulations 1930, tomatoes are graded as follows :—

A.1. Sound, firm, round, smooth-skinned fruit of sufficient maturity to ensure ripening during normal time of marketing and distribution, each fruit weighing from $\frac{1}{16}$ to $\frac{1}{3}$ lb. White tissue is used for packing this grade.

B. Sound, firm, uniformly-coloured fruit, too large or irregular in shape for A.1. grade. $\frac{1}{12}$ to $\frac{1}{4}$ lb. each. Blue packing-paper is used to denote this grade, and according to size the fruit may be labelled " Large Blues " or " Small Blues ".

B.N. Fruit in edible condition. May be irregular in shape and slightly blemished, but not sufficiently to affect keeping quality. $\frac{1}{12}$ to $\frac{1}{4}$ lb. each. Brown packing-paper is used to denote this grade.

B.W. Sound, firm, small fruit, unsuitable for other grades. Below $\frac{1}{12}$ lb. in weight. Blue and white packing paper denotes this grade.

Under the National Mark tomatoes are graded :—

A.1. Sound, firm, uniformly coloured, mature fruit of the following weights : 3 to 6 to the lb. ; 5 to 8 to the lb. ; 8 to 12 to the lb. ; 11 to 14 to the lb. ; and 13 to 16 to the lb. Pink packing-paper is used for the first and second sizes, pink and white for the next two sizes, and white for the last.

The fruit should be carefully packed into padded and lined packages, the colour of the packing-paper denoting the grade of the fruit. The fruit should be placed in layers, eye upwards.

### Marketing

Tomatoes are usually sent up in 12-lb. boxes, No. 12 chip-basket, No. 3 veneer box and the strike. In the early part of the season 6-lb. boxes, No. 6 chip-basket, No. 4 veneer box and the

6-lb. wicker handle basket are sometimes employed, but the 12-lb. weight is more satisfactory for large quantities. All packages should be fully labelled.

## Diseases and Pests

The tomato is subject to attacks by numerous diseases and pests. *Tomato Collar Rot*, *Tomato Root Rot*, *Tomato Sleepy Disease*, and *Botrytis* are diseases which must be taken seriously and dealt with drastically. *Collar Rot*, which name describes the disease, appears to be due to high soil temperature combined with low atmospheric temperature; *Root Rot*, known amongst growers as " Fusarium ", is most dangerous where borders are cold and the atmosphere of comparatively high temperature; *Sleepy Sickness* usually occurs in heavily manured borders, and is seldom seen where humus content is low; *Botrytis*, an autumnal disease, attacks fruit at calyx and leaves and stems through wounds. Increase fire heat and air temperature. Diseased plants should be destroyed by burning as soon as the fruit is gathered. *Tomato Black Stripe*, *Mildew*, *Buckeye*, *Tomato Blight*, *Mosaic* (frequently confused with Chlorosis) and *Chlorosis* may occur, but these are not usually so serious, and are usually due to atmospheric conditions, or bad cultivation.

The pests that seriously affect tomatoes under glass are not numerous, but each can be devastating if neglected. Above ground a sharp lookout must be kept for *Caterpillars*, *Red Spider*, or *White Fly*; and underground *Eelworms* and *Wireworms* may cause damage. Although cultivation costs may be considerably increased, there is no insuperable difficulty in getting rid of *Red Spider* or *White Fly*. It is just a matter of setting about the job in a businesslike manner with proper insecticides. A minute chalcid wasp (*Encarsia formosa*), a successful parasitic enemy of *White Fly* under glass, has in recent years been widely distributed among growers through the agency of the Cheshunt Glasshouse Research Station, and the distribution of growers' stock has carried the parasite to innumerable greenhouses. *See* section on Diseases and Pests, page 600.

If the houses are clean when the crop is planted and the correct cultural practice is followed, neither *Red Spider* nor *White Fly* should prove troublesome.

## Varieties

*Britain's Best*, *Best of All*, *Evesham Wonder*, *Golden Queen*, *Perfection*, and, for early sowing, *Craig* (not Ailsa Craig), *Market King*, *M.P.*, *Sutton's Earliest of All*, *Sutton's Early Market*, and *Sunrise*.

# CHAPTER XVI

# ALPHABETICAL LIST OF GREENHOUSE PLANTS

NOTE.—*The words in the brackets following the species and varieties indicate first the colour of the flowers, then the time of blooming, and lastly the average height in inches, unless otherwise indicated, to which the plants may be expected to grow.*

**Abelia,** *Caprifoliaceæ.*—Hardy and half-hardy evergreen and deciduous shrubs, which in mild, sunny, sheltered positions may be grown out-of-doors. Elsewhere they require to be grown under glass.

*Culture.*—Take cuttings with a " heel " in late summer and strike in a frame or layer in August. Plant out in March or October in a sunny position against a south wall and in well-drained peat, loam, and leaf-mould, or pot-up for the cool greenhouse (temperature 45–65° F. winter, 55–65° F. summer).

*Pruning.*—Trim to keep in shape only, cut off dead blooms and thin out old wood after flowering. The flowers are borne on the current year's growth.

*Species.*—*A. floribunda* [Mexico] (purplish rose, June–July, 48 in.); *A. triflora* [Himalayas] (pinkish white, Aug.–Sept., 10–12 ft.); *A. Schumannii* [West China] (rosy pink, June–Aug., 36–40 in.); and the hybrid *A. grandiflora* [garden origin] (pinkish white, Aug.–Sept., 36–48 in.).

**Abroma augusta,** *Sterculiacea.*—A warm greenhouse evergreen shrub from Madagascar, with purple flowers during July and August. Use loam and peat in equal proportions. Seed should be sown in heat in March or cuttings of half-ripened wood in April, placed under a bell-glass in strong heat. Pot-on when rooted (temperature 65–75° F. summer, 50–55° F. winter).

**Abrus precatorius** (Crab's-eye Vine or Weather Plant), *Leguminosæ.*—Native of the Tropics, with rose and white flowers from March to May, seeds bright scarlet with a black spot, used in bead-work; climber for the warm greenhouse. Cuttings may be struck in sand under glass or seed sown in the spring in ordinary soil. Cut out the old and weak wood in the spring.

**Abutilon** (Indian Mallow or Flowering Maple), *Malvaceæ.*—A genus of handsome, half-hardy shrubs excellent for decoration in the greenhouse or for sheltered beds and borders. There are many beautiful hybrids, but they are not so commonly grown at the present day. In the greenhouse it forms a good pillar subject or is useful for training along the roof of the conservatory if planted out. The flowers are pendant from the stalk, and the petals being generally incurved at the top, the flowers assume a somewhat globular form. All flower from August to November, and grow 18–72 inches high. Some varieties have beautifully variegated foliage.

*Culture.*—For bedding-out increase by means of cuttings of young wood, 5 inches in length, struck in moderate heat (60° F.), during the previous autumn, or early in February. Grow on, and, if for summer bedding, plant out about the end of May. Otherwise pot-up into 6- to 8-inch pots in March. Two parts fibrous loam to one part of peat and sand makes a suitable compost. Greenhouse temperature should range from 60–65° F. in summer to 45–55° F. in winter. Seed may be sown in pans in a warm greenhouse (70° F.) in March and the seedlings potted-on and hardened off. Plants in pots must be well-drained and freely watered. A little liquid manure may be given during the summer months. Abutilons are subject to attacks of Hollyhock Rust (*Puccinia malvacearum*).

*Pruning.*—Trim and cut out old wood in February.

*Species and Varieties* (most of which are hybrids of *A. Darwinii*).— *A.* " Boule de Neige " (white); *A. Darwinii* [Brazil] (orange, with blood-red veins, summer, 36–48 in.); *A.* " Firefly " (scarlet); *A.* " Golden Fleece" (yellow); *A. insigne* [Colombia] (white or rose, with heavy veining and markings, red and purple, autumn and winter, good for roof of conservatory); *A. megapotamicum* [Brazil] (red and yellow, 24–30 in.; does not require so much heat); *A.* " Milleri" (orange, mottled foliage); *A.* " Red Gauntlet " (dark red); *A.* " Royal Scarlet " (shining scarlet); *A. Savitzii* (yellow and green foliage); *A. Sellovianum* [Brazil] (light purple); *A. striatum* var. *Thompsonii* (mottled green-and-yellow foliage); *A. venosum* [Mexico] (golden orange, veins blood-red); *A. vitifolium* [Chile] (lavender-blue, nearly hardy, can be grown against a wall in the south; leaves turn golden yellow in autumn).

**Abyssinian Banana** (see **Musa Ensete**).

**Acacia** (**Mimosa**), *Leguminosæ.*—Most of these evergreen trees and shrubs are greenhouse shrubs not sufficiently hardy to plant in the open, except in warm, sheltered borders during the summer months. *A. dealbata* is the feathery-leaved plant usually known as **Mimosa**, and bears its yellow, tassel-like flowers at about the New Year. It thrives well in the cool greenhouse. It is considered by many authorities to be a variety of *A. decurrens*, the Green Wattle.

*Culture.*—Sow seed when ripe, or take cuttings of half-matured wood with a " heel " and strike in a close frame in July or August in sandy peat or loam. The seed should previously be soaked in warm water for four or five hours. Pot-up seedlings singly as soon as possible and stand near the glass in a warm greenhouse. In the warm greenhouse (temperature 55–70° F. winter, 60–75° F. summer) *A. armata* and *A. Riceana* will flower in early spring. Pot-up in summer after blooming, in 6- to 10-inch pots, using a compost of equal parts of loam and peat (or leaf-mould) with a little sand. Water freely, except in winter. Give liquid manure or soot-water while growing. Stand in a sheltered position out-of-doors in summer and take in again in September.

*Pruning.*—Cut back straggling shoots after flowering.

*Species.*—*A. armata* (Kangaroo Thorn) [Australia] (yellow, Jan.–March, 3–10 ft.); *A. Baileyana* [Australia] (yellow, Jan.–May, 3–20 ft.); *A. dealbata* (Mimosa or Silver Wattle) [Australia] (yellow, Jan.–May, 3–50 ft.); *A. Drummondii* [Australia] (pale yellow, Feb.–May, 4–6 ft.);

*A. hastulata* (pale yellow, Feb.–April, **3–4** ft.) ; *A. lineata* [New South Wales] (solitary yellow flowers in March, compact bush, **3–5** ft.) ; *A. longifolia* (Golden Wattle) [Australia] (yellow, April–May, **12–50** in.) ; *A. longifolia* var. *mucronata* [Australia] (yellow, Jan.–March, **18–50** in.) ; *A. platyptera* [Swan River] (solitary yellow flowers in March ; branches broadly winged, **3–4** ft.) ; *A. Riceana* (Tasmania) (lemon-yellow, Feb.– April, **18–40** in.).

**Acalypha,** *Euphorbiaceæ.*—Handsome foliage plants for the warm greenhouse, with the exception of *A. hispida*, which is remarkable for its long spikes of crimson flowers. All succeed in a mixture of loam and leaf-mould, and are propagated by cuttings of half-matured growth taken below a joint. They root readily in a little warmth. These should be grown as young plants for effect.

*Species and Varieties.*—*A. Godseffiana* [New Guinea] (foliage plant, leaves green with yellow margin, 10 in.) ; *A. hispida* (*Syn. A. Sanderi*) (Red-hot Cat-tail) [E. Indies and Burma] (has long spikes of red flowers, sometimes 18 in. long) ; *A. Wilkesiana* [South Sea Islands] (bronzy-green leaves mottled red ; there are several well-marked varieties of this species).

**Acantholimon,** *Plumbaginaceæ.*—Dwarf evergreen plants suitable for the alpine house, with sharp-pointed leaves. They succeed best in dry soil. Raised by cuttings early in the autumn or by layers in the spring ; may also be raised from seed as soon as ripe.

*Species.*—*A. acerosum* [Armenia] (pink flowers, June–July, 4 in.) ; *A. glumaceum* [Asia Minor] (pink flowers, June and July, 6 in.) ; *A. venustum* [Cilicia] (pink, June and July, 9 in.).

**Acanthophippium** (see Chapter on **Orchids**).

**Acanthus** (Bear's Breech), *Acanthaceæ.*—A hardy perennial useful for beds, borders, and for decoration in the cold greenhouse, specially noted for the beauty and luxuriance of its foliage. It is claimed that it was the leaves of this plant that suggested the Corinthian style of architecture. It likes a sunny, sheltered site with light soil.

*Culture.*—Sow seeds in heat in February, or propagate by means of division in April or October. Pot-up and place in the greenhouse.

*Species.*—*A. mollis* [S. Europe] (lilac, pink, or white, Aug., 40 in.) ; *A. mollis* var. *latifolius* (rose, summer, 24 in.) ; *A. spinosus* [S. Europe] (purplish pink or white, July and Aug., 40 in.).

**Acer,** *Aceraceæ.*—Of the family, the Japanese Acers are very decorative as pot-plants for the cool greenhouse. Plant in a good loamy compost with leaf-soil and sand. Propagated by budding or grafting on the common species, which are raised from seed. They are also propagated by layers. *Acer negunda variegata.*—The popular variegated maple commonly known as the "Box Elder". A decorative pot-plant for the cool greenhouse. Can be planted outside during the autumn and winter.

*Species and Varieties.*—*A. palmatum* (Japanese Maple) ; *A. palmatum atropurpureum* ; *A. palmatum dissectum* ; *A. palmatum ornatum* ; *A. palmatum reticulatum.* All decorative as foliage plants.

**Achillea,** *Compositæ.*—This genus includes one or two dwarf-growing perennials that are useful for cultivation in shallow pans in the alpine house (see Chapter on the **Alpine House,** page 141).

**235**

*Species and Varieties.*—*A. ageratifolia* [Greece] (white, May and June, 6 in.) ; A. *Herba-rota* [France] (white, May, 6 in.) ; *A. Kellereri* [garden origin] (white flowers and fine grey foliage, May and June, 6 in.) ; *A. moschata* [Italy] (white, June, 6 in.) ; *A. tomentosa* [Europe] (yellow, June and July, 8–10 in.) ; *A. umbellata* [Greece] (white, June, 4–5 in.).

**Achimenes,** *Gesneraceæ.*—A genus of beautiful, tuberous-rooted plants suitable for the living-room or greenhouse, and especially adapted for culture in hanging baskets. They combine great individual beauty with a variety of rich and brilliant colours rarely to be met with. Some of them are remarkable for their peculiar markings, others for their large, handsome, tubular flowers, while all are so effective as amply to recompense the amateur for his care and attention. The hybrid varieties are numerous, and the blooms are white, orange, rose, crimson, scarlet, blue, and purple, some being diverse in colour and beautifully marked and veined.

*Culture.*—Use a compost of equal parts of leaf-mould, loam, and silver sand. Plant five to six tubers 1 inch deep in a 5- or 6-inch pot in February, with growing ends inclined towards the centre and their root-ends towards the circumference of the pot, cover them with about an inch of compost, and place in a house with a temperature of 55–60° F. Shade from the hot sun and feed with liquid manure when well rooted. To keep up a succession commence starting them in heat in January and continue until May. The stems should be supported, or they will fall down and become injured. Dry-off after flowering, and when the foliage is dead lift the rhizomes and store.

*Propagation.*—Propagate by offsets in February, or by cuttings in May under glass in a temperature of 55–65° F. Seed may be sown in winter or early spring in shallow pans of sandy loam and peat. They should be covered with glass and placed in slight bottom heat.

*Species.*—*A. coccinea* [Jamaica] (scarlet) ; *A. grandiflora* [Mexico] (red, summer, 15 in.) ; *A. Harveyi* [Mexico] (scarlet, summer, 12 in.) ; *A. longiflora* [Mexico] (blue) ; *A. longiflora alba* (white) ; *A. tubiflora* [Mexico] (white, March).

*Varieties.*—*A. Admiration* (reddish purple) ; *A. Celestial* (pale mauve) ; *A. Pink Perfection* (rose-magenta). All grow from 12 to 18 inches high, and flower normally from July to September, but in the warm house they flower somewhat earlier.

**Acidanthera,** *Iridaceæ.*—A group of beautiful bulbous plants for a cool greenhouse, thriving in well-drained soil, and increased by offsets in the spring or seed sown in the spring.

*Species.*—*A. bicolor* [Abyssinia] (creamy-white flowers blotched with chocolate, Sept. and Oct., 18–24 in.) ; *A. b.* var. *Murielæ* is a much larger flowered variety ; *A. capensis* [S. Africa] (whitish, Sept. and Oct., 12–18 in.).

**Acis** (see **Leucojum**).

**Acokanthera spectabilis** (Winter Sweet), *Apocynaceæ* [S. Africa].—Clusters of Jasminum-scented white flowers during January and February. *A. venenata* (*Toxicophlæa Thunbergii*) [Bushman's Poison] (clusters of sweet-scented flowers, Feb. and March). A charming plant for the warm greenhouse. Propagated by seeds sown in spring or cuttings of half-ripened wood. Cut back after flowering, and pot-up in compost of three parts loam, one part sand, one part leaf-soil.

**Acradenia Frankliniæ,** *Rutaceæ* [Tasmania].—A cool greenhouse shrub, 4–6 feet, with white flowers and trifoliate leaves. Cuttings of side shoots in spring should be placed in a closed propagating frame. When rooted, pot-up in a good loamy mixture.

**Acriopsis** (see Chapter on **Orchids**).

*Species.—A. floribunda* [Philippine Islands] (green, pink, April and May) ; *A. latifolia* [Straits Settlements] (whitish yellow with reddish-purple stripes and spots, April and May).

**Acroclinium** (see **Helipterum**).

**Acrostichum aureum,** *Polypodiaceæ* [Tropics].—A handsome, strong-growing fern for the warm greenhouse, and best treated as an aquatic (40–60 in.). For Culture see **Ferns**.

**Acrostichum crinitum** (see **Elaphoglossum crinitum**).

**Acrostichum latifolium** (see **Elaphoglossum latifolium**).

**Acrostichum scandens** (see **Stenochlæna palustris**).

**Ada aurantiaca** (see **Orchids**).

**Adam's Needle** (see **Yucca**).

**Adders Tongue Fern** (see **Ophioglossum vulgatum**).

**Adenandra,** *Rutaceæ.*—Small, semi-hardy shrubs which do well in the cool greenhouse in a compost of sandy peat.

*Culture.*—Pot-up when new growth starts and stand in semi-shade. Water well while growing and syringe overhead. Keep just moist when dormant.

*Pruning.*—The flowers are borne on the ends of last year's shoots, and they must be pruned accordingly : prune hard back after flowering (summer).

*Propagation.*—Strike cuttings of young shoots in sandy peat in a frame in spring or sow seed when ripe.

*Species.—A. amœna* [S. Africa] (red) ; and *A. fragrans* (Breath of Heaven) [S. Africa] (rose-pink).

**Adenanthera pavonina,** *Leguminosæ* [Tropical Asia].—A shrub for the warm greenhouse (yellow and white, July, 36–40 in.).

*Propagation.*—Can be propagated by seeds sown or cuttings, in sandy loam and placed in a warm temperature.

**Adenocarpus viscosus (A. frankenioides),** *Leguminosæ* [Canaries].—Allied to the Cytisus or Broom, and at one time included with them. It requires the same treatment, and bears showy yellow flowers in April and May.

*Culture*—Seeds are sown in March, and cuttings may be struck in May or June, and kept under glass.

**Adiantum Capillus veneris** (Maidenhair Fern), *Polypodiaceæ.*—This is one of the most beautiful ferns we possess, and is suitable for growing in the cool and cold greenhouse.

*Culture.*—Pot-up firmly in March, using a compost composed of two parts peat to one part of loam, sand, and charcoal. Shade and water liberally in summer, but moderately in winter. (See Chapter on **Ferns**.)

**237**

*Propagation.*—Propagate by means of spores sown under glass in March, or by division during the same month. In dividing do not pull the roots apart, but cut them with a sharp knife. (See also **Ferns.**)

*Species.*—*A. cuneatum* [Brazil]. This and its varieties are the most popular of all Maidenhair Ferns for warm or cool house. *A. Moorei* [Peru], a graceful fern (12–18 in.). *A. pedatum* [N. America] is one of the hardiest of Maidenhair Ferns, ideal for the cool greenhouse (12–15 in.); *A. peruviana* [Peru] (20–30 in., warm greenhouse); *A. rubellum* [Bolivia] (reddish, 18–20 in., warm greenhouse); *A. trapeziforme* [Tropical America]. A very handsome fern with fronds 30–40 inches long, warm greenhouse. (For cultivation, see Chapter on **Ferns.**)

*Variety.*—*A. Farleyensis* [Barbados], a very handsome fern, requires a warm, moist atmosphere.

**Adonis amurensis** (Pheasant's Eye), *Ranunculaceæ* [Manchuria].— A useful little perennial recommended for cultivation in the alpine house (which see).

*Species.*—*A. pyrenaica* (yellow, March and April, 12 in.); *A. vernalis* (Spring Adonis) [Europe] (yellow, March, 10 in.).

**Ærides** (see Chapter on **Orchids**).

**Æschynanthus** (see **Trichosporum**).

**Æthionema,** *Cruciferæ.*—This is a very attractive group for the alpine house, grown in pans in well-drained soil, with three parts of loam, one part of leaf-soil, and one part equal proportions of sand and mortar-rubble. Increased by seeds sown as soon as ripe and stood in cold frame, or by cuttings of young shoots placed uuder a hand light in July.

*Species.*—*A. armenum* (pink, May and June, 3–4 in., dwarf, somewhat resembling *A. pulchellum*); *A. grandiflorum* [Palestine] (pink or rose, in long racemes, 9–18 in.); *A. iberideum* [E. Mediterranean] (white, April–June, 6 in.); *A. pulchellum* [Persia] (rose, May–June, 5 in.).

**African Corn Lily** (see **Ixia**).

**African Honeysuckle** (see **Halleria lucida**).

**African Violet** (see **Saintpaulia ionantha**).

**Agapanthus,** *Liliaceæ.*—Beautiful African lilies blooming outdoors in August and September, and combining graceful foliage with large, handsome heads of blossom. They grow to a height of from 18 to 40 inches. The blue species *A. africanus* is very lovely, and when mixed with gladioli the effect is unique. *A. a. albus,* a white variety, forms a good companion and makes an excellent contrast. *A. a.* var. *minor,* a dwarf, small-flowered form, is also useful, especially for pots. These plants will thrive in the open in warm, sunny borders in rich sandy loam and leaf-mould, but are more suitable for greenhouse. In the warm greenhouse *A. africanus* may be had in flower in midsummer.

*Culture.*—Pot-up in March, using compost of two parts loam to one part leaf-mould, rotten manure, and sand. A 9-inch pot will be sufficiently large for a good strong plant, but a large pot or tub is required for several plants. This is the most effective way of growing these plants, and they will go for several years without re-potting.

During summer give abundance of water and liquid manure twice a week. In winter protect from frost, and give water sparingly. Greenhouse temperature 45–65° F. winter, 60–65° F. summer. Large plants may be stood out during the summer.

*Propagation.*—Sow seed under glass or propagate by means of division in March.

*Species.*—*A. africanus* (blue); *A. africanus albus* (white); *A. africanus maximus* (light blue); *A. africanus minor* (blue).

**Agapetes,** *Ericaceæ.*—A beautiful group of evergreen shrubs bearing a profusion of brilliant tubular flowers.

*Culture.*—Succeeds best in the moister part of the cool greenhouse. Thrives in peat, three parts fibrous loam, one part sand. Like most members of the *Ericaceæ*, it objects to lime in any form.

*Propagation.*—Propagated by cuttings of half-ripened wood under glass in a warm greenhouse; can be successfully grafted on roots of *Macleania* in early spring, and should be kept close in a warm greenhouse.

*Species.*—*A. buxifolia* [Himalayas] (rich red, 12–36 in.); *A. macrantha* (syn. *Thibaudia macrantha*) [India] (white veined with red marking, 12–30 in.); *A. setigera* [Himalayas] (deep red, 12–30 in.).

**Agathea cœlestis** (see **Felicia amelloides**).

**Agathosma fœtidissima** (see **Barosma fœtidissima**).

**Agave,** *Amaryllidaceæ.*—The best-known kind is the *Agave americana* or American Aloe, which in the cool greenhouse usually grows from 20 to 40 inches high, though much larger plants are obtainable. It is a slow-growing plant, consisting of a number of broad, fleshy, bluish-green leaves with sharp points, and throwing up from the centre a long flower-spike, from which proceed branchlets sustaining white flowers tinted with a yellowish-green colour. The popular belief that the plant dies after flowering is a fallacy. The main stem does, certainly, but offshoots from the base carry on the growth. It is chiefly used for the ornamentation of terraces when placed in tubs or large pots, and is equally effective for this purpose in the greenhouse. (Average temperature 45° F. winter, 60° F. summer.)

*Culture.*—Pot-up firmly every four or five years in a well-drained compost of two parts of rich fibrous loam to one part of leaf-mould, sand, and brick-rubble. Water freely in summer, but keep on the dry side in winter. The plants may be stood out-of-doors in summer.

*Propagation.*—Propagate by means of seed sown in heat in February, or by offsets with a piece of root in the summer. Seedling plants will take two to three years to become of effective size.

*Species.*—*A. americana* [Mexico] (20–40 in.); *A. americana variegata* (variegated); *A. densiflora* [Mexico] (40 in.); *A. filifera* [Mexico] (24–36 in.); *A. guttata* (see *Manfreda guttata*); *A. maculosa* (see *Manfreda maculosa*); *A. variegata* (see *Manfreda variegata*); *A. Victoriæ-Reginæ* [Mexico], an attractive foliage plant; *A. virginica* (see *Manfreda virginica*).

**Agave Cactus** (see *Leuchtenbergia principis*).

**Ageratum** (Floss Flower), *Compositæ.*—A delightful little Mexican plant, best treated as a half-hardy annual, covered all through the summer with dense masses of blue-and-white flossy flowers. They make excellent pot-plants for growing in the cold greenhouse.

*Culture.*—Sow seed thinly in light soil late in April or in May, in a warm, sunny spot outdoors or under glass, in pans or deep boxes of half loam and half leaf-mould. Prick off as soon as possible, and pot-up for flowering. Cuttings may also be struck in a frame in August.

*Varieties.*—*Blue Perfection* (amethyst-blue); *Houstonianum* (lilac-blue); *Imperial Dwarf* (deep blue); *Lavender Band* (lavender); *Little Blue Cloud* (dwarf blue); *Little Dorrit* (pale blue); *Snowflake* (white).

**Aglaonema,** *Araceæ.*—Handsome foliage plants for the warm greenhouse, many of them bearing bright-red berries during the winter. They require a warm, moist atmosphere, and a compost of fibrous loam, peat, and leaf soil, with some sand added. Propagate by means of cuttings struck in sandy peat, or by division. Also by seed.

*Species.*—*A. costatum* [Moluccas], foliage plant, shining green leaves, midrib ivory-white and blotches of white; *A. pictum* [Sumatra], foliage plant, dark-green leaves blotched with white.

**Albizzia lophantha,** *Leguminosæ.*—[Australia] (pale yellow, 6 ft.). Same cultural conditions and treatment as **Acacia.**

**Albuca Nelsonii,** *Liliaceæ* [Cape of Good Hope].—Greenhouse bulb which bears white flowers with reddish-brown stripe, almond scented (24–36 inches).

*Culture.*—Place in sandy soil with a little warmth.

*Propagation.*—Suckers can be taken from the old bulb, or leaves taken off with a scale, or they can be raised from seed.

**Aletris capensis** (see **Veltheimia viridiflora**).

**Allamanda,** *Apocynaceæ.*—A handsome group of stove evergreens, mostly climbers.

*Culture.*—These can be either planted out in the border or in pots. They require a rich loam with addition of leaf-soil and sand. Temperature 50–60° F. winter, 60°–70° F. summer. The plants should be kept dry during autumn and winter.

*Propagation.*—Cuttings root readily in sand with bottom heat and moist atmosphere.

*Pruning.*—They should be pruned back in the winter or early spring.

*Species.*—*A. cathartica* [S. America] (yellow climber); *A. c.* var. *Hendersonii* [Guiana] (yellowish orange), climber; *A. c.* var. *Schotii* (rich yellow, striped throat); *A. neriifolia* [Brazil] (golden yellow), bush or half climber; *A. violacea* [Brazil] (light violet), climber.

**Allium,** *Liliaceæ.*—A genus of hardy, bulbous plants which grow from 6 to 18 inches high, and bloom from May to July. When grown in the open they like a sunny position and light loam to which a little sand and leaf-mould have been added. *A. molle* [S. Europe] (yellow, March and April, 10 in.) is useful in the cold or alpine house. Pot-up in pan in well-drained soil in October. *A. neapolitanum* (Daffodil Garlic) [Europe] (white, 12–18 in.), may be grown in pots and forced in the early spring. Propagate by means of seed in frame in slight heat in March, or by offsets in October.

**Alloplectus,** *Gesneraceæ.*—Useful evergreen plants for the warm greenhouse (temperature 50–60° F. winter, 65–75° F. summer). They

**PLATE 9**
A variety of *Pelargonium* with strongly
variegated leaves in the first stages of flowering.

are allied to *Gesnerias*, and require similar treatment and light rich soil. They root readily from cuttings in sandy soil with bottom heat.

*Species.—A. Schlimii* [Tropical S. America] (flowers yellowish scarlet, shading violet) ; *A. sparsiflorus* [Brazil] (foliage plant, leaves green above, violet or purplish violet beneath).

**Allosorus crispus** (see **Cryptogramma crispa**).

**Almond** (see **Prunus Amygdalus**).

**Alocasia,** *Araceæ.*—Handsome stove foliage plants.

*Culture.*—Pot in rough, fibrous loam, peat, and sand. A little chopped-up sphagnum moss may also be used. The plants require heat and moisture with liquid manure when growing, and should be shaded during bright weather.

*Propagation.*—Propagated by offsets and division in the spring. Some may be raised from seed sown in pots and placed in a warm house.

*Varieties.—A. Lowii* [Borneo] (olive-green leaves with silvery bands, underside purple) ; *A. Sanderiana* [Philippines] (sagittate leaves, glossy green with metallic shadings, white margins, and veins). There are also many beautiful hybrids, e.g. *A. hybrida, A. Chelsonii,* and *A. Sedenii.*

**Aloe,** *Liliaceæ.*—A large genus of greenhouse, evergreen, succulent plants with thick, fleshy leaves, generally in the form of a rosette. The flowers are borne in clusters on straight, upright stems. All the species contain a bitter principle known as Aloin, which is used in medicine as a purgative.

*Culture.*—Plant firmly in summer, in pots or tubs, in a compost or sandy loam, peat, and well-rotted manure. Stand in a sunny position, and water freely in summer, but sparingly in winter, during which time the plants should be kept in a temperature of 45–60° F.

*Propagation.*—Propagate by means of suckers in spring or sow seed in heat (temperature 60° F.).

*Species and Varieties.*—There are many of these, including *A. arborescens* [S. Africa] (leaves pale bluish green borne in rosettes on stems 12 ft. high) ; *A. brevifolia serra* [S. Africa] (leaves bluish green with serrated margins) ; *A. ciliaris* [S. Africa] (red and green, half climber), all the year round ; *A. concinna* [Zanzibar] (leaves serrated and spotted white) ; *A. laterita* [Tropical Africa] leaves reddish brown spotted yellow and pale green) ; *A. Perryi* [Socotra] (red, yellow, and green, 12 in.), said to be the source of Bitter Aloes of commerce ; *A. spicata* [S. Africa] (leaves green, spotted yellow, and edged with orange spines) ; *A. variegata* (Partridge-breasted Aloe) [S. Africa] which succeeds in a cool greenhouse or as a window plant ; *A. vera* [Atlantic islands] (yellow).

**Alonsoa** (Mask Flower), *Scrophulariaceæ.*—A pretty, half-hardy, chiefly dwarf annual suitable for sunny beds in the open or for pot culture in the cool greenhouse.

*Culture.*—Sow seed thinly in February or March under glass, using a compost of half leaf-mould and half sandy loam (temperature 55° F.). Propagation may also be effected by means of cuttings of young wood struck in sandy loam in bottom heat (temperature 55–60° F.) in March or August. If some of the plants are " stopped-back " periodically

Q

through the summer, they can be lifted and potted-up in September for flowering indoors during autumn and winter.

*Pot Culture.*—Pot-up in 5- to 6-inch pots, keep close (temperature 60–65° F.) for three weeks, then give ample light and air, but eliminate all possibility of draughts. Pinch out young shoots occasionally to encourage bushy growth. Water carefully and give weak liquid manure until the buds show colour.

*Species and Varieties.*—*A. incisifolia* [Peru] (greenhouse shrub) ; *A. linearis* [Peru] ; *A. Mutisii* [Peru], and *A. Warscewiczii* [Peru]. All are scarlet-flowered, except *A. Mutisii*, which is salmon-pink and grows some 18 inches high.

**Aloysia** (see **Lippia**).

**Alpine Rose** (see **Rhododendron ferrugineum** and **R. hirsutum**).

**Alpinia** (Gingerwort), *Zingiberaceæ.*—Herbaceous perennials for the warm greenhouse. Apart from their beautiful flowers, some are remarkable for their beautiful foliage. They like moisture and pot room in the growing season, and should be planted in rich, sandy soil and peat.

*Propagation.*—This is effected by seeds or by division, placed in a warm, moist atmosphere.

*Species.*—*A. mutica* [E. Indies] (bright yellow, crimson, and white, 30–40 in.) ; *A. Sanderæ* [New Guinea], beautiful variegated foliage ; *A. speciosus* (*Syn. A. nutans*) (Shell Flower) [E. Indies] (yellow and pink, 36–50 in.) ; *A. vittata* [South Sea Islands] (flowers red, foliage pale green with yellow bars or stripes).

**Alsophila**, *Cyatheaceæ.*—A graceful group of tree ferns for the cool house.

*Culture.*—Use peat and loam.

*Propagation.*—From spores (see Chapter on **Ferns**).

*Species.*—*A. Cooperi* [Queensland], of smaller stature than many, suitable for small greenhouse ; *A. excelsa* [Norfolk Islands and Australia] ; *A. oligocarpa* [Colombia] ; *A. Rebeccæ* [Australia], the cold house.

**Alstrœmeria** (Herb Lily or Peruvian Lily), *Amaryllidaceæ.*—Tuberous-rooted perennials, some of which are hardy and suitable for sunny borders in the open, but both hardy and half-hardy kinds are useful for pot cultivation in the cool greenhouse.

*Culture.*—Propagate by means of division in autumn, and pot-up singly in well-drained 7–8-inch pots, using a compost of rich and light loam and leaf-mould with a little sand and old mortar-rubble in it. Water freely and feed with liquid manure in summer when growing, reduce water gradually after flowering and keep just moist, but secure from frost in winter. Do not re-pot every year, but top dress with a layer of new soil. Seed may be sown in gentle heat from March to September (temperature 45–50° F.), the seedlings being pricked off singly into small pots and subsequently potted on in the following May or June.

*Species.*—*A. aurantiaca* [Chile] (orange-red, May–Aug., 30–36 in.) ; *A. chilensis* [Chile] (red, pink, or yellow, July, 30 in.) ; *A. pelegrina* * [Chile] (pinkish with purple spots, July, 12–18 in.).

* Greenhouse species.

242

# GREENHOUSE PLANTS

**Amarantus,** *Amarantaceæ.*—Half-hardy annuals growing from 12 to 36 inches high and flowering in the open from July to October. They thrive in sunny beds or borders with shallow, light soil, or in the cool greenhouse where they are useful for decorative purposes.

*Culture.*—Sow seed thinly in March in gentle heat (50° F.). Pot-up singly in sandy loam, harden off in May, and plant out in a sunny position in June or pot on for flowering in the cold greenhouse in 6-inch pots using a compost of two parts loam to one part of leaf-mould and a little sand.

*Species.*—*A. caudatus* (Love-lies-bleeding) [from the tropics of the Old World] (crimson, July–Oct., 10–40 in.) ; *A. c.* var. *ruber* (crimson with carmine foliage, July, 30 in.) ; *A. c.* var. *tricolor* (Joseph's Coat) (crimson, with red, yellow, and green foliage, July, 36 in.) ; *A. hypochondriacus* (Prince's Feather) [N. American annual with crimson plumes].

**Amaryllis Belladonna** (Belladonna Lily), *Amaryllidaceæ.*—This beautiful species is very variable in the size and colour of its flowers, frequently producing flowers variously shaded from white to a reddish or purplish hue. There is only one species which comes from Cape Colony. Some of the varieties are *A. Belladonna rubra major, A. Belladonna pallida,* and *A. Belladonna Parkeri,* a cross between *A. Belladonna* and *Brunsvigia Josephinæ.* This plant succeeds outdoors in well-drained soil at the foot of warm plant-house walls. The bulbs should be planted during the summer, when they are dormant, being covered with about 6 inches of rich, loamy soil mixed with leaf-mould and silver sand. If planted too deep they do not flower freely. The blooms are produced during August and September, and the leaves, in common with those of many South African bulbs, during the winter and spring. Leave the bulbs in the ground, but protect with fibre in winter.

*Greenhouse Culture.*—If grown in the greenhouse they require very large pots or pans. Even so, they do not flower freely ; thus in the colder parts of the country they should be planted out in raised beds in a cool greenhouse, or in a cold frame.

*Propagation.*—This may be carried out by means of seed sown in spring or summer in pots or pans of peaty loam in a warm greenhouse, the seedlings being potted up singly as soon as fit to handle.

**Amasonia calycina,** *Verbenaceæ.*—Tropical American sub-shrub, with yellow flowers with scarlet bracts in the autumn, 18–24 inches high, somewhat resembling **Clerodendron** and requiring the same treatment. *A. erecta* has white flowers with scarlet bracts.

**Amazon Lily** (see **Eucharis grandiflora**).

**Amelanchier canadensis, oblongifolia,** *Rosaceæ.*—These may be had in bloom in February in the cold greenhouse. A Canadian tree or shrub with white flowers which are followed by attractive purplish-black berries in summer. It should be put in a pot or tub in the autumn and brought under glass early in the New Year. *A. lævis* [N. America], has white flowers with red bracts, the unfolding leaves being bronzy-red.

*Culture.*—Plant from November onward to early March in moderately light, moist, chalky soil in full sun. Prune only to cut out hard wood, and thin when necessary.

**243**

*Propagation.*—Sow seed when ripe in a frame, or strike cuttings 10–12 inches long in the open in October or November.

**American Cowslip** (see **Dodecatheon**).

**American Laurel** (see **Kalmia**).

**American Lotus** (see **Nelumbo lutea**).

**Amherstia nobilis**, *Leguminosæ*.—One of the noblest of flowering trees, a native of India, where it reaches a height of 40 feet. Succeeds best when planted out in a border in the stove house. The rich vermilion-coloured flowers only last about three days. It should be planted in strong loam. Place cuttings of half-ripened wood under glass with a bottom heat of about 80° F. A plant for the specialist.

**Amorphophallus titanum**, *Araceæ*.—This native of Sumatra is a most remarkable species of a genus of warm greenhouse plants which have tuberous rootstocks. It is a perennial, and produces a large inflorescence, followed by a solitary, much-branched leaf, 10 feet high. The spathe and spadix forming the inflorescence are blackish purple in colour, the former being about 3 feet across, and the latter 6 feet or more high. When fully developed the flowers emit a most objectionable odour.

*Culture.*—Large pots or tubs are necessary to accommodate the plants, and they require a rich, loamy compost with leaf-soil and sharp sand During the growing season copious supplies of water and generous feeding are necessary to build up the tuberous rootstock, which must be rested in a semi-dry condition during the winter months.

*Propagation.*—Propagate by seeds, offsets, or by division.

*Species.*—There are several other species of *Amorphophallus* in cultivation, the best known being *A. campanulatus* [India] (brownish red and black, 3 ft.); and *A. Rivieri* [Cochin China] (green, spotted with rose, 3 ft.).

**Amphicome emodi**, *Bignoniaceæ*.—An attractive, half-hardy little plant from India, some 12–18 inches in height, bearing pink, funnel-shaped flowers with orange-yellow throats in late summer. *A. arguta* [Himalayas] is a taller-growing species up to 36 inches in height, with pink or red flowers.

*Culture.*—Sow seed in slight heat (50–55° F.) in March in sandy loam. Transplant when fit to handle, pot-up singly for flowering in 3-inch pots of loam and leaf-mould with a little sand. Cuttings made from young side shoots may also be struck in slight heat in March, and potted on for flowering indoors.

**Amygdalus communis** (see **Prunus Amygdalus**).

**Anagallis** (Pimpernel), *Primulaceæ*.—Half-hardy, dwarf-growing annuals, suitable for a warm, sunny rock garden, for the alpine house or for the greenhouse.

*Culture.*—Sow seed thinly under glass in March (temp. 50° F.). Prick out 4 inches apart in boxes as soon as fit to handle. Pot on as required.

*Species.*—*A. indica* (blue-flowering annual from Nepal, trailer, summer); *A. linifolia* (W. Mediterranean region), a biennial or perennial; *A. linifolia* var. *collina* (rose or purplish, summer, 6 in.), can be propagated by cuttings taken in July or August. These thrive in sandy soil in a frame, placed under a bell-glass.

# GREENHOUSE PLANTS

**Ananas sativa** (Pine-apple), *Bromeliaceæ.*—Native of Tropical America. *A. s. variegata* is a very decorative foliage stove plant, with green leaves striped with white, cream, yellow, and red. (For Cultivation, see Pine-apple in **Fruit Under Glass.**)

**Andromeda** (Marsh or Wild Rosemary), *Ericaceæ.*—Hardy, evergreen, heath-like shrubs, which thrive in the sun in boggy or moist, peaty soil, and also make good pot-plants for the cold greenhouse. The flowers, borne in sprays at the end of the branches, are, in effect, like those of the Lily of the Valley.

*Culture.*—Pot-up in October. The roots should never be quite dry, but they will grow in well-drained fibrous loam if ample moisture is provided and no lime is present.

*Propagation.*—Propagate by means of ripe seed in pans or boxes under glass in October, or divide the roots or layer in September.

*Species.*—*A. polifolia* [Northern and Arctic regions] (rose-white, May and June, 20 in.).

*Varieties.*—*A. p. augustifolia* and *A. p. major.* These varieties of this attractive native shrub differ chiefly in the size or colour of the flowers or foliage.

**Andromeda floribunda** (see **Pieris floribunda**).

**Andromeda formosa** (see **Pieris formosa**).

**Andromeda japonica** (see **Pieris japonica**).

**Andropogon citratus** (see **Cymbopogon citratus**).

**Androsace** (Rock Jasmine), *Primulaceæ.*—This genus contains one or two choice little alpine plants suitable for growing in shallow pans in the alpine house. (See Chapter XI.)

**Androsace vitaliana** (see **Douglasia vitaliana**).

**Anemia,** *Schizæaceæ.*—There are several species of this handsome dwarf-growing fern suitable for the warm greenhouse.

*Culture.*—Use a compost of fibrous peat, leaf-soil, and sand.

*Propagation.*—Carried out by spores sown in sterilised soil, which when large enough are pricked out. (See Chapter on **Ferns.**)

*Species.*—*A. adiantifolia* [Tropical America] (15 in.) ; *A. hirsuta* [Tropical America] (12 in.) ; *A. Phyllitidis* [Tropical America] (18 in.) ; *A. rotundifolia* [Brazil] (18–24 in.).

**Anemone** (Windflower), *Ranunculaceæ.*—Several of the tuberous-rooted anemones are useful for flowering in the cold greenhouse or alpine house. They thrive in the sun or semi-shade, in a moist, light, rich, sandy loam.

*Culture.*—Pot-up in autumn in 6-inch pans and stand in a cold frame or greenhouse. Dress annually with fertiliser. Lift and store dry when the foliage dies down. Propagate by means of seed sown in a frame in October or March, or by division of the tuberous roots.

*Species.*—*A. alpina* [Europe] (purple and white, 10–15 in.) ; *A. alpina* var. *sulphurea* (yellow, 10–15 in.) ; *A. blanda* [Greek Anemone] (blue, rose, and white flowers, Jan.–March, 6 in.) ; *A. capensis* (white, tinged with pink, March, 12 in., cool greenhouse) ; *A. fulgens* [Greece, S. Europe, etc.] (scarlet flowers, March, 12 in.) ; *A. Hepatica* (Hepatica) [Europe] (red, white, and blue flowers, Feb., 6 in.) ; *A. hortensis* [S. Europe] (purplish-rose and whitish flowers, April, 8–10 in.) ; *A. palmata* [Mediterranean region] (golden yellow, May, 6 in.) (there are also pale yellow and white varieties) ; *A. Pulsatilla* (Pasque Flower) [Europe] (blue to reddish purple, March and April, 9–12 in.) ; *A. vernalis* (Shaggy Windflower) [Europe] (purple and whitish, March and April, 6 in.). All the species mentioned are suitable for the alpine house, and should be grown in pans, and kept plunged in a cold frame, except when in the alpine house in flower. (See Chapter on **The Alpine House.**)

**Anemopægma clematideum** (see **Pithecoctenium cynanchoides**).

**Angelonia** (Whispering Bells), *Scrophulariaceæ*.—There are several species, chiefly perennials. They are useful, easily grown greenhouse plants, suitable for table decoration, flowering most of the summer. *A. grandiflora* is an excellent winter-flowering plant, particularly the var. *alba*.

They succeed in light turfy loam, with peat, leaf-soil, and sand.

*Propagation.*—Cuttings of young shoots, in spring, strike readily under a hand light ; or they may be plunged in the propagating bed and given plenty of air daily. Seed sown in September will give a fine display in the late spring and summer. For a later display sow in the early spring. Prick out seedlings into small pots, later transfer to a 5-inch pot.

*Species.*—*A. cornigera* [Brazil] annual, (rich purple velvet dotted, 12 in.) ; *A. grandiflora* [S. America] (lilac, 20–24 in.). The variety *alba* is a very dainty plant. Can be had by sowing at intervals. *A. salicariæfolia* [S. America] (deep blue, Aug., 24–30 in.).

**Angiopteris evecta,** *Marattiaceæ* [India, Madagascar, etc.].—A handsome fern for the warm greenhouse, but suitable only for a large house where it can have plenty of room to develop. Its fronds grow from 6 to 10 feet long.

*Culture.*—The pots should stand in 2–3 inches of water. Spores are freely produced, but it is doubtful if seedlings have been raised in cultivation.

*Propagation.*—It can be easily propagated by the fleshy scales at the base of each frond. Each scale contains two dormant buds. These scales complete should be placed in sand, covered with sphagnum, and kept in a close case from three to five months. When the roots have formed they should be potted-up. Spring is the best time to plant the scales.

**Angræcum Sanderianum** (see Chapter on **Orchids**).

**Angræcum sesquipedale** (see **Macroplectrum sesquipedale**).

**Anguloa** (see Chapter on **Orchids**).

**Anhalonium Williamsii** (see **Lophophora Williamsii**).

**Anigozanthos coccinea** (Australian Sword Lily or Kangaroo's Foot), *Amaryllidaceæ* (red, June, 36 in.).—A cool greenhouse perennial which thrives in a turfy compost of peat and loam. Increased by division of the roots in the spring, or by sowing the seed in sandy soil in a cool house. A variety is *A. Manglesii* (green and red, 24–30 in.).

**Aniseed Tree** (see **Illicium**).

**Anœctochilus** (see Chapter on **Orchids**).

**Anogramma schizophylla (Gymnogramma schizophylla),** *Polypodiaceæ* [Jamaica].—Tropical fern. (For treatment see Chapter on **Ferns.**)

**246**

**Anomatheca** (see **Lapeyrousia**).

**Anopterus glandulosus,** *Saxifragaceæ.*—A greenhouse evergreen shrub from Tasmania which is nearly hardy, and bears drooping racemes of white flowers in the spring. It makes a useful pot plant, or it may be planted out in the border. Use a compost of sandy loam and peat, mixed in equal proportions. It may be propagated by cuttings of half-ripened wood struck in sandy soil, in a close frame, with a little bottom heat.

**Ansellia** (see Chapter on **Orchids**).

**Anthericum Liliago** (St. Bernard's Lily), *Liliaceæ.*—Hardy, tuberous-rooted perennials, which thrive in a warm, sunny border with moist, light, rich soil. In the cold greenhouse they grow to a height of 30 inches and carry white flowers in early summer. *A. L.* var. *Major* is larger than the type.

*Culture.*—Sow seed in the open in April, or propagate by means of division in October. Pot-up in a 6-inch pot in the autumn, using the above-mentioned soil, and place in the cold greenhouse. Give plenty of water in summer, but little in winter.

**Anthurium,** *Araceæ.*—A genus of stove and greenhouse perennials, several of which have highly decorative spathes; others have very beautifully marbled and decorative leaves.

*Culture.*—A humid atmosphere and a temperature of between 60° and 70° F. are required. The best compost is a mixture of lumps of fibrous peat, four parts of sphagnum moss, one part turfy loam, two parts silver sand, half part charcoal, and a few broken crocks. Good drainage is essential, and the plant should be inserted so that its crown is on a cone 3 inches above the pot. Water freely at the roots and syringe frequently.

*Propagation.*—Propagated by division in January, or by seed sown and placed in heat. This last method, however, is rather a slow process.

*Species and Varieties.*—*A. Andræanum* [Colombo] (orange-red flowers, summer, 12 in.); *A. grande* [garden origin], and *A. magnificum* [Colombo] (both handsome foliage plants). *A. Scherzerianum* (Flamingo Flower) [Central America] (scarlet, summer, 15–18 in.); and *A. Veitchii* [Colombo] (another handsome foliage plant).

**Anthyllis Barba-Jovis** (Jupiter's Beard), *Leguminosæ.*—A greenhouse, silky, evergreen shrub, with whitish or straw-coloured, clover-head-like flowers (March–April, 24–36 in.). It thrives in well-drained soil. *A. montana* [S. Europe] is a charming rock plant, suitable for pans in the alpine house (purple, June and July, 6–12 in.). The var. *rubra* is equally attractive, with reddish flowers. It is increased by seed or cuttings sown in sandy soil.

The alpine species is propagated by root division in the spring or autumn.

**Antigonon leptopus** (Mountain Rose or Love's Chain), *Polygonaceæ.*—An elegant greenhouse climber from Mexico with rose-coloured flowers, suitable either for pots or for planting out in the greenhouse border.

*Culture.*—Plant in good sandy loam and train shoots near the glass. Water freely when growing, but keep on the dry side when resting.

**247**

# THE GREENHOUSE

*Propagation.*—It is readily raised from seed sown in the spring and the resulting plants potted on when large enough; or from cuttings of half ripened growth placed in a warm propagating case in sandy soil.

**Antirrhinum** (Snapdragon), *Scrophulariaceæ.*—Herbs or semi-shrubs, of which several species are very popular garden plants, both for the outdoor garden and for the greenhouse. The most popular are the common varieties in many colours of *Antirrhinum majus*, which are particularly valuable as pot-plants for the greenhouse. Seed sown in August or September gives a good display in the spring. It should be sown in January or February for the following summer.

*Culture.*—They should be given a light, rich soil in a 5-inch pot and grown cool. Fine spikes are obtained by pinching off the side-growth.

*Propagation.*—All the species are readily raised from seed in a little heat. They should be pricked out when large enough and grown cool. They can also be raised from cuttings placed under a bell-glass in a little warmth. Some species are very suitable for pans in the alpine house.

*Species.*—*Antirrhinum Asarina* [S. Europe] is a procumbent plant with cream flowers, occasionally tinged with red. Suitable for the alpine house or for a basket in the greenhouse. *A. glutinosum* [Spain] (pale yellowish, white and striped red, 4–5 in., alpine house); *A. majus* (Common Snapdragon) [Europe] (various colours). Apart from the many coloured varieties, it also has peloric forms : *A. maurandioides* (*Maurandia antirrhiniflora*) [Mexico] (flowers violet or purple, 30–60 in.), a perennial climber, and a charming plant for the roof of a greenhouse. Plant in a 10-inch pot. *A. sempervirens* [Pyrenees] (creamy-white flowers, 5–6 in.), suitable for the alpine house. *A. speciosum* [California] scarlet or coral-red, 24–36 in.), a small evergreen shrub.

**Aotus gracillima,** *Leguminosæ* [W. Australia].—Pretty little early-summer-flowering, half-hardy, evergreen plants for the cool greenhouse, growing some 30–36 inches high and bearing spikes of yellow and red pea-shaped flowers in late spring.

*Culture.*—These plants like a sunny position and a mixture of sandy loam and peat for compost. Re-pot in summer after flowering, when necessary, and water well. Keep just moist in autumn and winter. Prune after flowering and syringe overhead to encourage new growth.

*Propagation.*—Strike cuttings of semi-ripe side-shoots in the shade, in sandy peat, in late summer.

**Aphelandra,** *Acanthaceæ.*—A genus of tropical plants, many of them very handsome both in flower and in foliage.

*Culture.*—Pot-up in the spring and grow in a compost of equal parts of fibrous loam, leaf-soil, and peat, with a good proportion of sand, in a warm, moist temperature (65° F.). The blossom-spikes appear during the summer and autumn, and they will benefit from gentle feeding with liquid manure. They should be removed to a warm, dry atmosphere, when they will last in perfection much longer.

*Propagation.*—Cuttings should be made in the spring from young shoots taken off with a " heel ". These should then be inserted in pots of sandy soil and plunged in heat. When rooted pot-on into 5- or

248

6-inch pots, and if they are not pinched off they will flower the same year.

*Species and Varieties.—A. aurantiaca* [Mexico] (orange, 12–24 in.); *A. fascinator* [New Grenada] (orange-scarlet, 15–18 in.); *A. nitens* [Colombia] (vermilion-scarlet, 18 in.); *A. squarrosa* [Brazil] (orange-scarlet, 12–15 in.); *A. s.* var. *Leopoldii* [Brazil] (citron-yellow, 12–18 in.); *A. tetragona* [Colombia] (brilliant scarlet, 2–4 ft.), the finest of the genus.

**Aphelexis** (see **Helichrysum,** in which this genus is now included).

**Aponogeton,** *Aponogetonaceæ.*—Ornamental, aquatic perennials grown in pots or tubs in good, rich, loamy soil. *A. distachyum* (Cape Pond Weed or Water Hawthorn) of the Cape of Good Hope is the best known. It can be increased by seed sown in pots and stood under tepid water, or by division taken off in spring. Being almost hardy, it can be grown in quite a cool house, and does grow outdoors in some parts of the country. It bears white, scented flowers throughout the summer. *A. fenestralis (Ouvirandra fenestralis)* (Lattice-leaf or Lace-leaf) [Madagascar]. This is a very interesting plant. The leaves are a curiosity in plant life, consisting of a tracery of nerves and cross-veins, or skeletonised leaves. It requires a warm greenhouse, but is un-successful in a jar or glass aquarium, owing undoubtedly to the excessive light. It should always be grown in the shadiest part of the house in a temperature of 65–70° F. A few water-snails or tadpoles can be placed in the water, as these help to keep down the Confervæ. When the plant is active in the spring it can be divided, using a rich compost such as that recommended for water-lilies. It should then be plunged not more than 15–18 inches below soft water. Hard water is injurious. The flowers are white, but great beauty lies in the submerged skeleton leaves.

**Aporocactus flagelliformis (Cereus flagelliformis)** (Rat's-tail Cactus), *Cactaceæ* [Tropical America].—This is a well-known greenhouse or window plant with prostrate stems and red or pink flowers, which is easily grown.

*Culture.*—It requires well-drained soil and a cool temperature. It is often grafted on to other cacti, and sometimes worked in various designs. It delights in full sun, and should be watered liberally during the summer.

*Propagation.*—Effected by seed or cuttings in light, sandy soil in a little warmth. *A. Mallisonii* is a hybrid of *A. flagelliformis* and *Heliocereus speciosus* (fiery-red flowers, June and July, 30 in.).

**Apple** [*Malus pumila—Pyrus Malus*] (see **Fruit under Glass).**

**Apricot** [*Prunus Armeniaca*] (see **Fruit under Glass).**

**Aquilegia** (Columbine), *Ranunculaceæ.*—Hardy herbaceous perennials and biennials, that thrive in rather shady borders in the open, in moist, cool, well-drained, deep loam and leaf-mould. The newer long-spurred hybrids have now ousted the old *A. vulgaris* from popularity, and should be grown in preference to it. They are also useful for green-house culture.

*Culture.*—Sow seeds in spring or summer in sandy soil under glass, transplant when fit to handle, and pot-up as required for flowering in

**249**

the greenhouse. These plants will flower the following May and June. Although truly perennials, columbines should be treated as biennials, and some should be raised annually, as a few invariably die out each year.

*Species and Varieties.*—*A. alpina* [Europe, etc.] (violet-blue, May and June, 10 in.) ; *A. cœrulea* [N.W. America] (pale blue and white, May–July, 12–18 in.) ; *A. chrysantha* [New Mexico] (golden yellow, May–July, 39 in.) ; *A. flabellata* [Japan] (bright lilac, pale purple, or white, 12–15 in.) ; *A. f. nana-alba* is a dwarf white variety. *A. longissima* [N. America] (pale yellow, 18–24 in.) ; *A. Skinneri* (N. America] (crimson and gold, 18 in.).

**Arabian Jasmine** (see **Jasminum Sambac**).

**Arabis alpina,** *Cruciferæ*. (For Culture see Chapter on **Alpine House.**)

**Arabis** (Rock Cress).—Showy spring-flowering plants, chiefly for the rock garden, but several are useful for growing in pans for the alpine house.

*Culture.*—They require a well-drained soil, and when not in bloom should be plunged in ashes in a cold frame.

*Propagation.*—Cuttings of young growth should be taken after the flowers are over, and placed in sandy soil in a close frame or handlight. Also seed can be sown as soon as ripe and placed in a cold frame.

*Species.*—*A. androsacea* [Taurus] (white, 2 in., foliage covered with silky hairs) ; *A. aubretioides* [Cilician Alps] (pale pink, 4 in.) ; *A. muralis* (*A. rosea*) [Italy] (rosy purple, 10 in.).

**Arachnanthe moschifera** (see **Renanthera** in Chapter on **Orchids**).

**Aralia,** *Araliaceæ*.—A genus of hardy and greenhouse foliage shrubs. The latter thrive in the cool greenhouse in a compost of two parts of loam to one part of leaf-mould and peat with a sprinkling of sand added, and also make good room plants. *A. chinensis* (Chinese Angelica) is a handsome Chinese foliage plant growing to a height of 40–50 inches. *A. japonica* (see *Fatsia japonica*). *A. spinosa* (Hercules Club or Devil's Walking-stick) is a North American shrub, with handsome foliage, of sub-tropical appearance.

*Culture.*—Pot-up in 5- to 6-inch pots in March and re-pot when necessary.

*Propagation.*—Strike cuttings in sandy soil in a propagating case in March. Pinch back to make bushy and pot-on as required.

**Aralia elegantissima** (see **Dizygotheca elegantissima**).

**Aralia Sieboldi** (see **Fatsia japonica**).

**Aralia Veitchii** (see **Dizygotheca Veitchii**).

**Araucaria excelsa** (Norfolk Island Pine), *Coniferæ*.—An ornamental foliage plant suitable only for culture in the cool greenhouse or living-room. It makes an excellent room plant, and has bright green, flat branches emanating from the main stem so as to form horizontal platforms, the one practically equidistant above the other. Other greenhouse kinds are *A. Bidwillii* (Bunya-Bunya Pine) [Moreton Bay] ; *A. Cunninghamii* [Australia], and *A. Rulei* [New Caledonia].

*Culture.*—Pot-up in March in a comparatively small pot, using a compost of two parts of sandy loam to one part of leaf-mould (tem-

# GREENHOUSE PLANTS

perature 50° F. winter, 40° F. summer). Give plenty of fresh air, and water well in summer; never let the roots get too dry or too wet.

*Propagation.*—Propagate by means of cuttings of the leading shoots 5–6 inches long in heat (temperature 60° F.) in October, or by " ringing ". Seed may be sown under glass (temperature 50° F.) in March.

**Araujia (Physianthus albens), Asclepiadaceæ** *sericofera* [S. Brazil].—A half-hardy summer-flowering climber for cultivation in the cold greenhouse. It thrives in a mixture of sandy loam and leaf-mould, running up to a height of 18 feet or more, and bearing small white flowers in summer.

*Culture.*—Strike cuttings of young shoots in a propagating case in March. Pot-on as required and give ample water. Prune established plants in early spring, cutting side-shoots well back to direct strength into the main stem.

**Arctocalyx Endlicherianus** (see **Solenophora Endlicheriana**).

**Arctotis,** *Compositæ.*—A group of beautiful plants, most of which may be grown outside during the summer. A number of them, especially the half-shrubby kinds, are charming pot-plants for the cool greenhouse, flowering April to July.

*Culture.*—They require a well-drained soil, and most can be propagated by cuttings at almost any time of the year, pricked in pots of very sandy soil and placed in gentle warmth, but they should be kept uncovered and moderately dry, or they will rot. *A. aureola*, which does not propagate very readily from cuttings, should be grafted on the more robust *A. aspera arborescens*, which roots readily. They can be raised from seed, which should be sown as soon as ripe in very sandy soil. Prick out at an early stage and grow on cool.

*Species and Varieties.*—*A. aspera* var. *arborescens* [S. Africa] (white above, pink beneath, summer, 20–24 in.) ; *A. aureola* [S. Africa] (rich orange with dark centre, summer, 20–24 in.) ; *A. revoluta* [S. Africa] (deep golden yellow).

**Ardisia,** *Myrsinaceæ.*—These are evergreen shrubs, several species of which will flourish and fruit in a moderately warm greenhouse (temperature 55–65° F.). *A. crenulata* [China] is a favourite species. In winter its bright-red berries, which last nearly six months, and its evergreen leaves render it invaluable in the greenhouse.

*Culture.*—Pot-up in March into 5- or 6-inch pots, using a mixture of loam and peat for the soil. Water regularly while growing, and keep just moist in winter. Prune only to keep the plant a good shape, cutting back over-long side branches in March.

*Propagation.*—Propagate by means of cuttings struck in sand under glass in March. Seed may also be sown in January in a propagating case. Pot-up singly into small pots as soon as possible. Re-pot as necessary, and finally move into 5- or 6-inch pots. The seedlings take from three to four years to reach a useful size.

**Areca** (Betel-nut Palm), *Palmaceæ.*—These are greenhouse palms with long, bright-green feathery leaves, which grow from 10 to 25 feet high. They thrive in the shade in a compost of two parts loam to one part leaf-mould and sand.

*Culture.*—Pot-up annually in March or April, using 6- to 10-inch pots. Sponge the leaves frequently with warm soft water, and give water in moderation, but regularly. Temperature of the house 50° F. in winter to 60° F. in summer.

*Propagation.*—Sow seed 1 inch deep in heat in March.

*Varieties.*—*A. Aliceæ* [Australia] and *A. Catechu* [Tropical Asia].

**Areca Baueri** (see **Rhopalostylis Baueri**).

**Areca lutescens** (see **Chrysalidocarpus lutescens**).

**Areca sapida** (see **Rhopalostylis sapida**).

**Aregelia,** *Bromeliaceæ.*—A group of plants with ornamental foliage allied to the pine-apple and suitable for a warm, moist greenhouse. They are mostly natives of Guiana and Brazil, and not of very much horticultural value.

**Arenaria** (Sandwort), *Caryophyllaceæ.*—Dwarf-growing rock plants, several of which are suitable for growing in pans in the alpine house, needing the same treatment as **Arabis.**

*Species.*—*A. grandiflora* [Europe] (white, 6–8 in.), usually solitary white flowers; *A. montana* [S.W. Europe] (6 in.), large solitary flowers; *A. purpurascens* [Pyrenees] (purplish flowers, 3 in.), foliage forms a mossy carpet.

**Arisæma fimbriatum** (Fringed Calla), *Araceæ* [E. Indies].—A striking and handsome pot-plant for the warm greenhouse during the summer. It grows to a height of 12 inches, with a purple-and-white-striped spathe, the spadex ending with a graceful, pendulous, feather-like appendage. Dry off the tubers when the leaves turn yellow, after flowering. Pot-up in the spring in rich soil when growth commences. Propagate by offsets or by seed, which should be sown and stood in a warm temperature.

**Aristea corymbosa** (see **Nivenia corymbosa**).

**Aristolochia,** *Aristolochiaceæ.*—A genus of hardy, deciduous, and greenhouse perennial climbers. Some species, such as *A. macrophylla* (*A. Sipho*), the "Dutchman's Pipe" (brown and yellow, June–July, 20 ft.), are hardy in sheltered situations and thrive in the cold greenhouse, but others are suitable only for the warm house.

*Culture.*—*A. macrophylla* (*A. Sipho*) [N. America]. Sow seed under glass in March, or take cuttings under glass in April. Plant out in the following March in a warm, sheltered situation, or in a tub or bed in the greenhouse, in a mixture of light, sandy loam and leaf-mould. Water well while growing, and keep just moist when dormant. Thin out unwanted and weak wood during the spring.

*Greenhouse Species.*—*A. elegans* (Calico Flower) [Brazil] (purple and yellow); *A. Goldieana* [W. Africa] (green and yellow); *A. grandiflora Sturtevantii* (Pelican Flower) [W. Indies, Central and S. America] (purplish white). The flowers of the latter are often as much as 12 inches across and 24 inches or more long, terminating in a long, slender, ciliated tail.

**Armeria** (Sea Pink or Thrift), *Plumbaginaceæ.*—Although perfectly hardy in the rock garden, several of them are useful when grown in pans for the alpine house. They should be potted up in the autumn or early spring, in well-drained soil, and plunged in a cold frame until they commence to flower. Propagated by seed sown as soon as ripe, or by division after the flowers are over.

*Species.*—*A. argyrocephala* [Greece] (white, May–June, 6 in.); *A. cæspitosa* [Spain, Portugal] (pink, April, 3 in.).

**Artemisia** (Wormwood), *Compositæ.*—Aromatic herbs or small shrubs which are suitable for pans in the alpine house, their silvery foliage being very attractive.

*Species.*—*A. argentea* [Madeira] (12 in.); *A. frigida* [Siberia and N. America] (10 in.); *A. pedemontana* [Piedmont] (5 in.); *A. sericea* [Siberia] (5 in.).

**Arum Lily** (see **Zantedeschia**).

**Arum palæstinum** (Black Calla or Solomon's Lily), *Araceæ* [Palestine].—The spathe is greenish outside, blackish purple within. It has handsome leaves, and is the most popular of the **Arum**, being grown in pots as an oddity. Cultivation the same as **Amorphophallus**.

**Arum sagittifolium** (see **Xanthosoma sagittifolium**).

**Aruncus sylvester** (**Spiræa Aruncus**) (Goat's Beard), *Rosaceæ* [N. America, N. Europe, etc.].—An ornamental perennial bearing large, showy panicles of white flowers, 30–40 inches long, in May and June. Requires the same treatment as **Astilbes**.

**Arundina bambusæfolia** (see Chapter on **Orchids**).

**Arundinaria**, *Gramineæ.*—A genus of bamboo, the hardy species of which thrive in the open in a moist climate and in a deep, rich loam, holding ample leaf-mould, with plenty of protection from north and east winds. All species save *A. japonica* quickly suffer from drought, and it is essential that they receive attention in dry weather if planted where the soil is apt to dry quickly.

*Culture.*—Propagate by means of division in May and plant in sheltered positions. Cut out dead wood in April. (See also **Bambusa** and **Phyllostachys**).

*Species.*—There are many half-hardy species for the warm greenhouse, such as *A. aristulata* [Brazil] (10 ft.); *A. Fortunei* [Japan] (30–36 in.); *A. Fortunei* var. *aurea* with yellow variegation, and *A. F.* var. *variegata alba* (24–30 in.) are both very pretty plants.

**Arundo** (Great Reed), *Gramineæ.*—An ornamental perennial grass which thrives in the open in semi-shade on slightly swampy banks, in light, rich loam, and grows to a height of 10 feet. It is very attractive, and some forms, such as *A. Donax* [S. Europe] and *A. D. variegata*, are much grown as pot-plants for decoration in the cool greenhouse (temperature 45–55° F. winter, 60–65° F. summer). *A. Donax* has sturdy, upright stems and long, narrow, bluish-green leaves. *A. D. variegata* has leaves striped with white.

*Pot Culture.*—Pot-up in March in large pots or half barrels in a compost of half-loam and half leaf-mould and a little sand. Water liberally from May to October, but keep only just moist in winter. Propagate by means of division in May.

**Asclepias curassavica** (Blood Flower), *Asclepiadaceæ* [Tropical America].—A showy and attractive half-hardy perennial, some 18–36 inches in height with erect clusters of bright-reddish orange-scarlet flowers in summer and early autumn. It thrives in the cool greenhouse when treated as an annual. Although *A. tuberosa* (Butterfly Weed or Pleurisy Root) is hardy, it makes a very handsome pot-plant, bearing bright-orange flowers in summer and autumn.

*Culture.*—Sow seed thinly in sandy soil in March and pot-up singly as soon as fit to handle in a mixture of loam and leaf-mould with a little peat added, and pot-on as required. After flowering the plants may be preserved if desired. Keep almost dry through the winter, and start again in early spring, first cutting back last year's shoots. As soon as new growth commences re-pot, pinching off the ends of the new shoots to encourage bushy growth. Cuttings of new shoots may be rooted in a propagating case in April if so desired.

**Asparagus** (Asparagus Fern), *Liliaceæ.*—This genus contains a number of hardy and greenhouse evergreen and deciduous climbing and trailing plants, which thrive in a compost of two parts loam to one part of leaf-mould, peat, and sand. The delicate, fern-like branches make these plants excellent for table decoration and for clothing the walls of the greenhouse.

*Pot Culture.*—Pot-up in March, using 6- to 10-inch pots. Syringe and water well in summer. The vigorous climbers—such species as *A. plumosus* and *A. asparagoides* (*Myrsiphyllum asparagoides*) [the **Smilax** of florists]—should have their stems trained up strings or wires stretched from the ground to the roof of the house, and running up within 3 or 4 inches of the back wall. *A. crispus*, *A. scandens*, and its var. *deflexus* (*A. deflexus*) and *A. Sprengeri* make excellent basket-plants. but care must be taken to see that the roots never become too dry. All species mentioned above are natives of South Africa.

*Propagation.*—Propagate by means of seed sown in March in heat (temperature 60–65° F.), by cuttings in a propagating case at the same period, or by division in March. If raised from seed, pot-off singly as soon as the seedlings can be handled. Give plenty of light, and keep the temperature steady at about 60° F. The hardy species do well in the open in a warm, sunny position in rich, sandy soil. (See also **Smilax.**)

*Species.*—*A. asparagoides* [S. Africa]; *A. crispus* [S. Africa]; *A. plumosus* [S. Africa] and var. *nanus*; *A. plumosus* var. *tenuissimus*; *A. retrofractus* [S. Africa]; *A. scandens* [S. Africa]; *A. Sprengeri* [Natal]; *A. verticillatus* [Persia].

**Asperula arcadiensis,** *Rubiaceæ* [Greece].—A charming plant for the alpine house. *A. Gussoneii* (Woodruff) [Sicily]. Pretty little alpine plants. (For Culture see Chapter on **Alpine House.**)

**Aspidistra** (Parlour Palm), *Liliaceæ.*—These are plants bearing dark-green, broad, lanceolate, and leathery leaves on long stalks. They usually accommodate themselves to indoor conditions, and are therefore favourite room and greenhouse plants. The flowers are very small and insignificant and grow close to the ground.

*Culture.*—Pot-up moderately firmly triennially in April, using a compost of two parts of peat and loam to one part of leaf-mould and sand. The pots should not be too large. Stand in the shade (temperature 50° F. winter, 60° F. summer). Sponge the leaves with warm, soft water when dusty, and water well and regularly during the summer.

*Propagation.*—Propagate by means of division in April.

*Species.*—*A. lurida*, the best known, is one of the few plants that remain uninjured by the fumes of gas, and is very popular as an indoor plant. There is also a variegated form, *A. l. variegata*. *A.* var. *punctata* has small whitish spots on the leaves.

**Asplenium** (Spleenwort), *Polypodiaceæ*.—Hardy and greenhouse evergreen ferns, growing from 2 to 36 inches high. The greenhouse varieties thrive in the shade in a mixture of half peat and half sandy loam and leaf-mould.

*Pot Culture.*—Pot-up in March, using a compost as above, and water liberally during the summer (temperature 50° F. winter, 60° F. summer). Propagate by means of spores under glass in July. (See Chapter on **Ferns.**)

*Species and Varieties.*—*A. Adiantum-nigrum* [Europe and Britain]; *A. bulbiferum* [Australia]; *A. caudatum* [Tropics]; *A. dimorphum* [Norfolk Is.]; *A. fontanum* [Europe and Central Asia]; *A. lunulatum* [S. Africa]; *A. myriophyllum* [S. America]; *A. Nidus* (Bird's Nest Fern) [Tropics of the Old World]; *A. Ruta-muraria* [Europe and Asia]; *A. septentrionale* [Europe and N. Asia]; *A. Trichomanes* [temperate regions].

**Aster, China** (see **Callistephus**).

**Astilbe,** *Saxifragaceæ*.—Although perfectly hardy, they are very useful decorative herbaceous plants for the greenhouse, either for forcing or for the cold house. They have fern-like foliage and bear graceful plumes of flowers. They are generally but erroneously called **Spiræa.**

*Species.*—*A. astilboides* [Japan] (white, 24 in.); *A. chinensis* [China] (flowers yellowish-white and pink with blue anthers, 18 in.); *A. Davidii* [China] (magenta to red, 3 ft.); *A. japonica* [Japan] (white, 18–24 in.). This is the plant usually grown in the greenhouse under the name of *Spiræa japonica*. *A. rosea* is a hybrid between *A. chinensis* and *A. japonica*. It bears pink flowers. There are several well-known hybrids of this, the best of which are " Peach Blossom " (light pink), and " Queen Alexandra " (deeper pink).

*Culture.*—They should be potted up as early as possible in the autumn in 5- or 6-inch pots in rich, well-drained soil. The pots should afterwards be plunged in ashes or fibre outside, when they will soon commence to root. They can then be placed in heat and forced as required, or grown on cool. Always give plenty of water. The pots can be stood in saucers of water when the plants are well furnished with growth.

*Propagation.*—They can be propagated by division in the spring. Plants which have been heavily forced should be planted out and rested for at least one year.

**Asystasia bella (Mackaya bella),** *Acanthaceæ* [Natal].—A beautiful evergreen shrub which can be grown either in pots or in the greenhouse border. It bears tubular white flowers, striped or netted red. It requires a compost of leaf-mould and loam in equal proportions, with a little sand added. During the winter it should be rested. Propagation is effected by planting cuttings of young shoots in April, in sandy soil in a close frame.

**Atamasco Lily** (see **Zephyranthes atamasco**).

**Athyrium Felix-fœmina** (Lady Fern), *Polypodiaceæ* [Europe and N. America].—A very graceful fern which, although hardy, is most useful

**255**

for the cold greenhouse. By many authorities the genus **Athyrium** is now included in **Asplenium**.

**Attalea amygdalina** (see **Maximiliana regia**).

**Aubergine** (Egg Plant) (see **Solanum Melongena** var. *esculentum*).

**Aubrieta (Aubrietia)** (Purple Rock-cress), *Cruciferæ*.—A useful group of plants for the rockery or dry wall. Some of the varieties make a very bright display planted in pans for the alpine house. They are mostly forms of *A. deltoidea*, a species from South Europe and Asia Minor.

**Aucuba japonica** (Spotted or Variegated Laurel), *Cornaceæ*.—A hardy, evergreen shrub, growing some 8 feet high, and well suited for shady places and town gardens in which the air is often close and smoky. It may also be grown in large pots for decorative purposes, in the cold or cool greenhouse, but it thrives out-of-doors in the shade in well-drained ordinary soil. There are many useful varieties with spotted and deep-green foliage. The male and female flowers are borne on separate bushes, and the two sexes should be grown near together. The female bush produces large bright-red berries in autumn. *Pot Culture.*—Pot-up from April to November, using a 6- to 12-inch pot and a good loam for soil, and place in the greenhouse with an average temperature of 45° F. winter, 60° F. summer. Cut back long weak shoots in May. To propagate, take cuttings and strike in frames or in the open in autumn, or sow seeds in a frame when ripe.

**Audoninia capitata (Diosma capitata)**, *Bruniaceæ*.—An ornamental greenhouse shrub, native of South Africa. It thrives under similar conditions to those afforded the South African Heaths, and should be given a potting compost consisting of sandy peat and loam. It forms a very useful subject for conservatory decoration, and will continue to flower over a lengthy period. The flowers, which are purplish mauve, are freely produced in crowded oblong spike-like terminal heads during spring. *Culture.*—Propagate by means of cuttings made from the small half-ripened side shoots inserted in sand under a bell-glass or in a small propagating frame. Re-pot after flowering or in September.

**Auricula** (Primula Auricula), *Primulaceæ*.—Auriculas are divided into two classes—namely, Show Auriculas and Alpine Auriculas, the latter being more hardy and easier to grow. Show Auriculas are classed according to the colour of the edge, there being *White-edged*, *Green-edged*, and *Grey-edged* varieties. If there is no edge beyond the ground colour, it is called a *Self*. Thus, there are four classes of Show Auriculas, all of which flower in the latter half of April and require the protection of a greenhouse. In the Alpine Auriculas, which may be single or double, the eye is yellow, cream or white; there is no edge, but the ground beyond the eye is generally shaded to a darker colour round the edge. Other flowers among the alpine species are self-coloured. The alpine varieties are very suitable for culture in the cold greenhouse. The flowering period is from March to May. The best compost is a good fibrous, rather heavy loam, adding a little decayed manure and leaf-mould, with a liberal addition of silver sand and a sprinkling of charcoal or wood ashes. *Culture.*—(Show Auriculas.) Sow in pans in a warm house on the

**PLATE 10**
A pot of *Saintpaulia* (African Violet). These
little perennials from Africa have become
very popular in recent years.

surface of a compost of half loam and half leaf-mould and gritty sand, when ripe, or from January to March. Moist moss should be kept over the surface of the soil until the seedlings are up, in order to prevent it from drying too quickly, and the moss should be kept moist by sprinkling with a fine syringe. When the seedlings have three or four leaves, transplant into 3-inch pots. The pots must be well-drained, and small ones must be used, the Auricula never doing so well in large pots as in small ones—4- to 5-inch pots are large enough for full-sized plants. It will take about two years from the time of sowing to raise plants sufficiently advanced to bear flowers. Where it is essential that the flowers shall come true to type, and in the case of choice specimens, it is better to propagate by means of offsets or root division in February or March, when vigorous growth is being made, or in August, when fresh growth is commencing after re-potting. If the offsets can be removed with roots attached, so much the better. They may be placed singly in 3-inch pots, or three in a larger pot. Keep the pots in the open in a cool, sheltered site, and remove to the cool greenhouse at the end of September.

The Auricula blooms, and is in full growth from February to June, when the plants should be removed from the glazed shelter under which they have been flowering, and placed in the open air on a shelf or stage having a north or north-east aspect. Under a north wall or ledge is a good situation. The plants should not stand on the ground itself, and will benefit if some glass lights can be rigged up overhead to prevent the rain from washing the waxy " powder " from the foliage, but this must not hinder the free circulation of air. In August, when the fresh growth commences, the plants should be re-potted, the tap roots being shortened with a sharp knife. A depth of 1½ inches should be first filled with small pieces of broken pot, and on this some decayed leaves should be placed. The plant should then be introduced, and the pot filled with compost to about ½ an inch from the rim of the pot. Care should be taken not to allow the collar of the plant to be below the soil. Press firmly, give a little water to settle the soil about the roots, and at the expiration of seven or eight days water again sparingly, and then leave the plants to themselves until November. Then place the plants under the shelter of a glass roof, but do not prevent a free circulation of air from reaching them. When they begin to grow in February or a little later, they should be watered sparingly, the quantity being increased when the blooming period commences. Keep the plants within 18 inches of the glass, but shade from direct rays of the sun. When cold east winds are prevalent in March, close the ventilators on that side of the house and let in the air from the opposite quarter. Never allow water to fall on the foliage or to settle on the leaves at the base, as this frequently causes decay, and all dead and decaying leaves should be removed from the plants. Very little artificial heat is required, and a close atmosphere is fatal. Keep a look out for *Auricula Root Aphis (Pentaphis auricular)*.

(Alpine Auriculas.) Sow seed in a light, sandy soil in a little heat in March, and just cover with sand. Prick-off into boxes as soon as four leaves have formed. Harden-off in a shady cold frame at the end of

May. Plant out 6 inches apart in September or October in a partially shaded position facing north, in well-drained rather heavy loam and cow-manure, or pot-up for flowering in the alpine or cold house. Lift, divide, and re-plant triennially after flowering.

*Varieties* (Show).—White-edged : *Acme, Heather Bell,* and *White Lady.* Green-edged : *Dr. Horner, Mystic,* and *Prince Charming.* Grey-edged : *George Rudd, George Lightbody,* and *Grey Friar.* Self : *Canary, Gordon Douglas, Harrison Weir,* and *Odin.* Alpines : *Admiration, Day Dream, Firefly, Majestic, Roxborough,* and *Silver Wood.*

**Australian Bean Flower** (see **Kennedya**).

**Australian Blue-bell Creeper** (see **Sollya heterophylla**).

**Australian Brush Cherry** (see **Eugenia myrtifolia**).

**Australian Fuchsia** (see **Correa**).

**Australian Lilac** (see **Hardenbergia**).

**Australian Mint Bush** (see **Prostanthera**).

**Australian Pitcher Plant** (see **Cephalotus follicularis**).

**Australian Turmeric Tree** (see **Zieria**).

**Azalea,** *Ericaceæ.*—The Azaleas, which are now frequently grouped with Rhododendrons, are among the most brilliant of our early-flowering plants. Those common to our gardens are deciduous shrubs, varying from 2 to 6 feet or more in height. With Azaleas, as with Rhododendrons, the best garden varieties are hybrids. Azaleas are distinguished as Ghent (deciduous), molle (deciduous), and Indian (evergreen). The former two are suitable for open-air culture as well as for pot culture, but the latter for greenhouse decoration only.

*Soil.*—A compost of sandy peat and loam, or two-thirds fibrous loam and one-third leaf-mould, is suitable for all varieties, but they will grow quite well in almost any soil that does not contain lime or chalk. For use in the greenhouse *V. indica* and its hybrids can be had in bloom from December to May.

*Pot Culture.*—Pot these plants up firmly from October to November, using 6- to 10-inch pots and the compost mentioned above. Keep in a cold frame until late November, then move in succession into the house (temperature 55–65° F.), and gradually acclimatise to moist, warm conditions. After flowering, prune straggling shoots and remove all dead blooms. Re-pot if necessary (usually every second or third year), place the pots in the warmest corner (temperature 60–65° F.) and syringe overhead. When the growths have matured stand in the open in a cool, sheltered position in a bed of ashes or shingle from June to September, water liberally, and syringe overhead morning and evening in dry, warm weather. In September return to the cold house or frame. They are sometimes attacked by *Azalea Galls (Exobasidium japonicum)*. *A. molle,* although hardy, is also useful for the warm greenhouse, where it may be had in flower from February to March (temperature 45° F. winter, 65° F. summer). Keep warm and moist from November until it flowers. Syringe and give liquid manure.

*Forcing.*—For flowering in December an early habit must be induced, which may be effected by merely placing the plants in the greenhouse in the autumn in a temperature of 55–60° F. After forcing, the plants should have all the dead blooms picked off. They should be re-potted immediately or stimulated with weak liquid manure once a week. They must be trimmed into shape, but not pruned too severely, and kept in the warm, and syringed daily overhead when the weather is fine. The plants may be removed from the house in June and transferred to a cold frame, or they may be plunged in an open border until October, when they should again be brought into the cool greenhouse. Before housing them for the winter, examine the plants and dip them in a tubful of equal parts of soot-water (made by throwing half a bushel of soot into soapsuds) and tobacco-water. Repeat this dose three times, and every thrip will either disappear or die. Red spider is also very troublesome if the plants are in a dry position. Frequent syringing will materially help to eradicate this as well as the thrip. Indian Azaleas bear forcing well.

*Propagation.*—To propagate, take cuttings of half-matured wood early in summer and strike in a frame (50–60° F.) ; sow in moist heat (60–65° F.), in fine, sandy peat in spring ; or layer.

*Species.*—*A. calendulaceæ* [N. America] (orange-red) ; *A. molle* [Japan] (red, yellow, etc.) ; *A. lutea* (*A. ponticum*) [yellow]; *A. nudiflora* [N. America] (pink or white) ; *A. occidentalis* [California] (pink and white) ; all of which are hardy, but can be grown in pots. There are also endless numbers of beautiful hybrids and varieties known as **Japanese Azaleas,** *R. amoenum, R. obtusum* valuable for the greenhouse.

*Greenhouse species.*—*A. indica* (many shades of colour from white, pink, rose and red to deep blood-red, in both single and double-flowered varieties). They flower from Christmas to May, according to the temperature of the greenhouse, and grow from 1 to 3 feet high, or more with age. Named varieties are numerous and growers' catalogues should be consulted.

**Azalea procumbens** (see **Loiseleuria procumbens**).

**Azara,** *Flacourtiaceæ.*—Ornamental shrubs grown for their evergreen foliage and sweet-scented, inconspicuous flowers. Although these are hardy in some parts, they make useful pot-plants for the cool greenhouse. They should be grown in a sandy compost of loam and leaf-soil. They may be propagated by seed or by cuttings of ripe wood in autumn, under glass, with a little bottom heat.

*Species.*—*A. microphylla* [Chile] (flowers greenish in small clusters, Feb. and March, 3–10 ft.). It bears small orange berries and has graceful, evergreen foliage. *A. Gillesii* [Chile] (yellow flowers in dense, nodding heads, Feb. and March, 4–10 ft.) ; *A. lanceolata* [Chile] (yellow flowers in erect inflorescences).

**Azolla,** *Salviniaceæ.*—A small, floating aquatic, which multiplies rapidly by self-division and will grow readily in any water that contains a little nutriment. The plant grows very close together and has a lovely feathery or mossy appearance. In the open in the summer it takes on a beautiful coloured effect of green and red. The species generally in cultivation is *A. filiculoides*, native from California to Chile, but has escaped to streams in some parts of England.

**Babiana** (Baboon-root), *Iridaceæ.*—Dwarf, half-hardy bulbs with brilliantly-coloured flowers of great beauty, and pale-green, " hairy " leaves. The plants grow from 6 to 10 inches high, and bloom in the cool greenhouse from May to June. They are natives of the Cape of Good Hope, and can be grown in a warm, sheltered position in the open, but are better suited to a cold greenhouse. There are many varieties and all shades of colours; reds, blues, and purples predominating.

*Culture.*—Plant in October, 4 inches deep and 4 inches apart, in a warm, sheltered bed, or put four bulbs in a 4½-inch pot in a compost of sandy loam mixed with leaf-mould and cow-dung. Place in a temperature of 40–45° F. When the bulbs are sending up leaves and flowers they should be kept thoroughly moist. After blooming feed with weak liquid manure water until the leaves turn yellow, then stop the water, and dry off in the pot, or lift from the bed. *B. plicata* has lilac or red flowers and a pink-like scent (10–12 in.). *B. stricta rubrocyanea* has blue flowers with carmine centres, and is most attractive.

**Baboon-root** (see **Babiana**).

**Ballon Vine** (see **Cardiospermum Halicacabum**).

**Balsam Apple** (see **Momordica Balsamina**).

**Balsam Pear** (see **Momordica Charantia**).

**Bambusa** (Bamboo), *Gramineæ.*—There are three great classes of bamboos—namely, *Arundinaria*, *Bambusa*, and *Phyllostachys*. Most species do well in the open, especially if the soil is of a moist, deep, light, loamy nature, and contains some peat or leaf-mould, but in exposed situations they require some protection, particularly in the north and east.

*Pot Culture.*—Pot-up in March in a well-drained compost of two-thirds loam and one-third leaf-mould and sharp sand. Water liberally, syringe well overhead in summer, and give weak liquid manure twice a week during the growing period. Keep the roots just moist in winter. A moist and moderately warm atmosphere is essential. For sub-tropical species, temperature 50° F. winter, 60° F. summer.

The dwarfer kinds, such as *Arundinaria Fortunei variegata* (striped with silver, 24 in.), *A. pumila* (12–24 in.), *A. vagans* (12–18 in.), and *Phyllostachys ruscifolia* [Japan] (12–24 in.) are most suitable as pot-plants in the greenhouse. The taller kinds can, of course, be grown under similar conditions, in tubs or borders, but large structures are needed to house them. Propagate by offsets (division) in March. Cut out dead canes in April.

*Species.*—(Hardy) *B. disticha* [China and Japan] (24 in.); *B. palmata* [Japan] (2–4 ft.); *B. quadrangularis* [China and Japan] (4–8 ft.), and *B. tessellata* [China and Japan] (3–4 ft.).

**Banana** (see **Musa**, also **Fruit under Glass**).

**Banksia** (Australian Honeysuckle), *Proteaceæ.*—A genus of Australian evergreen shrubs with beautiful foliage. They are suitable for a cool airy greenhouse or conservatory, but their culture demands careful treatment, particularly with regard to watering. For this reason it is most essential that the pots should be thoroughly drained and that the compost used should be open and contain plenty of sharp sand and crock chippings. Although over-watering must be avoided, it is essential that the plants never suffer from lack of moisture, for if allowed to flag, they seldom fully recover. *Banksias* are not too easy to propagate, either from seeds or cuttings. For the latter, choose well ripened shoots, and insert them in pots of sand under a bell-glass in a cool propagating frame. When rooted, pot them carefully into small receptacles, and harden off gradually.

*Species.—B. collina* (yellow, 6–8 ft.); *B. dryandroides* (foliage and stems with reddish-brown hairs).

**Barbados Gooseberry** (see **Pereskia aculeata**).

**Barbados Lily** (see **Hippeastrum equestre**).

**Barbados Nut** (see **Jatropha Curcas**).

**Barberry** (see **Berberis**).

**Barbertown Daisy** (see **Gerbera Jamesonii**).

**Barosma,** *Rutaceæ.*—Evergreen, heath-like shrubs, all natives of the Cape of Good Hope, requiring a cool greenhouse. They thrive in a mixture of sandy loam and peat (temperature 60° F. summer, 35–40° F. winter). Propagate by cuttings of half-ripened wood in June in a cool, close frame.

*Species.—B. fœtidissima* (*Agathosma fœtidissima*) is an attractive little shrub, the foliage of which is rather strong smelling (white or pinkish white, June, 24–36 in.); *B. pulchella* is the species most generally grown (purple, June, 12–36 in.).

**Bauera rubioides,** *Saxifragaceæ* [New South Wales] (pink or white, 15–18 in.).—A handsome little shrub for the cool greenhouse, flowering most of the year, particularly during the winter and spring months. A cool greenhouse with a temperature of 40–50° F. suits them, and when growing they benefit from a watering of soot-water once every four waterings.

*Propagation.—Bauera* are readily propagated from half-ripened wood in the spring, inserted in small pots of equal parts of fine sifted peat and sand, covered with a bell-glass in a temperature of 55–60° F. Give a good watering at the time of inserting, and they should root without further watering. When the cuttings are rooted they should be potted in 2-inch pots in the same mixture as before, and kept in a tight case for a few days. When they begin to grip the soil the young plants should be cut back to about an inch above the pot to form bushy plants. Bauera should never be allowed to become pot-bound until the plants have reached the desired size. Afterwards they can be kept in good shape by cutting back the strong growths. During the summer months they are best plunged in ashes outside.

**Beaucarnea** (see **Nolina**).

**Bead Tree** (see **Melia Azedarach**).

**Bear's Grass** (see **Yucca**).

**Beaufortia,** *Myrtaceæ.*—Small, heath-like, Australian, evergreen shrubs with clusters of scarlet or purple flowers in early summer. They grow from 18 to 24 inches in height, and are suitable for cultivation in the cool to warm greenhouse.

*Culture.*—Pot-up in March in well-crocked pots of sandy loam, peat, and leaf-mould, and stand in the warm greenhouse (temperature 60–65° F.). Keep moist and when well established move to the cool greenhouse. Water well while growing and sparingly when dormant. Prune when necessary to keep the plants shapely in March.

# THE GREENHOUSE

*Propagation.*—Cuttings made of semi-mature side-shoots may be rooted in sandy soil in slight heat in June or July.

*Species.*—*B. decussata* [New Holland] (scarlet); *B. purpurea* [Australia] (purple); *B. sparsa* (*B. splendens*) [W. Australia] (scarlet).

**Beaumontia grandiflora,** *Apocynaceæ* [India].—A handsome twiner for the warm greenhouse, with large, whitish, trumpet-shaped flowers. It succeeds best when planted out in the border of the greenhouse in good loam and peat. It should be trained to the roof for full light, which is so necessary, as the wood must be well ripened to produce an abundance of winter bloom. Pruning should be done after flowering, to provide lateral shoots for next season's bloom. Propagated by cuttings of half-ripened wood placed in sand with bottom heat.

**Beech Fern** (see **Phegopteris polypodioides**).

**Begonia,** *Begoniaceæ.*—These plants, sometimes called " Beefsteak Plant " or " Elephant's Ear ", have made great headway during recent years, and are now among our most popular flowers. Both single and double varieties are to be obtained. The plants grow from 6 to 20 inches high, and flower nearly all the year round. They thrive in sunny beds and borders with rich loam, and are also extremely useful in the greenhouse. There is a delicious fragrance about some of the species which particularly recommends them for cultivation; others are grown for their richly variegated foliage and graceful habit, and they all hybridise with great facility.

*Culture* (tuberous-rooted).—For bedding out or for greenhouse decoration from June to October. Sow in February, under glass (temperature 65° F.) in a finely-sifted and just moist compost of two-thirds loam and one-third leaf-mould and sand. Water before sowing, and keep the seed-pan moist by covering with a piece of glass until germination takes place. Prick-off the seedlings into shallow boxes. Pot-off singly into pots or transplant into boxes or frames. Plant out in May or June or pot-up into 5-inch pots for the greenhouse. Keep near the glass and shade when the sun is hot. Occasional spraying overhead when the weather is warm will help them. These young plants should flower in the late summer.

*Starting Tubers.*—When starting tubers they should be planted flat or hollow side uppermost in February or March, being just covered in shallow trays, in heat (60° F.), with moist, sandy loam and well-rotted manure for soil. Water in moderation until growth commences. If for summer bedding, harden-off in May in a cold frame and plant out in June, or, if for the greenhouse, pot-up in 4-inch pots in a compost of two-thirds loam and one-third leaf-mould, well-rotted manure, and sand, re-potting when pot-bound into 7- to 8-inch pots. Water well in summer, shade from hot sun, and when the roots have filled the pots, feed with weak manure-water twice a week. Stake any shoots that need support and pick off all dead blooms (greenhouse temperature 55° F. winter, 70° F. summer). If grown in the open as bedding plants, tubers should be lifted in October, when the frost has turned the foliage black. If they must be removed from the beds before this, lift them with a good " ball " of soil, pack in boxes, and place in a sheltered spot to finish ripening. Then shake away the soil and foliage from the

262

roots, allow them to dry for a day or so, and store in dry soil in boxes in a cool but frost-proof place. Start them again the following February or March in a tray of damp fibre in heat, and when sufficient growth has been made pot-up with the crown of the tuber level with the surface of the earth.

Tuberous Begonias in pots must be gradually dried off and stood in a frost-proof shed or frame for the winter, or they may be shaken out of their pots and soil and stored in dry sand.

*Propagation.*—Particular varieties may be propagated in spring by means of leaf-cuttings, which consist of well-matured leaves cut with the point of a sharp knife across the larger veins of the lower side. These should be laid on sand or coconut fibre in a propagating case and held in place by small pieces of broken pot. Bulblets will form at the end of the nerves, and these, when large enough, must be removed and potted up singly. Ordinary stem cuttings may also be taken in spring and summer.

*Culture* (Fibrous-rooted Species).—This is a very large and varied class, including as it does a large number of species and varieties of a sub-shrubby habit, which require an intermediate or greenhouse temperature. Some of them flower more or less all the year round, but a few of them may be used for summer-bedding. The most important for this purpose are the many beautiful varieties of *B. semperflorens*, which may be raised from seed sown during January in a temperature of 60° F., or by means of basal cuttings from plants lifted and potted-up and kept in a warm house over the winter. The sub-shrubby and perennial species generally are propagated by means of ordinary cuttings, or by means of leaf-cuttings, in a temperature of from 60–70° F. In the case of leaf-cuttings, they are usually pegged down on boxes of sandy fibre, the principal veins being scored in places with a sharp knife. The winter-flowering section, which is represented by *Gloire de Lorraine* and its varieties, may be increased by means of leaf-cuttings or by young basal shoots. They are usually secured from plants that have flowered and that have been rested for a few weeks. These are then partly cut back and started in a temperature of from 65–70° F., cuttings being secured during March. The other winter-flowering section, which is represented by varieties raised from crossing the species *B. socotrana* with the tuberous-rooted varieties, are by no means easy to grow successfully, and require very careful management during their resting period. After flowering, they should be stood in a house with a temperature of from 55–60° F. They should have very little water at the root; on the other hand, they must not suffer, for it is important that their foliage should, so far as possible, be retained in a fresh condition until they start to throw up young shoots from the base in May. They should then be given more water at the root. When the young shoots are about 3 inches in length they should be secured as cuttings, and inserted singly in small pots of sandy compost. They root readily in a close case with a bottom heat of 70° F. During the summer months they should be grown in an average temperature of from 55–65° F. During the summer they enjoy ample atmospheric moisture, and must be shaded during the hottest

# THE GREENHOUSE

part of the day. All Begonias are very subject to attacks of Begonia mite " rust ". This must be guarded against by spraying with a nicotine compound, or by the use of a sulphur vaporiser.

*Culture of Ornamental and Variegated-leaved Species.*—Pot-up in March or April in a compost as already recommended, keep in a moist atmosphere, never letting the temperature fall below 50° F., and shade from the strong sun. At that time, water liberally, and give a little weak liquid manure. Decrease the water supply in winter, but do not dry off entirely. Propagate by means of seed, leaf-cuttings, or by cuttings of unflowered shoots (temperature 60–65° F.).

*Species and Varieties.*—(Fibrous). *B. acuminata* [Jamaica] (white, tinted red) ; *B. albo-coccinea* [India] (white and red) ; *B. coccinea* [Brazil] (red), the well-known *B. " President Carnot "* is an offspring of this species ; *B. Dregei* [South Africa] (white) ; *B. echinosepala* [Brazil] (pink and white) ; *B. fuchsioides* [Mexico] (scarlet) ; *B. Lucerna* [hybrid] (deep pink) ; *B. manicata* [Mexico] (shell-pink) ; *B. semperflorens* [Brazil] (many varieties) ; *B. socotrana* [Socotra] (bright rose) (this species and *B. Dregei* are the parents of the winter-flowering *Gloire de Lorraine*).

WINTER-FLOWERING : *B. Gloire de Lorraine* (reddish pink) ; *Turnford Hall* (blush white) ; *Mrs. L. de Rothschild* (soft pink) ; *Glory of Cincinnati* (pink) ; *Mrs. Petersen* (dark foliage, flowers rosy red) ; *Eges Favourite* (red) ; *The Fairy* (pale pink) ; *Bath Belle* (large bright pink) ; *Agatha* (rosy pink). All the foregoing are varieties of *Gloire de Lorraine*.

The following are some of the hybrids between *B. socotrana* and tuberous-rooted varieties, viz. : *Mrs. Heal* (carmine) ; *Fascination* (orange-salmon) ; *Exquisite* (pink and white) ; *Emita* (orange-scarlet) ; *Optima* (salmon) ; *Her Majesty* (coppery orange) ; *Altrincham Pink* ; *Clibran's Crimson* ; *Clibran's Red* ; *Duchess of Westminster* (soft pink) ; *Scarlet Beauty* ; *The Gem* (rosy scarlet); *Van der Meer's Glory.*

Other winter-flowering Begonias are : *B. Carrieri* [from *B. semperflorens* and *B. Schmidtii*] ; *Gloire de Sceaux* [from *B. socotrana* and *B. subpeltata*] (pink with dark foliage) ; *B. manicata* [Mexico] (pink) ; *B. Digswelliana* [from *B. fuchsioides* and *B. semperflorens* var.] (red) ; *B. Froebelii* [Ecuador] (scarlet) ; *B. nitida* [Jamaica] (flesh) ; *B. nitida alba* (white) ; and *B. Corbeille de Feu* [from *B. semperflorens* and *B. fuchsioides*] (red).

FIBROUS-ROOTED FOR BEDDING AND GREENHOUSE : *B. ascotensis* (from *B. fuchsioides* and *B. semperflorens*) ; *B. semperflorens* in many varieties, some of the best being : *Bonfire* (scarlet) ; *Scarlet Bedder* (scarlet) ; *Pink Profusion* (pink) ; *Prima Donna* (pink) ; *Glory of Erfurt* (pink) ; *Erfordia grandiflora* (silvery pink) ; and *Triumph* (white).

TUBEROUS-ROOTED : *Albatross* (white) ; *Canary Bird* (yellow) ; *F. C. Calthorpe* (scarlet) ; *General Allenby* (red) ; *Hilda Langdon* (rose-pink) ; *James Baird* (cardinal-red) ; *Lady Carew* (cerise) ; *Millicent* (flesh-pink) ; *Mrs. J. S. Brunton* (lilac-rose) ; *Mrs. F. C. Calthorpe* (salmon-pink) ; *Peace* (cream and yellow) ; *Sir J. Reid* (orange). These are all varieties of *Begonia tuber-hybrida*. *B. weltoniensis* [from *B. Sutherlandii* and *B. Dregei*] (pink), is often seen in cottage windows.

**264**

# GREENHOUSE PLANTS

FOR HANG BASKETS: *B. foliosa* [Colombia], frond-like growth of glossy leaves, flowers white, tinged with pink; *B. kewensis* [a *coccinea* hybrid] (white); *Alice Manning* (yellow); *Betha* (salmon-pink); *Golden Shower* (yellow); *Lena* (rosy crimson); *Meteor* (scarlet); and *Rose Cactus* (rose-pink). These are pendulous varieties of garden hybrids.

ORNAMENTAL-LEAVED: *Begonia Rex* [Himalayas] in many varieties; *B. Rajah* [Malaya], a beautiful species with leaves mottled green, brown, and red; *B. imperialis* [Mexico] (olive and greyish green); *B. maculata* [Brazil] (silver and green); *B. Cathayana* [China] (crimson and green). This species has been hybridised with *B. Rex* and has produced many very richly coloured foliage varieties.

Other species worth growing are *B. Haageana* [Brazil] a handsome, strong-growing plant with rosy-pink flowers; *B. boliviensis* [Bolivia] (scarlet, 20–30 in.); *B. Evansiana* [Java, China, etc.] (flesh coloured, 18–24 in.), an almost hardy species; *B. luxurians* [S. America], attractive foliage, cream-coloured flowers; *B. Pearcei* [Bolivia] the only yellow-flowered tuberous species in cultivation. Chiefly responsible for the many yellow, buff, and orange-coloured garden forms.

**Beloperone guttata,** *Acanthaceæ* [Mexico] (white, summer, 18–30 in.). —A very useful plant for the warm greenhouse, the graceful, drooping spikes of rich, salmon-coloured bracts, which almost cover the flowers, being very attractive during the summer and autumn. Cuttings root at almost any time in sandy soil with some bottom heat. Pot them on when ready, and finally transfer them to 6-inch pots in a good loamy mixture.

**Berberidopsis corallina** (Coral Barberry), *Flacourtiaceæ* [Chile].—A half-hardy, evergreen, climbing shrub, which thrives in a cool greenhouse, or in a border in the south, in well-drained light loam. against walls facing south or west, and partly shaded. It carries drooping bunches of coral-red flowers in June, and grows to a height of 20 feet.

*Culture.*—Take cuttings early in summer, or propagate by means of layering in October. Plant out in April and October, or pot-up in well-drained pots of light, peaty loam. Water well while growing, and thin out branches when overcrowded.

**Berberis** (Barberry), *Berberidaceæ.*—Beautiful, hardy, flowering shrubs, there being both evergreen and deciduous species, among which are some of the most useful and attractive shrubs in cultivation. The stems are very thorny, and many species bear lovely orange or yellow flowers in spring or early summer, and in autumn carry handsome black, purple, or red fruit.

*Culture.*—Pot-up in November, using 8- to 10-inch pots and a compost of two parts of sandy loam to one part of leaf-mould and rotten manure. Thin out shoots when overcrowded after flowering or in winter after fruiting, and trim to shape. Most species are propagated by means of seed sown in the open in October, by half-matured cuttings in a frame in July or August, or by layering in August.

*Species.*—*B. Darwinii* [Chile] (orange, April–May, 8–10 ft.); *B. linearifolia* [Chile] (orange, April–May, 6–8 ft.); and *B. lologensis* [Chile] (a natural hybrid between the two former species, having larger flowers

265

than *B. Darwinii* with some of the fine colouring of *B. linearifolia*) are useful evergreen species for pot culture in the cold greenhouse.

**Bergenia (Saxifraga** or **Megasea).** *Saxifragaceæ.*—A handsome foliage group of Saxifraga with thick, leathery leaves, most of which are perfectly hardy, but are useful for shady parts of the cold house. They thrive in ordinary well-drained soil, and are propagated by division in autumn or after flowering in the late spring.

*Species.*—*B. cordifolia* [Siberia] (clear rose, March–May) ; *B. ligulata* [Himalayas] (white, rose or purple, March–May) ; *B. ligulata* var. *ciliata* [Himalayas] (white and rose), the most beautiful of all ; considered a separate species by some authorities ; *B. purpurescens* [Himalayas] (rose to purple, April–May).

**Bertolonia,** *Melastomaceæ.*—Chiefly from Brazil. Includes some of the most beautiful foliage plants, from 6–8 inches high, for the warm greenhouse. To grow them successfully a humid atmosphere is required. In order that the atmospheric conditions may be more easily regulated, bell-glasses or glass cases should be provided. Although they require a fair amount of moisture at the roots, overhead sprinkling or syringing is not advisable. They are propagated by cuttings which strike readily in a moderately close case filled with clean, sharp sand. When rooted they should be put in clean, well-drained pots in a good open compost and stood back for a time in the close case. They can also be grown from seed sown in the spring, under conditions recommended for cuttings. They thrive in dense shade.

*Species and Varieties.*—*B. Houtteana* (*B. Van Houtte*), rich coloured leaves, deep purple beneath ; *B. Hrubyana*, white bars and spots on the upper surface of the leaves ; green instead of purple beneath ; *B. maculata*, dark velvety-green leaves, often spotted, rose-coloured flowers ; *B. marmorata*, upper surface of leaf vivid green, marked with streaks of pure white, under surface uniform purple ; *B Rodeckiana*, distinguished from all others of this group by the dark-red colour on the upper surface of the leaf, veins on the underside being green.

**Bertolonia guttata** (see **Gravesia guttata**).

**Beschorneria,** *Amaryllidaceæ.*—Succulent desert plants allied to **Agave** and requiring the same treatment as **Agave** and **Aloes.**

*Species.*—*B. bracteata* [Mexico] (24–36 in.), flowers at first green, turning yellowish-red when mature, with large, scariose, reddish bracts ; *B. yuccoides* [Mexico] (30–40 in.), flowers dark green tinged with yellow, with rich, rosy-red bracts, and slender, coral-red scapes.

**Bessera elegans** (Mexican Coral Drops), *Liliaceæ.*—Flowers scarlet outside, with white corona (July–Sept., 15–20 in.). An exceedingly pretty, bulbous, summer-flowering plant, requiring a compost of loam, leaf-soil, peat and sand with good drainage. During the growing season it requires a plentiful supply of water, but it should be kept cool and quite dry during the resting season.

It is usually propagated by means of offsets taken off and potted-up in the spring.

**Bestera pulchella** (see **Tassacia pulchra**).

**Bifrenaria** (see Chapter on **Orchids**).

# GREENHOUSE PLANTS

**Bignonia** (Trumpet Flower).—Some of these are fine, half-hardy, perennial climbers, closely allied to the **Tecoma,** which see.

There are several species, most of which are natives of tropical countries. *B. capreolata* [N. America], with beautiful orange-scarlet flowers in April and May, succeeds in sheltered, warm positions out of doors, and is suitable for the cool house. *B. Chamberlaynii* (*Anemopægma Chamberlaynii*) [Brazil] is one of the most beautiful and freest of the tropical climbers, and is suitable for a small house (clusters of bright yellow flowers, April–Oct.). *B. Unguis-cati* (*Macfadyena dentata*) [Argentina] is a climber with three-parted, claw-like tendrils, suitable for the cool house (Allamanda-like, bright yellow flowers, summer).

*Culture.*—Propagate by means of matured side-shoots struck in sand under a bell-glass in the hot-house in autumn, or by root cuttings treated in the same manner in spring or autumn. When fairly advanced in growth these plants may be trained over the roof of the greenhouse. They must be given a position in full sun and ample ventilation. Loam, leaf-mould, and rotten manure forms a suitable soil, and ample water is needed in spring and summer, but the drainage must be excellent. Keep the roots fairly dry in winter. Pot-up in March, and in spring and summer syringe overhead daily in fine weather. Each year in January prune back all weak growths by at least half their length and cut in also even the more vigorous stems by one third.

**Bignonia buccinatoria** (see **Phædranthus buccinatorius**).
**Bignonia callistegioides** (see **Clytostoma callistegioides**).
**Bignonia muricatum** (see **Pithecoctinium muricatum**).
**Bignonia pandorea** (see **Pandorea australis**).
**Bignonia purpurea** (see **Clytostoma purpurea**).
**Bignonia venusta** (see **Pyrostegia venusta**).
**Bilberry** (see **Vaccinium**).

**Billardiera,** *Pittosporaceæ.*—Tender, evergreen twiners or climbers, which can be grown outside in some favourable parts of the country, but which are quite attractive for the cool greenhouse, particularly when in fruit. They are best planted out in the greenhouse border, but are not always successful in soil that is calcareous. Cuttings root easily if put under a bell-glass with a little warmth, and they can be raised from seed sown in the spring and placed in a little warmth.

*Species.*—*B. longiflora* [Tasmania] (Flowers greenish yellow, changing to purple, berries deep blue) ; *B. scandens* [Australia] (flowers greenish yellow, violet, or purple, May–Aug.).

**Billbergia nutans** [Brazil].—Attractive, half-hardy, evergreen plants with long, narrow, grass-like foliage and spikes of greenish yellow and blue flowers, with rose-coloured bracts in late winter and early spring. They thrive in the cool greenhouse or room window in a mixture of about three parts of light loam to one part of well-decayed leaf-soil or brown fibrous peat, with a little clean, coarse sand added.

*Culture.*—Pot-up in well-drained pots after flowering is over in spring. Water well and maintain a moist atmosphere while growing Propagate by means of suckers at re-potting time.

*Species.*—Other species less frequently met with are *B. Bakeri* [Brazil], with greenish-yellow and violet flowers ; *B. speciosa* [Brazil],

# THE GREENHOUSE

with carmine and violet flowers, and *B. zebrina* [S. America], with green or yellowish-green flowers, and salmon and rose bracts.

**Bird of Paradise** (see **Strelitzia Reginæ**).
**Bird Plant** (see **Heterotoma lobelioides**).
**Bird's Nest Fern** (see **Asplenium Nidus**).
**Bird's Tongue Flower** (see **Strelitzia**).
**Bitter Cassava** (see **Manihot utilissima**).
**Black Calla** (see **Arum palæstinum**).
**Black-eyed Susan** (see **Thunbergia alata**).
**Black-throated Calla** (see **Zantedeschia melanoleuca**).
**Bladder Fern** (see **Cystopteris**).
**Bladder Nut** (see **Staphylla colchica**).
**Bladderwort** (see **Utricularia**).

**Blakea trinervia,** *Melastomaceæ* [Jamaica].—Warm greenhouse shrubs with large solitary pink or rose-coloured flowers during the summer. They thrive in loam or peat and require a liberal amount of water during the growing season. Cuttings of ripe wood root freely in sand under a bell-glass over moist heat.

**Blandfordia,** *Liliaceæ.*—Half-hardy, bulbous or rhizomatous-rooted evergreen perennials from Australia and New Zealand suitable for the cool greenhouse. They grow from 12 to 18 inches in height, and bear pretty tubular-shaped flowers in summer.

*Culture.*—Pot-up or re-pot in autumn in well-crocked pots of sandy loam and peat. Keep on the dry side until growth commences in the following spring. Stand in a sunny position and water regularly until blooming is finished. Propagation is carried out by means of division in autumn.

*Species.*—*B. aurea* (rich yellow); *B. flammea* (deep yellow); *B. grandiflora* (crimson); *B. nobilis* (orange).

**Blechnum** (Hard Fern), *Polypodiaceæ.*—Hardy and greenhouse evergreen ferns growing from 10 to 30 inches high. The hardy species, which are excellent subjects for the rock garden, thrive in shady positions in a mixture of sandy loam and leaf-mould containing no lime.

*Greenhouse Species.*—Pot-up in March, using a compost of half-peaty loam and half leaf-mould and sand. Stand in the shade, and water liberally with soft (not hard) water in summer. Temperature 50° F. winter, 60° F. summer. Propagate by means of spores sown under glass in July.

*Species.*—*B. brasiliense* [Brazil] is a small tree fern. Stem 12 inches or more, fronds 20–30 inches long (warm greenhouse). *B. gibbum* [New Caledonia] has stems 24–36 inches high, with 20–30 inch fronds (warm greenhouse). The fertile pinna is narrow. *B. occidentale* [W. Indies] (12–18 in.) has young fronds which are sometimes coloured pink. Suitable for the cool greenhouse. *B. pennae maxina* (*Lomaria alpina*) [temperate regions] has fronds 4–8 inches long. *B. spicant* [Europe, etc.] (12–18 in.) is hardy, but worth growing in the cold greenhouse.

**Bleeding Heart** (see **Dicentra spectabilis**).
**Bletia hyacinthina** (see Chapter on **Orchids**).
**Blood Apple** (see **Pereskia aculeata**).

268

# GREENHOUSE PLANTS

**Blood Flower** (see **Asclepias curassavica**).

**Blood Lily** (see **Hæmanthus**).

**Blood-root** (see **Sanguinaria canadensis**).

**Bloomeria,** *Liliaceæ*.—Half-hardy, bulbous-rooted plants, natives of California, which may be grown in the open in a warm, sheltered rock garden. In more exposed places, however, they should be kept indoors. They do well in a sandy soil, growing from 10 to 15 inches high, and flowering in May and June.

*Culture*.—Plant or pot-up in September or October, 2 to 3 inches deep, placing three or four bulbs in a 5-inch pot. Keep on the dry side until growth commences, then water regularly until the flowers fade. Propagate by means of offsets in September. *B. aurea* (golden yellow) and *B. Clevelandii* (yellow) are among the best species.

**Blue Amaryllis** (see **Griffinia hyacinthina** var. **maxima**).

**Blue Bell** (see **Scilla nonscripta**).

**Blue-Dawn-Flower** (see **Ipomæa Learii**).

**Blue Gum** (see **Eucalyptus globulus**).

**Blue Marguerite** (see **Felicia amelloides**).

**Blue Moonwort** (see **Soldanella alpina**).

**Blumenbachia lateritia (Cajophora lateritia)**, *Loasaceæ* [Chile].—An attractive climber, with brick-red flowers, for the roof of the green-house. It is best treated as an annual. Seed should be sown in the spring, three or four plants being grown in an 8-inch pot.

There are several other attractive species, but, as most of them are covered with stinging hairs, they are not to be recommended as pot-plants.

**Bog Violet** (see **Pinguicula**).

**Bollea** (see Chapter on **Orchids**).

**Bomarea,** *Amaryllidaceæ*.—A South American group of handsome, half-hardy, herbaceous twiners, with terminal, pendulous clusters of bright flowers, suitable for the cool greenhouse. They thrive in rich fibrous soil and require plenty of watering. During the growing season, which commences in the spring, an occasional manure watering is essential. Although useful pot-plants, their full beauty is developed only when planted out in a sunny position in the greenhouse border. Their terminal clusters of pendulous flowers hanging from the roof will give a good display all the summer. Propagation may be effected by seed, which should be sown, as soon as ripe, in shallow pans and placed in a warm propagation house. When large enough the seedlings should be potted-up singly. The old plant may also be divided when new growth commences in the spring, taking care that each part has some roots attached. These should then be potted-up and placed in the warmth until established, when they can be planted out.

*Species*.—*B. Carderi* (pale pink, slightly tinged with greenish white, and spotted with brown) ; *B. Caldasiana* (reddish brown and bright yellow, very free flowering) ; *B. patacocensis* (bright red with a few spots, in large clusters) ; *B. Wercklei* (vermilion, orange and yellow).

Several hybrids have been raised and are now in cultivation.

**Bonatea speciosa** (see Chapter on **Orchids**).

**Boronia,** *Rutaceæ*.—Handsome and fragrant evergreen shrubs which grow from 12 to 24 inches high and flower from February to March. They do best in the cool greenhouse (temperature 45–55° F. winter, 60–65° F. summer) in a compost of equal parts of sandy loam, peat, and leaf-mould. All are natives of Australia.

*Culture.*—Pot-up from April to May in 5- to 7-inch pots. Stop back young plants to make nice bushy plants. Place near the glass and give ample air. Applications of liquid manure should be given while growing. Prune after flowering, and stand outdoors from June to September. To propagate, take cuttings of young shoots in May and strike in sand, peat and charcoal, under glass (60° F.).

*Species.*—*B. elatior* (carmine) ; *B. heterophylla* (cerise) ; *B. megastigma* (brownish purple and yellow); *B. serrulata* (pink or rose); *B. tetrandra* (pink).

**Bottle Brush** (see **Callistemon**).

**Bottle Gourd** (see **Lagenaria leucantha**).

**Bougainvillea,** *Nyctaginaceæ.*—These are excellent shrubby climbers for the cool greenhouse, and grow well in pots of sandy loam and leaf-mould in a sunny position. Cut laterals hard back in February. These climbers will run up to a height of 15 feet or more, and when possible should be planted in a border in the greenhouse. The actual flowers of Bougainvilleas are insignificant, the decorative part being the showy, conspicuous bracts which surround the flowers.

*Culture.*—Plant in a well-drained prepared hole in the greenhouse border in a compost of two parts sandy loam to one part of leaf-mould, or pot-up in a large pot or small tub in spring or autumn. Water well while growing, and rest in winter. Prune after flowering. Cuttings of semi-mature shoots may be rooted in heat (65–70° F.) in a propagating case in spring.

*Species and Varieties.*—*B. glabra* [Brazil] has bright rosy-red bracts. The variety *B. g. Sanderiana* carries rose-purple bracts in summer ; *B. spectabilis* [Brazil] has brick-red bracts in June and July. Two other varieties of garden origin, *B. "Mrs. Butt"*, with a profusion of rich, crimson red bracts, and *B. "Orange King"*, with bright orange-salmon bracts, bear their bracts from June to August.

**Bouvardia** (Jasmine Plant), *Rubiaceæ.*—A pretty evergreen shrub with fragrant, waxy flowers which, given warm house treatment, can be made to bloom indoors from October to January. The plants are dwarf, and may be successfully grown in small pots. They grow to about 20 inches in height outdoors, and like a mixture of fibrous loam, leaf-mould, peat, and a little well-rotted cow manure.

*Pot Culture.*—Pot-up in March in 5- to 8-inch pots, using a compost as mentioned above. Keep in a frame from June to September, and during this period water liberally and syringe in the evening in fine weather. In September return to the greenhouse (temperature 50–60° F. winter, 60–65° F. summer), and give liquid manure when the buds begin to form.

*Pruning.*—Cut hard back after flowering, and stop back young shoots until August.

*Propagation.*—Propagate by means of cuttings of young shoots 2 inches long, or root cuttings in February and March in heat (70° F.).

# GREENHOUSE PLANTS

*Species and Varieties.—B. Humboldtii* [probably a hybrid] (large fragrant white flowers the whole summer) ; *B. jasminiflora* (white, free flowering) ; *B. leiantha* [Mexico] (scarlet, 18–24 in.) ; *B. triphylla* [Mexico] (scarlet, 24 in.). The last two are probable parents of the garden Bouvardias.

*Named Varieties.—Alfred Neuner* (double white) ; *Bridal Wreath* (white) ; *King of the Scarlets* (scarlet) ; *Mrs. R. Green* (single salmon) ; *President Cleveland* (scarlet) ; *President Garfield* (double pink) ; *Priory Beauty* (pink).

**Bower Plant of Australia** (see **Pandorea australis**).

**Bow-string Hemp** (see **Sansevieria**).

**Brachycome iberidifolia** (Swan River Daisy), *Compositæ.*—A beautiful, summer-flowering, dwarf-growing, half-hardy annual, covered during the greater part of the summer with a profusion of pretty cineraria-like flowers. It grows about 9 inches high, and makes a very effective subject for decoration in the cold greenhouse.

*Culture.—*Sow seed thinly in light rich soil in March or April, in gentle heat. Pot-up singly in 4-inch pots, or three or four in a 6-inch pan, and stand in a sunny position about the end of May.

*Varieties.—White Star ; Blue Star ; Red Star.*

**Brachysema,** *Leguminosæ.*—Greenhouse evergreen climbing plants with brilliant flowers from March to May, very ornamental in appearance, and suitable for pillars and trellis-work. All are natives of Australia.

*Pot Culture.—*Pot-up or plant in February in a compost of sandy loam, peat, and leaf-mould. Train the shoots up the trellis or pillars on wires running parallel with the glass and only 9–12 inches from it. Water well and regularly while growing but in moderation after flowering (temperature 50° F. winter, 60° F. summer).

*Propagation.—*To propagate, take cuttings of half-ripened shoots in June or July and place them in a propagating case. Layering may be carried out during the same period, or seed may be sown in slight heat in a compost of sand, loam and peat, in March.

*Species.—B. acuminatum* (bright red) ; *B. lanceolatum* (crimson, yellow, and white) ; *B. latifolium* (crimson) ; *B. subcordatum* (red) ; *B. undulatum* (violet).

**Brachystelma,** *Compositæ.*—A group of tuberous perennials from the Cape of Good Hope. Suitable for the cool greenhouse. They thrive in fibrous loam. Propagated by cuttings placed in sandy soil in heat, or by division of the root.

*Species and Varieties.—B. Arnottii* (brown, green, Aug., 5–6 in.) ; *B. Barbaræ* (purple speckled with yellow, Aug., 6 in.) ; *B. tuberosum* (purple, June, 15–18 in.).

**Brasenia Schreberi (Brasenia peltata),** *Nymphæaceæ.*—An interesting aquatic plant from North America, suitable for the cool aquarium. It has floating leaves, and bears purple flowers in the summer. It can be grown in a pot and submerged to a depth of from several inches to a foot under water. It is easily propagated by division of the roots in spring.

**Brassavola** (see Chapter on **Orchids**).

271

# THE GREENHOUSE

**Brassia** (see Chapter on **Orchids**).

**Bravoa geminiflora** (Twinflower), *Amaryllidaceæ.*—A half-hardy bulbous plant from Mexico, which likes a sunny, sheltered position in rich, light soil mixed with old leaf-mould, and is useful for decoration in the cold or cool greenhouse. It grows about 15 inches high, and carries rich orange red flowers in July and August.

*Culture.*—Plant in a warm border or pot-up two or three bulbs in a 5- to 6-inch pot, previously well-crocked. Stand in a cold frame, protected from frost, in September. Move into the greenhouse about mid-January, and water while growing. Dry-off after flowering and rest again during winter. Propagate by means of offsets when re-potting.

**Brazilian Spider Flower** (see **Tibouchina semidecandra**).

**Bredia hirsuta,** *Melastomaceæ.*—An ornamental greenhouse plant with rosy-pink flowers, growing about 12 in. high. A native of Japan.

*Culture.*—Grow in well-drained pots in a compost of loam, leaf-mould, peat and sand. Propagate by cuttings of ripened shoots inserted in sandy soil in a warm propagating case.

**Brevoortia Ida-Maia (Brodiæa coccinea)** (Crimson Satin Flower or Floral Fire-cracker), *Liliaceæ.*—A native of California, dark crimson and green, flowers in summer, 20 inches. For culture, see **Brodiæa.**

**Bridal Wreath** (see **Francoa racemosa**).

**Briza** (Quaking Grass), *Gramineæ.*—Although these graceful grasses are hardy, they make very attractive pot-plants. *B. maxima* [S. Europe] is an annual 18 inches high, and is very suitable for conservatory or greenhouse, while *B. minor*, a dwarf annual, 6–8 inches, is very attractive when grown in pans for the alpine house. Seeds can be sown in the spring for display in the summer. If sown in September it will flower the following spring.

**Brodiæa** (Californian or Missouri Hyacinth), *Liliaceæ.*—Beautiful hardy and half-hardy bulbous plants with hyacinth-like foliage, amidst which the cup-shaped flowers of various colours are borne on stems, but very little taller than the leaves. They grow, according to species, from 6–40 inches high, and mostly flower in summer.

They thrive in well-drained, deep, sandy soil, mixed with leaf-mould, in sunny borders, in the cool greenhouse, in the alpine house, or in the rock garden.

*Culture.*—Plant or pot-up in October, 3 inches deep. Protect with ashes during the winter, and lift the bulbs from the soil every fourth year only. Propagate by means of offsets in October.

*Species.*—*B. grandiflora* [California] (violet-blue, June and July, 15 in.); *B. ixioides* [S. California] (yellow, summer, 6 in.); *B. Ipheion uniflora* (Spring Star Flower) [Argentina] (white or blue, April–May, 6 in.); *B. volubilis* [*syn. Stropholirion californicum*] (climber, rosy purple, summer, 24 in.).

**Brodiæa coccinea** (see **Brevoortia Ida-Maia**).

**Bromelia,** *Bromeliaceæ.*—A group of warm greenhouse plants allied to the Pine-apple. Some of them have brilliant flowers or foliage. They require the same treatment as **Billbergia.** *B. Pinguin* [Jamaica]

272

Achimenes *var.*            Auriculas (*mixed*)

*Photos*]                    [*Sutton & Sons Ltd. and Alexander & Brown*
Acroclinium roseum *var. album*    Aquilegias (long spurred)

[*Thomsons (Photography*) *Ltd.*

Camellia in an Unheated Greenhouse

has reddish flowers in a dense panicle, with foliage becoming pink and red with age.

**Brompton Stock** (**Matthiola incana** var. *autumnalis*) (see **Stocks**).

**Broughtonia sanguinea** (see Chapter on **Orchids**).

**Browallia,** *Solanaceæ.*—Handsome, profusely flowering, half-hardy annuals and perennials, growing from 12–24 inches in height, and covered with beautiful flowers during autumn, winter and early spring. They thrive in warm, sunny borders in the milder localities in rich soil, or in the cool greenhouse.

*Culture.*—Sow seed thinly in March, under glass, in gentle heat (60° F.). Pot-up singly in light rich soil, pot-on into 5- to 6-inch pots and use for greenhouse decoration in autumn. Seed sown in summer will furnish plants for winter and spring flowering. Feed with weak liquid manure when the buds are forming. Perennial species may also be propagated from cuttings inserted in sandy soil in a propagator during spring or autumn.

*Species.*—(Annuals) *B. demissa* [S. America] (bluish violet, 8–16 in.); *B. grandiflora* [Peru] (pale blue or white, 18–24 in.); (perennials) *B. speciosa* [Colombia], and the var. *major* (blue, white throat, 24 in.).

**Brownea,** *Leguminosæ.*—Handsome stove evergreen shrubs or trees, with dense terminal clusters of bright red flowers, suitable for a large house. They attain a height of 20 feet or more, and thrive in a mixture of loam, peat, and sand, but care should be taken not to over-water them in the winter. Cuttings of ripened wood should be taken and placed in sand, under glass and in strong bottom heat (temperature 50–55° F. winter, 60–80° F. summer).

*Species and Varieties.*—*B. Ariza* (*B. Princeps*) [Bogotá] (richest scarlet, summer; requires a large house to get its full beauty); *B. Crawfordii* (a beautiful garden hybrid between *B. grandiceps* and *B. macrophylla*, scarlet, summer); *B. grandiceps* [Caracas] (red, summer); *B. macrophylla* [Colombia] (rich scarlet in large heads); *B. Rosa-de-Monte* [S. America] (crimson-scarlet, June).

**Brugmansia** (see **Datura**).

**Brunfelsia,** *Solanaceæ.*—Elegant free-flowering shrubs for the warm greenhouse. They flower during the spring and summer. After flowering they should be re-potted if necessary in a mixture of loam, leaf-soil, peat, and sand, and placed in a moist atmosphere, with a temperature of 60–65° F. to encourage new growth. Where growth is finished, keep them drier, both at the roots and overhead, and place them in a temperature of 50–55° F. Cuttings of fairly firm wood root readily in sandy soil, in a close case, with bottom heat. Pot-up in small pots when rooted, and grow on as already mentioned.

*Species and Varieties.*—*B. americana* [Tropical America] (white, shading with age to yellow, sweet-scented, June, 36 in.); *B. calycina* [Brazil] (rich purple, fading with age, June, 18–24 in.); *B. c.* var. *eximia* (free flowering, intermediate between type and var. *macrantha*); *B. c.* var. *macrantha* (has larger flowers and a white eye, and is one of the finest shrubs for a warm greenhouse); *B. undulata* [Jamaica] (has white flowers with undulate petals and long corolla tubes).

S

# THE GREENHOUSE

**Bryanthus Breweri** (see **Phyllodoce Breweri**).

**Bryanthus empetriformis** (see **Phyllodoce empetriformis**).

**Bryophyllum,** *Crassulaceæ.*—A small group of warm greenhouse plants of a succulent character, which thrive in pots of rich, loamy soil. Perfect drainage is essential, but very little water is needed at any time. Seed should be sown in sandy soil and placed in a little warmth. Leaves taken from the plant and laid on a damp surface will throw out young plants round their margins. When the small plants have reached a stage large enough to handle they can be taken from the parent plant and potted-up, and this is perhaps the best method of propagation.

*Species.*—B. *crenatum* [Madagascar] (yellowish, April and May, 20–30 in.) ; B. *pinnatum* (B. *calycinum*) [Mexico] (yellowish-red flowers, pendulous, with inflated calyx, 24–36 in.).

**Bryophyllum uniflorum** (see **Kitchingia uniflora**).

**Buddleia,** *Loganiaceæ.*—Beautiful hardy and half-hardy flowering shrubs, natives of India, Africa, China and S. America. Some species are not quite hardy enough to endure severe weather out-of-doors, but flourish in well-drained, deep, ordinary soil or good loam, in warm, sunny, sheltered positions, on a wall, or in the cold greenhouse, and flower profusely.

*Culture.*—Plant or pot-up B. *globosa* in March or October, the others from November to March. Do not prune B. *globosa*, merely cut out a little old wood after flowering, but in the case of B. *Davidii* (B. *variabilis*) cut the last year's shoots back to within a few inches of the old wood in February. If space is a consideration, B. *globosa* may also be cut back as advised for B. *Davidii*, but this will postpone its flowering until August or September. B. *alternifolia* carries pale purple flowers in June on the previous year's growth. The clusters of small flowers are borne close in to the long, drooping and slender stems. Prune this directly after flowering, and cut out the stems that have flowered.

*Propagation.*—This is effected by means of cuttings in a frame in late summer or autumn, or by means of seed when ripe.

*Species.*—B. *globosa*, commonly called " Orange Ball Tree ", is hardy. It grows about 10 feet high, and is remarkable for its pretty sprays of ball-shaped orange blossoms in May and June, also for its lanceolate leaves, pale green above and whitish below. It will do well in any soil, even near the sea, and is semi-evergreen. B. *Davidii* (B. *variabilis*) and vars. which are hardy, grow to about 15 feet in height and produce honey-scented inflorescens of lilac flowers in August. A dwarf form, B. *D. nanhœnsis*, rarely exceeds 4 feet in height. Other species are B. *alternifolia* (pale purple, June, 4–6 feet) ; B. *asiatica* [China, India, etc.] a most desirable greenhouse shrub, with slender spikes of fragrant white flowers in winter ; B. *caryopteridifolia* [W. China] a deciduous shrub, the young growth of which is covered with pure white wool. It bears fragrant lavender-coloured flowers, in May, on the previous year's growth, and attains a height of 8–10 feet. B. *Colvillei* [Himalayas] (rose to crimson, July, 20 ft.), which is the most beautiful of the genus, but one which requires a large house so that it can be planted out. B. *madagascariensis* [Madagascar] (terminal panicles of orange yellow flowers during the winter, 10–20 feet). The last three are, strictly

274

speaking, the only ones that need a greenhouse, although the others are useful for growing indoors.

**Bugle Lily** (see **Watsonia**).

**Bulbine bulbosa,** *Liliaceæ.*—This (12–18 in.) and *B. semi-barbatum* (24 in.) are both half-hardy, and bear yellow flowers.

**Bulbocodium** (Spring Meadow Saffron), *Liliaceæ.*—A pretty little hardy bulb, with crocus-like blooms, which likes a well-drained, sandy soil and a sunny position in a warm border, in the rock garden ; or it may be grown in the alpine or cold greenhouse. They grow about 5–6 inches in height and flower in early spring.

*Culture.*—Plant or pot-up in August, placing four or five bulbs in a 5-inch pot or pan, and stand in a light, airy position. Water regularly while growing, and dry off and rest after flowering. Lift from the soil every fourth year, and propagate by means of offsets in August. *B. vernum* (purplish red, Jan.–March, 5 in.) is the best species.

**Bulbophyllum** (see Chapter on **Orchids**).

**Burbidgea nitida,** *Zingiberaceæ.*—An attractive, stove, herbaceous perennial from N. Borneo, 24–30 inches high, with bright orange-scarlet flowers during the summer. Thrives in sandy loam, leaf-mould and a little fibrous peat, well drained. A moist atmosphere is essential. It is increased by division of the roots in the spring, or by seed sown when ripe, and placed in a warm temperature.

*B. schizocheila* [Malaya] is a dwarf, more compact than the above, and has orange yellow flowers. It requires the same treatment.

**Burchellia capensis,** *Rubiaceæ.*—An evergreen shrub from S. Africa, with rich, dark green foliage and brilliant scarlet flowers in terminal clusters (March and April, 3–5 ft.). It requires fibrous loam and sandy peat in equal proportions. It does best when planted out in the greenhouse border, although it is quite a good pot-plant. Firm cuttings of young shoots root readily in May and June, when placed under a bell-glass, in a warm temperature. Pot-on as required.

**Burlingtonia fragrans** (see **Rodriguezia** in Chapter on **Orchids**).

**Bushman's Poison** (see **Acokanthera venenata**).

**Buttercup** (see **Ranunculus**).

**Buttercup Tulip** (see **Calochortus**).

**Butterfly Flower** (see **Schizanthus**).

**Butterfly Iris** (see **Moræa**).

**Butterfly Pea** (see **Clitorea ternatea**).

**Butter-wort** (see **Pinguicula**).

**Cabbage Palm** (see **Oreodoxa oleracea**).

**Cabbage Palmetto** (see **Sabal Palmetto**).

**Cabomba** (Fanwort), *Nymphæaceæ.*—Interesting aquatic plants for the aquarium. The floating leaves differ from the submerged ones in that the latter are very finely dissected. They succeed best in water free from lime. *C. caroliniana*, which is a very common plant for fish-bowls and small aquaria, and which is a good oxygenator, is readily propagated from cuttings placed in soil and submerged in water, with a temperature of 55–65° F. It is often sold in bunches with a weight at the bottom. It will last for five or six weeks, and should then be replaced.

# THE GREENHOUSE

*Species.—C. aquatica* [Tropical America] (flowers yellow, spring, floating leaves, peltate and roundish). Requires a warm temperature. *C. caroliniana* [N. America] (flowers white with yellow spots at the base of the petals, floating leaves oblong). A much hardier plant than *C. aquatica* and the one most usually seen.

**Cacti** (includes all members of *Cactaceæ*) (see Chapter on **Cacti**).

**Cactus Melocactus (Melocactus communis)** [Melon Cactus or Turk's Cap], *Cactaceæ.*—An interesting succulent plant from the West Indies. It requires a high temperature, plenty of drainage, very porous soil and little water. It is increased by seed sown as soon as ripe in well drained sandy soil, in a temperature of 60–70° F.

**Cajophora lateritia** (see **Blumenbachia lateritia**).

**Calabash Gourd** (see **Lagenaria leucantha**).

**Caladium,** *Araceæ.*—Attractive tuberous-rooted foliage plants with large and beautifully coloured leaves, suitable for cultivation in the hot-house.

*Culture.*—Start the tubers in February in a tray or shallow box of leaf-mould, and pot-up singly, when growth commences, in a compost of two parts of turfy loam to one part each of leaf-mould and peat. Pot on into 6-inch pots and feed with doses of weak liquid manure. Water well while growing, and keep a warm moist atmosphere of never less than 75° F. during the summer, and 55° F. during the winter. Keep dry when dormant.

*Propagation.*—Divide the tubers when potting up in the spring.

New forms are raised from seed. This operation is an exceedingly easy one, as **Caladiums** cross-fertilise very readily. Seed should be sown as soon as ripe, and the pots plunged in moist heat. Seedlings at first have green foliage, and it is not until they have produced a number of leaves that the colouring appears.

*Species.—C. bicolor* [S. America] (green and red leaves) ; *C. Chantinii* [Pará] (green and yellow leaves) ; *C. Humboldtii* (*C. argyrites*) [Pará] (green and white leaves) ; *C. picturatum* [Brazil] (green and yellow leaves). There are numerous named varieties available.

**Calampelis scaber** (see **Eccremocarpus scaber**).

**Calandrinia,** *Portulaceæ.*—A group of plants suitable for the warm greenhouse or alpine house, where they require a well-drained, light, sandy soil. They are readily raised from seed in April, and even the hardy kinds like a little protection during the early stages. Cuttings also strike freely with a little warmth.

*Species.—C. discolor* [Chile], warm greenhouse (bright light purple flowers, summer, 15–18 in.) ; *C. grandiflora* [Chile], similar to above, warm greenhouse (purple, summer, 15–18 in.) ; *C. umbellata* [Peru] cumbels of bright crimson flowers, summer, 6 in.), suitable in pans for the alpine house.

**Calanthe Harrisii** (see Chapter on **Orchids**).

**Calathea,** *Marantaceæ.*—Handsome foliage plants allied to **Marantas,** with which some species have been confused. They require a moist stove house, where the temperature does not fall below 65° F., rising to 90° F. during the day. They should be potted in turfy loam, peat, sand, and well-rotted manure. Good drainage and plenty of pot room

276

are essential. When well established, liquid manure may be administered once a week, but artificial fertilisers should never be used. They may be increased by division of the crowns during the spring, or by placing cuttings of the kind that make secondary growth in a propagating case.

*Species.*—*C. argyrophylla* [garden hybrid] (foliage silvery white and pale green; under-surface red, 12–36 in.); *C. Chantrieri* (**Maranta Chantrieri**) [Brazil] (dark-green stripes on greyish-green ground, 18–24 in.); *C. eximia* [Central America] (foliage striped rich orange, green and silver; under surface wine-red, 12–36 in.); *C. illustris* [Ecuador] (foliage dark olive-green, with bluish metallic lustre over the whole leaf, midrib being feathered on either side with dull silvery white); *C. ornata* [Guiana] (rich shining green above, in the adult stage, dull purplish red beneath); the leaves in the juvenile stage are all beautifully striped with pink or rose between the principal veins, which in the intermediate stage changes to white, and finally green in the adult stage; this changing has led to the forms being distributed under separate names, all of which at times can be found on one plant; *C. zebrina* (Zebra Plant) [Brazil] (foliage velvety green, striped pale yellowish green, 12–36 in.).

**Calceolaria** (Slipper Flower), *Scrophulariaceæ.*—There are three distinct kinds of Calceolaria: the *herbaceous Calceolaria* (*C. herbeo-hybrida*), raised and reared under glass for flowering in May and June; the *shrubby Calceolaria*, grown for bedding-out or greenhouse decoration; these thrive in fibrous loam mixed with leaf-mould and sand. The third type, being hardy herbaceous perennials and annuals, make excellent subjects for the rock garden.

The flowers of the former through cultivation have attained an enormous size and a rich variety of markings, the ground colour being for the most part yellow, blotched or spotted with brown or crimson. The blossoms of the *shrubby Calceolarias* are small but very numerous, forming large trusses of flowers, and are either orange, yellow, or a deep, rich, velvety brown in colour, thus presenting an effective contrast when grown in clumps or masses.

*Culture.*—(*Herbaceous or Greenhouse Calceolarias*). Sow lightly and thinly in well-drained pots or pans in a cool greenhouse or frame during June. Pot-up singly in July, and keep in a frost-proof frame, preferably with a north aspect and with the bottom covered with ashes. Re-pot into 3- or 4-inch pots in September, and take into the greenhouse. See that they get plenty of fresh air by day. Keep warm and moist by night, and maintain a steady even temperature. A moist temperature of from 45–50° F. suits them admirably. A hot, dry atmosphere only predisposes to attacks from red spider, and is unnecessary, but the temperature must not fall below 45° F. Pot-up finally in February or March (before the flower-buds begin to move), using 7- to 8-inch pots and a compost of two parts loam to one parf leaf-mould and sand, and keep near the glass in a cool greenhouse. Stake securely, shade from the strong sun, and allow the plants plenty of space and air, and do not over-water. Keep the soil just moist and the temperature even. Weak liquid manure should be given at fortnightly intervals, as soon

# THE GREENHOUSE

as the buds appear. Fumigate on the slightest suspicion of greenfly. They are also subject to wilt, the plants suddenly collapsing. This is probably due to a species of Phytopthora. For this the soil should be sterilised.

*Propagation.*—Propagate by means of division in March or October. Seed should be sown afresh each year to obtain the best results.

*Herbaceous Species.—C. arachnoides* [Chile] (dull purple, woolly leaves, 12 in.) ; *C. corymbosa* [Chile] (yellow, marked with red lines in the throat, 24–30 in.) ; *C. crenatifolia* [Chile] (yellow with orange-brown spots, 18–24 in.) ; it is from this species that we probably derive the spots of Calceolaria flowers ; *C. Sinclairii (Jovellana Sinclairii)* [New Zealand] (lilac or fresh-colour spotted, 18 in.).

*Herbaceous and Hybrids.—C. herbeohybrida,* many beautiful strains of garden origin ; *C. multiflora nana,* dwarf compact strain similar to above.

*Culture.—*(Shrubby Calceolarias).—Take cuttings of vigorous young shoots in September and strike 2 inches apart, in pots, in well-drained, sandy soil under glass, or in a warm north border, and cover with a hand-glass. If the weather turns frosty, throw some covering over the hand-glass. The cuttings cannot be taken until fresh shoots have broken out from the base, as shoots that have flowered are useless for cuttings. Press the earth well round them and water well. The most favourable conditions for all cuttings is when a change to moist growing weather succeeds within two or three days the dry weather during which the cuttings have been taken. About the middle of February the cuttings must have their growing points pinched back to produce bushy plants. A fortnight later they may either be potted or kept as cool as possible, 3 to 4 inches apart in the pit. Finally they should be transferred to the garden or greenhouse, and set about 9 inches apart towards the end of May or early in June. Seed may also be sown under glass in March (temperature, 50–60° F.). Transplant the seedlings into boxes as soon as they can be handled, and next pot-up singly in 3- to 4-inch pots. Transfer to a cold frame in May, and before the plants become pot-bound, re-pot into 5- to 6-inch pots if for greenhouse use, or, if for summer bedding, harden off, and plant out early in June.

*Shrubby Species.—C. alba* [Chile] (white, summer, 12 in.) ; *C. amplexicaulis* [Chile] (pale yellow) ; *C. bicolor* [Peru] (sulphur-yellow, white, 12 in.) ; *C. fruticohybrida* (locality unknown] (yellow, summer, 15 in.) ; *C. hyssopifolia* [Chile] (sulphur-yellow, summer, 12 in.) ; *C. integrifolia* [Chile] (yellow, summer, 24–72 in.) ; *C. Pavonii* [Peru] (rich golden yellow) ; *C. violacea (Jovellana violacea)* [Chile] (mauve-purple).

*Shrubby hybrids.—C. Allardii* (golden yellow, 15 in.) ; *C. " Banksii "* (orange-bronze) ; *C. " Burbidgei "* (yellow) ; *C. " Bronze Prince " ; C. " Dulcia "* (pinkish mauve, 24 in.) ; *C. "gracilis "* [John Innes Strain] (pink to mauve and cream, 6–24 in.) ; *C. " Milkmaid "* (white, 24 in.) ; *C. " Profusa "* [*C. " Clibranii "*] (deep yellow, May–Sept., 9–36 in.) ; *C. " Sparkler "* (bronze and yellow) ; *C. " Sultan "* (maroon) ; *C. " Topaz "* (orange red, 15 in.) ; *C. " Veitchii "* (creamy white). All these flower from May to September and are useful greenhouse plants, growing from 9 to 36 inches in height.

**278**

Several Calceolarias are ideal for the alpine house, grown in pans in good turfy loam, leaf-soil, and sand. They are increased by seed sown as soon as ripe, which should be plunged in a cool frame. They may also be propagated by division, which should be done as soon as the plants have finished flowering. They should be kept on the north side of a wall in a cold frame when not in flower.

*Alpine Species.*—*C. acutifolia* (*C. polyrrhiza*) [Chile] (yellow, 6 in.) ; *C. biflora* [Chile] (yellow, 12 in.) ; *C. Darwinii* [Magellan region] (orange and brown, 4 in.) ; *C. tenella* [Chile] (yellow, spotted, 6 in.).

**Calendula** (Pot Marigold), *Compositæ.*—Beautiful hardy annuals which thrive in beds or borders in almost any soil. They grow about 18 inches high, and their bright flowers from March to October make them useful in the greenhouse.

*Culture.*—Sow seed in ordinary soil in a sunny position in March, and later, at intervals, up to September. Pot-up as required and take indoors, where they may be had in flower throughout the summer and autumn. Regular attention as regards watering is all that they require, and the prompt removal of dead flower-heads.

*Named Varieties.*—*Chrysantha* (buttercup-yellow) ; *Favourite* (sulphur-yellow) ; *Lemon Queen* (lemon-yellow) ; *Orange King* (bright orange) ; *Prince of Orange* (orange, striped pale yellow) ; *Radio* (orange) ; and *Yellow Queen* (golden yellow).

**Calico Bush** (see **Kalmia latifolia**).

**Californian Bluebell** (see **Phacelia Whitlavia**).

**Californian Hyacinth** (see **Brodiæa**).

**Californian Lilac** (see **Ceanothus**).

**Californian Pitcher Plant** (see **Darlingtonia californica**).

**Callianthemum anemonoides,** *Ranunculaceæ.*—An attractive plant from the Tyrol, which, although hardy in the rock-garden, will be found a useful subject for the alpine house. It should be grown in pans in ordinary soil of loam, leaf-mould, and sand. In June it bears anemone-like flowers, white or tinted rose, which look very charming above its Rue-like foliage (4–6 inches high). *C. Kernerianum* [Europe] is a dainty little plant with bluish-grey, fern-like foliage and large lilac-white flowers (June, 4–5 in.).

**Callicarpa,** *Verbenaceæ.*—Attractive berried-evergreens, and although most of them are hardy, they will be found very useful for the cool greenhouse during the late summer and autumn, with their lilac, violet, red, and occasionally white fruits. Cuttings strike readily in a little bottom heat, and should be potted-on gradually in a mixture of two parts good loam to one part of peat and sand in equal proportions, and kept in a temperature of 45–50° F. during the winter.

*Species and Varieties.*—*C. rubella* (*C. purpurea*) [China and Himalayas] (flowers pink, fruit lilac-violet) ; *C. Giraldii* [W. China] (flowers pink, fruit violet) ; *C. japonica* [Japan] (flowers pink or whitish, fruit violet, August) ; *C. j.* var. *leucocarpa* (white fruits). All the above grow from 24 to 36 inches in height)

**Calliphruria Hartwegiana,** *Amaryllidaceæ.*—This beautiful greenhouse bulbous plant from New Grenada is related to **Eucharis**. It bears greenish-white flowers in May and June, and grows to a height of 12 inches. As soon as new growth begins it should be re-potted firmly in a compost of sandy loam, a little peat, some leaf-soil and sand. It is propagated by offsets.

**Callipsyche,** *Amaryllidaceæ.*—Showy bulbous plants for the cool greenhouse requiring shade, particularly when in flower. They should be potted in a good compost of turfy loam, with a little leaf-soil and sufficient sand to make it porous; with good drainage. They require plenty of water when growing, but as the leaves turn yellow this should gradually be withheld. They should never be allowed to become dust dry, however; even when at rest, there should be just enough moisture to prevent the bulbs from shrivelling. They are propagated by offsets, which should be taken off when potting, or by seed sown as soon as ripe and placed in a warm temperature.

*Species.*—C. *aurantiaca* [Andes of Ecuador] (deep golden yellow, 20–24 in.); C. *eucrosioides* [Mexico] (scarlet and green, 24 in.); C. *mirabilis* [Peru] (greenish yellow, 30–36 in.).

**Callistemon** (Bottle-brush Plant), *Myrtaceæ.*—Very attractive greenhouse evergreen shrubs which thrive in full sun, in a cool house, in equal parts of sandy peat and loam. They carry beautiful crimson and golden flowers in May and June on stems from 3 to 6 feet in height.

*Culture.*—Pot-up in June (biennially) in 6- to 10-inch pots; stand out of doors from June to September, and trim after flowering. Water well and give occasional doses of liquid manure while growing. The Callistemon needs full sun and should be kept well up near the glass.

*Propagation.*—To propagate, take cuttings of matured wood in the late spring and strike in a frame. Seed may be sown when so desired in sandy soil in pots in March or April, but seedlings take some years to mature into flowering plants.

*Species.*—C. *citrinus splendens* [Australia] (scarlet); C. *linearis* [Australia] (scarlet); C. *salignus* [Australia] and C. *speciosus* [W. Australia] (scarlet).

**Callistephus chinensis** (China Aster), *Compositæ.*—A beautiful, half-hardy, summer and autumn-flowering annual, particularly adapted for small beds, edgings, the rock-garden, or for pot culture in the cold greenhouse.

The Aster is not only one of the most popular, but is also one of the most effective of our late summer and autumn flowers, producing blooms in profusion in which richness and variety of colour are combined with the most perfect and beautiful form. The colours range from scarlet, through pink, purple, lavender, and blue, to white. The Aster is indispensable in every garden and greenhouse where a late summer and autumnal display is desired.

In pots as single plants and for colour grouping it stands unrivalled. The plants grow from 6 to 24 inches high.

The Aster may be divided into two sections. One has flat petals either reflexed or incurved; the former resembling the **Chrysanthemum,** with flowers of white, blue, rose, scarlet and crimson; whilst the latter, turning its petals towards the centre of the flower, forms when well grown, a perfect ball, and is best described by its resemblance to the **Pæony;** these are crimson, pink, blue and white in colour. The other varieties are quilled with tubular florets, and the most perfect flowers are surrounded by a circle of flat or guard petals, as in the **Hollyhock.** The flowers of these are particularly admired for the exquisite symmetry of their form. A beautiful strain is the *Ostrich Plume*, with double flowers with fine curled petals—these grow to about 18 inches in height and make excellent subjects for cutting. The *Comet* type bear large flowers with broad florets like the **Chrysanthemum,** grow to about 2 feet in height and make splended bedding or edging plants. Equally admired is the *Victoria* strain, whose flowers are white, yellow, blue, rose or crimson; these grow to a height of about 15 inches and have double flowers from 4 to 6 inches in diameter. The *Giant Ray* varieties are chiefly grown for cutting. The single-flowered *A. chinensis* must not be overlooked; this is a great garden favourite which provides good cut blooms on stems about 18 inches high. Other varieties are *Firefly* (scarlet-crimson), *Southcote Beauty* (mixed colours), *Venus* (an early variety resembling a pink Verbena).

All varieties thrive in a deep, rich, light soil in hot, dry weather, and they should be frequently supplied with manure-water.

*Culture.*—The seed should be sown in a sheltered spot in light, rich soil, in the open, about the first week in April, and sown twice more at intervals of a fortnight for succession; or it may be sown in March in boxes or pans in light, rich soil, and placed under glass in an airy and sunny position (temperature 60° F.). When the seedlings are large enough to handle, about the end of April, prick-off and transplant about 4 inches apart into soil containing a good proportion of leaf-mould in a cold frame, and harden off. Pot-up three plants in a 6-inch pot in a compost of two-thirds fibrous loam and one-third well-decayed manure. Stand in the open on a hard bed of ashes or on slates, and cover to the rims of the pots with a layer of fibre. Until the buds begin to form a little weak liquid manure may be given with advantage. In dry weather a thorough soaking with water must be given, not just a sprinkling, or the roots will be drawn to the surface. Transfer under glass as soon as the buds begin to colour.

*Varieties of C. chinensis* [single] (18 in.) : *Chrysanthemum-flowered* (12 in.); *Comet* [broad florets] (24 in.); *Dwarf Bouquet* (6–9 in.); *Giant Ray* [stiff and prominent florets] (18 in.); *Mignon* (10 in.); *Ostrich Plume* [branching with double flowers] (18 in.); *Quilled* (tubular florets); *Pæony-flowered* (incurving florets) (18 in.); *Victoria* (double) (15 in.).

**Callitris Whytei** (see **Widdringtonia Whytei**).

**Calocephalus Brownii** (see **Leucophyta Brownii**).

**Calochortus** (Butterfly Tulip, Star Tulip, and Mariposa Lily), *Liliaceæ.*—Beautiful, half-hardy, bulbous plants that thrive in warm sheltered situations in full sun and in sandy leaf-mould They are also useful for cultivation in the cold greenhouse.

*Pot Culture.*—Pot-up 10 bulbs in a 4- to 5-inch pot in November in a compost of two-thirds sandy loam and one-sixth part each of peat and leaf-mould. Keep covered with fibre in a cold frame until late December, then transfer to the greenhouse; water regularly while growing and dry off after flowering.

*Propagation.*—Propagate by means of offsets in November. Seed may be sown in a frame, but seedlings are slow in reaching maturity.

*Species.*—*C. Howellii* [Oregon] (white, July–Aug., **18** in.); *C. pulchellus* [Central California] (yellow-orange, July–Aug., **12** in.); *C. venustus* and vars. [California] (yellow and red, July–Aug., **15** in.).

**Calodendron capensis** (Cape Chestnut), *Rutaceæ.*—This is said to be one of the most handsome trees of the Cape of Good Hope. It bears large panicles of white or rose-coloured flowers, sometimes **7** inches across and **6** inches deep, and has attractive evergreen foliage. Owing to its size, it requires a large greenhouse, and succeeds in a mixture of loam and peat. Cuttings of half-ripened wood root in sand placed under a bell-glass in gentle bottom heat.

**Calonyction** (Moonflower), *Convolvulaceæ.*—This genus is sometimes united with *Ipomæa*, but is distinguished by the shape of its flowers, the arrangement of its style and stamens, and its night-blooming habit. They are twining perennial herbs, useful for the walls or roof of the greenhouse, and they will grow in ordinary soil of loam, leaf-mould, and sand. They are readily raised by seed placed on a hot bed, or by cuttings placed under a bell-glass over bottom heat. The young plants should be potted-on finally giving them a **12**-inch pot, or, if possible, plant out in the border.

*Species.*—*C. aculeatum* (*Ipomæa Bona-nox*) [Tropical America] (white, July–Aug., **10** ft., commonly known as the " Moon-flower "); *C. muricatum* [Himalayas] (purple, summer, **10** ft.).

**Calycanthus floridus** (Carolina All-spice), *Calycanthaceæ.*—A hardy deciduous shrub from California which likes a partially shaded, moist position in any ordinary good soil. It carries purplish-red flowers in May and June, and grows to a height of **5** feet or more. It is sometimes introduced into the greenhouse on account of its fragrance.

*Culture.*—Plant or pot-up in November and cut out dead wood after flowering. Propagate by means of cuttings or layering in summer.

**Calypso borealis** (see Chapter on **Orchids**).

**Camarotis rostrata** (see Chapter on **Orchids**).

**Camellia,** *Ternstrœmiacea.*—The *Camellia japonica* and its varieties and hybrids is a very old favourite which was at one time supposed to be essentially a greenhouse plant. It has been found, however, that it is quite hardy and easy of culture outdoors. These lovely flowering evergreen shrubs thrive in sheltered and semi-shaded positions, and in practically any soil, provided it is lime-free.

The Camellia's robust constitution, dark, glossy, evergreen foliage, and lovely, wax-like flowers render it essential to the amateur's greenhouse. It is most useful when grown as a shrub **2–3** feet in height, but it will run up to a height of **20** feet if permitted. All Camellias bloom between February and May, at a time when flowers, comparatively speaking, are apt to be scarce. In the warm house it may be had in flower earlier.

*Culture.*—Pot-up firmly in May, when young growth is about **1** inch long, using **8**- to **12**-inch pots, according to the size of the plant. It should not be too big, as the Camellia does best when under-potted. Use a compost of one-half part turfy loam and a quarter part each of

**282**

# GREENHOUSE PLANTS

sand and peat or leaf-mould. As soon as re-established, gradually harden off, stand out-of-doors in partial shade on a firm base of ashes or bricks. Although partial shade is necessary, they must not be exposed to the drip from trees. Examine the pots occasionally and keep the roots moist, but not too wet. If allowed to become " dust dry ", the flower-buds will probably drop at a later date, although from the present state of the foliage it may appear that little damage has been done. This dryness at the roots is the most frequent cause of the all-too-common " bud dropping ", which causes such keen disappointment to amateurs. Move the plants into cold frames or the cold house in September, and keep the temperature at between 40° and 50° F. When the flowering season approaches raise the temperature 5°, and in another ten days 5° more, but as soon as the flowers open lower the temperature again by about 5°, so as to extend the blooming period of the plant. Sufficient circulation of air must be maintained, or the buds will drop. Keep the roots moist when the buds are forming, and top dress with leaf-mould and well-rotted manure, or give weekly applications of weak manure-water. Trim back all straggling shoots after flowering, and syringe daily to encourage new growth to break. Re-pot, if necessary, when new growth is about an inch in length. Sponge the leaves occasionally and disturb the roots as little as possible.

*Propagation.*—This is carried out by experts by means of grafting in a close propagating frame in early spring, using seedling *C. japonica* as a stock, or by cuttings of half-matured shoots in a frame in August or September. When the cuttings have struck give a moist heat of about 70° F. for a few weeks to encourage growth, then grow on in a temperature of 50–60° F., through the winter. Seeds may be sown 1 inch deep in a mixture of sandy peat (two-thirds) and leaf-mould (one-third), and the seedlings raised in moist heat (65° F.). Germination may take as long as two years, and the compost should never become dry. Most amateurs prefer to purchase young pot-plants.

*Species.*—*C. japonica* [China and Japan] (red, pink to white flowers and shining leaves). There are many beautiful named varieties of this species, such as *C. alba plena* (white, double) ; *C. anemoniflora* ; *C. Chandleri elegans* (double pink) ; *C. Donckelari* (rose) ; *C. Henri Favre* (rose-salmon) ; *C. Lady Clare* (pink) ; *C. Jupiter* (rosy red, single) ; *C. magnoliæflora* (pale rose, semi-double) ; *C. Mathiotiana* (rose-red, double, and alba, white) ; and *C. Waltham Glory* (scarlet). Another species is *C. reticulata* [China] (rose-crimson, semi-double flowers, dull leaves). There is a double-flowered variety of this species ; *C. Sasanqua* [China and Japan] (white, pink, or red flowers). There are various forms of this plant, including one in which the leaves are variegated green and white, with flowers pink and white.

**Campanula** (Bellflower), *Campanulaceæ.*—A comprehensive genus, including annuals, biennials, and perennials, providing plants for the alpine house, cold greenhouse, border, and rock-garden. They are characterised by the variety of their colours—usually shades of mauve, pink, blue, and white, single and double—and the profusion and duration of their bloom. Some of them are remarkable for their stately growth, others for their close, compact habit.

**283**

# THE GREENHOUSE

Of the tall-growing perennials, *C. pyramidalis* (the Chimney Bell-flower), from Europe, produces a most striking effect, and is undoubtedly the most useful and ornamental species for culture in the greenhouse. It attains a height of 6 feet or more, and carries glorious spikes of blue or white, bell-shaped flowers, grown in the open from June to September, in pots. The popular Canterbury Bell, *C. Medium*, is a very useful pot-plant for the greenhouse. Plants should be potted-up in 8-inch pots in the autumn and kept in a cool house or frame. They will then give a fine display of flowers during May and June, without any heat. *C. Vidalii* [Azores] is a useful shrubby species for flowering in the autumn, with white, waxy flowers. It can be propagated by seed or cuttings, and the plants are best in their second year.

Of the dwarf species, also perennials, some are grown in pots or baskets in the greenhouse. *C. fragilis* [Italy], *C. isophylla* [Italy] (blue or white) and *C. Mayi* (china blue) are trailing plants, excellent for hanging-baskets, and for growing so that they may hang over the edge of the greenhouse staging. In the warm house they bloom in summer. They are best grown in 4½- to 5-inch pots in the cool greenhouse, and will bloom from midsummer until the autumn. These plants love plenty of sun, and should be watered liberally while growing in summer, but in winter must be kept nearly dry. After flowering, cut the trailing shoots hard back.

*Pot Culture.—(C. pyramidalis)*. Sow in small pots, and place in a well-ventilated frame. Move into 5- or 6-inch pots in October, and keep in a frost-proof frame for the winter. Pot-up again in March, using 7- to 8-inch pots, and a compost of two-thirds sandy loam and one-third leaf-mould, rotted cow-manure, and a little old mortar-rubble; harden-off, and stand in the open. Stake as the flower-spikes form, move into the house about July, and give liquid manure when the buds form.

*(C. Medium)*. Seed sown outside in the spring and pricked off will make fine plants for potting-up in the autumn. There are single and double varieties, also *C. Medium* var. *calycanthema*, or Cup and Saucer. Varieties of *C. persicifolia* (Peach-leaved Campanula), both blue and white, as well as semi-double, make excellent pot-plants for the cool greenhouse. They may be kept outside all the summer, but must be given the protection of a cold frame during the winter.

*C. Allionii* [W. Alps] (blue, white, and pink, 3 in.); *C. alpina* [Europe] (light-blue flowers, July–Aug., 4 in.); *C. arvatica* [Spain] (light-blue flowers, June–Sept., 4 in.); *C. cæspitosa* [Austria] (June–Aug., 4 in.); *C. cenisia* [Switzerland] (blue, June, 4 in.); *C. cochleari-folia syn. pusilla* (deep blue or white, June–Sept., 3 in.); *C. garganica* [Italy] (blue, July–Aug., 5 in.); *C. pulla* [Europe] (violet, June–Sept., 3 in.); *C. Raddeana* [Caucasus] (purple, July–Sept., 8 in.); *C. Raineri* [Italy] (blue, June–Aug., 3 in.); and *C. Zoysii* [Austrian Alps] (June–Aug., 3 in.) are lovely little alpines for the alpine house. Pot-up in March or September in 4–5-inch pans of loam, peat and leaf mould (no lime). Keep on the dry side in winter in a cold frame. Keep a good look out for slugs, as they are partial to Campanulas. Propagate by means of seed in March or August, or by division in March or September.

284

# GREENHOUSE PLANTS

*Greenhouse Trailing Species.*—Propagate by means of seed in heat in March, by cuttings in a frame in August, or by division in March.

**Campsis grandiflora (Tecoma grandiflora)** [Chinese Trumpet Flower] *Bignoniaceæ.*—A climbing shrub from China, which bears orange, tubular-shaped flowers in August. It will bloom when quite small and can be grown as a pot-plant in fibrous loam, leaf-mould, and sand. It should be cut back hard in the winter. It is propagated by cuttings of the shoots, or by pieces of the root in shady soil, under a bell-glass with a little warmth.

**Camptosema,** *Leguminosæ.*—Showy greenhouse climbers either for the border or large pot. They require a compost of fibrous loam, leaf-mould, and sand. Propagation is effected by means of seed or cuttings in sandy soil in a little heat.

*Species.*—*C. pinnatum* [Brazil] (reddish-purple flowers, July); *C. rubicundum* [Argentina] (ruby-red, summer); *C. splendens* [S. America] (scarlet, summer).

**Canada Tea** (see **Gaultheria procumbens**).

**Canarina Campanula,** *Campanulaceæ.*—A beautiful, greenhouse, herbaceous perennial from the Canary Islands. It thrives in a compost of loam, leaf-mould, and sand in equal parts. Adequate root space and good drainage are essential. When new growth commences, a little heat is beneficial, as this assists the development of the flowers. Water should be given freely during the growing season. It is propagated by seed or cuttings in sandy soil, or by division of the roots when re-potting in January.

**Canary Creeper** (see **Tropæolum**).

**Candle Plant** (see **Kleinia articulata**).

**Candollea,** *Dilleniaceæ.*—Cool greenhouse, evergreen shrubs from Australia, which thrive in sandy peat and good fibrous loam. Cuttings root readily in sandy peat under a hand-glass.

*Species.*—*C. cuneiformis* (yellow, July, 6 ft.); *C. Huegelii* (yellow, May, 5–6 ft.); *C. tetrandra* (yellow, June, 6 ft.).

**Candytuft** (see **Iberis**).

**Canistrum,** *Bromeliaceæ.*—Showy epiphytes for the warm green-house. They are allied to the Pine-apple, and require the same culture as **Billbergia,** which see.

*Species.*—*C. aurantiacum* [Brazil] (orange-yellow flowers with orange-red bracts, June–Sept.); *C. amazonicum* [Brazil] (flowers white with green tube, in dense heads, handsome rosette of brownish leaves, May and June).

**Canna** (Indian Shot), *Cannaceæ.*—This beautiful half-hardy perennial is more especially a greenhouse plant, and, as such, its stately growth, combined with its reddish or deep-green foliage and rich, many-coloured flowers, render it very striking. When mixed with other plants it gives quite an oriental aspect, and is much used for summer bedding in warm, sunny beds and borders, with well-manured rich loam.

*Culture.*—Sow seed thinly ½ inch deep in well-drained, sandy loam and leaf-mould in a propagating case (temperature 75° F.), in February or March (the seed having previously been soaked for a day in warm water). The germination is very erratic, and some seeds will sprout

**285**

several weeks in advance of the others. Transplant each seedling into a single pot as soon as possible, leaving the seed-bed intact so that the other seeds may germinate at their leisure. The seed-bed must be kept uniformly moist. Pot-up singly as soon as possible, or propagate by means of division of roots in the spring, dividing them so that each section of root contains an eye, and sinking the pots in a box of fibre stood over the hot-water pipes. Pot-up early in March or April in single pots and, if for outdoor culture, plant out in June about 24 inches apart. If for greenhouse culture, pot-up into 6- to 12-inch pots, using a rich and porous compost of one-half loam and one-quarter part each of rotten cow-manure and sandy leaf-mould. Do not over-water until growth commences, but water freely and regularly in summer, and moderately in winter. The temperature of the greenhouse should be from 50° F. winter to 70° F. summer. During the winter the fleshy roots must be kept just moist and frost-proof. At the end of September pot-up those grown out of doors, and winter under glass. Keep moderately dry, and allow the leaves and stems to dry off gradually.

*Named Varieties.—Assaut* (scarlet); *Beethoven* (orange); *Italia* (orange and yellow); *Oiseau de Feu* (Fire Bird) (scarlet red); *President* (scarlet); *J. B. Van der Schoot* (yellow-spotted); and *R. Wallace* (canary-yellow). All flower in the open from August to October, and grow to a height of from 3 to 6 feet. In the cool or warm greenhouse they may be had in flower in summer.

**Canterbury Bell** (see **Campanula Medium**).

**Cantua buxifolia (Cantua dependens)**, *Polemoniaceæ.*—Attractive evergreen shrubs, natives of Peru, and one of the choicest of evergreen shrubs for culture in the cool greenhouse. They grow from 3 to 4 feet in height, and in April and May carry pendant clusters of pink to red, funnel-shaped flowers. *C. pyrifolia*, from S. America, has clusters of primrose coloured flowers and is a strong-growing climber.

*Culture.*—Pot-up in March, using well-crocked 8- to 10-inch pots and a compost of sandy loam and leaf-mould, or plant out in the greenhouse border. Water freely while growing, and keep just moist when dormant. Prune back to shape the plant after flowering, and cut out dead wood in spring. Re-pot or top dress annually. Both species are subject to red spider if grown in too dry an atmosphere.

*Propagation.*—Cuttings of new shoots may be rooted in sandy soil in slight heat (55° F.), preferably under a bell-glass, in April and May.

**Cape Cowslip** (see **Lachenalia**).

**Cape Daisy** (see **Dimorphotheca**).

**Cape Honeysuckle** (see **Tecomaria capensis**).

**Cape Hyacinth** (see **Galtonia candicans**).

**Cape Jasmine** (see **Gardenia jasminoides**).

**Cape Lily** (see **Crinum**).

**Cape Pond Weed** (see **Aponogeton distachyon**).

**Cape Primrose** (see **Streptocarpus**).

**Cape Shamrock** (see **Oxalis**).

**Capparis** (Caper Tree), *Capparidaceæ.*—Attractive evergreen shrubs for the greenhouse. The buds of *C. spinosa* when preserved are known as capers, and are used in caper sauce. They thrive best in a compost of well-drained, sandy loam, and should be grown in full sun. They may be readily increased by seed sown in sandy soil and placed in a warm house, or by cuttings of ripe shoots struck in sandy soil under a bell-glass, placed in moist heat.

*Species.*—*C. odoratissima* [Caracas] (violet, sweet-scented flowers, summer, 6 ft.) ; *C. spinosa* (common caper) [S. Europe] (flowers white, tinged on the outside with red, with conspicuous purple filaments, June, 3–4 ft.). The var. *rupestris* is a spineless form.

**Capsicum,** *Solanaceæ.*—Some species are very ornamental for green-house decoration in winter, while others have long been in cultivation for use in a green state for pickles, and, when ripened and ground, for Cayenne pepper. The smallest pods are the hottest and best suited for making Cayenne pepper, and are generally known as chillies. Seed should be sown in March and April in pots or pans and placed in heat. As soon as the seedlings are large enough, pot-off into 3-inch pots, still keeping them in heat until well rooted. Pot-on into 6-inch pots when the 3-inch pots are becoming full of root. They do best in a light, rich loam. Plenty of water and frequent syringing should be applied, as the plants are very liable to injury from red spider and other insects if this is neglected. The fruit will remain on the tree for a long time, especially if kept in the cool greenhouse. For pickling, the fruit should be gathered immediately it is ripe.

*C. annuum* (Common Capsicum), is an annual, and although it is never found wild, but as an escape from cultivation in the Old World Tropics, it is the principal species to which many of the various forms cultivated belong. These are often described by the shape of their fruits—e.g. Long Yellow, Long Red, Round Red, Red Cluster, etc. Little Gem, with erect red pods, and Prince of Wales, with yellow hanging pods, are attractive pot-plants.

**Caralluma,** *Asclepiadaceæ.*—Low-growing, succulent, plants, some-what resembling **Stapelias** (which see), requiring the same treatment.

*Species.*—*C. adscendens* [Coromandel] (flowers variegated with purple and yellow, summer, 12–18 in.) ; *C. affinis* [Mediterranean region] (reddish purple, striped yellow, 10–12 in.) ; *C. fimbriata* [Burma] (flowers fringed, pale yellow beneath, purple above, summer, 6–8 in.) ; *C. Sprengeri* [Abyssinia] (gold-bronze with white eye, 12–14 in.).

**Cardiospermum Halicacabum** (Balloon Vine), *Sapindaceæ.*—A popular and interesting, rapid-growing climber from the Tropics, for the cool greenhouse (temperature 45° F. winter, 60° F. summer). It is remark-able for its inflated seed-vessels, which are about an inch across. Although a perennial, it is best treated as an annual. Seed may be sown in the autumn and grown in a cool house, or sown in the spring, placed in warmth, and pricked out when large enough. Finally three plants should be placed in an 8-inch pot.

**Carex** (Sedge), *Cyperaceæ* (*C. japonica variegata, C. tristachya varie-gata*).—This is a useful, half-hardy, ornamental, herbaceous grass from Japan. It has striped green-and-white leaves, and is suitable for cultivation in the greenhouse (temperature 45° F. winter, 60° F. summer). It should be potted up in March, using a compost of half

**287**

loam and half leaf-mould with a little sand added. Water well while growing.

**Carludovica,** *Cyclanthaceæ.*—A group of low-growing, palm-like plants from Tropical America. They require the stove-house with a temperature of 50–55° F. in winter and 60–80° F. in summer. They succeed in rich, turfy loam, leaf-soil, and sand, in a moist atmosphere. They are increased by division, which should be carried out early in the spring. The roots should be placed in a warm, close, moist house, and potted-on when necessary.

*C. palmata,* the species most met with under cultivation, is a very graceful plant. It has dark-green, palm-like leaves, and grows to a height of from 3 to 5 feet. This plant is the source of the Panama hats. *C. rotundifolia* is similar to the above, but larger, the lobes of the leaves being very gracefully pendant.

**Carnation (Dianthus Caryophyllus),** *Caryophyllaceæ.*—This native of Southern Europe is one of our most popular and sweetest-smelling flowers, and is closely allied to the **Picotee** and the **Pink,** which are described elsewhere. The chief distinction between the Carnation and the Picotee is that the colour of the former is disposed in unequal stripes going from the centre to the outer edge ; that of the Picotee is disposed on the outer edges of the petals, radiating inwards and uniformly disposed. Carnations are classified as Selfs, Flakes, Bizarres, and Fancies.

*Selfs* are carnations of one colour only, without marks or shading. They are lavender, salmon, apricot, rose, yellow, cream, or white in colour.

*Flakes* are those the ground colour of which—be it what it may— is striped with one other colour only. In these the ground is generally white and striped with scarlet, rose, or purple. They are distinguished as scarlet, rose, or purple flakes, according to the colour of the stripes.

*Bizarres* are those the ground of which is marked and flaked with two or three other colours ; these are distinguished as scarlet, crimson, pink, or purple Bizarres, according to the predominance of the colour found in the markings.

*Fancies* are varieties that do not come within the other classes. The ground may be white, yellow, apricot, or mauve, spotted, striped or flaked with one or two other colours. The edges of the petals of the Carnation are smooth, those of the Pink are generally jagged or notched. The Pink for the most part has a dark eye, and sometimes a zone of the same colour as the eye midway between the base of the petal and the edge.

Carnations, Picotees, and Pinks are all propagated by seeds, layers, and cuttings.

*Carnations in the Border.*—Three weeks before planting time the bed (well-drained medium loam) should be double-dug, and a little well-rotted stable-manure should be dug in to at least 6 inches below the surface, but manuring must not be overdone. Plant in September or early in October, but in heavy and cold soils it is often wise to keep the young plants in a frame until May and then plant out. In April the flowering-stems should be supported, and as soon as it is apparent that

**288**

## Layering Carnations

1. Cutting the "tongue" in the shoot to be layered.   2. Shoot prepared for layering, showing a cut through the joint.   3. Pegging down the layer with the "tongue" open and well in contact with the soil.   The layering of carnations is best done in July and August.   See page 290.

Campanula pyramidalis
(*Chimney Bellflower*)

Campanula Medium
(*Canterbury Bells*)

Photos]                    [*Sutton & Sons Ltd., F. G. Preston, and Alexander & Brown*

Celmisia insignis
(*New Zealand Daisy*)

Calceolaria herbeohybrida

the principal bud is a healthy one the less important of them should be removed. A small dose of weak liquid manure or soot-water should be given twice a week, after watering, from the time the buds begin to form until the colour shows. These Carnations are perennials, and the beds may, if desired, be replanted only every third year. It is, however, usual to layer every year, in order to maintain a stock of healthy young plants.

*Carnations under Glass.*—Flowers of better size, quality, and colour are obtained under glass than in the open, as less leaf-growth is made and more vigour is imparted to the flowering stems. Carnations under glass need ample light, free ventilation in hot, bright weather, and at all times a good " buoyant " atmosphere. Without these no hope of success can be entertained. In September or early in October pot-up the young layers singly into 3-inch pots in a compost of two-thirds turfy loam and one-third well-rotted leaf-mould and coarse sand. Loam and leaf-mould used for potting should be sifted through a half-inch sieve, and must always be sterilized by baking over an iron sheet.

Stand the pots in a cold frame for the winter. Keep the frame fairly close until the plants are established, then give ample ventilation when the weather is good. Maintain the soil slightly moist, but no water must settle on the leaves, or " damping off " will certainly occur. In March re-pot into 6-inch pots, adding a little well-decayed manure and old mortar-rubble to the compost. Keep close for about ten days after potting, until established, then gradually give more air as the weather improves, and finally remove the lights. In May re-pot into 8-inch pots in a compost similar to that previously used, and return to the frame for a fortnight until the roots are established. Then stand in the open in a sheltered position on a firm bed of ashes or on slates or bricks. Water liberally, syringe overhead morning and evening in dry weather. Stake, manure, and as soon as it is apparent that the principal bud is a healthy one, the less important buds on the shoot should be removed, so as to concentrate and divert strength to develop the main bud. When the young plants are some 6 inches high the heads should be pinched off, to encourage sturdy and bushy growth. When the side shoots produced as a result of this pinching are from 6 to 8 inches long, they will, in turn, require pinching back; not later than mid-June, however, for ordinary July-flowering Carnations, or mid-August for perpetual-flowering species for autumn and winter blooms. Transfer to a light position in the cool greenhouse as soon as the flowers show colour (about July). Artificial heat should be used only to prevent the temperature of the house falling below 45° F. at night, and in damp, foggy weather to keep the atmosphere " buoyant " and dry. During the winter water must be given sparingly and in the morning. Keep a sharp look-out for diseases and pests, such as Black Mould, Carnation Fly, Carnation Maggot, Red Spider, and Rust, and at the slightest suspicion treat the disease or fumigate against the pests.

*Propagation.*—Choice varieties should be raised from cuttings or layers.

*Seed.*—When propagating by means of seed, the seeds should be sown 1 inch apart in April or May, in pots, small boxes, or seed-pans, in a

T

compost of two-thirds loam from decayed turf, one-third well-decom-posed cow-dung, and a little old mortar-rubble and bonemeal, and placed in a sheltered part of the garden. Some growers prefer to keep them in the cold house and harden off before planting out. When the plants show five or six leaves plant out to the same depth from 10 to 15 inches apart in sunny, well-drained beds composed of the same rich soil. Protect during winter with a cold frame. In cold and heavy soil some gardeners prefer to sow in August, winter in a cold frame, and plant out in spring. A little liquid manure, diluted until it is the colour of weak tea, will be beneficial if given at fortnightly intervals as soon as the buds appear. When the colour shows this must be discontinued. Carnations should be kept fairly dry, but the hoe must be used frequently. Remove all but the chief bud on each stem, except in the case of the Marguerite class.

Carnations should not be crowded with other plants, and their flowering-shoots should be staked in good time. Three or four stakes may be stuck in the ground round the plant, so that raffia tied round them will support the plant, or, in the case of choice blooms, each flower-stalk can be staked separately. Seedlings are more vigorous than plants raised from cuttings or layers, but if named varieties are desired, these latter methods of propagation must be resorted to. Propagation by layers is the more satisfactory.

*Layering.*—The season for this is in July or August. Having selected the basal shoots or " grass " to be layered, prepared pegs for pegging them down, and made a small trench 1 inch deep in the soil for their reception, add a little sand where the layers are to be placed, working it into the soil. Prepare each shoot by trimming off all the leaves with a sharp knife, except 5 or 6 inches at the top. Then, with a thin-bladed knife, make an incision half through the shoot with an upward cut, beginning below the joint and passing it through for about an inch or so. Bend the layer down into the sandy soil prepared for it, pegging it firmly in that situation in such a manner as to keep the slit or " tongue " open, and cover it with rich, light soil. Two days afterwards, when the wound is healed, a gentle watering will be beneficial. Let the layers remain in position until early in September, when they may be set out in their flowering quarters, or potted-up into 3-inch pots and taken into the greenhouse.

*Cuttings.*—Cuttings may be struck in a frame with a bottom heat of 60° F. at any time from November to February (the best time is January). Early in March, these cuttings, if struck in January, will need potting-on into larger pots.

*Perpetual or Tree Carnations.*—These are so called from the peculiar habit of the side-shoots, which are produced on the main stem. These hoots are long and straggling, with an upward tendency, and require training on sticks or a trellis of bars between two side-pieces. Although the flowers are somewhat smaller and less fragrant than those of the ordinary Carnation, they are invaluable for winter blooms. If well managed they may be had in flower nearly all the year round. The cultivation and requirements as to soil are much the same as for the ordinary Carnation, good fibrous loam, liberally sprinkled with leaf-mould, bonemeal, and old mortar-rubble making an excellent compost. The cuttings, which will be furnished by the side-shoots, should be from 2 to 3 inches in length, and may be struck in silver sand in February, August, or September, in gentle heat (55° F,), or the non-flowering shoots of the old plant may be laid down in a cold shaded frame in the last-mentioned month. When rooted (in about a month), pot-up in 2½-inch pots, and winter in a cool greenhouse near the glass, giving ample air (day temperature 60° F., night temperature 55° F.). The following summer the plants should be given two shifts—first into 6-inch pots and then into 8-inch pots, potting being more firm at each move. This will repress any tendency to bloom, and when they have made six pairs of leaves the heads should be nipped out, to encourage shrubby growth. During the summer the plants should be stood out-doors in a cool, sheltered position, on a bed of ashes, and carefully staked and trained. About the beginning of September the plants may be taken into the house, and watered occasionally with weak liquid manure or soot-water as soon as the roots have filled the pots. Air must be freely admitted, and they must be securely staked at an early period. Syringing overhead on bright days is helpful, but water should be applied to the roots only when dry. Give ample air, and keep the temperature at about 50° F. Under this management they will bloom freely during the winter and early spring months, and if planted out in the border early in May and watered well, will continue to flower throughout the summer. Perpetual-flowering Carnations may also be raised from seed sown in gentle heat (55° F.) in February. These seedlings will flower the same autumn or winter. One-year-old plants should be trimmed back slightly in late February, given a temperature of 55° F., and must be syringed overhead on bright, warm days. In about a month's time the new growth will break. When this occurs the plants should be potted-on into 9- to 10-inch pots for blooming the following autumn and winter.

*Malmaison Carnations.*—These have long been favourites because of the quality, size, and perfume of their blooms, which are crimson, salmon, blush-pink, cream, and white. They have been crossed with the Perpetual-flowering or Tree Carnation, the result being the Per-petual-flowering Malmaison. They are easy for the amateur to grow, and require treatment as detailed for border Carnations, but only one " stopping "; a second " stopping " would too much retard the com-mencement of blooming, which extends in the greenhouse from March to August. They also require a cooler atmosphere than the Perpetual-flowering or Tree Carnation, and the winter temperature should rarely rise above 45° F. Excessive watering must be guarded against at all times, especially in winter, when the roots must be kept almost dry. The paths and staging must never be " damped down " in winter. Another point in which the culture of the Malmaison varieties differs from that of the ordinary Carnation is that it should not be placed in the open in the summer. This would soften the foliage and expose it to attacks of fungoid diseases and insect pests. A glass covering is essential all the year round, but the plants must be kept as cool and airy as possible in summer, and when in bloom must be shaded from the direct rays of the sun. Propagation is usually effected by layering in a frame in July and August, or by cuttings struck in a propagating frame with bottom heat in May or June.

*Clove Carnations* are a hardy and vigorous class of scented border Carnations, and can be had in an almost unending selection of delicate colours. They should be potted-up and treated in the same manner as described for Carnations under Glass

*Varieties.*—Border, SELF.—*Bookham Apricot*; *Blush Clove* (blush-white); *Bookham Clove* (crimson); *Bookham Rose*; *Bookham Scarlet*; *Border Yellow*; *Coral Clove* (coral-pink); *Crystal Clove* (white); *Fiery Cross* (scarlet); *Glamour* (yellow); *Janet* (pink); *Margaret Keep* (bluish pink); *Orangeman* (orange-apricot); *Purple Clove*; *Royal Scot* (scarlet); *Salmon Clove*; *The Grey Douglas* (heliotrope); *Trumpeter* (rose-madder); *White Clove.*

FANCIES.—*Centurion* (yellow and scarlet); *Endymion* (canary-yellow, streaked blood-red); *Highland Mary* (primrose-yellow and rose-pink); *Kelso* (golden apricot and bluish grey); *Linkman* (yellow and scarlet); *Mona* (buff and rose); *Mrs. Hawksbee* (white and rose-crimson); *Ravenswood* (white and maroon-crimson); *Saracen* (slate-grey, striped crimson and rose); *Steerforth Clove* (white and crimson-maroon); *The Cadi* (rose-madder, striped blue and scarlet); *Viceroy* (yellow and carmine-crimson).

PERPETUAL BORDER.—*Sussex Avondale* (salmon-pink); *Sussex Beauty* (heliotrope); *Sussex Bizarre* (peach, flaked heliotrope); *Sussex Crimson*; *Sussex Maid* (white, flaked rose-pink); *Sussex Pink.*

PICOTEES.—(*Yellow Ground*). *Exquisite* (scarlet edge); *Her Majesty* (purple edge); *Margaret Glitters* (rosy scarlet edge); *Mrs. J. J. Kean* (rose-pink edge); *Niel Kenyon* (rose edge); *Togo* (crimson edge).

TREE OR PERPETUALS.—*Baroness de Brienen* (salmon-pink); *Coronation* (cerise); *Dairymaid* (white, flaked pink); *Edward Allwood* (scarlet); *Eileen Low* (salmon-pink); *Freda* (light pink); *Jenny* (light mauve); *Laddie* (salmon-pink); *Lady Northcliffe* (salmon-pink); *Mikado* (heliotrope); *Mary Allwood* (reddish salmon); *Mrs. A. J. Cobb* (crimson); *Orange Laura* (yellow and orange-red); *Peter Fisher* (rose-pink); *Saffron* (yellow); *Sunray* (deep yellow); *Tangerine* (flame-apricot); *Tarzan* (scarlet); *Topsy* (scarlet); *White Enchantress.*

MALMAISONS.—*Baldwin* (pink); *Calypso* (soft-flesh); *Duchess of Westminster* (rose-pink); *Maggie Hodgson* (crimson); *Nell Gwynne* (white); *Princess of Wales* (pink).

*Carnations, Marguerite.*—Attractive and free-flowering, half-hardy annuals, which have the appearance of a cross between a Pink and a Carnation. The flowers, which are mostly double, are delightfully fragrant. The plants thrive in open beds and in rich, gritty loam. They grow about 18 inches high, and flower from August to October.

*Culture.*—Sow seed thinly in February under glass (temperature 60° F.). When large enough to handle, prick off into 2- to 3-inch pots, and plant out early in June, or, if for indoor decoration, pot-on as required. If lifted before damaged by the frost—say, in September—they will furnish flowers in the greenhouse throughout the winter and spring. When the plants are lifted and potted, cut off all blossoms, and keep in a close frame for a short time to allow the formation of new buds, then move into the greenhouse. Pot-up in a compost of two-thirds fibrous loam and one-third of leaf-mould and sand mixed in equal proportions, using 6-inch pots. Water well after potting, then keep almost dry until the roots are established. They also make excellent plants for growing entirely in the greenhouse (temperature 55° F.).

**Carnegiea gigantea (Cereus gigantea),** *Cactaceæ.*—A native of Arizona, which bears white flowers in the summer, and grows to a height of from 4 to 25 feet. It requires the same culture as **Cereus,** which see.

**Carolina Allspice** (see **Calycanthus floridus**).

**Carolina Yellow Jessamine** (see **Gelsemium sempervirens**).

**Carpenteria californica,** *Saxifragaceæ.*—This native of California, although hardy against a wall in most parts of the country, succeeds best in such places when the soil is well drained, light, and sandy. It dislikes moisture during the winter but nevertheless is a very useful plant for the cold greenhouse, and benefits from being stood outside during the late summer and autumn. It is propagated from cuttings, in the summer, of half-ripened wood, by suckers which are occasionally produced, or by seed sown in the spring and placed in a little warmth.

**Carrion Flower** (see **Stapelia**).

**Caryopteris,** *Verbenaceæ.*—An attractive group of deciduous shrubs which produce lavender-blue or violet-blue flowers during the autumn. They are hardy in many parts of the country when grown in a sheltered position, but are also useful pot-plants for the cold house. They require well-drained sandy soil, and their pots should be plunged in ashes and stood in a warm, sheltered, sunny position when not in the greenhouse.

*Species.*—*C. incana* (*C. Mastacanthus*) [China and Japan] (bluish violet, 30–50 in.); *C. mongolica* [Mongolia and N. China] (blue, 20–30 in.); *C. tangutica* [China] (violet-blue, sweet scented, 30–50 in.); *C. clandonensis* is an attractive hybrid between *C. incana* and *C. tangutica,* with grey-tinted foliage, brilliant blue flowers. Seedlings from this give a variety of attractive forms.

*Propagation.*—All are propagated readily from cuttings of half-ripened wood placed in sandy soil under a hand-glass, and potted-on when rooted. Seed may also be sown in the spring.

**Caryota** (Fish-tail Palm), *Palmaceæ.*—A group of attractive stove palms which have graceful spreading fronds in their native habitat. They are of great economical importance, producing a highly nutritious Sago, also Toddy or Palm Wine. Some species produce suckers. They are best raised from seed which should be sown in a warm temperature of 65–75° F. Pot-on the seedlings as they develop into a mixture of rich, sandy loam and peat (temperature 50–55° F. winter, 60–80° F. summer).

*Species.*—*C. Cumingii* [Philippines] is a slender stem palm, 10 feet high. *C. Rumphiana* [Malaya and Australia] is a handsome and distinct species which produces leaves up to 8 feet long. *C. sobolifera* [Malacca] is an elegant dwarf species which produces suckers freely, *C. urens* [India and Malaya] is the Wine or Toddy Palm. It is probably

# THE GREENHOUSE

the largest growing species, but is useful for decoration in a young state.

**Cassia,** *Leguminosæ.*—Half-hardy, evergreen greenhouse plants which thrive in the cool or warm house. If given warm-house treatment, *C. corymbosa* [Argentine] which reaches a height of 10 feet, will produce its clusters of bright-yellow flowers almost all the year round. *C. grandis* (Pink Shower) [Panama] has pink flowers and reaches a height of 4 feet. *C. stipularis* [Chile] has deep orange flowers and makes a large floriferous bush. *C. tomentosa* [Mexico] is a winter-flowering species, with deep yellow flowers, growing to a height of 6 feet.

*Culture.*—Pot-up in March, using 6- to 10-inch pots and a compost of peaty loam or sandy leaf-mould. Prune back and start into growth in early spring. Keep quite dry in winter.

*Propagation*—Propagate by means of seed or cuttings in a close propagating case during the spring. Another useful species is *C. marylandica,* a herbaceous perennial with yellow flowers, 3–4 feet high.

**Cassiope,** *Ericaceæ.*—Small evergreen shrubs, which, although hardy in many parts of the country, are very attractive for growing in pans for the alpine house. Drought and warm air are fatal to them, and, except when standing in the alpine house, they appreciate having their pans plunged in sand or ashes. They require a peaty and sandy, moist but well-drained soil, and similar conditions to **Heaths.** They are readily raised from cuttings of mature wood in August, under glass, as well as by layering, or from seed, when they should be treated like **Ericas.**

*Species.*—*C. fastigiata* [Himalayas] (white, June, 6–12 in.); *C. hypnoides* [Arctic regions] (moss-like growth and white flowers with red calyx, May and June, 3–6 in.); *C. tetragona* [Arctic regions] (white, March–April, 6–8 in.).

**Castor Oil Plant** (see **Ricinus communis**).

**Catasetum** (see Chapter on **Orchids**).

**Catmint** (see **Nepeta**).

**Cat's Thyme** (see **Teucrium Marum**).

**Cattleya** (see Chapter on **Orchids**).

**Cavendishia acuminata,** *Ericaceæ.*—An evergreen climber from South America suitable for the cool greenhouse, whose scarlet-tipped, yellowish-green flowers are produced most of the year. It requires a compost of peat and sand Cuttings of nearly ripe wood root readily in a close case, with mild bottom heat.

**Ceanothus** (Californian Lilac), *Rhamnaceæ.*—Although these handsome flowering Californian shrubs are mostly grown outdoors, some species, such as *C. papillosus* (deep-blue flowers in May), *C. rigidus* (purplish-blue flowers in April), and *C. Veitchianus* (a natural hybrid with blue flowers in May and September), all of which are evergreen, may be grown in the cold house or on a wall facing south or west.

*Culture.*—Pot-up in October, using 6- to 10-inch pots and an ordinary potting compost and stand in the cold greenhouse. Give ample water in summer but little in winter. Trim to shape after flowering.

There is a semi-evergreen group of hybrids, with blue, pink, and white flowers chiefly between *C. americanus* and other species. Some of the

294

most distinctive of these are "*Gloire de Plantieres*", dark blue, "*Gloire de Versailles*", bright blue, "*Marie Simon*", flesh coloured. These flower on the new growth (July to September), and should be pruned back in the winter or early spring.

**Celmisia,** *Compositæ.*—Evergreen perennials from New Zealand which, although grown successfully out-of-doors in a few favoured localities, are generally more suited for the cool greenhouse. They are very useful for growing in pans, either as flowering plants or for their foliage for the alpine house. They should be kept plunged in ashes in a cold frame when not wanted for such. They require a well-drained soil, and are increased by seed, when obtainable. This should be sown as soon as ripe, and placed in a little warmth, and pricked out into small pots when ready.

*C. coriacea, C. holosericea, C. Monroei,* and *C. spectabilis* all have white flowers with yellow discs in the summer, and are from 6 to 12 inches high.

**Celosia** (Prince of Wales' Feathers, or Cockscomb), *Amarantaceæ.*— Free-flowering, half-hardy annuals, producing the greatest profusion of feathery spikes of most beautiful flowers. Some of the varieties have long flower-spikes, which may be dried for winter decoration; others have feathery or mossy plumes. They thrive if planted out in June in a warm, sheltered situation in southern districts but are not hardy enough to stand the open climate in the more northern counties. Grown in pots in the greenhouse, they may, with a little management, be had in flower the whole winter. They are useful for dinner-table decoration. The Cockscomb of the florists is *C. cristata*, native of the Tropics, remarkable for its large, deep, crimson blossom, which appears on the top and sides of the broad expansion into which the stem develops at the top and which resembles a large cockscomb.

*Culture.*—Sow seed thinly in pans in March, in rich, sandy loam and leaf-mould with bottom heat (70° F.), and just cover with very fine soil. These plants are gross feeders, and even as seedlings require a little well-rotted and finely-sieved manure in the sowing compost. Transplant into boxes as soon as possible, and when big enough pot singly into 2-inch pots, which should be placed on a shelf close to the glass. Syringe the seedlings constantly, give free ventilation, and do not keep the roots too moist. Re-pot frequently, harden off, and plant out 4–12 inches apart in June, or pot-up for the greenhouse as required, using 5- to 7-inch pots and a well-sieved compost of one-half part rich loam and one-half leaf-mould and sand. Keep the seedlings in a warm, moist, and fairly close atmosphere, not too wet at the roots, until the flowers appear in the late summer. As soon as the buds form, water twice a week with weak liquid manure until the colour shows (temperature 45–55° F. winter, 60–65° F. summer).

*Species and Varieties.*—*C. argentea* [India] (silvery); *C. cristata* [Cockscomb] (crimson, 18 in.); *C. cristata coccinea* (scarlet); *C. cristata* var. *pyramidalis* (scarlet, crimson and gold plumes, 30 in.).

**Celsia** (**Mullein**), *Scrophulariaceæ.*—Half-hardy annuals, biennials and perennials which thrive in the cool or warm greenhouse, in a compost of sandy loam and a little leaf mould.

*Culture.*—Pot-up annually using 5- to 6-inch pots, and stand on a bed of ashes in the greenhouse (temperature 45° F. winter, 65° F. summer). Keep fairly dry. Propagate *C. Arcturus* (half-hardy perennial) by means of cuttings of young wood in the spring, or by seed sown in heat in March or April. *C. cretica* (half-hardy biennial) should be propagated by means of seed sown in heat in March (for autumn flowering), or August (for winter and spring flowering). *C. sinuata* (half-hardy annual) is easily raised from seeds sown in March. The best results are obtained when several plants are grown together in each receptacle. Pot-up the seedlings when large enough to handle. In mild districts some species may be planted out in the open. Indoors move on into 6- to 8-inch pots for flowering in the greenhouse. *C. Arcturus* should be grown entirely in the house. They require ample water and free ventilation while growing, and weekly doses of liquid manure are beneficial.

*Species.*—*C. Arcturus* [candida] (deep yellow, spotted purple, June–Nov., 20 in.) ; *C. cretica* (Cretan Mullein) [Crete] (golden-yellow, spotted brown, June–July, 60 in.). *C. sinuata* [Mediterranean Region] (yellow, purple anthers, 15 in., annual).

**Centaurea,** *Compositæ.*—A large genus comprising hardy annuals, biennials, and perennials, all of which thrive in a sunny position and in any good garden soil. *C. Cyanus* (Cornflower) [S.E. Europe], 6–36 inches high, with white, pink, or blue flowers, and *C. moschata* (*C. suaveolens*) [Sweet Sultan], up to 36 inches in height, with white to yellow, rose, and purple flowers, both from July to October, are annuals worth growing under glass. *C. Cineraria* [Dusty Miller] (syn. *candidissima*) from South Italy, *C. gymnocarpa* and *C. ragusina* with their silvery foliage are perennials useful in the cold greenhouse and for summer bedding.

*Pot Culture.*—Sow annuals thinly, ½ inch deep, in a frame in March, and transplant singly into pots as soon as possible. Seed sown in September and grown cool during the winter will be very valuable for the cool greenhouse during March and April. The perennials should be potted-up in March in loamy soil, in 6- to 8-inch pots (temperature 45° F. winter, 65° F. summer). Water well while growing. To propagate, sow in heat in January and August, or take cuttings in September.

**Centradenia,** *Melastomaceæ.*—Showy and desirable evergreen plants for the warm greenhouse, some being excellent for table decoration. Cut sprays last in perfect condition for some time. They thrive in a compost of one part sandy loam and two parts rough peat. Cuttings of side shoots should be inserted in March or April. Pot-on when rooted, finally into a 5- or 6-inch pot. Strong plants benefit from a liquid manure, which gives better colour to flower and fruit.

*Species.*—*C. floribunda* [Mexico] (lilac, April and May, 15–18 in.) ; *C. grandifolia* [Mexico] (light rose, winter flowering, useful for cutting, 24 in.) ; *C. inæquilateralis* [Mexico] (pink, Jan.–April, 15–18 in.).

**Centropogon Lucyanus,** *Campanulaceæ.*—This supposed hybrid of garden origin makes a very useful winter-flowering plant for the warm greenhouse, either in pot or for hanging-basket. It bears rosy-carmine, tubular flowers tipped with white, and succeeds in a mixture of fibrous peat or leaf-soil and loam in equal proportions, with a little sand. When growing it requires a temperature of 60–65° F. and a fair amount of moisture. Conditions should be cooler and drier when resting. It is readily increased by cuttings, or by division of the root in April. These should be placed in a close case in a temperature of 60° F. They will make good flowering plants, 12–15 inches high in 5-inch pots, the following winter. Old plants cut back, shaken out, and re-potted make good specimens, 24–30 inches high.

*C. fastuosus* [Mexico] said to be one of the parents of the above hybrid, is well worth growing, producing its rose-coloured flowers throughout the winter, on plants up to a height of 24 inches.

**Cephalocereus senilis (Pilocereus senilis)** (Old Man Cactus), *Cactaceæ.* —An interesting succulent from Mexico, generally found in collections. It has a columnar stem, growing several feet, covered with white, finely waved bristles. It bears red and reddish-white flowers, followed by violet fruits. It requires the same treatment as **Cereus,** which see.

**Cephalotus follicularis** (Australian Pitcher Plant), *Cephalotaceæ.*— An interesting little insectivorous plant, with rhizomatous roots. It grows about 5 inches in height, and, in addition to its ordinary hairy, oval, green leaves, it produces a second form of leaves coloured and shaped like tiny pitchers, in which it traps insects. The actual flowers are insignificant. A shady spot in the cool greenhouse in a compost of half turfy peat and half live sphagnum moss is most suitable.

*Culture.*—Pot-up in a well-crocked 5-inch pot or shallow pan in March. The plant benefits if the pan is plunged into a larger pan of sphagnum and covered with a bell-glass. Water well while growing, and keep moist when dormant. Propagate by division of the roots in March.

**Cerasus (Cherry)** (see **Prunus Cerasus).**

**Ceratopteris thalictroides,** *Ceratopteridaceæ.*—A succulent, aquatic. fern, from the Tropics of the Old World, useful for growing in the mud, or in pots submerged in the aquarium. It is raised from spores, which should be sown in pots stood in water. It is also readily increased from the numerous bulbils formed on the larger fronds. (See Chapter on **Ferns.**)

*C. cornuta* is a floating variety of the above, which increases readily by offsets which form on the old fronds.

**Ceratozamia mexicana,** *Cycadaceæ.*—A handsome foliage plant from Mexico. It thrives in loam in the warm greenhouse.

**Cereus,** *Cactaceæ.*—A genus of cacti suitable for greenhouse culture, many of them being night flowering. The species vary greatly in form and size : some are dwarf in habit, some are of giant stature, while others are climbers. The stems are usually very spiny, and angular or round in shape. These plants like a sunny, warm position in a compost of two parts of turfy loam to one part of sand and brick-rubble. The average temperature of the house during summer should be 80° F. day, 70° F. night. During the winter, 60° F. day, 50° F. night.

*Culture.*—Pot-up triennially in March in well-drained pots. When they begin to grow, water freely. Keep dry in winter. There are a number of cristate forms of various species which are usually grafted.

*Propagation.*—Propagate by means of seed sown in heat in March, by cuttings in July, or by grafting in March.

*Species.*—*C. azureus* [S. Brazil] (reddish brown and white, 20–100 in.) ; *C. peruvianus* (white, May–July, 20–100 in.) ; *C. variabilis* [Brazil] (white, summer, 20–200 in.) ; *C. versicolor* [Peru] (yellow, 10–60 in.).

**Cereus amecænsis** (see **Heliocereus amecænis**).

**Cereus Baumannii** (see **Cleistocactus Baumannii**).

**Cereus flagelliformis** (see **Aporocactus flagelliformis**).

**Cereus grandiflorus** (see **Selenicereus grandiflorus**).

**Cereus Macdonaldiæ** (see **Selenicereus Macdonaldiæ**).

**Cereus Nycticaulis** (see **Selenicereus pteracanthus**).

**Cereus senilis** (see **Cephalocereus senilis**).

**Cereus speciosus** (see **Heliocereus speciosus**).

**Cereus spinulosus** (see **Selenicereus spinulosus**).

**Cereus triangularis** (see **Hylocereus tricostalus**).

**Ceropegia,** *Asclepiadaceæ.*—A genus of twining or erect plants with tuberous roots, thriving in warm greenhouse conditions. They require a compost of fibrous loam, peat and leaf-soil in equal portions with sand to ensure porosity. Several of the species are excellent when growing in hanging baskets. Propagation is achieved by cuttings of the small side shoots inserted during April in sandy peat in a warm propagating case. Careful watering is necessary during the dormant season.

*Species.*—*C. elegans* [India] (purple) ; *C. Gardneri* [Ceylon] (creamy white) ; *C. Woodii* [South Africa] (purple).

**Ceropteris,** *Polypodiaceæ.*—A group of ferns that in the past has been classified under **Gymnogramma,** but which are now considered sufficiently distinct to be separated. They are the group usually known as Gold and Silver ferns, having the under-surface of the fronds covered with a coloured powdery wax, silver, white, or bright yellow. They require the temperature of a warm greenhouse, and although they must not be grown in a dry atmosphere, care should be taken not to damp the fronds by syringing or any other method.

*Species.*—*C. argentea* (*Gymnogramma argentea*) [Madagascar] (white powder) ; *C. calomelanos* [W. Indies to Brazil] (stalks and rachises nearly black, white powder) ; *C. chrysophylla* (*Gymnogramma chrysophylla*) [W. Indies to Brazil] (powder golden yellow) ; *C. peruviana* (*G. peruviana* )[Mexico] (white powder. The var. *argyrophylla* is silvery on both sides). *C. tatarica* (*G. tatarica*) [Tropical America] (white powder).

**Cestrum (Habrothamnus),** *Solanaceæ.*—Handsome evergreen climbing shrubs, with clusters of yellowish-pink or red, tubular-shaped flowers in June and July, suitable for the cool greenhouse. They may be grown outdoors on a wall in a very sheltered position.

*Culture.*—Pot-up annually in March in a compost of two-thirds fibrous loam and one-third leaf-mould, well-rotted manure, sand, and a little old mortar-rubble. Water well while growing, and give liquid manure when the buds form, but keep the roots dry in winter (temperature 40–45° F. winter, 60° F. summer). Train the shoots on the wall of the house or up to the roof.

*Pruning.*—Prune fully grown plants back to within two buds of the old wood in February; younger plants should be allowed to retain about a third of the new wood each year.

*Propagation.*—Propagation is effected by means of cuttings struck in a temperature of from 60–65° F., in late summer.

*Species.*—*C. auranticum* [Guatemala] (golden yellow); *C. elegans* [Mexico] (red); *C. Newellii* [garden origin] (scarlet); and *C. Smithii*, a variety of *C. elegans* (soft pink).

**Chænomeles,** *Rosaceæ.*—Very useful plants for growing in pots for the cold house. With such protection they can be had in bloom in winter. This group of plants is more generally grown and known as **Cydonia,** the most popular being *C. lagenaria*, erroneously called *C. japonica* (the true *C. japonica* is the plant often grown as *C. Maulei*). Grown in an 8- to 12-inch pot it should be plunged outside in ashes, being brought under glass when the buds appear in early winter.

*Pot Culture.*—Pot-up in November in 8- to 10-inch pots, using well-manured ordinary soil for compost, and take into the cold greenhouse. Keep fairly dry until growth starts, then water moderately. Prune out weak wood and dead flower-shoots after flowering, and sink the pots to their rims in ashes outdoors, in a sunny, sheltered spot, from May to November. Propagation may be carried out by means of seeds, budding, layering, suckers, or cuttings in October.

*C. lagenaria* (*Cydonia japonica*), the Japanese Quince, from China, has many coloured forms, from deep crimson to pure white : *alba-rosea* (white, partly pink); *cardinalis* (deep scarlet); *grandiflora* and *nivalis* (white); *Simonii* (dark crimson). All 3–5 feet.

*C. japonica* (*Cydonia Maulei*), is a dwarf, compact bush from Japan, with brick-red flowers, which grows to a height of from 1 to 3 feet.

**Chænostoma,** *Scrophulariaceæ.*—Useful greenhouse plants, annuals or perennials, all natives of South Africa. Seeds of the annual kinds should be sown in March, in a little warmth, and several of them pricked out into a 5-inch pot in ordinary potting-soil for flowering in the summer. For spring flowering they should be sown in September. Cuttings of perennials may be taken in August, and grown on in a cool greenhouse for flowering the following year. Seed should be sown in March.

*Species.*—*C. fœtidum* (annual, white, June and July, 15–18 in.); *C. hispidum* (perennial, sub-shrubby, blush white, 10–18 in.). This is a useful vase and window plant.

**Chain Fern** (see **Woodwardia**).

**Chalcas exotica** (Orange Jessamine), *Rutaceæ.*—An attractive, warm greenhouse, evergreen plant from Polynesia. It has abundant, fragrant, white, orange-like flowers and red fruits, often produced together during July and August. Its leaves are large and glossy. It thrives in a compost of turfy loam and peat, and needs an abundance of water in the summer when the plant is established. It is increased by seed sown and placed in a warm house, or by cuttings of ripened wood placed under a bell-glass, in moist bottom heat, and grown on into 6-inch pots. This plant has been used as a stock for lemons, with success.

**Chamæcyparis (Cupressus)** [Cypress], *Pinaceæ.*—Most of the plants contained in this large genus of beautiful conifers are too big for greenhouse cultivation, but some species, such as *C. funebris* (the Funeral Cypress), an elegant, slender plant from China, in their younger forms are extremely useful for cold greenhouse or conservatory. Some of the dwarf varieties of *C. Lawsoniana*, such as *ericoides*, *Fletcheri*, *Olbrichii*, *Wisselii*, and a number of the dwarf forms of *C. L. nana*—i.e. *alba*, *glauca*, *minima*—are useful in their young state for the alpine house.

*Culture.*—Pot-up in a well-crocked 5- to 6-inch pot of loam and leaf-mould in spring or autumn, and grow near the glass. Pot-on as required until eventually they have to be planted outdoors. No pruning is necessary.

*Propagation.*—For indoor culture raise from seed sown in March or April in well-drained pans in slight heat (60–65° F.). All may be propagated in the autumn from cuttings taken with a " heel " and placed in sand.

**Chamædorea,** *Palmaceæ.*—Quick-growing, ornamental palms for the warm greenhouse. They are increased by seed, when obtainable, which should be sown and placed in a frame over bottom heat. Several may be increased by suckers, which should be placed in heat. Both seedlings and suckers should be potted-on as required, in peat and sandy loam, in equal parts, and a little charcoal.

*Species.*—*C. elegans* [Mexico] (graceful pinnate leaves, clusters of orange coloured flowers) ; *C. Ernesti-Augusti* [Mexico] (leaves simple, 3–4 ft.) ; *C. glaucifolia* [Guatemala] (leaves pinnate, 6–12 ft.). This is one of the most ornamental for decorative purposes.

**Chamæranthemum,** *Acanthaceæ.*—Stove foliage plants which thrive in equal proportions of well-drained peat and fibrous loam, with some sand added. Cuttings of young shoots root in the spring in sand. They should be placed in heat and grown on into 5- or 6-inch pots.

*Species.*—*C. argenteum* [New Britain] (leaves with silvery veins, 6–10 in.) ; *C. igneum* [Peru] (yellow flowers, red-veined leaves, 5–6 in.) ; *C. pictum* [Brazil] (green leaves, with a large, silvery blotch, and orange edge, 6–8 in.).

**Chamærops excelsa** (see **Trachycarpus excelsa**).

**Chamærops Fortunei** (see **Trachycarpus excelsa**).

**Chamærops humilis,** *Palmaceæ.*—The Chamærops, or Fan Palm, is the only palm native to Europe. It is a splended plant of oriental appearance, producing a striking effect if planted out on lawns or in the pleasure-grounds. It is also invaluable for greenhouse decoration, and succeeds best in the shade, in a compost of two parts loam to one part of leaf-mould and sand. It requires no protection in winter.

*Culture.*—Pot-up annually, using 6- to 12-inch pots. Sponge the leaves frequently with warm, soft water, and water regularly, but in moderation (temperature 50° F. winter, 65° F. summer).

*Propagation.*—This is carried out by means of suckers from the base

300

of the parent plant in September, or seed may be sown 1 inch deep in heat in March.

**Chaste Trees** (see **Vitex Agnus-castus**).

**Cheilanthes,** *Polypodiaceæ.*—A group of ferns of easy cultivation. They enjoy a position near the glass, but dislike strong heat or watering overhead, as most of the species grow naturally in dry, rocky situations.

*Species.*—*C. gracillima* (Lace Fern) [California], has graceful fronds, 2–4 inches long. *C. tomentosa* [Arizona] is covered with brownish-white hairs. It grows from 12–20 inches high.

**Cheiranthus Cheiri** (Common Wallflower), *Cruciferæ.*—For spring gardening these hardy annuals, biennials, and perennials are indispensable, and because of the delicious fragrance of their beautiful flowers, they are especial favourites, producing a splendid effect in sunny open beds, in mixed borders, in crevices in the wall-garden, in the rock-garden, or in the cold greenhouse. They grow from 6 to 24 inches in height, and flower during late winter and early spring, or in spring and summer. They thrive in an open and sunny position in dry, light, and sandy loam with some lime in it. On account of their variety much interest is excited in raising them from seed.

The single Wallflowers bear flowers varying from rich yellow and yellow striped with red to a deep blood-red, and even to purple. The double Wallflowers are usually yellow or a rich velvety reddish brown. The latter do not seed, and must be raised from cuttings. The Double German varieties, however, are raised from seed.

Grown in pots, Wallflowers are excellent for winter-flowering in the cool greenhouse, particularly the annual kinds, such as *Early Paris* and its coloured forms.

*Culture.*—They should be sown in the open exactly as plants to be flowered in the open, but should be potted-up—one in a 5-inch pot, or three in a 6-inch pot—early in September, and taken into the house, or stood in a frame for a time and taken into the house later. The potting-soil should not be too rich, and only sufficient heat should be applied to exclude the frost. The middle of December should see the first blooms. The dwarf-growing species, 6–12 inches in height, are excellent for the rock-garden or alpine house.

BIENNIALS.—Sow seed thinly in early June, in drills 12 inches apart, in an open position, or take cuttings (double varieties) in September and strike in a frame in sandy soil. Transplant the seedlings when 2 inches high to 10 inches apart, water well, and nip out the centres as soon as the plants are established. Plant out in position for flowering early in October.

PERENNIALS.—Sow seed in the open in April, in drills 10 inches apart, or take cuttings in September and strike in sandy soil. Plant out in permanent position in October. The perennial species, however, are usually grown as biennials. For pot culture *C. kewensis* is especially suitable.

*Species, Hybrids, and Varieties.*—*C. Allionii* [Hybrid] (bright orange, 10 in.) ; *C. alpinus* [N. Europe] (pale yellow, 4 in.) ; suitable for the alpine house : *C. kewensis* [Hybrid] chestnut-brown, 12 in.) ; *C. Marshallii* [Hybrid] (orange-yellow, 6 in.) ; the last two should be grown from cuttings. *C. mutabilis* [Madeira] (white, cream-coloured yellow, becoming darker). All April to June flowering. *Named Varieties.*—(*C. Cheiri*) : *Primrose Dame* (pale yellow) ; *Cloth of Gold* (bright yellow) ; *Harpur Crewe* (golden yellow, double) ; should be increased by cuttings. *Ivory White* ; *Orange Bedder* ; *Eastern Queen* (apricot) ; *Blood Red* ; *Vulcan* (crimson) ; *Harbinger* (brown) ; *Purple Queen* ; *Fire King* (bright orange) ; *Scarlet Emperor* (orange-scarlet) ; *Bacchus* (wine red).

**Cherry** (**Prunus avium** and **Prunus Cerasus**) (see Chapter on **Fruit under Glass**).

**Cherry Pie** (see **Heliotropium**).

**Chickweed Wintergreen** (see **Trientalis europæa**).

**Chilean Bellflower** (see **Lapageria rosea**).

**Chilean Crocus** (see **Tecophilea eyanocrocus**).

**Chimonanthus præcox** [**C. fragrans**] (Winter Sweet), *Calycanthaceæ.* —A winter-blooming, hardy, deciduous shrub from China, which likes a sunny, sheltered position and deep, moist, sandy loam. It bears fragrant, pale-yellow flowers, stained purple in the centres, in January and February, and reaches a height of 7 feet or more if trained on walls.

*Pot Culture.*—Plant in October or March, or pot-up for the greenhouse. When grown as a climber, cut back side-shoots to within five or six " eyes " of the main stems after flowering. Propagate by means of layering in August, or by suckers or seeds in March.

*C.* var. *grandiflorus* has larger and more showy yellow flowers.

**China Aster** (see **Callistephus hortensis**).

**China Berry** (see **Melia Azedarach**).

**Chincheringchee** (see **Ornithogalum thyrsoides**).

**Chinese Angelica** (see **Aralia chinensis**).

**Chinese Trumpet Creeper** (see **Campsis**).

**Chinese Wistaria** (see **Wistaria sinensis**).

**Chionanthus** (Fringe Tree), *Oleraceæ.*—Hardy deciduous shrubs or small trees, which like a sheltered position and a well drained, moist loam. They bear white flowers in June and July. *C. virginica* [N. America] with white flowers from July to August, may be had in flower in the greenhouse at Easter. See **Forcing.** *C. retusa*, from China, has white sweet-scented flowers in May.

*Culture.*—Pot-up in October or November, and trim to shape after flowering if required. Propagate by means of layering in September, or strike cuttings of half-ripe shoots in a close frame during July and August.

**Chionodoxa Luciliæ** (Glory of the Snow), *Liliaceæ.*—This bulbous plant from Asia Minor requires similar treatment to that accorded to bulbs generally, and thrives in sun or semi-shade, and sandy loam in the open. It is also useful for pot culture in the alpine house or cold greenhouse. The plants bear some five or six star-shaped, blue, white, or mauve blooms on stems from 6 to 9 inches tall.

*Pot Culture.*—Pot-up in the autumn, in a compost of sandy loam and leaf-mould, putting about ten bulbs into a 6-inch pot, stand in a cold frame, or plunge in ashes outside. Move into the cold greenhouse

**302**

when the buds appear. After blooming place in a frame, and continue to water until the foliage dies down; keep quite dry in summer. When overcrowded lift and re-pot when leaves die down. Propagate by offsets in October, or raise from seed.

*Species.*—*C. Luciliæ gigantea* (soft mauve, blue, and white, March 9 in.); *C. Luciliæ grandiflora* (lavender-blue, white centre, March–April, 9 in.); *C. sardensis* (deep blue, March–April, 6–8 in.).

**Chirita,** *Gesneraceæ.*—Useful plants for the warm greenhouse, requiring the same cultural treatment as **Gloxinia.** Like most members of *Gesneraceæ* they can be increased by leaf cutting.

*Species.*—*C. barbata* [India] (bluish lilac and yellow, March–April, 18–24 in.); *C. lavendulacea* [Indo-Malaya] (lavender, spring, 36 in.); *C. Marcanii* [Siam] (orange, summer, 24 in.); *C. Moonii* [Ceylon] (purple, July, 24–36 in.); *C. sinensis* [China] (lilac, May–July, 6 in.). This last will succeed in a cooler temperature.

**Chironia,** *Gentianaceæ.*—Soft-wooded greenhouse shrubs from South Africa which thrive in a mixture of three parts peat to one part fibrous loam, with some sand and charcoal. Small pots and good drainage are essential. They are propagated by cuttings inserted in sandy soil in a little heat, in spring. Pot-on gradually, and finally into 4½- or 5-inch pots.

*Species.*—*C. baccifera* (flowers pink in June. These are followed by a display of red, berry-like fruits, 12–18 in.); *C. floribunda* (rose, June, 12 in.); *C. linoides* (red, July, 15–20 in.).

**Chlidanthus fragrans,** *Amaryllidaceæ.*—A fragrant, half-hardy, bulbous plant from the Andes, that thrives in well-drained, warm, sunny borders or in pots in the greenhouse in a mixture of peaty loam leaf-mould, and sand. It grows about 9 inches high, and flowers in May and June. Flowers are yellow. *C. Ehrenbergii* [Mexico], yellow flowers, is taller than the above, and is perhaps a form of it.

*Culture.*—Plant or pot-up in April, 3½ inches deep, with three bulbs in a 5-inch pot. Water well while growing, and rest when dormant. Propagate by means of offsets in April.

**Chlorophytum elatum var. variegatum,** *Liliaceæ.*—A greenhouse foliage plant growing about 15 inches high. The long leaves, much like those of the **Aloe,** are green, striped with whitish yellow. The small flowers are of no importance. It likes a compost of two parts of fibrous loam to one part of leaf-mould and sand. Pot-up in March and place in a cool greenhouse (temperature 40–50° F.). Water and syringe well during the spring and summer and never allow the roots to dry up. A useful plant for sub-tropical bedding.

*Propagation.*—Sow seed in a frame (temperature 55–60° F.) or divide the roots in March.

**Choisya ternata** (Mexican Orange Blossom), *Rutaceæ.*—A half-hardy, evergreen shrub, which, if grown outdoors, likes a wall or a sunny sheltered position and sandy loam, otherwise it does well in the cold greenhouse. It grows from 6 to 10 feet high, and from May to September bears clusters of small, fragrant, white flowers.

*Pot Culture.*—Pot-up in the spring, when the young shoots are forming, using a 6- to 8-inch pot, and a compost of half peaty loam

# THE GREENHOUSE

and half leaf-mould and sand. Keep moist while growing, and syringe daily.

*Pruning.*—Prune straggly shoots after flowering, and put out in the open with the pot sunk in ashes, from July to October.

Propagate by means of layering in August, or by cuttings in a frame in August.

**Chondrorhyncha** (see Chapter on **Orchids**).

**Chorizema,** *Leguminosæ.*—Greenhouse evergreen shrubs from Australia, growing from 24 to 40 inches high and carrying red or yellow blossoms, shaped like those of the pea, almost the whole year round. They thrive best near the glass in the cool greenhouse (temperature 45° F. winter, 55° F. summer), in a compost of two parts of sandy peat to one part of fibrous loam. Good ventilation is at all times essential.

*Culture.*—Pot-up in the spring (biennially) using 6- to 8-inch pots. Keep dry until growth starts, and then water moderately, giving occasional doses of liquid manure. Stop back during the first and second years, to make bushy plants.

*Pruning.*—Prune out weak wood and remove dead flowers after flowering by cutting the plants back into shape, and stand outdoors from June to September.

*Propagation.*—Seed may be sown under glass in spring in small, well-drained pots of soil as above, and potted-on as required, or propagation may be carried out by means of cuttings of half-ripened wood, 3 inches long, taken with a " heel " under glass in June.

*Species.*—*C. cordatum* (scarlet, red, and purple), and *C. ilicifolium* (orange red) are good species, of which there are several varieties.

**Christmas Rose** (see **Helleborus**).

**Chrysalidocarpus lutescens,** *Palmaceæ.*—A very decorative feather palm from Madagascar for the stove or warm greenhouse, and a popular florist palm in a young state, although it will grow to 25 or 30 feet. The seed should be sown in boxes or pans, where they can remain until they have made two or more leaves. If potted too early they are subject to damping off. The receptacles for the seed should have a good layer of gravel at the bottom, as the roots work freely among it and are easily disentangled when potted. After potting they should be kept for a few days in a house with extra warmth and humidity. They thrive in loam, peat, and sand, and a warm, humid atmosphere.

**Chrysanthemum.**—The Chrysanthemum is one of the hardiest plants, but owing to the fact that it flowers somewhat late, its beautiful blooms are subject to injury from the weather when grown out-of-doors. They soon lose their freshness, and are injured in form and dimmed in colour under the adverse influences of rain and frost. To keep the blooms of chrysanthemums at their best it is desirable that they should at least have protection overhead, if it is nothing more than an awning of waterproofed calico. The best protection, however, is afforded by a cold greenhouse, because such a building admits of free entrance of light, which the semi-opacity of an awning will to a certain extent prevent.

*Classification.*—Speaking generally, chrysanthemums are classified as *Japanese, Japanese Reflexed, Japanese Incurved, Incurved, Reflexed,*

304

Annual Chrysanthemum

Chrysanthemum (The Melba)

Calendula (Double)
(Golden Beam)

Crocus

[F. G. Preston

Chionodoxa Luciliæ          Eustoma Russellianum

Photos]          [Sutton & Sons Ltd.

Cyclamen persicum "Triumph"          Cineraria stellata

# CHRYSANTHEMUMS

*Decoratives, Singles, Cascades, Korean, Pompons, Japanese Pompons, Anemones,* and *Anemone Pompons.* The distinctions between each class are easily recognized.

The *Japanese or double-flowering Exhibition* variety is marked by its irregularity. The large, handsome flower forms almost a ball, 8–10 inches in diameter, and its petals are tossed wildly about in every direction in charming disarray, which offers a remarkable contrast to the neatness and regularity in the other varieties.

*Reflexed* chrysanthemums are those whose florets are bent back and turn upwards towards the flower stalks.

In the *Incurved* varieties the arrangement is just the reverse, the florets turning upwards and away from the flower-stalks and curving inwards, so that in **many cases** the flower assumes the form of a ball composed of imbricated florets, so disposed as to lap over one another like tiles on a roof.

The *Decorative* class is in many ways very like the Japanese, and is extremely popular, owing to the great variety of the colours available. The flowers are of medium size, but very beautiful, and excellent for cutting. With care a succession of bloom may be had from October right through to January.

The *large-flowered Singles* are also great favourites, flowering from October to November, and providing good cut blooms often 6–7 inches in diameter—these are obtained by disbudding; if the plants are merely thinned out they will furnish numerous blooms of moderate size, while if left to grow naturally, many varieties will carry clusters of daisy-like flowers.

*Cascades* are of recent introduction, and are chiefly singles of various shades. Trained to hang down over the pots, they are very graceful and decorative.

*Korean Chrysanthemums* are a new race in brilliant colours, there being single and double-flowered varieties. Although they are hardy many of the varieties are very decorative for the cool greenhouse during the late summer. They require the same treatment as the *Decorative* varieties.

*Pompons* are varieties that do not attain the height of the tall, large-flowering chrysanthemums, and whose button-like blooms are smaller —about the size of half a crown. They are the hardiest of all varieties.

When the term *hybrid Pompon* is used it is taken to denote varieties which are not small enough to be ranked among the true Pompons and not large enough to be placed among the large-flowering varieties.

The true *Pompons* are suitable and beautiful for front shelves in greenhouses, or beds and borders out of doors. Being of compact, close growth, and having flowers about the size of very large daisies, and rivalling the large ones in colour, they are at once the neatest and most ornamental plants for decorating the greenhouse.

The *Anemone-flowered varieties* differ from all the others in having a centre of quilled florets, almost like a sunflower, but still more like an Anemone, surrounded by a fringe or edging of large loose ray florets. The *Anemone Pompons* are merely dwarf varieties of the Anemone-flowered varieties.

U

Chrysanthemums of all varieties may be classified, according to the time of their blooming, as : early-flowering, blooming from July to October ; semi-early, blooming in September and October in the open ; and ordinary, or late-flowering, flowering in November and December ; but this is merely useful as denoting the time when each individual variety will flower.

The culture and management of the chrysanthemum throughout the year are not difficult.

**Culture of Indoor Chrysanthemums.**—If seed is used it should be sown as soon as ripe (February) in a pan of sandy soil, in a temperature of 60° F. Transplant and pot-on as necessary.

*Propagation by Cuttings.*—The favourite method of increase by the best cultivators is by cuttings. Few plants strike so easily as the chrysanthemum. In any soil at any season put a growing shoot in any place where it does not freeze or scorch, and it is almost sure to root.

After the plants have finished blooming, the stems and all weak shoots from the base should be cut down to within a few inches of the soil, the pots being given a position in the cold greenhouse or in a frost-proof frame. A half-inch mulch of fine loam and leaf-mould and a little water will help the old roots to throw up sturdy young shoots for cuttings. In a month or so cuttings should be taken from these vigorous stems which emerge from the soil at a little distance from the main stem of the plant. These will be found to root more easily, and will go ahead better from the beginning than cuttings taken from the main stem itself, as these latter are apt to produce buds too early. Where cuttings have to be made from the main stem, and not from suckers, they should be from 2½ to 3 inches long, not too straggly, with good healthy buds. The lower leaves should be removed, and they should then be taken in their entire length, rootlets as well, and planted out half a dozen in a pot in 3-inch pots, or singly in thumb pots, in the case of Japanese varieties, in a mixture of well-rotted leaf-mould, grit or silver sand, and fibrous loam, in equal parts, and a dusting of wood ashes, all well sieved. A light sprinkling of sand should be placed on the surface of the soil in the pot, so that when the hole is made for the insertion of the cutting, a little of the sand may run into the hole. The holes for the cuttings should be just deep enough for the first leaf-joint to touch the soil, and the cutting must rest on the bottom of the hole drilled for it. The compost used should be moist enough not to need immediate watering, a good soaking being given a few hours after potting. The best way of starting these cuttings is to place the pots in fibre in a frame, in a temperature of from 40–45° F. Keep the frame close for about fourteen days, but wipe the moisture from the lights every morning, or it will drip and cause the cuttings to " damp-off ". Then gradually admit a little more air. When the cuttings have rooted (in from three to five weeks), stand the pots near the glass in a frost-proof frame, and give ample ventilation in fine weather. Cuttings of Japanese types must be taken in December or January, the cuttings must be labelled as soon as they are inserted, or the varieties may become mixed. Most Chrysanthemum shows are held early in November, and cuttings of early-flowering varieties are

**306**

struck rather late, and those of late-flowering varieties somewhat early, so as to have them as far as possible blooming simultaneously for the shows.

*Best Time for Cuttings.*—Nearly all growers differ as to the best time for striking cuttings of the " Decorative " types. Some recommend November ; some succeed admirably by inserting them in May ; the latter date only when propagating plants to flower in small pots in December. Perhaps it is better to make a compromise by striking in February or March.

*Potting-on.*—December-struck cuttings should be well rooted by the middle of February, and should then be potted-up into 3- or 3½-inch pots, adding to the compost one-third part well-rotted manure. They should receive their next shift into 5- or 6-inch pots about the first week in April. Disturb the roots as little as possible, and add a little more manure and a dusting of bonemeal and powdered charcoal to the compost, which do not sieve. The cultivation should be continued in a frame or on a shelf near the glass. Shade from hot sun, then in about a fortnight's time harden-off, stand out-of-doors by the middle of May, and give a final shift a month later.

*Summer Treatment.*—The pots should be stood in the open on slates or a bed of ashes in a sheltered position, facing south or west. As soon as the pots are full of roots the plants should be placed in 8- to 9-inch pots ; about the middle of June is a good time to complete the final potting-up. No soil is better for them than a compost of two-thirds lumpy fibrous loam, one-sixth well-rotted cow-dung, and one-sixth leaf-mould and a little old mortar rubble and sharp sand liberally coloured with bonemeal and soot. There should be good drainage, 2 inches of crocks in the bottom of each receptacle being an average amount.

*Staking and Tying.*—As soon as the final potting has been completed the plants must be staked with a cane or stick strong enough and tall enough to support the plant when full-grown. Let the base of the stake be pointed, and do not thrust it in too near the main stem. The main growth below the branches is usually tied to the stake in two places, and the branches are then tied loosely but securely to the stake with raffia, making the ties between the leaf-joints. In training, the fewer stakes used the better, but for show plants at least three stakes are necessary. If the pots are set out in rows—which should run north and south if possible—a strong post can be placed at each end of the row so that two wires may be strung between them. The stakes in each pot are tied to these wires, which must be some 3 and 5 feet above the ground, so that the pots cannot be blown over in a strong wind. The pots should be far enough apart—say 12 inches—so that the foliages do not touch, as the plants need ample air and sun to mature their stems and leaves.

*" Stopping " and Disbudding.*—If bushy plants are to be grown, pinch out the tip of the central shoot, when the plants are some 5 or 6 inches high. A second " stopping " will be necessary in early summer when each of the resulting shoots has made some 5–6 inches of growth. The first " stopping " should take place about the middle of April or at the

end of that month, according to varieties, some needing earlier treatment than others. Pinching-back, however, should be discontinued by the middle of June in the case of plants to bloom in November, and a month later when a December show is required. If you grow blooms for exhibition only, no stopping will be needed until the " break-bud " appears in early summer. Pinch-out this bud and all the young shoots just below it, except the three strongest and best placed, and concentrate the whole strength of the plant into these stems, and the strength of these stems into a single bud at the top by rubbing off other buds and shoots as they appear. That bud cannot then fail to become a prodigious flower. In the middle of July or early in August the " first-crown " bud forms at the point of each of these three shoots. In some varieties this forms the best bloom, and should be retained, all others being pinched off; with other varieties, however, it is better to nip off this bud and allow other " second-crown " buds to form at the top of the shoot and take its place, all other shoots surrounding it being pinched out. It is, of course, impossible to state here which of the numerous varieties are best grown either on the " first " or the " second-crown " bud, and the reader is advised to refer to a nurseryman's catalogue, in which a complete key to the stopping and timing of varieties is given, once he has decided on the varieties he wishes to grow.

*Feeding and Autumn Treatment.*—From first to last the plants should never flag, and once the plants are established in their flowering pots, but not before, water should be given liberally in dry weather. The plants should never become " dust dry ", and in hot weather they should be inspected at least three times daily to see if water is needed. From early in August the plants should be fed two or three times a week alternately with sulphate of potash and with weak manure-water. Feeding must cease as soon as the blooms are three-parts open, and early in October the plants should be moved under glass. Any plants showing colour in the flower-buds before this must at once be taken into the house. The plants in the house must have ample room, and must be raised on inverted pots or on staging to bring the buds near the glass. This is a critical change for them, and the leaves should be kept well syringed, *except in dull, damp weather*, two or three times a day for a few weeks, or it is probable that they will either discolour or fall off. In damp, dull weather the floors and stagings should be kept as dry as possible, and all overhead spraying must be discontinued, or there will be a risk of " damping off ". In such weather keep the pipes just sufficiently warm to maintain the temperature at 50° F., but no higher. In fine weather the plants must be kept as cool as possible and ample ventilation must be given—a little at night even. As a measure of safety against insect pests fumigate every two or three weeks, and dust the plants with flowers of sulphur at the slightest sign of mildew. All dead and decaying leaves should, of course, have been removed at the time the plants were moved into the house. Late-flowering varieties, that normally flower in December, should be kept in the open as long as possible. They must, however, be protected from frost. When this is no longer possible in the open they should be taken into the house, but must be kept as cool as possible, or they will flower before their time. If the blooms are opening too quickly the plants should be removed from the house and placed in a dark but dry and frost-proof shed, the temperature of which ranges from 40–45° F. This will retard the plants. The temperature of the house in which Chrysanthemums are being grown should never be allowed to rise above 55° F.

The chief pests to keep a look-out for are : aphides, black-fly, earwigs, leaf-eelworm, leaf-miners, leaf-spot, mildew, and rust. For their prevention and treatment see Chapter on **Diseases and Insect Pests.**

There are so many varieties of Chrysanthemum that it is difficult to recommend any particular kinds, but below is given a selection of good and popular sorts, and readers are recommended also to consult growers' catalogues.

*Varieties.*—GREENHOUSE, *Japanese Exhibition.*—*Aquitania* (chestnut and gold) ; *Eva Woollard* (lemon-yellow) ; *Henry E. Trueman* (white) ; *Henry Woolman* (reddish crimson) ; *Lancashire* (yellow) ; *Lorna* (strawberry) ; *Louisa Pockett* (white, tinted pink) ; *Majestic* (golden amber) ; *Mrs. A. Holden* (crimson scarlet) ; *Mrs. Gilbert Drabble* (marble-white) ; *Mrs. Jessie Powell* (salmon-rose) ; *Mrs. R. Luxford* (Indian red) ; *Mrs. Nelson Wyles* (golden amber) ; *Nan Luxford* (silvery pink) ; *Queen Mary* (white) ; *Red Majestic* ; *Rise of Day* (apricot) ; *Robert Radcliffe* (pink) ; *Shirley Primrose* (primrose yellow) ; *Thos. W. Pockett* (silvery pink) ; *Winn Quinn* ; *Yellow Henry Trueman* ; *Yellow Majestic.*

*Japanese Decorative.*—*American Beauty* (white) ; *Baldock's Crimson* ; *Blanche du Poitou* (creamy white) ; *Blanche Poitevene* (white) ; *December Gold* (yellow) ; *Exmouth Crimson* ; *Friendly Rival* (deep yellow) ; *Golden Ace* (golden bronze) ; *Golden Butterfly* (yellow) ; *Golden Marvel* (yellow) ; *Heston White* ; *In Memoriam* (crimson) ; *Jean Pattison* (copper-bronze) ; *Pearla* (pink) ; *Pink Pearl* ; *Southern Beauty* (Indian red) ; *The Favourite* (white). There are also *Amber Favourite Bronze Favourite, Golden Favourite, Pink Favourite, Yellow Favourite,* all good-coloured forms.

*Incurved Varieties.*—*Buttercup* (yellow) ; *Embleme Poitevene* (orange-yellow) ; *James Agate* (red) ; *H. W. Thorpe* (white) ; *J. W. Streeter* (primrose) ; *Mrs. Sidney Dove* (silvery pink) ; *Percy N. Dove* (pure white) ; *Progress* (silvery mauve) ; *Romance* (rich yellow) ; *Silver Sheen* (white).

*Single Varieties.*—*Absolute* (orange-amber) ; *Avondale Pink* (rich pink) ; *Ceddie Mason* (crimson) ; *Exmouth Pink* ; *Mensa* (white) ; *Golden Masons* (canary-yellow) ; *Golden Mensa* (yellow) ; *Golden Seal* (deep yellow) ; *Hon. Edith Smith* (pink) ; *Kitty Bourne* (yellow) ; *Lady Astor, M.P.* (crimson) ; *Lady St. Audries* (crimson and gold) ; *Mason's Bronze* (orange) ; *Miss Joyce Moore* (crimson) ; *Mrs. H. Woolman* (orange-yellow) ; *Mrs. W. Higgs* (pink) ; *Nona* (white) ; *Phyllis Cooper* (orange-gold) ; *Portia* (bronze-red) ; *Tangerine* (bright scarlet).

*Anemone-centred Singles.*—*Aphrodite* (mauve-pink) ; *Beautiful Lady* (bright pink and white) ; *Caleb Cox* (deep amber and golden bronze) ; *Elspeth* (mauve) ; *Golden Nymph* (straw-yellow and gold) ; *Mary*

*Godfrey* (pink) ; *Thora* (rose-pink) ; *Triumph* (mahogany-red) ; *Winsome* (crimson).

**Pompons.**—*Ball of Gold* (bright yellow) ; *Billie Burke* (golden orange) ; *Bright Eyes* (blush-white and orange-apricot) ; *Ethel* (bronze) ; *Golden Fringe* (bright yellow) ; *Golden West* (golden yellow) ; *Hilda Canning* (bronze) ; *Mlle. Elsie Dordan* (silvery pink) ; *Nemo* (white) ; *Thyra* (deep pink).

**Cascade.**—*Fugino* (white) ; *Kyokmachi* (rose and white) ; *Shojo* (red) ; *Swallow* (cream) ; *Yuson* (yellow).

**Korean.**—*Apollo* (bronze-red and gold) ; *Ceres* (yellow) ; *Ember* (coral and bronze) ; *Indian Summer* (copper orange) ; *King Midas* (yellow and bronze) ; *Romany* (bronze-red) ; *Saturn* (orange-bronze and yellow) ; *The Moor* (wine-red) ; *Venus* (rosy salmon pink).

**Chrysanthemum anethifolium** (Glaucous Marguerite), **Chrysanthemum frutescens** (Marguerite or Paris Daisy).—These are popular, half-hardy shrubby plants, both from the Canaries. They like a soil that is not too rich. They are extremely useful in the cool or warm house, where they flower almost all the year round. *C. Mawii* is another variety from Morocco.

*Culture.*—Sow under glass in April or strike cuttings of young shoots about 4 inches in length in sandy soil in a cold frame in September. No artificial heat is necessary, but mats should be used over the frames in severe weather to keep out the frost. Young seedling plants and those raised from cuttings should be periodically " stopped " during the spring, and also during the summer in the case of those grown on for pot culture, and bloom the following spring. They should be potted-up into 4-inch pots in March, grown on, then hardened off and planted out about 20 inches apart, towards the end of May. If they are to be grown on in pots for greenhouse decoration the following spring, they should be re-potted late in May into 6-inch pots, hardened off, and stood on ashes in the open until September, then moved into 7-inch pots and transferred to a cool but frost-proof house for the winter. Water liberally in summer, and give bi-weekly doses of weak liquid manure-water when the buds form about March. A succession of bloom will continue all through the summer.

Varieties of *C. frutescens* are *Brussonetii* (white, single), *Etoile d'Or* (yellow), and *Queen Alexandra* (white, double).

*Species.*—*C. indicum* [China and Japan] (yellow, Oct. and Nov., 15–18 in.) ; *C. morifolium* [China] (white, pink, or lilac rays, Oct. and Nov., 24–30 in.). These two last-named species are said to be the source of the florist or garden Chrysanthemum. *C. ornatum* [Japan] (white rays with yellow disc, Nov., 24 in.). All three require the same treatment as the florist Chrysanthemum.

Several species are grown on the rock-garden, and are useful in pans for the alpine or cool house. They can be raised from seed sown as soon as ripe and kept in a cold frame. Prick out into pans or small pots when large enough, keeping them plunged in the open, or in a cold frame when not in flower. Divide in the spring or autumn.

*Species.*—*C. alpinum* [Europe] (white, July, 6 in.) ; *C. arcticum* [Arctic regions] (white, July, 6 in.) ; *C. argenteum* [Levant] (white, silver foliage, 12 in.) ; *C. tomentosum* [Corsica] (white, July, downy foliage, 2 in.).

**Chrysurus aureus** (see **Lamarkia aurea**).

**Chysis** (see Chapter on **Orchids**).

**Cibotum,** *Cyatheaceæ.*—A group of tree ferns. For culture see Chapter on **Ferns.**

*Species.*—*C. Barometz* (Scythian Lamb) [China and Sub-Tropical Asia] ; *C. glaucum* [Hawaiian Isles] ; *C. regale* [Mexico]. This in a young state is grown by florists for decoration.

**Cineraria (Senecio Hybrida),** *Compositæ.*—Beautiful greenhouse perennials which are generally treated as biennials. With careful management they may be had in flower from November to May, though February and March are the months in which they flower most easily. The old-fashioned Cineraria was a round, smooth-edged flower, but the more modern types are the large single-flowered *C. grandiflora* the star-flowered *C. stellata*, and the cactus-flowered *C. radiata.* The flowers of the single-flowered plants are some 4–5 inches in diameter, and form a large head to the short, sturdy plant,

Available colours are : maroon, purple, red, rose, pink, blue, white, and in some varieties the flowers are self-coloured ; in others they are edged with white or with a second colour. *C. stellata*, the star-flowered type, grows to a height of from 18 to 42 inches, and, with its graceful heads of small, star-shaped and curiously coloured flowers, is very useful for decoration in the greenhouse and for cutting. The cactus-flowered varieties are similar in habit to *C. stellata*, but the sides of the petals curve downwards, and give them a spiky and pointed appearance, very like that of the **Cactus Dahlia.** Most of the garden Cinerarias are hybrids raised from various species, *C. cruenta, C. Heritieri, C. populifolia*, and perhaps others, all of which are natives of the Canary Islands, and are botanically known as Senecios.

Few plants, however, are so effective for decorative purposes. They thrive in a compost of two parts fibrous loam to one part of leaf-mould, well-decayed cow-manure, and a little sand and old mortar rubble, and are best grown from seed.

*Culture.*—The first sowing should be made in April, in pans filled with equal parts of loam and leaf-mould and one-sixth part of sand. They should be well drained, made firm, the seed should be lightly covered, and the pans placed in slight bottom heat. Cover with glass and paper, and keep slightly moist. Stand the seedlings in partial shade, move into 3-inch pots as soon as possible, gradually harden off, and remove the lights of the frame entirely by day from July to the end of September. Shift the young plants into 4½- to 5-inch pots as required, and give them their final shift in September into 6- to 8-inch pots. After each potting keep the frame closed until the plants are re-established, then again gradually admit full air. Keep moist, and syringe every afternoon in hot weather ; then towards the end of September the plants should be placed in a cool greenhouse, and weak liquid manure or soot-water given alternately with water. Another sowing may be made in a cold frame in May, and a third in June. Pot-on as above, but at proportionately later dates. Keep a watch for diseases and pests, the

**311**

principal ones being Chrysanthemum Leaf Miner, Mildew, and Rust, and deal with any of them as soon as they appear. In the warm house Cinerarias may be had in flower in winter and in early and late spring.

*Species and Varieties.*—*Senecio cruenta*, *S. Heritieri*, and *S. populifolia* (*Cineraria*), of which there are many varieties, usually divided into the following classes—viz. the large-flowered florist's varieties, the intermediate, and the stellata varieties [Star Cineraria] (Various colours, winter and spring, 18–30 in.).

**Cineraria maritima** (see **Senecio Cineraria**).

**Cirrhopetalum** (see Chapter on **Orchids**).

**Cissus,** *Vitaceæ.*—A genus of stove or greenhouse and hardy climbers, allied to **Vitis,** and by some authorities united to it. They are grown for the beauty of their foliage, of which *C. discolor* is the most attractive. They succeed in any good loam, leaf-soil, and sand. They are readily propagated from cuttings placed in a close case in heat during the summer.

*Species.*—*C. adenopodus* (*Vitis adenopoda*) [Uganda] is a quick-growing climber. The young shoots and leaves are covered with bright-red hairs. It bears greenish-yellow flowers, and its fruit when ripe is round and black. It is suitable for the warm greenhouse.

*C. discolor* (*Vitis discolor*) [Java] is sometimes known as Trailing Begonia owing to the brilliancy of its foliage, which is reddish beneath, velvet-green and mottled with silvery-white above. Thrives in a rich soil and a moist temperature of 75° F. *C. gongylodes* (*Vitis gongylodes*) [Brazil] is a vigorous climber for large greenhouses, giving a tropical appearance. In a moist atmosphere it sends down long, bright-red aerial roots. If the branches are stopped, tubers 5 or 6 inches long are formed, giving it the appearance of a bell-rope. From these tubers new plants are produced.

**Citrus sinensis** (Sweet Orange), *Rutaceæ.*—The dwarf fruiting species, which are usually grown in the cool greenhouse, are grafted plants. They thrive in a compost of three-quarters turfy loam and one-quarter leaf-mould, rotten manure, and sand.

*Culture.*—Pot-up when young, early in March, and re-pot annually until established in a large tub or 10- to 12-inch pot. Water regularly, and feed with occasional doses of liquid manure in summer. Shade from strong sun. In winter they need full sun. Trim to shape only. The trees may be propagated by seed sown in gentle heat (65° F.), by budding in July, or by grafting in March ; but cuttings struck in the spring produce bushes which fruit earlier.

The culture of the grapefruit (*C. paradisi*), the lemon (*C. Limonia*), the Seville orange (*C. Aurantium*), the lime (*C. aurantifolia*), and the citron (*C. Medica*) is identical with that of the orange. Although now grown in most of the temperate parts of the world, the Citrus originally came from Tropical and sub-Tropical Asia and the Malayan Archipelago. All the species have given rise to many varieties and hybrids.

**Clarkia,** *Onagraceæ.*—The Clarkia is a very showy annual which grows freely from seed, and blooms profusely in almost any circumstances. When planted in fairly rich, moist soil and properly attended to, they rank among the most effective of annuals for the border or for decoration in the cold greenhouse; their large, handsome flowers, which are useful for cutting, and their shrub-like habit of growth render them strikingly effective.

*Culture.*—For the greenhouse, sow seed thinly, ¼ inch deep, in light, rich soil in a frame in August. Thin out to 12 inches apart when large enough to handle, and pinch out the main shoots to encourage bushy growth. Pot-up as required, using 6- to 7-inch pots for three plants, A few sticks will be required as supports. Winter in the cool house, well up near the glass. The plants will bloom here from January to March. In the open, the plants will grow from 18 to 24 inches in height, and flower from July to October.

*Clarkia elegans*, a native of California, has given rise to many beautiful double varieties : *Brilliant Rose* (rose) ; *Firefly* (crimson) ; *Marginata* (pink, margined white) ; *Orange King* (orange) ; *Scarlet Beauty* (scarlet) ; *Purple Queen* (purple) ; *Salmon Queen* (salmon) ; and *Snowball* (white).

**Cleistocactus Baumannii (Cereus Baumannii)**, *Cactaceæ.*—A tall, columnar cactus from S. America, sometimes reaching a height of 6 feet. It bears red or orange flowers, and requires the same treatment as **Cereus,** which see.

**Clematis** (Virgin's Bower), *Ranunculaceæ.*—One of the most beautiful of our hardy climbers, these plants, which grow from 5 to 20 feet high, and flower in the summer or autumn, according to variety, do well against walls and on trellises, facing north, east, or west. They also make excellent climbers for the greenhouse, if planted in March in a well-drained border, or in large pots in a compost of two-thirds loam to one-third well-rotted manure, leaf-mould, and sand. They need ample space and sun, and if planted in a sunny position, the lower part of the stems require shade. The following species are very useful in this connection : *C. Armandii* [Central and W. China] with white flowers, also several varieties with shades of pink ; *C. Flammula* [S. Europe], with white flowers in September ; *C. florida* [Japan], with creamy-white and purple flowers, and its variety *bicolor* (*C. Sieboldii*) ; *C. indivisa* [New Zealand], with white flowers, and its variety *lobata*, both of which are winter flowering ; *C. montana* [Himalayas], which bears white flowers in May, and its variety *rubens*, with pink flowers and reddish foliage ; and *C. tangutica* [W. China], with yellow flowers in June and August. Although not particular as to soil, they prefer light to heavy land, if it has been well manured ; a mixture of well-drained loam, well-rotted manure, and old mortar-rubble is the most satisfactory compost.

*Culture.*—Propagate by means of layering in summer. Plant or pot-up in March. Cut away dead and weak wood, giving ample light and air to the growths retained, as overcrowded plants soon become weak. Fasten the shoots up securely. Propagation may also be carried out by means of grafting, by cuttings or by seed.

*Pruning.*—Most varieties require pruning after flowering, but the *C. Vitalba* section, which includes *C. balearica*, native of Minorca and Corsica, and *C. cirrhosa*, from South Europe, is best pruned in March, while *C. Jackmanii* and *C. Viticella* vars. should be cut down to 6 inches in

**313**

November, or to a foot in spring. Established plants are pruned back hard in February to within an inch of the old wood.

When potting use 5- to 10-inch pots and a compost of two parts fibrous loam to one part of leaf-mould, well-rotted manure, mortar rubble and sand. Place in a cool or cold greenhouse early in the year. Water liberally while growing, and keep well thinned, or they will grow in such profusion that they will block out the light from other plants.

*Hybrids and Varieties.*—*Early-flowering* (Florida Group) : *Belle of Woking* (silvery mauve) ; *Countess of Lovelace* (lavender-blue) ; *Duchess of Edinburgh* (double white).

*Late-flowering.*—*Gipsy Queen* (purple) ; *Jackmanii* (purple) and *J.* var. *Snow White* (white) ; *Prince of Wales* (violet, purple, red vars.) ; *Crimson King* (crimson) ; *Lawsoniana* var. ; *Henryi* (white) ; *Beauty of Worcester* (bluish violet) ; *Fairy Queen* (flesh-pink) ; *Lady North-cliffe* (deep lavender) ; *Mrs. Pope* (lavender) ; and *Nellie Moser* (mauve with pink bars) ; *Madame Van Houtte* (pale blue) ; *Duke of Edinburgh* (purplish violet) ; *Miss Bateman* (white) ; and *The Queen* (lavender) ; *C. Ascotiensis* (azure-blue) ; *Ville de Lyon* (carmine) ; and *C. Viticella alba* (white, semi-double).

**Cleome spinosa** (Giant Spider Plant), *Capparidaceæ.*—This native of Tropical America is an attractive annual for the open, but it may be used to good effect in the cool greenhouse. Seed may be sown in March in a little warmth. Prick out when large enough and grow on, planting finally in 6-inch pots in ordinary potting-soil of loam, leaf-soil, and sand. They will flower in June and July. Seeds may be sown in September and grown on in a cool house. They will flower in March and April. Flowers are rosy purple, varying to white, 36–48 inches.

**Clerodendron,** *Verbenaceæ.*—Beautiful deciduous, flowering shrubs or small trees, growing from 6 to 12 feet high and bearing purple, red, or white flowers from July to September. They thrive in a sunny, sheltered position in well-drained, rich loam. *C. fragrans* * [China and Japan] has white fragrant flowers in September and October. *C. fœtidum* [China], which grows from 3 to 6 feet high, carries purple flowers. Both these are good plants for outside, but they are also useful for the cold greenhouse. *C. fallax* [Java], which grows well in a cool greenhouse, bears orange-scarlet flowers. It requires an even temperature of about 55° F. Sow seed in gentle heat in March, and again in July for succession. Grow on, and flower in 5- to 6-inch pots. *C. macrosiphon* [Zanzibar] is an elegant, erect shrub for the warm house, with conspicuous pure white flowers, relieved by the long purple, thread-like filaments (May, June, 18–30 in.). *C. splendens* [Tropical Africa] is a handsome evergreen climber for the warm greenhouse or stove house, with scarlet flowers. It should be planted out in a border. *C. Thomsonæ* (*C. Balfouri*) [W. Africa] has crimson and white flowers. It needs the same temperature, and it also makes a useful pot-plant. *C. ugandense* [Tropical Africa], with its violet-blue flowers in the autumn and early winter is a useful pot plant, 2 to 3 feet high, for the greenhouse. If planted out in a border it may be trained up a pillar or under the roof and will reach a height of 20 feet.

* This type has semi-double flowers.

**314**

Propagate by means of seed, cuttings, or half-ripened shoots in a frame, or by root cuttings.

**Clethra** (Sweet Pepper Bush), *Clethraceæ.*—Choice, hardy and half-hardy flowering shrubs that, with the shelter of a wall, will thrive in a warm, sunny position in the south and west of England. They grow to a height of 5 to 6 feet, and carry fragrant, white, lily-of-the-valley-like flowers on the current year's growth from July to September.

*Culture.*—A compost of rich, moist loam and leaf-mould or peat suits them. Pot-up from November and stand in the cold greenhouse. Water well while growing. Propagate by cuttings of semi-matured shoots in a frame, in June, or by division. *C. alnifolia* [N. America] may be had in flower from February to April in the greenhouse.

**Clianthus,** *Leguminosæ.*—A genus of fine, free-flowering, evergreen, climbing shrubs, which includes " Parrot's Bill " and " The Glory Pea ", with elegant foliage and brilliantly coloured, singularly shaped flowers, which are produced in splended clusters. They attain a height of from 4 to 6 feet. *C. puniceus* var. *magnificus* (red) and var. *carneus,* " Parrot's Bill " or " Lobster's Claw " blossom freely out of doors against a trellis or south wall; *C. Dampieri* Australia " Dampiers or Glory Pea " succeeds best when planted in pots or baskets in the greenhouse, where it carries red flowers in summer. The flowers of *C. puniceus* [New Zealand] are crimson, and are borne from June to September. Those of *C. p. carneus* are flesh-coloured. There is also a white variety, *albus.*

*Culture.*—Seed sown in February blossoms the first year, and succeeds best in sandy peat and fibrous loam in a warm, sunny border of a cool greenhouse (temperature 50° F. winter, 65° F. summer). Sow seeds in February, singly in pots, and when 3–4 inches high move to 4½-inch pots, and keep in these until ready for planting out in April, or, in the case of *C. Dampieri* (Glory Pea) into a border in the house, or into a good large pot or large basket. In summer the plants must be kept well watered, but the soil must never become stagnant or sour. The great thing is to grow these plants on without a check. Once the roots become over-dry they will not recover; they are also impatient of disturbance. Protect from frost, and water sparingly in winter. Syringe house-plants daily in hot, dry weather, and train the shoots up trellis-work or wires placed some 10 inches from the glass, and trim back straggling shoots after flowering. They may also be raised by means of cuttings with a " heel " in sandy soil in a frame (temperature 70° F.) in May or June. *C. Dampieri* is a difficult plant to grow on its own roots, and does best when the young seedlings are grafted on seedling stocks of the " Bladder Senna ", **Colutea arborescens.** The seeds of this should be sown ten days or a fortnight in advance, the seedlings being cut off just above the cotyledons or seed-leaves. The Clianthus seedlings, while still in the cotyledon stage, are separated from the root, and their base cut in the shape of a wedge. This is then inserted into a slit made in the stem between the cotyledons of the Colutea seedlings, and carefully tied with wool or other soft material. While the union is taking place they should be put under a bell-jar in a warm greenhouse.

**Cliff Brake Fern** (see **Pellæa**).

**Climbing Dahlia** (see **Hidalgoa Werckleri**).

**Climbing Fern** (see **Lygodium**).

**Climbing Hempweed** (see **Mikania scandens**).

**Clitoria ternatea** (Butterfly Pea), *Leguminosæ.*—A beautiful warm greenhouse twining annual, with rich blue flowers. It is readily raised from seed sown in sandy soil and placed in a little warmth. Plant out either in a border or in 8-inch pots in sandy peat, fibrous loam, and sand. They will grow from 6 to 12 feet in height. Flowers are borne from June to August. There is also a white variety, *alba*.

**Clivia** (**Imantophyllum**), *Amaryllidaceæ.*—Beautiful evergreen plants, with long, strap-like, bright-green leaves, suitable for the greenhouse. They grow about 20 inches in height, and bear erect spikes on which are lily-like blooms in March and April. Scarlet, brick-red, and orange-yellow are the shades most frequently seen. Clivias make very useful room plants. A large number of improved varieties have been raised, many of which have been given varietal names.

*Culture.*—Plant in February in 9-inch pots, in a mixture of rich, sandy loam, leaf-mould, and old manure. Keep in a cool place, and let the roots fill the pots, as the plants flourish best when root-bound. Water well in summer, keep cool (45° F.) and on the dry side during winter, and sponge the leaves occasionally with tepid water. Weak manure-water should be given twice a week while the buds are forming.

*Propagation.*—Propagate by means of division of suckers in February, or by seed sown when ripe.

*Species.*—*C. miniata* and vars. (orange-scarlet to yellow); *C. nobilis* (red and yellow); and *C. cyrtanthiflora*, a beautiful hybrid from the two previous species.

**Club Moss** (see **Lycopodium**).

**Club Rush** (see **Scirpus**).

**Clusia,** *Guttiferæ.*—Stove evergreen shrubs, with coriaceous leaves and conspicuous wax-like flowers. They require a warm, moist atmosphere and rich, loamy sand. A large pot is not required, as quite a large plant can be grown in a 10-inch pot. They are raised from cuttings of half-ripe shoots in sand under a bell-glass, with plenty of bottom heat.

*Species.*—*C. flava* [Jamaica] (pale yellow, summer, 24–60 in.); *C. grandiflora* [Guiana] (rose and white flowers, 6–8 in. across, plant 2–10 ft. high). This is one of the most beautiful of all the genus.

**Clytostoma,** *Bignoniaceæ.*—Beautiful evergreen stove-house climbers grown for their magnificent flowers. They are allied to **Bignonia** (which see), and require the same treatment.

*Species.*—*C. callistegioides* (*Bignonia callistegioides*) is a strong climber from Brazil. It bears pale purple flowers, the tube being yellowish, streaked with purple, in summer. *C. purpureum* (*Bignonia purpurea*) [Uruguay] has tubular mauve flowers, with a white eye, in summer.

**Cobæa** (Cup-and-saucer Plant), *Polemoniaceæ.*—Beautiful, evergreen, rapid growing climbers, which thrive in the cool or warm greenhouse. They grow to a height of 20 feet, and flower under glass in summer. *C.*

*scandens* [Mexico] has beautiful bell-shaped, purple and greenish-white flowers, and *C. macrostoma* [Guatemala] has large, greenish-white, star-shaped blooms, and is a most prolific flowerer. There is also a variegated form of *C. scandens*, *C. s. variegata*, a beautiful greenhouse climber, which must be propagated by means of cuttings. The two former will also thrive in the open in warm, sheltered positions in the south and west of England; in more exposed situations they must be treated as annuals and raised afresh each year.

*Culture.*—Sow seed thinly under glass (temperature 45° F.) in light, rich soil in February, and press the seed gently into the soil. Pot-up into 3- to 4-inch pots as soon as possible. Harden off, and if for growing in the open, plant out 24 inches apart in June in equal parts of loam, leaf-mould and sand, or grow on in pots and keep in the cool greenhouse.

*Propagation.*—Propagation by cuttings is better than by seed, and cuttings of young shoots 3–4 inches in length should be taken in January or February and raised in a propagating case to be potted on later as described for seedling plants. In February, prune laterals back to two buds, and cut out all weak growth. Water well while growing. They do equally well in the cool or warm house. Average temperature 45° F. winter, 60° F. summer.

**Cobweb House Leek** (see **Sempervivum arachnoideum**).

**Cobwigia coccinea** (see **Stenomesson coccineum**).

**Cobwigia incarnata** (see **Stenomesson incarnatum**).

**Cochlioda** (see Chapter on **Orchids**).

**Cochliostema odoratissimum,** *Commelinaceæ.*—A curious stove perennial from Ecuador, of easy culture. It thrives in a warm, moist atmosphere in a mixture of two parts loam and one part of peat, with a little well-decayed cow- or sheep-manure when potting the mature plant. It requires a plentiful supply of water during the growing season, and at no time should it be allowed to get too dry.

*Propagation.*—It is increased by division of the root. To obtain seed the flowers should be fertilised artificially, although this can sometimes be accomplished by shaking the flower-stalk, and if done at the right time seed is freely produced. These should be sown in light, peaty soil as soon as ripe. Pot the seedlings singly in small pots, and grow on, potting them as required. They will flower in eight to twelve months. The flowers are blue with rose-coloured bracts and scape, 18 inches.

**Cockscomb** (see **Celosia**).

**Cockspur Flower** (see **Plectranthus**).

**Coconut** (see **Cocos nucifera**).

**Cocos,** *Palmaceæ.*—A group of decorative palms, of which *C. Weddelliana* is the most popular from an ornamental point of view, great quantities of these being grown and sold in 3- to 4-inch pots for house and table decoration. Their culture is easy, they grow slowly, and retain their beauty for a long time. Seeds, which should be retained in their fibrous husk, should be sown in a hot bed in spring, and potted-on as required in two parts of rich, loamy soil, one part peat, and one part sand. Copious supplies of water should be given during the summer, gradually reducing the amount as winter approaches. Temperature 65–75° F. summer, not below 50° F. winter.

*Species.*—*C. australis* [Buenos Aires] is a slow-growing ornamental palm, attaining a height of 20 feet. *C. nucifera* (Coconut Palm) [Tropical America] is the most important, from an economic point of view, of all cultivated palms. *C. plumosa* [Central Brazil] has long, narrow, plume-like leaves, 10–12 feet in length. *C. Romanzoffiana* [Central Brazil] has graceful arched leaves of deep green, and is very attractive. *C. Weddelliana* [Tropical Brazil] is a graceful palm, useful for greenhouse or table decoration, particularly in a small state. It will grow up to 10 feet.

**Codiæum** (Croton, or Variegated Laurel), *Euphorbiaceæ.*—Beautiful stove evergreen shrubs with variegated leaves, which are generally known as Crotons, both in gardens and nurseries. Among ornamental foliage plants few, if any, are more beautiful than the different varieties, with their magnificently coloured leaves, ranging through light and deep yellow, orange, pink, red, and crimson, in the most charming combinations. In some cases one colour predominates. Some are also remarkable for their singular form. They are valuable both for room and table decoration, the narrow-leaved varieties being most suitable for this purpose. These should be grown with a single stem and kept in 5-inch pots. They are equally valuable for furnishing conservatories and other cool houses during the summer and autumn, a time when foliage plants can be employed to good effect. For this purpose, as for house or table decoration, they must be gradually hardened off, as a sudden change in temperature will cause their leaves to fall off. Large specimens for decoration or exhibition, which can be obtained up to 6 feet high, should be encouraged to make plenty of side branches, by pinching the end of the leading shoot, if they do not start freely without. To bring out to the fullest extent the rich markings of the leaves they require a very moist, warm temperature (60–70° F., in winter). They should be given plenty of light by standing them on inverted pots so as to raise them above other plants among which they may be growing, and kept moist by syringing them frequently. This also helps to keep down red spider, which is one of the worst enemies the plants have to contend with, though thrip is equally as bad. The most effective antidote for the latter is to dip the heads of the plants in strong tobacco-water, which destroys the insects and their eggs. For red spider there is nothing so effective as hand-washing with a soft sponge and soapy water.

*Propagation.*—Cuttings of the young tops root readily in sand, loam, and peat. They should be placed singly in small pots, and stood in a close frame with strong, moist heat. They should receive a little air when well rooted, and this should be gradually increased until they are fully exposed, when they can be potted on into 3-inch pots in good fibrous loam with an ample sprinkling of sand. The plants should be kept in a warm, moist atmosphere, and should be afforded plenty of light. Pot-on as required, taking care not to overpot, for the advantage of growing Codiæums is that they can be kept in small pots for quite a long time, provided they do not suffer for want of water.

**318**

# GREENHOUSE PLANTS

The many cultivated forms are generally considered to be from one species, *C. variegatum*, a species from Malaya. The following are a few : *C. " Carrierei "*, broad leaves, orange, yellow, and green ; no red. *C. " Baron F. Scilliere "*, broad leaves, brilliant green, centre yellow turning white ; pink under-surface. *C. " Earl of Derby "*, trilobed leaves, suffused with bright red ; midrib bright yellow. *C. " Multi-color "*, leaves, when young, light green and yellow ; when mature, dark green blotched with yellow, deep orange, and crimson ; red midrib. *C. " Pictum "*, ground colour rich crimson, blotched and spotted with bright green and black. *C. " Triumphant Harwoodi-anum "*, deep green, yellow network with bright crimson ; when mature the leaves become rich greenish bronze with intense rosy crimson, very bright and effective.

**Cœlogyne cristata** (see Chapter on **Orchids**).

**Coix Lacryma-Jobi** (Job's Tear), *Graminæ*.—Ornamental greenhouse grass with bead-like inflorescens, from Tropical Asia. The beads or " tears ", which are pearly white to lead colour, are used for ornament or as a curiosity, and are used as beads and made into necklaces. They are raised by seed sown in pots and stood in saucers of water. When large enough, place five or six plants in an 8-inch pot, and keep in a saucer of water ; or they may be placed round the sides of the indoor aquarium. There is a variety, *aurea zebrina*, with yellow-striped blades.

**Colchicum,** *Liliaceæ.*—Hardy, bulbous, *poisonous* plants usually grown in the rock garden. They are also useful in the cold greenhouse.

*Culture.*—Plant or pot-up in July or August in moist, cool loam, in 6-inch pots or pans—three to four bulbs in each, according to size. Transplant triennially in August to increase.

*Species.*—*C. autumnale* (Meadow Saffron or Autumn Crocus) [Europe] (lilac-rose, Sept.–Oct., 6 in.) ; *C. crociflorum* [Central Asia] (white-and-purple striped, Feb. and March, 3–4 in.) ; *C. luteum* [W. India] (this is a spring-flowering species which produces its flowers and foliage together, it is a very desirable plant, and the only species with yellow flowers) ; *C. montanum* [Mediterranean region] (lilac or white, Sept.–Oct., 4 in.) ; *C. speciosum* [Caucasus] (crimson, purple or white eye, Sept.–Oct., 10 in.) ; *C. speciosum* var. *album* (white).

**Coleonema,** *Rutaceæ.*—Ornamental, heath-like evergreen shrubs, from the Cape of Good Hope, useful for the cool greenhouse in the autumn and winter. They should be stood outside during the summer. They should be potted firmly in two parts loam, one part peat, and some sand. Prune lightly in the spring.

*Propagation.*—Cuttings of young shoots getting firm at the base root readily if placed under a bell-glass in a little heat.

*Species.*—*C. album* (white, 16–24 in.) ; *C. pulchrum* (red, 24–36 in.).

**Coleus Blumei** (Fire-nettle), *Labiatæ.*—Beautiful half-hardy plants rom Java, grown for the sake of their foliage, which is highly variegated and of diverse strongly contrasting colours—crimson, white, dark and light green, bronze, maroon, and yellow. The leaves are generally of one of these colours, broadly fringed or undulate edged, banded, mottled, tinted or blotched. The plants are useful for bedding-out in the open in summer and for decorative purposes in the cool greenhouse (temperature 65° F.). They are highly sensitive to cold, and if kept through the winter the temperature must never be allowed to fall below 55° F.

*Culture.*—The plants can be raised from seed sown in heat (70° F.) in March or summer. Named varieties must be propagated by means of cuttings, 3 inches long, put in at any time from spring to autumn, struck singly in pots sunk to their rims in fibre, in a frame with good bottom heat (70° F.) and in a moist atmosphere; the best time to do this is March. These plants like a light, rich soil, two parts of loam to one part of leaf-mould and sand being recommended. Place near the glass, but shade from strong sun. When rooted the young plants should be re-potted into 3-inch pots and pinched back to encourage shrubby growth. Pot-on until they are finally in 5- to 6-inch pots, or 10-inch ones if large specimens are required. Ventilate freely, taking care that the temperature does not fall below 55° F. Syringe and water well in warm weather, and dress with fortnightly applications of weak liquid manure. When grown from seed it will be apparent as soon as germination takes place that many of the seedlings are purely green-leaved. These are useless as foliage plants, and should at once be weeded out. Pot-up firmly into thumb pots as soon as possible. When the plants become pot-bound, shift them into 3-inch pots, and later again into 5- to 6-inch pots, which are usually large enough to grow the plants in. Some few of the genus are annuals, but they are mostly perennials. The chief pests are *Mealy Bug* and *Scale*.

*Varieties.*—*Beckwith's Gem ; Countess of Dudley ; Decorator ; Golden Ball ; Nigger ; Pride of the Market ; Picturatum ; Princess Elizabeth ; Roi de Noire ; Sunset ;* and *Verschaffetii*. Many of the varieties are used in summer bedding schemes. All flower in the summer and grow from 6 to 24 inches high. *Coleus Autranii* [Tropical Africa], *C. Fredericii* [Angola], *C. shirensis*, and *C. thyrsoideus*, both from Central Africa, are winter-flowering greenhouse species, with beautiful blue flowers of various shades, and are propagated by means of seed or cuttings.

**Collinsia** (Collins's Flower), *Scrophulariaceæ*.—Showy hardy annuals which are easy to grow, and suitable for sunny beds and borders, or for cultivation in the greenhouse. They will soon cover any ugly bare space with a mass of bright colour, and provide excellent cut flowers. The plants grow to about 12 inches in height, and carry small Antirrhinum-like flowers, with double lips, from July to October. The most popular species is *C. bicolor* from California.

*Culture.*—Sow seed thinly ¼ inch deep from March to June, or in September, and thin out to 6 inches apart when fit to handle. Pot-up as required in 5- or 6-inch pots in well drained ordinary soil and stand in a light, airy position. Water regularly while growing.

**Colocasia,** *Araceæ*.—A small group of stove herbaceous plants grown for their handsome foliage either for the greenhouse or for planting out in the sub-tropical garden when their large leaves give a very pleasant effect. They do best in rich, damp soil, and are perhaps more suitable for planting out than for potwork. *C. antiquorum* [India] has large handsome green peltate leaves, and grows to a height of 3 feet. There

Conandrum ramondioides

*Photos*]

[*R. A. Malby*

Chlidanthus fragrans

Dicentra spectabilis

*Photos*] Acocanthera spectabilis [*F. G. Preston*

are several varieties of this : *C. a. esculenta* (Elephant's Ear) [Hawaii and Fiji] has handsome peltate-cordate leaves, and is largely planted in sub-tropical gardens. *C. a.* " *Illustris* " (Black Caladium) has green leaves, with blackish-green spots ; the leaf-stalks are purple.

**Columbine** (see **Aquilegia**).

**Columnea,** *Gesneraceæ.*—An attractive, warm-house evergreen, very suitable for baskets or for rambling up old fern-stems. Several of them bear very brilliantly coloured flowers. They require the same treatment as **Trichosporum.**

*Species.*—*C. Banksii* [garden hybrid] (deep red, free flowering, summer, 12–18 in.) ; *C. gloriosa* [Costa Rica] (scarlet and yellow, summer, 15–20 in.) ; the variety *purpurascens* has attractive purple leaves. *C. magnifica* [Costa Rica] (flame-scarlet, summer, 15–20 in.) ; *C. microphylla* [Costa Rica] (bright scarlet, very small leaves, summer, 24–36 in.) ; *C. Schiedeana* [Mexico] (scarlet, striped with yellow summer, 15–20 in.).

**Combretum,** *Combretaceæ.* Evergreen climbers or shrubs suitable for the warm greenhouse, being very attractive in flower. Although they can be grown in large pots, the best method of cultivation is to plant them in the border of the greenhouse, and train them up a pillar or the rafters. They should be planted in three parts peat to one part of loam and one of sand, taking care that they have a plentiful supply of water during the summer. Syringing in the spring is beneficial, and after the flowers are over the plants should be pruned and thinned.

*Propagation.*—They can be propagated from the stiffish side-shoots with " heel " attached, put in sand under a bell-glass, and placed in heat.

*Species.*—*C. coccineum* (*C. purpureum*) [Madagascar] (brilliant red flowers, summer, climber, 15–20 ft.) ; *C. grandiflorum* [Tropical Africa] (scarlet, May to July, can be treated as bush or climber, 4–5 ft.) ; *C. racemosum* [Tropical Africa] (white, March–July, climber, 12 ft.).

**Commelina** (Day Flower), *Commelinaceæ.*—Herbaceous perennials or evergreen trailers, some of which may be grown outdoors during the summer. The stove or greenhouse kinds require a light soil, and are readily propagated from cuttings in March or April, placed under a handlight in a warm house. The trailers are very useful as basket-plants or for covering the border in the greenhouse around and under other taller plants. *C. cœlestis*, a tuberous rooted species with beautiful blue flowers, is the best of the herbaceous species, and can be grown outside in the summer. The tubers should be lifted in the autumn, but should not be allowed to get too dry during the winter. It is readily raised from seed sown in the spring, or by division of the tubers. It is also very useful for the cool greenhouse, either planted out in the border or in pots.

*Species.*—*C. benghalensis* [Bengal] (sky-blue flowers, May and June, warm greenhouse trailer) ; *C. cœlestis* [Mexico] (sky-blue flowers, Aug. and Sept., 12–18 in.) ; *C. tuberosa* [Mountains of Mexico] (rich blue, June and July, 12 in.).

**Comparettia** (see Chapter on **Orchids**).

X

321

# THE GREENHOUSE

**Conandron ramondioides,** *Gesneraceæ.*—A pretty tuberous-rooted plant from Japan, somewhat allied to **Ramonda,** 6 inches high, with clusters of purple flowers in the summer. Not quite hardy, it should be grown in the alpine or cool house in a shady position. It should be planted out in a well-drained border, among lumps of sandstone if possible, with peat and loam in equal proportions, with sand and charcoal added. Or it may be grown in pans of the same compost and plunged in a shady, slightly heated frame, removing it to the alpine house when in bloom.

**Coniogramme japonica (Gymnogramme japonica),** *Polypodiaceæ.*— An interesting, strong-growing fern, 18–24 inches high, with a rather distinctive appearance, which, although it can be grown in the cool house, develops much better in a temperature of between 55 and 60° F. It needs an open, well-drained soil of a peaty nature, and it thrives planted out, on a raft or in a pot or pan. It is increased by division in the spring.

**Conostephium pendulum,** *Epacridaceæ.*—An ornamental evergreen greenhouse shrub from Western Australia. It grows 10–18 inches high, and bears attractive red flowers in April and May, which are followed by edible berries, known in Australia as " Nature Currant." It thrives in a compost of peat and sandy loam in a temperature of 60–70° F. in summer ; winter 40–50° F. Cuttings of young shoots taken in April will root readily in sand.

**Convallaria majalis** (Lily of the Valley), *Liliaceæ.*—To grow Lilies of the Valley well, the roots should be set in bunches a foot apart, in a mixture of sandy loam, leaf-mould and old manure, in a partially shaded position ; they can hardly be treated too liberally. The plants, natives of Asia and Europe, grow 9–10 inches high and flower from April to June.

*Culture.*—Plant each crown about 5 inches apart in October, only just covering with soil, and mulch with a 2-inch layer of leaf-mould, which should be removed in the spring. Dress annually in summer with leaf-mould and rotten manure, and water liberally in dry weather. Lift from the soil every fourth year, when the blooms become small, and propagate by means of division in October. It is advisable to lift a portion of the crowns each year, and not the whole of them in any one year ; a steadier succession of good bloom is thus obtained.

*Pot Culture.*—If grown in pots for the greenhouse, by a little management a succession may be kept in bloom until June, it takes about five weeks to force the crowns into flower. Plump retarded crowns should be potted-up, 1 inch apart, in November, using 5- to 6-inch pots and a compost of sandy loam and leaf-mould, the crowns being pressed gently into the soil so that only the tops protrude. Water well, and keep in a cool frame for a few days after potting, then take into the warm house in batches as bloom is required. The pots must be kept in the dark until the shoots are 5 or 6 inches in height ; after this gradually admit light, raise the temperature to between 60° and 70° F., and give warm water in increasing amounts as growth proceeds. If only plump crowns are selected when potting-up, a cluster of flowering spikes will be thrown up in each pot. After flowering, plant the crowns

322

in the border, where, in all probability, if they have not been forced too much, they will flower the following year.

To span the gap between the last of the border lilies and those to be forced in the greenhouse, " retarded " crowns can be bought and potted-up as above. Treatment is exactly the same as recommended for forced plants, except that the house temperature should be 5–10° lower and the plants must be carefully shaded from strong sun. The crowns will flower in just under a month from the time they are potted-up.

**Convolvulus,** *Convolvulaceæ.*—Annual and perennial herbs (mainly), most of which may be grown outdoors, although some require greenhouse culture, and are very decorative therein. They thrive in good, well-drained, fibrous soil, and, where possible, the twiners should be planted out in the border to allow them to develop, training them up pillars or along wires under the roof. They are increased by cuttings placed in sand, or by division in the spring, or by seed. They are usually rapid growers, and need attention or they soon entwine round themselves and form a tangled mass. If grown in pots, generous feeding is necessary when they are well rooted.

*Species.*—*C. californicus* [California] has creamy-yellow flowers. The plant is densely white-villose, and is suitable for growing in a basket. *C. canariensis* [Canary Isles] has violet-purple flowers in summer. It is a twiner. *C. Cneorum* [S. Europe] is a compact silver-leaf shrub with white- or pink-tinged flowers. Although it may be grown against a wall in the open, it makes a charming pot-plant for the conservatory or the alpine house. It readily roots from cuttings struck in sand. *C. mauritanicus* [N. Africa] is a free-blooming, blue-flowered, herbaceous trailer, which will succeed in the open in a sunny, warm spot, but also makes a useful basket-plant for the cool greenhouse. *C. tricolor* [S. Europe] is an annual, usually grown outside, but one which makes a beautiful basket plant for the conservatory. Sow seed in February, pot in small pots, and make up the baskets when the plants are large enough.

**Cooperia** (Evening Star), *Amaryllidaceæ.*—Half-hardy, bulbous-rooted plants, natives of the Texas to Mexico region, suitable for greenhouse culture. They grow from 9 to 12 inches high, and flower in July and August. They are night flowering and have a delicious fragrance.

*Culture.*—Pot-up in February, using a compost of peaty loam, leaf-mould, and sand, and stand in the greenhouse. Water liberally while growing, but keep dry in the pot after flowering. Propagate by means of offsets in February.

*Species.*—*Cooperia Drummondii* has white flowers, tinged with red on the outside, and grows to a height of 12 inches. *C. pedunculata* (Giant Prairie Lily) is larger than the previous species, and the flowers last several days longer. It also attains a height of 12 inches.

**Coprosma,** *Rubiaceæ.*—Half-hardy, evergreen, berry-bearing shrubs with attractive foliage. They thrive in the cold or cool greenhouse in a mixture of sandy loam and leaf-mould, but, on account of their somewhat unpleasant odour, they have fallen into disfavour, and are rarely met with nowadays.

They are propagated by means of cuttings under a bell-glass in early autumn. When rooted, pot-on, taking care never to over-pot. Prune to shape just before the new growth commences. They may be stood outside during the summer. *C. acerosa* [New Zealand] has white flowers and sky blue berries. It is low growing. *C. Petriei* [New Zealand] is a creeping shrub bearing purplish fruit.

**Coptis,** *Ranunculaceæ.*—Pleasing little plants which can be grown outside in the bog-garden or peat-bed in a shady position, but which are charming when grown in pans for the alpine house. They should be grown in lime-free soil. They are propagated by division after flowering, or by seed sown in the spring.

**Coral Barberry** (see **Berberidopsis corallina**).

**Coral-berried Duckweed** (see **Nertera depressa**).

**Coral Bush** (see **Templetonia retusa**).

**Coral Plant** (see **Russelia juncea**).

**Coral Tree** (see **Erythrina**).

**Cordia,** *Boraginaceæ.*—Warm-greenhouse shrubs with showy flowers, some of them being of considerable beauty. They are of easy culture, thriving in a mixture of two parts loam, one part peat, and one part sand. Propagation is effected by means of imported seeds. Cuttings of firm young wood, however, root readily when planted in sand **if** they are placed in heat with a hand-glass over them. *C. decandra* [Chile] is a handsome shrub with white flowers in summer, attaining a height of 3 feet. *C. Greggii* var. *Palmeri* [Mexico] bears large, sweet scented, white flowers in clusters in August, and also grows to 3 feet. *C. nivea* [Brazil] bears white flowers in clusters in August, and grows to a height of 3 feet.

**Cordyline** (Dracæna Palm), *Liliaceæ.*—These are handsome foliage plants. Some species are suitable for living-rooms, but others require a greenhouse.

*Culture.*—Pot-up in March, using 6- to 10-inch pots and a mixture of one-half peat and one-quarter part each of sand and loam, or two-thirds fibrous loam and one-third leaf-mould (temperature 50° F. winter, 60° F. summer). Water well, and syringe daily in fine weather during the summer. Sponge the foliage with soft warm water and shade from the hot sun.

Among the best species are *C. australis ; C. australis* var. *atro-purpurea* (purple-leaved) ; *C. australis* var. *aureo-striata* (variegated-leaved) [New Zealand] ; *C. indivisa* (green and yellow) [New Zealand] ; *C. terminalis* [E. Indies]. This requires a warmer and moister atmosphere than the previous species. There are many beautiful varieties of this species with rich-coloured leaves, e.g. *amabilis, Cooperi, metallica, Youngii*, etc. In warm, sheltered positions *C. australis* may be grown outdoors in the South and West of the British Isles. Plant out from September to March in a moderately dry, sunny position and in good loam. Propagate by seed sown 1 inch deep, in heat (60–70° F.) in March, by root-cuttings in fibre in a hot-bed, by cuttings, or by " ringing " in the spring. As, after a time, these plants become rather " leggy ", the last operation is a useful one.

**Corn Flag** (see **Gladiolus**).

**Coronilla glauca,** *Leguminosæ.*—A handsome, free-flowering, half-hardy shrub with evergreen glaucous foliage and pretty, yellow, pea-shaped flowers dispersed in little tufts, like coronets, in spring and summer. They are easily cultivated and succeed against a south wall, with a little winter protection. *C. valentina* [S. Europe] has deep yellow flowers, which are very fragrant at night. It has large, round, conspicuous stipules. It flowers from March to November, and grows to a height of 24–30 inches. Both are valuable for the cool greenhouse.

*Pot Culture.*—Pot up in March, using 6- to 8-inch pots and a compost of two parts sandy loam to one part of peat. Place in a cold greenhouse and give plenty of air and sun. Water well while growing, syringe on fine, warm days in spring.

*Pruning.*—Prune into shape and cut out old and dead wood in February. Stand in the open after flowering until September, then keep the roots only just moist until growth again begins (average temperature 50° F. winter, 60° F. summer).

*Propagation.*—To propagate, sow seed in a frame in March, or take cuttings of young wood 2–3 inches long in April and strike in a frame (temperature, 60° F.).

**Correa,** *Rutaceae.*—Half-hardy, evergreen, Australian shrubs. *C. alba*, the hardiest species, grows from 4 to 6 feet in height, and carries white, tubular flowers from April to July. It may be grown outdoors in warm, sheltered situations, but is most suited to the greenhouse. *C. speciosa* (*C. cardinalis*) are elegant shrubs with scarlet and green flowers in the spring. They grow 24–36 inches high. There are several forms of this species.

*Culture.*—Pot-up in April or May in pots according to the size of the plant, in a compost of sandy loam with peat and leaf-mould added. Little pruning is required, apart from shortening back the flowering shoots after flowering, to keep well-formed plants. Increase by means of cuttings made of the ends of partially ripe shoots 2–2½ inches long in midsummer. There are other species, but they are not much grown nowadays.

**Coryanthes** (see Chapter on **Orchids**).

**Corydalis,** *Fumariaceæ.*—This genus of hardy annual and perennial plants includes the perennials *C. cheilanthifolia* [China] (yellow flowers and fern-like foliage, May–June, 8 in.), *C. thalictrifolia* [China] (yellow, July–Sept., 12 in.) and *C. Wilsonii* [China] (deep canary-yellow, 8 in.), all of which are excellent for the cool greenhouse or alpine house.

*Culture.*—Seed should be sown in the open or in pots under glass in April, or propagation may be carried out by means of division in October. Pot-up in comparatively poor soil as soon as fit to handle and use for greenhouse decoration. Stand in semi-shade.

**Corylopsis,** *Hamamelidaceæ.*—Hardy, deciduous, free-flowering shrubs with fragrant yellow flowers borne in pendant clusters on the leafless branches in February, March, and April. *C. pauciflora* [Japan], which grows from 3 to 4 feet in height, and bears large primrose-yellow flowers in February and March, is useful for cultivation in the cold greenhouse. So is **C.** *spicata* [Central China], which reaches a height of from **5 to 6** feet and produces drooping racemes of yellow flowers in

**325**

February and March. C. *Veitchiana* [W. China] attains a height of from 4 to 5 feet, and bears fragrant primrose-yellow flowers in April.

*Culture.*—Pot-up from October to January, using 6- to 8-inch pots and a compost of turfy loam. Sink the pots to their rims in ashes in a sunny, sheltered spot in the open from May to December, and then take into the cold greenhouse, and keep fairly dry until growth commences. Then water moderately, but regularly.

*Pruning.*—Prune out weak wood and dead shoots after flowering.

*Propagation.*—Propagate by means of cuttings 2–3 inches long, made of side shoots with a " heel " in July or August, and insert in sandy soil in a close frame.

**Corypha**, *Palmaceæ.*—Fan-leaved, warm greenhouse palms that thrive in a compost of two parts of loam to one part of leaf-mould and sand (temperature 60° F. winter, 75° F. summer). *C. elata* [India] is a handsome fan-leaved palm whose leaves are used by the natives for thatching and making baskets. *C. umbraculifera* (Talipot Palm) [Malabar and Ceylon] is another handsome palm, but one which can only be grown in a large greenhouse. It is of economic interest and is used by the natives of Ceylon for making large fans, umbrellas, tents, and many other things.

*Culture.*—Pot-up bi-annually from March to April, using 8- to 12-inch pots, or larger, according to the requirements of the plant. Stand in the shade, and sponge the leaves frequently with warm soft water. Water regularly and in moderation. Propagate by means of seed sown in heat in March.

**Costus** (Spiral Flag), *Zingiberaceæ.*—Stove herbaceous perennials of easy growth, some with handsome flowers. They thrive in any rich, moist, sandy soil, under partial shade. They are readily propagated by cutting the stems into pieces an inch or two long, placing them in heat in a frame, in fibre, sifted peat, or fine moss and sand, covering them slightly, and potting-up when rooted. They can also be divided, but this is a slow method. They may also be increased by seed.

*Species.*—C. *igneus* [Brazil] (orange-red, Sept., 18–24 in.) ; C. *Malortieanus* [Costa Rica] (golden-yellow, orange-red bands, summer, 24–30 in.) ; C. *speciosus* [E. Indies] (white flowers, red bracts, Aug., 36 in.).

**Cotyledon**, *Crassulaceæ.*—A group of succulent plants, many of which have beautiful metallic or glaucous green foliage, and which bear mainly red and yellow flowers. Some authorities divide them into **Echeveria, Pachyphytum Umbilicus** and **Pistorinia.** Others group them all under **Cotyledon.** More recent revision has excluded the American species from Cotyledon, reinstating Echeveria, Pachyphytum for some of these, while others have been placed in new genera—i.e. **Dudleya, Stylophyllum, Oliveranthus,** etc.—but as the difference is merely botanical, and the culture of the groups identical, for convenience they are all included under Cotyledon.

Although a few are hardier than the others, the majority enjoy a warm greenhouse where the atmosphere is kept on the dry side during the winter months. They need no shading, but in bright weather during the spring, summer and autumn plenty of air is necessary.

**326**

They should never be put in large pots, as very few roots are formed. They thrive in sandy loam with a little old mortar rubble mixed with it, and good drainage is essential. A good supply of water may be given in summer, but an occasional watering is sufficient for the remainder of the year.

*Propagation.*—Propagation is carried out by seed sown in sandy soil in the spring and placed in a warm house. Those producing offsets are readily increased by placing them in small pots. Many can be increased by pulling off the outside leaves in the autumn and placing them in the greenhouse, where the atmosphere is dry. The young plants which form at the base should be potted when large enough to handle. Cuttings are placed out to dry before being inserted.

The principal pests are *Mealy Bug, Scale,* and *Woodlice.* The two former must be sponged off with a weak solution of methylated spirits. Do not use nicotine in any form on any succulents.

*Species.—C. atropurpurea* (*Echeveria sanguinea*) [Mexico] (bright flowers, purple and glaucous leaves, summer, 12 in.); *C. coccinea* (*Echeveria coccinea*) [Mexico] (scarlet and yellow, summer). *C. fulgens* (*E. fulgens*) [Mexico] (red and yellow flowers, 6–8 in.); *C. gibbiflora* (*E. gibbiflora*) [Mexico] (flowers yellowish with red tips, summer, 12–24 in.). Several varieties have glaucous purple leaves with metallic reflections. *C. Pachyphytum* [*Pachyphytum bracteosum*] (Silver Bract) [Mexico] (red, summer, 12 in.); *C. pulverulenta* (*Dudleya pulverulenta*) [S. California] (pale scarlet or coral, silver-green leaves, very mealy, Sept., 10 in. high, up to 12 in. diameter); *C. chrysantha, C. Pestalozzæ, C. Sempervivum, C. Umbilicus* are useful in pans for the alpine house, and are sometimes included under **Umbilicus.**

**Cow-Horn Orchid** (see **Schomburgkia tibicinis**).

**Crab's Eye Vine** (see **Abrus**).

**Cranberry** (see **Vaccinium**).

**Crane's Bill** (see **Geranium**).

**Craspedia,** *Compositæ.*—A drawf perennial which can be grown on the rock-garden, but which is also suitable for growing in pans for the alpine house. It thrives in loam, leaf-mould and sand, and should be kept plunged in a frame during the winter. It is increased by seeds sown as soon as ripe, or by division in the spring.

*Species.—C. alpina* [New Zealand] (white, June, 3–4 in.); *C. uniflora* [New Zealand] (May and June, 4 in.).

**Crassula,** *Crassulaceæ.*—These plants grow to a height of from 6 inches to 3 feet and carry red, rose, or white flowers in summer or winter, according to species. They have succulent stems and foliage and make good greenhouse plants. Crassulas grow well in a compost of two-thirds sandy loam and one-third crushed brick and old mortar-rubble.

*Culture.*—Pot-up in August or September. Keep fairly dry in winter. (temperature 45° F. winter, 65° F. summer). Water carefully, and keep the foliage dry while growing. These plants bloom well for several years.

*Propagation.*—Propagate by means of cuttings, stem and leaf, in sand on a sunny shelf in the house in the summer, or by division in the spring. The cuttings should be dried in the sun for two or three days before insertion.

*Species.*—*C. aborescens* [S. Africa] (white to pink, in clusters, 3 ft.; the giant of the genus forming a round bush 3 ft. in diameter); *C. falcata* [S. Africa] (bright crimson flowers, June–Sept., 12–36 in., a handsome plant); *C. lactea* [S. Africa] (white, 10–20 in., also a good room plant); *C. sarcocaulis* (red, July–Sept., 12 in.). These are good species and are hardy in most parts of the British Isles. They are recommended for culture in the alpine house. Pot-up in March in a 4- to 5-inch pan in compost mentioned, and treat as stated. *C. spathulata* [S. Africa] (flowers flesh coloured, winter and spring). This is a valuable winter flowerer, and is useful for baskets.

**Crassula coccinea** (see **Rochea coccinea**).

**Crassula elegans** (see **Oliveranthus elegans**).

**Craterostigma pumilum,** *Scrophulariaceæ.*—An attractive dwarf, perennial herb from East Africa, suitable for the warm greenhouse. It is allied to and somewhat resembles **Torenia.** It grows to a height of 3 inches, and bears lilac flowers blotched with purple and veined with white, in summer. It thrives in loam, leaf-mould, and sand. Seed should be sown in the spring and placed in a warm greenhouse.

**Crawfurdia,** *Gentianaceæ.*—Attractive cool-greenhouse twining herbs. They should be planted in pots or in the open border so that they can twine up pillars or wires up the roof of the greenhouse. They thrive in a mixture of loam, sand, and peat, with thorough drainage. They are increased by cuttings or by seed. The latter should be sown in the spring and placed in gentle heat. The seedlings should be grown in a light position. *C. fasciculata* [Himalayas] attains a height of 4 feet, and bears bluish-purple flowers in August. *C. luteo-viridis* [Sikkim Himalayas] also grows to 4 feet, and carries greenish-yellow flowers. The leaves and stem turn red with age. It is a very showy twiner when laden with brilliant red fruit.

**Creeping Forget-me-not** (see **Omphalodes verna**).

**Creeping Jenny** (see **Lysimachia nummularia**).

**Crepe Fern** (see **Todea barbara**).

**Cress** (see **Lepidium sativum**).

**Crinodendron** (see **Tricuspidaria**).

**Crinum** (Cape Lily), *Amaryllidaceæ.*—A half-hardy, bulbous plant with handsome, ribbon-like leaves and lovely trumpet-shaped flowers, blooming in June, July and August. Excellent subjects for the cool or warm greenhouse. *C. longifolium, C. Moorei,* and *C. Powellii,* as well as their varieties *album,* will grow outdoors in a sunny, sheltered, moist border, in well-drained, deep, and rich sandy loam and peat. They flower in the autumn. The most popular variety for pot culture is *C. Moorei,* which grows about 24 inches in height and carries rose-coloured flowers. In the warm house this and *C. Powellii* may be had in flower in summer.

*Pot Culture.*—Pot-up in the spring (triennially), one bulb in each 9- to 10-inch pot, in a compost of two parts fibrous loam to one part sandy peat. Propagate by means of offsets in March.

*Species.*—*C. americanum* (Florida Swamp Lily) [S. America] (creamy

**328**

white, spring and summer, occasionally in the winter) ; *C. asiaticum* [Tropical Asia] (white flowers tinged with green, will often bloom several times in a year—there are several hybrids and varieties of this evergreen Crinum) ; *C. erubescens* [Tropical America] (flowers reddish outside, white inside, tube red, warm greenhouse, summer) ; *C. giganteum* [Tropical Africa] (pure white, large, scented flowers) ; *C. Johnstonii* [British Central Africa] (fragrant flowers, white, tinged with pink on the outside, warm greenhouse) ; *C. longifolium* (*C. capense*) [S. Africa] (pink or white) ; *C. Moorei* [S. Africa] (pink and white) ; *C. Powellii* (rose-red or white—this is a hybrid of *C. longifolium* and *C. Moorei*). All grow from 24 to 36 inches in height.

**Crocus,** *Iridaceæ.*—The chief self-coloured varieties of crocus are white, yellow, blue, and purple ; the striped varieties present three colours in every variety of distribution. They grow from 3 to 4 inches high.

Besides those which bloom in the early spring (usually in February), there are species and hybrids that flower in the autumn and winter. These lesser-known kinds, of which the violet-blue September-flowering. *C. speciosus* is one of the most lovely, are rather more delicate in shape and colouring, and somewhat smaller. They are extremely beautiful, and should be much more popular than they are at present. Size, shape, and distinctness of colour in the bloom constitute the chief points in a good crocus. Nothing can be easier than their culture.

*Culture*—They like a good light soil to which a little bonemeal has been added, and thrive in sun or shade in a warm rock-garden, borders or in pots in the cold greenhouse or alpine house, and are also useful for naturalising in grass or for the wild garden. Crocuses are increased by offsets or by seed, the former being the usual method.

*Pot Culture.*—Plant about seven corms half an inch deep in a 5- to 6-inch pot or pan in autumn, using a compost of good, fairly light, sandy loam and leaf-mould, and keep covered with ashes or fibre in a frame until growth commences, then water and transfer to the cool house. Stand out in the open and keep dry in summer, and re-pot in September.

*Species.*—EARLY SPRING-FLOWERING.—*C. biflorus* [S.W. Europe] (white, veined violet—there are several beautiful varieties of this) ; *C. chrysanthus* [Asia Minor] (orange-yellow and red—also many beautiful varieties of this) ; *C. Imperati* [S. Italy] (lilac or buff and black) ; *C. mœsiacus* (*C. aureus*) [Asia Minor] (golden-yellow) ; *C. Sieberi* [Greece] (lilac-blue and gold) ; *C. versicolor* [S. France] (white, feathered purple) ; *C. vernus* and vars. [S. Europe] (various). AUTUMN FLOWERING.—*C. asturicus* [Spain] (purple) ; *C. byzantinus* (*C. iridiflorus*) [S.E. Europe] (lavender) ; *C. ochroleucus* [Syria] (yellow) ; *C. pulchellus* [Greece] (lavender-blue, with orange throat) ; *C. sativus* (saffron-crocus) [Asia Minor] (violet, mauve, and orange) ; *C. speciosus* [S.E. Europe] (violet-blue and orange) ; *C. zonatus* [Cilicia] (lilac-pink, with orange throat). All the above species and varieties are charming for the alpine house, while the following named varieties or florist crocus are valuable for the cool greenhouse or conservatory : *Grandeur Triomphante* (white and blue) ; *King of the Whites* (white) ; *Large Yellow* (yellow) ;

*L'Unique* (lilac-pink) ; *Van Speyk* (purple, veined white) ; and *Yellow Hammer* (yellow).

**Crossandra,** *Acanthaceæ.*—Beautiful, evergreen, free-flowering, soft-wooded shrub for the warm greenhouse. They have dense terminal spikes of flowers with conspicuous bracts, and remain in bloom for most of the year. They are of easy culture, and thrive in loam and peat, in equal proportions, with a good sprinkling of sand. They are readily propagated from cuttings at almost any time of the year if placed in sand and given a little bottom heat. Or they may be raised from seed sown in the spring, placed in warmth.

*Species.*—*C. flava* [Tropical W. Africa] (yellow, summer, 6–8 in.) ; *C. guineensis* [Guinea] (pale lilac, Sept.–Oct., 3–6 in.) ; *C. subacaulis* [E. Tropical Africa] (orange, summer, 9 in.) ; *C. undulæfolia* [India] (scarlet-orange, summer, 12–24 in.).

**Crotalaria** (Rattle Box), *Leguminosæ.*—A group of shrubs or herbaceous plants for the greenhouse. Some species are very free blooming, the flowers being chiefly yellow.

They all succeed in a good light soil, and some species may be put outside during the summer. Cuttings of the shrubby kinds root freely in a pot of sand under a bell-glass and stood in a cool house. But as seeds are usually freely produced they are easily increased. Seed should be sown in spring after being soaked in warm water. When potting-on the seedlings must be **placed separately in small pots.** Crotalaria is very subject to attacks of red spider.

*Species.*—*C. capensis* [S. Africa] (shrub, yellow flowers, summer, 3–8 ft.) ; *C. Cunninghamii* [Australia] (shrub, large greenish-yellow flowers, 8 ft.) ; *C. incana* [S. Africa] (woody perennial, yellow, summer, 24–36 in.) ; *C. longirostrata* [W. Mexico] (herbaceous, flowers yellow, striped with red, Dec. to March, 24–36 in.).

**Crotons** (see **Codiæum**).

**Crowea,** *Rutaceæ.*—Half-hardy, dwarf-growing, evergreen shrubs, some 2–2½ feet in height, with attractive little flowers in spring or summer, suitable for culture in the cool greenhouse.

*Culture.*—Pot-up in March in well-crocked pots of sandy loam and peat. Water regularly while growing, but keep fairly dry while dormant. Shorten back new growths to keep a good shape and bushy.

*Propagation.*—Cuttings of new shoots may be rooted in sandy soil under a bell-glass if given slight bottom heat in March and April.

*Species.*—*C. augustifolia* [W. Australia] (red) ; *C. saligna* [New S. Wales] (pink).

**Crow Foot** (see **Ranunculus**).

**Cryptochilus** (see Chapter on **Orchids**).

**Cryptogramma,** *Polypodiaceæ.*—A small group of sub-alpine ferns which, although hardy, are very attractive in pans for the cool or alpine house, in fern or wardian case, with sterile and fertile fronds usually different. The most popular species is the Parsley Fern (*C. crispa*). They are of easy cultivation, but are more successful when grown in lime-free soil with plenty of sandstone, and in a cool, moist position. They are increased by division in the spring or by spores. (See Chapter on **Ferns.**)

*Species.*—*C. acrostichoides* (Rock Brake) [N. America] (8 in.) ; *C. Brunoniana* [Himalayas, etc.] (somewhat resembles our native Parsley Fern, but is less hardy) ; *C. crispa* (Parsley Fern) [Arctic and North Temperate Regions, Great Britain] (one of the most charming of our native ferns, 10–12 in.).

**Cryptophoranthus** (see Chapter on **Orchids**).

**Cryptostegia,** *Asclepiadaceæ.*—Handsome stove evergreen climbers which succeed in a mixture of loam and peat in equal proportions. Better results are obtained if the plants can be planted out in the border of the greenhouse, although they can quite successfully be grown in large pots. The plants should be pruned back in the winter. Cuttings root freely if planted in sand under a glass in heat. *C. grandiflora* (*Nerium grandiflorum*) [E. Indies] attains a height of 20 feet, and bears large, reddish-purple (becoming lilac or pale pink), bell-shaped flowers in July. The juice of this plant when exposed to the sun produces caoutchouc. *C. madagascariensis* [Madagascar] grows to a height of from 8 to 10 feet and carries pale-pink or whitish flowers in June. It is a very showy greenhouse climber.

**Cucumis,** *Cucurbitaceæ.*—Although the Cucumber and Melon are the most popular known of this genus, there are several others that are very decorative as well as of interest, especially when in fruit. They need the same culture conditions as **Cucumber,** and are attacked by the same pests and diseases. *C. Anguria* (Bur Cucumber or Gooseberry Gourd) is a climbing annual from the American Tropics. It should be trained up the roof of the warm greenhouse, where the freely produced, gooseberry-like gourds look very attractive during the summer and autumn. Height, 6–10 feet. The fruit can also be used for pickling. *C. dipsaceus* (Hedgehog Gourd) are annual climbers from Arabia and Africa. Their habit and growth are similar to those of the Melon. The fruit is egg-shaped, and becomes hard and dry and covered with long scales or bur-like hairs, looking very ornamental during the summer and autumn. *C. metuliferus* (Horned Cucumber) [S. Africa], is a climber growing up to 20 feet high and has scarlet fruits covered with horny outgrowths.

**Cucumis Melo** (Melon) (see Chapter XIII).

**Cucumis sativas** (Cucumber) (see Chapter XIII).

**Cup and Saucer** (see **Cobæa scandens**).

**Cup Flower** (see **Nierembergia**).

**Cuphea** (Cigar Flower), *Lythraceæ.*—This genus of profusely-blooming plants contains a number of hardy and half-hardy annuals, perennials and shrubs, all best treated as half-hardy. *C. cyanea* [Mexico] is a branching, half-hardy shrub with yellow, violet, and blue flowers most of the year. The plant is more or less hispid, has an erect stem, and grows to a height of 12–15 inches. *C. ignea* (*C. platycentra*) [Mexico] perhaps the best known, is a graceful, branching, half-hardy shrub some 12 inches in height, covered in summer with splendid scarlet, bluish-black and white, tubular-shaped flowers. *C. micropetala* [Mexico] is a sub-shrubby plant, with scarlet, yellow, and greenish flowers during the autumn. Height, 12–18 inches. These are all popular greenhouse plants. Of the annuals, *C. lanceolata* (*C. Zima-*

**331**

*panii* [Mexico] with reddish-violet flowers, and *C. miniata* [Mexico], with calyx green, purple and scarlet wavy petals, are useful. Both may be treated like ordinary half-hardy annuals, and need rather poor soil to bring out their best flowering capabilities. Both grow about 24 inches high.

*Culture.—Annuals.*—Sow seed in spring in a temperature of 70° F. Pot-off as soon as possible, and grow on for greenhouse use. If pinched back once or twice, these will make nice bushy plants. *Shrubby Species.*—Propagate by cuttings of young wood in bottom heat (70°F.) in spring. Trim in the following January and re-pot, if necessary as soon as the new growth is breaking in February. Immediately the cuttings have struck, gradually give more light, placing on a shelf near the glass. Pot on until in 3½- or 4½-inch pots, using a compost of two-thirds sandy loam and one-third leaf-mould. Syringe the young plants morning and evening in fine weather, and pinch back two or three times in spring to induce bushy growth. The plants should flower about June, after which they should be kept dry at the roots.

**Curculigo,** *Amaryllidaceæ.*—Warm-house or conservatory foliage plants, with the habit of a young palm. They are very ornamental plants for the warm greenhouse, although useful in pots. But to see them at their best they should be planted out in a bed or border, where they will grow 4 or 5 feet high.

*Culture.*—The soil should be two parts loam, one part rotted cow-manure, and some sand. Drainage is very important, as the plant needs plenty of water.

*Propagation.*—This is effected by division. If the portions taken off are placed for a few days in the sand-case of a warm propagating house, they will rapidly make new roots. They can then be potted-up.

There are variegated varieties, and they are among the best of variegated plants, and although they are not so robust as the green-leaved kinds, they are more suitable for pot culture. *C. latifolia* [Malaya] has leaves 18–24 inches long, and bears clusters of bright-yellow flowers just above the ground. It is a beautiful and useful house plant, said to be more useful than palms, where there is no conservatory. *C. recurvata* [Tropical Asia] has handsome, dark-green, graceful, arching leaves, and clusters of bright-yellow flowers at the base of the leaves. It grows 24–36 inches high. Var. *striata* has a central band of white; and var. *variegata* has longitudinal bars of white.

**Curcuma,** *Zingiberaceæ.*—Showy and somewhat curious herbaceous plants, with a thick, tuber-like root-stock, from which rise spikes of flowers with conspicuous concave bracts, the latter being perhaps the most attractive or showy part of the plant.

*Culture.*—In spring the rhizomes should be shaken out of the old soil and re-potted in a fresh mixture of light loam, leaf-soil, and turfy peat, with good drainage. The pots should be placed in a warm pit or frame in bottom heat. After flowering, the water should be gradually withdrawn, but even during the resting period the soil should never be allowed to get quite dry, or the tubers may shrivel. It is propagated by division in the spring at the time of potting.

# GREENHOUSE PLANTS

Rhizomes of some of the species yield a kind of Arrowroot, while other species produce Tumeric.

*Species.*—*C. cordata* [Burma] (pink and yellow flowers, rich violet bracts with deep red spots, July, 12 in.); *C. petiolata* (Queen Lily) [India] (pale-yellow flowers, rosy-purple bracts, Sept., 15–18 in.) perhaps the most beautiful of the Curcumas; *C. Roscœana* [E. Indies] (pale-yellow flowers, bracts gradually changing from green to scarlet-orange, Aug., 12 in.).

**Curly Palm** (see **Howea**).

**Cushion Pink** (see **Silene acaulis**).

**Cyanathus,** *Campanulaceæ.*—Although hardy and usually grown on the rock garden, they can be grown in pans for the alpine house. They must be kept in a cool position in a frame under the north side of a wall or in semi-shade. The pans should be filled with turfy loam, leaf-mould, peat, and sandstone, suitable for the stems to nestle among. Cuttings in the summer can be struck in sandy peat, or propagation may be effected by division of the roots in the spring, or by seed sown as soon as ripe and plunged in ashes in a cold frame.

*Species.*—*C. incanus* [Himalayas] (soft azure-blue flowers, Aug., 3–4 in.); the var. *leiocalyx* [Yunnan] has yellow flowers. *C. lobatus* [Himalayas] (bright blue, Aug.–Sept., 4 in.).

**Cyanella,** *Amaryllidaceæ.*—Attractive little bulbs from South Africa. They make charming cold greenhouse plants, are almost hardy, and require the same treatment as **Ixia.**

*Species.*—*C. capensis* (purpled on branched stems, July and Aug., 12 in.); *C. lutea* [*C. odoratissima*] (yellow, less branched than *C. capensis*, Aug., 12 in.).

**Cyanophyllum magnificum** (see **Miconia magnifica,** also Greenhouse Foliage Plants).

**Cyanotis,** *Commelinaceæ.*—These are closely allied to **Tradescantia.** A few species are suitable for the stove-house or greenhouse. They require a rich, loamy soil and good drainage, and are quite attractive as basket-plants or in pans. They are chiefly propagated by cuttings placed in sandy soil in brisk heat.

*Species.*—*C. barbata* [India, China] (dark blue, summer, 3 in.); *C. hirsuta* [Abyssinia] (rose coloured and blue, soft, hairy foliage, 6–8 in.); *C. kewensis* [E. Indies] (rose, leaves and stem fleshy and covered with reddish hairs, 3 in., creeper).

**Cyathea.**—This is a genus comprising stove and warm greenhouse evergreen tree-ferns. The most useful species to associate with palms and flowering plants for conservatory decoration are: *C. dealbata* [New Zealand], *C. excelsa* [Mauritius], *C. insignis* [Jamaica] and *C. medullaris* [New Zealand].

*Culture.*—A compost of a light fibrous loam and peat in equal proportions, with about one-quarter part coarse grit, is a suitable soil. Pot-up in well-crocked pots or tubs in spring or autumn, or, if the house is large enough, plant in the warm greenhouse border, sufficiently far from the sides of the house to ensure that the fronds are in no way hindered from developing properly. Water while growing, keeping the stems syringed, and keep only just moist when dormant.

333

THE GREENHOUSE

**Cycad Family** (see **Ceratozamia, Cycas, Dioon, Encephalartos,** etc. also Greenhouse Foliage Plants).

**Cycas,** *Cycadaceæ.*—Interesting and ornamental palm-like plants, most of which are arborescent. The trunk or stem is usually simple, although occasionally branched, and is marked with the scars of fallen petioles, and terminated with a crown of pinnate leaves like that of a palm or tree-fern. Cycads are among the most ornamental of plants for the decoration of large conservatories or stove-houses, and are very effective when used in tropical or sub-tropical gardens. The leaves are also used in a cut state by florists.

*Culture.*—They thrive in good fibrous loam, and coarse sand. Potting is required at very rare intervals, consequently it is important to see that the pots are well drained, to prevent stagnation. During the growing season they should be given plenty of water, being kept dry as the leaves mature. Plants should be well syringed during the spring and summer, as several species are subject to mealy bug and scale. Frequent syringing with an emulsion of soft soap and paraffin will help to keep these pests down.

*Propagation.*—Propagation takes place by seed, which should be sown in sandy soil and placed in a temperature of 60–70° F., potting-on the young plants when ready. They should be grown on in a warm, moist, shady position. Occasionally young plants can be obtained by suckers, which are taken off, potted-up, and placed in a warm, moist atmosphere, first removing the leaves to guard against transpiration. Propagation is also effected by scales.

*C. circinalis* (Fern Palm) [E. Indies] is a palm-like tree with dark shining green leaves 5–8 feet long; stems 4–8 feet high. *C. revoluta* [S. Japan] is the most popular of all Cycads, the dark-green leaves, 2 to 4 feet long, being used for decoration by florists, and in some instances being used as palm leaves on Palm Sunday. It has nut-like seeds, bright red; stems 4–6 feet long.

**Cyclamen** (Sowbread), *Primulaceæ.*—A genus of winter- and spring-blooming, tuberous-rooted plants with pretty foliage, useful alike for rock-garden, border, and for greenhouse culture. Of the hardy Cyclamen there are two types, the spring-blooming and the autumn-blooming.

*C. coum* (*C. vernum*) [S.E. Europe to Persia] (3 inches) with purplish-red or white flowers from January to February, and *C. ibericum* (*C. vernale*) [Caucasus] (3 inches) with rose-purple and crimson, or white and crimson flowers from February to April, make useful little plants for growing in 4- to 5-inch pans in the alpine house. *C. persicum* [Greece to Syria], which grows from 6 to 10 inches in height and flowers from November to March, is the species used for pot culture, and varieties in shades of colour are obtainable, ranging from white, through rose and scarlet, to crimson. In some strains the flowers are scented, in others the petals are crimped or fringed.

*Pot Culture.*—(*C. persicum*). Soak the pot and tuber, that have previously been dried off, in water, and stand on a shelf in the greenhouse until growth begins. Pot-up in August, placing one tuber in a 5-inch pot in a fresh compost of rich sandy loam and leaf-mould with

334

# GREENHOUSE PLANTS

the tubers just above the surface. Keep close for a few days, then give ample air and not too much heat (60° F.). Moist, steady heat and shade are essential. Water moderately when growth begins, and increase the supply until the plants bloom. This occurs about November with some plants, and lasts until March. Give manure-water when in bloom. After flowering decrease the water supply, dry off, and keep the roots cool and almost dry until next potting-up. Keep the plants indoors from September to May, and in a cold frame, with the pots on their sides, from June to August. Use the same tubers for pot culture for only two years in succession. One-year-old plants give the finest flowers. Cyclamen are therefore best raised annually from seed. The chief pests to watch for are *Cyclamen Mite* (also known as *Begonia Mite*), *Green-fly*, *Thrip*, and *Vine Weevil*.

*Propagation.*—To propagate, sow seed thinly in pans in a finely sieved compost of two-thirds loam and one-third leaf-mould and sand, at any time between early August and late November. Cover only thinly with earth, and place in a cold frame or on a shelf near the light in the cool greenhouse (temperature 50–60° F.). Prick-off into pans, then pot-up singly into thumb pots, and subsequently into larger pots, with the tops of the tubers level with the surface of the soil—in the compost mentioned above—until (in July) they are in 5- to 6-inch pots, in which they may be flowered. Shade from strong sunlight, and maintain a moist, even temperature of about 50° F. Syringe every evening in fine weather.

*Species.*—*C. coum* (purple, red, and white, Jan.–March, 3 in.); *C. europæum* [Central and S. Europe] (red and white, July–Nov., 3 in.); *C. neapolitanum* [S. and E. Europe] (rose, white, and purple throat, Aug.–Sept., 3 in.). All these are useful for growing in pans in the alpine house, keeping the pans plunged in a cold frame in shade when not wanted for the house.

**Cycnoches** (see Chapter on **Orchids**).

**Cydonia japonica** (see **Chænomeles lagenaria**).

**Cydonia Maulei** (see **Chænomeles japonica**).

**Cymbidium** (see Chapter on **Orchids**).

**Cymbidium Sandersonii** (see **Ansellia gigantea**).

**Cypella,** *Iridaceæ.*—Very pretty half-hardy, bulbous plants from South America. Although they can be grown outdoors by planting in the spring and lifting in the autumn, they may also be grown in pots or pans for the cool house. They thrive in light soil, and until wanted for the house (i.e. when the buds appear), the pots or pans should be plunged in ashes. After flowering they should be gradually dried off. They are propagated by offsets, or by seed sown as soon as ripe and placed in a cool house.

*Species.*—*C. Herbertii* [S. Brazil, etc.] (yellow, varying from light yellow to deep chrome, spotted or barred with deeper colour, July, 12 in.); *C. peruviana* [Peru] (bright yellow, spotted reddish brown, July–Aug., 12–18 in.).

**Cyperorchis** (see Chapter on **Orchids**).

**Cyperus alternifolius** (Umbrella Plant), *Cyperaceæ.*—This is a rapidly growing greenhouse perennial from Madagascar, with stems 15 inches high. These stems are headed with tufts of ribbon-like leaves and spikes of brown flowers which last nearly the whole year through.

*Culture.*—Pot-up in March in 5- to 6-inch pots, using a compost of two parts rich loam to one part of leaf-mould and sand. Water well and syringe with rain-water in warm weather after potting, and once the roots are established, even stand the pots in saucers of water in hot weather. Shade from strong sun.

*C. a. variegatus* is a variegated form needing similar treatment, except that the soil for this should be on the poor side, to bring out the full beauty of the variegations of the foliage.

*Propagation.*—Propagate by means of seed sown in sandy soil in a propagating case with a moist bottom heat of at least 70° F., or by division of the roots in March.

*C. Papyrus* (Egyptian Paper Plant or Papyrus) is an interesting species, best planted out in a bed adjoining a warm aquarium where the soil is always damp. The fine, handsome stem, 6–10 feet high, with its pendulous, umbel rays at the top, makes a very bold feature in a large greenhouse. If grown in tubs it may be placed in the pond or aquarium outside, for the summer. The tubs should be only just submerged. It can also be grown in a large pot or tub half filled with rich loam and decayed cow-manure. The tub should then be filled with water, or, if a pot is used, it should be stood in a saucer of water. It is increased by division of the roots in the spring. The papyri of the ancient Egyptians was made from the culm or stem of this plant.

**Cypress** (see **Chamæcyparis**).

**Cypripedium** (Lady's Slipper) (see Chapter on **Orchids**).

**Cyrtanthus**, *Amaryllidaceæ.*—South African bulbous plants, most of which are useful for decorating the cool greenhouse or conservatory, requiring the same treatment as **Hæmanthus**.

*Species.*—*C. lutescens* (pale yellow, Feb.–March, 12 in.) ; *C. Mackenzii* (pure white, sweet scented, spring, 12 in.) ; *C. sanguineus* (bright red and yellow, Aug., 9 in., a handsome flower) ; *C. uniflorus* (white, with red stripe, summer, 6 in.).

**Cyrtomium falcatum** (Holly Fern).—A handsome fern from Japan and India 24–30 inches high with ovate, falcate, glossy pinnæ. Culture as for Polystichum to which it is closely allied.

**Cyrtosperma Johnstonii**, *Araceæ.*—A handsome, warm-house, foliage plant from the Solomon Islands. It has hastate, olive-green, beautifully red-veined leaves, the petioles of which are olive-green spotted with rose and covered with spine-like warts. It grows 18–30 inches high, and requires the same treatment as **Alocasia**.

**Cystopteris** (Bladder Fern), *Polypodiaceæ.*—Dainty little ferns which, although perfectly hardy, make charming pans for the alpine house, or they may be planted out on the rock-garden of a cold greenhouse. The pans should be plunged in ashes in a shady position. They succeed in sandy loam, peat, leaf-mould, and a little mortar-rubble. They are readily increased by spores when ripe, or by division of the plant in the spring.

*Species.*—*C. alpina* [Europe] has graceful little fronds 6 inches long, 2 inches broad, with the main rachis winged. *C. bulbifera* [N. America]

**PLATE 11**
*Saintpaulia* (African Violet). Many new
varieties of this plant have been
developed in a good range of colours.

has large, fleshy bulblets which are formed in the axils of the upper pinnæ; these fall to the ground and become new plants. *C. fragilis* [Temperate regions] is an elegant little fern adaptable for growing in fern-cases. There are several distinct varieties. *C. montana* [Mountains of the Northern Hemisphere] has fronds 8–9 inches long and 5–6 inches wide.

**Cytisus** (Broom), *Leguminosæ.*—A genus of shrubs, mostly hardy and deciduous, which thrive in a dry, sunny position. For pot culture, *C. racemosus*, evergreen, often grown under the name of *C. canariensis,* which is a different plant (probably the parent of *C. racemosus*) [*Genista formosa*], which grows from 3 to 6 feet in height, and bears yellow flowers, is the favourite. In the warm greenhouse (temperature 55–70° F. winter, 60–75° F. summer) it may be had in bloom from January to March. There are other good species and varieties which appreciate and respond to cold or cool greenhouse treatment. *C. racemosus* var. *elegans*, with greyish-green foliage, *C. filipes* [Teneriffe], a drooping species with white flowers, and *C. monspessulanus* [Mediterranean region], a semi-evergreen with yellow flowers in late spring, are all to be recommended. There are also *C. sessilifolius* [Europe], growing to a height of from 4 to 6 feet, with yellow flowers in May and June, and *C. supranubius* [Canary Islands], growing to the same height, bearing white flowers tinged with pink in May. Many of the beautiful-coloured forms of *C. Dallimorei* and *C. scoparius* var. *Andreanus* (Firefly, etc.) are also very useful. They may be grown in pots and plunged outside in ashes, bringing them into the cool house in the spring.

*Pot Culture.*—Pot-up in May, after flowering, using a compost of two parts turfy loam to one part lumpy leaf-mould and coarse sand. Prune hard back after flowering, then keep in the warmth, and syringe in fine weather. Harden off, and sink the pots in ashes outdoors from May to October, then move into the cool greenhouse. Keep fairly dry until growth starts; then water moderately, and give weekly doses of weak liquid manure as soon as the buds start to form.

*Propagation.*—To propagate sow seeds in the open in September or take cuttings in March or August, and strike in a frame, and grow in pots near the glass until ready for potting on or planting out. Young plants need occasional " stopping-back ". This should be done after flowering.

The **Cytisus** is closely allied to the **Genista.**

Several of the dwarf Brooms grown in pans will be found of great value for the alpine house. They should be potted-up in the autumn, plunged in ashes in a cold frame until the buds appear in the early spring, and after flowering they can be cut back into shape, top dressed, or repotted if necessary. They should be kept syringed for a time. All are readily increased from cuttings taken with a " heel " and placed in sand.

*Species.*—*C. Ardoinii* [S. France] (golden yellow, April–May, 12 in.); *C. Beanii* [hybrid] (bright golden yellow, April, 8–10 in.); *C. kewensis* [hybrid] (creamy white, April–May, pendulous habit).

**Dædalacanthus nervosus (Eranthemum nervosum, E. pulchellum),** *Acanthaceæ.*—A very pretty Indian, winter- and spring-flowering shrub

Y

for the warm greenhouse. Its attractive bright-blue flowers are not very common in winter-flowering plants. It is an easy plant to grow, succeeding in a mixture of fibrous loam, leaf-mould, and sand. It is readily raised from seed or by cuttings in the early spring, inserted in sandy loam and leaf-mould in a close case in bottom heat. The young plants should be potted-on when rooted, and occasionally pinched back in summer. *D. macrophyllus* is a similar shrub responding to the same treatment.

**Daffodils (Narcissus Family).**—No spring flower is fairer or more graceful than the Daffodil or Narcissus. Technically speaking, the terms Daffodil and Narcissus are synonymous, for Daffodil is merely the English for Narcissus. The word *Daffodil* is, however, popularly applied to those types of Narcissi with long, trumpet-like coronas; and the term *Narcissi*, which really includes the whole genus, is reserved for those kinds with short cup-shaped corollas. For cultural details see **Narcissus.**

**Dalechampia,** *Euphorbiaceæ.*—Although there are about sixty species in this genus, only a few are of horticultural value. *D. Roezliana*, from Mexico, is well worth cultivating for the warm greenhouse, forming an attractive plant with its brilliant rich carmine-rose coloured bracts and waxy-looking yellow flowers. The plants are erect and branching in habit and grow to about 18 inches high. The species thrives in well-drained pots filled with a mixture of loam, peat, and leaf-soil in equal parts, with plenty of silver sand to ensure porosity. Propagation is by means of cuttings which should be inserted in spring in sand under a bell-glass or in a warm propagating frame.

**Dancing Girls** (see **Mantisia Saltatoria**).

**Daphne,** *Thymelæaceæ.*—Beautiful, dwarf-growing, deciduous, evergreen shrubs, remarkable for their fragrant, waxy flowers and for their bright-red, *poisonous* berries. *D. Mezereum* [Europe], which is usually propagated by means of seed, is the best known of the hardy deciduous species. It grows to a height of from 24 to 48 inches, and the fragrant flowers which appear on the leafless branches from December to February are purple, rose, or white, according to variety. It thrives in ordinary garden loam, but needs shading from the hot sun. If trimming is necessary it should be done in April. It may be grown in the greenhouse if preferred. But here such species as *D. odora* [China] (pink, 24 in.); and *D. odora alba* (white), often but wrongly named *D. indica*, are more usually selected. These are too tender for the open air, except in the south-west. In the cool house (temperature 45° F. winter, 65° F. summer) they may be had in flower in December.

*Culture.*—Pot-up in April, using 5- to 7-inch pots and a compost of peaty loam and sand. Plunge the pots in a cool, shady position outdoors from May to September, syringe daily in fine weather, and keep the soil only just moist. Move into the cool house in September and gradually give more heat. Treatment as advised for Forcing (p. 97), will bring the blooms out by December. Propagate by means of cuttings under glass from April to July.

For the alpine house the following are to be recommended : *D. alpina* [Europe] (white, fragrant, April–May, 18–24 in.); *D. Cneorum* (Garland Flower) [Europe] (pink, April and Sept., 12 in.); *D. Genkwa* [Japan]

**338**

# GREENHOUSE PLANTS

(lilac, April, 24–30 in.) ; *D. petræa* (*D. rupestris*) [Tyrol] (pink, April and May, 3–4 in.) ; and *D. retusa* [W. China] (light pink, 4–6 in.). Pot-up in February in 4- to 5-inch pans with a compost of two parts loam to one part of peat and sand, with a little lime added, and treat as above. The choice dwarf species are often grafted on stocks of some of the more common kinds.

**Darlingtonia californica** (Californian Pitcher Plant), *Sarraceniaceæ.*— An interesting little half-hardy insectivorous plant for the cold greenhouse. The hollow, stem-like leaves springing from the base to a height of from 18 to 24 inches, thicken out at the tops and turn over to form the pitcher-shaped traps with which they catch insects to obtain their nitrogenous food.

*Culture.*—Pot-up in March or April in well-drained pans containing a compost of sandy peat, sphagnum moss and limestone chips. Water well and regularly while growing and keep just moist during winter.

*Propagation.*—The plants are increased by means of seed sown in shallow pans under glass in spring, or by means of young detached sideshoots in early summer. The latter should be potted-up singly, and protected until roots have formed and new growth is noticeable.

**Darwinia,** *Myrtaceæ.*—A group of Australian, heath-like, evergreen shrubs that grow well in the warm greenhouse. The flowers are chiefly red or white. They should be potted in equal parts of fibrous peat and loam with sharp sand. Cuttings of young shoots root readily in sand, placed under a bell-glass. *D. Hookeriana* grows to a height of from 18 to 24 inches, has red bracts and greenish-white flowers in June, and is smaller in every way than *D. macrostegia*, which has bell-shaped flowers, in June. It has creamy-white bracts splashed and streaked with red, and grows from 24 to 30 inches high.

**Dasylirion,** *Liliaceæ.*—Attractive, half-hardy, evergreen, foliage plants for cultivation in the cold greenhouse. They grow from 5 to 10 feet in height, the short stems being headed by a tuft of long, narrow leaves. The clusters of whitish-green, lily-like flowers are borne only on mature plants.

*Culture.*—Pot-up in March in a compost of two parts loam to one part of sandy peat and powdered brick-rubble, in pots according to the size of the plant, taking care not to overpot, and stand in a sunny position. Water regularly and well in summer, and keep just moist in winter.

*Propagation.*—Increase by means of seed sown in shallow pans of sandy loam in slight heat (55° F.) in April or May, and pot-on as required.

*D. acrostichum* [E. and Central Mexico] has narrow leaves and prickles which are pale yellowish brown at the tip. *D. graminifolium* [E. and Central Mexico] has glossy green leaves with yellowish-white prickles.

**Date Palm** (see **Phœnix dactylifera**).

**Date Plum** (see **Diospyros Kaki**).

**Datura** (**Brugmansia**), *Solanaceæ.*—Highly ornamental evergreen shrubs, producing large, sweet-scented, trumpet-shaped flowers of the most attractive character. It is with these shrubby plants that we are concerned for indoor culture. They are propagated by means of cuttings in the spring. These Angels' Trumpets flowers, as they are

339

called, are evergreen, half-hardy shrubs bearing huge and gorgeous fragrant, trumpet-like, white, yellow or red blooms in May and June, or August and September, according to species. At times two crops are borne, one at each period mentioned above. The plants have large bright-green leaves, and grow to a height of 10 to 12 feet, and are therefore suitable only for large greenhouses.

*Culture.*—The plants thrive in a compost of turfy loam, peat, or leaf-mould, coarse sand, and well-rotted manure. Re-pot occasionally, and water freely in summer. As soon as the buds have formed apply weak manure-water every ten days. After blooming stand in the open until the end of September. Water sparingly in winter. Prune in closely into the main stem in March, syringe to encourage new growth, and re-pot if necessary as soon as the young shoots appear (temperature 50° F. winter, 60° F. summer).

*Shrubby Species.*—*D. chlorantha* [origin unknown] (yellow); *D. sanguinea* [Peru] (red); *D. suaveolens* [Mexico] (white); *D. s.* var. *Knightii* (double white).

**Davallia,** *Polypodiaceæ.*—This includes several species, all of which are very beautiful and suitable for culture in hanging pots or baskets, for growing on rafts, or for growing in rooms.

*Culture.*—Pot-up in March in a compost of one part sandy loam to two parts peat, leaf-mould, and a little charcoal. Keep in a semi-shaded position, and water liberally in summer (temperature 50° F. winter, 60° F. summer).

*Propagation.*—This may be carried out by means of spores sown under glass at any time, or by division of the roots in March.

*D. bullata* [India, Java, etc.] has fronds 8 to 12 inches long, and is often grown in the form of balls and other shapes. *D. canariensis* (Hare's Foot Fern) derives its popular name from the form of rhizome, which is covered with close brown hair. It can be grown in a cool greenhouse, and is also a good room-plant. *D. elegans* [Old-World Tropics] has graceful fronds, 12–18 inches long, and is a warm-house plant. *D. fijiensis* [Fiji Islands] is one of the finest species. It has graceful, plume-like fronds, and requires a warm house. *D. solida* [Malaya] has broad, tripinnate segments. In the var. *superba* the young fronds are tinted red.

**Davidsonia pruriens,** *Saxifragaceæ.*—A handsome, Australian, warm-greenhouse foliage plant of great beauty, the leaves when young being covered with bright-red hairs. It thrives in fibrous loam and peat, with some sand. It may be raised from cuttings of the stem placed in sand, in a close case, with bottom heat. These should be taken frequently, to procure healthy young plants for their colouring.

**Day Flower** (see **Commelina**).

**Delphinium** (**Larkspur**) (Annual Delphinium), *Ranunculaceæ.*—A showy and branching hardy annual, with gorgeous spikes of flowers, both double and single, on stems 12–40 inches high in summer. The colours range from white, through rose-pink, scarlet, blue and mauve to purple. The dwarfer kinds (12 inches) are excellent for massing or for use as edgings, and the taller species (36 inches, should be grouped in mixed borders. There are now several strains: the Emperor,

Rocket, Hyacinth-flowered, and Stock-flowered. The Emperor strain is particularly free and branching. Larkspurs are excellent for pot-plants.

*Culture.*—Sow seed from March to May under glass or in the open. Thin out moderately when 3 inches high. Seed may also be sown in a frame in August : in this case pot-up in October or November in 5- to 6-inch pots, and winter well up near the glass in a cool greenhouse.

*Species.*—*D. cardiopetalum* [Mediterranean region] (blue) ; *D. Consolida* [Europe] (purplish blue) ; *D. Gayanum* (syn. *Ajacis*) [Europe] (blue : there are many coloured forms of this with both single and double flowers). *D. paniculata* [Mediterranean region] (purplish blue)

**Dendrobium** (see chapter on **Orchids**).

**Dendrobium muricatum** var. **munificum** (see **Inobulbon munificum**).

**Dendrochilum** (see Chapter on **Orchids**).

**Dendromecon rigida** (Tree Poppy), *Papaveraceæ.*—An attractive Californian shrub which is hardy outside against a warm south or south-west wall in some parts of the country, but which is more suitable in other parts for the cold house. It should be put in a light, airy position, where it will bear bright-yellow flowers most of the summer. It is an excellent subject for planting against a pillar.

*Culture.*—It thrives in a light, loamy soil, and is more suitable for planting out than for pots. It is propagated from seed, which germinates very slowly, or by cuttings of ripe wood in sand, with gentle heat. Prune out old weak growths and, if height is limited, the tall growths can be cut out, and new growths will start at the base.

**Dennstædtia,** *Polypodiaceæ.*—Handsome greenhouse ferns which are, by some authorities, included in **Dicksonia,** which differ from **Dennstædtia** in being tree ferns, as well as in other ways. They are suitable for the cool fernery, and can be increased by spores, or by division of the root-stock in the spring. They thrive in fibrous peat and loam with some sand (see Chapter on **Ferns**).

*Species.*—*D. cicutaria* [Tropical America] (3–4 ft., fronds 24–30 in.) ; *D. cornuta* [Central Brazil] (30–40 in.) ; *D. decomposita* [Costa Rica, Mexico] (3–4 ft., fronds 24–36 in.) ; *D. punctilobula* [N. America] is the only hardy species of the genus. It has a delightful scent, and is sometimes known as Hay-scented Fern. It is suitable for the cold house, and grows from 12 to 20 inches high.

**Dermatobotrys Saundersii,** *Scrophulariaceæ.*—A deciduous, warm-greenhouse, winter-flowering shrub from Zululand. It bears clusters of red and yellow, tubular, trumpet-shaped flowers, and grows from 12 to 24 inches high. Pot in the spring when necessary, using a mixture of equal portions of turfy loam and peat, with some sand. Propagated by seed sown in sandy loam and placed in a warm house ; or by cuttings of half-ripened wood in sand, in a close case, with bottom heat.

**Desfontainea spinosa,** *Loganiaceæ.*—A hardy evergreen shrub which forms an admirable plant for greenhouse or conservatory decoration. It is very attractive even when out of flower, and will thrive in a compost consisting of turfy loam and peat in equal parts with sufficient sand to keep it open. Propagation is achieved by means of cuttings inserted in a mixture of sandy loam and peat, and placing the receptacles under a bell-glass in a frame with bottom heat.

**341**

**Desmodium** (Tick Trefoil), *Leguminosæ.*—This genus includes a number of greenhouse deciduous shrubs which thrive in the cool house. *D. nutans* [E. Indies] has bluish-lilac flowers in July on pendulous branches, and grows 18–30 inches high. *D. tiliæfolium* throws up in spring greyish, hairy spikes, some 40 inches in height, which carry, from July to October, lilac coloured inflorescences nearly a foot in length. The leaves of both species are composed of three round leaflets borne on a short, slender stem. The most interesting member of the genus is *D. gyrans* (Telegraph Plant), the lateral leaflets of which move up and down either steadily or in jerks, being conspicuous in bright sunshine. These require a warm temperature.

*Culture.*—Pot-up in March in a compost of sandy loam and peat, and keep in the cool greenhouse (temperature 45° F. winter, 65° F. summer). Water well in summer, and keep moist only in winter.

*Propagation.*—Propagate by means of cuttings in a frame or from seed.

**Deutzia,** *Saxifragaceæ.*—A genus of beautiful, hardy, deciduous, flowering shrubs of upright growth, from 3 to 6 feet in height, and covered with clusters of pretty, snowdrop-like white, rose, or purple flowers (single or double) when in bloom (May to June). They thrive in a sheltered, partly shaded position in rich, well-drained ordinary soil in the shrubbery, or in the greenhouse.

*Pot Culture.*—Pot-up from September to November in rich, sandy loam, using as small a pot as convenient. Keep cool, but frost-proof. Then in December or January move into the greenhouse, and gradually raise the temperature to 65° F. As soon as the buds form, water with weak manure-water, or dress with artificial manure once a week until the colour of the flowers is visible. Thin out well, and cut away weak and old wood after flowering, and plant the shrubs out in the open in May or June, at which time the roots may be divided if they are getting too large. Deutzias, particularly *D. gracilis*, are well adapted for forcing. In the warm greenhouse they may be had in bloom in the late spring, but they should be exempted from this process every alternate year.

*Species and Varieties.*—*D. discolor grandiflora* (pink); *D. d. major* (white) [both from Central China]; *D. gracilis* [Japan] (white); *D. Lemoinei* [a hybrid of *D. gracilis* and *D. parviflora*] (a handsome shrub with panicles of pure white flowers, more vigorous and showy than *D. gracilis*); *D. longifolia* var. *Veitchii* [Central China] (rose-purple); *D. magnifica* (garden hybrid] (double white); *D. rosea* [a hybrid of *D. gracilis* and *D. purpurascens*, sometimes called *D. gracilis rosea*] (rose-coloured flowers); *D. scabra* (*D. crenata*) [Japan and China] *fl. pl.* (double pink); *D. Vilmorinæ* [China] (white); and *D. Wilsonii* [Central China] (tall white).

**Devil's Walking Stick** (see **Aralia spinosa**).

**Diacrium bicornutum** (see Chapter on **Orchids**).

**Diamond Flower** (see **Ionopsidium acaule**)

**Dianella** (Flax Lily), *Liliaceæ.*—Half-hardy perennials with decorative, grass-like foliage, flowers, and berries. They grow from 18 to 50 inches in height, and the blue flowers, which appear in the late spring and summer, are followed by blue berries. In the warmer districts they may be grown outdoors, but elsewhere the protection of a frost-proof greenhouse is necessary.

*Culture.*—Pot-up in spring in a compost of two to three parts of peat to one part of sandy loam. They may be raised from seed under glass, or by division in March.

*Species.*—*D. cœrulea* [Australia] (18–24 in.) *D. intermedia* [New Zealand] (18 in.); *D. lævis* (*D. strumosa*) [Australia] (18–36 in.); *D. tasmanica* [Tasmania and Australia] (24–36 in.).

**Dianthera nodosa,** *Acanthaceæ.*—A semi-prostrate greenhouse perennial bearing tubular pink flowers during the summer months. In common with other genera belonging to the *Acanthaceæ*, *Dianthera nodosa* enjoys warm greenhouse conditions and thrives in a compost of equal parts loam, peat and leaf-soil with sand. Propagate by cuttings made from side shoots inserted in sandy soil in a warm propagating case during spring or summer.

**Dianthus,** *Caryophyllaceæ.*—A beautiful and extensive genus, which embraces the **Carnation, Picotee,** and **Pink,** also the beautiful coloured forms of *D. Heddewigii* (Chinese Pink). See paragraphs under **Carnation** and **Picotee.** One or two of the dwarf-growing Pinks are recommended for culture in shallow pans in the alpine house: *Dianthus alpinu* [Europe] (rose or purplish crimson spotted; also a white variety, 3–4 in.); *D. arenarius* [Dalmatia] (fimbriate white flowers, 9–12 in.; *D. glaucus* is a variety of this); *D. cæsius* (Cheddar-pink) [Europe] (rose coloured, 9–12 in.); *D. Freynii* [Mountains of S. Europe] (pink, 3–4 in.); *D. neglectus* [S. Europe] (rose-pink, 4 in.); this is considered by some to be a variety of *D. glacialis.*

**Diapensia,** *Diapensiaceæ.*—Compact, evergreen alpine plants, the two best-known species coming from widely separated parts of the world. Both are attractive for the alpine house, grown in pans in sandy peat, and plunged in a cold frame, in a moist but not too bright position during the summer. May be increased by seed, which should be sown as soon as ripe, or by division of the plant in spring, the divisions being kept in a close frame for a time. *D. himalaica* [Sikkim] is dense tufted. The solitary bell-shaped flowers are white or rose-red, and appear from June to July. It grows to a height of 2 inches. *D. lapponica* [Northern regions] forms a dense cushion of leaves from which spring the white, solitary, bell-shaped flowers in July and August. It reaches a height of from 1 to 2 inches, and is an interesting alpine, but not often grown.

**Diascia Barberæ,** *Scrophulariaceæ.*—A pretty little half-hardy annual with rosy flowers on stems 12 inches in height, in the early autumn. It prefers a fairly good soil and a sunny situation, and thrives either in the greenhouse or in the open.

*Culture.*—Sow seed under glass (60° F.) in March, and thin out as soon as possible. Pot-up four or five plants in a 6-inch pot in a compost of two parts of sandy loam to one part of leaf-mould. Stand in a light, airy position, and water regularly while growing.

**Diastema,** *Gesneraceæ.*—Dwarf, warm-greenhouse plants, allied to **Achimenes** and **Isoloma.** They thrive in a compost of loam, peat, and some sand. They are propagated by cuttings of young shoots when 2 or 3 inches long (temperature 45–55° F. winter, 60–75° F. summer).

*Species.*—*D. Lehmannii* [Colombia] (white spotted and lined violet, July, 15 in.) ; *D. ochroleucum* [New Granada] (yellowish white, many flowers, Aug., 12–18 in.) ; *D. quinquevulnerum* [Colombia] (white, with five rosy spots, Aug., 5–7 in.).

**Dicentra,** *Papaveraceæ.*—The old and still popular name is **Dielytra.** The best known of the family is *D. spectabilis,* or Bleeding Heart, from Japan. It is a very handsome plant, both in habit and in foliage, as well as in flowers. These are of a peculiar wing-like shape, growing in long, drooping racemes on arching stems, reaching a height of 24 inches There are two forms of this plant : one with rosy-pink blossoms, the other with white. They are hardy perennials, and thrive in a sheltered, sunny site, and in a light, dry soil containing ample leaf-mould. They produce masses of fern-like foliage, above which rise long, tapering stems. From these hang the most charming little heart-shaped flowers, of exquisite colour. Although hardy, it is safer to winter them in a cold frame. In the open the flowers are borne from May to July. These plants are often forced in the greenhouse in late winter.

*Pot Culture.*—Pot-up in September in well-manured sandy loam, stand in the cold frame plunged in ashes, and keep just moist until November, then move into the warm greenhouse (55° F.). After flowering, continue to water until the stems die down, and stand in the open from May to September. Dicentras require ample moisture, and when making full growth the pots may be stood in saucers of water.

*Propagation.*—This is carried out by seed or division in April or September, and the plants should be planted-out or potted-up during those months.

In the greenhouse the flowers are usually borne in March and April, but they may be had earlier if the plants are taken into the house a little earlier and slightly more heat used. By introducing the pots to the heat in batches a succession of bloom can be kept up from midwinter until the end of April.

*Species.*—*D. Cucullaria* (Dutchman's Breeches) [N. America] (white, tipped creamy yellow, 5 in.) ; *D. eximia* [N. America] (rose or pink, 15 in.) ; *D. formosa* [N.W. America] (rose-purple, 9 in.) ; *D. spectabilis* [Japan] (red or white, 24 in.).

**Dichæa picta** (see Chapter on **Orchids**).

**Dichorisandra thyrsiflora,** *Commelinaceæ.*—A handsome, tropical, herbaceous perennial from Brazil. It has handsome foliage and rich blue flowers ; it will grow up to 4 feet high, and is one of the best of autumn-flowering stove plants. It succeeds in loam and peat in equal proportions, with some sand and leaf-mould.

*Propagation.*—It can be increased by division when growth commences when re-potting is done. This should be done annually, using 8-inch pots. Seed should be sown in the pan and placed on a hot bed, potting the seedlings on as required. When the flowers commence to expand, the plants can be placed in a warm greenhouse, where they will remain in bloom for six weeks or more.

**Dichrotrichum ternateum,** *Gesneraceæ.*—A showy stove perennial from the Moluccas, bearing loose cymes of crimson, tubular flowers during

# GREENHOUSE PLANTS

July. It is closely allied to, and requires the same treatment as **Æschynanthus** (which see).

**Dicksonia,** *Cyatheaceæ.*—A genus of stove and greenhouse ferns of easy culture in a moist, heated greenhouse. The best-known and most useful species for conservatory decoration are two tree ferns : *D. antarctica* [Australia and Tasmania] and *D. squarrosa* [New Zealand and Chatham Is.]. As a potting compost use equal proportions of light, fibrous loam and peat, adding to this about one-fourth part coarse grit. (See also **Ferns.**)

**Dictyanthus Pavonii,** *Asclepiadaceæ.*—A pretty, warm greenhouse, autumn-blooming climber from Mexico. It bears whitish flowers, spotted and elegantly veined with brown. It succeeds with the same cultural treatment as **Passiflora** (which see).

**Dictyosperma,** *Palmaceæ.*—Desirable greenhouse and table palms. sometimes included under **Areca,** being closely allied to them and requiring the same treatment. *D. alba* [Mauritius] has whitish petioles and whitish-green veined leaves, and grows to a height of 6 to 10 feet. This is the best of the genus, and is often sold as **Areca alba.** *D. aurea* [Seychelles] has orange or yellow petioles and veins. *D. rubra* [Mauritius] closely resembles *D. alba*, but the veins and petioles are dark red Young plants of this grow quickly, being very attractive in the young stage, and useful for table decoration.

**Didiscus** (see **Trachymene**).

**Didymochlæna lunulata,** *Polypodiaceæ.*—This native of Tropical America is a distinct fern, forming a short trunk a few inches high, but with fronds 3–5 feet long, and covered with brown chaffy scales. It is attractive in a small state only. See Chapter on **Ferns.**

**Dieffenbachia,** *Araceæ.*—Handsome evergreen stove plant with strikingly green leaves, sometimes irregularly marked with white or yellowish spots. They require the same rooting medium and cultural treatment as for **Crotons.** They form a thick, succulent stem and healthy, luxuriant growth, especially when grown in a high, moist temperature. As the stems grow, the leaves often become smaller ; the top should then be taken off, with a portion of the stem, and placed in a sand-bed in a warm house, where it will quickly throw out roots. If the remainder of the stem is cut up into portions 2 or 3 inches long, dried for a day or two, and then placed in boxes of sand and kept warm, every piece will throw out shoots, from the base of which roots will be produced. These can be potted-up as soon as roots are formed. When cutting up the stem care should be taken not to place any part in the mouth, as the juice is very acrid and poisonous, causing the tongue to swell and the sufferers possibly to lose their speech. Thus *D. Sequine* is called Dumb-cane, because those who chew it may lose the power of speech for some days. This plant was formerly used for torturing slaves in this way. *D. Chelsonii* [Colombia] has deep, satiny-green leaves, blotched with yellow, the middle feathered grey. *D. Fournieri* [Colombia] has leathery leaves with spots and blotches of white on a dark-green background. *D. magnifica* [Venezuela] has dark-green leaves, blotched and spotted with white along the veins ; the petioles are also variegated. *D. picta* [Tropical America] has

**345**

numerous irregular oblong or linear spots between the veins. There are several attractive varieties of this species. *D. Regina* [S. America] is greenish white, profusely mottled with light and dark tints, and is a very attractive plant. *D. Sequine* (Dumb-cane) [W. Indies] is green with white stripes and spots. It has a number of variegated varieties.

**Dielytra** (see **Dicentra**).

**Dierama pulcherrima** (**Sparaxis pulcherrima**), *Iridaceæ.*—These handsome South African, corm-rooted plants are suitable for the cool greenhouse, and are very attractive during the early autumn. They carry pendulous, bell-shaped flowers, varying in colour from dark blood-red, purple, rose, to white, on panicled spikes and remotely branched scapes. They grow from 3 to 6 feet high. The leaves are long, narrow, and sword-shaped. They are readily raised from seed, and require the same cultural treatment as **Ixia**.

**Diervilla** (Bush Honeysuckle or Weigela), *Caprifoliaceæ.*—Beautiful, hardy, deciduous shrubs which thrive in sun or semi-shade, and in almost any soil, though moist, fibrous loam and leaf-mould suits them best. They usually grow from 3 to 6 feet in height, and bear white, pink, or crimson bell-shaped flowers, over an inch in length in summer. The flowers are borne on the previous year's growth.

*Culture.*—Plant in October or November, and after flowering cut out old and straggly wood. To propagate, strike cuttings of soft wood in June in a frame, or matured cuttings in the open in October. *D. rosea* (rose-pink) which grows some 4 feet in height, may be had in flower in early spring in the warm greenhouse (temperature 55–70° F. winter, 60–75° summer) ; or it will flower in March in the cool greenhouse (temperature 45–55° F. winter, 60–65° F. summer). Pot-up annually in October, using 8- to 12-inch pots, and a compost of two parts sandy loam to one part leaf-mould and rotten manure. Water moderately, and give liquid manure while growing. Plant out in June after flowering, and do not re-pot for at least two seasons, as Diervillas will not stand forcing for two successive years. Prune as above.

*Species and Varieties.*—D. " *Abel Carriere* " (carmine-red, April–May, 5 ft.) ; *D.* " *Conquete* " (deep rose, 5 ft.) ; *D. coræensis* (*D. amabilis*) [Japan] (pale rose, April–May, 6 ft.) ; *D.* " *Eva Rathke* " (crimson-purple, May–Sept., 3–4 ft.) ; *D. floribunda* (*D. multiflora*) [Japan] (pale rosy pink, June, 6 ft.) ; *D. florida* [China] (deep rose, 5–6 ft.) ; *D. f. candida* (white) ; and *D. f. foliis purpureis* (purple foliage) ; *D. Middendorfiana* [Siberia] (greenish yellow, 3 ft.) ; *D. Styriaca* [garden origin] (deep rosy red, June–July, 3–4 ft.).

**Digitalis canariensis** (see **Isoplexis canariensis**).

**Dillwynia**, *Leguminosæ.*—Half-hardy, Australian, evergreen, shrubby, heath-like plants with orange-red and yellow flowers in late spring or early summer. They thrive in the cool greenhouse in a mixture of peat and sandy loam, three to four parts of the former to one part of the latter.

*Culture.*—Plants that have flowered have their side-shoots cut back to about one-third. Re-pot when new growth commences in summer. Plunge the pots outdoors to their rims in ashes from August to October and transfer to the cool greenhouse. Water regularly while growing.

**346**

*Propagation.*—Cuttings of semi-mature shoots may be rooted under a bell-glass in the greenhouse in late summer, or seed may be sown in the spring.

*Species.*—*D. ericifolia* (orange and yellow, May, 18–30 in.) ; *D. floribunda* (yellow, April, 24–36 in.) ; and *D. juniperina* (orange, striped red, March, 12–24 in.).

**Dimorphotheca aurantiaca** (Cape Daisy or Star of the Veldt), *Compositæ.*—A beautiful half-hardy annual that grows to a height of about 12 inches and bears a profusion of orange-yellow, marigold-like flowers, with a black disc in the centre, from July to September. There are also several hybrid varieties arising from *D. aurantiaca* and *D. pluvialis,* both from South Africa The latter bears white flowers on stalks 1 foot tall, the petals being dark maroon below. These hybrids are salmon, pale yellow, or rosy cream in colour. They like a sunny position and a light soil, and are extremely useful subjects for decoration in the greenhouse. Shrubby Dimorphothecas, also very useful in this respect, are *D. chrysanthemifolia* (yellow, summer, 18–24 in.) ; *D. cuneata* (orange, summer, 20 in.) ; *D. Ecklonii* (white above, purplish beneath, summer, 24 in.) They require cool-house treatment and are readily propagated from seed or cuttings.

*Culture.*—Sow seed thinly in May in a sunny position and in a light soil, or sow in March, under glass, ¼ inch deep, in boxes in a compost of sandy loam, and plant out or pot up and stand in the greenhouse early in June.

**Dionæa muscipula** (Venus Fly Trap), *Droseraceæ.*—(Carolina and Florida).—An exceedingly interesting herbaceous perennial requiring a mixture of peat and live sphagnum and broken crocks. The pots should be stood in saucers stuffed with moss and filled with water, particularly during the growing season. A bell-glass should be placed over the plant, but prevented from being shut close down. It is increased by division in the spring, although healthier plants are usually obtained from seed, which should be sown as soon as ripe and placed in a warm, moist atmosphere. If leaves are laid in damp moss under glass a young plant will sometimes form at their margins (temperature 50–60° F. winter, 60–75° F. summer).

**Dioon edule,** *Cycadaceæ.*—A handsome, Mexican, palm-like plant for a large warm house, or for standing outside in the summer. It is allied to **Cycas**, and requires the same cultural treatment. The seeds, which are as large as a chestnut, are eaten by the natives, being powdered up into a form of arrowroot. Propagation is effected by seed sown and placed in a warm house.

**Diosma,** *Rutaceæ.*—Half-hardy, evergreen, heath-like flowering shrubs from South Africa, suitable for the cold greenhouse. They grow 18 to 24 inches in height and bear pink to white flowers in spring.

*Culture.*—Plants that have flowered are trimmed back by about a third and re-potted when new growth commences in early summer. The most suitable compost is a mixture of sandy peat and a little loam. Water well while growing, and expose to full sun when established.

*Propagation.*—Cuttings of semi-mature side-shoots taken with a " heel " may be rooted in sandy soil under a bell-glass.

*Species.*—*D. capitata* (syn. *Audoninia capitata*, which see); *D. ericoides* (whitish pink, 24 in.).

**Diospyros Kaki** (Date Plum), *Ebenaceæ.*—This native of Japan and China is a large bush or small tree up to 20 feet high. It is cultivated for its large edible fruits which somewhat resemble a tomato in size and appearance. They are reddish or orange, and delicious when ripe, and are now obtainable on the market. In favourable localities it may be grown outside against a south wall. Much better fruits, however, are obtained from growing it inside an ordinary fruit-house, with apples and plums. It should be grown in pots, and in the same type of soil as the apple, and should be pruned in a similar manner. When the fruits are set the plant should have plenty of water, but should be kept on the dry side during the winter. Cuttings of soft, young shoots may be rooted in a warm, close case in the spring, or seed may be sown in a warm temperature at almost any time. There are a number of varieties; these are grafted on stocks of the typical plant, which are raised from seed.

**Diplacus** (**Mimulus**), *Scrophulariaceæ.*—Half-hardy, evergreen, shrubby plants, some 24–36 inches in height, with rich, orange, trumpet-shaped flowers in summer, and useful for culture in the cold or cool greenhouse. They are sometimes included under **Mimulus.**

*Culture.*—Pot-up in spring in pots containing a well-drained compost of sandy loam, leaf-mould, and peat, and, when so doing, cut back the shoots to form compact, bushy specimens. If preferred, leave the leading shoots long, and train them to pillar, wall, or supports. Water well while growing, and feed occasionally with weak manure-water. Full sun is desirable when established.

*Propagation.*—Cuttings of new shoots may be rooted under a bell-glass in sandy soil in April.

*D. glutinosus* (Bush Musk) [California] (orange-red) is a very variable plant, and has the following varieties: *albus* (white); *coccinea* (red) and *puniceus* (orange-red).

**Dipladenia,** *Apocynaceæ.*—A charming group of greenhouse twiners with large, more or less funnel-shaped flowers, many with purple or rosy shades and brilliant yellow throats, being among the best of green-house plants. At one time it was thought that they required a high temperature, but such is not the case, as they do much better in an intermediate temperature (60–70° F. summer, 55–65° F. winter), but the atmosphere must be moist during the growing season and dry during the winter.

*Culture.*—A suitable compost is fibrous peat, broken up with sufficient sand to keep it open, and thus ensure a free passage of water. It is very important to see that the drainage is good, for few flowering plants show the effects of a waterlogged soil quicker than these. Young plants should be grown-on without " stopping " and trained to some kind of support, such as wire or a trellis, or to a stake if it is intended to plant them out to train to supports under the roof-glass, which is the best way to show off the flowers of Dipladenias. Flowers will be produced most of the summer on the current year's wood, which should be removed at the end of the summer unless it is intended to extend the

348

plant. Plenty of syringing is beneficial during the growing season. When the pots are filled with roots they appreciate some help in the way of liquid manure. In February shake out the old soil of those grown in pots and re-pot in the same size pot, placing the plants in a little higher temperature (not less than 65° F.) until they have commenced to take root in the new soil, when the temperature may be lowered by 10°.

*Propagation.*—Cuttings can be taken in the early spring just as growth is about to commence—pieces of fairly strong growth with two or three leaves, and about an inch of stem under the lowest leaf. These should then be planted singly in small pots, in peat, sand, and charcoal, placing the pots in a propagating case, with a temperature of 70° F. When rooted—which will be in about a month—admit air occasionally during the day.

*Species.*—*D. amabilis* [garden hybrid] (rosy crimson); *D. atropurpurea* [Brazil] (purple-crimson); *D. Brearleyana* [garden hybrid] (rich crimson, very floriferous); *D. Martiana* (syn. *D. crassinoda*) [Brazil] (rose coloured, an old favourite); *D. insignis* [hybrid] (rosy purple); *D. nobilis* [hybrid] (rosy purple to orange-red); *D. Sanderi* [Brazil] (pink, yellow throat and base).

**Dipladenia flava** (see **Urechites suberecta**).

**Dipladenia Harrisii** (see **Odontadenia grandiflora**).

**Disa** (see Chapter on **Orchids**).

**Disocactus biformis (Phyllocactus biformis),** *Cactaceæ.*—An interesting cactus from Honduras, with two forms of branches. It has purplish-red flowers and requires the same cultural treatment as **Epiphyllum** (which see).

**Dissotis,** *Melastomaceæ.*—Evergreen soft-wooded shrubs for the stove greenhouse, some of them worthy of a place in choice collections as pot plants, particularly in some cases as basket-plants. The long, trailing, attractive growth hangs down 4 or 5 feet and bears a number of flowers most of the year. They thrive in a warm, moist temperature, in a mixture of loam, peat, and sand. Cuttings of half-ripened wood root readily in a close case with bottom heat. *D. incana* [S. Africa] grows 30–36 inches high and bears rosy-purple flowers. *D. Mahonii* [Uganda] has rosy-purple flowers and long, trailing shoots which are hispidly hairy. *D. plumosa* [Tropical Africa] has magenta-rose flowers, and is very similar in habit to the above.

**Dittany** (see **Origanum Dictamnus**).

**Diuris** (see Chapter on **Orchids**).

**Dizygotheca,** *Araliaceæ.*—Graceful stovehouse plants, grown chiefly for their foliage, usually known as **Aralia.**

*Culture.*—They require a light, rich soil with a mixture of equal parts of sandy loam and peat or leaf-mould. They need plenty of water and a moist atmosphere.

*Propagation.*—They are propagated by cuttings in a close case with bottom heat.

The specific rank of the many cultivated kinds is unknown, including those mentioned below. This can be settled only when they have flowered, which hitherto they have not done. They may be the juvenile forms remaining in a juvenile condition. *D. elegantissima* [New Hebrides] is an elegant plant with graceful leaves and mottled white petioles. *D. Kerchoveana* [S. Sea Islands] has slender stems of beautiful habit ; the edges of the leaflets are undulate, with serrate margins. *D. Veitchii* [New Caledonia] is one of the most handsome and desirable plants, with leaflets shining green above, red beneath. The variety *gracillima* has still narrower leaflets with a white rib.

**Dodecatheon** (Shooting Stars, American Cowslip), *Primulaceæ.*— Small perennial herbs with cyclamen-shaped flowers. Although quite hardy, they can be grown in pans for the alpine house. They should be potted-up in early autumn in moderately rich but well-drained soil ; the pans can then be plunged in a shady place either in the open or in a cold frame. They do not need to be disturbed every year. They are increased by seed sown as soon as ripe or by division of the roots in the autumn.

*D. Clevelandii* [S. California] grows from 15 to 18 inches high, has purple flowers with yellow bases and a few purple spots, in April and May. *D. Jeffreyi* [Mountains of California] has deep reddish-purple flowers in May, and attains a height of 16–18 inches. *D. Meadia* [N. America] has rose-coloured flowers with a white base. This is the best-known species, of which there are a number of beautiful forms.

**Dog's Tooth Violet** (see **Erythronium**).

**Dombeya,** *Sterculiaceæ.*—Ornamental warm-greenhouse trees or shrubs producing showy flowers in terminal or axillary inflorescences. Some thirty species have been described of which only one or two are generally cultivated outside botanic gardens to-day. They thrive in a compost of sandy loam and turfy peat. Propagate by cuttings inserted in sand in a warm propagating case.

*Species.*—*D. Burgessiæ* [S. Africa] (rosy white, Aug.–Nov., 10 ft.) ; *D. Mastersii* [Tropical Africa] (white, Aug.–Oct., 8 ft.) ; *D. Wallichii* [Madagascar] (scarlet, Aug.–Sept., 10–12 ft.).

**Dondia Epipactis** (see **Hacquetia Epipactis**).

**Doodia,** *Polypodiaceæ.*—A genus of greenhouse ferns which grow from 5 to 10 inches in height and thrive in a compost of two parts of loam to one part of leaf-mould and sand.

*Culture.*—Pot-up in March, and water liberally during spring and summer (temperature 45° F. winter, 65° F. summer).

Propagate by means of spores at any time in moderate heat, or by division of the roots.

*Species.*—*D. aspera* [Temperate Australia] (9 in.) ; *D. caudata* [Australia and New Zealand] (10 in.) ; and *D. media* [Australia and New Zealand] (10 in.).

**Doryopteris** (Lace Fern), *Polypodiaceæ.*—Attractive little pot ferns with oddly pretty fronds. They are sometimes included under **Pteris,** and require the same cultural treatment. *D. decipiens* [Hawaiian Islands] grows 8–12 inches high, and has much-divided leaves. It somewhat resembles a Geranium. *D. nobilis* [S. Brazil] has graceful bipinnate leaves, 12 inches long. *D. pedata* [Tropical America] has much-divided leaves, with the fertile fronds still more divided. The var, *palmata* from the West Indies has wider triangular lobes.

**Douglasia Vitaliana (Androsace Vitaliana)**, *Primulaceæ.*—A dwarf evergreen rock plant from the Alps and Pyrenees. Grown in pans, it is very suitable for the alpine house, where the bright-yellow, stalkless flower, borne just above the tuft of leaves, is very attractive during April and May. It is allied to **Androsace,** and requires the same cultural treatment. It is not very successful in a calcareous soil.

**Draba Aizoon** (Whitlow Grass), *Cruciferæ.*—[Europe] (yellow, April, 3 in.).

*Species.*—*D. imbricata* [Caucasus] (April, 3 in.) ; *D. olympic* [*D. bruniæfolia*] (deep golden-yellow, May–June, 4 in.). See Chapter on **Alpine House.**

**Draba pyrenaica** (see **Petrocallis pyrenaica**).

**Dracæna,** *Liliaceæ.*—These are chiefly attractive stove and hot-house foliage plants, most of which are now included under **Pleomele** by some authorities. They thrive in a mixture of fibrous loam, leaf-mould, sand and peat, in a warm, moist atmosphere, which should never fall below 60° F.

*Culture.*—Pot-up young plants in February or March in well-drained 5- to 6-inch pots, and stand in a semi-shaded position in the hot house. Water well, syringe, and sponge the leaves occasionally with lukewarm water while growing. Pot-on as required. Established plants in large pots or tubs should be top dressed with new soil instead of being re-potted. Occasional doses of weak liquid manure are beneficial.

*Propagation.*—Cuttings made of the tops of old plants may be rooted in a propagating frame in March or April. Seed may be sown in heat (60–65° F.), or the plants may be increased by means of root-cuttings or short pieces of the stem of an old plant in a propagating case in a moist, warm atmosphere.

*Species.*—*D. fragrans* [Guinea] has green leaves. There are many beautiful variegated varieties of this, e.g. *Massangeana*, with a broad yellow stripe along the centre of the leaf, and *Victoriæ* with beautiful stripes of yellow and green. *D. Godseffiana* [Congo] is an erect plant, with narrow, stiff leaves, which are green with white spots. *D. Goldieana* [W. Tropical Africa] has green and silver foliage. *D. Lindenii* is of a green and cream colour, and by some is considered a variety of *D. fragrans*. *D. Sanderiana* [Congo] is a slender plant, with narrow leaves which are glossy green, margined with white. (See also **Cordyline,** with which this genus is often confused.)

**Dracæna Palm** (see **Cordyline**).

**Dracophyllum,** *Epacridaceæ.*—Cool-greenhouse, hard-wooded plants from Australia, which, although of rather straggling habit, are of con-siderable beauty.

*Culture.*—They should be potted firmly in a mixture of two-thirds sandy peat and one-third finely chopped loam, with a few small pieces of charcoal added. After flowering they should be cut back hard and placed in a closer atmosphere to encourage new growth. Plenty of water should be given at all times, but care must be taken to see that the drainage is good.

*Propagation.*—The tips of the young shoots can be taken off and dibbled into sand, covered with a bell-glass, and placed in a little heat.

The glass should be lifted off daily and wiped dry to prevent the cuttings from damping-off.

*Species.*—*D. capitatum* (pure white in terminal heads, April–May, 18–24 in.) ; *D. gracile* (snow-white, fragrant, especially in the evening, June–July, 20–24 in.) ; *D. secundum* (white, tubular, funnel-shaped flowers on one side of the shoot, April–May, 18–24 in.).

**Drosera** (Sundew or Youthwort), *Droseraceæ.*—A genus of curious dwarf-growing insectivorous plants whose leaves are covered with glandular hairs which appear to be laden with dew. The leaves contract on contact so as to entrap insects settling on them. They grow in boggy situations, which are almost devoid of nitrogenous food. The plants depend on these glandular hairs to trap small flies, which are dissolved by a digestive fluid. The nitrogen contained in these insects is then absorbed by the plant as food. They mostly thrive in a warm, sheltered position in the bog or wild garden. *D. binata* [Australia and New Zealand] has white flowers and forked leaves. The var. *dichotoma* has double-forked leaves ; in both cases the segments are reddish green. They are easily grown, and increased by division, or by root-cuttings placed in chopped sphagnum in a warm house in the spring. *D. capensis*, the Cape Sundew, is also an interesting plant for the greenhouse, bearing vivid purple flowers. They do best in a compost of living sphagnum moss and a little peat and sand. The long, flat, ribbon-like, hairy leaves catch an extraordinary number of flies. *D. rotundifolia* [Europe], growing to a height of 4 inches, with white flowers in June and July, is useful in the alpine house. It does well in a 4- to 5-inch pan of compost as above. Plant in September and rest in winter. Stand the pots or pans in saucers of water and expose them fully to the sun.

**Drosophyllum lusitanicum,** *Droseraceæ.*—A cool-greenhouse insectivorous plant from South West Europe and North Africa, with the habit of Droseras. The plants are covered with sticky glands, and hold the insects that alight on them. The flowers are yellow, and appear in summer. It succeeds in sandy loam, kept on the dry side, and the plant should be exposed to sunlight. It is increased by seed sown in the spring in sandy soil.

**Dryas octopetala** (Mountain Avens), *Rosaceæ.*—[Northern Temperate regions]. For culture see Chapter on **Alpine House.**

**Drymoglossum** (Wood-tongue Fern), *Polypodiaceæ.*—Small, warm-greenhouse ferns with creeping habit, which can be grown on lumps of wood covered with peat, or placed to climb up a tree-fern stem. *D. carnosum* [E. Himalayas] is a creeper with fleshy fronds. *D. heterophyllum* (*D. piloselloides*) [Tropical Asia] has small fronds of various shapes, the young rhizomes being hairy.

**Drynaria,** *Polypodiaceæ.*—Handsome stove-ferns with either two forms of fronds, like the **Platycerium,** or the base of the fertile one being separately lobed. The fertile ones are often finely netted or veined. They are striking foliage plants, and are best grown on rafts built up with lumps of loam and peat. Many of them are suitable only for a large greenhouse. They are increased by division in the spring. *D. quercifolia* [E. Indies], grows to a height of 24 to 36 inches, and has

**PLATE 12**
Imperial Hybrids of *Scabiosa*.
Flowers from May to September.

basal or sterile fronds resembling oak leaves. *D. propiqua* [Tropical Asia] attains a height of 18–24 inches. The barren fronds, 8 to 9 inches long, are cut for half or three-quarters of their length into acute or bluntish lobes. (See Chapter on **Ferns.**)

**Dryopteris** (Wood Fern), *Polypodiaceæ.*—A group of widely distributed, handsome ferns with dissected foliage. Our native species can be grown outside and in the cool house, and in some cases are ideal for the alpine house. Those from warmer regions are decorative under glass.

*Culture.*—They succeed in a compost of two parts of sandy loam to one part of leaf-soil and peat (temperature 45° F. winter, 60° F. summer). Pot-up in March and water liberally during the summer. They are propagated by means of spores and by division of the old plants.

*Species.*—*D. æmula* (Hay-scented Fern) [Europe, Madeira] (12 in.) ; *D. cana* [Sikkim] (an attractive fern for the cool house, 12–18 in.) ; *D. crenata* [Mexico to Brazil] (margins of pinnæ bluntly lobed, warm house, 18–24 in.) ; *D. dissecta* (*Lastræa membranifolia*) [Tropics] (a handsome fern with broad segments, 24–50 in.) ; *D. effusa* [Brazil] (creeping root-stock, fronds 36–48 in.) ; *D Filix-mas* [Male Fern] (our handsome native fern, and its variety *cristata*) ; *D. Linnæana* (Oak Fern) [Europe to Asia, etc.] (the variety *Robertiana* has the scent of *Herb Robert* [*Geranium Robertianum*]) ; *D. oreopteris* (Mountain Fern) [Europe, Britain] (there are many varieties of this, e.g. *cristata, gracilis, montana rampcoronana*) ; *D. parasitica* (*Nephrodium molle*) [Tropics] (the easiest of ferns to grow inside) ; *D. patens* [Tropics and Sub-tropics] (24–36 in.) ; *D. rigida* [Europe, Britain] ; *D. setigera* [Japan, Tropical Asia] (24–36 in.) ; *D. spinulosa* (one of the rarest and yet most beautiful of our native ferns, for the cool fern house. There are several varieties, e.g. *dilatata, remota*). See Chapter on **Ferns.**

**Dryopteris Phegopteris** (see **Phegopteris polypodioides**).

**Duchesnea indica** (**Fragaria indica**), *Rosaceæ.*—Interesting trailing plants from Southern Asia, which make attractive basket plants for the cool greenhouse. They have solitary bright-yellow flowers which are borne on the runners, and small, bright, strawberry-like fruits which are produced nearly all the summer. They are increased by seed or by runners, and can be grown outside in favourable parts of the country.

**Dudleya** (see **Cotyledon**).

**Dumb Cane** (see **Dieffenbachia Sequine**).

**Dusty Miller** (see **Senecio Cineraria**).

**Dutchman's Breeches** (see **Dicentra Cucullaria**).

**Dutchman's Pipe** (see **Aristolochia macrophylla**) (**A. Sipho**).

**Duvalia,** *Asclepiadaceæ.*—A group of leafless succulents, chiefly from South Africa, with pecularities similar to **Stapelia,** and requiring the same cultural treatment. *D. Corderoyi* (*Stapelia Corderoyi*) has olive-green and reddish-brown flowers fringed with purplish mauve hairs, and grows to a height of 4–6 inches. *D. elegans* has dark purplish-brown flowers with long purple hairs, attaining a height of 3–4 inches. *D. Pillansii* has flowers which are greenish outside and purplish brown within, a yellow eye, and reddish hairs, 3–4 inches high. *D. polita* grows to a

Z

height of 2½–3 inches, and its flowers are greenish and dark brownish red.

**Dyckia,** *Bromeliaceæ.*—Small dwarf succulents, with rosettes of elegant foliage, and ornamental habit. They succeed under the same conditions as **Agave,** and bear yellow or orange flowers. *D. rariflora* [Brazil] has greyish-green leaves with small spines at the margins. The orange-coloured flowers are scattered, and appear in summer. It reaches a height of 18–24 inches. *D. sulphurea* [Brazil] has sulphur-yellow flowers in summer.

**Eccremocarpus scaber (Calampelis scaber),** *Bignoniaceæ.*—A half-hardy, Chilean climber of great beauty, with lovely foliage. It bears rich, orange-red or rosy-red, bell-shaped flowers from July to September. It grows to a height of about 10–20 feet and thrives in any well-drained light loam, against south walls, trellises, and pillars, and is also useful as a greenhouse climber.

*Culture.*—Propagate by means of cuttings in a frame in autumn, or sow seed in heat in January; plant-out in April or pot-up in 8-inch pots for decoration in the cold greenhouse. After flowering, cut away dead wood, and protect the roots in winter.

*Species.*—*E. scaber* (orange-red); *E. scaber* var. *roseus* (rosy red); *E. scaber* var. *luteus* (yellow).

**Echeveria** (see **Cotyledon**).

**Echidnopsis,** *Asclepiadaceæ.*—Leafless succulents allied to **Stapelia,** requiring the same cultural treatment. It is sometimes known as Viper Plant, owing to its trailing, serpent-like stems.

*Species.*—*E. Bentii* [Arabia] (large crimson flowers, June, 5–6 in.); *E. cereiformis* [S. Arabia] (flowers in fascicles, brownish outside, yellow inside, summer to autumn, 8–12 in.); *E. Dammanniana* [Eritrea] (similar to above, brownish purple, summer, 10–14 in.); *E. somalænsis* [Somaliland] (flowers sessile, dark purple, spotted with yellow, summer, 5–6 in.).

**Echinocactus,** *Cactaceæ.*—A genus of cacti, natives of Mexico, Texas, and California, suitable for greenhouse culture. Their thick stems are deeply ribbed, globular, and stumpy, and are covered with clusters of stout but often brilliant bristles and spines, which are usually grey, red, or yellow. They like a sunny, warm position in a compost of two parts of turfy loam to one part of sand and brick rubble (average temperatures: winter, day 60° F., night 50° F.; summer, day 80° F., night 70° F.).

*Culture.*—Pot-up triennially in March in well-drained pots of suitable size, according to the size of the plant, taking care not to over-pot. Water weekly in summer, and monthly during the rest of the year. Propagate by means of seed sown in heat in March, by cuttings (dried a few days before being inserted) in July, or by grafting in March.

*Good species* are :—*E. cornigerus* [Mexico] (reddish purple, June 9 in.); *E. cylindraceus* [Lower California] a half-hardy species, with green and yellow flowers in summer, and red spines, may be grown in the open in a sunny, warm, sheltered position. It is useful for window boxes; *E. electracanthus* [Mexico] (yellowish green, summer, 18 in.);

**354**

# GREENHOUSE PLANTS

*E. Grusonii* (Golden Barrel) [Central Mexico] (golden and yellow spines, sometimes reddish turning to white and later to grey, flowers brown and yellow, 15–24 in.); *E. ingens* (yellow, summer, 10–12 in.); *E. uncinatus* [N. Mexico] (purplish red, yellow stamens, April, 9 in.).

**Echinocactus Fiebrigii** (see **Rebutia Fiebrigii**).
**Echinocactus Haselbergii** (see **Notocactus Haselbergii**).
**Echinocactus Lecontei** (see **Ferocactus acanthodes**).
**Echinocactus Mamillarioides** (see **Pyrrhocactus centeterius**).
**Echinocactus minusculus** (see **Rebutia minuscula**).
**Echinocactus rhodophthalmus** (see **Thelocactus bicolor**).
**Echinocactus Simpsonii** (see **Pediocactus Simpsonii**).
**Echinocactus Wislezenii** (see **Ferocactus Wislezenii**).

**Echinocereus,** *Cactaceæ*.—A group of Cacti that was at one time included under **Cereus**, and still is by some authorities. Their stems are condensed, globular, cylindrical or prostrate, usually very spiny. The flowers are funnel shaped, and are various shades of pink, red, and purple, very rarely yellow. They are borne from May to July, opening by day, lasting in bloom for several days and are very attractive. For culture, etc., see **Cereus**.

*Species.*—*E. amœnus* [Mexico] (pink and green flowers very freely produced, 2–3 inches across, elongating with age); *E. cæspitosus* [Texas and Mexico] (rose, May–June, 4–10 in.); *E. coccineus* [S. United States] (fiery scarlet, yellowish at base, 2–2½ in. across); *E. pulchellus* [Mexico] (pink, free flowering, 1½–2 in. across); *E. rigidissimus* (Rainbow Cactus) (Mexico and Arizona] bears purple flowers with a white centre in summer. It has whitish or pale pink spines, reddish or brownish in alternate zones, 2½–3½ inches across. The plant attains a height of 12 inches.

**Echinopsis** (Sea Urchin Cactus), *Cactaceæ*.—A genus of round and prickly Cacti which bear brilliant flowers and are suitable for warm to hot greenhouse culture. They like a warm, sunny position in a mixture of equal parts of turfy loam, coarse sand, brick-rubble, and mortar (average temperatures: winter, day 60° F., night 50° F.; summer, day 80° F., night 70° F.).

*Culture.*—Pot-up triennially in March in well-drained pots. Water weekly in summer, and monthly for the rest of the year. Propagate by means of seed sown in heat in March, by cuttings taken from June to September, or by grafting in April.

*Good species* are :—*E. Decaisneana* (red, May–July, 6–12 in.); *E. Eyriesii* [S. America] (greenish white, March–July, 4–6 in. across, plant 12–18 in. high. The hardiest species will grow outside in some districts); *E. Eyriesii* var. *Muelleri* (pink, May–July, 10–15 in.); *E. formosa* [Argentina] (golden yellow and white flowers, reddish or flesh-coloured spines, May–July, 12–18 in.); *E. oxygona* [S. Brazil] (rose and white, summer, 10 in.); and *E. tubiflora* [S. Brazil and Argentina] (white, May–July, 10 in.).

**Echium** (Vipers Bugloss), *Boraginaceæ*.—A genus of handsome shrubby and herbaceous greenhouse and hardy plants. Flowers in spiked or panicled racemes. All the species are of easy culture and thrive in ordinary compost. Propagation is by seeds or cuttings.

**355**

*Species.*—*E. candicans* [Madeira] (bluish white, May, 2–4 ft.) ; *E. creticum* [Crete] (reddish violet, July, 2 ft.) ; *E. plantagineum* [S. Europe] (blue, July, 2–4 ft.) ; *E. Wildpretii* [Canaries] (violet-blue, summer, 2–3 ft.).

**Edelweiss** (see **Leontopodium**).

**Edraianthus (Hedrænthus),** *Campanulaceæ.*—By some authorities these are all included under **Wahlenbergia,** which see, others retain only the single-flowered members of the group in Wahlenbergia. They are a very attractive group of alpine plants, with showy, bell-shaped flowers, and although hardy on the rock-garden in a well-drained position, they are also very useful for the alpine house when grown in pans. They are best raised from seed sown as soon as ripe. The seedlings should be pricked out, and three or four grown-on in small pots during their first year, making up the pans in the following spring when the young plants show bud. They should be put in well-drained, gritty soil, three or four small pots to each pan, according to size. After flowering, the pans should be plunged in ashes in a cold frame. *E. graminifolius* [Dalmatia] has large purple flowers in bunches in June and July. It grows 3 to 4 inches high, and there are a number of forms of this species. *E. Pumilio* [Dalmatia] has compact tufts of narrow, bluish-grey-green leaves. It carries large lilac-blue flowers from May to June, and grows from 2 to 3 inches high. *E. serpyllifolius* [Dalmatia] has a tuft of narrow, deep-green leaves, and bears large purple flowers on long, trailing stalks in June and July, growing to a height of from 4 to 6 inches. The variety *major* has larger and perhaps more brilliant flowers.

**Edwardsia grandiflora** (see **Sophora tetraptera**).

**Eel Grass** (see **Vallisneria spiralis**).

**Egg Plant** (see **Solanum Melongeana**).

**Egyptian Paper Plant** (see **Cyperus Papyrus**).

**Eichornia,** *Pontederiaceæ.*—An interesting tropical aquatic with showy flowers, requiring a tank in the warm greenhouse. It should be floated, or planted in loam and leaf-soil in pots plunged just below the rim. *E. azurea* [Brazil] is a plant which creeps along the water, sometimes 5–6 feet. It has bright pale-blue flowers, with a heart-shaped spot of yellow and a white margin. *E. crassipes* (Water Hyacinth) [Brazil] is the one usually grown, and should be placed so that the plant floats on the water ; the lower portion of the leaves then becomes swollen and forms globular bladders. When growing in shallow water, or rooted in mud, or even when allowed to grow too quickly, the swollen part of the leaf only becomes partly developed, and the leaves elongate ; the plant thus loses some of its interest. It increases very quickly by division, and should be kept thinned out. It carries spikes of pale-violet flowers in summer, and grows to a height of 12 inches.

**Elæocarpus cyaneus,** *Elæocarpaceæ.*—This is a very handsome greenhouse shrub or small tree, native of Australia. It bears white fringed flowers in axillary racemes, during July. These are followed by attractive blue berries. It thrives in a compost of equal parts loam, peat and leaf-mould, with sufficient sharp sand to keep it open.

Propagate by cuttings made from ripened shoots inserted in sandy soil in a propagating case with bottom heat. Seeds may also be sown in heat.

**Elaphoglossum,** *Polypodiaceæ.*—A group of ferns for the warm greenhouse. These were previously included under **Acrostichum.** They require a warm, moist atmosphere, abundant water at the root, and a good open compost. The winter temperature should not go below 50° F. It is increased by spores or by division. *E. crinitum* (Elephant's Ear Fern) [W. Indies] has large fronds with dense, scaly stalks; the fertile fronds are smaller. It reaches 9–18 inches. Omit sand in compost and avoid over-watering. *E. latifolium* [Mexico and Brazil] has a thick, creeping, woody rhizome, and long, erect, leathery fronds, the fertile ones being narrower than the barren ones. Height, 12–18 inches. *E. villosum* [Mexico and W. Indies] has the rhizome and fronds covered with slender brown scales. The fertile fronds are half the size of the sterile ones. Height, 6–9 inches.

**Elephant's Ear Fern** (see **Elaphoglossum crinitum**).

**Elephant's Foot** (see **Testudinaria**).

**Elisena longipetala,** *Amaryllidaceæ.*—A handsome greenhouse bulb from Lima, which flowers in May, and requires a light, loamy soil with sand generously added. It needs the same treatment as **Hymenocallis.** It bears white flowers, in clusters of about six on a long scape, somewhat resembling the Peruvian Daffodil (**Ismene**). It is increased by offsets.

**Elk's Horn Fern** (see **Platycerium**).

**Elleanthus** (see Chapter on **Orchids**).

**Elodea** (Water Thyme), *Hydrocharitaceæ.*—Aquatic herbs grown in aquaria, of no attractive value except as an underwater plant. It is desirable for aquaria, being a good oxygenator. *E. canadensis, E. crispa, E. densa* are all natives of America. The last two have white, floating flowers. The former, of which the pistillate form only is seen, and which was at one time a great nuisance in streams and ponds, is a very rapid grower, but has now ceased to be so vigorous. Ducks, geese, and swans are fond of it. It can be used for manure when sufficient quantities are available.

**Embothrium coccineum,** *Proteaceæ.*—A cool-greenhouse evergreen shrub or tree up to 25 feet high from Chile. It bears orange-scarlet flowers and flower-buds, both of which are highly decorative during the summer, although in some of the milder parts of the country it can be grown outside. It thrives in fibrous loam and sandy peat, either planted out in bed or border, or in pots. It is increased from cuttings of ripened wood struck in sandy soil and placed under glass; also by layering the lower branches.

**Emmenanthe penduliflora** (Yellow or Golden Californian Bells), *Hydrophyllaceæ.*—An annual for the cool greenhouse, forming bushy plants with branches of creamy-yellow, bell-shaped, pendulous flowers. Sow seed under glass in the spring, and grow the plants on in the cool house. They will bloom in the summer and reach a height of from 18 to 24 inches.

**Encephalartos,** *Cycadaceæ.*—Handsome Cycads, with a palm-like aspect, from East, Tropical, and South Africa. They may be grown for their evergreen foliage for the greenhouse or conservatory, or they may be used with good effect in summer in the sub-tropical garden.

**357**

They grow slowly unless grown in a high temperature. Each plant is either a male or female one, *i.e. Diœcious*. The cones when developed are always interesting, and often decorative. They are increased by seeds, which generally have to be imported. These should be sown and placed in heat. Another method of propagating is by suckers, which should be taken off and potted-up separately. When making new growth they should be given plenty of water. (For culture see **Cycas**). *E. Altensteinii* [Cape of Good Hope] has pinnate, shining, dark-green leaves. The petioles are much swollen at the base. It grows 24–60 inches high. *E. cycadifolius* [S. Africa] has long, arching leaves and crowded pinnæ. It grows from 24 to 30 inches high, and somewhat resembles a Cycas, as its name implies.

**Epacris** (Australian and New Zealand Heath), *Epacridaceæ.*—Heath-like, early-flowering, evergreen shrubs from **Australia and New Zealand**. They thrive in the cold greenhouse and carry long spikes of small, cylindrical flowers ranging in colour from red, through rose to white, usually from December to February. They reach a height of from 18 to 24 inches.

*Culture.*—Pot-up firmly when growth re-commences (about May), using clean, dry, well-drained 5-inch pots and a compost of sandy peat. Keep in a close atmosphere until established, then stand in a good light in a cool greenhouse during the summer months (temperature 45° F. winter, 65° F. summer). Ventilate freely. Water moderately, and give liquid manure while growing, but do not syringe ; the great thing being to give sufficient light and air thoroughly to ripen the growths before the plants are again taken into the house. Cut long shoots back to within an inch or so of the base of the current year's growth after flowering and thin out any unwanted growth. Rest in a frame from July to September, or stand in a sunny position in the open on a hard bed of ashes or brick.

*Propagation.*—Propagate by means of cuttings of young wood 2 inches long, which strike easily in sand, under hand-lights with a little bottom heat, in spring ; or sow seed in pots of sandy peat during March.

*Species.*—*E. hyacinthiflora* (whitish red) ; *E. impressa* (red and white) ; there are many beautiful forms of this species ; *E. impressa* var. *longiflora* [*E. grandiflora* and *E. miniata*] (red and white) ; *E. purpurescens* [*E. onosmæflora*] (white, flushed red). There are also many beautiful garden varieties.

**Epicattleya** (see Chapter on **Orchids**).

**Epidendrum** (see Chapter on **Orchids**).

**Epidendrum Medusæ** (see **Nanodes Medusæ**).

**Epidendrum tibicinis** (see **Schomburgkia tibicinis**).

**Epigæa,** *Ericaceæ.*—Dwarf, trailing, sweet-scented evergreens, thriving only in a moist peaty soil, in a semi-shady spot in the rock-garden. They are very charming in pans for the alpine house. Put in pans in the autumn and plunge in a cold frame or pit during the winter. They are propagated chiefly by layering. *E. asiatica* [Japan] has clusters of pink flowers in June and July. *E. repens* (May Flower) [N. America] bears white flowers tinged with red in June and July.

# GREENHOUSE PLANTS

**Epilælia** (see Chapter on **Orchids**).

**Epiphronites** (see Chapter on **Orchids**).

**Epiphyllum,** *Cactaceæ.*—Spineless, upright, flat-stemmed Cacti, with large, showy flowers (many of them nocturnal), in shades of rose, white, yellow, crimson, and red. Some of them are popular as house- or window-plants. They are often known under the name of **Phyllocactus,** a genus not now generally recognized. There are many beautiful hybrids in cultivation, while crosses have been made with them and other Cacti. They are of easy cultivation, preferring a rather dry, warm greenhouse, but they will suceed even in a window, when once established.

*Culture.*—The most suitable soil is a light, porous loam with some leaf-mould and brick-rubble mixed. Drainage should be to the extent of one fourth, and rather small pots should be used in proportion to the size of the plant. When the pots are well filled with roots the plants benefit from an annual top dressing of soil and dry cow-manure, and during the growing season a little liquid manure can be given. Watering should be carefully done during the winter, as the roots soon die if kept too wet or in too great a bulk of soil.

*Propagation.*—Cuttings of the mature shoots about 6 inches long, taken before growth commences in spring, and inserted singly in small, well-drained pots, will root in a short time if placed in a temperature of 60° F. They should not be covered or watered, beyond a slight syringing to prevent the soil from becoming very dry. Seed should be sown in the spring, and placed in the same temperature as cuttings. When seedlings appear they should be placed in a light position until large enough to be potted-off singly.

*Species.*—*E. Ackermannii* [garden origin] (rich crimson, summer, 24–36 in.), the most free flowering of all, probably of generic origin; *E. crenatum* [S. Mexico] (white or cream-coloured flowers, drying yellow, fragrant, summer, 24–30 in.), the parent of many beautiful hybrids; *E. oxypetalum* [Mexico] (night-flowering climber, large white flowers, 10–15 ft.), one of the best species cultivated; *E. phyllanthoides* [S. Mexico] (rose and white, June, 12–24 in.), a beautiful species and one of the most floriferous; *E. Pittieri* [Costa Rica] (free-flowering, green and white, tinged with pink, with the perfume of Hyacinths, summer, 12–30 in.). There are also many beautiful named varieties and hybrids of the above species, ranging in colour from pure white, pink, yellow, mauve, red, crimson, orange, and violet.

The plants often grown under *Epiphyllum Gaertneri* and *E. Russelliana* are now included under **Schlumbergera,** which see.

**Epiphyllum truncatum** (see **Zygocactus truncatus**).

**Episcia,** *Gesneraceæ.*—Choice and interesting warm-house plants. Some have attractive foliage, and, as they grow successfully in shade, some of the creeping kinds may be used for growing on the borders between the paths and hot-water pipes. They require good fibrous loam, peat, leaf-soil, and sand. Cuttings inserted in sandy soil and kept for a while in a close case or bell-glass will root at any time of the year. Heat, moisture, and some shade, particularly in summer, are necessary to grow them successfully. *E. chontalensis* [Nicaragua] has

**359**

white flowers in July. Its foliage is green with regular purple patches, and it grows from 6 to 8 inches in height. *E. cupreata* [Nicaragua] carries scarlet flowers in June and July. Its foliage is copper-coloured on the upper side. It has creeping stems which root at the joints. This is charming as a basket-plant, or for growing on a mound. *E. fulgida* [Colombia] bears bright-red flowers in July, and has dark-green leaves. It is a beautiful creeping plant covered with soft pubescence. It also makes a useful basket-plant.

**Epistephium Williamsii,** *Orchidaceæ.*—A beautiful stove Orchid from South America, closely allied to **Sobralia.** It requires fibrous loam and sand, and a good water-supply during the growing season and reaches a height of 15 to 18 inches. It bears bright-reddish-purple flowers in large terminal spikes in the summer. It is increased by division when new growth commences.

**Eranthemum,** *Acanthaceæ.*—Handsome stove or warm-greenhouse plants, some grown for their flowers and others for their foliage. They require a compost of two parts loam to one part each of peat and leaf-soil, with sufficient sand added to keep it porous. Avoid over-potting. Cuttings root readily any time from March to June in sandy peat in a close frame or bell-glass, with a bottom heat of 70° F. When rooted, pot-up singly in 3-inch pots and place again in bottom heat to encourage the plants to root and grow rapidly, potting them on as required. After flowering, the plants can be cut back, kept on the dry side for a time, and then potted-on for another season.

*Species.*—*E. Andersonii* [Trinidad] (white flowers, partly dotted with thick crimson lake, November); *E. cinnabarinum* [Burma] (reddish pink, winter, 24–36 in.). This is a very handsome plant. There is a pretty variety, *E. c. ocellatum*, having crimson flowers with a white eye; *E. laxiflorum* [Fiji] (purple, winter, 24–36 in.); *E. reticulatum* [Polynesia] (white flowers, spotted blood-red, leaves netted and veined yellow, 30–40 in.); *E. Wattii* (purple, winter, 15 in. A comparatively recent introduction from Tropical Africa).

**Eranthemum nervosum** (see **Dædalacanthus nervosus**).

**Eranthemum pulchellum** (see **Dædalacanthus nervosus**).

**Eranthis** (Winter Aconite), *Ranunculaceæ.*—Dwarf, early-flowering, tuberous-rooted perennials, with buttercup-like flowers of deep yellow, which open from January to March. They make quite a pretty show if potted-up and used for providing early bloom in the cold greenhouse.

*Culture.*—Pot-up in October, in well-drained, moist, sandy loam, and leaf-mould, putting four or five tubers in a 5- to 6-inch pot Water regularly while growing, but gradually dry off and rest after flowering. Propagate by means of division in October.

*Species.*—*E. cilicica* [Smyrna] (yellow with brownish tinge); *E. hyemalis* [W. Europe] (yellow, greenish tinge); and a handsome hybrid *E. Tubergenii* (cross between *E. cilicica* and *E. hyemalis*; it has larger flowers).

**Eria** (see Chapter on **Orchids**).

**Erica,** *Ericaceæ.*—This is an important genus of hardy and greenhouse evergreen flowering shrubs, often known as Heath or Heather, and comprising several hundred species and varieties. They are

**360**

invaluable in the greenhouse, many of them flowering at a time when other blooms are scarce.

*Culture.*—(Greenhouse species.) Propagate by means of cuttings made of the tender tops of young shoots in March or April, or in September (temperature 50° F.). The cuttings should be an inch or so in length, and should be inserted in well-drained pots or pans, filled with sandy peat, moistened and firmly pressed down. Pot-up into 2-inch pots as soon as rooted. Keep in a close frame for ten days, then gradually give more air, and when they have made a few inches of growth, " stop-back " to make bushy plants. Re-pot in September into 5-inch pots, and transfer to a light, airy position in the greenhouse with sufficient heat to exclude the frost. Re-pot into 6-inch pots if need be, in March, and summer on a hard bed of ashes in a cold frame in full sun. Mature plants should be potted-up in September in 6- to 7-inch pots, in a compost of sandy loam and peat, in equal proportions, and should be stood in the cold greenhouse. Give plenty of air and light, and water regularly, but in moderation, and never allow the soil to become dust-dry, or the fine, fibrous roots will be damaged. Syringe twice daily during growing season (April to October). Trim after flowering. The winter-flowering kinds should be turned out into the frames after hardening off in April; the summer-flowering species in July, when they have finished blooming. As much air as possible should be given, and the lights of the frame should only be kept on to protect from heavy and excessive rain.

In the warm house *E. bucciniflora* [S. Africa] (white and pink) flowers from December to March; *E. gracilis* [S. Africa] (reddish purple) flowers in November and December; *E. g. nivalis* (white) flowers from December to January; *E. g. vernalis* (reddish purple) flowers from December to March; and *E. hyemalis* [garden origin: a very popular market plant] (purplish pink) flowers from December to February. *E. Cavendishiana* [hybrid] (yellow); *E. Massonii* [S. Africa] (red, white, and green, summer); *E. melanthera* [S. Africa] (white, March, April); *E. Pageana* [S. Africa] (yellow, March, April); *E. persoluta* [S. Africa] (white, summer). There are a number of beautiful named varieties of this species); *E. propendens* [S. Africa] (purple); *E. regerminans* [S. Africa] (pink, spring); *E. ventricosa* (Porcelain Heath) [S. Africa] (rose); and *E. Wilmorei* [garden origin] (purple and white), both summer flowering.

The soil best adapted for these plants is that obtained from a locality where the wild heath grows luxuriantly, taking care that it is lime free and not dug too deep. The turf must not exceed 4 inches—rather less. The summer is the proper season to procure and store up a heap, which may safely be used after having a summer and winter's seasoning.

In selecting plants it is of the utmost importance to choose healthy, dwarf-growing robust specimens. (See also **Calluna.**)

Other species that are useful for growing in pans in the alpine house are : *E. carnea* [Central and S. Europe] (carmine crimson and white, Nov.–April, 6–12 in.); *E. cinerea* [W. Europe] (rosy purple, Sept., 9 in.); *E. c. alba* (white, Sept., 9 in.); *E. c. pallida* (very pale pink, Sept., 9 in.); *E. darleyensis* (rosy red, Nov.–April, 12–18 in.); *E.*

THE GREENHOUSE

*mammosa* (reddish purple, autumn, 24 in.) ; *E. mediterranea* [W. Europe] (lilac-rose, March–May, 36–48 in.) ; *E. m. alba* (white, March–May, 24 in.) ; *E. tetralix* [N. and W. Europe] (pink, May and June, 12 in.) ; *E. t. alba* (white) ; and *E. vagans* (Cornish Heath) [W. Europe] (rosy purple, July–Oct., 12–18 in.). When not required for the alpine house the pans should be plunged in sand or ashes to prevent the pans getting dry. They appreciate a little shade in the hottest part of the summer. Most of them can be raised from cuttings of half-ripened growth struck in the summer, or by division of the roots in the spring.

**Ericinella Mannii,** *Ericaceæ.*—Shrubs allied to **Erica**, and requiring the same cultural treatment. They are natives of the Cameroon Mountains, and bear dull-red flowers in small clusters at the top of branchlets in July. They grow to a height of 4–6 feet.

**Erigeron,** *Compositæ.*—All are perfectly hardy, and several species are attractive rock plants, but may be grown in pans for the alpine house. They require a good soil with adequate drainage. When not in flower the pans should be plunged in ashes in an open position. The plants are increased by seed sown as soon as ripe, or by division in early spring or autumn.

*Species.*—E. *aurantiacus* [Turkestan] (orange, July–Aug., 9 in.) ; *E. alpinus* [Northern regions] (bluish purple, summer, 4–8 in.) ; *E. glaucus* (Beach Daisy) [Pacific Coast] (purple, summer and autumn, 6–9 in.).

**Erinacea pungens** (Hedgehog Broom), *Leguminosæ.*—This native of South-West Europe likes limestone soil and a sunny well-drained position. It makes a charming plant in a pan for the alpine house, with its violet-blue, pea-shaped flowers in June and July, followed by a large, inflated calyx, which is also ornamental ; and even out of flower its compact, spiny appearance makes it decorative.

*Culture.*—It requires good loam with leaf-soil and sand and some mortar-rubble, and it should be potted-on only when pot-bound. The pans should be kept plunged in ashes in a frame when not wanted in the alpine house. *Propagation.*—It is increased by seed sown as soon as ripe, or from cuttings of half-ripened wood taken with a " heel ", placed in sand under a bell-glass.

**Erinus alpinus,** *Scrophulariaceæ.*—This lovely little alpine plant from the mountains of Western Europe, grows 2–3 inches high, and carries purple flowers from April to June. When once established on the rockery it will seed about, and these seedlings stand the winter best. It makes attractive plants in pans for the alpine house. Seedlings or cuttings may be pricked out in small pots and grown-on for making up pans the following spring, and, as seedlings are subject to variation, more even pans can be made up this way. When not required for the alpine house, the pans should be plunged in ashes and kept in a cold frame. Propagation is effected by seed, which should be sown as soon as ripe, or by cuttings inserted in sandy soil and kept in a close frame. There are a number of varieties : *albus* (white) *carmineus* (crimson), *hirsutus* (violet, red), the latter being more vigorous and hairy. There are other named varieties which should be increased by cuttings or division.

**Eriochilus** (see Chapter on **Orchids**).

**Eriocnema** (see **Bertolonia**).

**Eriopsis** (see Chapter on **Orchids**).

**Eriospermum,** *Liliaceæ.*—Pretty greenhouse bulbous plants from Tropical and Central Africa. They are easy of cultivation in a compost of sandy loam. They require a resting period during the winter. They are increased by offsets, which should be taken off when potting-up the old bulbs in the spring. Several flowering bulbs can be grown in a 5-inch pot.

*Species.*—*E. Bellendenii* (light blue, June–Aug., 12 in.) ; *E. Mackenii* (bright golden-yellow, July, 10–12 in.) ; *E. pubescens* (white, green, June, 12 in.).

**Eriostemon,** *Rutaceæ.*—An interesting genus of greenhouse evergreen shrubs from Australia, handsome in appearance and producing beautiful star-shaped blossoms, white, pale pink, and rose in colour, from April to June. They thrive best in a compost of two parts fibrous peat with one part of rich loam and silver sand mixed in equal proportions.

*Culture.*—Re-pot annually in March, and water well from April to September, decreasing the quantity afterwards, but never letting the roots become " dust-dry " (temperature 45° F. winter, 60° F. summer). Stand in the open after flowering from July to September and cut back straggly shoots in February before re-potting. Propagation is best carried out by means of cuttings of young wood in March (temperature 60° F.), or of semi-matured wood in August.

*Species.*—*E. buxifolius* (pink) ; *E. densiflorus* (white, probably a white form of the former) ; *E. myoporoides* (white, sometimes pink) ; *E. pulchellus* (white) ; *E. salicifolius* (soft pink) ; and *E. scaber* (white with pink tint).

**Eritrichium nanum,** *Boraginaceæ.*—An alpine gem which so far has defeated all efforts to cultivate it successfully, but it is always worth trying as a pan for the alpine house.

*Culture.*—Plant it in a mixture of coarse sand, grit, granite dust, and a little fibrous peat. Round the neck of the plant sink pieces of granite, or slate or stone, to assist in keeping moisture away from the collar of the plant, and to help keep the foliage dry a piece of glass may be fixed over the plant ; this keeps off any moisture overhead. It requires no moisture during the winter, but during the summer it needs moisture at its roots, but none on its leaves. Perhaps the best way would be to dip the pan to the brim.

*Propagation.*—It can be raised from seed, and these are more likely to succeed than are imported plants.

It makes tufts of very small woolly leaves, about 1½ inches high, from which rise in spring small Forget-me-not-like flowers of dazzling azure blue, with a yellow eye. A gem indeed, and worth any trouble to obtain success.

**Erlangea tomentosa,** *Compositæ.*—Half-hardy greenhouse plants from Tropical East Africa, rather like the **Ageratum,** which thrive in a mixture of leaf-mould and loam in equal proportions. They carry lilac flowers from February to May in the cool greenhouse (temperature 45° F. winter, 65° F. summer).

*Culture.*—Pot-up as required, using 6- to 8-inch pots. Stop back several times to encourage bushy growth. Feed occasionally with liquid manure. Cut down established plants after flowering, and winter in a frost-proof house. Re-pot when renewed growth commences. Propagation may be carried out by means of cuttings in a warm frame in June or July; or by seed sown in the spring, placing the pots in a warm house, pricking the seedlings out when large enough, and growing them on, as stated for cuttings.

**Erodium** (Heron's Bill), *Geraniaceæ.*—Dwarf-growing alpines, which, although hardy on the rock garden, make very effective plants when grown in pans, with their finely cut foliage and flowers. They should be grown in well-drained soil, and when not required for the alpine house the pans should be plunged in ashes in a cold frame in an open position.

*Propagation.*—They are increased by seed, which should be sown as soon as ripe, and the seed-pots plunged in ashes in a cold frame, pricking out the seedlings singly into small pots, and either potting them on or putting them in pans, one, two, or three plants in a pan, according to size. Cuttings can also be taken in July and put in sand in a frame, which should be kept closed. The roots can also be divided in the early spring or early autumn.

*Species.*—*E. amanum* [Syria] (pure white flowers and hoary foliage, May–July, 6 in.); *E. chrysanthum* [Greece] (sulphur-yellow, male and female flowers being borne on separate plants, June and July, 4–6 in.); *E. chamædryoides* [Balearic Islands] (white, veined rose, May–June, 2–3 in.); *E. corsicum* [Corsica] (rosy pink, veined deeper colour, May–July, 2–5 in.); *E. macradenum* [Pyrenees] (violet-pink, with deep-purple markings, June–July, 4 in.); *E. petræum* [W. Mediterranean region] (purple, violet, or rose, June, 5 in.).

**Erpetion reniforme** (see **Viola hederacea).**

**Erysimum** (Hedge Mustard), *Cruciferæ.*—Although perfectly hardy, some of the dwarf perennial kinds are very suitable for pans in the alpine house. They only require good, ordinary, well-drained soil, and are readily increased by seed, cuttings, or by division.

*Species.*—*E. alpinum* [Scandinavia] (sulphur-yellow, sweet-scented flowers, April and May, 6 in.); *E. linifolium* [Spain] (lilac, summer, 6–10 in.); *E. pumilum* [S. Europe] (pale sulphur, fragrant flowers, summer, 2–3 in.).

**Erythrina Crista-galli,** *Leguminosæ.*—This plant, which grows some 4 or 5 feet in height, bears racemes of beautiful, dark red, pea-shaped flowers in summer and is an excellent subject for decorating the cool greenhouse.

*Culture.*—In April the plants, which should have been almost dried off for the winter, should be given a good soaking, when growth will soon commence. Re-pot, using a compost of half loam, and half leaf-mould and well rotted manure, with a little sand added. Water regularly while growing and feed occasionally with liquid manure. Place the plants out-of-doors from June to September in a sheltered sunny position.

*Propagation.*—Propagation may be carried out by means of seed, or by

364

taking cuttings of young shoots springing from the large perennial stem when about 3 inches in length. Cut them away from their base and set them in light sandy soil in a propagating case.

**Erythronium,** *Liliaceæ.*—The Dog's Tooth Violet or Adder's Tongue, as it is sometimes called, is a pretty little bulbous plant usually with beautifully spotted leaves, and delicate pendulous, cyclamen-like blooms on stems from 6 to 12 inches high. The flowers, borne from March to May, are purplish rose, yellow, cream, or white. It does well in any light soil and is useful as an edging to borders, or for early bloom in the cold greenhouse, where it commences to flower in February.

*Pot Culture.*—Plant 4–6 inches deep in August in 5- to 6-inch pots, using a compost of loam, peat, and leaf-mould, and keep in a cold frame during the winter, giving but little water until growth commences. Then increase the supply and take into the cold greenhouse. Stand in partial shade. Propagate by means of seed in a frame in August. Thin-out, but do not plant the seedlings out until the third September after sowing. The plants are also increased by offsets.

*Species.*—*E. citrinum* [S. Oregon] (yellow); *E. dens-canis* [Europe] (rose, rose-purple, or lilac, foliage beautifully mottled); *E. grandi-florum* [N.W. America] (bright yellow); *E. Hartwegii* [N.W. America] (creamy white); *E. revolutum* [N.W. America] (pink). Most of these species have beautiful named varieties.

**Escallonia,** *Saxifragaceæ.*—Very decorative evergreen shrubs, nearly all of which may be grown outside, either against a wall or in the open in most parts of the country. They are very useful for the cool greenhouse, either planted out or growing in pots, as they flower most of the summer and autumn. They succeed in any good potting soil and should not be disturbed at the roots more often than is necessary. They are readily propagated by cuttings of half-ripened wood inserted in sandy loam and placed under a bell-glass. Pruning should be done in the early spring by cutting back some of the leading growth to keep the bushes compact.

*Species and hybrids.*—*E. Ingramii* [garden hybrid] (rose-pink, summer); *E. Iveyi* [garden hybrid] (white, summer, 4 ft.); *E. langley-ensis* [garden hybrid] (rose tinted, summer, 4–5 ft.); *E. macrantha* [Chile] (crimson-red flowers, glossy leaves, June–July, 4–5 ft.); *E. montevidensis* [S. America] (large white flowers, late summer and autumn, 4–6 ft.); *E. organensis* [Organ Mountains] (beautiful rose-coloured flowers, autumn, 4–5 ft.; very beautiful, but more tender than most species.

**Eucalyptus** (Gum Tree), *Myrtaceæ.*—Half-hardy evergreen greenhouse trees, natives of Australia and Tasmania, which, with one or two exceptions—namely, *E. Gunnii* (*E. whittinghamensis*) [Australia and Tasmania], and *E. urnigera* [Tasmania]—can be grown outside only in mild localities. They are grown chiefly as foliage plants, their glaucous, silvery foliage serving as a foil to the brilliant hues of the brightest flowers or other plants. Their own flowers are of no account. They thrive in the cool greenhouse in a compost of two parts of fibrous loam to one part of leaf-mould and charcoal.

*Culture.*—Pot-up in March, using 6- to 8-inch pots and stand indoors

**365**

(temperature 50° F. winter, 60° F. summer). Water well in summer and plant outdoors in a sunny position from June to September.

*Propagation.*—To propagate, sow seed in gentle heat (60° F.) in early spring, or strike cuttings of mature shoots 3 inches in length under glass in June.

*Species* —*E. coccifera* [Tasmania] (purple, Oct.–Nov., 4 ft.) ; *E. ficifolia* (Crimson-flowered Eucalyptus) [Australia] ; *E. globulus* (the Blue Gum) [Australia] (white, July–Aug., 4 ft.) ; *E. maculata* var. *citriodora* (the Lemon-scented gum) [Australia] (white, Sept.–Oct. 3 ft.). All these species are well known.

**Eucharis** (Amazon Lily), *Amaryllidaceæ.*—Warm-greenhouse bulbous plants of great beauty and delightful fragrance, blooming in winter and spring, and, with a little management, they can be had at other times,

*Culture.*—The soil should consist of two parts rich loam, one part of leaf-soil and dry cow-manure, a sprinkling of bonemeal, with some charcoal added, to keep it open. Except for a short time during the autumn, when the bulbs should be rested, abundance of water should be given. For flowering at other times the bulbs should be kept longer on the drier side, provided they are strong and healthy, but they should never be kept so dry as to lose their foliage entirely, as this weakens the bulbs. When growing, the plants should be syringed freely, as this helps to keep down mealy bug and thrip, the plants being subject to both these. They should be grown in fairly large pots, to allow freedom to the roots, say three bulbs to a 6-inch pot. Frequent potting should be avoided, as they are impatient of root disturbance. They are increased by division in the spring, but when they are first divided do not give much water, until growth starts, when liquid may be given.

*Species.*—*E. grandiflora* (*E. amazonica*) [New Granada] (white, 18–24 in., will bloom two or three times during the year) ; *E. Sanderi* [New Granada] (white and yellow, March, 18 in. ; similar to *E. grandiflora*, and equally beautiful) ; *E. s.* var. *multiflora* is very free flowering but the flowers are smaller than the type.

**Eucomis punctata** (Pineapple Flower and King's Flower), *Liliaceæ.*—An ornamental half-hardy bulb from South Africa, with curious spikes of flowers. It grows about 24 inches high, and flowers in the open during the summer. In the cold greenhouse, where it grows to advantage, it may be had in flower a little earlier.

*Greenhouse Culture.*—Pot-up in March in 5-inch pots, using a compost of two parts of fibrous loam to one part of sand and a little well-rotted manure. Water liberally in spring and summer, but decrease the supply in autumn, and keep quite dry, with the pots lying on their sides under the staging in winter. Re-pot triennially, and propagate by means of offsets in March.

**Eucrosia bicolor,** *Amaryllidaceæ.*—An interesting greenhouse bulbous plant from Peru. It is coloured red and rose and striped with green. It likes a strong loam and a warm temperature, and should be rested in winter. It is increased by offsets placed in rich sandy loam and grown in a warm temperature (winter temperature, 35–40° F.).

**Eucryphia glutinosa (Eucryphia pinnatifolia),** *Eucryphiaceæ.*—A hardy, evergreen shrub of rather slow growth, from Chile. It eventually reaches a height of up to 20 feet. It produces beautiful white flowers in late summer, and may be grown out of doors or in the cold greenhouse. Outdoors it requires a sunny, sheltered position, and well-drained, non-limey, light, loamy or peaty soil.

*Culture.*—If grown as a pot plant in the greenhouse, it should be given a compost of two-thirds fibrous loam, and one-third leaf-mould, together with a sprinkling of sand and, if possible, a little peat.

*Propagation.*—To propagate, sow seed when ripe, or increase by means of layering.

Another species, but not so hardy, is *E. cordifolia* [Chile] (white, July–Aug., 25 ft.). *E. nymansensis* is a beautiful hybrid between the two species above (July–Aug.).

**Eugenia,** *Myrtaceæ.*—Evergreen shrubs, some of which are quite decorative for the greenhouse. They bear white or creamy flowers, and in some instances the many stamens are yellowish. They can be grown in pots, or may be planted out. They succeed in loam, three parts, to one part of peat, with some sand. Pot-on when necessary. Cuttings of firm shoots root readily if given a little bottom heat. The " Cloves " of commerce belongs to this genus, being the flower-buds of *Eugenia aromatica.* The fruits of most species which are beautifully coloured in shades of pink, rose, red, violet and white are edible, and are used for jelly-making and confectionery.

*E. Jambos* (Rose Apple) [E. Indies] has greenish-white flowers from February to July, and reaches a height of from 24 to 48 inches. It is grown for its handsome foliage and showy flowers. *E. myriophylla* [Brazil] is a foliage plant with fine, elegant leaves, growing from 12 to 24 inches high. *E. myrtifolia* (Australian Brush Cherry) [Australia] has white flowers in summer. The young growths are tinged with red, giving the plant a very attractive appearance.

**Eulalia** (see **Miscanthus**).

**Eulophia** (see Chapter on **Orchids**).

**Eulophiella** (see Chapter on **Orchids**).

**Eupatorium** (Hemp Agrimony), *Compositæ.*—Most of the species belonging to this genus are evergreen shrubs suitable only for culture in the greenhouse.

*Culture.*—(Shrubs)—Propagate by means of cuttings in heat in spring. Keep the cuttings warm and near the glass, harden off, and plant outdoors in the sun in June. Stop-back occasionally until July, and water well in summer. Cut old plants well back after flowering. Pot-up in September, using 6- to 8-inch pots and a compost of rich loam with some peat in it, and place in a cool house (temperature 45° F. winter, 65° F. summer). In the warm house, *E. Purpusii* may be had in bloom during April and May.

*Species.*—*E. atrorubens* [Mexico] (reddish purple, Jan.–Feb., 12–30 in.); *E. ianthinum* [Mexico] (lilac, Jan.–Feb., 15 in.); *E. micranthum* (*E. Weinmannianum*) [Mexico] (white, Sept., 24–48 in.); *E. Purpusii* (*E. petiolare*) [Lower California] (white, 30–40 in.); *E. riparium* [Mexico] (white, Feb., 24 in.); and *E. vernale* [Mexico] (white, Jan.-Feb., 24–36 in.).

**Euphorbia** (Spurge), *Euphorbiaceæ.*—A large genus, including annuals, biennials, and perennials. The latter group includes a number of succulent plants for the cool or warm greenhouse. *E. pulcherrima,* commonly known as Poinsettia, may be had in flower in winter when given warm house treatment. (See **Poinsettia.**)

Another winter-flowering species is *E. fulgens* (*E. jacquiniæflora*), Scarlet Plume [Mexico]. It succeeds in a warm house in pots, or it may be planted out and trained against a wall. Cuttings should be taken in June, when the old plants break into growth. Keep in a warm frame till rooted, and then continue growing with heat; afterwards disturb the roots as little as possible. Several plants may be grown in one pot. When in flower they should be grown cooler. After flowering, the plants should be kept dry for a few months, starting them into growth in May and June. They are excellent for cutting, the sprays remaining fresh for a long time.

*Culture.*—Pot-up in spring in well-crocked pots, according to the size of the plant, containing a compost of two parts of sandy loam to one part of crushed brick, oyster-shell, and coarse sand. Water well and regularly while growing, but keep only just moist when resting. Grow up near the glass.

*Propagation.*—Cuttings may be rooted in slight bottom heat after callus has been allowed to form at the base.

*Species.*—*E. bupleurifolia* [S. Africa] (thick stem, leaf cushions doubly spiral, needs moist position in summer, dry in winter; never in full sun, 4–5 in.); *E. Caput-Medusæ* [S. Africa] (short stem, serpentine branches, requires sun in summer, and warmth in winter, 6–8 in.); *E. fulgens* (Scarlet Plume) (a Mexican species bearing small scarlet flowers on slender arching stems, 2–3 feet high. The variety *E. f.* var. *pallida* bears pale orange flowers); *E. heptogona* [S. Africa]; *E. meloformis* [S. Africa]; *E. obesa* [S. Africa] (a very curious plant and diœcious); *E. pulcherrima* (Poinsettia) [Mexico] (the most popular species for greenhouse decoration, where it is much prized for its large scarlet bracts. There are varietal forms with pink and white bracts); *E. splendens* [Bourbon] (one of the most beautiful plants for the greenhouse, flowering most of the year, chiefly in the spring. A sturdy branching habit, with strong prickles); and *E. Susannæ* [S. Africa]. They are all succulent plants of variable appearance, both interesting and curious, many of them mimicking other plants of an entirely different family. There are many large succulent species in South Africa ranging in size from a few inches up to 30 feet high. The juice is very poisonous and is used in medicine under the name of *Gum Euphorbia.*

**Eurya japonica,** *Ternstrœmiaceæ.*—A half-hardy, evergreen plant, with handsome foliage, which thrives in the cool greenhouse, or in warm, sunny, sheltered situations outdoors. The flowers are similar to those of the **Camellia,** but small and insignificant.

*Culture.*—It requires a soil of sandy peat and loam. Pot-up in March, and water well until after flowering, then decrease the quantity. Propagation is carried out by means of cuttings of half-matured wood struck in heat in summer. *E. latifolia variegata* has cream-white and green foliage, and is a very attractive greenhouse foliage plant.

Cephalotus follicularis

Echium plantagineum

Chimonanthus præcox

Eranthis cilicica

Eranthis Tubergenii

**Euryale ferox,** *Nymphæaceæ.*—An attractive aquatic plant from China. It is a miniature *Victoria regia*, but since the introduction of the latter the Euryale has not attracted so much attention. It has the advantage of being more suitable for smaller tanks. Treated as an annual, the seeds, which should have been stored in cold water, should be sown and the pots stood a few inches under warm water. It requires the same cultural treatment as greenhouse Nymphæas. The flowers, which open by day, are prickly outside, and are reddish and purple, while the leaves, which are from 12 to 36 inches across and circular in form, are purple and spiny-ribbed beneath, the upper surface being green and uneven.

**Eustegia hastata,** *Asclepiadaceæ.*—A greenhouse, evergreen trailer from South Africa, producing white flowers in the summer. It is allied to **Ceropegia,** and requires the same treatment. It is increased by cuttings struck in sandy soil.

**Eustoma Russellianum (Lisianthus Russellianus),** *Gentianaceæ.*—A very handsome Texan greenhouse plant, with lavender-purple flowers during July and August. Although strictly a perennial, it is best treated as a biennial. The seed should be sown in May, and when the seedlings are large enough they should be pricked out singly into small pots and placed in a light, airy position in a temperature of not less than 45° F. Great care should be given to the watering, keeping the seedlings, if anything, on the dry side. It is important that the seedlings should be in a rosette stage during the winter. In the early spring the seedlings can be potted-on, one in a 5-inch pot, or two in a 6-inch pot, or three in an 8-inch pot. Use a compost of three parts loam, one part peat or leaf-soil, and one part sand. The mistake is often made of sowing the seeds too early, when the seedlings attempt to bloom the same summer, and are a failure.

**Eutaxia,** *Leguminosæ.*—Greenhouse evergreen shrubs from Australia, requiring the treatment of **Chorizema.**

*Species.—E. empetrifolia* (yellow, May, 18–24 in.) ; *E. myrtifolia* (yellow and dark orange, July–Aug., 18–30 in.).

**Eutoca sericea** (see **Phacelia sericea**).

**Evening Primrose** (see **Œnothera**).

**Evening Star** (see **Cooperia**).

**Exacum,** *Gentianaceæ.*—A group of pretty, erect, greenhouse plants, those generally grown being treated as either annuals or biennials. Seedlings must be sown in heat, and as they are quickly subject to damp, good drainage and careful watering are essential. They thrive best in a compost of fibrous loam and peat in equal proportions, with a good sprinkling of sand. They flower in the summer and autumn. If specimens in 5-inch pots are required, seed should be sown in March ; but if larger specimens are required, sow in August of the preceding year. The plants should be kept in a cool but not draughty greenhouse, and shaded from fierce sunlight. They can also be increased from cuttings placed in sandy soil and given bottom heat.

*Species.—E. affine* [Socotra] has purple and violet, scented flowers, and grows 12–15 inches high. *E. macranthum* [Ceylon] has larger flowers than the former species, dark purplish-blue with golden anthers,

A A

and they are borne during the summer and autumn. It is the best of the genus and grows 18–30 inches high.

**Exocorda** (Pearl Bush), *Rosaceæ*.—Ornamental, hardy shrubs which can be used for growing in pots for the cool house. With their racemes of white flowers, they are very valuable during the early spring. They should be potted up in the autumn in good, loamy soil with good drainage in the pots. These should be large enough to allow sufficient root room to make re-potting unnecessary for at least two or three years, and they should be plunged outside in ashes until the early spring, when they may be brought inside. If forced rather hard they should be rested one season, like other forced shrubs. They are propagated by seed or by soft wooded cuttings from forced plants. Taken in the summer from the open, they root slowly. They can also be increased by means of layering.

*E. Giraldii* [W. China] is a species of recent introduction producing large white flowers in May and June. *E. Korolkowii* (*E. Albertii*) [Turkestan] is one of the earliest to flower, and the white flowers can be obtained in February or March without very much heat. It grows 3–5 feet high. *E. macrantha* is a hybrid of *Korolkowii* × *racemosa*. It is a very vigorous, upright bush which flowers in March, and grows 4–6 feet high. *E. racemosa* (*E. grandiflora*) [China] bears pure white flowers 2 inches across in March and April. This species is one of the showiest shrubs blooming outside in May.

**Fabiana** (False Heath), *Solanaceæ*.—These are handsome, half-hardy, evergreen, summer-flowering shrubs, somewhat resembling the Heath in bloom and habit. They are suitable for outdoor culture in sandy loam with some peat in it, in warm, sheltered situations, or in the greenhouse. In exposed situations and the northern counties they should be grown only in the cool greenhouse. The white, tubular blossoms are borne in May and June.

*Pot Culture.*—After flowering, cut back weak and straggling stems, and pot-up, using a compost of two parts of sandy loam and one part of leaf-mould. Summer in the open on a bed of hard ashes. Return to the house in September. Water liberally in spring and summer.

*Propagation.*—Propagate in July or August by means of cuttings of young shoots in sandy soil in a warm frame, or sow seed in heat in March.

*Species.*—*F. imbricata* [Chile] white (3–6 ft.) ; *F. violacea* [S. Chile] has violet-coloured flowers of various shades, but is probably a geographical form of *F. imbricata* and is much hardier than the type.

**Fadyenia Fadyenii** (**Fadyenia prolifera**), *Polypodiaceæ*.—An interesting little Jamaican Fern, very suitable for growing in a Wardian case. It will succeed in ordinary soil suitable for ferns, in the warm greenhouse. The sterile fronds root at the apex.

**Fairy Lily** (see **Zephyranthes**).

**Fairy Primrose** (see **Primula malacoides**).

**Falkia repens**, *Convolvulaceæ*.—A pretty little creeping plant from South Africa. Suitable for the cool greenhouse, it may be grown either in a pan or treated as a basket plant. It thrives in a compost of loam, peat, and sand. It is increased by seed sown and placed in a warm greenhouse, by cuttings inserted under a bell-glass (temperature 58–60° F. in April), or by division in the spring. It bears convolvulus-shaped flowers in May and June, coloured rosy pink and white. Leaves are grey and heart-shaped.

**False Heath** (see **Fabiana**).

**False Solomon's Seal** (see **Smilacina**).

**False Spikenard** (see **Smilacina racemosa**).

**Fan Palms** are all palms with fan-shaped leaves (see **Chamærops, Latania, Livistona, Trachycarpus, Washingtonia**).

**Farfugium** (see **Ligularia** and **Senecio**).

**Fatsia japonica** (syn. **Aralia japonica**) [Japanese Aralia], *Araliaceæ.*— An evergreen shrub, almost hardy, from China and Japan. It thrives in sheltered town gardens and in the cool greenhouse. Only in good loam, in warm, sheltered positions will it grow out-of-doors. This plant will reach a height of about 12 feet, and bear clusters of creamy-white flowers in October and November.

*F. Moseri* is a dwarf, compact variety. *F. papyrifera* (Rice-paper Tree) [Formosa] is a handsome, half-hardy shrub, useful for the cool greenhouse and the sub-tropical garden, growing from 4 to 6 feet high.

*Culture.*—Plant in March or April, or pot-up in March, using a compost of two parts of loam to one part of leaf-mould and sand, and stand in the greenhouse (temperature 50° F. winter, 60° F. summer). Water well, syringe daily in spring and summer, and shade from the sun. Cut away dead flower spikes in January.

*Propagation.*—To propagate, sow seed when ripe, in heat (70° F.), insert 2-inch pieces of stem in sandy soil in a propagator, in spring or September, or increase by " ringing ".

**Feathered Hyacinth** (see **Muscari comosum** var. *monstrosum*).

**Feijoa Sellowiana,** *Myrtaceæ.*—An evergreen shrub from Brazil and Uruguay. It has leathery leaves, and bears white flowers with conspicuous red stamens. Although it can be grown in some places outside against a wall, in others it requires the protection of a greenhouse, where, either planted out or grown in a pot, it makes an attractive plant. It requires a mixture of loam, peat, and sand. It is increased by layers, or by cuttings of half-ripened wood struck in sand with a little heat, or by seed. The fruits are edible and aromatic.

**Felicia,** *Compositæ.*—Herbs, or sub-shrubs, chiefly from South Africa. The two annuals can be sown out in the open ground, but the evergreen one requires the protection of a cool greenhouse. The principal species is *F. amelloides*, an old favourite greenhouse plant often known as **Agathæa cœlestis.** It succeeds under the same conditions as **Cineraria.** It is easily raised from cuttings placed under a hand-light, and if batches are raised at different periods a display of flowers may be obtained for a large part of the year. The cuttings should be potted-on, and useful plants can be grown in 5-inch pots. When the old plants have finished they should be cut back into shape, placed in a little warmer temperature, and will soon give a further display. They succeed in an ordinary compost of loam, leaf-soil, and sand.

*Species.*—*F. amelloides* [*Agathæa cœlestis*] (Blue Daisy or Blue

Marguerite) is a native of South Africa, and is an attractive half-hardy plant, some 12–18 inches in height, bearing blue, daisy-like flowers, from February to October. It is an elegant pot plant and useful for bedding in protected places. *F. echinata* [S. Africa] has lilac flowers in spring, and grows 12–20 inches high. *F. petiolaris* [S. Africa] has rose-coloured flowers, becoming bluish in summer. It is prostrate, but is very useful for a hanging basket.

**Ferns** (see **Adiantum,** etc., also Chapter on **Greenhouse Ferns**).

**Fern Balls** (see **Davallia bullata**),

**Fern Palm** (see **Cycas circinalis**).

**Ferocactus,** *Cactaceæ.*—A group of spiny, globular to cylindric cacti allied to Echinocactus and requiring the same cultural treatment. *F. acanthodes* (*Echinocactus Lecontei*) (bell-shaped, orange to yellow) [California] ; *F. Wistizenii* (*Echinocactus Wistizenii*) (yellow) [W. Texas and Mexico].

**Ferraria** (Black Iris), *Iridaceæ.*—Hardy and half-hardy South African bulbous plants which grow about 8 inches high and flower from April to July. They thrive in sunny, well-drained borders with rich, sandy loam. The half hardy species are suitable for the cool greenhouse.

*Culture* (Half-hardy Species).—Plant the bulbs in pots in a cool greenhouse in November, using a mixture of sandy loam and peat for a compost. Water sparingly until growth commences, and then more regularly until June. No water is required after flowering.

*Propagation.*—Propagate by means of offsets.

*Species.*—*F. atrata* (bright dark purple, fringed with brownish green) ; *F. uncinata* (greenish brown) ; *F. undulata* (greenish brown, March and April).

**Ficus Carica** [Common Fig.] (see Chapter on **Fruit**).

**Ficus elastica** (India-rubber Plant), *Moraceæ.*—Greenhouse or room plants from Tropical Asia, that thrive in the shade in a compost of two parts of sandy loam to one part of peat (temperature 50° F. winter, 65° F. summer). One of their chief drawbacks is that they lose the leaves on the lower part of their stems. These leggy plants should be " ringed " ; the tops will then provide nice young plants, and the lower stems if cut back will soon " break " and provide new branches. *F. elastica* and *F. e. variegata* are those usually grown. *F. Parcellii* is a fine species from Polynesia that enjoys the moist growing conditions of a warm greenhouse or stove. It has very handsome white and green variegated foliage and attractive striped fruits. Another species, from China and Japan, *F. pumila* (*F. repens*) (Creeping Fig) is a creeping plant used for covering rock-work and dark walls in the greenhouse ; this latter plant, however, is not very interesting. It changes from a creeping habit to a tree-like habit when fruiting. The variety *minima* has smaller leaves, and is useful for hanging-baskets.

*Culture.*—Pot-up in March, using pots as small as possible in proportion to the size of the plant (6- to 8-inch). Sponge the leaves when dusty, and water well and syringe overhead daily in fine weather, in spring and summer, but not too freely in autumn and winter.

*Propagation.*—Propagation is carried out by means of cuttings in a propagating case in March, or by " ringing " in the case of leggy plants

**Fig (Ficus Carica)** (see Chapter on **Fruit**).

**Fig Marigold** (see **Mesembryanthemum**).

**Filipendula** (Meadow-Sweet), *Rosaceæ*.—A handsome herbaceous plant with white, pink, purple, or carmine flowers, hardy and very valuable for growing in the moist border, along the edge of ponds, or in the bog garden. It is sometimes included under **Spiræa,** from which it differs in having one-seeded carpels which are indehiscent, while the carpels of the Spiræa have several seeds and dehisce. There are also other botanical differences.

*Culture.*—Filipendulas can be grown in 6- or 8-inch pots, and are very decorative during the summer for the cool greenhouse. They should be potted-up in the autumn, giving them a rich compost of fibrous loam, dry cow-manure, and some sand. The pots can be either plunged in ashes outside or stood in a cold frame. Bring them into the house when the flowering shoots begin to show colour, although they can be forced. Much better-coloured inflorescences are obtained if the plants are grown cool. Forced plants should be grown one year outside and allowed to rest from flowering. At no time should the plants be allowed to get dry. They should be given plenty of water when growing, and benefit from being stood in a saucer of water when in flower.

*Propagation.*—They are propagated by division in the autumn or spring, or by seed sown in the autumn, in pans or boxes stood in the cool greenhouse.

*Species.*—*F. hexapetala* (Meadow-sweet Dropwort) [Europe, etc.] (a British plant, creamy white, June–July, 12–30 in.); the var. *floro-pleno* has double flowers. *F. palmata* (*F. digitata*) [Siberia, etc.] (pale pink, changing to white, July, 18–30 in.); *F. purpurea* [Japan] (carmine or deep pink, June–Aug., 18–36 in.); this species is often grown under the name of **Spiræa palmata** and **Filipendula palmata,** this is undoubtedly the finest species of the genus, and a very charming pot plant. There are varieties of it and probably hybrids. *F. rubra* [*Spiræa lobata*] (Queen of the Prairie) [N. America], (pink, June–July, 24–60 in.).

**Fire Nettle** (see **Coleus**).

**Fish Tail Palm** (see **Caryota**).

**Fittonia,** *Acanthaceæ*.—Ornamental foliage creeping perennials, valued for the brilliant variegation made by red or white venation in their leaves. The soil should be rich, light, and peaty. When growing, they require heat and moist atmosphere, with plenty of water, at the same time good drainage and shade from the bright sun are essential. Fittonia may be grown in conjunction with other foliage plants, and will help to cover up bare places on beds or borders; even under the stages of the stove-houses or other shady places their beautiful foliage always attracts attention. They can also be used for covering the tubs or large pot of palms or other plants. The best time for taking cuttings is the spring, and this should be done annually, as after a year the plants have rather a straggling appearance. The cuttings should be placed in sand with bottom heat. When rooted, put into small pots, and later put several of them into the pans in which they are intended to be grown, and raise the compost in the pan : this gives the plant a mound-like effect. They may also be planted out in their permanent

**373**

place. The plants should be pinched back once or twice to encourage side-growths. When fully grown they benefit from an occasional watering of soot-water; this also tends to bring out the brilliance of the markings.

*Species.*—*F. argyroneura* [Peru] (leaves vivid green with white veins, 3–5 in.); *F. gigantea* [Peru] (shining green leaves with carmine red veins, stems reddish violet, 12–15 in.); *F. Verschaffeltii* [Peru] (leaves dull green, often yellowish, carmine veins, 8–12 in.); *F. V.* var. *Daveana* (light-centred foliage with a dark-green border); *F. V.* var. *Pearcei* (bright-green leaves with bright carmine under-surface).

**Flame Nasturtium** (see **Tropæolum speciosum**).

**Flamingo Flower** (see **Anthurium Scherzerianum**).

**Flax** (see **Linum**).

**Flax Lily** (see **Dianella**).

**Floral Fire Cracker** (see **Brevoortia Ida-Maia**).

**Florida Moss** (see **Tillandsia usneoides**).

**Floss Flower** (see **Ageratum**).

**Flowering Currant** (see **Ribes**).

**Flowering Moss** (see **Pyxidanthera barbulata**).

**Foam Flower** (see **Tiarella cordifolia**).

**Forget-Me-Not** (see **Myosotis**).

**Forsythia** (Golden Bell Tree), *Oleaceæ.*—Free-flowering, hardy, deciduous shrubs, carrying golden-yellow, bell-like flowers in March and April. They are chiefly native to China and Japan, and grow from 6 to 10 feet in height, thriving in a sunny position. *F. suspensa* var. *Sieboldii* has graceful, arching stems which carry the flowers, and look well when grown against a wall or over pergolas and arbours; and *F. spectabilis*, a variety of *F. intermedia*, is useful for decoration in the cold greenhouse.

*Culture.*—If to be grown in the greenhouse, pot-up from October to December, using an 8- to 10-inch pot and a compost of two parts of loam to one part of leaf-mould and sand. Sink the pot in ashes outdoors in a sunny spot from May to December, and water sparingly; then take into the cold greenhouse.

*Species and Varieties.*—*F. intermedia* (a hybrid of *F. suspensa* × *F. viridissima*; it has several beautiful varieties) vars. *densiflora, primulina* and *spectabilis*; *F. ovata*; *F. suspensa* var. *Fortunei*; and *F. viridissima*.

**Fragaria indica** (see **Duchesnea indica**).

**Francoa ramosa** (Bridal Wreath), *Saxifragaceæ.*—A graceful plant with long, slender spikes of small white or rosy-red flowers in late summer. A cool greenhouse (temperature 45° F. winter, 60° F. summer) suits it well.

*Culture.*—Sow seed in March with slight bottom heat (55° F.), or propagate by means of cuttings under glass in June. Pot-up from February to March, using 6- to 8-inch pots and a compost of equal parts of sandy loam and leaf-mould. Keep the seedlings in a cool, airy frame during the summer, and then transfer them to the cool greenhouse in autumn. Water well in spring and summer, but very sparingly in winter. Discard the old plants, and raise a fresh batch annually, as these provide the best bloom.

*Other Species.*—*F. appendiculata* and *F. sonchifolia,* with pink flowers spotted with red. They are natives of Chile, and succeed under the same conditions.

**Freesia,** *Iridaceæ.*—A genus of almost hardy cormous plants from South Africa which form pretty plants for the warm, sunny border or greenhouse. The tubular blooms exhale a delicious fragrance, and are useful and beautiful as cut flowers. In addition to the well-known white type, *F. refracta alba,* there are now many lovely coloured varieties which are hybrids between *F. refracta* × *F. Armstrongii.* They carry their flowers on stems from 15 to 20 inches tall. In the warm greenhouse (temperature 55–70° F. winter, 60–75° F. summer) they may be had in flower in winter and early spring. *F. Armstrongii* [S. Africa] (magenta to pink), 24 to 30 inches.

*Culture.*—Indoors. Pot-up in succession from July to December, 1 inch deep and 2 inches apart, in a compost of equal parts of sandy loam, leaf-mould, and rotten manure. Six corms, which should all be of equal size, may be placed in a 6-inch pot. Place the pots, which must be well drained, under a south wall, or in a frame in the case of coloured varieties, until the bulbs begin to grow (about six weeks). Little water is required until growth starts. Then, if standing in the open, transfer to a cold frame, increase the water supply, and in a fortnight place on a shelf near the glass (temperature 50–60° F.). Thin stakes are necessary to support the fragile shoots and leaves, and must be inserted as soon as 3 inches of growth has been made. They require bi-weekly doses of liquid manure as soon as the buds form. The corms will bloom from January to April. After flowering gradually withhold the water supply and keep dry in a sunny frame from May to July to ripen the bulbs. Shake clear of soil and pot-up each year.

*Propagation.*—They can be increased easily from seed. Soak the seed for twenty-four hours before sowing. Sow the seed when ripe, in August or September, in 5-inch pots, in well-sieved sandy loam and leaf-mould, and place in a cool frame exposed to the sun's rays. Thin-out to leave five or six plants in each pot. Freesias do not like transplanting. They may also be propagated by means of offsets in July or August. This is the method for the named varieties.

*Named Varieties.*—*Purity* (white); *Excelsior* (cream); *La France* (cream and mauve); *Lemon King* (yellow); *Orange King* (orange-yellow); *Sunset* (brownish yellow); *La Charmante* (rose-apricot); *Rose Beauty* (rose); *Wistaria* (mauve).

**Fremontia californica,** *Sterculiaceæ.*—A beautiful, free-flowering, Californian shrub, 6–10 feet high, with bright-yellow flowers. Although it can be grown outside in some of the more favoured parts of the country, it makes a charming pot plant for the cool greenhouse. In May, after the flowers are over, the plants should be stood outside and the pots plunged in ashes until the autumn. It thrives in sandy loam with good drainage, for it dislikes an excess of moisture, particularly in the winter. It is propagated by seed or by cuttings of young growth placed under a bell-glass in summer. *F. mexicana* (Mexico) is a plant very similar to the above, said to be more tender, and to flower at an earlier stage. It may be a geographical form.

**Fringed Calla** (see **Arisæma fimbriatum**).

**Fringed Lily** (see **Thysanotus**).

**Fringed Tree** (see **Chionanthus virginica**).

**Fringed Violet** (see **Thysanotus**).

**Fritillaria** (Fritillary), *Liliaceæ.*—A genus of hardy, bulbous plants which succeed in any garden soil, although a dry, deep, rich (*F. Meleagris* moist), sandy loam gives the most satisfactory results. Some species are excellent for pot culture in the cold greenhouse, or alpine house.

*Pot Culture.*—Plant in the autumn, in 4- to 5-inch pots, in a mixture of loam, peat, leaf-mould, rotten manure, and sand, and give occasional doses of liquid manure when the buds form. Propagate by means of bulbous offsets in October; or by seed sown as soon as ripe, and the pots plunged in a cold frame.

*Species.*—*F. armena* [Armenia] (purple, April, 8–10 in.); *F. aurea* [S.W. Asia] (golden yellow, March, 8 in.); *F. citrina* [Asia Minor] (yellowish green, April–May, 8–12 in.); *F. lutea* [S.W. Asia] (yellow, sometimes suffused with purple, March–April, 8–10 in.); *F. Meleagris* (Snake's Head Fritillaria) (purple or white, March–May, 10 in.); *F. pudica* [N.W. America] (solitary, dark yellow, rarely purple); *F. recurva* [California] (bright red outside, brilliant yellow, spotted red inside, 8–18 in.); and *F. verticillata* [Altai Mts.] (white or yellow, spotted); an interesting plant, the leaves terminating in a tendril-like tip.

**Fuchsia,** *Onagraceæ.*—Few flowers are more pleasing either in form or colour than the fuchsias. The plants have a grace and beauty peculiar to themselves. They grow in almost any soil, and are excellent for the cold greenhouse or the open border in summer. Turfy loam and leaf-mould in equal proportions, with some broken charcoal, old mortar-rubble, and sand, suits them very well. Feeding them with weak manure-water of any kind is preferable to mixing manure with the soil, and after they are well rooted, they should never be watered with clear water, but should always have a stimulant. A carefully-shaded house, guarded against the ingress of bees, is the best place for them when in blossom. In such a situation they will continue to bloom for three months if the seedpods are constantly picked off.

*Culture.*—Sow in heat (70° F.) in the spring, but the more satisfactory way is to take cuttings in spring or autumn. Fuchsias, even as seedlings, are gross feeders, and need a little well-rotted and finely-sieved manure in the sowing compost.

*Propagation by Cuttings.*—Plants that have been at rest during the winter should be started in February or March, and large early-flowering specimens will be produced by cutting down the old plants and re-potting them in good, rich compost. When re-potted keep them in a temperature of 55° F., and syringe overhead daily in fine weather. Insert cuttings taken from these plants when the young shoots are 2–3 inches long in pots filled with two-thirds fibrous loam and one-third leaf-mould, well-rotted manure, and old mortar-rubble, or with peat and silver sand in equal parts to within an inch and a half of the top. Place over this three-quarters of an inch of silver sand and level the surface to make it firm. Then insert the cuttings and plunge the pots in a bottom heat of 60° F. In three weeks they may be potted into 3-inch pots and re-plunged in the same bed, keeping the temperature from 50° to 60° F. As soon as necessary shift into fresh pots, until they receive their final shift into 6-, 9-, or 12-inch pots towards the end of June; or into the open about the end of May, if for summer-bedding. The size of the pot must be regulated by the period at which they are wanted to bloom. If in July, a 6- to 9-inch pot will suffice; if in September or October, a 12-inch pot will not be too large. Cuttings can also be taken of semi-matured wood in August. The procedure is the same as for spring-struck cuttings. These autumn-struck cuttings make good standard plants if the main stem is allowed to grow unchecked. The cuttings should be kept in a frost-proof frame through the winter, and should be potted-on frequently to encourage quick growth.

" *Stopping* " *and Training.*—During the period of growth, the plants should be kept close up to the glass, and will require " stopping " at least six times, care being taken never to stop the shoots immediately preceding or directly after the operation of shifting into larger pots. If the standard form of growth is adopted, the plants from the first must be trained to a single stem, all side-shoots being rubbed away until the main stem is 3½ feet high, and all the side-shoots which form the head must be " stopped ". *The Earl of Beaconsfield, Mrs. Marshall,* and *Rolla* all form excellent standards. If the bush or pyramid form is wanted, the whole of the shoots should then be " stopped " at every third joint until enough branches are secured to form the bush or pyramid. They should then be trained into the desired shape. Never " stop " a plant within two months of the time it is required to bloom, or it will have no chance to form its flower-buds. A regular, moist temperature, never exceeding 60° F., must be maintained during the entire period of growth, and the foliage should be sprayed overhead during warm weather. During bright sunshine the glass should be slightly shaded with tiffany or other material. The delicate leaves are easily injured, and the plants should never receive the slightest check by being allowed to flag. In July or August the plants should be stood in a sunny position in the open, to ripen the wood. After September they must be kept in a frost-proof house, and should be rather dry at the roots in winter. The principal pests are *Greenfly, Mealy Bug, Red Spider, Thrips,* and *White Fly.*

*Species.*—F. *cordifolia* [Mexico] (red and green); *F. corymbiflora* [Peru] (scarlet); *F. excorticata* [New Zealand] (purple); *F. fulgens* [Mexico] (scarlet); *F. procumbens* (Trailing Fuchsia) [New Zealand] (orange and dark purple, blue anthers, glaucous red berries). There are several varieties of this species, and it is an interesting plant suitable for a hanging basket. *F. splendens* [Mexico] (scarlet, tipped with pale green); *F. triphylla* [Mexico] (scarlet). All flower from July to September and grow from 5 to 6 feet in height. There are numerous named double and single varieties of garden origin, sometimes known as *F. speciosa.*

**Funkia** (see **Hosta**).

**Furcræa,** *Amaryllidaceæ.*—Succulent plants, somewhat resembling

**Agave,** differing only botanically, and requiring the same cultural treatment, except that Furcræas need more heat and water. They usually flower only once, and then die without producing suckers, but when flowering they usually produce a large number of bulbils which can be used for propagation. Plants from these bulbils are said to flower earlier than seedlings. Seed is not often produced.

*Species.*—*F. cubensis* [Tropical America] has greenish flowers and rosettes of rigid bright-green leaves, armed with pungent, horny, brown spikes. This is one of the best-known species. The variety *inermis* is almost free from marginal teeth or spines. *F. longæve* [Mexico] has whitish flowers and rosettes of dense, narrow leaves. The stem is 3–4 feet long. It is probably the most handsome of the genus, and can be grown with less heat.

**Gagea,** *Liliaceæ.*—Neat little bulbous plants, mostly hardy. They are suitable for growing in pans for the alpine house. Most of them prefer a light soil, but our own native species, *G. lutea,* thrives better in a moister soil. Propagation is carried out by offsets in the autumn or by seed sown as soon as ripe and placed in a little warmth.

*Species.*—*G. bracteolaris* (*G. stenopetalus*) [Europe] (pale yellow, April, 6 in.) ; *G. Liotardii* (Gold Star) [S.E. Europe] (yellow, March, 6 in.) ; *G. lutea* (Yellow Star of Bethlehem) [Europe and Asia] (yellow and green, April, 6 in.).

**Galanthus** (Snowdrop), *Amaryllidaceæ.*—This is one of the most lovely of spring flowers, and may be had in flower in the greenhouse at a very early period, its white blossoms contrasting beautifully with the rich hue of the Crocus. A row of Snowdrops is very effective in juxtaposition with a row of blue Crocuses. Snowdrops grow from 6 to 12 inches high, and flower in winter or early spring, according to species. They thrive in the shade in well-drained, moist, gritty loam, and are excellent for beds, for the rock garden, for growing in pots, or for naturalising in grass. *G. Elwesii,* the Giant Snowdrop, is the most effective and valuable species for pot culture.

*Pot Culture.*—Plant 1 inch deep in September or October, using 4- to 5-inch pots or pans and a compost of two parts of ordinary soil to one part of leaf-mould and sand, and keep in a cold frame slightly covered with ashes or fibre until growth commences (about six weeks) Then take them into the cold greenhouse or alpine house, and water moderately until the flowers fade. They should then be stood in a cold frame, and plunged in ashes. Decrease the amount of moisture and dry off as soon as the leaves turn yellow. Propagate by means of offsets or by means of seed sown as soon as ripe and plunged in ashes in the open or in a cold frame.

*Species.*—(Early) : *G. Elwesii* [Asia Minor] (white, marked green, Jan., 8 in.) ; *G. nivalis* [Europe] (white, Jan., 6 in.) ; there being several varieties of the Common Snowdrop, *corcyrensis, flavescens, octobrensis, reflexus,* as well as the popular double Snowdrop, *G. nivalis* var. *fl. pl. G. plicatus* [Crimea] (white, Jan., 12 in.). (Late) : *G. Iikariæ* [Island of Nikaria] (white, March–April, 8 in.). (Winter) : *G. Fosteri* [Asia Minor] (white, 8 in.).

# GREENHOUSE PLANTS

**Galax aphylla,** *Diapensiaceæ.*—An attractive little North American perennial, 4–6 inches high, very suitable for the shady parts of the rock-garden. When grown in pans it is very useful for the alpine house, for, apart from the beauty of its dense, spike-like racemes of white flowers in July, its stiff, bronzy leaves are very beautiful and decorative, particularly in the autumn and winter. Use a compost of three parts of leaf-mould, one part of loam, and some sharp sand. Increase by division of large clumps in the early autumn.

**Galaxia,** *Iridaceæ.*—Bulbous plants from the Cape of Good Hope, which, although nearly hardy, are best grown in the cool greenhouse. They should be planted in the autumn in pots or pans of loam and sandy peat in equal proportions, with a small quantity of sand. They are increased by seed sown and placed in a little heat, or by offsets in the autumn.

*Species.*—*G. graminea* (yellow, July, 6 in.); *G. ovata* (dark yellow, July, 6 in.).

**Galeandra** (see Chapter on **Orchids**).

**Galtonia candicans (Hyacinthus candicans)** (Cape Hyacinth), *Liliaceæ.*—Beautiful, tall, hardy, bulbous plants from South Africa, growing about 40 inches high and flowering in August and September. Each flower-spike carries some thirty or forty drooping, bell-shaped, ivory-white flowers like large snowdrops. They do well grouped in a sunny border and with well manured, deeply-dug sandy loam and leaf-mould for soil, or they may be grown in pots in the cold greenhouse. *G. princeps* [S. Africa] is somewhat like *G. candicans*, but has fewer flowers and a shorter raceme.

*Pot Culture.*—Place one bulb half an inch deep in a 6-inch pot, using a compost of sandy loam, leaf-mould, and well-rotted manure, and set in a cold greenhouse; or it may be planted out in the beds or borders of such a greenhouse. Water when growth starts, and give liquid manure when about to bloom. Only grow in a pot for one year, after which plant out.

*Propagation.*—Propagate by means of seed sown in the open as soon as ripe, or by offsets in autumn.

**Gardenia,** *Rubiaceæ.*—Beautiful evergreen flowering shrubs, suitable for hothouse or warm greenhouse, and remarkable for their lovely, sweet-scented, single or double flowers. The various species bloom at different seasons—summer, autumn, and winter—and so provide bloom over a long period. Late flowering may be encouraged by removing the flower-buds as they form in summer. They require much heat and plenty of water when growing and coming into flower. They thrive in a compost of equal parts of peat, loam, and rotten manure, with a little charcoal added. If peat is not available, a compost of two parts good loam, one part leaf-mould, and one part coarse sand may successfully be used.

*Culture.*—Prune into shape and pot-up in February or March, putting year-old plants into 5- to 6-inch pots; 8-inch pots should be large enough for old specimens. Water well while growing, syringe daily, and give liquid manure when the buds form. Decrease water after flowering (temperature 55° F. winter, 70–80° F. summer). Propagate

**379**

in February or March by means of shoots stripped from the plant with a " heel " struck in sandy peat in well-drained pots, in a propagating frame with a bottom heat of 70–80° F.  Pinch back the young shoots as soon as a few inches of growth have been made, to encourage bushy growth.  A 5- to 6-inch pot is quite large enough for a year-old plant, which should bear an excellent crop of bloom, as young plants flower better than older specimens.

*Species.*—G. *amœna* [China] (white, with purple on the lobes, June) ; G. *jasminoides* (G. *florida*, G. *radicans*) [Cape Jasmine], both single and double flowered forms.  The variety *Fortuniana* carries larger flowers than the type, in July and August, and G. *Thunbergii* [Central and S. Africa] (white, Jan.–March).  This species makes a large bush or small tree up to 15 feet high.

**Gardenia citriodora** (see **Mitriostigma axillare**).

**Gardenia macrantha** (see **Randia macrantha**).

**Gardenia Stanleyana** (see **Randia maculata**).

**Garland Flower** (see **Daphne Cneorum**).

**Gasteria,** *Liliaceæ.*—Small, evergreen, succulent plants with racemes of bright-red flowers often produced in the winter.  The thick, succulent leaves are also attractive, being often barred, mottled or warty.  They are closely allied to **Aloe**, and require the same cultural treatment.

*Species.*—G. *acinacifolia* [S. Africa] (orange flowers, glossy dark green leaves with scattered pale dots, 12–20 in.) ; G. *pulchra* [S. Africa] (scarlet flowers, glossy dark-green leaves with oblong white spots, 24 in.) ; G. *verrucosa* [S. Africa] (scarlet and green, leaves rough and grey, covered with tubercles).

**Gaultheria,** *Ericaceæ.*—Ornamental evergreen shrubs grown for their attractive flowers and fruits as well as for their handsome evergreen foliage.  Like most members of *Ericaceæ*, they are unsuccessful in soil containing lime.  They are increased chiefly by seed or by layers. Some kinds grown in pots or large pans in peaty soil are useful shrubs for the greenhouse, while other dwarf kinds are charming plants for the alpine house.

*Species.*—G. *ferruginea* [Brazil] (pink flowers, June, 36–48 in.) ; G. *fragrantissima* (Himalayas and Ceylon) (white, June).  Both species are greenhouse plants.

The following species are suitable for the alpine house : G. *nummularioides* [Himalayas] (white or pink flowers, dense hairy foliage, 6 in.) ; G. *procumbens* (Canada Tea, Winter Green) [N. America] (flowers white, July, bright red berries later, 6 in.) ; G. *pyrolæfolia* [Himalayas] (white or pink flowers, May and June, large, bluish-black fruit later, 5–8 in.) ; G. *trichophylla* [Himalayas] (pink flowers, May–June, blue fruit, 4–6 in.).

**Gazania** (Treasure Flower), *Compositæ.*—A showy, summer bedding-plant growing to a foot in height, with yellow and bronze flowers from June to October.  They are also useful for cool greenhouse decoration.

*Culture.*—Propagate by means of basal cuttings in summer in a cold frame ; plant out in June in a sunny position.  Protect from frost in winter.  For indoors, pot-up in March or April in a mixture of sandy loam and peat.  Water moderately while growing, but decrease the quantity of water after flowering until March the following year, when the plants should receive a good soaking, and after an interval of a day or so be re-potted. Keep in a sunny position in a cool greenhouse.

*Species.—G. Pavonia* (yellow, brown and white); *G. rigens* (yellow and black); *G. splendens* (orange); *G. splendens*, var. *variegata* (orange).

**Gelsemium sempervirens** (Carolina Yellow Jessamine), *Loganiaceæ.*— A North American, glabrous, climbing, evergreen shrub, with yellow flowers, which are very fragrant. It is a very desirable twiner for the conservatory, either for trailing up pillars, the back wall, or the roof, planted out in the border, or for growing in large pots. It thrives in a rich, loamy soil, but good drainage is essential. It is increased by cuttings of half-ripened wood under a bell-glass with a little heat.

**Genetyllis** (see **Darwinia**).

**Genista canariensis** (see **Cytisus canariensis**).

**Genista fragrans [Genista formosa]** (see **Cytisus racemosus**).

**Gentiana** (Gentian) : *Gentianaceæ.*—Choice little rock plants from Europe, China, the Himalayas, and New Zealand suitable for culture in the alpine house. They all thrive in a light open mixture of equal parts of rich loam, peat and sand.

*Species.—G. acaulis* (Gentianella) [Europe] (large blue trumpet, March–May, 3–4 in.) ; *G. Farreri* [Eastern Alps, W. China] (Cambridge-blue, Aug.–Sept.) ; *G. sino-ornata* [W. China] (azure-blue, Sept.) ; *G. Veitchiorum* (sapphire-blue, Aug.) ; *G. verna* [Europe] (deep azure-blue, April–May, the most popular of all). Many other species are in cultivation.

**Gentianella** (see **Gentiana acaulis**).

**Geodorum** (see Chapter on **Orchids**).

**Geranium** (Crane's Bill), *Geraniaceæ.*—The term Geranium is sometimes taken to cover both sections of plants to which the names Geranium and Pelargonium are usually applied. The former should be applied to the hardy perennial kinds, mostly self-coloured, being white, blue, salmon, scarlet, crimson, cerise, etc., and single or double ; while the latter term includes all the show varieties, in which the two upper petals are generally distinct in colour and markings from the three below.

*Species.—G. argenteum* [Carnic Alps], 4 inches, with rose-pink flowers from June to September, *G. cinereum* [Pyrenees] pale-red flowers with dark stripes, in June, with a height of 6 inches, and the beautiful white variety *alba*, *G. Farreri* [China], 4–6 inches, with pale pink flowers in July and August, and *G. subcaulescens* [Dalmatia], 5 inches, with rose-purple flowers from June to September, are useful subjects for culture in the alpine house.

*Culture.—*Pot-up in March in 4- to 5-inch pans of well-drained, sandy loam, and stand in a sunny, open situation. Rest in winter. Propagation is by means of seed sown in March, cuttings placed in a frame in August, or by division from March to October. For details and culture of half-hardy greenhouse bedding plants and show varieties see **Pelargonium**.

**Gerbera Jamesonii** (Transvaal or Barbertown Daisy), *Compositæ.*— Half-hardy perennials from South Africa, which grow some 9–12 inches

**381**

in height and carry orange-scarlet, daisy-like flowers during summer. There are numerous hybrids and varieties, both double and single, with colours ranging from white through cream to red and purple. They may be grown outdoors in mild localities, but are chiefly cultivated for decoration in the cold greenhouse, and are now being grown for the market, being excellent for cutting, and remaining fresh in water for a long time.

*Culture.*—Sow seed in spring in sandy soil. Prick-off when fit to handle and pot-on as required, using a compost of sandy loam, peat, and leaf-mould, until the plants are in 5-inch pots. Stand in a light, airy position and water regularly while growing. Re-pot established plants in March or April. Propagation may be carried out by means of detaching and potting-up young basal shoots at the time of re-potting.

**German Ivy** (see **Senecio mikanioides**).

**Germander** (see **Teucrium**).

**Gesneria,** *Gesneriaceæ.*—Showy hothouse, tuberous-rooted and herbaceous plants with beautiful foliage and flowers. They grow from 1 to 2 feet in height, and in summer and autumn carry spikes of pendulous flowers, scarlet, orange, yellow, white, pink, etc.

*Culture.*—Pot-up the tubers from March to June for early and late flowering, using 5-inch pots well drained, and a compost of peat, rich loam, and sand (temperature 55° F. winter, 85° F. summer). An even heat is necessary. Give liquid manure when the buds form, and water well. Decrease the water supply after flowering, and keep dry until the time of re-potting. Leaf cuttings may be taken if desired, or seed may be sown in January. These plants will flower the following November.

*Species.*—*G. cardinalis* [Brazil] (bright scarlet, 12–18 in.); *New Hybrids* (white, yellow, orange, pink, etc., 12–18 in.).

**Gesneria cinnabarina** (see **Nægelia cinnabarina**).

**Gesneria zebrina** (see **Nægelia zebrina**).

**Giant Arrow-head** (see **Sagittaria montevidensis**).

**Giant Forget-Me-Not** (see **Myosotidium nobile**).

**Gilia** (**Ipomopsis**), *Polemoniaceæ.*—Hardy annuals and half-hardy biennials, which thrive in ordinary soil, in warm, sunny borders, or as pot plants in the cold greenhouse, where they furnish bloom from June to September.

*Pot Culture.*—Sow seed thinly, ¼ inch deep, from March to May, and thin out to 3 inches apart when fit to handle. Pot-up as required in well-drained pots, in light, warm soils. By this method a September sowing may be made. Water regularly while growing, and discontinue after flowering. (Biennials, also known as Ipomopsis).—Sow seeds under glass in June, grow on in pots, and stand in the greenhouse They require the protection of a slightly heated frame in winter.

*Species.*—(Annuals): *G. androsacea* [California] (pink, lilac, or white); *G. densiflora* [California] (lilac-pink, 12 in.); *G. liniflora* [California] (white or blush, 10–20 in.); *G. micrantha* var. *aurea* [California] (yellow, 5 in.); *G. tricolor* [California] (pale purple, white, and yellow, 10–20 in.). (Biennials): *G. aggregata* (*Ipomopsis elegans*) [N. America], and *G. coronopifolia* (*G. rubra*) [S. California] (crimson scarlet, 24–28 in.). There is also a shrubby species, *G. californica*

**382**

[California] (dwarf, much-branched shrub [not hardy], pink or rose, 12–18 in., increased by seed or cuttings).

**Ginger-wort** (see **Alpinia**).

**Gladiolus** (Sword Lily and Corn Flag), *Iridaceæ*.—The hybrid varieties of the Gladiolus are very numerous and very beautiful, and the colours range from white, through yellow, orange, salmon, pink, red and lavender, to deepest purple, or the principal species used in the origin of these hybrids being: *G. cardinalis* [S. Africa] (bright scarlet); *G. primulinus* [S. Africa] (primrose-yellow); and *G. psittacinus* [S. Africa] (yellow, striped with red).

Gladioli are divided into two sections—namely, the early-flowering and the later-flowering species. Of the early-flowering kinds, *G. Colvillei* [hybrid of garden origin] (bright red with purple spots, 18 in.) may be taken as an example. There are a number of beautiful varieties: " *Blushing Bride* " (rose-crimson, with yellow blotch); " *Delicatissimus* " (soft pink and white lilac); " *Peach Blossom* " (delicate blush); " *Spitfire* " (scarlet-vermilion); " *The Bride* " (white). All are valuable for the greenhouse. They should be potted-up in the autumn and grown in a cool house or frame. Will flower in March and April, but may be induced to flower earlier if placed in a warmer house.

The late-flowering hybrids, of which *G. gandavensis* (various) and *G. blenchleyensis* (scarlet) (both hybrids of garden origin, between *G. cardinalis* × *G. psittacinus*), as well as the *primulinus* hybrids are good representatives, bloom in August and September. These late-flowering species should again be subdivided into two classes. The first contains those kinds with large flowers placed in two rows down the stout stems and all pointing more or less in the same direction; to this group the two above-mentioned hybrids belong. The *primulinus* group form the other subdivision, their blooms being smaller and their stems more slender. These Gladioli are excellent for vases and for growing in pots. There is yet another " Intermediate " section between the large-flowered types and the *primulinus* group, in which the *primulinus* hybrids have been crossed back on some of the large-flowered hybrids. In these the blooms are large, and yet are as graceful as those of the *primulinus* section.

*Pot Culture.*—Place three corms 2 inches deep in a 6-inch pot, in a compost of two parts sandy loam to one part of leaf-mould and rotten manure and ample sharp sand, in October or November; cover with fibre until growth starts, and keep in a frame until March. Then put in a light, airy position in a cold greenhouse to bloom. Each flower-spike will need secure staking. Water well while growing, and give weak liquid manure as soon as the buds begin to form, but discontinue this as soon as the colour shows. Dry-off after flowering, store, and keep dry and frost-proof from May to October.

*Propagation.*—Examine when lifting, when numerous scaly-looking little objects will be found having the appearance of pieces of rubbish; these are young gladioli cormlets. Draw a drill 2–3 inches deep on a piece of rich soil in the reserve garden, and sow the cormlets thinly in March. If kept moist, some of these will flower late in autumn if

**383**

allowed to do so, although when the corm is so small it benefits from the removal of the flower-spike. Many will flower the second year, and all the third year. These young cormlets require exactly the same treatment as the old ones. Gladioli may also be raised from seed in May. Seed should be sown in a compost of equal parts of loam and leaf-mould, together with a liberal sprinkling of coarse sand, in a deep box in a cold frame. When the seedlings are sturdy, place the boxes in the open. In September or early October lift the small corms and store for the winter. Plant out again early in April, but, if the best blooms are desired, do not allow the plants to flower again until the third season. If, however, it is desired that all the young plants shall come " true to type ", propagation must be effected by offsets. Named varieties are innumerable, and catalogues should be consulted.

**Gleichenia,** *Gleicheniaceæ.*—Handsome and distinct ferns with much-branched fronds and thin, wiry, creeping stems, which ultimately form dense bushes. The temperature of a warm, moist greenhouse suits them, and they should always be given plenty of surface room. Large shallow pans or tubs are most suitable, with a compost of sandy peat, some charcoal, a few pieces of sandstone with some sphagnum moss, and good drainage. They should, however, be watered liberally during the growing season. They are increased by division in the spring, or by spores (see Chapter on **Ferns**).

*Species.*—*C. circinata* [Australia, New Zealand] (48–60 in., there are several beautiful forms) ; *G. flabellata* [Australia] (36–48 in.) ; *G rupestris* [Australia] (36–48 in.). The **var.** *glaucescens* is of thicker texture and glaucous on both sides.

**Globba,** *Zingiberaceæ.*—Pretty stove perennials with attractive bright flowers. They are easy to cultivate in a warm, moist stove-house, in sandy loam. They are increased by division of the roots in spring when potting-up.

*Species.*—*G. atrosanguinea* (*G. coccinea*) [Borneo] (red and yellow, most of the summer, 12–15 in.) ; *G. Schomburgii* [Siam] (golden yellow and orange-red, Aug., 8–12 in.).

**Globe amaranth** (see **Gomphrena**).

**Globe Flower** (see **Trollius**).

**Globe Hyacinth** (see **Muscari**).

**Globe Mallow** (see **Sphæralcea**).

**Globe Tulip** (see **Calochortus**).

**Globularia,** *Globulariaceæ.*—Pretty plants for the rock garden, with globular heads of blue flowers. Several are very useful for the alpine house when grown in pans of rather moist but well-drained soil; all benefit from sun. They are propagated by seed or by division in the spring.

*Species.*—*G. cordifolia* [S. Europe] (summer, 3–4 in.) ; *G. incanescens* [S. Europe] (blue flowers, greyish-blue foliage, summer, 3 in.) ; *G. nana* [Europe] (summer, 2 in.) ; *G. vulgaris* [S. Europe, Caucasus] (summer, 6–8 in.).

**Gloriosa,** *Liliaceæ.*—Weak-stemmed, tuberous-rooted climbers, supporting themselves by means of tendrils at the tips of their leaves. They require a warm greenhouse, and are quite easy to grow. The

Hippeastrum rutilum *var*. fulgidum

Gloxinias in the Greenhouse

Hybrid Cineraria grandiflora in the Greenhouse

flowers are borne in summer, when plenty of water should be given. Rest the tubers during the early part of the winter, and start to pot-up from January to March. Good drainage is always essential, as is an open soil, composed of loam and peat in equal proportions, with some sand added. They require a warm, moist atmosphere during the summer, but as growth ripens water should be gradually withheld, and the soil kept dry throughout the winter, when the pots should be laid on their sides in a warm place. The resting season is as important as the growing season. Since gloriosas resent root disturbance, even when resting, owing to their brittleness, great care should be taken.

*Propagation.*—They are increased by seed sown and placed in a warm, moist atmosphere; also by offsets, which should be taken off carefully at the time of starting into growth.

*Species.*—*G. Carsonii* [Central Africa] (brick-red and yellow); *G. Rothschildiana* [Tropical Africa] (crimson and purple); *G. superba* [Tropical Asia and Africa] (yellow, red, and scarlet); var. *grandiflora* (yellow, turning red with age); *G. virescens* (*G. Plantii, G. simplex*) [Mozambique] (orange and greenish yellow).

**Glory of the Snow** (see **Chionodoxa**).

**Glory of the Sun** (see **Leucocoryne**).

**Glory Pea** (see **Clianthus Dampieri**).

**Gloxinia** (**Sinningia speciosa**), *Gesneriaceæ.*—A genus of beautiful, tender, tuberous-rooted, perennial plants, producing trumpet-like flowers of most beautiful velvety colours. They thrive best in a fibrous, peaty loam, mixed with leaf-mould, cow manure, sharp sand, and charcoal. There are already many hybrid varieties, with flowers ranging from the purest white to the deepest crimson, most of them being marked and dabbled with spots and blotches, generally of a deeper colour on the inside of the blossom. The plants grow about 10 inches high and flower from June to October.

*Culture.*—Start the tubers in succession from January to April by placing them, with their crowns just above the surface, in a 2-inch layer of the above compost in a well-drained box. Maintain a temperature of 60–65° F. Keep just moist, and when from 2 to 3 inches of growth have been made plant one tuber in each 4-inch pot in the above-mentioned compost. Maintain the same heat and moisture, shade from the sun, and water liberally when well rooted. Pot-up into 5-inch pots as soon as pot-bound, and again into 6-inch pots when the buds are forming. Immediately the buds open, lower the temperature and give less water. After flowering, dry off gradually, and store the tubers in peat or coconut fibre in a temperature of about 50° F.

*Propagation.*—Propagate at the end of January by means of seed in a compost of peat, sand, and fine rich loam, thinly covered with coarse sand only, and exposed to a bottom heat of about 70° F. Water by immersing the box nearly to the edge in a bath of lukewarm water, and prick-off 1 inch apart as soon as possible. Keep the atmosphere moist, and never allow the little seedlings to become too dry, or they will shrivel up. A week or so after pricking-off gradually reduce the temperature to 60–65° F. Immediately the plants again tend to become overcrowded and each seedling can be handled, pot-up in 4-inch pots, with the lower leaves just touching the soil. Place the pots near the glass, and maintain the above temperature. Keep the atmosphere moist by means of damping down the staging, but do not allow the moisture to touch the leaves, or they are liable to rot. Give the plants ample room and air, but maintain an equable temperature, and guard against cold draughts. Pot-up by stages into larger pots as the plants become pot-bound, until the flowering pots (5–7 inches) are reached. Give these an ample depth of drainage, and keep the water away from the leaves and stem when watering. As soon as the buds mature give a weekly dressing of weak liquid manure. Seed may also be sown in a cold house in June. Old tubers, when started in heat in February in boxes of damp fibre, supply shoots from which cuttings may be made ; these should be placed in a close propagating frame and subjected to moist and gentle heat. Another method of propagation is by means of leaf-cuttings taken at any time, although seed is preferable, unless one wishes to increase some very choice variety. Partly matured, medium-sized leaves, with a small portion of leaf-stalk attached, should be inserted in an ordinary propagating case, where, if kept rather on the dry side, they will quickly root and form tubers, when they may be potted-up and grown on.

When carefully grown, Gloxinias are particularly free from fungoid diseases or insect pests, and the same tubers can be grown for a number of years. The chief pests are *Thrips*, which injure the leaves and flower-stalks. These are difficult to eradicate if once established, but they can be kept in check by maintaining a moist atmosphere during the time that the plants are growing.

*Varieties.*—*Mauve Queen* (mauve) ; *Beacon* (crimson) ; *Cyclops* (rose-scarlet and white) ; *Pink Beauty* (pink).

**Gnidia polystachya,** *Thymelæaceæ.*—A handsome greenhouse shrub from South Africa, growing 3–4 feet high, with graceful sprays of bright-yellow flowers. It should be grown in pots in a compost of loam and peat in equal proportions, with some sand ; good drainage is very important. It is propagated by young shoots 2 or 3 inches long, struck in sandy peat under a bell-glass. Other species worth growing are *G. denudata* (pale yellow, May–July, 15–18 in.) ; *G. pinifolia* (creamy white, fragrant, March–April, 12–15 in.) ; *G. tomentosa* (pale yellow, March–April, 24–36 in.).

**Godetia,** *Onagraceæ.*—Beautiful hardy annuals, from 6 to 24 inches in height with various-coloured flowers, according to species and variety, from June to October. They make extremely useful pot plants for introducing colour into the cold greenhouse.

*Culture.*—Sow seed thinly in the open in March, April, or May for summer flowering, or in the autumn for spring flowering. Thin out as soon as large enough to handle, pot-up as required and stand in the cold greenhouse.

*Named Varieties.*—*Apple Blossom* (pink) ; *Duchess of Albany* (white) ; *Duke of York* (red and white) ; *Kelvendon Glory* (salmon and orange) ; *Lady Albemarle* (crimson) ; *New Lavender* (mauve) ; *Sybil Sherwood* (salmon-pink and orange) ; and *Azalea-flowered* (various).

**Golden Barrel** (see **Echinocactus Grusonii**).

386

**Golden Bell Tree** (see **Forsythia**).

**Golden Calla** (see **Zantedeschia Elliottiana**).

**Golden Chain** (see **Laburnum**).

**Golden Drop** (see **Onosma stellatum** var. **tauricum**).

**Golden Rain** (see **Laburnum**).

**Golden-rayed Lily** (see **Lilium auratum**).

**Golden Spider Lily** (see **Lycoris aurea**).

**Golden Vine** (see **Stigmaphyllon ciliatum**).

**Goldfussia anisophylla** (see **Strobilanthes anisophyllus**).

**Goldfussia isophylla** (see **Strobilanthes isophyllus**).

**Gompholobium**, *Leguminosæ*.—Half-hardy, Australian, evergreen shrubs for culture in the cold greenhouse. They grow from 2 to 3 feet in height and thrive in a mixture of sandy peat and loam with the addition of a little charcoal.

*Culture.*—Pot-up in spring, and stand in a light, airy position. Water regularly while growing, and keep only just moist when dormant. After flowering trim off dead flower-heads and shape the bushes.

*Propagation.*—Cuttings of new growth may be struck in sandy soil under a bell-glass in spring.

*Species.*—*G. grandiflorum* (yellow, June, 18–24 in.) ; and *G. venustum* (purple, May–June, 24–36 in.).

**Gomphrena** (Globe Amaranth), *Amaranthaceæ*.—A half-hardy annual which thrives in the cool greenhouse (temperature 45° F. winter, 65° F. summer) in a compost of sandy loam, leaf-mould, and rotten cow-manure. There are several varieties of the well-known *G. globosa*, with small red, purple, orange, or white " everlasting " flowers on stems a foot high, which can be had in flower from April to September.

*Culture.*—Sow seed in pots in March, April, or May (temperature 70° F.), and transplant 1 inch apart as soon as they can be handled. Move on singly into 5-inch pots by June, and place near the glass to flower. Water liberally. Give liquid manure when the buds begin to form. If seed is sown in September and treated as above, there will be bloom in April.

**Gongora** (see Chapter on **Orchids**).

**Goodyera**, *Orchidaceæ*.—Dwarf terrestrial Orchids ; apart from their flowers they have very attractive foliage. (See Chapter on **Orchids**.)

**Gooseberry Gourd** (see **Cucumis Anguria**).

**Gordonia**, *Theaceæ*.—Handsome shrubs with glossy foliage and large white flowers which are borne on quite young plants. Although some kinds can be grown outside in parts of the country, in most districts they are more satisfactory in the cool greenhouse. When potting is necessary it should be done in the spring in a compost of peat, leaf-soil, and sand with a little loam. They require plenty of water, as they grow naturally in swampy soil.

*Propagation.* They are propagated by seed sown and placed in a warm, moist temperature, by layers, or by cuttings of half ripened wood placed under a hand-light.

*Species.*—*G. alatamaha* (*G. pubescens*) [N. America] (white flowers, Aug., scarlet foliage, autumn, 4–5 ft., deciduous) ; *G. axillaris* (*G. anomala*) [S. China] (creamy-white, Nov., 36–48 in., evergreen) ; *G.*

**387**

*Lasianthus* (Loblolly Bay) [S. United States] (white, July–Aug., 48–60 in., evergreen).

**Grammangis** (see Chapter on **Orchids**).

**Grammanthes dichotoma** (**G. gentianoides**), *Crassulaceæ.*—A beautiful little succulent annual from South Africa. It bears orange, yellow, or creamy-white flowers, often marked on the petals with a darker V-shaped mark. It is a charming little plant for growing in pans for the alpine house. The seed should be sown thinly in a warm greenhouse in the spring, in well-drained pans of sandy loam. Plenty of air, and careful watering are very important features in the cultivation of this charming little plant. There are several varieties.

**Grammatophyllum** (see Chapter on **Orchids**).

**Grape** (**Vitis vinifera**) (see Chapter on **Fruit**).

**Grapefruit** (see **Citrus grandis**).

**Grape Hyacinth** (see **Muscari**).

**Graptophyllum,** *Acanthaceæ.*—Ornamental, evergreen, warm-greenhouse shrubs, attractive for their flowers and variegated foliage. They succeed in a compost of peat and loam in a temperature of 50–55° F. winter, 55–70° F. summer. Cuttings of young shoots, just becoming firm, with a " heel " of older wood, root in sand under a bell-glass in heat. *G. Earlii* [Australia] has clusters of rich red flowers in summer, and grows 6–8 feet high. *G. hortense* (*G. pictum*) [Tropical Asia] bears racemes of crimson flowers in July and August. The leaves are irregularly marked with yellow.

**Gravesia guttata** (**Bertolonia guttata**), *Melastomaceæ.*—A dwarf, warm-house, foliage plant from Madagascar. It has leaves of a rich, dark-green colour, dotted with rose-coloured spots arranged in lines. There are several beautiful foliage varieties : var. " *Alfred Bleu* ", brilliantly spotted with red ; var. " *margaritacea* ", dark olive-green, faintly shaded with purple, pearly-white spots, under-surface bright ; var. " *superba* ", olive-green, with large reddish-purple spots irregularly arranged.

It is allied to **Bertolonia,** and requires the same cultural treatment.

**Great Reed** (see **Arundo Donax**).

**Grevillea robusta** (Silk Bark Oak), *Proteaceæ.*—A graceful, shrubby, evergreen plant, cultivated for the sake of its silky, fern-like foliage. Although it makes a useful " dot " plant outdoors in sunny, dry, and sheltered situations when planted in sandy loam, it is generally grown in the greenhouse or living-room. If unrestrained it will grow to a height of as much as 15 feet, though indoor plants are usually kept much smaller.

*Pot Culture.*—Pot-up every two or three years in March, using 5- to 8-inch pots and a compost of fibrous loam and coarse sand (temperature 50° F. winter, 65° F. summer). Ventilate freely, and prevent the soil from becoming " dust-dry ".

*Propagation.*—Sow seed in a frame with gentle bottom heat in March, or take cuttings of half-ripened shoots in summer and strike under hand-lights. Seeds are very erratic in their germination, and may sometimes take a year or more to germinate. Special care must therefore be taken to see that the seed-pans are well drained.

*G. elegantissima* is a variegated form. Some species not very often met with, however, are grown for the beauty of their flowers alone. The best of these are : *G. alpestris* [Australia] (red and yellow) ; *G. glabrata* [Australia] (white) ; *G. rosmarinifolia* [Australia] (rosy red) ; *G. sulphurea* [New South Wales] (pale yellow) ; and *G. Thelemanniana* [Australia] (pink and green). All these make plants from 15 to 20 inches high, and flower in May and June. They require similar treatment to *G. robusta*, except that young plants should be " stopped " occasionally to form bushy plants. They can be increased by cuttings of newly ripened shoots placed in sand under a bell-glass or in a propagating case. The cuttings should be given some bottom heat as soon as they have callused. They may also be grafted on seedlings of *G. robusta*.

**Griffinia,** *Amaryllidaceæ.*—Beautiful bulbous plants from Brazil, with distinctive flowers and foliage, somewhat resembling **Amaryllis.** They thrive in well-drained, fibrous loam and peat with some sand. They flower in spring and summer, and after growth is completed water should be withheld, so that the bulbs may be thoroughly ripened. During the growing season they require a temperature of 60–80° F., with plenty of moisture When at rest the temperature should be 40–50° F. Sow the seed in heat, either as soon as ripe or in the spring, and take offsets in the spring when the older bulbs are being started into growth. *G. Blumenavia* grows 12–20 inches high, and bears white-striped pale-rose flowers on a scape. *G. hyacinthina* grows 12–15 inches high, and carries blue-and-white flowers. The var. *maxima* sometimes called the " Blue Amaryllis " is probably the best garden form.

**Gromwell** (see **Lithospermum**).

**Ground** or **Moss Pink** (see **Phlox subulata**).

**Ground Rattan Cane** (see **Rhapis**).

**Guatemala Rhubarb** (see **Jatropha podagrica**).

**Guelder Rose** (see **Viburnum Opulus** var. **sterile**).

**Gum Tree** (see **Eucalyptus**).

**Gymnogramma.**—At one time this covered a group of ferns, including those known as Gold and Silver Ferns, but these are now included under **Ceropteris** and **Anogramma,** which see.

**Gymnogramma calomelanos** (see **Ceropteris calomelanos**).

**Gymnogramma japonica** (see **Coniogramma japonica**).

**Gymnogramma schizophylla** (see **Anogramma schizophylla**).

**Gynura aurantiaca** (Velvet Tree), *Compositæ.*—Attractive greenhouse plants from Java, covered with bright-violet or purple hairs. They have very handsome foliage, and grow from 12 to 18 inches high. They are readily propagated from cuttings, and succeed in light soil and a warm, moist atmosphere, shaded from bright sunshine. The flowers are orange or yellow, the chief beauty being their coloured foliage and stems. As young plants give the best colour, it is advisable to put cuttings in occasionally.

**Gypsophila,** *Caryophyllaceæ.*—These plants are perfectly hardy, and are often used for cutting in the herbaceous border or the rock garden. Some of the dwarf kinds are very attractive when grown in pans, and are useful for the alpine house. They like a light, rich soil containing chalk or old mortar-rubble. Pot-up in the spring, and stand the pans plunged in ashes in a cold frame in full sun.

*Propagation.*—Propagate by means of seed sown as soon as ripe, by cuttings of young shoots placed in sand under a bell-glass, or by division of the old root.

*Species.*—*G. aretioides* [Persian Alps] has a cushion of greyish-green foliage starred with pearl-like flowers in July. Grows 2 to 3 inches high. *G. repens* [European Alps] grows to a height of 6 inches and carries white or pale-rose flowers from July to September. *G. elegans* [Caucasus] is an annual, charming for cutting. Seed sown in September in pots, boxes, or pans, and grown in the cool house will be found valuable for cutting the following spring. Another batch of seed sown in January or February will continue the supply. There is also a rose-coloured variety.

**Haberlea,** *Gesneriaceæ.*—A pretty alpine perennial with flowers like **Streptocarpus,** very charming for the alpine house when grown in pans, nestling among pieces of rock. It is allied to **Ramonda,** and succeeds under the same cultural conditions. It is propagated by seed sown as soon as ripe. Stand the seed-pot in a saucer of water and cover with glass. Or it may be increased by dividing the crowns, and also by leaves inserted in sand and kept under a hand-light. *H. Ferdinandi-Coburgi* [Bulgaria] has lilac-lavender flowers in April, and is probably a fine form of *H. rhodopensis* [Balkans] which is 4–5 inches high and carries lilac flowers in April. *H. rh.* var. *virginalis* is a beautiful white form.

**Habrothamnus** (see **Cestrum**).

**Hacquetia Epipactis (Dondia Epipactis),** *Umbelliferæ.*—A pretty but curious little European plant, 3–5 inches high, with heads of minute yellow flowers surrounded by a frill of green leaves. Grown in pans of sandy soil it is very interesting for the alpine house during April. It is propagated by division of the roots before growth starts in the spring. Only strong clumps should be divided.

**Hæmanthus** (Blood Lily), *Amaryllidaceæ.*—Attractive, African, half-hardy, bulbous-rooted plants, related to the **Amaryllis** group. They thrive in the cool greenhouse in a compost of sandy loam and leaf-mould.

*Culture.*—Pot-up when necessary as new growth commences in early spring. Water regularly and feed with weak liquid manure occasionally while growing, dry off and rest when dormant, except in the case of those with evergreen foliage.

*Propagation.*—Propagation is carried out by means of offsets when re-potting.

*Species.*—*H. albiflos* [S. Africa] (white, autumn, 12 in.) ; *H. coccineus* [S. Africa] (scarlet, autumn, 12 in.) ; *H. Katherinæ* [S. Africa] (bright red, Aug., 18–24 in.). Several species are natives of West Africa and require moist, tropical conditions.

**Hæmaria** (see Chapter on **Orchids**).

**Halleria lucida** (African Honeysuckle), *Scrophulariaceæ.*—A greenhouse, ornamental, evergreen shrub from South Africa, 3–4 feet high, with clusters of tubular, drooping flowers, red, sometimes yellowish, during June. It thrives in a pot in a compost of loam, leaf-soil, and sand in equal proportions and will grow for a number of years without being disturbed. Cuttings root freely under glass, or it can be increased by seed. It bears a roundish, deep purple berry which is edible.

**Hamamelis** (Witch Hazel), *Hamamelidaceæ.*—Small, deciduous flowering trees or shrubs which thrive in sunny positions and in moist, but well-drained loam with peat and leaf-mould in it. They are suitable subjects, when small, for providing winter colour in the cold greenhouse.

*Culture.*—Plant in October and November. Keep the plants outside in an open position when not in flower, plunging the pots in ashes. Just thin out and trim the branches in April when overcrowded.

*Propagation.*—To propagate, sow seed when ripe in a frame, layer in late summer, or graft.

*Species.*—*H. japonica* [Japan] (yellow, Jan.–Feb., 8–15 ft.); *H. j. arborea* (yellow, Jan.–Feb., 15–20 ft.); *H. j. Zuccariniana* (pale yellow, Dec.–Feb., 3–6 ft.); *H. mollis* [Central China] (golden yellow, Dec.–Feb., 8–10 ft.).

**Hardenbergia Comptoniana (Kennedya Comptoniana),** *Leguminosæ.*—An attractive, Australian, half-hardy, evergreen climber with bunches of purple, pea-like flowers in late spring. They grow from 9 to 12 feet in height, and thrive in a mixture of sandy loam and peat in the cool greenhouse.

*Culture.*—Plant in the greenhouse border or in large pots. Keep only just moist during the winter, prune in March, thinning out old and unwanted shoots and cutting back others. Water regularly while growing.

*Propagation.*—Cuttings made of new shoots (3–4 inches long) may be rooted in sandy soil under a bell-glass in March or April. Another species, *H. monophylla*, is very similar to *H. Comptoniana*, the leaves in the latter consisting of from three to five leaflets, and in the former usually only one.

**Hare Bell Poppy** (see **Meconopsis quintuplenervia**).

**Hare's Foot Fern** (see **Davallia canariensis**).

**Hare's Tail** (see **Lagurus ovatus**).

**Hart's Tongue Fern** (see **Phyllitis Scolopendrium**).

**Hartwegia** (see Chapter on **Orchids**).

**Hatchet Flower** (see **Pelecyphora aselliformis**).

**Haworthia,** *Liliaceæ.*—A genus of dwarf-growing succulent South African plants for the cool greenhouse. They thrive in full sun in a mixture of sandy loam and brick rubble.

*Culture.*—Pot-up when necessary in March or April. Water regularly while growing and keep only just moist during winter.

*Propagation.*—Seed may be sown in spring and covered with glass.

*Species.*—*H. albicans* (green and rosy, 3 in.); *H. arachnoides* (rosy, 9–12 in.); *H. cymbiformis* (coral-red, 3 in.); *H. lætevirens* (green and pale rose, 5 in.).

**Haylockia pusilla,** *Amaryllidaceæ.*—An attractive little bulbous plant

# THE GREENHOUSE

from Buenos Aires, somewhat resembling a Crocus, and closely allied to **Zephyranthes.** It is charming when grown in pans for the cool house or alpine house, but must be kept in a frame in the winter. It requires sandy loam with a little peat or leaf-soil, and is increased by offsets. The flowers are yellowish, whitish, or pale rose, produced in the summer. The leaves appear after the flowers are over.

**Hay Scented Fern** (see **Dryopteris æmula**).

**Heaths** (see **Erica**).

**Heather** (see **Erica**).

**Hebeclinium** (see **Eupatorium,** the name by which this is now known).

**Hebenstretia comosa,** *Selaginaceæ.*—A half-hardy perennial, usually treated as an annual, growing about 18 inches high, with fragrant semi-double, orange-red and white flowers from July to September.

*Culture.*—Sow seed thinly in March in pots or pans under glass in a cool house, or in April in the open. Plant out in June or pot-up singly in well-drained pots (4½ or 5 inches) of light ordinary soil for the greenhouse.

**Hedgehog Broom** (see **Erinacea pungens**).

**Hedgehog Cactus** (see **Pediocactus Simpsonii**).

**Hedgehog Gourd** (see **Cucumis dipsaceus**).

**Hedgehog Juniper** (see **Juniperus communis** var. **echiniformis**).

**Hedge Mustard** (see **Erysimum**).

**Hedræanthus** (see **Edraianthus**).

**Hedychium** (Butterfly Lily), *Zingiberaceæ.*—Half-hardy, rhizomatous-rooted evergreens, some 3–4 feet in height with fragrant flowers in summer. They thrive in the cool greenhouse in a compost of sandy loam and leaf-mould.

*Culture.*—Propagate by means of division of the roots and pot-up in March. They require ample and regular water while growing.

*Species.*—*H. coccineum* [Himalayas] (orange-scarlet); *H. coronarium* [Tropical Asia] (white); *H. Gardnerianum* [India] (yellow); *H. Greenii* [Himalayas] (scarlet).

**Hedyscepe Canterburyana** (Umbrella Palm), *Palmaceæ.*—This handsome palm from Lord Howe's Island somewhat resembles **Howea** (**Kentia**). It will succeed with the same conditions, but as a house plant it is smaller and spreads more, and is a lighter shade of green. It requires plenty of water and a rich heavy loam. It is propagated by seed sown in heat.

**Heeria elegans** (see **Schizocentron elegans**).

**Heeria rosea** (see **Heterocentron roseum**).

**Heliamphora nutans,** *Sarraceniaceæ.*—This interesting, curious plant from British Guiana somewhat resembles **Sarracenia,** having leaves in the shape of pitchers. It requires a warm, moist temperature, and should be grown in pots in a mixture of fibrous peat, sphagnum, some bits of charcoal, and sand. The surface should be covered with sphagnum, and the pots should be plunged up to their rims in a pan filled with moss and kept under a bell-glass. It is propagated by division of the crowns, or seed may be sown round the old plants.

392

# GREENHOUSE PLANTS

**Helichrysum** (Everlasting Flowers), *Compositæ.*—These are mostly half-hardy or hardy perennials or annuals, which thrive in sunny positions and in gritty loam. They are mostly suitable for borders, or as pot plants indoors, while the dwarf species make excellent rock plants.

*Culture.*—(Annuals) : Sow seed thinly, in February or March, under glass in moderate heat, using a compost of one-half loam, one-quarter leaf-mould, and one-quarter well-decayed stable manure. Prick out 3 inches apart and harden off. Transplant in mid–May, 9–12 inches apart, or pot-up and stand in the greenhouse. Hardy species may be sown in the open in April or under glass in March. (Perennials) : Propagate by means of division in the spring, or take cuttings in April and strike in gentle heat. Pot-up for greenhouse as required.

*Species.*—(Half-hardy Annuals) : *H. bracteatum* [Australia] and vars. (white, brown, red, pink, and yellow, July–Oct., 36 in.) ; *H. orientale* [S. Europe and Asia Minor] (yellow, July–Oct., 24 in.). (Hardy Perennials) : *H. bellidioides* [New Zealand] (white, July–Oct., 5 in.) ; *H frigidum* [Corsica] (white, foliage grey, July–Oct., 2–3 in.). These are suitable for the alpine house.

**Heliconia,** *Musaceæ.*—Handsome foliage plants for the warm greenhouse, some with interesting flowers and showy bracts.

*Culture.*—They can be either grown in pots or planted out, and require a rich, well-drained, loamy soil. Plenty of water should be given during the growing season, but this should be reduced, as the plants die down in the winter. They need a warm, moist temperature, and shade should be provided during the summer, as the foliage is easily damaged by the sun.

*Propagation.*—They can be propagated by seed sown in moist heat, but better plants are obtained by dividing the root-stock in the spring. Pieces may be inserted in a 5-inch pot and placed in a warm, moist temperature ; they may then be potted-on when necessary.

*Species.*—*H. aureo-striata* grows 3–5 feet high, and has deep-green leaves beautifully striped with yellow. It is probably a form of *H. Bihai* (*Balisier*) [W. Indies]. This carries orange or red flowers in July and August, and its blossom-sheath is scarlet and black. It has large, handsome, banana-like leaves, and grows 4–6 feet high. *H. " Illustris "* is probably a form of the last-named. The ribs and veins are marked pink. *H. psittacorum* [Jamaica] has orange flowers in August and grows to a height of from 4 to 5 feet.

**Heliocereus,** *Cactaceæ.*—All very beautiful and desirable flowering Cacti. They are easy to cultivate, and thrive both in half-shade and in full sunshine. It has slender stems that need support. It is allied to and sometimes included in **Cereus,** requiring the same cultural treatment. *H. amecænsis* (*Cereus amecænsis*) [Mexico] is a remarkable and very beautiful plant, with white flowers. *H. speciosus* (*C. speciosus*) [Mexico] has purplish-red flowers. This species has been hybridised with species of **Epiphyllum** and has given origin to most of the beautiful varieties once grown under the generic name of **Phyllocactus.**

**Heliosperma alpestre** (see **Silene alpestre**).

**Heliosperma quadrifida** (see **Silene quadrifida**).

**Heliotropium peruvianum,** *Boraginaceæ.*—Profusely flowering and sweet-smelling, soft-wooded shrubs, commonly called *Heliotrope* or *Cherry Pie,* valuable for summer bedding, rustic baskets in the greenhouse or pot culture. They grow from 12 to 36 inches in height and flower from May to September, succeeding best in light rich loam or leaf-mould.

*Culture.*—Sow seed thinly in spring in moderate heat, and this will provide good plants for summer and autumn decoration. Pot-off in April into 4-inch pots, pinch back when 3–4 inches high, harden off and plant out about 12 inches apart in June. The finest plants are obtained from cuttings taken in the same way as for Verbenas and bedding Calceolarias. Take the cuttings in spring or autumn (preferably late August) and strike in boxes in a frame with moderate heat. Syringe overhead every afternoon in hot weather, and in five or six weeks pot-up into 3- or 4-inch pots and move into the cool house. They are very sensitive to frost, and like an average temperature of 60° F. from October to early June.

*Pot Culture.*—Pot-up annually in March, using 6- to 8-inch pots and a compost of two parts loam to one part of leaf-mould and sand. " Stop " back to make bushy, and prune well back annually in February. Standard Heliotropes can be trained as advised for standard Fuchsias. As soon as the flower-buds form, give bi-weekly dressings of weak liquid manure. Water well while growing, but keep dry during winter (temperature 45° F. winter, 60° F. summer).

*Named Varieties.*—*Lord Roberts ; Mrs. J. W. Lowther ; President Garfield ; Swanley Giant ; The Speaker ;* and *White Lady.*

**Helipterum,** *Compositæ.*—These half-hardy annuals, which now include the **Acroclinium** and **Rhodanthe,** are everlasting or Immortelle, valuable alike for decoration in the greenhouse (Rhodanthes) and flower-garden. Their neat compact growth renders them suitable for flower-beds, while their richly coloured blooms, carried in great profusion, make them very attractive. They grow from 12 to 18 inches in height and flower outdoors from June to October. Under glass bloom should commence about April. They succeed best in a light, rich soil, and in warm sheltered positions.

*Pot Culture.*—Sow seed ¾ inch apart under glass in a temperature of 50° F. in a compost of two parts loam to one part each of leaf-mould and well-rotted stable manure in August, and just cover with soil. Place the pots near the glass as soon as seedlings appear, and keep fairly dry at first, but increase the water supply as the plants grow ; when in full growth give ample water. These plants resent root disturbance, and should therefore be potted as soon as possible into the pots in which they are to flower.

*Species.*—*H. Manglesii* [Australia] (rose and silver) ; *H. M.* var *maculatum* (pink, yellow, or white) ; *H. roseum* [Australia] (rose).

**Helleborus** (Hellebore or Christmas Rose), *Ranunculaceæ.*—The various species of this charming genus form one of the garden's greatest assets, for they flower at a time when there is little else. They are hardy perennials which thrive in well-dug, light, and moist soil in a border facing preferably east or west, or in a cool greenhouse.

**394**

*Pot Culture.*—Sow seed in a frame in March or October, or propagate by root division in July. Pot-up in October, using 6- to 8-inch pots, and a compost of two parts fibrous loam to one part of rotten manure. Water liberally while growing, and in summer and autumn give doses of weak liquid manure. Select fresh plants annually, planting the old ones out in April or May.

Perhaps the finest species are *H. niger* (Christmas Rose) [Europe] (white, Oct.–April, 6–12 in.), with its several good varieties, *angustifolius*, *altifolius* (*maximus*), *præcox*, and *H. orientalis* (Lenten Rose) [Asia Minor] (Jan.–April, 18–24 in.). There are many colour forms of this species.

*Named Varieties.*—*Admiration* (white, spotted red); *Bluebird* slaty blue); *Bronze Beauty*; *Darkness* (red); *Eastern Queen* (yellow); *Gertrude Jekyll* (white).

**Helonia bullata** (Swamp Pink), *Liliaceæ.*—A pretty, hardy, perennial bog plant from North America, which can be grown in pans or pots for the alpine house. It should be planted in fibrous loam and peat with some chopped sphagnum, and kept in a shady place. Keep the pans plunged in ashes in a cold frame when not in flower. It is increased by seed or by division of the root in the spring. It bears purplish-rose flowers in the summer, and attains a height of 12 inches.

**Helxine Soleirolii**, *Urticaceæ.*—This is a pretty little perennial creeping plant from Corsica, with attractive green foliage and inconspicuous flowers. It makes an excellent subject for cultivation in the paved or rock garden, or it may be grown in pots in the alpine house or cold greenhouse. It thrives in semi-shade or shade, in gritty loam.

*Culture.*—Pot-up in well-drained pots in spring, and water well and regularly while growing.

*Propagation.*—This is best carried out by means of division of roots in the spring.

**Hemigraphis colorata**, *Acanthaceæ.*—This Javanese plant is an excellent subject for hanging-baskets, for covering the surface of large palms and other plants, and for growing under the staging. Its purplish foliage and white flowers are very attractive. It is readily propagated from cuttings in the spring, and succeeds in a warm, moist atmosphere.

**Hemimeris montana**, *Scrophulariaceæ.*—An attractive South African annual for the conservatory, with scarlet flowers in June and July. It is easy to cultivate.

**Hemionitis**, *Polypodiaceæ.*—A group of attractive warm-greenhouse ferns, of dwarf habit, with fertile and sterile fronds. For cultivation see Chapter on **Ferns.**

*Species.*—*H. elegans* [Mexico] grows 6–10 inches high. *H. palmata* [West Indies] has palmate fronds covered with down on both surfaces. It is reproduced by numerous buds as well as by spores. *H. pinnata* [Jamaica] has distinctly forked fronds, 5–6 inches long, dark chestnut-brown in colour, with soft, yellowish hairs.

**Hemp Agrimony** (see **Eupatorium**).

**Hemp Tree** (see **Vitex Agnus-castus**).

**Hepatica** (see **Anemone**).

**Herbertia,** *Iridaceæ.*—Pretty, half-hardy, bulbous plants whose flowers are unfortunately rather fugitive. They are natives of Texas and Chile. They succeed in sandy loam and peat and are propagated by seed or by offsets.

*Species.*—*H. cærulea* [Texas] (blue and white, July, 6 in.) ; *H. pulchella* [S. Brazil] (lilac and white, July, 9 in.).

**Herb Lily** (see **Alstrœmeria**).

**Hercules Club** (see **Aralia spinosa**).

**Hercules Club Gourd** (see **Lagenaria leucantha** var.).

**Heron's Bill** (see **Erodium**).

**Herpestis Monnieria,** *Scrophulariaceæ.*—A creeping, fleshy perennial from Texas useful only for growing in or along the side of the aquarium, in soil just under water, either in submerged pots or in shallow parts of the tank, where it will creep along the surface of the water. It carries pale-blue flowers in summer, and may be propagated by cuttings or division in the spring.

**Heteranthera reniformis** (Mud Plantain), *Pontederiaceæ.*— A tender, aquatic perennial, with white or pale-blue flowers, and kidney-shaped floating leaves. It can be grown in submerged pots, and given the same treatment as other greenhouse aquatics. It is propagated by division in the spring or by seed sown in pots submerged in a warm tank.

**Heterocentron roseum (Heeria rosea),** *Melastomaceæ.*—A warm greenhouse plant from Mexico with bright, showy, rose-coloured flowers during the autumn and early winter. It is very suitable for growing in hanging baskets and succeeds in sandy loam and peat. Propagation is readily achieved by means of cuttings which should be taken in February and March, and grown on in a warm temperature. Pot them on, when ready.

**Heterotoma lobelioides** (Bird Plant), *Campanulaceæ.*—A very attractive, ornamental greenhouse plant from Mexico, with blood-red and yellow flowers. It needs a rich, open soil, and is propagated by cuttings taken in the autumn and grown-on in the warm greenhouse.

**Hexaglottis,** *Iridaceæ.*—Attractive little bulbous plants from South Africa requiring the same treatment as **Ixia** and other such bulbs.

*Species.*—*H. longifolia* (yellow, May, 15–18 in.) ; *H. virgata* (yellow, May, 24 in.).

**Hexisea bidentata** (see Chapter on **Orchids**).

**Hibbertia,** *Dilleniaceæ.*—Greenhouse, evergreen, sub-shrubby or climbing plants carrying golden-yellow flowers from January to July. They are useful for decoration in the greenhouse (temperature 45–55° F. winter, 60–65° F. summer).

*Culture.*—They do best when planted in the greenhouse border, but with a confined root-run, although they can be grown in pots, in a compost of equal parts of peat and loam, with a little brick-rubble and coarse sand. Water freely in summer, and keep free from insect pests. Give liquid manure when approaching bloom and prune out old wood after flowering.

*Propagation.*—Propagate by means of 3-inch cuttings under glass in May.

**396**

# GREENHOUSE PLANTS

*Species.*—*H. dentata* [New South Wales] (climber, yellow, spring and summer) ; *H. perfoliata* [W. Australia] (trailer, pale yellow, summer) ; *H. volubilis* [Queensland] (climber, yellow, unpleasant scent, summer).

**Hibiscus** (Rose, Shrubby or Syrian Mallow), *Malvaceæ.*—The members of this genus are for the most part beautiful hardy and half-hardy plants. Whether the hardy sorts are planted in the shrubbery or mixed border, or the more tender species grown for indoor decoration, they are all alike characterised by the size and varied colour of their flowers. They grow from 7 to 10 feet in height, and in the cool greenhouse flower during late spring and throughout the summer. Even the hardy shrubby kind when grown in pots are showy for the cold greenhouse.

*Culture.*—Pot-up or plant in the greenhouse border in spring in a compost of fibrous peat and rich fine loam, with a large proportion of sand ; a little charcoal in the soil is often beneficial.

Do not prune, merely keep in shape by " stopping " and by removing dead blooms.

*Propagation.*—Propagate these from seed sown over gentle heat, or by cuttings struck early in spring in a close frame.

*Species.*—HARDY ANNUALS : *H. Trionum* (yellow and brown, July–Sept., 24–48 in.). WARM-GREENHOUSE SHRUBS : *H. coccineus* [Florida] (bright scarlet, Aug.–Oct., 48–60 in.) ; *H. diversifolius* (yellow with purple centre, June–July, 48–60 in.) ; *H. pedunculatus* [Natal] (rosy pink, Aug.–Oct., 36 in.) ; *H. rosa-sinensis* [China] (rose-red, 36–60 in.) ; there are several beautiful named varieties of this with double and semi-double flowers of various shades ; also var. *Cooperi* with variegated leaves. *H. schizopetalus* [Tropical Africa] (orange-red fimbriated petals—a beautiful plant) ; *H. Archeri* (red), is a hybrid of the two previous species. HARDY SHRUBS : *H. syriacus* [Asia] and vars. SINGLE : *cœleste* (light blue) ; *Hamabo* (white, crimson blotch) ; *rubis* (ruby-red) ; *totus albus* (white). DOUBLE : *amplissimus* (vinous-rose) ; *Duc de Brabant* (red) ; *Jeanne d'Arc* (white and rose).

**Hidalgoa Wercklei** (Climbing Dahlia), *Compositæ.*—An attractive plant from Costa Rica, climbing by means of leaf petioles. It is suitable for the cool greenhouse, and, like the Dahlia, can be grown outside during the summer. It succeeds in a good loam, and although it may be grown in pots, much better results are obtained when it is planted out. The dazzling, orange-scarlet, single, dahlia-like flowers are produced all the summer. It is increased by cuttings in the autumn, which should be grown-on in a warm greenhouse.

**Hippeastrum** (Equestrian Star), *Amaryllidaceæ.*—A large genus of strong-growing, bulbous plants, chiefly from the tropics and sub-tropics of South America. They are very gorgeous and attractive during the winter and spring, particularly some of the hybrids, which are of the richest crimson and blood-red hues, to nearly white, including stripes, spots, and many lovely shades of rose and pink. The flowers are borne on stout, erect stalks. They are often grown under the name of **Amaryllis.** They are more or less evergreen, and although they require a season of rest, they should never be kept entirely dry. When once established, and when the bulbs are of sufficient size, they usually flower annually, and their culture is generally easy.

*Culture*.—The growing season is from early spring, after they have flowered, until about September, in a minimum temperature of 60° F., with sufficient water, syringing, and air to assist with ripening. After September they should be rested and kept in a moderately dry house in a temperature of 45–50° F. until February, when the flower-scapes appear. For early flowering, batches of bulbs can be brought into heat from the end of December. Young bulbs should be potted if they require it. Just as growth is about to start shake out the old soil and fill in firmly with fresh compost. Established bulbs should be top-dressed annually when growth commences; this is generally sufficient with the aid of manure-water during the growing season. Good heavy loam with charcoal and bone-meal should be used, and it is very important to have good drainage. They require plenty of light and, except when in flower, all the sunshine possible.

Mealy bug is often a very serious pest, and should be guarded against most carefully, or the bulbs will soon be ruined.

*Propagation by Offsets*.—This method is adopted to increase named species or varieties. Take the old bulb from the pot and carefully remove the offsets without damaging the roots. This should be carried out when the bulb is at rest, and not done more often than is necessary, as Hippeastrum resent root disturbance. Offsets should be placed singly in pots in a compost of two parts loam, one part decayed manure, and half a part of sand, taking care not to over-pot. Keep the bulb two-thirds above the level of the soil, and plunge the pot in coconut fibre with bottom heat. It should be placed in a light position and syringed freely, but watered sparingly until growth has started. They should be kept growing the first year or two, to build up good flowering bulbs. Later give the same treatment as to established plants.

*Propagation by Seed*.—This method is for raising new varieties, and is the usual óne for producing bulbs for ordinary decoration. Seed should be sown as soon as ripe in pans of loam and leaf-soil in equal proportions, with sufficient sand to keep it open. Place the pan in a temperature of 60–70° F., shading it from the hot sun. When the seedlings appear give them plenty of light and a moist atmosphere. Keep the seedlings in the pan until a few leaves appear, then pot them up singly in small, well-drained pots in a similar compost, but slightly rougher than that used for the seed. Seedlings should not be rested in their early stages, but kept growing to build up good bulbs, as in the case of young offsets. Seedlings may be had in flower two to three years from the sowing of the seed. Can also be increased by scales.

*Species and Hybrids*.—*H. Ackermanni* [garden hybrid] (crimson, 18–24 in.); *H. aulicum* (Lily of the Palace) [Brazil] (red, 18–24 in.); *H. equestre* (Barbados Lily) [Mexico] (bright red and green, 18–24 in.); *H. Johnsonii* (red with white stripes), this is the oldest hybrid Hippeastrum and makes a good window plant; *H. pardinum* [Peru] (greenish yellow, spotted red, 20–24 in.); *H. pratense* [Chile] (scarlet, 18–20 in., nearly hardy); *H. procerum* [Brazil] (pale mauve, 24–36 in.); *H. vittatum* [S. Africa] (striped pink and white, 20–24 in.). There are also many beautiful hybrids in which some of the above species and hybrids have played an important part.

**Hippeastrum formosissimum** (see **Sprekelia formosissima**).

**Hoffmannia,** *Rubiaceæ.*—Warm-greenhouse, evergreen shrubs, some of which are attractive as flowering plants and some as foliage plants. They may be grown in the open in summer if planted in sandy soil, but they must have a warm greenhouse during the winter. They succeed in fibrous loam with one part of peat and sand. Old plants should be cut back hard, or they become ungainly. Mealy bug is their worst pest. Cuttings of half-matured wood-shoots root readily in sand in a close case with bottom heat.

*Species.*—*H. discolor* [Mexico] grows 6–9 inches high, has small red flowers, and leaves which are satiny green above and light purple to green beneath. *H. Ghiesbreghtii* [Mexico] grows 24–36 inches high, and bears yellow and red flowers. The leaves are strongly veined, purplish red beneath, dark velvety-green above. The var. *variegata* has handsome mottled leaves. *H. refulgens* [Mexico] carries pale-red flowers. Its leaves are pale red or wine-colour beneath, while the upper surface is dull green with shades of purple or brown.

**Hoheria populnea,** *Malvaceæ.*—Half-hardy flowering evergreen shrub from New Zealand, which will thrive in the conservatory or temperate greenhouse, although in the milder parts of the country it is quite hardy out-doors. It should be planted out in a border of prepared soil or placed in large pots or tubs. A very distinct species with pure white flowers, borne in masses during August.

*Propagation.*—Propagation is achieved by half-ripened cuttings inserted in sandy soil under a bell-glass or hand-light in July, with gentle bottom heat.

**Holothrix** (see Chapter on **Orchids**).

**Homalomena Wallisii,** *Araceæ.*—A warm-greenhouse, variegated foliage plant from Colombia, somewhat resembling **Diffenbachia,** and requiring the same cultural treatment. The leaves are blotched pale yellowish green, becoming greenish grey.

**Honey Bell** (see **Mahernia verticillata**).

**Honey Flower** (see **Melianthus**).

**Honeysuckle** (see **Lonicera**).

**Hoodia,** *Asclepiadaceæ.*—Greenhouse succulent plants chiefly from South Africa. They are allied to **Stapelia,** and require the same cultural treatment.

*Species.*—*H. Bainsii* [S. Africa] (dull yellow, reddish when fading, July–Aug., 5–6 in.); *H. Gordonii* [S. Africa] (buff-purple, July–Aug., 10–12 in.); *H. Juttæ* [S.W. Africa] (greenish yellow and brown, darker veins, 8–10 in.).

**Horned Rampion** (see **Phyteuma comosa**).

**Horse Brier** (see **Smilax rotundifolia**).

**Hosta (Funkia)** [Plantain Lily], *Liliaceæ.*—A genus of fine, hardy, herbaceous plants, suitable for the border, rock-garden, shrubbery, or cold greenhouse. They are remarkable for their broad leaves and spikes of bell-shaped, fragrant flowers, mostly white, with a tinge of lilac. Some species have varieties with variegated or glaucous foliage, and these are most ornamental in the greenhouse. They thrive in sun or shade, growing to a height of from 12 to 24 inches, and flowering from July to September.

*Culture.*—Propagate by means of division in spring or autumn. Pot-up in March, using 8-inch pots and a compost of two-thirds sandy loam and one-third well-rotted manure. Place in a cold greenhouse, and water well in spring and summer. Give liquid manure when the buds form. Seed may be sown in summer if preferred. The seedlings should be pricked out and potted-up as soon as large enough to handle.

*Species.*—*H. Fortunei* [Japan] (mauve flowers, glaucous foliage, there being several well-marked varieties); *H. grandiflora* [Japan] (white, autumn, 18 in.); *H. ovata* [Japan and N. China] and var. *variegata* (lilac-blue, July–Aug., 12–18 in.); *H. plantaginea* [Japan] (white, July–Sept., 18 in.); *H. Sieboldiana* [Japan] (pale lilac, July–Aug., 12–18 in.).

**Hottentot's Bread** (see **Testudinaria**).

**Hottentot's Head** (see **Stangeria eriopus**).

**Houlettia** (see Chapter on **Orchids**).

**House Leek** (see **Sempervivum**).

**Houstonia,** *Rubiaceæ.*—Attractive little plants for the rock garden, flowering most of the year round. When grown in pans under cold-frame treatment they are very useful for the alpine house, with a carpet of foliage beneath the pretty flowers of blue, white, or purple. They require a good loam, with leaf-soil and sand, and need to be kept moist. When not required for the alpine house, the pans should be kept plunged in ashes in a partially shaded position. Increased by seed sown as soon as ripe, or by division in the early autumn. *H. cærulea* (Bluets or Quaker Lady) [N. America] grows 3–4 inches high, and bears flowers varying from blue to white with a yellow eye, in summer. *Millards* variety is a very fine form of the above species. *H. serpyllifolia* [N. America] is a creeping plant, bearing deep violet-blue, occasionally white, flowers in early spring.

**Houttea,** *Gesneriaceæ.*—Stove shrubs from Brazil, allied to **Gesneria,** and requiring the same cultural treatment.

*Species.*—*H. Gardneri* (red, July–Aug., 24 in.); *H. pardina* (orange-red, Aug.–Oct.).

**Hovea,** *Leguminosæ.*—Beautiful, half-hardy, evergreen shrubs from Australia which thrive in the cool greenhouse in a compost of sandy peat and loam. They grow from 1–10 feet in height, and bear clusters of lovely blue or purple, pea-like flowers in spring.

*Culture.*—Pot-up in spring after the flowers are over. Water regularly while making growth, but keep only just moist in winter. Stand outdoors during the summer months with the pots sunk to their rims in ashes. Trim to shape after flowering.

*Propagation.*—Cuttings made of young shoots may be rooted in sandy soil in a propagating case in spring, or seed may be sown in slight heat (50–55° F.).

*Species.*—*H. Celsii* (blue, June, 3 ft.); *H. chorizemifolia* (purple, April, 1–4 ft.); *H. longifolia* (purple, July, 8–10 ft.).

**Howea (Kentia),** *Palmaceæ.*—The two species of this genus are undoubtedly the most popular, and at the same time the most satisfactory palms for general decorative work, consequently every year enormous numbers are raised and vast quantities of seed are imported.

*Culture.*—The seed should be sown as soon as received. It can be

Hibiscus Manihot        Helichrysums bracteatum

*Photos*]        [*Sutton & Sons Ltd. and Dobbie & Co.*

Fuchsia        Gloxinia "Triumph" strain

*Photos*]                                                      *[Sutton & Sons Ltd. and Dobbie & Co.*

1. Incarvillea Delavayi            2. Larkspurs (Delphinium
3. Brodiæa uniflora (Tritelia)                 Gayanum)
4. Fritillaria Meleagris              5. Ixias

sown in pots, pans, or boxes, or sown on a bench covered with about 1 inch of soil, kept moist, with a bottom heat of 75–80° F. The seed sometimes germinates irregularly, some of it germinating in two months. The seedlings should be potted into small pots when the first leaf is expanded; they should be kept moist, and placed in a temperature of not less than 65° F. The young plants should be potted-on as they require it, and from then the temperature need not be quite so high. Howeas are not particular about soil; a rich, light loam suits them, while a little help in the way of a fertiliser during the growing period will be beneficial.

Scale insects are the most troublesome, and these should be removed as soon as noticed, or the foliage will become disfigured. Large specimens in pots or tubs can remain a number of years without root disturbance, but they should have plenty of water, and an occasional watering with soot-water, liquid manure, or fertilizer will help them. No palms are more suitable for room decoration than Howeas.

*H. Belmoreana* [*Kentia Belmoreana*] (Curly Palm) has leaf-segments more arching, is more compact in growth, and is probably more popular than *H. Forsteriana* [*K. Forsteriana*] (Flat or Thatch-leaf Palm), which has flatter leaf-segments. Both are natives of Lord Howe's Island.

**Hoya,** *Asclepiadaceæ.*—Hoyas, or Wax Flowers, are a genus of greenhouse, climbing, evergreen plants remarkable for their wax-like flowers, which assume the form of clusters of tubular florets, mostly of a white or pink colour, and borne between July and October. The best known is *H. carnosa* [S. China and Australia], with greyish-white flowers.

*Culture.*—Pot or plant in a hanging basket in March in a compost of umpy peat and loam containing a little coarse sand and charcoal. A pot rather on the small side should be used, and once the plant has become fairly mature it should only be necessary to re-pot it every five or six years, even then giving it only a slightly larger pot. In the years when no potting is done a little of the old soil should be removed from the top of the pot and a little fresh compost added. Hoyas may also be grown up a pillar or along wires on the roof if planted in a well-drained greenhouse border or in 8-inch pots. Water well while growing, and keep dry in winter (average temperature 45° F. winter, 65° F. summer).

*Propagation.*—Propagation is easier by means of layering in spring or summer, though cuttings of the previous year's shoots, 4 inches long, may be taken and struck in sandy soil in a temperature of about 75° F. in spring or early summer. Do not cut off the spurs that remain after the flowers have passed, as these spurs will flower again.

There is a variegated-leaf variety of *H. carnosa*. Other species are *H. bella* (*H. Paxtonii*) [India] (pure white and violet, 15–20 in.); it requires a warmer house than *H. carnosa ; H. imperialis* [E. Indies] (dull purple and white), requiring rich soil and a high temperature; and *H. multiflora* [*Centrostemma multiflora*] (straw-yellow, tipped white).

**Huckleberry** (see **Vaccinium**).

**Huernia,** *Asclepiadaceæ.*—Cool-greenhouse, dwarf succulents, most of which are suitable for growing in rooms, although the odour of the

C C

flower is not very desirable there. They are perennials, chiefly from South Africa, and somewhat resemble **Stapelia,** differing in their bell-shaped flower. They require the same cultural treatment, but too large a pot should not be used, and they should be watered very carefully.

*Species.*—*H. barbata* (cream coloured, variegated with purple spots, Aug., 6 in.) ; *H. campanulata* (yellow, July–Oct., 6 in.) ; *H. oculata* (violet-purple and white, summer, 3–4 in.) ; *H. reticulata* (yellow, dotted with purple, Aug., 6 in.).

**Humea** (Incense Plant), *Compositæ.*—A handsome foliage plant, invaluable for decorative purposes. Planted in the centre of sunny beds and borders, its graceful appearance renders it most effective and striking. In long mixed borders, if placed at intervals in irregular positions, it breaks the monotonous appearance which most persons so dislike. The leaves when slightly rubbed yield a powerful odour. When well grown it has been known to reach a height of as much as 8 feet and be as much as 4 feet in diameter. It succeeds in light, rich, sandy loam and leaf-mould, and flowers from July to October.

The best-known species is *H. elegans* [Australia], a half-hardy biennial with drooping racemes of brownish-red, crimson, or pink flowers in July and August. The Humea makes a good plant for the large greenhouse if grown in an 8-inch pot.

*Culture.*—Sow seed in July under glass in a little heat. Prick out as soon as possible, pot-up as soon as necessary, and winter in a frost-proof house, keeping the pots near the glass and the soil moderately dry. Plant out in the open for flowering in the following June, or pot-up and stand in the greenhouse. Germination is very irregular, and each seedling should be pricked off singly when large enough to handle, the remaining seeds being left to germinate at their leisure. Do not water until the roots are established in the new pot, and keep cool (50° F.), and shade from strong sun.

There is a whitish-flowered form, var. *albida*, and var. *gigantea* is taller than the type with a larger panicle of flowers.

**Huntsman Cup** (see **Sarracenia**).

**Hutchinsia alpina,** *Cruciferæ.*—Although hardy, this plant, with its mass of pure white flowers in March and April, makes an attractive pan for the alpine house. It appreciates a little shade, and is readily rooted from cuttings, or by seed sown when ripe.

**Hyacinthus candicans** (see **Galtonia candicans**).

**Hyacinthus orientalis** (Hyacinths), *Liliaceæ.*—These natives of Syria and Asia Minor may be divided into two classes: the *early-flowering Roman Hyacinths* (*H. orientalis* var. *albulus*), so useful for pot work and for forcing, and the *Common* or *Dutch Hyacinths*, also good for pot work, but especially suitable for spring bedding. The Dutch section includes types with large flower-spikes and also miniature varieties with smaller flower-heads. The best soil for Hyacinths is a well-manured, sandy loam containing leaf-mould, but they will grow in almost any soil or in coconut fibre, moss, water, or sand.

*Pot Culture.*—An early planting in August will provide a show of bloom at the beginning of December, if the bulbs are given a tem-

# GREENHOUSE PLANTS

perature of 60–65° F. as soon as the flower-heads appear. If the bulbs are planted in succession from the above month until November it should be possible to have a few Hyacinths in flower as late as the beginning of April.

*Compost.*—To cultivate the Hyacinth successfully in pots, a free, porous, and well-mixed compost, prepared some time before it is required, is indispensable, and one composed of two parts of turfy loam to one part of well-rotted manure, leaf-mould, and sand, thoroughly incorporated and passed through a rough sieve, is undoubtedly the best compost for the production of handsome flowers.

*Size of Pot.*—The size of the pot must be regulated by the accommodation and requirements of the cultivator. For one bulb a 4½- to 5-inch pot will suffice ; for three bulbs a 5½-inch pot will be adequate. Here it may be said that Hyacinths cultivated in groups are much more effective than when grown singly.

*Planting.*—Fill the pots with the prepared soil to within an inch of the top, placing the bulb in the centre, or, if three, at equal distances apart, pressing them well into the soil, and filling up, leaving only the crown of the bulbs uncovered. The compost immediately below the bulb should not be too firm, but the soil round the bulb may be well pressed down.

*Subsequent Treatment.*—Water moderately, and place them in a sheltered position out-of-doors on coal-ashes, or anything that will secure good drainage and at the same time be objectionable to worms. Cover with 6 inches of coconut fibre, ashes, or sand. In five or six weeks the pots will be full of roots, and when about an inch of top growth has appeared they may be transferred to the cold greenhouse (temperature 45° F. winter, 65° F. summer). Shade for a few days at first, then move nearer to the glass, and water well while growing. Any side-growth springing from the bulbs must at once be cut away.

To obtain a few early blossoms, some pots may be removed at the end of three or four weeks and placed in a gentle hot-bed in a warm greenhouse or forcing-pit, but they should be kept close to the glass to prevent them from growing tall and unsightly. At first they should be forced very gently, and should be only gradually exposed to full daylight. When the buds begin to appear give bi-weekly doses of weak liquid manure ; the stimulant should cease as soon as the colour shows.

After flowering, Hyacinths must be lifted from the soil. Cut down the flowered stems as soon as the flowers have withered, and when the leaves have also turned yellow lift the bulbs, remove the foliage, and shake clear of soil, and place for a fortnight or three weeks in the reserve garden under a 2- to 3-inch layer of soil to mature. Then store the bulbs in a dry, cool, airy shed.

*Miniature Hyacinth (Cynthella).*—These Roman Hyacinths are small-sized bulbs of the ordinary Dutch Hyacinth. They are excellent for growing in groups in pans, bowls or pots. They should be planted close together and treated in the same way as the large Hyacinths in pots.

*Hyacinths in Sand.*—To assure an effective display when the Hyacinth is grown in sand it is necessary to plant thickly. Push the bulbs into the dry sand, leaving only the top visible, and, to fix the sand, the vessel should be immersed in a pail or bath of water. To prevent any subsequent displacement of the sand, and to secure for the plants a sufficient sully of moisture, this operation should be repeated once a week, a bath of two or three minutes duration being sufficient. An occasional watering of tepid water overhead, through a fine rose, will free the plants from dust and keep them healthy and vigorous.

*Hyacinths in Water.*—Growing Hyacinths in water is a method which is not recommended, because this method of culture so exhausts the bulb that it becomes either useless for transfer to the borders or takes so long in recovering itself that it is some years before it is in a condition to send up a decent flower-spike. If they are to be grown in this way, however, use rain-water or pond-water rather than spring-water. Place the bulb on the glass and let the water just touch its base. For four or five weeks keep it in the dark in a cool situation, but avoid a damp, close atmosphere. When the roots have grown two inches, remove the water half an inch from the base of the bulb, and gradually expose more and more of the bulb to the light and air. All possible disturbance of the roots should be avoided ; therefore never change the water while it remains sweet, but make good the loss by evaporation ; as a purifier place a piece of charcoal in the glass. Avoid a close, hot room, for the heat and closeness tends to induce long stems and small flower spikes. Choose an airy situation and place the glass in the lightest and sunniest position, turning it once a day.

*Hyacinths in Moss.*—To grow Hyacinths in moss, fill a china bowl or other vessel with fresh green moss cleared of all impurities. Let this be well wetted and lightly pressed down ; in it plant the Hyacinth bulbs, covering them lightly with some of the greenest moss. As soon as the Hyacinths are planted place the bowl in a dark, cool place for about three weeks ; afterwards keep it near a window where the bulb will have plenty of light and air. Be careful that the moss is always kept damp and that the top moss round the bulb is changed frequently in order that the surface may be kept green. The moss best suited to this purpose is that found on banks, or grown upon the roots of old trees.

*Hyacinths in Fibre.*—To grow Hyacinths in fibre, fill the vessel used nearly to the top with well-damped " fibre ", lightly pressed down ; plant the bulbs and cover with more damp " fibre ". Sprinkle with water and stand in a cold, dark place and leave until growth commences. See that the fibre does not become too dry. When growth commences gradually expose to more and more light and air. See also **Bulbs in Fibre,** page 122, and general cultural details under **Bulbs in Pots,** page 119.

*Propagation.*—Propagation is carried out by seed to raise new varieties, but to increase already existing varieties bulbs are cut or damaged, thus encouraging bulblets to form. When the bulbs are lifted in June they are cut across the bottom three or four times. They are then set out, bottom upwards, and covered with light, sandy soil for about three weeks, by which time the cuts have opened out and the wounds healed. They are then kept in a store-house until October, when they are planted out. In the following June little or nothing of the parent bulb remains but dry skin, to which the young bulbs are attached. These are picked off, and so grown-on; in about four years' time they will have developed into saleable bulbs. Another method is to hollow out the bottom of the bulb to the centre. More bulbs are obtained this way, but they are smaller and take a year or two longer to reach maturity.

*Named Varieties.*—*L'Innocence* (white); *City of Haarlem* (yellow); *Charles Dickens* (pink); *Roi des Belges* (red); *Lord Balfour* (mauve); *King of the Blues* (dark blue); *Duchess of Westminster* (purplish blue). But a list of good varieties can be obtained from a catalogue.

*Hyacinthus amethystinus* [Spain] grows 6 inches high and carries light-blue flowers in February and March. *H. azureus* (*Muscari azureum*) [Mediterranean region] is a dwarf-growing species, some 4 inches high, with lovely blue flowers in February. It is well worth growing in a 5-inch pot or pan for the alpine house.

**Hydrangea,** *Saxifragaceæ.* The common Hydrangea (*H. macrophylla*), perhaps better known as *H. hortensis*, is a half-hardy, deciduous shrub, native of China and Japan. It flowers in the open in June, July, and August on the ends of the previous year's shoots, and thrives in a well-drained and richly-manured sandy loam. Even in warm districts it requires, in the open, a sheltered position. It grows well in large tubs or vases, but needs plenty of water and generous feeding. *H. paniculata* [China and Japan] and its variety *grandiflora*, with large, pyramid-shaped heads of creamy-white flowers in July, August, and September, are quite hardy in any part of England and are among the best of our autumn-flowering shrubs. It may also be grown as a pot plant in the greenhouse, but it should always be remembered that it is hardy, and therefore must have ample air and not too much heat.

*Culture.*—The same treatment, both indoors and out, will suit these species, bearing in mind that although *H. paniculata* is quite hardy, *H. macrophylla* (*hortensis*) is not entirely hardy, and must be protected from frost in cold districts. The two species also require different treatment as to pruning. *H. macrophylla* should be pruned in summer, and should have all weak wood cut out. The stems should be thinned and dead flower-heads cut off. The strong shoots that are left should then be cut back to within six or seven buds of the old wood. *H. paniculata* should be pruned in March, the stems being thinned out to from six to twelve on each plant, according to the size of the bush. All remaining shoots should then be cut hard back to within a couple of eyes of the hard wood.

*Pot Culture.*—Pot-up from February to March, using 5- to 12-inch pots, and a compost of two parts rich loam and one part of rotten manure and sand. For the cultivation of blue-flowered Hydrangeas use peat or leaf-mould instead of loam, as the latter usually contains lime. When grown in small pots one stem only is encouraged, and this will carry a fine head of bloom. Plants in the larger pots will, of course, be large and bushy, and will carry masses of bloom: forty heads or more. Water abundantly while growing, and give liquid manure occasionally until the flowers show colour. After flowering, stand in the open in a sheltered position until September. *H. macrophylla* is also suitable for forcing in the warm greenhouse, and if transferred from the frame or cold greenhouse to the warm house as required, a succession of bloom can be had from March to September (average temperature 65° F.). The stems should be staked as soon as the flower-head forms, as these are very heavy and soon weigh down their stalks.

*Blue Hydrangea.*—Blue Hydrangeas are much admired. It is some peculiarity in soil and situation that produces this variety. Blue flowers may be procured by planting in a lime-free soil, and by watering copiously with a weak solution of alum (one teaspoonful in one gallon of rainwater), or with 3 oz. of aluminium sulphate in one gallon of water. Both these solutions should stand for at least twelve hours before use.

*Propagation.*—To propagate, strike cuttings of young wood, three to four joints long, in May, or cuttings of strong matured shoots, 6 inches long, that have not flowered, in August. Strike both in a frame. Cuttings struck in autumn should be wintered in a frame with an even temperature of 40° F., and ventilation must be ample in fine weather. Keep the roots moderately moist, and pot-on in the following spring. *H. petiolaris*, also grown in nurseries as *H. scandens*, is a climber which ascends trees, walls, or whatever support it has, in much the same way as ivy does.

*Named Varieties of H. macrophylla* (*H. hortensis*).—*Etincelant* (carmine); *Helge* (dark rose); *Krimhild* (salmon rose); *Le Cygne* (white); *L. Marne* (mauve) *Mme. Mouillere* (white); *Mme. de Vries* (apple-blossom pink); *Marie Matthes* (rose); *Parsival* (deep red); *Peer Gynt* (rose, red); *Rubis* (red); *Triumph* (rose-pink). Good varieties for bluing are: *Blue Prince; Goliath; Mme. A. Riverain; Niedersachsen;* and *Vicomte de Vibraye.*

**Hydrocleis nymphoides** (**H. Commersonii**) (Water Poppy), *Butomaceæ* [Brazil].—A handsome aquatic with large yellow flowers most of the year. It is an excellent plant for the inside aquarium, and should be grown in a large submerged pot, or it may be grown in a tub two-thirds full of moderately good soil. If two or three plants are inserted the tub will soon be furnished with the floating, glossy leaves, and bright-yellow flowers which continue for a long time, although the individual flowers last only one day. It is readily increased by cuttings placed in a pot just submerged, or by division in the spring.

**Hydrolea,** *Hydrophyllaceæ.*—Attractive cool-greenhouse plants, which require a damp, almost boggy position. They can be grown in pots stood in water round the edge of the aquarium, or in saucers of water.

*Propagation.*—Propagation is effected by seed sown in spring and stood in water in a warm greenhouse, by cuttings in the summer, or by division in the spring.

*Species.*—*H. corymbosa* [Florida] (blue, summer, 12–18 in.); *H. spinosa* [S. America] (pale blue, June–July, 12–15 in.).

**Hylocereus tricostatus** (**Cereus triangularis, C. tricostatus**), *Cactaceæ* [Mexico].—A climbing Cactus which can be easily grown in a greenhouse, for, with its numerous aerial roots, it can adhere to walls or other supports, its stems reaching from 10 to 20 feet. Its large white flowers, which are nocturnal, are very attractive. It requires the same cultural treatment as **Cereus.**

**Hymenanthera crassifolia,** *Violaceæ.*—A small evergreen shrub, native of New Zealand, which although nearly hardy, does best when grown in the cool greenhouse. It bears yellow flowers in spring and these are followed by clusters of spiny white berries.

A pretty and very charming subject that will thrive when given a compost of sandy peat and loam.

*Propagation.*—Propagation is achieved by cuttings inserted in sandy peat under a bell-glass during summer. Re-pot or plant out in spring.

**Hymenocallis** (Spider Lily or Sea Daffodil), *Amaryllidaceæ.*—Bulbous plants with large, fragrant flowers. Some species are winter-blooming, and these should be partly rested during the summer, while those flowering in the summer should be partly rested during the winter. No special treatment is required apart from a warm temperature ; the same bulbs if treated with care may flower year after year. They should have good turfy soil and drainage.

*Propagation.*—Propagation is carried out by offsets.

*Species.*—*H. Amancæs* (syn. *Pancratium Amancæs*) [Chile and Peru] is a greenhouse plant, growing 18–24 inches high, and is the only species with yellow flowers. *H. calathina* [syn. *Pancratium calathinum*] (Peruvian Daffodil) [Brazil] is also to be cultivated in the greenhouse. It bears white fragrant flowers in March and April. *H. macrostephana* is allied to *H. speciosa*, and is probably a hybrid of it. It grows 24–30 inches high in the warm greenhouse, and carries large white flowers in February and March. *H. speciosa* (syn. *Pancratium speciosum*) [W. Indies] is a winter-flowering species, in the warm greenhouse, and has large, pure-white, fragrant flowers. The last two named are the most showy of any.

**Hymenophyllum,** *Hymenophyllaceæ.*—Dwarf-growing, half-hardy or hardy, filmy ferns, some 4–12 inches in height, which thrive in the shade in the cool or warm greenhouse. They require moist, peaty loam and leaf-mould, with sand and charcoal in it, and need the shelter of a case, unless the locality has a very moist atmosphere. They are more successful when planted out among sandstone.

*Pot Culture.*—Plant or pot-up in March in a mixture of sandy peat, live chopped sphagnum, and small pieces of sandstone. They may also be grown upon blocks of peat, sandstone, or portions of tree-root, and need no soil, as long as they have a little packing of sphagnum or small pieces of peat. Hymenophyllums must have a constantly moist atmosphere, almost at saturation point, so that close cases are therefore necessary. Water freely in summer, but moderately in winter, and do not syringe. Only soft water should be used.

*Propagation.*—Propagation is carried out by means of spores sown under glass at any time, or by division in March.

*Species.*—*H. caudiculatum* [Peru and Chile] (6 in.) ; *H. demissum* [New Zealand] (4–6 in.) ; *H. dichotomum* [S. America] (4–6 in.) ; *H. pulcherrimum* [New Zealand] (6–12 in.) ; *H. tunbridgense* [Europe, Britain, N. Africa, S. Australia, etc.] (2 in.).

THE GREENHOUSE

**Hyophorbe,** *Palmaceæ.*—Attractive ornamental palms, worthy of more attention. They are rather slow-growing and require more heat and moisture than some palms. They have large, handsome leaves which are often tinged with purple maroon in a young state. The soil should be made up of three parts loam, one part dried cow-manure, and some sand. Pot firmly.

*Species.*—*H. amaricaulis* (*Areca speciosa*) [Mauritius] has leaves 3–4 feet long, midribs lined with orange, and the stem and petiole often purple maroon. *H. Verschaffeltii* (*Areca Verschaffeltii*) [Mauritius] has leaves 3–4 feet long, with white midribs. In older plants of both species the stems become swollen in the centre.

**Hypericum** (St. John's Wort), *Hypericaceæ.*—The shrubby species *H. patulum* [Japan] (18–36 in.) and *H. Moserianum* (Gold Flower) [hybrid of garden origin] (12–18 in.), and the variety *tricolor* with variegated leaves of white, green, and red, are useful for decoration in the cold greenhouse. They carry yellow flowers from July to August. Although *H. patulum* is itself only half-hardy, several varieties, notably *H. p. Forrestii* (golden yellow), and *H. p. Henryi*, both introduced from China, are perfectly hardy and will make bushes up to 6 feet high and 6 feet in diameter.

*Pot Culture.*—Pot-up in September, using 6- to 8-inch pots and a compost of two parts of sandy loam to one part of leaf-mould (temperature 40° F. winter, 60° F. summer).

*Dwarf Species.*—*H. balearicum* [Majorca] (yellow, 6–10 in.); *H. coris* [Europe] (yellow, procumbent, 5–8 in.); *H. empetrifolium* [Greece] (clusters of yellow flowers, fine foliage 8–10 in.); *H. fragile* [Greece] (large yellow flowers, 6–8 in.); *H. polyphyllum* [Cilicia] (yellow, 6–8 in.); *H. reptans* [Himalayas] (yellow, prostrate). All these are useful for growing in pans for the alpine house, flowering from May to July.

**Hypocyrta,** *Gesneriaceæ.*—A stove shrub allied to **Gesneria,** succeeding with the same cultural treatment. *H. glabra* [S. America] has rich scarlet flowers in June and July, and grows 8–10 inches high. *H. strigillosa* [Brazil] bears scarlet and yellow flowers in May and grows 20–24 inches high.

**Hypoxis** (Star Grass), *Amaryllidaceæ.*—Interesting greenhouse plants with hard rootstock or corm. They thrive in sandy loam and leaf-mould with good drainage. They need a dry atmosphere, and are quite successful in a succulent house. They are increased by means of seed or offsets. They are interesting but not showy.

*Species.*—*H. elata* [Natal] (golden yellow, June, 12–15 in.); *H hirsuta* [N. America] (yellow, 18–20 in.); *H. stellata* [S. Africa] (white with green stripes, 9 in.).

**Iberis** (Candytuft), *Cruciferæ.*—Hardy annuals and perennials both of which succeed in any soil with lime in it, but which prefer dry sandy loam, and a sunny position.

*Culture.*—ANNUALS : Sow in the open or under glass in spring or early summer for summer and autumn bloom, or in autumn for spring flowers, under glass. Pot-up when fit to handle, one plant in a 5-inch pot, or three plants in a 6-inch pot. PERENNIALS : Sow in well-drained

408

pots or pans or strike cuttings in sandy soil in a frame in summer. Pot-on as required.

*Species.*—ANNUALS : *I. amara* var. *coronaria* (large-flowered white Rocket Candytuft) ; *I. umbellata* [S. Europe] (purple, crimson, and pink, July–Oct., 12 in.). PERENNIALS : *I. gibraltarica* [Spain and Morocco] (lilac pink, May–July, 12 in.) [this needs a warm sheltered position] ; *I. saxatilis* [S. Europe] (white, April–May, 4–5 in.) ; *I. sempervirens* [S. Europe] (white, May–June, 6–12 in.) ; *I. Tenoreana* [Naples] (white, May–June, 6 in.). The perennials are valuable when grown in pans for the alpine house.

**Ice Plant** (see **Mesembryanthemum [Cryophytum] crystallinum**).

**Illicium** (Aniseed Tree), *Magnoliaceæ.*—A half-hardy evergreen shrub, with beautiful fragrant flowers, which, although it can be grown outside during the summer, needs the protection of a cool greenhouse during the winter in all but the most genial parts of the country. It is about as hardy as the **Camellia.** Pot-up in the autumn in a compost of sandy loam and peat.

*Propagation.*—It is propagated from cuttings of half-ripened wood in sandy soil under a bell-glass during the summer.

*I. anisatum* (*I. religiosum*) grows 3–4 feet high, and bears yellowish and white clusters of flowers in summer. The Japanese hold this tree as sacred and use it to make wreaths for decorating the tombs of their deceased friends. *I. floridanum* [Florida] grows 4–8 feet high, and bears flowers from April to June which are deep red or purple in colour and have the appearance of being semi-double.

**Imantophyllum** (see **Clivia**).

**Impatiens** (Balsam), *Balsaminaceæ.*—Greenhouse annuals and perennials, with succulent, brittle stems. They are valuable greenhouse plants, as they bloom most of the year. The annuals are readily raised from seed, and thrive in any ordinary light soil. *I. Balsamina* (Garden Balsam) is the most popular, and although easy to cultivate, good well-grown specimens are too rarely seen.

*Culture.*—ANNUALS : Seed should be sown thinly in March in pots or pans of rich, sandy soil and placed in a gentle bottom heat of 65° F. Pot-up into 3-inch pots when the rough leaf appears, potting them on as required, finally into 8- or 10-inch pots. During the whole time the plants should be kept near the glass. To obtain fine specimens use a rich compost of equal parts of loam and rotten cow-manure, with some leaf-soil and sand. The plants must receive no check, and the flower-buds should be removed from the main stems and the base of the side-growth, until the plants are of sufficient size, when they should be allowed to bloom. They will continue for some time, particularly if the plants are liberally supplied with liquid manure. There are several forms of Garden Balsam, e.g. *Camellia-flowered,* and *Rose-flowered,* each of which contains striped, spotted, and self-coloured blossoms. They all make charming plants for the cool greenhouse, or the window, while they can also be used for bedding out. PERENNIALS : The stove and greenhouse species are readily propagated from seed when obtainable, but generally from cuttings in a propagating frame with a little bottom heat. Use a compost of two parts of good fibrous loam to one

**409**

THE GREENHOUSE

part each of leaf-mould, dry cow-manure and sand, and pot them on
when necessary into different-sized pots, according to kind. *I. Hawkeri*,
*I. Holstii*, *I. kewensis*, *I. Petersiana*, and *I. Sultanii* need 6-inch pots,
and *I. Hookeriana*, and *I. Oliveri* will require larger pots. All will
benefit from an occasional watering with liquid manure when the pots
are getting filled with roots.

The chief pests are Mealy Bug, Mite, Scale, and sometimes the leaves
are attacked by Mildew.

*Species and Varieties.*—*I. Balsamina* [Tropical Asia] (rose-coloured,
18–24 in., double and single, as well as *Camellia* and *Rose-flowered*,
various colours). *I. Hawkeri* [S. Sea Islands] (deep carmine, with
white eye, summer, 18–24 in.). This requires an intermediate temperature. *I. Holstii* [E. Tropical Africa] (scarlet, summer, 20–24 in.).
*I. Hookeriana* [Ceylon] (white, with purple spot, autumn, 30–36 in.).
It blooms best when established and requires moderate heat. *I.
kewensis* (a hybrid between *I. Holstii* and *I. Herzogii*) is an excellent
plant, bearing light scarlet flowers over a lengthy period. *I. Oliveri*
[Tropical E. Africa] (pale lilac or rose), flowering continuously over a
long period, is an excellent cool greenhouse plant, which should never
be allowed to become pot-bound. It is extremely suitable for the
greenhouse border and will produce a bush 10 feet high and as much
through. *I. Sultanii* [Zanzibar] (scarlet, summer, 12–24 in.). *I.
Sultanii* var. *Episcopi* is a perpetual-flowering variety with purple-
carmine flowers marked with rose, often grown in greenhouses as *I.
Sultanii*. *I Sultanii* var. *alba* is a white-flowered variety sometimes
grown in gardens under the name of *I. flaccida alba*.

**Incarvillea,** *Bignoniaceæ.*—An attractive herbaceous plant with
large, trumpet-shaped flowers. It is almost hardy in most places,
although, if grown outside, it should be given a warm, sheltered position
in a sunny place. It is eminently suited to the cold greenhouse, grown
in pots in a mixture of loam, peat, and sand. Pot-up in the spring,
and during the winter the pots can be plunged in ashes to the rim in a
cold frame, covered with mats or other material during severe weather,
and kept on the dry side until growth commences. It will go for a
number of years in the same pots, needing little attention apart from
an annual top dressing.

*Propagation.*—It is propagated by seed sown as soon as ripe, and
placed in a little heat; or by division of the roots just as growth is
about to commence.

*Species.*—*I. Delavayi* [China, etc.] (rosy purple and yellow, summer,
18–24 in.—a handsome foliage plant) ; *I. grandiflora* [Yunnan, China]
(rose-red, summer, 12–15 in.) ; the var. *brevipes* has large crimson flowers.

**Incense Plant** (see **Humea elegans**).
**Indian Corn** (see **Zea**).
**Indian Cress** (see **Tropæolum**).
**Indian Rice** (see **Zizania palustris**).
**Indian Shot** (see **Canna**).
**Indiarubber Plant** (see **Ficus elastica**).
**Inobulbon munificum** (**Dendrobium muricatum** var. **munificum**) [see
Chapter on **Orchids**].

410

# GREENHOUSE PLANTS

**Iochroma,** *Solanaceæ.*—Attractive dwarf, shrubby plants suitable for the cool greenhouse, with clusters of long, tubular or trumpet-shaped flowers. These flowers are purple, blue, scarlet, yellow, or white in colour and remain in bloom for most of the late summer and autumn. They require the same cultural treatment as **Cestrum.**

*Species.*—*I. coccineum* [Mexico] (scarlet, Aug.–Sept., 40–50 in.) ; *I. flavum* [Colombia] (pale yellow, Aug.–Sept., 50–60 in.) ; *I. fuchsioides* [Peru] (orange-scarlet, Aug.–Sept., 30–40 in.) ; there is also a white variety of *I. fuchsioides. I. grandiflorum* [Peru] (rich purple, Aug.–Sept., a climber up to 30 ft.) ; *I. tubulosum* [Colombia] (deep blue, Aug.–Sept., 30–40 in.).

**Ionopsidium acaule** (Violet Cress or Diamond Flower), *Cruciferæ.*—An attractive dwarf annual, 2–3 inches high, from Portugal and North Africa. It will often establish itself in the rock-garden, and also makes charming pans for the alpine house.

*Culture.*—Seed may be sown either in July or August. Prick the seedlings out when large enough and keep in a cool frame during the winter. They will flower in February or March. Seed can be sown in February or March, and these will follow on with a display in May or June. It succeeds in any good sandy soil with adequate drainage.

**Ipomœa** (Moon Flower, Morning Glory, etc.), *Convolvulaceæ.*—A large genus of half-hardy climbing plants, closely allied to the **Convolvulus.** It contains one or two species suitable for culture in the greenhouse. The best known is *I. tricolor* (*I. rubro-cærulea* [Mexico] commonly called Morning Glory. This makes a handsome plant some 8–10 feet in height, with lovely sky-blue flowers from June to September. The flowers are fully open in the morning and close as the day advances.

*Culture.*—Sow seed singly in April, in small pots under glass (temperature 55–60° F.). Harden off and plant out 24 inches apart in May or June against a trellis or sunny wall, or pot-on for greenhouse purposes. They should flower in 6- to 8-inch pots.

*I. Horsfalliæ* [West Indies] is a strong-growing perennial climber and the best winter-flowering species. It bears rich magenta crimson flowers. It is best planted out, but can be grown in a large pot in a warm greenhouse.

*Propagation.*—It is propagated by stem cuttings, or by grafting on pieces of its own root, or of some other species. *I. Horsfalliæ* var. *Briggsii* is also an excellent strong-growing climber with deeper coloured flowers. *I. Learii* (Blue Dawn Flower) [Tropical America] bears blue flowers turning to purple. It is a perennial climber, best planted out in the border of the greenhouse and allowed to hang from the roof. It is a beautiful plant which bears its flowers from August to October. *I. versicolor* (*Mina lobata*) more generally known now as *Quamoclit lobata*, is a pretty, half-hardy, annual climber from Tropical America, with red and yellowish flowers. It likes a warm, sunny, sheltered position, and a rich, well-drained soil.

**Ipomœa Quamoclit** (see **Quamoclit pinnata**).

**Ipomopsis** (see **Gilia**).

**Ipsea** (see Chapter on **Orchids**).

**Iresine,** *Amaranthaceæ.*—Half-hardy, ornamental, foliage plants with reddish leaves, suitable for edging to warm, sunny, and sheltered beds in the open, or for pot culture in the greenhouse (temperature 55° F. winter, 65° F. summer). They grow about 18 inches high and thrive in ordinary soil.

*Culture.*—Strike cuttings of young shoots in sandy soil in a frame in late summer or in spring. Plant out in June, 8 inches apart, or pot-up in March, using 5- to 8-inch pots and a mixture of peat, loam, leaf-mould, and sand, and use for greenhouse decoration.

*I. Herbstii* [S. America] has purplish-red foliage. The variety *aureo-reticulata* has yellow veins. *I. Lindenii* [Ecuador] has blood-red foliage, more pyramidal than the preceding species.

**Iris,** *Iridaceæ.*—A genus of hardy plants with bulbous or long running tuberous or rhizomatous roots, and flowers of beautiful colours, mostly white, yellow, or brown, blue and purple, having six petals—of which the three outer ones are drooping or reflexed, and the three inner ones erect. They are usually divided into two sections—namely, the bulbous, and non-bulbous or rhizomatous-rooted. To the latter class belong the Flags, or Bearded Irises, the Kæmpferi or Japanese group, and the Sibirica Irises. To the bulbous class belong the English, Dutch, and Spanish Irises. These are smaller in every way, being shorter and having smaller flowers, which are, however, brilliant in colour and pencilling. The Dutch Iris comes into flower in the open about the middle of May. It is followed in June by the Spanish, and later in June comes the English Iris.

The cultivation of Irises is simple, the plants succeeding in a sunny position in any light, rich, garden soil, though sandy loam with 50 per cent. peat or leaf-mould is most suitable for the bulbous species. The English Iris needs a heavier and cooler soil than the Dutch and Spanish species, and it is necessary to lift the bulbs of the last two triennially, rest them for a few months, and then replant.

*Pot Culture.*—BULBOUS-ROOTED : Many of the bulbous Irises make good pot-plants ; among these are *I. alata, I. persica, I. reticulata,* and the English and Spanish kinds, of which there are many beautiful coloured forms. They need a compost of two-thirds fibrous loam, and one-third leaf-mould and sand. Plant five bulbs in a 6-inch pot or pan in September or October. These Irises require the same treatment as the Hyacinth (which see) when grown in this way. They also make fine flowers for cutting, but the blooms should not be cut until fully open.

*Propagation.*—They may be propagated by offsets in October. Most spring- and autumn-flowering species require to be lifted from the ground in August ; summer-flowering kinds should be lifted every third year, in October, after the plants have died down. English Irises should be left undisturbed ; the Dutch Irises need just the same treatment as the Spanish.

Although the Iris is subject to many diseases, the chief pest of Irises grown in pots is the *Iris Ink disease,* which attacks mainly the *I. reticulata* group. Botrytis is also to be watched for ; flowers, leaves bulbs (or rhizome) can be affected.

*Species and Varieties.*—BULBOUS-ROOTED, SPRING-FLOWERING : *I.*

412

*Danfordæ* [Asia Minor] (yellow, brown dots, Feb., 5 inches); *I. Histrio* [Asia Minor] (lilac-blue and yellow, Jan.–Feb., 6 in.); *I. orchioides* [W. Turkestan] (yellow, lilac spots, March–May, 20 in.); *I. persica stenophylla* [Cilician Taurus] (purple, yellow, and green, March, 4 in.); *I. reticulata* [Caucasus] (rich violet and bright-orange markings); and the beautiful varieties *Cantab* (light blue), *histrioides* (bright blue, yellow markings), and *Krelagei* (purple, red, and orange, Jan.–Feb., 8 in.). The above Irises are charming when grown in pans for the alpine house. Other suitable ones are *I. cristata* [S.E. United States] (pale lilac, May–June, 6 in.); *I. gracilipes* [N. Japan] (lilac, white, and gold, April–May, 10 in.); *I. lacustris* [N. America] (lilac, May, 4–6 in. *I. verna* [N. America] (violet-purple, with gold markings). The last four are rhizomatous.

SUMMER-FLOWERING : *I. xiphioides* (English Iris) [France and Spain] (purple, mauve, pink, and blue, July, 10–25 in.); *I. xiphium* (Spanish Iris) [Spain] (blue, yellow, and white, June, 20 in.).

AUTUMN-FLOWERING : *I. alata* (Scorpion Iris) [Mediterranean region] (sky-blue and yellow, Nov.–Jan., 4 in.); *I. unguicularis* (*I. stylosa*) [S. Europe and N. Africa] (blue, purple, and white, Nov.–April, 9–12 in.).

**Isertia coccinea,** *Rubiaceæ.*—A handsome stove evergreen shrub with panicles of scarlet flowers during July and August. It succeeds in a compost of peat and loam with the addition of a little charcoal and silver sand.

*Propagation.*—It is increased by cuttings struck in sandy soil in heat, in spring or summer.

**Ismene,** *Amaryllidaceæ.*—A group of handsome, free-flowering, sweet-scented, summer-blooming plants, suitable for the warm, sheltered borders in the open, or for indoor decoration in the cold greenhouse. They are now included under **Hymenocallis** (which see).

**Isochilus linearis** (see Chapter on **Orchids**).

**Isolepsis gracilis** (see **Scirpus cernuus**).

**Isoloma,** *Gesneriaceæ.*—Ornamental warm-greenhouse herbs, most of which have creeping rhizomes. This group also includes the plants sometimes known as **Tydæa.** They are closely allied to **Gesneria** and **Achimenes,** but they differ from the former in the absence of properly formed tubers, and from the latter in the more tubular flowers and lobed disc. They require the same cultural treatment as Achimenes and Gesneria.

*Species.*—*I. amabile* (*Tydæa amabilis*) [Colombia] (dark rose, dotted with purple); *I. bogotense* (*I. pictum, Tydæa picta*) [Colombia] (upper half of the flower red, lower half yellow, dotted with red, summer, autumn, 15–20 in.); *I. erianthum* [Colombia] (orange-red, or cinnabar red, lower part of the flower spotted, summer, 20–30 in.); *I. Ceciliæ* [Colombia] (somewhat resembles *I. amabile*, but the leaves are marked with violet and silvery blotches, flowers pale rose with purple spots, throat striped) *I. hirsutum* [West Indies] (has scarlet flowers dotted with purple and yellow. It is one of the best species for greenhouse decoration). All have handsome foliage, which, even without the flowers, is decorative.

413

# THE GREENHOUSE

**Isoplexis,** *Scrophulariaceæ.*—Pretty and interesting cool-greenhouse shrubs with racemes of small Foxglove-like flowers during June and July.

*Culture.*—They thrive in a compost of sandy loam and leaf-mould in 6- to 8-inch pots, according to the size of the plant. They are increased by seed or by cuttings of half-ripened shoots in summer, placed in sand under a bell-glass.

*Species.*—*I. canariensis* (*Digitalis canariensis*) [Canary Islands] (golden yellow, June, 3–4 feet); *I. Sceptrum* [Madeira] (yellowish brown, July, 30–42 in.).

**Itea virginica** (Virginian Willow), *Saxifragaceæ.*—An attractive, hardy, deciduous shrub from the Eastern United States. It grows some 2–5 feet in height and bears fragrant white flowers when forced in March (see **Forcing**).

**Ixia** (African Corn Lily), *Iridaceæ.*—Pretty, half-hardy South African plant, producing graceful, star-like flowers on stems some 15 inches tall, n the greatest profusion in May and June. The colours range from green, through white, yellow, and pink to red. They thrive in warm, dry, sunny borders or in the rock-garden in rich sandy loam, and leaf-mould or peat, or they may be grown to advantage in pots in the cold greenhouse.

*Pot Culture.*—Pot-up from August to September, placing six corms in a 6-inch pot, in a compost of two parts turfy loam to one part each of leaf-mould, rotten cow-manure, and sand. The crowns of the corms should be an inch below the surface of the soil. Keep cool but frost-proof during the winter. In early spring move to the cool greenhouse (temperature 45° F. winter, 65° F. summer) and give light and air. Water well after blooming until the foliage dies, then dry off with the pots laid on their sides near the glass in a sunny frame or greenhouse.

*Propagation.*—Propagate by means of seed sown in a frame in September or by offsets in October. The former process is rather lengthy, however, as it takes three years before the seedlings are large enough to bear flowers.

*Species.*—*I. aristata* (pink or white, April, 10–12 in.); *I. flexuosa* (red or lilac, April, 12–15 in.); *I. paniculata* (yellow and white, May, 12 in.); *I. speciosa* (crimson, July, 12 in.); *I. viridiflora* (green, May, 12–15 in.).

(*Named Varieties.*—*Alice* (pale yellow and lavender); *Azurea* (blue, purple centre); *Bridesmaid* (white and carmine); *Excelsior* (red); *King of the Yellows* (yellow); *Queen of the Roses* (rose) are among the best of the named sorts.

**Ixiolirion montanum** (Ixia Lily), *Amaryllidaceæ.*—A genus of nearly hardy bulbous plants from Syria, having lilac or different shades of blue flowers in June. The plants grow about 15 inches high, and thrive in well-drained sandy loam in a warm, sunny border or rock-garden. If grown in pots they should be kept dry during the winter, and five or six bulbs potted-up in a 6-inch pot in a good, well-drained compost, and grown on in a cold frame.

**Ixora,** *Rubiaceæ.*—Handsome and desirable stove-greenhouse ever-green shrubs with showy clusters of flowers, coloured white, yellow, orange, rose, or scarlet. They are perhaps the best stove-greenhouse

414

plants, that combine the showiest flowers with fine evergreen foliage. They are easy to cultivate, and should be more often seen. They require perfect drainage, as they are apt to suffer from soil sourness. They need a high temperature, and if given plenty of moisture will soon grow.

*Culture.*—Use a compost of two parts of fibrous loam, one part of fibrous peat, one of leaf-soil, and a generous addition of silver sand. Syringing will be found beneficial, as will shading from the bright sunshine. Young plants may be flowered in 6-inch pots. Start them in a temperature of 75° F. early in the year, and as soon as growth commences any potting or top dressing required should be attended to. While the plants are in bloom during the summer they should be given a high temperature, with a moist atmosphere. This should be drier and cooler during the winter. When the pots are filled with roots and the flower-buds developing, liquid manure should be frequently given. Careful pruning and pinching will prevent unnecessary hard cutting or training.

*Propagation.*—They may be propagated at almost any season, but young growth in spring is perhaps best ; young shoots with four pairs of leaves are suitable. These should be placed singly in 2-inch pots in two parts of sand and one part of peat. Plunge the pots in a propagating case in a temperature of about 70° F., shading them from the sun. Pot-on as required, taking care not to let the plants become pot-bound until the required size pot is reached. Large plants in pots will do well for some years, but must be kept well fed during the growing season.

*Pruning.*—Pruning should be done after flowering, and the plants should be allowed to dry for about a month. This helps to make the wood firm. The plants should be cut back to one joint, unless it is desired to obtain large specimens, or to shape the plant.

*Species.*—*I. acuminata* [Himalayas] (white, summer, 3–6 feet) ; *I. chinensis* [Moluccas and China] (orange-scarlet, summer, 20–40 in.) ; *I. coccinea* [India] (scarlet, summer, 3–4 feet) ; *I. congesta* (*I. Griffithii*) [India] (orange-yellow to reddish, July, 20–40 in.) ; *I. macrothyrsa* (*I. Duffii*) [E. Indies] (deep red and crimson, 30–50 in.). This is one of the finest of the genus and should not be pinched back. *I. splendens* [origin unknown, but probably hybrid] (bright coppery scarlet, summer, 20–40 in.).

There are many beautiful hybrids and varieties : " *Amabilis* " (pinkish, suffused orange) ; " *Chelsonii* " (bright salmon orange) ; " *Decora* " (yellow) ; " *Incarnata* " (flesh colour) ; " *Reginæ* " (violet-salmon) ; " *Splendida* " (crimson-orange).

**Jacaranda ovalifolia (J. mimosæfolia),** *Bignoniaceæ.*—A most useful subject for conservatory decoration and also for summer bedding displays. Young plants in small pots are excellent for use as pot plants among other flowering and foliage plants grown for conservatory embellishment, the fern-like foliage being extremely light and decorative. This Jacaranda bears very beautiful lavender-blue flowers on large established specimens when planted out in a border of rich soil, or grown in large pots.

# THE GREENHOUSE

*Propagation.*—Propagation is easily achieved by means of seeds sown in light sandy soil in well-drained pots in a temperature of 70–75° F. Cuttings made of firm side shoots also serve as a means of increase and root readily in sandy soil in a warm propagating case.

**Jacobæan Lily** (see **Sprekelia formosissima**).

**Jacobinia (Justicia)**, *Acanthaceæ.*—Beautiful hothouse shrubs, with brilliant flowers, growing from 12 to 60 inches in height, and thriving in a mixture of loam, peat, leaf-mould, and sand, in well-drained pots.

*Culture.*—Pot-up about the end of March and water liberally while growing (temperature 50–60° F. winter, 65–75° F. summer). Give liquid manure when the buds form. Prune shoots close to the base after flowering.

*Propagation.*—Propagation is by means of cuttings of young shoots struck in sandy soil in pots from April to June.

*Species.*—*J. carnea* [Brazil] (pink, summer); *J. chrysostephana* [Mexico] (yellow, winter); *J. coccinea* [Brazil] (crimson, summer); *J. Ghiesbreghtiana* (red, winter); *J. pauciflora* (*Libonia floribunda*) [Brazil] (scarlet and yellow, summer), a very floriferous plant which succeeds in a lower temperature; *J. penrhosiensis* (*Libonia penrhosiensis*) is similar to *J. pauciflora* but larger and showier. It is a hybrid between *J. pauciflora* × *J. Ghiesbreghtiana*. *J. Pohliana* [Brazil] (pink, summer); *J. spicigera* [Mexico] (scarlet and yellow, summer).

**Jamaica Honeysuckle** (see **Passiflora laurifolia**).

**Jamaica Sago Tree** (see **Zamia integrifolia**).

**Jankæa Heldreichii (Ramonda Heldreichii)**, *Gesneriaceæ.*—This native of Thessaly is recommended for culture in the alpine house (see Chapter XI). It is closely allied to **Ramonda** and requires the same cultural treatment.

**Japanese Aralia** (see **Fatsia japonica**).

**Japanese Snowball Tree** (see **Viburnum tomentosum**).

**Japanese Wistaria** (see **Wistaria floribunda**).

**Jasmine Nightshade** (see **Solanum jasminoides**).

**Jasmine Plant** (see **Bouvardia**).

**Jasminum** (Jasmine or Jessamine), *Oleaceæ.*—*J. nudiflorum* and *J. primulinum*, both from China have yellow flowers in winter, and are useful in the cold greenhouse. Given warm house treatment *J. grandiflorum* [India] will thrive and flower nearly all the year round. *J. polyanthum* [China] (white flowers, reddish outside), is a useful plant for the cool greenhouse. There are also several beautiful hothouse species. *J. Maingayi* [India] (white, very fragrant, requires warm temperature). *J. Rex* [Siam] (pure white flowers, 2 in. across; a valuable climber for the warm greenhouse); *J. rigidum* [India] (white, fragrant, also requires warm temperature); and *J. Sambac* (Arabian Jasmine) [India] (white, turning purple when they die). There is a double-flowered variety of *J. Sambac* sometimes known as *trifoliatum*. Both are deliciously scented and flower most of the year. They require a warm temperature.

*Pot Culture.*—Cold House : Pot-up in February or March, using 6- to 8-inch pots and a compost of two-thirds loam and one-third leaf-mould and well-rotted manure with a little sand. Or they may be

416

Hæmaria discolor

[R. A. Malby

Jasminum primulinum

[H. Smith

Jeffersonia

planted out in the border and either trained up pillars or to the roof; but the advantage of pots for those grown for the cool greenhouse is that they can be stood outside when not in flower. Give weak liquid manure twice a week as soon as the buds form.

WARM GREENHOUSE: Temperature 55–70° F. winter, 60–75° F. summer.—Pot-up in March. Keep moist and syringe frequently until the plants have bloomed; then keep moderately dry. The warm-greenhouse species are subject to Mealy Bug, but if preventative measures are taken they can easily be kept clean.

**Jatropha,** *Euphorbiaceæ.*—Tropical herbs or shrubs, flowering most of the year, which are cultivated in the warm greenhouse for their ornamental, curious leaves and flowers. Like most of the family of *Euphorbiaceæ*, all parts of the plant contain milky juice, and many of them are grown in the tropics for their economic uses.

*Culture.*—They thrive in a compost of two parts of fibrous loam, and one part each of peat and sand.

*Propagation.*—Cuttings of firm young shoots dried before insertion will readily strike in sandy soil under a bell-glass in brisk heat, or by seed sown and placed in heat.

*Species.—J. Curcas* (Barbados Nut, or Purging Nut) [Tropical America] (greenish yellow, many flowers, ivy-like leaves, shrub, 20–30 in.); *J. multifida* (Coral Plant) [Texas to Brazil] (scarlet leaves, deeply cut, 24–36 in.); *J. pandurifolia* [W. Indies] (scarlet, leaves somewhat fiddle-shaped, and beautifully coloured beneath); *J. podagrica* (Guatemala Rhubarb, Tartago) [Central America] (orange-red flowers, attractive peltate leaves, stem swollen at the base, 18–24 in.).

**Jeffersonia diphylla** (Twin-leaf, Rheumatism Root), *Berberidaceæ.*—An attractive, North American, hardy plant with solitary white flowers, and mostly bi-lobed leaves, suitable for the sheltered and shady part of the rock garden. It can also be grown in pans for the alpine house. It requires sandy, peaty soil, and the pans, when not in the alpine house, should be plunged to their rims in a shady position.

*Propagation.*—It is propagated by division, which should be done just as growth is about to commence, or by seed which should be sown as soon as ripe and placed in cool conditions.

**Jerdonia indica,** *Gesneriaceæ.*—A small herbaceous perennial from the Neilgherri Mountains, suitable for the stove-house. It carries crimson rosy-lilac flowers during October and November. The leaves are dark green blotched with pale green along the ribs and veins.

*Culture.*—It thrives in sandy loam and leaf-mould, with a moist atmosphere. It requires a lower temperature and drier conditions during the winter.

*Propagation.*—It is propagated by seed sown in bottom heat, or by cuttings of new growth struck in sandy soil, and placed in a case in heat.

**Jessamine** (see **Jasminum**).

**Jew Bush** (see **Pedilanthus tithymaloides**).

**Jew's Mallow** (see **Kerria**).

**Job's Tear** (see **Coix Lacryma-Jobi**).

**Joseph's Coat** (see **Amaranthus caudatus** var. **tricolor**).

**Jubæa spectabilis,** *Palmaceæ.*—A handsome Chilean palm, suitable for the cool greenhouse under such conditions as would suit **Chamærops humilis,** requiring the same cultural treatment. In general appearance it somewhat resembles a **Phœnix.** It is a handsome palm and can be used for indoor decoration or for sub-tropical bedding. It is readily increased by imported seed and a fair germination can be expected, providing they are started in a warm greenhouse and kept moist. This palm yields a sugary sap which the Chileans call palm honey.

**Jujube** (see **Zizyphus**).

**Juniper** (see **Juniperus**).

**Juniperus** (**Juniper**), *Pinaceæ.*—Although chiefly ornamental trees or big shrubs, quite a number of the dwarf compact kinds that are suitable for the rock-garden are also very valuable for growing in pans for the alpine house, particularly some of the dwarf forms of *J. communis*, such as *J. c. compressa*, compact cone-shaped, slow-growing, a plant 20 years old often being not more than 15 inches high. *J. c.* var. *echiniformis* (Hedgehog Juniper) (12–24 in.) ; *J. procumbens* (Japan) (prostrate habit, very ornamental, only a few inches high) ; *J. squamata* (Himalayas) (prostrate and decumbent, 12–20 in.) ; *J. virginiana* var. *compacta* (dwarf, bright green) ; *J. v. dumosa* and var. *humilis* are very similar. They prefer a sandy loam, moderately moist soil, but will succeed in rocky or gravelly soil. Most of the Junipers like limey soil.

*Propagation.*—They may be propagated by cuttings of nearly ripened wood in the autumn under glass, either outside or in the greenhouse. Usually those with needle-like leaves will be found to root more easily than those with scale-like leaves. The prostrate ones can be increased by layers. Seeds may also be sown in pots of sandy soil and placed in a cold frame or cool greenhouse.

**Jupiter's Beard** (see **Anthyllis Barba-Jovis**).

**Jussiææ** (sometimes written **Jussieua**) (Primrose Willow), *Onagraceæ.*—Warm-greenhouse herbs or shrubs with flowers similar to those of **Œnothera.** They require moist conditions or a marshy situation among aquatics, although they can be grown in pots on the bench, providing the plants are kept well watered. They require loamy soil.

*Propagation.*—Propagation is effected from cuttings of young shoots, by division, or by seed, the pots of which should be stood in water. *J. longifolia* [Brazil] has yellow flowers in summer, and is best treated as an annual. *J. Sprengeri* (Argentina) bears canary-yellow flowers, and is one of the most beautiful of aquatics, growing equally well with less moisture.

**Justicia** (see **Jacobinia**).

**Justicia calycotricha** (see **Schaueria calycotricha**).

**Justicia flavicoma** (see **Schaueria flavicoma**).

**Justicia nervosa** (see **Dædalacanthus nervosus**).

**Justicia speciosa** (see **Peristrophe speciosa**).

**Kæmpferia,** *Zingiberaceæ.*—Ornamental, herbaceous, stove-greenhouse perennials, with fleshy, tuberous rootstock, producing terminal spikes of flowers during the summer. Re-pot in the spring, when growth commences, in a light mixture of two parts of fibrous peat, one part of loam, and some sand in well-drained pots or pans. During the

**418**

growing season they require an abundance of water, but as the leaves turn yellow this should be entirely withheld, and the pots kept dry during the winter. They are increased by division at the time of potting, or by seed sown and placed in heat.

*K. Gilbertii* [Burma] has crimson heads with purple and white flowers. The leaves are green bordered with white, and the margins wavy. It is a very desirable variegated plant, and grows 12 inches high. *K. Kirkii* [Tropical Africa] grows 6–8 inches high, and has pale rose-purple flowers with yellow markings, The variety *elatior*, from Rhodesia, is a taller plant, with bright-rose flowers, with a yellow blotch and purple markings. *K. Roscoeana* [Burma] produces white flowers in October; leaves variegated above; height 9 inches. *K. rotunda* [India] has fragrant lilac or reddish and white flowers in July and August, and grows to a height of 12 inches.

**Kaffir Lily** (see **Schizostylis coccinea**).

**Kalanchoë,** *Crassulaceæ.*—Half-hardy, succulent plants with interesting foliage and clusters of pretty red, pink, yellow, or white flowers from March to July. They grow about 18–24 inches in height and thrive in a sunny position, some in a warm greenhouse, others in the cool greenhouse, in a mixture of sandy loam, leaf-mould, and brick rubble.

*Culture.*—Pot-up the young seedlings or cuttings in large 60 pots, in the spring when new growth starts. The pots must be well drained and water applied sparingly until the plants are well rooted again. Then finally pot-on into 6-inch pots. Water regularly and well while making growth, and keep only just moist during winter (temperature 45–50° F. winter, 60–65° F. summer).

*Propagation.*—Seed may be sown in pots or pans of sandy soil in slight heat (60–65° F.) in March, or cuttings made of new shoots and dried for a few hours may be rooted in early autumn in slight heat 65° F.).

*Species.*—*K. Blossfeldiana* (syn. *K. globulifera coccinea*) [Madagascar] (bright red, spring); *K. carnea* [S. Africa] (pink); *K. Dyeri* [Tropical Africa] (white); *K. flammea* [Tropical Africa] (bright red); *K. marmorata* (*K. grandiflora*) [Abyssinia] (white flowers, foliage has brown markings, spring); *K. thyrsiflora* [S. Africa] (yellow, spring); and hybrids *K. felthamensis* (orange red) and *K. kewensis* (pink).

**Kalmia** (American Laurel), *Ericaceæ.*—Pretty, hardy, evergreen shrubs, which should be treated the same as the **Rhododendron,** which see. They are suitable for gentle forcing, and *K. glauca* may be had in flower in April in the warm greenhouse. In this case it should be treated the same as **Azalea.**

*Pot Culture.*—Pot-up in October, using 8- to 10-inch pots and a compost of two parts of sandy loam to one part of leaf-mould or peat and well rotted manure. Keep the atmosphere moist (temperature 45–55° F. winter, 60–65° F. summer). Water well while growing and give liquid manure. As soon as the buds open, reduce the temperature by 10°. Prune and remove old flower-heads after flowering. Re-plant in the open and leave for two years before forcing again.

*Propagation.*—To propagate sow seed in a frame in spring; strike cuttings in a frame in October, or layer in October.

**419**

*Species.*—The best known are *K. augustifolia* (Sheep Laurel) [E. North America], which makes a bush some 3 feet in height and bears clusters of rosy-red flowers in June; *K. latifolia* (Calico Bush or Mountain Laurel) with its rose-and-white flowers in June, and which grows to a height of 8–15 feet; *K. polifolia* (Swamp Laurel) [E. North America] with its purple flowers in April and May, which grows about 2 feet high. There are several varieties of each of the three species, all of which are worth growing. *K. polifolia* and its varieties are very useful for the alpine house when grown in pans and treated as other alpine house plants.

**Kalosanthes** (see **Rochea**).

**Kangaroo's Foot** (see **Anigozanthus**).

**Kangaroo Thorn** (see **Acacia armata**).

**Kendrickia Walkeri,** *Melastomaceæ.*—This stove-greenhouse climber is said to be one of the loveliest and most desirable of Cingalese plants, tingeing the forest with its bright-red flowers. The calyx is rose-purple, the leaves dotted white, and the stems self-clinging. It thrives in a mixture of peat, sandy loam, and sandstone. It can be planted to climb up pillars or other tall plants. Prune back in spring. Cuttings root easily in a case with bottom heat.

**Kennedya** (Australian Bean Flower), *Leguminosæ.*—An Australian greenhouse, evergreen, climbing plant of neat habit, with beautiful pea-shaped flowers. It requires partial shade and a compost of peaty loam and ample sand, together with a little charcoal.

*Culture.*—Pot-up or plant in a greenhouse border or basket in a cool greenhouse (temperature 45–55° F. winter, 60–65° F. summer) in March. Syringe daily from April to August, and water well in summer, but keep fairly dry in winter. Trim back straggly shoots and cut off dead flower-heads in the autumn.

*Propagation.*—Propagation may be carried out by means of seed (soaked for 12 hours before sowing) sown in heat in March or April, or by cuttings of young shoots (in heat) in spring or summer.

Among the best species are *K. coccinea major* (scarlet, June, 10 ft.); *K. nigricans* (violet, May–June, 4 ft.); and *K. prostrata* var. *major* (*K. Marryattæ*) (scarlet, May–June, 4 ft.); *K. rubricunda* (scarlet, summer, 4–6 ft.).

**Kennedya Comptoniana** (see **Hardenbergia Comptoniana**).

**Kentia Belmoreana** (see **Howea**).

**Kentia Forsteriana** (see **Howea**).

**Kentia Lindenii** (see **Kentiopsis macrocarpa**).

**Kentiopsis macrocarpa** (**Kentia Lindenii**), *Palmaceæ.*—A handsome Australian palm, the young leaves having a reddish tinge. It somewhat resembles **Howea** (**Kentia**), and requires the same cultural conditions.

**Kerria** (Jew's Mallow), *Rosaceæ.*—Hardy, deciduous shrubs, throwing up long, slender branches, sending out short twigs furnished with pretty, light green, serrated, lanceolate leaves, and bearing orange-yellow flowers in March and April. *K. japonica* [China] (4 ft., single); *K. japonica flore pleno* (8–9 ft., double); and *K. japonica aurea variegata* (yellow-margined leaves) are the only species and varieties. As climbers they run up to double the heights mentioned.

**420**

# GREENHOUSE PLANTS

*Pot Culture.*—In the cool greenhouse (temperature 45–55° F. winter, 60–65° F. summer) *K. japonica flore pleno* may be had in flower in February, or even earlier in the warm house. Pot-up annually in October, using 8- to 10-inch pots, and a compost of two parts of sandy loam to one part of leaf-mould and rotten manure. Prune out weak wood and dead flower-shoots after flowering and plant outdoors.

*Propagation.*—Propagate by means of cuttings of the young shoots inserted in a frame in late summer, or by division of the roots in autumn.

**Killarney Fern** (see **Trichomanes radicans**).

**Kitchingia uniflora (Bryophyllum uniflorum)**, *Crassulaceæ.*—A charming little prostrate, sedum-like plant from Madagascar, 1–2 inches high, with fleshy, crenate, bright green leaves. It is allied to **Bryophyllum,** and during April and May bears large solitary, rosy-purple, tubular flowers. It is an ideal plant for growing in pans, or for a suspended basket in a warm, moist greenhouse. It succeeds in a mixture of peat and loam and roots readily from cuttings, and as it produces roots at the joints, rooted pieces are easy to obtain.

**Kleinia** (see **Senecio**).

**Klugia zeylanica (K. Notoniana)**, *Gesneriaceæ.*—This warm-greenhouse, fleshy-stemmed evergreen from Ceylon has blue flowers during the summer. It regularly succeeds in a mixture of equal parts of sandy loam and peat, and requires plenty of moisture while growing. It is increased by seed or by cuttings.

**Kniphofia (Tritoma)** (Red-hot Poker, Flame Flower, Torch Lily), *Liliaceæ.*—Showy, free-flowering, tall, hardy perennials, with long, graceful leaves and large stems, from 3 to over 7 feet in height, crowned by densely flowered spikes of brilliant bloom, which are produced outdoors during the summer and autumn months. They thrive in well-drained, deep, sandy soil, in sunny or partly shaded borders, and may also be potted-up and grown in the cold greenhouse (temperature 45–50° F. winter, 60–65° F. summer).

*Culture.*—Sow seed indoors during March or April, or propagate by means of division in March, and plant out from 18 to 30 inches apart ; or pot-up in April or November, using 8- to 10-inch pots and a compost of sandy, well-manured soil. Keep in the cold greenhouse : water well while growing, but keep fairly dry in winter, and protect the plants from frost.

*Species.*—*K. Macowanii* [S. Africa] (orange-scarlet, summer, 24–30 in.) ; *K. modesta* [S. Africa] (white, May–Sept., 30 in.) ; *K. Nelsonii* [S. Africa] (bright scarlet, summer, 18–24 in.) ; *K. Northiæ* [S. African coastal regions] (rose and pale yellow, May–Sept., 60 in.) ; *K. Uvaria grandiflora* (orange-red, July–Sept., 70 in.).

*Named Varieties.*—" Golden Spur " ; " Harkness Hybrid " ; " Mount Etna " ; " W. G. Mills " ; " Royal Standard ".

**Kochia** (Summer Cypress), *Chenopodiaceæ.*—Half-hardy annuals, useful for summer bedding, for mixed borders, and for decoration in the cold greenhouse. They have a soft, feathery, fern-like foliage, bright green in summer, crimson in autumn. They grow from 2 to 3 feet in height, and the insignificant flowers are borne from July to October.

*Culture.*—Sow seed in March under glass in moderate heat (temperature 60° F.). Pot-up singly in 4-inch pots, harden off, and plant out 12 inches apart in borders at the end of May, or stand in the greenhouse (temperature 45° F. winter, 65° F. summer). They benefit from an occasional pinching while growing; just remove all the tips to keep a stiff, well-shaped plant.

*Species.*—*K. scoparia* (Belvedere) [Central Europe] and *K. trichophylla* [China].

**Kœllikeria argyrostigma,** *Gesneriaceæ.*—A tuberous, warm-greenhouse plant from Tropical America. It grows 12 inches high, and bears white or cream-coloured flowers spotted with red during the summer, and has dark, velvety-green leaves dotted white. It succeeds with the same cultural treatment as **Achimenes.**

**Kyllinga monocephala,** *Cyperaceæ.*—A grass or sedge-like plant which is quite attractive in the warm greenhouse during the summer, with its terminal, cone-shaped, silky, white flower-heads.

*Culture.*—Pot-up in 5-inch pots in the spring in good loamy soil, giving it an abundance of water during the growing season; or it may be planted around the edge of the aquarium. It is increased by division in the spring.

**Lablolly Bay** (see **Gordonia Lasianthus**).

**Labrador Tea** (see **Ledum grœnlandicum**).

**Laburnum** (Golden Rain or Golden Chain), *Leguminosæ.*—Pretty, hardy, deciduous trees bearing a profusion of long, drooping, yellow flowers in the open in May. Almost any soil and a sunny position suit them well. In the cool greenhouse (temperature 45° F. winter, 65° F summer) they will flower from February to April, and earlier in a warm house.

*Pot Culture.*—Pot-up in October, using 8- to 10-inch pots and a compost of two parts sandy loam to one part of leaf-mould and rotten manure. Trim back weak shoots after flowering, and plant out in the open. Cut out dead wood in winter. Do not re-pot for forcing for two seasons, but rest the plants in the nursery.

*Propagation.*—To propagate sow in a frame in spring. Budding and grafting are sometimes resorted to.

*Species and Hybrids.*—*L. alpinum* (Scotch Laburnum) [Mountains of S. Europe]; *L. anagyroides* [*L. vulgare*] (Common Laburnum) [S. Europe]; *L. Vossii ; L. Watereri* [hybrids of garden origin]. *L. Adamii,* the Purple Laburnum, is a graft hybrid or *chimæra* between Common Laburnum and *Cytisus purpureus.*

**Lace Fern** (see **Doryopteris**).

**Lace Leaf** or **Lattice Leaf** (see **Aponogeton fenestralis**).

**Lachenalia** (Cape Cowslip or Leopard Lily), *Liliaceæ.*—South African, bulbous-rooted flowering plants, suitable for greenhouse culture. They grow from 6 to 10 inches high and produce tubular, usually white, yellow, red, or greenish-blue flowers, in early spring in a warm house, or in February and March in a cool greenhouse.

*Culture.*—Pot-up in August, ½ inch deep, in a compost of peaty loam, with decayed cow-manure and sand. Pot one bulb in a 4-inch pot, or five bulbs in a 6- to 7-inch pot. Keep in a cold but frost-proof frame until early December, watering only when the soil becomes dry, then transfer to a shelf near the glass in the greenhouse (50° F.) and water as growth commences. A little liquid manure given occasionally as the buds form will be beneficial, but this must be discontinued immediately the colour shows. Keep quite dry in pots in a sunny frame from May to August.

*Propagation*—Propagate by means of offsets in August, or from seed sown as soon as ripe. The plants will thrive without repotting, provided they are annually top-dressed with a little fresh compost.

*Species and Named Varieties.*—*L. glaucina* (white, red, yellow, or tinged blue) ; *L. orchioides* (white, yellow, red, or blue) ; *L. pendula* (red and yellow with purple tip) ; *L. tricolor* (yellow, green, and purplish red) ; *L. t.* var. *luteola* (yellowish green, tipped red) ; *L. t.* var. *Nelsonii* (golden yellow) ; *L. t.* var. *quadricolor* (red, yellow, green, and purplish red).

**Ladder Fern** (see **Nephrolepsis**).

**Lady Fern** (see **Asplenium Filix-fœmina**).

**Lady's Slipper** (see **Cypripedium, Paphiopedilum** and **Phragmopedium**).

**Lælia** (see chapter on **Orchids**).

**Læliocattleya,** *Orchidaceæ.*—A group of beautiful bi-generic Orchids, some of which are natural hybrids, and others are raised artificially. Many are of such a vigorous constitution that they seem to be nearly always in growth. For culture see Chapter on **Orchids.**

**Lagenaria leucantha [Lagenaria vulgaris]** (Calabash Gourd), *Cucurbitaceæ.*—A tender, climbing, annual gourd, producing ornamental, hard-shelled fruit, used in the manufacture of utensils, drinking-cups, water-jugs, pipes, etc. The fruits vary in shape and are given common names accordingly, e.g. *Bottle Gourd, Calabash, Hercules Club, Sugar Trough.* They will succeed under the same conditions as cucumbers, and are also subject to the same pests and diseases.

**Lagerstrœmia indica,** *Lythraceæ.*—Half-hardy, summer-flowering, evergreen shrubs from China, suitable for the cool greenhouse. They grow from 8 to 10 feet in height, and when thoroughly mature bear terminal clusters of pink, red, magenta, or white flowers.

*Culture.*—Plant in the greenhouse border or pot-up in a large pot or tub in March, using a compost of sandy loam and peat, and seeing that the pots or tubs are well drained. Top dress annually. Water well and regularly while making growth in summer, and feed with occasional doses of weak liquid manure. Keep only just moist in winter. Prune established plants in February, cutting back the side-shoots by about a third.

*Propagation.*—Cuttings of new growth (3–4 in. long) may be rooted in a mixture of half peat and half silver sand in heat (65° F.) in April, under a bell-glass. Pot-up singly as soon as established and stop-back to encourage bushy growth.

**Lagurus ovatus** (Hare's Tail Grass), *Gramineæ.*—A pretty, annual grass from the Mediterranean regions and Western Europe. It has soft, white, woolly heads, and, although quite hardy, it is very decorative as a pot-plant. The seed can be sown thinly in 5- or 6-inch pots in

February and grown in a cool house; thin out the seedlings and grow cool. Or the seed may be sown the same day in September and kept in a cool greenhouse during the winter. Decorative plants will then be obtained for the conservatory in April and May, 12–15 inches high.

**Lamarckia aurea [Chrysurus aureus]** (Golden Top), *Gramineæ.*—A handsome annual grass from the Mediterranean region, with feathery golden-yellow heads, growing 6–10 inches high. As a pot-plant it should be given the same treatment as **Lagurus.**

**Lantana** (Surinum Tea Plant), *Verbenaceæ.*—Although some of the Lantanas range from 6 to 10 feet in height, they may be described as a genus of dwarf, bushy, half-hardy, evergreen shrubs, 6–8 inches high, flowering from June to September. They are useful for the greenhouse and flower-garden.

*Culture.*—Pot-up as soon as the young shoots break after pruning (about March), using 6- to 7-inch pots and a compost of two parts of loam to one part of leaf-mould, well-rotted manure, and sand. Syringe overhead twice daily in spring and summer, and water well while growing, but keep fairly dry in winter, allowing only sufficient water to prevent the stems from shrivelling up (temperature 45° F. winter, 65° F. summer). Cut the shoots well back to within a few inches of their base in February. If planted out during the summer, they must be wintered indoors.

*Propagation.*—Seed sown in heat (75° F.) in March makes the summer- and autumn-blooming plants. They are also propagated in spring or autumn by cuttings of half-matured wood in heat. Stop-back young shoots and pot-up into larger pots as the plants become pot-bound. Lantanas are attacked by White Fly and Mealy Bug.

*Species.*—*L. Camara* (*L. aculeata*) [Tropical America] (flowers opening yellow or pink, changing to orange or scarlet; there are several varieties); *L. salvifolia* [Tropical and S. Africa] (lilac or pink, aromatic plant); *L. Sellowiana* (Trailing Lantana) [S. America] (rosy lilac, a profusion of blooms, winter and summer, charming for hanging basket).

*Varieties.*—*Chelsonii* (scarlet and yellow); *Delicatissima* (pale pink); *Globe d'Or* (yellow); *Favorita* (yellow and red); *La Neige* (white); and *Magenta King* (purplish red).

**Lapageria** (Chilean Beliflower), *Liliaceæ.*—A beautiful evergreen climber for the cool greenhouse, producing clusters of pretty, waxy, bell-like white, rose, or red flowers. The plants require a well-drained, turfy loam, plentifully mixed with sand, an equal portion of peat, and a little charcoal, free from lime. They grow to a height of 10 feet, and flower in October and November. They are suitable for walls or rafters in a cool greenhouse with moist atmosphere. There is only one species—*L. rosea*, a native of Chile.

*Culture.*—Propagate by means of seed sown as soon as ripe in gentle heat (temperature 50° F.), or by layers after flowering, the latter being the best way of obtaining strong, quick-growing plants. The pots in which they are grown must be well drained. Pot firmly or plant in the border in March, shade and water well. Syringe twice daily in spring and summer, when not in flower (temperature 45° F. winter, 65° F. summer). Ventilate freely in summer and autumn. Cut out weak shoots only after flowering; otherwise do not prune. Keep fairly dry in winter.

*Species and Varieties.*—*L. rosea* (rose); *L. r.* var. *albiflora* (white); *L. r.* var. *Nash Park* (rosy red); *L. r.* var. *superba* (brilliant rich crimson).

**Lapeyrousia [Anomatheca]** (Flowering Grass), *Iridaceæ.*—Bulbous plants, growing about 15 inches high, and flowering outdoors from June to September. They do well in the sun and in warm, sunny borders, or they may be used for decoration in the cold greenhouse. *L. cruenta* [Transvaal] (red) and its var. *L. c. alba* (white), both 6–10 inches high, and *L. grandiflora* [Zambesi] (flowers larger than *L. cruenta*, 10–16 in.) are the only kinds grown to any extent.

*Culture.*—Plant or pot-up placing four or five bulbs in a 5-inch pot, in a compost of light, sandy loam, and leaf-mould, in October. Stand in a cold frame covered with coconut fibre until growth commences, then move into the greenhouse and water regularly. Dry off gradually after flowering, and rest during the winter.

*Propagation.*—Propagation is usually carried out by means of offsets in October, or by seeds sown in sandy soil in spring to produce plants to flower the following winter. They will grow outside in some districts in a warm border by the greenhouse.

**Larkspur** (see **Delphinium**).

**Lasiandra macrantha** (see **Tibouchina**).

**Lastrea.**—Most of the ferns included under this genera at one time are now included under **Dryopteris,** which see.

**Lastrea membranifolia** (see **Dryopteris dissecta**).

**Latania,** *Palmaceæ.*—Handsome warm-greenhouse palms (with fan-shaped leaves, which require an abundance of water and moderate shading most of the year.

*Culture.*—A light, well-drained compost with a little bone-meal added is most suitable, and as the roots are rather delicate, it will be found beneficial at the time of potting if the temperature of the soil is the same as that of the house. They like a night temperature of 60–65° F.

*Propagation.*—They are propagated by imported seed, which should be sown over bottom heat, and the seedlings should be grown on in a warm, moist atmosphere.

*Species.*—*L. Commersonii* [Mauritius] is an attractive palm, the leaf-stalks and ribs of its fan-like leaves being bright crimson, particularly in the young foliage. *L. Verschaffeltii* (*L. aurea*) [Rodriguez Island] has the leaf-petiole tinted orange, with the ribs a golden colour. Both species grow to 7 feet in height.

**Lathyrus,** *Leguminosæ.*—Annual or perennial decorative climbers, the most popular and best known being the Sweet Pea. Although most of the genus is perfectly hardy, some species are very decorative for the cool greenhouse, where they can be trained up pillars, etc., and where they will give a good display. They may also be grown for cut flowers, particularly the white Everlasting Pea (*Lathyrus latifolius* var. *albus*), which is very valuable to florists who want white flowers during the early summer.

*Culture.*—They are best planted out in the bed or border of the house, although they can be grown in pots by giving sufficient root room;

such plants can then be stood outside when the flowers are over. They succeed in any good garden soil.

*Propagation.*—They are raised from seed sown and placed in a cold frame or in the cool greenhouse. Perennials are propagated by division of the roots, or special varieties by cuttings of the young growths after the flowering season or in the spring. Because the roots of the perennials are long and somewhat fleshy, they should not be disturbed more than necessary, and will continue for years without attention.

*Species.*—*L. latifolius* var. *albus* is the white form of the well-known Everlasting Pea (white, summer, 4–6 ft.). *L. pubescens* [Temperate S. America] (Lilac-blue, April, 3–5 ft.). This is a beautiful, not very hardy plant which requires either a cool greenhouse or, if outside, a warm south wall. *L. splendens* (Pride of California) [S. California] (carmine-red, April, 5–7 ft.). This is probably the most beautiful species of the genus, but it is not hardy, and is therefore decidedly a plant for the cool greenhouse.

**Lathyrus odoratus** (see **Sweet Pea**).

**Lattice Leaf** or **Lace Leaf** (see **Aponogeton fenestralis**).

**Laurustinus** (see **Viburnum Tinus**).

**Lavandula** (Lavender), *Labiatæ.*—The best-known species, *L. Spica* (mauve to white), the common Lavender, thrives in light and well-drained soil, and in sunny, open positions. It grows about 3 feet high, and flowers in July and August. On account of its delightful fragrance, it is frequently introduced into the cold greenhouse. Other species for the cold greenhouse are *L. dentata* [Mediterranean region]; *L. multifida* [Canary Islands]; *L. Stœchas* [Mediterranean region].

*Culture.*—Plant or pot-up in large pots or tubs in March or September, and clip after flowering.

*Propagation.*—To propagate, strike cuttings in October.

**Lavender** (see **Lavandula**).

**Leadwort** (see **Plumbago**).

**Ledum,** *Ericaceæ.*—Low, ornamental, evergreen shrubs, the leaves of which are fragrant when bruised. Although hardy, they make decorative plants when grown in pots for the cold greenhouse.

*Propagation.*—They are propagated by seed sown in spring in sandy peat, by cuttings or by layers. They require the same cultural treatment as **Rhododendron.**

*Species.*—*L. glandulosum* [W. North America] (white, May, 2–4 ft.); *L. grœnlandicum* [*L. latifolium*] (Labrador Tea) [N. America, including Greenland] (white, April–June, 24–30 in.); *L. palustre* (Wild Rosemary) [N. Arctic regions] (white, April–May, 12–30 in.).

**Leea,** *Ampelidaceæ* (*Vitaceæ*).—These plants are cultivated in the warm greenhouse in a young state for their foliage, which is very decorative. They are allied to **Vitis,** but do not climb. They are handsome when trained to a pillar, and do exceedingly well planted out They can also be grown as trained specimens in pots. In all cases they should be rested and kept partly dry during the winter.

*Culture.*—They succeed in a good, light loam with leaf-mould or peat and sand, with good drainage, but should be given plenty of water during the growing season.

*Propagation.*—They are propagated by cuttings struck in sandy soil and placed in a close propagating case.

*Species.*—*L. amabilis* [Borneo] (velvety leaves, bronzy green striped white, young leaves pinkish brown, 36 in.); *L. coccinea* [Burma] (scarlet flowers in bud, opening to pink, green pinnate, leaves, 30–36 in. One of the few species with attractive flowers. *L. Micholitzii* [New Guinea] (pinnate leaves, rich green, marked bright red and white on the young leaves, 36 in.).

**Leiophyllum buxifolium** (Sand Myrtle), *Ericaceæ.*—An ornamental, dwarf, evergreen shrub from North America, suitable for the rock-garden. Grown in pans it is a valuable plant for the alpine house. It bears pinkish-white flowers from April to June, and grows to a height of from 12 to 30 inches.

*Culture.*—It thrives in a peaty or sandy, loamy soil that is lime-free.

*Propagation.*—It is propagated by seed sown in pans and placed in a cool frame; by layers pegged down in the autumn; or by cuttings of half-ripened wood struck in sandy soil under a bell-glass.

**Lemon** (see **Citrus Limonium**).

**Lemon Scented Verbena** (see **Lippia citriodora**).

**Leonotis Leonurus** (Lion's Tail), *Labiatæ.*—An excellent winter-blooming, tender shrub from South Africa, with scarlet-orange flowers. Cuttings should be taken in early spring and grown on; they should be stood outside at the end of May, or planted in the open ground, being frequently pinched to obtain a well-shaped plant, otherwise they are apt to become a straggling bush. If planted out, lift in October and bring inside to flower during November or December. Good plants can be grown in 8-inch pots.

**Leontopodium alpinum** (**Edelweiss**), *Compositæ.*—An interesting perennial herb with silvery-grey foliage and flowers from the Alps of Europe and Northern Asia, a popular flower, sought after by tourists to the Alps. It is perfectly hardy and usually grown on the rock-garden, but when grown in pans it makes an interesting plant for the alpine house.

*Propagation.*—It is readily raised from seed, which should be sown as soon as ripe, plunging the pots in a cold frame. Prick out the seedlings when large enough in gritty or sandy loam. When in their flowering pots or pans the plants should be tightly wedged between pieces of stone or old mortar. Division of the plant is not very satisfactory.

*L. sibiricum* [Russia] is similar to *L. alpinum*, but will grow more readily at a lower elevation.

**Leptopteris**, *Osmundaceæ.*—A group of beautiful filmy ferns, allied to **Todea**, and at one time included in that genus. It requires the same treatment as **Hymenophyllum** and **Trichomanes**.

*Species.*—*L. hymenophylloides* (*Todea hymenophylloides*) [New Zealand] (feathery fronds, 12–24 in. long); *L. superba* (*Todea superba*) [New Zealand] (a dwarf tree fern with beautiful dense fronds, 18–36 in. long). This is a splendid fern for exhibition. The variety *plumosa* is denser and more dwarf.

**Leptosiphon** (see **Gilia**).

# THE GREENHOUSE

**Leptospermum,** *Myrtaceæ.*—Cool-greenhouse, evergreen shrubs which grow from 2 to 8 feet high and flower in midsummer. They succeed in a compost of two parts peat to one part of loam and a little sand. *L. scoparium* [New Zealand] (white), although only half-hardy, may be grown outdoors in a sunny, sheltered situation in the milder districts; elsewhere it is best indoors; this species and some very beautiful varieties of it provide us with some highly valuable and attractive shrubs.

*Culture.*—Pot-up in a large pot or tub in spring. Stand outdoors after flowering until September.

*Propagation.*—Propagate by means of cuttings (with moderate bottom heat of about 60–65° F.) in May, or by seed sown in slight heat in March.

*Species and Varieties.*—*L. flavescens* [Australia] (white, 48–60 in.); *L. scoparium* [New Zealand] (white); *L. s.* var. *Boscawenii* (cherry-red in bud, opening white, 20–50 in.); *L. s.* var. *Chapmannii* (rose-scarlet, 20–50 in.); *L. s.* var. *Donard Beauty* (red, margined rose, 50 in.); *L. s.* var. *grandiflorum* (white, 30–60 in.); *L. s.* var. *Nichollsii* (carmine, purple leaves, 20–50 in.).

**Leptotes bicolor (Tetramicra bicolor)** [see Chapter on **Orchids**].

**Leschenaultia,** *Goodeniaceæ.*—Half-hardy, dwarf-growing, heath-like, evergreen shrubs with tiny red or blue flowers in summer. They thrive in the cool greenhouse in a mixture of sandy peat. *L. biloba* [W. Australia] grows 12–18 inches high and has blue flowers in May, June, and July. *L. b.* var. *grandiflora* has larger and brighter flowers and is a better grower. *L. linarioides* [Australia] is a branched shrub bearing terminal inflorescences of yellow flowers in August.

*Culture.*—Pot-up in March, and stand in a light, airy position. Water regularly while making growth, and keep only just moist in winter. Remove dead flower-heads and trim to shape after flowering.

*Propagation.*—Cuttings of young shoots may be rooted in sandy soil in a propagating case in March or April.

**Leucadendron argenteum** (Silver Tree), *Proteaceæ.*—This is the celebrated Silver Tree of Table Mountain, Cape Town. It is an interesting tree, and quite decorative in a young state, with its silky leaves. It is readily raised from seed, but care must be taken of the seedlings, or they quickly damp off. It requires good drainage, and when potting must be handled gently, as it resents root disturbance. It is best to crack the pot it occupies and pot-on the cracked pot attached to the ball of soil.

**Leuchtenbergia** (Agave Cactus), *Cactaceæ.*—A characteristic plant, forming a long, parsnip-like root, and a thick stem which becomes woody with age. It is an easy plant to grow, requiring full sunshine and warmth, and is readily raised from seed. It is similar and closely allied to **Echinocactus** and **Mammillaria,** requiring the same cultural treatment. *L. principis* [Central and N. Mexico] grows 9–12 inches high, and has yellow flowers in June.

**Leucocoryne ixioides** (*L. odorata*) (Glory of the Sun), *Liliaceæ.*—A charming bulbous plant from north of Santiago, Chile, with white, lavender-lilac, or pale blue flowers. It makes a charming cut flower.

428

It is readily raised from seed, but hitherto has not been grown too successfully in this country. It may be so with the cultural treatment given to **Ixia.**

**Leucojum** (Snowflake), *Amaryllidaceæ.*—Hardy bulbs, with bell-like blossoms, which thrive in any garden soil in semi-shade, and are useful for growing in pots in the cold greenhouse or alpine house.

*Culture.*—Plant or pot-up in September for the spring- summer- and winter-flowering kinds, and in the spring for the autumn-flowering kind. Put four or five bulbs in a 5-inch pot of sandy loam and stand in a shaded cold frame. Move into the greenhouse when growth commences, keeping the soil moist. Gradually dry off after flowering and re-pot.

*Propagation.*—Propagate by means of offsets or by seed.

*Species.*—*L. æstivum* (Summer Snowflake) [Europe] (white, spotted green, May, 15 in.); *L. autumnale* [*Acis autumnalis*] (Autumn Snowflake) [S.W. Europe] (white, Oct., 10 in.); *L. hyemale* (Winter Snowflake) [Maritime Alps] (April, 6 in.); *L. vernum* (Spring Snowflake) [Central Europe] (white, March, 9 in.); the variety *carpathicum* has white flowers with yellow tips.

**Leucophyta Brownii (Calocephalus Brownii),** *Compositæ.*—An easily-grown, white, woolly plant from Australia, suitable for the cool greenhouse. It has a silvery appearance, and is much used in bedding schemes either as a carpet plant pegged to the ground, or as a pot-plant with others.

*Propagation.*—It is propagated by cuttings, and may be wintered in a cool greenhouse.

**Leucopogon,** *Epacridaceæ.*—Handsome, greenhouse, evergreen shrubs. They require the same cultural treatment as **Epacris.** They are chiefly natives of Australia and New Zealand.

*Species.*—*L. australis* (pure white, winter and early spring, 24–36 in.); *L. lanceolatus* (white, winter to summer, 5–8 ft.); *L. Richei* (erect spikes of pure white flowers, winter and early spring, 30–40 in.); *L. verticillata* (white or pink, summer, 36–50 in.—young growth is a lovely rose colour).

**Lewisia,** *Portulacaceæ.*—Beautiful little plants with fleshy leaves, some of which are sometimes included under **Calandrinia.** They are all suitable for warm, sunny, sheltered spots in the rock-garden in a well-drained position.

*Culture.*—They are ideal plants for growing in pans for the alpine house in a mixture of loam, peat, and sand, with a little brick-rubble and good drainage. They are more safely grown under such conditions. They should be kept on the dry side during winter, but require a good supply of water when growing.

*Propagation.*—They are increased by seed, which should be sown as soon as ripe and placed under glass.

*Species.*—*L. brachycalyx* [Western N. America] (white or pink, April–May, 4–6 in.); *L. Cotyledon* [Mountains of N. California] (white flowers with pink veins, leaves in dense rosette, April–May, 8–10 in.); *L. Howellii* [S.W. Oregon] (deep-rose flowers, rosettes of leaves, 6–10 in.); *L. rediviva* (Bitter Root) [Western N. America] (rose and white, June–

July, 3–5 in.). This should be carefully watered even when growing. The root is eaten in the spring by the Indian; the bark of the root, which is very bitter, slips off easily when boiled. *L. Tweedyi* [Washington] (pink, May–June, 8–12 in.). There are many beautiful named hybrids raised from the different species, some of which seem to hybridise quite readily.

**Libertia,** *Iridaceæ.*—Ornamental perennial herbs with dainty, Iris-like leaves, and white or bluish flowers. Many of them can be grown outside, particularly in the milder parts of the country. They are very decorative for the cool greenhouse, either in pots or planted out. They will succeed in ordinary well-drained soil. They are increased by seed sown as soon as ripe and placed in a cool greenhouse, or by careful division in the spring.

*Species.*—*L. cærulescens* [Chile] (blue, summer, 18–24 in.); *L formosa* [Chile] (white, May, 16 in.); *L. grandiflora* [New Zealand] (pure white, summer, 30–36 in.); *L. ixioides* [New Zealand] (white, summer, 18–24 in.).

**Libonia,** *Acanthaceæ.*—Half-hardy, winter-flowering, evergreen plants for the warm greenhouse. They grow from 18 to 24 inches in height, and require similar treatment to that recommended for **Jacobinia,** with which genus they are now included.

*Species.*—*L. floribunda* (scarlet and yellow), see **Jacobinia pauciflora;** *L. penrhosiensis* (scarlet and yellow), see **Jacobinia penrhosiensis.**

**Licuala,** *Palmaceæ.*—Handsome, warm-greenhouse, dwarf fan-palms, some of which are grown commercially. They like a tropical temperature and abundant moisture, and should be shaded from strong sunshine to obtain foliage of a rich, deep green. They are easily damaged, consequently they are not very suitable for room decoration, but as exhibition plants few palms are more striking.

*Propagation.*—Propagation is effected by fresh seeds sown in bottom heat and grown on as for **Howea.**

*Species.*—*L. elegans* [Sumatra] (36–48 in.); *L. grandis* [New Britain] 36–42 in.).

**Lietzia brasiliensis,** *Gesneriaceæ.*—A handsome but remarkable tuberous-rooted stove-plant, from Brazil. The terminal racemes of flowers, produced in summer, are green spotted with brown. It requires a well-drained compost of light, fibrous loam, leaf-mould, and sand. It is increased by means of cuttings, seed, or tubers, with bottom heat in each case.

**Lilac** (see **Syringa**).

**Lilium** (Lily), *Liliaceæ.*—There are many different species and varieties of Lilies, but they are for the most part hardy, bulbous perennials requiring practically the same management. Lilies thrive in deep, well-dug garden soil, or in a moist, well-drained, fibrous loam with well-decayed leaf-mould and gritty sand in it. A few, such as *L. auratum, L. giganteum, L. speciosum,* and most of the American Lilies, like a peaty soil, but with some the presence of peat in their soil will cause failure. Although very few are really successful on a calcareous soil, *L. candidum, L. Henryi, L. Martagon, L. pyrenaicum, L. regale,* and *L. testaceum* are exceptions. The best soil is porous, with moisture for the root-run, and humus in the form of leaf-mould, peat, spent hops or worn-out farm- or stable-manure.

Most species are suitable for cultivation under glass as well as in the open. In the warm greenhouse *L. longiflorum* will bloom in late spring, while *L. speciosum* and *L. auratum* flower in summer. Lilies which form roots from the base of the stem as well as from the bulb should be planted among low-growing shrubs, which will afford shade to the base of their stems. These particular lilies may be planted at any time, and somewhat deeper than the non-stem-rooting kinds. As Lily bulbs dry up very quickly, it is a good plan to keep them covered with cool, damp fibre for about ten days previous to planting. When in bloom all Lilies must be carefully staked, and all dead flowers must at once be removed, but the stems must not be cut down until they have died off.

*Pot Culture.*—Plant in late autumn. A 12-inch pot will take six bulbs; a large bulb of *L. auratum* would require a 10-inch pot to itself. A bulb of *L. longiflorum* or *L. speciosum* would require a 5- to 6-inch pot. Such species as *L. candidum* and *L. tigrinum* need a 6- to 8-inch pot. The bulbs should be covered by 1 inch of soil, which should be made firm, and care must be taken that the bulbs do not touch the sides of the pots. They should be treated in their first stages of growth in exactly the same way as Hyacinths grown in pots, except that the pots must be only partly filled with soil. The pots should remain buried in ashes or fibre in a frame until the plants begin to grow. As the stems grow, the pots are gradually filled up to within about an inch of the rim. Those intended to flower early should be placed under glass in a temperature of 45–50° F., until growth is well started, when heat should be increased to 60–70° F. Lilies so treated should flower about twelve to fourteen weeks after being brought into the greenhouse. Watering should be done very carefully, and not commenced until the plants have started; and then only sufficient should be administered to keep the earth moist. When the buds appear, weak liquid manure may be given once a week for a week or two, then twice a week, increasing the strength.

A good stimulant can be made by mixing some cow-manure and soot and placing one bushel in a bag in 15 gallons of rain-water, or one ounce of nitre of soda to a gallon of rain-water. When the colours of the flower begin to show, stop giving the liquid manure and remove the plant to a lower temperature (about 50° F.). This ensures perfect flowers, and they will last longer.

Late bloomers should remain outdoors in a sheltered situation.

*Lily Disease* is caused by the mould *Botrytis cinerea*. *Mosaic Disease* as well as *Bulb Mite* are two pests to guard against.

*The Madonna Lily* (*L. candidum*) and the *Nankeen Lily* (*L. testaceum*), require different treatment. Transplant these lilies in August. They like deep, well-dug loam and cow-manure for soil. They resent disturbance, and should be lifted only when necessary. Top-dress with well-rotted manure each spring.

*Propagation.*—Propagation is carried out by means of offsets in October, by planting scales from bulbs in sandy soil in a cold frame, or by seed in pans in a cold frame in August. Seedlings will flower when they are from two to five years old, according to species. The seedlings of such Lilies as *L. formosanum*, *L. philippinense*, and *L. regale*, however, usually flower in their second year (the first two sometimes within the year) and are therefore suitable for raising from seed.

*Species and Varieties.*[1]—*L. aurantiacum* [*L. croceum*] \* (orange, July–Aug., 9–14 ft.) ; *L. auratum* [golden-rayed or Japanese Lily] \* S.R. (white, yellow, and crimson, Aug.–Sept., 40 in.) ; *L. candidum* [White Madonna Lily] \* (white, June–July, 50 in.) ; *L. carniolicum* [Carniolan Lily] (scarlet with black spots, July, 30 in.) ; *L. chalcedonicum* [Turk's Cap] (bright scarlet, July–Aug., 40 in.) ; *L. croceum* (see *L. aurantiacum*) ; *L. elegans* [*L. Thunbergianum*] \* (red, shades of yellow with black spots, May–June, 20 in.) ; *L. formosanum ;* *L. longiflorum* [Trumpet Lily] \* S.R. (white, July–Aug., 30 in.) ; *L. Martagon* (rosy violet, wine-red and white, July, 40 in.) ; *L. philippinense* (white, tinged green, streaked red, July–Sept., 12–40 in.) ; *L. pumilum* [*L. tenuifolium*] \* (sealing-wax scarlet, June, 18 in.) ; *L. pyrenaicum* [Pyrenean Lily] (yellow and black, May and June, 30 in.) ; *L. regale* \* (white and yellow, July, 24–40 in.) ; *L. speciosum magnificum* and vars. [Japanese Lily] \* S.R. (carmine, margined white, Aug.–Sept., 50 in.) ; *L. sulphureum* [*Wallichianum superbum*] S.R. (sulphur-yellow, Sept.–Oct., up to 10 ft.) ; *L. testaceum* (syn. *excelsum*) [Nankeen Lily] \* (nankeen-yellow, anthers scarlet, June–July, 60 in.) ; *L. tigrinum splendens* [Tiger Lily] (scarlet-orange, dark-purple spots, Aug.–Sept., 50 in.) ; *L. umbellatum erectum* [*L. dauricum*] (orange scarlet, spotted with black, June and July, 20 in.).

**Lily of the Palace** (see **Hippeastrum aulicum**).

**Lily of the Valley** (see **Convallaria**).

**Limatodes rosea** (see Chapter on **Orchids**).

**Lime** (see **Citrus aurantifolia**).

**Limnobium stoloniferum (Trianea bogotensis),** *Hydrocharitaceæ.*—A neat, floating, aquatic herb, suitable for aquaria or for growing in glass vessels or tubs, even outside during the summer. It is advisable to prevent it from becoming crowded, so that the leaves may grow upright. It should be grown inside during the winter in a temperature not lower than 40° F. It is increased by division.

**Limonium [Statice]** (Sea Lavender), *Plumbaginaceæ.*—These extremely beautiful " Everlasting " flowers thrive in sunny borders or in the rock-garden, in well-drained, sandy loam and leaf-mould. If preferred, they may be potted-up and flowered in the cold greenhouse.

For drying, the flowers should be cut as soon as they are fully opened, tied in bunches, and hung up to dry in a cool, well-ventilated room.

*Culture.*—ANNUALS : For growing indoors the hardy species are best treated as half-hardy, and should be sown under glass in March (temperature 55° F.). Prick out 4 inches apart when large enough to handle, harden off at the end of April, and pot-up in a compost of two-thirds fibrous loam and one-third peat, to which a little leaf-mould and sand, and some well-decayed cow-manure have been added. Pot-on as the roots fill the pots, until 8- to 9-inch pots are reached.

[1] S.R. = stem-rooting.   \* = suitable for forcing.

Lewisia Howellii

*Photos*]

Lewisia Tweedyi

[*R. A. Malby*

[F. G. Preston

Monstera deliciosa
*Showing Flower and Fruit*

PERENNIALS : Sow seed in the open in April, take cuttings in the spring or summer, and strike in sandy soil in a cold frame, or propagate by means of division in April, or by root-cuttings in September, and pot-up as above.

*Species.*—HALF-HARDY ANNUALS : *L. Bonduellii* [Algeria] (yellow) ; *L. sinuatum* [Mediterranean region] and *L. sinuatum hybridum* (mauve, white, and rose, June–Oct., 15–30 in.) ; *L. Suworowii* [Turkestan] (rosy purple or white, June–Oct., 12–18 in.).

HALF-HARDY PERENNIALS : *L. brassicæfolium* [Canary Islands] (purple and yellowish, white, summer, 12–18 in. ; *L. macrophyllum* (blue and white, summer, 18–24 in.) ; *L. profusum* [hybrid] (violet purple and white, summer, up to 30 in.) ; a handsome greenhouse plant.

**Linaria** (Toad Flax), *Scrophulariaceæ.*—The name of a genus containing many species, hardy annuals, and hardy herbaceous perennials. They grow on rock-work in the wild or woodland garden, or in any well-drained soil and cool, semi-shaded position. The taller sorts are excellent for cutting. *L. vulgaris* (Butter and Eggs, or the common Toad Flax) [Europe] is indigenous to Britain, also *L. Cymbalaria* (Kenilworth Ivy) which is often found as a trailer on old walls. It has a pretty, indented leaf and a lilac-and-yellow flower, resembling that of a Snapdragon in shape. *L. bipartita splendida* [Portugal and N. Africa] is a useful annual with red, white, or purple flowers, which makes an excellent pot-plant for the cold greenhouse. It grows about 12 inches high and thrives in light, sandy loam in dry, sunny positions. *L. triornithophora* [Spain and Portugal] (violet and purple, striped with orange) is an interesting pot-plant for the cool greenhouse.

*Culture.*—Sow seed thinly in a frame in August. Pot-up the seedlings singly when large enough to handle, or put three in a pot and transfer to the cold greenhouse, where they will flower from March to May the following year. *L. Cymbalaria* [Europe], with lilac and yellowish flowers, is a useful little perennial trailing plant for hanging-baskets, while *L. alpina* [Alps], *L. Cymbalaria* var. *maxima* (*L. pallida*), and *L. origanifolia* [S. Europe] are charming when grown in pans for the alpine house.

**Lindenbergia grandiflora,** *Scrophulariaceæ.*—A valuable winter-flowering perennial from the Himalayas. It might be termed a bush musk, with its large, yellow, mimulus-like flowers, which give a good display for quite three months during the winter.

*Culture.*—Cuttings may be taken in April or May, and stood under a hand-light with a little warmth. Pot-on when rooted into small 60 pots, in a compost of equal parts of loam, leaf-mould, and sand. Pot-on into 5-inch pots, and finally into 8-inch pots in a compost of two parts loam, one of soil, and one of sand. To obtain bushy specimens the plants should be pinched two or three times during the growing season.

**Linnæa borealis** (Twin Flower), *Caprifoliaceæ.*—Sub-shrubby trailing plants from North Europe and North Asia with slender, thread-like stems, and pinkish or white, bell-shaped flowers, suitable for the shady parts of rockeries, and charming in pans for the alpine house. They should be planted in porous, peaty soil. When not in flower the pans should be plunged in ashes or sand to their rims and kept in a shady frame.

E E

*Propagation.*—They are propagated by division, or by cuttings of half-ripened shoots in sandy peat placed under a hand-light.

**Linum** (Flax or Linseed-oil Plant), *Linaceæ*.—A fine genus of hardy annual and perennial plants which thrive in dry, light soil in a sunny position

*Species.*—*L. arboreum* [Crete], a small shrub, with clear yellow flowers in May and June, growing 8–12 inches high, and *L. salsoloides* [Mediterranean Alps], bearing white flowers with a purple eye in June and July, and growing 8–10 inches high, are very useful perennials when grown in pans for the alpine house. *L. flavum* is a showy and attractive sub-shrubby perennial, some 10 inches high, with a profusion of golden-yellow flowers from June to September. When not in flower they should be plunged in ashes in a cold frame. *L. grandiflorum* [N. Africa], with bright-red flowers, and *L. perenne*, with beautiful pale blue flowers, are two lovely species. Both grow from 12 to 24 inches in height, and flower from May to September. Both these are also useful as pot-plants.

*Culture.*—PERENNIALS : Sow seed in pots as soon as ripe, and plunge the pots in a cold frame ; or sow seed in the open in April ; or take cuttings and strike in sandy soil in July. Pot-up in March or April, using 5- to 6-inch pots and a compost of loam and peat with a little sand mixed. Water well from March to October, and give weak manure-water when in bloom. Decrease the water supply after October.

*Pruning.*—Prune back the previous year's growth in February or March to within one inch of the base.

**Linum trigynum** (see **Reinwardtia trigyna**).

**Lion's Tail** (see **Leonotis Leonurus**).

**Liparis** (see Chapter on **Orchids**).

**Lippia** (Sweet Verbena), *Verbenaceæ*.—Only one kind of this sweet-smelling deciduous shrub is grown to any extent—*L. citriodora*, with purple blooms in August. It can be grown in the open or against a wall in the south and west of England, and in other parts it is suitable for the cold greenhouse, but it requires protection from the frost in winter, even under shelter.

*Culture.*—Re-pot into a smaller pot in the spring in rich mould, loam, sandy peat, or leaf-mould for preference ; when well rooted, transfer to a larger pot. It succeeds also in the warm greenhouse, where it flowers in summer.

*Pruning.*—Cut young shoots hard back to the old wood in February, and pinch back the young shoots from time to time, but not later than June.

*Propagation.*—Propagate by means of cuttings of young wood in gentle heat (temperature 60° F.) in spring.

**Lippia nodiflora.**—This is a dwarf-growing perennial, about 6 inches high, and carrying white, pink, or purple flowers from May to September. It is suitable for the rock-garden, but can also be grown in a pan with other alpine plants, where it will be interesting in the alpine house. It does best in the sun and in gritty loam.

*Propagation.*—It is propagated by means of division in March.

434

**Liriope spicata (Ophiopogon spicatus)**, *Liliaceæ.*—A cool greenhouse or half-hardy plant, a native of China and Japan. The average height is from 9 to 12 inches. The spikes of violet-blue flowers push up freely among the arching green leaves in autumn. As an ornamental pot-plant, var. *variegata*, with yellow and green leaves, is more useful than the green-leaved type.

*Culture.*—The plants thrive in a sandy, loamy potting compost, are readily increased by division of the clumps in spring, and should be grown on in the cool greenhouse (temperature 50–60° F.).

**Lisianthus** (see **Eustoma**).

**Lissanthe sapida,** *Epacridaceæ.*—A pretty little evergreen shrub from New South Wales, with racemes of flowers, white, tipped with green, during June, followed by red edible berries. It is allied to **Epacris,** and requires the same cultural treatment.

**Lissochilus** (see Chapter on **Orchids**).

**Listrostachys** (see Chapter on **Orchids**).

*Species.*—*L. bidens* [W. Tropical Africa] (flowers sweet-scented, white or pinkish, May–June, 10–15 in.) ; *L. pertusa* (*A. Pescatoreanum*) [Sierra Leone] (white, tinged yellow, May–June, 12 in.).

**Lithospermum** (Gromwell), *Boraginaceæ.*—Although most of these plants are quite hardy (some of them being grown in rock-gardens), they are equally valuable for growing in pans for the alpine house. They thrive best in a well-drained, sandy loam, and are propagated by seed, which should be sown as soon as ripe, by cuttings of half-ripened wood placed in sand in a cold frame, or by division in the spring.

*Species.*—*L. canescens* (Puccoon, or Red-root) [N. America] (orange, June–July, 8–12 in., leaves covered with silky hairs) ; *L. diffusum* (*L. prostratum*) [S. Europe] (deep gentian blue, summer, 8–15 in.). This is a favourite evergreen rock-garden sub-shrub, which should be planted in lime-free soil. There are forms of which " *Heavenly Blue* " is perhaps the best known. *L. fruticosum* [E. and S. Spain] (purple-azure, summer, 8–12 in.). This is a woody branching bush ; an erect *L. diffusum* which is said to stand lime better. *L. Gastonii* [Western Pyrenees] (bright sky-blue, with white eye, summer, 6–10 in.). This is a very desirable plant, with flowers twice the size of *L. fruticosum*. *L. graminifolium* [Italy] (soft pale blue, May–June, 6–12 in.). This is one of the best, being prolific, a lime lover, and one which will spread by layering. *L. oleifolium* [Spanish Pyrenees] (deep and pale blue and violet, May–June, 6 in.). A beautiful plant with few but rather large flowers.

**Lithospermum petræum** (see **Moltkia petræa**).

**Littonia modesta,** *Liliaceæ.*—An elegant, South African, warm-greenhouse plant which climbs by means of the tendril at the tips of its leaves. It somewhat resembles **Gloriosa,** and requires the same cultural treatment. It bears pretty, rich-orange, bell-shaped flowers in early summer.

**Livistona,** *Palmaceæ.*—These are undoubtedly the most common of fan-leaved palms, some of which are very easy to grow, and fairly hardy, as in the case of *L. australis* and *L. chinensis*, succeeding in a strong loam, with good drainage, and an abundance of water. Some of the more tender species, such as *L. humilis, L. olivæformis,* and *L.*

**435**

*rotundifolia*, require a lighter soil and more shade to obtain the rich green colour of a healthy Livistona.

*Culture*.—They thrive in good fibrous loam, with sufficient sand to keep it open, and a small portion of ½-inch bones added for old plants. Young plants are best planted in tan or fibre over hot-water pipes, keeping the house close and moist. Growth is then more rapid, and fine plants are more quickly obtained.

*Propagation*.—They are propagated by imported seeds sown in heat as soon as received.

*Species*.—*L. australis* [Australia], a form in South Australia with the young petioles and leaves blood red, known as *L. Mariæ*. *L. chinensis* [China], is often grown in the trade as *Latania borbonica*, and is the best-known representative of the genus. *L. Hoogendorpii* [Java] has rich, dark-green leaves which form a complete circle. *L. humilis* [N. Australia] has dark-green, deeply divided leaves, and is a handsome palm, in a young state, for decoration. *L. olivæformis* [Brazil] has rich, deep green leaves which are rather flabellate, and the margin is divided into broad segments. *L. rotundifolia* [Java] has dark-green leaves which are divided into many elongated segments. It is pretty in a young state for decoration.

**Loasa lateritia** (see **Blumenbachia lateritia**).

**Lobelia,** *Campanulaceæ*.—A genus of pretty, profusely blooming plants, half-hardy annuals and herbaceous perennials, of which the low-growing kinds are suitable for edgings. The various species grow from 5 to 36 inches in height, and bloom from July to October, and thrive in sunny positions with deep, well-manured, and moist soil.

*L. gracilis*, a half-hardy annual, from its bush-like habit and profusion of celestial blue flowers in July is extremely beautiful in pots, beds, or when used as an edging. All the varieties of the greenhouse annual *L. Erinus* (blue, white, and red), as well as others with yellowish or bronzy foliage; the double flowered variety known in gardens as *Kathleen Mallard ;* and *L. tenuior* (*L. ramosa*) [W. Australia] another annual with blue and white eye, flowering from July to October, and growing 15–18 inches high, are valuable for edging, for intermixing with other plants in the greenhouse, for hanging baskets, or for rustic-work vases, over whose edges they droop in graceful manner. Treat all these as half-hardy annuals. The tall perennial species, *L. cardinalis* [N. America] (scarlet, 24–36 in.); *L. fulgens* [Mexico] (scarlet); and *L. syphilitica* [N. America] (blue and white), with their handsome spikes of flowers, are very ornamental and valuable for pot culture, too. There are also a number of beautiful varieties and hybrids of these species.

*Culture*.—ANNUALS: Sow seed thinly under glass (temperature 60° F.) in March, on the surface of pans of very fine, moist, sandy soil, that have been soaked well before sowing. Prick off 1 inch apart in boxes, harden off in a cold frame in April, and plant out early in May. If required for greenhouse use pot-up singly into 3- or 4-inch pots, using a compost similar to that mentioned below (see Pot Culture).

PERENNIALS: Sow seed in a frame in April, take cuttings of young growth in March, or propagate by means of division in late April, and

436

plant out in rich, moist soil to which a dusting of bonemeal has been added, or pot-up for greenhouse use. Water liberally while the plants are making growth. As soon as the foliage is dead in autumn the stems should be cut down and the roots lifted and stored in boxes of dry soil in a frost-proof frame. Water should be given in March to re-start growth, and late in April the roots should be divided and the most vigorous planted out.

*Pot Culture.*—(*L. cardinalis, L. fulgens* and vars.). Pot-up in March, using 6- to 8-inch pots and a compost of fibrous loam, leaf-mould, rotten manure, and sand. Keep in a well-ventilated frame on ashes until about to bloom, then transfer to the cool greenhouse (temperature 45–55° F. winter, 55–65° F. summer). After blooming cut down flower-stems, return to the frame in October, and cover with ashes in winter. Give a good watering in February to start growth again, and a month later divide and re-pot if necessary.

*Species and Varieties.*—ANNUAL : *L. Erinus* [S. Africa] (blue). There are many garden forms of this species of which the following are the best : *Barnard's Perpetual* (dark blue and white) ; *Celestial* (cobalt-blue) ; *Crystal Palace* (dark blue) ; *Imperial Blue* (dark) ; and *Waverley* (light blue). All flower from July to October and grow about 6 inches in height. *L. E.* var. *hamburgia* and *L. E.* var. *Paxtoniana*, both bright blue, with white eye and slender trailing habit, are charming basket plants. *L. gracilis* [Australia] (celestial blue, 12 in.) ; *L. tenuior* [Australia] (blue, white eye, 12 in.). PERENNIAL : *L. cardinalis* [N. America] (crimson-scarlet, 24–36 in.) ; *L. fulgens* [Mexico] (scarlet, 30 in.) ; *L. syphilitica* [N. America] (blue and white, 24–30 in.). All flower from June to September. NAMED PERENNIAL VARIETIES : *Kimbridge* (magenta) ; *B. Ladhams* (scarlet) ; *Queen Victoria* (red) ; *Purple Emperor ; Salmon Queen.* HYBRID PERENNIALS : *Gerardii* (purple-violet) ; *Milleri* (violet).

**Lobelia littoralis** (see **Pratia angulata**).

**Lobster's Claw** (see **Clianthus puniceus**).

**Lockhartia** (see Chapter on **Orchids**).

*Species.*—*L. elegans* [Trinidad] (yellow, spotted red, June, 6–8 in.) ; *L. verrucosa* [Guatemala] (yellow, barred and spotted red, 10–12 in.).

**Loddigesia oxalidifolia,** *Leguminosæ.*—An interesting, much-branched, evergreen, greenhouse shrub from the Cape of Good Hope. It grows 15–30 inches high, has trifoliate leaves, and bears pink and purple pea-shaped flowers in June. It succeeds in a mixture of equal quantities of peat and loam, with a liberal amount of sand.

*Propagation.*—It is propagated by cuttings of young growth in April, placed in sandy peat under a bell-glass.

**Loiseleuria procumbens** (**Azalea procumbens**), *Ericaceæ.*—A low-growing, evergreen shrub from the alpine regions of the Northern Hemisphere, suitable for growing in the rock-garden. When grown in pans it is very useful for the alpine house. It requires an open position, appreciates being shaded during the midday sun, and likes a plentiful supply of moisture during the summer. It should be grown in sandy peat with good drainage, and the pans should be plunged in ashes when not in the alpine house.

*Propagation.*—It is propagated by division, or by layers which root readily.

**Lomaria alpina** (see **Blechnum penna-marina**).

**Lomatia,** *Proteaceæ.*—Half-hardy, evergreen foliage shrubs for the cold or cool greenhouse. They thrive in full sun in a mixture of sandy loam and peat.

*Culture.*—Pot-up annually in March, and water well while growing. Keep just moist in winter. Trim to shape in early spring.

*Propagation.*—Cuttings or mature shoots may be rooted in sandy soil in heat, 65–70° F., in summer.

*Species.*—*L. ferruginea* [Chile] (yellow and scarlet, 8–9 ft.) ; *L. longi-folia* [Australia] (greenish white, 10 ft.) ; *L. obliqua* [S. America] (cream, 10 ft.) ; *L. silaifolia* [Australia] (white, 3 ft.) ; *L. tinctoria* [New South Wales] (white, 3 ft.).

**Lonchitis,** *Polypodiaceæ.*—A group of pretty ferns, requiring a warm greenhouse, succeeding under usual fern conditions.

*Species.*—*L. occidentalis* [Tropical Africa] (fronds 24–36 in.) ; *L. pubescens* [Mauritius] (fronds 24–40 in.). There are several forms of this species.

**Lonicera** (Honeysuckle), *Caprifoliaceæ.*—A genus comprising all the trailing and climbing, hardy and half-hardy, deciduous or evergreen plants known as Honeysuckles. These thrive in any good, moderately dry, garden soil and frequently in shaded positions. Some of them are valuable under glass.

*L. sempervirens* (Trumpet Honeysuckle) [N. America], with coral-red and yellow flowers, forms a beautiful greenhouse climber ; the var. *superba* has more brilliant scarlet flowers. *L. Standishii* [China], and *L. fragrantissima* (Bush Honeysuckles) [China], both having almost delicious fragrance, may be had in flower in the cool greenhouse in winter, filling the house with their perfume. There are a large number of shrubby species in cultivation.

*Pot Culture.*—Pot-up in the late autumn, in a compost of sandy loam, leaf-mould, and rotten manure, and keep in a cold greenhouse until February, then move to a sunny position in the cool house. After flowering, cut away old wood and trim back shoots. The plants may be stood outdoors from June to October.

*Propagation.*—To propagate, strike cuttings of ripe shoots in the open in late summer ; let the cuttings stand in the bed for a year, then plant out from October to April. If preferred, propagate by layering or from seed.

**Lophocereus Schottii** (**Pilocereus Schottii**), *Cactaceæ.*—A stout columnar-growing Cactus from North-west Mexico, the flowering stems of which develop tufts of long, hair-like bristles. The stems are 10–12 feet high, often of a violet or purplish colour, branching at the base. The flowers, which are nocturnal, are greenish, reddish inside with white stamens, and followed by red fruits. They require the same cultural treatment as **Cereus.**

**Lophophora Williamsii** (**Anhalonium Williamsii**), *Cactaceæ.*—This native of Mexico and Texas is a distinctive plant, with a globular flattened stem, 2–3 inches in diameter and equally tall. The flowers

**438**

are pinkish from the centre of the crown, followed by pinkish fruits, which usually mature the following year. It delights in full sunshine and the same cultural treatment as **Mammillaria.** The plant has a tendency to become wrinkled and soft during the winter, but recovers in the spring. It is highly esteemed by some Indian tribes on account of its narcotic properties, and is the "mescal button" of the Indian used in religious rites.

*Propagation.*—It is propagated by seed sown in sandy soil and placed in heat.

**Loropetalum chinense,** *Hamamelidaceæ.*—An ornamental evergreen shrub from Central and South-eastern China, very desirable for the cool greenhouse, and one which should be grown in sandy, peaty soil. It bears clusters of white flowers in the early spring, somewhat resembling **Hamamelis.**

*Propagation.*—It is propagated by seed, cuttings, and sometimes grafted on Hamamelis.

**Lotus,** *Leguminosæ.*—The hardy perennial species of this plant, which grow well in ordinary soil, are well suited for sunny borders, for the rock-garden, or for growing in pans for the alpine house ; while the trailers make charming plants for growing in baskets for the cool greenhouse.

*Species.*—*L. Bertholettii* [*L. peliorhynchus*] [Canaries] (scarlet, June, 10 in.) ; *L. Jacobæus* [Cape Verde] (dark purple) ; and *L. mascænsis* [Teneriffe] (like *L. Bertholettii*, but with yellow flowers). Both the latter are charming as basket plants.

*Culture.*—Pot-up in March using a compost of half loam and half leaf-mould and sand, with a little charcoal added. Stand in a sunny position. Water very sparingly in autumn and winter and give only a moderate amount even in summer (average temperature 50° F. winter, 60° F. summer).

*Propagation.*—Propagate by means of cuttings struck in a frame in July, or sow seed in a temperature of from 50-60° F. in March.

**Lotus, Sacred** (see **Nelumbo**).

**Lourya campanulata,** *Liliaceæ.*—An interesting plant from Cochin-China, resembling an **Aspidistra.** It has a creeping rhizome from which rise handsome leaves and dense heads or spikes of pale yellow flowers, followed by large blue fruits. It should be grown in the warm greenhouse in fibrous loam, leaf-mould, some sand, and a little well-rotted manure.

*Propagation.*—It is propagated by seed or by division when new growth commences.

**Love's Chain** (see **Antigonon leptopus**).

**Love-in-a-Mist** (see **Nigella**).

**Love-lies-bleeding** (see **Amarantus caudatus**).

**Luculia,** *Rubiaceæ.*—Beautiful half-hardy evergreen shrubs with attractive foliage and large clusters of fragrant white or pink flowers in autumn. They grow from 8 to 14 feet in height, and thrive in the cool greenhouse in a mixture of sandy loam and peat.

*Culture.*—Plant in the greenhouse bed in April or pot-up in 6- to 7-inch pots or large tubs. Good drainage is essential. Water regularly

**439**

while growing, and feed with occasional doses of liquid manure. Keep only just moist when dormant. Cut well back in early spring, after flowering, and rest for a month or two before again potting-up with fresh soil. Plants in beds should be top dressed.

*Propagation.*—Cuttings of semi-mature shoots, 2–3 inches long, may be rooted in sandy soil in a propagating case with slight bottom heat (70° F.) in summer, or seed may be sown.

*Species.*—*L. gratissima* [Temperate Himalayas] (pink, 8–14 ft.) ; *L. Pinceana* [Khasia Mts.] (white, changing to cream, with rosy tinge, 8–10 ft.).

**Luffa cylindrica** (Dishcloth Gourd, or Vegetable Sponge), *Cucurbitaceæ.*—An interesting climbing annual from Tropical Africa. It grows 10–15 feet in height and bears white or soft yellow flowers, which are followed by long, strong, ribbed fruit with fibrous interior, which, when dried, bleached, and prepared, are used as bath sponges (Luffa), hence the name " Vegetable Sponge ". It is usually grown as an ornament or a curiosity, by the same treatment as **Cucumber** and **Melon.**

**Lycaste cristata** (see **Paphinia cristata**).

**Lycaste Skinneri** (see Chapter on **Orchids**).

**Lychnis** (**Viscaria**), *Caryophyllaceæ.*—Some of these are among the best known of garden flowers for the hardy border or rock-garden. *L. Cœli-rosa* (Rose of Heaven) [Mediterranean region] is also very useful for growing in pots for the cool greenhouse. Seed may be sown either in the autumn, and kept in a cool house, finally growing several plants in a 5- or 6-inch pot which will give a good show with its rosy flowers in April and May ; or seed may be sown in January or February to give a later display than the autumn-sown. There is a white-flowered variety, *alba*, and also the variety *fimbriata*, which has toothed petals. *L. alpina* [European Alps] is suitable for the alpine house. It should be grown in well-drained, sandy soil, and the pans plunged in ashes in a cold frame in a sunny position when not in flower. It is readily raised from seed, and grows 5–6 inches high, bearing pink flowers in spring.

**Lychnis Lagascæ** (see **Petrocoptis Lagascæ**).

**Lychnis pyrenaica** (see **Petrocoptis pyrenaica**).

**Lycopersicum esculentum** (**Tomato**) (see **Fruit Under Glass**).

**Lycopersicum pimpinellifolium** [**L. racemigerum**] (Currant Tomato).—An ornamental climber for the cool greenhouse during the summer and autumn. The long racemes of currant-like, red berries are very attractive, particularly when the plant is trained up the roof. It requires the same cultural treatment as the Tomato.

**Lycopodium** (Club Moss), *Lycopodiaceæ.*—Stove, greenhouse, or hardy, evergreen, perennial plants, the leaves of some species being needle or thread-like, and others imbricated scales. Several can be grown in Wardian or fern cases. Most of the stove and greenhouse species should be grown in baskets to allow the plants to hang down.

*Propagation.*—They are propagated by cuttings, or by division in the spring, or by spores. All species need special attention, and should be shaded from the sun. They require a rough, fibrous loam and spongy peat.

*L. cernuum* [Tropics] grows 10–30 inches high, and is a handsome stove-plant with much-forked light-green branches. *L. Phlegmaria* (Tropics of the Old World] grows 6–24 inches high, and is a stove-plant of pendulous habit, having forked branches, elegant and slender, with tasselled-like appearance. *L. squarrosum* [E. Indies] has pendulous stems, 12–24 inches long.

**Lycoris,** *Amaryllidaceæ.*—Attractive, bulbous plants, all of which produce their flowers after the leaves have died down. Most of them need a greenhouse, although *L. squamigera* can be grown in a warm, dry border, or sheltered nook under a south wall.

*Culture.*—They succeed under the same cultural treatment as that given to **Hippeastrum,** and require a compost of equal parts of loam and leaf-mould, with a good proportion of sand. Well-drained pots are essential.

*Propagation.*—They are propagated by offsets and by seed.

*Species*—*L. aurea* (Golden Spider Lily) [China] (bright yellow, Aug., 12 in., cool greenhouse) ; *L. radiata* [China and Japan] (deep pink, approaching red, June, 15–18 in., cool greenhouse) ; *L. squamigera* [Japan] (rosy lilac, July–Aug., 18–20 in.). This last is the most popular species. It should have the cool greenhouse, but it can be grown outside.

**Lygodium** (Climbing Fern), *Schizæaceæ.*—A genus of greenhouse climbing ferns which thrive in the shade in a compost of two parts of sandy loam to one part of peat, with a little charcoal added.

*Culture.*—Pot-up in March, and water liberally during the summer.

*Propagation.*—Propagate by means of spores sown under glass in heat at any time, or by division in March (temperature 45° F. winter, 60° F. summer).

*L. circinatum* (*L. dichotomum*)has forked fronds, and will grow to a height of 6–8 feet. It requires a temperature of 55–65° F. *L. japonicum* [Japan] will grow to a height of 5 feet. *L. palmatum* (Hartford Fern) [N. America] has palmate-cordate leaves in pairs and requires the same temperature as *L. japonicum. L. scandens* [S. China to Ceylon] is an attractive, free-growing climber for the warm greenhouse. (See also **Ferns.**)

**Lysimachia Nummularia,** *Primulaceæ.*—This is the well-known perennial creeper commonly called Creeping Jenny. It is an excellent subject for carpeting in the rock-garden and for growing in hanging-baskets in the cold greenhouse. It thrives in semi-shade, in moist, rich, ordinary soil, and produces its pretty yellow flowers during summer and early autumn. The var. *aurea* has yellow foliage.

*Culture.*—Propagate by means of division in April or October, and pot-up as required for the greenhouse. No protection is required during the winter.

**Lysionotus,** *Gesneriaceæ.*—Handsome, warm-greenhouse, soft-wooded shrubs, with long, tubular flowers.

*Culture.*—They thrive in a compost of peat and loam, with some sand, and in a warm, moist atmosphere. They mostly have thick, fleshy roots, so they can be kept on the dry side during winter.

**441**

*Propagation.*—They are propagated by seed sown in sandy soil and placed in brisk heat, or by division of the root in the spring.

*Species.*—*L. carnosa* [China] (white, tinged lilac, 12–15 in.) ; *L. serrata* [India] (pale lavender or white, July–Aug., 12–24 in.).

**Mackaya bella** (see **Asystasia bella**).

**Macleania,** *Ericaceæ.*—Half-hardy, evergreen, semi-trailing plants, with attractive foliage and flowers, which thrive in the cool greenhouse in a compost of sandy loam and peat.

*Culture.*—Pot-up in well-drained pots as soon as new growth commences in early spring, or plant out in the greenhouse bed, or preferably in a border with shallow soil, particularly such as *insignis*, *pulchra*, and *punctata*, and top-dress annually. Water carefully and regularly while growing, decreasing the quantity in winter. Also trim and train climbers as required, and prune back plants grown in pots in March.

*Propagation.*—Cuttings made of new shoots 3–4 inches long may be rooted in sandy soil under a bell-glass in slight heat (temperature 65° F.) in spring.

*Species.*—*M. insignis* [Mexico] (red foliage and scarlet flowers in late spring), can be cut back and grown as a pot-plant ; *M. longiflora* [Peru] (red, 48–60 in.) is a good pot-plant. *M. pulchra* [Colombia] (red and yellow, up to 10 ft.), is best planted in a prepared site in a bed and allowed to climb. *M. punctata* [Ecuador] (semi-climber, red and yellow, up to 10 ft.) ; *M. speciosissima* [Colombia] (semi-trailer, red and yellow) is best grown in a hanging basket.

**Macodes** (see Chapter on **Orchids**).

**Macradenia** (see Chapter on **Orchids**).

**Macroplectrum sesquipedale [Angræcum sesquipedale]** (see Chapter on **Orchids**).

**Macrozamia,** *Cycadaceæ.*—Cycas-like plants, decorative as single specimen plants. They are all natives of Australia, and are easy to cultivate, requiring sandy loam and peat, an ordinary greenhouse temperature, with plenty of water during the growing season and rest during the winter.

*Propagation.*—They are propagated by imported seeds, which should be sown in heat, and also occasionally by offsets.

*Species.*—*M. Fraseri* (stem 3–4 ft., dark-green, pendulous leaves, a handsome species) ; *M. Paulo-Guilielmi* [*M. plumosa*] (leaves spirally twisted, 20–30 in., stems 24–48 in., a very beautiful plant, distinctive and elegant) ; *M. spiralis* (bright, shining green leaves—a very decorative plant in a young state).

**Madagascar Periwinkle** (see **Vinca rosea**).

**Madonna Lily** (see **Lilium candidum**).

**Magnolia,** *Magnoliaceæ.*—A genus of trees and large shrubs, some of which are hardy, some only half-hardy deciduous, and others are evergreen. All bear beautiful, large, cup-shaped flowers, with fleshy petals, which are usually white, creamy-white, or have a purple tinge, and are borne singly at the end of the shoots. They grow from 3 to 10 feet, and even up to 60 feet in the open, and flower during spring and summer.

**442**

# GREENHOUSE PLANTS

*Culture.*—In the cold greenhouse *M. denudata* (*M. conspicua*), *M. liliflora* (*M. obovata*), and *M. stellata* may be had in flower in March. They are also useful for forcing in the cool or warm greenhouse. Pot-up in October or November, using 8- to 12-inch pots and a compost of sandy loam, leaf-mould, and rotten manure. They are rather impatient of root disturbance, so great care should be taken when potting. Transplanting in the open is best carried out when the new growth starts in the late spring. Keep fairly dry in a cold greenhouse (temperature 45–50° F. winter, 55° F. summer), until growth commences, then water moderately. After flowering prune out weak wood and dead flower-shoots. Sink the pots to their rims in ashes outdoors from May to December, when the pots should be moved into the house.

*Hardy Species.*—*M. Campbellii* [Himalayas] (white, pink, or red) ; *M. denudata* (*M. conspicua*) [Central China] (white) ; *M. mollicomata* [Tibet, Yunnan] (creamy white, stained purple) ; *M. parviflora* [Japan] (white, claret centre) ; *M. salicifolia* [Japan] (white) ; *M. Soulangeana* [garden origin] (white, stained purple) ; *M. Soulangeana* var. *Lennei* (rosy purple) ; *M. stellata* [Japan] (white) ; *M. Veitchii* [hybrid] (white, stained rosy red) ; *M. Watsonii* [Japan] (creamy white, claret centre) ; *M. Wilsonii* [W. China] (white, claret centre).

**Mahernia verticillata** (Honey Bell), *Sterculiaceæ.*—An evergreen sub-shrub from South Africa, very suitable for the cool greenhouse—with its fragrant, yellow, bell-shaped flowers during winter and spring. Being of rather a straggling habit, the young growth should be frequently stopped to encourage lateral growths.

*Culture.*—It is of easy cultivation in a compost of equal parts of loam, leaf-mould, and peat, with some sand.

*Propagation.*—It is propagated readily by cuttings of young growth placed under glass during the summer. Being of a flexible nature, the plant can be easily trained to any shape. It is also useful for hanging-baskets.

**Maianthemum bifolium (M. Convallaria),** *Liliaceæ.*—A hardy little plant from the Northern Temperate regions, valuable for growing in a shady position. When grown in pans of any good, fertile soil it makes an attractive plant for the alpine house. The pans should be plunged in a shady position when not in flower. It is increased by division in the spring. It should be divided every three or four years, or the pans become overcrowded and few flowers are produced.

**Maidenhair Fern** (see **Adiantum**).

**Maize** (see **Zea Mays**).

**Malayan Jessamine** (see **Trachelospermum jasminoides**).

**Male Fern** (see **Dryopteris Filix-mas**).

**Malope trifida,** *Malvaceæ.*—Although a perfectly hardy annual, this native of Spain and North Africa is very decorative for the cool greenhouse.

*Culture.*—The seed may either be sown in September in 3½-inch pots, thinning to four seedlings, which can then be kept in a cool greenhouse during the winter ; after which they should be potted-on in 6-inch pots : or three plants may be potted in an 8-inch pot early in the new year. It will give a good show in April and May, with its rose and purple flowers. Seed may also be sown early in the new year, to follow on after the autumn-sown seedlings. There are various forms : *grandiflora* is superior to the type ; *alba* has white, and *rosea* rose-coloured flowers.

**Malpighia,** *Malpighiaceæ.*—Interesting stove-greenhouse, evergreen shrubs, with clusters or corymbs of red, pink or white flowers. Some species are quite ornamental, with holly-like leaves.

*Culture.*—They thrive best in a compost of fibrous loam and sandy peat, in a warm, moist temperature.

*Propagation.*—They are propagated by cuttings of half-ripened shoots inserted with the leaves intact, under a bell-glass with bottom heat during the summer.

*Species.*—*M. aquifolia* [S. America] (pale pink, Aug., 40–50 in.) ; *M. coccifera* [S. America] (pink, June–Aug., 20–30 in.) : *M. nitida* [S. America] (pink, March–July, 50–60 in.).

**Malus,** *Rosaceæ.*—A genus of hardy, deciduous trees, sometimes included under **Pyrus,** most species of which bear delicate blossom and handsome fruit. Many of the species and hybrids can be grown in the cool or warm greenhouse, and thus be had in flower from March until the end of April.

*Species.*—*M. Eleyi,* a beautiful hybrid with very deep carmine flowers and purplish leaves ; *M. floribunda* [Japan], pink and white ; *M. f. atro-sanguinea ; M. purpurea* [garden hybrid] ; and *M. spectabilis* [N. China] rose, semi-double.

*Pot Culture.*—Pot-up young trees in October, using 8- to 12-inch pots and a compost of two parts of sandy loam to one part of leaf-mould and rotted manure ; sink the pots in ashes outdoors from May to December. They will not require re-potting for two or three years, but should be top dressed, and drainage should be attended to annually. They benefit from an occasional feeding with liquid manure when the pots are getting filled with roots.

*Propagation.*—Propagate by means of seed, grafting or budding in the open.

**Malva umbellata** (see **Sphæralcea umbellata).**

**Malvastrum hypomadarum,** *Malvaceæ.*—A South African, free-flowering, greenhouse shrub with white and rose-purple flowers. It succeeds in a 6-inch pot in a compost of equal parts of loam, leaf-mould, and sand

*Propagation.*—It is propagated by cuttings under glass in late spring which will flower the following season. This plant has been cultivated for many years as *M. capense,* which is a different plant.

**Malvaviscus mollis,** *Malvaceæ.*—A fine old warm-greenhouse shrub from Mexico, with bright-scarlet flowers during the autumn. Although it will grow into a large bush, useful-sized plants can be grown in 6-inch pots. It should be given a good light soil of fibrous peat and loam.

*Propagation.*—It is propagated by cuttings of side-shoots placed under a bell-glass, in heat.

**Mammillaria,** *Cactaceæ.*—A varied genus of tender and half-hardy Cacti with succulent, knobbly, and very spiny stems. They are mostly of dwarf growth, and rarely exceed 15 inches in height, many being only an inch or two tall.

**444**

# GREENHOUSE PLANTS

*Compost.*—They like a warm, sunny position, in a mixture of equal parts of fibrous loam, coarse sand, and brick-mortar rubble.

*Culture.*—Pot-up triennially in March in pots that are not too large (average temperature winter: 50° F. night, 60° F. day; summer: 70° F. night, 80° F. day). Ventilate freely, and water weekly during summer, but keep on the dry side in winter.

*Propagation.*—Propagate by means of seed sown in heat in March or by cuttings made of tops in March.

*Species.*—*M. bicolor* [Mexico] (purple, May–July, 4 in.); *M. elegans* [Mexico] (insignificant white, summer, 3 in.); *M. elephantidens* [Guatemala and Honduras] (violet-edged, white and pink centre, Aug.–Oct., 15 in.); *M. elongata* [Central Mexico] (white, summer, 6–9 in.); *M. elongata* var. *stella-aurata* (yellow, spines golden yellow and in rosettes, May, 3 in.); *M. Grahamii* [Texas] (rose-pink, June–Aug., 4–6 in.); *M. Heyderi* [Texas] (rosy purple, summer, 6 in.); *M. Heyderi* var. *applanata* (white, tinged red, July–Aug., 4–6 in.); *M. mutabilis* [Mexico] (purple, summer, 4–6 in.); *M. pusilla* [W. Indies] (yellowish white, May–June, silver spines, 3 in.); *M. rhodantha* var. *fuscata* (purple, summer, 6 in.); *M. r.* var. *sulphurea* (yellow, summer, 3 in.); and *M. viviparus* [S. America] (purple, spines purple and white, May–July). *M. radiosa* var. *arizonica* (pink), and *M. setispina* [Lower California] (pink, summer, 9 in.), which have white and brown, and white spines respectively, are half-hardy, and may be grown in the open in warm, sunny, and sheltered positions in some of the milder districts. They are also suitable for window-boxes.

**Mandevilla suaveolens,** *Apocynaceæ.*—Beautiful deciduous climbing plants which in the warm greenhouse run up to 15 or 20 feet in height, and in summer bear clusters of fragrant, white, jasmine-like flowers. They are best planted out in the greenhouse bed and trained up pillars and along roof wires.

*Culture.*—Plant in a well-drained site at the base of a pillar, in a compost of sandy peat and loam in spring. Water and syringe regularly while growing. A little powdered charcoal added to the soil when planting is beneficial. Cut out old and unwanted shoots after flowering and trim side shoots back according to requirements, leaving leaders full length. Keep on the dry side during winter.

*Propagation.*—Cuttings made of young side shoots about 3 inches in length may be rooted in pots of sandy soil in a propagating case with slight bottom heat in April or May, or ripe seed, when available, may be sown in slight heat (65–70° F.) in spring.

**Manettia,** *Rubiaceæ.*—A genus of evergreen twining plants which in the cool greenhouse reach from 12 to 14 feet in height, and in spring, summer, or early autumn produce red, white, or yellow flowers.

*Culture.*—Pot-up or plant in the greenhouse border, in March, in a well-drained site, in a mixture of sandy loam and peat, adding a sprinkling of powdered charcoal. Place in semi-shade and water and syringe regularly. Trim the plants to shape only after flowering.

*Propagation.*—Cuttings of young shoots about 3 inches in length may be rooted in pots of sandy soil in a propagating case with slight bottom heat, in spring or early summer.

*M. bicolor* [Brazil] has flowers which are red below and yellow towards the top. *M. inflata* [Paraguay] has red and yellow flowers, resembling *M. bicolor*, and is often grown under that name. It differs in its leafy reflexed calyx lobes; the base of the flower is swollen, and the yellow part is much smaller.

**Manfreda,** *Amaryllidaceæ.*—Tuberous plants with nocturnal greenish-or purplish-white flowers, somewhat resembling a tuberose. They are allied to **Agave,** and require the same cultural treatment.

*Species.*—*M. guttata* (*Agave guttata*) [Central America] (purplish, green and white, leaves mottled); *M. maculosa* (*Agave maculosa*) [Texas] (leaves glaucous and mottled); *M. variegata* (*Agave variegata*) [S. Texas and Mexico] (leaves channelled and mottled); *M. virginica* (*Agave virginica*) [S. United States] (hardy, suitable for the rock-garden or alpine house, leaves green, strongly-scented flowers). The variety *tigrina* has mottled leaves.

**Manihot,** *Euphorbiaceæ.*—Evergreen shrubs or herbaceous plants, some of which are grown in the warm greenhouse for the decorative effect of their foliage. They require a light but rich soil, and are propagated by seed placed in a warm temperature, or from cuttings of young but firm wood placed in sandy peat, under glass, with bottom heat.

*M. dulcis* [S. Brazil] is a handsome foliage shrub with deeply lobed leaves. The variety *Aipi* (Sweet Cassava) has reddish roots which are sweet and wholesome. The variety *multifida* has beautiful lobed leaves. *M. utilissima* (Bitter Cassava or Tapioca Plant) [Brazil] is of shrubby habit, and quite an attractive foliage plant with lobed leaves. This plant has been cultivated by the natives of Brazil since prehistoric times. The large, fleshy or tuberous roots contain a great quantity of starch, which give it its food value. They also contain more or less hydrocyanic acid, which makes the roots poisonous in a raw state. This is rendered harmless by heating, or pressed out with the juice. From the deposit after heating the Tapioca of our shops is obtained, also Brazilian Arrowroot. There is a beautiful variety, *M. u.* var. *variegata*, with bright yellow and green striped foliage.

**Mantisia saltatoria** (Dancing or Opera Girls), *Scitamineæ.*—An interesting stove herbaceous perennial from the East Indies. It bears pale violet and yellow flowers with numerous purple bracts during May and June.

*Culture.*—It succeeds in a compost of sandy peat and fibrous loam, but must have good drainage. Although it requires a good supply of water during the growing season, it should be kept fairly dry during winter.

*Propagation.*—It is propagated by division at the time of potting in the spring, when the new growth commences.

**Maranta,** *Marantaceæ.*—A genus of attractive, rhizomatous-rooted, ornamental foliage plants, suitable for cultivation in the warm greenhouse or moist stove house.

*Culture.*—Pot-up in spring in well-drained pots of sandy loam and peat and stand in semi-shade. Water regularly and syringe while growing. Occasional doses of weak liquid manure are beneficial. Keep only just moist during winter.

**446**

*Propagation.*—Propagation is carried out by means of division of the roots in spring.

*Species.*—*M. arundinacea* [Tropical America] (white, summer, 24–40 in.); there is a form with yellow and green variegated leaves—quite an attractive foliage plant. *M. arundinacea* is one of the sources of arrowroot, which is obtained from the roots. *M. bicolor* [Brazil] (light green, with dark green spots, 12 in.); *M. leuconeura* [Brazil] (light green, veined with white); *M. splendida* [Brazil] (dark green, marked with transverse bars, violet-red beneath, 18–30 in.).

**Maranta Chantrieri** (see **Calathea Chantrieri**).

**Maranta Porteana** (see **Stromanthe Porteana**).

**Marattia,** *Marattiaceæ.*—Stove or warm-greenhouse evergreen ferns, of a fair size and stately habit; consequently they are only suitable for a large greenhouse.

*Culture.*—They succeed in a compost of equal parts of loam, peat, and sand. Growing naturally in marshy places, they require plenty of water, and when possible they should be placed partly in water, where they will grow luxuriantly.

*Propagation.*—They are propagated by spores, which, although freely produced, rarely germinate, so they are generally increased by detaching the plump basal scales from the frond stem and laying them on a moist bed of fibre or sphagnum in peat. The scales quickly throw out roots and side-growths, which form small plants.

*M. alata* [W. Indies] has fronds 48–60 inches long, and is one of the most handsome of the genus, which will also succeed in a cool greenhouse. *M. fraxinea* [W. Africa, etc.] has fronds 5–10 feet long. There are several forms, of which the variety *elegans* is one of the best, and a good cool-greenhouse fern.

**Marguerite** (see **Chrysanthemum frutescens**), **Blue Marguerite** (see **Felicia amelloides**).

**Margyricarpus setosus** (Pearl Fruit), *Rosaceæ.*—A low-growing Peruvian evergreen, with narrow leaves, small, insignificant green flowers, and small, attractive white fruits. It is usually grown on rockeries, although it can be raised in pans for the alpine or cool greenhouse. It succeeds in a rich light soil, such as loam, leaf-mould, and sand in equal proportions.

*Propagation.*—It is readily propagated by cuttings taken in summer and placed in sand under a bell-glass.

**Marica,** *Iridaceæ.*—Tender, rhizomatous-rooted perennials, growing some 12–24 inches in height, and, in the warm greenhouse, bearing blue, white, violet or yellow, Iris-like flowers in summer.

*Culture.*—Pot-up in February, or, if preferred, plant in a greenhouse rockery in a compost of sandy loam and leaf-mould. Water regularly while growing, and feed with occasional doses of weak liquid manure. Keep only just slightly moist when dormant.

*Propagation.*—Divide the roots in spring, re-planting only the newer and most healthy portions.

*M. cærulea* [Brazil] grows 24–30 inches in height, has bright blue or lilac flowers, variegated at the base with bars of yellow, white, or brown. *M. gracilis* [Mexico to Brazil] grows 12–18 inches high, and bears white

# THE GREENHOUSE

flowers with yellow and brown cross marks at the base. The inner segments are blue.

**Marigold** (see **Calendula**).

**Maripose Lily** and **Maripose Tulip** (see **Calochortus**).

**Marjoram** (see **Origanum**).

**Marsh Rosemary** (see **Andromeda**).

**Marsilea,** *Marsileaceæ.*—Greenhouse aquatic plants related to ferns. The silky fronds, consisting of four leaflets, are sometimes mistaken for four-leaved Shamrock. They succeed in turfy loam and leaf-mould, requiring plenty of water at all seasons. If the pans or pots can be partly submerged in water or stood in saucers of water, so much the better.

*Propagation.*—They are readily increased in spring by division at the time of potting.

*M. Drummondii* [Australia] has leaflets thickly clothed with silky hair. *M. quadrifolia* [Europe and Asia] is a creeping plant, rooting as it runs. It is hardy in some parts of the country. The young leaflets close at night.

**Martinezia,** *Palmaceæ.*—Ornamental, feather-leaved, stove palms, with spiny trunks which, although they make good house palms, are unpopular because of their spiny nature.

*Culture.*—They do not require a lot of soil. Potting should be firm to retain small plants, which are of more decorative value. Light sandy loam with plenty of sharp sand is best, but they require an abundance of moisture and a stove temperature.

*Propagation.*—They are propagated by imported seed sown in heat. They are more decorative when young.

*M. caryotæfolia* [Colombia] has leaves which resemble those of the fish-tail palm, **Caryota,** but are light green. It differs from most palms in showing its adult leaves at an early stage. *M. erosa* [W. Indies] has needle-shaped spines on midrib and veins. This species makes a better specimen at 5 or 6 feet high than when small.

**Martynia** (Elephant's Trunk or Unicorn Plant), *Martyniaceæ.*—A half-hardy annual growing from 10 to 20 inches in height, and bearing beautiful, scented, Gloxinia-like flowers during August. It thrives in warm, sunny borders or in the cold greenhouse.

*Culture.*—Sow seed 2 inches apart in the open in April, and transplant when large enough to handle, or sow singly in small pots in March under glass. Harden off and plant out 12 inches apart in June, or pot-up into 5- to 6-inch pots by June, using a compost of loam, leaf-mould, rotten manure, and sand, and stand in the cold greenhouse (temperature 45° F. winter, 65° F. summer) to flower. Water well while growing, and apply liquid manure when the buds appear.

*Species.*—*M. fragrans* [Texas to Mexico] (violet and orange, Aug., 10–18 in.); *M. Louisiana* (Common Unicorn Plant) [Texas to New Mexico] (white or yellowish, with purple or yellow spots, summer, 18–24 in.); and *M. lutea* [Brazil] (orange yellow, Aug., 15–20 in.).

**Marvel of Peru** (see **Mirabilis**).

**Masdevallia** (see Chapter on **Orchids**).

**Mask Flower** (see **Alonsoa**).

[*F. G. Preston*

Nelumbium Nelumbo (N. speciosum)
*Showing Bud, Flower and Seed Vessel*

Giant Mimulus                    Linum rubrum

Photos]                        [*Sutton & Sons Ltd., Dobbie & Co., and Alexander & Brown*
Tropæolum (Golden Gleam)        Myosotis alpestris

# GREENHOUSE PLANTS

**Matilija Poppy** (see **Romneya**).

**Matthiola** (Stocks), *Cruciferæ*.—These are beautiful half-hardy annuals and biennials, which thrive in the sun and in a rich and not too dry soil with lime in it ; this is best supplied by the addition of lime-rubble. The Stock is one of the most popular and important of our garden favourites ; its delicious fragrance, the brilliant and diversified colours, the profusion and duration of its bloom, make it invaluable for flower-beds and borders, for edgings and for pot-culture in the greenhouse. There are several strains, the most important of which we mention below. By growing some of each, bloom can be had practically the whole year round.

Before being potted-up, seedlings should be examined to see that they are double, the single-flowered being discarded. Seedlings that will produce double-flowered plants generally have long, pale green, concave leaves ; while the foliage of the single-flowered are, as a rule, deeper in colour, somewhat convex and more rigid.

The *Ten-weeks' Stock* (*Matthiola incana* var. *annua*) is a favourite for bedding. This half-hardy annual grows 6–24 inches high, and usually blooms ten or twelve weeks after being sown. The colours available are purple, mauve, lilac, blue, crimson, pink, yellow, and white. When cultivated in rich soil, and occasionally watered with very weak guano-water, they throw out an immense quantity of lateral spikes of bloom.

*Culture.*—Sow seed thinly ⅛ inch deep in March, in a compost of loam, leaf-mould, and sand, in boxes, under glass (temperature, 60° F.). The seedlings must not be over-watered or given too much heat. Prick off, as soon as possible, 3 inches apart, into boxes ; when large enough pot into 3-inch pots ; harden off early in April, and finally pot-on into 6- or 7-inch pots for blooming. The over-vigorous seedlings should be thrown away, as they are usually single-flowered. Ample water will be required throughout the hot weather, and a weekly dose of weak liquid manure will be very beneficial.

*Intermediate Stocks.*—These furnish flowers in the borders from June to October, and are excellent in a cold greenhouse for flowering in late winter and early spring. For spring-flowering, sow thinly in light soil in boxes or pots in a cold frame in August. Thin or transplant singly into small pots when fit to handle, using a compost of two parts of turfy loam to one part of well-rotted manure. Stand the pots in the open until frost is imminent, then transfer to a frost-proof frame. Pot-up from October to February, using 6- to 7-inch pots, transfer to the cold greenhouse in January, and keep near the glass, or if for summer-flowering in the open, keep them in a frame until April, and as flower-spikes begin to appear give them a weekly dose of liquid manure. If preferred, treat as Ten-weeks' Stocks.

*East Lothian Stocks.*—These are half-hardy biennials, and bloom from June to September. After the Ten-weeks' Stocks, they are the most popular kinds for bedding, for they are very lovely and deliciously fragrant, and are very valuable as pot-plants for the cool greenhouse. The available colours are white, pink, scarlet, lilac, and purple.

*Culture.*—To obtain a succession of bloom, seed should be sown at intervals throughout the summer ; the first batch being sown in May

F F

in a finely-sifted compost of two-thirds loam to one-third leaf-mould and sand, in a shaded frame. As soon as the seedlings can be handled they should be thinned out to 2–3 inches apart, and when established they should have ample ventilation and be watered liberally. When the seedlings have four rough leaves they should be potted-up singly into 3-inch pots in a compost similar to that referred to above, save for the addition of a little well-rotted manure. In a fortnight's time they should be placed in a sunny position in the open for the summer. Late in October they should be given the protection of a frost-proof frame, but afforded as much ventilation as possible, without allowing the plants to damp off or suffer from frost. In March commence weekly doses of weak liquid manure, and about mid-April they should be put into their final pots (6- to 8-inch), according to the size of the plants, continuing the doses of liquid manure. If preferred, these Stocks may be treated as half-hardy annuals and can be sown thinly under glass in March, the after treatment being the same as that described for Ten-weeks' Stocks.

*Brompton Stocks* (*Matthiola incana* var. *autumnalis*).—These are half-hardy biennials flowering in May, June, and July, the prevailing colours being white, pink, scarlet, and purple.

*Culture*.—Seed should be sown in July, in a light, sandy bed or border with an eastern aspect. It succeeds when sown thinly in drills about 6 inches apart. As soon as the plants show their second leaves they should be watered every evening with a fine-rose pot. When about 3 inches high they should be thinned out to at least 6 inches apart. They should be wintered in a cold frame, given ample ventilation in fine weather, and planted out in their flowering position or in flowering-pots the following March. Great care should be taken not to expose the roots during transplanting, and the new soil should be the richest possible. The plants will require shading from the sun until established, and watering with liquid manure until they begin to flower.

*Nice or Winter-flowering Stocks* (a form of *M. incana* var. *autumnalis*).—These are useful in the cool greenhouse. They are very fragrant and bear masses of bloom throughout the winter and early spring. Apart from growing them as pot-plants, they may be planted out in the beds or borders of the greenhouse, while some growers utilise the stages or benches after the early bedding plants have been removed to the frames. The benches are filled with soil, and the plants, which have been grown in pots from seed sown in December, are planted on them. Or Stocks may follow Chrysanthemums, if seed is sown in August. In either case valuable cut flowers may be obtained. For winter-flowering sow in a cold frame in June, pot-up three seedlings in a 5-inch pot, grow on in a frame, and transfer to the cool house early in December. For spring-flowering, sow in a frame in August, grow in a frame as above, and take into the house when the winter-flowering plants are over.

*Varieties*.—BROMPTON : *Cottager's White* (white) ; *Sunrise* (rose) ; *Old English Scarlet* (scarlet) ; *Cottager's Purple* (purple) ; *Improved Green* (green). EAST LOTHIAN : *White Wallflower-leaved* (white) ; *Crimson Wallflower-leaved* (crimson). INTERMEDIATE : *Crystal White* (white) ; *Queen Alexandra* (lilac) ; *Covent Garden* (scarlet). NICE OR

# GREENHOUSE PLANTS

WINTER FLOWERING : *Mont Blanc* (white) ; *Riviera Market* (white and rose) ; *Beauty of Nice* (white, rose, salmon, mauve, or crimson) ; *Yellow Prince* (pale yellow) ; *Empress Elizabeth* (pink) ; *Queen of the Belgians* (lilac). TEN-WEEK : *Snowdrift* (white) ; *Princess Mary* (primrose) ; *Salmon Beauty* (salmon) ; *Almond Blossom* (pale red) ; *Crimson King* (crimson) ; *Fireball* (scarlet) ; *Mauve Beauty* (mauve) ; *Violet Queen* (violet) ; *Celestial* (blue) ; *Giant Perfection, Perfection Ten-week*, and *Superb Bedding* (various).

**Maurandia** *Scrophulariaceæ.*—A genus comprising six or seven species of a beautiful but somewhat tender, deciduous climber, growing up to about 10 feet in height, and flowering throughout July to September.

The best-known species is *M. Barclaiana* [Mexico], with flowers of a violet-purple colour with a greenish tube, rather like those of a Foxglove. This, and other species such as *M. erubescens* (*Lophospermum erubescens*) [Mexico], with rose-coloured flowers and a whitish tube, and *M. scandens* (*M. semperflorens*) [Mexico], with lavender flowers and a white throat, are useful in the cold or cool greenhouse. They make ideal hanging-basket plants.

*Pot Culture.*—Pot-up in March, using 6- to 7-inch pots and a compost of two parts of loam to one part of leaf-mould and sand. Water well in spring and summer, and give bi-weekly doses of weak liquid manure as soon as the buds appear (temperature 45° F. winter, 65° F. summer). Trim straggly shoots in autumn, and keep dry in winter.

*Propagation.*—Sow seed in heat in March or take cuttings of young shoots, some 2–3 inches in length, in summer and strike in sandy soil under glass.

**Maurandia antirrhiniflora** (see **Antirrhinum maurandioides**).

**Maxillaria** (see Chapter on **Orchids**).

**Maxillaria decolor** (see **Xylobium decolor**).

**Maxillaria elongata** (see **Xylobium elongatum**).

**Maxillaria leontoglossa** (see **Xylobium leontoglossum**).

**Maxillaria squalens** (see **Xylobium squalens**).

**Maximiliana regia (Attalea amygdalina),** *Palmaceæ.*—An elegant Brazilian palm for a large house. It is allied to and somewhat resembles **Cocos,** and requires the same cultural treatment. It should be grown in stout wooden tubs to accommodate the roots, and needs plenty of head room.

*Propagation.*—It is propagated by means of imported seed, which should be sown in a propagating case in fibre as soon as received.

**May Flower** (see **Epigæa repens**).

**Mazus,** *Scrophulariaceæ.*—Dwarf, mostly creeping, hardy plants, suitable for the rock-garden. When grown in pans and kept in a cold frame they are very acceptable for the alpine house. They succeed in a well-drained, sandy loam, and form dense tufts.

*Propagation.*—They are propagated by division.

*Species.*—*M. pumilio* [Australia and New Zealand] (pale violet-white, yellow centre, summer, 2–3 in.) ; *M. radicans* (*Mimulus radicans*) [New Zealand] (white with yellow centre, summer, 2–3 in.) ; *M. reptans* [Himalayas] (purplish blue, blotched white and yellow, summer, 3–4 in.).

**Meadow Rue** (see **Thalictrum**).

451

**Meadow Sweet** (see **Filipendula**).

**Meconopsis,** *Papaveraceæ.*—Biennial or perennial, poppy-like herbs, all of which are hardy, but in most places they require partial shade, and usually succeed best in a lime-free soil, the blues being a better colour. They are very beautiful when grown in pots for the cool greenhouse, and the dwarf kinds are suited to the alpine house.

*Culture.*—Seed should be sown as soon as ripe. Sow thinly in pans in a light, rich compost of loam, leaf-mould, and silver sand ; keep in a cold frame or cool greenhouse in shade. If the seedlings have not appeared by the autumn plunge the pans in ashes outside, exposed to all the frost and snow that comes. In spring bring the pans under glass again. Prick off the seedlings, when large enough, into pans or boxes rich in leaf-mould, keep them growing, and when established plant out in their flowering position, or put some into 5-inch pots and grow on ; the stronger kinds may be potted-on into 6-inch pots. The final potting should consist of three parts of good, rich, turfy loam, one part of leaf-mould, one part of sand, and one part of well-decayed cow-manure, with a sprinkling of bone-meal. The pots can be plunged outside for the winter, and placed in a cold frame when growth commences in the spring. Meconopsis benefit from an occasional feeding with manure-water during the height of their growing season.

*Species.*—*M. aculeata* [Himalayas] (blue or purple flowers, glaucous prickly leaves, June, biennial, 15–20 in.) ; *M. betonicifolia* (*M. Baileyi*) [W. China] (sky-blue to pale or mauvish blue, golden-yellow centre, May–June, 12–36 in.—usually a biennial, or if a perennial, a short-lived one) ; *M. integrifolia* [W. China] (yellow, May–June, 18–24 in.) ; *M. quintuplinervia* (Harebell Poppy) [N.W. China] (lavender blue, May–June, perennial, 12–20 in.) ; *M. racemosa* [W. China] (deep purple to pale lilac, leaves with yellow prickles, 12–20 in.) ; *M. regia* [Nepal] (yellow, handsome rosettes of leaves covered with grey hairs, 24–50 in.) ; *M. superba* [Tibet] (similar to the above, but with golden hairs on the leaves, 24–50 in.) ; *M. Wallichii* [Himalayas] (light blue, mauve, or slate violet, June–July, 24–48 in.).

**Medeola asparagoides** (see **Asparagus asparagoides**).

**Medinilla,** *Melastomaceæ.*—Choice stove or warm-greenhouse shrubs with attractive flowers and in some cases showy bracts and foliage. They require plenty of light, but will not stand strong sunshine.

*Culture.*—A good fibrous loam with about one-third sand and some pieces of charcoal should be used. They should be potted moderately firmly, to encourage short growths and firmer wood. When potting, a good shift should be given, as they root freely, and require an abundance of water during the growing season, but great care must be taken with the drainage. They must be given a temperature of 65–70° F. and freely syringed on bright days, particularly the under-side of the leaves, to check red spider. During the autumn and winter the temperature should be lowered to 60° F., and only sufficient water should be administered to keep the leaves firm. This will encourage the wood to ripen for flowering. The atmosphere should be kept as dry as possible when the flowers are forming. After flowering they can be pruned into shape if necessary. Any necessary potting should be done then.

*Propagation.*—Propagation is most successfully accomplished by means of cuttings of half-ripened wood taken in the early summer. These should be potted singly in a suitable sized pot, in fine, sifted peat and sand, with a small quantity of powdered charcoal. The cuttings should be placed in a propagating case in a temperature of not less than 70° F., and kept fairly moist, taking care that the air does not become stagnant. As the cuttings root they can be given more air, and as growth develops they should be pinched back to encourage breaks.

*Species.*—*M. Curtisii* [Sumatra] (flowers ivory white, purple anthers, red stems, spring, 12–36 in.) ; *M. javanensis* [Java] (pale rose, purple anthers, leaves tinged red beneath, spring, winter, 20–40 in.) ; *M. magnifica* [Philippines] (rosy-pink flowers, large pinkish bracts, May–June, 12–30 in.) ; *M. m.* var. *superba* (large inflorescences of deep pink flowers and bracts). This is a very beautiful plant, and a large specimen in flower is a lovely sight. *M. Teysmannii* (*M. amabilis*) [Java] (flowers like *M. magnifica*, but without the coloured bracts, spring, 12–30 in.).

**Mediterranean Cress** (see **Morisia monantha**) (**M. hypogæa**).

**Mediterranean Lily** (see **Pancratium maritimum**).

**Melaleuca,** *Myrtaceæ.*—Warm-greenhouse, evergreen shrubs from Australia. They require the same cultural treatment as **Callistemon**.

*Species.*—*M. decussata* (lilac, Aug., 20 ft.) ; *M. fulgens* (dark red, July–Sept., 3–10 ft.) ; *M. hypericifolia* (scarlet, June–Aug., 6–12 ft.) ; *M. Leucadendron* [Cajuput-tree] (white, June–Aug., 15–20 ft.) ; *M. squarrosa* (yellowish white, June–Aug., 4–8 ft.) ; *M. Wilsonii* (red, July–Aug., 4–6 ft.).

**Melandrium Elizabethæ** (see **Silene Elizabethæ**).

**Melandrium Hookeri** (see **Silene Hookeri**).

**Melastoma,** *Melastomaceæ.*—Stove evergreen shrubs, some of which have large, showy flowers and handsome leaves. They require a high temperature, partial shade, and a fair amount of moisture, but are not difficult to grow.

*Culture.*—The compost should consist of equal parts of loam and peat and one-third part of sand, with some broken charcoal added. The plants require good drainage, because of the plentiful supply of water they need when growing. In winter they should be given a lower temperature and a rather drier atmosphere. During the growing period they benefit from an occasional syringing, particularly under the surface of the leaves, to discourage red spider.

*Propagation.*—Propagation is carried out by striking cuttings of half-ripened wood in equal parts of peat and sand, plunging them in a propagating case in a temperature of 70–75° F. When the cuttings are rooted, place near the light and pinch to encourage breaks. Pot-on the plants as required.

*Species.*—*M. denticulatum* [New Caledonia] (white, July, 36–48 in.) ; *M. malabathricum* [India, Malaya] (purple, July, 5–8 ft.) ; *M. sanguineum* (*M. decemfidum*) [E. Indies] (rose-coloured, Sept.–Oct., 36–48 in.).

**Melia Azedarach** (Bead Tree or China Berry), *Meliaceæ.*—Although this grows naturally into a large tree, plants can be grown in pots for

**453**

# THE GREENHOUSE

the cool greenhouse, where their fragrant, lilac-coloured flowers are very decorative during the summer, as are also their pinnate leaves. It succeeds in any good ordinary potting soil of sandy loam and leaf-mould.

*Propagation.*—It is propagated by seed or by cuttings placed in sand under a bell-glass, with a little bottom heat. The name of Bead Tree has been given to members of this genus on account of the nuts, which have a natural perforation through the centre, being threaded for beads, particularly in Catholic countries.

**Melianthus major** (Honey-flower), *Melianthaceæ.*—A flexuous, South African, evergreen shrub, 1–6 feet high, with attractive glaucous leaves. It is almost hardy, but is very decorative for the cool greenhouse as a pot-plant, or when planted out to train up a pillar in the greenhouse. It bears reddish-brown flowers in spring and summer. It requires a soil of sandy loam and leaf-mould, and is propagated by seed, or by cuttings which strike freely under a bell-glass. It is also very decorative when used for summer bedding.

**Melocactus communis** (see **Cactus Melocactus**).

**Melon (Cucumis Melo)** (see **Fruit under Glass**).

**Merendera sobolifera,** *Liliaceæ.*—A spring-flowering bulb from Asia Minor and Persia, allied to **Colchicum,** which, although quite hardy, can be grown in pans for the alpine house. It requires well-drained soil, and the same cultural treatment as **Crocus** and other small spring-flowering bulbs.

**Mertensia,** *Boraginaceæ.*—For Culture, see Chapter on the alpine house.

*Species.*—*M. alpina* [Rocky Mountains] (Blue flowers, glaucous foliage, May 3–4 in.); *M. maritima* (Oyster Plant) [N. Temperate Regions] (blue or whitish flowers, glaucous fleshy leaves, July 8–10 in.); *M. primuloides* [Himalayas] (indigo-blue, passing to white and yellow, June, 4–6 in.); *M. virginica* (Virginian Cowslip) (blue, March–May, 12–18 in.). This last is a charming pot plant for the cool greenhouse, requiring a good rich soil.

**Mesembryanthemum** (Fig Marigold), *Aizoaceæ.*—This is a very large genus of succulent plants, largely natives of South Africa and other parts of that continent. A few are found in New Zealand, Australia, the Canary Islands, and in the Mediterranean region. Generally, they may be regarded as greenhouse plants, although some of them are hardy and grow outdoors in favoured situations. While most of them are perennials, there are a few annual species which have for many years been fairly common in gardens, the best known being *M. criniflorum* (*Dorotheanthus criniflorus*), which resembles *M. gramineum*, but the leaves have red tips; *M. crystallinum* [*Cryophytum crystallinum*] (Ice Plant); *M. gramineum* (*M. tricolor*; *Dorotheanthus gramineus*) with rose, red, and white flowers; and *M. pomeridianum* (*Carpanthea pomeridiana*) with yellow flowers. Some of them are excellent for window-gardening, while many of the strong growing and sub-shrubby species are very suitable flowering plants for the cool greenhouse, or for hot, sunny positions outdoors during the summer months. The greenhouse specimens will flower during the spring and summer.

454

The genus has lately been revised and divided up into a number of genera, but for the sake of convenience they are all here included under Mesembryanthemum.

*Propagation.*—Most of them are readily propagated by means of seed, cuttings, or division.

*Culture.*—They thrive in a compost of good medium loam with a little leaf-mould, and enough sand, old mortar rubble, or broken bricks to keep the whole open and porous   Perfect drainage is essential, and water must be carefully afforded during the winter months (temperature 50° F.).

The following are a few of the most showy SUB-SHRUBBY SPECIES : *M. aurantiacum* (deep orange) ; *M. aureum* (orange) ; *M. blandum* (white, changing to rose and red) ; *M. Brownii* (purple, changing to reddish yellow) ; *M. coccineum* (scarlet) ; *M. falciforme* (purplish pink) ; *M. roseum* (rose) ; *M. spectabile* (red) ; *M. violaceum* (violet). All reach from 12 to 18 inches in height, and most of this type are still in Mesembryanthemum in the new revision.

The other section, with compressed stems and very thick, fleshy leaves, are very interesting on account of their many strange forms and coloration, which in many cases has a striking resemblance to the ground and stones or pebbles among which they grow.  The plants may be grown in pans in well-drained soil, or seed may be very thinly sown in the pans.  During the summer they appreciate a rather moister atmosphere, and during the late afternoon a slight syringing with a fine spray is beneficial (temperature 50–55° F. winter, higher in the summer).  On account of their small size, a large collection may be accommodated in quite a small greenhouse, while many may be successfully grown in sunny windows.  They are generally only a few inches high, and flowering is very uncertain.  In this section the growing period is, in most cases, during our winter.  This necessitates great care in giving them water, especially during spells of dull weather.  It is this group that has chiefly been rearranged.

The following are some of the fairly common and distinct species : *M. Bolusii* (*Pleiospilos Bolusii*), *M. calcarium* (*Titanopsis calcarea*), *M. ficiforme* (*Conophytum ficiforme*), *M. fissum* (*Rismaria dubia*), *M. fulviceps* (*Lithops fulviceps*), *M. Lesliei* (*Lithops Lesliei*), *M. pseudotruncatellum* (*Lithops pseudotruncatella*), *M. simulans* (*Pleiospilos simulans*), *M. testiculare* (*Argyroderma testiculare*), *M. thecatum* (*Conophytum minutum*), *M. tigrinum* (*Faucaria tigrina*), *M. truncatellum* (*Conophytum truncatellum*), etc.

**Mesospinidium sanguineum** (see Chapter on **Orchids**).

**Metrosideros** (Iron-wood, or Bottle Brush), *Myrtaceæ.*—Australian and New Zealand evergreen trees, shrubs, or climbers. They bear flowers in clusters with attractive long, red, crimson, or white stamens. They are closely allied to **Callistemon,** and will succeed with the same cultural treatment. They succeed in equal parts of good loam and peat, with some silver sand. Most of them develop into large bushes and require a large tub.

*Propagation.*—They are propagated by seed, or cuttings of side-shoots can be struck in early spring, if placed in sand under a bell-glass,

455

in a cool pit. When rooted they should be potted-up and grown on, taking care that they do not suffer from lack of water during hot weather, especially if plunged outside.

*M. florida* [New Zealand] bears orange-red flowers with scarlet stamens in the summer, and is a climber. There is also a variegated form. *M. scandens* (*M. buxifolia*) carries white flowers in August, and is a climber, and should be trained up a pillar or the stem of a tree fern. *M. tomentosa* (New Zealand Christmas Tree) has dark crimson flowers in summer. The plant usually grown in gardens as *M. floribunda* is generally *Callistemon lanceolatus*.

**Mexican Flame Leaf** (see **Poinsettia**).

**Mexican Foxglove** (see **Tetranema mexicana**).

**Mexican Orange Blossom** (see **Choisya ternata**).

**Mexican Twin Flower** (see **Bravoa geminiflora**).

**Michelia fuscata** (*Magnolia fuscata*), *Magnoliaceæ*.—A Chinese, cool-greenhouse, evergreen shrub, with handsome foliage. It bears brownish-yellow flowers, edged with purple, and gives off a strong banana fragrance. It succeeds in sandy loam and leaf-mould, and is propagated by seed, when obtainable, and treated as for **Magnolia**; or by cuttings of ripened wood placed under a bell-glass with bottom heat.

**Miconia,** *Melastomaceæ*.—Handsome, warm-greenhouse, shrubs, some of which have very beautiful foliage with conspicuous veins. The flowers are small, coloured white, yellow, purple, or rose. At one time they were known as **Cyanophyllum,** a name which is now generally dropped.

*Propagation.*—They are propagated by cuttings of firm wood in a propagating case over bottom heat. They should be protected from direct sunshine and be given plenty of moisture. For further cultural treatment see **Medinilla** and **Melastoma.**

*Species.*—*M. flammea* [Tropical America] has large, glossy green leaves, 15–20 inches long. It has a stem covered with rusty hairs, and makes a handsome foliage plant. *M. Hookeriana* (*M. pulverulenta*) [Peru] has deep olive-green leaves with silvery mid-rib; a very handsome and ornamental shrub. *M. magnifica* (*Cyanophyllum magnificum*) [Mexico] has leaves 20–30 inches long, lustrous green above, red beneath, and wavy edged, with prominent, white or rose-coloured veins. It is one of the most striking of greenhouse plants, and is at its best when 12–18 inches high. *M. spectanda* [Brazil] has leaves 12–15 inches long, lustrous green above, greenish red below, with a prominent grey midrib. *M. velutina* [Brazil] is probably a form of *M. magnifica*, the leaves being more bronzy.

**Microcachrys tetragona** (Strawberry fruited Cypress), *Taxaceæ*.—A low, somewhat straggling, greenhouse evergreen bush, with slender, whip-like, four-angled branches. The male and female flowers are borne on separate shoots of the same tree. The translucent cones are egg-shaped or roundish, fleshy, and bright red when ripe. It needs the support of a stake, or it may be trained up a pillar. It is confined to the mountains of Tasmania, and requires the protection of a cool greenhouse. A mixture of good sandy loam with some peat affords a suitable compost.

*Propagation.*—It is propagated by seed, when obtainable, and by cuttings of ripened shoots placed in sand under a bell-glass, with a little heat. It is a shrub which is more interesting than beautiful.

**Microstylis** (see Chapter on **Orchids**).

**Mignonette** (see **Reseda odorata**).

**Mikania scandens** (Climbing Hempweed), *Compositæ.*—A climber with yellowish-white flowers and heart-shaped, shining leaves. It is a suitable perennial for the cool greenhouse, either for growing against the wall or for training up a pillar. It may be grown outside during the summer, where it is very suitable for growing over trellis or other similar places. It is closely allied to **Eupatorium** and succeeds with the same cultural treatment given to the greenhouse kinds.

*Species.*—*M. Sanderi* is a climber with variegated leaves, bright green marked with dark purple blotches. It is an attractive plant, the origin of which seems to be little known.

**Mikania senecioides** (see **Senecio mikanioides**).

**Milkweed** (see **Asclepias**).

**Milkwort** (see **Polygala**).

**Miltonia vexillaria** (see Chapter on **Orchids**).

**Mimosa pudica** (Sensitive Plant), *Leguminosæ.*—This plant originally came from Brazil, but is now naturalised in most warm countries. It is usually cultivated as an annual, but is probably a perennial in its native habitat. It is an interesting plant owing to its sensitive foliage. On being touched, the leaves fall and the leaflets close. The reason for and advantage of these movements are not very clearly understood, but the movement is usually much quicker in young plants. The flowers are purplish, borne in globose heads during the summer. It is readily raised from seed on a hot bed, or in a warm house, the seed being sown in a small pot and potted-on, finally into 5-inch pots. They make interesting and attractive plants for the greenhouse.

**Mimulus** (Musk or Monkey Flower), *Scrophulariaceæ.*—A genus of handsome, profusely-flowering annuals, hardy and half-hardy, and hardy perennials, with singularly shaped and brilliantly coloured flowers, distinguished by their rich and strikingly beautiful markings. Seed of the annuals sown in autumn produces very effective early-flowering plants for the greenhouse. The Mimulus, which grows from 6 to 30 inches in height, according to species, and flowers outdoors in June, July, and August, likes a shady site with moist, rich, ordinary soil. They are useful for cutting. One of the best kinds for pot culture is Harrison's Musk, a large form of *M. moschatus* [Musk Plant] (yellow, 6 in.). In the warm greenhouse (temperature 55–70° F. winter; 60–75° F. summer) this may be had in flower in summer.

*Culture.*—Sow seed thinly in February under glass, harden off, and plant out in May, or pot-up for the greenhouse in May, using 5- to 6-inch pots and a compost of two parts of loam to one part of leaf-mould, peat and sand. Pinch back to make bushy plants, and water well in summer. Keep cool in winter. If for the warm greenhouse pot-up in March and treat as above.

*Species and Varieties.*—HARDY PERENNIALS : *M. cardinalis* [N America] (scarlet, 20 in.); *M. cupreus* [Chile] (orange, 12 in.); *M.*

*luteus* [N. America and Europe] (yellow, spotted, 9 in.) ; *M. l.* var. *Burnettii* (pale brown, 10 in.) ; *M. l.* var. *tigrinus* (yellow, spotted, June, 9 in.) ; *M. moschatus* [N. America] (yellow, 6 in.) ; *M. ringens* [N. America] (pale blue, 10 in.). *M. glutinosus* [California] has been dealt with under **Diplacus glutinosus,** but apart from its woody habit, it differs in no way from Mimulus.

**Mimulus radicans** (see **Mazus radicans**).

**Mina lobata** (see **Ipomœa versicolor**).

**Mirabilis,** *Nyctaginaceæ.*—A genus containing about ten or a dozen species of greenhouse and hardy perennials, of which the best known is *M. Jalapa* (Marvel of Peru), from whose roots the purgative Jalap is prepared. The flowers are various in colour, being yellow, crimson, or white, or one or other of these colours striped or spotted with another. They grow best in sunny positions and in a light, rich loam, but will do well in any well-drained garden soil. The plants grow from 24 to 36 inches in height, and flower from July to September.

They should be treated in much the same manner as **Dahlias,** the roots being taken up in October and stored in sand or fibre for the winter. Plant in April 3 inches deep and 4 inches apart.

*Propagation.*—They can be grown from seed sown in gentle heat from March to April, the seedlings being hardened-off and potted-up in May, or the roots may be divided in April, and grown on in 6- or 8-inch pots in good ordinary potting-soil. They should be kept in a cool frame or house, and taken into the greenhouse when in bud.

*Species.*—*M. Jalapa* [Tropical America] (red, pink, or white, July–Sept., 36 in.).

**Miscanthus [Eulalia]** (Zebra-striped Grass), *Gramineæ.*—An ornamental, hardy, perennial grass, resembling ribbon-grass in some respects, but slighter in every way, and of not so strong a growth. It is suitable for borders and for culture in the greenhouse.

*Greenhouse Culture.*—Pot-up in March, using a 6- to 8-inch pot and a compost of two parts of loam to one part of leaf-mould and sand. Stand in a shady position (temperature 50° F. winter, 60° F. summer) and water well from May to October.

*Propagation.*—It is easily propagated by means of division in March or April.

*Species and Varieties.*—*M. saccharifer* [*E. saccharifer*] (green with white midrib, 48–72 in.) ; *M. sinensis* var. *variegatus* [*E. japonica variegata*] (white and green striped, 48–72 in.) ; *M. sinensis albolineatus* [*E. j. albo-lineata*] (white, striped, 48 in) ; and *M s. zebrinus* [*E. sinensis* var. *zebrina*] (transverse yellow marking) are the kinds most grown.

**Mitchella repens** (Partridge Berry), *Rubiaceæ.*—Although hardy, and very suitable for growing in shady parts of the rockery or cool fernery, this North American plant is very attractive when grown in pans for the alpine house. The flowers are small, pinkish, and fragrant, and the leaves shining and evergreen, with white markings. The chief attraction, however, is the bright-scarlet berries, usually borne in pairs, which remain most of the winter. It is readily increased by division in the spring.

458

**Mitraria coccinea** (Mitre Flower), *Gesneriaceæ.*—A half-hardy, ever-green, scandent shrub from Chile, with bright, glossy green leaves, and orange-scarlet, pendant, trumpet-shaped flowers in May, June, and July. It grows from 3 to 5 feet in height, and is practically hardy enough to stand the winter in the open if grown on a south or west wall. In most localities, however, it is best grown in the cold greenhouse.

*Pot Culture.*—Pot-up in March in a compost of two-thirds turfy peat and one-third sand. Water liberally, and syringe overhead twice a day in spring and summer. Give doses of liquid manure every ten days as soon as the buds begin to form, but keep the pots on the dry side in winter. Trim to shape in autumn. Average temperature required 40° F. winter, 60° F. summer.

*Propagation.*—To propagate strike cuttings of young shoots in a frame in summer.

**Mitriostigma axillare (Gardenia citriodora),** *Rubiaceæ.*—A charming South African evergreen shrub for the warm greenhouse, bearing an abundance of flowers with the fragrance of orange-blossom. The flowers are white, tinged pink in the bud, and borne in axillary clusters during the spring and early summer.

*Culture.*—It succeeds in a compost of fibrous loam, peat, and sand, in equal proportions. It strikes readily from cuttings placed in sand with bottom heat, and kept close. Pot-up when rooted and grow on. Good plants can be grown in 6-inch pots. It also makes a desirable basket plant.

**Moltkia petræa (Lithospermum petræum),** *Boraginaceæ.*—Although generally grown on the rock-garden, this dwarf shrubby perennial from South East Europe is also suitable for growing in pots or pans for the alpine house. When not in flower it should be plunged in ashes in a cold frame in an open position. It likes a well-drained soil and appreciates some mortar-rubble mixed with the compost.

*Propagation.*—It is propagated by seed sown as soon as ripe, or by cuttings of half-ripened wood placed in sand, under a bell-glass. The flowers are pinkish purple at first, and violet blue when open. It blooms from June to July and attains a height of from 12 to 20 inches.

**Momordica,** *Cucurbitaceæ.*—Warm-greenhouse climbers with white or yellow flowers and curiously shaped fruits. Ornamental gourds are among some of the most decorative of climbers for growing in the warm greenhouse, particularly when the fruits, which are usually warty, begin to ripen. Momordicas are readily raised from seed, and require the same cultural treatment as cucumbers.

*M. Balsamina* (Balsam Apple) [Africa and Asia] has yellow flowers with blackish centres, and orange fruit. It is a pretty annual which can be grown outside in a favourable position for climbing over a trellis. It requires light sandy soil, and should have plenty of water during the growing season. *M. Charantia* (Balsam Pear) [Tropical Africa and Asia] has yellow flowers. The fruit is also yellow, and splits into three divisions, disclosing the bright scarlet covering of the seeds, which gives the fruit a very attractive appearance. *M. cochinchinensis* (*M. mixta*) [Tropical Asia] has flowers, the male and female of which are usually borne on separate plants, which are pale yellow with a purple eye. The fruit is highly decorative, large, red, and round or oval. *M. involucrata* [S. Africa] has white or creamy-white flowers which are often dotted dark green. The fruit is yellow, changing to scarlet. It is a very graceful climber and resembles *M. Balsamina*.

**Monanthes,** *Crassulaceæ.*—Dainty little succulents suitable for the cool greenhouse or for growing in a room. They like sandy soil and a moderate amount of water during the summer, and are easily propagated by cuttings. The flowers, borne in summer, are small, pink, yellow, or whitish green. The leaves are fleshy, crowded into rosettes at the end of the short branches.

*Species.*—*M. anagensis* [Teneriffe] (flowers yellowish green, leaves green or reddish, 1–2 in.) ; *M. atlantica* [Canary Isles] (golden-yellow flowers, speckled red, 1–3 in.) ; *M. polyphylla* [Canary Isles] (yellowish-white flowers, pale-green leaves with warty tips).

**Monkey's Comb** (see **Pithecoctenium**).

**Monochætum,** *Melastomaceæ.*—Half-hardy, evergreen shrubs, from 12 to 24 inches in height, with attractive flowers in winter and early spring, suitable for culture in the cool greenhouse (temperature 45–65° F. winter, 55–65° F. summer).

*Culture.*—Prune old plants in spring, and re-pot as soon as new growth breaks, using clean, well-drained pots and a compost of rich, sandy loam and leaf-mould. Stand in a light, airy position, and water and syringe regularly while growing. Feed with occasional doses of weak liquid manure. Keep only just moist when dormant.

*Propagation.*—Cuttings, 2–3 inches in length, made of new shoots in spring, may be rooted in pots of sandy soil in a propagating case with slight bottom heat. The young plants require pinching back to encourage sturdy and bushy formation. They must be potted-on as required, and the atmosphere kept moist.

*Species.*—*M. alpestre* [Mexico] (red) ; *M. Hartwegianum* (*M. dicrananetherum*) [Andes] (rose) ; *M. Humboldtianum* [Caracas] (red and purple) ; *M. Lemonianum* [garden origin] (rose) ; and *M. sericeum* [Amazon region] (mauve).

**Monsonia,** *Geraniaceæ.*—Interesting greenhouse herbs or sub-shrubs, allied to **Pelargonium.** They require a compost made up of two parts of sandy loam, one part of peat or leaf-mould, one part of sand, and good drainage. They are increased by cuttings placed in sandy soil, under a hand-light in the early autumn, or by seed sown and placed in gentle heat in spring. Pot-on as required.

*M. lobata* [S. Africa] grows 12 inches high and bears in the spring and early summer flowers which are greenish and variegated outside, and pale bluish inside, with a dark centre. The leaves are cordate. *M. speciosa* [S. Africa] has rose-coloured flowers with a dark eye, borne in spring and early summer. The leaves are palmate, and the plant grows from 6–10 inches high.

**Monstera deliciosa,** *Araceæ.*—A handsome, root climbing, greenhouse aroid, from Tropical America, often grown for its large, handsome, perforated leaves. Where it is given enough room to develop, it produces edible fruit, which, when ripe, has a flavour between that of the pineapple and the banana. The fruit is from 6 to 8 inches long, and resembles in appearance a long pine cone, the covering being composed of hexagonal plates which are green at first, turning yellow and falling away as the fruit ripens. It is one of the best plants for enduring the varying conditions of temperature, succeeding in a dwelling-house or with stove-house treatment, while its sub-tropical appearance makes it very effective when put outside during the summer.

*Culture.*—It is readily increased by division of the growing stems cut up into lengths, and placed in a propagating case in fibre in a temperature of 75–80° F. Pot-up when rooted and grow on in a compost of two parts of loam, one part of leaf-mould, and one part of dry cow-manure. It takes kindly to pot culture, but it is advisable to stand the pots in water, as it is a thirsty subject.

**Montbretia** (see **Tritonia**).

**Moræa** (Butterfly Iris), *Iridaceæ.*—Pretty, bulbous plants, somewhat resembling an Iris, growing from 6 to 18 inches in height, and flowering in spring and early summer. They may be grown outdoors in warm, sunny, sheltered situations, and thrive in light, rich, sandy loam ; but the best results will be obtained in pots in the cool greenhouse.

*Pot Culture.*—Plant four or five bulbs 4 inches deep in a 4½-inch pot in November, and protect from frost in a dark corner of the cool green-house ; gradually introduce to the light early in March. Water well during growth, but keep dry after the foliage fades (temperature 50–60° F. summer, 10° lower in winter).

*Propagation.*—Propagate by means of seed, which should be sown as soon as ripe, and placed in a warm house with a temperature of 55–60° F. They may also be increased by offsets. Any transplanting should be done after the foliage has died down.

*Species.*—*M. bicolor* [Cape Colony] (yellow with beautiful brown spots, 18–24 in.) ; *M. iridioides* [S. Africa] (white, marked yellow and blue, summer, 20–24 in.) ; *M. Robinsoniana* (Wedding Iris) [Australia] (white, spotted red and yellow, 36–48 in.) ; *M. Pavonia* [Cape Colony] (orange-red, with blue-black or greenish-black spots, May, 18–24 in.).

**Morisia monantha (M. hypogæa)** (Mediterranean Cress), *Cruciferæ.*—This native of Corsica has golden-yellow flowers in spring and early summer, and attains a height of 2–3 inches. For culture see Chapter devoted to the alpine house.

**Mormodes** (see Chapter on **Orchids**).

**Morning Glory** (see **Ipomœa**).

**Moschosma riparium,** *Labiatæ.*—A half-hardy South African perennial, growing up to about 36 inches in height, with panicles of small, creamy to pinkish-white flowers in winter. It is suitable for culture in the cool or cold greenhouse.

*Culture.*—Prune well back after flowering and pot-up again in March, using 6- to 8-inch pots and a compost of rich, sandy loam and leaf-mould. Water well and regularly from October to March, then gradually reduce the quantity, and keep only just moist until again making growth. From June to September the plants are best grown outdoors, plunging the pots to the rims in ashes in a sunny situation.

*Propagation.*—Cuttings made of young shoots, 2–3 inches long in spring, may be rooted in pots of sandy soil in a propagating case with a moist atmosphere and slight bottom heat. They should be stopped-back to form bushy specimens, and potted-on as required, reaching their flowering pots, say 6-inch, not later than the end of June.

**Moss Campion** (see **Silene acaulis**).

**Moss Pink** (see **Phlox subulata**).

**Mother of Thousands** (see **Saxifraga sarmentosa**).

**Mountain Avens** (see **Dryas octopetala**).

**Mountain Rose** (see **Antigonon leptopus**).

**Mountain Crowfoot** (see **Ranunculus Thora**).

**Mount Etna Lily** (see **Sternbergia lutea**).

**Mullein** (see **Celsia**).

**Murræa exotica** (see **Chalcas exotica**).

**Musa** (Banana), *Musaceæ*.—This group of plants can undoubtedly be considered the largest tree-like herbs grown for fruit, and also for the decorative appearance of their large, handsome foliage, for they give a most gorgeous tropical effect. For this reason they are of great value when planted out in the sub-tropical garden.

*M. Basjoo*, *M. Ensete*, and *M. superba* are some of the best for this purpose. All are more decorative in foliage than in flowers. To grow them to perfection they need a large greenhouse. When grown for ornament it is generally found most convenient to grow them in large tubs, as they are then more easily moved about, although they can be permanently planted out in houses with sufficient heat and space for their development.

*Culture.*—They are readily increased by suckers, which are found round the old plant. These should be potted-up firmly into 5- or 6-inch pots in a compost of three parts of fibrous loam, one part of decayed cow-manure, sufficient sand to keep it open and porous, and a good sprinkling of bone-meal. They should then be placed in a close, humid atmosphere of not less than 65° F. at night; this will encourage quick growth. When the pots are filled with roots, the plants should be shifted on into pots two sizes larger, making the compost richer, for they are rank feeders. Some species are raised from seed, which should be covered three or four times their depth and pressed firmly. The pans should be placed where they can get plenty of bottom heat. As the seedlings appear, pot them on singly and grow on with suckers. During the winter they should be kept where the temperature does not fall below 45° F. at night. At that time they will require less watering and syringeing.

For further cultural details see **Banana** in **Fruit Under Glass.**

*M. Basjoo* (*M. japonica*) [Japanese Banana] (Japan) is one of the hardiest species, and can be grown outdoors in some parts of the country in favourable situations. It grows 6–9 feet high, and bears brown flowers and bracts. It is a very decorative plant, and is cultivated in Japan for its fibre. *M. Cavendishii* (Chinese or Jamaican Banana) is a well-known dwarf species, 4–6 feet high, grown for its fruits, which are fragrant and seedless. It has yellowish-white flowers, and green leaves spotted and blotched with red when young. It requires less heat than many others. *M. Ensete* (Abyssinian Banana) [Abyssinia] is the largest known species, as well as one of the oldest, being repre-

462

sented in Egyptian sculpture. It has whitish flowers, dark-brown bracts, and large leaves with a red midrib. *M. superba* [India] grows 6–10 feet high, and has whitish flowers with handsome foliage. The last two species are not stoloniferous, but are propagated entirely from seed. *M. Uranoscopos* (*M. coccinea*) [S. China] is a very showy plant, growing from 3 to 5 feet in height, but which may be raised in a 10-inch pot for winter decoration in tropical houses. It has brilliant scarlet bracts tipped with yellow, and a yellow calyx.

**Muscari** (Grape Hyacinth), *Liliaceæ*.—Beautiful, hardy, bulbous plants, growing from 4 to 12 inches in height, and carrying spikes of bead-like flowers in February and March, or April and May, according to species and variety. They do well in good loam and are excellent for warm, sunny borders, for the rock-garden, and for growing in pots or pans in the cold greenhouse or alpine house. When once planted they will thrive for many years without attention.

One of the best varieties is *M. armeniacum* var. *Heavenly Blue*, which carries rich, sky-blue flowers on stems about 8 inches high in April and May. Its flowers last well when used as cut blooms. *M. botryoides* [E. Europe], with blue and also white flowers, is excellent for pot culture and for cutting. In the cold house it will flower from January to March. In *M. comosum monstrosum* (*M. plumosum*), the Feather Hyacinth, which grows about 10 inches in height and flowers in April and is also useful for pot culture, the small flowers have assumed a thread-like appearance and make the spikes look just like a pale violet-blue feather. Another good species is *M. racemosum* [Europe], which grows 6 inches high and bears deep blue flowers in April and May.

*Pot Culture.*—Pot each October, 1½ inches deep in 5-inch pots, in a compost of two parts of loam to one part of leaf-mould and sand. Water moderately while growing. Dry off in a cold frame after flowering.

*Propagation.*—Propagate by means of offsets in October.

**Muscari azureum** (see **Hyacinthus azureus**).

**Musk** (see **Mimulus moschatus**).

**Mutisia**, *Compositæ*.—Almost hardy climbing plants with pretty, star-like blossoms in July and August. Although some species may be quite hardy in some parts of the country, these plants are usually grown in the cold greenhouse, and are of very easy culture.

*Culture.*—Pot-up in the spring when growth is about to commence, in a large pot, or, better still, plant in the greenhouse border in a compost of two-thirds loam and one-third leaf-mould, with ample sand, and a little peat, with some small pieces of sandstone mixed in with the soil. Water liberally, and syringe overhead daily from May to July, but keep only moderately moist during the autumn and winter. The plants will benefit if they are surrounded by slabs of stone on the ground. Let the shoots run up the pillars of the house, or train them to wires stretched some 9 inches from the glass of the roof. Weak and straggling shoots should be cut away after flowering. (Average temperature 60° F. summer, 50° F. winter).

*Propagation.*—Propagate by means of cuttings of young shoots placed in gentle heat in March, or by seed sown as soon as ripe and placed in gentle heat.

*Species.*—*M. decurrens* [Chilean Andes], which reaches about 12 feet in height and carries orange-yellow flowers in July, is the most commonly-grown species. Other species are *M. Clematis* [New Grenada] (red, July–Aug., 20 ft.), and *M. ilicifolia* [Chile] (rose, July–Aug., 15 ft.) ; *M. speciosa* [Ecuador] (red, July, 10–15 ft.).

**Myoporum parviflorum,** *Myoporaceæ.*—A procumbent Australian shrub, with shoots growing up to 2 feet long, making an excellent subject for a basket-plant for the cool greenhouse. The pale-green branches, wreathed with sweet, snow-white flowers, will droop very gracefully.

*Propagation.*—It is propagated by cuttings in the spring placed under a bell-glass in the cool greenhouse. Pot-on when rooted or place directly in the basket.

**Myosotidium nobile** (Antarctic or Giant Forget-me-not), *Boraginaceæ* [Chatham Islands].—A nearly hardy herbaceous perennial which can be grown outdoors in favourable localities if planted in a sheltered position. It may be planted in a bed or border in the cool greenhouse, but resents root disturbance. It is rather short-lived, and needs to be renewed from seed. It grows 15–20 inches high, and in the spring bears flowers with a dark blue centre and lighter edges. There is also a white-flowered form.

**Myosotis** (Forget-me-not), *Boraginaceæ.*—There are biennial and perennial species inhabiting both the north and south temperate zones, but most of the cultivated forms are native to Europe. Some of the perennial species are grown as biennials. All thrive in the sun and in ordinary soil. They grow from 2 to 9 inches in height, and bloom in the spring and summer. Many are useful for potting-up and growing in the cool greenhouse, where they are very decorative, either alone or for mixing with bulbs in pots.

*Culture.*—BIENNIALS : Sow seed thinly from June to July in the open, cover very lightly with soil and thin out to 5 inches apart when large enough to handle.

PERENNIALS : Sow seed in the open from April to July, or propagate by means of division in October, and plant out 5 inches apart. Grow in the reserve garden during the summer. Pot-up in October, using 4- to 5-inch pots and sandy soil, and keep in a cold frame through the winter. Move into the cool house in early spring.

*Species.*—*M. alpestris* (*M. rupicola*) [Europe] (blue with yellow eye, April and May, 3–5 inches). *M. azorica* [Azores] (purple, eventually fading to blue with yellow eye, summer, 4–5 in.). Both the above species are charming plants for the alpine house, and should be grown in pans. *M. cæspitosa Rehsteineri* (blue, April–May, 2 in.) ; *M. dissitiflora* [Switzerland] (light blue, April–June, 6–9 in.) ; *M. pyrenaica* (syn. *M. alpestris*) [Europe] (blue, pink, and white, June–Aug., 6 in.) ; *M. scorpioides* (*M. palustris*) [Europe and Britain] (sky-blue and yellow, May–Sept., 6–9 in.).

**Myriophyllum proserpinacoides** (Parrot's Feather), *Haloragaceæ.*—A favourite half-hardy, aquatic plant with delicate, feathery foliage, used in aquaria, fountains, and pools. It requires mud to root in, and although the shoots are weak, they need no support ; all the pretty

**464**

**PLATE 13**
'Floradale Beauty', a variety of *Verbena*.

# GREENHOUSE PLANTS

shoots grow out of the water. It is readily rooted by inserting long shoots in the mud of the water. The insignificant flowers are borne on different plants. The one in cultivation is said to be entirely female.

**Myrmecodia Antoinii (M. echinata),** *Rubiaceæ.*—An interesting plant from the Torres Straits that is myrmecophilous, a group of plants that provides food and shelter for ants. The branches are thick and fleshy, deeply four-grooved, rising from a large tuber, which is tuberculate and spiny, and it is in these excavations that the ants find their shelter. The flowers are small and white. It requires the same treatment as epiphitic Orchids, and is best grown in an orchid-basket in the warm greenhouse. It is increased by seed sown and placed in a warm, moist atmosphere.

**Myrsiphyllum asparagoides** (see **Greenhouse Foliage Plants** and **Asparagus asparagoides.** This is another name for **Smilax** of the florist).

**Myrtus** (Myrtle), *Myrtaceæ.*—Beautiful, evergreen, greenhouse shrubs, with fragrant, dark, glossy green, ovate or lanceolate leaves, and bearing pretty, white blossoms. It is sufficiently hardy to grow outdoors in warm, sunny, and sheltered situations. It requires plenty of water, and when grown under glass the leaves should be frequently syringed in spring and summer.

*Pot Culture.*—Pot-up in March (triennially), using 5- to 12-inch pots and a compost of two parts of sandy loam to one part of leaf-mould. Water well during spring and summer, and syringe. Stand outdoors in partial shade from July to October, then take into the cold greenhouse. Keep fairly dry in winter, and prune in February.

*Propagation.*—To propagate, strike cuttings in a frame in July, or layer in September.

*Species.*—There are several species, but the best known is *M. communis,* the Common Myrtle [Mediterranean Region] (white, July–Aug., 5–10 ft.), of which there are several well known varieties, differing chiefly in the shape of the leaves, habit of the plants or colour of the fruits.

*M. Luma* (*Eugenia apiculata*) [Chile] (15–20 ft.) ; *M. Ralphii* [New Zealand] (3–6 ft.) ; *M. Ugni* (Ugni or Chilean Guava) [Chile] (4–6 ft.). Wood of the latter species is very hard, and is used in the making of special implements.

**Nægelia,** *Gesneriaceæ.*—Stove, herbaceous perennials, with catkin-like, scaly stolons. The flowers are showy, mostly red, sometimes yellowish white or suffused. They are exceedingly ornamental plants, on account of their floriferous habit and beautifully mottled foliage. The latter should be carefully preserved from drip, and when syringeing care should be taken to avoid using dirty water, as sediment collects on the tiny hairs, giving the plants an unsightly appearance.

*Culture.*—They are closely allied to **Achimenes,** and succeed with the same cultural treatment. The roots, when dry, should be stored in the same pots in which they have grown. It is a mistake to keep any tubers or roots of Gesneriaceæ in dry sand in a dry store-room. After being ripened they should be stood under the bench in the greenhouse. Keep clear of drip, but give an occasional watering.

**G G**

465

*Propagation.*—Propagate by increase of stolons, by cuttings of young stems in heat, or by matured leaves in a propagating case.

*N. cinnabarina* (*Gesneria cinnabarina*) [Mexico] has scarlet flowers spotted on the under side. The leaves are green, beautifully shaded with flame-coloured hairs. It is a handsome winter-flowering plant, growing 24 inches high. There is also a rose-coloured variety. *N. fulgida* [Vera Cruz] grows to a height of from 20 to 24 inches, has rich, dark-green leaves, and bears vermilion flowers in the autumn. *N. multiflora* (*N. amabilis*) [Mexico] carries white or cream flowers in the autumn and attains a height of 20–24 inches. *N. zebrina* (*Gesneria zebrina*) [Brazil] bears bright orange-scarlet and yellow flowers, dotted with red, in September. The leaves are dark and marbled, and the plant grows 24 inches high. There are several beautiful forms of this— *regalis, splendens,* and others.

**Nandina domestica** (Flowering Bamboo of Japan), *Berberidaceæ.*— A half-hardy, ornamental, evergreen shrub from China and Japan, some 3–6 feet in height. The white flowers, borne in summer, have yellow anthers, and are succeeded by red berries in the autumn.

*Culture.*—It thrives in the cold greenhouse in a mixture of sandy loam, peat, and leaf-mould. Plant in the greenhouse bed in April. It can be grown outside in a sheltered place in favourable districts.

*Propagation.*—Cuttings made of mature shoots, 2–3 inches long, may be rooted in summer in pots of sandy soil under a bell-glass.

**Nanodes Medusæ** (see Chapter on **Orchids**).

**Narcissus** (Daffodil), *Amaryllidaceæ.*—Beautiful, hardy, spring-flowering bulbs which are excellent for beds, borders, the rock-garden (some species), for naturalising in grass, or for growing in pots in the greenhouse.

This genus is a large one, embracing the *Trumpet Daffodils,* with large crown or trumpet, as long as the perianth segments ; the *Short-cup* or *Incomparabilis,* the cup or crown being not less than one-third ; the *Barri,* the crown being less than one-third the length. (The last two groups are known as the medium-crowned class). The *Poet's Narcissus ; Poeticus* or *Pheasant-eye Narcissus* (the small-crowned class) ; the "*Angel's Tears* " ; the *Cyclamen-flowered ; Jonquils ;* the *Tazetta* or *Polyanthus Narcissus ;* the *Hooped Petticoat,* and many others, including hybrids of the different groups, many of which are very beautiful. Most species thrive in well-dug and well-drained ordinary soil, though some few, notably the *Hooped Petticoat, N. Bulbocodium, N. asturiensis* or *N. minimus,* the smallest of all Daffodils, the *Cyclamen-flowered,* and the "*Angel's Tears*" prefer warm, deep, and moist sandy loam, and are charming when grown in pans for the alpine house. The *Polyanthus Narcissi* like a rather stiff soil. Partial shade is desirable, but they will grow well in full sun.

*Greenhouse Culture.*—Narcissi and Daffodils, with very few exceptions, will not stand forcing—in fact, the bloom is far better if no artificial heat is applied, and bulbs grown under glass without any forcing will bloom three weeks or a month earlier than those grown in the open. *N. Tazetta* var. *papyraceus* (Paper-white Narcissus) responds to cool- and warm-house treatment, and may be had in flower

**466**

# GREENHOUSE PLANTS

in winter, even before Christmas, and is one of the most useful of florist flowers at that time of the year.

Indoor culture is similar to that recommended for the **Hyacinth.** Pot-up in clean pots with good drainage from August to November, using a compost of half-fibrous loam to a quarter part each of sand and leaf-mould or rotten manure. Place from three large to twelve small bulbs in a 4- to 5-inch pot, with the tops of the bulbs just showing above the soil, and stand in the open in a cool, shady position, under a 3-inch layer of coconut fibre until growth commences. It usually takes about two months for growth to start. Then move the pots into the cool or cold greenhouse in batches, keeping the temperature low at first, and not raising it until the bulbs have been under glass for about ten days. Water well when the growth commences and give soot water when the buds appear. Water regularly after flowering, then rest and dry off when the foliage dies down. Plant out in the open the following year.

The bulbs of the *Polyanthus Narcissus* are large, and a 5-inch pot will be needed for a single specimen, and a 6-inch pot for three. A group of six in an 8-inch pot will produce a very beautiful effect.

*Growing Bulbs in Water or Pebbles.*—This culture is very simple, and may be carried out under dwelling-house conditions. The bulbs should be placed in shallow pans or saucers, with clean pebbles to hold them up. Sufficient water should be supplied to keep the roots submerged. *Paper-white Narcissus*, or the *Chinese Sacred Lily* (*N. Tazetta* var. *orientalis*) are the most popular and useful for this purpose.

*Propagation.*—Propagate by means of offsets at lifting time, re-planting the offsets immediately in a reserve or nursery garden, where they are grown on until they are mature. Seed may also be sown very thinly in pans or boxes in August. Keep the seed-boxes for two years in a cold frame, then transfer the bulblets to the nursery garden, where they should first flower between their fourth and sixth year. When they have flowered they may be planted out in the flower-garden. Do not divide too frequently, as when the bulbs are too small over-division produces weak stock.

*Species.*—*N. asturiensis* (*N. minimus*) [Spain] (pale yellow, early spring, 3–4 in.); *N. Bulbocodium* (Hooped Petticoat Daffodil) [S. France and Morocco] (white and yellow, Feb.–April, 6 in.); *N. B.* var. *monophylla* (creamy white, Feb.-April, 4–6 in.); *N. cyclamineus* (Cyclamen-flowered Daffodil) [Portugal] (yellow, dark trumpet, Feb.–April, 6 in.); *N. Jonquilla* (Jonquil) [Europe and Algeria] (yellow, spring, 12–16 in.); *N. odorus* (Campernelle Jonquil) [France and Spain] (yellow, early spring, 12–18 in.); *N. Tagetta* (Polyanthus Narcissus) of which there are many varieties including *N. T. orientalis*, *N. T. papyraceus* (white), *N. T. Grand Monarch*, etc. (orange-yellow, Feb.–March, 12–18 in.); *N. Pseudo-Narcissus* (Common Daffodil or Lent Lily) [Europe, and Britain] (yellow or white, Feb.–March, 6–9 in.); there are many beautiful forms of this, e.g. *N. P. bicolor*, *N. P. cernuus*, *N. P. Horsfieldii*, *N. P. muticus*, as well as double-flowered forms. *N. triandrus* (Angel's Tears) [Portugal] (white or yellow, early spring, 6–9 in.).

**Nasonia punctata (Nasonia cinnabarina)** (see Chapter on **Orchids).**

**Nasturtium** (see **Tropæolum**).

**Navel-Wort** (see **Omphalodes**).

**Nectarine** (**Prunus Persica** var. **Nectarina nucipersica**) (see **Fruit Under Glass**).

**Nelumbium speciosum** (see **Nelumbo nucifera**).

**Nelumbo nucifera** [**Nelumbium speciosum**] (East Indian or Sacred Lotus), *Nymphæaceæ*.—A strong-growing, beautiful greenhouse aquatic from the warm parts of Asia. It can be grown outside in a favourable locality, provided the rhizomes are quite a foot or even more below the surface of the water, and protected during the winter.

*Culture.*—It is essential that the roots be protected from frost; therefore the pond should be covered with boards, or, better still, a glass cover and litter during the hard weather may be sufficient. Remove the litter and finally the cover as growth develops. The plant can either be grown in submerged beds in an aquarium or in tubs. The thick, fleshy rhizomes should be placed horizontally a few inches to a foot beneath the surface of the water, and should be given a compost of rich loam and well-decayed manure. Any re-planting should be done in the spring, as growth commences, but it is advisable to leave the rhizomes as undisturbed as possible. Much better results are obtained from plants that are left undisturbed, but top dressed, than from those which are dug up every year, which never seem to get properly established.

*Propagation.*—This is carried out by division or by seed, which should be sown in a pot and submerged a few inches under water, in a temperature of not less than 65° F. To hasten the germination of the rather hard seeds they should be slightly filed.

The flowers are fragrant, usually pink, although there are a number of horticultural varieties: *alba* (white flowers), *grandiflora* (large flowers), *alba-striata* (edge of petals striped and tipped red), *alba plena* (double white), and many others. This plant is often called the Egyptian Lotus, but the Lotus of the ancient Egyptians is a **Nymphæa**. Nelumbo is not a native of the Nile region.

*N. lutea* (American Lotus) [S. United States] is also a bold, attractive aquatic, with pale sulphur-yellow flowers. It requires the same cultural treatment.

**Nematanthus,** *Gesneriaceæ*.—Ornamental, stove, evergreen climbing shrubs with large bell- or funnel-shaped flowers of considerable beauty.

*Culture.*—They succeed in a compost of turfy loam, peat, dried cow-manure, and some charcoal, They are excellent for training up pillars or tree fern stems (temperature 45–55° F. winter, 65–80° F. summer).

*Propagation.*—They are propagated by cuttings inserted in sandy soil placed in heat, but kept rather dry. They will also root from leaves.

*Species.*—*N. chloronema* [Brazil] (scarlet, July); *N. corticicola* [Brazil] (scarlet, summer); *N. longipes* [Brazil] (bright red, winter, stem erect, 24 in.).

**Nemesia,** *Scrophulariaceæ*.—Beautiful half-hardy annuals, growing about 12 inches in height, and flowering in the open from June to September. They make excellent bedding, rock-garden, or pot plants. In the greenhouse they will bloom in spring, summer, or winter.

**468**

*Culture.*—In March sow seeds thinly in deep boxes of moderately rich soil under glass (50° F.). Thin as soon as possible, harden off in a cold frame, and plant out 7 inches apart in May, or pot-up, placing a single plant in a 5-inch pot, and stand in a cool greenhouse. These will furnish summer flowers indoors. Seed may also be sown in a frame in August. If seed is sown in the pots in which the plants are to flower and superfluous seedlings removed, these will furnish winter bloom. Another batch may be sown in September in order to provide flowers in the spring, and should be treated in the same manner as those sown in March.

*Species.*—*N. floribunda* [S. Africa] (white and yellow); *N. strumosa* [S. Africa] (red, pink, orange, yellow, blue and white); *N. s.* var. *Suttonii* is a series of improved forms with large flowers; *N. versicolor* [S. Africa] (white and mauve); *Named Varieties*: *Aurora* (red and white); *Blue Gem*; *Cherry Red*; *Orange Prince*; and *Twilight* (mauve and white).

**Neobenthamia gracilis** (see Chapter on **Orchids**).

**Nepenthes** (Pitcher Plant), *Nepenthaceæ.*—These curious, handsome, and interesting stove evergreens are grown for their coloured pitcher or urn-like leaf appendages, to the opening of which is attached a kind of lid which can be raised and lowered. The pitcher is often found to contain a watery liquid, and in this cockroaches, ants, and other insects are caught; their bodies decompose and give off ammoniacal fumes, which aid in the nutrition of the plant. They thrive in a compost of two parts of good loam to two parts of fibrous peat and one part of sphagnum moss, with some charcoal, broken crocks, and sharp sand added.

*Culture.*—Pot-up or plant in a basket in February or March, and grow near the glass. Good moist bottom heat is necessary (temperature 65° F. winter, 85° F. summer). Water well while growing, but shade from the sun's rays. Syringe daily, and keep the air moist. The best pitchers are produced by stopping the shoots after five or six leaves have been made.

*Propagation.*—Propagation is carried out by means of sucker growths or cuttings of one-year-old ripened shoots in a bottom heat of 80° F. The usual method is to place the cutting through the hole of an inverted small flower-pot and stand in a propagating case. The cutting soon throws out roots in the moist air. Another method of increase is by seed sown on the surface of heavily drained pans of fibrous peat, sphagnum, and some charcoal.

*Species.*—*N. albomarginata* [Singapore] (light green and reddish pitchers with distinct white ring towards the mouth); *N. ampullaria* [Borneo] (bottle-shaped, light-green pitchers); *N. atro-sanguinea* [garden hybrid] (reddish-crimson pitchers, 6 in. long, slightly spotted with yellow); *N. bicalcarata* [Borneo] (large bag-shaped pitchers provided with two sharply toothed wings when developed and with two decurved spurs); *N. coccinea* [hybrid] (crimson pitchers, spotted yellow); *N. intermedia* [hybrid] (green pitchers, spotted red); *N. Rafflesiana* [Borneo] (greenish-yellow pitchers, with brown markings, very handsome); *N. Sedenii* [hybrid] (light-green pitchers, blotched and speckled with brownish crimson).

**469**

**Nepeta** (Catmint), *Labiatæ*.—This genus of hardy herbaceous perennials contains a little trailing plant, *N. hederacea variegata* (*N. Glechoma variegata*) with round leaves, variegated green and creamy white, useful for culture in hanging baskets in the cold or cool greenhouse.

*Culture.*—Propagate by means of division in spring or autumn. Layering may also be effected, without cutting the stems; if preferred, cuttings of the creeping stems, 3–4 inches in length, can be struck in sandy soil in August, wintered in a frame, and potted-up in ordinary potting soil in April. The old wood should not be cut back until the young growth has appeared the following spring.

**Nephelaphyllum** (see Chapter on **Orchids**).

**Nephrodium** (see **Dryopteris**).

**Nephrolepis** (Ladder or Sword Fern), *Polypodiaceæ*.—Half-hardy and warm greenhouse ferns, growing from 10 to 30 inches in height, which thrive in a compost of one part of sandy peat to two parts of leaf-mould and sand. They require a winter temperature of 50° F. and a summer temperature of 70° F.

*Culture.*—Propagate by means of division in March, or sow spores in heat at any time. Pot-up in March, and water liberally in summer.

*N. cordifolia compacta* is a useful plant for pots, as are some of the beautiful forms of *N. exaltata*: *N. e. elegantissima*, *N. e. magnifica*, *N. e. Piersonii*, *N. e. todeoides*, and *N. e. Whitmanii*. Well-grown specimens of these are very lovely both for pots or baskets, but if not carefully raised will show reversion to the type. The once-pinnate leaves should be removed as they appear. (See also Chapter on **Ferns.**)

**Nerine,** *Amaryllidaceæ*.—Beautiful bulbous plants which thrive in the cool greenhouse in rich loam, mixed with leaf-mould, cow-manure, and sand. They grow about 20 inches in height, and flower from September to December.

*Culture.*—Plant singly in August in 4- to 5-inch pots, so that the top of the bulb just shows above the soil. Water well when the vegetation appears, and feed with liquid manure. Continue this treatment until May, when the leaves turn yellow. Then gradually decrease the water supply, and keep the bulbs quite dry from June to August. During this time the pots must be exposed to the sun until the flower-shoots again rise above the soil. When this occurs the pots should be well soaked and a top dressing of soil similar to that described above should be given. There is no need to re-pot annually if this dressing is provided —re-potting every fourth year will be sufficient.

*Propagation.*—Propagate by means of offsets removed in August, or sow seed when ripe. To produce seed, however, the flowers must be hand fertilised.

*Species and Varieties.*—*N. Bowdenii* [Cape Colony] (pink); *N. curvifolia* [S. Africa] and var. *Fothergillii major* (scarlet); *N. flexuosa* [S. Africa] (pale pink, there are several named varieties); *N. pudica* (white); *N. sarniensis* [S. Africa] (pale salmon); *N. s.* var. *corusca* (orange-scarlet); *N. undulata* [S. Africa] (soft flesh); and *N. u.* var. *alba* (white). There are many beautiful named hybrids.

**Nerium,** *Apocynaceæ*.—The best known of this genus of evergreen shrubs is *N. Oleander*, the Common Oleander, with leaves and stems **much**

**470**

resembling those of the Willow, and which, except in **sheltered** sites in the milder localities of the British Isles, usually requires a greenhouse. In Southern Europe they flower beautifully out-of-doors. The blossoms and even the wood of the Oleander are *poisonous*.

*Species.*—*N. odorum* (sweet-scented Oleander) [Persia] is a less robust grower than the well-known Common Oleander; otherwise the difference is merely botanical. It has the same range of coloured varieties. *N. Oleander* [Mediterranean region] is usually rose or pink, but there are several coloured forms: *album, atro-purpureum, carneum,* creamy white, *roseum,* variegated; *N. O.* var. *Loddigesii*; also forms with double flowers. They bloom in the summer, and grow from 6 to 12 feet in height.

*Pot Culture.*—Pot-up when required in February, using 6- to 12-inch pots and a compost of two parts loam and one part of leaf-mould, peat, and a little sand. Top dress annually with a little fresh compost if the plants are not to be re-potted. Stand in a sunny position in the cool greenhouse, and water well in summer. The tough, lanceolate leaves, which grow in whorls, three in number, require frequent sponging, owing to the attack of Black Mould (*Capnodium fœdum*) to which Oleanders are subject, as well as Mealy Bug and Scale.

*Pruning.*—Remove the shoots at the base of all flower-buds and prune to within three buds of the old wood after flowering. Keep the plants warm and moist for a couple of weeks after pruning, to encourage the formation of new shoots (average temperature 50° F. winter, 60° F. summer). Summer in the open, until the autumn, when they must be protected from frost. Keep fairly dry during winter. It is advisable to force these plants alternate years only.

*Propagation.*—To propagate, place cuttings of well-ripened shoots in bottles of water in a sunny frame in summer, or in a warm propagating case. When well rooted, pot-up in light soil, and " stop " from time to time.

**Nerium grandiflorum** (see **Cryptostegia grandiflora**).

**Nertera depressa** (Coral-berried Duckweed), *Rubiaceæ.*—This is a dwarf-growing plant from New Zealand and temperate South America. It rarely exceeds 3 inches in height, creeps along the surface of the ground, and roots as it runs. It carries a quantity of green, small, ovate leaves and tiny greenish flowers, followed by orange-scarlet berries, and is well worthy of a place in the rock-garden in the South of England. The plants may also be grown in pots or shallow pans in the alpine house. They thrive in the shade in warm, moist, sandy loam, and leaf-mould, but must be protected from frost.

*Culture.*—Sow seed in heat in March or April, or propagate by means of division in a warm greenhouse in the spring. Plant out or pot-up, and water freely while growing.

*N. Cunninghamii* [New Zealand] resembles the preceding species, but is of a more slender habit, and has narrower leaves and smaller berries.

**New Zealand Flax** (see **Phormium**).

**New Zealand Christmas Tree** (see **Metrosideros tomentosa**).

**Nicotiana** (Tobacco Plant), *Solanaceæ.*—Although treated as annuals, tobacco plants are perennials, and if protected from frost the roots will come up again year after year.

**471**

Among the kinds usually grown are *N. alata* [Brazil] and *N. Sanderæ*, a hybrid of garden origin. The blossoms are tubular in shape, terminating in five-pointed segments turning outwards from the tube. The first has white flowers fragrant in the evening; the second bears rosy-red, bluish-red, or white flowers, but these are not so fragrant. They grow from 18 to 36 inches high, thrive in rich soil in sunny beds and borders, and are also useful for decoration and perfume in the greenhouse. *N. suaveolens* [Australia] is a pretty, dwarf species, with sweetly-scented white flowers excellent for pot work. *N. sylvestris* [Argentina] makes a very handsome pot-plant, 4–5 feet high, with its clusters of long, white tubular flowers and large, handsome leaves.

*Culture.*—In March sow seed thinly in fine soil under glass (temperature 60° F.), and merely cover with fine sand. Prick off 6 inches apart into boxes of fairly rich soil, harden off, and plant out 12 inches apart early in June, or pot-on and keep indoors. For greenhouse use during the early part of the year seed sown in a frame in August or September will furnish bloom from February to April.

**Nierembergia** (Cup Flower), *Solanaceæ.*—This genus includes several choice half-hardy perennials, which thrive in the cold or cool greenhouse in moist loam. *N. rivularis*, with creamy-white flowers streaked with purple, from June to August, when grown in pans is a useful little plant some 3 inches in height, and makes a good subject for the alpine house. *N. cœrulea* (*N. hippomaniaca*) [Argentina] is a close-growing, compact herb with numerous deep bluish-violet flowers during the summer. It is valuable for the alpine house, the greenhouse, or for planting outside, and grows 6–12 inches high. *N. gracilis*, with its white flowers tinged and veined with purple, is suitable for hanging-baskets. *N. frutescens*, which grows about 18 inches in height, together with the former species, make pretty plants for the cold greenhouse or mixed border outdoors. The latter is similar to *N. gracilis*, but bears larger flowers, which are blue with a yellow throat.

*Culture.*—Sow seed under glass in March, or take cuttings in August and strike in sandy soil under glass. Plant out or pot-up in 6- to 7-inch pans of moist sandy loam and leaf-mould in spring or early autumn. Stand in a sunny position. Water while growing, and top dress with cow-manure in December. Keep fairly dry during winter.

**Nigella** (Devil-in-a-bush, Love-in-a-mist, Jack-in-prison), *Ranunculaceæ.*—Beautiful hardy annuals, useful for sunny beds and borders or for providing bloom for the cold or cool greenhouse as pot-plants, from March to June. They grow about 18 inches high and in the open flower from June to September.

*Culture.*—Sow a few seeds $\frac{1}{4}$ inch deep, in the pots in which the plants are to flower, early in March or in autumn, under glass, and thin out the superfluous seedlings when large enough to handle, leaving one only to mature in each 5-inch pot. A mixture of sandy loam and leaf-mould makes a suitable compost.

*Species and Varieties.*—*N. damascena* [S. Europe] (deep purple); *N. d.* var. *Miss Jekyll* (deep blue, double); *N. hispanica* [Spain and N. Africa] (deep blue or white); *N. orientalis* [Asia Minor] (yellow, spotted red).

**Nivenia corymbosa (Aristea corymbosa, Witsenia corymbosa),** *Iridaceæ.*—An ornamental, cool-greenhouse, shrubby Irid from South Africa, with a tall free-branching stem, woody at the base, and clothed with tufts of erect, glaucous green, Iris-like leaves. It bears dense clusters of Cambridge-blue flowers in August and September. The flowers are very fugacious, but, as they are produced so freely, a good display is maintained.

*Culture.*—It thrives in sandy peat and loam in equal proportions, good drainage and careful watering during the winter being essential.

*Propagation.*—It is readily raised from seed, which is occasionally produced, and which should be sown as soon as ripe and placed in a little warmth. It may also be propagated from cuttings inserted in sand placed under glass, with a little warmth.

**Nolina (Beaucarnea),** *Liliaceæ.*—Attractive, Mexican, evergreen foliage plants, with narrow leaves, some 24–36 inches long, resembling those of the **Cordyline.** They require cool to warm greenhouse treatment, and quickly suffer if the temperature is allowed to fall below 50° F.

*Culture.*—Sow seed thinly in small, well-crocked pots of sandy loam and leaf-mould in March and stand in the warm greenhouse (temperature 60–65° F.). Water well while growing, and keep only just moist when dormant. Re-pot in the spring, annually. When seed is not available, cuttings made of young side-shoots may be struck in a propagating case in March.

*Species.*—*N. gracilis* [Mexico] (glaucous foliage and stem swollen at base) ; *N. recurvata* [Mexico] (drooping foliage) ; and *N. stricta* [Mexico] (glaucous foliage).

**Nopalea cochinellifera,** *Cactaceæ.*—This native of the West Indies is allied to and resembles **Opuntia,** and thrives with the same treatment. It is chiefly interesting in being one of the food-plants of the cochineal insect, large quantities being reared on it.

**Notholæna (Nothochlæna),** *Polypodiaceæ.*—An attractive group of warm-greenhouse ferns, usually small and of delicate appearance, with light, graceful fronds. Some species are covered with a golden or silvery, wax-like powder They require a rather different treatment from most ferns, and like a light, airy position.

*Culture.*—They should be given a good supply of water at the roots, but should have plenty of free drainage, and care should be taken to keep moisture from the fronds. They like a compost of fibrous peat and lumps of sandstone in equal parts, and a few pieces of fibrous loam, with some charcoal. In potting, the plant should be raised just above the surface. It is increased by spores, which germinate freely, or by division of the crowns in March.

*Species.*—*N. ferruginea* [W. Indies and Mexico] has fronds 6–12 inches long, the lower surface being densely covered with woolly hairs. *N. lanuginosa* [S. Europe and Australia] has broad, bi-pinnate fronds, 6–9 inches long. It is a handsome species, covered with dense, woolly tomentum. *N. Parryi* [California] has bi-pinnate fronds 5 inches long, and is densely covered with white hairs, brown beneath. *N. sinuata* [Mexico] has entire or pinnatifid fronds, 12–20 inches long, the lower surface of which is covered with rusty scales. It is a handsome, showy fern. *N. trichomanoides* [Jamaica and Cuba] is a beautiful greenhouse species, and decorative as a basket-plant. Its fronds are 6–12 inches long, and the lower surface is covered with white powder and fine, rusty, woolly hairs.

**Notocactus,** *Cactaceæ.*—A South American genus of cacti allied to **Echinocactus.**

**Nycterinia** (see **Zaluzianskya**).

**Nyctocerus,** *Cactaceæ.*—A slender-growing cactus of a climbing nature, which can be trained either up pillars or along the roof of the greenhouse. They are among the several kinds of night-flowering cacti, and require the same cultural treatment as **Cereus,** being at one time included under that genus.

*N. guatemalensis* [Mexico] has flowers which are pale carmine red or yellowish red outside, and white inside, and bloom in the summer. The fruit is red. *N. serpentinus* [Mexico] is free-flowering, and the one most commonly met with in cultivation, and has flowers which are pale rose outside and white inside.

**Nymphæa,** *Nymphæaceæ.*—A large family of handsome, stove-greenhouse, and hardy aquatics, commonly known as Water-lilies.

*Culture.*—The stove or greenhouse kinds are best grown in pots in a compost of three parts of turfy loam to one part of decayed cow-manure, with some coarse sand, all of which should be prepared some months before it is used. They should then be placed in the aquarium with the crown about 12 inches below the surface (temperature 65–75° F.), and the water heated to 60–65° F., and should be exposed to all the sun and light possible, if the other plants growing there can stand it. As the leaves ripen the temperature of the water and house should be owered, and the tubers should be left in the water until the time of re-potting, which should be about March.

*Propagation.*—They are propagated by seed sown in small pots submerged in a shallow, warm-water tank in spring. The seedlings will grow away well if properly treated, and will often flower the same year. They are also increased by division of the rhizomes when potting.

*Species.*—*N. cærulea* (Blue Lotus of Egypt) [Egypt, N. and Central Africa] has light blue and dull-white flowers with yellow anthers. It is morning-flowering and free blooming, but not showy. There are forms in Africa with white and also with bright-red flowers. *N. capensis* (Cape Water Lily) [S. Africa] has rich, sky-blue flowers with blue anthers. It is a very desirable day-flowering plant. *N. zanzibariensis* [Zanzibar] has deep purplish-blue flowers. *N. devoniensis* (hybrid), is morning-flowering, with brilliant red flowers. *N. gigantea* [Australia] is one of the loveliest and largest of the genus, day-flowering, with bright-blue flowers. *N. Lotus* (white Lotus) [Egypt] has white flowers suffused pink. There are several beautiful forms of this : *dentata, grandiflora, magnifica,* and *superba. N. stellata* (Blue Lotus of India) [S. and E. Asia] is morning-flowering with pale-blue flowers. There are white and pink forms in India. *N. mexicana* [Mexico] is day-flowering, with canary-yellow flowers. Of recent years much work has been done by the hybridiser, and many beautiful coloured hybrids are now grown.

# GREENHOUSE PLANTS

**Ochna,** *Ochnaceæ.*—Greenhouse shrubs from South Africa, with yellow flowers during the spring, but more attractive when in fruit, as the sepals, which are greenish when in flower, become bright red in fruit. They increase in size, and form a striking contrast to the black, seed-like bodies which are borne upon it during the summer. *O. atropurpurea,* a one-flowered species with purple calyx. *O. multiflora,* several flowers in racemes. Requisite temperature 45–60° F. winter, 60–80° F. summer. It succeeds in fibrous loam, leaf-mould, and sand, and is propagated by cuttings of half-ripened wood placed under a bell-glass in a warm greenhouse, or by seed.

**Odontadenia grandiflora (Dipladenia Harrisii),** *Apocynaceæ.*—A tall, tropical climber from Brazil and Trinidad. It is allied to **Dipladenia** and requires the same cultural treatment. It bears large, yellow, fragrant, funnel-shaped flowers shaded orange, which rival in beauty the popular greenhouse **Allamandas.**

*Propagation.*—It is propagated by cuttings of young shoots placed in bottom heat.

**Odontioda** (see Chapter on **Orchids**).

**Odontoglossum** (see Chapter on **Orchids**).

**Odontonema Schomburgkianum (Thyrsacanthus rutilans),** *Acanthaceæ.*—A stove or warm-greenhouse shrub from Colombia, growing up to 3 feet high. It bears long, pendulous, terminal racemes of bright-crimson, tubular flowers during the winter and spring. It thrives in a compost of equal parts of fibrous loam and leaf-mould, with some sand. It can be grown in a cool greenhouse or even a frame during the summer, but must have a stove temperature during the winter.

*Propagation.*—It is propagated by cuttings, which should be inserted singly in pots in spring, and placed in a warm case. As the young plants develop they should be pinched once or twice to encourage a bushy habit. Good plants can be grown in 5- or 6-inch pots.

**Œnothera [Godetia]** (Evening Primrose), *Onagraceæ.*—A genus of beautiful plants, annuals, biennials, and perennials, delightful for bedding, borders, or the rock-garden, and also grown in the greenhouse. All the species are free flowering, and thrive in rich, sandy loam, or any good soil, and in sunny positions; although the Evening Primrose group can be planted in partial shade, when they will be found to open their flowers during some part of the day. Ample **water** is needed during dry weather. For treatment of Annuals see **Godetia.** The biennials and perennials, which are commonly known as Evening Primrose, grow form 6 to 36 inches in height, according to species, and carry yellow, white to rose, and golden flowers from June to October.

*O. eximea* [Rocky Mts.] (white, June–July, 9 in.) ; *O. pumila* [Newfoundland] (yellow) ; and *O. tetraptera* (white and pink), with its var. *Childsii* (deeper rose) when grown in 5-inch pans are useful in the alpine house. Stand outdoors or in a cold frame when not in flower, and cut back straggling and weak shoots after flowering.

*Culture.*—BIENNIALS : Sow seed in the open in a shady spot in May. When 1 inch high thin out to 3 inches apart, and plant out in the shade in March or September, or pot-up for the greenhouse.

PERENNIALS : Sow seed in the open in April, or in gentle heat in

March, take cuttings of young shoots in spring and strike in sandy soil, or propagate (some species) by means of division in April. Plant out or pot-up for the greenhouse in April or September. Pot-up as required, using 6- to 7-inch pots and ordinary potting compost. Winter autumn-sown plants well up to the glass in a cold greenhouse.

*Species.*—BIENNIAL : *O. acaulis* [Chile] (white, tinted rose, 10 in.) ; *O. biennis grandiflora* (pale yellow, 30 in.). PERENNIAL : *O. cheiranthifolia* [California] (pale yellow, trailer) ; *O. glauca* [United States] (pale yellow), and its variety *Fraseri* (golden yellow, both 12–20 in.) ; *O. missouriensis* [United States] (yellow, trailer) ; *O. pumila* (yellow, 6 in.) ; *O. speciosa* [N. America] (white to rose, 30 in.).

**Oftia africana (Spielmannia africana),** *Myoporaceæ.*—A greenhouse, evergreen shrub from South Africa, with white solitary flowers marked with a blue streak at the base of the petals. It succeeds in any light, rich soil, and can be planted out in the greenhouse and trained up a pillar. It is also useful as a pot-plant in 6-inch pots. It flowers from February to November, and roots readily from cuttings placed in sand under a bell-glass in heat.

**Old Man Cactus** (see **Cephalocereus senilis**).

**Old Man's Beard** (see **Tillandsia usneoides**).

**Oleander** (see **Nerium Oleander**).

**Olearia Haastii** (New Zealand Daisy Bush, or Tree Aster), *Compositæ.*—Hardy, evergreen shrubs which grow from 4 to 9 feet high, and bear white flowers outdoors in late summer. The leaves are greyish green above and silvery underneath. They like a sheltered position and well-drained soil.

*Pot Culture of Greenhouse Species.*—*O. stellulata* (*O. Gunniana*) [Tasmania]. There are several coloured forms of this, some of which are very attractive. In a warm house (temperature 45–50° F. winter. 60–75° F. summer), these may be had in flower in early spring, or in the cool greenhouse they may be had in flower in March. Pot when required in October, using 5- to 7-inch pots, and a compost of two parts sandy loam to one part of leaf-mould and rotten manure. Sink the pots in ashes in a sunny spot outdoors from May to December, then take indoors, and keep fairly dry until growth starts.

*Pruning.*—Trim to shape when necessary in March, and every four or five years the shrubs will become stilted and somewhat bare at the base ; they should then be cut hard back, and will soon " break " again from the ground line.

*Propagation.*—To propagate, sow in a frame in March or strike cuttings in a frame in September.

**Oliveranthus elegans (Cotyledon elegans),** *Crassulaceæ.*—An attractive much-branched, summer-flowering plant from Mexico, with large, bright-red, yellow-tipped flowers (April–May, 12–20 in.). It requires the same cultural treatment as **Crassula.**

**Omphalodes** (Navel-wort), *Boraginaceæ.*—Low-growing, hardy herbs, with Forget-me-not-like flowers, usually grown in rock-gardens, although the dwarf kinds can be grown in pans for the alpine house.

*Culture.*—They like an open, loamy soil, with pieces of sandstone intermixed, among which the roots love to ramble. It is very important that the pans should be well drained.

476

# GREENHOUSE PLANTS

*Propagation.*—They are propagated by seed, which should be sown as soon as ripe and stood in a cool frame. Some species are increased by means of division in the spring.

*Species.*—*O. cornifolia* (*O. cappadocica*) [Asia Minor] (clear rich blue, white eye, spring, 6–8 in.) ; *O. Luciliæ* [Asia Minor] (blue, varying from light blue to pinkish purple, all with a white centre, spring and early summer, 6–8 in.). This species dislikes division, and usually produces seed freely. *O. verna* (Creeping Forget-me-not) [Europe] (light blue flowers in pairs, April–May, 3–4 in.). This species is increased by stolons soon forming a thick mass, and is readily divided. There is a white-flowered variety, which, though pretty, is not so attractive as the Forget-me-not blue of the type.

**Oncidium** (see Chapter on **Orchids**).

**Onoclea sensibilis,** *Polypodiaceæ.*—An easily-grown, hardy, deciduous fern, very suitable for growing in a cold greenhouse, particularly if it can be planted out in heavy loam in a moist, cool place. It can also be grown in pots, which should be stood in a saucer of water. It has two forms of fronds : the narrow, somewhat leafless one bearing the sporangia, or spores.

*Propagation.*—It is increased by division in the spring, or by spores sown as soon as ripe. (See Chapter on **Ferns.**)

**Onosma,** *Boraginaceæ.*—Hardy plants with tubular or urn-shaped flowers. They are suitable for the herbaceous border or rock-garden, but some of the dwarf, compact-growing kinds can be useful for the alpine house when grown in pans. The compost should be made up of sandy loam with some leaf-mould and mortar-rubble. Good **drainage** is essential.

*Propagation.*—Cuttings of the perennial kinds root readily if placed in sandy soil in a close frame during the summer, taking care not to keep the atmosphere too wet, or the foliage damps off. They may also be increased by seed, which should be sown as soon as ripe. The biennial and annual kinds must be sown each year.

*Species.*—*O. albo-roseum* [Asia Minor] (white, changing to rose and violet, summer, 6–8 in., perennial) ; *O. echioides* (Golden Drop) [S. Europe] (pale yellow to white, fragrant, summer, 6–9 in., biennial or short lived perennial) ; *O. Hookeri* [Sikkim] (violet, early summer, 4–6 in.) ; *O. nanum* [Alps of Cappadocia] (white, early summer, 3–4 in.) ; *O. stellatum* [S.E. Europe] (yellow, early summer, 8–10 in.) ; the var. *tauricum* [Caucasus] has citron-yellow flowers. Both are perennials.

**Onychium,** *Polypodiaceæ.*—Greenhouse evergreen ferns which thrive in the shade in a mixture of half peat and half sandy loam and leaf-mould.

*Culture.*—Pot-up in March. Keep the atmosphere moist, and water liberally in summer (temperature 50° F. winter, 60° F. summer).

*Propagation.*—Propagate by means of spores sown in heat at any time, or by division in March.

*Species.*—*O. auratum* [India] is an attractive fern, with fronds 12–15 in. long, finely divided, with golden-coloured sporangia. *O. japonicum* [India, China, and Japan] is a favourite species, growing from 10 to 15 inches high.

**Ophioglossum** (Serpent's or Adder's Tongue), *Ophioglossaceæ.*—A group of interesting stove greenhouse or hardy ferns. The sporangia are arranged so as to form a flattened spike, arising from the barren frond. They are increased by division. For cultural treatment see Chapter on **Ferns**.

*Species.*—*O. palmatum* [Cuba] is a warm-greenhouse species, with fronds in the shape of a **V**, and several fertile spikes. *O. reticulatum* [Tropical America] is a warm-greenhouse fern with fronds 6–12 inches long, distinctly veined. The fertile spike overtops the sterile segment, and the roots are tuberous. *O. vulgatum* (Common Adder's Tongue) [Europe, Britain, and America] has fronds 6–8 inches long. The sterile division is placed about half-way up the barren frond. It is hardy, but can be grown in the alpine house in pans of moist or peaty soil, and kept in a cool place.

**Ophiopogon** (Snake's Beard or Japanese Hyacinth), *Liliaceæ.*— Beautiful, half-hardy, perennial foliage plants of dwarf growth, with grass-like leaves, the variegated forms being striped with yellow or white. They thrive in a compost of two parts of loam to one part of leaf-mould and sand. The flower-spikes, borne between June and September, are like those of a miniature Hyacinth, and rise to a height of about 10–15 inches.

*Culture.*—Pot-up in March (only when pot-bound), using 6- to 7-inch pots. Water well, and syringe the leaves daily from May to October, but keep fairly dry in winter.

*Propagation.*—Propagate by means of division in March (temperature 40° F. winter, 55° F. summer).

*Species.*—*O. Jaburan* [Japan] (white to lilac flowers, **vars.** *variegated* have yellow-and-white-striped leaves); *O. japonicus* [Japan and N. China] (violet-purple to lilac); the variety *variegatus* has variegated leaves and is an attractive plant.

**Ophiopogon spicatus** (see **Liriope graminifolia**).

**Oplismenus,** *hirtellus* (the **Panicum** of the Florist), *Gramineæ.*— Delicate, creeping, branching grass, allied to **Panicum,** and occasionally known as *Panicum variegatum*. It is a very popular plant, particularly the form with white-and-pink-striped leaves. It is very valuable for the edging of beds or for hanging-baskets. It is increased by cuttings placed in a close frame with bottom heat, or by division of the root.

**Opuntia** (Prickly Pear), *Cactaceæ.*—This is the general name of a genus of Cacti from the arid and semi-arid regions of Mexico and Central America to the southern parts of South America, suitable for greenhouse culture. There are many species, including *O. Ficus-indica*, otherwise known as Indian Fig, the fruit of which is edible. This is an ornamental and interesting plant with many-jointed, fleshy, round, or flat stems covered with hair or spines, in the axil of the leaves. They have very minute leaves, and carry their flowers on the sides of the stems. Opuntias thrive in warm, sunny positions, in a mixture of equal parts of fibrous loam, coarse sand, mortar, and powdered brick rubble.

*Culture.*—Pot-up triennially in March. Water weekly in summer, every ten days in spring and autumn, and keep dry in winter (average

478

temperature : 60° F. day, 50° F. night, winter ; 80° F. day, 70° F. night, summer). Ventilate freely at all times when the weather is favourable.

*Propagation.*—Propagation may be carried out by means of seed sown in heat in March, by cuttings in June, or by means of grafting in April.

Among good species may be mentioned *O. aurantiaca* [Argentina] (orange, June, 30 in.) ; *O. basilaris* [N. Mexico] (purple, May–June, 10–20 in.) ; *O. cylindrica* [Chile] (red, summer, 12–50 in.) ; *O. Dillenii* (orange-red, Sept., 50 in.) ; *O. Engelmannii* [Mexico] (yellow, May–June) ; *O. Ficus-indica* (yellow, June, 30 in.) ; *O. grandis* [Mexico] (yellow, summer, 30–50 in.) ; *O. humifusa* [Central U.S.A.] (sulphur-yellow, June–Sept., 10 in.) ; *O. nigricans* [Mexico] (pink, Aug., 40 in.) ; *O. polyacantha* [W. Central U.S.A.] (yellow, May, 25 in.) ; *O. pulchella* [Nevada and Arizona] (purple, summer, 10 in.) ; and *O. vulgaris* (Barberry Fig) [East U.S.A.] (pink, May–June, 30 in.).

**Orange, Lemon and Lime** (see **Citrus**).

**Orange Jessamine** (see **Chalcas exotica**).

**Orchids** (see Chapter on **Orchids**).

**Oreodoxa,** *Palmaceæ.*—A small group of stove-palms with slender ringed stems. They succeed in a compost of loam with some peat and sand. They are useful for decoration in the greenhouse and in the dwelling-house, as well as for planting out in the sub-tropical garden, provided they are sheltered from winds. They require the same cultural treatment as **Phœnix.**

*O. oleracea* (Cabbage Palm) [W. Indies] has graceful, arched, pinnate leaves whose stems become swollen at the base. In Florida this palm is grown and cut down when three years old for the central leaves which are edible. *O. regia* (Royal Palm) [Cuba] is a slow-growing palm, somewhat resembling the former species. Although they have very distinct characters when adult, it is almost impossible to distinguish between the two when young plants. *O. Sancona* [Colombia] is a handsome, easily cultivated species, the leaf-stalk when young being of a reddish bronze. This species is much used for room decoration, particularly on the Continent.

**Origanum** (Marjoram), *Labiatæ.*—Herbs, some of which are suitable for the rock-garden, or, grown in pans, for the alpine house. They should be given a light, well-drained soil, and the pans should be plunged in the open in ashes or similar material when not in flower. All are easily raised from seed, by cuttings from young growth, or by division in the spring.

*O. Dictamus* (Dittany) [Crete] (flowers pink, leaves clothed with dense wool on both sides, summer, 8–10 in., rather tender) ; *O. pulchellum* [S.E. Europe] (flowers rose-coloured, with reddish bracts, the clusters of which resemble small hops ; quite a pretty plant, summer, 10–15 in.) ; *O. sipyleum* (*O. hybridum*) [Levant] (pink flowers, hispid or woolly leaves, summer, 8–10 in.).

**Ornithogalum** (Star of Bethlehem), *Liliaceæ.*—The plants belonging to this genus are numerous, and consists of various bulbous-rooted plants, bearing for the most part white or yellow, star-like flowers.

**479**

# THE GREENHOUSE

Some are hardy and fitted for the open, others are half-hardy and better suited to the greenhouse. They grow from 10 to 30 inches in height, according to species, and flower outdoors from April to July.

*O. arabicum* [Mediterranean region], which grows about 30 inches in height, and bears white flowers with black centres, is the species usually grown in the greenhouse where it flowers in early spring.

*Pot Culture.*—Pot-up from August to November, placing three bulbs in a 6-inch pot or singly in a smaller pot, and using a compost of two parts of turfy loam to one part of leaf-mould and sand. Grow near the glass in a cold greenhouse (temperature 35° F. winter, 50° F. summer).

*Propagation.*—Propagate by means of offsets in the autumn or by seed sown as soon as ripe.

Other species worth growing are *O. lacteum* (Chincheringchee) [S. Africa] which carries white flowers with a brown centre in early summer, and grows 12–18 inches in height. *O. thyrsoides* [Cape Province], which grows 6–10 inches high and bears white flowers with brown eye in early spring, is charming when grown in pans for the alpine or cool house. The var. *aureum* has golden yellow flowers. They require sandy loam and moist conditions during the growing season.

**Oryza sativa** (Rice), *Gramineæ.*—This is the well-known rice of commerce from the Tropics of the Old World. Although of no horticultural value, it is very effective when grown round the edge of tanks in which are grown greenhouse aquatics.

*Culture.*—It should be grown either in a bed of damp soil or in large pots or pans, which should be stood in the tanks. It is readily raised from seed, which should be sown in small pots and stood in shallow water in a warm greenhouse. Thin out the seedlings to about three in each pot, and when large enough, either plant out in the bed or into larger pots, putting three of the small pots into an 8- or 10-inch pot.

**Osbeckia,** *Melastomaceæ.*—Stove or warm-greenhouse shrubs or sub-shrubs. They bear showy, pink, violet, or reddish flowers, and quite handsome coriaceous leaves. They require the same cultural treatment as **Melastoma.**

*Species.*—*O. nepalensis* [Nepal] (purplish rose, June, 15–18 in.); the var. *albiflora* is a pretty, white-flowered form. *O. rostrata* [Bengal] (rosy pink, Oct., 24–30 in.); *O. stellata* [Himalaya] (lilac-red, July–Aug., 20–24 in.).

**Osmanthus,** *Oleaceæ.*—Hardy evergreen shrubs, some of which resemble hollies. *O. aquifolium* [Japan] is sometimes introduced into the greenhouse on account of the small but fragrant white flowers which it bears in autumn. *O. Delavayi* [China] (white, March–April, 4–6 ft.) is an evergreen, and is the best species for outdoor culture and the most decorative for under glass, where its pure white, fragrant flowers are of great value in the cool greenhouse during February and March.

*Culture.*—Pot-up or plant in the greenhouse bed in May or September, in sandy loam, in full sun or partial shade. No pruning is necessary, except to trim back any long and straggling shoots. This should be done in June. Pot-plants should be stood outside during the summer, the pots being plunged in ashes.

**PLATE 14**
'Cherrytime', a variety of cactus-flowered *Zinnia*.
The flowers average five inches in diameter.

*Propagation.*—Cuttings of mature shoots may be rooted in a frame in September, or layers may be put down in summer, or they may be grafted on to Privet (**Ligustrum**), but this is not advisable.

**Osmunda,** *Osmundaceæ.*—Chiefly hardy evergreen or deciduous ferns growing from 10 to 100 inches in height. The hardy species thrive in partial shade in a warm, sheltered rock-garden, or bog land, in moist, peaty loam, leaf-mould and sand.

Although best planted out, most of them are very useful in pots in the cool greenhouse or fernery. They should be grown in the shade, in a mixture of half peat and half sandy loam and leaf-mould. Pot-up in March. Keep the atmosphere moist, and water liberally during the summer.

*Propagation.*—Propagate by means of offsets in March, or spores may be sown under glass in July.

*Species.*—*O. cinnamomea* (Cinnamon Fern) [N. America] (24–48 in.) ; *O. Claytoniana* [N. America and Japan] (somewhat resembles the previous species) ; *O. regalis* (Royal Fern) [Europe, etc.] is a handsome fern which will sometimes grow to a height of 10 feet. There are several geographical forms.

**Osteomeles,** *Rosaceæ.*—Attractive, evergreen shrubs, with graceful, pinnate foliage and clusters of white, hawthorn-like flowers, followed by bluish-black, berry-like fruits. They can be grown in a sunny position against a wall in the open in favourable districts. In the cool greenhouse they may be raised either in pots, or they can be planted out in a border and trained up a pillar or against the wall. They should be given well-drained soil.

*Propagation.*—They are increased by seed sown when ripe, which is usually slow in germinating, often not until the second year ; or by cuttings of half-ripened wood in July, placed under glass in a warm greenhouse. They can also be grafted on to **Cotoneaster.**

*O. anthyllidifolia* [Hawaiian Islands] grows from 2 to 8 feet in height, and in the spring bears white flowers in corymbs. The leaves are grey with silky pubescence. *O. Schwerinæ* [China] is hardier than the previous species and the flowers, fruit and foliage are all very much smaller.

**Osteospermum,** *Compositæ.*—An ornamental, greenhouse, evergreen shrub with pretty flowers, the best-known species being *O. moniliferum* [S. Africa]. It grows to a height of from 2 to 3 feet, and thrives in any light, rich soil. The flowers of most species are yellow, and appear from April to August, according to species.

**Othonna crassifolia,** *Compositæ.*—A half-hardy, shrubby little, trailing, succulent perennial from South Africa, with yellow, daisy-like flowers in June and July. It is useful for cultivation in hanging-baskets in the cold or cool greenhouse, where it will withstand extremes of temperature and moisture.

*Culture*—Pot-up annually in March in well-drained pots, using a compost of one part sand and leaf-mould to two parts of fibrous loam. Little or no water is needed until the plants commence to make growth. Then stand the pot in a bowl of water until well soaked, and subsequently keep moist until after flowering.

*Propagation.*—Cuttings made of new shoots when growth commences

**H H**

in April may be rooted in pots in the cool greenhouse, or ripe seed may be sown from March to July. The seed should be covered with a sheet of glass, the seedlings being pricked off 2–3 inches apart, as soon as large enough to handle, and subsequently potted-up singly into small pots.

**Ourisia,** *Scrophulariaceæ.*—Dwarf, perennial alpine plants, usually grown in the rock-garden, in a sheltered, somewhat shady position, where the ground is moist, but sweet and well drained. They are charming when grown in pans in the alpine house. When not in flower the pans should be plunged in ashes in a cold frame that is shaded from the sun, as exposure to the hot sunshine is fatal to the plants. Slow surface creepers, they can be readily increased by division in the spring.

*Species.*—*O. coccinea* [Island of Chiloe] (scarlet, May–Sept., 6–12 in.) ; *O. macrophylla* (*O. robusta*) [New Zealand] (white, sometimes with purple streaks, spring, 12–18 in.).

**Ouvirandra** (see **Aponogeton**).

**Oxalis** (Cape Shamrock, Wood Sorrel), *Oxalidaceæ.*—A genus of pretty, hardy and half-hardy annuals, perennials, and bulbous plants, all of which have beautiful green, clover-like foliage, which forms a fine contrast to their richly coloured blossoms. These plants grow from 4 to 12 inches in height and flower in the spring, summer, and autumn, according to species. They are admirably adapted for pot culture. *O. adenophylla*, *O. enneaphylla*, *O. lobata*, and *O. magellanica*, grown in a 5- to 6-inch pan make useful little plants for culture in the alpine house. In the warm greenhouse autumn-flowering species may be had in bloom in summer. *O. Martiana* (*O. floribunda*) [Tropical America and Tropical Asia] is an ideal hanging-basket plant, and *O. Ortgiesii* [Peru], a free, yellow-flowering species, is a most useful subject for pot culture in the warm greenhouse They succeed in any well-drained, light, sandy soil mixed with leaf-mould ; the rock-garden species need a gritty loam and a semi-shaded position.

*Culture.*—ANNUALS : Sow seed thinly in March or April in a cool house. Prick off, 3 inches apart, in pots for the greenhouse, and again in May and June for flowering in the autumn.

*Propagation.*—Propagation is carried out by means of small bulbs removed from the parent and planted in September.

*Pot Culture.*—Pot-up in March, putting five bulbs $\frac{3}{4}$ inch deep, in a 5-inch pot, in a compost of two parts of sandy loam to one of leaf-mould. Keep cool, and water sparingly until growth commences, then water liberally. Gradually withhold water after flowering, and keep dry through the winter (average temperature 40–50° F.).

*Species and Varieties.*—ANNUAL : *O. rosea* [Chile] is a charming little annual with dainty rosy flowers, the veins of which are of a deeper colour. It makes a pretty little pot-plant for the cool greenhouse, growing 6–8 inches high, and blooming during the spring and summer. There are two varieties : *alba* with white flowers, and *delicata*, pale pink. PERENNIAL : *O. adenophylla* [Chile] (lilac-pink, dark eye, May–July, 5 in.) ; *O. Bowiei* [Cape Horn] (bright rosy red, autumn, 4–6 in.) ; *O. enneaphylla* [Falkland Islands] (white, May–Sept., 6 in.) ; *O. hirta* [S.

Africa] (deep rose to lavender, autumn, 9–12 in.) ; *O. lasiandra* [Mexico] (rosy crimson, May, 12–15 in.) ; *O. lobata* [S. America] (yellow, **Sept.**– Oct., 4 in.) ; *O. magellanica* [S. America] (pale pink, summer, 2–3 in.) ; *O. Martiana* (*O. floribunda*) [Tropical America] (red, rose, mauve, or white, March, 6 in.) ; *O. purpurata* [S. Africa] (carmine, Aug.–Sept., 8 in.) ; *O. tuberosa* [S. America] (rose, Oct.–Nov., 6 in.).

**Oxypetalum cæruleum (Tweedia cærulea),** *Asclepiadaceæ.*—A charming twining plant from Argentina, interesting on account of the changing colour of the flowers at the different stages of their existence. Opening pale blue, they later have a tinge of green, then purplish, fading to lilac. All shades are showing at the same time on a well-grown plant. It likes a rich, well-drained, loamy soil, and does best when planted out in the greenhouse with the shoots trained near the glass.

*Propagation.*—It is propagated by seed sown and placed in a warm greenhouse, or by cuttings placed under a bell-glass and given a little bottom heat.

**Pachyphytum** (see **Cotyledon**).

**Pæonia** (Peony), *Ranunculaceæ.*—Although hardy, some of the single and double forms of *P. lactiflora* are useful for growing under glass, either in a cool greenhouse or for forcing purposes, when they are valuable, used either for greenhouse decoration or for cutting. They should be lifted in September and placed in a cold frame, and brought into the house later. If the plants are to be forced they should be brought into a temperature of 55–60° F. in January. As the plants grow, feed well with liquid manure, and good blooms can be obtained in about eight weeks. To obtain extra fine blooms, particularly of the double varieties, the lateral buds should be removed as soon as they appear. Two years' rest should be given to plants which are forced. The Chinese *P. suffruticosa* (*P. moutan*) in variety can also be had in flower in February in the cold greenhouse, and are very decorative.

**Palms.**—These are among the most striking of foliage plants, and are of great decorative value. The foliage of the palms is of two kinds : the fan-leaved, in which the venation radiates from the centre, and the feather-veined, in which the leaf is frequently divided into long, narrow segments from the sides of the long midrib. Some species require a considerable amount of heat, but such species as the *Areca* (Betel-nut Palm), *Chamærops* (Fan Palm), *Oreodoxa* (Cabbage Palm), *Howea* [*Kentia*] (Curly Palm), and *Phœnix* (Date Palm) may be grown easily in a house merely protected from frost.

*Culture.*—Palms are usually bought by the amateur as small plants, and should be re-potted into pots of the same size, in a compost of fibrous loam and silver sand or fibrous peat and grit. Spring or early summer is the best time for potting. The roots must not be injured, and they must be planted firmly the same depth as before. Water well both summer and winter, sponge the leaves with warm, soft water, and syringe morning and evening in spring and summer. Partial shade is required in hot weather, and a little liquid manure made from cow-manure and soot is beneficial. Should the foliage turn yellowish, a small lump of sulphate of iron on the surface of the soil will remedy this.

*Propagation.*—Propagation is usually by means of **seed**, division in April, or by suckers in September. (See also section dealing with Palms in Chapter on **Greenhouse Foliage Plants.**)

**Pancratium calathinum** (see **Hymenocallis calathina**).

**Pancratium illyricum** and **P. maritimum** (Mediterranean Lily or Sea Daffodil), *Amaryllidaceæ.*—Semi-hardy, bulbous plants which thrive in light, rich loam and peat, in warm and well-drained borders, and in sunny, sheltered positions. There are also some stove and greenhouse species. Both plants bear fragrant white flowers in May and June on stems 18 inches high.

*Pot Culture.*—Pot-plants should not be re-potted too frequently, as better results are obtained from pot-bound specimens. Re-pot every third or fourth year (in March), placing the bulbs 5 inches deep in two-thirds loam to one-third well-rotted manure and a little sand. A top dressing may be given annually, taking care not to injure the roots. Dry off gradually, after blooming, and stand hardy species in the open from May to September.

*Propagation.*—Propagate by means of offsets in October or March.

**Pandanus** (Screw Pine), *Pandanaceæ.*—This is a large genus of warm-greenhouse and stove trees or shrubs. Botanists have described something like eighty species, but very few are grown outside botanic gardens. In fact the ones generally cultivated are *P. Sanderi* [Timor, Malay Archipelago], which is of a denser habit than *P. Veitchii*, the variegations being golden yellow, and instead of being at the margins are in narrow bands with green throughout the leaf; and *P. Veitchii*, a native of Polynesia, which has green leaves broadly bordered with white on the margins. *P. utilis* [Madagascar] in a juvenile state is an attractive plant, carrying green leaves with red spines. In the Tropics this is a valuable plant to the natives, the roots providing fibre for ropes, baskets, mats, etc., as also do the leaves. All are very attractive and useful plants for table decoration.

*Culture.*—Pot-up when necessary in clean, well-crocked pots in March (the size of the pot being determined according to the size of the plant), using a compost of sandy loam, leaf-mould, and peat, and stand in a shady position in the warm greenhouse until re-established. A little powdered charcoal may be added to the compost with advantage. Water and syringe regularly while growing, and maintain a moist atmosphere. Give ample light but shade from direct sun.

*Propagation.*—Offsets or suckers, which develop round the base of the plants, may be detached in spring or summer and potted-up singly in small thumb pots, placing them in a warm propagating case until rooted.

**Pandorea,** *Bignoniaceæ.*—Ornamental greenhouse climbers with handsome foliage and beautiful funnel or bell-shaped flowers. They were at one time included under **Tecoma,** but are allied to **Bignonia,** and require the same cultural treatment.

*Propagation.*—They are propagated by seed and by cuttings of young shoots placed under glass with bottom heat.

*P. australis* [*Bignonia Pandorea*] (Wonga-Wonga Vine) [Australia] bears yellowish-white flowers, spotted violet, in spring. The variety *rosea* has light, rose-coloured flowers. Although this plant has not such large, showy flowers as some species, it is worth cultivating for its foliage alone. Seedlings of this species, when young, have finely cut foliage somewhat resembling that of a fern, and they have been given the varietal name of *filicifolia*. The plant changes entirely as it gets older. *P. Brycei* [Rhodesia] is winter-flowering, and has light pink flowers, netted red, with a yellow throat. *P. jasminoides* (Bower Plant of Australia) is autumn flowering, and carries white flowers, sometimes tinged pink, with usually a rosy pink throat.

**Panicum** (Panick Grass), *Gramineæ*.—A large genus of stove, greenhouse, or hardy annual or perennial grasses of variable habit, chiefly grown in many parts of the world on account of their food value for man and beast, but several are quite useful for decorative purposes.

*Culture.*—Pot-up in the spring in 6- or 8-inch pots in a compost of sandy loam with peat or leaf-mould added, and grow in a warm, moist atmosphere.

*Propagation.*—Propagation is carried out by means of division in the spring. Place in sandy soil in a propagating case in spring or early summer, and pot-on in 5- or 6-inch pots when ready.

*Species.*—*P. plicatum* [Tropics] is a free-growing, green-leaved plant, 16–18 inches high, useful as a pot-plant or as undergrowth in a heated greenhouse. There is also a variegated form of this. *P. sulcatum* [Tropical America] is a handsome perennial grass, growing up to 6 feet high, useful for the greenhouse or for sub-tropical beddings.

**Panicum variegatum** (see **Oplismenus, hirtellus**).

**Pansy** (see **Viola**).

**Paphinia** (see Chapter on **Orchids**).

**Paphiopedelum** (see Chapter on **Orchids**).

**Papyrus** (see **Cyperus Papyrus**).

**Parrot's Bill** (see **Clianthus puniceus**).

**Parrot's Feather** (see **Myriophyllum**).

**Partridge Berry** (see **Mitchella repens**).

**Partridge-Breasted Aloe** (see **Aloe variegata**).

**Pasque Flower** (see **Anemone Pulsatilla**).

**Passiflora** (Passion Flower), *Passifloraceæ*.—A genus of beautiful ornamental climbing shrubs, with starry flowers which are produced in great profusion and in succession during the greater part of the year under glass. They are, indeed, among the most interesting, important and effective plants for training in conservatories, and will grow in almost any well-drained soil, though sandy loam is best. They should be given a position against a sunny wall facing south or west; the root-run should be restricted to encourage flowering.

*Greenhouse Culture.*—Plant in March in a compost of two parts of fibrous loam to one part of peat and sand, syringe and water well in summer, but keep fairly dry in winter (temperature 45° F. winter, 65° F. summer). Prune back to within two buds of the old wood in winter, and cut away all weak shoots in spring. Strike cuttings of young shoots in a frame in summer. Some species may be increased by seed sown in spring and placed in a temperature of 60–65° F. The plants should be potted-off when large enough.

# THE GREENHOUSE

*Species.—P. Allardii* (hybrid) white shaded pink, carona white and dark purple. *P. amabilis* [Brazil] (solitary bright-brick-red flowers with white filaments, May–June, 10 ft., warm greenhouse) ; *P. Banksii* [Australia] (brick-red, summer, 12–15 ft., cool greenhouse) ; *P. cærulea* [Brazil] (blue, June–Sept., 25 ft.) is the most hardy ; for the cool greenhouse, or a warm outside wall, the white variety *Constance Elliott* (June–Sept., 25 ft.) is recommended. *P. coccinea* [S. America] (scarlet and orange, Sept., 20 ft., warm greenhouse) ; *P. edulis* (round-fruited Granadilla) [Brazil] (white, tinted purple, with sweet edible fruit) ; *P. laurifolia* (Jamaica Honeysuckle) [Tropical America] (white and violet, red spots, Aug., 20 ft., warm greenhouse) ; *P. quadrangularis* (Common Granadilla of the Tropics) [Nicaragua] (Calyx lobes white, petals reddish violet, with a crowded row of corona petals bright blue mottled with white—one of the most beautiful of Tropical flowers. Fruits are large, edible, and full of sweet pulp) ; *P. racemosa* [Brazil] (scarlet, June–July, 12–15 ft.) ; *P. Watsoniana* [Brazil] (white, violet and lilac, summer, 12–15 ft., cool greenhouse). There are many beautiful hybrids between these species.

**Paullinia thalictrifolia,** *Sapindaceæ.*—A handsome, warm-greenhouse, climbing foliage plant. The leaves are much divided, resembling a Maidenhair Fern or **Davallia.** It is useful for covering unsightly palm tubs, etc., and can also be grown as an upright, fern-like plant. Unless shaded too much the leaves have a pretty, bronzy tint.

*Propagation.*—It is increased by cuttings of young growth in the spring placed under glass with bottom heat. Young plants should be pinched back, they will then branch out and make handsome plants in 5-inch pots.

**Pavetta,** *Rubiaceæ.*—Tropical stove evergreens, allied to **Ixora,** requiring the same cultural treatment. They succeed in a compost of three parts fibrous loam, two parts of peat, and one part of well-decayed manure. They should be given a summer temperature of 65–75° F., and be kept well syringed. Winter temperature should not be lower than 55° F. Cuttings of young growth taken in the early spring root freely, when placed in small pots plunged to the rim in a propagating case with plenty of bottom heat. Old plants may be cut down to obtain plenty of young shoots. Pot-on plants as required, giving liquid manure at intervals during the growing season. The plants should be headed back annually, and they will bloom for many years. They should be watched for scale and mealy bug.

*Species.—P. borbonica* (Isle of Bourbon) is a foliage plant whose dark-green leaves are mottled with light green, and have a salmon-red midrib. The flower of this plant is unknown in cultivation : it may not even be a Pavetta. *P. caffra* (S. Africa) is a beautiful greenhouse plant (white flowers, summer, 26–48 in.) ; *P. indica* [India] (white fragrant flowers, autumn, 36–48 in.).

**Pavonia rosea** (*Malvaceæ*).—A showy and interesting stove and warm-greenhouse plant from Tropical America. It is evergreen and bears solitary flowers in the upper axils to form a short terminal corymb. They are purplish red and very attractive.

*Culture.*—The plants thrive in a light rich compost of loam, peat,

486

and leaf-mould. Cuttings root readily when inserted in sand under a bell-glass or propagating frame. This species enjoys warm, moist growing conditions and when well rooted in the final pots, liberal feeding with diluted liquid manure is beneficial.

**Peach (Prunus Persica)** (see **Fruit Under Glass**).

**Peach-coloured Trumpet Flower** (see **Solandra grandiflora**).

**Pear (Pyrus communis)** (see **Fruit Under Glass**).

**Pearl Bush** (see **Exochorda**).

**Pearl Fruit** (see **Margyricarpus setosus**).

**Pedilanthus tithymaloides** (Slipper Spurge, Bird Cactus, Jew Bush), *Euphorbiaceæ.*—A dwarf succulent shrub from South America with bright-red, or purple flowers, in dense terminal cymes. The leaves are dark green and narrow. There is a variegated variety, the leaves of which are bordered with white.

Culture is the same as for the succulent **Euphorbias.**

**Pediocactus Simpsonii (Echinocactus Simpsonii)** (Snowball Cactus), *Cactaceæ.*—Pinkish, funnel-shaped flowers. Requires the same culture as **Echinocactus.**

**Pelargonium** (Stork's Bill), *Geraniaceæ.*—There is frequent confusion over the names *Geranium* and *Pelargonium*. The former name covers both sections of plants, but is correctly assigned to the hardy perennial sorts (see **Geranium**). The term " Pelargonium " includes all half-hardy greenhouse and bedding plants and the show varieties; but, of course, there are botanical differences. Pelargoniums are plants of various habits, some being fleshy and tuberous and requiring the same treatment as succulents. However, those commonly grown are erect or trailing leafy sub-shrubs with stems soft and succulent, or small and firm. Most Pelargoniums are natives of South Africa. They need a light, airy position and sufficient heat to keep out the frost.

In summer a moderate and regular amount of water is required, but in winter only sufficient moisture to keep the roots from becoming dust-dry is needed. Weekly doses of weak liquid manure or soot-water are beneficial to pot-plants when the flower buds are forming.

*Zonal Pelargoniums* popularly, but erroneously, called " Geraniums ", are greatly used as bedding plants; in fact the majority of the so-called Geraniums seen in garden beds during the summer are Zonal Pelargoniums. Although the so-called bedding Pelargoniums are thought to be of hybrid origin, probably between *P. inquinans* $\times$ *P. zonale*, improved by a careful selection of seedlings, thus getting a variation of colour in the flowers and foliage, they are generally included under the group of *P. hortorum*. They make excellent pot-plants for decoration in the greenhouse, and given cold-, cool-, or warm-house treatment they may be had in flower almost the whole year through. The varieties, some of which are double, vary in size almost as much as they do in colour, which ranges from brilliant crimson-red, to pink, and from salmon to white. The kinds with variegated leaves are most effective for summer bedding.

*Ivy-leaved Pelargoniums* or *P. peltatum.*—The various forms of this are attractive plants of straggling habit, with brilliant flowers of various colours, mostly red, rose, pink, or white, some varieties being double.

If used for summer bedding the growths will need pegging down, to make them run over the soil which should not be too rich. They make excellent plants for hanging baskets and for window-boxes and when used as pot-plants. Three plants in an 8-inch pot, when finally potted-up, will be found most satisfactory. They are also very suitable for running up the greenhouse wall or up the pillars.

*Regal* or *Show Pelargoniums*, *P. domesticum* distinguishes the garden type of florists' and fancy Pelargoniums, and are a group of hybrid origin, not used as bedding plants, but a great asset in the greenhouse, in view of the size and brilliance of the blooms, which vary from deep maroon to shades of red, pink, to pure white, and because they are so prolific in flowers. They bloom in early summer, from May to July. After flowering, and as soon as the wood has ripened, they should be cut hard back. When they commence to break they should be shaken out, the roots partly pruned, and replaced with new soil in a smaller pot, treated as young plants, and at the end of the year, or early in the new year, they should be transferred to their flowering-pots. In this way established plants may be grown for a number of years in pots of a similar size, the soil being renewed annually. Attention should be given to feeding with manure-water when the flowers are forming and the plants expanding. So treated they will flower well for several years.

*Scented-leaved Pelargoniums* have, as their name implies, fragrant foliage. They make fine pot-plants of almost any desired size, and can also be used with effect in bedding schemes and for indoor decoration, although their flowers are insignificant. They should be potted-on frequently to encourage active growth, and kept cool and dry, but free from frost during the winter.

*Propagation.*—About six months after cuttings are struck the plants should come into bloom. March-struck cuttings should therefore flower in autumn and winter; plants raised in July or August, in early spring (those to be used for bedding in the open should, of course, have their early flowers nipped off); while April and May should see the first blooms of September-struck cuttings. June and July are, however, the best months for taking cuttings. The pots are prepared in the usual manner, and filled with a compost of five-eighths of loam to three-eighths parts of sand and leaf-mould. The cuttings should be taken in dry weather when the parent plant has had no water for some days, and should be kept dry for twenty-four hours before potting. Place five cuttings round the edge of each 4-inch pot, with their stems inserted to a depth of about 1 inch or $1\frac{1}{2}$ inches. If the cuttings are struck in August or September the protection of a frame is not essential, and the pots may be sunk in a sheltered south border, where they will require no shading unless the sun is very hot. If a frame is used the lights should be put on only as a protection against heavy rain. When struck in a frame keep the atmosphere close, shade, and sprinkle the cuttings occasionally overhead till rooted. Afterwards give air gradually to harden-off the cuttings for potting-off into 3-inch pots as soon as they are rooted. If they grow too freely before it is time to take them into the house or frames (September) the top shoots should be broken off; in this way they will make strong bushy plants. These

488

tops may themselves be used to provide another batch of cuttings. In any case, it is a good plan just to rub out the tips, even if they are not sufficiently long to make cuttings. Through the winter months little water and just sufficient heat (50–55° F.) to exclude frost should be given. Pick off all flower-buds as they appear, and as the weather improves gradually give more air. Late in March or early in April the young plants will need re-potting very firmly into 5- or 6-inch pots, so that they may be grown on to be hardened-off and planted-out late in May or in early June. From April onwards plants grown for flowering in pots should receive weekly doses of weak liquid manure or soot-water, and should be grown near the glass in a cool greenhouse (temperature 50° F. winter, 65° F. summer), being pinched-back to make them bushy. Plants stopped-back not later than February will flower in May; when blooming is to be delayed until July, pinching-back may be continued until towards the end of April. The plants should be kept cool and shaded to prolong their flowering period. Give liquid manure while the buds are forming. After flowering, ripen the growth in the sun in the open, then cut the stems back to from 3–4 inches from the base in July and rest the plants with the pots on their sides in a frame for two months. Then pot-up in fresh soil, keep in the frame, and remove all buds until the plants are moved into the house early in September to provide another show of bloom through the coming autumn and winter.

*Care of Old Plants.*—To secure profusion of bloom, early growth and under-potting are of first importance. No matter how robustly a plant is grown, one eighteen months old cannot be made to flower so freely as one four or five years old. Early growth is of fore-most importance. Plants to flower in May should be cut down by the end of the previous June. Success depends on their chief growth being completed before Christmas. No after-management can compensate for the neglect of early growth. Any size of plant or leaf may be obtained at any period; but the flower will be scarce unless early growth is secured.

Under-potting is the next great point. Plants in general, and Pelar-goniums in particular, flower best when they are pot-bound—that is, when the roots are trying with all their strength to burst the pot asunder. Some varieties will scarcely flower at all unless their roots are in this condition. The reason seems to be that whatever tends to check the extension of other parts favours the development of flowers.

*Plants for Autumn and Winter Flowering.*—A further batch of cuttings taken from old plants "started" in gentle heat in the green-house, can, if desired, be struck in the spring (March). These two or three batches of cuttings will provide plants that will bloom, in the greenhouse, practically all the year round. March-struck cuttings should be potted-up singly into 3-inch pots about May. When these pots are full of roots, move the young plants into 4-inch pots; harden-off in a cold frame ready for setting out in the open on a hard bed of ashes in June, or into the open beds, if for summer-bedding, although autumn-struck cuttings make better bedding plants. Plants raised for flowering indoors in autumn and winter should be stopped-back in

July, and all flower-buds picked off until September. Early in August, move them into 6-inch pots and transfer to a light and airy shelf in the greenhouse at the beginning of September. As the season advances, a little heat (55° F.) will make the plants blossom more freely, but much forcing is a mistake. Zonal, Ivy-leaved, and ornamental-leaved Pelargoniums, if treated in this way, will flower in autumn and winter; Regals so treated, however, will not come into bloom until March, and will continue to flower until the middle of June. Plants may also be raised from seed, but this is rarely attempted by the amateur.

*Pelargoniums from Seed.*—For those who wish to try this process plants for spring flowering may be raised from seed sown in a frame in August. Cover the seed with ⅛ inch of soil, prick off as soon as the seedlings can be handled and pot-on as required until the plants are in the 5–6-inch pots in which they are to flower. Care must be taken to exclude both frost and damp during the winter, but no artificial heat is required. Another batch of seed may be sown in March to supply autumn-flowering plants.

*Varieties.*—REGAL and DECORATIVE: *A. E. Blake Amos, Bridesmaid, Charmer, Dazzler, Fondant, Gorgon, Market Favourite, Magpie, Nubian, Pearl, Princess Mary, Rose of Devon, Sugar Plum, Sunset.* ZONAL: Single-flowered for Pots: *Amarantha* (Amaranth); *Canopus* (scarlet); *Dick Smith* (vermilion); *Freyda* (rose-pink); *Harry Wood* (salmon); *Janet Scott* (orange); *Mrs. J. Foster* (pink); *Mrs. T. F. Bunting* (salmon); *Peach* (cherry-red); *Ryecroft Gem* (crimson-lake); *Snowstorm* (white); *W. A. Cull* (rosy pink). Double for Pots: *Edith Cartwright, Dr. Despres* (crimson maroon); *Emperor* (white, edged rose); *Fantome* (purple); *Fireworks* (cerise scarlet); *Gustav Emich* (orange scarlet); *Madame Landry* (salmon); *H. J. Rawlings*; *Ryecroft White* (white); *Sunbeam* (orange-scarlet). Bedding: *Fire Dragon* (crimson scarlet); *H. Greenhill* (rose-pink); *Paul Crampel* (scarlet); *Salmon Crampel* (salmon); *Dr. Nansen* (white); *Maxime Kovalesky* (orange-scarlet); *King of Denmark* (salmon); *Decorator* (red). IVY-LEAVED: *Madame Crousse* (rose); *Scarlet Crousse*, and *Sir Percy Blakeney* (scarlet); *Alliance* (cream); *L'Elegant* (white and purple); *Chas. Turner* (deep pink); *Galilee* (soft pink); *James T. Hamilton* (crimson). SCENTED-LEAVED: *P. crispum, P. odoratissimum, P. quercifolium,* and *P. tomentosum; Clorinda* (cerise); *fragrans* (nutmeg scented).

There are many beautiful hybrids raised between the different sections, particularly the scented-leaved group, i.e. *Ps. Clorinda, Fair Helen, Pretty Polly,* and *Scarlet Pet.* Although practically the whole of the genus needs protection *P. Endlicherianum* [Asia Minor and Syria] can be grown in a sheltered part of the rock-garden, and is very charming when grown in pans for the alpine house. It should be planted in well-drained soil and the pans plunged in ashes in a frame during the winter.

**Pelecyphora anselliformis** (Hachet Flower), *Cactaceæ.*—An interesting succulent from Mexico, closely allied to **Mammillaria,** requiring similar cultural treatment, and requiring very careful watering, particularly in the winter. The flowers are whitish outside with a carmine-violet centre, and they bloom in June. The plants grow 3–4 inches high. The variety *concolor* [Mexico] has purple flowers.

# GREENHOUSE PLANTS

*Propagation.*—They are readily raised from seed sown in sandy soil and placed in moderate heat. Offsets are rarely produced.

**Pellæa** (Cliff Brake Fern), *Polypodiaceæ.*—Greenhouse deciduous and evergreen ferns which thrive in the shade in a mixture of one half sandy loam and one half peat and leaf-mould with a little charcoal added (temperature 50° F. winter, 60° F. summer).

*Culture.*—Pot-up in March and water liberally during the summer.

*Propagation.*—Propagate by means of spores sown in heat at any time, or by means of division in March.

*Species.*—*P. falcata* [India to New Zealand], *P. hastata* [S. Africa], and *P. rotundifolia* [New Zealand], all growing about 10 inches in height, are the three species generally cultivated.

**Pellionia,** *Urticaceæ.*—Tender, creeping, handsome, foliage plants, suitable for baskets, for growing under the staging, or for covering the top of pots or tubs containing large palms, etc. They require a warm temperature and a moist atmosphere, with rich sandy loam.

*Propagation.*—They are readily propagated from cuttings or by division.

*P. Daveauana* [Burma and Cochin China] has dark bronzy, olive-green leaves, flushed red or violet, sometimes with light-green markings down the centre of the leaf. The var. *viridis* has bright-green leaves, with whitish blotches. *P. pulchra* [Cochin China] has leaves which are dull blackish along the midrib and veins, with bright-green inter-spaces on the under surface of the leaf, and pale-purplish stems tinged with a dull purple colour.

**Pentapterygium,** *Ericaceæ.*—Handsome greenhouse epiphytic shrubs suitable for growing either in baskets or in pots. They require well-drained peat and sand, and are propagated by means of cuttings inserted in sand under a bell-glass, with a little warmth.

*P. rugosum* (*Vaccinium rugosum*) [Himalayas] grows from 12 to 30 inches high, and bears in the spring, nearly white flowers, beautifully mottled with purple or blood-red bands. *P. serpens* [Himalayas] has bright-red flowers with V-shaped markings.

**Pentarhaphia,** *Gesneriaceæ.*—Warm-greenhouse evergreen shrubs or sub-shrubs, requiring the same cultural treatment as **Gesneria.**

*Species.*—*P. cubensis* [Cuba] (solitary tubular scarlet flowers, July, 18–24 in.) ; *P. floribunda* [Cuba] (red, summer) ; *P. libanensis* [Jamaica] (crimson, June, 3 in.).

**Pentas lanceolata (P. carnea),** *Rubiaceæ.*—An erect, cool-greenhouse, soft wooded shrub from South Africa, with pale purple flowers blooming most of the year.

*Culture.*—It is of easy culture in a compost of loam, leaf-mould, and a little sand.

*Propagation.*—It is propagated by cuttings of young shoots placed in sandy soil in a little heat, at almost any time of the year. The plants should be pinched back as they grow, to encourage a compact habit.

*P. l.* var. *kermesiæna* has carmine-rose flowers, tinted with purple in the throat. Other species useful for the greenhouse are *P. coccinea* [Tropical Africa] (scarlet, summer, 30 in.) ; *P. parviflora* [Tropical Africa] (orange, spring, 24 in.).

**Pentlandia miniata** (see **Urceolina miniata**).

**Peperomia,** *Piperaceæ.*—Tropical and sub-tropical herbs, with tails like catkins, some of which have very attractive foliage, and are suitable for growing in small pots or pans ; while some are of trailing habit and well adapted for hanging-baskets. For stove, conservatory, or house decoration, their stout, succulent leaves enable them to withstand the change. They should be grown in good fibrous peat and loam with some silver sand. Although they should be shaded from bright sunshine in summer, they should be given all the light possible during dull weather, particularly in winter.

*Propagation.*—They are increased by means of seed sown in a warm, moist temperature, or by cuttings of short shoots ; or pieces of stem with a leaf attached will root readily in the spring. They should be placed in sandy peat in a propagating house, but not in a close case, as the cuttings are apt to damp off if confined. Keep shaded and not too moist until rooted. Even then Peperomias do not require so much water as many stove plants, but the syringe should be kept going.

*Species.*—*P. brevipes* [Tropical America] has beautifully variegated foliage, brown and light green. It is useful for growing in baskets and is often raised in gardens under the name of *P. prostrata. P. eburnea* [New Granada] grows 12–15 inches high, and has brilliant green leaves veined with emerald-green, the leaf-stalk being ivory-white. It is an attractive perennial of tufted habit. *P. maculosa* [Tropical America] has shining green, fleshy leaves, mottled purple. It is suitable for a pan. *P. marmorata* [S. Brazil] has bright-green leaves, variegated with white. *P. metallica* [Peru] grows 12–15 inches high, and has blackish-green leaves, marked down the middle with white ; veins red. *P. Sandersii* var. *argyreia* [Brazil] has leaves which are thick and fleshy, striped bright green and metallic white. It reaches a height of 8–10 inches, and is often grown under the name of *P. arifolia* var. *argyreia.*

**Pepper** (see **Piper**).

**Pereskia,** *Cactaceæ.*—A grotesque but attractive genus, distinct from other cacti, in that the stems are woody and bear real leaves like those of the orange-tree. The flowers are borne in autumn and winter in panicles on the ends of the stems. These climbers are vigorous growers, and will run up to a height of 5 or 6 feet, and are therefore only useful for growing in large greenhouses.

*Culture.*—They thrive in a mixture of sandy loam, leaf-mould, and peat in an average temperature of 60° F. day, 50° F. night, winter ; and 80° F. day, 70° F. night, summer. Pot-up in March and keep the atmosphere warm and dry. Water liberally in summer and moderately in autumn and winter.

*Propagation.*—Propagate by means of cuttings placed in heat in March.

*Species.*—*P. aculeata* (Blade Apple, Barbados Gooseberry) [Tropical America] (white, Oct., 72 in.) ; *P. Bleo* [New Granada] (rose, Nov. 72 in.) ; *P. grandiflora* [Brazil] (white, Aug., 72 in.). The Pereskia is much used as a stock on which other kinds of cacti are grafted, especially **Schlumbergera** and **Zygocactus.**

**Pergularia,** *Asclepiadaceæ.*—Stove evergreen climbers allied to **Stephanotis,** requiring the same cultural treatment.

*Species.*—*P. minor* [India and China] produces very fragrant orange-yellow flowers during summer. *P. odoratissima* [China] bears very fragrant, greenish-yellow flowers in June. *P. sanguinolenta* [Sierra Leone] is free flowering and bears yellowish-green blooms in July. This plant is full of deep-red-coloured juice.

**Perilla,** *Labiatæ.*—Half-hardy annuals growing from 12 to 24 inches in height. Their flowers are of little beauty, but the dark-purple foliage is extremely useful for summer bedding purposes, and for decoration in the greenhouse, as it sets off to advantage any adjacent bright flowers.

*Culture.*—Sow seed thinly in March under glass. Harden off and plant out 12 inches apart in June, or pot-up in 5 inch pots and stand in the greenhouse.

*Species.*—*P. macrophylla compacta* and *P. nankinensis* are the best known. They are probably forms of *P. frutescens,* which is worthless from a garden point of view.

**Peristeria** (see Chapter on **Orchids**).

**Peristrophe speciosa (Justicia speciosa),** *Acanthaceæ.*—An attractive, greenhouse plant from the Himalayas, with bushy habit, and carmine-purple flowers. It blooms for a long period during the winter. It can also be grown as a window or room plant.

*Culture.*—Cuttings taken at any time when the shoots are soft will root readily if placed over a little bottom heat. When rooted and potted-up they may be removed to a lower temperature. Pot-on as required into a compost of rich loam and leaf-mould, with a little sand. They should have plenty of air, and should be pinched back occasionally to form good bushy plants. Good plants can be grown in 6-inch pots.

**Pernettya mucronata** (Prickly Heath), *Ericaceæ.*—Hardy, evergreen, Ericaceous shrubs from Chile, which do well in moderate sun, and in cool, moist, well-drained peaty loam, free from lime. All bear small white or pinkish flowers towards the end of May, and these are followed by small but brilliant globular berries in autumn and winter. They grow to a height of from 2 to 5 feet.

*Pot Culture.*—Pot-up in October or November, using 6- to 8-inch pots and a compost of two parts of peat to one part of leaf-mould and sand, and place in the cold greenhouse. Give ample water in spring and summer. Plant outdoors in full sun when the berries fall. No pruning is necessary.

*Propagation.*—To propagate, sow in a frame in March, take cuttings in summer, or divide the roots in autumn.

*Varieties and Colour of Fruit.*—*P. mucronata* (white); *P. m. atrococcinea* (deep purple); *P. m. lilacina* (pink); *P. m. speciosa* (crimson). *P. Pentlandii*, also from Chile, somewhat resembles *P. mucronata*, but the leaves are not spiny tipped, and the fruit is dark purplish-blue. *P. tasmanica* [Tasmania] is a dwarf, prostrate species, which forms a dense green cushion, upon which lies the large globose berry, which is usually red, although sometimes yellow or cream. This plant is charming for growing in pans for the alpine house, and in favourable districts, for the rock-garden.

# THE GREENHOUSE

**Persian Ranunculus** (see **Ranunculus asiatica**).
**Peruvian Daffodil** (see **Hymenocallis calathina**).
**Peruvian Hyacinth** (see **Scilla peruviana**).
**Peruvian Lily** (see **Alstrœmeria**).
**Peruvian Swamp Lily** (see **Zephyranthes**).
**Pescatoria** (see Chapter on **Orchids**).
**Petrea volubilis** (Purple Wreath), *Verbenaceæ*.—This plant, which is found from Cuba to Brazil, is one of the most distinctive and beautiful of stove climbers, either for training up the roof, a pillar, or to a balloon-shaped, or flat wire frame. The flowers are like a five-pointed star of lilac with a violet centre, and appear from March to May. Whether planted out or grown in pots it requires good drainage to prevent the compost becoming sour or stagnant.

*Culture.*—It should be planted in four parts of turfy loam, one part of turfy peat, and one part of well-decayed cow-manure, with a good sprinkling of sand. It succeeds best with a night temperature of 65–70° F. during the summer, and 10–15° warmer during the day, while the temperature in the winter should not fall below 50° F. at night. Syringeing should be given on bright days during the growing season, with a little ventilation to keep the air sweet.

*Propagation.*—It is easily propagated by cuttings placed in light, sandy soil, with bottom heat. Pot-on as required until they are in 8- or 10-inch pots.

**Petrocallis pyrenaica (Draba pyrenaica)**, *Cruciferæ*.—This charming little rock-garden plant, from the mountains of Southern Europe, bears flowers in April and May, which are white at first changing to rosy pink, and it makes a choice plant for the alpine house. It is sometimes included under **Draba**, and succeeds with the same cultural treatment. It grows 2–3 inches in height. There is also a variety *alba*, whose flowers remain white.

**Petrocoptis**, *Caryophyllaceæ*.—Attractive rock-garden plants which make very suitable pans for the alpine house. They are allied to and sometimes included under **Lychnis**, and succeed with the same treatment.

*Species.*—*P. Lagascæ* (*Lychnis Lagascæ*) [Pyrenees] (pale rose with white centre, April–May, 2–4 in.); *P. pyrenaica* (*L. pyrenaica*) [Pyrenees] (pale flesh or rose colour, April–May, 3–4 in.).

**Petunia**, *Solanaceæ*.—There is very little difficulty in the culture of this half-hardy, soft-wooded plant, which, although a perennial, is usually most satisfactory when treated as a half-hardy annual. There are single and double varieties, and the prevailing colours are white, rose, carmine, magenta, blue, and purple. They like a sunny position in moderately rich, light soil, and flower in the summer and autumn. Single varieties grow about 12 inches in height, and double varieties about 24 inches. Both are suitable for cultivation in the greenhouse. They are very beautiful in appearance and look well in sunny borders, used for bedding-out purposes, in hanging baskets and for pot culture, particularly the double varieties.

*Culture.*—Sow seed thinly in March under glass (temperature 65° F.), and only just cover with soil. Prick off about 4 inches apart early, and at the end of April harden off, and plant out 12–15 inches apart in

May and June. If pricked off into pots for the greenhouse they must not be allowed to get root bound, but must be potted-on frequently until they are in their flowering-pots. *Double varieties* may also be propagated by means of cuttings of young wood (in a temperature of 65° F.) in the spring, or of more mature shoots in a cold frame in August.

*Pot Culture.*—Pot-up in May, using 6- to 10-inch pots, and a compost of two parts loam to one part of leaf-mould and dry, well-rotted manure, and keep in the cool greenhouse. Pinch back to five joints from the old stem as soon as established in the flowering-pots. Early training and staking are essential. Flowering may be retarded by standing the plants in a cold frame or on a bed of ashes in the open any time after the middle of May.

*Species.*—*P. axillaris* (*P. nyctaginiflora*) and *P. violacea*, both species coming from the Argentine. They are seldom grown in gardens. The popular Petunias grown are probably of hybrid origin between *P. axillaris* × *P. violacea*.

**Phacelia (Eutoca)**, *Hydrophyllaceæ*.—Beautiful, dwarf-growing, hardy annuals, suitable for edging, border, rockery, or for growing in pots in the cold greenhouse. They do well in sun or semi-shade in ordinary soil.

*Culture.*—Sow thinly in the position in which they are to flower in spring or late summer, and thin out to 6 inches apart when large enough to handle. In small pots leave only one plant, and in pans thin out to three plants. Do not attempt to transplant.

*Species.*—*P. campanularia* [S. California] (deep-blue, campanula-like flowers, June–Aug., 8 in.) ; *P. sericea* (*Eutoca sericea*) [Rocky Mts.] (leaves silky on both sides, June, 5–10 in., perennial) ; it should be kept in a dry atmosphere during the winter. *P. tanacetifolia* [California] (pale mauve, June–Aug., 20 in.) ; and *P. Whitlavia* (California Bluebell) [California] (deep blue, June–Aug., 8–10 in.).

**Phædranassa chloracra** (Queen Lily) [Ecuador], *Amaryllidaceæ.*— Half-hardy, bulbous plants, growing about 18 inches high, and flowering in spring. They like a well-drained, deep, sandy loam, and thrive in sunny, sheltered positions in warm borders, or in pots in the greenhouse.

*Culture.*—If in a border plant 6–9 inches apart and 5 inches deep in March or October, and protect with fibre in winter. If in pots, place in a 5-inch pot. The bulbs should be rested after the leaves have died down. The flowers precede the foliage, which commences to develop when the plant is in flower.

*Propagation.*—Propagate by offsets in March or October.

**Phædranthus buccinatorius**, *Bignoniaceæ*.—An evergreen, summer-blooming, greenhouse climber from Mexico, with handsome foliage and terminal racemes of flowers which are blood red in colour and yellow at the base. It is sometimes included under **Bignonia,** and succeeds with the same treatment and conditions.

**Phænocoma prolifera**, *Compositæ*.—A half-hardy, South African, evergreen shrub with hairy stems and rose-purple, everlasting flowers in summer, sometimes included in **Helichrysum.** There is a var. *Barnesii*, which has heads of deep crimson.

*Culture.*—Pot-up in March as soon as new growth commences, after cutting well back, using well-crocked pots and a mixture of fibrous peat and silver sand in the proportion of two parts to one. Keep on the dry side until re-established, then water well and keep moist until after flowering. It needs a cool, airy house, and plenty of ventilation from spring to autumn. It benefits from some liquid manure during growth when the pots are full of roots.

*Propagation.*—Cuttings made of young shoots, 2–3 inches long, taken with a " heel ", may be rooted in small pots under a bell-glass.

**Phaius grandifolius** (see Chapter on **Orchids**).

**Phalænopsis** (see Chapter on **Orchids**).

**Phegopteris polypodioides [Dryopteris Phegopteris]** (Beech Fern) (see **Dryopteris**).

**Philadelphus** (Mock Orange), *Saxifrageæ.*—Hardy, deciduous, flowering shrubs known as **Syringa,** a name which properly belongs to the Lilacs. The scent emitted by the fragrant blossoms is considered to resemble that of the orange-flower, hence the name Mock Orange. The flowers of all species, hybrids, and varieties, save those of *P. Coulteri,* which has a red spot at the base of the petals and *P. purpureo-maculatus,* a hybrid from it, whose petals are splashed with purple, are white or yellowish-white. The leaves when crushed have an odour resembling that of the cucumber. They grow some 3–15 feet in height, and thrive in any good garden soil.

*Pot Culture.*—In the warm greenhouse (temperature 55–75° F. winter, 60–75° F. summer), *P. Lemoinei erectus* may be had in flower in March. Pot-up annually in October, using 8- to 10-inch pots and a compost of two parts of sandy loam to one of leaf-mould and well-rotted manure.

*Pruning.*—Thin out the shoots well immediately after flowering and cut back old and weak wood of the previous year to the young lateral growths at the base. If the shrubs are much overgrown, they should be cut back hard in March. The great thing is to thin out the wood rather than to trim it back ; the latter process will cause a total lack of bloom. Sink the pots to their rims in ashes outdoors from May to December, then take inside again and keep fairly dry until growth commences once more.

*Propagation.*—To propagate, strike cuttings in a frame in July and August.

*Species.*—*P. coronarius* [Caucasus] (white) ; *P. Coulteri* [Mexico] (white and red) ; *P. inodorus* [S.W. United States] (white) ; *P. mexicanus* [Mexico] (cream) ; *P. microphyllus* [Colorado] (white).

*Hybrids.*—*P. Burkwoodii* (white) ; *P. Lemoinei* (white). There are many beautiful forms of this hybrid, both double and single-flowered, e.g. " *Avalanche* ", " *Boule d'Argent* ", " *Bouquet Blanc* ", " *Gerbe de Neige* ", " *Mont Blanc* ", and " *Virginal* " (white double). *Nuce Blanche* (white) ; *purpureo-maculatus* (white and purple) ; and *Voie Lactee* (largest single white flowers 2 inches across).

**Philageria Veitchii**, *Liliaceæ.*—A bi-generic hybrid between *Lapageria rosea* × *Philesia buxifolia.* It has solitary pale rose-purple and bright-rose flowers, and, like its parents, requires a peaty soil and a moist, cool greenhouse. It is a straggling, half-hardy shrub with flexuous branches.

*Propagation.*—It is propagated by means of cuttings placed under a bell-glass in a cool house.

**496**

*Photos*]                                        *[Dobbie & Co. and Sutton & Sons Ltd.*

1. Nigella, Miss Jekyll
4. Nemesia strumosa

2. Petunia (Single)
3. Petunia (Dwarf, Single)
5. Dimorphotheca hybrids

G

1. Primula obconica      2. Phacelia campanularia

3. Double Begonias

4. Phlox paniculata      5. Ranunculus

**Philesia buxifolia,** *Liliaceæ.*—An interesting Chilean shrub, with showy, pendulous, red, lapageria-like flowers. It may be planted out in a cool, moist greenhouse, similar to a cool fern-house, or it may be grown in a large pot or pan, in peaty soil. It is a slow grower, and in some parts of Ireland and the South of England it will grow outside in favoured positions. Suckers are thrown up, from which the plant may be propagated. A certain percentage can also be rooted from ripened growth placed under a bell-glass in a cool temperature. Philesia is easily grown with cool, moist conditions, but refuses to be forced.

**Philibertia,** *Asclepiadaceæ.*—Warm-greenhouse twiners allied to **Ceropegia,** succeeding with the same cultural treatment.

*Species.*—*P. campanulata* [Peru] (bell-shaped flowers, greenish-yellow with purplish markings, Oct., 24–60 in.) ; *P. gracilis* (*P. grandiflora*) [Buenos Aires] (cream-coloured inside, dotted and streaked with purple, June, sub-shrubby climber).

**Philodendron,** *Araceæ.*—Stove- or warm-greenhouse plants, some of which have highly ornamental foliage. They are very useful for covering walls, pillars, tree-stumps, or tall palm-stems. They are easily grown where there is a high temperature and a moist atmosphere.

*Culture.*—They like an open compost of loam and peat to which some coarse sand and a lump of charcoal have been added. Plenty of water and frequent syringeing are necessary during the summer.

*Propagation.*—Propagate by dividing the stems into lengths consisting of three to four joints, and insert in a pot or in fibre in a propagating case, with brisk heat.

*Species.*—*P. bipinnatifidum* [S. Brazil] has reddish-brown, green, and white flowers, with double pinnate leaves, three to five lobes. *P. crassinervium* [Brazil] has pale yellowish-green and red flowers, long, narrow leaves with red margins, and red leaf-stalks. *P. Selloum* [Brazil] is similar to the last named, but is distinguished by the numerous parallel spots seen on both sides of the leaf. *P. verrucosum* [Costa Rica] is a handsome foliage plant with heart-shaped leaves, of a delicate satiny-green shaded with metallic-olive colour on the upper surface, the under surface being green with violet markings. The shoots when young are bright red, and covered with fleshy bristles and greenish hairs.

**Phlox,** *Polemoniaceæ.*—This magnificent genus of plants, both annual and perennial, is unrivalled for richness and brilliancy of the colours of the flowers, and the profusion and duration of the blooming. Phloxes grow from 3 to 40 inches in height, and flower in spring, summer, and autumn, according to species. They need a certain amount of sun, and enjoy an open position, but one sheltered from stray winds.

The *Phlox Drummondii* varieties—half-hardy annuals—make splendid bedding and pot-plants, for the cold greenhouse. They produce large flower-heads of brilliant colours. The varieties of *P. Drummondii compacta* (6 inches) are excellent edging plants. *Phlox paniculata* (*P. decussata*) and *P. maculata* are perennials. The modern garden Phlox or Summer Phlox, so popular in our gardens, and of which there are many named varieties is probably the issue of these two species. It is sometimes known as *P. pyramidalis*. They all produce a fine effect when planted in groups of five or six in mixed borders : and if grown

I I

# THE GREENHOUSE

in pots they may be brought into the cool greenhouse when in bud, where they add a beautiful bit of colour; while the dwarf-growing perennials or *Mossy Phloxes* such as *P. subulata* and its varieties make excellent subjects for the rock-garden. The latter also does well in the alpine house in 4- to 5-inch pans of sandy loam and peat. It should be potted-up in March or September, and stood in a cold frame in a sunny place. It is usually propagated by means of cuttings in July, or by division in March or September.

The annual and herbaceous kinds succeed best in sunny, sheltered positions, in deep, rich, moist, but well-drained loam, with a good dressing of rotted cow-manure worked into the bottom spit.

*Pot Culture.*—PERENNIALS: Seed from the modern garden Phlox or Summer Phlox should be sown in the open in April; this will eventually give new varieties. Otherwise take cuttings of the young growth of named varieties in the autumn, and strike in sandy soil, over a little bottom heat, under glass. In a fortnight pot-up singly in 4-inch pots in a compost of two-thirds loam to one-third well-rotted manure, together with a little coarse sand. Winter in the cool house, near the glass, and in March harden off in a cold frame ready for planting out in May. It is also possible to propagate by means of division in February, March, or October, and to plant out in permanent positions. A good plan is to make this division bi-annually. Stake early and thin out all weak growths. Pot-up in October using 5- to 6-inch pots and a rich, sandy soil. Stand in a sunny position outside with the pots plunged in ashes, taking the plants into the cool greenhouse when coming into flower. The season of flowering can be prolonged if some plants are pinched back slightly, which will delay their time of flowering. They should have water freely from April to October, then a decreasing supply. Give liquid manure from May to September.

HALF-HARDY ANNUALS: Sow seed thinly in the open in April, or in February and March under glass in slight heat. Prick out 4 inches apart as early as possible, harden off, and plant out from 12 to 18 inches apart early in June. If seed is sown in a frame in August, and the seedlings are potted-up and transplanted to the greenhouse blooms may be had from January to March, as well as the flowers in summer and autumn from the February or March sown seed.

*Species.*—ANNUAL: *P. Drummondii* [Texas] (various, June–Oct., 6–12 in.); PERENNIAL: *P. maculata* [N. America]; *P. paniculata* [*P. decussata*] (various, July–Oct., 40 in.). *Named Varieties of P. paniculata* [*P. pyramidalis*] (Herbaceous or Summer Phlox)—*Tapis Blanc* (white); *Crepuscule* (silvery mauve); *Elizabeth Campbell* (pink); *Etna* (orange-scarlet); *Selma* (pink with crimson eye); *Thor* (flame and crimson eye); *America* (salmon); *Coquelicot* (orange-scarlet); *Imperator* (crimson); *Albert Vandal* (mauve); *Sherriff Ivory* (rose-crimson eye). *Phlox Arendsii*—Hybrids between *P. divaricata* and *P. paniculata*—*Amanda* (lilac); *Charlotte* (white and lilac); *Hanna* (rose); *Marianne* (bluish violet). All flower from July to September and reach a height of from 12 to 18 inches. ALPINE: *P. amœna* [Eastern U.S.A.] (carmine-pink, May–July, 6 in.); *P. divaricata* [N. America] (lavender-blue, May–July, 6–12 in.); *P. Douglasii* [N. America] (purple lilac or

498

white) ; *P. Hoodii* [N. America] (pale lilac) ; *P. mesaleuca* [N. America] (rosy pink to white) ; *P. ovata* [N. America] (red, May–July, 10 in.) ; *P. pilosa* [N. America] (lilac-white, July–Aug., 8–15 in.) ; *P. subulata* and *vars.* [U.S.A.] (light blue, pink, or white, May–June, 4 in.) ; there are many forms of this, e.g. *annulata* (whitish blue and purple) ; *lilacina* (lilac) ; *Nelsonii* (white and rose) ; *nivalis* (white) ; *P. stolonifera* [N. America] (rose-purple, June, 6 in.).

**Phœnix,** *Palmaceæ.*—Beautiful, feathery-leaved, greenhouse palms which thrive in a compost of two parts of fibrous loam to one part of leaf-mould and sand.

*Culture.*—Pot-up annually in March or April, using a comparatively small pot and not too much soil (temperature 50° F. winter, 65° F. summer). Keep in the sun, water moderately but regularly, and sponge the leaves frequently. The soil should be kept just moist in winter.

*Propagation.*—Propagate by means of seed sown 1 inch deep in heat in March.

Good species are *P. canariensis* [Canary Islands] ; *P. dactylifera* (Date-palm) [Arabia and N. Africa] ; *P. reclinata* [Tropical and S. Africa] ; *P. Rœbelenii* [Assam] (dwarf) ; and *P. rupicola* [Sikkim], perhaps the most popular of all.

**Pholidota** (see Chapter on **Orchids**).

**Phormium** (New Zealand Flax), *Liliaceæ.*—Tall perennials with handsome foliage, which require a fairly sheltered, sunny position, and a well-drained loam, and which flower from June to September. In the colder districts they are grown in large pots or tubs, and watered indoors.

*Culture.*—Sow in a frame in March, or propagate by means of division of the roots in April. Pot-up or plant out from March to April and keep well watered while making growth. Take indoors again about the end of September, or early in October.

*P. Cookianum* [Small Flax lily] (yellow, 60 in.), var. *variegatum* has yellowish-white striped leaves ; and *P. tenax* (crimson, 70 in., the leaves of which have bright red or brownish margins), of which there are a number of varieties, differing chiefly in the colour of their leaves, including some variegated forms, are very good species.

**Phragmopedilum** (see Chapter on **Orchids**).

**Phyllagathis,** *Melastomaceæ.*—Stove- or warm-greenhouse plants with attractive flowers and handsome foliage. From February to May the temperature should be gradually raised to 70° F. at night, and kept at this temperature throughout the summer ; then it should be gradually reduced so that the night temperature during the winter does not fall below 55° F. During the growing season they require plenty of water, and as the days lengthen syringeing should be increased to provide a moist atmosphere. Slight shading is necessary during very bright sunshine.

*Culture.*—Re-potting should be done in the early part of the year, using a compost of four parts fibrous loam, one part fibrous peat, one part well-decayed cow-manure, with some sand.

*Propagation.*—Propagate by means of cuttings of young shoots in February or March, placed in small pots in a mixture of loam, peat and

**499**

sand in equal parts. These should be placed in a propagating case with a bottom heat of 80° F. They can also be increased by leaf-cuttings placed in a propagating case with the petiole of the leaf inserted in sand, the leaf lying flat on the sand. Keep moist, and in a short time growth will break out from different parts of the leaf. Rooted plants should be potted-on as required until they reach 8- or 10-inch pots. They will then produce good plants.

P. *gymnantha* [Borneo] bears close heads of pink flowers in summer, and has glossy green leaves. P. *rotundifolia* [Sumatra] is a beautiful foliage plant, carrying dense, crowded heads of reddish flowers with purple scales. The glossy leaves are of a rich metallic-green colour, tinged red above and dark red beneath.

**Phyllanthus,** *Euphorbiaceæ.*—Greenhouse shrubs or sub-shrubs cultivated for their graceful and curious foliage. They succeed in a compost of equal parts of sandy loam, fibrous peat, to which has been added some dry cow-manure and charcoal with coarse sand. Good drainage is essential. Most of them enjoy warm-greenhouse treatment.

*Propagation.*—They are propagated by cuttings of half-ripened wood of side-shoots inserted in sand under a bell-glass, in heat. Some kinds are raised from seed.

P. *grandifolius* (P. *juglandifolius*) [W. Indies] is a handsome foliage plant whose leaves have a metallic lustre. P. *nivosus* (Snow Bush) [South Sea Isles] is a wiry-branched shrub. The leaves are variegated green and white, and sometimes at the tips of the shoots they are quite white. The variety *roseo-pictus* has leaves mottled red and pink, as well as green and white, while the var. *atropurpurea* has dark-purple leaves. P. *nivosus* is sometimes useful for bedding out during the summer, and can be grown readily from root-cuttings. P. *pulcher* (syn. *Reidia glaucescens*) [Malaya] is a handsome plant suitable for indoor house decoration as a table plant. It has yellow flowers and dark-green foliage and grows to a height of 48 inches. P. *speciosus* (*Xylophylla latifolia* [Jamaica] is a small shrub with branches flattened into leaf-like organs. The greenish-white flowers are produced along the margins in September.

**Phyllitis (Scolopendrium),** *Polypodiaceæ.*—Greenhouse and hardy ferns, commonly called Hart's Tongue Ferns, growing from 5 to 20 inches high. The hardy kinds thrive in the shade in a sheltered rock-garden, or on moist banks in sandy loam, peat, and leaf-mould, with a little mortar in it. There are many frilled varieties, notably P. *crispum* and its various forms. Others are tasselled, while some are both frilled and tasselled. P. *Scolopendrium* (S. *vulgare*) is the common Hart's Tongue. All are decorative in the cold fernery or the alpine house.

P. *Delavayi* [S. China] is an attractive little fern with reniform fronds. P. *rhizophyllum* [N. America] has long, tapering fronds, often rooting at the tips and forming young plants. Both species are suitable for the cool fernery.

*Greenhouse Culture.*—The greenhouse species do best in the shade in a mixture of two parts of loam and peat to one part of sand and mortar-rubble. Pot-up in March and water liberally in summer.

*Propagation.*—Propagate by means of division in March, or by spores sown under glass at any time.

**Phyllocactus** (see **Epiphyllum**).

**Phyllocactus biformis** (see **Disocactus biformis**).

**Phyllodoce,** *Ericaceæ.*—A small genus of pretty, interesting, small shrubs sometimes included in **Bryanthus**. Although hardy, they are very suitable for growing in pans for the alpine house.

*Culture.*—Pot-up in the autumn or early spring, in sandy, peaty soil, and plunge the pans in a semi-shady place.

*Propagation.*—They are propagated by means of cuttings struck in sandy peat, under a hand-light in July.

*Species.*—*P. Breweri* (*Bryanthus Breweri*) [California] (purplish red, May, 6 in.) ; *P. empetriformis* (*Bryanthus empetriformis*) [N.W. America] (reddish purple, May and June) ; *P. nipponica* [Japan] (white and pink, May, 4–8 in.).

**Phyllotænium Lindenii** (see **Xanthosma Lindenii**).

**Phymatodes,** *Polypodiaceæ.*—Stove ferns allied to **Polypodium,** and sometimes included in that genus. They require the same cultural treatment as stove Polypodium.

*Species.*—*P. glaucum* [Philippines] (fronds 12–16 in., glaucous) ; *P. muscæfolium* [E. Indies] (fronds, 12–30 in., very distinct, veins over the whole surface) ; *P. nigrescens* [India] (fronds 20–30 in.) has dark-green, wart-like surface projections due to the sori being sunk in deep cavities.

**Physianthus** (see **Araujia**).

**Phyteuma comosum** (Horned Rampion), *Campanulaceæ.*—This plant is charming for the rock-garden and for growing in pans, in well-drained soil. Slugs are very fond of it, and steps must be taken to protect it from them. For further details and cultural treatment see chapter devoted to the alpine house.

**Picotees.**—These are a kind of carnation, distinguished by a narrow, dark-coloured edging to the petals, or by the petals being covered with tiny dots ; the ground colour is usually white or yellow. Both are grown in the greenhouse, but the yellow-ground Picotees alone are grown in the open border, as the white-ground varieties are not quite hardy enough to stand the dampness of our winters in the open. The cultivation is in every respect the same as for the **Carnation,** which see.

**Pieris,** *Ericaceæ.*—These shrubs, although hardy, are very decorative for growing in pots for the cold greenhouse. They will also stand forcing, particularly *P. japonica,* as it makes a very handsome and graceful pot-plant for inside decoration, with its racemes of pure-white flowers. Pieris, like other Ericaceæ, require moderately moist, well-drained soil, free from lime ; they also dislike heavy clay.

*Culture.*—Plants in pots should be plunged in ashes in a shady place when not in flower, being brought into the greenhouse as the flower-buds make their appearance. If used for forcing it will be found advisable to give them at least one year's rest, forcing them about every other year. They require much the same cultural treatment as **Rhododendron,** and allied genera.

*Propagation.*—Propagation is by seed, treated as for Rhododendron, by layers, or by cuttings taken in August, placed under a bell-glass in a cool house, and kept there during the winter. Cuttings of forced plants will be found to root more freely than others.

*Species.*—*P. floribunda* (*Andromeda floribunda*) [U.S.A.] is an ever-green with upright panicles of white flowers (April–May, 10–40 in.); *P. formosa* (*A. formosa*) [E. Himalayas] is an evergreen with deep-green leaves, and drooping, spreading panicles of white flowers, sometimes tinged with pink, borne in April and May. It is a charming plant for the cold greenhouse. *P. Forrestii* [Yunnan and Upper Burma] bears waxy white and pendulous flowers in April. It is an evergreen, the young shoots being often red, sometimes quite rich, adding extra beauty to the plant. It is not quite so hardy as some, and may benefit from the protection of a cold house. *P. japonica* (*A. japonica*) [Japan] is an evergreen resembling *P. formosa*. The white flowers are borne in pendulous panicles in April and May. This is one of the most graceful of early spring evergreens, and the best of the genus for forcing.

**Pilea muscosa** (Artillery Plant), *Urticaceæ.*—A well-known greenhouse plant, with graceful, curving shoots, fine, close foliage and compact habit. It is very useful for growing along the edges of the staging to screen the pots, and in such a position in the Orchid house it tends to equalise the moisture conditions.

*Culture.*—It is easy to grow, being readily propagated by cuttings, and succeeds in ordinary potting soil, enjoying an abundance of water. If the plant is grown in a sunny place the staminate flowers when ripe discharge their pollen forcibly and visibly, particularly if the foliage is sprayed, hence the name of Artillery Plant.

**Pilocereus** (see **Cephalocereus**).

**Pilocereus Schottii** (see **Lophocereus Schottii**).

**Pilocereus senilis** (see **Cephalocereus senilis**).

**Pimelea** (Rice-flower), *Thymelæaceæ.*—Attractive, half-hardy, free-flowering shrubs, some 3–4 feet in height, with terminal clusters of tiny white or pink flowers in early summer. They thrive in the cool greenhouse in a soil of sandy peat.

*Culture.*—Cut back the shoots by about two-thirds of their length when flowering is finished (middle to the end of June). Stand in a warm corner of the house, and water and syringe until new growth commences. Re-pot into a slightly larger pot without undue dis-turbance of the roots. Little water is necessary, but the soil must not be allowed to become bone dry even during winter. Water regularly once more when the plants again show signs of " breaking ".

*Propagation.*—Cuttings of new shoots, 2–3 inches long, with a " heel " of the old wood, may be rooted in pots under a bell-glass in spring.

*Species.*—*P. ferruginea* (*P. decussata*) [Australia] (pink, 24–36 in.); *P. Gnidia* [New Zealand] (red, 1–4 ft.); *P. hispida* [Australia] (pink, 24–36 in.); *P. hypericina* [Australia and Tasmania] (white, 4 ft.); *P. lingustrina* [Australia] (white, 48 in.); *P. rosea* [Australia] (pink, 24–36 in.); *P. spectabilis* [Australia] (white and pink, 4 ft.); *P. Traversii* [New Zealand] (pink, 2–4 ft.).

**Pimpernel** (see **Anagallis**).

**Pincushion Flower** (see **Scabiosa**).

**Pineapple** (see **Ananas sativa** and **Fruit under Glass**).

**Pineapple-scented Sage** (see **Salvia rutilans**).

**Pine-Barren Beauty** (see **Pyxidanthera barbulata**).

# GREENHOUSE PLANTS

**Pinguicula** (Bog Violet or Butterwort), *Lentibulariaceæ*.—An interesting genus not often met with under cultivation. One of the most interesting species is the Mexican Butterwort, *P. caudata*, by reason of the characteristics of its flowers and leaves. The plant produces two kinds of growth : the resting, where the plant forms a dense rosette, 1 inch in diameter, and the growing type, with leaves 4 or 5 inches long. *P. gypsicola* and *P. Rosei* are two other Mexican species.

*Culture.*—They should be potted-up in February in pans or pots. Three plants can be put in a 6-inch pan, in a compost of two parts of peat, one part of fibrous loam, one part of silver sand, and some chopped sphagnum, with plenty of drainage. When growing, the plants should be stood in saucers of water to avoid watering overhead, which destroys the dew-like deposit of the leaves. They should be stood in a warm house during the summer. In October they should be stood at the cool end of the house to rest. It is said that these three species are used by Orchid-growers, who find them excellent traps for the tiny, midge-like fly, *Sciara pectoralis*, which lays its eggs in Orchid seedlings when they are very young.

*Propagation.*—Propagation is carried out by means of seed sown either round the old plants or in a similar compost, and placed in the same temperature, or by leaves in the resting stage broken off from the main stem. The leaves should be laid flat on sand and placed under a bell-glass ; in four to six weeks the young plants will be ready for potting-up.

*Warm Greenhouse Species.*—*P. caudata* [Mexico] (deep carmine, Aug., 5–6 in.) ; *P. gypsicola* [Mexico] (purple, Aug., 4–5 in.) ; *P. kewensis* [hybrid–*P. caudata* × *P. Rosei*] (rosy purple, summer, 6 in.) ; *P. lutea* [N. America] (yellow, June, 3 in.) ; *P. Rosei* [Mexico] (deep violet-purple, summer, 3–4 in.).

*Hardy Species.*—*P. grandiflora* [S.W. Ireland] (violet-blue, summer, 4 in.) ; *P. vulgaris* [Europe] (violet, summer, 3 in.). These last two species are suitable for the alpine house, requiring the same compost as mentioned before, but grown under frame conditions.

**Pink Root** (see **Spigelia marilandica**).

**Piper** (Pepper), *Piperaceæ*.—Although many are of economic value, there are a few species that are decorative in the stove or warm greenhouse. They are usually of easy cultivation, requiring a warm temperature, a humid atmosphere, and an ordinary compost of loam, leafmould and sand.

*Propagation.*—They are readily propagated by cuttings of half-ripened shoots inserted in sandy soil, under a bell-glass with bottom heat.

*P. ornatum* [Celebes] is an ornamental climber which can be trained over a wire frame. The upper surface of the young leaves is glossy, and covered with pinkish spots. The older leaves become duller and have white spots. *P. porphyrophyllum* [Malay Peninsula] is a handsome, climbing, foliage plant, with cordate leaves which are purple beneath and bronzy-green and pink spotted above. *P. rubronodosum* [Colombia] is a distinctive stove shrub with deep-green leaves, which, when young, are frosted over with silvery grey.

**Pistia Stratiotes** (Water Lettuce), *Araceæ*.—This small, tender, floating perennial from the Tropics is suitable for the tropical aquarium or pond. The wedge-shaped, slightly concave leaves are of a delicate pea-green colour, forming a rosette which floats on the water, sending down long, feathery roots. The greenish-white flowers are borne at the base of the leaves, and although small, show at a glance their relation to the **Arum** family.

*Propagation.*—The plant sends out several runners, at the ends of which similar plants are formed; these in turn send out runners, so that it increases rapidly. It can also be raised from seed, which at the time of collecting should be placed in a jar of water and stood in a warm water tank in a stove temperature. As the seeds germinate, the young seedlings float to the top; they can then be taken out and floated on the tank.

**Pistorinia** (see **Cotyledon**).

**Pitcairnia,** *Bromeliaceæ.*—Stove perennials with narrow or sword-shaped leaves having spiny margins. They require similar cultural treatment to that accorded **Billbergia.** All the species are natives of South America.

*Propagation.*—They are easily increased by means of division of the offshoots, which should be inserted in small pots at almost any time of the year.

*Species.*—P. *Andreana* (yellow and red, summer, 12 in.); *P. aphelandræflora* (red, summer, 12 in.); *P. beycalena* (*P. muscosa*) (red, winter, 12 in.); *P. punicea* (scarlet, summer, 12 in.). Altogether there are over forty other species, but they are chiefly of botanical interest.

**Pitcher Plant** (see **Nepenthes**).

**Pithecoctenium** (Monkey's Comb), *Bignoniaceæ.*—Warm-greenhouse, evergreen climbers, cultivated for their showy flowers. The leaves are trifoliate, the terminal leaflet developing into a tendril. They are closely allied to **Bignonia** and require the same cultural treatment.

*Species.*—P. *cynanchoides* (*Anemopægma clematideum*) [Argentina and Uruguay] has a few tubular, funnel-shaped, white flowers in terminal racemes, in the summer. *P. muricatum* (*Bignonia echinata*) [Mexico] bears flowers which are white outside with a yellow throat, in many-flowered racemes, in the summer.

**Plantain Lily** (see **Hosta**).

**Platycerium** (Stag-horn Fern), *Polypodiaceæ.*—An interesting group of ferns with two forms of fronds, the sterile, flat, round, expansions which in their natural habitat grow around the branches and the stems of trees, and collect leaves and other debris upon which they live and obtain their food supply. The fertile fronds are thick and irregularly lobed, the sori forming large patches on the upper half of the lower surface.

They are amongst the most beautiful and distinctive of ferns with their noble stag-horn appearance.

*Culture.*—Being distinct epiphytal ferns they thrive in baskets or shallow pans of rough peat and sphagnum, with plenty of drainage. They may also be grown on a large block of wood, or attached to a portion of tree-fern stem. They are fastened to such supports by means of wire, having previously attached some fibrous peat, sphagnum moss, bone-meal, and charcoal. A little moss may be added every year or two. They all like a warm, moist atmosphere, although this should be reduced during the winter.

*Propagation.*—They are increased by division or by suckers at the roots, or by means of spores sown as soon as ripe. (*P. grandis* does not produce suckers, but must always be increased by spores.) (See Chapter on **Ferns.**)

*Species.*—*P. angolense* [Angola] has fertile fronds which are not divided into lobes, but just wavy at the margins, often twice as long as wide. *P. biforme* [Java] has very long, frequently forked fertile fronds. *P. bifurcatum* (*P. alcicorne*) (Elk's Horn Fern) [Temperate Australia] has several times forked fertile fronds. It succeeds in a cooler and drier atmosphere than most other species. *P. grandis* [N. Australia] is distinguished by the sterile as well as the fertile fronds being forked. Fertile leaves are carried in pairs. *P. Stemaria* [Guinea] barren fronds rounded, fertile ones pendant and twice forked.

**Platyclinis** (see Chapter on **Orchids**).

**Plectranthus** (Cockspur Flower), *Labiatæ.*—Stove or greenhouse herbs or sub-shrubs, closely allied to **Coleus,** succeeding with the same cultural treatment. Any light, rich soil is suitable, and they are readily propagated from cuttings.

*Species.*—*P. albocæruleus* [Tropical Africa] (white and bluish) ; *P. chiradzulensis* [Tropical Africa] (lavender-blue, 24–30 in.) ; *P. fruticosus* [S. Africa] (blue, summer, 24–36 in.) ; *P. Mahonii* [Tropical Africa] (racemes of many small violet-blue flowers) ; *P. saccatus* [Natal] (flowers deep blue in bud, pale blue when open, Oct., 12–24 in.) ; this is the largest flowered and most ornamental of the genus.

**Pleiocarpa mutica,** *Apocynaceæ.*—A beautiful stove flowering shrub or small tree, native of Tropical Africa. It produces masses of sweetly scented small white flowers on the old wood. They are almost sessile and generally produced along the main stem and branches, often from just above soil level. No flowers are produced on the young wood. It thrives under similar conditions and treatment to that afforded **Ixoras.**

*Propagation.*—Vegetative propagation is by no means easy, although cuttings of half-ripened wood, inserted with a " heel " in sand in a warm propagating frame, will occasionally root quite well. Often, however, excessive callus is formed instead of roots.

**Pleione** (see Chapter on **Orchids**).

**Pleomele** (see **Dracæna**).

**Pleroma** (see **Tibouchina**).

**Plumbago** (Leadwort), *Plumbaginaceæ.*—A genus comprising about ten species of plants, mostly perennials, some suitable only for the greenhouse, and others hardy. The most noteworthy for greenhouse culture is *P. capensis* (Cape of Good Hope), an admirable pillar plant, often running up to 30 feet or more in height, and capable of being trained to the rafters of a greenhouse. Its flowers, borne in September, are of a beautiful pale lavender-blue colour, and in form are very like (those of the **Phlox.**)

In the warm greenhouse this may be had in flower earlier [summer]. Almost as popular is *P. capensis* var. *alba* (white). *P. rosea* E. Indies] is a fine winter-flowering plant with rosy-scarlet flowers, requiring more heat than *P. capensis*. It is very adaptable to pot culture. *P. rosea* var. *coccinea* has larger scarlet flowers.

*Culture.*—Pot-up annually in March in 6- to 8-inch pots, or plant in the cool-house border. A compost of two parts of loam and one part of leaf-mould and coarse sand is best. Water well and syringe in warm weather, but keep dry from October to March. Young pot plants (not climbers) should be pinched back once or twice. In the case of bushes cut back the shoots to within 10 inches of the previous year's growth in October. Climbers should be trained in a single stem in much the same manner as a vine, and kept from 1 foot to 2 feet from the glass. Cut back all laterals of climbers to within 5 inches of their base after flowering, and prune back again to within 2–3 inches of their base early in February. If grown in the greenhouse border, mulch annually in spring with well-rotted manure. (Average temperature 45° F. winter, 65° F. summer.)

*Propagation.*—Propagate by means of cuttings of semi-matured shoots 2–3 inches in length, struck in fine loam and sand, with gentle bottom heat, in spring or early summer, or by means of basal shoots which have rooted in the surrounding soil. Root cuttings also serve as a means of increase. Pieces of the more fleshy roots cut in 1-inch lengths and laid in pans of very sandy soil in a warm propagating case in early spring, will quickly form small embryo plants. (See also **Ceratostigma.**)

**Plumeria (Frangipani),** *Apocynaceæ.*—Stove trees or shrubs with thickish branches and showy, waxy, funnel-shaped, fragrant flowers equalling tuberose **Jessamine** and **Gardenia** with their scent. They are decidedly summer-growing plants, and should be kept rather dry during the winter. They thrive in a compost of sandy loam and fibrous peat, with a little sand.

*Propagation.*—They are propagated by means of cuttings during February and March inserted in sand under a bell-glass in heat.

*Species.*—*P. acutifolia* (Temple Flower) [Mexico] (flowers white flushed with pale yellow, summer, 20–50 in.) ; *P. Jamesonii* [Ecuador] (rich yellow tinged with red, July, 20–50 in.) ; *P. rubra* [W. Indian Red Jasmine) [Mexico, etc.] (golden with bright-red tips, summer) ; *P. tricolor* [Peru] (white with rose margin, yellow throat, July–Oct., 4–10 ft.).

**Poinsettia [Euphorbia pulcherrima]** (Mexican Flame Leaf), *Euphorbiaceæ.*—This showy, evergreen greenhouse plant from Mexico, has bright-scarlet bracts, often a foot in diameter, in autumn and early winter. The bracts retain their beauty for several weeks.

*Culture.*—Poinsettias grow well in a 6-inch pot in a well-drained compost of sandy loam and leaf-mould, in the warm house, and in summer need ample water at the roots, and syringeing overhead twice daily in fine weather (temperature : 65° F. day, 55° F. night, winter ; 80° F. day, 70° F. night, summer). After the bracts fade, gradually reduce the water supply, and keep the roots quite dry in mid-winter and early spring.

*Pruning.*—Cut back the previous year's growth to within three or four buds of the old wood.

*Propagation.*—Take cuttings with a " heel " of the young shoots that " break " in the spring. Dry the cuttings on a shelf in the greenhouse for two or three days, then insert them singly in pots in sandy soil, using a little sphagnum moss at the bottom of the pots for the roots to grip, and plunge them into gentle bottom heat.

*Species.*—*Euphorbia pulcherrima*, the most common species, makes a bush up to 8 feet in height.

**Polianthes tuberosa** (Tuberose) [Mexico], *Amaryllidaceæ.*—Half-hardy bulbous plants growing 24–36 inches high, and flowering in the cool or warm greenhouse in September. The flowers, which are useful for cutting, have a very strong, sweet perfume. They thrive in sunny positions in sheltered warm borders, or they may be flowered in pots in the greenhouse. The Tuberose, as cultivated, is not found in a wild state. The kinds most generally grown have double flowers. There are several varieties, such as *Double African, Double American,* and *The Pearl,* the last named being the most popular.

*Pot Culture.*—Plant bulbs singly, 6 inches deep, in 4- to 5-inch pots, (African kinds) late autumn, (American kinds) early spring, in a mixture of sandy loam, leaf-mould, and well-rotted manure, and plunge the pots to their rims in fibre in a warm frame (bottom heat 65° F.). Give little or no water until they begin to grow. When their roots fill the pots, re-pot, and repeat the treatment until the buds appear, then shift to the cool or warm greenhouse, in a slightly cooler temperature for flowering. The bulbs only flower for one season.

*Propagation.*—Propagate by means of offsets. It is not, however, easy in this country, and it is better to purchase fresh bulbs annually.

**Polyanthus.**—This usually refers to **Primula polyantha,** a group of plants derived from *P. elatior* and its allies, although forms of *Narcissus Tazetta* and a type of Rose are sometimes known as such.

**Polygala** (Milk-wort), *Polygalaceæ.*—Useful plants, mostly shrubby, tender evergreens, or hardy dwarf perennials, which thrive in a mixture of cool, moist, gritty loam and peat, or leaf-mould, and in partial shade in sheltered positions. The hardy species are excellent for the rock-garden, border, or wild garden, and require no protection in winter. If grown in pans they are very useful for the alpine house. The pans should be plunged in ashes in a sunny position when not in flower. Tender species are useful for decoration in the greenhouse.

*P. myrtifolia* [S. Africa] is a densely-branched shrub, 2–5 feet high, with rich purple flowers. *P. virgata* [S. Africa] grows 2–5 feet high and bears purple or flesh-coloured flowers.

*Pot Culture.*—It is these shrubby species that are, as a rule, grown in the greenhouse, and very showy plants they make. Pot-up in March in a compost of one-half peat, one-quarter fibrous loam, and one-quarter sand. Shade from direct sun and syringe. Remove all dead flower-heads, and after flowering cut the shoots of the current year back to within 6 inches of the old wood. If the plants have become very straggly, cut the shoots hard back to bring the bushes into shape. Syringe the plants overhead to encourage new growth to break, then stand the plants in the sun in a frame or in the open to ripen the new wood; water liberally. Remove to the house in September and ventilate freely, merely excluding frost and damp. At this time and until growth commences in the spring, the roots should be kept only just moist. Any straggling shoots should again be cut in spring (average temperature 45° F. winter, 60° F. summer).

*Propagation.*—Shrubby species are increased by cuttings of young shoots struck in coarse sand in a propagating case in spring.

*Hardy Species.*—*P. calcarea* [Europe] (purple, blue, mauve, or rose, May–Sept., 5 in.); *P. Chamæbuxus* [Europe] (purple and yellow, June–July, 3 in.); *P. Vayrediæ* [Spain] (reddish purple and yellow, May–Sept., 4 in.).

**Polygonatum multiflorum** (Solomon's Seal), *Liliaceæ.*—Although perfectly hardy, this native of Europe and Northern Asia is a good subject for forcing or for growing in pots for the cool greenhouse.

*Culture.*—The plants are grown in the open during the summer, and the large, fleshy rootstocks potted-up into 6-inch pots. When the tops have died down after flowering they can be transferred again to the open ground. If forced, it is best to allow the plants to have at least one year's rest from forcing. Large numbers are imported each year for this purpose.

*Propagation.*—They are propagated by division or by seed. This plant is also known as " David's Harp " or " Lady's Seal ".

**Polypodium** (Polypody), *Polypodiaceæ.*—Greenhouse and hardy deciduous evergreen ferns, very ornamental, growing from 6 to 15 inches in height.

*P. aureum* [Tropical America] (handsome green, glossy fronds, 36–48 in.); *P. fraxinifolium* [Colombia] (attractive ash-leaved fronds, 24–36 in. long); *P. Heracleum* [Java] (large, Heracleum-like fronds, 12–24 in. long); *P. Knighteæ* [Australia] (graceful fronds with frilled edge, 24–36 in. long); this makes a handsome basket plant. *P. pectinatum* [Tropical America] (lobed fronds, 9–28 in. long).

*Culture.*—The greenhouse species do best in the shade in a mixture of a half part turfy peat to a quarter part each of loam and sand. Pot-up in March. Keep the temperature moist, and water liberally in summer (temperature 45° F. winter, 60° F. summer).

*Propagation.*—Propagate by means of spores sown under glass at any time, or by means of division in March.

Hardy species and varieties suitable for the cold greenhouse or alpine house should be grown in pans, plunged in ashes, and kept in a shady position when not required for the house.

*P. californicum* [California] has fronds with cut pinnæ resembling *P. vulgare. P. vulgare* (Wall Fern or Polypody) is a British fern of which there are many beautiful varieties, e.g. *cambricum, cornubiense, elegantissimum,* and *pulcherrimum.*

**Polystichum (Aspidium)** (Shield Fern), *Polypodiaceæ.*—A large genus of hardy and greenhouse ferns, deciduous and evergreen, including amongst the greenhouse varieties *P. aristatum* (Tropical Asia) (10 in.) and *P. capense* [S. Africa, S. America, and New Zealand], 2–3 feet.

*Pot Culture.*—Pot-up in March, using a compost of two parts of loamy peat to one part of sand and a little charcoal. Stand in the shade and keep moist, watering liberally and regularly (temperature 50° F. winter, 60° F. summer).

*Propagation.*—Propagate by means of spores sown under glass in July. (See Chapter on **Ferns.**)

**Pomaderris elliptica** (Kumarahon, Golden Tainui), *Rhamnaceæ.*— A small evergreen tree or shrub from New Zealand and Australia. It bears numerous axillary inflorescences of pale-yellow flowers during early spring. The species thrives in a compost of sandy loam, peat, and leaf-soil. A temperature of 50–55° F. is suitable.

*Propagation.*—Young stock may be propagated by means of cuttings. These should be made from young firm shoots and inserted in pots of sandy peat in a warm propagating frame. Seeds may also be employed.

*P. phylicæfolia*, a heath-like species, native of New Zealand, is also an interesting plant for the greenhouse. It bears numerous small yellow flowers during early spring.

**Pomegranate** (see **Punica**).

**Poor Man's Orchid** (see **Schizanthus**).

**Portlandia,** *Rubiaceæ.*—Ornamental stove shrubs, with large, funnel-shaped flowers. They require moist, tropical heat, and a mixture of loam and leaf-mould in equal parts with a good quantity of sand.

*Propagation.*—They are propagated by means of cuttings of firm shoots inserted in sand, under a bell-glass with brisk bottom heat.

*Species.*—*P. coccinea* [Jamaica] (scarlet with yellow anthers, June, 20–30 in.) ; *P. grandiflora* [W. Indies] (whitish, reddish at the throat, very fragrant at night, June–Aug., 6–10 ft.) ; *P. platantha* [Tropical America] (pure white, summer, 20–30 in.).

**Posoqueria,** *Rubiaceæ.*—Stove- or warm-greenhouse ornamental shrubs with terminal corymbs of fragrant flowers, some of which have a very long tube. They will grow from 5 to 6 feet or more, and succeed with the same cultural treatment as **Gardenia.**

*Species.*—*P. densiflora* [Brazil] bears white flowers, turning to yellow in the summer. *P. fragrantissima* [Brazil] bears very fragrant white flowers in July. The leaves are glossy, with yellow veins. *P. longiflora* [French Guiana] is a free-flowering plant carrying in summer waxy-white, very fragrant flowers. *P. versicolor* [Cuba] bears in August fragrant flowers of various colours, changing from white, through pink to crimson.

**Pothos,** *Araceæ.*—Much-branched stove- or warm-greenhouse evergreen climbers grown as foliage plants. They are very suitable for planting against damp walls, clinging by means of their cord-like roots. They require the same cultural treatment as **Philodendron.**

*Species.*—*P. argenteus* [Borneo] has silvery-grey leaves with a deep-green margin and centre. *P. aureus* [Solomon Islands] has bright green leaves, mottled and blotched creamy-yellow. It should not be grown in too dark a position, as the markings have a tendency to disappear. *P. celatocaulis* [Borneo] is a handsome climber, lying perfectly flat upon the surface up which it is climbing. It bears handsome scarlet berries, and is an ideal plant for covering walls or tree-fern stems.

**Pratia,** *Campanulaceæ.*—Slender, prostrate or creeping herbs, several of which are grown on rock-gardens. The same, and several of the more tender kinds can be grown in pans for the cool greenhouse or alpine house.

*Culture.*—They succeed in a lime-free fibrous loam, peat, or leaf-mould, with some sand. If in pans they should be plunged in ashes in a partly shaded position when not in flower.

*Propagation.*—They are readily propagated from cuttings placed in a cold frame any time from July to September. Pot-up in small pots when rooted. They may also be increased by means of division in the spring, or by seed sown when ripe with a little warmth.

*Species.*—*P. angulata* (**Lobelia littoralis**) [New Zealand] grows 1–2 inches high, and bears white flowers with purple streaks in the summer. These are followed by purplish-red berries. The variety *arenaria* from the Falkland Isles is a strong grower, with larger leaves, and white, star-shaped flowers. Both are hardy and suitable for planting in a shady place in the rock-garden. *P. begonifolia* [Nepal] has greenish flowers marked with pink in the summer. The berries are black. It grows 1–2 inches high, and is not really hardy, so should be grown indoors. *P. repens* [Falkland Islands] bears white flowers with a violet tint, from June to October. It grows 1 inch high, is hardy, and is therefore suitable for planting in a sunny, moist position in the rock-garden.

**Prickly Heath** (see **Pernettya mucronata**).

**Prickly Pear** (see **Opuntia**).

**Pride of California** (see **Lathyrus splendens**).

**Primrose** (see **Primula**).

**Primrose Willow** (see **Jussiæa**).

**Primula,** *Primulaceæ.*—A large genus, including some of the most popular flowers, the Auricula, the Cowslip, the Polyanthus, and the Primrose. In the greenhouse, in the rock-garden or bog-garden, in beds, and growing wild in the woods, the Primula is one of the most useful genera that exist. The majority thrive in rich, deep loam, and appreciate the admixture of leaf-mould and grit with the soil, with the exception of the higher alpine species, which appreciate a compost containing a quantity of old mortar rubble and like a position in the sun. *P. marginata* (blue) is an example of this class. They are all moisture-lovers, but must have a well-drained soil. The majority like partial shade, unless unlimited moisture is available in hot weather.

*Pot Culture.*—Pot-up firmly in the case of the hardy species in autumn, winter, and early spring. In the case of the greenhouse species in September or October, using 5- to 6-inch pots and a compost of half loam and half leaf-mould, rotted manure, and coarse sand, and keep in a frame until November, pinching-off any flower-buds that form; then transfer to the cool greenhouse for flowering. Water moderately and regularly (temperature 45–50° F. winter, 65° F. summer). A little soot-water may be given from time to time while the buds are forming. Discard the plants after flowering, except choice varieties.

*Propagation.*—Sow seed in pots or pans, under glass, in May, in a compost of equal parts of loam, leaf-mould, and sand, all sieved through a ½-inch mesh, and well mixed. Cover thinly with fine, sandy soil, and keep in a temperature of 60° F. Prick-off 1 inch apart into pans as soon as possible, and in about three weeks pot-up singly into 3-inch pots, harden off, and keep on a bed of hard ashes in a shaded frame. Transfer to 5- to 6-inch pots in September. Propagate also by means of division in September, or in spring.

*Species.*—*P. malacoides* (Fairy Primrose) is a good pot-plant for a warm greenhouse (temperature 55–70° F. winter, 60–75° F. summer). It is dainty and very free-flowering, and will bear masses of pale mauve-pink or white blooms in whorls in winter and almost all the year. It should be treated as an annual. The flowers are produced when the stems are 2–3 inches in height, and continue until they reach a height of 7–8 inches. *P. obconica*, another excellent species for the greenhouse, is practically perpetual-flowering ; the large blooms being white, lilac, rose or crimson in colour. To this flower there is the objection that the leaves irritate the skin, if they are allowed to touch it ; care should therefore be taken to wear gloves when handling these primulas. *P. floribunda* [Himalayas] (yellow) and *P. f.* var. *Isabellina* (primrose yellow), both free-flowering ; *P. kewensis* (golden yellow), a hybrid between *P. floribunda* and *P. verticillata* ; *P. sinensis* (Chinese Primrose) [China], which is the most valuable and decorative of the greenhouse Primulas, with its wonderful range of colour varieties ; and the variety *stellata*, with its tall, graceful branching stems, and star-like flowers in tiers ; and *P. verticillata* (sulphur-yellow), all make a wonderful display in the greenhouse from late autumn to early spring. All these greenhouse species need similar treatment, and that detailed above will suit them all.

*P. polyantha* (*P. variabilis*) [Polyanthus] is said to be derived from a cross between the Cowslip (*P. officinalis*) and the Primrose (*P. vulgaris*), partaking of the former in the number of its florets and of the latter in their form. They are generally classified as : *Gold-Laced*, these having flowers with a brilliant yellow edge round the outer part of the petals ; *Fancies*, and *Selfs*. They make an excellent show, especially during April and May, in partly shaded beds and borders, or they may be grown in pots in the cool greenhouse. They need a moist, deep, good loam. There are innumerable named varieties. The *Munsted* strain is excellent : the colours are numerous, and the flowers are borne from March to June on 8-inch stems.

*Pot Culture.*—Sow seed thinly under glass in April or May, prick off into boxes, and place in a cold frame. Harden off and plant out 9 inches apart in June, and pot-up singly in 8-inch pots in October, and keep in a cold frame until just before bloom is required, when transfer to the cool house. The Polyanthus may also be propagated by division immediately after flowering. Ample ventilation must be given while in the cold frame, but frost must be excluded. Keep the plants just moist, and as soon as the buds begin to form give doses of weak liquid manure every ten days. (See also **Auricula.**)

Alpine Primulas are of great value in the rock-garden and bog-garden, and some of the choicer species are excellent for cultivation in the alpine house. They should be re-potted every two or three years (but top dressing and drainage must be attended to annually), after flowering. in 4- to 6-inch pans in a compost of two parts of fibrous loam to one part of leaf-mould, silver sand and rotted manure. Stand in a cold frame or under a north wall in summer and rest in autumn and winter. Some of the candelabra Primulas, e.g. *P. Beesiana, Bulleyana*, and *pulverulenta* are valuable for the alpine house. They are chiefly rampant feeders and require a rich compost; being short lived, fresh pans should be made up every year or so.

*Species and Varieties.*—*P. Allionii* * [Maritime Alps] (rose-pink and white, March, 1–2 in.); *P. Beesiana* * [Yunnan] (rose-carmine, yellow eye, May–June, 12–18 in.); *P. Bulleyana* * [China] (reddish orange, May–June, 12–18 in.); *P. capitata* * [Himalayas] (blue, April–June, 6–12 in.); *P. Cockburniana* * [W. China] (orange, May–June, 6–12 in., slender); *P. denticulata* * [Himalayas] (lilac and white, Feb.–April, 12–18 in.); *P. Edgeworthii* * [Indian Himalayas] (pale lavender, grey foliage, May, 6 in.); *P. farinosa* * [Northern regions] (rose-purple, May, 6 in.); *P. floribunda* (buttercup-primrose) [Himalayas] (yellow, April–May, 6–9 in.); *P. f.* var. *Isabellina* (a primrose-yellow form of *P. floribunda*); *P. Forrestii* * [Yunnan] (yellow, May, 12–18 in.); *P. hirsuta* * [Pyrenees] (lilac, rose, or white, April, 3–4 in.); *P. japonica* [Japan] and vars. (various, May–Aug., 12–24 in.); *P. kewensis* [hybrid of garden origin] (pale yellow, April, 15 in., half hardy); "Linda Pope" * [hybrid], a superb plant (flowers lilac turning to lavender); *P. Littoniana* * [Yunnan] (violet-blue, fragrant, June–July, 10–15 in.); *P. malacoides* [China] (pale mauve, pink or white, Sept.–May, 12–24 in., half hardy); *P. marginata* * [Alps] (lavender-blue, margined white, Feb.–March, 6 in.); *P. minima* * [S.E. Europe] (rose or white, 1 in., a dainty little plant); *P. nutans* * [Yunnan] (powder-blue heads of drooping flowers, June–July, 9–15 in.); *P. obconica* [China] and vars. (various, spring, 9–12 in., tender); *P. Palinuri* * [S. Italy] (deep yellow, March–April, 8–10 in.); *P. pulverulenta* * [W. China] (deep rose-purple, flower-stalks covered with farina, May–June, 12–18 in.); *P. rosea* * [W. Himalayas] (rosy pink, March–May, 4–7 in.); *P. Sieboldii* * [Japan] and vars. (red, purple, lilac, May–June, 12 in.); *P. sinensis* [China] and the var. *stellata* (various, Sept.–May, 12–24 in., tender); *P. sonchifolia* * [S.W. China] (violet, mealy calyx, June, 6 in.); *P. verticillata* [S. Arabia] (yellow, spring, 12 in.); *P. viscosa* * [Pyrenees] (violet or red, April, 4 in.); *P. viscosa* var. *Mrs. G. H. Wilson* * (dark blue, April–May, 4–7 in.); *P. vulgaris* * (primrose) [Europe] (yellow, cream, or white, March–April, 3–5 in.); *P. Winteri* * [Himalayas] (pale lavender or mauve, with yellow eye, grey foliage). Those without distinguishing marks are for the greenhouse.

**Primula Auricula** (see **Auricula**).

**Pritchardia**, *Palmaceæ.*—A small group of ornamental, fan-leaved palms succeeding in a compost of equal parts of loam and peat, or leaf-mould, with some sand. They prefer a warm, moist atmosphere of 70–85° F. in the summer and a night temperature of not less than 50° F. in the winter. They require a liberal amount of water in the summer.

*Species.*—*P. Martii* [Hawaiian Isles] is a dwarfer plant than some species, with dark-green leaves. *P. pacifica* [Pacific Islands] has rich, dark-green, arching leaves. The young leaves are densely covered with

* Species thus marked are alpine house subjects.

*By courtesy of*]                                    [*Sutton & Sons Ltd.*

Primulas: stellata, obconica, malacoides, japonica, sinensis, Double
and Single

Salpiglossus sinuata

*By courtesy of* ]                    [*Carters' Tested Seeds Ltd.*

Gloxinia (sinningia speciosa)

whitish-brown felt, which later disappears. It is a fine palm, and the best of the genus.

**Pritchardia filamentosa** (see **Washingtonia filifera**).

**Prostanthera** (Australian Mint Bush), *Labiatæ*.—Australian evergreen shrubs or sub-shrubs, suitable for growing in the cool greenhouse. Being plentifully studded with resinous glands, they are strongly scented. They succeed in fibrous loam and peat in equal parts, with plenty of sand, and it is important that they should have good drainage.

*Culture.*—They are propagated by means of cuttings of young shoots, which root readily under a bell-glass with a little heat. Grow on in a cool house. Young plants should be pinched back occasionally to obtain good shape, and useful plants may be grown in 5- or 6-inch pots. Pot-on into larger pots if large specimens are required.

*Species.*—*P. lasianthos* (white, tinged or spotted red, June); *P. nivea* (snow-white or tinged with blue, July, 12–50 in.); *P. rotundifolia* (purple, July, 1–5 ft.); *P. Sieberi* (lilac-mauve, March–April, 1–8 ft.); *P. violacea* (bluish purple, June, 12–40 in.).

**Protea,** *Proteaceæ.*—Evergreen shrubs with thick, leathery leaves, requiring cool-greenhouse treatment. The flowers are usually solitary, and are often surrounded by coloured bracts in the form of a dense capitate head; this can be either globose, oblong, or cone-like, perhaps more interesting than brilliant. The beauty of the flowers arises from their curious structure.

*Culture.*—They require a light, airy greenhouse, fully exposed to the sun, but they are not easy to cultivate, the one great danger being excessive watering. They resent root disturbance and in this respect great care is necessary when re-potting. It is a good plan to place the pot in which the plant is growing inside a larger pot, and fill up the space with silver sand, always keeping it moist. They should be potted in fibrous loam, peat, and sand, in equal proportions, with some broken brick and charcoal mixed in, taking care to allow plenty of drainage. They can sometimes be induced to flower by permitting the plants to become pot-bound.

*Propagation.*—Propagate by means of cuttings of half-ripened wood inserted in sandy peat, and placed under a bell-glass, with a little warmth; or by imported seed sown as soon as received.

*P. cynaroides* [S. Africa] has flower-heads somewhat resembling those of the globe artichoke. The bracts are bright pink, the centre of the flower having whitish hairs. Bushes grow up to 6 feet high. It is said that when the heads of the flowers of this species first open they are full of honey, and they are known in South Africa as honey-pots. The next species seems more entitled to that name. In any case, the flowering of the honey-pots is said to be celebrated by picnics. *P. mellifera* (*P. repens*) [S. Africa] has whitish-green bracts, with pinkish or rosy-pink tips. The flowers are whitish, the centre being covered with golden hairs. The var. *rubra* is deeper in colour, some parts of the bracts being dark red.

**Prunus,** *Rosaceæ.*—This genus includes several lovely, deciduous spring-flowering, small trees which lend themselves admirably to culture under glass. *P. Amygdalus [Amygdalus communis]* (almond) and *P. nana* (Russian Almond) [S. Russia], a dwarf-growing species, some 12–18 inches in height, with masses of lovely blossom in April thrive in the cold greenhouse as do *P. Cerasus* and vars.; *P. japonica* (*P. sinensis*) [China] (rose-pink or white, double and single flowers, March–April); and *P. subhirtella*, a plant much cultivated in Japan and known as the Cherry of Japan (white, tinged red, Feb.–March). In the warm greenhouse Prunus may be flowered early : *P. Lannesiana* [Japan] and its many beautiful forms, so popular in our gardens, known as Japanese Flowering Cherries (white and pink, double and single, Jan.–April); *P. Persica* [Peach] (red and white, double, Jan.–April); *P. serrulata* (Japanese Cherry) [China and Japan] (early spring); *P. Sieboldii* (*P. Watereri*) [China and Japan] (pink, March); *P. triloba* (rosy pink, double, Jan.–April).

*Culture.*—Pot-up young trees specially purchased or propagated for pot culture in October or November, using clean, well-drained, 6- to 8-inch pots for dwarf plants, 10–12-inch for larger plants, in a compost of two parts of sandy loam to one part of leaf-mould and rotten manure. Plunge the pots outdoors to the rims in ashes. Prune to shape only in December, and transfer to the greenhouse when growth commences unless they are required earlier for forcing. Pruning proper should be done as soon as the flowers are over. Cut out weak wood and shorten old flowering-wood. Keep in a good open place, with pots plunged in ashes, and water regularly while growing, and feed with liquid manure. Keep moist only when dormant.

**Psoralea affinis,** *Leguminosæ.*—A small South African shrub requiring the protection of a cool greenhouse. It may be raised either as a pot plant or it may be planted out in the border of the greenhouse, where it will attain a good size and be a very attractive object in the early spring, with its many clusters of blue and purple, pea-shaped flowers. It succeeds in a compost of fibrous loam and sandy peat, in equal proportions, good drainage being essential.

*Propagation.*—It is propagated by means of seed, or by cuttings in April and May of half-ripened wood, inserted in sand under glass.

**Pteridium aquilinum [Pteris aquilina]** (Common Bracken), *Polypodiaceæ.*—This is very common in many parts of the country, but it is very decorative when grown in large pots for the cold greenhouse.

*Propagation.*—It is propagated by means of spores or by placing lumps of peat containing the rhizome in pots. In some parts of the world, particularly in New Zealand, this plant is used for food.

**Pteris** (Ribbon Fern), *Polypodiaceæ.*—Greenhouse and hardy ferns growing from 12 to 40 inches high. The hardy sorts thrive in shady situations in sandy loam and peat.

*Greenhouse Culture.*—Pot-up in March and water liberally in summer (temperature 50° F. winter, 60° F. summer).

*Propagation.*—Propagate by means of spores sown in heat at any time. Prick out when ready, and grow on. Pot-up at that time for the greenhouse; these roots will come up into leaf the following spring. The old roots are very difficult to move and re-establish. Propagation by division is, therefore, not advisable.

514

*Species.*—*P. cretica* [temperate regions]. This species and its many forms are some of our most popular ferns. Some are crested, others variegated. *P. quadriaurita* [Tropics] is a beautiful fern with fronds 6–30 inches long. *P. q.* var. *argyræa* has a band of white down the centre of the frond, and *P. q. tricolor* is similar, but with a tinge of red in addition. *P. serrulata* (Ribbon Fern), half hardy, is an excellent room fern, some 20 inches in height. *P. tremula* [Australian Bracken] is also half hardy, and is of equal height.

**Pteris aquilina** (see **Pteridium aquilinum**).

**Pterostylis** (see Chapter on **Orchids**).

**Punica Granatum** (Pomegranate), *Punicaceæ.*—A half-hardy, deciduous shrub or small tree which loves a light, rich, loamy soil, and in the open requires the protection of a south wall; even then fruits rarely develop. In most districts it is better grown in pots or tubs in the cold greenhouse. It bears large, bright-red flowers in late summer, and these are followed, in favourable conditions, by the well-known, apple-shaped fruits. Although the fruit may not develop, the flowers are extremely decorative in themselves.

The variety *nana* makes a charming pot-plant, and is the best for greenhouse use. For ornament the double-flowered forms are best in both cases.

*Culture.*—Propagate by means of cuttings made of semi-mature shoots in summer and strike in sandy soil in slight heat, or graft in March. Cut out dead and weak wood in autumn after flowering is over.

**Purple Bells** (see **Rhodochiton volubile**).

**Purple Rock Cress** (see **Aubrieta**).

**Purple Wreath** (see **Petrea volubilis**).

**Puschkinia scilloides** (Striped Squill), *Liliaceæ.*—An attractive Oriental, dwarf, hardy, bulbous, spring-flowering plant, suitable for growing on the rock-garden or in the open border. It is also valuable for growing in pans in the alpine house.

*Culture.*—It should be planted in sandy loam and leaf-mould, and the pans plunged to the rims in ashes in an open position, until the flower-buds appear. It is increased by division of the bulbs, which should be done every two or three years.

**Pycnostachys Dawei,** *Labiatæ.*—This native of Uganda is a handsome, erect, winter-blooming perennial, with cobalt-blue flowers, in short, terminal, crowded spikes. It is a useful cool-greenhouse plant, closely allied to **Coleus,** and succeeds with the same cultural treatment.

*Propagation.*—Cuttings of young growth should be taken about June and grown on, occasionally pinching back to obtain a compact habit; otherwise they become somewhat straggling plants, particularly if the cuttings are taken too early. They can also be propagated from seed, which is usually produced freely.

*P. urticifolia* is another good species from Tropical Africa that is useful for the conservatory. It produces erect inflorescences of dark blue flowers in winter, and grows to a height of 3–4 feet.

**Pyrenean Primrose** (see **Ramonda Myconi**).

**Pyrostegia venusta** (**Bignonia venusta**), *Bignoniaceæ.*—A handsome Brazilian climber, with drooping panicles of tubular crimson and orange flowers. At one time it was included with **Bignonia,** and it is treated as such. It is one of the best rafter plants for a warm greenhouse, and blooms profusely in early winter.

**Pyrrhocactus centeterius (Echinocactus mammillarioides),** *Cactaceæ* [Chile] (see **Echinocactus**).

**Pyrus** (see **Malus**).

**Pyrus floribunda** (see **Malus floribunda**).

**Pyrus japonica** (see **Chænomeles lagenaria**).

**Pyrus Maulei** (see **Chænomeles japonica**).

**Pyrus spectabilis** (see **Malus spectabilis**).

**Pyxidanthera barbulata** (Flowering Moss, Pine-Barren Beauty), *Diapensiaceæ.*—A New Jersey, evergreen, creeping, sub-shrub, 2 inches high, forming moss-like cushions. These are studded during April and May with solitary, sessile, white or rose-coloured, star-like flowers. It is a pretty little plant for the rock-garden, and is also a choice and charming plant to grow in pans for the alpine house. It is closely allied to **Diapensia** and **Galax**. It appears to thrive best in a light, sandy, lime-free soil, in an open position.

*Propagation.*—It is propagated by means of cuttings placed in sandy soil in a close, but not heated frame.

**Quamoclit pinnata** (Cypress Vine, Indian Pink), *Convolvulaceæ.* —A pretty, annual species, of climbing habit. It bears red flowers in summer and will grow up to 6 feet in height ; a native of the Tropics and easily propagated from seeds

**Queen of the Prairie** (see **Filipendula**).

**Quisqualis indica** (Rangoon Creeper), *Combretaceæ.*—A warm-greenhouse climber from Malaya, best planted out in the greenhouse border, although it can be grown in a large pot.

*Culture.*—It should have a compost of two parts of loam, one part of peat, and some sand.

*Propagation.*—It is propagated by means of soft-wood cuttings taken with a " heel ", and placed in sand under a bell-glass, with bottom heat.

The flowers are blood red, rose coloured or white, and sweetly scented, from May to August.

**Raffenaldea primuloides,** *Cruciferæ.*—An attractive, North African, perennial herb, flowering in the winter or early spring, which, although hardy in favourable situations, is best grown in pans, where it gets some protection either in the alpine house, or in a frame, where the pans should be plunged to the rims in ashes. Although larger, it somewhat resembles in appearance **Morisia monantha,** from which it differs in the structure of the fruit. It succeeds under the same cultural conditions.

*Culture.*—It is best grown in a deep pot, owing to its long, stout, fleshy tap-root, from the crown of which rises a rosette of bright-green leaves. From the axils of these spring flowers, which are primrose-yellow in colour, with darker veins, and which are produced over a long period.

*Propagation.*—It is propagated by means of seed, which should be sown as soon as ripe and should be removed from the pod ; if sown in the pod it will sometimes take two years to germinate.

**Ramonda Myconi [R. pyrenaica]** (Pyrenean Primrose or Rosetta Mullein), *Gesneriaceæ*.—A choice little alpine with purple flowers, suitable for the rock-garden, or when planted in pans is charming for the alpine house. It should be planted among lumps of stone, the crinkled leaves hugging them closely. It should be grown in the shade and given a good, peaty soil.

*R. serbica* [Serbia] (violet) and its variety *Nathaliæ* with bright lavender-blue flowers are equally attractive.

*Propagation.*—They are propagated by means of seed or by leaf-cuttings.

**Ramonda Heldreichii** (see **Jankæa Heldreichii**).

**Randia,** *Rubiaceæ*.—Stove- or warm-greenhouse evergreen shrubs or climbers with funnel or bell-shaped flowers, white, yellowish and sometimes rose. They are closely allied to **Mitriostigma** and **Gardenia,** requiring the same cultural treatment.

*Species.*—*R. dumetorum* (*R. floribunda*) [Tropical Asia] (white and greenish yellow, fragrant, July); *R. macrantha* (*Gardenia macrantha*) [Tropical Africa] (white, greenish yellow, fragrant, June); *R. maculata* (*Gardenia Stanleyana*) (purple with white lobes).

**Rangoon Creeper** (see **Quisqualis indica**).

**Ranunculus (Buttercup-Crowfoot),** *Ranunculaceæ*.—Although most of these are perfectly hardy, some of the dwarf, choicer kinds, usually grown in the rock-garden, will be found very suitable for growing in pans for the alpine house. *R. asiaticus* and its varieties are very decorative for the conservatory and *R. cortusæfolius* is quite a good conservatory plant.

*Culture.*—*R. asiaticus* is tuberous-rooted, and after the foliage has died down the plant should be lifted and kept in a cool, frost-proof shed until the planting time. Early in January it can be potted- or panned-up, putting several tubers in a 5- or 6-inch pot or pan of light soil, placing the tubers at least 1 inch below the surface. Place the receptacles in the coolest house, and the plants will commence to flower in April. If batches are planted at various times, a supply will be maintained over a period.

They are increased by means of seed, but imported tubers are quite cheap.

*R. alpestris, R. amplexicaulis, R. glacialis, R. gramineus, R. montanus, R. rutæfolius,* and *R. Thora* can all be grown in pans for the alpine house. They prefer a good, open, well-drained soil and plenty of water during the growing season.

They are increased by division as new growth is about to commence, or by seed sown as soon as ripe, plunging the pots or pans in ashes in a cool frame.

*Species and Varieties.*—*R. asiaticus* (Persian Ranunculus) [Asia Minor, Persia, etc.] is available in various colours, both single and double. The Persian varieties are compact, and the flowers very beautiful. The var. *africanus* (Turban Ranunculus) is larger in all its parts, coarser in growth, but hardier. *R. alpestris* [Pyrenees, etc.] (white, May–June, 4–6 in.); *R. amplexicaulis* [Pyrenees, etc.] (white, April–May, 4–8 in.); *R. cortusæfolius* [Teneriffe, Canary Isles] (yellow, May, 12–36 in.); *R.*

*glacialis* [Mts. of Europe] (white, or reddish suffused with purple, May–June, 4–6 in.) ; with age the flowers become coppery red.  *R. gramineus* [S.W. Europe] (yellow, April–June, 8–12 in.) ;  *R. montanus* [Europe, etc.] (yellow, April–June, 5–6 in.) ;  *R. rutæfolius* [Higher Alps] (yellow, May–July, 3–4 in.) ;  *R. Thora* (Mountain Crowfoot) [S. Europe] (white, June–July, 3–6 in.).

The last two are not easy to grow successfully.

**Rat's-tail Cactus** (see **Aporocactus flagelliformis**).

**Rattle Box** (see **Crotalaria**).

**Ravenea Hildebrandtii,** *Palmaceæ.*—This graceful, ornamental palm from the Comoro Islands is suitable for the stove-house, as it does not exceed 10 feet in height when mature.  It requires the same cultural treatment as **Areca.**

**Rebutia,** *Cactaceæ.*—Small plants which somewhat resemble a Mammillaria.  They are not ribbed, but have spirally arranged warts or tubercles, and small spines.  Flowers appear at the sides, and sometimes even at the base, and are large in comparison with the plant. Rebutia was at one time referred to as **Echinocactus,** and succeeds with the same cultural treatment.

*Species.*—*R. Fiebrigii* (*Echinocactus Fiebrigii*) [Bolivia] has orange-red flowers with white stamens.  The spines are white, the longest ones having brownish tips.  It is a beautiful, free-flowering species of easy cultivation.  *R. Haagei* [N. Argentina] has clear-pink flowers, and is a small, free-branching plant.  *R. minuscula* (*Echinocactus minusculus*) [N. Argentina] has bright-crimson flowers, which are yellowish at the base and have yellow stamens.  Numerous flowers are borne.

**Red Root** (see **Lithospermum canescens**).

**Rehmannia,** *Scrophulariaceæ.*—Beautiful, half-hardy, herbaceous perennials growing from 18 to 36 inches in height, with spikes of Foxglove-like flowers in summer.  They thrive in pots in the cold greenhouse in light sandy loam.

*Culture.*—Sow seed thinly in May in well-drained pans or boxes and just cover with fine soil.  Prick off as soon as large enough to handle and pot-on singly until they reach their flowering pots (6–7 inch) about the end of the following March.  Water regularly and feed with occasional doses of weak manure water when the flowers are developing. Cut the dead flower-spikes down and keep only just moist in winter.

*Propagation.*—Propagation may be carried out by means of cuttings made of base shoots in autumn.

*Species.*—*R. angulata* [China] and vars., with pink or rose flowers, 24–48 inches ;  *R. Henryi* [China] pale-yellow, spotted red ;  and *R. glutinosa* [China] yellowish buff and purple, both 6–8 inches high, suitable for the alpine house, are the most popular kinds.

**Rein Orchid** (see **Habenaria**).

**Reinwardtia,** *Linaceæ.*—Warm-greenhouse sub-shrubs closely allied to **Linum.**  They are very showy plants with bright-yellow flowers borne in great profusion during the winter, making them very valuable decorative plants, particularly as yellow at that time of the year is scarce.

*Culture.*—Cuttings should be taken from strong shoots, preferably from the base, and placed in sand in a propagating case in April. When rooted they should be potted-up singly in a warm temperature until established in 5- or 6-inch pots. They should frequently be pinched back to encourage a compact habit. They can then be grown in a cooler atmosphere and given plenty of air and sun to ripen the shoots well for flowering the following winter. Being very subject to red spider, the plants should be frequently syringed during the growing season, thus obtaining a moist atmosphere. Old plants may be cut back and potted-on and grown a second year. They require a temperature of 55–60° F. during the flowering season to encourage the flowers to open.

*Species.*—*R. tetragyna* [India] (flowers lemon-yellow, styles usually four, 12–18 in.) ; *R. trigyna* (*Linum trigynum*) [India] (flowers orange-yellow, styles three, 12–24 in.).

**Renanthera** (see Chapter on **Orchids**).

**Reseda odorata** (Mignonette), *Resedaceæ.*—This is a sweet-scented, North African, branching, annual herb, much grown for its strong and agreeable fragrance. It develops rapidly, and flowers very quickly from seed. Mignonette grows from 9 to 18 inches in height, and flowers outdoors from July to September. It makes a useful pot-plant in the greenhouse, where it responds to cool- and warm-house treatment, and flowers almost all the year round. If well thinned out as soon as large enough, it will grow stronger and produce larger racemes of bloom. It likes a fairly rich soil with lime and a sunny position.

*Pot Culture.*—Sow seed thinly, $\frac{1}{4}$ inch deep, in pots under glass, in March, June, August, and September, using a compost of two parts of oam to one part of rotted cow-manure and a little crushed lime rubble and sand, and place several seeds in each 6-inch pot. Thin to four plants in each pot, and stand near the glass or grow in a frame. When well rooted, feed liberally with liquid manure. Cut off all dead flowers and prune back straggly shoots.

*Named Varieties.*—*Crimson Giant* ; *Golden Gem* ; *Pearl* (cream) ; *Machet* (buff) ; *Salmon Queen* (salmon-pink) ; *Giant Red* (red).

**Resurrection Plant** (see **Selaginella lepidophylla**).

**Rhabdothamnus Solandri,** *Gesneriaceæ.*—An uncommon cool-greenhouse plant or small shrub, native of New Zealand. It forms a bushy specimen from 1 to 3 feet in height and produces its rich orange flowers which are longitudinally striped with reddish brown, very freely over a period of several months.

*Propagation.*—Propagation is by seeds or cuttings and a light loamy compost with peat added, is suitable.

**Rhapis** (Ground Rattan Cane), *Palmaceæ.*—Greenhouse palms with fan-like leaves borne on slender stems, which thrive in a compost of two parts of sandy loam to one part of leaf-mould and sand. *R. flabelliformis* and *R. humilis*, both natives of China, and both growing to 7 or 8 feet in height, are the commonly grown species.

*Culture.*—Pot-up in March using a comparatively small pot and not too much soil. Water well in spring and summer (temperature 50° F. winter, 60° F. summer). Shade from the sun and syringe twice a day from May to October.

*Propagation.*—Propagate by means of suckers in August, or sow ¾ inch deep (in heat) in March.

**Rheumatism Root** (see **Jeffersonia diphylla**).

**Rhexia virginica,** *Melastomaceæ.*—This native of Massachusetts is a pretty, low-growing, tuberous-rooted plant 10–12 inches high. Although it can be grown outside in some favourable situations, it makes a charming plant for the alpine house when grown in pans, with its attractive rosy-coloured flowers during July and August. As it grows wild in the sunny swamps in company with *Sarracenia purpurea,* the same cultural treatment as for that plant will suit it.

*Propagation.*—It is increased by means of seed and by tubers, which should be potted-up in the autumn and kept in a cold frame.

**Rhipsalis,** *Cactaceæ.*—A genus of South American Cacti suitable for greenhouse culture. The stems are slender and either round or flattened. The flowers are small and of little decorative value, and the plants are grown for the mistletoe-like berries which they bear. They like a partly shaded position in a mixture of equal parts of peaty loam, sand, and charcoal.

*Culture.*—Pot-up in April. Water well and keep in a warm, moist atmosphere. Shade from the strong sun. Keep slightly moist in winter (average winter temperature, day 55° F., night 50° F.; summer, day 65° F., night 50° F.).

*Propagation.*—Propagate by means of seed sown in heat in March, or by cuttings in June.

Good species are *R. Cassytha* (Mistletoe Cactus) [Central and S. America] (white flowers and white berries, April, 15–40 in.); *R. Houlletiana* [Brazil] (creamy white or yellow flowers, red berries, 10–24 in.); and *R. salicornioides* (*Hatiora salicornioides*) [Brazil] (pale-yellow flowers, white berries, April–May, 10 in).

**Rhodanthe** (see **Helipterum**).

**Rhodochiton volubile,** *Scrophulariaceæ.*—A free-flowering, graceful Mexican climber for the cool greenhouse, during the spring or summer. It is closely allied to **Maurandia** and **Lophospermum,** and sometimes known under the latter name. When grown up the roof of the greenhouse, the curious, distinctive, pendulus, dark-red flowers look very effective, with a wide saucer-shaped pink or rose coloured calyx, which enhances their beauty and contrasts with the dark-red corolla. Bloom is obtained the first season from seed, and it is best treated as an annual. It requires the same cultural treatment as **Maurandia,** which see.

**Rhododendron,** *Ericaceæ.*—Among the most handsome and finest of all our flowering shrubs are the hardy Rhododendrons. Several of the early flowering species are useful cool-greenhouse plants, as they furnish bloom from January to early March. Chief among these are *R. dauricum* [N. Asia], *R. moupinense* [W. China], *R. mucronulatum* [China], *R. parviflorum* [Siberia and China], and *R. præcox* [hybrid of garden origin], all hardy plants. In addition to the hardy and half-hardy species, such as the Himalayan species and their hybrids, which do well in a cool greenhouse when the temperature is kept a few degrees above freezing point in the winter, the Javanese species and hybrids are choice greenhouse kinds which require moist warmth all the year

**520**

on account of their continual growing and blooming. These are best kept under glass all the year round with a minimum temperature in the winter of 50° F., and, like other greenhouse Rhododendrons, should, if possible, be planted out in the beds or borders of the greenhouse in a porous, peaty soil, with good drainage.

The following species must not be overlooked for culture in the alpine house : *R. Forrestii, R. hippophæoides, R. impeditum, R. intricatum,* and *R. lepidotum,* all natives of China, as well as *R. ferrugineum* and *R. hirsutum,* both European, and known as " Alpine Rose ". These two do not object to limestone. They grow about 6–8 inches in height, and in April and May produce lovely bluish-purple, carmine, or red flowers. They should be potted-up in autumn in a 5- to 6-inch pan of turfy peat and silver sand. Rhododendrons must be carefully chosen which are suitable for each situation. For Pot Culture see **Azalea.**

*Propagation.*—To propagate hybrids, graft (on stock *R. ponticum*) under glass from January to May, layer well-matured shoots in late summer, or take cuttings. Species may be increased by means of seed sown thinly in March or April in pans, in chopped sphagnum or a compost of equal parts of well-sieved leaf-mould, or peat, and coarse sand in a cold frame. Most species may be raised from cuttings of semi-matured shoots struck in a frame with slight bottom heat, and practically all species can be layered in summer.

*Javanese Species, Hybrids, and Varieties.*—*R. jasminiflorum* [Java] (white, slightly tinged rose, May) ; *R. retusum* [Java] (bright scarlet outside, yellow inside tube, May–June) ; " *Brilliant* " (scarlet) ; " *Ceres* " (tawny yellow) ; " *Exquisite* " (light fawn-yellow) ; " *Little Beauty* " (carmine-scarlet) ; " *Maiden's Blush* " (blush, with yellow eye) ; " *Triumphans* " (crimson-scarlet).

*Himalayan Species and Hybrids.*—*R. arboreum* [Himalayas] (white, rose, or blood colour, March–May) ; there are a number of forms and varieties of this. *R. barbatum* [Sikkim] (blood-red) ; *R. Falconeri* [Sikkim] (white, numerous but small, May) ; *R. Fortunei* [China] (pale rose, fragrant, May) ; *R. Griffithianum* [Sikkim] (yellowish and rose, May) ; one of the largest flowers of the genus. *R. Loderi,* a beautiful hybrid between the two last-named species, pure white or faintly tinged with pink. *R. Maddenii* [Sikkim] (pure white with a faint blush, June–Aug.) ; *R. triflorum* [Sikkim] (greenish yellow, May–June). *Hybrids and Varieties.*—" *Alice* " (rich rosy pink) ; " *Charles Dickens* " (dark scarlet) ; " *Duchess of Connaught* " (white with yellow spots) ; " *Gomer Waterer* " (white, large) ; " *Lady Armstrong* " (pale rose spotted) ; " *Mrs. F. Hankey* " (salmon, spotted red) ; " *Old Port* " (plum colour) ; " *Pink Pearl* " (pink) ; " *Sappho* " (white with maroon blotch). There are many more species and varieties, also hybrids, in cultivation and many of them may be used for greenhouse or conservatory decoration.

**Rhodothamnus Chamæcistus,** *Ericaceæ.*—A dwarf, much-branched, evergreen shrub from the Alps of Eastern Europe. In habit and flowers it resembles **Azalea.** The solitary pink flowers are borne at the tips of the branches. Although quite hardy, it is suitable for growing in pans for the alpine house. It should be planted in peaty soil mixed with broken sandstone, given good drainage and kept in partial shade.

**521**

*Propagation.*—It is propagated by means of seed, which should be treated as for **Rhododendron,** by layers, or by cuttings of ripened shoots with a " heel ", struck in sandy peat and placed under a bell-glass. It is not always one of the easiest plants to cultivate.

**Rhoeo discolor (Tradescantia discolor),** *Commelinaceæ.*—A striking foliage plant for the warm greenhouse, with leaves which are deep purple beneath, and lighter above. The white flowers appear in boat-shaped, spathe-like structures. The var. *vittata* has its leaves striped above with yellow. It prefers a warm, moist atmosphere, and is readily rooted from cuttings, or from the stem cut into lengths and placed in a propagating case with bottom heat.

**Rhopalostylis,** *Palmaceæ.*—Pinnate leaf-palms, somewhat resembling **Howea,** and succeeding with the same cultural treatment. They are very useful for decorating the conservatory, growing in quite a low temperature. They should be raised in shade, as the young leaves readily scorch in the sun.

*Propagation.*—They are propagated by means of imported seed.

*Species.*—*R. Baueri* (*Areca Baueri*) [Norfolk Islands] (flowers ivory-white, leaves stout and rigid) ; *R. sapida* [*Areca sapida*] (Nika Palm) [New Zealand] (flowers pinkish, plant not so tall or stout as *R. Baueri*).

**Rhynchanthera grandiflora,** *Melastomaceæ.*—A handsome, Brazilian, stove evergreen shrub, with panicles of large, showy, purple flowers during the autumn.

*Culture.*—It should be given a compost of rich fibrous loam and sandy peat in equal proportions, good drainage being very essential.

*Propagation.*—It is propagated by means of cuttings of young shoots in sandy soil, placed in heat under a bell-glass, slightly raised to prevent damping off.

**Rhynchospermum** (see **Trachelospermum**).

**Rhynchostylis** (see Chapter on **Orchids**).

**Ribbon Fern** (see **Pteris**).

**Ribes** (Flowering Currant, etc.), *Saxifragaceæ.*—A genus of pretty, hardy, deciduous shrubs akin to the currant and gooseberry, bearing in spring red, rose, white, yellow and green florets, clustered together in pendulous racemes. *R. aureum* [N.W. America], with golden-yellow flowers, and *R. sanguineum* [California], with pinkish-red flowers, sometimes deepening to light crimson, are suitable for culture in the greenhouse. In the warm house (temperature 55–70° F. winter, 60–75° F. summer) they may be had in flower from January to March.

*Culture.*—Pot-up in November, using 8- to 10-inch pots and poor, ordinary soil, and re-pot annually. Thin out well and cut out old wood after flowering.

*Propagation.*—To propagate take cuttings of matured wood in October and strike in the open, or layer in September.

**Rice** (see **Oryza sativa**).

**Rice Flower** (see **Pimelea**).

**Rice Paper Tree** (see **Fatsia papyrifera**).

**Richardia** (see **Zantedeschia**).

**Ricinus communis** (Castor-oil Plant), *Euphorbiaceæ.*—This is a magnificent and highly ornamental, half-hardy annual from the Tropics of the Old World, whose picturesque foliage and stately growth, combined with the brilliant coloured fruits, impart to sub-tropical bedding plantations, shrubbery or greenhouse, quite an oriental aspect. They thrive in rich loam in warm beds, or in the cold greenhouse.

*Species.*—One of the best varieties is *R. c. Gibsonii*, with its large, handsome, dark-red or bronzy-purple foliage.

*Culture.*—Sow each seed in a separate pot in March under glass (temperature 45° F.). Pot-on into 5-inch pots, harden off, and plant out in June from 2 to 3 feet apart, or pot-on into 6- to 8-inch pots and keep indoors (temperature 45° F. winter, 60° F. summer). Shade from the sun and water moderately but regularly.

**Rivina** (Blood Berry, Rouge Berry), *Phytolaccaceæ.*—Evergreen berry-bearing plants, suitable for the warm greenhouse.

*Propagation.*—Propagate by seeds sown in early spring in heat. Grow in small pots filled with a light open compost. Cuttings may also be employed if desired.

*Species.*—*R. humilis* is the species most generally grown. It has white flowers which are followed by bright scarlet fruits. *R. aurantiaca* with yellow fruits is also good. Both are natives of Tropical America.

**Rochea (Kalosanthes)**, *Crassulaceæ.*—Succulent, shrubby, early summer-flowering plants for the greenhouse, with clusters of tubular white, pink, scarlet, or yellow flowers. They are all natives of South Africa, and are sometimes included with **Crassula.** They are allied to the House Leek, and are readily propagated from cuttings.

*Culture.*—If single plants are desired, cuttings about 4 inches long should be taken in March and potted-up in sandy, peaty soil. The pots should be placed near the glass in a night temperature of 50° F. Care should be taken not to keep the plants too wet, or they are liable to rot. When rooted the plants should be pinched back to encourage them to break. After a few days pot the plants on into pots two sizes larger in a compost of two parts of fibrous loam to one part of sand and one part of broken charcoal, adding one-fifth of dried sheep- or cow-manure. They should be stood near the glass in a night temperature of about 40° F. Keep them in a cool house just free from frost during the winter, and in the spring pinch back again to encourage further breaking. Pot-on again shortly afterwards. They can be flowered the second summer from cuttings. If larger specimens are required the plants should be cut back after flowering to 6 inches from the pot, and potted-on when they break. Fine specimens may be obtained in 10- or 12-inch pots. The plants should have an abundance of fresh air at all times.

*Species.*—*R. coccinea* (scarlet, July–Aug., 12 in.); there are some beautiful hybrids of this plant in cultivation; *R. falcata* (see *Crassula falcata*); *R. jasminea* (white, April–May, 9–10 in.); there are hybrids of this and the previous species. *R. odoratissima* (pale yellow or creamy white, sometimes rose, June, 12 in., sweet scented).

**Rock Cress** (see **Arabis**).

**Rockfoil** (see **Saxifraga**).

**Rock Jasmine** (see **Androsace**).

**Rodriguezia** (see Chapter on **Orchids**).

# THE GREENHOUSE

**Romneya** (Matilija Poppy), *Papaveraceæ.*—Tall, showy, flowering sub-shrubs or perennial herbs, growing from 5 to 8 feet in height and flower-ing in the open from June to September.  They are almost hardy and thrive in the sun, and in well-drained, sandy, enriched loam, in a sheltered position or under a south wall.

*R. Coulteri* [California and Mexico] has silver-grey leaves, and large, snowy-white, poppy-like flowers with golden-yellow centres, often more than 6 inches in diameter.  It reaches a height of about 5 feet, and is one of the best to grow.  *R. trichocalyx* [California] has flowers of a similar colour, and during the same period, but is not quite so tall, the calyx being covered with fine bristles or hair.  It is equally desirable. The Romneya is rather difficult to establish, but once settled it will be a joy for many years.

*Pot Culture.*—Pot-up in April when required, but do not disturb the roots more than is necessary.  The compost should consist of three parts of good fibrous loam, one part of leaf-mould, and one part of sand. They should be potted-up fairly firmly in 6- to 7-inch pots for the first year or so, but much larger pots will be required as the plants become established.  Water moderately in summer, but very sparingly in winter (average temperature, 50° F.).  Keep the plants in a frost-proof shed or a cool greenhouse in the winter.

*Pruning.*—Cut out all dead wood in the spring or cut back hard to the old wood and remove all weak shoots as new growth develops, as the flowers are borne on the new shoots of the current year.  In severe winters protect the crowns with straw, bracken, or sacking, if the pots are plunged in ashes outside.  In the North of England these plants must be grown all the year round under glass, and are well worth attention.

*Propagation.*—To propagate, divide the roots in March, or strike root cuttings 4 inches long in a frame in the autumn.  Pot-on the young plants when rooted and grow-on in a frame.

**Rondeletia (Rogiera),** *Rubiaceæ.*—Stove or warm-greenhouse ever-green shrubs with white, yellow, or red flowers, some of which are very pretty and well worth a place.  They are rather slow growers, and it will be found an advantage to keep young plants warmer to encourage them to grow.

*Culture.*—They are readily propagated from half-ripened shoots inserted in 3-inch pots in a mixture of finely sifted peat and sand, and stood in a propagating case in a temperature of 70° F.  When rooted they should be potted-up into small pots in a mixture of fibrous peat and sand.  When they commence to grow, pinch them back to about two joints above the soil, to encourage them to break.  When well rooted pot-on in pots 2 inches larger, in a compost of loam and peat in equal proportions and some sand.  Although they would flower in these pots, it is advisable to grow them on for the first year until they are put into 8-inch pots, in the same compost as before, allowing them to flower in these pots, where they can remain for two years.  If the dead flowers are removed, the plants will often bloom a second time the same year.  Should they require potting they should be cut back hard. As new growth commences, and after they show three or four pairs of

524

leaves, pinch back; this gives a very much more shapely plant, and yields more flowers.

*Species.*—*R. cordata* [Guatemala] (pink, summer, 12–40 in.); *R. gratissima* [Tropical America] (rosy pink, summer); a beautiful, sweet-scented plant for a cool stove house. *R. odorata* (*R. speciosa*) [Cuba and Mexico] (crimson to bright vermilion, yellow eye, autumn); the var. *major* has larger flowers.

**Roses.**—Roses may be grown either in pots or in a border prepared in the house. If a whole house can be devoted to them, so much the better; if not, they can be brought on with other flowers.

Roses grown under glass can be brought into bloom considerably earlier than those planted in the open. If raised in an unheated house, bloom may be expected in April and May; should a little heat be available, flowers may be had much earlier. Newly potted plants, however, must not be forced; only established roses that have been grown in pots for a year in the house or in the open may be so treated, and these should receive but little heat.

*The Compost.*—An important part of the process is the preparation of the compost in which the plants are to grow. This should be prepared in September, in order that it may have a clear month in the open under cover to amalgamate. It should be composed of a barrow-load of leaf-mould, one of drift sand, one of old mortar rubbish, one of rotted manure, and five of good, well-rotted, turfy loam, which should not be sifted too finely, for roses like a lumpy soil. This is further enriched by the addition of two gallons of bone-meal, and another gallon or so of some good fertiliser. A bushel of quarter-inch bones is also mixed in the compost.

*Potting.*—If the roses are not bought from the nurseryman already potted-up, about the middle of October, when the leaves commence to drop, the bushes should be lifted from the ground and potted-up in 7- or 8-inch pots. They must be taken out of the soil while it is fairly dry, so that their roots may be easily freed from it. The stem is held in the left hand, while with the right a short, pointed stick is used among the roots to loosen the soil as much as possible, taking great care not to break the root fibres. The ball of roots should be shaken from time to time during this process. When the roots are as free as possible from soil they should be carefully looked over, all woody and long, fleshy roots being removed with clean cuts made by a sharp knife, leaving all the useful fibrous ones untouched. The pots used should always be large enough to allow of the fibrous roots lying out horizontally in the soil, but so long as this is possible, the smaller the pot the better.

All pots should, of course, be clean and dry, as should the crocks for drainage. A good layer of these is placed in the bottom of the pot, and is covered with a little soil. The ball of the tree is set firmly in the centre, and the upper two-thirds of the fibrous roots are held upwards with the left hand, while with the right the compost is rammed down very firmly and evenly over the bottom third in the pot. A wooden rammer is used for this purpose. A few more roots are then laid out, and covered with firmly rammed soil, and so on until the pot is almost full, a space of 2 inches being left at the top for future top-dressings.

# THE GREENHOUSE

*The Border.*—If the roses are to be grown in a border in the house and not in pots, a month or five weeks before planting the border should be dug out to a depth of from 2½ to 3 feet, and should, where space is available, be about 3 feet wide. At the bottom of the border place about 6 inches of broken-up chalk or concrete. On this base should be laid a compost similar to that already described. On the broken chalk and other drainage, turves a couple of inches thick should be laid, grassy side downwards, and on this the mixed soil should be placed.

*Pruning Roses after Planting.*—When roses are planted during the autumn and winter months, their first pruning should be left until the spring, but when spring-planted, it should be done at the time of putting in. The trees should be gone over carefully and all dead wood cut clean out, together with weak and sappy, unripened wood, also any shoots which have received injury. Standards should then be cut back to within about 4 inches of their union with the stock, bush trees being dealt with a little less severely, having about 6 inches of every shoot left above the ground. This pruning is only meant to be carried out the first time after planting. The subsequent treatment varies with the variety.

*Pruning Established Roses.*—The time of pruning roses differs with the variety, and the times mentioned are for those grown for the cold house ; for early flowers, pruning must be done earlier, according to requirements. Hybrid Perpetuals, both dwarf and bush, as well as standards and Hybrid Teas, are pruned during February, bush and standard Teas and Noisettes during March, while the climbing roses, Hybrid Perpetuals, Hybrid Teas, Teas, and Noisettes should be looked over twice in the year, being well thinned as soon as they have flowered in the summer and pruned properly in March. If required for exhibition, the plants must be pruned much harder than plants for bedding or garden decoration. As a general rule weak-growing varieties should be pruned hard, and strong-growing sorts lightly.

Roses may be roughly divided into classes for purposes of pruning. The first with which we are concerned is that of the Hybrid Perpetuals, Hybrid Teas, Teas, and Noisettes, which require hard pruning. All dead, unripe, and weak shoots should be cut clean out, and the centre of the plant thinned well to allow good room either with a sharp knife or the secateurs. The shoots retained should be cut back to from four to six buds. Examples of this type are: *Phyllis Gold; Fashion; President Hoover; Lady Forteviot; Happiness; Sir Henry Segrave; Mrs. Wemyss Quin; Marcia Stanhope; Rev. F. Page-Roberts; Lady Sylvia; Peace;* and *Wheatcrofts Gold.*

The Hybrid Perpetuals, Hybrid Teas, Teas, and Noisettes, which require moderate pruning, are the next class. These should have the dead unripe and weak shoots cut clean away. The shoots which cross, or may cross when full grown, should be cut out, the plant never being allowed to get crowded in the middle. The strong, well-ripened last year shoots which are left should be cut back to from six to eight eyes. Examples of roses needing this treatment are : *Augustus Hartmann ; Betty Uprichard ; Captain Hayward ; Clarice Goodacre ; Covent Garden ; Earl Haig ; Emma Wright ; General McArthur ; George Dickson;*

# GREENHOUSE PLANTS

*Lady Hillingdon; Los Angeles; Mabel Morse; Mrs. A. R. Barra-clough; Mrs. Henry Bowles; Mrs. John Laing; Mrs. Herbert Stevens; Red Letter Day; Shot Silk; Picture; Christopher Stone; Mrs. Edward Laxton; The Doctor; Frensham; Dainty Maid; Poinsettia; Goldi-locks;* and *Dainty Bess.*

There are also varieties of Hybrid Perpetuals, Hybrid Teas, Teas, and Noisettes which require light pruning. They should be treated as the previous classes, but still less wood should be cut away. The centre of the plant should be kept open, but beyond this the strong shoots from the base should be left about 8 inches long, while the other shoots should be cut back till on their laterals or side shoots there are from one to three buds left. The base shoots should be left 12 inches long, while the laterals on the older wood may be reduced to four or five eyes. Roses needing pruning of this kind are such plants as *Caroline Testout, Frau Karl Druschki, Hugh Dickson, Gustave Regis, Lady Waterlow, Mme. Jules Gravereaux, Pax, Vanity,* and *Madame Albert Barbier.* Very strong-growing varieties are best pegged down, the shoots being left from 3 to 6 feet in length.

The next section includes the climbing kinds of Hybrid Perpetuals, Hybrid Teas, and Teas, as well as some of the other climbers. These roses need very little pruning, most of them doing best if left to grow naturally. The necessary thinning out of dead wood and of the shoots which are likely to overcrowd the plant, together with the worn-out wood of over two years' growth, will keep the plants in full vigour and blossom. The removal of the old worn-out wood is as well done in the summer, directly after the plants have done blooming, and the young shoots should at once be tied in to take the place of those removed. It is at this time that any necessary re-shaping of the rose should be done, crowded growths being thinned and the branches re-spaced over the wall or trellis so as to keep as much flowering wood as possible. Where the base of the plant becomes bare, as often happens with climbing roses, the space may be filled either by bending down one or more of the lower shoots to cover the bare space or by shortening one or two of the base shoots to induce them to throw out laterals. Among these climbing roses are : *Climbing Caroline Testout; Mme. Edouard Herriot (Daily Mail Rose); Irish Fireflame; Climbing Lady Hillingdon; Sunburst; Wm. Allen Richardson; Chaplin's Pink Climber; Paul's Scarlet Climber; Paul's Lemon Pillar; Climbing Lady Sylvia; Climbing Crimson Conquest.*

*Wintering in the Open.*—The bushes, when potted, should be watered and plunged to the rim of the pots in ashes in a sheltered, but sunny position in the open so that they may finish ripening their new wood. To make doubly sure that the frost does not get to the roots, cover the pots with a layer of litter 6–10 inches in depth. This should be done not later than the first week in November, and if possible earlier by a fortnight. At the end of the year they should be placed in a cold frame, and will then require little further care or attention until February, when they are pruned and moved into the house.

*Moving into the House.*—Before bringing in the roses at the beginning of February the greenhouse should be thoroughly cleaned, the glass washed, the woodwork brushed, and the brickwork limewashed. Ample fresh air is required when the weather is fine, for which the ventilating facilities of the house will be all called into play. Keep the temperature as even as possible and avoid draughts at all costs, for they are a sure source of mildew. Close down the ventilators in the early afternoon to conserve some of the sun's heat. Roses grown in the borders and, therefore, not moved out of the house in summer and autumn, should be given as much ventilation as possible, even through the winter, or they will become tender and weakly. If grown in a house by themselves, even a few degrees of frost will do them no harm, but if grown with other flowers, this, of course, is not generally permissible. A watering with clean water is also needed occasionally. During the whole period of the indoor life of the plants, with the exception of the flowering period and that in late summer and autumn when the wood is ripening, they should be syringed daily in the morning in fine and sunny weather with water that has been exposed to the air of the house for at least twenty-four hours. A warm, humid atmosphere encourages the formation of young growth, and is especially necessary in the case of climbing roses grown under glass. A daily inspection of the pots is essential. Early in the season only a little water is required, but as the young growth appears and the weather becomes warmer, watering must be more frequent—as often as twice a day in the middle of summer, but be careful not to over-water.

*Forcing.*—If heat is available, some of the roses can be forced, and may be pruned and taken into the house early in November with a temperature of between 40–50° F. After a fortnight or three weeks the temperature may be raised to 55° F. by day and 45° F. by night. Through March the temperature should be increased by another 5°, while through April a day temperature of 65° F. and a night temperature of 55° F. should be aimed at. This will entail careful ventilation on hot sunny days. Try to produce conditions similar to those obtaining in the open in June and July. When the sun is out and the weather is very mild, it may be necessary, at times, to have all the ventilators open, and the doors as well, in order to keep down the temperature in the house, but care must be taken not to lower the temperature unduly, or the flowering period will be delayed. It is of the utmost importance that the plants should not be in a direct draught. Bear in mind that in forcing roses *as little artificial heat as possible should be used.* If the weather is fine, syringe the plants as advised for roses grown in the cold house, but avoid doing this when the sun is strong, as beads of water will burn the tender foliage. The pots should be sunk in ashes in the open as soon as bloom is finished. Roses for forcing should not be re-potted annually, but a couple of inches of the soil from the top of the pot should be removed and replaced with some fresh compost and a little fertiliser in January.

*Fumigation.*—It may be necessary to fumigate the house, to destroy any young greenfly that there may be. These are most harmful to roses. Two successive nights should make the fumigation effective. Never should roses grown under glass be sprayed to kill off greenfly, for the foliage and blooms would be irrevocably spoilt. Red spider and

**PLATE 15**
'Snowtime', a variety of cactus-flowered *Zinnia*.
The flowers average five inches in diameter.

thrips are not likely to give much trouble if the atmosphere is kept moist, but a look-out must be kept for *Grey Mould, Rose Mildew, Rose Rot,* and *Rose Rust.*

Disbudding should be carefully attended to, if good blooms are desired. As with outdoor plants, the rose trees should be kept clear of ingrowing and blind shoots, and to get good blooms the trees should not be allowed to carry too many growths. Weak liquid manure should be given weekly as soon as the buds appear, but must be discontinued as soon as the buds show colour.

After all the flowers have been picked, anyhow not later than the beginning of July, all the trees should be moved out of the house on to a spare piece of ground where they should remain, plunged to the rims of the pots, until the re-potting, if necessary, again takes place. They must be shaded from the strong sun when first put out in the open; after a week or so, they will enjoy all the sun they can get to ripen the wood. Watering must still be carefully attended to.

**Rose Apple** (see **Eugenia Jambos**).

**Rose of Heaven** (see **Lychnis Coeli-rosa**).

**Rosette Mullein** (see **Ramonda Myconi**).

**Roupellia grata,** *Apocynaceæ.*—A stove climber from Sierra Leone, with dense cymes of very fragrant, pale-rose flowers during May. It can either be planted out in the border or grown in a large pot in a compost of fibrous loam and peat, in the proportion of two to one, with plenty of drainage. The leaves are thick and nearly 12 inches long, and have a short red leaf-stalk. Cuttings of young shoots root readily, if placed in sand, under a bell-glass with heat.

**Royal Fern** (see **Osmunda**).

**Royal Palm** (see **Oreodoxa regia**).

**Royal Water Lily** (see **Victoria regia**).

**Ruellia (Stephanophysum),** *Acanthaceæ.*—Warm-greenhouse herbs or sub-shrubs. They are very pretty and free flowering, and thrive in any light rich soil, in a warm moist atmosphere.

*Propagation.*—They are readily increased by means of cuttings of young shoots placed in sand under a bell-glass in heat. Young plants should be pinched once or twice when growing to obtain nice bushy plants. Good flowering-plants may be obtained in 5- or 6-inch pots.

*Species.*—*R. acutangula* [Brazil] (bright orange-scarlet, with yellow throat, May, 8–20 in.); *R. amœna* [Brazil] (sprays of bright red flowers, summer, 9–18 in.); *R. Baikiei* [Brazil] (scarlet, summer, 12–20 in.); *R. formosa* [Brazil] (showy scarlet flowers, summer, 12–25 in.); *R. macrantha* [Brazil] has large, trumpet-shaped flowers, purplish rose in colour, with purple veins. It will grow into a fair sized shrub, 4 to 5 feet high, is of easy culture and is one of the best greenhouse flowering plants.

**Ruscus androgynus** (see **Semele androgyna**).

**Russelia,** *Scrophulariaceæ.*—Showy, stove, evergreen shrubs, with slender pendulous branches, and showy red flowers. They are of easy cultivation, and some, particularly *R. juncea*, make excellent basket-plants. Although evergreen in some species, the leaves are little more than fine scales.

L L

*Culture.*—They thrive in a mixture of equal parts of fibrous loam and peat with some sand, in a warm, moist atmosphere, good drainage being essential.

*Propagation.*—They are readily increased by means of seed or by cuttings inserted in sandy soil under a bell-glass in heat.

*Species.*—*R. juncea* (Coral Plant) [Mexico] bears flowers in loose, remote racemes, in July. The shoots are twiggy and rush-like. *R. sarmentosa* (*R. multiflora*) [Central America] grows 24–50 inches high, and bears terminal racemes of bright-red flowers in July. *R. elegantissima* and *R. Lemoinei*, both very floriferous, particularly in the winter, are hybrids of the two first-named species.

**Sabal,** *Palmaceæ.*—Stove or greenhouse fan-leaved palms, and although some grow to large trees, some are useful for decoration when grown in large pots or tubs. They succeed under the usual cultural conditions for **Palms.** The soil should consist of a rich loam with the addition of grit.

*Propagation.*—They are propagated by means of imported seed, although some species form suckers which can be taken off.

*Species.*—*S. Blackburniana* (*S. umbraculifera*) [Bermuda] is a useful palm when small, suitable as a room or window-plant. *S. glabra* (*S. Adansonii*) [Southern U.S.A.] is a dwarf stemless greenhouse palm, hardier than some. *S. Palmetto* (Cabbage Palmetto) [Southern U.S.A.] is a good greenhouse palm.

**Saccharum,** *Gramineæ.*—Tall grasses, which, though rarely grown for ornament, make bold specimens, and are well worthy of a place. The most important species is the Sugar-cane (*S. officinarum*) which is extensively cultivated in the tropics and sub-tropics for the production of sugar.

*Culture.*—They are easy to cultivate, succeeding in a light, rich soil, with good heat, and plenty of water during the growing season.

*Propagation.*—Propagation is effected by means of suckers or by cuttings of the stems. These will send out growths at their joints when laid on fibre in a propagating case with plenty of bottom heat.

*Species.*—*S. ægyptiacum* [Algeria] is free flowering, bearing flowers in silvery panicles in July. It is a vigorous cold-greenhouse plant, rivalling bamboo and pampas grass. *S. officinarum* (Sugar-cane) [E. Indies] has long, broad leaves, hanging in graceful curves. The stem is yellowish green. The var. *violaceum* has rich violet or plum-coloured stems.

**Saccolabium** (see Chapter on **Orchids**).

**Sacred Lotus** (see **Nelumbo nucifera**).

**Sadleria cyatheoides,** *Polypodiaceæ.*—A small tree-fern from the Sandwich Islands. It resembles a small **Cyathea** or a **Blechnum,** and has a stem 3–4 feet long. It thrives with the same treatment as for other stove ferns.

**Saffron Crocus** (see **Crocus sativus**).

**Sage** (see **Salvia**).

**Sagittaria montevidensis** (Giant Arrow-head), *Alismaceæ.*—A handsome, South American, free-flowering, water-side plant, not hardy, but suitable for growing in an indoor aquarium. It can be planted either in the mud at the side of the aquarium, or in pots of loamy soil, which should be stood in the water. It may also be grown in a tub and stood outside during the summer. It grows 3–5 feet high, and in summer bears white flowers with a crimson spot.

**St. Bernard's Lily** (see **Anthericum Liliago**).

**St. John's Wort** (see **Hypericum**).

**Saintpaulia ionantha** (African Violet), *Gesneriaceæ.*—Beautiful little half-hardy perennials from Tropical Africa, some 3–4 inches in height, with large purple, violet-like flowers in summer, autumn, and winter. They are suitable for pot culture in the cool or warm-greenhouse. There is also a white-flowered variety, *S. i. albescens.* The var. *grandiflora* has larger flowers of intense blue. The var. *variegata* has leaves variegated with yellow turning to white. *S. kewensis* (E. Tropical Africa] is closely allied to *S. ionantha*, and is often confused with it, but it is a shaggier plant with white hairs.

*Culture.*—Sow seed in clean, well-crocked pots in February, in a propagating case, in a compost of sandy loam, leaf-mould and fibrous peat, just covering the seed lightly with a sprinkling of sand. Prick off as soon as possible 2 inches apart, and subsequently move on and pot-up singly until they reach their flowering-pots (4–5-in.) about the end of May. Water regularly to keep the soil moist while growing and a moist atmosphere by means of occasional damping down. The temperature of the house should not be allowed to fall below 50° F.

*Propagation.*—This may also be carried out by means of leaf-cuttings in a propagating case (see Chapter on **Propagation**), or by division in the spring.

**Salpiglossis sinuata** [**S. variabilis**] (Scalloped-tube Tongue), *Solanaceæ.* —A very lovely half-hardy annual from Chile, with large, quaintly-veined, funnel-shaped flowers of rich shades of deep violet, purple, crimson, scarlet, pink, gold, yellow, or white, suitable for sunny beds or for pot culture in the greenhouse, and useful for cutting. The plants grow to about 20 inches in height, and flower outdoors from July to September.

*Culture.*—Sow seed thinly in light, rich soil early in March, under glass, with moderate heat (temperature 50° F.). Pot-up as soon as possible in 3-inch pots in light, rich, sandy soil. Harden off, and plant out 9 inches apart or pot-on for flowering in May and June. A few twigs, a foot or so high, should be used to stake the plants. Autumn-sown seed potted-up and transferred to the greenhouse, and sown near the glass, will produce blooms from January to March, while seed sown in January will continue the display throughout April and May. Seeds of separate colours can now be obtained.

**Salvia** (Sage), *Labiatæ.*—There are many species belonging to this genus ; some are annuals, some biennials, and others perennials. They are grown in the greenhouse or in the garden as ornamental bedding plants, and mostly provide masses of brilliant flowers. Examples of these are : *S. patens* and *S. splendens.* There are some species, how-ever, which are not grown for their flowers, but for the beauty of their foliage. Salvias grow from 12 to 70 inches in height, and bloom from

June to September. Given warm-house treatment, they may be had in flower in the autumn.

For the greenhouse a good selection would be *S. coccinea grandiflora* [N. and Tropical America] (rosy red), a half-hardy annual; *S. cærulea* [S. Africa] (deep blue, Aug.–Sept., 2–3 ft.); *S. fulgens* [Mexico] (scarlet, July–Aug., 24–30 in.), a shrubby perennial; *S. gesneræflora* [Columbia] (scarlet, Aug.–Sept.); this sub-shrubby perennial closely resembles *S. fulgens* and is considered by many to be only a variety of it. *S. involucrata* [Mexico] and the var. *Bethellii* (rose), a half-hardy perennial; *S. leucantha* [Mexico] (white flowers with densely tomentosed violet or lavender calyx. Stem and leaves also slightly grey with wool covering); *S. patens* [Mexican Mts.] (blue, summer, 12–20 in.); a half-hardy herbaceous perennial with thick, tuberous roots. It is widely used in summer bedding schemes. *S. Pitcheri* [*azurea grandiflora*] (blue), a hardy perennial; *S. rutilans* [Pineapple-scented Sage] (bright scarlet, autumn and winter, 20–30 in.); a sweet-scented foliage sub-shrub, of uncertain origin. *S. Sessii* [Mexico], a tall growing species (4–5 ft. high) producing scarlet flowers in winter. *S. splendens* vars. *Harbinger* and *Pride of Zurich* (both scarlet), half-hardy perennials. All thrive in the sun in rich ordinary soil.

*Pot Culture.*—Sow in moderate heat in February, prick off early, and pot-on as required, never allowing the plants to become pot-bound, and using eventually 6- to 8-inch pots and a compost of two-thirds turfy loam and one-third coarse sand, leaf-mould, and well-rotted manure. Grow-on in an average temperature of 60° F., harden off in a cold frame, summer with the pots plunged in ashes in the open, and take into the cool house early in October. Pinch back occasionally until August, and syringe daily. After blooming, keep the roots fairly dry and cool until March, then give more moisture and slight heat. Rather than raise from seed, however, strike cuttings of young wood in August, September, or February and March.

**Salvinia,** *Marsiliaceæ.*—Interesting plants for the aquarium, allied to ferns. They grow and float on the water in a similar way to **Azolla.** The mature plants are made up of slender stems clothed in fern-like leaves, arranged in threes, two being complete, and the other being submerged, divided and resembling roots with root functions, the plant having no real roots.

*Culture.*—They are rapidly increased by division, but during the winter the temperature must not be allowed to fall below 55° F. If it does the plants should be placed in large, water-tight, shallow pans containing water and three parts filled with soil. They should be kept in a warm house during the winter.

*Propagation.*—They may also be increased by means of spores when these are obtainable. They should be sown in mud and placed in a warm greenhouse.

The two best-known species are *S. auriculata* [Tropical America], which has floating, nearly circular leaves, densely matted with brown hairs; and *S. natans* [Europe, Central China, and N. India], which has oblong floating leaves, smaller than those of the preceding species. This is the one most generally grown.

**Sanchezia nobilis,** *Acanthaceæ.*—An ornamental foliage, warm-green-house plant from Ecuador, grown both for its flowers and foliage. The flowers are yellow, borne in panicles, with bright-red bracts. The handsome leaves are pinnately veined. The variety *glaucophylla* has variegated leaves with yellow or white along the veins. It is an attractive foliage plant when well grown, and succeeds with the same cultural treatment as **Codiæum.**

**Sand Myrtle** (see **Leiophyllum buxifolium**).

**Sandersonia aurantiaca,** *Liliaceæ.*—A pretty, South African, tuberous-rooted, erect-growing herb, with solitary, urn-shaped or globose, orange-coloured flowers. It requires the same cultural treatment as **Gloriosa,** blooms in summer, and grows 24–40 inches high.

**Sandwort** (see **Arenaria**).

**Sanguinaria canadensis** (Blood-root), *Papaveraceæ.*—A dwarf, North American, perennial herb, with thick, prostrate root-stock, and white, handsome flowers during April and May. It is quite hardy, and is usually grown in the rock-garden, but can be used for growing in pans for the alpine house. It prefers a light, sandy, loamy soil, and the pans should be plunged to their rims in ashes until the flower-buds appear. It grows 6 inches high.

*Propagation.*—It is propagated by means of division, which should be done when the leaves have died—about August. The var. *plena* has an extra number of narrow petals.

**Sansevieria** (Bow-string Hemp), *Liliaceæ.*—Tender, decorative, green-house plants, useful for growing in pots for room or window decoration. Although beautiful in flower, they are usually grown for their foliage, which is erect, stiff, and usually variegated, barred or striped.

*Culture.*—They are interesting plants, thriving in good, sandy loam, with abundant water during the summer, but little in winter. They will last for a number of years without being re-potted.

*Propagation.*—They are readily increased by division, or they may be raised from leaf-cuttings, made about 3 inches long and inserted in sandy soil. Roots appear after three or four weeks, and later a bud is formed which produces a new plant.

*Species.*—*S. cylindrica* [Tropical Africa] has whitish flowers in August, and cylindrical, solid, dark-green leaves, often banded with lighter lines, 30–40 inches long. *S. thyrsiflora* (*S. guineensis*) [Tropical Africa] bears fragrant, greenish-white flowers in September. Both surfaces of the leaves are marked with pale-green, transverse bands, which become paler with age. The leaves are 30–40 inches long. *S. zeylanica* [Ceylon] has leaves which are 15–25 inches long. They are dark green, variegated, with transverse whitish markings, and darker-green longitudinal lines on the back, the margins being distinctly red-lined. It carries greenish-white flowers in September. A plant grown as *S. z.* var. *Laurentii,* from the Belgian Congo, has long, narrow leaves, longitudinally striped with golden yellow.

**Saponaria** (Soapwort), *Caryophyllaceæ.*—This genus includes the beautiful hardy annual *S. Vaccaria,* sometimes known as *Vaccaria pyramidata,* a native of Europe, which grows about 20–24 inches in height and carries delicate clusters of rose-pink or, in the case of *S. V. alba,* white flowers in late summer or late spring in the open or in the cold greenhouse. They are excellent as cut flowers.

*Culture.*—Sow seed in the open in April or under glass in September. Transplant when large enough to handle and pot-up, placing four or five seedlings in a 4- to 5-inch pot of dry, light, gritty loam, and stand in a sunny position. Winter September-sown plants in a cold frame. Give ample air, and keep the roots moist.

Several dwarf species are charming for the alpine house. They should be grown in pans of well-drained soil and plunged in a cold frame in a sunny position when not in flower.

*Species.*—*S. cæspitosa* [Pyrenees] (rose, May–June, 3–6 in.) ; *S. lutea* [Alps] (yellow, June, 3–5 in.).

**Sarcocaulon,** *Geraniaceæ.*—An interesting group of South African, succulent or fleshy, greenhouse sub-shrubs with purple flowers, armed with spines, which are the remains of persistent and hardened leaf-stalks.

*Culture.*—They thrive in a cool house with plenty of air during the summer, with similar conditions to those given to other succulent plants. The compost should consist of loam, leaf-mould, and sand, with good drainage.

*Propagation.*—They are propagated by means of seed sown in sandy soil, by cuttings of young shoots placed in sand under glass, or by root-cuttings.

*Species.*—*S. Burmanii* grows 6–10 inches high, and blooms in May. The leaves are fleshy, and the petals are twice the length of the sepals. *S. Patersonii* grows 16–20 inches high, and also flowers in May, but the flowers are smaller than those of the preceding species, and the petals are not twice the length of the sepals.

**Sarmienta repens,** *Gesneriaceæ.*—A glabrous, creeping, greenhouse shrub from Chile, with thin, wiry stems, and solitary, urn-shaped, scarlet flowers.

*Culture.*—It should be planted in a small pan or Orchid basket, given plenty of drainage, in fibrous peat mixed with chopped sphagnum and charcoal. It can also be successfully grown on pieces of tree-fern stem. It requires plenty of water during the summer, shade from the bright sunshine, and a position near the glass in a cool, moist greenhouse. A house in which **Lapageria** will grow suits it.

*Propagation.*—It is increased by means of cuttings of half-ripened shoots placed in sandy peat under a bell-glass in a cool house, or by division of the shoots, which root at the nodes as they run.

**Sarracenia** (Side-saddle Flower, Trumpet Leaf, etc.), *Sarraceniaceæ.*—Interesting and curious half-hardy perennial herbs from North America. The radical leaves are hollow and pitcher-shaped, and are usually provided with a lid or expanded blade. The flower is rather strange, with a five-partite, umbrella-shaped style. With the exception of *S. purpurea*, which can be grown outside in favourable districts, they all need a cool greenhouse, and one that is kept rather moist. A moderately cool house with a moist, close atmosphere is essential, and the temperature may fall almost to freezing point in the winter.

*Culture.*—Pot-up in a mixture of three parts of fibrous peat, one part of chopped sphagnum, and some charcoal. Plenty of drainage is

**534**

necessary to ensure that the compost does not become sour from the amount of water it needs during the growing season. Alkaline water being detrimental, soft water should always be used, and occasional liquid manure will be appreciated. Less water is required during the winter, but the plants should never be allowed to become dry. When growing they should have a bright, sunny exposure, and be kept near the glass; in such a position better-coloured pitchers are obtained. It is a good plan to stand the pot permanently in a saucer of water.

*Propagation.*—Propagation is effected by means of division in the early spring, at the time of potting before the growth becomes active. These should be kept in a close frame for a few weeks, as the plants resent disturbance. They can also be raised from seed, and it is quite a good plan to sow them in the pot round the old plant if there is room. They germinate in about four weeks. As the young pitcher leaves appear, the seedlings should be pricked out.

*Species.*—*S. Drummondii* grows 10–30 inches high, and has pitchers richly purple veined, variegated white. It is the richest in colour and the most striking of all. The var. *alba* has green pitchers with pure-white variegation. *S. flava* grows 10–25 inches high, and has yellowish-green pitchers, reddish at the base and netted with purple veins. *S. purpurea* (Huntsman Cup) has spreading pitchers, inflated, contracted at the throat, varying in colour from green to dark purple. The sunnier the position the more purple the pitchers. This is the hardiest species, and can be grown outdoors in some districts.

There are other species as well as many beautiful hybrids that have been artificially raised.

**Satin Flower** (see **Sisyrinchium**).

**Satyrium** (see Chapter on **Orchids**).

**Sauromatum,** *Araceæ.*—Curious, warm-greenhouse, or half-hardy, tuberous-rooted, herbaceous perennials. Although the two species mentioned may be grown outside in a sheltered position, they are generally grown in a cool house. The spathe, which is produced before the foliage, is usually purple and variously spotted. The handsome, solitary leaves are pedately parted. Pot them up in the autumn in fibrous loam, and peat or leaf-mould in equal proportions, with some sand.

*Propagation.*—Propagation is effected by means of offsets taken from the parent plant at the time of planting.

*Species.*—*S. guttatum* [Himalayas] (spring, leaf-stalk not spotted, 30–36 in.); *S. venosum* [Himalayas] (spring, leaf-stalk spotted, 40 in.).

**Saxifraga** (Saxifrage or Rockfoil), *Saxifragaceæ.*—This large genus contains many choice plants suitable for growing in pans in the alpine house, where they give a wonderful display during February, March, April, and May. Botanically they are divided into a number of groups, but only certain species of these groups are touched upon from a garden point of view. These will be dealt with, together with any special treatment they may need.

*General Culture.*—Saxifrages are all readily increased by seed, which is generally best sown as soon as ripe, or by cuttings or division, which can easily be cared for in a cold frame, either in sand or in pots of sandy soil. Young plants should be grown-on in small pots, which should be kept plunged in ashes in a cold frame in such a position as each group should require. When the plants are established they should be selected for making up the pans, preferably when in flower, as any variation can then be detected, rather than have a mixture in the pan. The compost should be open, and according to the various requirements of certain groups, and the pans should be well-drained. Three plants should go to a 5-inch pan or four to a 6-inch pan. Pieces of rock-stone (either limestone or sandstone, according to the groups), greatly add to the appearance, as well as being beneficial to the plants. Such pans will give a good display for a number of years with nothing else but an annual cleaning, top dressing, and attention to drainage. With regard to the large rosette kinds, one plant in a 5- or 6-inch pot gives the best results.

*Dactyloides Group, or Mossy Saxifrage.*—These make compact, mossy tufts and are of easy cultivation. They are very valuable not only on account of the wealth of flower in the summer, but also because of their evergreen foliage, which is very beautiful even in the depth of winter. They prefer a mixture of loam, leaf-mould, and silver sand and a cool, half-shady position. The red-coloured varieties retain their colour best when grown in the shade, and better results are obtained by dividing the plants annually; or, if cuttings are taken after blooming, pricked out thickly in pans, and stood in a close frame until rooted, they make well-furnished pans the following spring, giving a mass of flowers during the following early summer. There are many varieties, with white, pink, and red flowers.

*Species.*—*S. cæspitosa* [Northern and Arctic regions] (white, June, 3–5 in.); *S. Camposii* [*S. Wallacei*] (white, June–July, 4–6 in.); this is an attractive plant whose showy flowers can be used for cutting. *S. decipiens* [Europe] (white or pink, May–June, 4–6 in.); this is a very variable plant in cultivation and is the source of some of the red, mossy Saxifrages, e.g. vars. *bathoniensis*, *Clibranii*, *grandiflora*, etc. *S. moschata* [Central and S. Europe] (yellowish, occasionally rose or purple, May–June, 4–5 in.); this is also a very variable plant which includes several good red-coloured forms, e.g. *atropurpurea*, *Guildford Seedling*, *Rhei*, *Rhei superba*, and *versicolor*.

*Euaizoonia Group or Encrusted Saxifrages.*—These form flat rosettes more or less encrusted with a silvery deposit, chiefly on the edge of the leaves. From the rosettes rise tall, loose spikes of flowers. This group requires a sunny position, well-drained, gritty loam, and a fair supply of lime rubble. They are mostly easy to cultivate, and are increased by means of seed or division, producing no offsets.

*Species.*—*S. Aizoon* [Northern and Arctic regions] (yellowish white, June, 6 in.). The following two are varieties and geographical forms of this species : *S. catalaunica* [Spain] (white, May–June, 12–18 in.); and *S. cochlearis* [Maritime Alps] (white, June–July, 6–8 in.); *S. Cotyledon* [mts. of Europe] (white tinged rose, May–July, 10–30 in.); the side rosettes of this species should be removed as they develop, continually growing the one rosette on; a handsome plume of flowers is thus obtained. There are several handsome varieties, e.g. var. *icelandica*, perhaps the largest form; var. *pyramidalis*, with large pyramidal panicles of white flowers speckled with crimson; var. *pyrenaica*, with shorter plumes of pure white flowers. All the varieties respond to the treatment of *S. Cotyledon*. *S. lingulata* [S. Europe] (white, June–July, 18–24 in.). There are several popular varieties of this species, e.g *australis*, *Bellardii*, and *lantoscana*. *S. longifolia* (Queen of Saxifrages) [Pyrenees] (white, June–July, 18–24 in.); has a handsome rosette of greyish-green leaves with silvery edge. The true *S. longifolia* does not produce offsets. *S. Tumbling Water* is a superb hybrid of *S. longifolia* with probably *S. lingulata*. It forms a magnificent rosette of silver leaves, finally producing a handsome plume, 24–30 inches long, of pure snow-white flowers. The rosette dies, but offsets are freely produced. *S. Macnabiana* (white, heavily speckled with pink to purple, May–June, 10–12 in.); a beautiful hybrid.

*Kabschia Group, or Cushion Saxifrages.*—This is an important group containing many of the most beautiful of our Rockfoils. They form compact cushions, and commence flowering in February. Many beautiful hybrid Kabschia Saxifrages have been raised in recent years. They like a light, gritty, well-drained loam, and when making up the pans pieces of rock should be wedged amongst the plants. They prefer an open position, although the *Burseriana* set seems to appreciate a little shade. The species may come true from seed, but hybrids are unlikely to do so. Cuttings are made of single rosettes taken after the plant has flowered. They should be struck in sand, although some of the stronger-growing kinds may be increased by division.

*Species and Hybrids.*— × *S. apiculata* [garden origin] (yellow, Feb., 3–4 in.); one of the oldest and the best of the hybrid Kabschias. There is also a white variety. *S. Burseriana* [Central European mts.] (Jan.–April, 2–4 in.); a variable plant, but one of the loveliest of all the Kabschias, with its domed cushions of pointed, bluish-green leaves and pure white flowers on bright red stems. *S. Burseriana* and its varieties, *brookside*, *crenata*, *gloria*, and *sulphurea*, and the beautiful hybrids of it, e.g. *bursiculata*, *Elizabethæ*, *Irvingii*, *Jenkinsæ*, *Kellerei*, *kewensis*, and others are among the most beautiful of our early-flowering Saxifrages for the alpine house. *S. diapensioides* [Alps] (flowers large and white, March–April, 3 in.); forms hard, dense cushions. *S. Grisebachii* [Macedonia] (spikes of pinkish flowers with crimson-velvet bracts, March, 4–6 in.). The *Wisley variety* (*S. G. wisleyana*) is a distinct form. The flower-spikes are thicker and bolder and the velvety colouring much brighter. *S. lilacina* [W. Himalayas] (rosy lilac or purple, March–April, 1 in.). This makes a good pan specimen for the alpine house. This plant has taken a very important part as a parent in the production of many of the beautiful pink- and rose-coloured Kabschia hybrids of recent years. *S. media* [Pyrenees] (flesh colour or purplish, June, 3 in.); *S. Rocheliana* [S.E. Europe] (white, April–May, 2–3 in.); *S. sancta* [Macedonia] (orange-yellow, June, 2 in.); *S. scardica* [Balkans] (pure white, March, 3–4 in.); *S. Stribrnyi* [Bulgaria] (flowers carmine, calyx reddish purple, Feb.–April, 4–5 in.); *S. thessalica* [E. Europe and N.E. Asia Minor] (violet-purple. April, 2–5 in.). There is great confusion regarding the name of this plant : it is sometimes known as *S. porophylla*, but the correct name is probably *S. Frederici-Augusti*.

*Porphyrion Group or Creeping Saxifrages.*—This group is limited to a few species, of which *S. oppositifolia* is the best known. They form close mats of creeping stems, and will be found to succeed best in lime-free soil. A little shade is beneficial, particularly in the drier parts of the country. They prefer a light, gritty loam; if the soil is too rich they will make too much leaf and will not flower well. They are increased by means of cuttings or division after flowering.

*Species.*—*S. biflora* [Mts. of Europe] (deep violet or purplish crimson, April–June, 2 in.); *S. oppositifolia* [Northern and Arctic regions] (violet, lilac, or rosy purple, May–June, trailing). An excellent little rock-plant of which there are many beautiful varieties : *alba* (white) *coccinea* (rich purple), *latina* (rosy purple), *major* (rich crimson-red), *speciosa* (pale rose), *splendens* (purplish crimson). *S. retusa* [S. European Alps] (ruby to purplish red, May–June, 1–2 in.).

Apart from those already mentioned, many beautiful hybrid Saxifraga have been raised in recent years, some giving a wonderful range of delicate shades of rose or pink, others yellow and white. All the following are more or less connected with the Kabschia group, and require the same cultural treatment.

× *S. "Arco-Valleyi"* (shell-pink, March, 1 in.); × *S. "Boydii"* (yellow, March, 1–2 in.); × *S. "bursiculata"* (white, March, 3 in.); × *S. "Cherry Trees"* (pale yellow, 1–2 in.); × *S. "Delight"* (deep pink, Feb., 2 in.); × *S. "Faldonside"* (lemon-yellow, Feb.–March, 2 in.); × *S. "Haagei"* (golden yellow, March–April, 2–3 in.); × *S. "His Majesty"* (white, red centre, March, 3 in.); × *S. "Irvingii"* (pink, March, 1 in.); × *S. "Jenkinsæ"* (soft pink, Feb.–March, 1 in.); × *S. "Myra"* (deep pink, March, 1–2 in.); × *S. "Riverslea"* (rich crimson, Feb.–March, 1 in.); *S. "Salomonii"* (white, Feb.–March, 1–2 in.).

Other Saxifraga worth growing in the alpine house are : *S. Brunoniana* [Himalayas], which bears yellow flowers in June and July and reddish, threadlike runners, which produce young plants. It prefers light loam, free from lime, and a semi-shady position. *S. Fortunei* [Japan] (white, Sept.–Oct., 12–20 in.); an attractive, autumn-flowering plant, and useful for the greenhouse. *S. sarmentosa* (Mother of Thousands) [China and Japan] is an old-fashioned greenhouse or window plant, and an ideal basket-plant. It is more suitable for the conservatory or cool greenhouse, and is attractive the whole year round. The flowers, borne in summer, are white with yellow and scarlet spots. The var. *tricolor*, with creamy-white and red variegation, is a handsome greenhouse foliage plant, but more tender than the type. Both can be readily increased by runners.

**Scabiosa** (Scabious or Pincushion Flower), *Dipsacaceæ.*—This genus of flowers, consisting of a disc studded with numerous stamens, which have obtained for them the name of "Pincushion Flower", and surrounded with petals of blue, lavender, rose, purple, or yellow-white, is fairly large, and comprises many beautiful annuals, biennials, and perennials. They grow from 6 to 60 inches in height, and bloom from

May to September, thriving in sunny, open borders, and in well-drained, rich, light soil. They also make good pot-plants (particularly *S. atropurpurea* and its varieties) for bearing winter bloom. For this purpose seed should be sown in June or July. The plants, when large enough, should be potted-off and grown on in a cool frame, and taken into the greenhouse in September. The flowers, especially those of the annuals, are useful for cutting.

*Culture.*—ANNUALS : Sow seed of Sweet Scabious thinly, early in March under glass in slight heat, and prick-off into boxes about three weeks later. Keep in a warm frame. Pot-up singly in April, and pot-on into 5- or 6-inch pots. Seed sown in September, pricked out into small pots for the winter and potted-on in the spring give a good display in the greenhouse in April and May, and very valuable cut flowers.

BIENNIALS : Sow seed in June in Boxes. When 1 inch high plant out 3 inches apart in the reserve garden for the summer, pot-up in the autumn, and protect in a frame during the winter. Pot-on in flowering-pots in the early spring. Several of the perennial species are better treated as biennials.

PERENNIALS : Sow seed in the open in July, lift in October and winter in a frame, put into 6- or 8-inch pots in March. To ensure trueness to type propagate by division in March or October, and plant out in positions 12 inches apart in warm borders of light rich soil. Cover the crowns with small conical piles of ashes or fibre during severe winters.

*Species.*—ANNUAL : *S. atropurpurea* [S. Europe]. *Named Varieties.* —*Black Prince* (maroon) ; *candidissima* (white) ; *Coral Pink* (pink) ; *Fairy* (pale lavender) ; *Fire King* (crimson) ; *Scarlet King* (scarlet) ; and *Yellow Prince* (yellow). All grow 24–36 inches high. PERENNIAL : *S. caucasica* [Caucasus] and vars. *Named Varieties of S. caucasica* : *Annie* (pale lavender) ; *Collarette* (violet) ; *Diamond* (violet-blue) ; *Edith* (silver-lavender) ; *Elsie* (pale blue) ; *Isaac House* (deep blue) ; *Mrs. House* (white) ; and *Princess* (deep lavender). All 24 to 36 inches. *S. lutea* (yellow, June–Oct., 60 in.).

**Scaphosepalum** (see Chapter on **Orchids**).

**Scarborough Lily** (see **Vallota purpurea**).

**Scarlet Plume** (see **Euphorbia fulgens**).

**Schaueria,** *Acanthaceæ.*—A half-shrubby stove plant with erect branches. The flowers are borne in erect, feathery panicles, yellow, orange, or red. They are closely related to **Jacobina,** and require the same cultural treatment.

*Species.*—*S. calycotricha* (*Justicia calycotricha*) [Brazil] (yellow, Feb., 18–24 in.) ; *S. flavicoma* (*J. flavicoma*) [Brazil] (light yellow, Feb., 24 in.). There has been a great deal of confusion regarding these two plants, as they greatly resemble each other. The former has a greenish-yellow calyx, minutely downy. In the latter the calyx has yellow glandular hairs and the leaves are longer and narrower.

**Schizanthus** (Butterfly Flower, Fringe Flower, Poor Man's Orchid), *Solanaceæ.*—Half-hardy Chilean annuals which thrive in a compost of two parts of fibrous loam to one part of leaf-mould and a little pounded mortar-rubble.

*Pot Culture.*—Sow several seeds in a 5-inch pot in September, and keep moderately moist in a temperature of 60° F. Thin out to five seedlings in each pot, and top the young plants occasionally. Winter on a sunny shelf near the glass in a cold greenhouse, and in February pot-up with three plants in 6- or 7-inch pots, staking carefully. Three weeks later nip out the heads. Or the seed **may** be sown thinly in a large 60 pot, thinning out to three seedlings and finally to one, and treating as above. Only slight heat is needed to bring the plants into bloom.

*Species.*—*S. Grahamii* (rose and orange); *S. pinnatus* [*S. grandiflorus*] (purple and white); *S. retusus* and vars. (salmon-rose and orange); × *wisetoniensis* (various). All flower from March to October, according to the time of sowing, and grow to a height of 18–48 inches.

**Schizocentron elegans (Heeria elegans),** *Melastomaceæ.*—A low, creeping plant forming a dense carpet, and rooting at the joints. A dainty ornamental plant for the cool greenhouse, suitable for growing on a tree-fern stem, as a basket-plant or on the top of large tubs containing palms and similar plants. The flowers are deep purple, and during May and June, when in full flower, make a striking display. It thrives best in a compost consisting of equal parts of loam and peat, with some sand.

*Propagation.*—It is propagated by cuttings of young shoots placed in sandy soil under a bell-glass in the warm greenhouse; or by division of the creeping plants, which root as they run.

**Schizostylis coccinea** (Kaffir Lily, Crimson Flag, or Winter Gladiolus), *Iridaceæ.*—This is a half-hardy South African plant, which increases freely by means of underground stolons or rhizomes. There is a fine rose-coloured variety named *Mrs. Hegarty*. These plants grow from 20 to 30 inches high, and flower in October and November. They thrive in sunny, sheltered borders with a south aspect, and moist but well-drained, light, rich soil. They are also useful for pot culture in the cool greenhouse.

*Pot Culture.*—Plant in November in a compost of two-thirds loam and one-third leaf-mould, well-rotted manure, and coarse sand. Stand in a cold frame, giving no water until growth commences. Sink the pots outdoors in a sunny position in summer, and late in September, when the buds show, transfer to the cold house. Dry off gradually after flowering, and keep partly dry in a frost-proof frame during the winter. Re-pot if necessary in March, and set out again in the open for the summer. Lift and divide the roots every few years in March, and propagate by means of offsets during that month.

**Schlumbergera,** *Cactaceæ.*—A genus of Cacti, often referred to as **Epiphyllum,** suitable for greenhouse culture, and, from their pendant habit of growth, useful for hanging-baskets. The brilliant succulent flowers are borne from March to May at the extremities of the short, jointed and flat stems. These plants grow from 10–24 inches in height. The most usual colours are violet, crimson, scarlet, and rose-pink.

*Culture.*—These plants like a partly shaded position in a mixture of equal parts of sand, fibrous loam, peat, and leaf-mould, with a little charcoal (average temperature 60° F. day, 50° F. night, winter;

80° F. day, 70° F. night, summer). Pot-up in well-drained pots (not too large) in March. Water well in summer and place in a warm, moist atmosphere. Keep slightly moist in winter.

*Propagation.*—Propagate by means of cuttings, four or five joints in length, taken just before the start of new growth in spring, and insert in sandy loam and crushed brick. Another method of increase is by grafting in March on *Pereskia aculeata, Selenicereus,* or *Hylocereus undulatus.*

Good species are : *S. Gærtneri* [*Epiphyllum Gærtneri*] (Easter Cactus) from Southern Brazil, (scarlet or rosy red, April–May) ; *S. Russelliana* (*Epiphyllum Russellianum*) [W. Brazil] (rosy red or violet-purple, April–May). There are various forms of both species.

**Schomburgkia** (see Chapter on **Orchids**).

**Schubertia grandiflora (Araujia grandiflora),** *Asclepiadaceæ.*—A climbing Brazilian shrub, for the warm greenhouse. It has loose umbels of large white flowers, the yellowish-coloured branches being covered with reddish-brown hairs. It succeeds with the same cultural treatment as **Stephanotis.**

**Scilla (Squill),** *Liliaceæ.*—The species of this genus are very numerous and easily grown, the best known being *S. nonscripta* (*S. nutans*), otherwise known as the Bluebell or Wild Hyacinth of Western Europe. They are hardy, spring-flowering, bulbous plants. Most species do well in warm, sunny borders, in the rock-garden or in pots in the greenhouse. Some of the dwarf kinds, such as *S. bifolia, S. sibirica,* and *S. verna,* are charming when grown in pans for the alpine house. They are also very useful for naturalising in grass and woodland.

*Pot Culture.*—Pot-up from August to November, placing about eight bulbs in a 5- to 6-inch pot, with the tops of the bulbs ½ inch below soil level, and use a compost of two parts of light rich loam to one part of leaf-mould. Keep the pots in a frame until growth starts, then transfer to the cold greenhouse (temperature 50° F.). Plunge the pots or pans in the open after flowering. Re-pot or top dress in the autumn.

*Propagation.*—Propagate by means of offsets in September.

*Species.*—*S. bifolia* [Europe and Asia Minor] and vars. (white, pink, blue, Feb.–March, 6 in.) ; *S. hispanica* and vars. (Spanish Squill) [Spain and Portugal] (white, pink, blue, April–May, 15–20 in.) ; *S. peruviana* (Peruvian Hyacinth) [Mediterranean region] (purple, lilac, or white, May–June, 6–10 in.) ; *S. sibirica* (Siberian Squill) [Russia and Asia Minor] (blue, white, March, 6 in.) ; and *S. verna* (Sea Onion) [W. Europe] (blue, spring, 6 in.), are amongst the best for pot culture.

**Scirpus** (Club Rush, or Bulrush), *Cyperaceæ.*—Hardy perennial marsh or aquatic plants of which *S. lacustris,* the Common Bulrush, is the best known.

*Pot Culture.*—*S. cernuus* (*S. gracilis*) [Cosmopolitan] is a greenhouse species thriving in a compost of two parts of loam to one part of leaf-mould and sand. It is a pretty little evergreen perennial with drooping, grass-like foliage, also known as *Isolepsis gracilis.* It is useful for cultivation in hanging-baskets and for the cool to warm greenhouse staging. Pot-up when required in March in a 6-inch pot and water liberally (average temperature 55° F. winter, 65° F. summer).

**541**

*Propagation.*—Propagate by means of division in March.

**Scolopendrium** (see **Phyllitis**).

**Scorpion Iris** (see **Iris alata**).

**Screw Pine** (see **Pandanus**).

**Scutellaria** (Skull-cap, Helmet Flower), *Labiatæ.*—Stove, greenhouse or hardy plants, including some of the most decorative plants for the stove or warm greenhouse.

*Species.*—*S. coccinea* [Colombia] (bright scarlet, summer, 18–24 in.) ; *S. costaricana* [Costa Rica] (rich bright scarlet, June, 18–30 in.) ; *S. Lehmannii* [Colombia] (bright scarlet, summer, 12–24 in.) ; *S. Mociniana* [Mexico] (bright red, yellow, summer, 15–18 in.) ; *S. splendens* [Mexico] (scarlet, autumn, 12–25 in.) ; *S. violacea* [India and Ceylon] (rich violet-blue, summer, 18–24 in.).

All are beautiful plants of easy culture, and may be grown in a warm greenhouse. Cuttings root readily in the spring, or at almost any season, in a warm propagating case. Young plants when growing should have their tips taken out once or twice to encourage a bushy habit, which means more flower. Nice little plants may be grown in 5-inch pots.

*Culture.*—They should have a compost of two parts of fibrous loam and one part each of leaf-mould and decayed manure, with a good sprinkling of sand. Several dwarf kinds which are attractive rock-garden plants can be grown in pans for the alpine house. They should be given a good open compost and drainage, and the pans should be plunged to their rims in a cold frame in a sunny position.

*Propagation.*—Propagation is effected by means of seed sown as soon as ripe, or by cuttings of young shoots placed in sand under a bell-glass in July.

*Alpine-house Species.*—*S. alpina* [Europe and Central Asia] (purple and yellow, Aug., 9 in.), and the vars. *alba*, *cærulea*, and *rosea*. *S. indica* var. *japonica* [Japan] (purple lilac, June–July, 4–6 in.) ; *S orientalis* [Altai Mts.] (yellow, or yellow and purple, Aug., 8–12 in.).

**Scuticaria** (see Chapter on **Orchids**).

**Scythian Lamb** (see **Cibotium Barometz**).

**Sea Lavender** (see **Limonium**).

**Sea Onion** (see **Scilla verna**).

**Sea Pink** (see **Armeria**).

**Sea Urchin Cactus** (see **Echinopsis**).

**Sedum** (Stonecrop), *Crassulaceæ.*—Sedums are very easy to cultivate, usually thriving in sandy soil. For the greenhouse, *S. Sieboldii* [Japan] and its variety *variegatum*, also *S. spectabile* [China and Japan] are general favourites. Most of the dwarf kinds make charming pans for the alpine house.

*Propagation.*—The majority of them are readily propagated from cuttings or divisions placed in sandy soil, as well as by seed sown as soon as ripe.

*Species.*—*S. brevifolium* [Mediterranean regions] (pinkish-grey foliage, 4 in.) ; *S. cæruleum* [Mediterranean regions] (blue, annual, 3 in.) ; *S. dasyphyllum* [Europe] (flowers white and pink, leaves studded with pimples) ; the var. *glanduliferum* is densely covered with hair, 2–3 inches,

*S. kamtschaticum* [Korea and Japan] (yellow, 6–8 in.) ; *S. Midden-dorffianum* [Amurland] (yellow, 6–12 in.) ; *S. obtusatum* [California] (flowers yellow, foliage reddish green, 2–5 in.) ; *S. pilosum* [Caucasus] (rose-pink, compact rosettes, biennial, 3–4 in.) ; *S. reflexum* [Europe] (yellow, trailing, 7–10 in.) ; *S. sempervivoides* [Asia Minor] (scarlet, 3–6 in.), a biennial with handsome rosettes.

**Selaginella,** *Selaginellaceæ.*—An extensive genus of stove, greenhouse, or hardy evergreen plants, resembling mosses, and allied to ferns. But, unlike ferns, the Selaginellas are readily increased by cuttings.

*Culture.*—Pot-up in spring, using well-crocked pots, and in the case of trailers, shallow pans, in ordinary loamy potting compost with plenty of coarse grit and a little peat or leaf-mould added. Water and syringe regularly while growing, and preserve a moist atmosphere by means of occasional damping down. Shade from strong sun.

The best-known hardy species is *S. helvetica* [Europe]. Eight useful cool greenhouse kinds are : *S. apus* [N. America] (dwarf) ; *S. Braunii* [W. China] (12–18 in.) ; *S. hæmatodes* [Venezuela] (handsome, fern-like, 9–15 in.) ; *S. Kraussiana* [Madeira] (trailer, for hanging-basket) ; *S. Martensii* [Mexico] (9–12 in.) ; *S. lepidophylla* (Resurrection Plant) [Texas and Mexico], often sold in a dry state, but if placed in a saucer of water the absorption of water will cause the ball to expand as though living ; *S. uncinata* [China] (trailer for hanging-basket) ; and *S. Watsoniana variegata* [garden origin]. Seven species for stove culture are *S. atroviridis* [India], *S. caulescens* [E. Indies], *S. Galeottei* [Mexico] (a beautiful basket-plant), *S. plumosa* [India and Ceylon], *S. serpens* [W. Indies], *S. Vogellii* [Africa], and *S. Willdenovii* [India], a climbing plant growing with age to a height of from 15 to 20 feet. It is one of the finest species with glaucous blue foliage.

**Selago,** *Selaginaceæ.*—Greenhouse, heath-like shrubs or sub-shrubs with flowers in terminal spikes. They can be grown in a cool green-house, and are of easy cultivation in sandy loam, leaf-mould, and sand.

*Propagation.*—They are propagated by means of cuttings of half-ripened shoots placed in sandy soil under a bell-glass with a little bottom heat. They should be pinched back once or twice to obtain bushy plants, and they can be grown in 5- or 6-inch pots. They are summer-flowering.

*Species.*—*S. corymbosa* [S. Africa] (white, 18–24 in.) ; *S. Gillii* [S. Africa] (pink, 6–8 in.) ; *S. serrata* [S. Africa] (blue, 12 in.).

**Selenicereus,** *Cactaceæ.*—Slender trailing or climbing cacti with fragrant nocturnal flowers. Allied to **Cereus,** they are sometimes included in that genus, and require the same cultural treatment.

*Species.*—*S. grandiflorus* (*Cereus grandiflorus*) [Jamaica] has large white flowers with yellow centres. The flowers are very beautiful, and when fully open measure nearly 12 inches in diameter. The stems are bluish-green with brownish spines. *S. Macdonaldiæ* (*C. Macdonaldiæ*) [Honduras] bears large white flowers in July. It is one of the largest flowers of the cacti family. *S. pteracanthus* (*C. nycticaulis*) [Mexico] has large white fragrant flowers, and is one of the commonest and best of the night-flowering species. *S. spinulosus* (*C. spinulosus*) [Mexico] carries white flowers with a pink tinge.

**Selenipedilum (Selenipedium)** (see **Phragmopedilum** and Chapter on Orchids).

**Selliera radicans,** *Goodeniaceæ.*—A dwarf creeping herb, rooting as it runs, bearing white, axillary, sessile flowers during the summer. It is almost hardy, and can be grown in a damp place in the rock-garden. When grown in pans it makes an interesting plant for the alpine house. It should be planted in retentive soil.

*Propagation.*—It is propagated by division in the spring, and grows 1–2 inches high.

**Semele androgyna [Ruscus androgynus]** (Climbing Butcher's Broom), *Liliaceæ.*—An ornamental, greenhouse, evergreen climber from Madeira and the Canary Islands. It has leaf-like, flattened branches, which function as leaves, upon whose sides are produced during April clusters of greenish-white flowers. These are followed later by red, globose berries. The plant is a strong grower, reaching 10–30 feet in height, or even more. It succeeds in a rich soil, and is increased by seed or by division.

**Sempervivum** (Houseleek), *Crassulaceæ.*—A large genus of curious, succulent plants, mostly hardy perennials, although some require the protection and warmth of a greenhouse. They are well suited to sunny chinks or bare ledges in the rockery. *S. arachnoideum* [Mts. of Europe], the Cobweb Houseleek, with its cobweb-like white down, is perhaps the best known. It grows about 5 inches high, and bears reddish-pink flowers in June. Other species are *S. calcareum* [France] (pale red); *S. ciliosum* [Bulgaria] (pale green); *S. glaucum* [Central Europe] (red); *S. montanum* [Pyrenees]; *S. soboliferum* (Hen and Chicken Houseleek) [Europe] (yellow); *S. tectorum* (Common Houseleek) [Europe] (pale red). They all make charming pans for the alpine house. They should have well-drained soil and be kept in an open, sunny position when not required inside. For culture of Sempervivums see Chapter devoted to the **Alpine House**, page 149.

**Senecio** (Groundsel or Ragwort, sometimes called **Farfugium, Jacobæa, Kleinia,** and **Cineraria**), *Compositæ.*—A large genus of annual and perennial plants, some hardy and others suitable only for the greenhouse, including the garden Cineraria (*Senecio hybrida*). The hardy types in cultivation like a moist, deep, and moderately light loam, and a sunny position, and are very suitable for growing in the marsh-garden or by the edge of water. They grow from 3 to 60 inches high, and flower in summer and autumn.

The kinds mostly grown in the greenhouse are half-hardy evergreen shrubby species with silver-grey, white, or ivy-like foliage, and yellow flowers, while others have large, handsome leaves, as in *S. grandifolius* and *S. Petasites*. Certain other species have angular, terete, or fleshy stems, often found among collections of succulent plants, and sometimes known as *Kleinias*.

*Greenhouse Culture.*—Pot-up in March in a compost of two-thirds fibrous loam, one-third sand, leaf-mould, and a little well-rotted manure, with the exception of the Kleinia group, which requires an open, well-drained, sandy soil and no manure. Water liberally in spring and summer, but keep fairly dry in autumn and winter. These

544

**PLATE 16**
The magnificent bloom of a pot-grown *Begonia*.

climbing kinds, such as *S. macroglossus* (Cape Ivy) and *S. mikanioides* (German Ivy), both from South Africa, may be trained up the pillars and along the roof of the greenhouse (average temperature 50° F. winter, 60° F. summer).

*Propagation.*—Propagate by means of seed sown and placed in a temperature of 60–65° F., or by cuttings struck in spring, in a frame, with slight bottom heat.

*Species.*—*S. articulatus* [*Kleinia articulata*] (Candle Plant) [S. Africa] (white, 12–18 in.) ; it has glabrous fleshy stems, the branches being swollen at intervals. It is the commonest Kleinia in cultivation, usually grown with South African succulents. *S. Cineraria* [*Cineraria maritima*] (Dusty Miller) [Europe], is white and woolly, and makes a useful pot-plant ; it is also used for summer bedding. *S. cruentus* [Canary Islands] (purplish red, spring, 24–30 in.). This is said to be the source of the florist's Cineraria. *S. fulgens* (*Kleinia fulgens*) [S. Africa] (bright-orange vermilion, May), a succulent sub-shrub. *S. Galpinii* (*Kleinia Galpinii*) [S. Africa] (orange, summer, 10–15 in.), a succulent sub-shrub. *S. grandifolius* [Mexico] is a shrub with large leaves and a big terminal head of yellow flowers during the winter, growing 4–12 feet high. *S. Grantii* (*Kleinia Grantii*) [E. Tropical Africa] (vermilion, summer, 10–12 in.) ; it resembles *S. fulgens*. The last three are very handsome plants. *S. Haworthii* [S. Africa] (yellow, July) ; a small, succulent greenhouse sub-shrub, covered with soft, snow-white wool. *S. Heritieri* [Canaries] is a small-leaved, scandent plant bearing white flowers tinged with pink. It is a parent of the well-known hybrid Senecio (Cineraria) *Beauty of Cambridge*, also of the more recent hybrids *Camden*, *Granta* and *Veronique*. *S. macroglossus* [S. Africa] is an evergreen climber with Ivy-like leaves. *S. mikanioides* [*Mikania senecioides*] (German Ivy) is a greenhouse evergreen climber with Ivy-shaped leaves. The last two species have yellow flowers. *S. Petasites* (Velvet Groundsel) [S. Mexico] is a handsome winter-flowering plant with large terminal heads of bright-yellow flowers and large, soft, velvety leaves. It somewhat resembles *S. grandifolius* *S. incanus* [European Alps], with its silvery leaves, and stems white with adpressed hairs. Charming in pans for the alpine house.

**Senecio hybrida,** the Cineraria of the florist (see **Cineraria**).

**Sensitive Plant** (see **Mimosa pudica**).

**Serpent** or **Snake Gourd** (see **Trichosanthes Anguina**).

**Shaggy Windflower** (see **Anemone vernalis**).

**Sheep's Laurel** (see **Kalmia angustifolia**).

**Sherwoodia** (see **Shortia**).

**Shooting Stars** (see **Dodecatheon**).

**Shortia** (**Sherwoodia**), *Diapensiaceæ.*—This genus contains one or two little creeping plants for culture in the alpine house.

*Culture.*—They require humus and leaf-mould and absolutely lime-free soil. They can be grown in pans, which should be kept in semi-shade, and on no account should the plants be allowed to get dry. They are worth growing for their foliage alone.

*Propagation.*—They are propagated by division or by means of seed, when obtainable.

M M                                                                    545

# THE GREENHOUSE

*Species.*—*S. galacifolia* [N. America] (white, spring, 4–8 in.). There is a rose-coloured variety. *S. uniflora* [Japan] (rosy pink, March–April, 3–6 in.) ; this is a more beautiful plant. The var. *grandiflora* has larger flowers. The foliage of both species assumes a rich crimson colour in autumn and winter.

**Siberian Squill** (see **Scilla sibirica**).

**Sibthorpia,** *Scrophulariaceæ.*—This genus includes one or two little creeping perennial plants, useful for hanging-baskets in the cold greenhouse.

*Culture.*—Take cuttings in August and strike in sandy soil in a frame, or propagate by means of division of the roots in April and plant out or pot-up for greenhouse decoration, or grow in pans for the alpine house.

*Species.*—*S. europæa* [Europe] (yellow, 1 in.) ; *S. e. variegata ;* and *S. peregrina* [Mauritius] (yellow, July).

**Side-saddle Flower** (see **Sarracenia**).

**Silene,** *Caryophyllaceæ.*—This genus includes some species that are sometimes placed under **Melandrium** and **Heliosperma.** Most of this genus is perfectly hardy, and the dwarf kinds are beautiful, valuable rock-garden subjects, most of which can be grown in pans for the alpine house.

*Culture.*—They should be planted in a good, loamy, well-drained soil, and the pans should be plunged in an open position in a cold frame.

*Propagation.*—They are propagated by means of seed sown as soon as ripe, by cuttings in July placed in sand under a bell-glass, or by division.

*Species.*—*S. acaulis* [Cushion Pink, or Moss Campion] (pink, sometimes white, June–Aug., 2 in.) ; *S. alpestris [Heliosperma alpestre]* (white, May–July, 5–6 in.) ; *S. Elizabethæ (Melandrium Elizabethæ)* [Italy] (rose, July, 9 in.) ; *S. Hookeri (Melandrium Hookeri)* [California] (pale pink, May, 5–6 in.) ; a beautiful alpine plant. *S. quadrifida (Heliosperma quadrifida)* [E. Europe] (white, May–June, 3–4 in.) ; *S. Schafta* [Caucasus] (rose or purple, June–August., 6–8 in.).

**Silk-bark Tree** (see **Grevillea robusta**).

**Silver Tree** (see **Leucodendron argenteum**).

**Sinningia,** *Gesneriaceæ.*—Stove- or warm-greenhouse, tuberous-rooted plants, with handsome, tubular flowers, all natives of Brazil. They are allied to **Isoloma** and **Gesneria,** and require the same cultural treatment. The cultivated *Gloxinia*, which is *Sinningia speciosa,* or hybrid offsprings of it, is dealt with under **Gloxinia,** which see.

*Species.*—*S. concinna* is a neat little plant with purple flowers, yellowish beneath and spotted inside. They bloom in summer and autumn. The var. *grandiflora* is larger, with lilac-blue flowers—a handsome greenhouse plant. *S. Helleri* [Brazil] produces flowers with a red calyx and a white corolla spotted with red, in June. *S. Regina* [Brazil] has drooping, pale-violet flowers in clusters of four to six. The leaves are velvety on the upper surface, with white veins. *S. speciosa* [Brazil] has violet or purple flowers. It is a variable plant, giving rise to several beautiful and interesting forms. This species is one of the parents of the garden Gloxinia, which see.

**Sisyrinchium** (Satin Flower, Rush Lily), *Iridaceæ.*—Hardy perennials,

546

useful in the border, the rock-garden or the alpine house. A cool and fairly moist loam, with one-third part leaf-mould and sand, or sandy peat, suits them best. They produce graceful, satiny, bell-shaped flowers of yellow, blue, or purple, from April to June.

*Pot Culture.*—Pot-up annually in the above compost in September and place in a sunny position in the cold greenhouse or frame. Keep moderately dry until growth commences in the spring, then water liberally. After blooming, keep in a cold frame until re-potting time again comes round.

*Propagation.*—Propagate by means of seed sown in the spring or by division of the roots in February or September.

*Species.*—S. *angustifolium* [N. America] (light blue, May–July, 5–10 in.) ; S. *Bermudianum* [Bermuda] (deep blue, May–June, 10 in.) ; S. *californicum* [California] (yellow, May–July, 12–18 in.) ; S. *filifolium* [Falkland Islands] (white, March–May, 6–8 in.) ; S. *grandiflorum* [N. America] (purple, March–May, 10 in.) ; S. *iridifolium* [Chile] (creamy yellow, June–July, 12–24 in.).

**Skimmia,** *Rutaceæ.*—Hardy evergreen shrubs, some 2–3 feet in height, with small, fragrant flowers in April, followed in autumn and winter by clusters of attractive scarlet berries. S. *Foremanii*, a hybrid of the common species S. *japonica* [Japan] and S. *Fortunei* [China], makes a useful pot-plant for decoration in the cold greenhouse. As Skimmias are mostly unisexual, it will be necessary to have some staminate plants growing among the pistillate plants to ensure pollination and a good display of berries ; or the female flowers can be cross-pollinated by hand, from a male plant that may be growing in the open.

*Culture.*—Pot-up in March or October, using well-crocked pots, the size required varying according to the size of the plants, and a compost of rich loam. No pruning is necessary. Stand in a sunny position.

*Propagation.*—Propagate by means of cuttings or layers in the summer.

**Skull Cap** (see **Scutellaria**).

**Slipper Flower** (see **Calceolaria**).

**Slipper Spurge** (see **Pedilanthus tithymaloides**).

**Smilacina** (False Solomon's Seal), *Liliaceæ.*—Perennial herbs with creeping root-stock. They are easily cultivated in any good soil, but prefer a moist, though not wet, position, preferably in partial shade. They are handsome plants both in flower and foliage, the flowers being whitish green, borne in terminal panicles or racemes. Although quite hardy, they are very decorative for the cold greenhouse, and by slow forcing may be had in flower during the early spring.

*Culture.*—Pot-up in the early autumn in a compost of fibrous loam, leaf-mould, and sand. The pots should be kept outside in a partly shaded position until they are required in the house. Give an occasional watering as growth develops, and when well established allow plenty of water. They are increased by division.

They were at one time known as **Vagnera,** a name not now recognised.

*Species.*—S. *paniculata* [Mexico] (panicles of snow-white flowers, May, 30–40 in.) ; S. *racemosa* (False Spikenard) [N. America] (dense panicles of numerous white flowers, May, 15–30 in.) ; this species is probably the most attractive and the best for forcing. *S. stellata* [N.W. America] (dense racemes of white flowers, May–June, 20–30 in.).

**Smilax,** *Liliaceæ.*—Beautiful, quick-growing, evergreen, climbing plants with attractive foliage. They thrive in the cool greenhouse in a mixture of two parts of loam to one part of leaf-mould and sand, and are very useful for indoor decoration when cut.

*Culture.*—Pot-up in March, using 10- to 12-inch pots, stand in semi-shade, syringe and water well morning and evening in hot weather (average temperature 50° F. winter, 60° F. summer). Train the climbing stems up strings or wires stretched from the ground to the roof of the house and running up within 3 or 4 inches of the back wall. Or they may be planted out in the greenhouse border, although their roots should be restricted. Cut old plants right back each March.

*Propagation.*—Propagate by means of seed sown during the spring in a temperature of 60–65° F., or by division in March.

*Species.*—There are a number of hardy climbing Smilax, the best-known being *S. aspera* [S. Europe] (white, sweet-scented flowers, red berries) ; *S. lanceolata* (Florida Smilax) [N. America] (berries remain on during winter) ; and *S. rotundifolia* (Horse-Brier) [N. America] (bluish-black berries).

**Smilax of Florist** (see **Asparagus asparagoides**).
**Snake's Beard** (see **Ophiopogon**).
**Snake's Head** (see **Fritillaria Meleagris**).
**Snake's Tongue** (see **Ophioglossum vulgatum**).
**Snapdragon** (see **Antirrhinum**).
**Snowball Tree** (see **Viburnum Opulus sterile**).
**Snowbush** (see **Phyllanthus nivosus**).
**Snowdrop** (see **Galanthus**).
**Snowflake** (see **Leucojum**).
**Soapwort** (see **Saponaria**).
**Sobralia macrantha** (see Chapter on **Orchids**).
**Solandra,** *Solanaceæ.*—Beautiful climbers for the warm greenhouse, with large, trumpet-shaped flowers. They can either be grown up the wall or used for training up a pillar. If room permits they may be planted out, but if given too much space they will grow rampant without blooming. They can be grown successfully in large pots, and will be found to flower quite freely.

*Culture.*—They like plenty of light and sunshine all the year round, and will thrive in any good sandy loam with plenty of drainage. They should have an abundance of water during the growing season, but this should be withheld until the leaves commence to fall, and the plants kept dry for a time. This drastic treatment generally induces the plants to flower freely. Thin out the old exhausted wood occasionally.

*Propagation.*—They are propagated by means of cuttings of firm young shoots taken with a " heel ", placed in bottom heat in sandy soil, and if cuttings of flowering shoots are taken, they will give small flowering plants.

*Species.*—*S. grandiflora* (Trumpet Flower) [Tropical America] grows 10–15 feet high and bears fragrant flowers which are greenish in bud, white when open, and rich brownish yellow as they age. *S. Hartwegii*

[Mexico] grows 10–20 feet high, and in the spring bears large yellow flowers, which are brownish purple inside.

**Solanum Capsicastrum** (Berried Solanum or Star Capsicum), *Solanaceæ*. —Beautiful, evergreen, greenhouse shrubs, which do well in a compost of rich loam, peat, and sand, in the warm house, and which in winter bear red, cherry-like berries. There are several very good forms and varieties grown for their large berries. Of these, the hybrid known as *Weatherillii* is excellent. All the hybrid forms are crosses between *S. Capsicastrum* and *S. Pseudo-capsicum* (Jerusalem Cherry).

*Culture.*—Sow seed in March (temperature 60° F.), or strike cuttings of young growth in February in moderate heat. Pinch back when 4 inches high, pot-up in June in 5-inch pots, and stand outdoors in a sunny, sheltered position for the summer, as the flowers will be found to pollinate more readily outside. Pinch back again two or three times before July, and early in October move into the house, and place near the glass. Syringe overhead when the weather is warm and bright, and feed twice a week alternately with weak manure water and soot-water (temperature 45–55° F.).

*Pruning.*—Cut back shoots of old plants in February.

**Solanum jasminoides** (Jasmine Nightshade).—A half-hardy, climbing perennial from Brazil, which should be grown in leaf-mould, sand, and loam, mixed in equal proportions, and in warm and sheltered positions, or in a greenhouse in cold districts. It carries light-blue flowers from June to October. *S. j.* var. *album* has pure white flowers. *S. Seaforthianum* [Brazil] is a beautiful, dainty, slender climber or twiner, resembling the previous species, but not so rampant. The flowers are light purple or blue, and bloom from July to October. The plant grows 3–6 feet high, and makes a good pot-plant. There is also a white variety. *S. Wendlandii* [Costa Rica] is a magnificent climber for the roof of the cool greenhouse. It is a handsome plant with large trusses of pale lilac-blue flowers during the summer. It should be planted in poor soil or otherwise have its roots restricted, as it is a rampant grower. It should be cut back hard each year before growth commences.

*Propagation.*—It is readily propagated from cuttings.

*Culture.*—All are propagated by means of cuttings of young wood in a frame with bottom heat during March. Cut back any weak shoots during February.

*S. crispum* [Chile] hardy in many parts, can be grown under similar conditions, and is an attractive climber or shrub up to 10 feet or more, and carries bluish-purple flowers from June to September. *S. marginatum* [Abyssinia] grows 2–3 feet high, and its leaves, spines and stem are silvery white. *S. Melongena* var. *esculentum* (Common Egg Plant, or Aubergine) [India]. Although used for greenhouse decoration in 5- or 6-inch pots, it is extensively grown as a vegetable, requiring the temperature and conditions of a tomato house, but care must be taken to protect it from red spider and mite. To ensure large fruit, the flowers should be artificially pollinated. There are a number of forms, differing in shape or colour of fruit, e.g. black, purple, striped, or white. All are readily raised from seed sown in heat. *S. pyracanthum* [Africa] grows 2–3 feet high and has handsome leaves and orange spines. *S. Warsce-*

*wiczii* [S. America] grows 3–4 feet high, and has handsome leaves and greenish-yellow spines. All are handsome plants, and treated as annuals are decorative and valuable for the conservatory or for sub-tropical bedding.

**Soldanella,** *Primulaceæ.*—Pretty little dwarf perennial herbs from the mountains of Europe. Although hardy, and useful for the rock-garden, they can be grown successfully in pans for the alpine house.

*Culture.*—They should be planted in well-drained, lime-free soil, consisting of loam, peat, and sand, and a quantity of granite chippings, with good drainage. They should be given plenty of water during the summer, but should be kept dry during the resting season, although never allowed to become quite dry.

*Propagation.*—They are propagated by division directly after flowering, when any potting or top dressing should be done ; or by means of seed sown as soon as ripe in fine peat and sand. Plants should be kept in a cold frame during the winter to keep off the wet, which is detrimental.

*Species.*—*S. alpina* [Blue Moonwort] (violet with dark streaks, May, 3–4 in.) ; *S. minima* (very small, pale-lilac flowers, striped purple inside, spreading fringe, April, 2 in.) ; *S. montana* [E. Europe] (purple, very deeply cut fringe, April–May, 3 in.) ; *S. pusilla* (coppery to blue, wavy, May, 4–6 in.) ; *S. p.* var. *alba* is a pretty white-flowered form.

**Solenophora Endlicheriana (Arctocalyx Endlicherianus).** *Gesneriaceæ.*—A Mexican, stove, evergreen shrub, with beautiful orange-coloured flowers with purple markings, leaves large and hairy, the stems erect and purplish. It requires warm, moist conditions and a compost of fibrous loam, leaf-mould, and sand.

*Propagation*—It is propagated by means of cuttings of matured wood placed in a close case with bottom heat. It grows to a height of from 12 to 20 inches, and blooms in April.

**Sollya heterophylla** (Australian Bluebell Creeper), *Pittosporaceæ.*—Half-hardy Australian evergreen climbing plants, some 6–7 feet in height, with clusters of rich blue flowers in late spring and summer. They are suitable for growing on pillars or trellis in the cool greenhouse.

*Culture.*—Pot-up or plant in a prepared site in the greenhouse bed in March, or in well-drained 5- or 6-inch pots of sandy loam and peat. Water regularly, and syringe while growing. Keep just moist in winter.

*Propagation.*—Propagation may be carried out by means of cuttings made of new shoots in spring or summer, and struck in pots of sandy soil under a bell-glass.

*S. Drummondii* has flowers in pairs or solitary, and is very similar to *S. heterophylla* and *S. parviflora*, but is more slender and twining.

**Solomon's Seal** (see **Polygonatum**).

**Sonerila,** *Melastomaceæ.*—Stove herbs or small shrubs, some of which are attractive foliage plants which can be grown all the year round.

*Culture.*—They thrive best in a close, moist atmosphere in a temperature of not less than 75° F. The compost should consist of fibrous peat, broken small, a small quantity of chopped sphagnum, and some sand, to which should be added some bits of charcoal or crocks. They are shallow-rooting plants, and should be given plenty of drainage. They prefer partial shade, and should never be syringed ; care should be taken to see that water never remains on the leaves.

*Propagation.*—Propagation is effected by means of cuttings of ripened growth placed under a bell-glass in a mixture of fine peat, silver sand, and some fine-chopped sphagnum, in a bottom heat of 70–80° F. Care should be taken to prevent condensation on the glass falling on to the foliage. When the plants begin to flower, water should be gradually withheld, and they may be kept a little cooler. They can also be increased by means of seed, often freely produced ; and by division.

*Species.*—*S. margaritacea* [Java] has rose-coloured flowers. The upper surface of the leaves is dark-green with rows of oval, pearly-like spots ; the under surface is purple, and the stems are bright red. The var. *argentea* has leaves surfaced with silver-grey, and is one of the parents of most of the forms with silvery foliage. The var. *Hendersonii*, with dark olive-green and white-spotted leaves, is responsible for the irregular blotches on many of the garden forms. *S. speciosa* (*S. elegans*) [India] (purple or rose, spring, 12 in.) is a species grown entirely for its flowers. There are also many garden forms and hybrids.

**Sophora tetraptera (Edwardsia grandiflora)** *Leguminosæ* [N. Zealand]. Evergreen shrub with golden-yellow, pea-shaped flowers. Excellent for the cold greenhouse. Culture as for **Acacia.** Propagation by seed.

**Sophrocattlælia** (see Chapter on **Orchids**).

**Sophrocattleya** (see Chapter on **Orchids**).

**Sophronitis grandiflora** (see Chapter on **Orchids**).

**South African Hemp** (see **Sparmannia africana**).

**Sowbread** (see **Cyclamen**).

**Spanish Bayonet** (see **Yucca**).

**Sparaxis,** *Iridaceæ.*—Half-hardy, South African, bulbous plants, which may be grown in the open in sunny positions, in warm, sheltered borders, and in well-drained, sandy soil, or in pots in the greenhouse. They grow from 10 to 20 inches high, and carry brightly-coloured, bell-shaped flowers in April and May.

*Pot Culture.*—Pot-up in September, placing six bulbs 2½ inches deep in a 5-inch pot, and stand in a cold frame covered with a layer of coconut fibre until growth commences. Little water should be given until top growth has been made. The culture of these plants is very similar to that required for **Ixia** (which see).

*Species.*—*S. grandiflora* and vars. (violet, white, or crimson, 18 in.) ; *S. tricolor* (orange-red and purple, 20 in.).

**Sparmannia africana** (South African Hemp), *Tiliaceæ.*—Greenhouse, evergreen shrubs, growing from 3 to 6 feet high and bearing white (single or double) flowers from November to January. They thrive in the cool greenhouse (temperature 45° F. winter, 65° F. summer), in a compost of two parts sandy loam and peat to one of rotten manure.

*Culture.*—Pot-up from March to April, using 6- to 12-inch pots, and from June to September stand in the open and give weekly doses of weak liquid manure ; also syringe well during dry weather. Water well in summer, moderately in winter. Prune hard in February.

*Propagation.*—Propagate by means of cuttings made of young as well as of semi-matured shoots, rooted in sandy soil with heat (55–60° F.) in March or April.

**Spathiphyllum,** *Araceæ.*—Stemless, or very short-stemmed plants, with leaf-like spathe, usually grown for their foliage, in the stove or warm greenhouse.

*Culture.*—They succeed in a compost of equal parts of fibrous loam and peat, with some sand and pieces of charcoal. They require plenty of drainage, abundance of water, and a moist atmosphere.

*Propagation.*—Propagation is carried out by seed sown on a hot bed, but chiefly by means of division in the spring. Some of the small species are very useful and attractive.

*Species.*—*S. Patinii* (*S. candicans*) [Colombia] (spathe pure white, 9 in.) ; *S. cannæfolium* [W. Indies] (spathe green outside, white inside, leaves dark green, shining, 12–15 in.).

**Spathoglottis** (see Chapter on **Orchids**).

**Speedwell** (see **Veronica**).

**Sphacele,** *Labiatæ.*—Cool-greenhouse shrubs or sub-shrubs which can sometimes be grown in the open in favourable localities. They require the same cultural treatment as the greenhouse **Salvia.**

*Species.*—*S. chamædryoides* (*S. campanulata*) [Chile] (pale blue, July, 20–30 in.) ; *S. Lindleyi* [Chile] (purplish violet, July, 30–40 in.).

**Sphæralcea** (Globe Mallow), *Malvaceæ.*—Ornamental greenhouse or hardy herbs, sub-shrubs, or shrubs, closely allied to **Abutilon.** They require a well-drained, loamy soil, and a light, airy position near the glass.

*Propagation.*—They are readily increased by means of cuttings of young growth inserted in sandy soil under a bell-glass, leaving them until they are rooted. They may also be propagated by means of seed sown in sandy soil and placed in a little warmth.

*Species.*—*S. acerifolia* [N.W. America] (pink, July, 30–40 in.) ; *S. cisplatina* (*S. miniata*) [S. America] (brick-red, May–July, 24–36 in.) ; *S. Munroana* [S. America] (scarlet or cinnabar red, July, 12–20 in.) ; *S. umbellata* (*Malva umbellata*) [Mexico] (red and white, 36 in.) ; *S. u.* var. *tricolor* has reddish-purple flowers striped rose and white.

**Spider Lily** (see **Hymenocallis**).

**Spider Plant** (see **Cleome**).

**Spiderwort** (see **Tradescantia**).

**Spielmannia africana** (see **Oftia africana**).

**Spigelia marilandica** (Pink Root), *Loganiaceæ.*—A handsome, North American, perennial herb, which, although hardy, is very charming for the cold greenhouse, either planted out or for growing in pots. It bears long, tubular, red flowers, with a yellow throat. It should be planted in a compost of good turfy loam and peat, where it will grow to a height of from 12 to 20 inches, and bloom in July. It is increased by means of cuttings of young growth placed in sand and peat under a bell-glass.

*S. splendens* [Mexico] is a beautiful warm-greenhouse plant, growing 12–18 inches high, and bearing bright-scarlet flowers in July.

**Spiræa,** *Rosaceæ.*—A genus of graceful and attractive plants, both herbaceous and woody perennials, with fern-like foliage and pyramidal feathery spikes of red, pink, or white flowers. They thrive shaded from the hottest rays of the sun, and require plenty of water. They grow 1–15 feet in height, and flower, some between February and May, others in July, August, and September. They are excellent in the open border, for forcing in the greenhouse, and as room plants, with flowers suitable for cutting. For forcing use *S. arguta*, a garden hybrid which blooms in May, and which is the showiest and freest flowering of the earlier Spiræas; *S. japonica* [China and Japan] and vars. (pink, June and July, leaves purple in a young state); *S. multiflora*, another handsome shrub of garden origin, similar to *S. arguta*, but producing its pure white blooms later in the year; *S. Thunbergii* [China] (May, 3–5 ft.); and *S. Van Houttei*, a garden hybrid growing 3–5 feet high, probably the most beautiful of the early kinds.

*Pot Culture.*—Pot-up in October, using 8- to 10-inch pots and a compost of two-thirds sandy loam and one-third leaf-mould and a little well-rotted manure. Keep almost dry in a frost-proof frame until growth starts, then take into the cool or warm house in succession as bloom is required. A fortnight later raise the temperature by 5° or so, and give bi-weekly doses of weak liquid manure. In hot weather stand in a saucer of water. Harden off in a frame, and sink the pots in ashes outdoors from May to October, then re-pot if necessary.

*Pruning.*—Care must be taken in the pruning of the shrubby Spiræas, since those which flower in the spring require different treatment from those which flower in the summer. The former bloom on the wood made in the previous year, and require no regular pruning. It is merely necessary to thin out the older wood of spring-flowering shrubs after flowering, if the bushes have become unshapely. Shrubs that flower between July and September, such as the *japonica* set, should have all weak wood cut completely away in February, and all other shoots that have flowered must be cut back by at least one half.

*Propagation.*—Propagate by means of division in March or October. Cuttings of young wood may also be taken in autumn and struck in sandy soil in a frame.

*Other Species.*—SHRUBS: White Flowers.—*S. bracteata* [Japan] (4–8 ft.); *S. canescens* [Himalayas] (6–10 ft.); *S. prunifolia fl. pl.* (6–8 ft.). Pink Flowers.—*S. Douglasii* [N. America] (4–6 ft.); *S. japonica*, *S. Bumalda*, "*Anthony Waterer*", [garden hybrid] (1–3 ft.); *S. Margaritæ* [garden Hybrid] (4–5 ft.); *S. Menziesii triumphans* [N. America] (4–6 ft.).

The herbaceous plant usually known as *Spiræa japonica* and grown in the greenhouse, also used for forcing, is **Astilbe japonica,** which see.

**Spiræa Aruncus** (see **Aruncus sylvestris**).

**Spiræa lobata** (see **Filipendula rubra**).

**Spiræa hexapetala, palmata, rubra,** etc. (see **Filipendula**).

**Spiral Flag** (see **Costus**).

**Spiranthera odoratissima,** *Rutaceæ.*—A handsome, Brazilian, stove, evergreen shrub, with white, sweet-scented flowers in July. It succeeds in a compost of equal parts of sandy loam and peat, with some sand.

*Propagation.*—It is propagated by means of cuttings of half-ripened wood inserted in sand under glass. This should be removed to prevent the cuttings from damping off, which they are very prone to do.

**Spironema fragrans,** *Commelinaceæ.*—An interesting Mexican warm-greenhouse plant, with white, fragrant flowers and robust creeping habit. It can be grown in a border in the greenhouse, or is fairly successful under the staging. It should be given a light, rich soil, and is propagated by division.

**Spleenwort** (see **Asplenium**).

**Sprekelia formosissima** (Jacobæan Lily), *Amaryllidaceæ.*—A half-hardy, bulbous-rooted plant from Mexico and Guatemala, with large, bright-red or crimson flowers in summer, related to **Hippeastrum,** and requiring similar cultural treatment.

**Spurge** (see **Euphorbia**).

**Squill** (see **Scilla**).

**Stachys corsica,** *Labiatæ.*—An attractive dwarf rock-garden plant from Corsica and Sardinia which may be grown in pans for the alpine house.

*Culture.*—It should be planted in well-drained pans of sandy loam, leaf-mould, and sand, or granite chippings, and the pans plunged to their rims in ashes in a sunny position, in a cold frame, when not in flower.

*Propagation* —It is increased by means of seed sown as soon as ripe, by cuttings of half-ripened growth in July placed in sand under a bell-glass, or by division in the spring. The plant grows 1–2 inches high ; the flowers are pinkish white and bloom in July.

*S. lavendulæfolia* [Caucasus] is another beautiful rock plant, growing 3–4 inches high, and bearing purplish-red flowers in summer. It requires the same treatment as the previous species.

**Stag's Horn Fern** (see **Platycerium**).

**Stangeria eriopus (S. paradoxa)** (Hottentot's Head), *Cycadaceæ.*—An interesting, South African Cycad, differing from all others in the arrangement of the leaf-veins. This is so pronounced that before the fruits were known it is said to have been described as a fern. It requires the same cultural treatment as **Cycas.**

**Stanhopea** (see Chapter on **Orchids**).

**Stapelia** (Carrion Flower), *Asclepiadaceæ.*—A genus of botanically interesting, succulent-stemmed plants, which, on account of their somewhat unpleasant smell, are little grown by amateurs. The plants produce a number of fleshy leafless stems some 6–12 inches in height, and large purple and yellow star-shaped flowers borne low down near the ground.

*Culture.*—Re-pot only when necessary, as these plants do best when the roots are restricted. A compost of two-thirds sandy loam and one-third crushed brick and old mortar-rubble forms a suitable mixture for growing-in. Water carefully and regularly while making growth, and keep just moist when dormant. They like plenty of air and full sun, and thrive in the cool greenhouse or in a room with an even temperature.

*Propagation.*—The plants may be increased by means of division—that is, detaching new shoots with roots, cuttings inserted in small pots after being dried for about 24 hours previously, or ripe seed sown in sandy soil in slight heat (55–60° F.). Pot-up singly in small pots as soon as fit to handle.

*Species and Hybrids.*—× *S. bella* [garden hybrid] [purplish red and whitish, 5–6 in.); *S. gigantea* [Tropical and S. Africa] (pale purple, light yellow, and crimson, 5–7 in.); *S. grandiflora* [S. Africa] (purplish brown, white base, with purple hairs, 8–10 in.); *S. nobilis* [S. Africa] (reddish purple, light yellow, with crimson markings); *S. variegata* [S. Africa] (green and yellow with dark purplish-brown spots, 3–5 in.); there are a number of varieties of this species.

**Stapelia Corderoyi** (see **Duvalia Corderoyi**).

**Staphylea** (Bladder Nut), *Staphyleaceæ.*—Beautiful, hardy, deciduous shrubs from the Caucasus, which like a semi-shaded position in well-drained loam. Given the protection of glass, their white flowers, which in the open are seen in May and June, appear from December to March.

*Species.*—*S. colchica* [Caucasus] is an elegant, erect shrub, 5–8 feet high, with white, sweet-scented flowers. *S. holocarpa* [Central China] is a handsome shrub which flowers before the leaves appear. It bears white or pink flowers in May or June, and is probably the most beautiful species. There is also a variety *rosea*. *S. pinnata* [Europe and W. Asia] bears greenish-white flowers in May and June.

*Culture.*—Plant when small in a large pot or tub and stand outdoors on a hard bed of ashes during the summer; take indoors early in October, and water regularly. *S. colchica* and *S. holocarpa* are both excellent for forcing. Occasional doses of weak liquid manure will help to produce a good show of bloom. Do not prune, but merely trim to shape after flowering.

The plants may be increased by means of seed, cuttings or layers in autumn.

**Star Capsicum** (see **Solanum Capsicastrum**).

**Star Grass** (see **Hypoxis**).

**Star Jessamine** (see **Trachelospermum jasminoides**).

**Star of Bethlehem** (see **Ornithogalum**).

**Star of the Veldt** (see **Dimorphotheca**).

**Star Tulip** (see **Calochortus**).

**Statice** (Sea Lavender) (see **Limonium**).

**Stauntonia hexaphylla,** *Lardizabalaceæ.*—A beautiful Japanese half-hardy climbing shrub closely related to the Berberis Family, suitable for cultivation in the cold or cool greenhouse. It bears clusters of small white, tinted violet flowers in late spring; these are followed by long, edible berries.

*Culture.*—Pot-up or plant in a prepared site in the greenhouse bed in a mixture of rich loam and leaf-mould. Water regularly while growing, and give occasional doses of liquid manure or other artificial fertiliser containing nitrogen and potash, and keep just moist in winter. Trim to keep the plant in shape only, after flowering.

*Propagation.*—Cuttings made from sound new shoots may be rooted in pots of sandy soil in summer in a cold frame.

**Stauropsis** (see Chapter on **Orchids**).

**Stemona** (**Roxburghia**), *Stemonaceæ.*—Interesting stove climbers with handsome flowers and leaves, although the flowers have a rather unpleasant odour. They thrive in light, turfy loam, and may be increased by suckers in the spring.

# THE GREENHOUSE

*S. Curtisii* [Penang] (flowers green, red, and yellow, leaves alternate, April) ; *S. tuberosa* (*Roxburghia gloriosoides*) [E. Indies] (flowers green, leaves opposite, summer, 50–60 in.).

**Stenochlæna,** *Polypodiaceæ.*—Tropical climbing ferns which are very effective when growing up palm stems and tree-ferns. They are readily increased by taking off the shoots, which root as they run.

*Species.—S. palustris* (*Acrostichum scandens*) [India] is a vigorous grower useful for growing in a cool fernery, with fronds 12–30 inches long. *S. sorbifolium* [Brazil, etc.] has a climbing rootstock, and the fronds are often prickly.

**Stenomesson,** *Amaryllidaceæ.*—Bulbous plants from Tropical America, suitable for growing either in a warm or a cool greenhouse.

*Culture.*—They require a good soil in a sunny house, with a temperature not below 45° F. They should be given plenty of water during the growing season, but should be kept practically dry when at rest. Potting should be done just as new growth is about to start, when all offsets should be removed from the old bulb. The offsets can be grown on. Stenomessons require the same cultural treatment as **Hippeastrum.**

*Species.—S. aurantiacum* (yellow, May, 12 in.) ; *S. coccineum* (*Coburgia coccinea*) [Peruvian Andes] (bright crimson, May, 12–15 in.) ; *S. flavum* [Peru] (bright yellow, May, 12 in.) ; *S. incarnatum* (*Coburgia incarnata*) [Peru] (crimson and green, but variable in colour, Aug., 24 in.) ; *S. vitellinum* [Lima] (yellow, April, 12 in.).

**Stenospermation popayanense,** *Araceæ.*—Stove- or warm-greenhouse evergreen perennial from Colombia, with ivory-white, boat-shaped spathe. It grows 12–18 inches high, and blooms in summer.

*Propagation.*—It is increased by division, and requires the same cultural treatment as **Spathiphyllum.**

**Stenotaphrum secundatum** var. **variegatum,** *Gramineæ.*—Attractive, half-hardy, ornamental, grass-like plants with rhizomatous roots, growing some 9–12 inches in height, sometimes known as **Stephanophorum.** They thrive in a mixture of sandy loam, peat, and leaf-mould in the cool greenhouse, and make decorative basket plants.

*Culture.*—Pot-up in March in well-drained pots (4–5 inch) and keep on the moist side while growing.

*Propagation.*—Propagate by means of division in spring.

**Stephanophorum** (see **Stenotaphrum secundatum** var. **variegatum**).

**Stephanophyllum** (see **Ruellia**).

**Stephanotis floribunda,** *Asclepiadaceæ.*—This is a beautiful evergreen twiner or climber from Madagascar, for the cool greenhouse (average temperature 55° F. winter, 65° F. summer). It will reach a height of 30 feet, and from May to July will bear clusters of fragrant, waxy-white flowers. A well-drained compost of fibrous loam and leaf-mould suits it well, and it can be grown either in pots or planted out in the greenhouse border, and trained up a pillar or over the rafters. An occasional syringeing should be given during the growing season. During the winter water should be reduced and syringeing cease. Cut out weak wood during the winter. Mealy bug and scale are certain to find Stephanotis.

*Propagation.*—Propagation is carried out by means of cuttings of the

556

previous year's wood struck in spring in sandy soil with bottom heat. Pot-on as required.

**Sternbergia** (Mount Etna Lily), *Amaryllidaceæ.*—Beautiful, half-hardy, bulbous plants, growing about 10 inches high, and bearing large, yellow, crocus-like flowers. They thrive in sunny positions in warm, well-drained borders, in the rock-garden, cold greenhouse, or alpine house. They need sandy soil mixed with a little leaf-mould and mortar-rubble.

*Pot Culture.*—Most of the species can be potted-up during July or August. Place the bulbs deep in the pots, and plunge these to the rim in ashes in a sunny, sheltered position. Protect from frost with fibre, and lift and re-pot not oftener than once every three or four years, as they resent disturbance.

*Propagation.*—Propagate by means of offsets in April.

*Species.*—*S. colchiciflora* [Hungary] (yellow, Aug.) ; *S. lutea* (Yellow Star Flower, Winter Daffodil) [Europe and Asia] (yellow, Aug.–Sept.) ; this is the most satisfactory of all—said to be the Lily of the Field, of the Bible. *S. Fischeriana* (yellow, Feb.–March).

**Steudnera,** *Araceæ.*—Attractive stove-plants, both in flower and foliage.

*Culture.*—They thrive in a compost of two parts of rich sandy loam, one part of leaf-mould, and some pieces of charcoal, with good drainage. A warm, moist atmosphere with a fair amount of water during the growing season is essential, but it is very important to see that they have a period of rest in winter, by withholding water and standing the plants in a cooler, drier atmosphere.

*Propagation.*—Propagation is effected by means of suckers, or by division of the root-stock in spring at the time of potting.

*S. colocasiæfolia* [Burma] grows 18–24 inches high, and bears in the summer flowers which are yellowish purple or reddish inside. The var. *discolor* has brownish-purple blotches on the leaves.

**Stewartia** (occasionally spelt **Stuartia**), *Ternstrœmiaceæ.*—Beautiful deciduous shrubs with showy flowers, some of which can be grown in the open in favourable localities, but generally speaking are best grown in the conservatory or cool greenhouse. They are very attractive during the summer with their large, conspicuous, cup-shaped, creamy or white flowers and bright green foliage, which turns to red, orange, or scarlet in the autumn.

*Culture.*—They succeed in a mixture of loam and peat in equal proportions, but must always have a lime-free soil.

*Propagation.*—They can be propagated by means of seed sown as soon as ripe and placed in a little heat with a piece of glass over the pot ; by layers, or by cuttings of nearly ripened wood inserted in sand under a bell-glass.

*Species.*—*S. Malachodendron* [Southern U.S.A.] (white with a violet blotch, April–June, 3–8 ft.) ; one of the showiest, but more tender than some species. *S. Pseudo-Camellia* (*S. grandiflora*) [Japan] (creamy white, silky, summer, 12 ft.) ; *S. pentagyna* [South eastern U.S.A.] (creamy white, petal margins wavy, May–July, 12 ft.) ; the var. *grandiflora* has very beautiful flowers with purple stamens.

# THE GREENHOUSE

**Stewartia grandiflora** (see **Stewartia Pseudo-Camellia**).

**Stifftia chrysantha,** *Compositæ*.—A fine, showy, interesting evergreen shrub, from Brazil, with heads of orange-coloured flowers followed by saffron-coloured pappus. It requires a well-drained, turfy loam and a light, airy position in a warm greenhouse.

*Propagation.*—It is propagated by means of cuttings of young shoots struck in sandy soil under a bell-glass, with bottom heat (Feb.–April, 12–60 in.).

**Stigmaphyllon,** *Malpighiaceæ*.—Handsome, warm-greenhouse, climbing shrubs. They will grow in a compost of loam, leaf-mould, and some sand, and can either be planted out in the border of the greenhouse or may be grown in pots.

*Propagation.*—They are propagated by means of cuttings of ripened wood struck in sandy soil, and placed under a bell-glass in heat.

*Species.*—*S. ciliatum* (Golden Vine) [Brazil] bears in autumn clusters of bright-yellow flowers, with beautifully fringed petals. The leaves of this climber are heart-shaped, with hairs on the margins. *S. littorale* [Argentina] is a climber which bears yellow flowers in autumn. The leaves are of various shapes with very long leaf-stalks.

**Stock** (see **Matthiola**).

**Stonecrop** (see **Sedum**).

**Strawberry [Fragaria]** (see Chapter on **Fruit under Glass**).

**Strawberry-fruited Cypress** (see **Microcachrys tetragona**).

**Streblorhiza speciosa,** *Leguminosæ*.—A cool-greenhouse, climbing shrub from Norfolk Island, which can be trained up pillars, against the wall, or up sticks, either in pots or planted out. If the latter method is adopted, care must be taken to see that the drainage is good.

*Culture.*—After potting, the plants should be kept in a close house for a few weeks and syringed daily. Plants in pots will need annual attention, either in potting or top-dressing in March or April, when the side shoots should be cut hard back and the leading shoots shortened. If planted out, abundant water must be given to the roots, and the syringe used freely.

*Propagation.*—It is propagated by means of seed or by cuttings.

**Strelitzia Reginæ** (Bird-of-Paradise Flower), *Musaceæ*.—Strikingly beautiful South African perennials with highly ornamental foliage and lovely orange and blue-purple flowers borne on long stems some 36 inches high in late winter and early spring, suitable for culture in the warm greenhouse.

*Culture.*—Pot-up in spring or autumn in well-drained 6- to 7-inch pots of sandy loam, peat, and leaf-mould, or plant in a prepared site in the greenhouse bed. Water regularly and well while growing, and give ample ventilation and full sun. Keep only just moist in winter.

*Propagation.*—Propagation may be carried out by means of seed, when obtainable, sown in pots of sandy loam and placed in a propagating case with bottom heat (temperature 65–70° F.) in early spring. Strelitzia may be induced to set seed if the flowers are hand fertilised ; the usual method of propagation being by offsets or new shoots.

# GREENHOUSE PLANTS

**Streptanthera,** *Iridaceæ.*—Dwarf, bulbous, greenhouse plants from South Africa, very pretty when in flower. They grow in pots or pans of sandy loam, with good drainage.

*Propagation.*—They may be increased by means of offsets removed at the time of potting in autumn or early spring; or by seed sown when ripe and placed in a little heat.

*Species.*—*S. cuprea* (yellowish copper, purple, and pale yellow, June, 9–10 in.); *S. elegans* (white, tinged blush, purple, black marked with yellow spots, spring, 9 in.).

**Streptocarpus** (Cape Primrose), *Gesneriaceæ.*—A genus of many species of dwarf perennial plants, suitable for culture in the greenhouse or conservatory. The flowers, which are freely produced, appear in autumn. They are of various colours, bell-shaped, spotted in the throat and somewhat similar to those of the **Gloxinia.**

*Culture.*—Pot-up annually in February or March, using 6-inch pots and a compost of equal parts of sandy loam and leaf-mould (temperature 45° F. winter, 65° F. summer). Give water sparsely until the roots are established, then water well while growing, but keep almost dry in winter.

*Propagation.*—Propagate by means of seed sown in gentle heat (60° F.) in February, by leaf-cuttings, or by division in March. If seed is sown, the small plants should be pricked off singly into small pots and gradually re-potted until they reach 6-inch pots. When once established in these pots the temperature can be lowered from 60° F. to 55° F. They must be kept moist and shaded from strong sun. Spring-sown plants flower in late summer, and if kept over the winter they make fine plants the following year, when they will bloom throughout the summer and autumn. They should be given weekly doses of weak liquid manure as soon as the buds begin to form. The large, one-leaved kinds, such as *S. Dunnii, S. grandis,* and *S. Wendlandii* should be stood on inverted flower-pots, in a temperature not too moist, otherwise the handsome leaves become damaged, where they come in contact with the staging.

*Species.*—*S. caulescens* [Tropical Africa] (soft shrubby or stem bearing habit, pale blue); *S. Dunnii* [S. Africa] (rose); *S. Galpinii* [Transvaal] (violet, mauve, and white); *S. Holstii* [E. Africa] somewhat (resembles *S. caulescens,* but has violet-blue flowers spotted with white); *S. Rexii* [S. Africa] (blue); *S. Wendlandii* [S. Africa] (violet-blue). There are many garden hybrids and varieties in varying shades of purple, blue, white, and rose. All flower from May to October and grow to a height of 10–20 inches.

**Streptosolen Jamesonii (Browallia Jamesonii),** *Solanaceæ.*—This is a favourite greenhouse evergreen climber from Colombia. It does not do well as a pot-plant, only as a small plant, but requires a deep border in a sunny greenhouse and a compost of two-thirds rich loam and one-third leaf-mould and sand. It needs a sunny, airy position, and in summer may be set out in a sunny, sheltered position in the open. Masses of drooping flowers are borne all through the summer—in fact most of the year—but are most profuse in June and July. The newly-opened buds are a yellowish pink, later becoming orange, then orange-red, and are most effective.

# THE GREENHOUSE

*Pruning.*—In November cut the older wood right back to the base, and keep the roots fairly dry during the winter. Streptosolens may also be grown as bushes or standards. The latter two forms should be pinched back once or twice in late spring to induce bushy growth. Re-pot annually in March, or, when this is not possible, mulch liberally with a dressing of rich soil and water, and until the flowers appear syringe overhead daily. Average temperature 50° F. winter, 65° F. summer.

*Propagation.*—They are readily propagated by means of cuttings inserted in sandy soil under glass. Side shoots should be selected in preference to terminal growth.

**Striped Squill** (see **Puschkinia scilloides**).

**Strobilanthes,** *Acanthaceæ.*—Sub-shrubby greenhouse plants grown or their flowers and foliage. As old plants become weedy and unattractive, it is advisable to have well-grown young plants.

*Culture.*—To get the most attractive foliage they should always be given a high temperature, abundance of moisture, and plenty of syringeing. They are of easy cultivation in light soil.

*Propagation.*—They are propagated by means of cuttings.

*Species.*—S. anisophyllus (*Goldfussia anisophylla*) [India] (purple and white, June, 20–30 in.) ; S. Dyerianus [Burma] (pale violet, 6–8 in.) ; this is a beautiful foliage plant when young, the leaves being variegated with tints of blue, lilac, and rosy purple. S. isophyllus (*Goldfussia isophylla*) [India] (blue and white, free flowering most of the autumn and winter, 12–20 in.).

**Stromanthe,** *Marantaceæ.*—Handsome stove perennials, grown chiefly for their foliage, their leafy stems rising from a thick, horizontal rhizome. They are closely allied to **Calathea** and **Maranta,** and require the same cultural treatment.

*Species.*—S. amabilis [Brazil] grows 12–15 inches high, and has leaves variegated with bands of light and dark green and markings of silvery grey. S. Porteana (*Maranta Porteana*) [Brazil] is a handsome dwarf plant, growing 20-40 inches high. Its leaves are bright green above with stripes or bars of silvery white, purple beneath. S. sanguinea (*Thalia sanguinea*) [Brazil] has leaves which are bright green above and purple beneath, with panicles of bright red, and red bracted flowers. The variety *spectabilis* has leaves which are partly coloured with green beneath.

**Strongylodon pseudolucidus,** *Leguminosæ.*—An attractive twining plant from Madagascar and Ceylon, for the conservatory or warm greenhouse. It bears racemes of bright-red flowers during the autumn. It may be planted out or grown in a pot, trained up a pillar, the wall, or along the rafters. It will succeed in loam, leaf-mould, and some sand.

*Propagation.*—It is propagated by means of seed sown and placed in heat, or by cuttings of young shoots struck in sandy soil under a bell-glass, placed in a little heat.

**Strophanthus,** *Apocynaceæ.*—Interesting and beautiful flowering shrubs, suitable for the stove or warm greenhouse. The flowers are shaped like a funnel, the top of which ends in five very long, twisted,

560

Silene orientalis  Hyacinth "Queen of the Pinks"

*Photos*]   [*Sutton & Sons Ltd. and Alexander & Brown*

Schizanthus  Lychnis Cœli-rosa (Viscaria)

Sparaxis "Fire King"        Polianthes tuberosa (Tuberose)

*Photos*]                    [*Sutton & Sons Ltd. and Alexander & Brown*

Scabiosa atropurpurea        Viburnum Opulus sterile
(Sweet Scabious)

tail-like appendages. They are easy to cultivate in a compost of sandy loam and peat, with some sand. Cuttings of young shoots root readily in sand under glass, with a little heat.

*Species.*—*S. dichotomus* [E. Indies] (whitish and purple, Feb.–March, 20–30 in., stove) ; *S. Petersianus* var. *grandiflorus* [Tropical and S. Africa] (purplish and creamy white, May–June, 40–50 in., stove climber) ; *S. speciosus* (*S. capensis*) [S. Africa] (creamy yellow or orange spotted red, June, 30 in., greenhouse).

**Stuartia** (see **Stewartia**).

**Stylophyllum** (see **Cotyledon**).

**Sugar Cane** (see **Saccharum**).

**Summer Cypress** (see **Kochia**).

**Summer Snowflake** (see **Leucojum æstivum**).

**Sundew** (see **Drosera**).

**Surinam Tea Plant** (see **Lantana**).

**Swainsona galegifolia**, *Leguminosæ.*—This delightful, Australian, greenhouse, evergreen shrub is semi-climbing in habit and grows to a height of between 2 and 4 feet. All through the summer, from May to September, it carries, on long stems, rose or deep red Sweet Pea-like flowers, and can be used as a pot-plant, or may be trained up the back wall of the greenhouse, or trained up a pillar there. If planted in the greenhouse border the root-run must be somewhat restricted, or the plant will prove too rampageous. There is a useful white variety, *S. g. alba*, as well as *S. g. violacea* which has rose-violet flowers and a smaller habit.

*Culture.*—Re-pot annually if grown in pots, in a well-drained compost of two-thirds fibrous loam and one-third peat and sand. Water liberally and syringe overhead daily in fine weather in spring and summer, and when the buds are forming give bi-weekly doses of weak liquid manure. In autumn ample ventilation is needed to ripen the wood and form buds for flowering the following summer. In dull weather and in winter little water should be given (average temperature 40° F. winter, 60° F. summer).

*Pruning.*—Early in spring all old wood should be cut out of the centre of the plants, all straggly shoots should be trimmed in, and the stouter young wood of the previous year should be cut back by nearly two-thirds. In summer small plants may be used for bedding in the open, and if pegged down to the soil they form an excellent groundwork.

*Propagation.*—Propagate by means of seed sown in a temperature of 70° F., in March, or by cuttings of young shoots struck in sandy soil in a propagating case during the same month. Pinch back the young shoots two or three times during the first two years to make nice bushy plants. Not until the third year should they be allowed to flower, and then pinching back should cease in May.

**Swamp Blueberry** (see **Vaccinium corymbosum**).

**Swamp Laurel** (see **Kalmia polifolia**).

**Swamp Pink** (see **Helonia bullata**).

**Swan River Daisy** (see **Brachycome**).

**Sweet Pea (Lathyrus odoratus)**, *Leguminosæ.*—No flower is more pleasing to grow than the Sweet Pea. It is colourful, a free grower, and possesses a delightful though delicate fragrance. Of all the numberless annuals, the Sweet Pea stands out conspicuously as the one really indispensable in all gardens. Provided it is not allowed to seed, it will flower for many weeks. As a cut flower, too, it ranks second to none for table decoration. Sweet Peas enjoy a rich soil properly prepared prior to sowing. A trench 2 feet wide should be dug out to a depth of from 2 to 3 feet, while a plentiful supply of well-rotted horse-manure should be worked into the lower strata some 10 inches below the surface. With the top spit may be incorporated a little leaf-mould, bonemeal, soot, and lime, but no stable manure. Under glass Sweet Peas can be sown at various times, according to the required flowering period. To secure the finest blooms outside, the seeds should be sown in late autumn or early in February in 5-inch pots, placing six seeds in each, or a single seed in a small pot. It is often beneficial to soak the seeds in warm water overnight, especially if the weather is very dry.

The seeds may also be sown some 2 inches apart in boxes about 4 inches deep, but the seedlings must be potted-off singly as soon as possible. A compost of two-thirds fibrous loam and one-third leaf-mould, to which a sprinkling of bonemeal, wood ashes, and coarse sand have been added, will be found most suitable. Raise the young plants on a shelf near the glass in a cool greenhouse or in a frost-proof frame. Before being planted out into the open, early in March, when the plants are about 4 inches high, the plants should be hardened off in a cold frame. One shoot, certainly not more than three growths, should be allowed to spring from each root, if exhibition blooms are desired. They should be planted out 1 foot apart in rows, and all tendrils kept cut off. The stems should be tied singly to tall canes, 8 or 10 feet high, and when the plants have grown to 3 or 4 feet high they should be given, after rain or a soaking with clear water, a little soot-water or weak liquid manure (the colour of weak tea), once a week. The application of the latter must not be overdone. Water applied to Sweet Peas must have been exposed to the air for at least twenty-four hours; cold water may cause the buds to drop. The tips can be pinched-out when they reach 6–8 inches above the top of the stakes, or they may be trained in a slanting direction along the top of the stakes. The soil between the plants should be kept continually stirred. Plants so raised should flower from early June to late September; if desired, April or early May blooms may be had by growing the peas throughout in the greenhouse, at a temperature between 50 and 60° F., and houses that have been used for Chrysanthemums may be used for Sweet Peas. The seeds are sown as stated, and when the seedlings are 3–4 inches high they are planted out 5 inches apart in the bed or border, prepared in the house, or may be potted-up into 10-inch pots. The compost should consist of two-thirds loam and one-third well-rotted manure, together with a little old mortar-rubble, and a dusting of bonemeal. Do not water too freely until growth becomes more rapid— about March—then more water may be given, and the heat of the greenhouse should be gradually reduced as the weather improves. The plants should have supports: string, such as binder's twine, being the best material to use under glass. The string should be attached to the posts of the house or to temporary posts, and tied to wires stretched along the roof. Flower-buds should appear towards the end of April, when weekly weak dressings of fertilisers or an occasional watering with soot-water or liquid manure (the colour of weak tea) may be given. If preferred, ½ oz. of phosphate of potash mixed with a gallon of water makes an excellent but rather costly manure, to be given occasionally. Peas do not need nitrogenous artificial manures, as they can themselves secure nitrogen from the soil. All stimulants must be kept at least 6 inches from the stem, and once a week is often enough to apply them, care being taken not to overdo it. Clear watering should be given when required, and always a good soaking instead of frequent small amounts. All shades are not entirely successful when grown under glass, but shades of orange, salmon, cream, white, mauve, and blue are usually satisfactory.

Blooms for exhibition may need shading, the blues and purples from the rain and the salmon and pinks from the sun, as they quickly fade. The chief pests which attack this plant are slugs and greenfly. The weekly application of soft-soap solution will banish the latter, while a little soot placed round the plants will prevent the former reaching them. The presence of slugs must be guarded against, especially when the young plants are coming through the ground. The after-attention is very simple, but it is of prime importance to keep the plants free from seeds. If seeds are required, a portion of the row or one clump may be reserved for the purpose. Named varieties are innumerable, and catalogues should be consulted.

**Sweet Pepper Bush** (see **Clethra**).

**Sweet-scented Verbena** (see **Lippia citriodora**).

**Sword Lily** (see **Gladiolus**).

**Synechanthus fibrosus,** *Palmaceæ.*—A slender, graceful palm from Central America, with a crown of spreading, pinnate leaves. It flowers in a small state, and bears clusters of orange-red fruits. It closely resembles **Chamædorea,** and succeeds with the same cultural treatment.

**Synnotia,** *Iridaceæ.*—Pretty, cool-greenhouse, bulbous plants with Ixia-like flowers, very attractive for spring decoration.

*Culture.*—The bulbs should be potted-up in October, placing six or eight in a 5-inch pot in well-drained, sandy loam, covering the bulbs with 1 inch of soil. The pots should be stood in a cool frame and given very little water during the winter, increasing the water as the plants grow and flowers develop; they should then be exposed to full light and plenty of air. After flowering, water should be gradually reduced, to obtain a gradual ripening. When the leaves die away, the bulbs should be kept dry until the autumn.

*Propagation.*—This is effected by means of offsets removed at the time of potting, or by seed sown in sandy soil as soon as ripe and placed in a cool frame.

*Species.*—*S. bicolor* [S. Africa] (violet and yellow, March, 6–9 in.); *S. galatea* [S. Africa] (yellowish and white, tinged red, March, 6–10 in.).

**Syringa** (Lilac), *Oleaceæ.*—Hardy, deciduous shrubs which thrive in the sun in moist, well-manured, well-drained, and rather heavy loam. They grow from 5 to 15 feet high and flower in the open in April and May. Several species (although most of those grown for pot work are varieties of *S. vulgaris*, the common Lilac) may be had in flower in the warm greenhouse from January onwards. Among the best varieties are *Charles X*, *Ellen Willmott*, *Marie Legraye*, *Madame Lemoine*, *Madame F. Morel*, *Persian*, *Souvenir de L. Spath*, etc.

*Culture.*—Plant in October or November.

*Pruning.*—Periodically cut away all suckers from the roots of grafted plants, dis-bud surplus buds in spring, and cut out old, weak wood after flowering, so as to allow ample air and light to penetrate to the centre of the plants, in order that the shoots may be ripened and able to form flower-buds for the next season. Care must be taken to cut the old wood right back to strong young shoots well down the stem. Never trim away the young or half-matured shoots just to bring the bush into shape, as this procedure will cause a total lack of bloom the following year.

*Propagation.*—Propagate by means of layering in June, by matured cuttings in the open in October, or by suckers in October.

*Forcing.*—For decoration in the greenhouse, pot-up in the spring and grow in pots plunged during the summer (giving plenty of water), or at the latest in October or November. This should be done preferably in the spring, as the check the plants receive from lifting will induce them to form new flower-buds during the summer and they will force with greater certainty. Use 6- to 10-inch pots and a compost of two parts sandy loam to one part of leaf-mould, and a little sand and bonemeal, stand in a sheltered, frost-proof position, and move into the house in succession as bloom is desired. For forcing, a strong heat is necessary, commencing at 60° F. for the first few days, then increasing to 75 or 80° F., with watering and syringeing several times daily. When the flowers begin to open the syringeing should cease, and when they are fully open remove the plants to a cool house to harden off. Here they will be useful for cutting, or as pot-plants for the room or greenhouse. As the season advances less heat will be required. The Persian Lilac is one of the most useful for forcing, owing to its abundance of bloom and delicate trusses, but to produce white flowers it should be forced in the dark. After flowering, remove all dead blooms, syringe, and continue the heat for three weeks or so, then harden off and sink the pots in ashes outdoors from May until October of the following year. Then take indoors and keep fairly dry until growth starts, when they should be watered moderately and regularly. Never force two years running. Prune as above. Named varieties are frequently increased by crown or cleft grafting in March.

*Named Varieties.*—*Madame Lemoine* (white, double) ; *Marie Legraye* and *Mont Blanc* (both white, single) ; the former being perhaps one of the best of all Lilacs for forcing. *Jeanne d'Arc* (cream, double) ; *Virginite* (pink, double) ; *Lucy Beltet* (flesh-pink, single) ; *Emile Lemoine* (rose, double) ; *Princess Marie* (rose, semi-double) ; *Souvenir de L. Spath* (deep wine-red, single) ; *Leon Simon* (blue, double) ; *Alphonse Lavallée* (blue, tinged violet, double) ; *President Grevy* (blue, double) ; *Charles X* (purple, single) ; *La Tour d'Auvergne* (purplish violet) ; *Lemoinei* (mauve, double) ; *Louis Van Houtte* (pale lavender, edged rose).

For **Mock Orange** or **Philadelphus coronarius** (commonly called **Syringa**) see **Philadelphus.**

**Syringodea pulchella,** *Iridaceæ.*—A pretty, autumn-flowering, bulbous plant from South Africa, suitable for the cool greenhouse. It grows 6 inches high, bears pale purple flowers, and requires the same cultural treatment as **Ixia.**

**Tacsonia,** *Passifloraceæ.*—Half-hardy, evergreen, climbing plants related to, and sometimes included under **Passiflora,** needing similar cultural attention. They bear pink or bright-red flowers in summer and autumn, and are also known as Red Passion Flower.

*Species.—T. exoniensis* [hybrid] (brick-red, rose-pink, white, with violet throat) ; *T. manicata* (Red Passion Vine) [Peru] (brilliant scarlet and blue) ; *T. Van Volxemii* [Colombia] (bright scarlet) ; one of the finest species.

**Tainia** (see Chapter on **Orchids**).

**Talauma Hodgsonii,** *Magnoliaceæ.*—A tender, evergreen tree from the Himalayas, with large, fragrant, Magnolia-like flowers, purplish blue on the outside, opening to ivory-white. It has large, glabrous, leathery leaves, sometimes up to 2 feet long. It can be grown in pots, but if the house is large enough it may be planted out in the border or bed of a cool greenhouse.

*T. Candollei* var. *Galeottiana* is a beautiful plant with fragrant, nodding, green and yellow flowers, a native of Java. It requires a warmer temperature, and should be grown in the stove house. A compost of fibrous peat with a little loam and sand is most suitable. It is propagated by means of cuttings of ripe shoots placed in sand under a bell-glass with bottom heat. A fair percentage can sometimes be rooted ; or they may be grafted, or inarched on **Magnolia obovata.**

**Talbotia elegans** (see **Vellozia elegans**).

**Tanakæa radicans,** *Saxifragaceæ.*—An interesting, Japanese, dwarf, creeping plant producing slender runners, with flowers resembling a miniature **Astilbe japonica.** Although probably hardy, it makes an attractive plant for the alpine house when grown in a pan, both with its thick, leathery leaves, as with its flowers. It should be grown in loam, peat, and sand, and kept plunged in ashes in partial shade in a cool frame.

*Propagation.*—It is propagated by means of runners.

**Tape Grass** (see **Vallisneria spiralis**).

**Tea Plant** (see **Thea sinensis**).

**Tecoma,** *Bignoniaceæ.*—Upright climbing shrubs with pinnate leaves and terminal clusters of usually yellow flowers. They are not quite hardy, but are excellent for the warm greenhouse or conservatory, for training up walls or pillars—all except *T. Smithii,* which is more suitable for pot culture.

*Culture.*—They should be planted in well-drained, sandy loam, and be given plenty of water in summer, but should be kept moderately dry at the roots during winter, when they should also have a lower temperature. They should have plenty of light and air at all times.

*Propagation.*—They are propagated by means of seed, which should be sown and placed in heat, by half-ripened shoots in sandy soil placed under a bell-glass in heat, or by root cuttings.

*Species.*—*T. mollis* [Mexico] (yellow, July, 5–6 ft.) ; *T. Smithii* [garden hybrid] (bright yellow tinged orange, Sept.–Jan., 2–4 ft.) ; it is well suited for growing in pots. *T. stans* (Yellow Elder) [S. America] (yellow, July–Sept., 10 ft.).

**Tecoma capensis** (see **Tecomaria capensis**).

**Tecoma grandiflora** (see **Campsis grandiflora**).

**Tecoma jasminoides** (see **Pandorea jasminoides**).

**Tecomaria capensis** (Cape Honeysuckle), *Bignoniaceæ.*—A half-hardy climber from the Cape of Good Hope, bearing orange-scarlet, trumpet-shaped flowers. It is allied to **Tecoma,** and requires the same cultural treatment, and, like *Tecoma Smithii*, is suitable for growing in pots. It blooms in August and September and grows up to 15 feet in height. There is a yellow-flowered form—*T. c.* var. *aurea.*

**Tecophilæa cyanocrocus** (Chilean Crocus), *Amaryllidaceæ.*—Half-hardy, bulbous plants with azure-blue flowers, each with a white throat. They thrive in sunny positions in well-drained, warm borders, in a mixture of peat, leaf-mould, and sand. They may also be flowered in pots in a frame or in the cold greenhouse.

*Culture.*—Pot-up in August 4 inches deep, placing four bulbs in a 5-inch pot, and plunge the pots to the rims in a sunny frame.

*Propagation.*—Propagate by means of offsets in August.

**Telegraph Plant** (see **Desmodium gyrans**).

**Telopea speciosissima (Waratah),** *Proteaceæ.*—An interesting, ever-green, greenhouse shrub from New South Wales, with dense, globular heads of crimson flowers, the brightest part of the flower being the crimson involucral bracts.

*Culture.*—It should be grown in a greenhouse with a rather dry atmosphere, in well-drained, sandy soil, and a bed or border with good drainage is most suitable. It requires abundant water in the summer, but should be kept nearly dry at the root during winter.

*Propagation.*—It is propagated by means of layers in pots during the winter, which should be left until rooted in the pots before being detached.

**Templetonia retusa** (Coral Bush), *Leguminosæ.*—An interesting, Australian, greenhouse shrub with red, sometimes white, pea-shaped flowers, thriving in a mixture of sandy loam and peat. It is propagated by means of cuttings of young growth struck in sandy soil under a bell-glass ; or by seed sown in sandy soil and placed in a little heat. It blooms from March to June, and grows 30–40 inches high.

**Testudinaria** (Hottentot's Head, Tortoise Plant, or Elephant's Foot), *Dioscoreaceæ.*—An interesting perennial plant, with slender, twining growths which rise from a solid, fleshy or woody hemispherical stem which is above ground. The plants are more curious than beautiful.

*Culture.*—They succeed in well-drained, sandy loam, and require a fair amount of water during the growing season, but should be kept quite dry during the period of rest.

# GREENHOUSE PLANTS

*Propagation.*—They are increased by means of seed, when obtainable, and by imported plants when resting.

*Species.*—*T. elephantipes* [S. Africa] (flowers greenish yellow, stem globular, July, 8–10 ft.) ; *T. paniculata* [S. Africa] (flowers greenish or pale yellow, scented ; stem oblong and flattened above ground, 8–12 ft.).

**Tetramicra bicolor** (see **Leptotes bicolor**).

**Tetranema mexicana** (Mexican Foxglove), *Scrophulariaceæ.*—A pretty, dwarf perennial for the warm greenhouse. The lovely purplish-violet flowers are borne in profusion during the summer, and with care it can be had in flower all the year round.

*Culture.*—Pot-up in spring in 5-inch pots or pans in a compost of loam, leaf-mould and sand, in equal proportions.

*Propagation.*—It is increased by means of seed sown and placed in a warm temperature, or by division at the time of potting.

**Tetrazygia,** *Melastomaceæ.*—Stove shrubs from the West Indies, requiring the same cultural treatment as **Melastoma.**

*Species.*—*T. angustiflora* (white, May, 10 ft.) ; *T. elæagnoides* (white or pink, June, 2 ft. or more).

**Teucrium** (Germander), *Labiatæ.*—Herbs, shrubs, or sub-shrubs, many of which are hardy. Some of he dwarf kinds, suitable for the rockery, may be grown in pans for the alpine house.

*Culture.*—They succeed in moderately good but well-drained soil.

*Propagation.*—They can be propagated by means of seed. The herbaceous kinds may be increased by division in the spring, while the shrubby ones may be propagated by means of cuttings inserted in sandy soil under a bell-glass, during the summer.

*Species.*—*T. Marum* (Cat Thyme) [Mediterranean region] (purplish flowers, leaves and shoots greyish, summer, 8–12 in.) ; cats have a great liking for this plant. *T. Polium* [Mediterranean region and Orient] (flowers white, yellow, or purple, leaves yellowish, hoary or golden, summer, 4–6 in.) ; a very variable plant.

**Thalia dealbata,** *Marantaceæ.*—An elegant aquatic from S. Carolina, which, although sufficiently hardy to be grown outside in some parts, is very suitable for the inside aquaria, either planted in a bed round the edge, in submerged pots, or in a water-filled tub planted in loam. It looks very stately, with its canna-like leaves and erect panicles of purple flowers, which continue from June to September. It grows 30–50 inches high, and is increased by division in the spring.

**Thalia sanguinea** (see **Stromanthe sanguinea**)

**Thalictrum** (Meadow Rue), *Ranunculaceæ.*—Hardy herbaceous perennials with fern-like foliage and pretty little flowers borne in umbels. A curious feature of these flowers is that they have no petals, but the sepals are coloured. They thrive in well-drained, rich, sandy loam, in sunny or shady borders, or by the side of a stream. The dwarf kinds, such as *T. alpinum* [Northern and Arctic regions] (5–8 in.) and *T. Chelidonii* [Himalayas] (lilac or purple, 6–8 in.), are charming in pans for the alpine house, and are also useful rock-garden plants. *T. minus* var. *adiantifolium*, which grows some 15–20 inches high, with beautiful, fern-like foliage, and carries yellow flowers from June to September, and *T. dipterocarpum*, from Western China, which grows from 36 to 50

567

# THE GREENHOUSE

inches high, and carries rose, purple, or white flowers from June to September, are excellent for the cold greenhouse.

*Pot Culture.*—Sow seed in the open in April, or propagate by means of division in March or root-cuttings in October, and plant out in a permanent position at either of those times. Pot up in November in 5- to 6-inch pots and a compost of equal parts of loam and leaf-mould.

**Thatch Palm** (see **Thrinax**).

**Thea,** *Ternstrœmiaceœ.*—Evergreen shrubs for the cool greenhouse, the most important member being *Thea sinensis*, whose leaves yield the well-known tea. This species requires a moister and warmer atmosphere than others. From a garden point of view it is of less ornamental value than some others of the genus which are grown for their handsome flowers and attractive evergreen foliage. They are allied to **Camellia,** and require the same cultural treatment.

*Species.*—*T. cuspidata* [China] (white, winter, up to 15 ft.); *T. maliflora* (*T. rosœflora*) [China] (pink, winter, up to 10 ft.); *T. sinensis* (Tea Plant) [China and India] (white and fragrant, winter, up to 10 ft.).

**Thelocactus bicolor (Echinocactus rhodophthalmus),** *Cactaceœ* [Texas and Mexico] has night-flowering purplish-pink, bell-shaped flowers. Same culture as **Echinocactus.**

**Thrift** (see **Armeria**).

**Thrinax** (Thatch Palm), *Palmaceœ.*—Useful, elegant, fan-leaved palms that are well adapted for growing in pots for room or greenhouse decoration. They grow slowly with little attention.

*Culture.*—They are propagated by means of seed, which, like all other palm seed, should be obtained when freshly imported and sown at once in well-drained pots of sandy loam and plunged in bottom heat. Plants when young succeed in a compost of loam, peat, and sand; as they get older turfy loam and sand will be found more suitable.

*Species.*—*T. argentea* (Silver Thatch Palm) [Panama] (leaves silvery grey, up to 12 ft.); *T. multiflora* [Santo Domingo] (young leaves covered with white woolly tomentosa, up to 8 ft.); *T. radiata* [Trinidad] (a popular palm with green leaves often downy beneath, up to 8 ft.).

**Throatwort** (see **Trachelium cœruleum**).

**Thunbergia,** *Acanthaceœ.*—A genus of slender and rapid-growing, evergreen climbers with pretty tubular flowers, white, yellow, and orange in colour, from June to September. They are valuable for growing up the roof or pillars of the warm greenhouse, and if planted out should have the root-room restricted to prevent rampant growth. The smaller kinds, either perennials or annuals, may be used for hanging-baskets and for decorating the front of the greenhouse staging. *T. coccinea* [India], a greenhouse perennial, produces clusters or racemes of orange-red flowers. The climbers should be cut back each autumn, training the young growth in the spring, as it develops. All may be propagated by means of cuttings struck in a warm case. Among the annuals may be named *T. alata* (Black-eyed Susan) [S.E. Africa], orange, with rich brown eye, and *T. alata alba*, white, also with rich brown eye. They will run up to a height of from 5 to 6 feet, and like a rich fibrous loam, plentifully mixed with leaf-mould and sand. *T. Gibsonii* [British E. Africa], a trailing plant, has brilliant orange-coloured

568

flowers, and is very beautiful. *T. grandiflora* [Bengal] bears racemes of light-blue flowers in autumn, and requires a large house. *T. natalensis* [Natal] bears in the summer large pale-blue flowers with a yellow throat. It is best treated as a herbaceous plant and cut to the ground in the winter. It can be grown in a border or in pots in the cool greenhouse.

*Propagation.*—It is increased by means of division in the spring, and from seed which is produced freely.

*Pot Culture.*—Sow seed in March in sandy soil in a temperature of 60° F., or propagate by means of cuttings subjected to gentle bottom heat. Pot-up singly as soon as the seedlings can be handled (or the cuttings have rooted) in a compost of two-thirds fibrous loam to one-third part of leaf-mould and sand. When the roots have filled the pots, pot-on for flowering into 4- or 5-inch pots, or harden off and set out in the open in June in a warm, sheltered bed.

**Thunia** (see Chapter on **Orchids**).

**Thymus,** *Labiatæ.*—Mostly hardy, dwarf, creeping plants or sub-shrubs, some of which are grown in the rock-garden or for covering dry, sunny banks. Quite a number, particularly forms of the common Thyme (*Thymus Serpyllum*), with its various-coloured flowers, make a good show when grown in pans for the alpine house.

*Culture.*—Thymus succeed in well-drained pans of light, sandy soil, and should be plunged in ashes in a sunny position when not wanted in the alpine house. They are increased by means of division in the spring; the creeping kinds by cuttings, which should be half-ripened shoots placed in sandy soil under a bell-glass in the summer; or by seed sown in March and April.

*Species.*—*T. heterotrichus* [Greece] (pale violet, summer, 4–6 in.); *T. Herba-barona* [Corsica] grows 3–5 inches high, and bears in summer purplish flowers with a white and red calyx. This plant has the strong fragrance of seed cake. *T. membranaceus* [Spain] is a compact, twiggy sub-shrub, up to 12 inches high, the growths of which are covered in late summer with long, white, tubular flowers intermixed with papery-white bracts. These are all choice plants for the alpine house, but need some protection during the winter.

**Thyrsacanthus rutilans** (see **Odontonema Schomburgkianum**).

**Thysanotus** (Fringed Violet, Fringed Lily), *Liliaceæ.*—Greenhouse perennials, some of which have thickened rootstock, grass-like foliage, and are very elegant when in flower. They thrive in sandy loam, and are increased by offsets.

*Species.*—*T. dichotomus* [Australia] (purple, July, 12–20 in.); *T. unceus* [Australia] (purple, Aug., 12–20 in.); *T. tuberosus* [Australia] (purple, June, 10–12 in.).

**Tiarella cordifolia** (Foam Flower), *Saxifragaceæ.*—Hardy, North American perennials which like a shady position in the border or rock-garden, and a moist, ordinary soil. They make useful little pot-plants for decoration in the cold greenhouse. They grow some 9 inches high, and carry creamy-white flowers from April to June.

*Pot Culture.*—Pot-up in November, using 5- to 6-inch pots or pans and moist ordinary soil, grow in the reserve garden in summer and give plenty of water in dry weather. Cold greenhouse or frame treatment during the winter and spring suits these plants well, and no artificial heat is needed. Sow seed in the open in April, or propagate by means of division in March.

**Tibouchina semidecandra [Pleroma macranthum, Lasiandra macrantha]** (Brazilian Spider Flower), *Melastomaceæ*.—Half-hardy, Brazilian, evergreen, shrubby plants, with lovely rich purple, blue, or violet flowers in summer. They may be grown as bushes in pots, care being taken never to allow them to become pot-bound. Pot-on, using good fibrous loam and one-sixth part sheep-manure, with some sand and charcoal. Or they may be planted out and allowed to climb up the pillars in the cool greenhouse. When exposed to full sunshine they flower freely.

*Culture*.—Pot-up or plant out in the greenhouse bed in autumn in a compost of sandy loam and peat with a few pieces of charcoal added. Keep just moist throughout the winter. Water regularly while making growth, and syringe the underside of the leaves to prevent red spider. After flowering prune according to requirements.

*Propagation*.—Cuttings of sound new shoots may be rooted in early spring in sandy soil in a propagating case. They must be stopped back and potted-on as required.

**Tiger Flower** (see **Tigridia Pavonia**).

**Tiger Iris** (see **Tigridia**).

**Tigridia** (Tiger Iris), *Iridaceæ*.—Half-hardy, bulbous plants which do best in a light, rich, sandy loam, and leaf-mould, in a warm, sunny position in a dry border or rock-garden, or in the cold greenhouse. The plants grow from 12 to 18 inches in height, and bear glorious spotted or blotched blooms either of carmine, scarlet, apricot, yellow, pink, or cream, from May to July.

*Pot Culture*.—Plant about the middle of April, 4 inches deep, letting the bulbs rest on sand. Six bulbs may be placed in a 6-inch pot, the latter being kept in a frame or cool house until growth has started, when more water and warmth can be given. If preferred, single bulbs can be flowered in small pots. Feed with weak liquid manure as they approach the flowering stage, and decrease the water supply afterwards.

*Propagation*.—Propagate by means of offsets in April.

*Species*.—*T. Pavonia* (Tiger Flower, or Shell Flower) [Mexico] (scarlet, marked yellow and purple, 15–20 in.). There are several beautiful varieties, *T. P.* var. *conchiflora* (yellow, purple spots); *T. P.* var. *grandiflora* (crimson, scarlet and yellow); *T. Pringlei* [N. Mexico] (crimson, orange, and scarlet).

**Tillandsia,** *Bromeliaceæ*.—An ornamental warm-greenhouse plant belonging to the pineapple family. They are mostly epiphytes, and in many of them the narrow entire leaves are so arranged as to form a cup, holding water, in which other small plants live. They are grown both for their foliage and their flowers, which bloom at almost any time. The foliage of many is beautifully marked, while the flowers of some are very showy, coloured either blue, violet, red, yellow, or white, and the combination in some cases is very lovely.

*Culture*.—Although in nature many of them are epiphytes, they are generally grown in pots in cultivation. There are a few exceptions, one of which is the Spanish or Florida Moss or Old Man's Beard

# GREENHOUSE PLANTS

(*Tillandsia usneoides*), which, having no roots, should be fastened to a piece of cork, bark, or soft wood, packed with some sphagnum to hold moisture. Those grown in pots should have lumps of rich fibrous peat and charcoal, and in some cases chopped sphagnum, with the pots half to three parts filled with drainage. During the summer they require a moist atmosphere : the syringe should be kept going, and a fair amount of water allowed. Very little water is required during the winter months, and the plants should be kept nearly dormant, but never completely dry.

*Propagation.*—They may be increased by means of seed sown and placed in a moist, warm atmosphere, and by suckers. The latter should be allowed to grow to a fair size before being detached ; they should be inserted singly in pots just large enough to hold them, in a compost of fibrous loam, peat, and sand, and confined in a close warm frame, kept moderately moist, and shaded. The best time for the operation is spring.

*Species.—T. anceps* [Costa Rica, Trinidad] (flowers blue or purple, leaves striped, June, 12 in.) ; *T. bulbosa* [W. Indies, etc.] (violet and white, Nov., 12 in.) ; the var. *picta* has the upper leaves and bracts scarlet. Both can be grown attached to cork or wood. *T. fasciculata* (*Vriesia glaucophylla*) [Central America, etc.] (blue flowers with greenish or red tinged bracts, 24 in.) ; it is a very variable plant. *T. Lindeniana* [Ecuador, Peru] (bluish purple flowers rising from carmine bracts, 8–12 in.) ; there are several forms of this species. *T. usneoides* (Spanish or Florida Moss, Old Man's Beard) [Tropical America] is a lichen-like plant, forming loose pendulous tufts sometimes several feet long, silvery or hoary grey. The flowers are said to be greenish with a tinge of red.

**Tillandsia carinata** (see **Vriesia carinata**).

**Tillandsia hieroglyphica** (see **Vriesia hieroglyphica**).

**Tillandsia psittacina** (see **Vriesia psittacina**).

**Tillandsia splendens** (see **Vriesia speciosa**).

**Toad flax** (see **Linaria**).

**Tobacco** (see **Nicotiana**).

**Todea barbara**, *Osmundaceæ.*—Greenhouse evergreen ferns from South Africa and New Zealand, with delicate and transparent fronds, which grow from 20 to 40 inches high and thrive in a compost of equal parts of sandy loam, leaf-mould, and peat, with a little charcoal in it (average temperature 50° F. winter, 60° F. summer).

*Culture.*—Plant in March and water liberally in summer.

*Propagation.*—Propagate by means of division in March, or by spores sown in heat at any time.

**Todea hymenophylloides** (see **Leptopteris hymenophylloides**).

**Todea superba** (see **Leptopteris superba**).

**Tomato [Lycopersicum esculentum]** (see Chapter on **Fruit Under Glass**).

**Torch Lily** (see **Kniphofia**).

**Torenia,** *Scrophulariaceæ.*—Beautiful, half-hardy annuals of trailing nature, which can be had in flower by various sowings from May to August, and are suitable for pots or for hanging-baskets in the warm greenhouse. They need a compost of sandy loam and leaf-mould.

# THE GREENHOUSE

*Culture.*—Sow seed in gentle heat in spring, and prick off 2 inches apart as soon as the seedlings can be handled. When large enough pot-up three plants in a 5-inch pot or four or five plants in a 6-inch pot, or plant in a hanging-basket previously lined with sphagnum moss. Water regularly while growing, give ample air and full sun when once established.

*Species.*—The most common are *T. flava* (*T. Baillonii*) [India] (yellow with brown throat, 6–10 in.), and *T. Fournieri* [Cochin China] (pale violet-blue, with yellow and white throat, 12 in.). There are several varieties of the latter : var. *alba* (White Wings) with pure white flowers, and var. *grandiflora*, which has larger flowers and blooms more freely.

**Tortoise Plant** (see **Testudinaria**).

**Townsendia,** *Compositæ.*—Dwarf rock-garden plants which may be grown in pans for the alpine house. They are of easy culture in a well-drained compost of loam, leaf-mould, and sand, with some granite chippings. They are readily raised from seed sown as soon as ripe and plunged in ashes in a cold frame, although they are rather short-lived plants.

*Species.*—*T. exscapa* [N. America] (white or purplish tint, April–May, 2 in.) ; *T. grandiflora* [N. America] (bright blue or violet, summer, 9–12 in.) ; *T. Wilcoxiana* [N. America] (yellow, May, 2 in.).

**Toxicophlæa Thunbergii** (see **Acocanthera venenata**).

**Trachelium cæruleum** (Throatwort), *Campanulaceæ.*—A half-hardy sub-shrubby perennial from Southern Europe, which prefers the treatment of a biennial, as young plants are more floriferous than old plants. It thrives in leaf-mould and sandy loam in sunny beds or borders. *T. cæruleum* is a fragrant and attractive pot-plant for the cool greenhouse. It grows about 18 inches high, and produces dense masses of light-blue flowers from June to August.

*Culture.*—Sow seed thinly in warm beds or boxes in a cold frame from February to June. Pot-up into single pots as early as possible, and prevent the plants being drawn up by the glass. Pot-on for flowering indoors when large enough. If preferred propagate by means of cuttings in March or October. Keep the plants moderately dry in winter. When growth begins in the spring, re-pot into 5- to 6-inch pots and keep moist but cool. After each re-potting, as soon as the plants are established, pinch back the young shoots to make nice bushy plants. Immediately the buds form, give bi-weekly doses of weak liquid manure, but discontinue this when the flowers begin to open. It can also be grown and used as a bedding plant outside.

**Trachelospermum (Rhynchospermum),** *Apocynaceæ.*—This is a small genus of evergreen twining shrubs with leathery leaves and fragrant flowers. Being on the borderland of hardiness, the Trachelospermums should be planted on a sheltered wall outside, or grown in cool and unheated greenhouses. *T. divaricatum*, with creamy-yellow flowers, is a native of China and Japan. *T. jasminoides* (Star or Malayan Jessamine) [S. China] has pure white flowers, from May to August, and its var. *variegatum* has leaves edged with creamy white, tinged red. In some gardens the name **Rhynchospermum** replaces Trachelospermum.

572

*Culture.*—Pot-up in a large well-drained pot or tub, or plant out in a prepared site in the greenhouse border in March in a compost of sandy loam, leaf-mould, and peat. Water and syringe regularly while growing and shade from strong sun.

*Propagation.*—Cuttings and layering provide ready means of increase in spring and summer. They should be placed in a propagating case with a bottom heat of 70° F. until established.

**Trachycarpus,** *Palmaceæ.*—Useful palms for the cool or cold house. *T. excelsa* may be grown outside in favourable localities, and produces flowers and seeds.

*Culture.*—They are of easy culture in a compost of rich loam with a small quantity of leaf-mould or peat, and some sand. Good drainage, together with an ample supply of water during the summer, are essential.

*Propagation.*—They are increased by means of seed, which should be sown fresh in heat, or by suckers, which are sometimes produced freely.

*Species.*—*T. excelsa* (*Trachycarpus Fortunei, Chamærops excelsa*) [Upper Burma, China, and Japan] is a popular fan-leaved palm, growing up to 60 feet in height. The trunk is clothed with old leaf-sheaths. *T. Martiana* [Himalayas, etc.] also grows up to 60 feet high, and has a slender trunk, naked for the most part, but showing leaf-scars.

**Trachymene cœrulea [Didiscus cœruleus]** (Blue Lace Flower), *Umbelliferæ.*—Beautiful little Australian half-hardy annuals, some 18–24 inches in height, with rich blue flowers in summer, suitable for culture in the cold or cool greenhouse.

*Culture.*—Sow seed under glass in slight heat (50–55° F.) in early spring. Pot-off singly as soon as large enough to handle, using a compost of fibrous loam, with a little leaf-mould and sand added. Pot-on into 5-inch pots for flowering. Water regularly while growing, and shade from strong sun. Seed may be sown at different times during the summer to maintain a display, or seed may be sown in September for flowering the following April and May.

**Tradescantia** (Spiderwort), *Commelinaceæ.*—A genus of pretty perennial foliage plants, some of which are hardy and suitable for planting outdoors, while others require the shelter and warmth of a greenhouse. Some are trailing plants, known as Wandering Jews, and are suitable for hanging-baskets or pots, or for growing under the greenhouse staging. The leaves are sometimes striped. They thrive in sun or shade in well-drained, good soil.

*Culture.*—Propagate by means of cuttings in a cold frame in August, or by division of the roots from March to October, and plant out or pot-up for indoor use. The greenhouse species require ample moisture and an average temperature of 65° F. summer, 55° F. winter. A com post of turfy loam, together with a little sand and peat, will suit these plants well.

*Species.*—*T. fluminensis* [Central Brazil] is one of the commonest greenhouse and basket plants, useful for growing under stagings; in spite of little light, it remains green. There are forms with yellow-and-white-striped leaves, but these should be grown in full sunlight

**573**

# THE GREENHOUSE

and not too rich a soil, to keep their variegation. In light places with a low temperature the leaves of the variegated forms become tinted with rose, making them very attractive. *T. Reginæ* [Peru] has purple-red leaves, margined with silver. *T. Warscewicsziana* [Guatemala] is an upright plant, 12 inches high, with violet flowers; it requires the temperature of a warm greenhouse.

**Tradescantia discolor** (see **Rhœa discolor**).

**Tradescantia zebrina** (see **Zebrina pendula**).

**Transvaal Daisy** (see **Gerbera Jamesonii**).

**Trapa natans** (Water Chestnut, Water Caltrops), *Hydrocaryaceæ* (*Œnotheraceæ*).—A dainty little aquatic from Europe and the Orient, which can be grown in inside aquaria, warm pools, or raised for tub culture. It has two kinds of leaves, submerged and floating. The former are slender, feathery, and root-like. The latter, often beautifully mottled, are rhomboidal in shape, in the form of a loose rosette, the leaf-stalk of which is swollen and spongy. The flowers are white and small, but the fruits are leathery or bony with four large spines, and are large compared with the size of the flowers and leaves.

*Culture.*—They are readily raised from seed, which should be kept in water or moist to retain its vitality until it is sown in pots and submerged in a tank or tub of water with a little warmth. When germinated they may be potted-on or planted in a tub or tank in rich, loamy soil. If in pots they should be submerged in water at least 9–12 inches deep. In some parts of Europe the fruits are roasted and eaten as chestnuts.

**Treasure Flower** (see **Gazania**).

**Tree Peony** (see **Pæonia suffruticosa**).

**Tree Poppy** (see **Dendromecon rigidum**).

**Trevesia,** *Araliaceæ.*—Decorative stove plants with handsome foliage. They succeed with the same treatment as **Dizygotheca.**

*Species.*—*T. eminens* [Philippines] has handsome leaves divided into a number of segments, each with a prominent mid-rib and serrate edge. It is probably a form of the next species. *T. palmata* [India] has large palmate leaves, and the shoots are covered with prickles and reddish hair. *T. Sanderi* (Malaya) has handsome deeply-cut leaves.

**Trianea bogotensis** (see **Limnobium stoloniferum**).

**Trichinium,** *Amarantaceæ.*—Small, curious little greenhouse perennials, natives of Australia, with oblong or globose heads of red, pink, yellow, or white flowers like tufts of hair on stems some 9–24 inches in height, in June. They thrive in the cool greenhouse in a mixture of sandy loam and leaf mould.

*Culture.*—Pot-up in well-drained pots and water regularly while growing. Shade from strong sun and give ample ventilation.

*Propagation.*—Propagation is effected by means of seed or root-cuttings.

*Species.*—*T. exaltatum* (red and yellow, 24 in.); and *T. Manglesii* (pink, 9 in.); the latter is perhaps the choicest species.

**Trichomanes,** *Hymenophyllaceæ.*—A genus of filmy ferns requiring a very humid atmosphere. For this reason they are usually grown under bell-glasses or hand-lights or in close glass cases on the north or shady side of a warm or cool greenhouse.

*Culture.*—The Trichomanes are best cultivated in either close cases with beds built up of lumps of sandstone, and a compost worked among them of fibrous peat and broken soft sandstone. Plenty of drainage must be given, but it is essential to keep a moist, close atmosphere. Or they may be grown in square pans or dwarf pots. Plenty of drainage is necessary, and the most suitable compost consists of fibrous peat and soft sandstone. This should be raised towards the centres of the pots or pans, so as to form mounds with small pieces of sandstone protruding. When re-potting is necessary it should be done in spring.

*Species.*—The most ornamental and generally cultivated species are : *T. alatum* [W. Indies] ; *T. javanicum* [India, Java, etc.] ; *T. parvulum* [Japan and China] ; *T. radicans* (Killarney Fern) [Temperate regions) ; *T. reniforme* [New Zealand] ; and *T. venosum* [Australia and New Zealand]. Those from the West Indies and Java are best grown in the warm house.

**Trichopilia suavis** (see Chapter on **Orchids**).

**Trichosanthes Anguina** (Serpent or Snake Gourd), *Cucurbitaceæ.*—A tall, slender, climbing, ornamental gourd with white-fringed flowers, followed by long, twisted, highly coloured, striped-red-and-white fruits from 2 to 3 feet long. These look very attractive hanging from the roof during the late summer and autumn. It requires the same cultural treatment as the **Cucumber.**

**Trichosma** [Hair Orchid] (see Chapter on **Orchids**).

**Trichosporum** (**Æschynanthus**), *Gesneriaceæ.*—Beautiful, free-flowering, twining stove shrubs, well worthy of extensive cultivation. They bear handsome flowers somewhat resembling **Columnea** and have attractive, deep green, fleshy leaves and a pleasant fragrance.

*Culture.*—They are easily grown, either on blocks of wood covered with moss or fibre, or attached to pieces of old tree-fern stem. They can also be grown in orchid baskets or shallow pans, in a loose, open compost of Osmunda fibre and sphagnum moss with plenty of broken charcoal, always taking care that they are given plenty of drainage, to allow the water, which should be copiously supplied during the summer, to pass freely through them. They require a moist, warm temperature of not less than 65° F. at night, although in the winter this can be allowed to fall 5 or 10 degrees, and sufficient water should be administered to prevent the plants from shrivelling.

*Propagation.*—They are readily propagated in spring from cuttings of pieces of half-ripened shoots cut into 2- or 3-inch lengths, with most of the leaves, except one or two at the top, removed. The cuttings should be struck in a light compost and placed in a propagating case with bottom heat (temperature about 70° F.). They soon root, and can be potted off singly, replaced in the case, and gradually hardened off. They should be potted-on or put in baskets, and not allowed to flower the first year, but grown on fast, being pinched back three or four times, thus securing a good foundation for a future plant. The second year they should not be stopped, but allowed to grow on to flower. When well rooted an occasional dose of liquid manure may be given. If in baskets, pans, or on blocks of wood they are best suspended from the roof near the glass, but a light shade should be given if the sun gets too strong.

*Species.—T.* Boschianum (*Æschynanthus Boschiana*) [Sumatra] (scarlet, July, 12 in.) ; *T. fulgens* (*A. fulgens*) [E. Indies] (orange-red, Oct., 12 in.) ; *T. grandiflorum* (*A. grandiflorus*) [E. Indies] (orange-scarlet, Aug., 50–60 in.) ; *T. pulchrum* (*A. pulcher*) [Java] (brilliant scarlet, June) ; a trailing plant. *T. speciosum* (*A. speciosa*) [Java] (orange-red, summer, 20–24 in.).

**Tricuspidaria,** *Elæocarpaceæ*, also known as **Crinodendron,** which is now generally considered the accepted generic name.—Although in favourable localities these plants may be grown outside, they are, generally speaking, more suitable for the cool greenhouse, either grown in pots or planted out in a bed or border. They are beautiful, evergreen shrubs, with large, cup-shaped, pendulous flowers.

*Culture.*—They succeed in cool, moist, sandy peat, or loam that is free from lime.

*Propagation.*—They are readily propagated from seed sown in sandy peat and placed in a little warmth, or by cuttings of half-ripened wood placed in a close frame with gentle bottom heat. When rooted, pot-on singly in small pots in a compost of loam, peat, and sand in equal parts. As the plants develop, pot-on as required, using the same compost.

*Species.—T. dependens* [Chile] (white, April–May, 2–10 ft.) ; *T. Patagua* (*Crinodendron Hookerianum, T. lanceolata*) [Chile] (red, April–May, 3–12 ft.) ; this species was for a long time grown under the name of *T. dependens.* The two plants are very distinct in habit, shape of leaf, and shape and colour of flower.

**Trientalis europæa** (Chickweed-Wintergreen), *Primulaceæ.*—This slender, creeping perennial, a native of Europe and Britain, has dainty, white, star-shaped flowers. It is sometimes grown in the shady parts of the rock-garden, but is very attractive when grown in pans of light, rich soil composed of loam, leaf-mould, and sand in equal proportions.

*Propagation.*—It is propagated by means of seed sown as soon as ripe in light, sandy soil, with a piece of glass placed over the pot. Another method is by division in the spring ; these should then be placed under a hand-light until established. The pans should be plunged in ashes in a shady position when not in the alpine house.

**Trillium** (Wood Lily or Trinity Flower), *Liliaceæ.*—Hardy, tuberous-rooted perennials which thrive in well-drained, moist, peaty soil, in partial shade in the border or rock-garden, or in pots in the cold greenhouse or alpine house. *T. grandiflorum* (Wake Robin) [N. America] which grows about 6–12 inches high, and bears white or rose-coloured flowers from May to July, is by far the most desirable species. It is much grown as a pot-plant in the cold greenhouse or alpine house, although the Trilliums force well, especially *T. grandiflorum.*

*Pot Culture.*—Pot-up in October, using 5- to 6-inch pots and a compost of moist peat and fibrous loam, and winter in a cold frame. Grow in a shady position in the cold greenhouse during the spring and summer.

**576**

Strobilanthes isophyllus

 [*G. H. Preston*

Reinwardtia trigyna

Saxifraga "Tumbling Waters"

*Photos*]                                                      [*R. A. Malby*

Ramonda Myconi (R. pyrenaica)

GREENHOUSE PLANTS

*Propagation.*—Propagate by means of seed sown in a frame in March, or in the open in June, or increase by division of roots in October

*Other Species.*—*T. erectum* [N. America] (deep purple, May–June, 5–10 in.) ; *T. ovatum* [California] (white, May–July, 8 in.) ; *T. sessile* var. *californicum* (purple, rose, or white, May–June, 8 in.).

**Trinity Flower** (see **Trillium**).

**Triteleia** (see **Brodiæa**).

**Tritoma** (see **Kniphofia**).

**Tritonia (Montbretia),** *Iridaceæ.*—A hardy, herbaceous bulb and plant which has much increased in favour during the last few years. These plants, which grow from 2 to 4 feet in height, and carry on delicate arching stems, orange, orange-red, or yellow blooms similar to those of the **Gladiolus,** but smaller, during July, August, and September, thrive in rich, sandy loam and leaf-mould in sunny positions in beds or borders. Tritonias are also grown in pots for the greenhouse, and the flowers are also useful for cutting.

*Pot Culture.*—Pot-up in April, placing five bulbs in a 7- to 8-inch pot, and using a compost of two parts of peaty loam to one part of leaf-mould and sand. Sink the pots to the rims in a bed of ashes in a cold but frost-proof frame ; water very little until growth commences, and transfer to the cold greenhouse early in June. No staking is necessary. Re-pot every fourth year only, because if disturbed more frequently the bulbs will be unlikely to flower. No artificial heat is required. When lifted, divide and save the younger and larger corms for replanting.

*Species.*—*T. Clusiana* [S. Africa] (orange, summer, 12 in.) ; *T. rosea* [S. Africa] (bright red, summer, 12–14 in.) ; *T. Pottsii* [S. Africa] (bright yellow, tinged red, summer, 16–24 in.) ; *T. crocosmæflora* is a hybrid of *T. Pottsii* and is the popular Montbretia of our gardens, and the origin of some of the beautiful varieties.

*Named Varieties.*—*Drap d'Or* (yellow) ; *Etiole de Feu* (orange) ; *George Davidson* (golden yellow) ; *His Majesty* (orange-scarlet) ; *Lady Hamilton* (Apricot) ; *Lord Nelson* (scarlet) ; *Phare* (crimson) ; *Prometheus* (orange-red) ; *rosea* (rosy pink) ; *Salmon King* (salmon) ; *Star of the East* (golden orange) ; *St. Botolph* (yellow).

**Trollius** (Globe Flower), *Ranunculaceæ.*—Hardy, herbaceous perennials which thrive in rich, moist loam, in shady borders or in the marsh-garden. They also make good pot-plants for the cool greenhouse. They grow from 10 to 40 inches high, and flower in April, May, and June.

*Pot Culture.*—Pot-up in November, using 6- to 8-inch pots and a compost of rich loam. Keep in a cool greenhouse, and give plenty of water in dry weather.

*Propagation.*—Sow seed in the open in April, or propagate by means of division of the roots in April or October (preferably) and plant out. Lift and divide the roots when overcrowded only.

*Species.*—*T. asiaticus* [Siberia] (yellow or orange, May–June, 24 in.) ; *T. europæus* [N. Europe] (lemon-yellow, May–June, 15 in.) ; and the var. *napellifolius* (orange, May–June, 30 in.) ; *T. Ledebouri* [Siberia] (golden yellow, April–May, 30–40 in.). There are also a number of beautiful hybrids or varieties : *Excelsior* (deep orange, 24 in.) ; *Fire Globe* (rich deep orange, 24 in.) ; *Moorheimii* (golden yellow, 15 in.) ; *Orange Crest* (deep orange, 18 in.) ; *Orange Globe* (light orange, 24 in.).

**Tropæolum** (Indian Cress), *Tropæolaceæ.*—This is the garden Nasturtium, but not that of the botanists. They are beautiful climbers, mostly half-hardy perennials or annuals, invaluable for covering trellises outdoors and for training up pillars and rafters in the cool greenhouse. The best known of the annuals are *T. majus*, *T. minus*, and *T. peregrinum* [*T. aduncum*] (Canary-bird Flower or Canary Creeper), all three natives of Peru.

*T. peregrinum* (*T. aduncum*).—This beautiful, well-known creeper flowers best in a rather poor dry soil and in a sunny position. It is half-hardy, and bears yellow flowers.

*Culture.*—Sow seed late in April very thinly in the open, or under glass in March in a cool greenhouse. If planted indoors, pot-off singly, harden off, and plant out 12 inches apart in May ; otherwise thin out when large enough to handle.

*T. majus* and *T. minus*.—Many varieties are well known as climbers, and suitable for training up the roof of the cool greenhouse, the shoots hanging down to form a curtain ; and some are useful for hanging-basket culture.

*Culture.*—Sow seed thinly from March to June, ½ inch deep, in light, poor soil, and thin out to from 12 to 18 inches apart when large enough to handle. Some of the double varieties do not seed, and cuttings must be struck in a cold frame in August or September.

For outdoor use *T. peregrinum* (*T. aduncum*) and *T. majus* are especially good, also the perennial species *T. polyphyllum* [Chile] (yellow, trailer), which is also suitable for trailing about the rockery. In this useful category, too, comes *T. speciosum* (Flame Nasturtium) [Chile].

*T. peltophorum* (*T. Lobbianum*) [Colombia] (orange-red flowers with long spur) is a climbing annual which blooms beautifully through the winter months in the warm greenhouse, and likes a light, but not too-rich soil.

*Culture.*—Pot-up from March to April, in 6- to 10-inch pots, and grow near the glass.

*Propagation.*—Propagate by means of seed, or by cuttings in heat in March or April.

There are also tuberous-rooted species of the Tropæolum, such as *T. azureum* [Chile], with azure-blue flowers, *T. pentaphyllum* [Argentina] (green and red), and *T. tricolor* (*T. tricolorum*) [Chile], with orange-scarlet flowers tipped with black, which flower from April to June. They are all interesting and attractive climbers, and are suited to the cool greenhouse.

*Culture.*—These should be potted-up in August, in 4- to 8-inch pots, and set 2 inches deep in a compost of sandy loam and leaf-mould. Water liberally as soon as top growth appears and provide supports up which the young shoots may run. Dry off the tubers gradually after blooming, and store the pots in a dry, warm position until it is time to pot-up again the following August.

# GREENHOUSE PLANTS

*Propagation.*—Propagate by means of seed sown in gentle heat in February or March, or by offsets at the time of potting-up.

**Trumpet Flower** (see **Bignonia**).

**Trumpet Leaf** (see **Sarracenia**).

**Tuberose** (see **Polianthes tuberosa**).

**Tulips (Tulipa),** *Liliaceæ.*—Beautiful, hardy, bulbous, spring-flowering plants, which look best massed in beds or borders, carpeted with other spring flowers. Choice of variety is not always easy, as so many lovely colours are available. The plants grow from 6 to 30 inches high, according to the type, and flower from March to the end of May. They make useful pot-plants in the cold greenhouse, or may be grown in bowls for decoration in the house during early spring. There are so many to choose from that it is a matter of taste. Fine for pot and bowl culture are the early single and double types, particularly the *Duc van Thols* when well rooted, while the Cottage and Darwin Tulips are strongly recommended. These can be had in bloom from January to May.

Several of the dwarf species of Tulip are useful for obtaining early colour in the rockery or alpine house. *T. Batalinii* [Bokhara] (yellow, April, 6 in.); *T. Clusiana* [Mediterranean region] (white, flushed red, with crimson eye, fragrant, April–May, 6–9 in.); *T. linifolia* [Bokhara] (bright crimson); *T. montana* [Persian Mts.] (bright red, May–June, 6 in.); and *T. patens (T. persica)* [Orient] (April–May, 6 in.), are all suitable.

*Pot Culture.*—The early single and double dwarf *Duc van Thol* Tulips are excellent for this purpose. They may be planted from three to five in a 5-inch pot, or six or eight bulbs in a 6-inch pot; but of the Darwin Tulips three bulbs are sufficient in a 5-inch pot. All Tulips require a good supply of water when in flower, and should be shaded from the sun; hard forcing will prevent flowering. The soil and treatment necessary for Tulips grown in pots are the same as recommended for **Hyacinths.**

*Propagation.*—Propagation is carried out by means of seeds or offsets, the latter separated from the bulbs when these are lifted in summer, and planted in September or October. (See also Chapter on **Bulb Culture**).

Named varieties are innumerable, and catalogues should be consulted.

**Tunica Saxifraga,** *Caryophyllaceæ.*—A dwarf, rock-garden perennial which can be grown in pans for the alpine house.

*Culture.*—It succeeds in rich, light, well-drained soil, including some mortar rubble, and apart from an annual top dressing needs little more attention. The plant has the habit and appearance of a dwarf **Gypsophila,** and is covered during July with a mass of white or lilac flowers. It grows 6–10 inches high.

*Propagation.*—It is propagated by means of seed sown as soon as ripe, or by division in the spring. There is a double-flowered form of both white and lilac plants.

**Turk's Cap Cactus** (see **Melocactus**).

**Tussacia,** *Gesneriaceæ.*—Stove perennials with creeping rhizomes and showy coloured, bell-shaped flowers, the calyx as well as the corolla

579

# THE GREENHOUSE

being brightly coloured. They are allied to **Gesneria,** and require the same cultural treatment.

*Species.*—*T. pulchra (Besteria pulchella)* [W. Indies] (yellow and red, July, 12 in.) ; *T. semi-clausa* [Brazil] (cinnabar-red, golden yellow, striped crimson-purple, stems spotted red, July, 12 in.) ; a showy plant, in some varieties of which the stems and leaf stalks are violet coloured

**Tweedia cærulea** (see **Oxypetalum cæruleum**).

**Twin Flower** (see **Linnæa borealis**).

**Twin Leaf** (see **Jeffersonia diphylla**).

**Tydæa amabilis** (see **Isoloma amabilis**)

**Tydæa picta** (see **Isoloma bogotense**).

**Tytonia natans** (Water Balsam), *Geraniaceæ.*—A beautiful stove aquatic from Tropical Asia, with variegated flowers, red, white, and yellow. It should be grown in rich, loamy soil, in large pots or pans of water, and placed in a warm part of the stove. It flowers from July to September. Seed should be sown in the spring in pots of soil, and stood in water. This plant is sometimes known as **Hydrocera triflora.**

**Umbilicus** (see **Cotyledon**).

**Umbrella Palm** (see **Hedyscepe Canterburyana**).

**Umbrella Plant** (see **Cyperus alternifolius**).

**Urceolina,** *Amaryllidaceæ.*—Attractive and interesting bulbous plants for the warm greenhouse, with umbels of pendulous, pitcher-shaped flowers during the autumn. They are easy to cultivate.

*Culture.*—Place one bulb with its top level with the surface of the soil in a 5-inch pot in the spring, just before growth commences. It requires good drainage and a light, rich, porous soil. Place the pots in a warm greenhouse, and when growth commences water freely until the leaves begin to turn yellow at the end of the summer, when water should be withheld. A few weeks later the flowers appear. After the flowers are over the bulbs should be placed in a lower temperature in a place where they will be kept dry. In the spring the bulbs should be shaken out and re-potted.

*Propagation.*—They are increased by means of seed sown as soon as ripe and placed in a warm house, or by offsets at the time of potting.

*Species.*—*U. miniata (Pentlandia miniata)* [Peru and Bolivia] (bright scarlet, September, 12 in.) ; *U. pendula (U. aurea)* [Peru] (yellow and green, July, 12 in.).

**Urechites suberecta (Dipladenia flava),** *Apocynaceæ.*—This native of Colombia is a woody semi-climber for the stove-house, bearing large, funnel-shaped, yellow flowers during May. It is closely allied to **Dipladenia,** and requires the same cultural treatment.

**Utricularia** (Bladder-wort), *Lentibulariaceæ.*—Interesting plants with bladders or pitcher-like bodies attached to the leaves or roots ; these are best developed in the aquatic species. They are of two distinct groups, one group of which is decidedly aquatic, such as *U. prehensilis* and *U. vulgaris* (the latter being a native, quite hardy, and best grown outside), and is grown in water ; while *U. cærulea* and *U. bifida* can be grown in mud at the water edge of the warm aquarium, or in pans of soil submerged just under water in a warm greenhouse. The other

580

group, which is terrestrial or epiphytic, often forms tubers, and has some of the most beautiful flowers, including such as *U. Endresii, U. Humboldtii, U. janthina, U. longifolia, U, montana*, and *U. reniformis*; these are grown in the warm greenhouse, often among Orchids, requiring a similar temperature and atmosphere.

*Culture.*—These do best in baskets of fibrous peat, sphagnum, and some charcoal, and although they require a fair amount of water when growing, they should be kept on the dry side when resting and given a slightly lower temperature. *U. Humboldtii* and *U. reniformis* can also be grown in a pot or pan of peat and partly stood in water.

*Propagation.*—Propagation is carried out by means of division, which should be done in the spring, at the time of potting, as growth is about to commence.

*Species.*—*U. cærulea* [India] (dainty, pale-blue flowers, summer, 3 in., warm greenhouse); *U. bifida* [India, Malay, etc.] (yellow and orange, summer, 2–3 in., warm greenhouse); *U. Endresii* [Costa Rica] (pale lilac and yellow, summer, 6–8 in., warm greenhouse); *U. Humboldtii* (dark purplish blue, summer, 6–8 in., stove); *U. janthina* [Brazil] (pale blue or lilac, yellow and dark-violet, kidney-shaped leaves, summer, 12–15 in.); *U. longifolia* [Brazil] (violet-purple and orange, summer, 12–18 in.); *U. montana* [Tropical America] (white and yellow, summer, 6–9 in.); *U. reniformis* [Brazil] (rose, with dark markings, kidney-shaped leaves, summer, 15–20 in.).

**Vaccaria pyramidata** is perhaps the correct name for **Saponaria Vaccaria,** which see.

**Vaccinium** (Bilberry, Cranberry, Huckleberry), *Ericaceæ.*—Evergreen and deciduous shrubs, all of which require lime-free soil. Many of them are perfectly hardy, yet some are very decorative for the cold greenhouse, while the more tender ones can be grown in the cool greenhouse, where they would obtain some warmth during severe weather Except in very hard weather they should be given a moist atmosphere. They should be grown in pots, to enable the plants to be stood in the open air during summer, thereby getting the wood well ripened. They are very attractive with their racemes of white, rose, or red flowers. The fruits of many are still more decorative, also edible, while some are very beautiful in foliage during the autumn.

*Culture.*—They all require a peaty or sandy acid soil, such as two parts peat, one part sandy loam, and one part sand, but on no account should it be rich. The plants should never at any time be allowed to get very dry. Potting should be done during autumn or early spring, and only when the plants require it.

*Propagation.*—They are readily raised from seed sown in the spring in sandy peat, or fine chopped sphagnum, and stood under glass, the seedlings being potted-off when ready. They can also be propagated by means of cuttings of half-ripened wood placed under a hand-light. Other methods are by means of suckers, division, and by rooting trailing stems.

*Species.*—*V. corymbosum* (Swamp Blueberry) [N. America] (flowers white or rose coloured, May, berries black covered with bloom, leaves beautiful shades of red during the autumn, 2–5 ft.); *V. erythrinum*

[Mountains of Java] (purple-red flowers, Dec.–Jan., evergreen with red twigs, 12–24 in., tender) ; *V. erythrocarpum* [Virginia to Georgia] (pink flowers, June, berries red turning darker, 24–48 in.) ; *V. Mortinia* [E. Andes of Ecuador] (rosy-pink flowers, red fruit, evergreen, April–May, tender, 24–48 in.) ; *V. vacillans* [N.E. North America] (pink flowers, May, blue-black fruit, 12–36 in.).

**Vaccinium rugosum** (see **Pentapterygium rugosum**).

**Vallisneria spiralis** (Eel Grass, Tape Grass), *Hydrocharitaceæ.*—A half-hardy, submerged, aquatic herb from the warm and temperate regions of the world. It grows in a depth of water anything from 1 to 6 feet, spreading by means of runners. It is useful only as an interesting aquarium plant, particularly to the botanical student. The pistillate stems are borne on long, spiral, thread-like stems which reach to the surface of the water. The staminate flowers are on short stalks at the bottom. When ready, the staminate flowers break away and float to the surface. Both are borne on separate plants in June and July. This plant has escaped into many rivers, ponds, etc., in many parts of the British Isles.

*Culture.*—They can be grown in a warm aquarium tank, in a tub, or in deep glass bowls, the last being the most suitable, provided they have depth, as they allow the plants to be seen. They should be planted in ordinary soil, either in the bottom of the container or in a pot, and sunk to the bottom.

*Propagation.*—They are readily increased by means of division in the spring.

**Vallota purpurea** (Scarborough Lily), *Amaryllidaceæ.*—These are handsome, half-hardy, bulbous plants, which thrive in a compost of two parts of sandy loam to one part of leaf-mould. They require the protection of the cool greenhouse or a sunny window ; and flower on stems 1–2 feet high in August and September.

*Culture.*—Plant in July or August, singly in 5- to 8-inch pots, with the crowns 6 inches below the surface. Water well when growth appears. Winter near the glass (temperature of house 45° F. winter, 65° F. summer), and give liquid manure when the buds form. Water moderately until the leaves die in spring, and keep fairly dry and exposed to the sun from May to September. Leave in the same pot for three or four years.

*Propagation.*—Propagate by means of seed in spring or by offsets in August.

There is also a bigeneric hybrid between *V. purpurea* × *Cyrtanthus sanguineus* named *Vallota hybrida* intermediate between the two parents, with bright-orange, vermilion flowers. It requires the same cultural treatment.

**Vanda** (see Chapter on **Orchids**).

**Vegetable Sponge** (see **Luffa**).

**Vellozia** (**Xerophyta**), *Velloziaceæ.*—Stove- or warm-greenhouse plants with stout, erect, woody fibrous stems, and tufts of narrow, rigid, sharp leaves, resembling a **Yucca**, often bearing beautiful flowers.

*Culture.*—They thrive in a compost of well-drained sandy loam and peat, with plenty of drainage to prevent over-watering. They succeed

582

in a temperature of 65–80° F. during summer, with a winter temperature of from 40–50° F., and do not require a moist atmosphere. Potting or top dressing should be carried out in the spring, although they can remain undisturbed for a number of years.

*Propagation.*—Propagation is carried out by means of seed sown in well-drained, sandy soil and given a little warmth. They can sometimes be increased by suckers.

*Species.*—*V. candida* [Brazil] (white, summer); a handsome stove plant. *V. elegans* (*Talbotia elegans*) [S. Africa] (pale lilac, May–June, greenhouse); *V. trichophylla* [E. Tropical Africa] (reddish lilac, summer, 3–5 ft.); a beautiful plant for the stove-house.

**Veltheimia,** *Liliaceæ.*—Beautiful, South African, half-hardy, bulbous, early spring-flowering plants, which thrive in the cool greenhouse in a compost of sandy loam and leaf-mould. The clusters of long, narrow, tubular flowers are borne at the head of tall stalks, 12–18 inches long, which spring from the basal rosette of large, broad leaves.

*Culture.*—Pot-up in a large pot or tub in autumn with the tips of the pear-shaped bulbs just showing above the soil. Water regularly while making growth, and gradually dry off after flowering. Doses of weak liquid manure are beneficial as the flowering period approaches.

*Propagation.*—Propagate by means of offsets when re-potting—every third or fourth year.

*Species.*—*V. Deasii* (pink-flushed green, leaves glaucous and undulated); *V. glauca* (red and yellow); somewhat resembles the first named, but is larger. *V. g. rubescens* (reddish); *V. intermedia* (pinkish); and *V. viridifolia* [*Aletris capensis*] (reddish and green).

**Velvet Groundsel** (see **Senecio Petasites**).

**Velvet Tree** (see **Gynura aurantiaca**).

**Venus Fly Trap** (see **Dionæa muscipula**).

**Verbena** (Vervain), *Verbenaceæ.*—Most of the plants belonging to this genus, half-hardy annuals, biennials, and perennials, provide masses of gorgeous colour, white, blue, lavender, rose-red, and purple, over a period of several weeks in summer and autumn, thriving in sunny beds and borders in light, rich, sandy loam.

The garden Verbena (*V. hybrida*), although a bedding plant, is also very decorative for the cool greenhouse, requiring the same cultural treatment as **Pelargonium.** The plants should be grown in 5-inch pots and pinched back once or twice, keeping the shoots either staked or supported with twigs.

*Pot Culture.*—Pot-up in March, using 5- to 6-inch pots and a compost of sandy loam and leaf-mould, and a little well-rotted manure. Stop back the young shoots to make bushy plants, and water well while growing. Keep fairly dry in winter.

*Propagation.*—Propagation may be carried out by means of cuttings made of sturdy shoots that have no flower-buds, rooted in a frame in spring or early autumn. Autumn-struck Verbenas are best left in the cutting pots until February; and, unlike Calceolarias, if sufficient old plants are wintered for stock, spring-struck cuttings are best.

*Species.*—*V. chamædrifolia* [S. Brazil, etc.] is a slender creeping

# THE GREENHOUSE

plant with dazzling red flowers, which, apart from being suitable for bedding or for growing on the rock-garden, makes a charming basket-plant for the conservatory, or in pans for the alpine house. *V. tenera* var. *Maonettii* [Argentina], with pink flowers rayed with white, is also attractive for the alpine house. *V. tridens* [Paraguay] is a shrubby species, some 36–60 inches in height, with sweet-scented, white to rosy-lilac flowers, and although hardy in a sunny position outdoors, it is useful for culture in the cool greenhouse.

**Verbena citriodora** (see **Lippia citriodora**).

**Veronica** (Speedwell), *Scrophulariaceæ.*—*Shrubby Species* (which are generally known by the generic name of **Hebe,** and most of which are natives of New Zealand).—The evergreen shrubs of this genus are amongst the most valuable of summer- and autumn-blooming plants. Their handsome mauve, red, pink, blue, and white spikes of flowers, which are produced in great profusion and in succession for months, make them invaluable for greenhouse culture and for prominent positions outdoors, where with a dry sub-soil, and somewhat sheltered, sunny situation, the plants will generally stand uninjured through the winter.

Some of the dwarf species, e.g. *V. Armstrongii, V. Astonii, V. Bidwillii V. bombycina* [Syria], *V. cupressoides, V. Hectori, V. salicornioides,* and *V. Teucrium* var. *prostrata* make useful and attractive pans for the alpine house.

*Pot Culture.*—Pot-up in the early summer, using 6- to 8-inch pots, and a compost of two parts of loam to one part of leaf-mould. Harden off and stand in the open from May to September, then take into the cold house. After flowering, prune severely in March, and place the pots near the glass.

*Propagation.*—To propagate shrubby kinds, strike cuttings of matured wood in a frame in August. The herbaceous ones are increased by means of division in the spring. The young shoots of the shrubby species or varieties should occasionally be pinched back, but no " stopping " must be done after June.

*Species and Varieties.*—*V. Andersonii* [hybrid of *V. speciosa*] (purple or blue, July–Sept., 24 in.); there is also a variegated variety used for bedding. *Autumn Glory* (deep violet, Sept.–Oct., 18 in.); another beautiful hybrid. *V. cupressoides* (violet-purple, July–Sept., 12 in.); *V. Hectorii* (pale lilac and white, July, 12 in.); *V. Hulkeana* (lilac or lavender, May–June); a slender, graceful pot-plant. *V. longifolia* var. *subsessilis* [Japan] (intense blue, Aug.–Sept., 24 in.); *V. speciosa* and vars. (red, rose, purple, mauve, blue, July–Sept., 36–60 in.).

**Viburnum,** *Caprifoliaceæ.*—Deciduous or evergreen shrubs, decorative in flower, and many of them beautiful in fruit during the autumn. *Viburnum Carlesii* [Korea] has clusters of pinkish-white, fragrant flowers which appear with the leaves. *V. fragrans* [China] has white flowers which are pinkish in bud. This is the earliest species to flower, and only needs the protection of a cold greenhouse to bloom in the winter. *V. Opulus sterile* (the Guelder Rose or Snowball Tree) [Northern Hemisphere], which has balls of white sterile flowers, *V. Tinus* (*Laurustinus*) [Mediterranean region], a well-known evergreen, useful in

**584**

pots for the cold house, and *V. tomentosum plicatum* (Japanese Snowbal Tree) [China and Japan], with large balls of white flowers, while all quite hardy in the open, may be had in flower from February to April in the warm greenhouse.

*Culture.*—Pot-up in October, using 7- to 10-inch pots and an ordinary loam potting soil. Prune after flowering, and plant out for two years in the open before again attempting to force.

*Propagation.*—Propagation is effected by means of green wood cuttings, by layering, or by grafting on *V. Lantana* and *V. Opulus.*

**Victoria regia** (Royal Water Lily), *Nymphæaceæ.*—A magnificent stove aquatic plant from British Guiana, and one of the most remarkable productions of the vegetable kingdom, with its enormous peltate leaves, often over 4 feet in diameter. As the leaves develop the edges turn up 2–6 inches. The underside is deep purple, with a number of short, horny prickles; the upper surface is usually green. The large flowers, often 1 foot across, are white on the outside, passing to purple in the centre at first, becoming a dull crimson about the second day. Although a perennial with a tuberous rhizome, it is best treated as an annual, it being impossible to keep the plant alive during our dull, sunless winters.

*Culture.*—It is propagated by means of seed, which should be sown in February in a pot of loam; this should be sunk a few inches below the surface in a tank with a temperature of not less than 85° F. When the seedlings appear, prick them out singly in small pots, gradually potting the plants on as they grow. In May they should be big enough to place out in the large tank, which should be at least 4 feet deep, and in as light a position as possible, close to the glass, and large enough to allow the plant to develop to its full size. A built-up brick frame, not watertight, but sufficiently tight to keep the compost together, should be built in the centre of the tank, with its top below the surface. This should be filled with good, strong loam to which has been added a fair proportion of rotted cow-manure and some bonemeal. The temperature of the water at this stage should not be below 85° F., but when the plant is well established this may be reduced to 80° F., but not lower. To keep the plant healthy it needs all the sunlight possible, so no artificial shading should be given. It can be grown only successfully in a large tank and with sufficient heat to maintain the aforementioned temperature.

*V. Cruziana* [Paraguay] does not require so much heat, and the up-turned margin of the leaves, from 6 to 8 inches high, is green.

**Victoria Rosemary** (see **Westringia rosmariniformis).**

**Villarsia reniformis,** *Gentianaceæ.*—An Australian, marsh-loving, greenhouse herb, with bright-yellow fringed flowers.

*Culture.*—It should be grown either in soil at the edge of the aquarium, or in pans stood in water. The most suitable soil is composed of equal parts of loam and peat, with the addition of some sand. It flowers from June to July and grows 8–24 inches high.

*Propagation.*—It is increased by means of seed sown as soon as ripe, and the pot stood in water, or by division in the spring.

**Vinca rosea** (Madagascar Periwinkle), *Apocynaceæ.*—A tender, some-what shrubby evergreen from the Tropics, for the warm greenhouse,

# THE GREENHOUSE

flowering most of the summer. It is as remarkable for its shining green foliage as for its handsome circular flowers, which are rose or white.

*Culture.*—It is propagated by means of cuttings of young shoots in the spring placed in sandy soil in a close case. When the young plants are established, pinch out the tips to make them bushy. They require a compost of fibrous loam with a little decayed manure and some sand. The old plants may be grown on a second year, cutting them back in the spring and growing them on. They can also be raised from seed sown in January or February in a temperature of 65–70° F.

*Vinca rosea* can also be used as a bedding-out plant.

**Viola** (Violets and Pansies), *Violaceæ.*—The Viola and Pansy are so similar in their cultural requirements that we treat them under the one heading. The flowers of the Pansy are larger and more vivid in colour, but the Viola bears many more flowers, which are usually softer in shade and more self-coloured. It also has a much longer period of bloom, and is more perennial in habit. Violas, sometimes called Tufted Pansies, are much used for bedding or as edging plants, where they will flower from May until well into November. They are also useful for growing in pots in the greenhouse. Any ordinary, deeply-dug, moderately rich loam will suit them. A sprinkling of good compost and a dressing of soot or bonemeal should be scattered on the top. A cool, but not damp position in partial shade is best.

*Pot Culture.*—Plants intended to be grown in pots should be struck from cuttings in July or August. When rooted, plant in 4-inch pots with a few crocks at the bottom, using the same kind of soil as recommended for the plants in beds ; then place in a cold frame, plunging the pots up to their rims in ashes or coconut fibre. Keep in the frame until the end of March or the beginning of April, giving plenty of air on warm days. Then shift into 8-inch pots and plunge in ashes or fibre as before. Keep close for a few days, then admit air gradually. All plants should be staked or supported with small twigs.

Apart from the Tufted Pansies, there are a number of Viola species and varieties very suitable for the alpine house. They should be grown in well-drained, fibrous loam, leaf-mould, and sand, in pans which should be plunged in ashes in a slightly shaded position when not wanted in the alpine house.

*Propagation.*—They are usually increased by means of seed sown as soon as ripe and stood in a sheltered position in partial shade ; or by cuttings of young basal growth.

*Species.*—*V. alpina* [E. Europe] is a rare and lovely mountain species, 2–3 inches high, bearing rich purple, blotched violet flowers in April and May. *V. gracilis* [Macedonia] bears small, purple, pansy-like flowers in the summer. *V. hederacea* [*Erpetion reniforme*] (Austrian Violet) is half-hardy, has kidney-shaped leaves, and carries blue-and-white flowers in June and July. *V. lutea* [Europe] bears yellow or purplish-violet flowers in spring and summer. *V. papilionacea* (*V. cucullata*) [N. America] is a handsome Violet growing 3–7 inches high. It bears deep-violet flowers with a white or greenish-yellow eye. *V. Patrinii* [Himalayas] is a dainty Violet with clear, lavender-blue flowers in May and June. *V. pedata* (Bird's-foot Violet) [N. America] carries pale-lilac

586

flowers in April and May. The variety *bicolor* has the two upper petals coloured dark violet, and a form with nearly white petals is known as var. *alba*. All are beautiful Violets. *V. rothomagensis* [W. Europe] has bright blue flowers, striped black, in the summer. *V. septentrionalis* [N. America] bears rich violet-purple or white flowers in the summer.

**Violet** (*Viola odorata*).—The common Violet (*Viola odorata*) is distributed over Europe as well as being a native of our own island. It is found wild, both purple and white. White Violets are generally found in well-shaded, moist, calcareous soils. Violets may be grown in pots by placing two or three runners or offsets in a pot in April or May and keeping them in a frame, slightly shaded from the hot sun in summer. Loam, leaf-mould, and sand suit them admirably, but the Violet is not particular as to soil, for that which will grow good vegetables will grow good violets. Russian Violets, and sometimes the Neapolitan, will flower from September to April, if given the protection of glass. True violets flower in March and April. There are many varieties, but their culture is so similar that they may all be considered together. The grower should start with good stock from a reliable source, and, although the violet is a perennial, it is best to replant the stock each year.

*Cultivation.*—They should be propagated by division or " runners " annually in May or June. When the plants have flowered, remove them from the soil, divide them into single crowns, cutting off unwanted runners and dead foliage and selecting the finest outside crowns only ; then plant-out the single varieties 15 inches apart each way, and the double kinds 10–12 inches apart, and press the soil firmly round the roots, but do not bury the crowns. A rich, well-dug, and well-drained bed of moderately light loam and ample leaf-mould (though the Violet is not very particular as to soil), and with an east aspect, where they can receive the morning sun, should be chosen. In such a situation they escape the ravages of the red spider and other pests, and produce larger and brighter flowers. The site should have been well dug the previous autumn, and if the soil was very heavy plenty of leaf-mould and a little well-rotted manure should have been added. Leaf-mould and vegetable humus will help in too light a soil. When the plants show signs of growth, stir the soil about their roots with a small hoe, water liberally, and syringe them in the evenings of dry, hot days. Pinch-off all runners as they appear—this is most important if large flowers are desired—and give a little shade from the sun in hot weather. Nothing more, save fortnightly doses of weak liquid manure or dustings with an artificial fertiliser and soot, is required for their culture during the summer months. The double varieties should be wintered in pots under glass or in a frame. Violets may also be propagated by cuttings struck in a cold frame in September or October.

*Pot Culture.*—To obtain bloom during the winter months, the best compost consists of four parts of turfy loam to one part each of rotted manure, leaf-mould, and sand, and a sprinkling of soot, well mixed together. In September, raise the violets from the bed in which they have been growing with as much earth on their roots as possible, and remove all side-shoots and runners. One strong plant should be put in each 6- to 7-inch pot with the crowns just above the soil. The pots

THE GREENHOUSE

should be well-drained with broken bones instead of potsherds, for the roots of the violets will lay hold of the bones, which give vigour to the plants and make them bloom more profusely. Having potted as many as necessary for a season, the pots should be well watered to settle the soil about the roots. A sufficient number of frames should be arranged in a sunny, sheltered, southern aspect, placing them in such a manner that the lights will throw off rain quickly. Put in a layer of old tan, about 4 inches thick, and in this the pots should be plunged in rows up to their rims. The bed of tan should be 6–9 inches higher at the back than at the front, and should be raised so that the plants are from 6 to 9 inches from the lights. Keep the frame almost closed for three or four days after planting, and shade if the sun is strong. After the first fortnight, and when the temperature is above 50° F., the lights may be removed during the day, and at night they should be tilted up at the back for the admission of air. When the temperature is below 50° F., the lights should be left on, but even then air should be admitted from behind during the day-time. If the temperature is below 40° F., the admission of air should be very partial, if it is admitted at all. At no time after the plants begin to bloom should the lights be entirely removed, except for the purpose of watering or gathering the flowers. When the weather is cold, a covering of mats should be applied at nights. In hard frosts, two mats should be put on as well as litter round the sides of the frame. Care must be taken to wet the leaves as little as possible.

*Frame Cultivation.*—Violets can also be planted out in frames. The plants should be lifted in September, planted in frames, facing south, and partly filled with well-prepared stable manure and leaves. About 6 inches of soil is necessary for planting them in ; this should be brought up as near to the lights as the foliage will allow, so as to obtain as much sun and light as possible during the winter. Give a good watering, and keep the frame closed for about a week after planting ; plenty of air may then be admitted on all favourable occasions during the winter. The lights should be removed entirely during sunshine and when there is no frost, also during mild weather. Fog is injurious to Violets, causing the leaves to damp and preventing the proper development of the flowers.

*Varieties.*—(Double)—*Comte de Brazza* (white) ; *Marie Louise* (lavender, blue, and white) ; *Madame Millet* (violet-pink) ; *Duchesse de Parme* (pale blue) ; *Mrs. Arthur* (dark blue, white throat). (Single)—*White Czar* (white) ; *Cœur d'Alsace* (rose pink) ; *Rosea Delicatissima* (rose, pink, and white) ; *Mrs. Lloyd George* (rose and lavender). (Semi-double)—*Admiral Avellan* (purple) ; *Princess of Wales* (violet).

**Violet, African** (see **Saintpaulia**).
**Violet Cress** (see **Ionopsidum acaule**).
**Violet, Dog's Tooth** (see **Erythronium**).
**Virginian Willow** (see **Itea virginica**).
**Virgin's Bower** (see **Clematis**).
**Viscaria** (see **Lychnis**).
**Vitex** (Chaste Tree, Tree of Chastity), *Verbenaceæ.*—Deciduous and evergreen shrubs, some of which are nearly hardy and can be grown

588

against a wall in most parts of Southern England, particularly in dry districts. They are very decorative for the cool greenhouse during the early autumn, with their panicled spikes of lilac or lavender flowers.

*Culture.*—They can be grown in pots in a sandy compost of loam and peat, but good drainage is essential. The plants should be plunged in ashes in an open sunny position until in bud, when they can be removed into the greenhouse. They will benefit from some protection during the winter. The plants should be pruned back in the spring to encourage strong growth, as these give the best display.

*Propagation.*—They are propagated by means of cuttings of half-ripened shoots placed under a bell-glass, by layers, and also by seed sown in the spring in pots and placed in a little warmth.

*Species.—V. Agnus-castus* [S. Europe and W. Asia] (lilac flower, greyish pinnate foliage, strong aromatic odour, July–Sept., 20–50 in.) ; *V. Negundo* [China and India] (lilac or lavender, foliage, etc., greyish, June–July, 20–36 in., tender) ; the var. *incisa*, from North China, has beautiful, laciniated, pinnate leaves and flowers later. It is hardier than the type and is often grown under the name of *V. laciniata* and *V. incisa.*

**Vitis adenopoda** (see **Cissus adenopodus**).

**Vitis discolor** (see **Cissus discolor**).

**Vitis gongylodes** (see **Cissus gongylodes**).

**Vitis vinifera** [Grape] (see Chapter on **Fruit under Glass**).

**Vriesea** (see **Vriesia**).

**Vriesia** (**Vriesea**), *Bromeliaceæ.*—Stiff-leaved, ornamental bromeliads, many with beautiful marbled or banded leaves and brightly-coloured bracts. They are sometimes included under **Tillandsia** and require the same cultural treatment.

*Species.—V. carinata (Tillandsia carinata)* [Brazil] grows 8–12 inches high, has yellow flowers in the autumn, and bracts which are scarlet at the base and yellowish green at the tips. *V. hieroglyphica (T. hieroglyphica)* [S. Brazil] has yellowish flowers ; the leaves are marked with dark green above and brownish purple beneath. These, together with its bracts, make it a handsome foliage plant forming a tuft several feet across. *V. psittacina (T. psittacina)* [Brazil] grows 10–12 inches high, and carries yellow and green flowers in summer. The bracts are bright red in the lowest part, and yellow above. *V. speciosa (T. splendens)* [Guiana] grows 12–20 inches high, and bears yellowish-white flowers. The bracts are bright red. The leaves are bright green above and lighter beneath, both sides being marked with dark brown transverse bands. There are also many beautiful hybrids of garden origin.

**Vriesia glaucophylla** (see **Tillandsia fasciculata**).

**Wachendorfia,** *Hæmodoraceæ.*—Half-hardy, tuberous-rooted, perennial plants from South Africa which can be grown in warm, sheltered, frost-proof, sunny positions in well-drained borders with rich, sandy loam, to which has been added a little peat, if possible. They may also be grown in pots in the cool greenhouse. The flowers are usually yellow or purple, and are borne on stems from 1 to 2 feet in height.

*Culture.*—Plant or pot-up in October, putting two or three plants in a 5- to 6-inch pot, in a mixture of sandy loam with a little peat, and stand

# THE GREENHOUSE

in a cold frame. Water well while making growth, and gradually dry off after flowering, and keep dry throughout the winter.

*Propagation.*—Propagation is carried out by means of offsets in October or at the time of planting in the spring.

*Species.*—*W. paniculata* (golden yellow, April–May, 18–20 in.) ; there is a variety *pallida* with pale-yellow flowers. *W. thyrsiflora* (yellow, June–July, 20–24 in.).

**Wahlenbergia,** *Campanulaceæ.*—These are chiefly perennials, suitable for the rock-garden, and also very attractive when grown in pans for the alpine house. They should be given well-drained, loamy soil, and the pans should be plunged in ashes in a sunny cold frame when not in flower.

*Propagation.*—They are increased by means of cuttings struck in sand n a close frame or by seed sown as soon as ripe.

*Species.*—*W. albo-marginata* [N. Zealand] (blue and white, summer, 5–8 in.) ; *W. hederacea* [Europe] (pale-blue lilac, summer, 4–8 in.) ; this plant is not happy in chalky soil ; *W. saxicola* [Tasmania] (bright light blue, summer, 2–4 in.) ; *W. vincæflora* [Australia, N. Zealand] (blue and white, summer, 12 in.) ; *W. Pumilio* (see **Edrianthus Pumilio**) ; *W. serpyllifolia* (see **E. serpyllifolium**), and *W. s. major* (see **E. serpyllifolium** var. major). (See Chapter devoted to the **Alpine House.**)

**Waitzia,** *Compositæ.*—Half-hardy Australian annuals growing about 20 inches high and blooming in the open in the late summer—July to September. *W. aurea* and *W. grandiflora*, both with golden-yellow flowers are the best-known species. If grown in the greenhouse they will flower in May and onwards to September. They are among the best of Everlasting Flowers.

*Culture.*—Sow seed thinly in September for the early batch, and in February for those to flower later. Pot-up singly as soon as possible and re-pot as necessary, growing the young plants in a light, dry position near the glass. Water moderately.

**Wake Robin** (see **Trillium**).

**Wall Fern** (see **Polypodium vulgare**).

**Wallflower** (see **Cheiranthus**).

**Wandering Jews** (see **Tradescantia**).

**Waratah** (see **Telopea speciosissima**).

**Warrea discolor** (see **Warscewiczella**).

**Warscewiczella** (see Chapter on **Orchids**).

**Washingtonia filifera** (**Prichardia filamentosa**), *Palmaceæ.*—A handsome, Californian, fan-leaved palm, with leaves bearing at the margins abundant thread-like filaments. It will succeed in a lower temperature than many palms, and will stand living-room conditions quite well.

*W. gracilis* [Lower California] differs from the former by its more slender stem, has leaves which are less divided and hardly any threads from the margins.

*Propagation.*—It is readily raised from fresh seed sown and placed in heat. For further cultural treatment see **Chamærops.**

**Water Balsam** (see **Tytonia natans**).

**Water Caltrops** and **Water Chestnut** (see **Trapa natans**).

**Water Hawthorn** (see **Aponogeton distachyus**).

590

# GREENHOUSE PLANTS

**Water Lettuce** (see **Pistia Stratiotes**).

**Water Lily** (see **Nymphæa**).

**Water-Rice** (see **Zizania palustris**).

**Watsonia** (Bugle Lily), *Iridaceæ*.—Half-hardy, South African, bulbous plants, which should be grown in sunny positions in warm, sheltered borders, and in sandy loam, peat, and leaf-mould, or in the cold greenhouse.

*Culture.*—Plant in October or March, 3 inches deep and 4 inches apart. Pot-plants should be kept dry in winter. If planted out in a pit or frame where they are protected from frost they will flower much more strongly than in pots.

*Propagation.*—Propagate by means of offsets in October or seed sown when ripe.

*Species.*—*W. coccinea* (scarlet, 20 in.) ; *W. densiflora* (pink, 15 in.) ; *W. iridifolia* (rose or pinkish, July–Aug.) ; *W. i.* var. *O'Brienii* (*W. i. Ardernei*) has pure white flowers. *W. Meriana* (rose, purple, or scarlet, 20 in.). All June to August flowering.

**Wattle** (see **Acacia**).

**Wax Flower** (see **Hoya**).

**Wedding Iris** (see **Moræa Robinsoniana**).

**Weigela** (**Weigelia**) (see **Diervilla**).

**Weldenia candida,** *Commelinaceæ*.—An interesting, choice, tuberous-rooted herb from Mexico and Guatemala, 12 inches high, with snow-white flowers in April. It is suitable for the cool greenhouse, and should have the protection of such during the winter, for it needs more protection than a cold frame.

*Culture.*—It succeeds in well-drained pots or pans, in a compost of loam and leaf-mould in equal proportions and some sand. It requires a liberal amount of water when growing, which should be gradually reduced as the leaves start to turn yellow. It should be kept dry when resting. Re-pot or top dress the dormant plant just before growth is about to commence.

*Propagation.*—It is propagated by means of seed which should be sown fresh and placed in a little warmth ; also by offsets.

**West Indian Red Jasmine** (see **Plumeria rubra**).

**Westringia,** *Labiatæ*.—A handsome, half-hardy, Australian, evergreen shrub bearing white or pale-blue flowers usually in June or July, although some species bloom in September. Westringias are usually grown in the cool greenhouse. They grow from 2 to 4 feet in height, and thrive in a mixture of sandy loam and leaf-mould.

*Culture.*—Pot-up in March in well-crocked pots and stand in the cool house. Water regularly while making growth, and keep just moist in winter.

*Propagation.*—Propagation may be carried out by means of cuttings taken from young shoots and placed in sandy soil in a frame.

*Species.*—*W. rosmariniformis* [Victorian Rosemary] (light blue, July) ; *W. triphylla* (white, Sept.).

**Whispering Bells** (see **Angelonia**).

**Whitlow Grass** (see **Draba**).

**Widdringtonia,** *Pinaceæ*.—Half-hardy evergreen shrubs, which in a

591

young state make attractive foliage plants for the cool greenhouse or conservatory, with their upright habit and fresh, bright-green foliage, either as dot plants or mixed with other tall-growing plants.

*Propagation.*—They are readily propagated by means of cuttings with a " heel " inserted in the autumn in sand, under a hand-light, and placed in a cool pit. They may also be increased by means of seed sown in sandy soil and placed in a little warmth.

*Species.—W. cupressoides* [S. Africa] is bright green, with a pyramidal compact habit. *W. juniperoides* [S. Africa] is glaucous green with spirally arranged leaves. *W. Whytei (Callitris Whytei)* [S.E. Africa] in a juvenile state resembles the former species.

**Wigandia caracasana,** *Hydrophyllaceæ.*—A handsome, erect sub-shrub from S. Mexico, Venezuela, and Colombia, grown more for its foliage than as a flowering plant, although its lilac or violet flowers, the inflorescence of which is covered with golden, silky down, are quite attractive. Its fine foliage and bold habit make it useful for sub-tropical bedding. It often reaches a height of 6–10 feet in a summer, and can be used for decorating the conservatory, but it is not really satisfactory. Its great drawback are the leaves, which are covered with stinging hairs.

*Culture.*—It is best treated as an annual, although roots can be kept over the winter if protected from frost. Cuttings can then be taken in spring from the new growth, and inserted in sandy soil with bottom heat, being carefully shaded until rooted. Seed should be sown in early spring in heat and the seedlings grown-on in rich, sandy loam ; they should then be hardened off for planting out in June.

The var. *macrophylla*, from Mexico, has larger leaves, is a taller plant, and the inflorescens are covered with white silky down. It is the plant which is generally cultivated.

**Wild Hyacinth** (see **Scilla nonscripta**).

**Wild Rosemary** (see **Ledum palustre**).

**Winter Aconite** (see **Eranthis**).

**Winter Daffodil** (see **Sternbergia lutea**).

**Wintergreen** (see **Gaultheria procumbens**).

**Winter Sweet** (see **Chimonanthus præcox**).

**Wistaria** (see **Wisteria**).

**Wistaria (Wisteria),** *Leguminosæ.*—Hardy, deciduous climbers that do well in any good garden soil, but which prefer moist, deep, and well-drained, sandy loam. They are highly ornamental on a house, wall, pergola, or tree-stump, both for their foliage, which somewhat resembles that of the Ash, and for their long racemes of purple, mauve, or white flowers, which in form are very like the blossoms of the Laburnum. They grow from 3 to 20 feet high, and will cover an enormous space if allowed to grow unrestricted. When grown in the open they come into flower in May.

The best-known species is *W. floribunda* [Japanese Wistaria] (violet or violet-blue) ; there are several coloured forms of this, *alba rosea*, as well as double-flowered varieties, while *W. floribunda* var. *macrobotrys* (*W. multijuga*), a newer form, has racemes of bloom sometimes as much as 3 feet in length. *W. floribunda* and its forms bloom about ten days

Platyclinis glumacea

Nerine hybrid "Nena"

[*J. E. Downward*

# GREENHOUSE PLANTS

later than *W. sinensis* (*W. chinensis*), the Chinese Wisteria (blue-violet), the white form being the last to flower.

*Pot Culture.*—In the warm greenhouse (temperature 55–70° F. winter, 60–75° F. summer), *W. sinensis* will flower from February to April. Pot-up in October, using 8- to 12-inch pots and a compost of rich, sandy loam. Sink the pots to their rims in ashes outdoors in a sunny spot from May to December.

*Propagation.*—Propagate by means of layering young wood in the summer.

*Pruning.*—Prune in January or February, cutting back straggly shoots to within an inch of the base.

**Witch Hazel** (see **Hamamelis**).

**Witsenia corymbosa** (see **Nivenia corymbosa**).

**Wood Fern** (see **Dryopteris**).

**Wood Lily** (see **Trillium**).

**Woodsia,** *Polypodiaceæ.*—Greenhouse and hardy deciduous ferns growing from 3 to 6 inches high. The hardy species, i.e. *W. alpina, W. ilvensis,* and *W. obtusa,* thrive in the shade in a sheltered rock-garden or on a moist bank, in a mixture of sandy loam and leaf-mould, and may be grown in pans for the alpine house.

*Greenhouse Culture.*—The greenhouse species do best in the shade in a compost of equal parts of loam and peat with a little charcoal added (average temperature 45° F. winter, 55° F. summer). Pot-up in March and water liberally in summer.

*Propagation.*—Propagate by means of spores sown in heat at any time, or by division of the roots in March.

*Species.*—*W. alpina* (*W. hyperborea*) [Arctic Europe] is a dainty British fern forming dense tufts 3–6 inches high. *W. ilvensis* [Europe and N. America] has fronds 4–8 inches long, the lobes of which are crenate. *W. mollis* [Mexico, etc.] is an attractive warm-greenhouse species. *W. obtusa* [N. America] is a dainty fern, 6–9 inches high.

**Wood-tongue Fern** (see **Drymoglossum**).

**Woodwardia** (Chain Fern), *Polypodiaceæ.*—Cool-greenhouse, evergreen ferns which thrive in a compost of equal parts of loam and leaf-mould (average temperature 45° F. winter, 55° F. summer).

*Culture.*—Pot-up in March; water liberally and syringe daily in summer.

*Propagation.*—Propagate by means of division of roots in March, or as in the case of *W. radicans,* by bulbils or scaly buds, which are formed at the apex of the leaf, or by spores sown in heat at any time.

*Species.*—*W. areolata* [U.S.A.] has barren and fertile fronds 9–12 inches long. *W. radicans* [S. Europe, etc.] is an interesting fern with fronds 3–5 feet in length. The Japanese variety, *W. r. orientalis* is a larger plant. *W. spinulosa* [Temperate America] resembles *W. radicans* but has narrower fronds.

**Wormwood** (see **Artemisia**).

**Xanthoceras sorbifolia,** *Sapindaceæ.*—A handsome deciduous shrub from North China, sometimes developing into a tree, with fine pinnate foliage, and bearing in May erect racemes of flowers, white, spotted yellow and red. It is usually grown outside, and at its best there are

P P

**593**

few more beautiful shrubs. It is very useful for growing in pots for the greenhouse, and for some years large quantities have been imported into the country for forcing early into flower.

*Culture.*—They should be potted-up in the autumn, and the pots plunged in ashes in the open, bringing them into the house as required. If forced very hard it is advisable to rest the plants one year, forcing every other year. During the summer the plants should be stood outside in a sunny position and their pots plunged in ashes. Any pruning —which means chiefly cutting into shape—should be done after flowering. It succeeds in a compost of two parts of sandy loam, one part of leaf-mould, and one part of sand, good drainage being very important.

*Propagation.*—It is propagated by means of seed which should be stratified and sown in the spring ; also by means of root-cuttings placed in gentle heat in April.

This plant is seldom attacked by insect pests, but is very subject to coral-spot fungus. Any branches affected should be cut out and burnt, and the cut painted over with coal tar.

**Xanthosoma,** *Araceæ.*—Handsome stove foliage perennials, some of which have beautiful variegated leaves.

*Culture.*—They thrive in a rich, light, well-drained soil consisting of fibrous loam, leaf-mould, and sand, in equal proportions, a warm, moist atmosphere and plenty of water during the summer. Both heat and water should be reduced during the winter, but the plants should never be allowed to get quite dry. Although stove plants, they will stand more rough usage than is generally supposed, the leaves being of a firmer texture than those of Caladiums. They can be used for decorating the greenhouse, or even for the living-room. They should be grown in the warm, moist atmosphere of the stove until a number of leaves have developed ; thereafter they will maintain a good appearance under cooler conditions.

*Propagation.*—They are propagated by means of division of the rootstocks into small portions ; these should be placed in light, sandy soil, or coconut fibre, in bottom heat.

*Species.*—*X. Lindenii* (*Phyllotænium Lindenii*) [Colombia] has deepgreen leaves variegated ivory-white. *X. mirabilis* [S. America] has green leaves, spotted yellow, with primrose-yellow flowers. *X. sagittifolium* (*Arum sagittifolium*) [Tropical America] has large sagittate leaves, tinted bluish. *X. violaceum* [W. Indies] has green leaves with a bluish tint, the leaf stalks being brownish violet. The flowers are pale violet and yellowish white.

**Xerophyta** (see **Vellozia**).

**Xylobium** (see Chapter on **Orchids**).

**Xylophylla latifolia** (see **Phyllanthus speciosus**).

**Yellow Star of Bethlehem** (see **Gagea lutea**).

**Youth and Age** (see **Zinnia**).

**Yucca** (Adam's Needle, Bear's Grass, Spanish Bayonet), *Liliaceæ.*— These inhabit the southern United States, Mexico, and Central America, and most of them are practically hardy. They are evergreen plants of quaint appearance, forming striking objects when planted on lawns,

594

# GREENHOUSE PLANTS

banks, or in the rock-garden. They are also useful for winter bedding. Yuccas do best in sheltered, sunny positions, and in well-drained ordinary soil. The more choice kinds may be grown in the cool greenhouse.

*Pot Culture.*—Pot-up in March or April in a compost of two-thirds fibrous loam, one-sixth coarse sand, and one-sixth finely-crushed brick rubble. Cut away dead leaves in March and dead flowers in October.

*Propagation.*—They are propagated by means of tops, with the leaves trimmed off, planted in pots of very sandy and porous soil, by rhizomes in spring, or by seed.

*Species.*—*Y. aloifolia* is a slender plant, having green glaucous leaves with whitish margins and reddish-brown tips. It requires the protection of a greenhouse. There are several beautiful coloured leaf varieties of this, e.g. *marginata*, *purpurea*, and *tricolor*. *Y. filamentosa*, is the species to which the common name of Adam's Needle applies. It has sharp-pointed leaves, from the sides of which are attached long, thread-like filaments. There is also a variegated variety, *Y. flaccida*, which somewhat resembles *Y. filamentosa*, but differs from it by its flaccid, recurving leaves, and is probably only a variety. *Y. glauca* (*Y. angustifolia*) is a hardy, more or less dwarf, evergreen species, with narrow, spear-like leaves, which radiate from the crown and form a rosette some 2 feet high. The white and green inflorescences or bell-shaped flowers rise in July to a height of 36 inches. This is an excellent species for a small garden. *Y. gloriosa* has long, stiff, sword-like leaves, is vigorous and quite hardy. Its inflorescences of greenish-white bell-shaped flowers appear in August. *Y. recurvifolia*, one of the best species for the garden, has graceful, drooping, dark-green leaves nearly 2 feet in length and produces greenish-white inflorescences some 3 feet in height in August and September.

All the above-mentioned species are highly decorative when in flower as they all produce a large number of creamy-white flowers on large erect panicles.

**Zaluzianskya [Nycterinia]** (Night or Star Balsam), *Scrophulariaceæ.*—Interesting little half-hardy annuals from South Africa, 6–12 inches in height, with white, yellow, or pink flowers opening at night during the summer. They are suitable for culture in the cool greenhouse.

*Culture.*—Sow seed thinly in shallow pans of sandy loam and cover with a piece of glass. Prick off into boxes when large enough to handle, or pot-up singly in thumb-pots and move on as required, until they reach their flowering pots about the end of May. If sown thinly in pans they are attractive for the alpine house.

*Species.*—*Z. capensis* (white or lilac, 9–12 in.); *Z. selaginoides* (white to lilac and pink, with yellow eye, fragrant at night, 3–5 in.).

**Zamia** (Jamaica Sago Tree), *Cycadaceæ.*—Tropical or sub-tropical plants resembling palms. The leaves are pinnate and the leaflets narrow.

*Culture.*—They require stove- or warm-greenhouse treatment, and will succeed in a compost of equal parts of good loam and peat with some sand. Good drainage is essential, and during the summer the plants should be placed where they do not get strong sunshine. They

# THE GREENHOUSE

require a fair amount of water at the root and overhead during summer, but this should be greatly reduced during winter, although the plants should never be allowed to get really dry, and the temperature should not fall below 60° F. Should the plants at any time look sick, they should be removed from the pot, all soil be shaken out, the roots washed, any decayed part removed, and be re-potted in fresh soil. The pot should then be plunged in bottom heat and carefully watered until new growth appears.

*Propagation.*—Zamias are propagated by means of seed sown in sandy soil and placed in bottom heat. Pot-on as required. They may also be increased by division when there is more than one crown. They are allied to **Cycas,** and succeed under the same conditions and with the same treatment.

*Species.*—*Z. angustifolia* [W. Indies] has four to eighteen leaflets on each side, usually alternate (stove). *Z. floridana* [S. Florida] has twelve to eighteen pairs of leaflets, 4–7 inches long, usually opposite, glabrous above with scattered hairs beneath (warm greenhouse). *Z. integrifolia* (Jamaica Sago Tree) [W. Indies] has six to sixteen pairs of alternate leaflets, 4–7 inches long (warm greenhouse).

**Zantedeschia [Richardia]** (Arum Lily), *Araceæ.*—The common Arum Lily, *Zantedeschia æthiopica*, often known as *Richardia africana*, and its varieties are easy to cultivate, either in the greenhouse or in a room. They usually flower from February to May.

*Culture.*—Re-pot every October in rich, light mould, preferably loam, with equal parts of sand and cow-manure, the offsets having been removed and the old soil well shaken out. A 6-inch pot may be used for each plant, or three may be placed in a 9- to 10-inch pot. From this time until June, or earlier if the plants have flowered, they should have ample water and occasional doses of liquid manure ; it is best to keep the pot always standing in a deep saucer full of water. After this, however, they must be planted out in rich soil, or stood in the open in semi-shade, kept moist, and given occasional doses of manure-water until October, when the same treatment should be repeated.

*Propagation.*—They are propagated by means of offsets.

The yellow species are less hardy, and thrive best in the warm greenhouse, where they may be had in flower in the winter.

*Culture.*—Pot-up in February. Withhold water gradually after flowering and keep the pot in a frost-proof frame throughout the winter.

*Species and Varieties.*—*Z. æthiopica* (*Richardia africana*) [S. Africa] (white, spring, 24 in.) ; *Z. a.* var. *Childsiana* ; *Z. a.* var. *minor* [Little Gem] (white, dwarf) ; *Z. Elliottiana* (Golden Calla) [Tropical Transvaal] (yellow, summer, 24 in.) ; *Z. melanoleuca* [*Richardia melanoleuca*] (black-throated Calla) [Natal] (purple and yellow, 24 in.) ; *Z. Rehmannii* (rose Calla) [Natal] (rose, pink, or white, 24 in.).

**Zea Mays** (Indian Corn or Maize).—This monotypic genus of *Gramineæ* is a half-hardy, Tropical American annual (the origin of which is uncertain), which thrives in ordinary soil, in warm, sunny situations and grows to a height of about 3 feet. Its variegated forms are useful for greenhouse purposes, and as " dot " plants in summer bedding.

596

Varieties of this plant are commonly grown in sub-tropical and tropical countries, as its seeds form a staple food for many races when ground into flour. Fruit clusters are often boiled as a vegetable and known as " corn-cobs ".

*Culture.*—Sow seed ¾ inch deep in April, harden off and plant out in June about 18 inches apart. If required for greenhouse decoration, pot-up from April to May using 6- to 8-inch pots and a compost of rich, sandy loam and leaf-mould. Water well in summer (average temperature 50° F. winter, 60° F. summer).

**Zebrina pendula,** *Commelinaceæ.*—One of the plants known under the name of Wandering Jew. It is a popular trailing greenhouse plant from Mexico, very useful for growing in baskets and for covering the ground under benches and other taller-growing plants. It is closely allied to and sometimes included under **Tradescantia,** and succeeds with the same cultural treatment. It differs botanically from this genus chiefly in its tubular perianth, instead of free petals.

*Propagation.*—It is readily increased by means of cuttings.

**Zenobia pulverulenta,** *Ericaceæ.*—A very handsome deciduous or sub-evergreen shrub from the Eastern United States. It grows 2–4 feet high, and bears racemes of Lily-of-the-Valley-like flowers, with glaucous white foliage and young shoots. It flowers in June and July, and is hardy in most parts of the country where it can have sandy peaty soil. It is also very valuable as a pot plant, either for growing in the cool greenhouse, or for forcing into bloom early in the spring.

*Z. speciosa,* also from the Eastern United States, resembles the former, but the foliage is not so glaucous, nor does it flower so freely, but it is quite a beautiful shrub.

*Culture.*—Plants should be potted-up in the autumn in a mixture of sandy, peaty soil or light, loamy, lime-free soil and decayed leaves, in equal proportions. The pots should either be plunged in ashes in a sheltered position, or stood in a cool house during the winter, or in a partly shaded place during the summer. After blooming, the flower-bearing parts of the shoots should be cut off if not required for seed.

*Propagation.*—They are propagated by means of cuttings of half-ripened wood placed in gentle heat during July. They may also be raised from seed treated as for **Rhododendron.**

**Zephyr Flower** (see **Zephyranthes).**

**Zephyranthes** (Zephyr Flower, Fairy Lily), *Amaryllidaceæ.*—Bulbous-rooted plants, some species of which are sufficiently hardy to thrive in warm, sunny borders and in rich, well-drained peaty loam. The more tender kinds should be grown in pots in the greenhouse.

*Pot Culture.*—Pot-up from August to November, placing four to five bulbs four inches deep in a 5-inch pot and using a compost of two parts of loam to one part each of leaf-mould and peat, with a little silver sand. Dry off gradually after flowering. Lift when over-crowded and propagate by means of offsets in October.

*Species.*—*Z. Atamasco* (Atamasco Lily) (N. America] is pure white, being the largest and most popular of the white flowered, spring-blooming species. *Z. candida* (Peruvian Swamp Lily) [Buenos Aires] (white, autumn) ; *Z. cardinalis* [America] has bright red flowers in summer, the leaves appearing in the autumn. *Z. carinata* [Mexico] (pale pink) is the largest and choicest of the rose-coloured species, and is summer-flowering. *Z. rosea* [Cuba] (rose) is smaller than *Z. carinata*, and is probably the most popular rose-flowered species. *Z. texana* [Texas] (yellow and coppery). They all flower from May to September, and grow to a height of 6–10 inches.

**Zeuxine regia** (see Chapter on **Orchids**).

**Zieria** (Australian Turmeric Tree), *Rutaceæ.*—A remarkably pretty evergreen shrub for the cool greenhouse. It succeeds best in a mixture of sandy loam and peat. It requires the same cultural treatment as **Boronia.** The flowers of nearly all species are white, and are borne in June; the height of the shrubs varies from 2 to 10 feet, according to species. There are not many species, however, and it is only necessary to name one of them here, viz.—*Z. Smithii,* also called Sandfly Bush and Tasmanian Stinkwood.

*Propagation.*—It is propagated by means of cuttings of young shoots placed in sand and struck in heat.

**Zinnia** (Youth and Old-age), *Compositæ.*—A grand genus of handsome, summer- and autumn-flowering, half-hardy annuals, combining the greatest richness and diversity of colour with unequalled profusion and duration of bloom. For warm, sunny beds the dwarfer kinds, such as *Z. Haageana* [Tropical America] (12 in., single or double), are valuable ; the taller kinds, which are chiefly single or double forms of *Z. elegans* and are nearly every colour except blue or green, are excellent for borders and the greenhouse, and are now grown as cut flowers. The plants grow from 9 to 40 inches in height, and can be had in flower from the end of March until October. They thrive in light, rich, well-drained soil.

The best known are *Z. elegans* [Mexico], 20–30 inches in height, with flowers of various colours—white, buff, orange, scarlet, rose, lilac, bronze, violet, and crimson—and its varieties, *coccinea* (scarlet) ; *flore-pleno* (double flowers) ; and *violacea* (purplish violet). In addition to these types there are the double " *Quilled* ", the "*Anemome-flowered* ", and the " *Cactus-flowered* ", all growing to about 20 inches in height. More striking still are the giant " *Dahlia-flowered* " strains, so called from their resemblance to that flower, and bearing flowers as much as 5 inches in diameter. The flowers are purple, crimson, scarlet, rose, orange-yellow, and white and are borne on stems 30–40 inches high. The " *Gallardia-flowered* " type bears flowers that are well named, and the " *Pompom* " or " *Button* " has small compact neat flowers.

*Culture.*—GREENHOUSE PLANTS : Sow early in January and again early in March under glass in boxes of two-thirds fibrous loam and one-third well-rotted manure and sand. Keep the temperature between 60 and 65° F., and the atmosphere moist. Keep drier as soon as the seedlings have germinated, and when they are large enough to handle pot-up the seedlings singly into small pots, or prick off in frames 4 inches apart. Give ample light and ventilate freely, but do not let the temperature fall below 60° F. Avoid cold draughts. More water will be needed as growth increases. Re-pot before the pots become pot-bound, to encourage steady growth. After this final potting reduce the temperature by 10 degrees, and as the buds appear water weekly with weak liquid manure and dress with bonemeal.

**Zizania palustris** (Water or Indian Rice), *Gramineæ*.—A handsome, North American, aquatic, annual grass which can be grown round the edge of ponds and lakes, being one of the handsomest of tall, hardy grasses. It is also very decorative when grown in pots for standing round the edge of the inside aquarium. It blooms in summer, and grows 2–5 feet high. It should be given the same cultural treatment as **Rice** (*Oryza sativa*).

**Zizyphus** (Jujube), *Rhamnaceæ*.—Pretty, fruit-bearing, hardy and greenhouse shrubs (mostly evergreen), with extremely graceful foliage, greenish or whitish flowers, and drupe-like, edible fruit, which is used for confectionery as well as for dessert. They succeed best in sandy peat and loam, and may be stood outside during summer.

*Propagation.*—They are propagated by means of cuttings of ripened wood struck under glass or by root buds in pieces of the root.

*Z. Jujuba* [N. Africa, India, and Australia] (orange or red, April–May, 10 ft.) or the Jujube Tree, is one of the best-known greenhouse species, and *Z. sativa* [*Z. vulgaris*] (Common Jujube) [S. Europe] (purplish green or black, Aug.–Sept., 5 ft.) of the hardy shrubs. *Z. Spina-Christi* (*Paliurus Spina-Christi*) [N. Africa and W. Asia] has red fruit, and is considered by some to have formed Christ's crown of thorns.

**Zygocactus truncatus (Epiphyllum truncatum)**, *Cactaceæ*.—A very handsome, Brazilian, warm-greenhouse plant, often grown under the name of **Epiphyllum**, to which it is allied, but it is more closely connected with **Schlumbergera**, and succeeds with the same cultural treatment. It is a very desirable plant, with flowers of various shades of red or pink, from October to January. It can be grown on its own roots as a hanging-basket plant, but is often grafted on species of **Pereskia, Selenicereus**, and **Hylocereus undatus**, to obtain standard plants, or to train up the rafters of the greenhouse. There are several beautiful varieties : *Altensteinii* (carmine-scarlet to crimson, a vigorous grower) ; *crenatus* (red and bluish violet) ; *delicatus* (white in bud, opening to delicate pink and crimson) ; as well as many beautiful hybrids between *Z. truncatus* and other closely allied genera.

**Zygopetalum** (see Chapter on **Orchids**).
**Zygopetalum aromaticum** (see **Warscewiczella aromatica**).
**Zygopetalum discolor** (see **Warscewiczella discolor**).
**Zygopetalum Wendlandii** (see **Warscewiczella Wendlandii**).

# CHAPTER XVII

# DISEASES AND PESTS

## Insect Pests

It cannot be too strongly impressed that every effort should be made to detect the presence of pests at the earliest possible moment, and to set about destroying them immediately. It should be borne in mind that every part of a plant, both above and below ground, is liable to be attacked by pests, and growers are advised to become acquainted with the different pests, their habits, and methods of feeding, as this will be a great help when applying control measures. Pests are more or less controllable if tackled immediately they make their appearance ; but if allowed to run unchecked will quickly multiply exceedingly and do untold harm. They are of two main types—i.e., biting and sucking. The former include Cockroaches, Beetles, and their larvæ, and the larvæ of Butterflies, Moths, Sawflies, etc. These are destroyed by use of stomach poisons, either dusted on their food or sprayed in the form of a wash or by some other method. The sucking type, such as Aphides, White-flies, Mealy-bugs, and Scale insects, all of which pierce the tissue and suck the sap in some form or other, are destroyed by the aid of contact washes or by fumigants, as it is impossible to poison their food.

## Fumigation

The best time for this important operation in the greenhouse is the evening in calm weather, about an hour before sunset. To prepare a house for fumigation, shut all ventilators, and cover with damp matting all broken or cracked lights and all roof ventilators which are at all likely to leak. See that the temperature of the house is not below 60° and maintain this level during the period of fumigation. A slight rise is preferred to a fall, so as to avoid condensation of water vapour. Where convenient, plants which are in full flower and known to suffer should be removed during the actual process, and if possible water-storage-tanks should be covered with boards. Most gardeners will find the fumigating or vaporising materials sold ready for use with the necessary apparatus for burning highly satisfactory ; the makers give detailed instructions, which should be closely followed. Where the house is badly infested with any insect pest it should be dealt with two or three times on successive evenings ; this is almost always necessary when extirpating Red Spider. Should the greenhouse be well away from any dwelling-house and badly infested with White-fly, Thrip, Scale, or other greenhouse pest, Hydrocyanic Acid Gas can be used, especially for houses of tomatoes, but the instructions should be very carefully carried out, owing to the deadly nature of the gas. Tetrachlorethane is not so dangerous and is perhaps more suitable for the amateur when dealing with White-fly. Special care should be taken when fumigating a house of mixed plants or tender foliage subjects—e.g. Ferns, etc.—as it

**600**

may be risky to use the gases just mentioned, and better to rely on nicotine fumigants. The next morning, or when the fumes have thoroughly cleared, open the doors and ventilators and go round the house with the syringe and warm soft water, and free all plants from dead insects, washing the bodies off the stems and leaves.

In the following pages it is intended to show the best ways of combating most of the pests and diseases that attack our greenhouse plants, and to complete the chapter by articles on Fumigants (soil and greenhouse) and Insecticides and Fungicides.

**Abutilon Rust** (*Puccinia malvacearum*).—This fungus causes discoloured spots on the leaves, at first reddish brown, darker later. Pick off diseased leaves, and spray weekly with Bordeaux Mixture of Potassium Permanganate.

**Ants.**—Ants, of which *Acanthomyops niger* is the commonest species, are garden pests for several reasons. They thrive in the warm, sheltered atmosphere of the greenhouse and, once established, are by no means easy to eradicate. The best time to get rid of them is in the early spring, when all the young brood is hatched and food is greatly in demand. Sprinkle sugar round their haunts, and they will reveal their nest by carrying the sugar into it. Saturate the nest with paraffin or some strong disinfectant, or destroy it with boiling water. Empty honey-jars or old treacle-tins make good traps for the little pests, and hundreds may be easily destroyed by plunging the infested traps into boiling water. Old pieces of sponge dipped in syrup are equally efficacious. Paris-green and sugar, or Arsenic and sugar are recommended for poisoning and destroying them. A slight dressing of Derris or Pyrethrum dust can be applied to the staging. Pots or pans with ants should be plunged to their rims in water. Plants most usually affected are those attacked by Aphis and Mealy-bug, as the ants act as carriers of these pests and their eggs from one plant to another. They are also a great nuisance in garden frames and propagating pits.

**Aphides.**—There are many species attacking different kinds of plants. The common name for all the many species of aphis is " Green-fly ", or " Plant lice ", probably from the brilliant green of the aphis affecting the rose. Many kinds of aphis are, however, coloured differently : white, reddish, and black aphides being as common as the green. Aphides are sucking, not chewing insects, so that in order to deal with them it is not enough merely to poison the surface of their food-plant, as is the case with Caterpillars and such creatures. The aphides pierce right through the poisoned surface and suck the juices of the plant, so, to deal with them at all effectively, the insecticide has to be applied directly to their bodies. The best way to do this is to fumigate the plants or to forcibly apply a contact wash, to the part where the insects are, as soon as possible after the pests are discovered. Choice greenhouse plants, where possible, should be gone over with a stiff paint-brush, all the Aphides being either brushed off or killed by squashing between thumb and finger. Alternatively, the infested shoots may sometimes be turned down and actually immersed in the insecticide. When spraying with a contact wash it is very important that the pests are struck forcibly by the insecticide, or disappointment will result.

# THE GREENHOUSE

The wash should also be directed to the under-surface of the leaves. The best contact washes are Nicotine and Pyrethrum Emulsions. Spraying should be carried out during a dull day or, better still, in the evening, when the sun has lost its power.

The insect which deposits the sticky substance known as " *Honey dew* " is an aphis, and on this gummy substance a fungus grows, known as " *Sooty Mould* ", which does a great deal to weaken the plant by blocking up the pores on the surface of the leaves, and thus suffocating the plant. Honey-dew producing aphides are especially vulnerable to a lime-wash applied in March. Special efforts should always be made to exterminate aphides in spring and autumn. Roses (or other plants) under glass attacked by Green-fly must never be sprayed, but should be fumigated (see p. 617).

Plants most usually affected are Apples, Arums, Calceolarias, Cherries, Cinerarias, Currants, Ferns, Peaches, Pelargoniums, Plums, Roses, and many other indoor plants. Some plants, such as Auriculas, are affected by *Root Aphis*, particularly when grown in pots. They cover the roots and collar of the plant with white, mealy threads. The first signs are a yellowing of the foliage, after which the plant commences to wilt. All plants infested should be shaken free from soil and the roots dipped in a diluted Nicotine Wash and then planted in a fresh, clean compost. Sometimes the trouble can be checked by watering the soil with $\frac{1}{4}$ oz. Nicotine in five quarts of water.

**Auricula Root Aphis** (*Pentaphis auriculæ*).—See under **Aphides.**

**Azalea Gall.**—This is caused by the fungus *Exobasidium vaccinii.*— The terminal buds and leaves near the tips become very much swollen and pink, later being covered with a white bloom. Remove and burn the galls before the white bloom—which is the spores—develops.

**Beetles.** See Cockroaches, etc.

**Begonia Mite** (*Tarsonemus pallidus*).—These tiny pests attack the foliage, buds, and open flowers of the tuberous and fibrous-rooted Begonia as well as Cyclamen, Gloxinias, and Fuchsias, and cause the leaves to become rusty in appearance, curled and brittle, particularly on Cyclamen.

*Treatment.*—Spray with Pyrethrum Mixture, weak Nicotine Solution, or dust with Pyrethrum Powder, Flowers of Sulphur, or Vaporise Sulphur, and repeat the treatment if necessary.

**Botrytis cinerea** (Grey Mould).—This attacks numerous plants belonging to widely separate families, and destroys leaves, shoots, flowers, and fruit. It appears as a greyish- or brownish-olive mould, often forming large patches. It is frequently found on old flowers, especially on double ones in the autumn—i.e. China Aster, Chrysanthemum, Dahlia, Rose, Zinnia, etc. Spray with Bordeaux Mixture, or with Liver of Sulphur. Leaves, old flowers, and fruit attacked should be collected and burnt. See also under Grey Mould on Pelargonium, Tomato, and Vine, etc.

**Bulb Mite** (*Rhizoglyphus echinopus*).—This dirty, reddish-white mite attacks bulbs and tubers, notably those of the Hyacinth, Liliums, Hippeastrum, Eucharis, and other bulbs grown indoors under glass. It causes the foliage to turn yellow and the bulb eventually to rot. It

# DISEASES AND PESTS

usually attacks bulbs, which have been previously damaged, and the presence of the mite on bulbs is an indication that they have been attacked by some other pest or disease.

*Treatment.*—Soak the bulbs for some twenty minutes in soapy water at a temperature of 125° F., planting the bulbs again at once. All badly infested bulbs should be burnt.

**Capsid Bug** (Tarnished Plant Bug) (*Lygus pratensis*). This pest is very destructive to many kinds of plants, especially Chrysanthemums, deforming and destroying buds, flowers, and foliage. The bug is about ¼ inch long, pale yellowish green, mottled reddish brown, and the larvæ are wingless and of a deeper green. The damage is usually done during the autumn.

*Treatment.*—Infested plants should be forcibly sprayed with a nicotine-soap Wash, taking care to wet the under-surface of the leaves; or Nicotine Dust may be applied. Clean cultivation in the matter of weed destruction and collecting dead leaves and other rubbish in the vicinity helps considerably.

**Carnation Black Mould or Fairy-ring** (*Heterosporium echinulatum*).— Fairy-ring-like spots which extend and grow together, destroying the tissues of the leaves. Remove all affected leaves close to the stem, and burn. Treat as for **Rust.**

**Carnation Maggot.**—This is the larva of the Carnation Fly (*Hylemyia brunnescens*). The tiny, yellowish-white maggots bore into the leaves and down through the centre of the stem, eventually killing the plants. Young plants, grown in the open, are chiefly attacked. The presence of the maggots may be noted by the appearance of wavy, whitish lines in the leaves. They usually attack Carnations and Sweet Williams in the open border, but occasionally Carnations under glass.

*Treatment.*—Spray occasionally with Paraffin Emulsion as a preventative, particularly in the spring and autumn, and root up and burn all affected plants. When only a few plants are affected the larvæ may be killed within the leaf by crushing between fingers and thumb, those in the stem by piercing with a long pin.

**Carnation Rust** (*Uromyces caryophyllinus*).—Patches of pale yellow or orange, powdery pustules appear grouped together on the stem and leaves. Great harm is often done to greenhouse carnations.

*Treatment.*—Give plenty of air, remove all diseased leaves and spray once in two weeks with a solution of Copper Sulphate, 1 oz. to 1¼ gallons of water. Keep the temperature low.

**Caterpillars.**—The caterpillars of numerous moths cause havoc to some greenhouse plants if a careful watch is not kept, as they are often carried inside with plants that have been standing in the open. They are all biters, and their food is easily poisoned by means of spraying.

*Treatment.*—Spray the foliage with Arsenate of Lead Solution (*poisonous*) in summer, or, if preferred, careful hand-picking may be resorted to. This is sometimes sufficient under glass.

**Cattleya Fly** (*Isosoma orchidearum*). This tiny pest, which is not often encountered here, attacks the new growth and causes abnormal swelling at the base of the newest pseudo bulb, and its eventual destruction. The grubs feed on the interior of the swelling.

*Treatment.*—Cut off and burn affected bulbs or root-points. Fumigate with some safe preparation to destroy the fly. Spray plant every other day for about a fortnight with Nicotine Insecticide. In purchasing freshly imported plants, reject those showing signs of having been affected by the fly.

**Chrysanthemum Leaf Eelworm** (*Aphelenchoides ritzema-bosi*). See under **Eelworms.**

**Chrysanthemum Leaf-miners** (*Phytomyza atricornis*). See **Leaf-miners.**

**Chrysanthemum Leaf Rust** (*Puccinia chrysanthemi*).—This fungus causes reddish-brown rust-pustules on the leaves and prevents them being of any service to the plants.

*Treatment.*—Remove and burn badly infected foliage, and spray the plants with a solution of 2 oz. of Liver of Sulphur in 6 gallons of water, or with a weak solution of Bordeaux Mixture as soon as the disease is noticed. It is a good plan to dip or spray the plants once or twice in their early stages and spray again before housing with a solution of Liver of Sulphur, ½ oz. to a gallon of water, the same solution being effective for mildew.

**Chrysanthemum Leaf-spot** (*Septoria chrysanthemi*).—Small dark-brown spots which increase in size, finally destroying the leaf. Treat as for Chrysanthemum Rust.

**Chrysanthemum Mildew** (*Oidium chrysanthemi*).—The affected parts become covered with a whitish mould. This disease is most common on greenhouse chrysanthemums, but may also attack plants grown in the open.

*Treatment.*—Dust the diseased parts with " Flowers of Sulphur " or spray with a solution of Liver of Sulphur, ½ oz. to the gallon of water, ventilate as freely as possible, and prevent cold draughts.

**Cineraria Rust** (*Coleosporium senecionis*).—Bright-orange patches appear on the underside of leaf, rarely seen above. Other species of Senecio are also attacked. Destroy by burning the affected plants. Spray others with Bordeaux Mixture. As the Scots Pine is the alternate host plant of this disease, keep the plants as far away from the Pines as possible.

**Cockroaches** (*Periplaneta americana*) and **Crickets** (*Gryllus domesticus*). —Spray paraffin into all likely crevices and cracks, and dust the shelves and floor with Borax Powder or Insect Powder. These pests can also be destroyed by placing portions of Phosphorous Paste near such crevices in which the pests are likely to hide, while small quantities of Olive Oil placed in glass jars (jam jars) and stood about the greenhouse will account for large numbers of cockroaches, etc. They should be removed from the oil each morning.

**Cress Disease.**—When grown inside, Cress will sometimes become attacked by the fungus *Pythium debaryanum.*—The stem at ground level dies and the seedlings fall over, finally forming a slimy mess. Sow thinly, careful ventilation and soil sterilisation are the best preventive methods.

**Cuckoo Spit** (*Philænus spumarius*).—A yellow insect known as the frog hopper causes this trouble. The female hopper lays her eggs on the plant, and the grubs suck the sap from the stems and leaves, covering themselves meanwhile with the well-known frothy substance known as "spittle" or "spit". They are prevalent from May to July, and greatly retard the development and growth of the plants.

*Treatment.*—Spray with Nicotine or Paraffin Emulsion. Project the spray as forcibly as possible to wash away the covering of froth, and thus enable the substance used for spraying to come in actual contact with the insects. This pest affects plants in the open more than in the glasshouses, although roses and other plants stood out for the summer may be attacked.

**Cucumber Canker.**—This is due to *Mycosphærella citrullina.*—The lower part of the stem becomes cankered, the upper part of the plant wilts. The plants should be burnt, and care should be taken to avoid using the soil again for Cucumbers, or Melons which are also affected.

**Cucumber Mildew** (*Erysiphe cichoraceorum*).—Whitish growths on the leaf-surface. Dust with flowers of sulphur. See also **Mildew.**

**Cucumber Scab** (*Cladosporium scabies*).—Dark spots on rind of fruit, which later crack, and often exude a gummy substance. Clean cultivation, destruction of affected parts, and good ventilation are the best preventives.

**Damping Off.**—This is a term applied to seedlings which die off suddenly in a young state, and is caused by various agents, one of the principal being *Pythium debaryanum*, which is more prevalent under glass than in the open ground. It is often brought about by overcrowding of the seedlings, particularly when they have become drawn and weak by careless watering, and especially by bad ventilation. Most members of the family of Cruciferæ as well as seedling tomatoes are subject to it in the early stages or when attacked by *Phytophthora* or *Rhizoctonia solani.* Thin seed-sowing, careful ventilation, and soil sterilisation are the best preventive measures. See also under **Cress.**

**Earwigs** (*Forficula auricularia*).—These do considerable damage in greenhouses, feeding on the foliage and flowers of such plants as Chrysanthemums and others during the night. They hide during the day among the leaves, in the hollow of bamboo canes among the flowers, etc.

*Treatment.*—They are easy to trap, owing to their propensity to hide in any sheltered spot during the day. Thus a handful of straw, shavings, or hay, pushed lightly into a flower-pot and stuck on a stick among the plants in the beds will be found full of earwigs in the morning, if they are present in any numbers. Crumpled paper, pieces of corrugated cardboard, hollow stalks, and similar things make effective earwig traps. A poison bait can also be applied consisting of 2 lb. Bran ; ½ pint Black Treacle ; ¼ lb. of Sodium Fluoride, and ½ gall. of Water. The Treacle should be dissolved in a little water, adding to it the Sodium Fluoride Solution, this can then be mixed with the bran so to form a mash. The bait should be applied in the evening on the floor and stages of the greenhouse. It is very important that all dead leaves at the bottom of plants, as well as any other rubbish which would provide any refuge or harbour for the insect, should be removed, as such provide a breeding-ground for the pest.

# THE GREENHOUSE

**Eelworms** (*Aphelenchoides and Heterodera*).—Eelworms, of which there are several species, attack different plants. They are very difficult to detect, as they are extremely small and almost transparent. They occur in large numbers together, and all fresh supplies of potting soil or new soil from any source should be carefully examined for them, as this is a common method of introduction. If possible, soil should be treated by some form of sterilisation. The Eelworm attacks the roots or leaves of the plants on which it feeds, penetrating them and sucking their juices. Many plants are liable to attack, among the commoner victims being Begonias, Coleus, Cucumbers, Melons, Phloxes, Strawberries, Tomatoes, Vines, which are usually attacked by the **Root-knot Eelworm** (*Heterodera marioni*). The roots of infected plants become swollen and galled. The **Chrysanthemum Leaf Eelworm** (*Aphelenchoides ritzema-bosi*) lives in the leaves and stem; the leaf turns dark brown and hangs on the plant for a long time; the buds and flowers are infected and become blind. The **Leaf Eelworm** (*Aphelenchoides olesistus*) attacks the foliage of Begonias, Coleus, Gloxinias, Salvias, and some of the ferns, turning them yellow. Frequent applications of a nicotine soap wash are said to check it.

The nature of the apparent injury varies with the species, both of plant and eelworm. Sometimes Cucumbers, Melons and Tomatoes, simply die, no reason being apparent until the roots are lifted and carefully examined. **Eelworms** cause the " *Cauliflower Disease* " in Strawberries, in which the stems become swollen and the buds crowded together, suggesting a cauliflower; other eelworms cause general decay of the roots and crowns. Vines often show a peculiar appearance just below the soil, where the bark may have disappeared. Most often the roots of plants affected by eelworm have small warty growths and nodules on them, showing the points of attack.

*Treatment.*—The only thing to be done with plants badly infected with eelworm is to dig them up and destroy them. Remove the soil all around, bury it deeply, and replace with fresh soil sterilised by pouring boiling water over it. The pest is comparatively easy to eradicate when it appears indoors, but in the garden it is a far more difficult matter. Cuttings from diseased plants are liable to be infected, and when rooted should be immersed in hot water at 110° F. for about twenty minutes. Infected root-stocks may also be immersed in hot water for twenty to thirty minutes, but the stems should be cut back as low as possible, and the roots washed clean of soil. Afterwards place the plants in cool water and pot in sterilised soil. In cases where Kainit can be used it will be found helpful, and should be forked into the affected soil in combination with twice its weight of Basic Slag.

If there is any fear of Eelworm, all new soil should be either lightly baked or scalded with boiling water before use.

**Erysiphaceæ.**—A group of Mildews, many of which derive their specific name from one of their host plants. See **Mildew**.

**Grey Mould.** See **Botrytis cinerea.**

**Hellebore Leaf-blotch** (*Coniothyrium hellebori*).—Attacks the leaves of *Helleborus niger*. Forms large, circular, brownish blotches, with a somewhat scorched appearance, covered with minute black dots.

606

# DISEASES AND PESTS

*Treatment.*—Cut off and burn affected leaves, and spray the remainder with Liver of Sulphur.

**Honey Dew.** See **Aphides.**

**Iris, Ink Disease** (*Mystrosporium adustum*).—This chiefly attacks the Reticulata Group. The outside scales of the bulbs become discoloured, as if stained with ink. The foliage is unhealthy and turns yellow during the growing season.

*Treatment.*—Slightly infected bulbs at the end of the growing season should be dried off and soaked for an hour in a 2 per cent. solution of Formalin, then dried and stored in sand for a period, and finally planted in fresh soil. In badly infested bulbs the discoloration may extend to the centre, and such bulbs should be destroyed by burning, together with the soil in which they were grown.

**Leaf Eelworm** (*Aphelenchoides olesistus*).—See under **Eelworms.**

**Leaf Hopper** (*Erythroneura pallidifrons*).—This pest attacks a number of plants—i.e. Calceolaria, Fuchsia, Geranium, Primula, Salvia, etc. This insect attacks the underside of the leaves and sucks the sap, causing a mottled appearance. The foliage fails to function and growth is stopped.

*Treatment.*—The pest can be controlled by thorough and forcible applications of Nicotine Soap or Pyrethrum preparation, taking care that the undersides of the leaves are well drenched with the wash.

**Leaf Miners** (*Phytomyza atricornis*).—These maggots hatch from the eggs of small flies that frequent the leaves of plants, such as Chrysanthemums and Cinerarias, and eat into the foliage, making pale streaks across the surface of the leaves or causing brown shrivelled patches.

*Treatment.*—As a deterrent, spray at least fortnightly both surfaces of the leaves with Paraffin Emulsion or Nicotine and Soap Wash. With such plants as Chrysanthemums, spraying with soot-water throughout the season is a good preventive. In the early stages, when the streaks on the leaves are first noticed, the maggots may be destroyed by means of pinching between the finger and thumb. Pick off and burn badly infested leaves.

**Lily Disease.**—This disease, which causes spotting of the foliage and buds, is caused by the mould *Botrytis elliptica.* The parts affected with the stem die and dry up and the flowers become distorted.

*Treatment.*—Spray affected plants with Liver of Sulphur or Bordeaux Mixture, and change soil and pot after flowering is over. Give the bulbs a dusting with sulphur.

**Lily Mosaic Disease.**—This is caused by inoculation of a virus by a species of aphis. It may attack any species of *Lilium*, but chiefly affects *L. longiflorum*, and its varieties; the leaves become mottled, distorted, and the petals of the flowers, instead of opening, remain together at the tips. There is no known cure, but fumigation will arrest the spread of the disease; all affected plants should be burnt As seed does not seem to carry the disease, it is advisable to propagate by seed only, for any vegetative propagation of infected plants will certainly transmit it.

See also under **Bulb Mite** (*Rhizoglyphus echinopus*) which can also be very troublesome to Lily bulbs grown in pots.

607

# THE GREENHOUSE

**Mealy-bug.**—The Mealy-bug is so called because a white, downy, waxy material grows on the bodies of the female insects. Mealy-bugs attack chiefly Figs and Grapes under glass, as well as a great variety of ornamental plants. The two most common species of Mealy-bugs that occur in plant houses are *Pseudococcus gahani*, and *P. citri*.

*Treatment.*—A constant watch should be kept on all glasshouses for any signs of Mealy-bug, and steps taken against them as soon as detected, so as to prevent vast colonies establishing themselves. If present in large numbers, fumigation with Hydrocyanic Gas is sometimes necessary, but usually a good spraying with Nicotine and Soap Solution, and the subsequent application of a little Methylated Spirit to the mealy-looking patches where the females congregate will help to wipe them out. Persistence with any form of treatment is particularly essential to eradicate this pest.

**Mice.** House Mice (*Mus musculus*) and Field Mice (*Arvicola riparia*). Much harm is done by these in the greenhouse to newly-sown seeds and to bulbs. They will also injure Cucumbers, Melons, Vegetable Marrows, etc. It is supposed that they are guided to the seeds by their acute sense of smell.

*Traps for Mice.*—Most gardeners use the common break-back trap with good effect. Perhaps the simplest and cheapest trap of any is a pickle-jar sunk to the brim, or very nearly so, in the earth. The rim and inside of the jar as far as the shoulder should be liberally smeared with grease, and the jar half filled with water. A little corn, lumps of grease, etc., may be placed on the earth in the immediate vicinity of the jar. Phosphorous Paste can also be placed about, but must be collected next morning to prevent other animals or birds from getting it.

**Mildew** (*Erysipheæ*).—In this disease, which is due to a fungus, the buds, leaves, small shoots, and stems are chiefly affected; they become covered with a whitish mould and eventually shrivel up. If conditions are favourable, the disease quickly spreads by means of spores blown from leaf to leaf.

*Treatment.*—Spray the affected parts with Lime Sulphur, and cut out all diseased portions in autumn while the effects of the mildew can still be seen. The hot-water pipes can be washed with a mixture of ¼ lb. of Flowers of Sulphur and ¼ lb. of Quick Lime in 3 gallons of water. The door of the house should be kept closed for an hour, and afterwards the place well aired. In the following spring any buds still affected must be pinched off and burned, and as a preventive measure the plants should again be sprayed. Mildew is often encouraged by bad ventilation and cold draughts, which should be attended to.

**Millepedes.**—The two most injurious species are *Blanjulus guttulatus*, with smooth cylindrical bodies, and *Polydesmus complanatus*, with broader, flattened bodies, often found between the scales of lilies and other bulbs. Millepedes attack all bulbs, roots and other vegetable matter, living and dead. They eat away the skin or hollow out the inside, usually following where Slugs and Wireworms have started. Decay sets in, and other pests get to work.

*Treatment.*—Work Powdered Naphthalene into the heap of stacked loam, or the mixed compost, or fumigate with Carbon Disulphide, in

608

Passiflora Allardii

Amaryllis Belladonna *var.* "Hathor"

# DISEASES AND PESTS

either case leaving it for a time before using it, allowing 1½ oz. to every square yard. Water after application. Place a turnip or potato tuber with the centre scooped out, or sliced mangold or carrot, on sticks just under the surface of the soil in the greenhouse or frame. The millepedes will enter these and feed. These traps should be frequently inspected and the pests destroyed.

**Nerium Black Mould** (*Capnodium neerii*).—Forms a black, velvety-like growth on the leaves of Oleanders, giving them a dirty appearance.

*Treatment.*—Spray as for Aphis, which is the cause of the honey dew upon which the fungus grows.

**Peach, Plum, and Nectarine Rust** (*Puccinia pruni*).—Causing small yellowish spots on the upper surfaces of the leaves with heaps of dark-brown pustules freely scattered over the under surface. This Rust also attacks *Anemone coronaria*, in which it becomes perennial and restricts flowering.

*Control.*—Spray with Bordeaux Mixture. Do not grow Anemones close to Peaches, etc.

**Peach Leaf-curl** (*Taphrina deformans*).—Leaves curl, wrinkle and turn red.

*Control.*—Spray with Lime Sulphur just as buds swell in spring.

**Peach Scale** (*Lecanium corni*).—See under **Scale.**

**Pelargonium Stem-rot** (*Fusarium pelargoni*).—The stems become blackened and decayed, the leaves turn yellow, pale, and pink-coloured spots sometimes appear on the blackened portion of the stems. The plants should be destroyed. Grey Mould (*Botrytis cinerea*) often appears on dying shoots and foliage of Pelargoniums. Remove and burn all decaying leaves and shoots ; maintain a drier atmosphere, and less close conditions.

**Plant Lice.**—See **Aphides.**

**Red Spider** (*Tetranychus telarius*).—The red spider mite is the most familiar of all greenhouse pests. It eats into the underside of the foliage of ornamental plants, Cucumbers, Tomatoes, Peaches, Vines, and particularly Violets in frames. It sucks at the sap, causing the leaves to turn yellow and later, if the attack is severe, whitish. The pest is encouraged by drought in the open, or by excessive heating and drying of the atmosphere of the greenhouse, and may be kept under by remedying these conditions.

*Treatment.*—Plants attacked in the open should be sprayed with Paraffin Emulsion or Lime-sulphur, but this must be done early, before the trees or bushes are badly damaged. On the first discovery of Red Spider in the greenhouse, all affected leaves should be sponged with soapy water, and the house fumigated with Naphthalene Vapour. Clean cultivation is very important, care should be taken to destroy all weeds around the plants and houses, especially in the autumn, as they are hosts to which the mites migrate. Such hosts are particularly Violets when grown in the vicinity. The walls of greenhouse and frames should be pointed and whitewashed to reduce shelter for these pests. White-oil-emulsions which are on the market under various proprietary names will help to control the Mites, but care must be taken not to apply these washes to tender-foliaged plants, or those with

Q Q

# THE GREENHOUSE

glaucous leaves such as Carnations, these should be sprayed with Liver of Sulphur and Soft Soap Wash. This should be applied as soon as mixed, but only in dull weather or during the evening, to avoid injury to the foliage. When spraying, it is essential to direct the wash with force to the undersides of the leaves where the mites are found and where they feed.

**Rose Mildew** (*Sphærotheca pannosa*).—A Mildew on new growth, see **Mildew.**

**Rose Rot.**—Plants grown under glass are occasionally attacked by a disease due to *Peronospora sparsa*. Brown spots rapidly spread over the leaves, bearing threads of greyish fungus on the lower surface. Destroy all fallen leaves by burning. Spray with Bordeaux Mixture on the first trace of the disease.

**Rose Rust** (*Phragmidium mucronatum*).—Yellow spots are scattered closely over the lower surface of the leaves followed by brown and black spots, often causing the leaves to fall easily. Collect and burn fallen leaves. Spray with Potassium Permanganate. Stand all pot roses in the open.

**Rust.**—A popular name given to the *Uredo* stage of certain Fungi which are highly destructive on wild and cultivated plants. The name refers to the pustules of rusty-orange-coloured spores which appear usually on the foliage, spreading very rapidly, and finally destroying the plant. Some kinds of rust require two host plants to complete their life-cycle, as in the case of the Cineraria Rust, which has one stage on various members of the family of Composites—i.e. Cineraria, Ragworts, Groundsel, the alternative host being the Scots Pine. Another example is the Peach and Anemone Rust. Such Rust fungi are known as heterœcious. Other Rusts restrict themselves to one or more genera of the same family, as the Hollyhock Rust (*Puccinia malvacearum*), attacking Abutilon and other members of Malvaceœ. All Rusts are very destructive and should be thoroughly dealt with, as directed under the following headings :

**Abutilon Rust** (*Puccinia malvacearum*) ; **Carnation Rust** (*Uromyces caryophyllinus*) ; **Chrysanthemum Rust** (*Puccinia chrysanthemi*) ; **Cineraria Rust** (*Coleosporium senecionis*), also attacks other species of Senecio ; **Peach Rust** (*Puccinia pruni*), also attacks Plums and Anemones ; **Rose Rust** (*Phragmidium mucronatum*) ; **Sempervivum Rust** (*Endophyllum sempervivi*) ; and **Viola Rust** (*Puccinia violæ*).

**Scale** (*Lecanium, Aspidiotus, Diaspis, Pinnaspis*).—There are several species of some of these, often deriving their specific name from one of their host plants. They attack a great variety of plants grown in temperate and tropical greenhouses. They are fairly inconspicuous, as their colour often tones with the plant on which they are feeding. They infest and do much injury to the shoots, stems, and leaves of many trees and plants. The tiny insects pierce the tissue and suck the sap from the plants, attacking first the older wood. They infest the young shoots only after all the larger branches have been covered. Badly affected trees, bushes, and herbs lose their leaves early in the season, and rarely carry good flowers ; the sucking of the sap soon drains their vitality. The males are in the form of small flies. The

610

females look like little plates or scales—whence the name—fixed to the bark and sometimes the leaves.

*Treatment.*—Scale is destroyed by scrubbing, in the case of tender-leaved plants, with the aid of a soft brush or pointed stick, but the leaves of Orchids or very tender plants should be sponged with Eucalyptus Oil Emulsion, taking great care to avoid injury to the foliage. Thorough spraying is recommended with strong soapy water in the proportion of 1 oz. of soap to 1 quart water; or with paraffin in the proportion of ¼ gill to 1 gallon of water; or with a lye of wood ashes or potash; or with nicotine wash; or with fish oil. As much of the old wood as possible should be cut away. The solutions should be applied in winter, and special attention should be given to the undersides of the branches. Routine fumigation, either by Nicotine Vapour or Hydrocyanic Acid Gas, will destroy young scale.

**Sempervivum Rust** (*Endophyllum sempervivi*).—Leaves of infected Houseleeks are covered with yellowish-brown spots. The fungus often causes the plants to take on an etiolated appearance. Burn all plants. No cure is known as the fungus is perennial, living within the plants, and appears every season.

**Shanking.** See **Grapes.**

**Slugs.**—Those most generally met in gardens are the **Garden** or **Black Slug** (*Arion hortensis*), and the **Grey Field Slug** (*Agrilolimax agrestis*), both of which are very destructive, feeding on seedlings, leaves, and shoots of plants, particularly in alpine frames; also *Milax sowerbii,* which does so much damage underground, particularly with bulbous plants and other underground parts of plants. Slugs bury themselves in the ground or under leaves and other rubbish, and come out at night to feed on young foliage. They are always more numerous and destructive after long, wet, mild winters. In the greenhouses these pests may be partly kept in check, if the houses are kept free from the heaps of stones, bricks, and rocks, used to form rockeries, all of which are favourite places for slugs and other pests. For prevention and treatment, see Snails. When found, a pinch or two of salt on the head and back is sufficient to kill a slug; or they may be gathered and dropped into salt water.

**Snails.**—The Large Garden Snail (*Helix aspersa*) and the Strawberry Snail (*H. rufescens*), which is much smaller, are the two most abundant in gardens, and although both snails and slugs would do quite a great deal of damage in the greenhouse once they got there, it is outside that they are such pests in gardens. Do not allow rubbish to accumulate in odd places; keep the garden and greenhouse tidy. Encourage frogs, toads and insectivorous birds, such as the thrush, which devour snails and slugs. Dust young growths over with a mixture of soot and lime to prevent the pests from devouring them. At night or early in the morning sprinkle lime thickly on the soil, and repeat the process two or three days in succession; this will kill numerous snails, but of course the effectiveness of these dressings is lost after rain, and they should be renewed. Others may be trapped in orange-skins, lettuce-leaves, or bran, of which they are very fond. A poison bait of " Paris Green and Bran " has proved successful, but great care must

# THE GREENHOUSE

be taken to prevent domestic animals coming in contact with it, as Paris Green is exceedingly poisonous. Mix 2 oz. of Paris Green with 3½ lb. of Bran either dry or with 1 qt. of water. This mixture should be spread about where the slugs and snails are known to feed ; it has no effect on slugs which feed underground. Much may be done by diligent searching in the early morning or late evening. A ring of cinders round choice plants will do a great deal to discourage the attentions of slugs and snails. There are several anti-slug and snail powders on the market, e.g. Powdered Blue Stone (Copper sulphate), most of which are very effective.

**Snowflies.** See **White-fly.**

**Sooty Mould.** See **Aphides.**

**Spit.** See **Cuckoo Spit.**

**Thrips.**—The two most common in greenhouses are *Heliothrips hæmorrhoidalis* and *Thrips tabaci*, which attack many kinds of plants. The latter is concerned with the introduction of the " *Spotted Wilt Disease of Tomatoes* " and other plants. These minute, blackish-grey winged insects infest and injure the flowers, leaves, and shoots, causing them to appear spotted, warped, and twisted out of place.

*Treatment.*—The best remedy against thrips is the plentiful application of salt water, tobacco water, strong soapy water, or any of the insecticides that are sold for the purpose of destroying insect life. Fumigation with Nicotine Vapour tends to reduce attacks, and Hydrocyanic Acid Gas is successful, but should be used carefully, and never be applied to a greenhouse near a dwelling-house. Thrips, like Red Spider, are most active when the atmosphere is too dry. Keep plants in good health. Attention to ventilation, prevention of draughts, constant and careful watering are the best preventive measures.

## Tomato Diseases and Pests

**Blight.**—This disease is caused by *Phytophthora infestans*, which is also responsible for the Potato Blight, and can be recognised by the formation of blackish-purple spots on the foliage and fruits. It rarely affects tomatoes in glasshouses, except in leaky or faulty structures.

*Treatment.*—Remove and destroy badly affected plants. Attend to atmosphere and ventilation, raise the temperature of the house and spray with Bordeaux Mixture as soon as the disease appears.

**Blossom End Rot.**—This is not associated with any organism, but is due to lack of sufficient soil moisture just after setting. To prevent the occurrence keep the soil uniformly moist.

**Buckeye** (*Phytophthora parasitica*).—Fruit growing low down on the plant, particularly near the ground, becomes blotched, and dull brownish patches form at the calyx or eye.

*Treatment.*—Keep the trusses tied up so that the organism is not carried on to the fruit by splashes from careless watering. Remove and destroy affected fruit and attend to atmosphere and ventilation. Spray soil with fungicide such as Cheshunt Compound. See page 619.

**Chlorosis.**—Yellow and pale-green blotching of the leaves similar to that encountered in Mosaic, for which this disease is frequently mistaken.

612

# DISEASES AND PESTS

*Treatment.*—Remove and destroy badly affected plants. Attend more closely to correct cultural details in regard to soil, watering, atmosphere, and ventilation.

**Foot Rot.**—This usually occurs in the planting-out stage, and is caused by the fungi *Phytophthora cryptogea*, *P. parasitica*, and *Rhizoctonia solani*. The base of the stem at soil level, and roots become diseased causing collapse of the entire plant.

*Treatment.*—Remove and destroy badly affected plants, earth up others at the base, and dress soil with Cheshunt Compound. All soil, pots, and boxes, should be sterilised. See page 619.

**Grey Mould** (*Botrytis cinerea*).—This attacks stems and fruit, and is usually due to faulty greenhouse management as regards heat and ventilation. If these are attended to by introducing a warm, dry atmosphere circulated freely among the leaves, it will not occur.

*Treatment.*—Spraying with Calcium Bisulphite Solution, Bordeaux Mixture, or Liver of Sulphur, 2 per cent. is beneficial. Affected fruits should be removed and burnt. Badly affected plants are best destroyed.

**Leaf Mould** (*Cladosporium fulvum*).—So familiar is this to growers that it needs no detailed description. It first appears as a greyish mould on the under-side of the leaves. This spreads rapidly, and changes to tawny-olive colour, finally to purple. The upper side of the leaf changes to pale yellow. In bad cases the foliage is destroyed. The disease also attacks the flower, but not the fruit itself. The disease does not usually appear before July. A high humid atmosphere aids the disease. A low temperature and adequate ventilation will sometimes control it. Any check to the roots of the plant assists the disease, so that the injurious effect of a dry subsoil should be avoided. Spray with Bordeaux or treat with Vaporised Sulphur.

**Mosaic.**—The foliage becomes patchy and mottled light green, and may be disfigured at the edges ; sometimes the leaf is reduced so that only the mid-rib with a fringe of tissue remains. Distortion sometimes appears in various parts of the flower and prevents the fruit setting.

*Treatment.*—Remove and destroy badly affected plants. Attend more closely to cultural detail. As it appears to have a serious effect on plants that possess a weak constitution, and not infrequently occurs with the presence of a stagnant subsoil, a well-balanced growth should be aimed at. Plants will benefit from one or two applications of Dried Blood Mixture, Sulphate of Ammonia 1 part, Nitrate of Potash 1 part, Superphosphate 3 parts, Dried Blood 5 parts.

**Root Rot.**—This may be due to various causes, and is generally brought about by conditions of the soil, which may be too compact, too cold, or too wet, and especially such as have been heavily manured for a number of years, which retards growth and renders the root system susceptible to infection by organisms that are not always harmful. By improving the soil by applications of spent hops and peat, the injury to the roots can sometimes be overcome. One form of Rot is due to the infection of the fungus *Colletotrichum atramentarium*, which destroys the roots, causing the plant to wilt. This disease can be recognised by the minute black bodies on the outside of the roots, which are really the resting bodies, and which lie in the soil during the winter. The fungus

THE GREENHOUSE

does not generally appear until the end of the season, so that the crop is not greatly affected; but it may develop at an earlier stage, and thus shorten the life of the plant. Its development is associated with cold, heavy, compact soil, and is less serious in such soils that remain open and porous. Sterilise the soil and add coarse organic material for future crops.

**Sleepy Disease or Wilt** (*Verticillium dahliæ*).—This disease is of fungoid origin, entering through the roots of the plants, and difficult to combat. It will often destroy an entire greenhouse full of fine tomato plants that a short time before appeared in perfect health. When the temperature is low, affected plants wilt rather suddenly and die prematurely; when the temperature is moderately high there is little wilting of the foliage, but the leaves develop yellow patches and slowly dry up from the base of the plant upwards. On cutting open a diseased stem it will be seen to be of a yellowish brown.

As soon as the Wilt appears the average temperature of the house should be raised to 70° F. Shading with a light dressing of whitening on the glass helps the plants to resist the disease. As little water as possible should be given to the roots, as an excess only aggravates wilting, although a light overhead damping helps wilting plants to recover. Encourage the plants to make fresh roots by placing fresh soil around the base of the stem. Burn all dead plants and infected material, spray or wash the whole house with some fungicide, and sterilise the soil before it is replanted.

Another parasitic fungus, **Fusarium,** will also cause Sleepy Disease or Wilt, and may be called a high-temperature disease, for it develops more readily at a temperature of 80–85° F. It is comparatively rare in this country, and occurs only at the height of summer. When necessary control can be secured by lowering the temperature.

**Stripe.**—This is a Virus disease. The leaves first become affected with pale yellow blotches, which turn brown, spread, and eventually form large wrinkled patches on the foliage. The stem becomes pitted with dark longitudinal streaks. The fruit also becomes infected, and is spotted with irregular sunken brown patches.

*Treatment.*—Water once in ten days with a solution of 1 oz. of Potassium Sulphide to every six gallons of water. Stable manure should only be given in moderation where attacks of this disease are to be expected. Burn the diseased portions removed from the plants, and wipe the blade of the pruning-knife with a cloth soaked in a diluted disinfectant, before passing on to a healthy plant after pruning a diseased one. For other Pests, see **Aphides, Caterpillars, Eelworms, Red Spider, White-fly,** and **Wireworms,** all of which are troublesome to Tomatoes.

**Vine Mildew** (due to *Uncinula necator*).—Leaves covered with whitish powder, later spotted. Fruit whitish, later marked with dark spots. Apply Flowers of Sulphur or Liver of Sulphur, raise the temperature, attend to ventilation, and avoid draughts.

**Vine or Black Weevil** (*Otiorrhynchus sulcatus*).—The mature weevils are nocturnal, and are found throughout the spring and early summer, doing considerable damage to the young shoots of the Grape Vine and other plants, including Roses grown in the greenhouse, alpine plants in

614

pots, particularly Saxifragas. These weevils, which are a third of an inch in length and black flecked with yellow, sometimes attack plants grown in the open. Plants attacked by them assume a sickly colour, and fail to develop properly. The larvæ, which are creamy white or light brown, feed on the roots and attack the bulb-corms and tubers of many greenhouse plants; Begonias, Cyclamen, Ferns, Primulas, as well as many alpine plants, Lewisias, Saxifragas, and Sedums.

*Treatment.*—Lay tarred cloths or paper under the trees or plants where possible, and shake the branches or shoots just before it gets dark. Numbers of weevils will fall and stick to the tar. Spray the foliage in summer with Arsenate of Lead. Clean up and destroy all rubbish in the neighbourhood, and in autumn dress the soil with a fumigant, such as Naphthalene, at the rate of 1½ lb. to the square rod. Pot-plants, if attacked, should be re-potted, the soil being shaken thoroughly out of the roots, so that a thorough hunt may be made for the larvæ of the pests in the soil. Pot the plant up in clean soil. Dry Lead Arsenate added to potting compost 4–8 oz. to each bushel will destroy the young larvæ. This is particularly advisable for plants such as Cyclamen, Primula, Saxifragas, and other alpine plants which will remain in their pots or pans for more than one year. The greenhouse itself should be carefully cleaned out, walls kept pointed up and lime-washed, and the weevils searched for by the aid of a light at night.

**Viola Rust** (*Puccinia violæ*).—Stem and leaves bear cup-shaped yellow spots, followed by brown rust. Destroy diseased plants and spray the remainder with Potassium Permanganate.

**Weevils.** See **Vine or Black Weevils.**

**White-fly** (*Trialeurodes vaporariorum*).—The Greenhouse White-fly, also known as the " Ghost Fly " is well known to most cultivators of greenhouse plants, especially to tomato-growers, to whom it has caused considerable financial loss. It is essentially a greenhouse pest, and, being a native of a warm country, cannot live outdoors during our winters, except possibly in very mild districts. The white colour is due to a covering of mealy wax, which acts as a protection and is very difficult to wet with spray.

*Life History.*—The female White-fly lays her eggs, usually in an incomplete circle, but sometimes in groups. Each egg is stalked, the stalk being inserted in a slit in the leaf, and presenting the appearance of a small black peg. The eggs hatch in from eleven to fourteen days, according to the temperature, and produce pale-green, flattish larvæ which crawl about for several days and then settle down with their sucking apparatus driven into the plant, and remain stationary until later on they become adult White-flies.

*Methods of Control.*—Where this pest is not present, great care should be taken in introducing fresh plants to see that they are not infested with White-fly. Spraying has so far proved of little use against this pest. Fumigation by means of Hydrocyanic Acid Gas and Tetrachlorethane, obtainable from most horticultural sundriesmen under various proprietary names, has proved most effective. The latter is less poisonous than Hydrocyanic Acid Gas, and therefore more suitable for the amateur; although effective and safe for Tomatoes, it

# THE GREENHOUSE

proves injurious to many greenhouse plants, Asparagus fern, Azalea, Chrysanthemum, Cineraria, Pelargonium, Salvia, and others, a list of which is usually given by the firm who supplies the fumigant. Hydrocyanic Acid Gas is the most satisfactory control, as it can be used fairly safely with some mixed collections of plants. Sodium Cyanide or Calcium Cyanide is generally used, the last named, a more recent introduction being mostly used, as it is in the form of a powder, and only requires to be sprinkled on the floor of the house or houses. In good air-tight houses $\frac{1}{4}$ oz. to 1,000 cubic feet is regarded as the standard dose ; in old houses more may be required. Fumigation should take place in darkness and on a calm night. It is important that there should be no moisture on the foliage, and also that the plants be as dry as possible at the roots. As the eggs of the fly are unharmed a second fumigation and even a third should follow the first, after about two to three weeks according to the temperature of the house. It must always be remembered that Sodium Cyanide, Calcium Cyanide, and Hydrocyanic Acid Gas are all deadly poisons, and great care must be taken to prevent accidents. The *Board of Agriculture and Fisheries* issue a leaflet with full instructions for fumigating by this method.

*Natural Enemies.*—It has recently been discovered that White-fly is parasitised by two very small chalcid wasps. One of them, *Encarsia ormosa*, has been bred in large quantities both at the Experimental Station, Cheshunt, and at the Royal Horticultural Society's Gardens, Wisley. From these quantities have been distributed to growers. This parasite has proved a complete control for White-fly on Tomatoes and many indoor plants.

**Wireworms.**—These are the grubs of " Click-beetles ". There are several species of this pest, *Agriotes lineatus* and *A. obscurus* being two of the most common which do serious damage by feeding on the roots and lower parts of the stems of many plants in pots or those planted out in beds or border. Wireworms have hard, polished skins, whitish yellow, turning brownish later, and can always be distinguished from other grubs by the fact that they have only three pairs of legs.

*Treatment.*—Sterilise the soil or dress with powdered Naphthalene. Pieces of potato, fixed to pieces of stick and buried in the soil, act as traps. Lift periodically, examine and destroy the pests. Or small heaps of clover covered with a board or tile, placed on the soil will aid, as the beetles congregate beneath the covering and may be collected and destroyed. A search for them should be made in the loam heaps, as this usually comes from meadowland, a good breeding-ground for them

**Woodlice or Pillbug** (*Armadillidium vulgare* and *Oniscus ascellus*).— These insects are very destructive, especially to seedlings. Indeed, where woodlice abound many persons are often under the impression that the seed has never come up at all. Woodlice congregate in rubbish, at the bottom of pots in a hotbed, and round the sides of wood edgings, fences, decayed staging, stones and bricks of the greenhouse walls if in a neglected state. They should be searched for every morning and destroyed by pouring boiling water over them. They may be trapped by means of small flower-pots filled with dry manure or old hay, with scooped-out potato and mangold root, or with half an orange placed

**616**

about the greenhouse. Powdered Borax or Pyrethrum Powder sprinkled in infested places will also do much to keep down this pest.

**Worms** (*Lumbricus*, of which there are many species).—Worms in pots are sometimes the cause of plants flagging and becoming sickly. The worms which act as efficient drainers in the open ground have the reverse effect in pots, causing fine earth to sink to the bottom of the pot and clog the drainage. Re-potting in fresh earth is the natural course to adopt. A weak solution of Smelling Salts or of Carbonate of Ammonia will bring them to the surface of the soil in a helpless state. This is best done in the evening. An infusion of Walnut Leaves is said to have the same effect. If plants are allowed to become rather dry and then watered with Lime-water, the worms will come out on the top and can be destroyed.

## Fumigants

These can be considered under two headings, as " Soil Fumigants " and " Greenhouse Fumigants ".

**Soil Fumigant.**—(i) Naphthalene which can be obtained either in a crude form, or " Drained salts ", or Flaked Naphthalene, the latter being more suitable than the former. The action of Naphthalene is rather to drive the pest from the soil, than as a deadly poison. It should be used at the rate of 3–4 oz. per sq. yd. for light soils, and double that amount for heavy soils. Apply evenly over the soil surface and lightly fork in so that it thoroughly mixes with the soil, and follow with a good watering.

Use for *Wireworm, Leather Jackets, Millepedes, Woodlice, Root Maggots*, and *Root-feeding Aphides*, in beds or borders, in glasshouses, where planting out is done.

(ii) *Carbon disulphide*.—This is a very highly inflammable, evil-smelling liquid, and special care must be taken that no naked flame comes near it ; even to smoke when using this fumigant is dangerous. It is very valuable for treating freshly stacked loam, or compost heaps infested with *Wireworm, Weevil-larvæ, Leather Jackets*, etc. : or for *Root Aphis* and *Root Mealy-bugs* on pot plants, when the plants should be knocked out of the pot and the liquid applied through an atomizer. After treatment the plants should be shaded for a day or two. The operation should be done out of doors.

**Greenhouse Fumigants.**—These are very suitable for dealing with pests in greenhouses that are not easily reached by means of wet sprays or dusting with insecticides.

Care must always be taken to ascertain the cubic capacity of the house, because only if this is determined can the operation of fumigation be carried out with success, as an underdose will be disappointing and an overdose may be disastrous to the plants.

(i) *Nicotine*.—This fumigant is obtainable from horticultural sundriesmen and others, either as cones, shreds, or in liquid form with full instructions given which should always be carefully carried out. Pure Nicotine should be used at the rate of $\frac{1}{8}$ fluid oz. to each 1,000 cu. ft. of space. This is vaporised in a small metal saucer placed over a methylated-spirit lamp. All forms are very poisonous.

**617**

# THE GREENHOUSE

(ii) *Hydrocyanic Acid Gas.*—This method of fumigation should be carried out with great care.   Owing to its poisonous nature, it should never be used in glasshouses adjoining or in the vicinity of dwelling-houses; neither is it advisable to use it in a greenhouse of mixed plants, but only in suitable houses where there are no possibilities of any danger.   *Hydrocyanic Acid Gas* is used for *White-fly, Aphides, Thrips, Scale*, and other glasshouse pests.

Full instructions for this method of fumigation are given in the *Ministry of Agricultural & Fisheries Advisory Leaflet* 92.

(iii) *Tetrachlorethane.*—This is much less dangerous to human beings, and is recommended to owners of small glasshouses instead of the more dangerous Hydrocyanic Acid Gas.   It is obtainable from horticultural sundriesmen, often under proprietary names with particulars of how to use it, and is in the form of liquid, which is poured along the paths of the greenhouse on a calm evening at the rate of from 3–5 fluid oz. per 1,000 feet.

This vapour controls *White-fly*, and may be used in houses of Tomatoes, but is risky to use in a house of mixed plants—more so even than the Hydrocyanic Acid Gas.   The following are affected : Asparagus Fern, Azaleas, Chrysanthemums, Cinerarias, Pelargoniums, Salvias, and others, a list of which is given by the firms who supply this type of fumigant.

(iv) *Naphthalene* Grade 16.—This is used for the infestations of *Red Spider, Mites,* and *Thrips.*   When used for *Red Spider* on Carnation it is volatilised by means of a special lamp.   For every 1,000 cu. ft. use 4–5 oz.   The house should be well damped down before fumigation, which should be commenced in the evening and continued for twelve hours, during which time the temperature should be kept 70° F. as near as possible.

For Thrips on Arums, Begonia, Cyclamen, etc., Naphthalene Grade 16 should be broadcast over the plants at the rate of 10 oz. per 1,000 cu. ft.

# INSECTICIDES AND FUNGICIDES
## When and How to Use

| Preparation. | How to Make. | How to Apply. | Principal Use. |
|---|---|---|---|
| **Arsenate of Lead.** | Dissolve 1 oz. arsenate of soda, 2½ oz. sugar of lead in 14 gallons of rain-water, then add 1½ lb. black treacle. Harmless to foliage. Can be purchased in paste, or as a fine powder ready for use. (*Poison.*) | During spring, in fine spray on fruit trees, as soon as petals have fallen and leaves have formed, and on flowers and roses, by means of knapsack machine. This insecticide poisons the food of the pests. As it is poisonous, never use where the spray is likely to fall on vegetables or fruit. | Fruit tree caterpillars, slug-worms, and vine or black weevil. |
| **Bordeaux Mixture.** | Dissolve 1 lb. sulphate of copper in boiling water; then slake 1 lb. freshly-burnt quick-lime in a little boiling water; mix well and dilute to 12 gallons with water. Stir well, and use at once. | Apply to plants when half-grown early in summer. An excellent fungicide. If necessary, make second and third applications at intervals of 3 weeks. | Black mould (Nerium), chrysanthemum leaf rust, chrysanthemum leaf spot, grey mould, lily disease, tomato blight, tomato canker, and vine mildew. |
| **Carbolic Emulsion.** | Dissolve ½ lb. hard soap in ½ gallon water, add ½ pint carbolic acid, boil, stirring meanwhile. Dilute with 25 parts water as wanted. Label bottle " Poison." | Useful for summer spraying and as fungicide. Good surface spray. | Weevils, eelworms, and leather jackets. |
| **Caustic Soda.** | Dissolve 12 oz. caustic soda in 8 gallons water. Use rubber gloves. | A good cleansing winter wash applied by means of knapsack sprayer. Cleans bark and destroys scale. Use only when trees dormant. | Aphis, buckeye in tomato, fungi, mealybug, red spider, tomato foot rot and weevils. |
| **Cheshunt Compound.** | Mix 5 oz. of finely-powdered fresh ammonium carbonate with 1 oz. of powdered copper sulphate and store in airtight stoppered bottle or jar. | Dissolve ½ oz. of the powder in ½ pint of hot water, turn into a bowl or pan containing a gallon of water and use at once. Do not use iron, tin, or zinc receptacle. | Soil fungicide for " damping off " diseases. |
| **Cleansing Washes.** | See **Caustic Soda** and **Lime Sulphur.** | | |
| **Derris Preparations.** | Should be purchased ready made. | As wet sprays, and dry dusting. | Ants, aphides, young caterpillars on tender-leaved plants. |
| **Lime Sulphur.** | Boil 5 gallons slaked lime and 5 lb. flowers of sulphur in water for about 1 hour, stirring meanwhile; make up to 25 gallons. Harmless to foliage. Best purchased ready for use. | Summer spraying on foliage; makes good combination with arsenate of lead. Strain solution before use, and do not use apparatus having copper fittings. Give second and third applications at 3-weekly intervals. A good fungicide, insecticide and cleanser. | Black beetles, flower-beetles, mildew, red spider, scale, scab, and weevils. |
| **Lime Wash.** | Slake 6 lb. of quick-lime with a little water, then dilute to 5 gallons. See that the lime is not air-slaked before use. Stir well. | A wash for applying to the trunks of fruit trees just before the bloom opens. A good insecticide, also an excellent cleansing wash. Strain two or three times before use in sprayer. | Aphides, scale, lichen and mosses on tree trunks, walls of greenhouses and frames. |
| **Liver of Sulphur.** | Dissolve 3½–5 oz. potassium sulphide (liver of sulphur) in 10 gallons water, add ½ lb. soft soap. Does not affect zinc paint. | For outdoor and greenhouse use as summer spray. Make fresh as wanted. | Cucumber and melon leaf blotch, grey mould, Helebore leaf blotch, lily disease, rose and vine mildew, and red spider. |

**619**

| Preparation. | How to Make. | How to Apply. | Principal Use. |
|---|---|---|---|
| **Nicotine Emulsion.** | Nicotine 98 per cent. ½—¾ oz., soft soap ¼ lb., and soft water 10 gallons. Boil the soap in 1 gallon of water, add the nicotine, and make up to 10 gallons. (*Poison.*) | Reliable insecticide for use at all times ; on fruit trees as soon as blossom has fallen and leaves have formed. Apply as coarse spray. One of the most effective " contact " poisons. Must be used at least 14 days before fruit or vegetables are to be gathered. | Aphides, begonia mite, caterpillars, cuckoo-spit, leaf hopper, leaf miners, and white-fly. |
| **Paraffin Emulsion.** | Boil 1 lb. soft soap in 1 gallon rain-water, while hot mix in 1 gallon of paraffin by means of syringe. When required for use dilute with rain-water to 20 gallons, mixing well. | Stringent summer wash and soil spray. | Aphides, carnation maggot, cockroaches, cuckoo-spit, leaf miners, mussel scale, red spider, and weevils. |
| **Paris Green.** | Mix ½ oz. Paris green with ½ lb. bran. Moisten with water until bran flakes adhere. Scatter with a wooden spoon over 120 sq. yards. | Poison bait for cut-worms. Apply before or after planting. | Ants, cut-worms, slugs, and snails. |
| **Pyrethrum Powder Emulsion.** | Dissolve 1 lb. of pyrethrum powder and ¼ lb. of soft soap in a little hot water for about 4 hours, dilute to 5 gallons and mix thoroughly. | Apply as fine spray. | Ants, aphides, caterpillars, cockroaches and weevils. |
| **Quassia Emulsion.** | Steep 1 lb. quassia chips in 1 gallon water for 12 hours, melt ½ lb. soft soap and add, make up to 8 gallons with water. | For use in warm weather after showers. | Aphides and red spider. |
| **Soda-Resin Wash.** | Boil 1 oz. washing soda and 8 oz. powdered resin in 1 pint of water ; dilute to 1 to 2 gallons. | Spring wash. | Mealy-bug, mussel scale, and oyster scale. |
| **Winter-washes.** | See **Caustic Soda,** and **Lime Sulphur** above. | | |

## D.D.T. PREPARATIONS

D.D.T. (dichloro-diphenyl-trichlorethane) is a powerful insecticide with a very wide range of usefulness, and has partly taken the place of lead arsenate, nicotine and derris. It is particularly useful in the control of various caterpillars, beetles and Capsid bugs, but is not effective against aphides and is quite harmless to Red Spider. It should be used with discretion and according to the maker's instructions.

# INDEX

Abelia, 233
Abroma augusta, 233
Abrus precatorius, 233
Abutilon, 233
Abutilon Rust, 601
Abyssinian Banana (see Musa Ensete, 462)
Acacia, 234
Acalypha, 235
Acantholimon 235
Acanthophippium, 167
Acanthus, 225
Acer, 235
Achillea, 235
Achimenes, 236
Acidanthera, 236
Acis (see Leucojum, 429)
Acokanthera spectabilis, 236
Acradenia Frankliniæ, 237
Acriopsis, 160, 167
Acroclinium (see Helipterum, 394)
Acrostichum aureum, 237
Acrostichum crinitum (see Elaphoglossum crinitum, 357)
Acrostichum latifolium (see Elaphoglossum latifolium, 357)
Acrostichum scandens (see Stenochlæna palustris, 556)
Ada aurantiaca, 173
Adam's Needle (see Yucca, 594)
Adder's Tongue Fern (see Ophioglossum vulgatum, 478)
Adenandra, 237
Adenanthera pavonina, 237
Adenocarpus viscosus, 237
Adiantum Capillis veneris, 237
Adonis amurensis, 238
Ærides, 160
Æschynanthus (see Trichosporum, 575)
Æthionema, 238
African Corn Lily (see Ixia, 414)
African Honeysuckle (see Halleria lucida, 390)
African Violet (see Saintpaulia ionantha, 531)
Agapanthus, 238
Agapetes, 239
Agathea cœlestris (see Felicia amelloides, 371)
Agathosma fœtidissima (see Barosma fœtidissima, 261)
Agave, 239
Agave Cactus (see Leuchtenbergia principis, 428)
Ageratum, 239
Aglaonema, 240
Albizzia lophantha, 240
Albuca Nelsonii, 240
Aletris capensis (see Veltheimia viridiflora, 583)
Allamanda, 240

Allium, 240
Alloplectus, 240
Allosorus crispus (see Cryptogramma crispa, 330)
Almond (see Prunus Amygdalus, 513)
Alocasia, 241
Aloe, 241
Alonsoa, 241
Aloysia (see Lippia, 434)
Alpine House, The, 141–150.
Alpine Rose (see Rhododendron ferrugineum and hirsutum, 520)
Alpinia, 242
Alsophila, 242
Alstrœmeria, 242
Amarantus, 243
Amaryllis Belladonna, 243
Amasonia calycina, 243
Amazon Lily (see Eucharis grandiflora, 366)
Amelanchier canadensis oblongifolia, 243
American Cowslip (see Dodecatheon, 350)
American Laurel (see Kalmia, 419)
American Lotus (see Nelumbo lutea, 468)
Amherstia nobilis, 244
Amorphophallus, 244
Amphicome emodis, 244
Amygdalus communis (see Prunus Amygdalus, 514)
Anagallis, 244
Ananas sativa, 245
Ancistrochilus (see Pachystoma, 164)
Andromeda, 245
Andromeda floribunda (see Pieris floribunda, 501)
Andromeda formosa (see Pieris formosa, 501)
Andromeda japonica (see Pieris japonica, 501)
Androsace, 245
Androsace Vitaliana (see Douglasia Vitaliana, 351)
Anemia, 245
Anemone, 245
Anemopægma clematideum (see Pithecoctenium cynanchoides, 504)
Angelonia, 246
Angiopteris evecta, 246
Angræcum Sanderianum, 160
Angræcum sesquipedale (see Macroplectrum sesquipedale, 169)
Anguloa, 167, 173
Anhalonium Williamsii (see Lophophora Williamsii, 438)
Anigozanthos coccinea, 246
Aniseed Tree (see Illicium, 409)
Anœctochilus, 160
Anomatheca (see Lapeyrousia, 425)
Anopterus glandulosus, 247
Ansellia, 160

621

# INDEX

*Anthericum Liliago*, 247
Anthurium, 247
*Anthyllis Barba-Jovis*, 247
*Antigonon leptopus*, 247
Antirrhinum, 248
*Antirrhinum Asarina*, 248
Ants, 601
*Aotus gracillima*, 248
Aphelandra, 248
Aphelexis (see Helichrysum, 393)
Aphides, 601
Aponogeton, 249
*Aporocactus flagelliformis*, 249
Apple, 181, 190
Apricot, 190
Aquarium, The Inside, 150–152
Aquilegia, 249
Arabian Jasmine, 416
Arabis, 250
*Arabis alpina*, 145
*Arachnanthe moschifera*, 160
Aralia, 250
*Aralia elegantissima* (see *Dizygotheca elegantissima*, 349)
*Aralia Sieboldii* (see *Fatsia japonica*, 371)
*Aralia Veitchii* (see *Dizygotheca Veitchii*, 349)
*Araucaria excelsa*, 250
Araujia, 251
*Arctocalyx Endlicherianus* (see *Solenophora Endlicheriana*, 550)
Arctotis, 251
Ardisia, 251
Areca, 251
*Areca Baueri* (see *Rhopalostylis Baueri*, 522)
*Areca lutescens* (see *Chrysalidocarpus lutescens*, 304)
*Areca sapida* (see *Rhopalostylis sapida*, 522)
Aregelia, 252
Arenaria, 252
*Arisæma fimbriatum*, 252
*Aristea corymbosa* (see *Nivenia corymbosa*, 473)
Aristolochia, 252
Armeria, 252
Artemisia, 253
Arum Lily (see Zantedeschia, 596)
*Arum palæstinum*, 253
*Arum sagittifolium* (see *Xanthosoma sagittifolium*, 594)
*Aruncus sylvester*, 253
*Arundina bambusæfolia*, 167
Arundinaria, 253
Arundo, 253
*Asclepias Curassavica*, 253
Asparagus, 93, 254
Aspect of Greenhouse, 23, 178
*Asperula arcadiensis*, 254
Aspidistra, 254
Asplenium, 254
Aster (see Callistephus, 280)
Astilbe, 255
*Asystasia bella*, 255
Atamasco Lily (see *Zephyranthes Atamasco*, 597)
*Athyrium Filix-fœmina*, 255

*Attalea amygdalina* (see *Maximiliana regia*, 451)
Aubergine (see *Solanum Melongena* var. *esculentum*, 549)
Aubrieta, 256
*Aucuba japonica*, 256
*Audoninia capitata*, 256
Auricula, 256
Auricula Root Aphis, 602
Australian Bean Flower (see Kennedya, 420)
Australian Bluebell Creeper (see *Sollya heterophylla*, 550)
Australian Brush Cherry (see *Eugenia myrtifolia*, 367)
Australian Mint Bush (see Prostanthera, 513)
Australian Pitcher Plant (see *Cephalotus follicularis*, 297)
Australian Turmeric Tree (see Zieria, 598)
Azalea, 258
Azalea Gall, 602
*Azalea procumbens* (see *Loiseleuria procumbens* 437)
Azara, 259
Azolla, 259

Babiana, 259
Baboon-root (see Babiana, 259)
Balloon Vine (see *Cardiospermum Halicacabum*, 287)
Balsam Apple (see *Momordica Balsamina*, 459)
Balsam Pear (see *Momordica Charantia*, 459)
Bambusa, 260
Banana (see Musa, 182, 462)
Banksia, 260
Barbados Gooseberry (see *Pereskia aculeata*, 492)
Barbados Lily (see *Hippeastrum equestre*, 397)
Barbados Nut (see *Jatropha Curcas*, 417)
Barberry (see Berberis, 265)
Barbertown Daisy (see *Gerbera Jamesonii*, 381)
Barosma, 261
*Bauera rubioides*, 261
Bead Tree (see *Melia Azedarach*, 453)
Beans, 93
Bear's Grass (see Yucca, 594)
Beaucarnea (see Nolina, 473)
Beaufortia, 261
*Beaumontia grandiflora*, 262
Beech Fern (see *Phegopteris polypodioides*, 496)
Beetles (see Cockroaches etc., 604)
Beetroot, 93
Begonia, 262
Begonia Mite, 602
*Beloperone guttata*, 265
*Berberidopsis corallina*, 265
Berberis, 265
Bergenia, 266
Bertolonia, 266
*Bertolonia guttata* (see *Gravesia guttata*, 388)

# INDEX

Beschorneria, 266
*Bessera elegans*, 266
*Bestera pulchella* (see *Tussacia pulchra*, 579)
Bifrenaria, 160
Bignonia, 267
*Bignonia buccinatoria* (see *Phædranthus buccinatorius*, 495)
*Bignonia callistegioides* (see *Clytostoma callistegioides*, 316)
*Bignonia muricata* (see *Pithecoctinium muricatum*, 504)
*Bignonia Pandorea* (see *Pandorea australis*, 484)
*Bignonia purpurea* (see *Clytostoma purpureum*, 316)
*Bignonia venusta* (see *Pyrostegia venusta*, 515)
Bilberry (see Vaccinium, 581)
Billardiera, 267
*Billbergia nutans*, 267
Bird of Paradise (see *Strelitzia Reginæ*, 558)
Bird Plant (see *Heterotoma lobelioides*, 396)
Bird's Nest Fern (see *Asplenium Nidus*, 255)
Bitter Cassava (see *Manihot utilissima*, 446)
Black Calla (see *Arum palæstinum*, 253)
Black-eyed Susan (see *Thunbergia alata*, 568)
Black-throated Calla (see *Zantedeschia melanoleuca*, 596)
Black Weevil, 614
Bladder Fern (see Cystopteris, 336)
Bladder Nut (see *Staphylea colchica*, 555)
Bladderwort (see Utricularia, 580)
*Blakea trinervia*, 268
Blandfordia, 268
Blechnum, 268
Bleeding Heart (see *Dicentra spectabilis*, 344)
*Bletia hyacinthina*, 173
Blight, 612
Blood Apple (see *Pereskia aculeata*, 492)
Blood Flower (see *Asclepias Curassavica*, 253)
Blood Lily (see *Hæmanthus*, 390)
Blood-root (see *Sanguinaria canadensis*, 533)
Bloomeria, 269
Blossom End Rot, 612
Blue Amaryllis (see *Griffinia hyacinthina* var. *maxima*, 389)
Bluebell (see *Scilla nonscripta*, 541)
Blue Dawn Flower (see *Ipomœa Learii*, 411)
Blue Gum (see *Eucalyptus globulus*, 365)
Blue Marguerite (see *Felicia amelloides*, 371)
Blue Moonwort (see *Soldanella alpina*, 550)
*Blumenbachia lateritia*, 269
Bog Violet (see Pinguicula, 503).
Bollea, 167
Bomarea, 269
*Bonatea speciosa*, 167

Borders and paths, **34–35, 178**
Boronia, 269
*Botrytis cinerea*, 602,
Bottle Brush (see Callistemon, 280)
Bottle Gourd (see *Lagenaria leucantha*, 423)
Bougainvillea, 270
Bouvardia, 270
Bower Plant of Australia (see *Pandorea australis*, 484)
Bow-string Hemp (see Sansevieria, 533)
*Brachycome iberidifolia*, 271
Brachysema, 271
Brachystelma, 271
*Brasenia Schreberi*, 271
Brassavola (see Lælia, 169)
Brassia, 161, 167, 173
*Bravoa geminiflora*, 272
Brazilian Spider Flower (see *Tibouchina semidecandra*, 570)
*Bredia hirsuta*, 272
*Brevoortia Ida-Maia*, 272
Bridal Wreath (see *Francoa ramosa*, 374)
Briza, 272
Brodiæa, 272
*Brodiæa coccinea* (see *Brevoortia Ida-Maia*, 272)
Bromelia, 272
Brompton Stock (see Matthiola, 449)
*Broughtonia sanguinea*, 161
Browallia, 273
Brownea, 273
Brugmansia (see Datura, 339)
Brunfelsia, 273
Brussels Sprouts, 94
*Bryanthus Breweri* (see *Phyllodoce Breweri*, 501)
*Bryanthus empetriformis* (see *Phyllodoce empetriformis*, 501)
Bryophyllum, 274
*Bryophyllum uniflorum* (see *Kitchingia uniflora*, 421)
Buckeye, 612
Buddleia, 274
Bugle Lily (see Watsonia, 591)
Bulbine, 269
Bulb Mite, 602
Bulbocodium, 275
Bulbophyllum, 161
Bulbs, culture, 118–123
Bulbs, forcing, 97
*Burbidgea nitida*, 275
*Burchellia capensis*, 275
*Burlingtonia fragrans* (see Rodriguezia, 165)
Bushman's Poison (see *Acokanthera venenata*, 236)
Buttercup Tulip (see Calochortus, 281)
Butterfly Flower (see Schizanthus, 539)
Butterfly Iris (see Moræa, 461)
Butterfly Pea (see *Clitorea ternatea*, 316)
Butterwort (see Pinguicula, 503)

Cabbage Palm (see *Oreodoxa oleracea*, 479)
Cabbage Palmetto (see *Sabal Palmetto*, 530)

**623**

# INDEX

Cabomba, 275
Cacti, Culture of, 138–140.
*Cactus Melocactus*, 276
*Cajophora lateritia* (see *Blumenbachia lateritia*, 269)
Calabash Gourd (see *Lagenaria leucantha*, 423)
Caladium, 276
*Calampelis scaber* (see *Eccremocarpus scaber*, 354)
Calandrinia, 276
*Calanthe Harrisii*, 161
Calathea, 276
Calceolaria, 277
Calendula, 279
Calico Bush (see *Kalmia latifolia*, 419)
Californian Bluebell (see *Phacelia Whitlavia*, 495)
Californian Hyacinth (see Brodiæa, 272)
Californian Lilac (see Ceanothus, 294)
Californian Pitcher Plant (see *Darlingtonia californica*, 339)
*Callianthemum anemonoides*, 279
Callicarpa, 279
*Calliphruria Hartwegiana*, 279
Callipsyche, 280
Callistemon, 280
*Callistephus chinensis*, 280
*Callitris Whytei* (see *Widdringtonia Whytei*, 591)
*Calocephalus Brownii* (see *Leucophyta Brownii*, 429)
Calochortus, 281
*Calodendron capensis*, 282
Calonyction, 282
*Calycanthus floridus*, 282
*Calypso borealis*, 173
*Camarotis rostrata*, 161
Camellia, 282
Campanula, 283
*Campsis grandiflora*, 285
Camptosema, 285
Canada Tea (see *Gaultheria procumbens*, 380)
*Canarina Campanula*, 285
Canary Creeper (see Tropæolum, 578)
Candle Plant (see *Kleinia articulata*, 544)
Candollea, 285
Candytuft (see Iberis, 408)
Canistrum, 285
Canna, 285
Canterbury Bell (see *Campanula Medium*, 283)
*Cantua buxifolia*, 286
Cape Cowslip (see Lachenalia, 422)
Cape Daisy (see Dimorphotheca, 347)
Cape Honeysuckle (see *Tecomaria capensis*, 566)
Cape Hyacinth (see *Galtonia candicans*, 379)
Cape Jasmine (see *Gardenia jasminoides*, 379)
Cape Lily (see Crinum, 328)
Cape Pond Weed (see *Aponogeton distachyus*, 249)
Cape Primrose (see Streptocarpus, 559)
Cape Shamrock (see Oxalis, 482)
Capparis, 286

Capsicum, 94, 287
Capsid Bug, 603
Caralluma, 287
*Cardiospermum Halicacabum*, 287
Carex, 287
Carludovica, 288
Carnation, 288
Carnation Black Mould, 603
Carnation Maggot, 603
Carnation Rust, 603
*Carnegiea gigantea*, 293
Carolina All-spice (see *Calycanthus floridus*, 282)
Carolina Yellow Jessamine (see *Gelsemium sempervirens*, 381)
*Carpenteria californica*, 293
Carrion Flower (see Stapelia, 554)
Carrots, 94
Caryopteris, 293
Caryota, 293
Cassia, 294
Cassiope, 294
Castor Oil Plant (see *Ricinus communis*, 522)
Catasetum, 161
Caterpillars, 603
Catmint (see Nepeta, 470)
Cat's Thyme (see *Teucrium Marum*, 567)
Cattleya, 167
Cattleya Fly, 603
Cauliflower, 94
*Cavendishia acuminata*, 294
Ceanothus, 294
Celery, 94
Celmisia, 295
Celosia, 295
Celsia, 295
Centaurea, 296
Centradenia, 296
*Centropogon Lucyanus*, 296
*Cephalocereus senilis*, 297
*Cephalotus follicularis*, 297
Cerasus (see *Prunus Cerasus*, 514)
*Ceratopteris thalictroides*, 297
*Ceratozamia mexicana*, 297
Cereus, 297.
*Cereus amecænsis* (see *Heliocereus amecænsis*, 393)
*Cereus Baumannii* (see *Cleistocactus Baumannii*, 313)
*Cereus flagelliformis* (see *Aporocactus flagelliformis*, 249)
*Cereus grandiflorus* (see *Selenicereus grandiflorus*, 543)
*Cereus Macdonaldiæ* (see *Selenicereus Macdonaldiæ*, 543)
*Cereus nycticaulis* (see *Selenicereus pteracanthus*, 543)
*Cereus senilis* (see *Cephalocereus senilis*, 297)
*Cereus speciosus* (see *Heliocereus speciosus*, 393)
*Cereus spinulosus* (see *Selenicereus spinulosus*, 543)
*Cereus triangularis* (see *Hylocereus tricostatus*, 406)
Ceropegia, 298
Ceropteris, 298

**624**

# INDEX

Cestrum, 298
Chænomeles, 299
Chænostoma, 299
Chain Fern (see Woodwardia, 593)
*Chalcas exotica*, 299
Chamæcyparis, 300
Chamædorea, 300
Chamæranthemum, 300
*Chamærops excelsa* (see *Trachycarpus excelsa*, 573)
*Chamærops Fortunei* (see *Trachycarpus Fortunei*, 573)
*Chamærops humilis*, 300
Chaste Tree (see *Vitex Agnus-castus*, 588)
Cheilanthes, 301
Cheiranthus, 301
Cherry, 193
Cherry Pie (see Heliotropium, 394)
Chickweed Wintergreen (see *Trientalis europæa*, 576)
Chicory, 94
Chilean Bellflower (see *Lapageria rosea*, 424)
Chilean Crocus (see *Tecophilaea cyanocrocus*, 566)
*Chimonanthus præcox*, 302
China Aster (see *Callistephus chinensis*, 280)
China Berry (see *Melia Azedarach*, 453)
Chincheringchee (see *Ornithogalum thyrsoides*, 479)
Chinese Angelica (see *Aralia chinensis*, 250)
Chinese Trumpet Creeper (see Campsis, 285)
Chinese Wisteria (see *Wisteria sinensis*, 592)
Chionanthus, 302
*Chionodoxa Luciliæ*, 302
Chirita, 303
Chironia, 303
*Chlidanthus fragrans*, 303
*Chlorophytum elatum* var. *variegatum*, 303
Chlorosis, 612
*Choisya ternata*, 303
Chondrorhyncha, 173
Chorizema, 304
Christmas Rose (see Helleborus), 394
*Chrysalidocarpus lutescens*, 304
Chrysanthemum, 304
*Chrysanthemum anethifolium* and *frutescens*, 310
Chrysanthemum Leaf Eelworm (see Eelworms, 606)
Chrysanthemum Leaf Miners (see Leaf Miners, 607)
Chrysanthemum Leaf Spot, 604
Chrysanthemum Mildew, 604
*Chrysurus aureus* (see *Lamarckia aurea*, 424)
Chysis, 168
Cibotium, 311
Cineraria, 311
*Cineraria maritima* (see *Senecio Cineraria*, 544)
Cineraria Rust, 604
Cirrhopetalum, 161

Cissus, 312
*Citrus sinensis*, 312
Clarkia, 312
*Cleistocactus Baumannii*, 313
Clematis, 313
*Cleome spinosa*, 314
Clerodendron, 314
Clethra, 315
Clianthus, 315
Cliff Brake Fern (see Pellæa, 491)
Climbing Dahlia (see *Hidalgoa Wercklei*, 397)
Climbing Fern (see Lygodium, 441)
Climbing Hempweed (see *Mikania scandens*, 457)
*Clitoria ternatea*, 316
Clivia, 316
Club Moss (see Lycopodium, 440)
Club Rush (see Scirpus, 541)
Clusia, 316
Clytostoma, 316
Cobæa, 316
Cobweb House Leek (see *Sempervivum arachnoideum*, 544)
*Coburgia coccinea* (see *Stenomesson coccineum*, 556).
*Coburgia incarnata* (see *Stenomesson incarnatum*, 556)
Cochlioda, 173
*Cochliostema odoratissimum*, 317
Cockroaches, 604
Cockscomb (see Celosia 295)
Cockspur Flower (see Plectranthus, 505)
Coconut (see *Cocos nucifera*, 317)
Cocos, 317
Codiæum, 318
*Cælogyne cristata*, 161, 173
*Coix Lacryma-Jobi*, 319
Colchicum, 319
Coleonema, 319
*Coleus Blumei*, 319
Collinsia, 320
Colocasia, 320
Columbine (see Aquilegia, 249)
Columnea, 321
Combretum, 321
Commelina, 321
Comparettia, 168
Compost, 67, 81–84, 183
Compost Heap, The, 56
*Conandron ramondioides*, 322
*Coniogramme japonica*, 322
*Conostephium pendulum*, 322
Construction of a Greenhouse, 23
Control of Pests, 50
*Convallaria majalis*, 322
Convolvulus, 323
Cooperia, 323
Coprosma, 323
Coptis, 324
Coral Barberry (see *Berberidopsis corallina*, 265)
Coral-berried Duckweed (see *Nertera depressa*, 471)
Coral Bush (see *Templetonia retusa*, 566)
Coral Plant (see *Russelia juncea*, 529)
Coral Tree (see Erythrina, 364).
Cordia, 324

R R

# INDEX

Cordyline, 324
Corn Flag (see Gladiolus, 383)
*Coronilla glauca*, 325
Correa, 325
Coryanthes, 168
Corydalis, 325
Corylopsis, 325
Corypha, 326
Costus, 326
Cotyledon, 326
Cow-horn Orchid (see *Schomburgkia tibicinis*, 165)
Crab's Eye Vine (see Abrus, 233)
Cranberry (see Vaccinium, 581)
Crane's Bill (see Geranium, 381)
Craspedia, 327
Crassula, 327
*Crassula coccinea* (see *Rochea coccinea*, 523)
*Crassula elegans* (see *Oliveranthus elegans*, 476)
*Craterostigma pumilum*, 328
Crawfurdia, 328
Creeping Forget-me-not (see *Omphalodes verna*, 476)
Creeping Jenny (see *Lysimachia Nummularia*, 441)
Crepe Fern (see *Todea barbara*, 571)
Cress Disease, 604
Crinodendron (see Tricuspidaria, 576)
Crinum, 328
Crocus, 329
Crossandra, 330
Crotalaria, 330
Crotons of Florists (see Codiæum, 318)
Crowea, 330
Crowfoot (see Ranunculus, 517)
Cryptochilus, 168
Cryptogramma, 330
Cryptophoranthus, 173
Cryptostegia, 331
Cuckoo Spit, 604
Cucumber, 94, 194
Cucumber Canker, 605
Cucumber Mildew, 605
Cucumber Scab, 605
Cucumis, 331
*Cucumis Melo* (see Melon, 212)
*Cucumis sativus* (see Cucumber, 194)
Cup and Saucer (see *Cobæa scandens*, 316)
Cup Flower (see *Nierembergia*, 472)
Cuphea, 331
Cupressus (see Chamæcyparis, 300)
Curculigo, 332
Curcuma, 332
Curly Palm (see Howea, 400)
Cushion Pink (see *Silene acaulis*, 546)
Cuttings, 64–68
Cyanathus, 333
Cyanella, 333
*Cyanophyllum magnificum* (see *Miconia magnifica*, 456)
Cyanotis, 333
Cyathea, 333
Cycad Family (see Ceratozamia, Cycas, Dioon, Encephalartos, etc., also Greenhouse Foliage Plants Chapter)
Cycas, 334

Cyclamen, 334
Cycnoches, 161
*Cydonia japonica* (see *Chænomeles lagenaria*, 299)
*Cydonia Maulei* (see *Chænomeles japonica*, 299)
Cymbidium, 173
*Cymbidium Saundersonii* (see *Ansellia gigantea*, 160)
Cypella, 335
Cyperorchis, 174
*Cyperus alternifolius*, 335
Cypress (see Chamæcyparis, 300)
Cypripedium, 174
*Cyrtomium falcatum*, 336
*Cyrtosperma Johnstonii*, 336
Cystopteris, 336
Cytisus, 337

*Dædalacanthus nervosus*, 337
Daffodils, 338
Dalechampia, 338
Damping off, 605
Dancing Girls (see *Mantisia saltatoria*, 446)
Daphne, 338
*Darlingtonia californica*, 339
Darwinia, 339
Dasylirions, 339
Date Palm (see *Phœnix dactylifera*, 499)
Date Plum (see *Diospyros Kaki*, 348)
Datura, 339
Davallia, 340
*Davidsonia pruriens*, 340
Day Flower (see Commelina, 321)
D.D.T., 620
Delphinium, 340
Dendrobium, 161, 168, 174
*Dendrobium muricatum* var. *munificum* (see *Inabulbon munificum*, 169)
Dennstædtia, 341
*Dermatobotrys Saundersii*, 341
*Desfontainia spinosa*, 341
Design of the Greenhouse, 13–15, 20
Desmodium, 342
Deutzia, 342
Devil's Walking-stick (see *Aralia spinosa*, 250)
*Diacrium bicornutum*, 174
Diamond Flower (see *Ionospidium acaule*, 411)
Dianella, 342
*Dianthera nodosa*, 343
Dianthus, 343
Diapensia, 343
*Diascia Barberæ*, 343
Diastema, 343
Dicentra, 344
*Dichæa picta*, 168
*Dichorisandra thyrsiflora*, 344
*Dichrotrichum ternateum*, 344
Dicksonia, 345
*Dictyanthus Pavonii*, 345
Dictyosperma, 345
Didiscus (see Trachymene, 573)
*Didymochlæna lunulata*, 345
Dieffenbachia, 345

626

# INDEX

Dielytra (see Dicentra, 344)
Dierama pulcherrima, 346
Diervilla, 346
Digitalis canariensis (see Isoplexis canariensis, 414)
Dillwynia, 346
Dimorphotheca aurantiaca, 347
Dionæa muscipula, 347
Dioon edule, 347
Diosma, 347
Diospyros Kaki, 348
Diplacus, 348
Dipladenia, 348
Dipladenia flava (see Urechites suberecta, 580)
Dipladenia Harrisii (see Odontadenia grandiflora, 475)
Disa, 174
Diseases and Pests, 188, 600
Disocactus biformis, 349
Dissotis, 349
Dittany (see Origanum Dictamnus, 479)
Diuris, 174
Dizygotheca, 349
Dodecatheon, 350
Dog's Tooth Violet (see Erythronium, 365)
Dombeya, 350
Dondia Epipactis (see Hacquetia Epipactis, 390)
Doodia, 350
Doryopteris, 350
Douglasia Vitaliana, 351
Draba Aizoon, 351
Draba pyrenaica (see Petrocallis pyrenaica, 494)
Dracæna, 351
Dracæna Palm (see Cordyline, 324)
Dracophyllum, 351
Drosera, 352
Drosophyllum lusitanicum, 352
Dryas octopetala, 352
Drymoglossum, 352
Drynaria, 352
Dryopteris, 353
Duchesnea indica, 353
Dudleya (see Cotyledon, 326)
Dumb Cane (see Dieffenbachia Sequine, 345)
Dusty Miller (see Senecio Cineraria, 544)
Dutchman's Breeches (see Dicentra Cucularia, 344)
Dutchman's Pipe (see Aristolochia Sipho, 252)
Duvalia, 353
Dyckia, 354

Earwigs, 605
Eccremocarpus scaber, 354
Echeveria (see Cotyledon, 326)
Echidnopsis, 354
Echinocactus, 354
Echinocactus Fiebrigii (see Rebutia Fiebrigii, 518)
Echinocactus Haselbergii (see Notocactus Haselbergii, 474)
Echinocactus Lecontei (see Ferocactus Lecontei, 372)

Echinocactus mamillarioides (see Pyrrhocactus centeterius, 516)
Echinocactus minusculus (see Rebutia minuscula, 518)
Echinocactus rhodopthalmus (see Thelocactus bicolor, 568)
Echinocactus Simpsonii (see Pediocactus Simpsonii, 487)
Echinocactus Wislezenii (see Ferocactus Wislezenii, 372)
Echinocereus, 355
Echinopsis, 355
Echium, 355
Edelweiss (see Leontopodium, 427)
Edraianthus, 356
Edwardsia grandiflora (see Sophora, 551)
Eel Grass (see Vallisneria spiralis, 582)
Eelworms, 606
Egg Plant (see Solanum Melongeana, 549)
Egyptian Paper Plant (see Cyperus Papyrus, 335)
Eichornia, 356
Elæocarpus cyaneus, 356
Elaphoglossum, 357
Electricity in the Greenhouse, 42–44
Elephant's Ear Fern (see Elaphoglossum crinitum, 357)
Elephants' Foot (see Testudinaria, 566)
Elisena longipetala, 357
Elk's Horn Fern (see Platycerium, 504)
Elleanthus, 162
Elodea, 357
Embothrium coccineum, 357
Emmenanthe penduliflora, 357
Encephalartos, 357
Endive, 94
Epacris, 358
Epicattleya, 168
Epidendrum, 174
Epidendrum Medusæ (see Nanodes Medusæ, 176)
Epidendrum tibicinus (see Schomburgkia tibicinus, 165)
Epigæa, 358
Epilælia, 174
Epiphronites, 168
Epiphyllum, 359
Epiphyllum truncatum (see Zygocactus truncatus, 599)
Episcia, 359
Epistephium Williamsii, 360
Eranthemum, 360
Eranthemum nervosum (see Dædalacathus nervosus, 337)
Eranthemum pulchellum, 360
Eranthis, 360
Eria, 162
Erica, 360
Ericinella Mannii, 362
Erigeron, 362
Erinacea pungens, 362
Erinus alpinus, 362
Eriochilus, 174
Eriocnema (see Bertolonia, 266)
Eriopsis, 168
Eriospermum, 363
Eriostemon, 363
Eritrichium nanum, 363

**627**

# INDEX

*Erlangea tomentosa,* 363
Erodium, 364
*Erpetion reniforme* (see *Viola hederacea,* 586)
Erysimum, 364
Erysiphaceæ (see Mildew, 608)
*Erythrina Crista-galli,* 364
Erythronium, 365
Escallonia, 365
Eucalyptus, 365
Eucharis, 366
*Eucomis punctata,* 366
*Eucrosia bicolor,* 366
*Eucryphia glutinosa,* 366
Eugenia, 367
Eulalia (see Miscanthus, 458)
Eulophia, 162
Eulophiella, 162
Eupatorium, 367
Euphorbia, 368
*Eurya japonica,* 368
*Euryale ferox,* 369
*Eustegia hastata,* 369
*Eustoma Russellianum,* 369
Eutaxia, 369
*Eutoca sericea* (see *Phacelia sericea,* 495)
Evening Primrose (see Œnothera, 475)
Evening Star (see Cooperia, 323)
Exacum, 369
Exocorda, 370

Fabiana, 370
*Fadyenia prolifera,* 370
Fairy Lily (see Zephranthes, 597)
Fairy Primrose (see *Primula malacoides,* 510)
*Falkia repens,* 370
False Heath (see Fabiana, 370)
False Solomon's Seal (see Smilacina, 547)
False Spikenard (see *Smilacina racemosa,* 547)
Fan Palms (see Chamærops, Latania, Livistona, Trachycarpus, Washingtonia)
Farfugium (see Senecio, 544)
*Fatsia japonica,* 371
Feathered Hyacinth (see *Muscari comosum* var. *monstrosum,* 463)
*Feijoa Sellowiana,* 371
Felicia, 371
Ferns (see Adiantum, etc., 237)
Ferns, Culture of, 130–135
Fern Balls (see *Davallia bullata,* 340)
Fern Palm (see *Cycas circinalis,* 334)
Ferraria, 372
Fertilizers, 55–58
*Ficus Carica* (see Fruit Chapter, 197)
*Ficus elastica,* 372
Fig, 197
Fig Marigold (see Mesembryanthemum, 454)
Filipendula, 373
Fire Nettle (see Coleus, 319)
Fish-tail Palm (see Caryota, 293)
Fittonia, 373
Flame Nasturtium (see *Tropæolum speciosum,* 578)
Flamingo Flower (see *Anthurium Scherzerianum,* 247)

Flax (see Linum, 434)
Flax Lily (see Dianella, 342)
Floral Fire Cracker (see *Brevoortia Ida-Maia,* 272)
Florida Moss (see *Tillandsia usneoides,* 571).
Floss Flower (see Ageratum, 239)
Flowering Currant (see Ribes, 522)
Flowering Moss (see *Pyxidanthera barbulata,* 516)
Flowering Shrubs, Forcing, 97
Flowers, Forcing, 96
Foam Flower (see *Tiarella cordifolia,* 569)
Foliage Plants, 124–129
Foot Rot, 613
Forcing
    Bulbs, 97
    Early vegetables, 93
    Flowering shrubs, 97
    Flowers, 96
    Fruit, 96, 185
    Other plants, 98
    Roses, 98
    Vegetables, 93
Forget-me-not (see Myosotis, 464)
Forsythia, 374
Foundations of the Greenhouse, 23–26
*Fragaria indica* (see *Duchesnea indica,* 353)
Frames, 53
*Francoa ramosa,* 374
Freesia, 375
*Fremontia californica,* 375
Fringed Calla (see *Arisæma fimbriatum,* 252)
Fringed Lily (see Thysanotus, 569)
Fringed Tree (see *Chionanthus virginica,* 302)
Fringed Violet (see *Thysanotus,* 569)
Fritillaria, 376
Fruit under Glass
    Aspect and Site of House, 178
    Border, 178
    Bruises, 188
    Compost, 183
    Diseases, 188
    Forcing, 96, 185
    Fumigation, 180, 186
    House, Type of, 182
    Housing, 185
    Manuring, 187
    Pollination, 186
    Pruning and Disbudding, 187
    Re-potting, 183
    Selecting Trees, 182
    Shading, 180
    Sterilising Soil, 189
    Temperature, 179
    Thinning, 187
    Training, 180
    Ventilation, 178
    Watering, 185
    Wintering in Open, 184
Fuchsia, 376
Fumigants, 617
Fumigation, 50, 180, 186, 600
Fungicides, 618
Funkia (see Hosta 399)
Furcræa, 377

# INDEX

Gagea, 378
Galanthus, 378
*Galax aphylla*, 379
Galaxia, 379
Galeandra, 162, 168
*Galtonia candicans*, 379
Gardenia, 379
*Gardenia citriodora* (see *Mitriostigma axillare*, 459)
*Gardenia macrantha* (see *Randia macrantha*, 517)
*Gardenia Stanleyana* (see *Randia maculata*, 517)
Garland Flower (see *Daphne Cneorum*, 338)
Gasteria, 380
Gaultheria, 380
Gazania, 380
*Gelsemium sempervirens*, 381
Genetyllis (see Darwinia, 339)
*Genista canariensis* (see *Cytisus canariensis*, 337)
*Genista fragrans* (see *Cytisus racemosus*, 337
Gentiana, 381
Gentianella (see *Gentiana acaulis*, 381)
Geodorum, 169
Geranium, 381
*Gerbera Jamesonii*, 381
German Ivy (see *Senecio mikanoides*, 544)
Germander (see Teucrium, 567)
Gesneria, 382
*Gesneria cinnabarina* (see *Nægelia cinnabarina*, 465)
*Gesneria zebrina* (see *Nægelia zebrina*, 465)
Giant Arrow-head (see *Sagittaria montevidensis*, 530)
Giant Forget-me-not (see *Myosotidium nobile*, 464)
Gilia, 382
Gladiolus, 383
Gleichenia, 384
Globba, 384
Globe Amaranth (see Gomphrena, 387)
Globe Flower (see Trollius, 577)
Globe Hyacinth (see Muscari, 463)
Globe Mallow (see Sphæralcea, 552)
Globe Tulip (see Calochortus, 281)
Globularia, 384
Gloriosa, 384
Glory of the Snow (see Chionodoxa, 302)
Glory of the Sun (see Leucocoryne, 428)
Glory Pea (see *Clianthus Dampieri*, 315)
Gloxinia, 385
*Gnidia polystachya*, 386
Godetia, 386
Golden Barrel (see *Echinocactus Grusonii*, 354)
Golden Bell Tree (see Forsythia, 374)
Golden Calla (see *Zantedeschia Elliottiana*, 596)
Golden Chain (see Laburnum, 422)
Golden Drop (see *Onosma stellatum* var. *tauricum*, 477)
Golden Rain (see Laburnum, 422)
Golden Rayed Lily (see *Lilium auratum*, 430)

Golden Spider Lily (see *Lycoris aurea*, 441)
Golden Vine (see *Stigmaphyllon ciliatum*, 558)
*Goldfussia anisophylla* (see *Strobilanthes anisophyllus*, 560)
*Goldfussia isophylla* (see *Strobilanthes isophyllus*, 560)
Gompholobium, 387
Gomphrena, 387
Gongora, 162
Goodyera, 169
Gooseberry Gourd (see *Cucumis Anguria*, 331)
Gordonia, 387
Grafting, 71–78
Grammangis, 162
*Grammanthes dichotoma*, 388
Grammatophyllum, 162
Grape, 201
Grapefruit (see *Citrus paradisi*, 312)
Grape Hyacinth (see Muscari, 463)
Graptophyllum, 388
*Gravesia guttata*, 388
Great Reed (see *Arundo donax*, 253)
Greenhouse, The
  Aspect of, 23
  Borders and Paths, 34–35
  Concrete, 19
  Construction of, 23
  Control of Pests in, 50
  Design of, 13–15, 20
  Electricity in, 42–44
  Foundations and structure, 23–26
  Frames, 53
  Fumigation, 50
  Gas in, 42
  Glass for, 29
  Heating, 36–44
  Heating frames, 54
  Hot-water systems, 38–40
  Lights; English, French and Dutch, 54
  Maintenance of, 47–49
  Metal, 18
  Oil burners, 41–42
  Overhaul, yearly, 50
  Pests in, 50
  Propagating cases in, 46–47
  Shading of, 31–33
  Size and Purpose of, 17
  Soil in, 23
  Soil sterilization in, 51
  Staging, 36
  Stoking, 40–41
  Types of, 15–17, 182
  Uses of, 44–46
  Ventilation of, 30–31
  Water supply of, 33–34
  Watering frames, 54
  Woodwork of, 27–29
*Grevillea robusta*, 388
Grey Mould (see *Botrytis cinarea*, 602), 613
Griffinia, 389
Groomwell (see *Lithospermum*, 435)
Ground or Moss Pink (see *Phlox subulata*, 497)

# INDEX

Ground Rattan Cane (see Rhapis, 519)
Guatemala Rhubarb (see *Jatropha podagrica*, 417)
Guelder Rose (see *Viburnum Opulus* var. *sterile*, 584)
Gum Tree (see *Eucalyptus*, 365)
Gymnogramma, 389
Gymnogramma calomelanos (see *Ceropteris calomelanos*, 298)
Gymnogramma japonica (see *Coniogramme japonica*, 322)
Gynura aurantiaca, 389
Gypsophila, 389

Habenaria, 162
Haberlea, 390
Habrothamnus (see Cestrum, 298)
*Hacquetia Epipactis*, 390
Hæmanthus, 390
Hæmaria, 163
Halleria lucida, 390
Hamamelis, 391
*Hardenbergia Comptoniana*, 391
Harebell Poppy (see *Meconopsis quintuplenervia*, 452)
Hare's Foot Fern (see *Davallia canariensis*, 340)
Hare's Tail (see *Lagurus ovatus*, 423)
Hart's Tongue Fern (see *Phyllitis Scolopendrium*, 500)
Hartwegia, 175
Hatchet Flower (see *Pelecyphora anselliformis*, 490)
Haworthia, 391
*Haylockia pusilla*, 391
Hay-scented Fern (see *Dryopteris Æmula*, 353)
Heather (see Erica, 360)
Heaths (see Erica, 360)
Heating Frames, 54
Heating the Greenhouse, 36–44
Hebeclinium (see Eupatorium, 367)
*Hebenstretia comosa*, 392
Hedgehog Broom (see *Erinacea pungens*, 362)
Hedgehog Cactus (see *Pediocactus Simpsonii*, 487)
Hedgehog Gourd (see *Cucumis dipsaceus*, 331)
Hedgehog Juniper (see *Juniperus communis* var., 418)
Hedge Mustard (see *Erysimum*, 364)
Hedræanthus (see Edraianthus, 356)
Hedychium, 392
*Hedyscepe Canterburyana*, 392
*Heeria elegans* (see *Schizocentron elegans*, 540)
*Heeria rosea* (see *Heterocentron roseum*, 396)
*Heliamphora nutans*, 392
Helichrysum, 393
Heliconia, 393
Heliocereus, 393
*Heliosperma alpestre* (see *Silene alpestris*, 546)
*Heliosperma quadrifida* (see *Silene quadrifida*, 546)
*Heliotropium peruvianum*, 394

Helipterum, 394
Hellebore Leaf-blotch, 606
Helleborus, 394
*Helonia bullata*, 395
*Helxine Soleirolii*, 395
*Hemigraphis colorata*, 395
Hemimeris montana, 395
Hemionitis, 395
Hemp Agrimony (see Eupatorium, 367)
Hemp Tree (see *Vitex Agnus-castus*, 588)
Hepatica (see Anemone, 245)
Herbertia, 396
Herb Lily (see Alstrœmeria, 242)
Hercules Club (see *Aralia spinosa*, 250)
Hercules Club Gourd (see *Lagenaria leucantha* var., 423)
Heron's Bill (see *Erodium*, 364)
*Herpestis Monnieria*, 396
*Heteranthera reniformis*, 396
*Heterocentron roseum*, 396
*Heterotoma lobelioides*, 396
Hexaglottis, 396
*Hexisea bidentata*, 169
Hibbertia, 396
Hibiscus, 397
*Hidalgoa Wercklei*, 397
Hippeastrum, 397
*Hippeastrum formosissimum* (see *Sprekelia formosissima*, 554)
Hoffmannia, 399
*Hoheria populnea*, 399
Holothrix, 169
*Homalomena Wallisii*, 399
Honey Bell (see *Mahernia verticillata*, 443)
Honey Dew (see Aphides, 601)
Honey Flower (see Melianthus, 454)
Honeysuckle (see Lonicera, 438)
Hoodia, 399
Horned Rampion (see *Phyteuma comosum*, 501)
Horse Brier (see *Smilax rotundifolia*, 548)
Hosta, 399
Hottentot's Bread (see Testudinaria, 566)
Hottentot's Head (see *Stangeria eriopus*, 554)
Hot-water systems, 38–40
Houllettia, 163
House Leek (see Sempervivum, 544)
Houstonia, 400
Houttea, 400
Hovea, 400
Howea, 400
Hoya, 400
Huckleberry (see Vaccinium, 581)
Huernia, 401
Humea, 401
Huntsman Cup (see Sarracenia, 534)
*Hutchinsia alpina*, 402
*Hyacinthus candicans* (see *Galtonia candicans*, 379)
*Hyacinthus orientalis*, 402
Hydrangea, 406
*Hydrocleis nymphoides*, 406
Hydrolea, 406
*Hylocereus tricostatus*, 406
*Hymenanthera crassifolia*, 407
Hymenocallis, 407

# INDEX

Hymenophyllum, 407
Hyophorbe, 408
Hypericum, 408
Hypocyrta, 408
Hypoxis, 408

Iberis, 408
Ice Plant (see *Mesembryanthemum* (*Cryophytum*) *crystallinum*, 454)
Illicium, 409
Imantophyllum (see Clivia, 316)
Impatiens, 409
Incarvillea, 410
Incense Plant (see *Humea elegans*, 402)
Indian Corn (see Zea, 596)
Indian Cress (see Tropæolum, 578)
Indian Rice (see *Zizania palustris*, 599)
Indian Shot (see Canna, 285)
Indiarubber Plant (see *Ficus elastica*, 372)
*Inobulbon munificum*, 169
Inorganic Artificial Manures, 57
Insecticides, 619
Insect pests, 600
Iochroma, 411
*Ionopsidium acaule*, 411
Ipomœa, 411
Ipomopsis (see Gilia, 382)
Ipsea, 169
Iresine, 412
Iris, 412
Iris, Ink Disease, 607
*Isertia coccinea*, 413
Ismene, 413
*Isochilus linearis*, 163
*Isolepsis gracilis* (see *Scirpus cernuus*, 541)
Isoloma, 413
Isoplexis, 414
*Itea virginica*, 414
Ixia, 414
*Ixiolirion montanum*, 414
Ixora, 414

*Jacaranda ovalifolia* (*J. mimosæfolia*), 415
Jacobæan Lily (see *Sprekelia formosissima*, 554)
Jacobinia, 416
Jamaica Honeysuckle (see *Passiflora laurifolia*, 485)
Jamaica Sago Tree (see *Zamia integrifolia*, 595)
*Jankæa Heldreichii*, 416
Japanese Aralia (see *Fatsia japonica*, 371)
Japanese Snowball Tree (see *Viburnum tomentosum*, 584)
Japanese Wisteria (see *Wisteria floribunda*, 592)
Jasmine Nightshade (see *Solanum jasminoides*, 549)
Jasmine Plant (see Bouvardia, 270)
Jasminum, 416
Jatropha, 417
*Jeffersonia diphylla*, 417
*Jerdonia indica*, 417
Jessamine (see Jasminum, 416)
Jew Bush (see *Pedilanthus tithymaloides*, 487)

Jew's Mallow (see Kerria, 420)
Job's Tear (see *Coix Lacryma-Jobi*, 319)
John Innes Composts, 58
Joseph's Coat (see *Amarantus caudatus*, 243)
*Jubæa spectabilis*, 418
Jujube (see Zizyphus, 599)
Juniper (see Juniperus, 418)
Juniperus, 418
Jupiter's Beard (see *Anthyllis Barba-Jovis*, 247)
Jussiæ, 418
Justicia (see Jacobinia, 416)
*Justicia calycotricha* (see *Schaueria calycotricha*, 539)
*Justicia flavicoma* (see *Schaueria flavicoma*, 539)
*Justicia speciosa* (see *Peristrophe speciosa*)

Kæmpferia, 418
Kaffir Lily (see *Schizostylis coccinea*, 540)
Kalanchoë, 419
Kalmia, 419
Kalosanthes (see Rochea, 523)
Kangaroo Thorn (see *Acacia armata*, 234)
Kangaroo's Foot (see Anigozanthus, 246)
*Kendrickia Walkeri*, 420
Kennedya, 420
*Kennedya Comptoniana* (see *Hardenbergia Comptoniana*, 391)
*Kentia Belmoreana* (see Howea, 400)
*Kentia Forsteriana* (see Howea, 400)
*Kentia Lindenii* (see *Kentiopsis macrocarpa*, 420)
*Kentiopsis macrocarpa*, 420
Kerria, 420
Killarney Fern (see *Trichomanes radicans*, 574)
*Kitchingia uniflora*, 421
Kleinia (see Senecio, 544)
*Klugia Notoniana*, 421
Kniphofia, 421
Kochia, 421
*Kœllikeria argyrostigma*, 422
*Kyllinga monocephala*, 422

Lablolly Bay (see *Gordonia lasianthus*, 387)
Labrador Tea (see *Ledum grœnlandicum*, 426)
Laburnum, 422
Lacæna, 163
Lace Fern (see Doryopteris, 350)
Lace Leaf or Lattice Leaf (see *Aponogeton fenestralis*, 249)
Lachenalia, 422
Ladder Fern (see Nephrolepis, 470)
Lady Fern (see *Athyrium Filix-fœmina*, 255)
Lady's Slipper (see Cypripedium, 174)
Lælia, 163, 169
Læliocattleya, 163, 169
*Lagenaria leucantha*, 423
*Lagerstrœmia indica*, 423
*Lagurus ovatus*, 423
*Lamarckia aurea*, 424
Lantana, 424
Lapageria, 424

# INDEX

Lapeyrousia, 425
Larkspur (see Delphinium, 340)
*Lasiandra macrantha* (see Tibouchina, 570)
Lastrea (see Dryopteris, 353)
*Lastrea membranifolia* (see *Dryopteris dissecta*, 353)
Latania, 425
Lathyrus, 425
*Lathyrus odoratus* (see Sweet Pea, 561)
Lattice Leaf or Lace Leaf (see *Aponogeton fenestralis*, 249)
Laurustinus (see *Viburnum Tinus*, 584)
Lavandula, 426
Lavender (see Lavandula, 426)
Layering, 68
Leadwort (see Plumbago, 505)
Leaf cuttings, 70
Leaf Eelworm, 606
Leaf Hopper, 607
Leaf Miners, 607
Leaf Mould, 613
Ledum, 426
Leea, 426
Leeks, 94
*Leiophyllum buxifolium*, 427
Lemon (see *Citrus Limonia*, 312)
Lemon-scented Verbena (see *Lippia citriodora*, 434)
*Leonotis Leonurus*, 427
*Leontopodium alpinum*, 427
Leptopteris, 427
Leptosiphon (see Gilia, 382)
Leptospermum, 428
*Leptotes bicolor*, 169
Leschenaultia, 428
Lettuce, 94
*Leucadendron argenteum*, 428
Leuchtenbergia, 428
*Leucocoryne ixioides* var. *odorata*, 428
Leucojum, 429
*Leucophyta Brownii*, 429
Leucopogon, 429
Lewisia, 429
Libertia, 430
Libonia, 430
Licuala, 430
*Lietzia brasiliensis*, 430
Lights; English, French and Dutch, 54
Lilac (see Syringa, 563)
Lilium, 430
Lily Disease, 607
Lily Mosaic Disease, 607
Lily of the Palace (see *Hippeastrum aulicum*, 397)
Lily of the Valley (see Convallaria, 322)
*Limatodes rosea*, 163
Lime (see *Citrus aurantifolia*, 312)
Lime, uses of, 59
*Limnobium stoloniferum*, 432
Limonium, 432
Linaria, 433
*Lindenbergia grandiflora*, 433
*Linnæa borealis*, 433
Linum, 434
*Linum trigynum* (see *Reinwardtia trigyna*, 518)
Lion's Tail (see *Leonotis Leonorus*, 427)

Liparis, 164, 175
Lippia, 434
*Lippia nodiflora*, 434
Liquid Manure, 90
*Liriope graminifolia*, 435
Lisianthus (see Eustoma, 369)
*Lissanthe sapida*, 435
Lissochilus, 164
Listrostachys, 164
Lithospermum, 435
*Lithospermum petræum* (see *Moltkia petræa*, 459)
*Littonia modesta*, 435
Livistona, 435
*Loasa lateritia* (see *Blumenbachia lateritia*, 269)
Lobelia, 436
*Lobelia littoralis* (see *Pratia angulata*, 509)
Lobster's Claw (see *Clianthus puniceus*, 315)
Lockhartia, 164, 437
*Loddigesia oxalidifolia*, 437
*Loiseleuria procumbens*, 437
*Lomaria alpina* (see *Blechnum Pennamarina*, 268)
Lomatia, 438
Lonchitis, 438
Lonicera, 438
*Lophocereus Schottii*, 438
*Lophophora Williamsii*, 438
*Loropetalum chinense*, 439
Lotus, 439
Lotus, Sacred (see Nelumbo, 468)
*Lourya campanulata*, 439
Love-in-a-mist (see Nigella, 472)
Love-lies-bleeding (see *Amarantus caudatus*, 243)
Love's Chain (see *Antigonon leptopus*, 247)
Luculia, 439
*Luffa cylindrica*, 440
Lycaste cristata (see *Paphinia cristata*, 176)
*Lycaste Skinneri*, 175
Lychnis, 440
*Lychnis Lagascæ* (see *Petrocoptis Lagascæ*, 494)
*Lychnis pyrenaica* (see *petrocoptis pyrenaica*, 494)
*Lycopersicum esculentum* (Tomato), 228
*Lycopersicum pimpinellifolium*, 440
Lycopodium, 440
Lycoris, 441
Lygodium, 441
*Lysimachia Nummularia*, 441
Lysionotus, 441

*Mackaya bella* (see *Asystasia bella*, 255)
Macleania, 442
Macodes, 164
Macradenia, 169
*Macroplectrum sesquipedale*, 169
Macrozamia, 442
Madagascar Periwinkle (see *Vinca rosea*, 585)
Madonna Lily (see *Lilium candidum*, 430)
Magnolia, 442
*Mahernia verticillata*, 443
*Maianthemum bifolium*, 443

632

# INDEX

Maidenhair Fern (see Adiantum, 237
Maintenance of the Greenhouse, 47–49
Maize (see Zea Mays, 596)
Malayan Jessamine (see *Trachelospermum jasminoides*, 572)
Male Fern (see *Dryopteris Filix-mas*, 353)
*Malope trifida*, 443
Malpighia, 444
Malus, 444
*Malva umbellata* (see *Sphæralcea umbellata*, 552)
*Malvastrum hypomadarum*, 444
*Malvaviscus mollis*, 444
Mammillaria, 444
*Mandevilla suaveolens*, 445
Manettia, 445
Manfreda, 446
Manihot, 446
*Mantisia saltatoria*, 446
Manures, 55–58
    Inorganic artificial manure, 57
    Natural manure, 55
    Organic manure, 55
Manuring, 187
Maranta, 446
*Maranta Chantrieri* (see *Calathea Chantrieri*, 276)
*Maranta Porteana* (see *Stromanthe Porteana*, 560)
Marattia, 447
Marguerite (see *Chrysanthemum frutescens*, 310)
Marguerite, Blue (see *Felicia amelloides*, 371)
*Margyricarpus setosus*, 447
Marica, 447
Marigold (see Calendula, 279)
Maripose Lily (see Calochortus, 281)
Maripose Tulip (see Calochortus, 281)
Marjoram (see Origanum, 479)
Marsh Rosemary (see Andromeda, 245)
Marsilea, 448
Martinezia, 448
Martynia, 448
Marvel of Peru (see Mirabilis, 458)
Masdevallia, 175
Mask Flower (see Alonsoa, 241)
Matilija Poppy (see Romneya, 524)
Matthiola, 449
Maurandia, 451
*Maurandia antirrhiniflora* (see *Antirrhinum maurandioides*, 248)
Maxillaria, 169, 175
*Maxillaria discolor* (see *Xylobium discolor*, 172)
*Maxillaria elongata* (see *Xylobium elongatum*, 172)
*Maxillaria leontoglossa* (see *Xylobium leontoglossum*, 172)
*Maxillaria squalens* (see *Xylobium squalens*, 172)
*Maximiliana regia*, 451
May Flower (see *Epigæa repens*, 358)
Mazus, 451
Meadow Rue (see Thalictrum, 567)
Meadow Sweet (see Filipendula, 373)
Mealy-bug, 608
Meconopsis, 452

*Medeola asparagoides* (see *Myrsiphyllum asparagoides*, 465)
Medinilla, 452
Mediterranean Cress (see *Morisia Hypogæa*, 461)
Mediterranean Lily (see *Pancratium maritimum*, 484)
Melaleuca, 453
*Melandrium Elizabethæ* (see *Silene Elizabethæ*, 546)
*Melandrium Hookeri* (see *Silene Hookeri*, 546)
Melastoma, 453
*Melia Azedarach*, 453
*Melianthus major*, 454
*Melocactus communis* (see *Cactus melocactus*, 276)
Melon, 212
*Merendera sobolifera*, 454
Mertensia, 454
Mesembryanthemum, 454
*Mesospinidium sanguineum*, 175
Metrosideros, 455
Mexican Flame Leaf (see Poinsettia, 506)
Mexican Foxglove (see *Tetranema mexicana*, 567)
Mexican Orange Blossom (see *Choisya ternata*, 303)
Mexican Twin Flower (see *Bravoa geminiflora*, 272)
Mice, 608
*Michelia fuscata*, 456
Miconia, 456
*Microcachrys tetragona*, 456
Microstylis, 170
Mignonette (see *Reseda odorata*, 519)
*Mikania scandens*, 457
*Mikania senecioides* (see *Senecio mikanoides*, 544)
Mildew, 608
Milkweed (see Asclepias, 253)
Milkwort (see Polygala, 507)
Millepedes, 608
*Miltonia vexilliaria*, 164, 170
*Mimosa pudica*, 457
Mimulus, 457
*Mimulus radicans* (see *Mazus radicans*, 451)
*Mina lobata* (see *Ipomœa versicolor*, 411)
Mint, 94
Mirabilis, 458
Miscanthus, 458
*Mitchella repens*, 458
*Mitraria coccinea*, 459
*Mitriostigma axillare*, 459
*Moltkia petræa*, 459
Momordica, 459
Monanthes, 460
Monkey's Comb (see Pithecoctenium, 504
Monochætum, 460
Monsonia, 460
*Monstera deliciosa*, 460
Montbretia (see Tritonia, 577)
*Moorea irrorata*, 170
Moræa, 461
*Morisia monantha*, 461
Mormodes, 175

**633**

Morning Glory (see Ipomœa, 411)
Mosaic, 613
*Moschosma riparium*, 461
Moss Campion (see *Silene acaulis*, 546)
Moss Pink (see *Phlox subulata*, 497)
Mother of Thousands (see *Saxifraga sarmentosa*, 535)
Mountain Aven (see *Dryas octopetala*, 352)
Mountain Rose (see *Antigonon leptopus*, 247)
Mountain Wolf's Bane (see *Ranunculus Thora*, 517)
Mount Etna Lily (see *Sternbergia lutea*, 557)
Mullein (see Celsia, 295)
*Murraya exotica* (see *Chalcas exotica*, 299)
Musa, 182
*Musa Ensete*, 462
Muscari, 463
*Muscari azureum* (see *Hyacinthus azureus*, 463)
Mushrooms, 94
Musk (see *Mimulus moschatus*, 457)
Mustard and Cress, 95
Mutisia, 463
*Myoporum parviflorum*, 464
*Myosotidium nobile*, 464
Myosotis, 464
*Myriophyllum proserpinacoides*, 464
*Myrmecodia Antoinii*, 465
*Myrsiphyllum asparagoides*, 128
Myrtus, 465

Nægelia, 465
*Nandina domestica*, 466
*Nanodes Medusæ*, 176
Narcissus, 466
*Nasonia punctata*, 176
Nasturtium (see Tropæolum, 578)
Natural Manures, 55
Navel-wort (see *Omphalodes*, 476)
Nectarine, 218
Nectarine Rust, 609
*Nelumbium speciosum* (see *Nelumbo nucifera*, 468)
*Nelumbo nucifera*, 468
Nematanthus, 468
Nemesia, 468
*Neobenthamia gracilis*, 176
*Neogyne Gardneriana*, 170
Nepenthes, 469
Nepeta, 470
Nephelaphyllum, 170
Nephrodium (see Dryopteris, 353)
Nephrolepis, 470
Nerine, 470
Nerium, 470
Nerium Black Mould, 609
*Nerium grandiflorum* (see *Cryptostegia grandiflora*, 331)
*Nertera depressa*, 471
New Zealand Flax (see Phormium, 499)
New Zealand Christmas Tree (see *Metrosideros tomentosa*, 455)
Nicotiana, 471
Nierembergia, 472
Nigella, 472
Nitrogenous Manures, 57

*Nivenia corymbosa*, 473
Nolina, 473
*Nopalea cochinellifera*, 473
Notholæna, 473
Notocactus, 474
Nycterinia (see Zaluzianskya, 595)
Nyctocerus, 474
Nymphæa, 474

*Ochna multiflora*, 475
*Odontadenia grandiflora*, 475
Odontioda, 176
Odontoglossum, 176
*Odontonema Schomburgkianum*, 475
Œnothera, 475
*Oftia africana*, 476
Old Man Cactus (see *Cephalocereus senelis*, 297)
Old Man's Beard (see *Tillandsia usneoides*, 570)
Oleander (see *Nerium Oleander*, 470)
*Olearia Haastii*, 476
*Oliveranthus elegans*, 476
Omphalodes, 476
Oncidium, 170, 176
Onions, 95
*Onoclea sensibilis*, 477
Onosma, 477
Onychium, 477
Ophioglossum, 478
Ophiopogon, 478
*Ophiopogon spicatus* (see *Liriope spicata*, 435)
*Oplismenus hirtellus*, 478
Opuntia, 478
Orange, 217
Orange Jessamine (see *Chalcas exotica*, 299)
Orchid Culture, 153–159
Orchids, List of, 160–177
Oreodoxa, 176
Origanum, 479
Ornithogalum, 479
*Oryza sativa*, 480
Osbeckia, 480
Osmanthus, 480
Osmunda, 480
Osteomeles, 481
Osteospermum, 481
*Othonna crassifolia*, 481
Ourisia, 482
Ouvirandra (see Aponogeton, 249)
Oxalis, 482
*Oxypetalum cæruleum*, 483

Pachyphytum (see Senecio, 544)
Pachystoma, 164
Pæonia, 483
Palms, 124, 483
*Pancratium calathinum* (see *Hymenocallis calathina*, 407)
*Pancratium illyricum*, 484
*Pancratium maritimum*, 484
Pandanus, 484
Pandorea, 484
Panicum, 485
*Panicum variegatum* (see *Oplismenus hirtellus*, 478)

# INDEX

Pansy (see Viola, 586)
Paphinia, 164, 176
Paphiopedilum, 164, 170, 176
Papyrus (see *Cyperus Papyrus*, 335)
Parrot's Bill (see *Clianthus puniceus*, 315)
Parrot's Feather (see Myriophyllum, 464)
Parsley, 95
Partridge Berry (see *Mitchella repens*, 458)
Partridge-breasted Aloe (see *Aloe variegata*, 241)
Pasque Flower (see *Anemone Pulsatilla*, 245)
Passiflora, 485
Paths and Borders, 34–35
*Paullinia thalictrifolia*, 486
Pavetta, 486
*Pavonia rosea*, 486
Peach, 218
Peach-coloured Trumpet Flower (see *Solandra grandiflora*, 548)
Peach Leaf-curl, 609
Peach Rust, 609
Peach Scale, 609
Pear, 183, 190
Pearl Bush (see Exocorda, 370)
Pearl Fruit (see Margyricarpus, 447)
Peas, 95
*Pedilanthus tithymaloides*, 487
*Pediocactus Simpsonii*, 487
Pelargonium, 487
Pelargonium Stem-rot, 609
*Pelecyphora anselliformis*, 490
Pellæa, 491
Pellionia, 491
Pentapterygium, 491
Pentarhaphia, 491
*Pentas lanceolata*, 491
*Pentlandia miniata* (see *Urceolina miniata*, 580)
Peperomia, 492
Pepper (see Piper, 503)
Pereskia, 492
Pergularia, 493
Perilla, 493
Peristeria, 164
*Peristrophe speciosa*, 493
*Pernettya mucronata*, 493
Persian Ranunculus (see *Ranunculus asiatica*, 517)
Peruvian Daffodil (see *Hymenocallis calathina*, 407)
Peruvian Hyacinth (see *Scilla peruviana*, 541)
Peruvian Lily (see *Alstrœmeria*, 242)
Peruvian Swamp Lily (see Zephyranthes, 597)
Pescatoria, 171
Pests, Control of, 50
*Petrea volubilis*, 494
*Petrocallis pyrenaica*, 494
Petrocoptis, 494
Petunia, 494
Phacelia, 495
*Phædranassa chloracra*, 495
*Phædranthus buccinatorius*, 495
*Phænocoma prolifera*, 495
*Phaius grandifolius*, 171

Phalænopsis, 165
*Phegopteris polypodioides* (see Dryopteris, 353)
Philadelphus, 496
*Philageria Veitchii*, 496
*Philesia buxifolia*, 497
Philibertia, 497
Philodendron, 497
Phlox, 497
Phœnix, 499
Pholidota, 171
Phormium, 499
Phosphate Manures, 58
Phragmopedilum, 165, 171
Phyllagathis, 499
Phyllanthus, 500
Phyllitis, 500
Phyllocactus (see Epiphyllum, 359)
*Phyllocactus biformis* (see *Disocactus biformis*, 349)
Phyllodoce, 501
*Phyllotænium Lindenii* (see *Xanthosoma Lindenii*, 594)
Phymatodes, 501
Physianthus (see Araujia, 251)
*Phyteuma comosum*, 501
Picotees, 501
Pieris, 501
*Pilea muscosa*, 502
Pilocereus (see Cephalocereus, 297)
*Pilocereus Schottii* (see *Lophocereus Schottii*, 438)
*Pilocereus senilis* (see *Cephalocereus senilis*, 297)
Pimelea, 502
Pimpernel (see Anagallis, 244)
Pincushion Flower (see Scabiosa, 538)
Pineapple, 225
Pineapple-scented Sage (see *Salvia rutilans*, 531)
Pine-barren Beauty (see *Pyxidanthera barbulata*, 516)
Pinguicula, 503
Pink Root (see *Spigelia marilandica*, 552)
Piper, 503
*Pistia Stratiotes*, 503
Pistorinia (see Cotyledon, 326)
Pitcairnia, 503
Pitcher Plant (see Nepenthes, 469)
Pithecoctenium, 504
Plant Lice (see Aphides, 601)
Plantain Lily (see Hosta, 399)
Platycerium, 504
Platyclinis, 165
Plectranthus, 505
*Pleiocarpa mutica*, 505
Pleione, 171
Pleomele (see Dracæna, 351)
Pleroma (see Tibouchina, 570)
Plum Rust, 609
Plumbago, 505
Plumeria, 506
Podochilus, 165
Poinsettia, 506
*Polianthes tuberosa*, 507
Pollination, 186
Polyanthus, 507
Polygala, 507

**635**

# INDEX

*Polygonatum multiflorum,* 508
Polypodium, 508
Polystichium, 508
*Pomaderris elliptica,* 509
Pomegranate (see Punica, 515)
Poor Man's Orchid (see Schizanthus, 539)
Portlandia, 509
Posoqueria, 509
Potash Manures, 57
Potatoes, 95
Pothos, 509
Potting, 80–89
Pratia, 509
Prickly Heath (see *Pernettya mucronata,* 493)
Prickly Pear (see Opuntia, 478)
Pride of California (see *Lathyrus splendens,* 425)
Primrose (see Primula, 510)
Primrose Willow (see Jussiæ, 418)
Primula, 510
*Primula Auricula* (see Auricula, 256)
Pritchardia, 512
*Pritchardia filamentosa* (see *Washingtonia filifera,* 590)
Propagating cases, 46–4.
Propagation methods
    Cuttings, 64–68
    Layering, 68
    Seeds, 60–63 (see also Grafting, Leaf cuttings, Offsets, Root cuttings, Root division, and Runners)
Prostanthera, 513
Protea, 513
Pruning and Disbudding, 187
Prunus, 513
*Psoralea affinis,* 514
*Pteridium aquilinum,* 514
Pteris, 514
*Pteris aquilina* (see *Pteridium aquilinum,* 514
Pterostylis, 177
*Punica Granatum,* 515
Purple Bells (see *Rhodochiton volubile,* 520)
Purple Rock Cress (see Aubrietia, 256)
Purple Wreath (see *Petrea volubilis,* 494)
*Puschkinia scilloides,* 515
*Pycnostashys Dawei,* 515
Pyrenean Primrose (see *Ramonda Myconi,* 517)
*Pyrostegia venusta,* 515
Pyrus (see Malus, 444)
*Pyrus floribunda* (see *Malus floribunda,* 444)
*Pyrus japonica* (see *Chænomeles lagenaria,* 299)
*Pyrus Maulei* (see *Chænomeles japonica,* 299)
*Pyrus spectabilis* (see *Malus spectabilis,* 444)
*Pyxidanthera barbulata,* 516

*Quamoclit pinnata (Ipomæa Quamoclit),* 516
Queen of the Prairie (see Filipendula, 373)
*Quisqualis indica,* 516

Radishes, 96
*Raffenaldia primuloides,* 516
*Ramonda Heldreichii* (see *Jankæa Heldreichii,* 416)
*Ramonda Myconi,* 517
Randia, 517
Rangoon Creeper (see *Quisqualis indica,* 516)
Ranunculus, 517
Rat's-tail Cactus (see *Aporocactus flagelliformis,* 249)
Rattle Box (see Crotalaria, 330)
*Ravenea Hildebrandtii,* 518
Rebutia, 518
Red Root (see *Lithospermum canescens,* 435)
Red Spider, 609
Rehmannia, 518
Rein Orchid (see Habenaria, 162)
Reinwardtia, 518
Renanthera, 165
Re-potting, 183
*Reseda odorata,* 519
Resurrection Plant (see *Selaginella lepidophylla,* 543)
*Rhabdothamnus Solandri,* 519
Rhapis, 519
Rheumatism Root (see *Jeffersonia diphylla,* 417)
*Rhexia virginica,* 520
Rhipsalis, 520
Rhodanthe (see Helipterum, 394)
*Rhodochiton volubile,* 520
Rhododendron, 520
*Rhodothamnus Chamæcistus,* 521
*Rhœo discolor,* 522
Rhopalostylis, 522
Rhubarb, 96
*Rhynchanthera grandiflora,* 522
Rhynchospermum (see Trachelospermum, 572)
Rhynchostylis, 165, 171
Ribbon Fern (see Pteris, 514)
Ribes, 522
Rice (see *Oryza sativa,* 480)
Rice Flower (see Pimelea, 502)
Rice Paper Tree (see *Fatsia papyrifera,* 371)
Richardia (see Zantedeschia, 596)
*Ricinus communis,* 522
Rivina, 523
Rochea, 523
Rock Cress (see Arabis, 250)
Rockfoil (see Saxifraga, 535)
Rock Jasmine (see Androsace, 245)
Rodriguezia, 165
Romneya, 524
Rondeletia, 524
Room Plants, 136–137
Root Cuttings, 69
Root Division, 63
Rose Apple (see *Eugenia Jambos,* 367)
Rose Mildew (see Mildew, 608)
Rose of Heaven (see *Lychnis Cæli-rosa,* 440)
Rose Rot, 610
Rose Rust, 610
Roses, 525

# INDEX

Roses, Forcing, 98
Rosette Mullein (see *Ramonda Myconi*, 517)
*Roupellia grata*, 529
Royal Fern (see Osmunda, 481)
Royal Palm (see *Oreodoxa regia*, 479)
Royal Water Lily (see *Victoria regia*, 585)
Ruellia, 529
Runners, 69
*Ruscus androgynus* (see *Semele androgyna*, 544)
Russelia, 529
Rust, 610

Sabal, 530
Saccharum, 530
Saccolabium, 165, 172
Sacred Lotus (see *Nelumbo nucifera*, 468)
*Sadleria cyatheoides*, 530
Saffron Crocus (see *Crocus sativus*, 329)
Sage (see Salvia, 531)
*Sagittaria montevidensis*, 530
St. Bernard's Lily (see *Anthericum Liliago*, 247)
St. John's Wort (see Hypericum, 408)
*Saintpaulia ionantha*, 531
Salpiglossis, 531
Salvia, 531
Salvinia, 532
*Sanchezia nobilis*, 533
Sand Myrtle (see *Leiophyllum buxifolium*, 427)
*Sandersonia aurantiaca*, 533
Sand-wort (see Arenaria, 252)
*Sanguinaria canadensis*, 533)
Sansevieria, 533
Saponaria, 533
Sarcocaulon, 534
*Sarmienta repens*, 534
Sarracenia, 534
Satin Flower (see Sisyrinchium, 546)
Satyrium, 172
Sauromatum, 535
Saxifraga, 535
Scabiosa, 538
Scaphosepalum, 177
Scarborough Lily (see *Vallota purpurea*, 582)
Scarlet Plume (see *Euphorbia fulgens*, 368)
Schaueria, 539
Schizanthus, 539
*Schizocentron elegans*, 540
*Schizostylis coccinea*, 540
Schlumbergera, 540
Schomburgkia, 165
*Schubertia grandiflora*, 541
Scilla, 541
Scirpus, 541
Scolopendrium (see Phyllitis, 500)
Scorpion Iris (see *Iris alata*, 412)
Screw Pine (see Pandanus, 484)
Scutellaria, 542
Scuticaria, 166
Scythian Lamb (see *Cibotium Barometz*, 311)
Seakale, 96
Sea Lavender (see Limonium, 432)

Sea Onion (see *Scilla verna*, 541)
Sea Pink (see Armeria, 252)
Sea Urchin Cactus (see Echinopsis, 355)
Sedum, 542
Seeds, 60–63
Selaginella, 543
Selago, 543
Selecting Fruit Trees, 182
Selenicereus, 543
Selenipedium (see Phragmopedilum, 165)
*Selliera radicans*, 544
*Semele androgyna*, 544
Sempervivum, 544
Senecio, 544
*Senecio hybrida* (see Cineraria, 311)
Sensitive Plant (see *Mimosa pudica*, 457)
Serpent or Snake Gourd (see *Trichosanthes Anguina*, 575)
Shading, 31–33, 180
Shaggy Windflower (see *Anemone vernalis*, 245)
Shanking (see Grape, 211)
Sheep's Laurel (see *Kalmia angustifolia*, 419)
Sherwoodia (see Shortia, 545)
Shooting Stars (see Dodecatheon, 350)
Shortia, 545
Siberian Squill (see *Scilla sibirica*, 541)
Sibthorpia, 546
Side-saddle Flower (see Sarracenia, 534)
Silene, 546
Silk-bark Tree (see *Grevillea robusta*, 388)
Silver Tree (see Leucadendron, 428)
Sinningia, 546
Sisyrinchium, 546
Size and Purpose of Greenhouse, 17
Skimmia, 547
Skull Cap (see Scutellaria, 542)
Sleepy Disease, 614
Slipper Flower (see Calceolaria, 277)
Slipper Spurge (see *Pedilanthus tithymaloides*, 487)
Slugs, 611
Smilacina, 547
Smilax, 548
Smilax of the Florist (see *Myrsiphyllum asparagoides*, 465)
Snails, 611
Snake's Beard (see Ophiopogon, 478)
Snake's Head (see *Fritillaria meleagris*, 376)
Snake's Tongue (see *Ophioglossum vulgatum*, 476)
Snapdragon (see Antirrhinum, 248)
Snowball Tree (see *Viburnum Opulus sterile*, 584)
Snowbush (see *Phyllanthus nivosus*, 500)
Snowdrop (see Galanthus, 378)
Snowflake (see Leucojum, 429)
Snowflies (see White-fly, 615)
Soapwort (see Saponaria, 533)
*Sobralia macrantha*, 172
Soil and Aspect of Greenhouse, 23
Soil Sterilisation, 51–53, 90–92, 189
Solandra, 548
*Solanum Capsicastrum*, 549
*Solanum jasminoides*, 549
Soldanella, 550

# INDEX

Solenophora Endlicheriana, 550
Sollya heterophylla, 550
Sonerila, 550
Sooty Mould (see Aphides, 601)
Sophrocatlælia, 172
Sophrocattleya, 172
Sophronitis grandiflora, 177
South African Hemp (see Sparmannia africana, 551)
Sowbread (see Cyclamen, 334)
Spanish Bayonet (see Yucca, 594)
Sparaxis, 551
Sparmannia africana, 551
Spathiphyllum, 552
Spathoglottis, 166
Speedwell (see Veronica, 584)
Sphacele, 552
Sphæralcea, 552
Spider Lily (see Hymenocallis, 407)
Spider Plant (see Cleome, 314)
Spiderwort (see Tradescantia, 573)
Spielmannia africana (see Oftia africana, 476)
Spigelia marilandica, 552
Spiræa, 552
Spiræa Aruncus (see Aruncus sylvester, 253)
Spiræa hexapetala, palmata, rubra, etc. (see Filipendula, 373)
Spiræa lobata (see Filipendula rubra, 373)
Spiral Flag (see Costus, 326)
Spiranthera odoratissima, 553
Spironema fragrans, 554
Spleenwort (see Asplenium, 255)
Sprekelia formosissima, 554
Spring Meadow Saffron (see Bulbocodium, 275)
Spurge (see Euphorbia, 368)
Squill (see Scilla, 541)
Stachys corsica, 554
Staging, 36
Stag's Horn Fern (see Platycerium, 504)
Stangeria eriopus, 554
Stanhopea, 166
Stapelia, 554
Stapelia Corderoyi (see Duvalia Corderoyi, 353)
Staphylea, 555
Star Capsicum (see Solanum Capsicastrum, 549)
Star Grass (see Hypoxis, 408)
Star Jessamine (see Trachelospermum jasminoides, 572)
Star of Bethlehem (see Ornithogalum, 479)
Star of the Veldt (see Dimorphotheca, 347)
Star Tulip (see Calochortus, 281)
Statice (see Limonium, 432)
Stauntonia hexaphylla, 555
Stauropsis, 166
Stemona, 555
Stenochlæna, 556
Stenomesson, 556
Stenospermation popayanense, 556
Stenotaphrum secundatum var. variegatum, 556

Stephanophorum (see Stenotaphrum secundatum var. variegatum, 556
Stephanophysum (see Ruellia, 529)
Stephanotis floribunda, 556
Sterilisation of Soil, 51–53, 90–92, 189
Sternbergia, 557
Steudnera, 557
Stewartia, 557
Stewartia grandiflora (see Stewartia Pseudo-Camellia, 557)
Stifftia chrysantha, 558
Stigmaphyllon, 558
Stock (see Matthiola, 449)
Stoking, 40–41
Stonecrop (see Sedum, 542)
Strawberry, 226
Strawberry-fruited Cypress (see Microcachrys tetragona, 456)
Streblorhiza speciosa, 558
Strelitzia, Reginæ 558
Streptanthera, 559
Streptocarpus, 559
Streptosolen Jamesonii, 556
Stripe, 614
Striped Squill (see Puschkinia scilloides, 515)
Strobilanthes, 560
Stromanthe, 560
Strongylodon pseudolucidus, 560
Strophanthus, 560
Stuartia (see Stewartia, 557)
Stylophyllum (see Cotyledon, 326)
Sugar-cane (see Saccharum, 530)
Summer Cypress (see Kochia, 421)
Summer Snowflake (see Leucojum æstivum, 429)
Sundew (see Drosera, 352)
Surinum Tea Plant (see Lantana, 424)
Swainsona galegifolia, 561
Swamp Blueberry (see Vaccinium corymbosum, 581)
Swamp Laurel (see Kalmia polifolia, 419)
Swamp Pink (see Hellonia bullata, 395)
Swan River Daisy (see Brachycome, 271)
Sweet Pea, 561
Sweet Pepper Bush (see Clethra, 315)
Sweet-scented Verbena (see Lippia citriodora, 434)
Sword Lily (see Gladiolus, 383)
Synechanthus fibrosus, 563
Synnotia, 563
Syringa, 563
Syringodea pulchella, 565

Tacsonia, 565
Tainia, 166
Talauma Hodgsonii, 565
Talbotia elegans (see Vellozia elegans, 582)
Tanakæ radicans, 565
Tape Grass (see Vallisneria spiralis, 582)
Tarragon, 96
Tea Plant (see Thea sinensis, 568)
Tecoma, 565
Tecoma capensis (see Tecomaria capensis)
Tecoma grandiflora (see Campsis grandiflora, 285)
Tecoma jasminoides (see Pandorea jasminoides, 484)

# INDEX

*Tecomaria capensis*, 566
*Tecophilæa cyanocrocus*, 566
Telegraph Plant (see *Desmodium gyrans*, 342)
*Telopea speciosissima*, 566
Temperature, 179
*Templetonia retusa*, 566
Testudinaria, 566
*Tetramicra bicolor* (see *Leptotes bicolor*, 428)
*Tetranema mexicana*, 567
Tetrazygia, 567
Teucrium, 567
*Thalia dealbata*, 567
*Thalia sanguinea* (see *Stromanthe sanguinea*, 560)
Thalictrum, 567
Thatch Palm (see Thrinax, 568)
Thea, 568
Thinning Fruit, 187
Thrift (see Armeria, 252)
Thrinax, 568
Thrips, 612
Throat-wort (see *Trachelium cæruleum*, 572)
Thunbergia, 568
Thunia, 166
Thymus, 569
*Thyrsacanthus rutilans* (see *Odontonema Schomburgkianum*, 475)
Thysanotus, 569
*Tiarella cordifolia*, 569
Tiger Flower (see *Tigridia pavona*, 570)
Tiger Iris (see Tigridia, 570)
Tigridia, 570
Tillandsia, 570
*Tillandsia carinata* (see *Vriesia carinata*, 589)
*Tillandsia hieroglyphica* (see *Vriesia hieroglyphica*, 589)
*Tillandsia psittacina* (see *Vriesia psittacina*, 589)
*Tillandsia splendens* (see *Vriesia splendens*, 589)
Toad Flax (see Linaria, 433)
Tobacco (see Nicotiana, 471)
*Todea barbara*, 571
*Todea hymenophylloides* (see *Leptopteris hymenophylloides*, 427)
*Todea superba* (see *Leptopteris superba*, 427)
Tomato, 96, 228
Tomato Diseases and Pests, 612
Torch Lily (see Kniphofia, 421)
Torenia, 571
Tortoise Plant (see Testudinaria, 566)
Townsendia, 572
*Toxicophlæa Thunbergii* (see *Acokanthera venenata*, 236)
*Trachelium cæruleum*, 572
Trachelospermum, 572
Trachycarpus, 573
*Trachymene cærulea*, 573
Tradescantia, 573
*Tradescantia discolor* (see *Rhœa discolor*, 522)
*Tradescantia zebrina* (see *Zebrina pendula*, 597)

Transvaal Daisy (see *Gerbera Jamesonii*, 381)
*Trapa natans*, 574
Treasure Flower (see Gazania, 380)
Tree Peony (see *Pæonia suffruticosa*, 483)
Tree Poppy (see *Dendromecon rigida*, 341)
Trevisia, 574
*Trianea bogotensis* (see *Limnobium stoloniferum*, 432)
Trichinium, 574
Trichocentrum, 172
Trichomanes, 574
*Trichopilia suavis*, 172
*Trichosanthes Anguina*, 575
Trichosma, 177
Trichosporum, 575
Tricuspidaria, 576
*Trientalis europæa*, 576
Trillium, 576
Trinity Flower (see Trillium, 576)
Triteleia (see Brodeæa, 272)
Tritoma (see Kniphofia, 421)
Tritonia, 577
Trollius, 577
Tropæolum, 578
Trumpet Flower (see Bignonia, 267)
Trumpet Leaf (see Sarracenia, 534)
Tuberose (see *Polianthes tuberosa*, 507)
Tulips, 579
*Tunica Saxifraga*, 579
Turk's Cap Cactus (see Cactus, 270)
Turnip, 96
Tussacia, 579
*Tweedia cærulea* (see *Oxypetalum cæruleum*, 483)
Twin Flower (see *Linnæa borealis*, 433)
Twin Leaf (see *Jeffersonia diphylla*, 417)
*Tydæa amabilis* (see *Isoloma amabilis*, 413)
*Tydæa picta* (see *Isoloma picta*, 413)
Types of Greenhouse, 15–17
*Tytonia natans*, 580

Umbilicus (see Cotyledon, 326)
Umbrella Palm (see *Hedyscepe Canterburyana*, 392)
Umbrella Plant (see *Cyperus alternifolius*, 335)
Urceolina, 580
*Urechites suberecta*, 580
Utricularia, 580

*Vaccaria pyramidata* (see *Saponaria Vaccaria*, 533)
Vaccinium, 581
*Vaccinium rugosum* (see *Pentapterygium rugosum*, 491)
*Vallisneria spiralis*, 582
*Vallota purpurea*, 582
Vanda, 166, 172
Vanilla, 166
Vegetable Marrow, 96
Vegetable Sponge (see Luffa, 440)
Vegetables, Early, 93
Vellozia, 582
Veltheimia, 583
Velvet Groundsel (see *Senecio Petasites*, 544)

# INDEX

Velvet Tree (see *Gynura aurantiaca*, 389)
Ventilation of Greenhouse, 30–31, 178
Venus Fly Trap (see *Dionæa muscipula*, 347)
Verbena, 583
*Verbena citriodora* (see *Lippia citriodora*, 434)
Veronica, 584
Viburnum, 584
*Victoria regia*, 585
Victorian Rosemary (see *Westringia rosmariniformis*, 591)
*Villarsia reniformis*, 585
*Vinca rosea*, 585
Vine Mildew, 614
Vine Weevil, 614
Viola, 586
Viola Rust, 615
Violet, 587
Violet, African (see Saintpaulia, 531)
Violet Cress (see *Ionopsidium acaule*, 411)
Violet, Dog's Tooth (see Erythronium, 365)
Virginian Willow (see *Itea virginica*, 414)
Virgin's Bower (see Clematis, 313)
Viscaria (see Lychnis, 440)
Vitex, 588
*Vitis adenopoda* (see *Cissus adenopodus*, 312)
*Vitis discolor* (see *Cissus discolor*, 312)
*Vitis gongylodes* (see *Cissus gongylodes*, 312)
*Vitis vinifera*, 201
Vriesia, 589
*Vriesia glaucophylla* (see *Tillandsia fasciculata*, 570)

Wachendorfia, 589
Wahlenbergia, 590
Waitzia, 590
Wake Robin (see Trillium, 576)
Wall Fern (see *Polypodium vulgare*, 508)
Wallflower (see Cheiranthus, 301)
Wandering Jews (see Tradescantia, 573)
Waratah (see *Telopea speciosissima*, 566)
*Warrea discolor* (see Warscewiczella, 177)
Warscewiczella, 177
*Washingtonia filifera*, 590
Water Balsam (see *Tytonia natans*, 580)
Water Caltrops (see *Trapa natans*, 574)
Water Chestnut (see *Trapa natans*, 574)
Water Hawthorn (see *Aponogeton distachyus*, 249)
Watering Frames, 54
Watering Fruit, 185
Water Lettuce (see *Pistia Stratiotes*, 503)
Water Lily (see Nymphæa, 474)
Water-rice (see *Zizania palustris*, 599)
Water Supply, 33–34
Watsonia, 591
Wattle (see Acacia, 234)
Wax Flower (see Hoya, 401)
Wedding Iris (see *Moræa Robinsoniana*, 461)
Weevils (see Vine-Weevils, 614)
Weigela (see Diervilla, 346)
*Weldenia candida*, 591

West Indian Red Jasmine (see *Plumeria rubra*, 506)
Westringia, 591
Whispering Bells (see Angelonia, 246)
White-fly, 615
Whitlow Grass (see Draba, 351)
Widdringtonia, 591
*Wigandia caracasana*, 592
Wild Hyacinth (see *Scilla nonscripta*, 541)
Wild Rosemary (see *Ledum palustre*, 426)
Winter Aconite (see Eranthis, 360)
Winter Daffodil (see *Sternbergia lutea*, 557)
Winter-green (see *Gaultheria procumbens*, 380)
Wintering Fruit Trees, 184
Winter-sweet (see *Chimonanthus præcox*, 302)
Wireworms, 616
Wistaria, 592
Wisteria, 592
Witch Hazel (see Hamamelis, 391)
*Witsenia corymbosa* (see *Nivenia corymbosa*, 473)
Wood Fern (see Dryopteris, 353)
Woodlice, 616
Wood Lily (see Trillium, 576)
Woodsia, 593
Wood-tongue Fern (see Drymoglossum, 352)
Woodwardia, 593
Woodwork in the Greenhouse, 27–29
Worms, 617
Wormwood (see Artemisia, 253)

*Xanthoceras sorbifolia*, 593
*Xanthosoma*, 594
*Xerophyta* (see Vellozia, 582)
*Xylobium*, 172
*Xylophylla latifolia* (see *Phyllanthus speciosus*, 500)

Yearly Overhaul of Greenhouse, 50–51
Yellow Star of Bethlehem (see *Gagea lutea*, 378)
Youth and Old-age (see Zinnia, 598)
Yucca, 594

Zaluzianskya, 595
Zamia, 595
Zantedeschia, 596
Zea, 596
*Zebrina pendula*, 597
*Zenobia pulverulenta*, 597
Zephyr Flower (see Zephyranthes, 597)
Zephyranthes, 597
*Zeuxine regia*, 167
Zieria, 598
Zinnia, 598
*Zizania palustris*, 599
Zizyphus, 599
*Zygocactus truncatus*, 599
Zygopetalum, 172
*Zygopetalum aromaticum* (see *Warscewiczella aromatica*, 177)
*Zygopetalum discolor* (see *Warscewiczella discolor*, 177)
*Zygopetalum Wendlandii* (see *Warscewiczella Wendlandii*, 177)